Encyclopedia of Modern French Thought

ENCYCLOPEDIA OF MODERN FRENCH THOUGHT

CHRISTOPHER JOHN MURRAY,
EDITOR

FITZROY DEARBORN

An Imprint of the Taylor & Francis Group
New York • London

Published in 2004 by
Fitzroy Dearborn
An imprint of the Taylor & Francis Group
29 West 35th Street
New York, NY 10001

Published in Great Britain by
Fitzroy Dearborn
An imprint of the Taylor & Francis Group
11 New Fetter Lane
London EC4P 4EE

10 9 8 7 6 5 4 3 2 1

First published in the USA and UK 2004

Library of Congress Cataloging-in-Publication Data

Encyclopedia of modern French thought / Christopher John Murray, editor.
   p. cm.
   Includes bibliographical references and index.
  ISBN 1-57958-384-9 (alk. paper)
  1. France—Intellectual life—20th century—Encyclopedias. 2.
France—Civilization—20th century—Encyclopedias. I. Murray,
Christopher John.
II. Title.
  DC33.7.E55 2004
  944.081′03—dc22

                                       2003014408

CONTENTS

Preface: Encyclopedia of Modern French Thought

French thought has had a profound impact on modern intellectual and cultural life, notably in the United States. It is an influence that has been keenly felt in (among other fields) philosophy, linguistics, political and social thought, cultural studies, history, psychoanalysis, literary theory and criticism, anthropology, the philosophy of science and technology, media studies, and in the theory and practice of the arts. Moreover, in recent decades French thinkers have played the leading role in attempting to characterize those profound changes in our intellectual, cultural, and moral life that have been labeled the "post-modern condition."

Though it is not possible to consider all the defining characteristics of modern French thought – the range of disciplines and themes is far too wide – there are several features that, though not universal, illustrate the unique significance of French thinkers.

The first is their response to German thinkers: Kant certainly, but also, and with dramatic impact, Hegel, Marx, Freud, Dilthey, Durkheim, Husserl, Jaspers, Heidegger, and – especially during the second half of the century, when faith in "big theorie" gave way to a radical skepticism – Nietzsche. Many of the most original interpretations of these major thinkers, interpretations that have in turn been influential in the United States, Britain, and elsewhere, are the work of French intellectuals.

A second and related feature is the key role played by French thinkers in the radical reappraisal of many of the central assumptions, concepts, and values of Western thought, notably those inherited from the Enlightenment. These include such closely related themes as the authority of reason – the degree to which it is limiting or even, as an agent of the dominant ideology, repressive; the unstable nature of the self – a questioning of the Cartesian *cogito*, the thinking self as autonomous and foundational; the pervasive and inescapable role of language in determining our understanding of ourselves and the world, and in determining the limits of thought; and the status of "grand narratives" such as religion, science, or Marxism in a postmodern world that is increasingly complex, skeptical, and pluralistic. During a century when traditional social, moral, and religious beliefs have been lost or greatly weakened, French thinkers have explored, among other things, the ethical implications of living in a world that seems to have no meaning or purpose; they have closely scrutinized the changing nature of political power and analyzed the individual's potential for resistance; and, largely through feminist, gay, and lesbian thinkers, they have helped to redefine our understanding of gender and sexuality.

Another important feature is the responsiveness of French intellectuals to the forces shaping the modern world. In part at least, modern French thought can be seen as a series of reflections on the major events of national and international history – on two world wars, on the rise of Fascism and Communism in the interwar years, on colonial struggles for independence, on the postwar rise and fall of revolutionary

Marxism, on the plight of minorities, on the social unrest reflected in the protests of May 1968, and on the spread of global capitalism. This responsiveness to events is also seen in a willingness to engage directly in social and political action, a characteristic role of French intellectuals since the eighteenth century that was given fresh impetus by the Dreyfus affair. Both right-wing and left-wing intellectuals have formed action groups, written for journals and newspapers, literally taken to the streets, and more recently used television in order to influence opinion on such issues as social injustice and the misuse of power; race, colonialism, and immigration; the need for revolution and the desire for stability; sexual politics; religious fundamentalism; the role of the mass media; and environmental issues.

French thinkers have also played a key role in French, and therefore Western, culture. It is difficult fully to appreciate twentieth-century French art and architecture, fiction, poetry and drama, music, cinema and photography without an understanding of French ideas. Often this is not simply a question of the inevitable influence of the prevailing intellectual trends: artists and writers have often consciously concerned themselves with exploring ideas through their art – the novelist François Mauriac was typical (in this, at least) when he described himself as "un métaphysicien qui travaille dans le concret." Moreover, French thinkers have themselves done likewise – the most celebrated example is Sartre, who wrote novels, plays, biography, criticism, and autobiography as an important complement to his formal philosophical works – and they have also shown a keen interest in the arts in terms of their own disciplines such as sociology, anthropology, political science, semiotics, and philosophy.

The *Encyclopedia of Modern French Thought* is intended to provide a wide-ranging guide to the wealth of ideas represented by these and other features, its scope being twentieth-century thought across disciplines. It will be of particular interest to those who study modern French life, ideas, and culture; but also, given the international significance of many French thinkers, to those interested in modern thought in general.

It does not include science, though it does include the philosophy of science. Novelists, dramatists, and poets are included only when they have made a contribution to debate through their essays, and have played a particularly important role in French intellectual life (for example, Breton, Gide).

By "French" thinkers is meant those who have engaged in French intellectual debates in French. This includes those born and perhaps educated elsewhere: examples include Kristeva and Todorov (Bulgaria), Greimas (Lithuania), Poulet and Irigaray (Belgium), Starobinski (Switzerland). It also includes francophone intellectuals from former colonies. This is not an unthinking form of cultural neo-colonialism. Many francophone writers have engaged in French intellectual debates and often in France itself, and most received a French education. Moreover, the entries were selected and written in the full knowledge that such writers were (or are) striving to fashion their own unique intellectual, historical, cultural, and political identity, a process that involves a systematic resistance to assimilation. By contrast, because of their very different intellectual, educational and colonial history, French-Canadian thinkers are not included.

Some 150 diverse scholars have shared their expertise to create the 234 entries in this *Encyclopedia of Modern French Thought*. The selection of entries, which range from 1,000 to 5,000 words, is based on a desire to balance range of subjects with depth of treatment. Most are on individuals, but there are also entries that provide a different and complementary focus by looking at specific disciplines (Anthropology, Classics, Linguistics. . .); at influential theories, belief, and methodologies (Catholicism, Feminism, Phenomenology . . .); and at a number of key themes and subjects that draw together several disciplines (Anti-humanism, Sexuality, Language . . .). There are also entries that provide the historical, social and political background to intellectual life (Colonialism, Journals, Historical Surveys . . .). A thematic table of contents delineating these can be found on page xv.

Because some recent French writers are notorious for the difficulty of their style, which is usually a way of trying to avoid easy assimilation in the dominant forms of understanding, contributors were asked to pay close attention to clarity of exposition. This is not an attempt, however, to reduce complex, challenging, and far-reaching theories to simple, predigested summaries; concerns about the subtle power of dominant ideologies, and also about the limits of the sayable, are important. The aim, rather, as with any such project, is to encourage both student and lay reader to turn to the works in question and engage directly with their authors' ideas and strategies.

Given the close relationship between intellectual developments and both cultural and social factors, we have provided the reader with a **Chronology** that provides a detailed timeline of works and events in several categories: ideas, literature, music, art and architecture, film, and political/social life. As a guide to the many writers, works, and subjects in the book, there is (as noted above) a **Thematic Table of Contents**, and also a comprehensive, analytical **Index** at the end of the book. The entries on individuals contain a **Biography** at the end of each article, thus focusing the entry itself on that person's ideas and their impact on French thought. The entries include **See Also** to identify key links and interrelationships and **Selected Writings and Further Readings**, which are bibliographies to guide readers through the ever-growing wealth of literature.

Acknowledgments

I'd like to thank the advisors and contributors for their advice, encouragement, and hard work. I'd also like to thank Gordon Lee of Fitzroy Dearborn for launching the project so efficiently, and Kate Aker of Routledge for guiding it so skillfully to port.

LIST OF ENTRIES

A

Alain (Émile-Auguste Chartier)
Althusser, Louis
Anthropology
Ariès, Philippe
Arkoun, Mohammed
Aron, Raymond
Art history, criticism, and aesthetics
Artaud, Antonin
Autobiography

B

Bachelard, Gaston
Badiou, Alain
Balibar, Étienne
Balibar, Renée
Bardeche, Maurice
Barrès, Maurice
Barthes, Roland
Bataille, Georges
Baudrillard, Jean
Bazin, André
Beauvoir, Simone de
Béguin, Albert
Benda, Julien
Benveniste, Émile
Bergson, Henri (Louis)
Berl, Emmanuel
Bernanos, Georges
Beyala, Calixthe
Binet, Alfred
Bloch, Marc
Blondel, Maurice Edouard
Bloy, Léon
Body
Bonnefoy, Yves
Bourdieu, Pierre Félix
Braudel, Fernand Paul
Breton, André
Breuil, Henri

Brunschvicg, Léon
Butor, Michel

C

Caillois, Roger
Camus, Albert
Canguilhem, George
Cassin, Barbara
Castoriadis, Cornelius
Catholicism
Cavaillès, Jean
Certeau, Michel de
Césaire, Aimé (-Fernand)
Chamoiseau, Patrick
Cioran, Émile Michel
Cixous, Hélène
Classics
Colonial and postcolonial experience
Culture

D

Debord, Guy
Debray, Régis
Deleuze, Gilles
Depestre, René
Derrida, Jacques
Didi-Huberman, Georges
Diop, Cheikh Anta
Djebar, Assia
Duby, Georges
Dufrenne, Mikel
Duhem, Pierre Maurice Marie
Dumazedier, Joffre
Dumézil, Georges
Durkheim, Émile
Duvert, Tony
Duvignaud, Jean

E

Economics
Educational theory

xi

List of Entries

THEMATIC LIST OF ENTRIES

Disciplines
Anthropology
Art history, criticism, and aesthetics
Classics
Educational theory
Historiography
Law
Linguistics
Literary theory and criticism
Philosophy
Philosophy of Science
Psychology
Sociology
Theology and religious thought

Historical, political and social contexts
Colonial and postcolonial experience
Francophonie, La
French Colonial Thought
French Thought in the United States
French-Jewish Intellectuals
German thought, influence of
Historical survey: 1870–1918
Historical survey: 1918–1939
Historical survey: 1939–1968
Historical survey: 1968–
Holocaust, the
Jewish question, the
Journals and periodicals
Political movements and debates

Individuals
Alain (Émile-Auguste Chartier)
Althusser, Louis
Ariès, Philippe
Arkoun, Mohammed
Aron, Raymond
Artaud, Antonin
Bachelard, Gaston
Badiou, Alain
Balibar, Étienne
Balibar, Renée

Bardeche, Maurice
Barrès, Maurice
Barthes, Roland
Bataille, Georges
Baudrillard, Jean
Bazin, André
Beauvoir, Simone de
Béguin, Albert
Benda, Julien
Benveniste, Émile
Bergson, Henri (Louis)
Bernanos, Georges
Beyala, Calixthe
Bloch, Marc
Blondel, Maurice Edouard
Bloy, Léon
Bonnefoy, Yves
Bourdieu, Pierre Félix
Breton, André
Breuil, Henri
Brunschvicg, Léon
Caillois, Roger
Camus, Albert
Canguilhem, George
Cassin, Barbara
Castoriadis, Cornelius
Cavaillès, Jean
Certeau, Michel de
Césaire, Aimé (-Fernand)
Chamoiseau, Patrick
Cioran, Émile Michel
Cixous, Hélène
Debord, Guy
Debray, Régis
Deleuze, Gilles
Depestre, René
Derrida, Jacques
Didi-Huberman, Georges
Diop, Cheikh Anta
Djebar, Assia
Duby, Georges
Dufrenne, Mikel

Thematic List of Entries

Subjects, Themes, Movements, Genres
Autobiography
Body
Culture
Poetry
Surrealism
Homosexuality
Humanism/anti-humanism
Intellectuals
Knowledge and truth
Language
Media
Modernism and post-modernism

Nationalism and identity
Sexuality
Subject (self and subjectivity)

Theories, Beliefs, and Methodologies
Catholicism
Existentialism
Feminism
Marxism
Phenomenology
Post-structuralism
Psychoanalytical theory
Structuralism

CHRONOLOGY

The timelines below guide readers to major developments in contemporary French thought. The academic timeline marks the publication of significant works by key authors, as well as foundation dates for notable institutions and schools of thought. The art and architecture timeline marks the composition date of influential works and seminal exhibits. The film timeline delineates the date of release of key French films of the modern and postmodern eras. The literature timeline traces the publication dates of works exemplifying the primary tendencies of modern French thought, and the founding dates for important journals or reviews, as well as notable honors won by seminal authors. The music timeline does the same for innovative and influential musical works of the modern and postmodern eras. The political and social life timeline supplies a context for principal developments in French thought and the arts in France over the course of approximately the last 100 years.

Academic Timeline

1896
Bergson, *Matière et mémoire*

1897
Durkheim, *Le Suicide*

1900
Bergson, *Le Rire*

1903
Gourmont, *Physique d'amour*

1907
Bergson, *Évolution créatrice*

1912
Durkheim, *Les Formes élémentaires de la vie religieuse*

1915
Bloy, *Jeanne d'Arc et l'Allemagne*
Rolland, *Au-dessus de la mêlée*

1916
Saussure, *Cours de linguistique générale*

1917
Gourmont, *Pendant la guerre*

1919
Gilson, *Le Thomisme*

1920
Maritain, *Art et scolastique*

1921
Alain, *Mars, ou la guerre jugée*
Brunschvicg, *L'idéalisme contemporain*

1922
Febvre, *La Terre et l'évolution humaine*

1925
Mauss, *Essai sur le don*

1927
Benda, *La Trahison des clercs*
Gide, *Voyage au Congo*
Maritain, *Primauté du spirituel*
Massis, *Défense de l'Occident*

1928
Febvre, *Un destin: Martin Luther*

1929
Annales founded

1930
Berl, *Mort de la Morale bourgeoise*

1932
Alain, *Idées*
Gilson, *L'Esprit de la philosophie médiévale*
Maritain, *Distinguer pour unir, ou les degrés du savoir*

Chronology

1934
Alain, *Les Dieux*
Blondel, *La Pensée*

1935
Marcel, *Être et avoir*

1936
Sartre, *L'Imagination*

1937
Céline, *Bagatelles pour un massacre*
Marcel, *Être et avoir*

Collège de Sociologie formed

1938
Bachelard, *La Psychoanalyse de feu*

1939–40
Bloch, *La Société feudal*

1940
Sartre, *L'Imaginaire*

1941
Grenier, *Inspirations méditerranéennes*

1942
Febvre, *Le Problème de l'incroyance au XVIe siècle, la religion de Rabelais*
Merleau-Ponty, *La Structure du comportement*

1943
Bataille, *L'Expérience intérieure*
Camus, *Le Myth de Sisyphe*
Sartre, *L'Etre et le néant*

1945
Merleau-Ponty, *Phénoménologie de la perception*

Les Temps modernes founded

1946
Sartre, *Réflexions sur la question juive*

1947
Kojève, *Introduction à la lecture de Hegel*
Sartre, *L'Existentialisme est un humanisme*

1948
Sartre, *Qu'est-ce que la littérature?*

1949
Bataille, *La Part maudite*
Beauvoir, *Le Deuxième Sexe*
Braudel, *La Méditerranée et le monde méditerranéen à l'époque de Philippe II*
Poulet, *Études sur le temps humain, I*

1950
Ricoeur, *Philosophie de la volonté*

1951
Camus, *L'Homme révolté*
Malraux, *Les Voix du silence*
Marcel, *Mystère de l'être*

1952
Fanon, *Peau Noire, masques blancs*
Sartre, *Saint Genet comédien et martyr*

1953
Barthes, *Le Degré zéro de l'écriture*

1955
Aron, *L'Opium des intellectuels*
Goldmann, *Le Dieu caché*
Lévi-Strauss, *Tristes tropiques*
Teilhard De Chardin, *Le Phénomène humain*

1956
Cioran, *La Tentation d'exister*
Sarraute, *L'Ère du soupçon*

1957
Barthes, *Mythologies*
Bataille, *La Littérature et le mal*, and *L'Érotisme*
Teilhard De Chardin, *Le Milieu divin*

1958
Bataille, *L'Érotisme*
Lévi-Strauss, *Anthropologie structurale*

1959
Diop, *L'Unité culturelle de l'Afrique noire*
Morin, *Autocritique*

1960
Ariès, *L'Enfant et la vie familiale sous l'Ancien Régime*
Merleau-Ponty, *Signes*
Ricoeur, first volume of *Philosophie de la volonté*
Sartre, *Critique de la raison dialectique*

Tel quel founded (–1983)

1961
Bataille, *Les Larmes d'Éros*
Bachelard, *La Poétique de l'espace*
Fanon, *Les Damnés de la terre*
Foucault, *Folie et Déraison: Histoire de la folie à l'âge classique*
Levinas, *Totalité et infini*

1962
Lévi-Strauss, *La Pensée sauvage*
Mandel, *Traité d'économie marxiste*

1963
Barthes, *Sur Racinebache*
Beauvoir, *La Force des choses*
Robbe-Grillet, *Pour un nouveau roman*

1964
Beauvoir, *Une Mort très douce*
Lévi-Strauss, *Le Cru et le cuit*
Goldmann, *Pour une sociologie du roman*

Lacan founds École Freudienne de Paris

1965
Althusser, *Pour Marx*, and (with Balibar) *Lire 'Le Capital'*
Duvignaud, *Sociologie du theatre*
Picard, *Nouvelle critique ou nouvelle imposture*
Vernant, *Mythe et pensée chez les Grecs*

1966
Canguilhem, *Le Normal et le pathologique*
Foucault, *Les Mots et les choses: Une Archéologie des sciences humaines*Greimas, *Sémantique structurale*
Lacan, *Écrits*

1967
Debord, *La Société du Spectacle*
Debray, *Révolution dans la révolution*
Derrida, *De la grammatologie*
Diop, *Antériorité des civilisations nègres*

1968
Baurillard, *Systèm des objets*
Deleuze, *Différence et répépetition*
Lefebvre, *La Vie quotidienne dans le monde moderne*
Lévi-Strauss, *L'Origine des manières de table*

1969
Foucault, *L'Archéologie du savoir*
Kristeva, *Séméiotikè: Recherches Pour une Sémanalyse*
Ricoeur, *Le Conflit des interprétations*

Psychoanalyse et politique (psych et po) group founded

1970
Aron, *Marxismes imaginaires*
Barthes, *S/Z*
Beauvoir, *La Vieillesse*
Derrida, *Positions; La Dissémination*
Duvignard, *Spectacle et société*
Monod, *Le hasard et la nécessité*

1971
Poulantzas, *Pouvoir politique et classes sociales*
Poulet, *La Conscience critique*
Veyne, *Comment on écrit l'histoire*

1972
Barthes, *Le Plaisir du texte*
Deleuze and Guattari, *L'Anti-Oedipe*
Derrida, *Positions*
Hocquenghem, *Le Désir homosexuel*

1973
Cioran, *De l'inconvénient d'être né*
Mudimbe, *L'Autre Face du royaume*
Nancy, *La remarque spéculative, un bot mot de Hegel*

1974
Derrida, *Glas*
Irigaray, *Spéculum de l'autre femme*
Laroui, *La Crise des intellectuals arabs*
Leclerc, *Parole de femme*
Levinas, *Autrement qu'être*
Lyotard, *Économie libidinale*

1975
Ariès, *Essais sur l'histoire de la mort en Occident du Moyen-Age à nos jours*
Barthes, *Barthes par Roland Barthes*
Ellul, *Sans feu ni lieu: Signification biblique de la Grande Ville*
Foucault, *Surveiller et punir: Naissance de la prison*
Lacan, *Le Séminaire XX: Encore*

Le Roy Ladurie, *Montaillou, village occitan, 1294–1324*
Lévi-Strauss, *La Voie des masques*
Ricoeur, *La Métaphore vive*

1976
Foucault, first volume of *Histoire de la sexualité* (–1984)

1977
Barthes, *Fragments d'un discours amoureux*
Baudrillard, *Oublier Foucault*
Canguilhem, *Idéologie et rationalité*
Glucksmann, *Les Maître-penseurs*
Irigaray, *Ce Sexe qui n'en est pas un*

1978
Lacoue-Labarthe and Mathieu Bénezet, *Misère de la littérature*
Todorov, *Symbolisme et interpretation*
Touraine, *La Voix et le regard*

1979
Baudrillard, *De la séduction*
Blanchot, *L'Écriture du désastre*
Bourdieu, *La Distinction*
Debray, *Le Pouvoir intellectuel en France*
Fourastié, *Les Trente glorieuses*
Lyotard, *La Condition postmoderne: rapport sur le savoir*

1980
Barthes, *La chambre claire*
Certeau, *L'Invention du quotidien*
Deleuze and Guattari, *Mille plateaux*
Derrida, *La Carte Postale*

1981
Baudrillard, *Simulacra et simulation*
Duby, *Le Chevalier, la femme et le prêtre*

1982
Levinas, *De Dieu qui vient à l'idée*
Mudimbe, *L'Odeur du père*
Todorov, *La Conquête de l'Amerique*

1983
Lévi-Strauss, *Le Regard éloigné*
Ricoeur, *Temps et récit*, vol 1
Vovelle, *La Mort et l'Occident (1750–1820)*

1984
Bourdieu, *Homo academicus*

1985
Vovelle, *La mentalité révolutionnaire*

1986
Baudrillard, *L'Amérique*
Lacoue-Labarthe, *L'Imitation des modernes*
Nancy, *La communauté désœuvrée*

1987
Derrida, *Psyché: inventions de l'autre*
Finkielkraut, *La Défaite de la pensée*
Kristeva, *Soleil Noir: Dépression et Mélancolie*
Rousso, *Le syndrome de Vichy*

1988
Balibar, *Race, nation, classe*
Nancy, *Expérience de la liberté*

1989
Bourdieu, *La Noblesse d'état*
Duvert, *Abécédaire malveillant*
Vernant, *L'Individu, la mort, l'amour: Soi-même et l'autre en Grèce ancienne*
Vovelle, *Les Aventures de la raison. Entretiens avec Richard Figuier*

1990
Derrida, *Mémoires d'aveugle*
Nancy, *Une pensée finie*
Serres, *Le Contrat naturel*

1991
Baudrillard, *La Guerre du Golfe n'a pas eu lieu*
Debray, *Cours de médiologie générale*
Deleuze and Guattari, *Qu'est-ce que la philosophie?*
Derrida, *Circonfession*
Todorov, *Face à l'extrême*

1992
Debray, *Vie et mort de l'image*

1993
Derrida, *Spectres de Marx*
Kristeva, *Les Nouvelles Maladies de l'Âme*
Serres, *La Légende des anges*
Vovelle, *Combats pour la Révolution française*

1994
Balibar, *Lieux et noms de la vérité*
Derrida, *Force de loi*

1996
Derrida, *Résistance à la psychanalyse*

1997
Irigaray, *Être deux*

1998
Bourdieu, *La Domination masculine*

1999
Eribon, *Réflexions sur la question gay*

2000
Lacoue-Labarthe, *Phrase*
Nancy, *Le regard du portrait*

2001
Balibar, *Nous, citoyens d'Europe? Les frontières, l'État, le peuple*

2002
Nancy, *La création du monde: ou la mondialisation*

Art and Architecture Timeline

1896
Redon, *Tentation de saint Antoine*

1897
Rousseau, *La Bohémienne endormie*

Gauguin, *D'où venons-nous? Que sommes-nous? Où allons-nous?*
Rodin, *Balzac*

1901
Maillol, *Le Méditerranée*
Picasso, *Femme au verre d'absinthe*

1903
Cézanne, *Les Grandes Baigneuses*

1904
Rodin, *Le Baiser*

Major Cézanne exhibition, Salon d'Automne

1905
Matisse, *Luxe, calme et volupté*
Picasso, *Famille d'acrobates au singe*
Vlaminck, *Paysage aux arbres rouges*

Les Fauves at Salon d'Automne

1906
Derain, *Les Deux péniches*

Exhibition of ancient Iberian art, Paris

1907
Picasso, *Les Demoiselles d'Avignon*
Rousseau, *Charmeuse de serpents*

1908
Braque, *Maisons à l'Estaque*

1910
Vlaminck, *Bords de rivière*
Utrillo, *Le Lapin agile*
Picasso, *Portrait d'Ambroise Vollard*

1911
Chagall, *Moi et le village*
Duchamp, *Nu descendant un escalier*
Matisse, *L'Atelier rouge*

1912
Delaunay (R), *Fenêtre*
Duchamp, *Nu descendant un escalier, No 2*
Perret, Théâtre des Champs-Élysées

1913
Apollinaire, *Les Peintres Cubistes*
La Fresnaye, *La Conquête de l'air*
Picabia, *Udnie (Jeune Fille américaine)*

1914
Delaunay (R), *Hommage à Blériot*
Delaunay (S), *Prismes électriques*

1915
Gris, *Nature morte au livre, à la pipe et aux verres*

1916
Modigliani, *Portrait de Max Jacob*

1917
Léger, *Partie de cartes*

1918
Rouault, *Miserere*

1919
Duchamp, *L.H.O.O.Q.*

1920
Ozenfant, *Composition*

L'Esprit nouveau launched by Le Corbusier and Ozenfant (–
    1925)

1921
Léger, *Le Grand Déjeuner*
Matisse, *L'Odalisque à la culotte rouge*
Picasso, *Trois Femmes à la fontaine*

1922
Picabia, *Nuit espagnole*
Valadon, *Nu au bord du lit*

1923
Gris, *Arlequin assis*
Le Corbusier, *Vers une architecture*
Perret, Church of Notre Dame, Le Raincy

1924
Picasso, *Mandoline et guitare*
Freysinnet, airship hangers, Orly

1925
Dufy, *Fête nautique au Havre*
Rouault, *L'Apprenti ouvrier (autoportrait)*
Soutine, *Le Boeuf écorché*

1928
Chagall, *Les Mariés de la Tour Eiffel*

1930
Giacometti, *La Boule suspendue*

1931
Le Corbusier, Villa Savoie, Poissy
Masson, *L'Enlèvement*

1932
Giacometti, *Les Cages*
Picasso, *Jeune Fille devant une glace*

1933
Bonnard, *Nu devant la glace*
Braque, *Nature morte à la mandoline*
Matisse, *La Danse*

1935
Le Corbusier, *La Ville radieuse*
Picasso, *Minotauromachie*

1936
Braque, *L'Oiseau et son nid*

1937
Picasso, *Guernica*

1938
Chagall, La Crucifixion blanche

1939
Masson, *La Terre*
Picasso, *Pêche de nuit à Antibes*

1940
Maillol, *Portrait de Dina*

1942
Balthus, *Le Salon*
Le Corbusier, *La maison des hommes*
Tanguy, *Divisibilité infinie*

1943
Fautrier, *Otages*

1945
Léger, *Acrobates et musiciens*
Richier, *L'Escrimeuse avec casque*

1946
Picasso, *La Joie de vivre*

1947
Dubuffet, *Dhôtel nuancé d'abricot*

1948
Matisse, *Saint Dominique*

1949
Giacometti, *Homme traversant une place*
Richier, *L'Ogre*

1950
Dubuffet, *Corps de dames*
Léger, *Les Constructeurs*
Picasso, *La Chèvre*

1951
Picasso, *Massacre en Corée*

1952
Le Corbusier, Unité d'Habitation, Marseille
Matisse, *La Tristesse du roi*
Staël, *Les Grands footballeurs*

1953
Richier, *Tauromachie*

1954
Balthus, *Le Passage du Commerce-Saint-André*
Dubuffet, *Vache la belle allègre*
Staël, *Les Martigues*

1955
Le Corbusier, Notre Dame du Haut, Ronchamp
Picasso, *Les Femmes d'Alger*

1956
Souleges, *Peinture, 14 avril 1956*

1957
Mathieu, *Cérémonies commémoratives de la deuxième
    condemnation de Siger de Brabant*
Vasarely, *Vega*

1958
Klein, *Le Vide* (exhibition)

Chronology

1959
Vasarely, *Album III*

1960
Giacometti, *Grand Femme à sa toilette*
Klein, *Anthropométries* (exhibition)

1962
Klein, *Feu couleur FC1*

1963
Saint-Phalle, *Hon*

1964
Masson, *Thaumaturges malveillants menaçant le peuple des hauteurs*

1965
Giacometti, *Caroline*

1966
César, *La Victoire de Villetaneuse*

1967
Dubuffet, *L'Hourloupe*
Vasarely, *Constellations*

1973
Dubuffet, *Don Coucoubazar*

1977
Piano and Rogers, Centre Pompidou, Paris

1980
César, *Compression murale, vélo*

1983
Saint-Phalle and Tinguely, fountain, Centre Pompidou

1984
César, *Hommage à Eiffel*

1986
Musée d'Orsay completed

1990
Von Spreckelsen, La Grande Arche, Paris

Film Timeline

1902
Méliès, *Le Voyage dans la lune*

1915–16
Feuillade, *Les Vampires*

1919
Gance, *J'accuse*

1922
Gance, *La Roue*

1923
Dulac, *La Souriante Madame Beudet*

1925
Duvivier, *Poil de carotte*

1927
Clair, *Un Chapeau de paille d'Italie*
Gance, *Napoléon*

1929
First talking movies

1930
Clair, *Sous les toits de Paris*
Vigo, *À Propos de Nice*

1933
Vigo, *Zéro de conduite*

1934
Pagnol, *Merlusse*
Vigo, *L'Atalante*

1936
Pagnol, *César*
Renoir, *Le Crime de Monsieur Lange*

1937
Duvivier, *Pépè le Moko*
Renoire, *La Grande Illusion*

1938
Carné, *Quai des Brumes*
Pagnol, *La Femme du boulanger*

1939
Duvivier, *La Fin du jour*
Renoir, *La Règle du jeu*

1942
Carné, *Les Visiteurs do soir*

1943
Clouzot, Le Corbeau

1945
Cocteau, *La Belle et la bête*
Carné, *Les Enfants du Paradis*
Pagnol, *Naïs*

1946
First Cannes film festival

1950
Cocteau, *Orphée*

1951
Cahiers du cinema founded

1952
Clair, *Les Belles-de-nuit*
Pagnol, *Manon des sources*

1953
Tati, *Les Vacances de Monsieur Hulot*

1956
Resnais, *Nuit et Brouillard*
Vadim, *Et Dieu créa la femme*

1958
Chabrol, *Le Beau Serge*
Malle, *Les Amants*
Tati, *Mon oncle*

1959
Godard, *À bout de souffle*
Renoir, *Le Déjeuner sur l'Herbe*
Resnais (Duras), *Hiroshima, mon Amour*
Truffaut, *Les Quatre Cents Coups*

1960
Chabrol, *Les Bonnes Femmes*
Malle (Queneau), *Zazie dans le Métro*

1961
Resnais (Robbe Grillet), *L'Année dernière à Marienbad*
Truffaut, *Jules et Jim*

1962
Godard, *Vivre sa Vie*
Robbe-Grillet, *L'Immortelle*
Truffaut, *Jules et Jim*
Varda, *Cléo de 5 à 7*

1963
Chabrol, *Landru*
Resnais, *Muriel, ou le Temps d'un Retour*

1964
Godard, *Une femme mariée*

1965
Godard, *Alphaville*

1966
Robbe-Grillet, *Trans-Europ-Express*

1968
Godard, *Weekend*
Chabrol, *Les Biches*

1969
Godard (Cohn-Bendit), *Vent d'est*

1971
Chabrol, *Le Boucher*
Ophuls, *Le Chagrin et la pitié*
Tati, *Traffic*

1973
Eustache, *La Maman et la putin*
Malle, *Lacombe Lucien*

1975
Truffaut, *L'Histoire d'Adèle H*

1976
Cassenti, *L'Affiche rouge*
Ferreri, *La Dernière Femme*

1977
Metz, *Le Signifiant imaginaire*
Varda, *L'une chante, l'autre pas*

1978
Truffaut, *La chamber verte*

1983
Robbe-Grillet, *Belle Captive*

1985
Charef, *Le Thé au harem d'Archimède*
Lanzmann, *Shoah*
Varda, *Sans toit ni loi*

1986
Resnais, *Mélo*
Beineix, *37°2 la matin*
Berri (Pagnol), *Jean de Florette*

1987
Malle, *Au Revoir les Enfants*
Varda, *Jane B. par Angès V.*

1989
Nuytten, *Camille Claudel*
Tavernier, *La vie et rien d'autre*

1991
Carax, *Les Amants du Pont-Neuf*

1992
Collard, *Les nuits fauves*

1993
Godard, *Hélas Pour Moi!*

1994
Chabrol, *L'Enfer*
Robbe-Grillet, *Un Bruit Qui Rend Fou*

1997
Besson, *Le Cinquième Élement*

1999
Carax, *Pola X*

Literature Timeline

1895
Valéry, *Le Soirée avec Monsieur Teste*

1896
Jarry, *Ubu Roi*

1897
Barrès, *Les Déracinés*
Gide, *Les Nourritures terrestres*

1902
Gide, *L'Immortaliste*

1904
Rolland, first volume of *Jean-Christophe* (–1912)

1905
Claudel, *Le Partage de midi*

1908
France, *L'Île des pingouins*

1909
Gide, *La Porte étroite*

La Nouvelle Revue Française (NRF) launched

1910
Claudel, *Cinq grandes odes*
Péguy, *Le Mystère de la charité de Jeanne d'Arc*

1911
Colette, *La Vagabonde*

Chronology

1912
France, *Les Dieux ont soif*

1913
Alain-Fournier, *Le Grand Meaulnes*
Apollinaire, *Alcools*
Cendrars, *La Prose du Transsibérien et de la petite Jehanne de France*
Proust, first volume of *À la recherche du temps perdu* (– 1927)

Vieux-Colombier theater set up by Copeau

1914
Gide, *Les Caves du Vatican*

1915
Rolland awarded Nobel Prize

1916
Apollinaire, *Le Poète assassiné*
Barbusse, *Le Feu*

1917
Duhamel, *Vie des martyrs*
Jacob, *Le Cornet à dés*
Valéry, *La Jeune Parque*

1918
Apollinaire, *Calligrammes*

1919
Reverdy, *La Guitare endormie*

1920
Colette, *Chéri*
Duhamel, first volume of *Vie et aventures de Salavin* (–1932)
Valéry, *Le Cimetière marin*

Théâtre National Populaire (TNP) created

1921
Anatole France awarded Novel

1922
Martin du Gard, first volume of *Les Thibault* (–1940)
Rolland, first volume of *L'Ame enchantée* (–1933)
Valéry, *Charmes*

1923
Radiguet, *Le Diable au corps*

1924
Breton, *Manifeste du surréalisme*
Saint-John Perse, *Anabase*

1926
Aragon, *Le Paysan de Paris*
Bernanos, *Sous le soleil de Satan*
Cendrars, *Moravagine*
Cocteau, *Orphée*
Éluard, *Capitale de la douleur*

1927
Green, *Adrienne Mesurat*
Mauriac, *Thérèse Desqueyroux*
Proust, last volume of *À la recherche du temps perdu* (1913–)

Bergson awarded Nobel Prize

1926
Gide, *Si le grain ne meurt*

1928
Bataille, *Histoire de l'oeil*
Breton, *Nadja*
Malraux, *Les Conquérants*

1929
Cocteau, *Les Enfants terribles*
Giraudoux, *Amphitryon 38*
Saint-Exupéry, *Courier Sud*

1930
Claudel, *Le Soulier de satin*
Desnos, *Corps et biens*
Éluard, Breton, and Char, *Ralentir travaux*

1931
Saint-Exupéry, *Vol de nuit*
Simenon, *Pietr-le-Letton* (first Maigret novel)

1932
Céline, *Voyage au bout de la nuit*
Mauriac, *Le Noeud de Vipères*
Romains, first volume of *Les Hommes de bonne volonté* (–1946).

Légitime Défense published in Paris

1933
Duhamel, first volume of *Chronique des Pasquier* (–1944)
Malraux, *La Condition humaine*

1934
Aragon, *Les Cloches de Bâle*
Char, *Le Marteau sans maître*
Drieu la Rochelle, *Comédie de Charleroi*

1935
Giraudoux, *La Guerre de Troie n'aura pas lieu*

L'Étudiant noir launched in Paris

1936
Bernanos, *Journal d'un curé de campagne*
Céline, *Mort à crédit*
Giono, *Les vrais richesses*
Montherlant, first volume of *Les jeunes filles* (–1939)

1937
Anouilh, *Le Voyageur sans baggage*
Jouve, *Matière celeste*
Martin du Gard awarded Nobel Prize

1938
Artaud, *Le Théâtre et son double*
Nizan, *La Conspiration*
Sartre, *La Nausée*

1939
Césaire, *Cahier d'un retour au pays natal*
Leiris, *L'Âge d'homme*
Sarraute, *Tropismes* (revised 1957)
Yourcenar, *Le Coup de grâce*

1941
Aragon, *Le Crève-coeur*

1942
Anouilh, *Antigone*
Camus, *L'Étranger*
Ponge, *Le Parti pris des choses*
Saint-John Perse, *Exile*
Vercors, *Le Silence de la mer*

1943
Bernanos, *Monsieur Ouine*
Saint-Exupéry, *Le Petit Prince*
Sartre, *Les Mouches*

1944
Camus, *Caligula*
Cassou, *33 Sonnets composés au secret*
Genet, *Notre-Dame-des-fleurs*
Sartre, *Huis Clos*

1945
Colette, *Gigi*
Guillevic, *Terraqué*
Sartre, *L'Age de raison*

1946
Char, *Feuillets d'Hypnos*
Genet, *Miracle de la Rose*
Gide, *Thésée*
Prévert, *Paroles*

1947
Camus, *La Peste*
Montherlant, *Le Maître de Santiago*
Sartre, *Les Jeux sont faits*
Vian, *L'Écume des jours*
Avignon festival founded
Diop launches *Présence africaine* in Paris
Gide awarded Nobel Prize

1948
Simenon, *Pedigree*

La Nouvelle Critique launched

1949
Queneau, *Exercices de style*
Sartre, *La Mort dans l'âme*
Senghor, *Anthologie de la nouvelle poésie nègre et malgache de langue française*
1950
Duras, *Un barrage contre le Pacifique*
Ionesco, *La Cantatrice chauve*
Michaux, *Passages*

1951
Beckett, *Malone meurt*
Sartre, *Le Diable et le bon dieu*
Yourcenar, *Mémoires d'Hadrien*

1952
Mauriac awarded Nobel Prize

1953
Anouilh, *L'Alouette*

Beckett, *En attendant Godot*
Bonnefoy, *De mouvement et de l'immobilité de Douve*
Laye, *L'Enfant noir*

1954
Beauvoir, *Les Mandarins*
Montherlant, *Port-Royal*
Sagan, *Bonjour tristesse*

1955
Adamov, *Le Ping-Pong*
Robbe-Grillet, *Le Voyeur*
Vailland, *325 000 francs*

1956
Butor, *L'Emploi du Temps*
Genet, *Le Balcon*
Senghor, *Éthiopiques*

1957
Antelme, *L'Espèce humaine*
Camus, *La Chute*
Robbe-Grillet, *La Jalousie*

Camus awarded Nobel Prize

1958
Beauvoir, *Memoires d'une jeune fille rangée*
Duras, *Moderato cantabile*
Jaccottet, *L'Ignorant*

1959
Queneau, *Zazie dans le métro*
Sarraute, *Le Planétarium*
Sartre, *Les Séquestrés d'Altona*

1960
Simon, *La Route de Flandres*

OULIPO (Ouvroir de Littérature Potentielle) founded

1961
Guillevic, *Carnac*
Rochefort, *Les Petits Enfants du siècle*

1963
Césaire, *La tragédie du roi Christophe*
Le Clézio, *Le Procès-verbal*

1964
Leduc, *La Bâtarde*
Sartre, *Les Mots*
Wittig, *L'Opoponax*
Sartre refuses the Nobel Prize
Théâtre du Soleil created by Mnouchkine

1965
Bonnefoy, *Pierre écrite*
Perec, *Les Choses*

1966
Rochefort, *Une Rose pour Morrison*

1967
Ponge, *Le Savon*
Tournier, *Vendredi ou les limbes du Pacifique*
Yacine, *Les Ancêtres redoublent de férocité*

Chronology

1968
Yourcenar, *L'Oeuvre au noir*

1969
Perec, *La Disparition*
Wittig, *Les Guérillères*

1970
Robbe-Grillet, *Projet pour une revolution à New York*
Tournier, *Le Roi des aulnes*

1971
Tournier, *Vendredi ou la vie sauvage*

1972
Beauvoir, *Tout compte fait*

1973
Duras, *India Song*

1975
Bonnefoy, *Dans le leurre du seuil*
Cardinal, *Les Mots pour le dire*
Perec, *W: ou le souvenir d'enfance*

1976
Robbe-Grillet, *Topologie d'une cite fantôme*

1977
Tournier, *Le Vent Paraclet*

1978
Jabès, *Le Soupçon Le Désert*
Perec, *La Vie mode d'emploi*

1980
Jabès, *L'Ineffaçable L'Inaperçu*
Navarre, *Le Jardin d'acclimatation*

Yourcenar first woman elected to Académie Française

1981
Ernaux, *La Place*

1983
Sollers, *Femmes*

1984
Duras, *L'Amant*

1985
Tournier, *La Goutte d'or*
Wittig, *Virgile, non*

Simon awarded Nobel

1987
Baroche, *L'Hiver de beauté*

1988
Char, *Éloge d'une soupçonnée*
Ernaux, *Une femme*
Rochefort, *La Porte de fond*

1990
Guibert, *A l'ami qui ne m'a pas sauvé la vie*
Kourouma, *Monnè, outrages et défis*
Kristeva, *Les Samouraïs*

1991
Guibert, *Mon valet et moi*

1992
Guibert, *Cytomégalovirus: journal d'hospitalisation*

1994
Kofman, *Rue Ordener, Rue Labat*
Robbe-Grillet, *Les derniers jours de corinthe*
Semprun, *L'Écriture ou la vie*

Music Timeline

1890
Satie, *Gnossiennes*

1894
Debussy, *Prélude à l'après-midi d'un faune*

1899
Ravel, *Pavane pour une infante défunte*

1900
Charpentier, *Louise*

1902
Debussy (Maeterlinck), *Pelléas et Mélisande*
D'Indy, Symphony No 2

1903
Debussy, *Estampes*
Satie, *Trois Morceaux en forme de poire*

1904
L'île joyeuse

1905
Debussy, *La Mer*

1907
Debussy, *Images*
Dukas, *Ariane et Barbe-bleue*
Fauré, *Vocalise*

1908
Ravel, *Gaspard de la nuit*

1910
Fauré, *Le Chanson d'Eve*

1911
Ravel, *Valses nobles et sentimentales*

1912
Ravel, *Daphnis et Chloé*
Roussel, *Le Festin de l'araignée*

1913
Debussy, *Jeux*

1915
Debussy, Sonata for cello and piano

1917
Cocteau (Diaghilev, Satie, Picasso) *Parade*
Fauré, Violin sonata No 2
Ravel, *Le Tombeau de Couperin*

1918
Varèse, *Amériques*

1919
Milhaud (Cocteau), *Le Boeuf sur le toit*
Poulenc (Apollinaire), *Le bestiaire*
Satie, *Socrate*

1920
Honegger, *Pastorale d'été*
Milhaud, *Saudades do Brazil*

1921
Fauré, *L'Horizon chimérique*
Roussel, *Pour une fête de printemps*

1923
Cantaloube, *Chants d'Auvergne* (first set)
Honegger, *Pacific 231*
Milhaud (Cendrars), *La création du monde*

1924
Poulenc, *Les biches*

1925
Auric, *Les Matelots*
Ravel (Colette), *L'Enfant et les sortilège*

1926
Milhaud, *Le Carnival d'Aix*
Mistinguett, *Ça c'est Paris*

1928
Honegger, *Rugby*
Ravel, *Boléro*

1929
Poulenc, *Aubade*

1930
Ibert, *Divertissement*

1931
Ravel, Piano concerto in D major

1934
Milhaud, *Concertino de printemps*
Reinhardt and Grappelli form the Quintette de Hot Club de
    France (–1939)

1936
Honegger, *Nocturne*

1937
Dupré, *Poèmes héroïque*
Milhaud, *Suite provençale*

1938
Messiaen, *Nativité du Seigneur*

1940
Françaix, *L'apostrophe*

1941
Messiaen, *Quatuor pour la fin des temps*

1942
Langlais, Organ symphony

1944
Honegger, *Chant de libéeration*
Jolivet, *Chant de Linos*
Messiaen, *Technique de mon langage musical*

1945
Trenet, *La Mer*
Poulenc (Éluard), *Figure humaine*

1946
Piaf, *La vie en rose*

1947
Duruflé, Requiem
Poulenc (Apollinaire), *Les Mamelles de Tirésias*

1948
Boulez (Char), *Le Marteau sans maitre*
Messiaen, *Turangalîla-Symphonie*

1950
Gréco, *Je hais les dimanches*
Tailleferre, *Il était un petit navire*

1952
Barraqué, Sonata
Milhaud, *David*

1955
Aznavour, *Sur ma vie*

1956
Messiaen, *Catalogue d'Oiseaux* (–1958)
Poulenc (Bernanos), *Les dialogues des Carmélites*

1957
Brel, *Quand on n'a que l'amour*

1958
Françaix, *Divertimento*

1960
Barraqué, *Au delà du hazard*
Messiaen, *Chronocromie*
Piaf, *Non, je ne regrette rien*

1962
Boulez, *Pli selon pli*
Brel, *Ne me quitte pas*

1963
Loussier, *Play Bach*

1965
Boulez, *Éclat*

1966
Barraud, *Symphonie concertante*

1968
Barraqué, Concerto for clarinet, vibraphone and six trios

1970
Dutilleux, *Tout un monde lointain*

1972
Boulez, *Explosante-Fixe*

1974
Boulez, *Rituel in memoriam Bruno Maderna*
Messiaen, *Des Canyons aux étoiles*

1976
Françaix, *Ouverture anacréontique*
Gainsbourg, *L'Homme à Tête de Chou*
Jarre, *Oxygène*

1981
Boulez, *Répons*

Radio Beur in Paris popularizes *raï*

1985
Dutilleux, *L'arbre des songes*

1986
Françaix, *Danses exotiques*

1989
Dutilleux, *Mystère de l'instant*

1991
Moumen, *Rih el Gharbi (Le vent d'ouest)*

Political and Social Life Timeline

1879–1940 Third Republic

1893
Dreyfus convicted of treason

1898
Zola, *J'accuse*

1899
Action Française movement launched

1900
Exposition universelle in Paris

Péguy launches *Cahiers de la Quinzaine* (–1914)

1901
Parti républicain radical et radical-socialiste founded

1904
Jaurès launches *L'Humanité*

1905
Legal separation of Church and state
Socialist part formed (*Section Française de l'Internationale Ouvrière*)

1906
Dreyfus rehabilitated
Marie Curie becomes first woman professor at the Sorbonne

1908
L'Action Française launched (–1944)

1909
Blériot flies across Channel

1911
Agadir incident (Morocco)

1912
Morocco becomes French protectorate

1913
President: Poincaré (–1920)

1914
July Jaurès assassinated
August World War I (–1918)

1916
Battle of Verdun (nearly 350,000 French casualties)

1917
Clemenceau becomes Prime Minister (–1920)

1918
November End of World War I

1919
Bloc national in power (–1924)

1920
Jeanne d'Arc canonized
French Communist party (PCF) established

1921
Rif uprising in North Africa
France occupies Rhineland

1922
Radio-Paris begins to broadcast

1923
France occupies Ruhr

1924
Cartel des Gauches in power (–1928)

1925
Rif War in North Africa (–1926)
Thérèse of Lisieux canonized

1928
Croix-de-Feu founded

1929
Work begins on Maginot Line

1931
Exposition coloniale

1932
First television broadcasts (in Paris)

1934
Stavisky affair
Front populaire formed
Political riots in Paris

1936
Front populaire in power under Blum (–1937)
Parti populaire français formed

1938
Daladier becomes Prime Minister (–1940)

1939
September World War II (–1945) (*les années noires*)
3 September France declares war
September 1939-May 1940 (*drôle de guerre*)

1940
10 May German offensive begins
14 June German troops enter Paris
1 July Vichy government set up under Marshal Pétain (–1944)
October: Anti-Jewish legislation (*le statut des juifs*) introduced

1941
Légion des volontaires français (LVF) formed
Law allowing confiscation of Jewish property

Combat launched (–1974)

1942
July 13,000 French Jews held in the Vél(odrome) d'Hiv(er) stadium before being sent to concentration camps
November German forces occupy south of France

1943
Free French headquarters set up in Algiers
Melice formed in Vichy
Compulsory call-up of men and women to work in Germany

1944
6 June Allies land in Normandy
25 August Paris liberated

1944 Provisional government under De Gaulle (–1946)

Women granted suffrage
Le Monde launched

1945
May End of World War II (in Europe)
August Beginning of war of independence in Indo-China (–1954)
October Laval executed

1946
De Gaulle resigns
French Guiana, Guadeloupe, Martinique, and Réunion become *départements*

1946–1958 Fourth Republic

1947
France accepts Marshall Aid
Rassemblement du peuple français (RPF) movement launched by De Gaulle

1949
France a founding member of NATO

1950
Regular television broadcasts in Paris area
Club Méd(iterranée) created

1953
Poujadist movement launched

1954
May Dien Bien Phu is lost to the Vietminh
July War of independence in Indo-China ends
November Beginning of Algerian war of independence (–1962)

1956
Morocco and Tunisia gain independence
Suez crisis

1957
Treaty of Rome lays foundation of European Economic Community
Valéry Giscard d'Estaing, *Lieutenent en Algérie*

1958
De Gaulle recalled over Algerian crisis
President: Charles de Gaulle (–1969)

1958– Fifth Republic

1959
Malraux appointed minister of culture (–1969)

1960
Manifeste des 121 condemns French campaign in Algeria
Parti socialiste unifié (PSU) formed
Sub-Saharan African colonies gain independence
France explodes atomic bomb

1961
April Failed *putsch* by army officers
OAS terror

1962
July Algeria gains independence

1966
France withdraws from NATO

1969
President: Georges Pompidou (–1974)

1970
Mouvement de liberation des femmes (MLF) created

1971
Manifeste des 343 calls for legalization of abortion

1972
Front National formed by Le Pen

1974
President: Valéry Giscard d'Estaing (–1981)
Age of majority reduced to 18

1975
Abortion legalized

1978
Success for the Right in general election

1981
President: François Mitterrand (–1995)
Death penalty abolished

1984
Le Pen elected to the European Parliament

1986
Le Pen elected to National Assembly

Chronology

1987
Klaus Barbie on trial in Lyon for 'crimes against humanity'

1988
As candidate for the presidency, Le Pen wins 14.4 per cent of the vote

1991
Édith Cresson becomes first woman Prime Minister

1992
Euro-Disney opens

1993
European Union established
Success for the Right in general election

1994
Le Pen reelected to European Parliament
Touvier put on trial for 'crimes against humanity'
Bill passed to protect French from influx of English expressions

1995
President: Jacques Chirac (–)

1997
Sans-papiers granted amnesty

2000
Corsica granted autonomy

2002
Franc replaced by Euro

ALAIN (ÉMILE-AUGUSTE CHARTIER)
Philosopher

Alain, an unconventional philosopher in both style and substance, chose his pseudonym in homage to the fifteenth-century Norman poet Alain Chartier. Beyond a common surname, the identification is doubly appropriate: Alain was himself a native of Normandy and a man of letters. For many years over three decades, he contributed short daily essays to *La Dépêche de Rouen* (Rouen Dispatch) under the general heading, "*Propos d'un Normand*" (1952–1960, Remarks of a Norman). The brevity and humane outlook of the propos established Alain's literary philosophical lineage: Montaigne, Pascal, and perhaps the first-person *Méditations* of Descartes. Five volumes of propos were published between 1908 and 1928, then collected and reprinted after Alain's death under the same title as his newspaper column.

Many of Alain's propos offer practical advice, often in the form of moral or psychological maxims and aphorisms; because he tends to identify happiness with self-mastery and freedom from pain, these propos usually involve matters of personal distress, not one's obligations to others. Stoicism is a prominent influence: "It is rain and storm, it is not part of me" (*Propos sur le bonheur*, revised 1928; *Alain on Happiness*, 1973). However, more broadly observed propos, together with longer essays and extended works, constitute a reflective record animated by a central philosophy. Like many of his contemporaries (notably Henri Bergson), Alain defends a philosophy of becoming, as opposed to "closed systems," claiming certainty on the basis of logical demonstration or protracted argument. The real is said to be always in process, as sensed by way of the richness and uncertainty of lived experience. Many propos reinforce this point stylistically: written as stories or conversations, they open up discourse, fashioning an outcome not logically predetermined.

Truth for Alain is not a question of the mind's collaboration with nature: Science holds no patent where truth is concerned. In *Entretiens au bord de la mer* (1931, Conversations by the Seashore), his wise old man finds it "more than strange" that anyone should expect the world to hold still for the observer, "to order, by the succession of objects, the succession of our thoughts." One philosopher's river is another's ocean; like Heraclitus, Alain likens time and experience to the constant motion of a body of water. There is no such thing as one wave "alongside of another." The sea, "refus[ing] all of our ideas," teaches us that "[all] forms are false." Thus, reason must fail in its attempts to ride the waves—to divide the indivisible, set limits to the unbounded. However, what Alain's oceanic metaphor excludes from consideration is scientific reason's historical success in mapping nature's regularity. (Oceanographers confidently classify and explain waves, currents, and tides.) For Alain, truth is "momentary," to be realized only through observation and insight in a lifelong process of dispelling errors and illusions through doubt. With such comments, he sustains his Cartesian skepticism, as in a propos of 1924: "To think is to say no"; doubt is "attached like a shadow to all of our thoughts."

In Alain's view, Plato's Allegory of the Cave is entirely compatible with a skeptical notion of truth. Although he shares Plato's goal of surpassing the blind opinion of cave dwellers, what Alain particularly admires about the allegory is its depth of meaning, always open to new interpretations. The Cave thereby serves his dominant intention—portraying knowledge as continual inquiry within the perceived world—in contrast to its traditional interpretation as a world separated from the realm of timeless, always-true Forms, or Ideas. Alain does, however, embrace Plato's image of the Good as a sun "at the horizon of intelligible things" that "makes all ideas knowable" (*Histoire de mes pensées* [1936, The Story of My Thoughts]).

One might then suppose that the Good's illumination serves to unify the three areas of spiritual expression with which Alain is largely concerned—morality, art, and religion. On the contrary, if there is one theme that unites his commentaries, it is not at all spiritual but bodily. Our sense of the real "has nothing to do with physical change" but relates directly to the "movement of growth," the child's sense of a changing world as his or her remembered past is acted out in the present and imaginatively projected toward the future. From *Les Dieux* (1934; *The Gods*, 1974): "[T]he real is what is expected, what is obtained and discovered . . . as being within our own power and always responsive to our own action." "There is a profound relationship between our human destiny and the functions of our body" (*Propos sur le bonheur*). This is to voice an idealist position—all knowledge as ultimately self-knowledge—in terms that anticipate Merleau-Ponty's phenomenology of the body. However, the philosophy is basically practical: "In moments of anxiety, do not try to reason, for your reasoning will only turn against you. Instead try . . . arm-raising exercises. . . . Thus the moralist sends You to a gymnast" (*Propos sur le bonheur*).

Having throughout his career said no to formal reason, Alain does specify a faculty to which to say yes—the imagination. Imagination chooses its own objects, creating its own reality in the form of literature, music, theater, and the visual arts. Again, the context is physiological: In his example, a person is shocked and frightened by having seen two cars that narrowly miss crashing. The effect of the imagined crash—an image drawn by "the movement of blood and muscle"—is as real as if the accident had actually occurred. This is to regard emotionally charged imagery as the somatic counterpart of a belief in something that did not occur that can then be creatively channeled. Still, Alain seems ambivalent: Is imagination bad (residence of false beliefs) or good (creative antithesis to reason)? Both, it seems; in the latter case, what makes the difference is said to be judgment, with which imagination enters into a corrective dialogue. Eloquent but disordered, "always wandering and sad," imagination needs to be objectified—transformed into "finished and durable works of art" (*Système des beaux-arts* [1926; System of the Fine Arts]).

Alain's approach to religion at first seems to parallel his analysis of moral and artistic activity: Religious doctrine, prayer, and ritual are forms that respond to human needs equally, likewise carrying no implication of transcendence. Desire and fear are ordered and calmed through story-telling, ritual, spectacle, and such physical acts as raising one's arms or kneeling with head in hands. Where this interpretation departs from its aesthetic counterpart is that Alain does not regard religion as imaginatively creative—he does not validate an observant life through association with judgment or the will to seek happiness. Instead, religion integrates prayer, dance, and music as natural elements that always recall man to himself; and through commemoration of good men and their deeds—respect for the past—religion offers examples of intrinsic worth that the individual comes to accept "as a duty, to oneself." Clearly it is Alain the humanist who allies himself with religion as it shares with art and morality the aspiration toward a life of value and meaning; but with a skeptical touch: "Religion . . . is a story, which, like all stories, is full of meaning. And one doesn't ask if a story is true" (*Les Dieux*).

BERNARD ELEVITCH

See also **Maurice Merleau-Ponty**

Biography

Alain was born on March 3, 1868, in Mortagne-au-Perche, Normandy. He studied with Alençon at the Lycée de Vannes and went on to attend the Ecole Normale Supérieure. On graduation, he took a post as an assistant professor of philosophy at the Lycée Corneille of Rouen. He later moved to the College Henri IV, in Paris.

Between 1908 and 1928, five volumes of his *propos* were published. In 1926, he published *Système des beaux-arts*. Several works followed, including *Propos sur le bonheur* (revised 1928) and *Histoire de mes pensées* (1936). Alain died June 2, 1951, in his house in Vésinet.

Selected Writing

Cent-un propos d'Alain, 5 vols, 1908–1920 (reprint: *Propos d'un Normand*, 1952–1960)
Système des beaux-arts, 1920
Mars, ou la guerre jugée, 1921; as *Mars, or the Truth About War*, translated by Dorothy Mudie and Elizabeth *Hill*, 1930
Propos sur l'esthétique, 1923

Propos sur le christianisme, 1924
Propos sur le bonheur, 1925, revised 1928; as *Alain on Happiness*, translated by Robert D. and Jane E. Cottrell, 1973
Sentiments, passions, et signes, 1926
Esquisses de l'homme, 1927
Les Idées et les âges, 2 vols, 1927
Entretiens au bord de la mer, 1930
Idées, 1932
Les Dieux, 1934; as *The Gods*, translated by Richard Pevear, 1974
Histoire de mes pensées, 1936
Minerve, ou de la sagesse, 1939
Préliminaires a l'esthétique, 1939
Éléments de philosophie, 1941
Morceaux choisis, 1960
Propos sur des philosophes, 1961
Esquisses, 2 vols, 1963–1964
Collected Éditions (Gallimard, Bibliothèque de la Pléiade)
Propos, 1956
Les Arts et les dieux, 1958
Les Passions et la sagesse, 1960

Further Reading

Bourgne, Robert, ed., *Alain, lecteur des philosophes*, Paris: Bordas, 1987
Foulquie, Paul, *Alain*, Paris: l'Ecole, 1952
Halda, Bernard, *Alain*, Paris: Éditions Universitaires, 1950
Maurois, Andre, *Alain*, Paris: Domat, 1950
Pascal, Georges, *Pour connaître la pensée d'Alain*, Paris: Bordas, 1946
Pascal, Georges, *L'Idée de philosophie chez Alain*, Paris: Bordas, 1970
Reboul, Olivier, *L'Homme et ses passions d'après Alain*, 2 vols, Paris: Presses Universitaires de France, 1968
Semin, Andre, *Alain: un sage dans le cité*, Paris: Laffont, 1985

ALTHUSSER, LOUIS
Philosopher, Political Theorist

The name of Louis Althusser has become a landmark in twentieth-century French thought, being associated predominantly with the structuralist school of Marxism. In Anglophone circles, this school even came to be known under his own name and was responsible for stimulating important discussions around the relative autonomy of the superstructures, the nonsubjective nature of the historical process, the validity of the concept of ideology and its permanence, the scientific nature of Marxism, and the mutual overlapping of politics and philosophy. There can be no dispute that Althusser's writings have had theoretical effects and consequences that he could not have anticipated, effects resonating from Western Europe to Latin America, through the disciplines of sociology and political and social theory, to gender and film studies, as well as to cultural and literary studies and, more obviously, Marxist economics and radical philosophy.

As his foreword to *For Marx* reminds us, many of Althusser's essays were shaped by the ideological and political conjuncture that saw the death of Stalin, the denunciation of the cult of personality, and the concomitant rise of a liberal-humanist Marxism galvanized to transcend Stalinist dogmatism with an ideology of the liberation of authentic man. Althusser condemned and fought hard against this ideological fusion of Marxism and humanism, claiming that the revolutionary character of Marx's philosophy was both hindered and threatened by such intraideological currents. It was this tension between science and ideology that was to dominate many of his writings, producing from his readers cries of theoreticism and the denial of concrete politics, as well as vindications of his sophisticated account of the complex reality of political societies.

Whatever place we might assign the historical specificity of Althusser's writings, it is clear that any assessment of his significance at the start of the twenty-first century will be quite different from one written in the 1970s or 1980s and guided by the so-called demise of Althusserianism (see Benton, 1984). This is not, as one may reasonably digress, because the political climate has rendered Marxism a different kind of ideological animal than it was several decades ago, and neither is it because of the tragedy of his final years, recorded in his autobiography (1993; Elliott, 1994). It is rather the result of the astonishing number of posthumous volumes of Althusser's writings that have now come to light. These afford a more nuanced, finely sketched picture of the sheer range and depth of his thought, which embraced among others the figures of Spinoza and Machiavelli as well as Marx, Freud, Lacan, and the French epistemological tradition. Althusser's structuralist approach to Marxism was so distinctive and powerful that we continue to feel its latent effects among so many poststructuralist thinkers who have continued to work both inside and outside a Marxist perspective (e.g. Balibar, Badiou, Foucault, and Rancière).

Against Humanism and Historicism

Althusser may share the title of "Western Marxist" with Korsch, Lukács, Gramsci, Sartre, and Merleau-Ponty, but it is one that fits him in name alone. In developing a structuralist method (albeit one attributable more to Spinoza than Lévi-Strauss, as we shall see below), Althusser endeavored to bring a new apparatus of thought to Marxism in the form of a science of history, freed from all evolutionary and historicist tendencies and autonomous in its object of analysis, its theory, and its method. Above all, this new science, which Althusser claims to recover in embryonic form in Marx's writings and build into an epistemological system himself, would be untainted by any of the ideological currents of Marxism, which continued, in his view, to compromise and weaken it. To this end, Althusser positioned himself against many of the Western Marxists noted above, claiming that there remained a residual Hegelianism in their readings of Marx. His project, he writes in *For Marx,* was "to draw a line of demarcation between Marxist theory and the forms of philosophical (and political) subjectivism which have compromised or threatened it" (1969, p. 12). Thus begins Althusser's diatribe against all forms of Hegelian Marxism; notably that of Lukacs with its attendant historicism and humanism as well as its residual idealism, but also against many other forms of humanism, particularly the Sartrean variety that ultimately remained tied to a conception of the subject as *cogito* (1969, p. 219–247; 1968, p. 119–144).

Although the recent publication of Althusser's early writings affords a more balanced consideration of Althusser's negotiation of Hegel, who was the subject of his 1947 Master's dissertation (see 1997, p. 36–169), by the 1960s his tendency was toward a largely negative reading of Hegel. Hegel's system is understood to correspond to an expressive totality in which the dialectical movements of the relations of the totality are inseparable from their own genesis as concepts. The totality is therefore circular: the Hegelian system is inseparable from its goal, which is given in the dialectical structure of its conditions of becoming. Transferred by Marxists to the realm of history, this Hegelian logic produced either teleological accounts of the subject's historical realization in the movement of history (Lukacs, Sartre) or mechanical, economic determinist accounts of the steady march of the productive forces toward their inevitable realization in communism (Kautsky and Luxemburg). The theoretical and political lesson to be drawn from this is a clear one. However much Marxist conceptions of totality try to counter Hegelian idealism by appealing to history, the component parts of this totality are "flattened out . . . into a variation of the Hegelian totality" (1968, p. 132). Furthermore, by collapsing the theoretical field of knowledge into the movement of real history, that is, by historicizing knowledge, Marxist forms of knowledge, like those associated with Hegelianism, are subjected to the ideological idiosyncrasies of the historical process.

It is against these ideological (and hence regressive and idealist) tendencies that Althusser pits his own symptomatic reading of Marx's *Capital,* analogous to the one performed by Jacques Lacan on Freud's writings. Such a reading attempts to recover the latent discursive structure underlying the text; it shifts the focus away from economism (the language of classical polit-

ical economy) and away from humanism and historicism (the language of Hegelianism), and isolates the new object of analysis inaugurated by Marx's "theoretical revolution": the mode of production. This invisible structure articulates all the elements of a social formation as a complex totality in which each element or instance (the legal, the ideological, the political) is understood as relatively autonomous, being determined only in the last instance by the (ever tardy) economic instance. Discussions as to whether a relation of reflection, determination, or homology characterizes the base–superstructure topography were to all intents and purposes displaced. As with structural linguistics, it was the difference between these various complex levels, rather than their underlying expressive unity, that takes on greater significance for Althusser. To emphasize the unevenness of structural relations and to analyze their historical complexity, Althusser used the Freudian concept of overdetermination, already repositioned in Lacan's structuralist reading of the psychoanalyst. Freud used this concept to refer to the multiplicity of dream-thoughts contained, by the censorship of psychic agency, within a single dream image.

Although Lacan reconfigured the concept in relation to language, Althusser repositions it in relation to the economy. Here it indicates that where a specific level may appear to determine the general form of the structure, it is itself "also determined in one and the same movement, . . . by the various levels and instances of the social formation it animates" (1969, p. 101). If, in every structural totality, there was always a "structure in dominance" that articulated the other levels, it was not determinant; this role was reserved for the economy even as it was once again overdetermined by the other levels. In this way, no simple Hegelian logic of contradiction can prevail; where effects are attributable to a single cause, overdetermination ensures the absence or deferral of any primary cause or uniform causality and renders each level mutually determining and determined, complex and decentered.

The antihumanism of this structuralist schema has far-reaching implications. No longer can the subject be considered as the origin or foundation of meaning or the author of history. Althusser displaces the subject from its function of determination; instead, a system of objective relations is understood to underpin and construct subjectivity. Thus, "considered as agents, human individuals are not 'free' and 'constitutive' subjects in the philosophical sense of these terms. They work in and through the determinations of the forms of historical existence of the social relations of production and reproduction" (1984, p. 134). With this antihumanist strategy, Althusser calls into question the metaphysical properties that tie the subject to empiricist and idealist conceptions of knowledge, as well as to individualist and voluntarist forms of politics. Each of these opposes an original subject (perceiving subject, subject of *praxis*) to an object (object of knowledge or social totality). Unsurprisingly, this claim tarnished Althusser's name in the French Communist Party and was greeted with condemnation by many Marxists (e.g., see Thompson, 1978).

Nevertheless, Althusser located such a preponderance of metaphysical elements in Marx's early, prescientific writings. Here, he argued, the influence of the German idealism of Feuerbach and Hegel, and their concepts of species–being, human essence, alienation, and consciousness, gave Marx's thought an anthropological, humanist content. It is not until 1845–1846, with the writing of *The German Ideology,* that the settling of accounts with German metaphysics takes place. Hence, the well-known formulation of the epistemological break identified by Althusser—itself more akin to a tension or tendency rather than a definitive break (1968; Balibar, 1993)—whereby Marx's writings became recognizably antihumanist and a new science, the continent of history, is opened up by him. No longer can history be viewed as the activity of subjects; history becomes a "process without a subject or goal," one which begins with the concrete determinants of the mode of production rather than with the ideological notion of the voluntary agent (1972, p. 161–186; 1984, p. 133–139).

Certainly, for postwar philosophical currents such as the phenomenological Marxism of Merleau-Ponty and the existential humanist Marxism of Sartre, the discourse of structuralism, with its antihistoricist and antihumanist arguments, proved distinctly unpalatable. For Althusser, the battle was clearly more than a war over concepts: It was about creating a scientific discourse for Marxism that could be insulated from the ideological residues of subjectivism and naive idealism. As a result, Marx's fledgling science of historical materialism would emerge more able to respond politically and analytically to the historical conjuncture of late capitalism, whereas the sturdy epistemological structure brought to it by Althusser would render Marxism autonomous of bourgeois socialist ideology and sufficient unto itself, its conditions of existence and its object of investigation now being wholly internal to its structure of knowledge. It is only when Marxism is able to distinguish its scientific basis from the ideology latent within it, to deal with the difference between them, that the consequences of this epistemological rupture with philosophy would be felt. For his critics, however, this rigorous attempt to isolate Marxism could only result in a dogmatic theoreticism, scientific idealism, and ahistoricism (Anderson, 1976).

Marxist Science in the Wake of Spinoza

Curiously, the theoretical novelty of Althusser's recasting of Marxist philosophy as a theory of theoretical practice is largely generated via non-Marxist sources. Although the theory of the discontinuity or break in Marx's *oeuvre* is provided by the epistemology of Bachelard and the imaginary structure of ideology furnished with recourse to Lacan's structuralist psychoanalysis, the antiempiricist theory of knowledge is constructed with close philosophical allegiance to the seventeenth-century Dutch rationalist philosopher Baruch Spinoza. If Althusser once noted his unusual affinity with the latter two thinkers, namely, their shared marginalization (all faced forms of excommunication as a result of their ideas), he also noted more pertinently that his alleged structuralism was to be attributed less to the Parisian intellectual fashion of the day and more to Spinoza's antihumanism (1976, p. 132). Similar to Althusser, Spinoza was critical of the authority imparted on the subject as the creator of knowledge (an authority that was, in its Cartesian form, guaranteed by religious faith). This led Spinoza toward a theory of knowledge that departed from a simple correspondence between the subject and the real and from an uncritical account of the role of representation (of both ideas and images) in the formulation of knowledge. Thus, according to Althusser, Spinoza constructed a theory that reflected on "the difference between the imaginary and the true" (1969, p. 17). He recognized, in other words, that the empiricist construction of the object gave rise to an imaginary or ideological formulation of knowledge. In *Reading Capital,* Althusser links empiricism with what he calls a "philosophy of vision," described there as "the logic of a conception of knowledge in which . . . the whole nature of its object is reduced to the mere condition of a given" (1969, p.19). The formation or structure of knowledge requires no separation or dislocation from the ideological impurities of the object because the object of knowledge is intrinsic to the real, empirical object. Empiricism invests in the kinds of dualisms that contravene its own efforts to isolate the kernel of objectivity (e.g., a conception of a divided subject split between mind and body, essence and appearance, the visible and the hidden). These dualisms, particularly the sovereign fundamental conflict between truth and fiction, are wholly internal to the structure of ideology, according to Althusser. Empiricism then is resolutely attached to the givenness of reality, and its critical distance from the concrete–real, for Althusser, the ideological, is henceforth denied.

For Althusser and Spinoza, knowledge of the "true" is not the result of a philosophy of reflection, whose mast is always empiricist; rather, it is derived *a priori,* according to conditions internal to the production of knowledge itself. Here the object of knowledge is entirely internal to thought and is to be distinguished from the empirical or real object of mundane reality. The derivation of scientific knowledge has three phases: generality I consists of the raw material or brute facts on which scientific theory labors. These facts are never pure and uncontaminated, but always carry conceptual residues from previous ideological interpretations (hence Marx's early negotiation of the ideological currents of Hegelianism). Science must maneuver a path between this dimension of the real, generality I, and generality III; namely, the theoretical field in which science produces and practices a distinct mode of knowledge. Sandwiched between these two regions, generality II is "an extremely complex and contradictory unity" that will always contain their ideological residues and their scientific possibilities. Generality II is the *problématique* of knowledge; it is the set of related concepts that must be worked on by science, and it will take markedly different forms depending on the degree of development of a knowledge at a specific point in its history. For an ideological practice to become a scientific one, then, the mode of framing the questions asked of knowledge must be transformed. It was precisely this reframing of the objects of analysis in *The German Ideology* (i.e., the creation of a new *problématique*) that, for Althusser, constitutes the immense theoretical revolution initiated by Marx that transforms Marxist philosophy into a science of history.

Althusser's epistemology has some difficult paths to negotiate in its journey away from the ideologies of humanism, historicism, and empiricism. It seems unclear whether the resources necessary to counter ideology have been developed adequately. Given that every science must emerge out of ideology, perhaps there can be no pure science but only a science of ideology (Macherey, quoted in 1969, p. 41). If science is the Other of ideology, then insofar as it tries to extricate itself from the clutches of the latter, it will be continually reinhabited and contaminated by it. In this way, the risk of the conceptual breakdown of science is implied from within, as its tautological structure will be riven with ideological residues. Thus, criticisms regarding Althusser's theoreticism and the alleged containment of science from the world of ideology (and, hence, its divorce from any other theoretical referent) must, to some degree, be misdirected fire, being anticipated already in the failed logic of his epistemology.

Ideology with no End

If Althusser's epistemological efforts were to banish all ideological elements from Marxism, his conclu-

sions in the realm of politics were diametrically opposed. Here he claimed ideology as an omnihistorical reality akin to the eternity of the Freudian unconscious, immutable in structure and form and secreted by all human societies (be they capitalist or communist) "as the very element and atmosphere indispensable to their historical respiration and life" (1968, p. 232). Ideology is at once a priori and timeless in that it is a necessary transhistorical structure without which there could be no society; at the same time, ideology is also endowed with a specificity that allows its historical variance and a necessary responsiveness to the needs of particular political and social formations. Any accusation that Althusser's structuralist analysis implied the displacement of the dimension of history *tout court* is an error of interpretation.

In keeping with his critique of empiricism and humanism, a formulation of ideology as an inversion or mystification of the real (as presented by the Marxist metaphor of the *camera obscura* in *The German Ideology*) must be rejected outright. Likewise, Althusser's critique of the subject precludes him from establishing an overly simplistic account of ideology as false consciousness, where the subject's experience of the world must become the source of knowledge necessary to transcend ideology. In his influential essay of 1972 "Ideology and Ideological State Apparatuses," Althusser's central focus is on precisely how ideology is able to reproduce the relations of production by establishing modes of identification for subjects (subject-positions) so that they may take up their allotted place in the social formation. The state, no longer viewed simply as the instrument or agent of the bourgeoisie against the proletariat, consists of ideological state apparatuses (church, school, family, political parties, communications, and so on) and repressive apparatuses (army, police) that secure the conditions of class domination by consent and force, respectively. This revision and elucidation of the operation of the state owes something to the reflection on the logic of consent and the role of the state in Western states presented by Gramsci in his *Prison Notebooks* (1971, part 2). It was also this aspect of Althusser's work that was to open up important discussions within feminism regarding the role of the family and the construction of gendered identity in the reproduction of capitalist relations of production (Barrett, 1988; Assiter, 1990).

How does ideology account for the constitution of the subject of ideology? Here Althusser's focus is the ideological mechanism through which thought, perception, and subjectivity are produced, or in other words, the representation of ideology within consciousness. Althusser understands the subjects' perceptions of their lived relations to be anchored resolutely to an imaginary relation. Thus, ideology "represents the imaginary relationship of individuals to their real conditions of existence" (1984, p. 36). This concept of the imaginary is invested with allusions to Spinoza and the psychoanalyst and philosopher Jacques Lacan. From Spinoza, Althusser takes the view of the imagination as a source of deception and illusion; from Lacan, he takes the view that the imaginary is a necessary form of misrecognition. It deceives subjects as to their relation to the symbolic social order, the place of the law, and the only possible place for speaking and acting subjects. According to Lacan, the imaginary only partially constitutes the subject with a fantasy of wholeness and containment. It leaves a dimension of experience, the real, that is forever foreclosed and cannot be represented in the symbolic except through its effects. Althusser's theoretical explanation for this process of constitution is the much more inclusive notion of interpellation. Interpellation performs a vital hailing function of identification for Althusser, enabling subjects to recognize themselves in the dominant ideology. That such a structure of recognition is a profoundly unconscious event remaining forever on the level of misrecognition (*méconnaissance*) is a necessary and essential counterpart to the receipt of consciousness, belief, action, and speech by the subject.

It is significant that ideology works not only to tame and discipline subjects but also, as Althusser's former student, Michel Foucault, would later explore in *Discipline and Punish,* to normalize and subject the body according to certain models of behavior. Dislocated from its association with the realm of ideas, ideology is inscribed in material practices and rituals that constitute subjects. In his example of religion, Althusser notes the modalities of kneeling, the discourse of prayer, the sign of the cross, and the gaze of the Absolute subject, all of which interpellate and insert the subject into the materiality of religious ideology. Althusser's analysis nonetheless stops short of a consideration of how the process of interpellation must be continuous if it is to produce and maintain self-disciplined subjects. There is no focus on the perpetual process of interpellation and, similarly, no discussion of the link between ISAs and the historically specific—and flexible—ways of constituting subjects of capitalism. The attempt to supplement Marxism with psychoanalysis did not extend to an elaboration of the possible relation between ideology and its profoundly unconscious effects. This was, as Althusser admits in an undated letter to a friend, "a limit that had not been crossed" (1996, p. 4–5).

For many of his critics, the net result of these theoretical weaknesses was not merely the death of the subject but the erasure of Marxism's revolutionary project. Althusser's structuralism was viewed as oscillating between an antihumanism, insensitive to the questions of resistance and transformation, and an ahistoricism, ignorant of the idiosyncrasies of the historical process. Poststructuralism's regard for the reinscription of subjectivity (albeit one vigilant to all metaphysical risks and without any determining power, hence essentially coming after Althusser), with a conception of history as genealogy, replaced Marx's role in this trajectory with the figure of Nietzsche. Althusser's later writings offer ample evidence of his continued preoccupation with the tensions that mark his thought, as well as anticipating some poststructuralist themes.

Although these final writings do not amount to a distinct theory or perspective, it is apparent that Althusser was moving toward a more dynamic conception of the subject as well as continuing his regard for the contingency of history, aspects of his structuralist position often overlooked by those preferring to emphasize his ahistoricism and antisubjectivism (see Elliott [1998] for a convincing assessment). Here Althusser traces a subterranean materialist tradition originating with Democritus and Epicurus and continuing by way of Hobbes, Spinoza, Machiavelli, and Marx (1994, p. 29–48). Under the idea of "aleatory materialism" Althusser gives weight to specter of the encounter, to the singular historical event that disrupts the course of historical necessity, thus introducing an element of contingency into the supposed authority of synchronic lawlike structures. Althusser's reflections on Spinoza and the concept of freedom similarly caution a too-hasty surmising of his apparent rejection of the subject:

> That one can liberate and recompose one's own body, formerly fragmented and dead in the servitude of an imaginary and, therefore, slavelike subjectivity, and take from this the means to think liberation freely and strongly, therefore, to think properly with one's own body, in one's own body, by one's own body, better: that to live within the thought of the conatus of one's own body was quite simply to think within the freedom and the power of thought. (1998, p. 12–13)

It is fair to say that Althusser's reading of Marx owes as much to Spinoza as it does to Marx. In this extract, we find evidence of Althusser thinking of knowledge and politics beyond the elusive difference between science and ideology. This is not to say that the thought of this influential Marxist philosopher was not structuralist or antihumanist in content, and neither is it to suggest that his thought is not plagued with unruly contradictions between voluntarism and determinism, contingent and structural necessity. It is to suggest, however, that it is only by thinking beyond these dualistic categories that the complex matrix of Althusserian Marxism is revealed.

CAROLINE WILLIAMS

See also **Alain Badiou, Etienne Balibar, Michel Foucault, Jacques Lacan, Claude Lévi-Strauss, Maurice Merlau-Ponty, Jacques Rancière, Jean-Paul Sartre**

Biography

Althusser was born in Algiers in 1918. He joined the Communist Party in 1948. In 1965, he published his influential work *For Marx*, which was followed by *Lenin and Philosophy* in 1969. In 1980, he murdered his wife; he was thereafter confined to an asylum until his death in 1990.

Selected Writings

Pour Marx, 1965; as *For Marx*, translated by Ben Brewster, 1969

Lenin, Philosophy and Other Essays, translated by Ben Brewster, 1971

Politics and History: Montesquieu, Rousseau, Marx, translated by Ben Brewster, 1972

Essays in Self-Criticism, translated by Graham Lock, 1976

Essays on Ideology, translated by Ben Brewster and Graham Lock, 1984

Philosophy and the Spontaneous Philosophy of the Scientists, translated by Ben Brewster, James H. Kavanaugh, Grahame Lock, and Warren Montag, 1990

The Future Lasts a Long Time and The Facts, translated by Richard Veasey, 1993a

Ecrits sur la psychoanalyse: Freud et Lacan, 1993b; as *Writings on Psychoanalysis*, translated by Jeffrey Mehlman, 1996

Sur la philosophie, 1994

Sur la reproduction, 1995

Ecrits philosophiques et politiques. Tome II, 1995

The Spectre of Hegel: Early Writings, translated by G. Goshgarian, 1997

The only materialist tradition, Part I: Spinoza, in *The New Spinoza*, edited by Warren Montag and Ted Stolze, Minneapolis: Minnesota University Press, 1998

With Etienne Balibar, Roger Establet, Pierre Macherey, and Jacques Ranciere, *Lire le Capital*, 1965

With Etiene Balibar, *Reading Capital*, translated by Ben Brewster, 1968

Further Reading

Anderson, Perry, *Considerations on Western Marxism*, London: Verso, 1976

Assiter, Alison, *Althusser and Feminism*, London: Pluto, 1990

Balibar, Etienne, The non-contemporaneity of Althusser, in *The Althusserian Legacy*, edited by Anne Kaplan and Micheal Sprinkler, London: Verso, 1993

Barrett, Michele, *Women's Oppression Today: The Marxist Feminist Encounter*, revised edition, London: Verso, 1988

Benton, Ted, *The Rise and Fall of Structural Marxism*, London: Macmillan, 1984

Callari, Antonio, and David F. Ruccio, eds., *Postmodern Materialism and the Future of Marxist Theory*, Hanover: Wesleyan University Press, 1996

Elliott, Gregory, Analysis terminated, analysis interminable: the case of Louis Althusser, in *Althusser: A Critical Reader*, edited by Gregory Elliott, Oxford: Blackwell, 1994

Elliott, Gregory, The necessity of contingency: some notes, *Rethinking Marxism*, 10(3), 1998, 74–79

Gramsci, Antonio, *Selections from the Prison Notebooks*, edited and translated by Quentin Hoare, London: Lawrence and Wishart, 1971

Thompson, E. P., *The Poverty of Theory and Other Essays*, London: Merlin Press, 1978

ANTHROPOLOGY

The opening of the Institut d'Ethnologie (Institute of Ethnology) at the Paris University in 1925 marked the institutionalization of a French anthropology that had until then been split into a myriad of organisms with no organic ties. Created by Marcel Mauss, Paul Rivet, and Lucien Lévy-Bruhl, under the patronage of Edouard Daladier, then Minister of the Colonies, the Institute was meant to serve colonization. The latter, however, paid little attention to it, as is demonstrated by the fact that field studies were financed mostly by the banker A. Khan and the Rockefeller Foundation. Right away, the Institute became the sole rightful owner of the discipline: Its creators held at the same time its means of transmission through teaching, of practice through the financing of expeditions (104 between 1928 and 1940), of publishing its results through the creation of the collection *Travaux and mémoires de l'Institut d'ethnologie* (Works and Papers from the Institute of Ethnology), and of museology with the Musée du Trocadéro followed by the Musée de l'Homme (Museum of Man) in 1937.

The creation of the institute synthesized five main currents of different intellectual traditions. The first dated at least from Bonaparte's expedition in Egypt (1798–99), when very erudite research in terms of humanities had developed, especially within the Institut des Langues Orientales (Institute of Oriental Languages), the Ecole Française d'Extreme-Orient (French School of the Far East), and the French Institute in Damas. For example, Cambodian inscriptions were being meticulously detailed, but almost nothing was reported on the country's inhabitants. The amount of knowledge accumulated on the folklore of the French regions was equally massive. After the publication of the works of Herder and the Grimm Brothers, Europe had been won over by anthologies of folktales and of popular beliefs, whereas the nationalist movements stirring across the continent were often associated with a search for origins in ethnic terms (Taine, 1875).

The second current, gravitating around the Société d'Ethnographie (created in 1859), involved newly created learned societies in the provinces that mixed research on popular lore, archeology, and prehistory. The results of this approach appeared in the works of Sébillot (*Le Folklore de la France*), then those of Saint-Yves (*Les Saints successeurs des Dieux: Essais de mythologie chrétienne*), as well as in *Saint-Besse, étude d'un culte alpestre* from the Durkheimian Robert Hertz and the eight volumes of the *Manuel du folklore français contemporain* (Handbook of Contemporary French Folklore) by Van Gennep.

A third contribution came from physical anthropology. In 1856, Quatrefages de Bréau transformed his chair of Anatomy and Natural History of Man at the Museum of Natural History into a chair of Anthropology and defined the program "to make known from all points of view the various human races" (de Quatrefages, 1889: V). Within this line of thought were the works of Broca, who founded the Paris school of anthropology and endowed it with *Bulletin et mémoire;* the works of Hamy, who created the Museum of Ethnography at the Trocadéro in 1878; and also of Verneau, a popularizer of the discipline who held the Museum's chair of anthropology before Rivet came to replace him in 1928.

A fourth contribution was made by colonial science. From the beginning of colonization, the military, administrators, and Church officials gathered an incredible amount of information. Thus, Faidherbe, after arriving in Gorée in 1852, wrote linguistics studies and monographs on the peoples of the region. Later works were written by Delafosse, Monteil, and Decary. The development of this knowledge was supported by the geographic societies (Lejeune, 1993). The first of such societies was created in Paris in 1821, and by the turn of the century their importance was remarkable. For example, the geographic society in the city of Lille alone counted two thousand members in 1905.

Aside from these four sources, the institute owed its origins mostly to the French School of Sociology, from which came Lévy-Bruhl and Mauss. Lévy-Bruhl held a chair of philosophy at the Sorbonne, and Mauss directed the study of the religions of primitive peoples in the 5th section and, starting in 1931, held a chair of sociology at the Collège de France. Often referred to as "primitive sociology," ethnography (and consequently ethnology) was dedicated to peoples with no writing systems according to Durkheimian positivist sociology. This is important because Karady noted that an average of 45 percent of the recensions published by *L'Année Sociologique* (The Sociological Year) had ethnological or exotic themes ("Le problème de la légitimité dans l'organisation historique de l'ethnologie française" and "Durkheim et les débuts de l'ethnologie universitaire"). Essentially, ethnography concerned itself with questions of "social morphology" and, to use Mauss's vocabulary, of "social physiology"; that is, the study of the categories at work in collective psychologies. This field of research was especially promoted by Lévy-Bruhl and Mauss and pursued on the Kanaka field by Leenhardt (*Gens de la Grande Terre*, 1937) with the same philosophical tone of inspiration, then by Griaule and his students with the African Dogons, Bambaras, Bozos, and Songrays to the point that for the longest time, French ethnology seemed especially concerned with the descriptions of perception systems (Balandier 1955).

The first generations of students from the institute graduated between 1928 and 1938. They included Griaule, Leiris, Mus, Métraux, Dieterlen, Gessain, Lifchitz, Victor, Lévi-Strauss, Paulme, Leroi-Gourhan, Soustelle, Cazeneuve, and Rodinson (Gaillard, *The Routledge Dictionary of Anthropologists*). In the 1930s there was a systematic effort at field studies. The most famous mission organized by the institute was the Dakar-Djibouti expedition, which, under M. Griaule's leadership, crossed Africa from west to east between 1931 and 1933. *L'Afrique Fantôme* (The Ghost Africa, 1934), the acerbic diary written by Michel Leiris, the expedition's secretary and archivist, was one of the large-scale literary works of French culture of the time. In its pages, Leiris denounced colonial compromising and its means of acquiring works of art. In fact, the expedition had brought back to France more than 3,500 objects because such undertakings were as much museological predatory and stocking-up endeavors as they were taking the census of the peoples, languages, and customs of the world.

Exoticism had been in fashion since the 1920s. The American troops that came at the end of World War I had brought jazz, which was followed by the *Revue Noire* with Josephine Baker (1925). Along with the surrealists and cubists, plastic artists were interested and inspired by the arts then called primitive. The novelist Pierre Loti gave in 1930 a giant head from Easter Island that still stands at the entrance of the museum. It was also the apogee of travel writers, such as Blaise Cendrars and Paul Morand, who wrote about life in the faraway countries of Africa or Asia, where the young Malraux would travel and that he would use as the topic of his first novels. Tristan Tzara published a *Poèmes Nègres,* made up of a compilation from the ethnology journal *Anthropos;* Georges Bataille started the journal *Documents,* with the subtitle: "Archeology, fine arts, ethnography, varieties" (financed by the art dealer Georges Wildenstein), in the third issue of which Mauss published an article on Picasso. *Le Minotaure,* a magazine that succeeded it, devoted its entire second issue to Dogon masks and Dakar-Djibouti; and, according to Maurice Agulhon's calculations, eight million French people visited the 1931 colonial fair (33 million in tickets), for a total population of about 40 million (Agulhon, 1997). The director of the small Museum of the Trocadéro since 1928, Rivet hired G.-H. Rivière to renovate it. Rivière, who had no diplomas, went from being a pianist in a bar called the Boeuf-sur-le-toît to being Rivet's assistant. Volunteers rushed to the museum; all of Paris visited its rooms, and wild parties were organized, such as the pareo-costumed evening. Paul Rivet, a Deputy and freemason, unlocked the funds that allowed the construction of the Musée de l'Homme. The new building, done in pure totalitarian style, replaced the Palais du Trocadéro and was inaugurated in 1937. A cantata with lyrics by Robert Desnos and music by Darius Milhaud was written.

Still, it is in this museum that the first network of French resistance was formed during the Occupation (Blumenson, 1979). Its members would be executed or deported (including Vildé, Lewitzky, Tillion, and Oddon, among others), whereas other anthropologists in danger or against the Vichy government fled to other countries or chose to go to London (including Soustelle, Lévi-Strauss, Rivet, Métraux, Caillois, and others). As a result of the Vichy government's anti-Semitic laws of June 2, 1941, Mauss was replaced by Leenhardt as the director of study of the primitive peoples in the 5th section of higher education (Fabre, 1997). During that same period, in 1942, the Sorbonne finally agreed to create a chair of ethnography, which Mauss had been demanding for years, and which was held by Griaule, the first person to defend a thesis of ethnology with Dogon masks as a main theme (Paris, Institut d'ethnologie, 1938). Many doctorates would follow: Denise Paulme (*La communauté taisible des Dogon* [The Dogon Family Community], 1942), Leroi-Gourhan (*Archéologie du Pacifique nord: Matériaux pour l'étude des relations entre les peuples riverains d'Asie et d'Amérique* [North Pacific Archeology, Materials for the Study of the Relations between Waterside Peoples of Asia and America], 1945), and Lévi-Strauss (*Les Structures élémentaires de la parenté* [Elemental Structures of Kinship,] Paris, Mouton, 1967 [1948cb]).

Three organizations created shortly before the war played an important part during the Liberation: the Centre National de la Recherche Scientifique (CNRS, National Center for Scientific Research), l'Organisation de la Recherche Scientifique Outre-mer (ORSTOM, Organization of Overseas Scientific Research), and l'Institut Français d'Afrique Noire (IFAN, French Institute of Black Africa). These organizations would allow not only numerous expeditions but also long-term stays in exotic fields. To complete the training offered by the Institute of Ethnology, Leroi-Gourhan created in 1946 a training center for ethnological research (Centre de Formation à la Recherche Ethnologique, CFRE), opened to students who had graduated from the Institute (Gaillard, 1989, 85–126). In a parallel move, with the financial support of the Ford and Rockefeller Foundations, an economics and social sciences section was created in 1947 within the practical school of higher education, constituting a 6th section (Mazon, 1988).

Rivet and Leenhardt retired in 1950. Specializing in "races," Vallois succeeded Rivet at the head of the Musée de l'Homme and hired Pales, a doctor-colonel. For the most part, the museum devoted itself to physical anthropology, but postwar research would be led by the works of Leroi-Gourhan, Bastide, Devereux—whose influence would be mostly retrospective—and above all, Griaule, followed by Lévi-Strauss's structuralism and, last, Balandier's dynamism.

Joining the development of the Negritude movement with the magazine *Présence Africaine* and the works of Aimé Césaire and L. S. Senghor (President of Senegal in 1960, but also a linguist and a graduate from the Institute of Ethnology), Griaule's research placed the Dogon cosmologies on the same level as the ones from classical civilizations. This was the main contribution of a life's work that would be continued by his disciples after his death (Lebeuf, de Ganay, Paques, and Zahan). Here it is worth mentioning the filming by Dieterlen and Rouch of the Sigui, a ceremony that only takes place once every sixty years. The Africanism of Griaule, who was bound to authenticity and so valued the civilization of the traditional Black Africa, would nevertheless soon be challenged by a new approach based on the notion of the "colonial situation." This idea, taken from Sartre, was created by Octavio Mannoni, who, in *Psychologie de la Colonisation* (published in 1950 by Le Seuil after having been serialized in the magazine *Esprit*), tried to describe both the transition from the old to the new Malagasy society and especially the psychological aspect of colonial dependency, which goes through the emergence of both a guilt and an inferiority complex.

The graduates from the training center were hired by ORSTOM and IFAN as early as 1946. They left to take up residency in overseas territories for many years. A first wave included Balandier, Mercier, Lombard, Guiart, and Condominas. By 1950, the first two suggested a new Africanism that began with the study of the growing cities as a "colonial sociology or ethnology" before becoming an anthropology of decolonization and finally a dynamic anthropology (Balandier, 1955b). One no longer looked at the African as the "first or original man" who would teach us something about ourselves but, rather, as a man in a situation within a society animated by antagonisms that could take the form of religious movements. More of a classicist, Lombard participated in the advent of an ethnohistory of the African state societies that would become one of the most remarkable aspects of French anthropology (works by Dampierre, Tardits, Izard, Adler, and Terray, among others). Guiart restarted an ethnology of contemporary Oceania, whereas Condominas took Asia away from the Belles-Lettres approach, as Dumont would do for India and Berque and Rodinson for the Arab and Eastern worlds. Most of them would start teaching at the 6th section of the EPHE Ecole Pratique des Hautes études on their return to France by the second half of the 1950s. There, they would create several research centers (center for African research, center for Indian research, center for South-East Asia research, etc.) that would soon be linked to laboratories at the CNRS that are still in existence today.

After taking over the direction of the primitive peoples study center (following Leenhardt's retirement in 1950) in the religious science section of the EPHE, Lévi-Strauss renamed it the "peoples without writing systems" study center and suggested a more in-depth theoretical research and a new opening to foreign scientific influences to which the members of the young generation adhered. In 1949, after having given new prominence to the study of kinship—ignored until then—and having imposed a new reading of Mauss, who favored the reciprocity principle though the triad duty of giving, duty of receiving, and duty of giving back, Lévi-Strauss launched an ambitious program for the discovery of the "innate structures of the human spirit," to begin with a "ready-made" exploration (structuralism) of the level of intelligibility (kinship, Amerindian mythology, dualistic system). This scientific goal was coupled with literary works, notably the magnificent *Tristes Tropiques*, whose first sentence, "I hate travelling and explorers," was a declaration of war against the exoticism still in place. French ethnology was now granted recognition through science. The Secretary of the International Social Sciences Counsel of the UNESCO since 1962, Lévi-Strauss was also the advisor of Braudel, the president of the EPHE's 6th section, who did not make a decision with regard to anthropology without consulting with Lévi-Strauss first. Next to structuralism, sometimes denounced as the ideology of the technocracy because the individual or collective object no longer played a role, other and less flamboyant works were being developed. The meticulous research of Leroi-Gourhan gave way to an ethnology of the techniques and the works of Bastide, who mostly focused on the study of syncretism in the Black Americas, leading to an ethnopsychiatry. The great works of Devereux, a scientist from Romania, belong to this latter field, as he proposed an ethno-

psychiatry of individual subjects *(Reality and Dream: The Psychotherapy of a Plain Indian)* as well as of collective myths, including Graeco-Latin ones *(Ethnopsychanalyse complémentariste* and *Tragédie et Poésie grecques)*. As a specialist on India, Dumont offered a global idea of the caste system, which he demonstrated as being based on the opposition between pure and impure in a religious whole that encompasses politics and economics *(Homo hierachicus: Le Système des castes et ses implications)*. To report it, he developed the concept of holism, which defines an ideology in which the individual is subordinate to the social whole, and that he opposed to individualism, the emergence of which in the Western world he would relate in several works.

Although Griaule had been teaching at the Sorbonne since 1942, the provincial universities were slow to take to ethnology. In 1945, Leroi Gourhan inaugurated in the city of Lyons a lectureship in colonial ethnology; in 1953, the Bordeaux University created a post of Senior Lecturer for Métais; Montpellier would do the same for Servier in 1958, and Zahan would be appointed Professor in Strasbourg in 1960. The lectureships would become chairs in the 1960s, which would create lectureships in the 1970s and, in the 1980s, departments of anthropology or social sciences where ethnology would be prominent. The Fouchier reform created in 1966 a "masters of ethnology," followed almost right away by the creation of a Bachelor's degree offered by the department of sociology and ethnology of the Nanterre-Paris X university—a department opened in 1967 and run by de Dampierre. By October 1968, the university of Jussieu-Paris VII offered training in ethnology dubbed "pirate" by its promoter, Jaulin, who denunciated the "criminal and soulless" Western world. Finally, in 1969, the Paris-VIII-Vincennes University offered the sociology department anthropology with strong Marxist characteristics (Gaillard, 2003).

Thanks to the support of the philosopher Merleau-Ponty, Lévi-Strauss was offered a Chair in 1959 at the Collège de France, which he called social anthropology. There, he created a laboratory and two journals: *L'Homme* (Man) and *Etudes rurales* (Rural Studies). In the second half of the 1960s, the success of structuralism pushed into the background Sartre's Marxist-flavored existentialism. It is to be noted that the film critic Metz, the linguist Greimas, and the psychanalyst Kristéva, as well as the essayists Todorov and Barthes, were all members of the social anthropology laboratory at the beginning of their careers. Ethnologists were also members of the laboratory, of course, including Françoise Héritier, who pursued Lévi-Strauss's works on kinship and succeeded him at the Collège de France, and Godelier, who, influenced by the ideas of Althusser, tried to bridge the gap between Marxism and structuralism and created an economics anthropology *(Rationalité et irrationalité en économie)* before going to live with the Baruya in New Guinea *(La production des grands hommes)*. It was also in Lévi-Strauss's laboratory that French Americanism reappeared—worth noting here are the works of Pierre Clastres, who was inspired by the philosophical thought of Gilles Deleuze. Directed against ethnocentrism, Clastre positively turned the "lack of State" that characterized most of the Amerindian societies into an act of will from its participants who refused the centralization of power and its consequence: the separation between dominating and dominated. The political and social blended because, "the primitive society is the place of refusal of a separate power, because [society] itself, and not the chief, is the real place of power" *(La société contre l'Etat)*. By asking "What is an order?" or "What is a law?" Clastres went beyond Marxism, which, triumphant in the first half of the 1970s, had brought the question of social order back to alienation and means of production *(Recherches d'anthropologie politique)*.

Far from leading to its rejection, decolonization gave anthropology a formidable impetus in the 1960s. To maintain its influence, France sent dozens of young graduates overseas who chose to accomplish their compulsory military service in the Cooperation services. Often sent to Africa, they found there fields of study that did not necessitate any further subventions, and Balandier created in 1960 *Les Cahiers d'études africaines* (African Studies Notebooks) where they could express themselves. Augé followed in these footsteps and, after African works, suggested an anthropology of the subway or of other places such as airports on his return to France. The situation of the civil volunteer ethnologists did not keep some of them from rejecting the word ethnology, which they associated with colonialism (everyone then preferred to be called an "anthropologist"), and from proposing a Marxist and revolutionary anthropology (Copans, Schlemmer, or Rey). The post-1968 years (between 1971 and 1978) followed C. Meillassoux *(Anthropologie économique des Gouro de Côte-Ivoire)* and were ruled by the theoretical hypotheses of the Marxist school (Terray, Godelier, and Bonte); as they looked to apply Marx's schema on societies then called precapitalist, they found means, tools, and returns of production determining specific dynamics.

In the second half of the 1960s, an ethnology of France was revived. After a strong start with the creation in 1937 of the Musée des Arts et Traditions Populaires (Museum of Folk Arts and Traditions), which initiated vast research, the ethnology of France fell into disrepute during the Occupation. With an anti-Semitic background set as a national tradition, G.-H. Rivière

and André Varagnac had agreed to actively collaborate with the Vichy government, which wanted to revitalize the "true French traditions." Thus, the ethnology of France only survived in the 1950s through very isolated works: L. Dumont's *La Tarasque, essai de description d'un fait local d'un point de vue ethnographique, Nouville, un village français* (1953) by Lucien Bernot and René Blancard, and *Village in the Vaucluse, An account of life in a French village* by the American Laurence Wylie. Such authors no longer emphasized tales, architecture, or folk dances, and they abandoned what looked like inventory for data collection requiring lengthy stays in small communities of which they tried to offer a global image, one that insisted on the relationships between individuals and communities.

In an attempt at synthesis, in 1962, R. Gessain organized a multidisciplinary research on the Plozévet isolate in Brittany, which monopolized over 150 researchers and contracted employees. It produced three books: *Commune en France, la métamorphose de Plozévet*, by Edgar Morin; *Bretons de Plozévet*, by Andrée Burguière; and *Goulien, commune bretonne du Cap Sizun*, by Charles Pelras. This crucible of renewal was followed by the creation in 1966 of the Centre d'Ethnologie Française (Center for French Ethnology) and research teams working on France: "France Est" (Eastern France) and "Recherche ethnographique sur un élevage transhumant dans les monts Aubrac." In the early 1980s, the researchers' retrospective outlook paid particular attention to the limits of the transition from "macrocosm to microcosm" that had been taking place since the 1950s (Bromberger, 1987). Researchers denounced falling back on small communities taken as frame and object of research, creating a global vision that was partially artificial. Thus, after the nostalgic or militant search for the past, the singularity of the differences prevailed without noting that it would be difficult to move toward comparative work. Gérard Althabe, on his return from Madagascar, began to work on neighborliness within tall buildings and put together a team devoted to urban anthropology. By the mid-1970s, the computerized handling of civil and parish registries stimulated the anthropology of kinship, giving it the means to superimpose on a large scale matrimonial strategies, kin relations, and estate systems (Cuisenier et al., 1970). Research was done in the Châtillonnais by Jura, Béarn, Eure, Finistère, Morvan, Pyrénées, and others.

Lévi-Strauss's lecture at Unesco in 1971 (Lévi-Strass, 1983a) gave at the same time a new legitimacy to the anthropology of France. In 1952, he was pleading to the same assembly for the mixing of cultures: conceptual and technological transfers were reciprocally enriching, and nothing was worse for a culture than "to find itself isolated" *(Race et histoire)*. With such mixing apparently reigning in 1971, Lévi-Strauss then invoked the dangers of cultural standardization and the need to protect particularities. In the following years, he developed the notion that "the greatest peril threatening humanity today is a universalization of the ways of life" and talked to the Assemblée Nationale in 1976 about it (Lévi-Strass, 1983b). Politicians, moved by his words, decided to protect endangered identity particularisms, trades, and knowledge, and in 1979, the Ministère de la Culture set up a think tank on the theme.

The year 1980 was declared the year of the national heritage. Promoted to concept, the words "national heritage" were defined, according to the structuralist system of opposition, as "everything that is the basis of a group's identity and differentiates it from another." A temporary counsel set up to help complete the report remained as a "Mission du patrimoine ethnologique" (Mission of the Ethnological National Heritage), a service subordinate to the minister of culture. By defining subsidized topics of research, it played a key role in the ethnology of France. The works of the 1980s, which resulted from the Mission bids, dealt with ethnology of the techniques, know-how, and their transmission. Research showcased regional heritages: salt production and shellfish breeding in Brittany (Delbos and Jorion, 1984), hunting in Eastern France (Hell, 1985), bourgeois culture (Le Wita, 1998), the slaughterhouses in Adour (Vialles, 1987), paper, leather, vineyards, and so on (Chevallier, 1990). In 1983, the Mission created the journal *Terrain*, which published studies belonging to an anthropology close to daily life, but that also gradually attempted to draw different fields closer (including exotic ones), with thematic issues devoted to objects that were in principle universal (drinking, the body, fire, time, sight, love, landscape, and so on). Simultaneously, a growing process of decentralization of power was taking place, and the regions' rise to power would be accompanied by the creation of eco-museums.

With regard to research at the beginning of the twenty-first century, the more classical fields are doing well: kinship (Bonte, Héritier, and Houseman), study of Amerindian thought systems (Menget, Tylor, and Descola), African thought systems (Jonckers, Henry, and Journet), or technology (Signault and Geistdoerfer)—all are still very dynamic fields. The evolutionist approach is getting stronger (Testard), the anthropology of law has its own journal (*Droit et Cultures;* Law and Cultures), and there are those who are attempting to apply concepts of psychoanalysis to ethnographic materials (Bidou, Juillerat, Gaillard, and Geffray). The discipline is also examining itself with works on its history by Blanckaert, Gaillard, and espe-

cially Jamin, who started the journal *Gradhiva* and the reprint collection of the same name. Last, promising new fields have emerged, such as medical anthropology (Benoit, Laplantine, Epelboin, Sindzingre, and Zempléni), development anthropology (de Sardan), cognitive anthropology (Sperber and Boyer), and anthropology of migration and globalization. The main element is that the division between anthropology or ethnology and the other social sciences, notably sociology, is nowadays often dismissed. The result is a scattered anthropological knowledge and, consequently, a possible end to an intellectual collectivity. Ethno-anthropology is far from being as successful today as it was in the 1960s–1980s, when structuralism controlled the whole intellectual field. Other disciplines, such as classical studies and especially history, are now more popular. Also happening is a certain fading of the social sciences, which did not keep their promises, and a great comeback of the novel, now popular with cultivated audiences.

GÉRALD GAILLARD

See also **Louis Althusser, Roland Barthes, Georges Bataille, Aime Cesaire, Gilles Deleuze, Arnold van Gennep, Algirdas Julien Greimas, Julia Kristeva, Michel Leiris, Claude Lévi-Strauss, Lucien Levy-Bruhl, Maurice Mauss, Maurice Merleau-Ponty, Jean-Paul Sartre, Tzvetan Todorov**

Further Reading

Agulhon, Maurice, "L'Exposition coloniale de 1931," in *Les Lieux de mémoire*, edited by P. Nora, Paris: Gallimard, 1997, 493–b515

Balandier, Georges, "France: Revue de l'Ethnologie en 1952–1954," New York, *Yearbook of Anthropology*, (1955a): 525–540

Balandier, Georges, *Sociologie actuelle de l'Afrique noire*, Paris: PUF, 1955b

Balandier, Georges, "Tendances de l'Ethnologie Française," in PuF, *Cahiers internationaux de sociologie*, Vol. 27, (1959): 11–22

Bastide, Roger, *Les Amériques noires*, Paris: Payot, 1967

Bastide, Roger, *Sociologie des maladies mentales*, Paris: Flammarion, 1965

Bernot, Lucien and René Blancard, Nouville un village Français Paris, Institut dethnologie, 1953.

Blumenson, Martin, *Le réseau du Musée de l'Homme. Les débuts de la résistance en France*, Paris: Le Seuil, 1979 The Book exist in Engllish as "the Vilde Affair" 1977.

Bromberger, Christian, "Du grand au petit. Variations des échelles et objets d'analyse dans l'histoire de l'ethnologie de la France," in *Ethnologies en miroir: La France et les pays de langue*, edited by Isac Chiva and Utz Jeggle, Paris: MSH, 1987: 67–94

Bromberger, Christian, "Bulletin du Musée d'ethnographie du Trocadéro," Paris: Jean-Michel Place, ré-édition Bulletin 1931–1935, 1988

Burguière, Andre, *Bretons de Plozévet*, Paris: Flammarion, 1975

Chevallier, Denis. *Savoir-faire et techniques. Répertoire des opérations 1980–90*, Paris: Ministère de la Culture, Mission du patrimoine ethnologique, 1990

Clastres, Pierre. *La société contre l'Etat*, Paris: Minuit, 1974

Clastres, Pierre, *Recherches d'anthropologie politique*, Paris: Le Seuil, 1980

Cuisenier, Jean, Martin Ségalen, Michel, de Virville, "Pour l'étude de la parenté dans les sociétés européennes: le programme d'ordinateur Archiv," *L'Homme*, 10, 3 (1970): 27–75

Delbos, G., and P. Jorion, *La transmission des savoirs*, Paris: MSH, 1984

Devereux, Georges, *Reality and Dream: the Psychotherapy of a Plain Indian,* New York: New York University Press, 1951, 2nd edition 1969

Devereux, *Ethnopsychanalyse complémentariste*, Paris: Flammarion, 1972

Devereux, *Tragédie et Poésie grecques*, Paris: Flammarion, 1975

Dumart, Louis, *La Tarague, Essai De Description D'un fait local d'un point de une ethnographique,* Paris, Gollimard, 1951

Dumont, L., *Homo hierachicus: Le Système des castes et ses implications*, Paris: Gallimard, 1966

Fabre, Daniel, "L'Ethnologie française à la croisée des engagements (1940–1945)" in *Résistants et résistance*, edited by Jean-Yves Boursier, Paris: L'Harmattan, 1997, 305–319

Gaillard, Gérald, "Chronique de la recherche ethnologique dans son rapport au Centre national de la recherche scientifique 1925–1980," *Cahiers pour l'histoire du Cnrs*, 3 (1989): 85–127

Gaillard, Gérald, *Images d'une génération: Elements pour servir à la constitution d'une histoire de l'anthropologie française (1950–b1970)*, Paris: Thèse, EHESS, 1988

Gaillard, Gérald, "Learning and Teaching Anthropology in France," in *Learning Fields: Teaching Social Anthropology across Europe*, edited by Dorle Dracklé and Iain Edgar, London: Blackwell, 2003, 172–193

Gaillard, Gérald, *Répertoire de l'ethnologie française, 1950–1970*, Paris: Editions du Cnrs, 1990; also available at http://www.univ-lille1.fr/bustl-grisemine/pdf/rapports/G2003-27-V1.pdf

Gaillard, Gérald, *The Routledge Dictionary of Anthropologists* London, Routledge, 2003

Godelier, Maurice, *La production des grands hommes*, Paris: Fayard, 1982

Godelier, M., *Rationalité et irrationalité en économie*, Paris: Maspero, 1969

Hell, Bernard, *Entre chien et loup: Faits et dits de chasse dans la France de l'Est*, Paris: MSH, 1985

Hertz, Robert, *Saint-Besse, étude d'un culte alpestre*, in Hertz, Mélanges & Sociologie religiense et de folkone (1928) Paris, Puf, 1970. (1913)

Jamin, Jean, "Le Musée d'ethnographie en 1930: l'ethnologie comme science et comme politique," in *La Muséologie selon G.H. Rivière: cours de muséologie, textes et témoignages*, Edited by l'Association des Amis de George-Hensi Rivière, Paris: Dunod, 1989: 110–119

Jamin, Jean, "Les objets ethnographiques sont-ils des choses perdues: A propos de la mission Dakar-Djiouti," in *Temps perdu, temps retrouvé*, edited by Jacques I Hainard Roland Kaehr, Neuchâtel: Musée d'ethnographie, 1985

Karady, Victor, "Durkheim et les débuts de l'ethnologie universitaire," *Actes de la recherche en sciences sociales*, 74 (1988): 21–32

Karady, Victor, "Le problème de la légitimité dans l'organisation historique de l'ethnologie française," *Revue française de sociologie*, 23,1 (1982): 17–35

Le Wita, Béatrix, *Ni vue ni connue. Approche ethnographique de la culture bourgeoise*, Paris: MSH, 1998

Leenhardt, Maurice, *Gens de la Grande Terre*, Paris: Gallimard, 1937

Lejeune, Dominique, *Les Sociétés de Géographie en France et l'Expansion Coloniale au XIXe siècle*, Paris: Albin Michel, 1993

Leroi-Gourhan, Andre, *L'Homme et la Matiéve*, Paris: A. Michel, 1943

Leroi-Gourhan, Andre, *Milieu et techniques*, Paris: A. Michel, 1945

Lévi-Strauss, Claude, *Race et histoire*, Paris: Unesco, 1952

Lévi-Strauss, Claude, "Race et cultures," in C. Levi-Strauss, Le Regard éloigné . . . *Le regard éloigné*, Paris: Plon, 1983a, 21–49

Lévi-Strauss, Claude, "Reflexion sur la liberté," in I Levi-Strauss, *Le regard éloigné*, Paris: Plon, 1983b, 317–382

Lévi-Strauss, Claude, *Tristes Tropiques*, Paris: Plon, 1955

Lewis, IOAN M., "G. Dieterlen," *Anthropology Today*, 16, 2 (2000): 25–26

Llobera, Josep, R., "The fate of anthropology in l'Année Sociologique," *Journal of Anthropological Society of Oxford*, 27 (1996): 235–251

Litteton, C. S. *The New Comparative Mythology: An Anthropological Assessment of the Theories of Georges Dumézil*, Berkeley: California University Press, 1982

Mannoni, Octario, Psychologie de la Colonisation, Paris, Le Senil, 1950

Mazon, Brigitte, *Aux Origines de l'Ecole des Hautes Etudes en Sciences Sociales: Le rôle du mécénat américain*, Paris: Le Cerf, 1988

Meillassoux, Claude, *Anthropologie économique des Gouro de Côte-Ivoire*, Paris: Mouton, 1964

Meillassoux, Claude, *Femmes, Greniers et capitaux*, Paris: Maspéro, 1975

Morin, Edgard, *Commune en France, la métamorphose de Plozévet*, Paris: Fayard, 1967

Needham, Rodney, "Introduction," in *Right and Left: Essays on Dual Symbolic Classification*, Chicago: Chicago University Press, 1978

Pelras, Christian, *Goulien, commune bretonne du Cap Sizun*, Rennes: Presses Universitaires de Rennes, 2001

Pinçon-Charlot, Monique I and Michel, *La chasse à courre: Ses rites et ses enjeux*, Paris: Payot, 1993

Rivière, Georges-Henri, ed. *L'Aubrac, étude ethnologique, linguistique, agronomique et économique d'un établissement humain*, Paris: CNRS, 1970–1982

Saint-Yves, Piere, *Les Saints successeurs des Dieux: Essais de mythologie chrétienne*, Paris: Nourry, 1907

Sébillot, Paul, *Le Folklore de la France*, Paris: Maisonneuve et Larose, 1968

Taine, Hypolite, *Des origines de la France Contemporaine*, 1976–1893, 6 vols. Reed 2 vols, Paris, Laffont, 1986.

Van Gennep, Arnold, *Manuel du folklore français contemporain*, Paris: Picard, (1937) Paris, Laffont, 1988

Vialles, Noélie, *Le sang et la chair: Les abattoirs des pays de l'Adour*, Paris: MSH, 1987

Wylie, Lawrence, *Village in the Vaucluse, An account of life in a French village*, Cambridge, MA: Harvard University Press, 1957

ARIÈS, PHILIPPE
Historian

Though often associated with the *Annales* school of social historians, most of whom had left-wing origins or leanings, Philippe Ariès belongs to that odd species, a right-wing social and cultural historian, and one moreover who never repudiated his early loyalties and commitment to *Action Française* in the 1930s. There was a clear link between the nostalgic politics of his family's royalism and his deployment of historical memory in his studies of the history of childhood and death in European culture. For him, memory constituted a permanent commitment, a kind of security against, and an alternative to, the fragmented and state-run lives of modern society.

Ariès, therefore, was not haunted by guilt at his involvement in the wartime educational program promoted by the Vichy—not for him the "Vichy syndrome" (Hutton, 1997). Nevertheless, he seems to have rejected the nationalist abuse of history imposed during that period while retaining confidence that historical memories remained a vital resource for the present. In his view, the community of the long historical past was ever present as current memory in French culture. This community was integrated in that the fundamental distinctions of rich and poor, young and old, kin and strangers, and the living and the dead were fused in open households in which public and private lives were seamlessly intertwined. This was in essence the grand household of his family's memory, but for Ariès, it also represented the cultural foundation that had been undermined by the subsequent historical changes that led to modernity.

In the study that made him internationally famous, translated as *Centuries of Childhood*, Ariès built up a picture of that disintegration of the social whole into age groups by setting out a model of the changing social role of children before industrialization. His early work had used demographic evidence as a reflection of family culture and custom, but in studying the concept of the child, he drew enterprisingly on figurative and symbolic sources in art, as well as personal memoirs and other documentary records. He was rather vague about the causation and timing of the sweeping changes in cultural attitudes toward, and social institutions designed for, children. Strikingly, he proposed that during the Middle Ages, when children were kept in the home as dependants during a long infancy, there was no concept of the child. In other words, whatever the private relationship between parents and children, there was no social recognition of the distinctive nature of childhood; someone too young to take part in social life was of no significance. It was only when a child entered the adult world, at about the age of seven years, that he or she was noticed, at which time the child left to go straight into training for adulthood. It was at that age, significantly, that they began to wear smaller versions of adult dress. Only with the segregation of children in schools and colleges in the later sixteenth and seventeenth centuries did distinctive children's and young people's clothes develop. This physical and symbolic separation of the age groups created a fissure in more than organization, for it also occasioned uncertainty of social attitudes toward children. At first treated with indulgence (coddling), children faced growing mistrust in society and were subjected to controlled development in a carefully rigorous educational curriculum. Uncontrolled, precocious development was viewed as unnatural because the young needed to pass through carefully phased stages of growth in schools before they were released onto the wider stage to join the adults. In this sense, the psychology of the young was invented along with their distinct social identity.

There are many problems with this model, which Ariès himself nearly admitted. However valid the model for some men of the early modern period, women of all classes continued to be kept at home and were dressed as little ladies until girls' schools were systematically implemented in the nineteenth century. In that period, too, the working class had "childhood" imposed on them and work and sexuality were seen as dangerous forms of exposure to the adult world. Later historians have therefore reinforced this skepticism by introducing more subtle complications into the original schema, pointing to elements of class control and political intervention in the creation of mass childhood. The image of the Middle Ages also attracted considerable criticism, as the medieval church showed a consistent educational concern for children as a distinct group (Wilson, 1980). However, the picture of the late twentieth century is strikingly close to that suggested by Ariès: segregated institutions, distinctive youth cultures, and specialist forms of dress and discipline, reinforced by commercial exploitation, all isolate the younger from the older age groups.

Ariès's subsequent work on death followed a similar approach and perhaps demonstrates the limitations of his method. At its heart again was culture embodied in custom and an emphasis on the intensely personal context of family and social life. His first version (*Western Attitudes towards Death*, 1974) proposed a sequence of phases of social changes in the culture of death, from an integrated world where death was familiar and omnipresent, the "tame death" for which we prepared, to a modern situation where death is both a forbidden topic and a virtually invisible process.

Medicalization has robbed us of control and participation. In between, in the early modern period, the primary obligation of drawing up a will, thus reconciling oneself to both God and society, meant that the individual had to take control of the deathbed scene, a process in which the deathbed speeches of the dying person, rather than the rituals of the bereaved, were central. Witnesses were required not to ensure the salvation of the dead so much as to organize the continuity of property and family afterwards. Ariès's subsequent elaboration on these themes (*L'Homme devant la mort*, 1977) adopted a more impressionistic qualitative approach, "more intuitive and subjective, but perhaps more comprehensive." (*The Hour of Our Death,* p. xiii) His cultures of death lasted many centuries, sometimes coexisting as contrasting practices. Contented resignation and preparation in the face of death were exemplified by actions in the *Chanson de Roland* and in twentieth-century English memoirs. Yet increasingly, under modernity, death was seen as an enemy to be fought and resented. Although elaborate funerals became less acceptable from the late seventeenth century except for monarchs and other national figures, private funerals led increasingly to more elaborate and extravagant monuments erected as memorials to those cruelly taken from the living. These themes are pursued with some brilliance, drawing on the history of art and architecture, with asides on the history of cemeteries and urban health policies, national monuments and ceremonies. The overall picture, however, is complicated and defies a simple historical schema. In the end, Aries suggests, the Anglo-Saxon cultures may be demanding the return of control of death and dying to those most affected—the dying and their relatives.

As an historian of *mentalités,* Ariès has been both inspirational and much criticized. The work of this "Sunday historian," as he called himself, has some parallels with that of Michel Foucault, whose work on madness Ariès was instrumental in seeing published. Both felt a deep unease about modernity and the social forms of intrusion and control that it imposes. Unlike Foucault, however, Ariès did not seek to denounce the many forms of power or locate roots of resistance. He perhaps sought a reintegration of society rather than a challenge to modern fragmentation, a return to the hidden tradition. In this sense, history could be both a living past and a hope for the future.

PETER RUSHTON

See also **Michel Foucault**

Biography

Ariès was born in 1914 and did not become a professional historian until after his major works on childhood and death were published, when in 1978 he was appointed at the École des Hautes Études, a post he held until his death in 1984. Before then, he was always what he himself called a "Sunday historian," working on his studies while employed in charge of the publications of an institute for trading in tropical fruits, the Institut Français de Recherches Fruitières Outre Mer. Paris intellectuals were reportedly shocked by the rumor that a banana importer had written a revolutionary study of childhood. His involvement as a reader with Plon publishers, however, allowed him wider influence on historical scholarship, for it was largely through his insistence that Michel Foucault's first book, the outcome of his doctorate on madness, was published.

Selected Writing

Les Traditions sociales dans les pays de France, 1943
Histoire des populations françaises et leurs attitudes devant la vie depuis le xviiie siècle, 1948 and 1976
Le Temps de l'histoire, 1954
L'Enfant et la vie familiale sous L'Ancien Régime, 1960; in English as *Centuries of Childhood,* 1962
Essais sur l'histoire de la mort en Occident du Moyen-Age à nos jours, 1975; in English as *Western Attitudes towards Death: from the Middle Ages to the Present,* 1974.
L'Homme devant la mort, 1977; in English as *The Hour of Our Death,* translated by Helen Weaver, 1981
Un Historien du dimanche, edited by Michel Winock, 1980
Essais de mémoire, 1983, includes *Le Temps de l'histoire*
The World of Children, 1966
With A. Benjin, *Western Sexuality: Practice and Precept in Past and Present,* 1985
With George Duby, *Histoire de la vie privée,* 5 volumes, 1985–1988; in English as *A History of Private Life,* 1989

Further Reading

Burton, Anthony, Looking forward from Ariès? Pictorial and material evidence for the history of childhood and family life, *Continuity and Change,* 4(2), 1989, pp. 203–229
Hutton, Patrick H., The problem of memory in the historical writing of Philippe Ariès, *History and Memory,* 4(1), 1992, pp. 95–22
Hutton, Patrick H., France at the end of history: the politics of culture in contemporary French historiography, *Historical Reflections,* 23(2), 1997, pp. 105–127
Hutton, Patrick H., The politics of the young Philippe Ariès, *French Historical Studies,* 21(3), 1998, pp. 475–495
Johansson, S. Ryan, Centuries of childhood/centuries of parenting: Philippe Ariès and the modernization of privileged infancy, *Journal of Family History,* 12, 1987, pp. 343–365
Morel, Marie-France, Reflections on some recent French literature on the history of childhood, translated by Richard Wall, *Continuity and Change,* 4(2), 1989, pp. 323–337
Vann, Richard T., The youth of centuries of childhood, *History and Theory,* 21, 1982, pp. 279–297
Wilson, Adrian, The infancy of the history of childhood: an appraisal of Philippe Ariès, *History and Theory,* 19, 1980, pp. 132–153

ARKOUN, MOHAMMED

Historian

A useful way to understand Arkoun's method and orientation is by examining the titles of some of his principal works. These include, in English, *The Unthought in Contemporary Islamic Thought* (2002) and *Rethinking Islam: Common Questions and Uncommon Answers* (1994) and, in French, *Lectures du Coran* (Readings of the Qur'an, 1982) and *Pour une critique de la raison islamique* (Toward a Critique of Islamic Reason, 1984). This is because Arkoun has described himself as a "historian-thinker," or someone who considers that whatever the personal costs, knowledge is an absolute right of all human beings. However, its pursuit requires that research has to be alive not only to yesterday's but also to today's problems because it is only by the proper situation of the past that it is possible to intervene in the present and thereby act as a counter-force to the usually distorting effects of official ideologies. Methodologically, like a number of his contemporaries in France (Pierre Bourdieu being one of these), he is concerned with the nature of the links among philosophy, the social sciences, and education and, therefore, the role that the engaged intellectual can play in society.

In considering his work, it is necessary to take into consideration three major contexts of influence. These are his Maghreb/Algeria/Kabyle roots, his early historical studies and the importance in their direction of Claude Cahen, and finally, French sociological writing wherein both Michel Foucault and Pierre Bourdieu have provided ways of working. In addition, his historical studies have also been influenced by the work of the *Annales* school and in particular, Lucien Febvre and Marc Bloch, whereas Arkoun's interest in the idea of an encompassing logosphere of the Mediterranean brings into focus Fernand Braudel's idea of total history. Perhaps two other influences can be highlighted: Jacques Derrida in respect of the very nature of language, and the nineteenth-century sociologist Emile Durkheim, whose notion of what is a social fact is reused by Arkoun to express two core problematics: the "Qur'anic fact" and the "Islamic fact." It is central to Arkoun's method that he explores the processes through which ideas and practice become established as fact. To achieve this work of deconstruction, it requires him to examine not only the nature of the text itself but also the social and political contexts within which the text emerged. As a result, two of Foucault's works are of particular importance—*The Archaeology of Knowledge* and *The Order of Things*. Two aspects of Arkoun's methodology link him to Foucault: the employment of Foucault's idea that understanding the nature of knowledge requires one to use similar techniques to the archaeolgist, that is, putting together the piecemeal fragments of a bygone age in such a way that it is possible to construct a coherent narrative; and the idea that philosophical discourse is the result of the bringing together of the different branches of knowledge that exist at any specified moment in time. This is the importance for Arkoun in insisting on an examination of the social, political, and economic contexts within which discourse developed around the core artifacts of the belief system of Muslims. Furthermore, the interpretation of these also has to be seen in terms of the changing social, political, and economic contexts within which Muslims operate.

What these opened up for Arkoun was the possibility of shifting from the "historico-transcendental thematic" that was the standard method of traditional Islamology to a different paradigmatic base that focuses on the structure of knowledge. Arkoun illustrates this method of textual analysis and the importance of the social, political, and economic contexts within which these were written and developed in his *Lectures du Coran*. The importance of Foucauldian ideas as a central influences on Arkoun's thinking is also apparent in *The Unthought in Contemporary Islamic Thought*. Arkoun's purpose, as the title suggests, is to explicitly explore what has been a recurring theme in his work: The effect of the "unthought" and the "unthinkable"; that is, until Muslims choose to explore what they have previously not thought to explore, it will be virtually impossible for them to move forward. In chapter 2, he sets up six triangles, or *topoi*, that he argues are required to be understood if there is to be a "critical reassessment of all living traditions." His six triangles are respectively a cognitive triangle of Language, History, and Thought that includes within it a triangle of Revelation, History, and Truth; a theological–philosophical triangle of Faith, Reason, and Truth; a hermeneutic triangle of Time, Narratives, and the Ultimate Absolute Truth; an empirical triangle of Mind, Society, and Power (authority); an anthropological triangle of Violence, Sacred, and Truth that he uses to focus on *Sura 9* of the Qur'an, most commonly referred to as "repentance," to explore what he calls "the so-called religious regime of truth;" and finally, a philosophical–anthropological triangle that he further defines as the "social institution of mind" and the "imaginary institution of society," in which the three elements of the triangle are Rationality, Irrationality, and Imaginary (or the *imaginaire*), the elements of which are also relevant to the subsidiary triangle of Revelation, History, and Truth. Of these triangles, it is the anthropological triangle of Violence, Sacred, and Truth that is perhaps the most important—particularly, first, for the understanding of the relationship between the West and Muslim societies as he subsequently illustrates through a discussion of the role of the "just war/*jihad*" idea as it was used first to explain the Crusades and, second, the naval confrontation between the Ottoman Empire and Venice at the Battle of Lepanto in 1571.

Finally, in both *Rethinking Islam* and *The Unthought in Contemporary Islamic Thought,* where he also uses the Violence, Sacred, and Truth triangle, Arkoun devotes a lengthy consideration to a discussion of what is understood to be the nature of the "person," both in the classical texts and in how these influence the understanding of the person in contemporary Muslim societies. However, this emphasis on the rereading of the text can be seen, as Robert D. Lee, the translator of Arkoun's *Rethinking Islam,* argues, as concerned with the search for "authenticity" in much the same ways as the writings of the antecedents of the contemporary Islamist movements like Sayyid Muhammad Qutb. Although this seems a valid criticism, nevertheless, in a very real sense, contemporary conflicts in Muslim countries are struggles over authenticity.

KAY ADAMSON

See also **Marc Bloch, Pierre Bourdieu, Jacques Derrida, Emile Durkheim, Lucien Febvre, Michel Foucault**

Biography

Born in 1928 at Taourirt-Mimoun in Little Kabylia, Mohammed Arkoun studied first at the University of Algiers. After he was nominated as a Professor of Arabic in Strasbourg in 1956 at the age of twenty-eight, he then studied with Claude Cahen, the eminent French historian who was teaching medieval history and who focused on the period from the origins to the Ottoman Empire. Both were nominated to Paris in October 1959, where Cahen would be the only holder of a mainstream post on medieval history outside of Europe and where Arkoun would undertake his *doctorat d'Etat* examining Arab humanism of the fourth century A.H. (tenth century A.D.) and, in particular, the work of the philosopher and historian al-Miskawayh. Arkoun established himself at Paris III (Sorbonne), where he specialized in the comparative history of religions and is an emeritus professor. He is also the long-time editor of *Arabica: Journal of Arabic and Islamic Studies,* which was originally founded by the prominent orientalist E. Lévi-Provençal, whose focus had been the history of Muslim peoples in Spain. Arkoun is also a member of the Institute of Ismaili Studies in London.

Selected Works

It is possible to follow the broad outline of Arkoun's thinking through his publications in English. These consist of, most recently, *The Unthought in Contemporary Islamic Thought.* The Institute of Ismaili Studies Web site also provides access to other material about and by Arkoun.

L'Humanisme arabe au IVe/Xe Siècle. Miskawayh, philosophe et historien, second edition, 1982
Lectures du Coran, 1982
Pour une critique de la raison islamique, 1984
Rethinking Islam: Common Questions, Uncommon Answers, translated and edited by Robert D. Lee, 1994
Islam, Europe and the West: meanings-at-stake and the will-to-power, pp. 172–189 in *Islam and Modernity: Muslim Intellectuals Respond,* edited by John Cooper, Ronald L. Nettler, and Mohamed Mahmoud, 1998
The Unthought in Contemporary Islamic Thought, 2002

Further Reading

Foucault, M., *The Archaeology of Knowledge,* London: Routledge, translated by A. M. Sheridan Smith, Eds. Gallimard 1969
Foucault, M., *The Order of Things. An Archaeology of the Human Sciences,* London: Routledge, Eds. Galllimard 1966
Lee, Robert D., Arkoun and authenticity, *Peuples Méditerranéens,* 50, 75–106, 1990

ARON, RAYMOND
Philosopher

A philosopher, sociologist, political scientist and commentator, teacher and academic, Raymond Aron belongs to a tiny group of figures who, through their fundamental excellence, surpass given categories of function and output. Raymond Aron enjoyed prestige within the world of politics through books and journalistic commentaries—of which de Gaulle was an avid reader—as well as in academia, where his superior analytical skills were acknowledged by academics from the humanities, sociology, and political science. Still, for most of his postwar career, Aron seemed a perennial outsider. Never acquiescent or docile, he refused—except as a Gaullist during a brief period after the Liberation—membership in any political party or theoretical school. As a liberal Frenchman and an individualist sociologist, he was a doubly paradoxical figure. His concern was not for structures, classes, or theoretical abstractions but, ultimately, for humanity's present reality: This commonsense perspective, which belies his philosophical insight and sophistication, explains how Aron, despite his huge effect in academic circles, was somewhat sidetracked in the Parisian Parnassus by the changing scholastic movements. It was not until his late years, in the 1970s, when the tide finally turned for the pro-Communists on the French intellectual scene, that Aron came to enjoy the reverence that in France befalls agenda-setting spirits.

Aron wrote several thousand editorials and several hundred academic articles, essays, and comments, as well as about forty books. Thematically, his diverse writings fall into two categories: the "international" as political phenomenon and meta-Marxist analysis of modern society are combined with a concern for the conditions, practices, and traditions of either thought or action—an oscillation somewhat comparable to Marx's own shifting between superstructure and basis. In his own words, the total oeuvre is a "reflection over the 20th Century in the light of Marxism and an attempt to clarify all parts of modern society: economy, social and class relations, political regimes, international relations and the ideological discussions" (*Le Spectateur engagé*, 1984).

Aron's central works include *The Opium of the Intellectuals* (1955), *Peace and War* (1962), *Clausewitz* (1976), and his *Mémoires* (1983). Yet the masterpiece, binding together all of the works by philosophically exploring the limits of historical intelligibility and thus developing the framework for historical sociology, is his main doctoral dissertation *Introduction à la philosophie de l'histoire. Essai sur les limites de l'objectivité historique* (1938, *Introduction to the Philosophy of History: An Essay on The Limits of Historical Objectivity*). An often-overlooked intellectual pearl of the twentieth century, the dissertation situates itself at the juncture between philosophy, historiography, and the social sciences. It contains a philosophical examination of the hermeneutic condition of human understanding, carefully balanced between History's relativistic insistence on particularism and Sociology's deterministic search for causal dependence. From this phenomenological starting point, Aron works his way back to the generalities and develops a methodology for historical sociology, which—through its demarcation of the conditions of understanding and emphasis on both regularities and accidents in history—also generates a political philosophy of action.

Because history has no prime mover, the dissertation points out that the future is never completely determined by the past, and because every historical work is always ambiguous and inexhaustible, the comprehension of history is always contingent on its analyst. As a consequence, the individual has a limited possibility of free action. This freedom makes us human, but it also imposes an obligation to act. The very impossibility of establishing a philosophy of history beckons both political moderation and liberal tolerance for diverging opinions. Against the backdrop of Durkheimian positivism (Brunschvicg and Simiand), Aron introduces the historical situatedness of German hermeneutics (from Dilthey to Weber) into the French context of transcendental philosophical analysis. Thus, unexpectedly, the latter's intertwining with German phenomenological speculation becomes the foundation of Aron's liberal individualism and historical sociology.

The dissertation begins and ends with the individual perspective—from the conditions for knowing oneself to the responsibility for political choices following the reflection over reality. The emphasis on the limits of reason and comprehension is profoundly Kantian. Even though Aron does not solve the philosophical riddle of relativism, he points to a pragmatic solution whereby the individual has the moral and political responsibility to keep searching for the truth to the best of one's ability. Aron thus transposes the epistemological dilemma from a transcendental to a moral domain in a profoundly secular, even Weberian, protestant fashion. Through the meticulous unfolding of its subject, the dissertation is both a worthy conclusion to the preceding century's differentiation of Sociology from History (thereby completing Max Weber's work) and an agenda-setter, still pertinent for today's epistemological battle that divides the social sciences and humanities. Furthermore, the dissertation is a cornerstone in Aron's production, as all of his later works are conceived within its confines and very often can be seen to perpetuate both its conclusions and discussions.

Aron's concern for the Marxist philosophy of history was not limited to the philosophical discussion and refutation of the *Introduction*. Through a number of works, he delivered sharp analyses of how the Marxist Left's constructed myths formed a quasi-religious belief-system. As is the case here, Aron's arguments are often worked out in shorter essays and then later developed into whole books. His writings on Marxism as a secular religion include, among others, a double article from 1944 and two selections of essays, *Polémiques (Polemics)* (1955) and *Marxismes imaginaires—d'une sainte famille à l'autre* (1968, *Imaginary Marxisms—From One Holy Family to the Next*). A high point in this liberal critique of ideology is *The Opium of the Intellectuals* (1955). The book was written on the backdrop of the geopolitical realities of the Cold War, which had left France on the fringe of world politics, as well as in reaction to the irresponsibility and naïveté of the "communizing" fellow travelers of the French intelligentsia.

Opium of the Intellectuals gave ideology its bad name. Its critique of the Marxist philosophy of history and the predilection of pluralism and openness share many elements with, for example, Hayek's *Road to Serfdom* (1944) and Popper's *Open Society and its Enemies* (1945). Aron's basically new move was to identify the wrongful convictions as something peculiar to the class of intellectuals whose attitude in France is determined by frustrated "national pride and a nostalgia for the universal idea." Basically, deploying a calm and empirical historical sociology of knowledge, Aron noted that those who preach the proletariat's cause are themselves of bourgeois origin. Moreover, their myths of the ever progressive Left, of the inevitability of the coming revolution, and of the irreconcilability of bourgeois and proletarian interests, are all leftovers of either Christianity's Messianic anticipation or the historical struggle against the aristocracy of *Ancién regime*. Intellectuals are particularly prone to fall for these myths because their special domain, rationalism, contains "a nostalgia for religious truth."

In the West, the days of the revolution are behind us, not before us; in reality, proletarians share the bourgeois aspirations, and the idea of the class struggle is merely a proposition denied by history. Negating immoderate and quasi-religious ideologies that lead to fanaticism, Aron set the ideal of an individual who "because he likes individual human beings, participates in living communities, and respects the truth [then] refuses to surrender his soul to an abstract ideal of humanity, a tyrannical party, and an absurd scholasticism." (p. 334) Aron thus shared the cautious attitude toward undue faith in science and progress with conservative critic of the excesses of the 1789 revolution, Edmund Burke, as well as with fellow analyst of international politics, Hans J. Morgenthau's *Scientific Man and Power Politics* (1945).

Precisely the field of international relations pairs Aron's concern for identification of the important long-term elements of the historical conjuncture with his sense for necessity of political acuity. One of Aron's finest legacies is the result of his historical sociological writings on international relations, from the weekly commentaries to *Peace and War* (1962). His teaching experience in 1930s Germany awoke the geopolitical instinct in the young intellectual of Jewish descent. This instinct was further refined through the war articles from London and later in journalism and lectures in Paris. The theoretical point of view of *Peace and War* was developed through a series of articles in the 1950s (reprinted in *Etudes politiques* [1972]). From the prolific climax of 1962 and through to his death, Aron never ceased to rework both his theoretical premises and his concrete political evaluations—especially in his penultimate great book, *Clausewitz* (1976) and the posthumous new introduction to the 1984 edition of *Peace and War*.

Aron defined international relations as the sustenance of relations between autonomous centers of decision—the states—in both war and peace. As a consequence, diplomacy and strategy are complementary and international relations can be defined as the field of diplomatic-strategic action. Praxeological international relations thus aims to identify the building blocks that actors, politicians, and analysts employ to account for material determinants and possible belief systems. In the United States, a set of pseudo-scientific propositions believed to contain the eternal wisdom of international relations has been tentatively subtracted from the herbarium of history into so-called realism. This scientific attempt fails, as it does not grasp the fundamental temporality of the human situation—and thus, the best thing a social scientist can obtain is not eternal laws, but regularities, bound to a given conjuncture. Although he also emphasized the empirical side of material determinants and especially the importance of how technological development is a crucial factor in changing the historical setting, Aron fundamentally offers a sociology of the two belief systems that constitute the "antinomies of the diplomatic-strategic type of action"; namely, the Machiavellian question of means and the Kantian question of peace (*Peace and War*, French 8th Ed. 1984, pp. 563–566). Even if Aron as such can be categorized as a "constructivist," he still insists on the realistic necessity of prudence.

Alongside Jean Touchard, René Rémond, Alfred Grosser, Maurice Duverger, and others, Aron was instrumental in the refounding of French political science that took place after the war—on the backdrop of the dynamism of American political and social science and in the institutional setting of the new Fondation Nationale de Science Politique (FNSP), which continues to educate the country's leading civil servants without primarily being a research faculty. Aron's clear and erudite style was ever emblematic of the methodological ambitions of the FNSP, which amounted to a "well-tempered aronisim" (Vineeut 1987, p. 209).

This position, combined with his antipositivistic stance in social scientific methodology, certainly played a role in the comparatively few nomothetical aspirations of French political science up until the end of the twentieth century, but it also demarcated a central tension within French social thought dating from 1945. Aron's style may come as a surprise to foreigners who have been introduced to French standards of expression through familiarity with the dense, literary prose of Sartre, Derrida, Foucault, or Bourdieu, but the method of exposition induced by the French *lycées* strives for a different type of clarity. Aron was a champion of this tradition whose concrete method always consists of a symmetrical structuring of the argument around a set of abstract concepts derived from the main question, *la problématique,* and each subpart plays harmonically into the whole through a meticulous unfolding and discussion of the subtopic's facets. In opposition to the drifting Anglo-Saxon essay, a French exposition of a subject matter is constructed around its *plan,* and Aron's works are all tributes to this principle.

In French social science, literary ambitions often turn the unfolding through precise description into origami through chiasmic circumscription. Aron, in response to a rather lofty dissertation defense, replied with the words, "Let's return to earth!" (Colquhoun 1986, Vol. II, p. 8) The exclamation also serves as a headline for his style and his emphasis on making an argument, a point, a case for or against something. In the 1960s, left-bank students guided by Structuralism and Marxism in various guises labeled Aron's moderate liberalism as reactionary and, as a paradoxical token to his superior skill or their own demise of reason, launched the incomparable slogan, "rather be wrong with Sartre, than right with Aron."

Aron's essential legacy is the honest, moderate humanism expressed in the style and content of his writing and analyses. A liberal free-thinker of the classic sort, he was cautiously rationalist: "If the civilizations, all ambitious and fragile, are to bring the prophets' dreams to life in a far future, which universal vocation could unify them aside from Reason?" (*Mémoires* p. 729). As such, he is a towering, yet lonely, figure in French thought since 1945.

HENRIK ØESTERGAARD BREITENBAUCH

See also **Pierre Felix Bourdieu, Leon Brunschvicg, Jacques Derrida, Emile Durkheim, Michel Foucault, Jean-Paul Sartre**

Biography

Raymond Aron (1905–1983) was born into an upper-middle class Jewish family. He graduated first in his class as agrégé in philosophy from the ENS (École Normale Supérieure) in 1928. Aron went to Germany as an academic for some years in the 1930s, where he discovered the German sociologists as well as the rising Nazi movement. Aron presented his doctorat d'Etat at the Sorbonne in 1938, then fled to London, from where he wrote analyses and comments for France Libre during the war. On his return, he worked in academia and journalism until the end of his life. He became Professor of Sociology at the Sorbonne in 1955, was named member of the Académie des sciences morales et politiques in 1962, was appointed to the Collège de France in 1970, and died a few weeks after publishing his Mémoires.

Selected Works:

La sociologie allemande contemporaine, 1935, as *German Sociology* Trans: Mary Bottomore and Thomas B. Bottomore
Introduction à la philosophie de l'histoire: Essai sur les limites de l'objectivité historique, doctoral dissertation, 1938
Le grand schisme, 1948, as *The Great Schism*
L'Opium des intellectuels, 1955, as *The Opium of the Intellectuals* Trans: Daniel J. Mahoney and Brian C. Anderson

La tragédie Algérienne, 1957
Dimensions de la conscience historique, 1961
Richard Howard & Anette Baher Fox *Paix er guerre entre les nations*, 1962, as *Peace and War*
Essai sur les libertés, 1965
Richard Howard & Helen Weaver *Les étapes de la pensée sociologique*, 1967, as *Main Currents of Sociological Thought*
"*What is a theory of international relations?*" Journal of International Affairs Vol. 21, No. 2, 1967.
Marxismes imaginaires—d'une sainte famille à l'autre, 1968
Etudes politiques, 1972
République impériale: Les Etats-Unis dans le monde 1945–72, 1973, as *The Imperial Republic; The United States and the World, 1945–1973*, Trans: Frank Jellinek
Clausewitz: Penser la guerre, 1976
Mémoires: 50 ans de réflexion politique, 1983

Further Reading

Baverez, Nicholas, *Raymond Aron, Un moraliste au temps des idéologues*, Paris: Flammarion, 1993
Colquhoun, Robert, *Raymond Aron, I: The Philosopher in History, II: The Sociologist in Society*, London: Sage Publications, 1986
Commentaire, 28/29, Hiver, 1985 (*in memoriam* special containing a number of articles)
Frost, Bryan-Paul, Resurrecting a neglected theorist: the philosophical foundations of Raymond Aron's theory of international relations, *Review of International Studies*, 23, 1997, 143–166
Hayek, Frederick A: The Road to Serfdom, Chicago: University of Chicago Press, 1944
International Studies Quarterly, 29,1, 1985 (*in memoriam* special containing a number of articles)
Judt, Tony, *Past Imperfect: French Intellectuals 1944–1956*, Berkeley: University of California University Press, 1992
Judt, Tony, *The Burden of Responsibility: Blum, Camus, Aron, and the French Twentieth Century*, Chicago: The University of Chicago Press, 1998
Morgenthau, Hans J., *Scientific Man Power Politics*, Chicago: University of Chicago Press, 1946
Popper Karl R., *Open Society and its Enemies*, London: Routledge & Kegan Paul, 1945
Vincent, Gérard, *Sciences—Po-Hisfoire d'une réussite*

ART HISTORY, CRITICISM, AND AESTHETICS

French art history and criticism has a long and impressive history, including practitioners, theorists, and philosophers such as Divert, Tine, Baudelaire, de Montesquieu, Zola, Proust, and Mâle. The preeminence of France—especially Paris—in the Fine Arts (at least since the mid-nineteenth century), explains the breadth and depth of debate.

Any account of contemporary aesthetics has to accept the enormous diversity in approaches, even within any particular school or group of critics. Even the very definition of aesthetics—the reflection on, sensibility to, and perception of art—has been disputed, deconstructed, and reconstituted in the second half of the twentieth century. There is a danger, then, of fragmentation. This is true more in Anglo-American thought, which since the late 1960s and early 1970s has seen the emergence of gay and feminist aesthetics, than in France, where Cultural Studies is seen as part of the communitarian tradition that French Republican values tend to discount. Important work has emerged, if not synthesis, from Hocquenghem, Irigaray, Guibert, Wittig (see Heathcote, Hughes, and Williams, 1998), and the move by Buci-Glucksmann (1986) to claim the baroque as feminine moved in this direction. Nevertheless, (working-)class-based aesthetic theories have appeared (Ragon, 1978; Bourdieu, 1979). The fragmentation is such that we are forced to say that every individual has his or her own aesthetic categories and, therefore, that no meaningful synthesis may be possible. It is with these caveats in mind that the main currents of art history, criticism, and aesthetics in postwar France need to be considered.

Periodization itself is a minefield, as prewar aesthetic concerns in France were carried through the Second World War, coming to dominate the debates of the 1950s. However, it is possible to say that 1945 saw a desire for and an assertion of a *tabula rasa* as far as art history and fine arts were concerned. The post-Holocaust world was never to be the same in any domain of the arts. Theodor Adorno's assertion that "no poetry is possible after Auschwitz" could be applied to the poetic nature of art in general. Hence, the spectacular growth of Abstract Expressionism, especially out of the United States, allegedly funded by the Central Intelligence Agency to undermine the politicized avant-garde movements (Dada, Constructivism, Surrealism, and the like) that had swept across the world in the aftermath of the Russian Revolution of 1917.

Ironically, the postwar period is often hailed as the moment when the world art capital moved from Paris to New York. Following the art movements of the last decades of the nineteenth century (Impressionism, Symbolism), Paris had consolidated the title during the first third of the twentieth century, mainly because of the exile of artists from Soviet Russia and Nazi Germany. Since the Second World War, however, the United States had begun to challenge France's preeminence for some historians because France clung so closely to the Iron Curtain, but France—especially Paris—was not happy to let this unofficial tag move west across the Atlantic. France had its own answers to the Jackson Pollacks of the 1950s. The Lettristes and Cobra group led by Isidore Isou laid the basis for the *Internationale Situationniste*. Nicolas de Staël showed that the prewar migration to Paris by talented artists from Eastern Europe had not yet finished. Matisse, Dubuffet, Léger, and Masson, not to mention

other fragments of Surrealism, were still active, and Picasso was happily working in the south of France.

Indeed, in the postwar period, France was producing new important artists such as Jean Hélion. The early 1960s saw crucial developments in the visual arts: the so-called new realism of Yves Klein, the pop art of Raymond Hains. Situationism and happenings saw art bursting out of the galleries into the streets in a prelude to the radical upheaval of May 1968. Niki de Saint-Phalle's early work and that of Christo (wrapping everything in plastic sheeting) contributed to the growing radicalization. Much of the art created in the 1960s worked with notions of the sacred (or to the debunking of old notions of the sacred) that had emerged from the work of Georges Bataille and, more conservatively, from that of Roger Caillois. Of course, the May events produced their own politicized artwork: the agitational poster, produced in long sessions at the Ecole des Beaux-Arts in Paris, and other more militant abstract work by artists such as Gérard Fromanger and performance artist Jean-Jacques Lebel.

Fromanger is considered in a work by the radical anti-psychiatry theorist Gilles Deleuze on Francis Bacon (1981), and even though Jacques Rancière has recently doubted the concept of a Deleuzian aesthetic, Deleuze's theories have been crucial in informing creativity since the 1960s. His forthright rejection of the dialectic leading to a positive conception of the philosophy of art has had a huge effect on artists, with his key concepts of rhizome, multitude, desire, and machine undermining traditional notions and metaphors of root, singularity, taste, and creativity. Indeed, the copying, borrowing, and general sending-up of serious modernism, so typical of today's postmodernism, was, in the 1960s, a deeply political challenge to the art institution.

Not surprisingly, aesthetic theories tend to run alongside artistic practices, to the point that it is nigh impossible to say which came first. Similarly, developments in critical theory in relation to literature can be seen in parallel with those in the visual arts in France. For example, Abstract Expressionism seemed to inform the aesthetics of the New Novel in the 1950s. The slow dematerialization of the art object across the 1960s (evident in the minimalist, pop art, and conceptual movements) is replicated in the literary theory of the time. Theorists of narrative attempted first to show how narrative texts are structured and then to deconstruct the literary text in a gesture that was further proof that the visual and the written arts have always and will continue to have a dialogue. Communist Party thinker Pierre Daix attempted to summarize the meeting of modern art with *la nouvelle critique* (1968). However, it is the art criticism of Marcelin Pleynet that was the important bridge.

Originally a poet and central figure in the avant-garde journal *Tel Quel,* Pleynet began in the late 1960s to specialize in art criticism. The use of Paul Valéry's Nietzschean expression for the journal's name was a hint of the radical formalism with which the old Collège de France poet was going to be associated. Pleynet analyzed painting dating from Cézanne (1971) in relation to ideology, displaying his freedom to dissent from established forms of art history and criticism. A champion of Support(s)-Surface(s), an important group of artists questioning the (physical and material) limits of art, he also played a crucial role in bringing American art into France, writing lucidly (1977) on Twombly, Motherwell, Francis, and minimal art. Similarly, Jean-Louis Schefer, also a onetime *Tel Quelian,* produced an important scenographic form of art criticism (1969), in which a painting was treated like a piece of theater and was analyzed structurally and semiologically, as if it were a narrative. In the wake of the 1960s theoretical explosion, Sarah Kofman produced a useful synthesis of Freudian aesthetics (1970); Nicos Hadjinicolaou (1973) produced a Marxist version of the history of art, building on the genetic-structural work of Lucien Goldmann (1970); and J. G. Merquior tried to summarize Claude Levi-Strauss's structuralist aesthetics (1977). An important dissenter against the perceived speculative nature of structuralism and semiology in art criticism was the Swiss theorist Philippe Junod (1976), whose work argued the case of the late nineteenth-century aesthetician Konrad Fiedler.

The art criticism of the 1960s was a fast-moving phenomenon. Nevertheless, there were attempts in the postwar period to transcend one's historical moment and erect monuments of art criticism. One of these was by the great French politician and novelist of the Chinese revolution and of political action, the future government minister of the Arts under General de Gaulle, André Malraux. Fine-art criticism was dominated by Malraux in the 1950s and early 1960s. His magisterial three-volume magnum opus, *La Psychologie de l'Art* (1947–1949), as well as *Les Voix du silence* (1951) and republished studies (1957, 1965), attempted to understand art globally, and his work has influenced subsequent art debates in France. The essayist Gaëtan Picon (1974) continued this erudite tradition in the 1960s and into the 1970s.

Other figures from the 1930s continued to play important roles in postwar aesthetics. Maurice Merleau Ponty (Johnson, 1993) and Jean-Paul Sartre influenced art-criticism debates with their differing versions of existentialism. Existentialist philosophy swept away the Bergson-inspired philosophy of art of the prewar period, dominated by Charles Mauron's work on the psychology of aesthetics (1935), by Emile Mâle's exhaustive efforts to understand how religious art is affected by other ideological spheres (1932), and by Henri Focillon's archaeological treatise on form in art (1934). Here, "form" and "content" were hotly debated. In arguing that technique in medieval art has obscured subject matter, Mâle was proposing an iconology that shows how in medieval (and presumably all) art, "every form clothes a thought" (1913), an approach that was to have a big influence on Erwin Panofsky and the Warburg school.

Alongside this more traditional approach in the 1920s and 1930s there emerged a more skeptical and yet more rigorous approach to art and aesthetics. Merleau-Ponty's *Phénoménologie de la perception* and Sartre's *L'Imaginaire* were key moments in the effort by Phenomenology to set up aesthetics as a branch of the sciences, rather than of the arts (Kaelin, 1966), as well as an opportunity for Sartre to settle scores with Alain. In the wake of Phenomenology's success, Etienne Souriau and Pierre Francastel were to become important theoreticians and art historians.

The 1960s thus saw a battle between a traditionalist school, represented by Etienne Gilson (1963, 1964), which tended to rely on a psychological and comparative approach—of which the artist René Passeron is a good example (1962)—and the emerging functionalists, of whom Souriau was the best-known. One-time director of the influential *Revue d'esthétique,* Souriau was eminent in his field, and his later work on the correspondence between the arts paralleled that in poetry of Gaston Bachelard (Cazeaux, 2000). Another phenomenologist, Mikel Dufrenne, who was originally influenced (like Merleau-Ponty) by Walter Benjamin, contributed to the "linguistic turn" debate. His *Esthétique et philosophie* (1967), asking whether art could be considered a language, was an important bridge between Structuralist and formalist aesthetics. The 1960s also saw, within the rise of sociology, significant studies of society's aesthetic preoccupations and practices, with regard to art (Francastel, 1965; Bourdieu, 1967; Duvignaud, 1967) and to photography (Bourdieu, 1965).

Tel Quel's materialist mysticism carried this spirit on, though in an altogether different vein, importing a heady mix of psychoanalysis, Structuralism, Russian formalism, and Marxism into the debate, drawing on Louis Althusser's rereading of Marx while promoting all things Chinese in a new form of (seemingly politically correct) orientalism. Barthes's novelistic writing of Japan (1970) from a deliberately superficial perspective contributed to this valorization of Far Eastern aesthetics, whereas his radical rereading and rewriting of a Balzac short story, in the enigmatically titled *S/Z* (1970), redrew the aesthetic map. On the one hand, Balzac's *Sarrasine* showed that the written, performing, and visual arts were one; on the other hand, that the viewer and the reader were now (ideally at least) producers of meaning and text. His work on pleasure (1973) in the decadent early 1970s then deployed Lacanian concepts to win back the concept from its ownership by the Right.

The dramatic events of May 1968 fractured the debate further, in a rush of politicized creativity that questioned the very definition of art. Pierre Gaudibert (1972), curator of the Musée d'Art Moderne de la ville de Paris, drew on Althusser, Wilhelm Reich, Paul Nizan, and Daniel Mothé to show that art and all cultural activities under capitalism were simply the Bourgeoisie's way of integrating and normalizing the working class into Neo-capitalism. The short-lived Maoist cultural hegemony in post-1968 France—which saw all art as bourgeois (and therefore fascist, rather curiously)—merely pulverized any aesthetic categories left standing. Aesthetics, like the very object it aimed to theorize, was considered compromised, as a form of bourgeois ideology, which merely gave a semblance of autonomy. In the 1980s, Kofman could write only about the melancholy aspect of art (1985). The French art world was similarly affected. However, the mess that art fell into in 1970s France, fueled by the perception that, like social revolution, the avantgarde was dead, helped American artists to become more appreciated (see Pleynet).

The 1980s shifted the artistic debates toward more functional media such as architecture, typified by the "grands projets" inaugurated by France's first socialist President for many decades, François Mitterrand (Ragon, 1986). The 1980s also saw more communitarian considerations arise, especially in relation to the bicentennial celebrations of the French Revolution (see Sayag and Julia, 1989). The consolidation of Trotskyist Marxism in France, following May 1968, allowed Michel Lequenne (1984) to unearth the Lukacsian approach to aesthetics, occulted by decades of Stalinism, socialist realism, and the Althusserian grip on the French intelligentsia.

It is often suggested that the debates within art history and criticism of this period, of the 1960s and since, have merely replayed those that had taken place in the 1920s. For example, Daniel Buren's installation work (since 1968) or Support(s)-Surface(s) experiments could be seen in the Dadaist and Surrealist excesses of fifty years before. Such a view, though easy to assert (the 1960s follow, by definition, the 1920s), is not only historically analogical—evacuating the content of the more recent debates, such as key developments in art history—but also fails to engage with the aesthetic preoccupations of the end of the twentieth century. A key area of these preoccupations is postcolonial aesthetics.

At the turn of the twenty-first century, a growing minority of art critics is reassessing certain art movements to expose their complicity in maintaining colonial and racial stereotypes. One need only compare the work of Archer-Shaw (2000) on the Parisian avantgarde of the 1920s with that of Jean Laudes (1968) of thirty years before. Bidima (1997) goes a stage further by showing that expropriation of African art in Western art markets, especially in Paris, has always constricted and continues to alienate all art forms created in Africa. Only an art that deconstructs all aspects of art and posits a new utopia, he argues (following Deleuze), is valid aesthetically; and thus, he has no truck with Afrocentric or male-centered viewpoints. Yves Michaud (2001), in contrast, considers that the utopia of art is now finished and that an aesthetic pluralism now dominates that promotes, in theory, a democratic and subjectivist approach and eschews all established aesthetic (or political) criteria (Michaud, 1997).

Another important development is the growing acceptance of photography into the arena of art criticism, and a burgeoning market of work on the photograph in all of its dimensions by theorists, essayists, and critics is evident in France at the start of the new century (Soulages, 1998). The theorization of photographic aesthetics relies heavily on phenomenologic methods of art criticism, helping to renew interest in Merleau-Ponty and even Sartre while maintaining a psychoanalytical dimension (see, for example, Barthes, 1980). The work of Régis Debray (1992) on the notion of "médiologie"—the study of how reality is mediated by images (photographic or otherwise)—helped bring photography into the center of aesthetic reflection.

If Lyotard's postmodern theories (1978, 1979) did little to stem the perceived decline of aesthetics in the late 1970s—Derrida's effort (1978) being more of an exception, in all senses of the word—then the 1990s showed a marked return of aesthetics. Philippe Lacoue-Labarthe, Jean-Luc Nancy, Jacques Rancière, and Giorgio Agamben, all based around the Collège International de Philosophie, as well as Jean-Marie Schaeffer, Luc Boltanski, and Gérard Genette have all helped to rekindle interest. Genette (1994) argues that poetics makes aesthetics redundant, showing transcendence to be the crucial category of art once immanence is excluded. Boltanski (1999), Nancy (1993), and Lacoue-Labarthe (1989) put forward politicized considerations, the former on how we (are forced to) adjust to (media) representation, the latter two more interested in the very limits of mimesis and representation. Paul Virilio (1980) and Jean Baudrillard (1991) have wrestled with understanding humanity now confronted with cyberreality. Virilio suggests that we are all subject to "picnoleptic" moments in which both time and image stand still, and Baudrillard suggests that the hyperreal nature of the virtual world is such that the Gulf War of 1991 was merely a televisual spectacle. Returning to a phenomenological approach, Georges Didi-Huberman has recently asked *how* we see an image (1990).

However, the most important contemporary philosopher of art in France is undoubtedly Jean-Marie Schaeffer. Heavily influenced by the analytical philosophical tradition, he has suggested controversially (1992) that aesthetics have too often excluded pleasure and taste, privileging high art over popular forms. He criticizes the German aesthetic tradition, from Hegel to Heidegger, for its view that art produces an "ecstatic" knowledge, and consequently, he has argued for a new form of aesthetics and criticism (2000) that seems to privilege description over evaluation.

Much of the fallout from 1960s radical theory still remains. Following the fascination with Lacanian bodily aesthetics in the 1980s, Christine Buci-Glucksmann wrote perceptively on the baroque (1986). Recent art criticism has continued the post-1968 fascination with psychoanalysis and desire into the 1990s, Damisch (1992) and Millet (1997) being fine examples of this, the latter in her steering of the journal *Art Press*. Louis Marin's work (1994) on representation in art has worked to combine structuralist and poststructuralist approaches. Meanwhile, Pierre Fresnault-Deruelle (1989) and the Groupe μ (1992), based in Liège in Belgium, have continued a rigorous semiological approach, attempting to produce a general grammar or rhetoric of the language of the visual, using the theories of Umberto Eco and Roland Barthes. The 1990s have also seen the attempt to understand the institutional and patrimonial nature of art and criticism. Recent studies by Luc Ferry (1993) and Marc Fumaroli (1991) are good examples of how the debate has shifted to one in which France's very cultural heritage, threatened by globalization, Americanization, and the triumph of English, needs, it seems, to be defended.

Aesthetics must today battle with the complexity, ambiguity, and contradictions of the modern world. Indeed, the stunning shift in material and physical artistic supports brought about by computers means that possibilities are nigh limitless, requiring a theorization in a Benjaminian perspective. Aesthetics seems to have separated itself today from criticism, which, in the best of cases, does not mean that there is no judgment or that others' judgments are ignored. For some, on the contrary, it means that spontaneous acts of judgment—or "taste"—are themselves ripe for normative reflection. Aesthetics in France today then tends—the final triumph of Kant over Hegel?—to be descriptive of these acts rather than normative in the wider social sense.

Furthermore, the act of designing an art history requires explanations and judgments. Therefore, Jimenez (1995, 1997) suggests that contemporary art criticism—similar to (because of?) art—is "sans repères" (without points of reference), a rudderless, chaotic, valueless activity. The turn toward an analytical philosophy, represented by Schaeffer, in which description replaces evaluation, is, Jimenez argues (1999), a function of the crisis of contemporary art. The next debate must surely be then whether (and if so, how) there can be a return to a politically committed form of art criticism and, of course, of art.

ANDY STAFFORD

See also **Entries on the individuals mentioned in this article**

Further Reading

Archer-Shaw, Petrine, *Negrophilia. Avant-Garde Paris and Black Culture in the 1920s*, London: Thames & Hudson, 2000

Barthes, Roland, *L'Empire des signes*, Paris: Seuil, 1970; as *Empire of Signs*, translated by Richard Howard, 1983

Barthes, Roland, *S/Z*, Paris: Seuil, 1970; as *S/Z*, translated by Richard Miller, 1975

Barthes, Roland, *Le Plaisir du texte*, Paris: Seuil, 1973; as *The Pleasure of the Text*, translated by Richard Miller, 1976

Barthes, Roland, *La Chambre claire. Note sur la photographie*, Paris: Seuil/Gallimard, 1980; as *Camera Lucida: Reflections on Photography*, translated by Richard Howard, 1984

Baudrillard, Jean, *La Guerre du golfe n'a pas eu lieu*, Paris: Galilée, 1991; translated by Paul Patton, Sydney: Power Publications, 1995

Bidima, Jean-Godefroy, *L'Art négro-africain*, Paris: Presses Universitaires de France, 1997

Boltanski, Luc, *Distant Suffering: Morality, Media and Politics*, translated by Graham Burchell, Cambridge: Cambridge University Press, 1999

Bourdieu, Pierre, *La Distinction. Critique sociale du jugement*, Paris: Editions de Minuit, 1979; translated by Richard Nice, 1984

Bourdieu, Pierre, Luc Boltanski et al, *Un art moyen. Essai sur les usages sociaux de la photographie*, Paris: Editions de Minuit, 1965; as *Photography: a middle brow art*, 1990

Buci-Glucksmann, Christine, *La Folie du voir. De l'Esthétique baroque*, Paris: Galilée, 1986

Cazeaux, Clive, *The Continental Aesthetics Reader*, London: Routledge, 2000

Daix, Pierre, *Nouvelle critique et art moderne*, Paris: Seuil, 1968

Damisch, Hubert, *Le Jugement de Pâris*, Paris: Flammarion, 1992

Debray, Régis, *Vie et mort de l'image*, Paris: Gallimard, 1992

Deleuze, Gilles, *Francis Bacon, logique de la sensation*, Paris: Editions de la Différence, 1981

Derrida, Jacques, *La vérité en peinture*, Paris: Flammarion, 1978

Didi-Huberman, Georges, *Devant l'Image*, Paris: Minuit, 1990

Dufrenne, Mikel, *Esthétique et philosophie*, Paris: Klincksieck, 1967

Dufrenne, Mikel, *Phénoménologie de la perception critique*, 2 volumes, Paris: Presses Universitaires de France, 1967

Duvignaud, Jean, *Sociologie de l'art*, Paris: Presses Universitaires de France, 1967; as *The Sociology of Art*, translated by Timothy Wilson, 1972

Ferry, Luc, *Homo Aestheticus. The Invention of Taste in the Democratic Age*, translated by Robert de Loaiza, Chicago: University of Chicago Press, 1993

Focillon, Henri, *La vie des formes*, Paris: Presses Universitaires de France, 1934

Francastel, Pierre, *Histoire de la peinture française*, 3 volumes, Paris: Gonthier, 1955

Francastel, Pierre, *La réalité figurative. Eléments structurels de la sociologie de l'art*, Paris: Gonthier, 1965

Fresnault-Deruelle, Pierre, *Les Images prises au mot (rhétorique de l'image fixe)*, Paris: Edilig, 1989

Fumaroli, Marc, *L'état culturel. Une religion moderne*, Paris: Fallois, 1991

Gaudibert, Pierre, *Action culturelle: intégration et/ou subversion*, Paris: Castermann, 1972

Genette, Gérard, *L'Œuvre d'art. Immanence et transcendance*, Paris: Seuil, 1994

Gilson, Etienne, *Introduction aux arts du beau*, Paris: Vrin, 1963

Gilson, Etienne, *Matières et formes*, Paris: Vrin, 1964

Goldmann, Lucien, *Structures mentales et création culturelle*, Paris: Anthropos, 1970

Groupe μ (Jean-Marie Klinkenberg, Philippe Minguet, Francis Edeline), *Traité du signe visuel. Pour une rhétorique de l'image*, Paris: Seuil, 1992

Hadjinicolaou, Nicos, *Histoire de l'Art et lutte des classes*, Paris: Maspero, 1973, translated by Louise Amal, 1978

Hamon, Françoise, and Philippe Dagen, dir., *Histoire de l'Art. Epoque contemporaine. XIXe–XX siècles*, Paris: Flammarion, 1995

Heathcote, Owen, Alex Hughes, James S. Williams, *Gay Signatories. Gay and Lesbian Theory, Fiction and Film*, Oxford: Berg, 1998

Jimenez, Marc, *La Critique. Crise de l'art ou consensus culturel?* Paris: Klincksieck, 1995

Jimenez, Marc, *Qu'est-ce que l'esthétique?* Paris: Gallimard, 1997

Jimenez, Marc, *L'Esthétique contemporaine*, Paris: Klincksieck, 1999

Johnson, Galen A., *The Merleau-Ponty Aesthetics Reader*, Evanston, Illinois: Northwestern University Press, 1993

Junod, Philippe, *Transparence et opacité. Essai sur les fondements théoriques de l'art moderne*, Lausanne: L'Age d'homme, 1976

Kaelin, Eugene F., *An Existentialist Aesthetic. The Theories of Sartre and Merleau-Ponty*, Madison: University of Wisconsin Press, 1966

Kofman, Sarah, *L'Enfance de l'art. Une interprétation de l'esthétique freudienne*, Paris: Payot, 1970

Kofman, Sarah, *La Mélancolie de l'art*, Paris: Galilée, 1985

Lacoue-Labarthe, Philippe, *Typography. Mimesis, Philosophy, Politics*, translated by Christopher Fynk, Stanford, California: Stanford University Press, 1989

Laudes, Jean, *La Peinture française (1905–1914) et "l'art nègre"*, Paris: Klincksieck, 1968

Lequenne, Michel, *Marxisme et esthétique*, Paris: Editions La Brèche, 1984

Lyotard, Jean-François, *Discours, figure*, Paris: Klincksieck, 1978

Lyotard, Jean-François, *La Condition postmoderne*, Paris: Editions de Minuit, 1979

Mâle, Emile, *Religious Art in France; Thirteenth Century: A Study in Medieval Iconography and its Sources of Inspiration*, London: Dent, 1913

Mâle, Emile, *L'Art religieux après le concile de Trente*, Paris: Armand Colin, 1932

Malraux, André, *La Psychologie de l'Art*, 3 volumes, Geneva: Skira, 1947–1949

Malraux, André, *Les Voix du silence*, Paris: Gallimard, 1951

Malraux, André, *La métamorphose des dieux* 2 volumes, Paris: Gallimard, 1957 and 1974

Malraux, André, *Le musée imaginaire*, Paris: Gallimard, 1965

Marin, Louis, *De la représentation*, Paris: Seuil, 1994

Mauron, Charles, *Aesthetics and Psychology*, translated by Roger Fry and Katharine John, London: Hogarth Press, 1935

Merquior, J.-G., *L'Esthétique de Levi-Strauss*, Paris: Presses Universitaires de France, 1977

Michaud, Yves, *La Crise de l'art contemporain*, Paris: Presses Universitaires de France, 1997

Michaud, Yves, The end of the utopia in art, in Jean-Marie Schaeffer, dir., *Think Art. Theory and Practice in the Art of Today*, Rotterdam: Witte de With, 1998, pp. 131–156.

Millet, Cathérine, *L'Art contemporain*, Paris: Flammarion, 1997

Nancy, Jean-Luc, *The Birth to Presence*, translated by Brian Holmes, et al., Stanford, California: Stanford University Press, 1993

Passeron, René, *L'Oeuvre picturale et les fonctions de l'apparence*, Paris: Vrin, 1962, 1974

Picon, Gaëtan, *1863: naissance de la peinture moderne*, Geneva/Paris: Skira/Flammarion, 1974

Pleynet, Marcelin, *L'Enseignement de la peinture*, Paris: Seuil, 1971

Pleynet, Marcelin, *Art et Littérature*, Paris: Seuil, 1977

Ragon, Michel, *L'Art: pour quoi faire?* Paris/Tournai: Castermann, 1978

Ragon, Michel, *Histoire de l'architecture et de l'urbanisme moderne*, 3 volumes, Paris: Seuil, 1986

Rancière, Jacques, Deleuze accomplit le destin de l'esthétique, *Magazine littéraire*, February 2002, pp. 38–40

Sayag, Alain, and Julia, Isabelle, Prefaces to *La France. Images of Women and Ideas of Nation, 1789–1989*, London: South Bank Centre, 1989

Schaeffer, Jean-Marie, *L'Art de l'âge moderne. L'Esthétique et la philosophie de l'art du XVIIIe siècle à nos jours*, Paris: Gallimard, 1992; translated by Steven Rendall, Princeton, New Jersey: Princeton University Press, 2000

Schaeffer, Jean-Marie, *Adieu à l'esthétique*, Paris: Presses Universitaires de France, 2000

Schefer, Jean-Louis, *Scénographie d'un tableau*, Paris: Seuil, 1969

Schor, Naomi, *Reading in Detail: Aesthetics and the Feminine*, New York: Methuen, 1987

Soulages, François, *Esthétique de la photographie. La perte et le reste*, Paris: Nathan, 1998

Souriau, Etienne, *La Correspondance des arts. Eléments d'esthétique comparée*, Paris: Flammarion, 1969

Virilio, Paul, *Esthétique de la disparition*, Paris: Balland, 1980; translated by Philip Beitchman, 1991

ARTAUD, ANTONIN
Dramatist, Actor, Poet

In a letter of 1946, Antonin Artaud writes about his works *The Umbilical* and *Nerve-Scales*: "At the moment, they seemed to me to be full of cracks, gaps, platitudes. . . . But after twenty years gone by, they appear stupefying, not as my own triumphs, but in relation to the inexpressible." He refers to the fact that after all those years, his work went its own way, "constituting a bizarre truth by themselves." Concerning that "bizarre truth," one cannot deny that his peculiar work gave rise to the most passionate, if not eccentric, commentaries. His writings are often made to bear witness, as an example or martyr, to clinical studies, cult-veneration, and biographies: Artaud became a legend. Moreover, his tragic life, for example, his internment in mental asylums, made of him a victim or a "suicide of society." As dramatist, actor, and poet, Artaud was certainly a pioneer of experimental theater and poetry, and the importance of his writings as such became more and more acknowledged, thanks to the edition of his collected works (twenty-two volumes); the critical and philosophical approaches of thinkers such as Blanchot, Derrida, or Deleuze; and some recent studies.

One of the central features of his work is certainly the anguish for dispossession: The stupefying fact that his own work seems to "lie in relation to the author" and constitute "a bizarre truth." It is not exaggerating to say that most of his writings are motivated by the obstinate desire to conjure that continuous awareness of dissociation, dispossession, the "loss" or "traps in our thoughts." The origin and urgency of his speech, which impelled him into expression, was precisely the suffering of a lack of "true communication with ourselves." He indefatigably described "something furtive" that separated him from his words and his thoughts. This *impouvoir* (powerlessness) appears thematically in his correspondence to Jacques Rivière, director of the NRF, who reproached the poems Artaud had sent to him for their lack of consistency and maturity. For Artaud, however, that lack is not accidental, caused by a simple impotence or a lack of inspiration and practice. In his famous answers to Rivière, he always stresses how much the "dispersiveness" of his poems and their "formal defects" are not to be attributed to a lack of mastery or intellectual development but to a "central collapse of the mind" (*effondrement*). He writes in one of his letters to Jacques Rivière (January 29, 1924), "There is thus something that is destroying my thinking, a something which does not prevent me from being what I might be, but which leaves me, if I may say so, in abeyance (*en suspens*). A *something furtive* which takes away from me the words which I have found." What is this "something furtive," which finally not only takes away from him his memory and his desires, but his body? Since even my body, thus Artaud, has been stolen from my birth. All his work, writings, and theater can be seen as a tentative to conjure that loss, the "abnormal separation" and dispossession, trying to restore a kind of life and of body no longer threatened by the "voids" and "orifices." He

writes in that context, "I am a man who has lost his life and who is seeking every way of re-integrating it in its proper place."

Hence, in *Nerve-Scale*, Artaud describes "true inspiration" as the spirit that would give him back speech and would enable him to re-establish that "true communication with myself." However, this inspiration can only be attained after having been able to overcome the dissociations occurring in normal speech, thinking, and writing (classical literature is "trash," "cochonnerie"). He must therefore get rid of everything that deprives him of his own nature. Words, for example, will have to be "physical signs" that do not "trespass towards concepts" but that "will be construed in an unconditional, truly magical sense." Or else his thinking will have to "whip his innateness" in favor of a "genitality" of thinking (Deleuze). This magical speech resembles an inspired incantation, "intellectual cries" (*des cris intellectuels*) as he says in *Position of the Flesh*, "cries which stem from the marrow's delicacy" (*des cris qui proviennent de la finesse des moelles*). In that sense, Artaud attempts to elaborate a real system of shouts, a system of gestures and "mysterious signs" that escape the classical systems of expressions and language, and that "correspond to some obscure reality which we here in Occident have completely repressed." That "obscure reality" is what he calls "the flesh," and his theater will have to be governed according the requirements of that kind of "physical signs" and writings. It is well known that he sought the themes for that "theory of theater" (elaborated in *The Theater and Its Double*) in non-Western forms of theater; for example, the ancient Balinese theater. He also used also the term "theatre of cruelty," meaning to define a new kind of "spectacle" that neutralized intellectual associations by minimizing the spoken word and relied instead on a combination of physical movement and gesture, sounds, and the elimination of conventional spatial arrangements and sets. Thanks to what he called the "hieroglyphs of breath," he tried to recover an idea of "sacred theater," where a real union with life was made possible. In *The Theater and Its Double*, he writes at this occasion, "It happens that mannerism, this excessively hieratic style, with its rolling alphabet, its shrieks of splitting stones, noises of branches, noises of the cutting and rolling of wood, compose a sort of animated material murmur in the air, in space, a visual as well as audible whispering. And after an instant the magic identification is made: *we know it is we who were speaking*." The theater of cruelty achieves a restoration of life, a repossession of thought and body, precisely because it restores a speech in immediate presence with flesh. This notion, however, has no ontological meaning and is deeply opposed to what a phenomenologist as Merleau-Ponty would have understood by it. It does not refer to some deeper dimension or "element" of being but to a "fluctuating center" that escapes all forms of thinking, of meaning and understanding. Moreover, what he means by body is not an animated unity or original subjectivity. The body he wants to restore is an unarticulated, exploded plurality of forces that can not organize themselves into a unity. A "body without organs": "The body is the body, it is alone and has no need of organs, the body is never an organism, organisms are the enemies of bodies." It is clear that in *The Theater and Its Double*, Artaud transcends the simple treatise on theatrical practice, as it means to be a global and nontheoretical "destruction" of the Western metaphysical premises (of duality between body and soul, sign and concept, and so on). But it is also clear that "destruction" is impelled by the inner obsession to conjure that continuous dissociation (and the metaphysical dualities it implicates) that is caused by that "something furtive" to which he referred in his letter to Rivière; the incantatory character of the writings in his "cahiers de Rodez," written in the asylum, are certainly a good illustration of it. In conjuring the separation, his writings gravitate around that "something furtive," origin of all dissociation. But precisely thanks to its intensive presence and thanks to the obsessive incantation it awakes, some unity seems to be achieved. As a consequence, it appears that the origin of the separation seems to be at the same place the origin of the recovered unity or the "re-established communication with one's self." That communication, he says in *Nerve-Scale*, presupposes "a certain flocculation of objects, the gathering of the mental gems about one as yet *undiscovered nucleus*."

ROLAND BREEUR

See also **Maurice Blanchot, Gilles Deleuze, Jacques Derrida, Maurice Merleau-Ponty, Jacques Riviere**

Biography

Antonin Artaud, French poet, dramatist, and actor, was born in Marseilles in 1896. Artaud went to Paris in 1920 and became a stage and screen performer. In 1927, he cofounded, together with Roger Vitrac and Robert Aron, the Théatre Alfred Jarry. Originally a member of the Surrealists, he was expelled after two years, in 1926. After a "mythical" journey in Mexico (cf. *D'un voyage au pays des Tarahumaras*) and Ireland (in 1936–1937), he underwent asylum internment from 1937 to 1946. During the internment years, his health greatly deteriorated because of prolonged starvation and electroshock treatments. However, his final two years of life were extremely productive (cf. the essay *Van Gogh the Suicide of Society* and the radio broadcast *To have done with the judgement of God*). He died in a Paris suburb in 1948.

Selected Writings

Oeuvres Complètes
Collected Works, 6 volumes, translated by Victor Corti
Antonin Artaud: Selected Writings, edited by Susan Sontag, translated by Helen Weaver, 1989

Further Reading

Barber, Stephen, *Antonin Artaud: Blows and Bombs*, London: Faber & Faber, 1993

Bermel, Albert, *Artaud's Theatre of Cruelty*, New York: Taplinger Publishing Co., 1977

Blanchot, Maurice, Artaud, in *Le livre à venir*, Paris: Gallimard, 1959

Deleuze, Gilles, Le schizophrène et le mot, *Critique*, 255–256, 1968, 731–746

Deleuze Gilles, and Félix Guattari, Comment se faire un corps sans organes? in *Mille plateaux*, Paris: Minuit, 1980, 185–204

Derrida, Jacques, La parole soufflée, in *L'écriture et la différence*, Paris: Editions du Seuil, 1967

Derrida, Jacques, Le théatre de la cruauté et la clôture de la représentation, in *L'écriture et la différence*, Paris: Editions du Seuil, 1967

Derrida, Jacques, *Artaud le moma: interjections d'appel*, Paris: Galilée, 2002

Garelli, Jacques, *Antonin Artaud et la question du lieu*, Paris: J. Corti, 1982

Virmaux, Alain & Odette, *Artaud*, Paris: Belfond, 1979

AUTOBIOGRAPHY

Autobiography has conventionally been defined as the biography, or life story, of the person writing that story, usually in the form of a first-person, chronologically ordered narrative. Over much of the twentieth century, reliance on such a conventional definition tended in France, far more than in many other national cultures, to reflect and reinforce a pervasive devaluation of the genre, with only the odd exception—such as Rousseau's *Confessions* (written in the 1760s)—being recognized as worthy of serious critical scrutiny. Lacking intellectual legitimacy, autobiography remained out of favor among both writers and critics for much of the twentieth century. Surrealism, for example, was based on a set of premises and values that, in promoting above all the cause of the lyrical subject, spurned pedestrian autobiography as much as it disowned the realist apparatus of the novel. It was only after the Second World War, with the advent of existentialism, that a group of writers and intellectuals eventually discovered in autobiography a global form eminently compatible with their theoretical preoccupations. As structuralism gradually took over from existentialism in the 1950s and 1960s as the key provider of new ideas and methods in the human and social sciences, autobiography was once more dislodged from the intellectual agenda. Only in the last quarter of the twentieth century, when the demise of structuralism opened the way for the broad cultural phenomenon known as the "return of the subject," did autobiography finally begin to attract widespread and sustained attention among contemporary writers and critics. Something of a misnomer, the "return" of the subject might more aptly be characterized as a process of refiguration because the survivor of the structuralist critique of the "founding" or "sovereign" subject resurfaces bearing the traces of its critique. Neither self-determining nor fully determined, the refigured subject or self is located (as opposed to disengaged), embodied (as opposed to unaffected), ongoing (as opposed to unchanging), and relational (as opposed to autonomous).

Under this new dispensation, autobiography has come to be studied both as a specific genre, synonymous with the developmental narrativity of "life-writing," and as a pervasive, scattered, cross-generic register, variously labeled "self-writing," "autography," or "the autobiographical." Reflecting the postmodernist turn to hybrid forms, autobiography in this more general yet more erratic sense is considered to manifest itself in a given text as one discursive ingredient among others. Coextensively, whether geared toward the generic or the cross-generic field, the study of autobiography as a key mode of research into the modalities of human identity has come to be informed by a broad spectrum of theoretical and methodological interests, ranging from linguistics, psychoanalysis, and ethnography to feminism and queer studies. As a result, the study of autobiography has never been more steeped in intellectual endeavor at large than over the last three decades of the twentieth century.

As happens with any major shift in intellectual outlook, the "return of the subject" has resulted in a significant revision of past literary history: in this case, a revision that seeks to incorporate, not always uncritically, all things autobiographical. Among French authors from the first half of the twentieth century whose work has been revisited in this light, the cases of André Gide, Colette, and Michel Leiris are perhaps the most noteworthy. Long considered a documentary resource for those interested in the author's background, Gide's *Si le grain ne meurt* (If It Die, 1926) is now regarded as a work of such compelling ambiguity and complexity that it demands to be treated on a par with his most strongly admired fictional output. The fact that the ambiguities in question arise through the oblique ways in which Gide negotiates the issue of his homosexual nature has led specialists in queer studies to highlight the value of this autobiography as a pioneering work of confessionalism whose confusions and evasions, initially suggestive of a sexually repressed mind, end up challenging any attempt to reduce the diverse facets of a subjectivity to a uniform, easily stereotyped, homosexual identity.

Colette is among a large number of women writers whose work was not taken seriously by the critical establishment until it was revisited by feminist critics. Autobiographical works such as Colette's *La Naissance du jour* (Break of Day, 1928) and *Sido* (1929) have benefited in particular from contemporary feminist studies, not least because feminism in the 1970s and 1980s, in reacting against structuralism's neglect of the gendered, embodied subject, was one of the key driving forces behind the return of the subject. Valued for the frank way in which it maps the donning of masks, disguises, and fictional selves on a stage of androgynous desire, Colette's autobiographical writing has come to be read, like Gide's, as another exemplary affirmation of dispersed identity.

Based on a thematic rather than chronological principle of organization, Michel Leiris's *L'Age d'homme* (Manhood, 1939) enacts a different—and innovative—kind of dispersal. Described by the author himself as a "collage," this work marshals a diverse set of aesthetic and intellectual imperatives drawn from surrealism, existentialism, ethnography, and psychoanalysis into the writing of a relentlessly lucid self-portrait. Through primarily sexual confession, Leiris aims to "liquidate" his past while remaining conscious that, in the very process, he is fatally destined to do little more than glamorize the tormented inner life he seeks to put behind him. Thus, *L'Age d'homme* not only anticipates contemporary interest in the genre of auto-ethnography but also proves compelling for an audience familiar with deconstructionist thought insofar as it acknowledges the ambiguous space opened up in autobiographical writing between intention and effect, writer and reader, self-writing and self-reading. Following *L'Age d'homme*, Leiris went on between 1948 and 1976 to write the four volumes of *La Règle du jeu* [The Rule of the Game], widely recognized as constituting one of the great works of twentieth-century autobiography.

In these revaluations of past autobiographical works, the principle of ambiguity or uncertainty emerges as a highly valued leitmotif. Under the sway of postmodernism, moreover, this motif has come to unsettle the question of genre itself. Insofar as one of the main axes of generic ambiguation in contemporary textual practice coincides with the shift from life-writing to more mixed and unstable forms of self-writing, contemporary critics have been encouraged to seek out forerunners of the latter. Thus, surrealism, rarely seen as a movement promoting the cause of autobiography, can nevertheless be construed to have engaged widely with the autobiographical. Opening on the question, "Qui suis-je?" (Who am I?), André Breton's *Nadja* (1928) announces the author's intention to explore some of the more irrational workings of subjectivity as prompted by a series of real-life incidents, many of which are incorporated into the narrative of a love affair. But Breton's ambition to write about himself is constantly supplemented, and beset, by a wider range of discursive ingredients that make the text as much an essay, a treatise, or a manifesto as it is an example of autobiography. Similar patterns of generic hybridity inform Breton's prose ventures in *Les Vases communicants* (Communicating Vessels, 1932), *L'Amour fou* (Mad Love, 1937), and *Arcane 17* (Arcane, 1944): texts that are all autobiographical in their appeal to the writer's own experience but that, in the long run, escape any unambiguous generic definition, including that of autobiography.

Because of their commitment to the lived experience of concrete individuals, writers associated with existentialism brought about a return to more conventional forms of autobiographical writing. Between the mid-1940s and the mid-1960s, works such as Jean Genet's *Journal du voleur* (A Thief's Journal, 1948), André Gorz's *Le Traître* (The Traitor, 1958), Simone de Beauvoir's *Mémoires d'une jeune fille rangée* (Memoirs of a Dutiful Daughter, 1958), and Violette Leduc's *La Bâtarde* (La Batarde, 1964) demonstrated in a rich variety of ways the need for a revaluation of autobiography as the most appropriate way of exploring the significance of human agency in terms of both its capacities and its limits. This was, of course, a "need" rendered all the more urgent by the collective experience of the Second World War. Among this group of writers, the key promoter of autobiography (and biography) at the theoretical level was Jean-Paul Sartre. Sartre's influential essay *Questions de méthode* (Search for a Method, 1957) replaces the traditional notion of a life's *fil conducteur* (main thread) with that of the *projet* (project), characterized as the dynamic orientation whereby a consciousness seeks to confront and overcome the constraining givenness of its environment. He then went on to apply his own theory to himself in a work that proved to be the high point of existentialist autobiography. In *Les Mots* (The Words, 1964), Sartre engages in a pitiless demystification of childhood and, with it, of the child he himself was, the family members who raised him, and the entire bourgeois society whose ideology his grandfather in particular foisted upon him. Rarely has childhood been treated in the context of autobiography with such cutting intellectual verve and stylistic flair by such a self-distant, "dissonant," narrator. Indeed, Sartre's irony in *Les Mots* goes so far as to encompass autobiography itself, as his brilliant critique of the "retrospective illusion" (near the end of the book) underlines. This is a problematization echoed in numerous external comments made by Sartre about his book, remarks to the

effect that *Les Mots* is as much a novel as an autobiography. In these and other ways, Sartre seems to anticipate, even to herald, the disqualification of autobiography implicit in the structuralist critique of the subject, already underway even as Sartre was adding the last touches to *Les Mots*.

Whether understood as a quasi-scientific methodology espousing Lévi-Strauss's "distant gaze," or as what Foucault called a "critical activity" stemming from a deconstructive outlook, structuralism constituted an intellectual paradigm that proved exceptionally inhospitable to autobiography. Ironically, however, as structuralism began to break up in the mid-1970s, the "return" of the subject in the wake of this demise was most tellingly announced by a vanguard of intellectuals formerly closely aligned with structuralist thought, most notably Roland Barthes. In his famous essay "La Mort de l'auteur" (The Death of the Author, 1968), Barthes offered one of the most extreme denunciations of the "founding subject" to be found in the library of structuralism. And yet, a few years later, we find him surprising his readers with a self-portrait, *Roland Barthes par Roland Barthes* (Roland Barthes by Roland Barthes, 1975). Composed of fragments, the text takes the form of what Barthes himself calls a "patchwork." Although the alphabetic ordering of the fragments serves to prevent any slide into sustained self-narration, Barthes does appeal recurrently to moments of personal experience. At the same time, he engages in essayistic forays into the kind of critical discourse for which he remains best known, juxtaposing these with memories, photographs, illustrations of his doodlings and amateur artwork, and numerous reflections of a confessional nature. An intellectual turning point, this self-portrait is written on a knife-edge between a "return" to autobiography and a still lively critique of autobiography, as is nowhere more evident than in the book's opening salvo: "Tout ceci doit être considéré comme dit par un personnage de roman" (All this must be regarded as spoken by a fictional character). Barthes subsequently ventured even further along the road of autobiographical writing with *Fragments d'un discours amoureux* (Fragments of a Lover's Discourse, 1977) and *La Chambre claire* (Camera Lucida, 1980), completing a kind of trilogy, broadly comparable in its hybrid mix of critical and personal registers to the aforementioned sequence of works by Breton.

A watershed year, 1975 also saw the publication of Georges Perec's *W ou le souvenir* d'enfance (W or The Memory of Childhood), an innovative work in which childhood autobiography alternates with the reconstruction of a fiction first written by the author at the age of thirteen. That autobiography was back on the map is a point strongly underlined by another work published in 1975, Philippe Lejeune's *Le Pacte autobiographique* (The Autobiographical Pact), a major theoretical study that almost single-handedly reignited critical interest in the genre. What Lejeune arguably failed to anticipate, however, was the turn toward hybrid forms of autobiographical writing already being signaled in the groundbreaking experiments of Barthes and Perec. This turn was quickly confirmed two years later by the publication of Patrick Modiano's *Livret de famille* (Family Record), at once a patchy autobiography, a series of biographical sketches, and a collection of short stories (a multi-generic mix echoed in Pierre Michon's superb *Vies minuscules* [Minuscule Lives, 1984]), and Serge Doubrovsky's *Fils* (Son/Threads), described in the author's own blurb as "fiction, d'événements et de faits strictement réels; si l'on veut, autofiction" (a fiction, made from strictly real events and facts; if you like, an autofiction). Indeed, as Doubrovsky first coined the term "autofiction," it has gained widespread recognition, both within and beyond the French-speaking world, as a suitable descriptor of a growing range of works seeking to demonstrate that, just as fiction is inevitably to some degree autobiographical, so autobiography cannot—and should not—disguise the fact that it is at least partly fictional. In France, most of the autobiographies produced from the late 1970s onward by the former *nouveaux romanciers*, most notably *Enfance* by Nathalie Sarraute (Childhood, 1983), *L'Amant* by Marguerite Duras (The Lover, 1984), and the three volumes of Alain Robbe-Grillet's *Romanesques* (Fictions, 1985–2001), can in various ways be construed as "autofictions."

Although the term "autofiction" has come to be understood as highly symptomatic of the postmodernist approach to autobiography, it should not for all that be mistaken for yet another variant of postmodern irony. The notion of autofiction has in fact come to be invested over the late twentieth century with an increasing sense of necessity. Our contemporary models of the refigured subject emphasize the uncertainties informing selfhood, identity, experience, and memory, and contemporary writers have responded to these models by producing more conjectural and conditional forms of autobiographical writing in which a pervasive sense of disquiet, encompassing questions of genre, gender, and self, is assumed as both an aesthetic

resource and an ethical safeguard. Fictionality is thus invoked by the vigilant autobiographer not only to assert the power of the imagination but equally to concede the limits of re-imagination. Whether evidenced through the foregrounding of loss and absence in Sophie Calle's photo-textual autobiography *Des Histoires vraies* (True Strories, 1994), or through the inscription of forgetting and trauma in works such as Jorge Semprun's *L'Écriture ou la vie* (Literature or Life, 1994) and Béatrice de Jurquet's *La Traversée des lignes* (Crossing the Lines, 1997), this concession has resulted in a generic "pact" between autobiography and fiction. Fiction no longer impinges as the counterforce or ironic undertow of autobiography but, rather, as the only opportunity we might have of bearing witness to our own, and others', lives. As so memorably described by the American writer William Maxwell in his poignant autofiction *So Long, See You Tomorrow* (1980), this is a fragile and always contestable opportunity, relying as it does on "the unsupported word of a witness who was not present except in imagination."

JOHNNIE GRATTON

See also **Roland Barthes, Simone de Beauvoir, Andre Breton, Michel Foucault, Andre Gide, Andre Gorz, Michel Leiris, Claude Levi-Strauss, Jean-Paul Sartre**

Further Reading

Anderson, Linda, *Autobiography*, London: Routledge, 2001

Eakin, Paul John, *Fictions in Autobiography: Studies in the Art of Self-Invention*, Princeton, New Jersey: Princeton University Press, 1985

Gratton, Johnnie, "Introduction: The Return of the Subject," in *Subject Matters: Subject and Self in French Literature from Descartes to the Present*, edited by Paul Gifford and Johnnie Gratton, Amsterdam: Rodopi, 2000, 1–27

Hughes, Alex, *Heterographies: Sexual Difference in French Autobiography*, Oxford: Berg, 1999

Keefe, Terry, and Edmund Smyth, eds., *Autobiography and the Existential Self: Studies in Modern French Writing*, Liverpool: Liverpool University Press, 1995

Lejeune, Philippe, *On Autobiography*, translated by P.J. Eakin, Minneapolis: University of Minnesota Press, 1989

Lecarme, Jacques, and Éliane Lecarme-Tabone, *L'Autobiographie*, Paris: Armand Colin, 1997

Schrag, Calvin O., *The Self after Postmodernity*, New Haven, Connecticut: Yale University Press, 1997

Sheringham, Michael, *French Autobiography: Devices and Desires*, Oxford: Clarendon Press, 1993

B

BACHELARD, GASTON

Philosopher

Bachelard first established his reputation as a philosopher of science. Over a period of three decades, beginning in 1927, he published over a dozen books and a number of articles, about half of which have been collected in three volumes. During this period he rose from the post of a science teacher in a provincial college in Champagne to a prestigious chair at the Sorbonne and became the leading philosopher of science of his generation.

The originality of Bachelard's thinking follows from his particular conception of rationalism. The standard view, one could say, is that rationalism is an effort to describe the nature of reality or to find criteria to establish truths about it, through the power of reason. Bachelard argues that rationalism's strength lies in its capacity to transcend reality as it presents itself; rationalism is an open-ended quest that creates new realities. Scientific thinking is rationalism at work; new inventions change and multiply the material and epistemological terrain in which scientists operate; "there is little thought that is more philosophically varied than scientific thought" (*Rationalisme appliqué*, 1949).

Following the tradition in French philosophy of science (Poincaré, Duhem, Meyerson) Bachelard's analyses are set in a historical context. To elucidate his views he most frequently used as an example the transition from classical mechanics to the theory of relativity and quantum physics (*Le Nouvel esprit scientifique*, 1934). The key to his argument is the specific role he assigns to mathematics in the new scientific developments.

This is a brief outline of how Bachelard presents these developments: The first breach in the order of Newtonian mechanics begins with the creation of non-Euclidian geometries (by Lobatchevsky and Riemann). Bachelard underlines that these constructions have nothing to do with a "description of reality" but begin as mathematical hypotheses. Should there be events that take place in the spaces suggested by the new geometries, they would violate the Newtonian laws. Such is indeed the world as conceived by Einstein's relativity, which cannot be understood within these laws. Quantum physics was also based on mathematical constructs, yet the outcome is a new, tangible, and hitherto unknown reality that is not only the domain of physicists but has also entered everyday lives. These developments demonstrate the "ontologizing" capacity of mathematics, "the power of mathematics to create reality" (*Le Nouvel esprit scientifique*, 1934).

What follows is that scientists do not deal with sets of given facts inserted in "nature" that are progressively discovered and understood. Instead, "we quit nature to enter a factory of phenomena" (*L'Activité rationaliste de la physique contemporaine*, 1951) To a scientist facts are constructs, they begin by an organization of objects of thought, a "noumenology," and progress to a collective "phenomeno-technique" that creates effects (Zeeman's effect, Compton's effect, etc.), manufacturing new matters such as artificial isotopes, for example.

In its evolution, science increasingly detaches itself from the world as it is commonly understood. The theory of relativity and quantum physics developed independently of such understanding and end up violating it. This, Bachelard holds, is the mark of reason gaining its autonomy, in the sense that it frees itself from the limited world that the senses give us. Science is not an accumulation of "objective knowledge" but develops through ruptures, corrections of errors, which are mostly induced by habits that have their roots in common knowledge.

Common knowledge is enslaved by the senses and by physical needs and are obstacles to scientific activities; therefore, for science to progress it has to separate itself from common knowledge and for this the scientific mind has to undergo a cleansing operation. It is necessary to undergo a process, which not unlike psychoanalysis discovers and eradicates all ordinary knowledge from the scientific idiom. Only then will the separation between the two types of knowledge be complete, and only through this the "Interests of life are replaced by interests of the mind" (*La Formation de l'esprit scientifique*, 1938). This program of purification is similar to Bacon's call for the renewal of science through purging the mind of non-scientific idolatry.

In 1938 Bachelard published *La Psychanalise du feu*. The book was meant to illustrate in detail the folly of pre-scientific thinking, in this case through examining theories that were advanced to explain the phenomenon of combustion. However, as the work progressed Bachelard's hostility to the confused unscientific thinking gave way to an appreciation of the effect fire has on imagination. This was the beginning of his investigations into the nature of the imaginary for which he is far better known to the English-speaking world.

His first work devoted specifically to the question of imagination was a study of Lautréamont's poem *Les Chants de Maldoror* (*Lautréamont*, 1939), one of the most violent poetic outpourings on offer. But it was the series of monographs that explored imagination in relation to water, air, and earth—thus returning to the ancients' fascination with the four elements—that brought Bachelard's work to the attention of the wider public. Reading through endless poets, alchemists, mythological texts, and any other sources that would supply striking images, he proposed a structure of the imaginary that is organized around the four elements. A work of the imaginary is usually bound by a particular element, forming a "poetic complex." Bachelard distinguished dynamic and material imagination, linking (loosely) the former to air and fire and the latter to water and earth.

In two later works, *La Poétique de l'espace* and *La Poétique de la rêverie*, Bachelard abandons attempts to group images around the elements (or, as he suggested in *Lautréamont*, to classify poetic images following procedures similar to the way mathematicians identify groups). An image is always alone and its depth can only be grasped when it is studied in isolation. The state of mind in which the imaginary faculty is alive is reverie. This is an ontological reverie, which is a heightened state of consciousness (unlike daydreaming, which is a diminishing consciousness). Reverie is the source of well-being.

Unlike scientific concepts that evolve historically and in a collective context, a poetic image has no history and it is an instant of solitude. A concept and an image belong to separate poles of the psyche, "between the concept and the image there is no synthesis . . . concepts and images belong to two divergent planes of spiritual life" (*La Poétique de la rêverie*, 1960. Nevertheless, in one important aspect the world of concepts and the world of the imaginary are similar—both are faculties that surpass physical reality. Just as the scientific concept develops independently of perception, the imaginary does not draw from a pool of images of objects perceived but it is a creative faculty, "A man should be defined by those tendencies which impel him to surpass the *human condition*" (*L'Eau et les rêves*, 1943). In this sense a mere representation of reality is in effect a betrayal of the spiritual life. But one more difference has to be noted. Scientific thought sees perception of everyday reality as an *obstacle* and works against it; the poetic imagination is just as free from this reality without, however, needing to destroy it (although it may want to as in the case of Lautréamont's poem).

There are two other important works, *L'Intuition de l'instant* and *La Dialectique de la durée*, published in 1932 and 1936, respectively. They deal neither with science nor the poetic image, but deal with the question of time. Both begin with a critique of Bergson's central thesis, namely, that time is duration, a single and continually changing flux that forms our *élan vital*, a life force that pushes us along, so to speak. Duration, argues Bachelard, is a fiction, it can be compared to the sense of perspective that we create in order to arrange objects in space; it is a fiction created by an inattentive mind. We cannot have an immediate experience of duration; the more attention is focused the more it will reveal that all thoughts, images, ideas are in their nature instantaneous. "Time has but one reality, that of an instant" (*L'Intuition de l'instant*, 1932), the only reality that we have is the "reality that the present instant presents us with" (*L'Intuition de l'instant*, 1932).

Bachelard does recognize a "lived time" that Bergson proposes and he refers to it as a transitive, or horizontal time and its flow, in his view, is identical with life processes. He opposes to this time a vertical, or "willed time" which is the time of instants. Instants are atoms of time, they cannot touch each other or dissolve into one another; they have no duration but vary in richness and density. Instants are separated by a void (which means that horizontal time does not bind them together), "the decisive centers of time are its discontinuities" (*La Dialectique de la durée*, 1936). It is out of the void that instants emerge. Willed time does not flow; it is a time of acts, it spurts out.

This atomist conception of time is an ontological basis for Bachelard's consistent antisubstantialism. So, although an atomist, Bachelard rejected as ill-conceived Democritus's atoms of bits of substance. He considered Bergson's conception of time substantialist, he rejected Descartes's "thinking substance." The modern physicists' matter, he reminds us, is not substance either. And to avoid any misunderstanding Bachelard specifically states that, although he often refers to the poets' four elements as matter, this should not be conceived as substance but only as a poetic orientation. What emerges from this is a world in which there is nothing to unfold, no substratum, and no transcendental reality. All acts of consciousness are instants, intermittent and discontinuous; it is a world of poetics where acts create the world rather than respond to it. Instants can be so rich that they have been likened to "eternity," which is why a singular act can have profound resonance; the human destiny is a poetic destiny (*La Dialectique de la durée*).

Such a conception of time seems without precedent in Western philosophy, but it is strikingly close to the views put forward by some Buddhist philosophers (particularly of the School of Dignaga), who also expounded a temporal atomism to argue against the concept of substance. Bachelard did not seem to know these. He took the notion of the instant from the historian Gaston Roupnel, and drew matter for his arguments from other nonphilosophers such as Janet and an obscure Brazilian psychologist, Lucio Alberto Pinheiro dos Santos. He also found support for his views in the new scientific developments.

Bachelard's importance in the philosophy of science in France can be compared with that of Popper's in Britain. For decades he was on the syllabus in schools and many leading philosophers of science of the following generation made a point of positioning themselves in relation to Bachelard's work. This often took the form of a criticism, particularly of his contention that for science to progress it has to reject all common knowledge. It has been argued that in this view science cannot serve the interests of life (Stengers), that Bachelardian epistemology degenerates into a Comtean catechism (Serres); and that once Bachelardian epistemologists rid science of all common knowledge there will be nothing left with which to do science (Latour).

Nevertheless, a number of his views have filtered through. The idea that science evolves unevenly and through ruptures, creating a proliferation of theories with differing epistemological standards and that, therefore, there cannot be a unified scientific method, as well as bringing to the fore the view that science does not deal with "nature" but creates its own subject matter in a collective context, have had a great impact in France. In this he also anticipated some aspects of the more recent historically oriented Anglo-Saxon philosophers of science (Kuhn, Feyerabend, Hacking, for example), although they did not seem to be aware of Bachelard's work (with the exception of Hacking). His influence was felt outside philosophy of science, too. Althusser's use of the concept of an epistemological rupture was quite famous, and Marxists were drawn to some of Bachelard's thinking (but were also critical). But it is the writings of Canguilhem and Foucault that are most clearly marked by Bachelard's epistemological investigations.

Bachelard's writings on the poetic imagination were received by academia with less enthusiasm but were (and still are) very widely read. They made a considerable impact on literary criticism. Barthes, Starobinski, Poulet were among those who expressed their admiration, and were to varying degrees influended by him. He was also criticized. Blanchot, for example, reproached him for concentrating too much on single images but losing sight of the narrative force of poetry. Bachelard's work also triggered some more systematic historical and philosophical studies on imagination (Durand, in particular).

His writings on time, although of great philosophical interest, have received less attention and have had little impact.

Largely due to his background (he did not pass through the École Normale Supérieure, nor did he study in Paris), Bachelard's approach was unorthodox and it is difficult to locate him within major philosophical currents. He seemed completely unaffected by Platonic or Aristotelian thought; the German philosophers (apart from Schopenhauer) had practically no influence on his thinking. One movement that expressed views that were very close to his was that of the Surrealists. Bachelard befriended some them; he was attracted to their poetry, and often commented on it. He referred to the thinking of modern physicists as a surrationalism, and the worlds they create surreality. His views on time and the spiritual necessity to create realities that defy the world of the senses could serve as a philosophical basis for Surrealism.

During his fifteen years at the Sorbonne, Bachelard had many students, some of whom became later distinguished philosophers. He taught at school level; he had, for a philosopher, a remarkably wide readership, references to his work come up in most unexpected places. Because of all this, he probably left a deeper mark than is generally realized.

But Bachelard was not a product of a "school" and he did not create one. In the next generation different trends began to dominate. There was an increased engagement with German thought; the end of metaphysics, or of philosophy *tout court*, among other things, began to be contemplated. This formed a large chunk of French philosophy (at least as seen from the Anglo-Saxon shores), and there was little place in it for Bachelard; his presence subsequently diminished. However, he remains one of the most original and significant figures in modern philosophical thought.

ZBIGNIEW KOTOWICZ

See also **Louis Althusser, Roland Barthes, Henri Bergson, Maurice Blanchot, George Canguilhem, Michel Foucault, Pierre Janet, George Poulet**

Biography

Gaston Bachelard was born on June 27, 1884 in Bar-sur-Aube, in Champagne. From 1903 until the outbreak of the First World War he worked for the postal service while pursuing his studies. In 1912 he received his degree in mathematics. In 1914 he was mobilized. For his service in the trenches he received the Croix de Guerre. In 1919 he took a post in the local college in Bar-sur-Aube teaching mathematics, physics, and chemistry. He obtained his degree in philosophy in 1920, aggregation in 1922, and his doctorate from the Sorbonne in 1927. His doctoral dissertations were directed by Abel Rey and Léon Brunschvicg.

In 1930 he was appointed to the chair of philosophy at the University of Dijon, and ten years later he succeeded Abel Rey to the chair of history and philosophy of science at the Sorbonne, where he remained until his retirement in 1954. The following year he was elected to the Acadèmie des Sciences morales et politiques and in 1961 he received the Grand Prix National des Lettres. Bachelard died in Paris on October 16, 1962 and was buried in Bar-sur-Aube.

Selected Writings

Essai sur la connaissance approchée, 1928
Etude sur l'évolution s'un problème de physique: la propagation thermique dans les solides, 1928
La Valeur inductive de la relativité, 1929
Le Pluralisme coherent dans la chimie moderne, 1932
L'Intuition de l'instant, 1932
Les Intuitions atomistiques, 1933
Le Nouvel esprit scientifique, 1934; as *The New Scientific Spirit*, translated by A. Goldhammer, 1984
La Dialectique de la durée, 1936; as *The Dialectic of Duration*, translated by Mary McAllester Jones, 2000
L'Experience de l'espace dans la physique contemporaine, 1937
La Formation de l'esprit scientifique, 1938

La Psychanalyse du feu, 1938; as *The Psychoanalysis of Fire*, translated by Alan C. M. Ross, 1964
Lautréamont 1939, new edition 1951; as *Lautréamont*, translated by R. S. Dupree, 1986
La Philosophie du non, 1940; as *The Philosophy of No*, translated by G. C. Waterston, 1968
L'Eau et les rêves, 1942; as *Water and Dreams*, translated by E. R. Farrell, 1983
L'Air et les songes, 1942; as *Air and Dreams*, translated by E. R. Farrell and C. F. Farrell, 1988
La Terre et les revêries de la volonté, 1948
La Terre et les revêries du repos, 1948
Le Rationalisme appliqué, 1949
L'Activité rationaliste de la physique contemporaine, 1951
Le Matérialisme rationnel, 1953
La Poétique de l'espace, 1957; as *The Poetics of Space*, translated by Maria Jolas, 1964
La Poétique de la revêrie, 1960; as *The Poetics of Reverie*, translated by Daniel Russell, 1969
La Flamme d'une chandelle, 1961; as *The Flame of a Candle*, translated by Joni Caldwell, 1988
Fragments d'une poetique du feu, 1988; as *Fragments of a Poetics of Fire*, translated by Kenneth Haltman, 1990

Further Reading

Bhaskar, Roy, "Feyerabend and Bachelard: Two Philosophies of Science", New Left Review, 94 (1975)
Chimisso, Cristina, *Gaston Bachelard: Critic of Science and the Imagination*, London: Routledge, 2001
Dagognet, Francois, *Gaston Bachelard, sa vie, son oeuvre, avec un exposé de sa philosophie*, Paris: PUF, 1965
Gaudin, Collete, *Gaston Bachelard. On Poetic Imagination and Reverie*, Dallas: Spring Publications, 1984
Graukroger, Stephen, "Bachelard and the Problem of Epistemological Analysis", Studies in History and Philosophy of Science, 7 (1976): pp. 189–244
Lecourt, Dominique, *Pour une critique de l'épistémologie (Bachelard, Canguilhem, Foucault)*, Paris: François Maspero, 1972
McAllester Jones, Mary, *Gaston Bachelard, Subversive Humanist: Texts and Readings*, Madison Wisconsin: University of Wisconsin Press, 1991
Perrot, Maryvonne, *Bachelard et la poetique du temps*, Bruxelles: Peter Lang, 2000
Quillet, Patrick, *Gaston Bachelard*, Paris: Seghers, 1964
Serres, Michel, "La Réforme et les sept péchés", L'Arc 42 (1970):
Therrien, Vincent, *La Revolution de Gaston Bachelard, en critique littéraire*, Paris: Klincksieck, 1970
Tiles, Mary, *Bachelard: Science and Objectivity*, Cambridge: Cambridge University Press, 1984

BADIOU, ALAIN
Philosopher

Unlike many of those schooled in the antihumanist principles of Althusser and Lacan, Badiou has never been tempted to celebrate the apparent end of philosophy, to question the possibility of metaphysics, or to qualify the classical attributes of truth: rigour, clarity,

and eternity. In his determination to take another step in the distinctly modern understanding of these attributes, he has devised the only truly innovative theory of subjectivation since Sartre.

Rather like Sartre, Badiou's chief concern is with the transformative power of radical commitment. Unlike Sartre, however, Badiou's peculiar understanding of commitment subordinates it to a process that in certain respects is antithetical to the notoriously imprecise existentialist notions of authenticity or project—the process that Badiou calls a *truth*, or truth procedure. As Badiou explains in detail in his major work to date (*L'Etre et l'événement*, 1988), truths are militant processes that, beginning from a specific time and place within a situation, pursue the step-by-step transformation of that situation in line with new forms of broadly egalitarian principles. Only a pure commitment, one detached from any psychological, social, or "objective" mediation, can qualify as the adequate vehicle for a truth, but reciprocally, only a properly universal truth qualifies as worthy of such a commitment. Only a truth can "induce" the subject of a genuine commitment.

Badiou's notion of truth is thus subjective for the same reason that it is universal: truth is a matter of actively *holding true* to a principle or cause that can, from within the constraints of a given situation, consistently solicit the adherence of every member of that situation. Though it develops from a particular place within the situation, a truth holds true without reference to the prevailing criteria of recognition, classification, and domination which underlie the normal organization of the situation: this "subtractive" condition of a truth-procedure applies, for example, as much to the invention of new means of mathematical formalization as it does to the implications of modernist art, the practice of radical politics, and the discipline of love. Withdrawn from its situation's general means of discernment, every truth is new by definition, and every subject is sustained by his or her contribution to its novelty.

Badiou's most general goal can be described, then, as the effort to expose and make sense of the potential for profound, transformative innovation in any situation. Every such innovation can only begin with some sort of exceptional (though invariably ephemeral) break with the status quo, an "event." An event can occur at any time but not in just any place; an event will generally be located close to the edge of whatever qualifies as "void" or indistinguishable in the situation, i.e., in that part of the situation where for literally fundamental reasons the prevailing forms of discernment and recognition cease to have any significant purchase. A truth then expands out of this "eventalsite" [*site événementiel*] insofar as it elicits the militant convic-

tion of certain individuals who develop the revolutionary implications of the event, and by doing so constitute themselves as the subjects of its truth. A subject is thus anyone carried by his or her fidelity to the consequences, as rigorous as they are haphazard, of an event, while a truth is nothing other than the cumulative collection of such post-eventual consequences. The laborious, case-by-case application of these consequences will then serve to transform the entire way the situation organizes and represents itself, in keeping with the implications of the event.

An ordinary individual or "some-one" only becomes a genuine subject insofar as he or she is caught up in a materially transformative procedure of this kind. By the same token (for reasons sketched in Badiou's most accessible short work, *L'Ethique* [1993]), subjects only remain subjects insofar as their fidelity is in turn equipped to resist the various sorts of corruption it must inevitably face: fatigue, confusion, and dogmatism. For example, those mobilized by the civil rights, feminist, or anticolonial movements remain true subjects insofar as these movements, initially sparked by certain events affecting particular groups of people in particular situations, call for the transformation of the situation as a whole in terms that can be directly and universally affirmed by its every inhabitant. But should such a movement seek simply the promotion of a particular group for its own sake, then its partisans act only as the proponents of an interest in competition with other interests. The identification of suffering victims is not by itself the sufficient basis, Badiou insists, for a genuine political movement. Like all truths, politics must proceed in a sphere of rigorous universality, on the basis of statements that literally anyone could make or affirm. This doesn't mean, however, that truth operates in the domain of consensus or communication. Every genuinely universal principle has its origin in an active and precisely situated *taking* of sides; every true affirmation of the universal interest begins as divisive. There is no philosopher more opposed to the "ethical" coordination of opinions or differences than Badiou.

A subject, in short, is someone who continues to hold true to a cause whose ongoing implications relates indifferently to all members of the situation, and which thereby considers these members as elements of an effectively indiscernible or "generic" collection.

Badiou distinguishes four general fields of truth, or four domains of subjectivation (which in turn operate as the four generic "conditions" of philosophy itself): politics, science, art, and love. These are the only four fields in which a *pure* subjective commitment is possible, that is, one indifferent to procedures of interpretation, representation, or verification. Badiou provides his most concise overview of the generic procedures

in his *Manifeste pour la philosophie* (1989). True politics is a matter of collective mobilization guided by a "general will" in something like Rousseau's sense, and not the business of bureaucratic administration or the socialized negotiation of interests. Within the limits of the private sphere, genuine love begins in the wake of an unpredictable encounter that escapes the conventional representation of sexual roles, continues as a fidelity to the consequences of that encounter, and is sustained through an unrepresentable exposure to what Lacan famously described as the "impossibility of a sexual relationship." True art and true science proceed in somewhat the same way, through a searching experimental fidelity to a line of enquiry opened up by a new discovery or break with tradition. Mathematics is then the most "truthful" component of science simply because, thanks to its axiomatic foundation in the basic postulates of set theory, it is the most securely abstracted from any natural or objective mediation.

For the same reason, as Badiou explains in the difficult opening meditations of *L'Etre et l'événement*, mathematics is the only discourse suited to the literal articulation of pure being-qua-being, or being considered without regard to being-this or being-that, being without reference to particular qualities or ways of being: being that simply *is*. More precisely, mathematics identifies what can be said of being-qua-being with *pure* multiplicity, meaning multiplicity considered without any constituent reference to unity or unification. (Why? Because the theoretical foundations of mathematics ensure that any unification, any consideration of something as *one* thing, must be thought as the *result* of an operation or counting-as-one; by the same token, these foundations lead us necessarily to presume that whatever was thus counted, or unified, is itself not-one, i.e., pure multiplicity.) Such pure multiplicity is by definition a medium in which no genuine change or innovation is possible. Every truth must therefore begin with a break in the fabric of being-as-being—an event is precisely "that which is *not* being-as-being." Truth and being cannot be said in one and the same discourse. In other words, by thus consigning the tasks of ontology to mathematics, Badiou frees philosophy proper from its ultimate coordination with Being, a coordination maintained in their different ways by Spinoza, Hegel, Heidegger, and Deleuze. Any actively inventive philosophy is conditioned by the varied truth procedures operative in its time, rather than by an essentially timeless mediation on being.

Badiou's many examples of a truth procedure are varied enough to include both St. Paul's militant conception of an apostolic subjectivity that exists only through proclamation of an event (the resurrection of Christ) of universal import but of no recognizable or established significance, and the Jacobin or Bolshevik

fidelity to a revolution which exceeds, in its subjective power and generic scope, the various circumstances that contributed to its occurrence. Mallarmé, Schoenberg and Beckett are foremost among the practitioners of a suitably subtractive or generic art, which is always an effort to devise new kinds of form at the very edge of what the situation considers formless or void. After Descartes and Galileo, Cantor and Cohen demonstrate what inventive scientific formalisation can achieve, at the limits of mathematical consistency. In the end, every truth is "founded" only on the fundamental "inconsistency" that Badiou discerns as the exclusive and insubstantial being of pure being-qua-being—the generic being of all that *is* simply insofar as it is, but that is only *exceptionally* accessible, through the rare commitment of those who become subjects in the wake of its eventual exposure.

It is not hard to understand why Badiou's work is only just beginning to get the general recognition it deserves. Though it relies on a minimum of technical knowledge, its reference to the austere rigor of contemporary mathematics distances it from readers more comfortable with the playful indeterminacy of poetry, sophistry, or rhetoric. Its sharp separation of philosophy from ontology alienates the disciples of both Heidegger and Deleuze. Its unyielding resistance to the linguistic turn will repel those who follow Wittgenstein or Habermas in the cautious supervision of language games and discourse ethics. Its subtractive orientation resists any nostalgia for the metaphysics of Presence, just as its ultimately literal or *formal* integrity frustrates any will to interpretation, figuration, or representation. Its explicit antihumanism, its enthusiastic affirmation of the revolutionary legacy of *la pensée soixante-huit*, is designed to confound our modern "Thermidorians"—all those who, invoking the authority of Kant, Tocqueville, or Rawls, effectively defend the status quo in the name of liberal democracy and a respect for human rights. Its trenchant universalism, finally, its insistence upon the difficult Platonic category of the Same, will alienate those who justify the retreat from radical political mobilization through an apparent respect for the Other, for community, or for cultural difference. It is precisely for these reasons that Badiou's work is perhaps the most promising contribution, in all of contemporary French thought, to the lasting renewal of philosophy.

PETER HALLWARD

See also **Louis Althusser, Gilles Deleuze, Jacques Lacan, Jean-Paul Sartre**

Biography

Born in Rabat, Morocco in 1937, Alain Badiou was a student of the L'Ecole Normale Supérieure in the

1950s. He taught at the University of Paris VIII (Vincennes/Saint Denis) from 1969 to 1999, when he returned to L'Ecole Normale as head of the philosophy department. He continues to teach a popular seminar at the Collège International de Philosophie, on topics ranging from the great "anti –philosophers" (Saint-Paul, Nietzsche, Wittgenstein, Lacan . . .) to the major conceptual innovations of the twentieth century. Much of Badiou's life has been shaped by his dedication to the consequences of the May 1968 revolt in Paris. Once a leading member of *Union des jeunesses communistes de France (marxistes-léninistes)*, he remains with Sylvain Lazarus and Natacha Michel at the center of *L'Organisation Politique*, a "post-Party" organization concerned with direct popular intervention in a wide range of issues (including immigration, labor, housing). He is the author of several successful novels and plays as well as more than a dozen philosophical works, of which the most of important are *L'Etre et l'événement* (1988), *Logiques des mondes* (2003), and *Théorie du sujet* (1982).

Selected Works

Théorie du sujet, 1982
Peut-on penser la politique?, 1985
L'Etre et l'événement, 1988; translated by Oliver Feltham, 2004
Manifeste pour la philosophie, 1989; translated by Norman Madarasz, 1999
Le Nombre et les nombres, 1990
Conditions, 1992
L'Ethique: Essai sur la conscience du mal, 1993; translated by Peter Hallward, 2001
Beckett: L'incrévable désir, 1995
Gilles Deleuze: "La clameur de l'Etre," 1997; translated by Louise Burchill, 2000
Saint Paul et la fondation de l'universalisme, 1997
Court Traité d'ontologie transitoire, 1998
Abrégé de métapolitique, 1998
Petit Manuel d'inésthétique, 1998
Le Siècle, 2002; bilingual edition, translated with commentary by Alberto Toscano
Badiou: Theoretical Writings, edited by Alberto Toscano and Ray Brassier, 2004
Logiques des mondes, 2005

Further Readings

Barker, Jason, *Alain Badiou: A Critical Introduction.* London: Pluto, 2002
Bosteels, Bruno, "Alain Badiou's Theory of the Subject: The Recommencement of Dialectical Materialism?" *Pli (Warwick Journal of Philosophy)* 12 (2001) 200–229
Bosteels, Bruno, *Badiou and the Political* [in preparation]. Duke University Press, 2004
Brassier, Ray, "Stellar Void or Cosmic Animal? Badiou and Deleuze" *Pli (Warwick Journal of Philosophy)* 10 (2000): 200–217
Clemens, Justin, "Platonic Meditations: The Work of Alain Badiou." *Pli (Warwick Journal of Philosophy)* 11 (2001): 200–229
Critchley, Simon, "Demanding Approval. On the Ethics of Alain Badiou" *Radical Philosophy* 100 (2000): 16–27
Hallward, Peter, *Badiou: A Subject to Truth.* Minneapolis: University of Minnesota Press, 2003
Hallward, Peter, ed., *Think Again: Alain Badiou and the Future of Philosophy.* London: Continuum Press, 2004
Jambet, Christian, "Alain Badiou: *L'Etre et l'événement*" in *Annuaire philosophique 1987–1988.* Paris: Seuil, 1989
Kouvélakis, Eustache, "La Politique dans ses limites, ou les paradoxes d'Alain Badiou" *Actuel Marx* 28, (2000): 39–54.
Lecercle, Jean-Jacques, "Cantor, Lacan, Mao, Beckett, *même combat*: The Philosophy of Alain Badiou," *Radical Philosophy*, 93 (1999): 6–13
Ramond, Charles (editor), *Alain Badiou: "La Pensée forte"* [papers given at the international conference on Badiou, Bordeaux, Oct. 21–23 1999], Paris: L'Harmattan, 2002
Riera, Gabriel (editor), *Alain Badiou: Philosophy Under Conditions.* (omit), Albany, NY: SUNY Press, 2004.
Simont, Juliette, "Le Pur et l'impur (sur deux questions de l'histoire de la philosophie dans *L'Etre et l'événement*)," *Les Temps modernes*, 526 (1990): 27–60
Toscano, Alberto, "To Have Done with the End of Philosophy," *Pli (Warwick Journal of Philosophy)* 9 (2000). 220 239
Žižek, Slavoj, "The Politics of Truth, or, Alain Badiou as a Reader of St Paul" in *The Ticklish Subject* (by Slavoj Žižek), London: Verso, 1999

BALIBAR, ÉTIENNE
Philosopher

Étienne Balibar's writings oscillate between philosophy and politics, merging investigations into the history of ideas with a resolute commitment to the present. In his early work, Balibar's major concern was historical materialism. As a student and close collaborator of Althusser, he coauthored *Lire le Capital* (1965), one of the most systematic attempts to read Marx philosophically. The book's aim was the elaboration of a "true science" of historical materialism, centered on the pivotal concept of *mode of production*, depicting the political economy as a complex and overdetermined structure. This anti-Hegelian reading broke with a prevailing teleological conception of history in postwar Marxism. Balibar's contribution confronted the theoretical problem posed by the refutation of historical determinism: the succession of different modes of production. All production is foremost a *reproduction* of social relations. The mode of production reproduces the elements' places within a given structure and is thus the fundamental concept of historical continuity. The immanent contradictions of one mode of production do not bring about a transition to another mode; they can only arrive at equilibrium. Far from tending toward demise, capitalism only reproduces itself and perpetuates its cycle. A consistent and nonteleological theory of transition hence requires a consideration of different temporalities articulated within a mode of production.

Balibar carried on the project of systematically reconstructing Marxism until the late 1970s. Among his main themes were questions regarding the philosophical and scientific status of historical materialism, the relation between the state and class struggle, and the function of ideology. His reflections on the state and historical transformations continued through *Sur la dictature du prolétariat* (1977), written in the context of the rise of Eurocommunism. Against the "revisionism" of the French Communist Party leadership, Balibar maintained that a genuine extension of democracy beyond the dominant classes required the dismantling of the state apparatus. His vocal critique of the Communist party's policies paralleled a theoretical shift away from historical materialism.

Although Balibar later rejected some of the positions he had upheld in the 1970s, the dialogue with Marx has remained a constant feature in his work. The critical disengagement that Balibar subsequently called a "deconstruction" of Marx set the stage for a new set of concerns clustered around the question of the *subject*: a research agenda that would lead him to focus on the question of *philosophical anthropology.*

This investigation of modern identities and subjectivities is highly influenced by Balibar's materialist reading of Spinoza (*Spinoza et la politique*, 1985), where he discovers a theory of *transindividual subjectivity.* Neither purely individual nor collective, subjectivity is constituted through communication, that is, through the imaginary. The mechanisms through which subjectivities are established are the focus of *Race, nation, classe* (1988, with Immanuel Wallerstein). Contemporary racism, Balibar suggests, functions as a meta-racism, as racism without races, where notions such as culture or immigration substitute for biological race. Racism, in Balibar's explanation of nationalism, operates as the production of a "fictitious ethnicity." The reproduction of the nation requires the individual to be socialized as a *homo nationalis*, by means of normalizing institutions and practices. Radicalizing Benedict Anderson's account of the nation as an imagined community, Balibar maintains that not only are communities imaginary, but "only imaginary communities are real." In his later *Masses, Classes, Ideas* (1994), Balibar expands on the crucial relation between the *imaginary* and the *real*, arguing that the imaginary is not an effect, but a cause. The imaginary, understood as the sphere of social relations, is not a reflection of underlying real processes, but retains its own autonomy and efficiency; in other words, the imaginary (and *a fortiori* ideology) should not be understood as a "superstructure," but as a "base."

When Jean-Luc Nancy asked the question "Who comes after the subject?" Balibar's response was unambiguous: the *citizen.* Both in political and philosophical terms, the revolutionary epoch of the late eighteenth century points to the displacement of the subject in favor of the citizen. Citizenship is indeed one of the leading themes in Balibar's recent work, often seized through the pivotal question of immigration. Political philosophy, as a reflection on the constitution of the public space, can no longer axiomatically suppose the categories of "belonging" and "reciprocity." What is at stake, then, is a rethinking of democracy, in terms of its *borders* (*frontières*). The polyseomy of the border stands both for the concrete political institution, where issues of identity, community, and citizenship are regulated, and for the conceptual question about the limit of politics. The national border is a privileged site, condensing processes of subjectivation and normalization while separating the exclusion of the foreigner from other schemes of anthropological differentiation. Counter to the prevailing politics of structural exclusion, Balibar proposes three models of politics: *emancipation, transformation, civility.* In their constitutive dissonance, they overdetermined a universal concept of the political (*La crainte des masses*, 1997). Emancipation is the name of an autonomous, unconditional politics, that of the self-determination of a people (understood as *demos*, not *ethnos*), articulated in the proposition of *égaliberté*, that is, in the inseparability of equality and liberty. Transformation stands for a heteronomous politics, a practice under given socio-economic conditions aimed at the alteration of these very conditions. Yet both politics as emancipation and as transformation is heteronomous in the sense that it is only possible within the absence of *ultra-violence.* A third concept, that of *civility*, is therefore necessary. As opposed to traditional conceptions of politics that externalize violence, civility takes the global proliferation of violence as its very object to create the necessary space for politics.

Influenced to some extent by Derrida, Balibar's later work is marked by an attention to textual problems, contradictions, and aporias. These are not semantic obstacles a hermeneutic approach to the text can overcome. Rather they define the specificity of philosophical writing, insofar as the philosophical text radicalizes the contradictions that go beyond it. In a sense, then, this "symptomatic reading" reveals a continuity of Balibar's method from the early days of *Lire le capital.* An example of this is his analysis of Marx and Engels's "vacillation" with regard to the necessary, yet impossible, notion of a proletarian ideology. Linking the very notion of politics to this vacillation, Balibar demonstrates that a mass revolutionary politics is always tied to a *conjuncture.*

Conjuncture is a key concept for Balibar: it is the condition of possibility for both emancipatory politics and truth. Arguing against the "metaphysics of truth and totality" that haunt historical materialism, Balibar contends that truth can only be the effect of a conjuncture. If ideology (as a subset of the imaginary) is part of the materiality of history, then truth can only appear as a moment from within ideology. Neither historically determined nor historically relative, truth is the very break that disrupts and suspends the governing configuration of the imaginary. In other words, truth is the effect of a critique that confronts and contradicts the dominant ideology and its criteria of universality. Although truth effects relate to their historical contexts, they are not predetermined by history, but imply a "non-contemporaneity" of critique and its conditions.

This conception of truth as a moment sheds light on two of the characteristic traits of Balibar's work. The first is the absence of a unified corpus. Balibar's writings present themselves almost exclusively under the form of dispersed yet related essays: singular texts that differentiate, dissociate, and displace their objects. Finally, it elucidates the twin aspect of his work, at once philosophical and political. A work that in its double articulation is fundamentally that of a public intellectual, committed to "philosophy as a practice."

YVES WINTER

See also **Louis Althusser, Jacques Derrida**

Biography

Born in Avallon, France in 1942, Étienne Balibar was a student at the Ecole Normale Supérieure in the early 1960s. He taught at the University of Algiers, Algeria from 1965–1967, before returning to France and taking up a position at the Lycée de Savigny-sur-Orge. From 1969 until the mid 1990s he taught at the University of Paris I (Sorbonne), interrupted by a stay in Leiden, Netherlands in the late 70s. From 1994 to 2002 Balibar held a chair in political and moral philosophy at the University of Paris X (Nanterre). In 2000 he was appointed Distinguished Professor in Critical Theory at the University of California, Irvine. He was a member of the French Communist Party from 1961 until 1981, when he was excluded for his public condemnation of the party's stance toward immigration. Balibar continues to be an outspoken critic of French and European immigration policies and a prominent advocate against exclusion. Étienne Balibar is the author and editor of over twenty books, the co-director of the series *Pratiques Théoriques* at Presses Universitaires de France, and the translator of works by Marx, Locke, and Antonio Negri.

Selected Writings

Lire le Capital (with L. Althusser, P. Macherey, J. Rancière, R. Establet), 1965; as *Reading Capital*, translated by Ben Brewster, 1970

Cinq études du matérialisme historique, 1974

Sur la dictature du prolétariat, 1976; as *On the Dictatorship of the Proletariat*, translated by Grahame Lock, 1977

Ouvrons la fenêtre, camarades! with G. Bois, G. Labica, J.-P. Lefebvre, 1979

Marx et sa critique de la politique with C. Luporini and A. Tosel, 1979

Spinoza et la politique, 1985; as *Spinoza and Politics*, translated by Peter Snowden, 1998

Race, nation, classe with I. Wallerstein, 1988; as *Race, Nation, Class*, translated by Chris Turner, 1991

Sterke posities in de politieke filosofie with G. Lock and H. Van Gunsteren, 1989

Écrits pour Althusser, 1991

Les frontières de la démocratie, 1992

La Philosophie de Marx, 1993; as *The Philosophy of Marx*, translated by Chris Turner, 1995

Masses, Classes, Ideas. Studies in Politics and Philosophy, translation of essays written between 1982 and 1991 by James Swenson, 1994

Lieux et noms de la vérité, 1994

La Crainte des masses. Politique et philosophie avant et après Marx, 1997; partially translated as *Masses, Classes, Ideas*, 1994 and as—politics and the other scene—, translated by David Hahn, 2002

Droit de cité. Culture et politique en démocratie, 1998

Identité et différence. John Locke: An Essay Concerning Human Understanding, II, XXVII. L'invention de la conscience, translated with an introduction by Étienne Balibar, 1998

Sans-papiers: l'archaïsme fatal, with J. Costa-Lascoux, M. Chemillier-Gendreau, E. Terray, 1999

Nous, citoyens d'Europe? Les frontières, l'État, le peuple, 2001

Further Reading

Benton, Ted, *The Rise and Fall of Structural Marxism: Althusser and his Influence*, London: Macmillan, 1984

Corredor, Eva L., "Interview with Etienne Balibar," in *Lukács After Communism*, by Eva L. Corredor, Durham, NC: Duke University Press, 1997

Duroux, Yves, "Inactuel Marx, remarques sur le noeud politique," *Critique*, 53 (1997): 601–602, 522–536

Elliott, Gregory, *Althusser: The Detour of Theory*, London and New York: Verso, 1987

Hindness, Barry and Paul Q. Hirst, *Pre-Capitalist Modes of Production*, London and Boston: Routledge and Kegan Paul, 1975

Hitchcock, Peter, "Metaphors of Materialism," in *Oscillate Wildly by Peter Hitchcock*, Minneapolis: University of Minnesota Press, 1999

Klein, Julie R., "Etienne Balibar's Marxist Spinoza," *Philosophy Today*, 44 (2000): 41–50

Lipietz, Alain, "From Althusserianism to Regulation Theory," translated by Erika Thomas in E. Ann Kaplan and Michael Sprinker, *The Althusserian Legacy*, London: Verso, 1993

Silverman, Maxim, "Race, Nation, Class," in *Race, Discourse and Power in France by Maxim Silverman*, Aldershot: Avebury, 1991

Sprinker, Michael, "The Legacy of Althusser," in *Depositions: Althusser, Balibar, Macherey, and the Labor of Reading*,

edited by Jacques Lezra, Yale French Studies, 88 (1995): 201–225
Zizek, Slavoj, "Badiou, Balibar, Rancière" in *The Ticklish Subject by Slavoj Zizekt*, London: Verso, 1999

BALIBAR, RENÉE
Literary Critic, Linguist

In 1974 Renée Balibar, a professor of literature at the University of Tours, published two books that were to have a lasting impact on literary sociology and the historical and sociological study of linguistics: *Les français ficitifs: Le rapport des styles littéraires au français national* (Fictitious French: The Relationship of Literary Styles to National French) written with Geneviève Merlin and Gilles Tret, and *Le français national: Politique et pratique de la langue française sous la révolution* (National French: The Politics and Practice of French Language during the Revolution) written with Dominique Laporte. *Les français fictifs* studies the relationship between French literature and the institution of an "official" French language by means of national education viewed as a "state ideological apparatus" (a concept made famous by Louis Althusser's *Lire le Capital*, written in collaboration with Etienne Balibar, Renée's son, and published in 1968). *Le français national* examines the linguistic policies of the First Republic, especially the creation of an idealized French language; not only as a means for the dissemination of centralized power throughout the nation, but also as a democratic tool allowing citizens from every province equal access to political participation. Balibar's originality resides partly in her transcendence of the critique, common in Marxist sociological criticism of the time, of written language's subjection to bourgeois ideology, by viewing it as a potential means of liberation from the artificial boundaries of class, nationality, and culture.

Les Français fictifs contains themes that dominate her research in subsequent years, including the creation of "national French" as two official, artificial languages: an ideal of direct communication among citizens on the one hand, and an obscure, elitist "literary" code on the other. The dissemination of these artificial languages occurs in the national school: primary education for the ideal of "direct communication" or transparency, secondary education for the opaque "code" embodied in the pedagogical literary canon.

Balibar applied her analysis of the educational system to literary texts. In *Les Français fictifs*, the author she refers to most is Flaubert. One characteristic of "literary" French imposed in secondary education by the idealization of seventeenth-century verse is the imitation of the sounds and structures of Latin. In Flaubert's *Un Coeur simple*, for example, Balibar claims that the phrase "*les bourgeoises . . . envièrent à Madame Aubain sa servante*" [the *bourgeoises* envied Mme Aubain her servant] is an allusion to Latin syntax, and therefore a sign of the difference between literary and nonliterary speech (111). The ability to "read" that sign is a privilege acquired during secondary education. A contrast to Flaubert is Albert Camus's narrator Meursault in *The Stranger*. On the surface, Flaubert's "fetishization" of Latin and of literary irony could not be more different than the literalness and lack of self-consciousness of Camus's anti-hero, whose education was interrupted before he became initiated into literary French at the *lycée*. Balibar shows, however, that Camus's work is no less "literary" than Flaubert's: not only does the substitution of "primary school French" for "secondary school French" by Camus merely replace one "fictitious" French with another, there is in fact a common misperception that Camus did not use the literary past tense, the *passé simple*, in his narrative. Balibar points out that there are in fact several uses of the *passé simple*, and that Camus' anti-style is simply traditional literary style in disguise.

In *Le Français national*, the ideological aspects of her thought are more evident. Her concern is not literature, so much as language policy as a means of political domination (a process in which literature does, however, play a role). She begins with a distinction: language policy under the Revolution was overtly deductive, imposing from the top down a particular linguistic and cultural practice upon each member of the nation; under its Third Republic custodians, it was ostensibly inductive, attempting to derive linguistic principles from the diversity of linguistic practices. The actual implementation of linguistic and pedagogic policy under the Third Republic, however, was in the end just as, if not more, oppressive than the unrealized policies of the First. Balibar and Laporte end the book with a radical vision: "*penser le français national à l'envers*" [to conceive of national French in reverse], to reclaim language as the collective artifact of humanity rather than a jealously guarded secret handed down by a caste of priest-pedagogues.

In 1985 she published *L'Institution du français: Essai sur le colinguisme des Carolingiens à la République* (The Institution of French: An Essay on Colingualism from the Carolingians to the Third Republic). She develops two concepts that dominate her later work: *colinguisme*, the relationship among various "official" languages, such as French and Latin in the national school system; and *grammatisation*, the attempt by society to impose a codified language on the population, thereby preventing it from taking control of the means of expression. The birth of *colinguisme* in France occurs with the simultaneous presence in Carolingian society of an "official" vernacular and of

Latin, the latter artificially maintained by a progressively rarefied elite. For Balibar, *colinguisme* begins at the moment when the speakers of a vernacular attempt to found it formally as a separate, official language with its own legal authority. This occurred with the creation of the first known French text, the *Serments de Strasbourg* in A.D. 842, an event that is a loss of innocence for the French language. By creating a *de facto* "state language," the authors of the *Serments* and other non-Latin legal (and literary) documents of the time were in effect dividing the vernacular into an oral language for the masses and a written one for the elite.

According to Balibar, schoolteachers ritualistically repeat the same founding gesture every day in their classrooms, and every French child in his or her first encounter with the school experiences on an individual level the same fall from grace that originally occurred on a collective scale in the ninth century. Furthermore, because the inauguration of the legal and artistic status of the French language constituted a foray onto the turf of Latin, the history of French *colinguisme* is the history of the re-latinification of the vernacular, a trend that has historically prevented French from being the unmediated expression of the masses. The legal and artistic capacities of French are therefore similar, as both coincide with the emergence of the written vernacular, a form that has always been more than the simple transcription of French as it was actually spoken.

Although Renée Balibar is best known for her Marxist critique of institutions licensed by the state to define and disseminate French language and literature, her contributions to the field of literary criticism are no less important. In addition to the readings of Flaubert and Camus, she contributed greatly to the criticism on Charles Péguy, the subject of her earliest publications in the 1960s, and whose school notebooks she researched for a 1990 article. Her constant return to individual literary texts and their pedagogical roots is one of the characteristics that distinguish her from the literary sociology that emerged in the wake of Lucien Goldmann, Pierre Bourdieu, and others.

M. MARTIN GUINEY

See also **Louis Althusser, Etienne Balibar, Albert Camus, Lucien Goldmann**

Biography

Renée Balibar was born Renée Charleux on January 18, 1915 in Le Creusot, in the Burgundy region. Her father died in World War I shortly after her birth. Her mother worked for the postal service in Paris, where Balibar studied at the Lycée Fénelon. She completed the *classes préparatoires* at the Lycée Henri IV, and in 1935 entered the *Ecole Normale Supérieure* at the rue d'Ulm. She was one of only a small number of women between the wars to have been admitted to the most prestigious "*ENS*" for men, as opposed to the ones for women situated in the suburbs of Sèvres and Fontenay-aux-Roses. She married fellow student Pierre Balibar, a mathematician, in 1937. They had four children: Etienne (1942), Marie (1943), Antoinette (1945), and Sébastien (1947). She intended to take the *concours de l'agrégation* for men, but the start of World War II interfered, and she took the exam for women instead. After the *agrégation* she taught for many years in the *lycée*, first in Auxerre, then Lyon, and from 1946 onward in Tours. She joined the University of Tours in the mid-sixties and stayed there for the remainder of her career. Renée Balibar died in 1998.

Selected Works

Les français fictifs: Le rapport des styles littéraires au français national, with Geneviève Merlin and Gilles Tret, 1974
Le français national: politique et pratique de la langue nationale sous la révolution, with Dominique Laporte, 1974
Histoire de la littérature française, 1991
L'Institution du français: Essai sur le colinguisme des Carolingiens à la République, 1985
"National Language, Education, Literature", in *Literature, Politics and Theory, edited by F. Barker* (Papers from the Essex Conference 1976–1984), 1986
"*O mère ensevelie hors du premier jardin:* La poésie des écoliers républicains" *Revue des Lettres Modernes*, 1990
Philosophies du roman policier, edited with Colas Duflo 1995

Further Reading

Branca-Rosoff, Sonia (editor), *L'institution des langues. Renée Balibar, du colinguisme à la grammatisation*. Paris: Editions de la Maison des sciences de l'homme, 2001
Coward, David, "Review of *Histoire de la littérature française* by Renée Balibar," *French Studies*, 47:3 (July 1993), 364.
Mackey, William, "Review of *L'Institution du français: Essai sur le colinguisme des Carolingiens à la République* by Renée Balibar," *History of European Ideas* 13 (1991): 1–2; 125–130.
Offord, M, "Le Colinguisme, Renée Balibar, l'orthographe française au temps de la Réforme," in *History of European Ideas*, 21:1 (1995): 119.

BARDÈCHE, MAURICE
Literary critic and political polemicist

Maurice Bardèche was the intellectual doyen of the French extreme right during the second half of the twentieth century. A man of letters more than of action, Bardèche distinguished himself as a literary scholar and a leading exponent of neofascism. Though he contributed to radical right-wing journals in the 1930s, his real political awakening dated from the liberation of France in 1944–45. The key event was the execution for treason in February 1945 of Bardèche's brother-in-law, the pro-Nazi writer Robert Brasillach. Due mainly to his close association with the latter, Bardèche was imprisoned for six months. The spectacle of Brasillach's execution and the liberation purges, he would later claim, determined his political engagement.

Bardèche's intellectual legacy derives from three distinct genres: scholarship, political polemic, and journalism. He co-wrote with Brasillach an acclaimed *Histoire du cinéma* (1935) and a pro-Franco *Histoire de la guerre d'Espagne* (1939). Appointed professor of literature at the Sorbonne (1941–42) and University of Lille (1942–44), he published notable and enduring works of literary criticism on Balzac (1941) and Stendhal (1947). These were followed by further studies of Balzac (1964, 1980), a work on Proust that won the Prix de la Critique Littéraire (1971), and studies of Flaubert (1975), Céline (1986), and Bloy (1989). Bardèche also edited the complete works of Balzac (1957–63) and of Flaubert (1971–76), together with those of Brasillach (1963–66), whose reputation he sought to rehabilitate.

Ostracized from academia, Bardèche attracted notoriety through his overtly political writings. Reacting to what he perceived as the injustice of the postwar judicial process, he published in 1947 his first major polemical work, *Lettre à François Mauriac*. Here he argued the essential legality of the Vichy regime and the illegitimacy of the Resistance, inveighing against the "lie" that had transformed resisters into patriots and collaborators into traitors. Pétain's government, Bardèche protested, had entered into collaboration with Nazi Germany as a necessity; it had sought rightly to exterminate its enemies in the pursuit of national unity. The Vichy administration had preserved France from extinction, while its Jewish Statutes had done more to protect than to endanger French Jews.

The following year, in *Nuremberg ou la terre promise* (1948), Bardèche turned his attention to Nazi war crimes. He challenged the authority of the war crimes tribunals—a cover, he charged, for Allied crimes such as the bombing of Dresden. He accused the Allies of largely fabricating the case against Nazi Germany and pointed the way for later revisionists by casting doubt on the evidence of the Holocaust, arguing that there had been no state-sponsored policy of genocide.

Although the *Lettre à François Mauriac* outraged a section of public opinion, it brought no legal proceedings against its author; as an apology for Nazism and a denial of Nazi war crimes, *Nuremberg ou la terre promise* was banned and saw Bardèche put on trial.

Defended by the former counsel for Pétain and Brasillach, he was sentenced to a year's imprisonment. He served only days of his sentence before being pardoned, in a controversial move, by President Coty.

Bardèche's writings and imprisonment marked him out as the standard-bearer of French and European neofascism. In 1951, he played a prominent role in the creation of a pan-European neofascist movement, the European Social Movement (MSE) or "Malmö International." The vision propounded by Bardèche and the MSE was that of a Europe of nationalist states, militarily and economically unified in the face of the superpowers and constituting a "third order" between liberal democracy and communism. This was the European neofascism to which Bardèche owed his ideological allegiance and for which he argued vigorously in *L'Oeuf de Christophe Colomb* (1951) and *Les Temps modernes* (1956).

Bardèche's political credo was nowhere more systematically defined than in his best-known book, *Qu'est-ce que le fascisme?* (1961). As a political thinker, this is his most important and lasting contribution. Here he proclaimed himself a "fascist writer" and endeavored to theorize a form of fascism stripped of the "errors and excesses" of the Italian and German models. Only thus, reasoned Bardèche, could fascism move beyond its discredited past and reinvent itself as a viable political alternative.

Described as the "catechism of post war fascism" (Algazy) and the *Mein Kampf* of the 1960s" (Del Boca and Giovana), the book was to have a profound impact on the ideological renewal of the French and European extreme right, appearing in several editions and translations. Through analyzing the failed fascist projects of the past, it sought to rescue some transcendent essence of fascism and articulate the elusive synthesis between nationalism and socialism. Mussolini's early fascism was admirable, with its public works, concern for social justice, and corporatism, before it lapsed into Caesarism. National Socialism, awesome in its mobilizing power, was vitiated by its revanchist impulses, its anti-Semitism (which had no place in the "fascist contract"), and its Germanocentric aspirations. Here, for Bardèche, lay the fatal weakness of the Italian and German experiments: both foundered on their essential nationalism, failing to attain any truly European or universal stature. The closest Bardèche came to recovering from the past a model for contemporary fascism was in Mussolini's Salò Republic of 1943–44, with its progressive program and social radicalism; its tragedy, for Bardèche, was that it was launched too late to revive Italian fascism.

Written a decade and a half after the defeat of fascism, Bardèche's book stands as a landmark in the development of the postwar extreme right in France. It provided the first critical assessment of Hitler's Germany and Mussolini's Italy from within the French neofascist community, and the most self-reflexive statement of the fundamental values around which this community coalesced ("nationalism, socialism, anticommunism, and authoritarianism"). It also offered an opportunity to cast a retrospective judgment on Pétain's regime, defined as a "pseudofascism" lacking the raw energy and transformative spirit that were the driving force of true fascism for Bardèche.

In confecting a selective, sanitized, "moderate" concept of fascism, Bardèche's work sought to dispel the opprobrium attaching to the extreme right. The strength of his analysis lay in its "third force" Europeanism and its critique of some classic features of fascism; its weakness lay in its utopian abstraction and ultimate disregard for practical politics.

In addition to his books (published mainly through his own publishing house, Les Sept Couleurs), Bardèche made a sustained contribution to extreme-right thought through the journal that he edited from 1952 to 1982. *Défense de l'Occident* was the most important organ of the postwar French extreme right, bringing together leading militants, intellectuals, and propagandists of the interwar and postwar generations. Vehemently anticommunist and antidemocratic, it promoted Bardèche's Europeanist neofascism, opening its columns to German, Italian, and other European contributors. Here again, Bardèche showed his independence of mind, articulating a nuanced position on the highly charged issue of French Algeria in particular. Less nuanced was the support extended by Bardèche's journal and publishing house to historical revisionists seeking to question, and ultimately to deny, the Holocaust.

A self-proclaimed "fascist," Maurice Bardèche was a bold, provocative, sometimes eccentric political thinker. Lucid and trenchant, his writings retain an intellectual rather than pragmatic appeal. With their Manichaean world view, they stand as a testament to the radicalizing effects on the French extreme right of occupation, liberation, and the Cold War.

J. G. SHIELDS

See also **Léon Bloy**

Biography

Maurice Bardèche was born October 1, 1907 in Dun-sur-Auron, Cher. He studied at the Lycée de Bourges, Lycée Louis-le Grand in Paris, and École Normale Supérieure. He married the sister of Robert Brasillach, Suzanne Brasillach (1934), with whom he had five children. Having acquired a doctorate on Balzac and a university teaching qualification, he taught French literature at the Sorbonne (1940–41) and University of Lille (1942–44). He was disqualified from teaching and imprisoned for six months at the liberation (1944–45), then imprisoned again briefly, in 1954, for the publication of *Nuremberg ou la terre promise* (1948). Bardèche founded the publishing house Les Sept Couleurs (1948–78), the journal *Défense de l'Occident* (1952–82), and co-founded the European Social Movement (1951). He was an influential figure behind various French extreme-right movements. He wrote mainly works of literary criticism and political polemic. He won the Prix de la Critique Littéraire for his study of Proust (1971). Bardèche died July 30, 1998.

Selected writings

Histoire du cinéma, with Robert Brasillach, 1935, 1943; revised by Bardèche, 1948, 1954, 1965
Histoire de la guerre d'Espagne, with Robert Brasillach, 1939
Balzac romancier, 1941
Stendhal romancier, 1947
Lettre à François Mauriac, 1947
Nuremberg ou la terre promise, 1948
Nuremberg II ou les faux-monnayeurs, 1949
L'Oeuf de Christophe Colomb, lettre ouverte à un sénateur d'Amérique, 1951
Les Temps modernes, 1956
Suzanne et le taudis, 1957
Qu'est-ce que le fascisme?, 1961
Une lecture de Balzac, 1964
Histoire des femmes, 1968
Sparte et les Sudistes, 1969
Marcel Proust romancier, 1971
L'Oeuvre de Flaubert, 1975, revised 1988
Balzac (biographie et étude de l'oeuvre), 1980
Louis-Ferdinand Céline, 1986
Léon Bloy, 1989
Souvenirs, 1993
Edited *Oeuvres complètes* of Balzac, 1957–63, of Robert Brasillach, 1963–66, and of Flaubert, 1971–76

Further reading

Algazy, Joseph, *La Tentation néo-fasciste en France 1944–1965*, Paris: Fayard, 1984
Algazy, Joseph, *L'extrême droite en France de 1965 à 1984*, Paris: L'Harmattan, 1989
Chiroux, René, *L'extrême droite sous la Ve République*, Paris: Librairie Générale de Droit et de Jurisprudence, 1974
Brasillach, Robert, *Notre avant-guerre*, Paris: Plon, 1941
Del Boca, Angelo, and Giovana, Mario, *Fascism Today*, London: Heinemann, 1969
Desbuissons, Ghislaine, "Maurice Bardèche, écrivain et théoricien fasciste?" *Revue d'histoire moderne et contemporaine*, 37 (1990): 148–59
Desbuissons, Ghislaine, "Maurice Bardèche: un précurseur du 'révisionnisme'," *Relations internationales*, 65 (1991): 23–37
Duprat, François, *Les Mouvements d'extrême droite en France depuis 1944*, Paris: Albatros, 1972

Kaplan, Alice Yaeger, *Reproductions of Banality: Fascism, Literature and French Intellectual Life*, Minneapolis: University of Minnesota Press, 1986

Milza, Pierre, *Fascisme français: passé et présent*, Paris: Flammarion, 1987

MAURICE BARRÈS

Writer, Politician

Maurice Barrès, who arrived in Paris in 1883, initially to study law, met here some of the foremost representatives of literary decadence, and succumbed to the general despondent mood. As he abandoned plans of a legal career, he made connections among the literati. He was introduced to Anatole France, and joined the Parnassian circle of Leconte de Lisle. At the same time, Barrès became familiar with such motorious works as Paul Bourget's *Essais de psychologie contemporaine* (1883), a compelling cultural analysis of the decadent condition, and Joris-Karl Huysmans's novel *À Rebours* (1884), whose hero Des Esseintes embodies the nihilism of his generation. Although deeply affected by these works (he wrote an influential article on Huysmans's novel that pointed to its decadent aesthetics), Barrès was trying to find his voice. He found it in *Le Culte du moi*, his first fictional trilogy, where he defines the cultivation of the self as a form of existential therapy, a redeeming virtue, and only source of happiness in a "barbaric" age plagued by uninspiring ideas, political mediocrity, and mass consumption. But beyond exploring the limits of existential freedom and aesthetic pleasure through the meditations of the young, partially autobiographic hero, Philippe, the novels that make up the trilogy—*Sous l'oeil des barbares* (1888), *Un homme libre* (1889), and *Le Jardin de Bérénice* (1891)—also seek solutions to the quandary posed by subjective idealism. How does one find continuity and renewed interest without linking the self to the greater community, and the individual ethos to a collective set of values? As the young hero returns to his native land, the Lorraine region, and muses on its sad fate and noble past, nationalism emerges as a response to the hero's self-searching. In Barrès' own life, as well as in his writings, the nation and its past will eventually provide the providential answer. In philosophical terms, the nation offers a reliable ontological support for the hesitating subject, an inextinguishable reservoir of energy and meaning going all the way back in time, and extending to the dimensions of the collective unconscious.

Barrès' good fortune or terrible luck, depending on how one looks at it, is that unlike other fin-de-siècle or modernist writers who only dabbled in politics, Barrès embraced politics as a career, as he later put in his *Cahiers*, as an escape from his ceaseless ruminations and existential doubts. Leaving aside the part of ambition that undoubtedly went into his choice, Barrès confesses, "I almost went mad . . . Politics saved my life." His restless imagination was soon captured by the political figure of Georges Boulanger, the general who became minister of war in 1886, and who embodied the hopes of all those who were dissatisfied with the parliamentary republic, of those who sought justice as well as power, and dreamed of *revanche* (revenge) and the faded glories of the nation. Boulanger mounted a coup to overthrow the republic, but the attempt ended in disaster. This pitiful episode did not diminish, however, Barrès's worship for his hero. Barrès's political career was marked throughout by his attachment to Boulanger. In 1889 Barrès chose to represent the Boulangist party in Nancy on a populist platform meant to carry the blue-collar vote by appealing to vague socialist promises and by raising the specter of foreign workers. Barrès won election to the Chamber of Deputies, a seat he held until 1893. He had already been active in political campaigning as editor of the patriotic journal *La Cocarde* (1894–95), which sought again an alliance between the Boulangists and the socialists. Although Barrès was active on the left of the party, his sentiments were never too far removed from the right wing of the movement, sustained by the virulent anti-Semitic pamphleteering of Edouard Drumont. In all his political capacities, Barrès was also following a personal agenda, implementing an existential and aesthetic program, and seeking self-promotion as much as political renewal. The confusion between the personal and the collective, social good and individual success never ceased to influence his career. In effect, as a member of the Chamber, Barrès was often more interested in rhetorical effects than tangible results, and as writer, especially in his later years, the propagandist often took over the fictional creator. Maurice Barrès's shift from Romantic revolt to nationalist dogma is not as remarkable as it may seem. Several important cultural historians have analyzed this particular phenomenon, Zeev Sternhell in *Maurice Barrès et le nationalisme français* (2000), among others. As Sternhell argued, the conceptual leap from radical subjectivity and individual difference to organic nationalism is already present in the works of German thinkers, such as Herder, Fichte, and Hegel with which Barrès was familiar in his youth. Although Barrès repudiated these foreign masters, as he became increasingly xenophobic and leery of "barbaric" influences, their effect on his thought was undeniable. But even without this direct influence, he could draw on indigenous sources from Michelet to Bergson, who had already absorbed a good dose of German philosophical idealism. Other intellectual trends favored Barrès's nationalist creed. Writers seemed especially sensitive to the antipositivist trends of the period, and many questioned the intellectual heritage of the Enlightenment, including its secular humanism and its belief in progress. The Wagnerian furor in France completed the formula of cultural nationalism, by giving it a popular appeal.

The Dreyfus affair crystallized the nationalist ideology in France. In 1894, the wrongful condemnation of a Jewish officer, Alfred Dreyfus, for treason, polarized French public opinion. Although many French intellectuals courageously sided with the wronged officer, and mounted a campaign for judicial revision, especially after Zola's publication of his famous pamphlet *J'accuse*, Barrès retrenched in his nationalist convictions, which from then on also took a distinctive anti-Semitic coloring. This racial influence was strengthened by other intellectual encounters. Through Jules Soury, a professor of psychology at the Sorbonne, and a militant ethnologist, Barrès became familiar with the tenets of social Darwinism, and its implications: racial warfare and national conservation. These pseudo-scientific teachings complemented Taine's mainly literary doctrine of the influences of *la race*, *le milieu*, and *le moment*, with which Barrès was familiar in his youth. The transition to an intolerant, racist form of nationalism is particularly evident in Barrès's second fictional trilogy, *Le Roman de l'énergie nationale*, comprising *Les Déracinés* (1897), *L'Appel au soldat* (1900), and *Leurs figures* (1902), and in *Scènes et doctrines du nationalisme* (1902).

Barrès's defining nationalist fiction, suggested by the metaphor of roots, and its negative counterpart, uprootedness, is presented in his novel, *Les Déracinés*. The destinies of the young Lorrainers who leave their native soil to seek their fortunes in Paris, much like the author himself, end up (with some exceptions) in tragic fashion: squalid poverty, moral decay, and death on the scaffold. The consequences of uprootedness and servile careerism are vividly displayed in an allegory which seems contradicted by the author's own life. But such contradictions seem minor in an ideology centered on the determinism of the soil, and the symbolic burden of the dead, *la terre* et *les morts*, which resonate, at least in part, with the national-socialist mystique of *Blut und Erde*, as Robert Soucy has argued.

For Barrès, the turn of the century is also the period of a retroactive assessment of the native Lorraine, which encapsulates for him the magic beauty and martyrdom of the nation. His traumatic childhood experiences in a land ravaged by an occupying army take renewed importance, as does regionalism as a whole. Barrès gives one of his most poetic descriptions of Lorraine in *La Colline inspirée* (1913), centered round the ancient shrine at Sion-Vaudrémont, where a group of priests tried to re-establish a popular cult at the be-ginning of the nineteenth century. In this reconsideration of the past, heredity (*la voix du sang*) becomes for Barrès a major formative principle in the makeup of the individual psyche, by stamping the self in an irreversible way. The subject is seen no longer as a self-sufficient entity, but as an echo chamber of the collectivity. It is true that in Barrès's thought education was called to reinforce the natural effect of heredity, and it comes as no surprise that his series of articles entitled, *Scènes et doctrines du nationalisme*, found approval with the nationalist movement in education (L'Éducation nationaliste). Moreover, as Barrès became more traditionalist in form, he also returned to the Catholicism of his youth, which now played an important role in his nationalist vision.

In Barrès's revised philosophy, the subject is thus defined *a priori* by the traditions of his forbears and has to protect against any outside influences that might contaminate its purity: no longer those peddled by native Barbarians, but by Jews and Germans. This is a far cry from Barrès's initial stance on the primacy of the ego, a form of self-betrayal in the eyes of some of his peers, André Gide, in particular, whose experiments in subjective freedom had taken him to distant and forbidden territories. If Barrès traveled far away, it was in the service of the French missionary schools in the Levant, whose "civilizing" mission was promoted by colonial France. In this late period Barrès produced a third fictional trilogy, *Les Bastions de l'Est* (1905–21): *Au service de l'Allemagne* (1905), *Colette Baudoche* (1909), *Le Génie du Rhin* (1921) centered on the provinces of Alsace and Lorraine, which stand as faithful bastions against any "barbaric" invaders from the East.

In politics, Barrès joined the anti-Dreyfusards in forming the League of Patriots dominated by the ultra-nationalist politician, Paul Déroulède. In spite of ideological differences with Charles Maurras, the founder of the Action Française, Barrès remained faithful to right-wing causes, especially in education. Sensing a change in the political mood in the first years of the twentieth century, he settled for a milder form of conservatism, which implicitly accepted the republican status quo and the heritage of the French Revolution, and thus reentered Parliament in 1906 as a deputy of Paris. The same year he was elected member to the Académie Française.

The Great War further enhanced Barrès's nationalist fervor; too old to serve, he threw himself with unbridled passion in the service of the country, by writing daily patriotic articles for the *Écho de Paris*. They were later collected in the fourteen volumes of *Chronique de la Grande Guerre* (1920–24). After the war, his patriotic passion mellowed, and his nationalist creed became increasingly mystical. *Un Jardin sur Oronte*

(1922) is a poetic allegory upholding the primacy of native place and religion over the strongest emotions of the subject. The romance between a Crusader and a bewitching Syrian girl (a thinly veiled portrait of the "foreign" poet Anna de Noailles, for whom Barrès nurtured a strong attraction) ended predictably with the sacrifice of love in the name of cultural allegiance. Published shortly before the end of his life, *Un Jardin sur Oronte* is perhaps Barrès's most personal novel. In revealing the dangerous attraction of the exotic Other personified by the oriental woman, he both accepted, and transcended in fiction, at least, the fearful seduction that inhabited his nationalist creed, as it did many similar ideological currents of the period.

The immediate posterity, represented by avant-garde and modernist writers, was unkind to Barrès. Even before his death, the Parisian Dadaists represented by André Breton, Louis Aragon, and Tristan Tzara organized a mock trial of Barrès as the embodiment of the most retrograde trends in recent French culture, but French writers on the Right found in Barrès a useful ally. A closer look at his influence on twentieth-century French writers finds, however, a more complicated picture, suggesting the ambiguous make-up of French intellectuals during this period. Even if Barrès's style were less exceptional than many French critics have asserted, his influence would be no less important. His writings have marked not only traditional, conservative writers, such as Mauriac, Montherlant, Bernanos, but also more liberal, if not politically opposite figures, such as Aragon, Malraux, and Cocteau. Even more importantly, Barrès was an inspirational figure for General de Gaulle, and later for François Mitterrand. One can only wonder to what extent the mixture of personal and collective grandeur in Barrès's writings plays a part in his posthumous seduction. Although shunned by the literary establishment in the aftermath of the Second World War, as an undesirable reminder of the role that native nationalism played in the constitution of the Vichy regime, Barrès made an unexpected comeback in the late 1960s, and his reputation has benefited from an appreciable number of new studies and biographies. Two recent biographies, by François Broche in 1987 and by Sarah Vajda in 2000, take a clear position against the anti-Barrès phenomenon. In their biographical studies the authors downplay or even defend (in Vajda's case) the excesses in Barrès nationalist philosophy, in the name of his literary importance or authentic patriotism. The history of Barrès's reception is certainly far from settled.

ALINA CLEJ

See also **Henri Bergson, Georges Bernanos, André Breton, André Gide, Charles Maurras**

Biography

Maurice Barrès was born in 1862, in the small town of Charmes-sur-Moselle, on the northeastern border of France. As a young child he witnessed the devastating effects of German occupation during the Franco-Prussian War (1870–71), and the humiliation of the French population in defeat. Frail and hypersensitive, Barrès suffered in his school years. In 1889 he was elected to the Chamber of deputies, where he represented the Boulangist party. Although he started on the left side of this populist movement, he became increasingly involved in nationalist, conservative causes. During the Dreyfus affair, he took the side of the army. Barrès was re-elected to the Chamber of deputies in 1906, and became member of the Académie Française the same year. The bellicose prewar atmosphere and the clamor for revenge (*Revanche*) accentuated the chauvinist aspect of his nationalist creed. In July 1914, he succeeded Paul Déroulède as Chairman of the Ligue des patriotes. During the war Barrès wrote daily patriotic articles for the *Écho de Paris*. Barrès died of a heart attack in 1923.

Selected Writings

Huit Jours chez M. Renan, 1888
Le Culte du moi: Sous l'oeil des barbares, 1888; *Un homme libre*, 1889; *Le Jardin de Bérénice*, 1891
L'Ennemi des lois, 1893
Du sang, de la volupté et de la mort, 1894
Le Roman de l'énergie nationale: Les Déracinés, 1897; *L'Appel au soldat*, 1900; *Leurs Figures*, 1902
Scènes et doctrines du nationalisme, 1902
Pages lorraines, 1903
Le Voyage de Sparte, 1906
Les Bastions de l'Est: Au service de l'Allemagne (1905); *Colette Baudoche*, 1909
Autour de Jeanne d'Arc, 1910
Greco ou le Secret de Tolède, 1911
La Colline inspirée, 1913
Les Diverses Familles spirituelles de la France, 1917
La Chronique de la Grande Guerre, 1920–1924
Un jardin sur l'Oronte, 1922
Une enquête aux pays du Levant, 1923
Mes cahiers, 1896–1923, 1930–1956

Further Reading

Aragon, Louis, *La Lumière de Stendhal*, Paris: Denoël, 1954
Aron, Raymond, *L'Opium des intellectuels*, Paris: Calmann-Lévy, 1955
Benda, Julien, *La Trahison des clercs*, Paris: Grasset, 1927
Berl, Emmanuel, *Mort de la pensée bourgeoise*, Paris: Grasset, 1929
Boisdeffre, Pierre de, *Métamorphose de la littérature: de Barrès à Malraux*, Paris: Alsatia, 1950
Boisdeffre, Pierre de, *Maurice Barrès*, Paris: Éditions universitaires, 1962
Bonnet, Margueritte, *L'Affaire Barrès*, Paris: Corti, 1987
Breton, André, "L'Affaire Barrès," [1921], in *Oeuvres complètes*, Vol. I, Paris: Éditions de la Pléiade, 1988

Brasillach, Robert, *Portraits*, Paris: Plon, 1935

Broche, François, *Maurice Barrès*, Paris: Éditions Jean-Claude Lattès, 1987

Camus, Albert, *L'Homme révolté*, Paris: Gallimard, 1963

Carroll, David, *French Literary Fascism*, Princeton University Press, 1995

Céline, Louis-Ferdinand, *Les Beaux Draps*, Paris: Nouvelles Éditions françaises, 1941

Cocteau, Jean, *Maurice Barrès*, Paris: La Table Ronde, 1948

Davies, Peter, *The Extreme Right In France, 1789 to the Present*, London; New York: Routledge, 2002

Domenach, Jean-Marie, *Barrès par lui-même*, Paris: Seuil, 1954

Fernandez, Ramon, *Barrès*, Paris: Éditions de livre moderne, 1943

Frandon, Ida-Maria, *L'Orient de Maurice Barrès*, Genève: Droz, 1952

Gaulle, Charles de, *Mémoires de guerre*, Paris: Plon, 1954

Gide, André, *Journal 1889–1939*, Paris: Bibliothèque de la Pléiade, 1948

Girardet, Raoul, *Le nationalisme français, 1871–1914*, Paris: Seuil, 1983

Maurras, Charles, *Maîtres et témoins de ma vie d'esprit*, Paris: Flammarion, 1954

Montherlant, Henri de, *Aux fontaines du désir*, Paris: Grasset, 1927

Noailles, Anna de, *Le livre de ma vie*, Paris: Hachette, 1932

Pétain, Le Maréchal, *Paroles aux Français*, Paris: H. Lardanchet, 1941

Rachilde, *Portraits d'hommes*, Paris: Mercure de France, 1930

Soucy, Robert, *Fascism in France. The Case of Maurice Barrès*, Berkeley: University of California Press, 1972

Sternhell, Zeev, *Maurice Barrès et le nationalisme français*, Paris: Fayard, 2000

Tison-Braun, Micheline, *La Crise de l'Humanisme, 1890–1914*, Vol. I, Paris: Nizet, 1958

Vajda, Sarah, *Maurice Barrès*, Paris: Flammarion, 2000

Weber, Eugen, *Action Française. Royalism and Reaction in Twentieth-Century France*, Stanford: Stanford University Press, 1962

Weber, Eugen, *The Nationalist Revival in France: 1905–1914*, Berkeley: University of California Press, 1959

Zeldin, Theodore, *A History of French Passions, 1848–1945*, Vol. I, Oxford: Clarendon Press, 1973

Zeldin, Theodore, *Maurice Barrès*, Actes du colloque organisé par l'Université de Nancy, *Annales de l'Est*, No. 24, Nancy 1963.

Zeldin, Theodore, *Barrès, une tradition dans la modernité*, Actes du colloque de Mulhouse, Bâle: Honoré Champion, 1991

BARTHES, ROLAND

Essayist, Literary Theorist and Critic, Philosopher of Culture

It would take a long time to cover the areas and the widely diverse approaches taken by Roland Barthes in his relatively short career. The tendency is to treat his body of work as within Literary or Critical Theory, particularly that of semiology and structuralism, informing areas as diverse as photography, literature and poststructuralist philosophy. However, it is also possible to see Barthes as a writer who, although never publishing any novels, was fascinated by the act of writing,

and, later on in his career, went on to become a practitioner of what he called the "novelistic." Indeed, the essayistic and novelistic tendencies in his writing are evident in his early work as a journalist.

Barthes's swift rise to fame clearly benefited from spanning two intellectual generations—the Sartrean one and then that of the postmodern. And yet it is (the relationship between) the literary and the political that fascinated him throughout his career. As Stafford (1998) suggests, Barthes's career can be divided up into three categories: journalist (1953–60), academic (1960–), and writer (1970–), and none of these is in any way exclusive, all are present within each other. One of the last intellectuals of the second half of the twentieth century, Barthes was heavily influenced by postwar intellectual culture. A keen reader of Sartre (by his own admission, 1971), in the postwar golden age of political engagement, he had also read the nineteenth century historian Jules Michelet just as thoroughly while ill during the War, and had also been influenced by Gide and Nietzsche in the 1930s. Mixing the historical and the historiographical, the empathetic historian of Michelet and the stern theorist of writing and acting in situation of Sartre, Barthes became fascinated by Brechtian theory and epic theater. He was a crucial leader in the moves in the 1950s to import the German dramatist's ideas and plays into France. At the same time, influenced by semiologist and fashion theorist Algirdas Julien Greimas, whom he had met in Alexandria in 1949, Barthes began a serious study and application of the ideas of Ferdinand de Saussure, the Swiss linguist and father of semiology. Into this heady mix of Sartre, Michelet, Brecht, and Saussure, Barthes added an unorthodox, Trotskyan version of Marxism, to produce his best-known work, *Mythologies* (1957).

Looking for a "*sociologie engagée*" (a "politicized sociology"), and drawing on his left-wing journalism which he had been publishing in *Les Lettres nouvelles* and *Esprit* just as the Algerian War for independence was beginning, his monthly mythological studies launched an ideological critique, both bitter and amusing, of France, as the country moved through the troubled and ideologically-controlled 1950s. This was a time when sociology as a discipline was only just beginning to grow. Barthes was influenced by the *Annales* thinkers, such as Lucien Febvre, who promoted "history from below" and a "*longue durée*" view of change. *Mythologies* was an acerbic and humorous collection of vignettes, which, in turn, praised, satirized, and exposed the values of 1950s France with a sophisticated, highly dialectical view of capitalist society. *Mythologies* has been hailed as a classic of Cultural Studies. Not only did it treat Racine and the new Citroën DS on an equal footing, but it also showed how anything from literature and photography to women's magazines, cooking recipes, and wrestling could be seen to have wider ideological functions. Barthes's avowed enemy was the petite bourgeoisie, whose tendency to convert History into Nature was a key element in maintaining the capitalist and colonialist status quo in France. The final essay, "Myth Today," showed Barthes to be a consummate theorist, deploying Saussure, Marx, and Brecht in equal measure, and is one of the earliest attempts to popularize semiology.

Barthes had also read and absorbed Lévi–Strauss's structural anthropology. The very act of writing could thus, for Barthes, be seen anthropologically. Seeing writing as part of the literary institution, he had developed the idea of *écriture* in relation to History, and considered that writing was tending toward, though not finding, a "degree zero" in which "style" was becoming absent (1953). His new literary history, based on this view, re-addressed ("Marxianized," Barthes claimed later, 1971) the area Sartre had ignored in his hurried *What is Literature?* of 1947. If for Sartre language was opaque, then political commitment on the part of the writer had to ignore questions of literary form. Barthes agreed with the political ethos of writing being politically situated. But, as his analysis of modern literature—a very limited selection, running from Flaubert to Camus—pointed out, the modern writer was torn between, on the one hand, using a language owned and created by the Bourgeoisie since the mid-nineteenth century, and, on the other, trying to express the fracture that modernity had visited upon the human psyche. Writing at a time when the Communist Party "socialist realist" line, perversely and in philistine fashion, decreed that militant and critical literature should avoid the artistic innovations associated with formalism (such as Surrealism), and considered all experiments with form as "bourgeois," Barthes was putting forward the opposite view. Literature had to recognize that it was rooted in society and history, but also so was the language that it employed.

His desire for an *engagement* of literary language and form led him in the 1950s to work on (and, at times, run) the radical popular theater journal *Théâtre Populaire* that was championing Jean Vilar's attempts at the TNP to bring the masses to enjoy a politically mature and questioning form of theater. Paradoxically, perhaps, this interest in form encouraged Barthes also to be one of the first advocates of the *Nouveau Roman*, especially the novels of Alain Robbe-Grillet, whose prose eschewed all traditional forms of narrative and story-telling (including that of political commitment), and showed, according to Barthes, that *chosisme* (the world of things) needed to be included in the novel. His collected essays (1964), drawn from journals such as *Critique*, were important catalysts for the ensuing debates over the renewal of the novel's aesthetic premises.

Barthes's introduction to the work of Michelet, which he had published in 1954, had caught the eye of the *Annales* historian Lucien Febvre. In it Barthes displayed a fascination with Michelet's "bodily" attachment to history and writing, anticipating Bachelard's existentialist and phenomenological poetic sensibility. And his deep knowledge of Michelet's post-romantic history-writing and treatises on natural science helped Barthes to earn temporary posts in the Sociology section of the CNRS during the 1950s. At one stage, he was working on the sociology of vocabulary in 1830s France, later on work and clothing with Georges Friedmann. He was also to play an important part in the founding of a new intellectual journal.

The growth of "the New Left" (following the Soviet invasion of Hungary in 1956) saw him set up, with Edgar Morin and Jean Duvignaud (a colleague from the journal *Théâtre Populaire*), the intellectual journal *Arguments*, one of the most important noncommunist publications of the intellectual left after the War. Following the success of *Mythologies* as well as his monograph on Michelet, Barthes claimed to have always been commissioned to write his many varied journalistic pieces. This was a golden state of affairs for a burgeoning, performative essayist, well versed as a journalist in how to operate in the publication revolution in France and within the growing discipline of the sociology of culture. It is here that he landed his first permanent post at the age of forty-five.

Appointed to a post in the "Sociology of Signs" at the Ecole Pratique des Hautes Etudes in 1960, alongside Fernand Braudel, Lévi-Strauss, Jean-Pierre Vernant, and having set up (with Morin) CECMAS (the Centre for the Study of Mass Communications) and its journal *Communications*, his fortune and fame could not but grow in the 1960s. Semiology, structuralism, and the heated debate over Racine and literary criticism, helped by a judicious attachment to the journal *Tel Quel* and its founder Philippe Sollers (1978), made Barthes into a household name.

Important articles now appeared on photography and advertising, on car culture and on the semiology of food. He held important seminars on rhetoric, arguing that the study of rhetoric, which had been excluded from school and university curricula since the late 1870s, needed to be rediscovered, in order for language in modern society to be fully understood. His magisterial study of rhetoric (written in 1966, but not published until 1970) was modestly subtitled an "*aide-mémoire*," but was in fact an erudite account that showed the finer workings of rhetoric from Ancient Greece to the present day.

This interest in the rhetorical nature of language affected his long and painstaking work on fashion. There was now a shift of emphasis in it. Having tried in the late 1950s to account for and explain how fashion forms changed, Barthes now accepted that this was nigh impossible, and that the only way to explain how an article of clothing became "fashionable" was by considering it to be written or verbalized (rather than simply "seen" or worn). And, though it was an important publication of his work of a decade (1957 to 1967), *The Fashion System* merely ended up confirming that fashion was a "poor" system, with only a small number of possible variants. This mirrored the inevitable conclusion on the structural analysis of narratives (1965) that had reduced the world's narratives, following the work of the Russian Formalist Vladimir Propp, to a small number of types. There was a realization then that structuralism had ended up showing narratives also to be a "poverty of forms." This realization foresaw an important shift which was to take place in the second half of the 1960s, in which narrative became to be considered as smaller than a story but longer than a few words, a crucial move toward poststructuralism which drew on the work of Chomsky, championed by Nicolas Ruwet. But Barthes could not have foreseen the episode that catapulted him into the limelight, the joust between himself and Sorbonne professor Raymond Picard.

Picard was a specialist of Racine, and the republication in book form of Barthes's various essays on the seventeenth century dramatist of tragedy (1963), sparked a series of rather malicious attacks on Barthes's deployment of new critical methodologies. The old was pitted against the new, the Sorbonne expert against the marginal literary critic and sociologist. Barthes's psychoanalytical and structuralist reading of Racine's world was only one among a rising number of readings, in what was loosely termed *la nouvelle critique*, which (broadly speaking) applied to the literature of (relatively) new epistemologies in the social sciences—Marxism, existentialism, psychoanalysis, structuralism, formalism. The row also raised important questions about the role of the critic. Barthes's response, *Criticism and Truth* (1966), was an important statement of the shift that taken place in his thought. It showed that literary criticism, far from looking for the truth of literature, was (or should be) looking rather for its validity. Barthes's influence on the rapidly-changing perspectives of literary criticism in France in this period can be gauged by the extraordinary regularity with which his ideas and formulations are invoked in the 1966 Cerisy Colloquium on contemporary criticism (Poulet 1968).

Nevertheless, Barthes's conception and deployment of semiology (1965) have been criticized by linguists and theorists alike. His claim that linguistics was merely a branch of semiology (rather than the other way around) annoyed semiologist and linguist alike.

Culler has criticized the conclusions on fashion. Indeed, Barthes's flights of fancy into various areas of the social sciences during the 1960s were not always appreciated, neither by technocratic specialists, nor by Marxist philosophers.

The search for validity over "Truth" in literature was an important change of perspective. He had already signalled his attachment to semiology (1965), but a key shift had appeared in the preface to his collected *Critical Essays* (1964). A belief that the act of writing was one of questioning rather than of affirmation, that writing was "intransitive," an end in itself rather than a means, joined with a growing anti-scientific approach towards structuralism, which would make him, alongside Foucault and Derrida, Deleuze and Lacan, a key 1960s theorist. But Barthes never let go of the Sartrean "situation"—dialectics. So, from high structuralist who analyzed stories on James Bond (1965) to theorist of the "adventure of the signifier," Barthes work saw a radicalization of his *écriture*. Having shown how "realism" in Flaubert was merely a set of codes guaranteed by some apparently insignificant signifiers (1968), Barthes now analyzed another short story for its codes. His choice of France's greatest literary writer, Honoré de Balzac, whose work still inspired numerous publications of literary criticism, cannot not have been innocent.

During 1968–69, while teaching a seminar on Balzac's curious, gothic story "Sarrasine", he wrote his analysis and published it as *S/Z* (1970). Based on his seminar with doctoral students, *S/Z* was a radical re-reading, even rewriting, of Balzac's story about a sculptor's love for an opera singer. Barthes showed, using close analysis of the codes deployed in the story, that the different levels of narration, the "economic" mystery of the family's fortune and the psychoanalytical level of desire, could be left as possible entries into the story, without any one being privileged. This "suspension" of judgment by the critic at the end of his reading mirrored the pensiveness of the character telling the yarn in Balzac's story. Barthes had finally undermined the high structuralist belief that there were a finite number of archi-narratives by showing that every reading of a narrative was a rewriting of it, thereby showing its difference from itself. He had also put into practice his belief that the author—or literary authority—was dead. Rather than a text's meaning being controlled by its creator, on the contrary, the reader was now the producer of meanings, necessarily plural as the subject doing the reading is always in a state of historical, psychic, and social flux. The "Death of the Author" (1983), published in late 1968, is perhaps the classic text of the 1968 democratization of literary culture in France. Yet *S/Z* also confirmed that this new freedom for the reader was not set to become a new form of literary scientism. The digressions sprinkled between the numbering of the various codes found in Balzac's story were speculative, provisional, and essayistic in the extreme, undermining any notion of a "science" of the text. Zen Buddhism was an important influence here. With *satori* acting as a search for peace and wisdom, Barthes used Japanese haïku (three-line poems with little discernible import) to show the re-writing of a Balzac story could undermine the production of singular meanings, which characterized Western literary criticism. Seeing in haïku a silence, or exemption of meaning, which seemed to escape the constraints of signification that language seemed to operate, Barthes was reiterating the Mallarméan poetic stance that language (especially poetry) is not simply communication. This interest in silence was a prelude to a more controversial comment that appeared in his 1977 inaugural lecture (1978): because language obliges us to speak, he argued, it is a form of "fascism."

Barthes's shift to avant-garde writer in the late 1960s paralleled that shift made by the group of writers running *Tel Quel*, whose theoretical fundamentalism and Maoist vanguardism is an enduring moment of the turbulent years 1967–1974 in France. He followed the *Tel Quel* fascination with Sade, Bataille, and Artaud, and was an important participant in the journal's establishment of a Theoretical Research Group (GET, "Groupe d'études théoriques"). He even supported the journal's curious *rapprochement* with intellectuals in the French Communist Party. But Barthes never endorsed *Tel Quel*'s Maoist rejection of bourgeois culture, as his literary interests at the time showed. From 1967 to 1972, he wrote acclaimed pieces on Flaubert, Proust, and Loti (1972), reading and writing on literature as if it were his own creative production, and supplying libertarian rereading of Sade, Fourier, and even the Jesuit spiritualist Loyola (1971). Indeed, he was simply carrying on his writerly habit, since the 1950s, of providing prefaces for editions of the classics of French literature (Stendhal, Hugo, Chateaubriand, La Bruyère, La Rochefoucauld, Fromentin).

One other important parallel with *Tel Quel*, other than the interest in and promotion of "theory," was the use of the Orient as critique of the West. After a number of visits to Japan, Barthes published his brilliant, if (self-avowedly) "superficial" account of Japanese culture (1970). Here, in fine poststructuralist fashion, he deliberately ignored social reality, revelled in his linguistic exclusion from Japanese culture, and described how he found decentered cities, haïku-led cultural practices, a world as if it were a literary text. But his stay in Morocco in 1969 was less fruitful, as he found himself, with his distinctly Proustian interests, considered part of the colonial and bourgeois French society against which the Moroccan students he was

teaching were in constant revolt. Nevertheless, he made important friends, such as the poets Abdelkebir Khatibi and Zaghloul Morsy, both involved with the radical, literary journal *Souffles*.

The return to unstable post–1968 France saw Barthes now theorize the power of the state to (re-)impose its will via the Doxa of everyday life. Though *Mythologies* had foreseen this, Barthes now moved to see this phenomenon as a function of language, not so much that of myth. Therefore, to undermine and escape the social Doxa, language itself had to be changed. The stereotype was one way of enacting this. Instead of seeing the stereotypical as a petite-bourgeois *simili* of bourgeois culture, he now advocated the stereotype as a way undermining the belief in the individual's original creativity in language. This strategy was not dissimilar to his urging in *S/Z* to re-read, as rereading could help to counter the capitalist encouragement towards regular and serial consumption of narratives. Finding ways of fighting society's control of language and language production was thus in the early 1970s the key aim of his writing.

In his next publication (1971), he showed how the libertarian Sade, the utopian Fourier, and the spiritualist Loyola were all examples of what he called "logothets," writers who had produced new, counter-doxal languages. The suggestion was that the Left in post-1968 France needed to work in this direction of recasting language, in order to combat the restrictions of the social idiolect, language's tendency to solidify to which we are all subject. One way was to "textualize" as much as possible. His dictionary entry, the "Theory of the Text" (1972), zigzagging through Freud, Marx, and Nietzsche, was anything but a scientific account of "text." Instead it was a playful but iconoclastic attempt to put this logothetic view into practice, by showing how textuality—the search, critique and re-writing (via writing) of language's production of meaning—can shake the status quo of contemporary society. Thus writing became Barthes's *praxis*. He had shown in *S/Z* how the students' desire to speak out (rather than write) had been a weak link in the mass protests of May 1968, and he now began work on an extensive history of writing, which was unfortunately published only posthumously (2000).

Barthes's unpredictability saw him then move, in the decadence of the early seventies, to an unsuspected area of research: a theorizing of the pleasure of literature (1973), which, for the sharp critic of bourgeois and petite bourgeois culture, seemed to many like a sudden change of heart. But the brief essay is a Lacanian attempt to show how his reading habits took shape, divided between *jouissance* (ecstasy) and pleasure, depending on whether the text being read was avant-garde (*scriptible*, and therefore fully rewritable by the reader), or merely classic and readable (*lisible*). Using notions of intertextuality, Barthes also recast literary history, not as one of progression, but of regression, in which Robbe-Grillet came *before* Flaubert, in formal, writerly terms, because Flaubert merely anticipated Robbe-Grillet's prose.

This concentration on pleasure was indicative of a return to the "subject," a term that the antihumanist structuralism of the sixties had seemingly ignored. Following his performative interview in *Tel Quel* in 1971, Barthes became more interested in the self. His writing insisted more on the place of the body within the act of writing that belonged to the "scripteur." The brilliant idea of writing his own biography, in the same series in which he had written on Michelet, was the polar opposite of egotism (1975). For Barthes now theorized the self—his self—in the third person, as if spoken in a novel. This was the crowning act of Nietzscheanism, of the avant-garde's cherished aim: to make life into literature. In this biography of the self, he playfully theorized his own image (in both the photographic and the media sense), displaying how writing the self could allow the self to escape society's pigeon-holing of the individual. Writing could even be a form of salvation against the attempts by society to constrain, contain, and immobilize the intellectual.

His work on the discourse of love (1977) continued this "literarization" of life, and once again saw the self as competing with language. In a series of well-observed vignettes, gesturing towards Goethe's romanticist story of unrequited love, the *Fragments* (as they are affectionately known) played out scenes of romantic conversations and missed meetings, in a theatrical manner that harked back to the passion for drama in his earlier career. Refreshingly, it used Winnicott, rather than Freud, for its psychoanalytical musings. *Fragments* is also the book that has consistently sold the best in Barthes's writing career, addressing a topic in mid-seventies France that was almost taboo on the intellectual left. Then again, Barthes did seem to have deserted confrontational writing and politics, just as the media assault by *nouveaux philosophes* such as Bernard-Henri Lévy and André Glucksmann began to dominate intellectual horizons in mid-seventies France. His slow acquiescence before the changing French political scene had been catalyzed by his trip to China in 1974 with the *Tel Quel* group, just as Maoism was becoming compromised as a totalitarian and corrupt regime. The trip was clearly not inspirational to him, neither for his writing nor his political views. His refusal on his return to comment on his trip became a suspension of judgment similar to the conclusion of *S/Z*. This suspension became the very subject of his essay on China (1975). Thus the thoroughly literary period of his career emerged just as the post-1968 *ennui* had become generalized.

Barthes now sought intellectual solace in his own creativity. He took up calligraphy, working more on music too, and he wrote numerous prefaces on the visual arts, introducing American painters into France such as Cy Twombly, and new French photographers such as Lucien Clergue and Daniel Boudinet. He still maintained a deep attachment to *écriture*, arguing in interviews that it was unfortunate that the vast majority of the population was excluded from it, and that, in order to read the world accurately (he suggested in a neat trademark, Barthesian paradox), one needed to be able to write. Here was an example of Barthes's skillful interview technique (1981).

Appointment in 1977 to a chair in literary semiology at the prestigious Collège de France now confirmed Barthes as a well-known intellectual figure and allowed him to pursue his interests. He gave lectures on Proust and the preparation of the novel, and on Proust and photography. But he also developed other finer areas of research such as the "neutral," which may seem ironic given the stark criticism (in *Mythologies* published twenty years before) of petite bourgeois ideology's tendency towards "neither-norism." He also worked on what he called, in the great French moralist tradition, an "ethology," a politics of living, in a series of lectures called "How to Live Together." The self had finally returned to the center stage of Barthesian writerly "performance." And in the Cerisy conference on him (1978), he could now proudly proclaim that his work was able to bridge the gap between idealism and materialism.

The return to the self was crowned by his final book, a wonderful essay on photography (1980), which confounded all the critics by skirting round a theory of photography (as language). His study was a romantic attempt to refind in a photograph his cherished mother who had recently died, in a deeply moving and essayistic account of the *numen* of photography, eschewing his trademark view of language as ubiquitous. Barthes's main point was that photography avoided the tangles of linguistic communication because it was a physical, material trace of existence, not (merely?) a referent. The problem was how to "read" photography, or rather how to avoid "reading" a medium that, by definition, had no referent, only the individual subject's affective and memorial input. Thus Barthes navigated his way through subjectivity and phenomenology, to produce an essay of moving proportions, and (paradoxically) of theoretical worth, as photography and death was shown to be deeply linked. He was dead within months of it being published, such, it is said, was his grief after his mother's death.

Fame brought with it some playful if pointless criticism. The "Roland Barthes Made Easy" by Burnier and Rambaud (1978) mimicked Barthes's writing style. And since his death he has caused nearly as much debate and argument as during his lifetime. The posthumous publication of his writings from time spent in Morocco in 1969 (1987) revealed notes surprising in their crudeness. And despite his delicate, anti-hysterical, modest side, *Incidents* showed a crude, homosexual side to his life. Then there was the court case over whether some of his lectures on the "neutral" could be published. More recently, and controversially, a Roland Barthes Institute has been set up in Paris. Much of the posthumous Barthes seems then to be at odds with the modest but maverick iconoclast that he was in his lifetime.

Barthes's wide interests have led him to be characterized in many different ways: as theorist and semiologist, utopian thinker, moralist, "deft and supple" intellectual mover, and high structuralist. Ultimately, he was a theorist of alienation who saw Literature, or the literary, as a means of dis-alienation. It may be that Barthes, the postromantic social theorist and literary critic, will endure also as a writer and essayist.

ANDY STAFFORD

See also **Georges Bataille, Albert Camus, Gilles Deleuze, Jacques Derrida, Jean Duivignaud, Lucien Febvre, Andre Gide, Andre Glucksmann, Algirdas Greimas, Jacques Lacan, Claude Levi-Strauss, Alain Robbe-Grillet, Ferdinand de Saussure, Jean-Pierre Vernant**

Biography

Born in Cherbourg (Normandy) in 1915, brought up in the Bayonne region of France, Roland Barthes was a classics student at the Sorbonne until tuberculosis interrupted his studies. This affected his future career dramatically. World War II saw him convalescing, and then emerging with no formal postgraduate qualification, only a degree in Classics. The 1950s saw a period of unstable employment, in which journalism became crucial, and during which he began various research posts in the burgeoning area of Sociology. *Le degré zéro de l'écriture* (1953) and *Michelet* (1954) were well received, but it was *Mythologies* (1957) that made his name. A series of essays from his left-wing journalism, the collection drew together his fascination with Brecht and his growing interest in Saussure and semiology. Work on clothes and fashion history then helped him in 1960 to secure a post in the VI section of the Ecole Pratique des Hautes Etudes, and led to his treatise on fashion (*Système de la Mode*, 1967). The attack launched in 1965 by Sorbonne professor Raymond Pi-

card, over Barthes's application of *la nouvelle critique* to Racine (1963), and the ensuing debate, summarized as the "old" university versus new critical theories (1966), made Barthes a household name; and his structuralist and semiological theories guaranteed his importance as an important intellectual figure of the 1960s. An iconoclastic reading of a Balzac short story and an ethnographic portrait of Japan (*S/Z* and *L'Empire des signes*, 1970) launched the final phase of his career, in which the themes of pleasure (1973), the self (1975), love's language (1977) and photography (1980) dominated. He was elected in 1977 to a Chair of Literary Semiology at the prestigious Collège de France in Paris. He died in 1980, after an accident.

Selected Writings

Barthes's *Complete Works*, prepared by Eric Marty and published by Les Editions du Seuil, cover the vast majority of Barthes's writings: *Œuvres complètes*, 3 vols, tome 1: 1942–1965 (1993), tome 2: *1966–1973* (1994), tome 3: *1974–1980* (1995); as *Selections from the Oeuvres Complètes*, New York: Hill & Wang, 2000

Le Degré zéro de l'écriture, 1953; as *Writing Degree Zero*, translated by Annette Lavers and Colin Smith, 1967

Eléments de sémiologie, 1965; as *Elements of Semiology*, translated by Annette Lavers and Colin Smith, 1967

Essais critiques, 1964; as *Critical Essays* translated by Richard Howard, 1972 *Alors la Chine?*, 1975

Mythologies, 1957; as *Mythologies*, translated by Annette Lavers, 1972, and as *The S/Z*, 1970; as *S/Z*, translated by Richard Miller, 1975

Sade, Fourier, Loyola, 1971; as *Sade, Fourier, Loyola*, translated by Richard Miller, 1976

Le Plaisir du texte, 1973; as *The Pleasure of the Text*, translated by Richard Miller, 1976

Roland Barthes par Roland Barthes, 1975; as *Roland Barthes by Roland Barthes*, translated by Richard Howard, 1977

Collective, *Prétexte: Roland Barthes/Colloque de Cérisy*, Paris: UGE, 1978

Eiffel Tower and Other Mythologies, translated by Richard Howard, 1979

Fragments d'un discours amoureux, 1977; as *A Lover's Discourse: Fragments*, translated by Richard Howard, 1979

Texte, théorie du', 1973; as "Theory of the Text," translated and edited by Ian McLeod in R. Young, *Untying the Text: A Post-Structuralist Reader*, 1981

"Introduction à une analyse structurale du récit," in *Communications*, 1965; as "Introduction to a Structural Analysis of Narrative", translated by Richard Howard, in *A Barthes Reader*, edited by Susan Sontag, 1982

Sur Racine, 1963; as *On Racine*, translated by Richard Howard, 1983

L'Empire des signes, 1970; as *Empire of Signs*, translated by Richard Howard, 1983

Système de la Mode, 1967; as *The Fashion System*, translated by Matthew Ward and Richard Howard, 1985

Michelet par lui-même, 1954; as *Michelet*, translated by Richard Howard, 1987

Critique et vérité, 1966; as *Criticism and Truth*, translated by Katrine Pilcher Keuneman, 1987

Nouveaux essais critiques, 1972; as *New Critical Essays*, translated by Richard Howard, 1990

Leçon, 1978; as "Inaugural Lecture, Collège de France," translated by Richard Howard, in *A Barthes Reader*, edited by Susan Sontag, 1982

La Chambre claire. Note sur la photographie, 1980; as *Camera Lucida: Reflections on Photography*, translated by Richard Howard, 1984

Le Grain de la voix: entretiens 1962–1980, 1981; as *The Grain of the Voice*, translated by Linda Coverdale, 1985

L'Obvie et l'Obtus, 1982; as *The Responsibility of Forms: Critical Essays on Music, Art and Representation*, translated by Richard Howard, 1985

Le Bruissement de la langue, 1984; as *The Rustle of Language*, translated by Richard Howard, 1986

L'Aventure sémiologique, 1985; as *The Semiotic Challenge*, translated by Richard Howard, 1987

Sollers écrivain, 1979; as *Sollers Writer*, translated by Philip Thody, 1987 *Incidents*, 1987; as *Incidents*, translated by Richard Howard, 1992

Variations sur l'écriture, 2000

Further Reading

Burnier, Michel-Antoine and Rambaud, Patrick, *Le Roland-Barthes sans peine*, Paris: Balland, 1978

Calvet, Louis Jean, *Roland Barthes: 1915–1980*, Paris: Flammarion, 1990; as *Roland Barthes: A Biography*, translated by Sarah Wykes, Oxford: Polity, 1994

Coste, Claude, *Roland Barthes, moraliste*, Lille: Editions du Septentrion, 1998

Culler, Jonathan, *Structuralist Poetics*, London: Routledge and Keegan Paul, 1975

Heath, Stephen, *Vertige du déplacement: lecture de Barthes*, Paris: Fayard, 1974

Knight, Diana, *Barthes and Utopia. Space, Travel, Writing*, Oxford: Oxford University Press, 1997

Knight, Diana (editor), *Critical Essays on Roland Barthes*, New York: G. K. Hall, 2000

Lavers, Annette, *Roland Barthes: Structuralism and After*, London: Methuen, 1982

Le Magazine littéraire, special nos.: February 1975, and October 1993

Lefebvre, Henri, *L'Idéologie structuraliste*, Paris: Editions Anthropos, 1975

Moriarty, Michael, *Roland Barthes*, Oxford: Polity, 1991

Nottingham French Studies 36:1 (Spring 1997)

Poulet, Georges, *Les Chemins actuels de la critique*, Paris: Union Générale d'Editions/10/18, 1968

Rabaté, Jean-Michel (editor), *Writing The Image After Roland Barthes*, Philadelphia: Philadelphia University Press, 1997

Roger, Philippe, *Roland Barthes, roman*, Paris: Grasset, 1986

Stafford, Andy, *Roland Barthes, Phenomenon and Myth. An Intellectual Biography*, Edinburgh: Edinburgh University Press, 1998

Tel Quel, Autumn 1971

BATAILLE, GEORGES
Writer

The writings of Georges Bataille are heterogeneous in the extreme, at times didactic and pedagogic, at others approaching a limit of sense in their opening toward experience, or silence. Bataille draws on philosophy, anthropology, economics, literature, painting, and on his own experience in a nonsystematic manner, creating a body of thought that it is difficult to synthesize or to unify. The difficulty of Bataille's thought does not lie in terminology or philosophical complexity, but in the fact that it addresses the relations between thought and experience, and constantly insists on the impossibility of resolving the tension between them. However, in the acuity of the exploration of this tension, in its heterogeneity, the plurality of its modes, and in the breadth of Bataille's interventions across nearly half of the twentieth century, Bataille rivals his contemporary Jean-Paul Sartre in importance and in force.

Bataille's thought is a sustained attempt to give an account of an experience of sacrifice. The attempt, however, constantly admits to its failure or its betrayal of the experience, and in this admission thought is closest to the account that is its aim. Sacrifice, according to Bataille, takes different forms. Indeed, it is difficult to say that one theme or premise remains at the center. Bataille displaces his own terms: transgression, eroticism, the acephalous, sovereignty, sacrifice . . ., and in this displacement thought dissolves its own authority and so is sacrificed. Thus, according to one moment, it is possible to say that the thought of sacrifice is a theory of limits. In sacrifice, a limited consciousness experiences the momentary suppression of its limits and is opened to an experience of limitlessness. The notion of transgression that is elaborated here is premised on a vision of human consciousness as necessarily limited, yet through its very limitation construing an "other side" of the limit. This other side is experienced through transgression as a violence (the sense of the rupture of the limit), as a dissolution of the limited person and an experience of the "totally other" (*tout autre*). The totally other is represented, historically and culturally, in different ways, but Bataille's term *the sacred* is intended to refer not only to the explicitly religious (which in some contexts is a betrayal of the sense of the sacred and its representation as a superior, transcendent but limited "person" or as God) but also to the erotic, or to an experience of immanence, which Bataille calls "inner experience" (see *L'Expérience intérieure*, 1942). Bataille insistently returns to erotic experience and to death as two instances of the dissolution of personal limits. Ultimately, however, both of these are flawed as experiences of sacrifice, and reveal sacrifice as a simulacrum. Erotic experience, which affords the subject an experience of self-dissolution, is nevertheless constrained within the physical dimension and, in erotic love, within the form of the couple (see *L'Erotisme*, 1957). The experience of death is unavailable to me as an experience of my own death, and so is given to me in the form of ritual or as representation. The subject of sacrifice in this case is not the victim that is killed but the witness of the death of the other, in which the subject "participates." The experience is mediated via an object that is destroyed. Sacrifice is thus, Bataille admits, a ruse or a subterfuge, because it is a spectacle (see "Hegel, la mort, le sacrifice"). At its core, Bataille confronts the impossibility of sacrifice, of the thought of sacrifice, and opens up a space in which thought admits to its own impotence and finitude.

Bataille attempts to account for sacrifice in several different modes. It constructs a fragmentary and not altogether empirical anthropological and historical narrative for humanity which hypothesizes the passage from animal to man as resting on the creation of taboos or limits, notably around sex and death, and the emergence of work as a system of reserve and economy which leaves behind the immediate form of animality but at the same time ritualizes the experience of this "lost" immediacy as the sacred (in *L'Erotisme*, for example). In a different mode, Bataille addresses the concept of economy, proposing that a "general economy" persists above and beyond any limited or reserved economy (see *La Part maudite*). The limited economy depends upon accumulation, usefulness, and commensurability. It is fundamentally an economy of exchange. But in the economic world there are instances that fall outside this understanding of human relations, instances of useless expenditure, loss, or destruction. These nevertheless accrue some value, in terms of prestige or honor. The general economy remains therefore an economy, and sacrifice remains an economic gesture as long as it is premised on the notion or the possibility of a return. Much of Bataille's thought thus addresses forms of human culture and activity which tend towards the unmediated experience of the totally other, but which fold this experience back within the mediated form of the economic. It is a question, Bataille says, of introducing into this world the most intense experience of the totally other *that it can bear*. Bataille nevertheless strains toward an exceeding of this limit, where sacrifice would be for and to nothing, where it would be in other words not itself; not a "sacrifice without sacrifice" or a sacrifice of sacrifice, but a space in which sacrifice collapses.

The dimension of sacrifice and the economic moment both inform Bataille's insistent focus on the notion of sovereignty (see particularly *La Souveraineté*). The sovereign is that which has its end in itself, in effect knows no end other than itself, no other authority than itself. Bataille's sovereign is one who may enjoy or consume an object beyond the purely necessary or useful; sovereign experience is beyond need or the demand to survive. The sovereign is not only, however, the king or the master, but any man, in the sense that the servile worker may from time to time experience some enjoyment beyond the useful, beyond work. Much of Bataille's writing of the postwar period is devoted to the exploration of the fortunes of sovereignty, construing a form of historical anthropology which charts the prominence and decline of instituted forms of sovereignty through religion, through to the situation of sovereignty in the postwar world, whose ultimate horizon Bataille locates in communism. Bataille looks to art and literature to provide, in the postreligious world, representations of the experience of sovereignty that are no longer mediated through these instituted forms. A crucial insistence throughout his work, and significantly through his consistent emphasis on the figure of Nietzsche, is that sovereignty as such is nothing. The experience of sovereignty that takes place beyond the domain of usefulness and production, of servitude in Bataille's terms, is an experience of liberation from the constraints of time, in the instant. It liberates from anxiety before death but remains an experience of man's finitude.

Bataille's thought is a sovereign experience both in the sense of thinking this experience and attempting to think, and to write, according to it. Thus Bataille's writing maintains a distance from philosophy properly speaking, although it may engage with it. As a writer, Bataille wants to avoid becoming constrained within the domain of philosophy that he sees as servile (limited by its nature as system or project). His postwar nonfictional works are thus characterized by a tension between pedagogic imperatives—to write in a way that establishes a communication with *any* reader around sovereign experience—and the failure and collapse of explanation and commentary. Bataille believed that discursive language itself forms a constraint and a system in which the experience of sovereignty cannot be communicated except as if in secret, or in the interruption of itself. Fiction, particularly narrative, offers Bataille a frame in which this tension between language and sovereign experience can be effected, and as such his fictional writings are to be read as significant elements of his thought (see *Le Bleu du ciel, Madame Edwarda, L'Abbé C.*). Poetry, for Bataille, is a limit at which thought and language most acutely confront their own dissolution, where the tension between meaning and sovereign experience is most demanding. He is thus critical of the everlasting potential fall of poetry into the decorative or sentimental, and his own poetry forms again a conjunct to his thought (see *L'Impossible*).

Bataille is not systematic, to the extent that one can say he elaborated *a* philosophy; his is a thought that lives off the relations that it engages with other bodies of thought. This is not to say that it is not original or singularly marked by a particular style of thinking. Bataille is a thinker who consistently addressed the relation of his own writing and thinking to those with whom he entered into relation, and addressed the discursive and existential status of his own thought in relation to other bodies of thought. Thus Bataille is not a "philosopher" though he engaged with the work of philosophers and wrote using philosophical concepts. He is not an anthropologist, an economist, nor a sociologist, although his work may certainly be seen as a heretical contribution to these disciplines. It is more appropriate to designate him as a thinker who undertook to engage with the prominent intellectual currents of his time from the perspective of his specific experience. His work is thus interrupted by moments of disruptive experience, by a Nietzschean laughter, which punctures and exposes the systems of thought with which he engages. His thought is not, however, an apology for unmediated experience at the expense of discursive seriousness; both components of the dynamic of transgression are necessary ("*Il faut le système et il faut l'excès*"). Moreover, given Bataille's status as the author of several highly structured and self-conscious fictions, is would be naïve to think of him as an apologist for experience over thought and writing; the incidence of these moments of violence within a discursive and often intentionally pedagogical and dogmatic writing suggests a rhetorical strategy rather than an affirmation of nondiscursive and "real" experience.

Bataille's engagement with the intellectual currents of his time may be considered in three classifications. Firstly, a relation to monumental philosophies without which Bataille's thought is inconceivable and incomprehensible, a relation such that it is through a specific relation with this philosophy that Bataille's thought reaches for its own specificity. Although writers and thinkers such as Durkheim, Freud, and Kierkegaard may be thought of as important for Bataille, this relation exists only with Nietzsche and Hegel. The notion of the death of God and of the instant of eternal return are crucial to Bataille, to his attempt to do justice to the atheological demand imposed by Nietzsche, and to the insistence on the instant of sovereign experience. A large part of Bataille's trajectory as a thinker is characterized by a desire to respond to the demand imposed on thought by these aspects on Nietzsche's writing, from the fragmentary and polemical articles of the journal *Acéphale* in the mid-1930s, to *Sur Nietzsche* and *Mémorandum* (a book consisting of citations from Nietzsche's work). Hegel is no less significant, however, and it is in Bataille's relation to Hegel that lie some of the most challenging and fascinating elements of his thought. The Hegel with whom Bataille was to engage, however, was the Hegel of the *Phenomenology of Spirit*, in so far it is this element of Hegel's philosophy that was presented, commented, and interpreted by Alexandre Kojève in his lectures at the Ecole Pratique de Hautes Etudes from 1933 to 1939. Hegel's importance for Bataille lies partly in the emphasis placed on death or negativity as that through which man's consciousness of himself must be mediated, the notion developed in *Phenomenology of Spirit* of a "sojourn with death." But while for Hegel this experience of negativity is put to work in the service of the dialectical movement of knowledge, toward *le savoir absolu*, for Bataille there remains a "*negativité sans emploi*" or a *non-savoir* that is not mediated and transformed (see the letter to Kojève published in *Le Coupable*). The pure negativity or death thus experienced constitutes the ruin of dialectics and of *le savoir absolu*, such that after the end of history as hypothesized by Kojève, for Bataille there remains an unemployable negativity that is experienced as sovereign. Through this relation to Hegel one can read Bataille as caught in a tension between different forms of mediation of this experience, or the putting to work of death (sacrifice being one), and a stress on the finitude and immanence of death.

A no less significant form of Bataille's engagement with his time is his involvement with groups, communities, and reviews. Through this involvement Bataille responds to the demands placed on him by his century, but also develops and explores a fascination with the possibility of community which has been the focus of recent interventions by Jean-Luc Nancy and Maurice Blanchot. Bataille's engagement with French sociology (the work of Durkheim, Mauss, and others), and his disgust with the fascism of the 1930s lead him, in the inter-war period, to become fascinated with the possibility of a community bound not by a leader, nor through the mediation of capital, nor through the quasi-religious forms of instituted sovereignty such as king or State. Bataille's prewar work develops particularly through his involvement with groups such as the review *Documents*, a non-polarized forum for work on the image, which is significantly opposed to and partly dissident from the Surrealist camp formed around André Breton. The transgressive materialism emphasized in Bataille's work for *Documents* develops in his interventions in the early 1930s in the review *La Critique sociale*, a more politically oriented journal of dissident Marxism under the direction of Boris Souvarine. Bataille's contributions to this journal, and his interventions in the group associated with it, the *Cercle Communiste Démocratique*, develop a form of heretical Marxism through an emphasis on unproductive expenditure (*dépense*) that does not fit easily with the orthodox Marxist stress on production. The domain of expenditure beyond relations of exchange and production, informed in Bataille's thought by encounters with Freudian psychoanalysis, French sociology, and German phenomenology, will be the basis for further analyses of the exploitation of this affective dimension in fascism. Thus Bataille articulates a politically engaged and urgent attempt to counter the rise of fascism in France, through a critical analysis of the affective violence that it exploits in the form of instituted power. Although this is announced as necessary given the incapacity of Socialism or Communism to confront fascism (through their inability to think beyond the limit of commensurate relations mediated by exchange or production), it runs the dangerous risk of complicity with the fascism against which it is directed. In the mid-1930s, specifically at the moment of the Popular Front and the rise of fascist leagues in France, Bataille was involved in activist politics through left-wing groups such as *Masses* (almost a political party which also involved a form of popular university) and *Contre-attaque* (founded by Bataille and André Breton, among others). The short-lived *Contre-attaque* represents an acute moment of political engagement intended to be on a mass scale, perhaps the last moment of explicit resistance to fascism. At this point in his intellectual trajectory Bataille and his intellectual interventions took the explicit and urgent form of resistance to fascism. But his subsequent exploration of forms of community, after the demise of *Contre-attaque*, are no less informed by an attempt to think and to establish a community based neither on the implicit servitude of the bourgeoisie nor on the incarnation of violence in the fascist leader, supported by military power. The community of Bataille's experiments is precisely *acephalous*, without a head, its bond effected through a relation to the experience of sovereignty. The communication that founds this community is not that of commensurate exchange but the fundamental communication of the experience of death. The "secret society" named "Acéphale" was reputedly an attempt to form such a community, but the apparent importance of sacrifice and of ritual, associating the community with forms of mythic or religious mediation, may be proposed to have led to its failure. Bataille is also constantly in flight from his own position as an intellectual, resisting being positioned as the "leader" or "head" of a group, a position that would betray the acephalous imperative of his thought, and of the community. The "Collège de sociologie," an extra-mural forum for debate which undertook to explore and to disseminate an analysis of a "sacred sociology"—bringing to bear the insights of French sociology on the contemporary forms of social and political life—shows Bataille engaged in a fraught relation with the other founding members of the Collège—Roger Caillois and Michel Leiris. Bataille's always eccentric position and the movement of his thought at this time toward his own experience of an atheological mysti-

cism led to the dissolution of the Collège in 1939 and Bataille's isolation from intellectual communities during the early years of the Occupation.

The impetus toward community is, however, also present in Bataille's encounter and relation to Maurice Blanchot, whom he met in 1941. The relation between Bataille and Blanchot is one of distant proximity, described by both thinkers as a relation of *friendship*, complicity or shared guilt in relation to the experience of sovereignty and the necessity of responding to its demand. Blanchot's presence is strongest in Bataille's *L'Expérience intérieure*, where Bataille marks Blanchot's crucial intervention through the phrase: "Experience itself is the authority, but this authority dissolves" ("*que l'autorité s'expie*"). Sovereign experience has its end in itself but is the dissolution of that end, of that authority. That authority is ruined in sovereign experience is an insight that at the same time responds to the prewar experience of fascism, and the war itself, and sets the agenda for Bataille's postwar writing on sovereignty and on literature and art.

A third type of engagement with the context is Bataille's consistent activity of *critique*, critical analysis, mostly in the form of articles, of current publications. The review *Critique*, which Bataille founded in 1946 and with which he was heavily involved until the mid-1950s, represents one of his most significant contributions to the postwar French intellectual context. His own publications in the review form the basis of many of his publications in book form and of other aborted projects such as the four volumes of *La Souveraineté*. *Critique* was intended and functioned as an intellectual forum opposed to and critical of the dominant intellectual tendency of Sartre and *Les Temps Modernes*. Bataille's book *La Littérature et le mal* consists predominantly of essays which were initially critical reviews of Sartre's essays on writers such as Baudelaire and Genet. If Sartre develops a philosophy of committed literature, and judges the writer's life on the basis of the success or failure of this commitment, Bataille insists in *La Littérature et le mal* that literature is its own end, that it is necessarily guilty of its disconnection from action. Bataille was relatively unknown for much of his life, perhaps the most prominent moment being Sartre's hostile review of *L'Expérience intérieure* in 1943; his influence and huge importance in the present is largely the result of the affirmation of his work by French writers and thinkers of the 1960s and 1970s for whom Bataille's position in distinction to Sartre, his critique of Hegel and to a lesser extent his interruptive and transgressive fictional texts were exemplary. Bataille thought informs, not without reserve, the work of Foucault, Derrida, Barthes, Lacan, Baudrillard, and perhaps particularly the *Tel Quel* group whose affirmation of Bataille was a significant factor in the posthumous notoriety he now enjoys.

PATRICK FRENCH

See also **Roland Barthes, Jean Baudrillard, Maurice Blanchot, Jacques Derrida, Emile Durkheim, Michel Foucault, Alexandre Kojeve, Jacques Lacan, Marcel Mauss, Jean-Luc Nancy, Jean-Paul Sartre, Simone Weil**

Biography

Georges Bataille was born in Billon, Puy-de-Dôme, in 1897. He entered the army in 1916, but was discharged due to tuberculosis in 1917. He studied at the École des Chartres, in Paris, from 1918 to 1922. Upon completing his studies, he received a fellowship to attend the School of Advanced Hispanic Studies in Madrid.

Bataille's first published work, *Notre Dame de Reims*, reveals the religious faith that dominated much of the early part of his life, a faith from which he was to radically sever himself in the early 1920s. During his time in Madrid and in Spain he witnessed the goring of the bullfighter Granero, an experience that would mark him. His early work with the philosopher Leon Chestov on Nietzsche and Tolstoy would also be influential. From the mid-1920s onwards he held a position in the Department of Coins and Medals at the Bibliothèque Nationale, a position he maintained for most of his life. Alongside this, however, he was introduced into the milieu of intellectual Paris and frequented groups such as that around the Rue Blomet, establishing lifelong friendships with Michel Leiris and the painter André Masson. In 1926 he undertook psychoanalysis with Dr. Adrien Borel, and as part of his cure wrote the book *Histoire de l'œil*, published under the pseudonym Lord Auch. Borel would show him the photograph of the "Torture of a thousand cuts"—the execution of a Chinese man—which would fascinate him and remain an obsessive reference point in his writing right up to the final book *Les Larmes d'Eros*. From this period also he was involved with the journal *Documents*. He was politically mobilized in the 1930s through involvements in a series of groups (see above) for which the most urgent task was the resistance to the rise of fascism. He planned but abandoned a book on *Le Fascisme en France*. He wrote the novel *Le Bleu du ciel* in 1935, on the eve of the Spanish Civil War, and in it confronted the tension between political commitment (symbolized partly by a fictionalized Simone Weil) and erotic excess. His movement toward an atheological mysticism in the late 1930s contributed to his isolation at the beginning the Second World War, an isolation compounded by the death of his lover Laure (Colette Peignot). During the war years, he wrote several volumes that were later to be collected under the title *La Somme athéologique*. A fiction, *Madame Edwarda*, is also published under the pseudonym Pierre Angélique. He was also plagued by illness, a condition that affected him throughout his life, and an experience that informed his thought. During the war he instigated a Collège d'Etudes Socratiques, where his main interlocutor was Maurice Blanchot. The Collège was abandoned, but the friendship and dialogue with Blanchot continued until his death. From 1945 on, Bataille was intensely involved in the polemics and intellectual life of his time, particularly through the review *Critique*, which he founded in 1946. His writing in this period was also voluminous, characterized by many aborted projects. Alongside major discursive works such as *La Part maudite*, *L'Érotisme*, and the substantially complete but unpublished *La souveraineté*, Bataille also write the novel *L'Abbé C*, the collection of narratives and poetry *L'Impossible* (originally *Haine de la poésie*), and works on art (*Manet, Lascaux ou la naissance de l'art, Les Larmes d'Eros*). At the end of his life he occupied a position in the Bibliothèque d'Orleans, and, beset by financial penury, was able to purchase an apartment in Paris thanks to a sale of paintings organized by his close associates. Bataille died in Paris on July 8, 1962.

Selected works

Madame Edwarda, par Pierre Angélique, 1941; as *The Naked Beast at Heaven's Gate*, translated by Audiart, 1956

Le Bleu du ciel, 1957; as *The Blue of Noon*, translated by Harry Mathews, 1978

Histoire de l'œil, par Lord Auch, 1928; as *Story of the Eye*, translated by Joachim Neugroschel, 1979

"La notion de dépense," 1933; as "The Notion of Expenditure" translated by Allen Stoekl, 1985

La Littérature et le mal, 1957, as *Literature and Evil*, translated by Alastair Hamilton, 1985

L'Expérience intérieure, 1943; as *Inner Experience*, translated by Leslie-Ann Boldt, 1988

Le Coupable, 1944; as *Guilty*, translated by Bruce Boone, 1988

La Part maudite, essai d'économie générale I. La consommation, 1949; as *The Accursed Share: Volume 1*, translated by Robert Hurley, 1988

Les Larmes d'Eros, 1961; as *The Tears of Eros*, translated by Peter Conor, 1989

"Hegel, la mort et le sacrifice," 1955; as "Hegel, Death and Sacrifice" translated by Jonathan Strauss, 1990

La Souveraineté, unpublished, 1953–4; as *The Accursed Share: an essay on general economy; vol. 2, Sovereignty*, translated by Robert Hurley, 1991

Sur Nietzsche, volonté de chance, 1945, as *On Nietzsche*, translated by Bruce Boone, 1992

L'Érotisme, 1957; as *Eroticism*, translated by Mary Dalwood, 2001

Further Reading

Blanchot, Maurice, *The Unavowable Community*, Barrytown, New York: Station Hill Press, 1988

Derrida, Jacques, "From restricted to general economy: a Hegelianism without reserve" in *Writing and Difference*, London: Routledge, 1978

Foucault, Michel, "Preface to Transgression" in *Language; Counter-Memory; Practice*, Ithaca, New York: Cornell University Press, 1977

Hill, Leslie, *Writing at the Limit: Bataille, Klossowski, Blanchot*, Oxford: Oxford University Press, 2001

Libertson, Joseph, *Proximity: Levinas, Blanchot, Bataille and Communication*, The Hague: Martinus Nijhoff, 1982

Marmande Francis, *Georges Bataille politique*, Lyon: Presses Universitaires de Lyon, 1985

Nancy, Jean-Luc, "The Unsacrificeable" in *Yale French Studies 79 (1991): Literature and the Ethical Question*, 20–38

Nancy, Jean-Luc, *The Inoperative Community*, Minneapolis: University of Minnesota Press, 1991

Richman, Michele, *Reading Georges Bataille: Beyond the Gift*, Baltimore: Johns Hopkins University Press, 1982

Sollers, Philippe, "The Roof" in *Writing and the Experience of Limits*, New York, Guildford: Columbia University Press, 1983

BAUDRILLARD, JEAN
Writer

Jean Baudrillard is one of the foremost critics of contemporary society and culture and is often seen as the guru of French postmodern theory. A professor of Sociology at the University of Nanterre from 1966–1987, Baudrillard took the postmodern turn in the mid-1970s, developing a new kind of social analysis that went beyond the confines of modern social theory. He is ultimately important as a critic of modern society and theory, who claims that the era of modernity and the tradition of classical social theory are obsolete, and that we need a novel mode of social analysis adequate to the emerging era of postmodernity.

A prolific author who has written over twenty books, Baudrillard has commented on the most salient sociological phenomena of the contemporary era. His commentary includes the erasure of the distinctions of gender, race, and class that structured modern societies in a new postmodern consumer, media, and high-tech society; the mutating roles of art and aesthetics; fundamental changes in politics and culture; and the impact of new media, information, and cybernetic technologies in the creation of a qualitatively different social order. For some years a cult figure of postmodern theory, Baudrillard moved beyond the problematic of postmodernism from the early 1980s to the present, and has developed a highly idiosyncratic mode of social and cultural analysis.

Baudrillard's 1960s and early 1970s studies of the consumer society and its system of objects drew on classic sociological theory and provided critical perspectives on everyday life in the post–World War II social order organized around the production, consumption, display, and use of consumer goods. His work on political economy merged semiological and neo-Marxian perspectives to provide deep insights into the power of consumption and how it was playing a crucial role in organizing contempobjects, needs, and consumerism. His 1970s studies of the effects of new communication, information, and media technologies blazed innovative paths in contemporary social theory and challenged reigning orthodoxies. Baudrillard's claim of the emergence of a radical break with modern societies was quickly appropriated into the discourse of the postmodern and he was received as the prophet of postmodernity in avant-garde theoretical circles throughout the world.

Baudrillard proclaimed the disappearance of the subject, political economy, meaning, truth, the social, and the real in contemporary postmodern social formations. This process of dramatic change and mutation, he argued, required entirely new theories and concepts to describe the rapidly evolving social processes and novelties of the present moment. Baudrillard undertook to explore this disturbing and original situation and to spell out the consequences for contemporary theory and practice. For some years, Baudrillard was a cutting-edge, critical social theorist, one of the most stimulating and provocative contemporary thinkers. He became a cult figure and media celebrity of postmodernism during the 1980s, and although he continued to publish books at a rapid rate, a noticeable decline in the quality of his work was apparent. In retrospect, he can be seen a theorist who traced in original ways the life of signs and impact of technology on social and everyday life.

In his mid-1970s work, Baudrillard posits a divide in history as radical as the rupture between premodern symbolic societies and modern capitalism. In the mode of classical social theory, he systematically develops distinctions between premodern societies organized around symbolic exchange, modern societies organized around production, and postmodern societies organized around simulation. Against the organizing principles of modern and postmodern society, Baudrillard valorizes the logic of symbolic exchange, as an alternative organizing principle of society. Against modern demands to produce value and meaning, Baudrillard calls for their extermination and annihilation, providing as examples, Mauss's gift-exchange, Saussure's anagrams, and Freud's concept of the death drive. In all of these instances, there is a rupture with the logic of exchange (of goods, meanings, and libidinal energies) and thus an escape from the logic of production, capitalism, rationality, and meaning. Baudrillard's paradoxical logic of symbolic exchange can be explained as expression of a desire to liberate him from modern positions and to seek a revolutionary position outside of modern society. Against modern values, Baudrillard advocates their annihilation and extermination.

Baudrillard's distinction between the logic of production and utility that organized modern societies and the logic of simulation that he believes is the organizing principle of postmodern societies postulates a rupture between modern and postmodern societies as great as the divide between modern and premodern ones. In theorizing the epochal postmodern rupture with modernity, Baudrillard declares the "end of political economy" and of an era in which production was the organizing principle of society. Following Marx, Baudrillard argues that this modern epoch was the era of capitalism and the bourgeoisie, in which workers were exploited by capital and provided a revolutionary force of upheaval. Baudrillard, however, declared the end of political economy and thus the end of the Marxist problematic and of modernity itself.

The discourse of "the end" signifies his announcing a postmodern break or rupture in history. We are now, Baudrillard claims, in a new era of simulation in which social reproduction (information processing, communication, and knowledge industries, and so on) replaces production as the organizing principle of society. From now on, capital and political economy disappear from Baudrillard's story, or return in radically new forms. Henceforth, signs and codes proliferate and produce other signs and powerful sign machines in ever-expanding and spiraling cycles. Technology thus replaces capital in this story and semiurgy, (the proliferation of images, information, signs) replaces production. His postmodern turn is thus connected to a form of technological determinism and a rejection of political economy as a useful explanatory principle—a move that many of his critics reject.

Baudrillard's postmodern world is also one of radical implosion, in which social classes, genders, political differences, and once autonomous realms of society and culture collapse into each other, erasing previously defined boundaries and differences. If modern societies, for classical social theory, were characterized by differentiation, for Baudrillard postmodern societies are characterized by de-differentiation, or implosion. For Baudrillard, in the society of simulation, economics, politics, culture, sexuality, and the social all implode into each other, such that economics is shaped fundamentally by culture, politics, and other spheres, while art, once a sphere of potential difference and opposition, is absorbed into the economic and political, and sexuality is everywhere. In this situation, differences between individuals and groups implode in a rapidly mutating dissolution of the social and the previous boundaries and structures upon which social theory had once focused. In addition, his postmodern universe is one of *hyperreality* in which entertainment, information, and communication technologies provide experiences more intense and involving than the scenes of banal everyday life, as well as the codes and models that structure everyday life. The realm of the hyperreal (i.e., media simulations of reality, Disneyland and amusement parks, malls and consumer fantasylands, TV sports, and other excursions into ideal worlds) is more real than real, whereby the models, images, and codes of the hyperreal come to control thought and behavior. Yet determination itself is aleatory in a nonlinear world where it is impossible to chart causal mechanisms and logic in a situation in which individuals are confronted with an overwhelming flux of images, codes, and models, any of which may shape an individual's thought or behavior.

In this postmodern world, individuals flee from the "desert of the real" for the ecstasies of hyperreality and the new realm of computer, media, and technological experience. In this universe, subjectivities are fragmented and lost, and a novel terrain of experience appears that for Baudrillard renders previous social theories and politics obsolete and irrelevant. Tracing the vicissitudes of the subject in contemporary society, Baudrillard claims that contemporary subjects are no longer afflicted with modern pathologies like hysteria or paranoia, but exist in

> a state of terror which is characteristic of the schizophrenic, an overproximity of all things, a foul promiscuity of all things which beleaguer and penetrate him, meeting with no resistance, and no halo, no aura, not even the aura of his own body protects him. In spite of himself the schizophrenic is open to everything and lives in the most extreme confusion

For Baudrillard, the "ecstasy of communication" means that the subject is in close proximity to instantaneous images and information, in an overexposed and transparent world. In this situation, the subject "becomes a pure screen a pure absorption and resorption surface of the influent networks."

Thus, Baudrillard's categories of simulation, implosion, and hyperreality combine to create a new postmodern condition that requires entirely original modes of social theory and politics to chart and respond to the novelties of the contemporary era. His style and writing strategies are also implosive, combining material from strikingly different fields, studded with examples from the mass media and popular culture in a new mode of postmodern theory that effaces all disciplinary boundaries. His writing attempts to simulate the new conditions, capturing its novelties through inventive use of language and theory. Such radical questioning of contemporary theory and the need for alternative theoretical strategies are thus legitimated for Baudrillard by the radicality of changes in the current era.

For instance, Baudrillard claims that modernity operates with logic of representation in which ideas represent reality and truth, concepts that are key postulates of modern theory. A postmodern society explodes this epistemology by creating a situation in which subjects lose contact with the real and they fragment and dissolve. This situation portends the end of modern theory that operated with a subject-object dialectic in which the subject was supposed to represent and control the object. In the story of modern philosophy, the philosophic subject attempts to discern the nature of reality, to secure grounded knowledge, and to apply this knowledge to control and dominate the object (i.e., nature, other people, ideas). Baudrillard follows here the poststructuralist critique that thought and discourse could no longer be securely anchored in *a priori* or privileged structures. Reacting against the logic of representation in modern theory, French thought, especially some deconstructionists (Rorty's "strong textualists"), moved into the play of textuality, of discourse, which allegedly referred only to other texts or discourses in which "the real" or an "outside" were banished to the realm of nostalgia.

In a similar fashion, Baudrillard, a "strong simulacrist," claims that in the media and consumer society, people are caught up in the play of images, spectacles, and simulacra, that have less and less relationship to an outside, to an external "reality," to such an extent that the very concepts of the social, political, or even "reality" no longer seem to have any meaning. And the narcoticized and mesmerized (some of Baudrillard's metaphors) media-saturated consciousness is in such a state of fascination with image and spectacle that the concept of meaning itself (which depends on stable boundaries, fixed structures, shared consensus) dissolves. In this alarming and novel postmodern situation, the referent, the behind and the outside, along with depth, essence, and reality, all disappear, and with their disappearance, the possibility of all potential opposition vanishes as well. As simulations proliferate, they come to refer only to themselves: a carnival of mirrors reflecting images projected from other mirrors onto the omnipresent television and computer screen and the screen of consciousness, which in turn refers the image to its previous storehouse of images also produced by simulatory mirrors. Caught up in the universe of simulations, the "masses" are bathed in a media massage without messages or meaning, a mass age where classes disappear, and politics is dead, as are the grand dreams of disalienation, liberation, and revolution.

In a sense, there is a parodic inversion of historical materialism in Baudrillard. In place of Marx's emphasis on political economy and the primacy of the economic, for Baudrillard it is the model, the superstructure, that generates the real in a situation he denominates the "end of political economy." For Baudrillard, sign values predominate over use values and exchange values; the materiality of needs and commodity use-values to serve them disappear in Baudrillard's semiological imaginary, in which signs take precedence over the real and reconstruct human life. Turning the Marxist categories against themselves, masses absorb classes, the subject of praxis is fractured, and objects come to rule human beings. Revolution is absorbed by the object of critique, and technological implosion replaces the socialist revolution in producing a rupture in history. For Baudrillard, in contrast to Marx, the catastrophe of modernity and eruption of postmodernity is produced by the unfolding of technological revolution. Consequently, Baudrillard replaces Marx's hard economic and social determinism with its emphasis on the economic dimension, class struggle, and human praxis, with a form of semiological idealism and technological determinism where signs and objects come to dominate the subject.

Baudrillard thus concludes that the "catastrophe has happened," that the destruction of modernity and modern theory, which he noted in the mid-1970s, has been completed by the development of capitalist society itself, that modernity has disappeared and a new social situation has taken its place. Against traditional strategies of rebellion and revolution, Baudrillard begins to champion what he calls "fatal strategies" that push the logic of the system to the extreme in the hopes of collapse or reversal, and eventually adopts a style of highly ironic metaphysical discourse that renounces opposition and the discourse and hopes of progressive social transformation. Baudrillard's *Fatal Strategies* (1983, translated in 1990) presented a bizarre metaphysical scenario concerning the triumph of objects over subjects within the "obscene" proliferation of an object world so completely out of control that it surpasses all attempts to understand, conceptualize, and control it. His scenario concerns the proliferation and growing supremacy of objects over subjects and the eventual triumph of the object. In a discussion of "Ecstasy and Inertia," Baudrillard notes how objects and events in contemporary society are continually surpassing themselves, growing and expanding in power. The "ecstasy" of objects is their proliferation and expansion to the Nth degree, to the superlative; ecstasy as going outside of or beyond oneself: the beautiful as more beautiful than beautiful in fashion, the real more real than the real in television, sex more sexual than sex in pornography. Ecstasy is thus the form of obscenity (fully explicit, nothing hidden) and of the hyperreality described by Baudrillard earlier taken to a higher level, redoubled and intensified. His vision of contemporary society exhibits a careening of growth and excrescence (*croissance et excroissance*), expanding and excreting ever more goods, services, information, messages, or demands—surpassing all rational ends and boundaries in a spiral of uncontrolled growth and replication.

Yet growth, acceleration, and proliferation have reached such extremes, Baudrillard suggests, that the ecstasy of excrescence is accompanied by inertia. As the society is saturated to the limit, it implodes and winds down into entropy. This process presents a catastrophe for the subject, for not only does the acceleration and proliferation of the object world intensify the aleatory dimension of chance and nondeterminacy, but the objects themselves take over in a "cool" catastrophe for the exhausted subject, whose fascination with the play of objects turns to apathy, stupefaction, and an entropic inertia.

In retrospect, the growing power of the world of objects over the subject has been Baudrillard's theme from the beginning, thus pointing to an underlying continuity in his project. In his early writings, he explored the ways that commodities were fascinating individuals in the consumer society and the ways that the world of goods was assuming new and more value through the agency of sign value and the code—which were part of the world of things, the system of objects. His polemics against Marxism were fuelled by the belief that sign value and the code were more fundamental than such traditional elements of political economy as exchange value, use value, production, and so on in constituting contemporary society. Then, reflections on the media entered the forefront of his thought: the TV object was at the center of the home in Baudrillard's earlier thinking and the media, simulations, hyperreality, and implosion eventually came to obliterate distinctions between private and public, inside and outside, media and reality. Henceforth, everything was public, transparent, ecstatic and hyperreal in the object world that was gaining in fascination and seductiveness as the years went by.

And so ultimately the subject, the darling of modern philosophy, is defeated in Baudrillard's metaphysical scenario and the object triumphs, a stunning end to the dialectic of subject and object which had been the framework of modern philosophy. The object is thus the subject's fatality and Baudrillard's "fatal strategies" project an obscure call to submit to the strategies and ruses of objects. In "banal strategies," "the subject believes it to always be more clever than the object, whereas in the other [fatal strategies] the object is always supposed to be more shrewd, more cynical, more brilliant than the subject." Previously, in banal strategies, the subject believed it to be more masterful and sovereign than the object. A fatal strategy, by contrast, recognizes the supremacy of the object and therefore takes the side of the object and surrenders to its strategies, ruses, and rules.

In his later writings, Baudrillard posited an "immanent reversal," a reversal direction of direction and meaning, in which things turn into their opposite. Thus, the society of production was passing over to simulation and seduction; the panoptic and repressive power theorized by Foucault was turning into a cynical and seductive power; the liberation championed in the 1960s became a form of voluntary servitude; sovereignty had passed from the side of the subject to the object; and revolution and emancipation had turned into their opposites, snaring one more and more in the logic of the system, thus trapping individuals in an order of simulation and virtuality. His concept of "immanent reversal" thus provides a perverse form of Horkheimer and Adorno's dialectic of Enlightenment, where everything becomes its opposite,—where Enlightenment becomes domination, where culture becomes culture industry, where democracy becomes a form of mass manipulation, and science and technology part of an apparatus of domination.

Baudrillard follows this logic and a perverse and nihilistic metaphysics based on this vision into the 1990s and to the present where his thought becomes ever more hermetic, metaphysical, and cynical. The texts of the past decade continue the fragmentary style and use of short essays, aphorisms, stories, and aperçus that Baudrillard began deploying in the 1980s, and often repeat some of the same ideas and stories. They contain few striking ideas or perspectives, but are often entertaining, although they can be outrageous and scandalous. These writings can be read as a continual commentary on current social conditions, along with a running dialogue with Marxism and poststructuralist theory. Yet after his fierce polemics of the 1970s against competing models of thought, Baudrillard's dialogue with theory now consists mostly of occasional asides and his mode of analysis consists of ruminating on contemporary events and trends.

In general, in Baudrillard's post-1990s musings, the postmodern condition is one of absorbing otherness, of erasing difference, of assimilating and imploding all oppositional or negative forces into a viral positivity, in which the positive radiates throughout every interstice of society and culture, irradiating into nullity any negativity, opposition, or difference. It is also an era in which reality has disappeared, constituting the "perfect crime," which is the subject of a book of that title. Baudrillard presents himself here as a detective searching for the perpetrator of the "perfect crime," the murder of reality, "the most important event of modern history." His theme is the destruction and disappearance of the real in the realm of information and simulacra, and the subsequent reign of illusion and appearance. In a Nietzschean mode, he suggests that henceforth truth and reality are illusions, that illusions reign, and that therefore we should respect illusion and appearance and give up the illusory quest for truth and reality.

Baudrillard has never been as influential in France as in the English-speaking world and elsewhere. He is an example of the "global popular," a thinker who has followers and readers throughout the world, though, so far, no Baudrillardian school has emerged. His influence has been largely at the margins of a diverse number of disciplines ranging from social theory to philosophy to art history, thus it is difficult to gauge his impact on the mainstream of social theory, or any specific academic discipline. He is perhaps most important as part of the postmodern turn against modern society and its academic disciplines. Baudrillard's work cuts across the disciplines and promotes cross-disciplinary thought. He challenges standard wisdom and puts in question received dogma and methods. While his early work on the consumer society, the political economy of the sign, simulation and simulacra, and the implosion of phenomena previously separated can be deployed within critical social theory, much of his post-1980s work quite self-consciously goes beyond the classical tradition and in most interviews of the past decade of the twentieth century Baudrillard distanced himself from critical social theory, claiming that the energy of critique has dissipated.

Baudrillard thus emerges in retrospect as a transdisciplinary theorist of the fin-de-millennium who produces signposts to the new era of postmodernity and is an important, albeit hardly trustworthy, guide to the new era. Baudrillard exaggerates the break between the modern and the postmodern, takes future possibilities as existing realities, and provides a futuristic perspective on the present, much like the tradition of dystopic science fiction, ranging from Huxley to cyberpunk. Indeed, Baudrillard's post-1970s work may be read as science fiction that anticipates the future by exaggerating present tendencies, and thus provides early warnings about what might happen if present trends continue. It is not an accident that Baudrillard is an aficionado of science fiction who himself has influenced a large number of contemporary science fiction writers.

In retrospect, Baudrillard's early critical explorations of the system of objects and consumer society contain some of his most important contributions to contemporary social theory. His mid-1970s analysis of a dramatic mutation occurring within contemporary societies and rise of a new logic of simulation that sketched out the effects of media and information on society as a whole is also original and important. But at this stage of his work, Baudrillard falls prey to a technological determinism and semiological idealism, which posits an autonomous technology and play of signs generating a society of simulation which creates a postmodern break and the proliferation of signs, spectacles, and simulacra. Baudrillard erases autonomous and differentiated spheres of the economy, polity, society, and culture posited by classical social theory in favor of an implosive theory that also crosses disciplinary boundaries, thus dissolving social theory into a broader form of social critique.

In the final analysis, Baudrillard is perhaps more useful as a provocateur who challenges and puts in question the tradition of classical social theory than as someone who provides concepts and methods that can be applied in social or cultural analysis. He claims that the object of classical theory—modernity—has been surpassed by a new postmodernity and that therefore new theoretical strategies, modes of writing, and forms of theory are necessary. While his work on simulation and the postmodern break from the mid-1970s into the 1980s provides a paradigmatic postmodern theory and analysis of postmodernity that has been highly influential, and that despite its exaggerations continues to be of use in interpreting present social trends, his later work is arguably of more literary and philosophical than sociological interest. Baudrillard thus ultimately goes beyond social theory altogether into a new sphere and mode of writing that provides occasional insights into contemporary social phenomena and provocative critiques of contemporary and classical social theory, but does not really provide an adequate theory of the present age.

Douglas Kellner

See also **Marcel Mauss, Ferdinand de Saussure**

Biography

Jean Baudrillard was born in the cathedral town of Reims, France in 1929. He told interviewers that his grandparents were peasants and his parents became civil servants. He also claims that he was the first member of his family to pursue an advanced education and that this led to a rupture with his parents and cultural milieu. In 1956, he began working as a professor of secondary education in a French high school (*Lyceé*) and in the early 1960s did editorial work for the French publisher Seuil. Baudrillard was initially a Germanist who published essays on literature in *Les temps modernes* in 1962–63 and translated works of Peter Weiss and Bertolt Brecht into French, as well as a book on messianic revolutionary movements by Wilhelm Mühlmann. During this period, he met Henri Lefebvre, whose critiques of everyday life impressed him, and Roland Barthes, whose semiological analyses of contemporary society had lasting influence on his work.

In 1966, Baudrillard entered the University of Paris, Nanterre, and became Lefebvre's assistant, while studying languages, philosophy, sociology, and other disciplines. He defended his *"These de Troisième Cycle"* in sociology at Nanterre in 1966 with a dissertation on *"Le système des objects,"* and began teaching sociology in October of that year. Opposing French and United States intervention in the Algerian and Vietnamese wars, Baudrillard associated himself with the French Left in the 1960s. Nanterre was the center of radical politics and the "March 22 movement," associated with Daniel Cohn-Bendit and the *enrageés*, began in the Nanterre sociology department. Baudrillard said later that he was at the center of the events of May 1968 that resulted in massive student uprisings and a general strike that almost drove de Gaulle from power. Baudrillard continues to devote his time to university teaching, writing, traveling, and producing books.

Selected Writings

The System of Objects, 1968
The Consumer Society, 1970
For a Critique of the Political Economy of the Sign, 1972
The Mirror of Production, 1973
Simulations, 1983
In the Shadow of the Silent Majorities, 1983
"The Ecstacy of Communication," in *The Anti-Aesthetic*, edited by Hal Foster, 1983
America, 1988
Cool Memories, 1990
Fatal Strategies, 1990
Symbolic Exchange and Death, 1993
The Transparency of Evil, 1993
Simulacra and Simulation, 1994
The Illusion of the End, 1994
The Gulf War Never Happened, 1995
The Perfect Crime, 1996
The Vital Illusion, 2000
Impossible Exchange, 2001

Further Reading

Best, Steven, and Kellner, Douglas, *Postmodern Theory: Critical Interrogations*, London and New York: MacMillan and Guilford Press, 1991
The Postmodern Turn, New York: Guilford Press, 1997
Debord, Guy, *The Society of the Spectacle*, Detroit: Black and Red, 1970
Frankovits, Alan, (editor), *Seduced and Abandoned: The Baudrillard Scene*, Glebe, New South Wales: Stonemoss 1970
Gane, Mike, *Baudrillard. Critical and Fatal Theory*, London: Routledge 1991
Gane, Mike (editor) *Baudrillard Live. Selected Interviews*, London: Routledge, 1993
Genosko, Gary, *Baudrillard and Signs*, London: Routledge, 1994
Kellner, Douglas, *Jean Baudrillard: From Marxism to Postmodernism and Beyond*, Cambridge and Palo Alto: Polity Press and Stanford University Press, 1989
Kellner, Douglas (editor), *Jean Baudrillard. A Critical Reader*, Oxford: Basil Blackwell, 1994
Rokek, Chris and Bryan Turner (editors), *Forget Baudrillard*, London: Routledge, 1993
Stearns, William and William Chaloupka (editors), *The Disappearance of Art and Politics*, New York and London: Saint Martins and Macmillan Press, 1992

BAZIN, ANDRÉ
Film critic and theorist

André Bazin passionately argued for a vision of cinema that conveyed the meaning of human experience in the encounter with the objective fact of material existence. Through an attentive and compassionate gaze, the cinematic image discovers the "authentic" appearance of reality. It intercedes on behalf of the mundane world to restore a sense of the identity of things as they are, but only through the intervention of a subject who recognizes its own agency in reference to the historical, social, and psychological conditions of its being-in-time. Cinema, therefore, must fulfil an ethical, political, aesthetic, and philosophical imperative: to show, rather than to interpret or explain, the "hidden meaning in people and things without disturbing the unity natural to them."

Bazin developed a theory of cinema that was based on the fundamental capacity of film to record and preserve an image of the world through purely mechanical means. It is in this sense that the invention of photography realizes the age-old dream of art to create the illusion of resemblance. But the image reproduced by the camera possesses the qualities of a natural phenomenon, despite its origin as an automatic copy, because it bears the trace of living things in the form of a "luminous imprint." Bazin claims in "The Ontology of the Photographic Image" that the indexical properties of photography permit "transference of reality from the thing to its reproduction." After the manner of a death mask or a fingerprint, the image shares "a common being" with its model. Cinema merely extends their identity into the realm of time and motion. Just as the ancient Egyptians embalmed the dead body in a protective cocoon to insure the survival of the immortal soul, so cinema sustains its phantom existence by imbuing the image of things with the semblance of life. Film mummifies change and endlessly projects the passage of time as a movement between presence and absence.

The ontological premises of his theory of representation led Bazin to develop a critical position as regards the course of film history. Accordingly, he favored a film practice that tended toward the achievement of realism. The mimetic qualities of the cinematic image contribute to the production of a more or less complete picture of reality or, as he calls it in an essay of the same name, "the myth of total cinema." But, despite the referential claim of the image, the basic technical and formal elements of the medium may be used to frame or focus the presentation of an event on screen. The construction of a shot or a sequence establishes a set of visual and pictorial relationships that shape the content and form of the film image for narrative or dramatic purposes. Bazin, however, opposes the tradition of filmmaking that applies the creative resources peculiar to cinema—the stylistic procedures of composition, lighting, set design, performance and, particularly, editing—toward modifying or manipulating the raw material of reality.

To varying degrees, German Expressionism, Soviet montage, and the classic Hollywood style submit the spatial and temporal unity of appearances to a process of abstraction. The meaning of an image no longer resides in its "objective" status but is derived from its association with other images. Their organization increases the psychological or polemical impact of a scene. Bazin, on the other hand, insists upon a cinematic method that maintains the integrity and autonomy of the object or action depicted. He sought an aesthetic form that would respect the ambiguous structure of reality. The work of Flaherty, Murnau, Stroheim, and Dreyer suggests an approach to realism that "reveals" the perceptual structure of the visible world, rather than describes or interprets it. Ultimately, though, deep-focus photography and the long take provided Bazin with an expressive technique that would reconcile the paradoxical strain of materialism and idealism that inflected his theory of film. The internal consistency of the image retains its dynamism and density in the films of Jean Renoir and Orson Welles because the significance of narrative events unfolds within a mobile and multiply focused frame. In the case of Rossellini and De Sica, the factual dimension of space and time remains accessible because the emotive force of a dramatic situation emerges within a transparent and neutral *mise-en-scéne*. Each method places spectator and author alike in a relation to the real that demands a more concentrated level of affinity. Therefore, Bazin celebrated *Citizen Kane*, *La Règle de jeu*, and neorealism in general not just as significant advances in film style but as final affirmation of the power of cinema to deliver the "truth" through the concrete substance of an image.

Bazin has been criticized for a naive belief in cinematic presence over filmic representation, for privileging authenticity and essence over construction and convention. In the 1970s and 1980s, his reputation suffered at the hands of the theoretical model that dominated film studies in the United States and United Kingdom: a structural-semiotic account of the "film apparatus" that sought to demystify its ideological effects. In

France too, his ideas engendered considerable debate, beginning with Jean Mitry's denial of the "natural" relation between film and reality independent of cultural mediation, and including Jean-Louis Comolli's political revision of the role of the subject in securing the meaning of an image. But it would be a misconception to reduce Bazin's critical position to a simple issue of reference and resemblance, a direct equation of appearance and reality. He places as much emphasis on mind as matter, on consciousness and perception as concrete evidence or physical fact. His thinking on cinema was forged in the intellectual context of existentialism and phenomenology, and inherits a Bergsonian attitude to experience and the Personalist perspective on human agency. Perhaps for this reason echoes of Bazin's metaphysical belief in the transformative potential of realism, stripped of the analogical bond between being and image, return in the theoretical writings of Gilles Deleuze, Jean-Louis Schefer, and Nicole Brenez.

Bazin always arrived at his theoretical insights through an analysis of specific films. The latest popular movie or the more challenging innovations in film language and style served as the pretext for a rigorous critical inquiry into the relationship of cinema to painting, theater, and the novel; the social and symbolic significance of particular genres like the Western and the gangster film; the mythic appeal of the star; eroticism and censorship; religion and film; the work of important figures like Charlie Chaplin, Renoir, Welles, and Robert Bresson; the state of contemporary French cinema. The venue for these reflections was not just limited to the pages of film journals. Bazin pursued his cultural program in the public arena by organizing a network of cine-clubs and discussion groups across France, speaking at screenings and lectures, agitating and arguing for the films and directors he loved at festivals and conferences. His ideas and personal example directly influenced the next generation of French film critics who worked under his tutelage at *Cahiers du Cinéma* and eventually formed the *nouvelle vague*. By the end of his life, Bazin had established cinema as a serious field of artistic and intellectual activity and a necessary key to the understanding of French cultural life and modern thought.

ALAN WRIGHT

See also **Henri Bergson, Gilles Deleuze**

Biography

Born in 1918 in Angers at the end of World War I, André Bazin spent his childhood years in La Rochelle. He studied at the École Normale Supérieure with the intention of pursuing a career in education, but a serious stammer and the onset of an intellectual and religious crisis prevented him from becoming a teacher. In the early years of World War II, he became involved with a number of cultural groups influenced by the ideas of Christian activists like Marcel Legaut, Emmanuel Mounier, and Teilhard de Chardin. While working at the Maison des Lettres, Bazin discovered cinema and started to organize public screenings, lectures, and journals. His first essays date from this period. Between 1945 and 1950, he wrote numerous articles and reviews as a film critic in *Le Parisien Libéré*, *L'Ecran Française*, *Esprit*, and *Les Temps Moderne*. He also helped launch the national film academy, IDHEC Institut des Hautes Etudes Cinématographiques, and directed the cinema arm of *Travail et Culture*, where he ran educational programs in factories and schools. As the cultural ferment after the Liberation waned, Bazin found it increasingly difficult to reconcile his political and aesthetic ideals with the Communist party line, and devoted his time to promoting film culture in cine-clubs, festivals, and his own writings. He encouraged a group of young cineastes, which included François Truffaut and Jean-Luc Godard, who later wrote for *Cahiers du Cinéma*, the influential film journal he founded with Jacques Doniol-Valcroze in 1951. He continued to work tirelessly as his health declined. He was diagnosed with leukemia in 1954 and died on November 11, 1958.

Selected Writings

Qu'est-ce que le cinéma?, 4 volumes, 1958–1962; as *What is Cinema?*, 2 volumes, translated by Hugh Gray, 1967, 1971
Jean Renoir, 1971; as *Jean Renoir*, translated by W. W. Hasley II and William H. Simon, 1973
Orson Welles, 1972; as *Orson Welles*, translated by Jonathon Rosenbaum, 1978
Le Cinéma de l'occupation et de la résistance, 1975; as *French Cinema of the Occupation and Resistance*, translated by Stanley Hochman, 1981
Cinema de la cruauté, 1975; as *The Cinema of Cruelty*, translated by Sabine d'Estrée, 1982
Bazin at Work: Major Essays and Reviews of the Forties and Fifties, translated by Alain Piette and Bert Cardullo, 1997

Further Reading

Andrew, Dudley, *André Bazin*, New York: Oxford University Press, 1978
Andrew, Dudley, "André Bazin" in *The Major Film Theories*, New York: Oxford University Press, 1976
Henderson, Brian, "Bazin Defended Against His Devotees", *Film Quarterly*, 32, 4 (1979): 26–37
Michelson, Annette, "What is Cinema?", *Performing Arts Journal*, 17 (May–Sept, 1995): 20–29
Rosen, Philip, "Subject, Ontology, and Historicity in Bazin" in *Change Mummified*, Minneapolis and London, University of Minnesota Press, 2001

Staiger, Janet, "Theorist, yes, but what of? Bazin and History", *Iris*, 2, 2 (1984)
Velvet Light Trap, 21 (Summer, 1985), Special Issue on Bazin
Wide Angle, 9, 4 (1987), Special Issue on Bazin
Williams, Christopher, (editor), *Realism and the Cinema*, London: Routledge, 1980

BEAUVOIR, SIMONE DE
Writer

Simone de Beauvoir was one of the most influential French thinkers of the twentieth century. When she died in 1986, she was mourned not only by her intimate friends in France, but by women throughout the world who had taken courage, inspiration and, most of all, hard-headed argument from her *oeuvre*. As the preeminent foundational theorist of twentieth-century feminism and as female intellectual icon extraordinaire, her name had become synonymous with the women's movement for millions. But Simone de Beauvoir's contribution to the development of modern thought was much broader than this. She also is remembered for the pivotal part that she played in one of the most exciting and influential periods of French intellectual history, the emergence of French existentialism following World War II. The ideas she developed as a Parisian existentialist philosopher provided her with much of the analytical framework that she used to such fine effect as a feminist theorist.

The debate regarding Simone de Beauvoir's own place in French intellectual history is illustrative of and runs parallel to the recent history of women's struggle for equal rights. So far there have been three eras in Beauvoir scholarship, each distinguished by its methodology. The first, and oldest, treated Beauvoir as a disciple of her life-long friend and companion, Jean-Paul Sartre. It found Beauvoir's writings interesting and worthy mainly because they offered exemplifications of what were presumed to be the ideas of Sartre. The second era of Beauvoir scholarship began in the 1970s. Inspired by the international feminist movement and at ease with the notion of the intellectually creative woman, it sought to identify ideas and themes found in Beauvoir's writing but not in Sartre's. By focusing on this residual thought, scholars succeeded in creating an intellectual persona for Beauvoir distinct from Sartre's. This early feminist approach, however, shared with its predecessor the *a priori* assumption that the distinctive ideas shared by Beauvoir and Sartre could only have originated with him. The third and most recent era of Beauvoir scholarship features a completely traditional methodology. It seeks to determine on the basis of empirical evidence the individual contributions made by Beauvoir and Sartre to their common fund of ideas. Initially this research program suffered from a shortage of documentary evidence. But from the mid-1980s on, Beauvoir and Sartre's private letters, diaries, and notebooks became available to scholars. These documents show that Beauvoir was, at the least, an equal partner with Sartre in the development of their shared philosophical ideas. It is from this recently established historical basis that commentary on Beauvoir's place in the history of ideas and of French culture must begin.

In many ways, Simone de Beauvoir, her thought and its orientation, can only be understood in terms of the twentieth-century Parisian intellectual tradition. Beauvoir began her university studies at the Sorbonne in 1926. There she read Plato, Schopenhauer, and Bergson, developed an enthusiasm for Nietzsche, was deeply influenced by the Cartesian rationalism associated with the teaching of Alain, worked closely on Kant and Hume, and prepared a dissertation on Leibniz. She excelled as a student, coming second to Simone Weil, but ahead of Maurice Merleau-Ponty, on the pass list for the moral science and psychology examinations of 1928. Intrigued, Merleau-Ponty introduced himself to Beauvoir. They quickly became close friends and philosophical associates and, for a while, enjoyed daily dialogues in the Luxembourg Gardens. This was the first stage in the building of the influential intellectual circle that would ultimately include Beauvoir and Merleau-Ponty, but also Sartre, Raymond Aron, Albert Camus, Boris Vian, Jean Genet, and Claude Lanzmann.

Two salient characteristics of Beauvoir as philosopher are her phenomenological approach and her use of fiction as a means for developing philosophical ideas. Her student diaries show that she became converted to these methods following her early reading of Henri Bergson, whom Edmund Husserl credited as being "the first phenomenologist." In a diary entry from 1926, Beauvoir comments on Bergson's *Time and Free Will: An Essay on the Immediate Data of Consciousness* (1899) as follows: "whereas in reading other philosophers I have the impression of witnessing more or less logical constructions, here finally I am touching palpable reality and encountering life." For the phenomenologist, the challenge is not to develop philosophical systems but rather to find a way through the constructs that the intellect has imposed between consciousness and reality. In *Time and Free Will* Bergson identifies fiction, with its focus on the concrete and the particular, as a literary form especially well suited to this philosophical task and imagines some "bold novelist" of the future as the one who achieves this unveiling. The teenage Beauvoir took Bergson's challenge to heart. In a diary entry from 1927, she wrote "I must . . . write 'essays on life' which would not be a novel, but philosophy, linking them together

vaguely with a fiction. But the thought would be the essential thing . . . ."

After university, employed as a schoolteacher, Beauvoir persisted in addressing herself to Bergson's methodological challenge, and produced several apprentice novels, slowly developing her skills at writing philosophical fiction. She finished *Quand prime le spirituel*, a set of five interlocking short stories that develops her then novel view of the self as a narrative construct, in 1937, but the book did not find a publisher until 1979. Originally offered to Gallimard, it was turned down on the grounds that Beauvoir's very honest "essays on life" from women's points of view would undermine their reputation. Her debut in print was thus delayed until the publication of her novel *L'Invitée* in 1943.

Begun in 1937 and finished in 1941, this novel takes up the philosophical questions that had fascinated Beauvoir as a student and develops a set of answers that served as the underlying conceptual framework for her later works, including *Le Deuxième sexe* (1949). These foundational principles must be noted, before tracing their development in her fiction and essays of the 1940s.

Beauvoir pursued her philosophical investigations from the point of view of a situated individual consciousness, which, in the tradition of Franz Brentano, she identifies as a relation (rather than as a substance or being) that some objects, most notably humans, have to the world. This relational approach to consciousness divides being into two primary categories, but ones that are very different from those of Descartes. The most elementary, nonconscious being or being-in-itself, includes anything that can be made an object of consciousness. This category, much wider than material objects, embraces not only the meanings of words and concepts, but also memories, including moments of consciousness reflected upon. Beauvoir's other primary category of being, conscious being or being-for-itself, is synonymous with human being in her work. It is an assemblage of nonconscious being, especially a body and a past, which possesses the power of consciousness.

Beauvoir identifies two primary dimensions of human reality, which she calls *transcendence* and *immanence*. It is important to understand how this distinction accords with the history of modern philosophy. Kant, in the eighteenth century, shifted philosophers' attention away from cosmic reality and on to humankind, especially onto the nature of human being. But his analysis remained abstract and excluded individual existents in favor of the notion of a universal ego. Half a century later, this concept was rejected by the Danish philosopher, Kierkegaard, thereby opening philosophy's door to the indeterminacies, the concrete particularities, the social constructions and, therefore, the differences in human existence. This turning led to new philosophical questions that became the key questions for the existential-phenomenological tradition and for Beauvoir in particular. Of these, the most fundamental is: What is the relation between individuals' freedom and the givens of their situations, or, in Beauvoir's terminology, between their power of transcendence and their immanence?

From one point of view, one is free to make choices about one's being; from another, one is predetermined. The individual faces different possibilities, about which she or he cannot keep from making choices. But juxtaposed to the dimension of freedom are the givens of an individual's existence, most especially the body. Everyone is embodied, which means having fixed attributes, including sex and race, and being always located at a single and unique point in physical space and time. Everyone also possesses a unique past. In addition, they hold images of themselves generated by the people around them and by the social categories to which they find themselves assigned.

Beauvoir's innovation was that she tied this split between transcendence and immanence in human existence to her ontological categories of conscious being and nonconscious being and to the principle of intentionality, a feature of Brentano's relational view of consciousness. If consciousness is not a kind of receptacle for perceptions and images, but rather a relation to the world, then consciousness is always consciousness *of* something. Whereas immanence is self-evidently a universal property of nonconscious being and, thus, also of conscious being, the ontological basis of transcendence or freedom had remained unclear prior to Beauvoir and Sartre. Beauvoir, especially, identified the origin of transcendence with consciousness and its property of intentionality. If transcendence is a process of "forever going beyond what is" (*Pyrrhus et Cinéas*, 1944), then according to the principle of intentionality, consciousness is intrinsically a continuous process of transcendence, a deliberate positing of one object of consciousness after another. Beauvoir identifies this transcendent nature of consciousness as that which compels human beings endlessly to project their existences beyond the present and as that which makes transcendence an essential dimension of human existence. "One never arrives anywhere," she says in *Pyrrhus et Cinéas*, "there are only points of departure."

Although Beauvoir's contributions to delineating the basis of human freedom, the structure of consciousness, and the implications of embodiment are significant, it is her solution to the problem of other minds and, through it, her exploration of the realm of intersubjective relations, especially between the sexes, for which she is most remembered. Indeed, "the problem

of the 'Other' " was, as she indicated on several occasions, her central philosophical obsession from her student days onward.

Beauvoir argued that our belief that other people are conscious beings like ourselves is based, not on the philosopher's traditional argument from analogy, but rather on the phenomenological event of experiencing oneself as the object of another's look. Her fiction emphasizes situations where being looked at or judged by another person (for example, being caught in an unseemly act) causes a metamorphosis in one's consciousness, in the sense of being made aware that one has another self, an objective self that exists for someone else. One's "self-for-the-Other" is revealed to one as an awareness that they exist as an object in a world whose center of reference is another person's consciousness rather than one's own. The experience of being an object, argues Beauvoir, entails the "Other-as-subject," because only another consciousness could cause this decentering of one's sense of self.

This ever-present possibility of experiencing a transformation in one's mode of consciousness, from experiencing oneself wholly as a subject to an object in a world organized by someone else's consciousness, provides the ontological basis and the dynamism of Beauvoir's theory of intersubjectivity. Rather than holding the traditional view of the self as a fixed entity residing in consciousness and knowable by introspection, Beauvoir perceives the self as an ongoing project that other people continuously and unpredictably influence.

In interpersonal encounters, a person experiences not only one's self as subject, but also one's self as the other person's object. Over time, an individual experiences and remembers many of these encounters. But under the relational view of consciousness none of these selves is ever more than an object of consciousness, and, therefore, none of them is ontologically privileged. Thus the Beauvoirian notion of selfhood is far removed from the self-identity of the Cartesian subject.

Her theory of intersubjectivity, with its central subject/object relation, extends naturally to cover sociological relations. Rather than two individuals, the terms of the binary relation may be an individual and a group or two groups, for example, men and women, or colonialists and colonized. Thus analysis of intersubjectivity provides a foundational basis for social theory applicable to every level of aggregation.

The asymmetry of Beauvoir's subject/object relation is inherently reversible. X may cause Y to experience them as X's object, but Y may subsequently do the same to X. The potential for reversibility holds whether X and Y are individuals or groups. Thus Beauvoir's intersubjective social theory is not only integrally dynamic, but also provides a theoretical understanding of the processes and possibilities of deliberate liberational change.

Beauvoir's first published novel, *L'Invitée* (1943), provides a paradigmatic example of her literary-philosophical method, inspired by her student reading of Bergson. The novel takes place in the bohemian Paris of the late 1930s and is centered on the lives of five young people variously involved in the arts. Most of the narrative takes the point of view of Françoise, who is thirty and an aspiring writer. The book opens with Françoise personifying well-known positions regarding two important philosophical questions: the relation of body to consciousness, and the possible relations between one's own consciousness and those of other persons. Françoise then undergoes a series of lived situations that test these and other hypotheses, the metaphysical drama of the novel being coextensive with the philosophical argument. The events of the first half of the book falsify the traditional positions, while the second half develops Beauvoir's own theories further, with constant testing against the characters' experiences.

In the mid-1940s Beauvoir published two book-length philosophical essays. The first, *Pyrrhus et Cinéas*, was rushed into print following the Liberation of Paris in 1944 and became a major vehicle for the introduction of "Existentialism" to the French reading public. She followed these two years later with *Pour une morale de l'ambiguïté* (1947), which develops ethical arguments based on the ontological framework that she had developed in earlier works. These included her novels *Les Sang des autres* (1945), which explores social and ethical implications of intersubjectivity, and *Tous les homes sont mortel* (1946), which charmingly examines the existential significance of mortality. Her semi-autobiographical novel *Les Mandarins*, which appeared in 1954 and won that year's *Prix Goncourt*, also explored these issues while providing an intimate representation of Parisian intellectual life at mid-century.

In 1947 Simone de Beauvoir traveled to the United States, where her reputation as an important new French intellectual had preceded her. Indeed, American universities eagerly opened their doors to her. In a period of three months Beauvoir lectured on philosophy at twenty three if America's leading institutions, including Harvard, Vassar, Yale, Princeton, and Berkeley. The following year her social and philosophical essays that had appeared in *Les Temps Modernes* were collected in *L'Existentialisme et la sagesse des nations* (1948).

Beauvoir published the two volumes of her classic study of the condition of women, *Le Deuxième sexe*, in 1949. With a good claim to being judged the twentieth century's most important feminist text, the book remains one of the landmark political, social, and philosophical studies of its era. And while the impact of the book can only be judged adequately in the international arena which is its proper territory, it is very much a product not only of directions in philosophy in modern France, but of French culture in that it draws on the history and culture of French women for the greater part of its examples of the condition of women in general. The book continues to attract the kind of passionate, engaged debate that is only afforded to works of great significance.

The ideas that inform *Le Deuxième sexe* come directly from Beauvoir's philosophical explorations of intersubjectivity and the nature of the Other in *L'Invitée*, *Pyrrhus et Cinéas*, *Pour une morale de l'ambiguïté*, and the rest of her early fiction. The thought deployed in the text is also closely related to Beauvoir's exploration of the social and cultural fabric of the United States, which forms the topic of her book, *L'Amerique au jour le jour* (1948), an account of her postwar journey to America in 1947, which vividly registers the problematic conditions of race and racism for the first time in her writing. In addition, Beauvoir herself stressed a characteristic autobiographical impulse that contributed to the decision to write the book. As she considered the possibilities for a new project after the completion of *Pour une morale de l'ambiguïté*, it was her realization that she herself belonged to the category "woman," that this was the first thing that she would need to say about herself in any autobiography, that led her directly to her topic. It took Beauvoir only two years to research and write her study of women. When it appeared *Le Deuxième sexe* was not only an instant classic, it was an instant international best seller. It made Beauvoir's name not only in France but also around the world. It was, Beauvoir said in old age, "possibly the book that has brought me the greatest satisfaction of all those I have written."

The pivotal philosophical theme in *Le Deuxième sexe* is the question of the "Other." Just how central this is can be seen in the two alternate titles Beauvoir considered for her study: *The Other, the Second* and *The Other Sex*. Beauvoir's thesis is that the condition of women, throughout history, has been governed by their social construction as the inessential "Other" in relation to the full "Self" granted to the human male. This thesis is illustrated exhaustively, as Beauvoir draws on biology, psychology, history, law, anthropology, classics, mythology, and religion to provide harmonious examples of the ways in which woman has been consistently relegated to a secondary position in all of these areas of intellectual and imaginative endeavor, despite the violently incompatible propositions regarding women this has entailed. Throughout the history of culture and ideas, woman has been judged too pacific, too violent; too spiritual, too physical; too forceful, too timid; too practical, too vague. In the great chain of historical binary illustrations that Beauvoir provides regarding the definition of woman at different times and in different places, the only constant is that woman is always judged to occupy the less valued of the dualistic positions. This is one of the most influential strains in Beauvoir's text, and one which provided a fruitful starting point for the next generation of French feminist thinkers such as Helene Cixous, Luce Irigaray, and Monique Wittig, who pursue the notion of the social impact of binary thought in a variety of ways. For *Le Deuxième sexe*, the idea of the construction of woman as the eternal "Other" remains one of its key points. But the contribution of *Le Deuxième sexe* to the history of ideas neither begins nor ends with this argument. The text is dense with quotations, full of voices speaking about women across the centuries. And, as a writer who refused to accept the ordinary distinctions between philosophers, memorialists, and writers of fiction, Beauvoir's authorial voice aligns itself equally with a great diversity of precursors. In terms of philosophy, *Le Deuxième sexe* resonates with concepts drawn from or developed from those of Bergson, Merleau-Ponty, Sartre, Levi-Strauss, Husserl, Kierkegaard, Heidegger, and, especially, Hegel. But Beauvoir is equally indebted to diarists such as Marie Bashkirtsev, and writers of fiction such as Virginia Woolf and Katherine Mansfield. Beauvoir draws as well on previous feminist thought from Poulain de la Barre to Mary Wollstonecraft to Susan B. Anthony to make her points. One of the most engaging aspects of *Le Deuxième sexe* is the historical honesty and cultural generosity in its great panoply of works and individuals cited as working and having worked counter to the relegation of women to a secondary place. This aspect of the text is crucial, not only because it allows Beauvoir to present herself as joining rather than initiating an important fundamental challenge to the oppression of women, but it also enacts the second great point made by the study, by providing examples of those who have challenged or violated the norm to which they were supposedly destined to conform.

This point is best summed up in the most famous and most often cited sentence in the text: "One is not born, but rather becomes a woman." It is Beauvoir's profound contention that the epiphenomena associated with the enactment of individuals' biological sex in each age are social and cultural constructs rather than natural givens. The ramifications of this idea have been deeply influential, particularly in the Anglophone world, where the distinction between sex and gender, based directly on Beauvoir's work in *Le Deuxième sexe*, has provided a fundamental point of departure for two generations of feminist thinkers, best repre-

sented by Kate Millett in the late 1960s and 1970s with her ideas of sexual politics, and by Judith Butler, in the 1980s, with her equally influential notion of the performance of sex. In *Le Deuxième sexe* itself, Beauvoir deploys this concept in support of her argument for the need to move away from the unequal ascription of subjectivity to men and women, to a position in which both are granted full subjectivity, and work toward associations which are based, not on dominance and dependency, or on poles characterized by fullness of being for men and its lack for women, but on intersubjectivity, reciprocity, and full recognition of the equal sharing of the status of Other. The means to bring this about, argues Beauvoir, are psychological, social, and political. Women must refuse complicity with their victimization, and both men and women must work, in all areas of life, to bring about the sexual equality from which, as *Le Deuxième sexe* demonstrates, they will both benefit. The philosophically informed cultural and political analysis in *Le Deuxième sexe* has profoundly influenced feminist thought and practice throughout the world, with Christine Delphy's social materialist analysis in France, and Alice Schwarzer's broad-based feminist campaigns in Germany being two important examples.

The same principles that animate *Le Deuxième sexe* are utilized by Beauvoir in her study of the treatment of the elderly, *La Vieillesse*, which appeared in 1970. Along with Beauvoir's final interviews with and brutal but loving meditations on the death of Jean-Paul Sartre in *Le Cérémonie des adieux* (1981) and powerful reflections on the death of her mother in *Une mort très dòuce* (1964), this work forms part of Beauvoir's work on the ways in which individuals are excised from the body of society and exiled to its margins. In these cases, it is the position of those whose bodies are failing which interests Beauvoir, and to whom she applies her philosophical analysis of the ways in which cultures deploy the category of "otherness" to relegate to a social wilderness those who have the misfortune to be placed in that category. That wilderness, as Beauvoir demonstrates in *La Vieillesse*, is full of dangers for the elderly, who are at risk of both mental and physical death because of the cultural habit in the West of declaring the nonproductive worker nonhuman and therefore nothing but a drain on the resources of society in general. As in *Le Deuxième sexe*, but even more convinced, as she explained, of the importance of the material conditions of those assigned to the social categories she discusses, Beauvoir looks at the ways in which the elderly are defined as Other before being denuded of dignity, support, and sometimes life itself. As in *Le Deuxième sexe*, Beauvoir is interested in the psychology of consenting to be defined as Other, and examines the ways in which the relinquishing of the ability to devise projects and imagine goals for one's activities soon sets those who accept the definition of old outside the scope of human endeavor. Beauvoir's existential emphasis on choice and action is clearly in play in her analysis, but in ways that once again bring to the fore her idiosyncratic and original interest in the intersubjective and reciprocal aspects of experience.

Like *Le Deuxième sexe*, *La Vieillesse* is a text that functions in a number of ways. It is, from one point of view, a philosophical study of the ontology and ethics of old age. From another, it is a sociological and cultural history of the treatment of the aged. From yet another, it is a rich psychological survey of the experience of age, an experience, which is only now, with the demographic changes in the West accentuating the aged, receiving the kind of attention it needs. It interrogates and analyses the representation of the elderly in art. Finally, and in this it is also similar to *Le Deuxième sexe*, it is a fine piece of polemic, a kind of philosophical study which is also a call to action in the tradition of Paine and Rousseau. And again Beauvoir stresses the way her life, her thought, and her passions coincided in the selection of her topic. In the opening to the book, Beauvoir underscores the outrage she caused by addressing the "forbidden subject" of her own aging at the end of the third volume of her autobiography, *La Force des choses*, in 1963. In *La Vieillesse*, she says, she aimed to "break the conspiracy of silence" about aging, to challenge society on its treatment of the aged, to confront her readers with the voices and lives of those who are subjected to the barbarous treatment reserved for the old in modern society. Once again, the study illustrates the ways in which Beauvoir enacted her philosophically informed refusal to draw boundaries between the kinds of material that might appear in any one text. Philosophy and polemic, autobiography and fiction, are all mixed in *La Vieillesse* to Beauvoir's usual fine effect.

Beauvoir's interest in aging and in women, along with her categorical refusal to segregate any element of her work from other elements, served her particularly well in her late fiction. In particular, *La Femme rompue* (1968), her collection of three stories concerned with women who feel themselves to be growing old and who are subjected to the humiliations reserved for the aging woman in sexist society, draws brilliantly on her philosophical principles and political commitments in the compelling presentation of the psychological and social experiences commensurate with the marginalization based on sex and age. This intersection of the political, the personal, the philosophical, and the psychological also worked exceptionally well for Beauvoir in her novel, *Les Belles Images* (1966), like *La Femme rompue*, a strong and excellent piece of work that provides one of the finest critiques of technology in modern fiction. That critique, and indeed Beauvoir's critique of life in the twentieth century, is given its fullest rein in the volumes of her autobiography which she published intermittently from the end of the 1950s to the beginning of the 1970s. *Memoires d'une jeune fille rangée* (1958), *La Force de l'age* (1960), *La Force des choses* (1963), and *Tout compte fait* (1972) form an extraordinary quartet of texts which have largely been read for the fascinating detail Beauvoir provides about her life and that of her friends in one of the most important intellectual circles of the century. However, these volumes are also of great interest not only because of the historical detail they provide regarding the texture of life in Paris, one of the world's great cities, in the context of a century racked by wars which were themselves underpinned by ideologies of race and fueled by technologies of violence previously unknown, but because they, too, provide illustrations of the ways in which Beauvoir's ideas regarding reciprocity and intersubjectivity inform her personal experience of life and of the politics of her time.

In all of her work, Beauvoir builds on the radical conceptions of the ontology of reciprocity and the embodiment of consciousness that she developed in her earliest writing. These philosophical foundations provided her with an extraordinary platform from which to survey some of the most widespread and seemingly intractable abuses in human culture. By attending to the effects of social practices on consciousness, and the ability of the individual to act freely as an agent, Beauvoir produced a striking body of ethically informed work which continues to engage readers interested in existentialism, ethics, and ideas attuned to the promotion of justice for previously marginalized groups.

KATE FULLBROOK AND EDWARD FULLBROOK

See also **Raymond Aron, Henri Bergson, Albert Camus, Maurice Merleau-Ponty, Jean-Paul Sartre**

Biography

Simone Lucie Ernestine Marie Bertrand de Beauvoir was born on January 9, 1908 in Paris. Her schooling took place at the Catholic girls establishment, *Cours Désir*, until she took her baccalauréat in philosophy and mathematics in 1926. She completed her license and obtained a certificate in philosophy in 1927. In 1928 she began studying for the agrégation in philosophy at the Sorbonne. During her studies she met her lifelong companion, Jean-Paul Sartre, and they took the two top places in the examination in 1929. In 1931 she was appointed to a teaching post in Marseilles and in 1932 to a post in Rouen. She taught in Paris at the

Lycée Molière from 1936 to 1939 and at the *Lycée Camille Sée* from 1939 to 1941. From then on she lived as a writer producing novels, essays on ethics, polemics, and serving as a founding editor of the influential journal, *Les Temps Modernes*. Her novel, *The Mandarins*, was awarded the Prix Goncourt in 1954 and her classic feminist study, *The Second Sex*, appeared in 1949. She died in Paris on April 14, 1986.

Selected Works

L'Invitée, 1943
Pyrrhus et Cinéas, 1944
Les Bouches inutiles (play), 1945
La Sang des autres, 1945
Tous les hommes sont mortels, 1946
Pour une morale de l'ambiguïté, 1947
L'Amérique au jour le jour, 1948
L'existentialisme et la sagesse des nations, 1948
Le Deuxième sexe (2 vols.), 1949
America Day by Day, translated by Patrick Dudley, 1952
Must We Burn Sade?, translated by Annette Michelson, 1953
Les Mandarins, 1954
Privilèges, 1955
La Longue Marche, 1957
The Long March, translated by Austryn Wainhouse, 1958
Mémoires d'une jeune fille rangée (memoirs), 1958
La Force de l'âge (memoirs), 1960
Brigitte Bardot and the Lolita Syndrome, 1960
Memoirs of a Dutiful Daughter, translated by James Kirkup, 1963
La Force des choses (memoirs), 1963
Une mort très douce (biography), 1964
The Blood of Others, translated by Yvonne Moyse and Roger Senhouse, 1964
The Prime of Life, translated by Peter Green, 1965
Les Belles images, 1966
La Femme rompue, 1968
Force of Circumstance, translated by Richard Howard, 1968
A Very Easy Death, translated by Patrick O'Brian, 1969
La Vieillesse, 1970
The Ethics of Ambiguity, translated by Bernard Frechtman, 1970
The Second Sex, translated by H. M. Parshley, 1972
Tout compte fait (memoirs), 1972
Old Age, translated by Patrick O'Brian, 1977
All Said and Done, translated by Patrick O'Brian, 1977
Les écrits de Simone de Beauvoir (unpublished writings), 1979
Quand prime le spirituel, 1979
La Cérémonie des adieux suivi de Entretiens avec JeanPaul Sartre (biography and conversations, 1981.
Who Shall Die? translated by Claude Francis and Fernande Gontier, 1983
When Things of the Spirit Come First: Five Early Tales, translated by Patrick O'Brian, 1983
The Mandarins, translated by Leonard M. Friedman, 1984
She Came to Stay, translated by Yvonne Moyse and Roger Senhouse, 1984
The Woman Destroyed, translated by Patrick O'Brian, 1984
Les Belles Images, translated by Patrick O'Brian, 1985
Adieux, translated by Patrick O'Brian, 1985
Lettres à Sartre, vol. I, 1930–1939; vol. II, 1940–1963, edited and annotated by Sylvie Le Bon de Beauvoir, 1990
Journal de guerre, Paris: Gallimard, 1990
Letters to Sartre, edited and translated by Quintin Hoare, 1991
All Men are Mortal, translated by Leonard M. Friedman, 1992

Further Reading

Bair, Deirdre, *Simone de Beauvoir: A Biography*, London: Jonathan Cape, 1990
Bergoffen, Debra, *Gendered Phenomenologies, Erotic Generosities: The Philosophy of Simone de Beauvoir*, New York: SUNY Press, 1996
Delphy, Christine et Chaperon, Sylvie (editors), *Cinquantenaire du Deuxième sexe*, Paris: Syllepse, 2001
Evans, Mary, *Simone de Beauvoir: A Feminist Mandarin*, London: Tavistock, 1985
Fallaize, Elizabeth, *The Novels of Simone de Beauvoir*, London: Routledge, 1988
Francis, Claude and Gontier, Fernande, *Simone de Beauvoir*, translated by Lisa Nesselson. London: Mandarin, 1989
Fullbrook, Kate, and Fullbrook, Edward, *Simone de Beauvoir and Jean-Paul Sartre: The Remaking of a Twentieth-Century Legend*, Hemel Hempstead: Harvester Wheatsheaf, 1993; New York: Basic Books, 1994
Fullbrook, Edward, and Fullbrook, Kate, *Simone de Beauvoir: A Critical Introduction*, Cambridge and Cambridge, MA: Polity Press, 1998
Kruks, Sonia, "Gender and Subjectivity: Simone de Beauvoir and Contemporary Feminism," *Signs*, 8, 1 (Autumn 1992): pp. 89–109.
Le Doeuff, Michèle, *Hipparchia's Choice: An Essay Concerning Women, Philosophy, etc.*, translated by Trista Selous, Oxford: Blackwell, 1991
Lundgren Gothlin, *Sex and Existence: Simone de Beauvoir's "The Second Sex,"* London: Athlone, 1996
Marks, Elaine, *Simone de Beauvoir: Encounters with Death*, New Brunswick, NJ. Rutgers University Press, 1973
Moi, Toril, *Feminist Theory and Simone de Beauvoir*, London: Blackwell, 1990
O'Brien, Wendy and Embree, Lester (editors), *The Existential Phenomenology of Simone de Beauvoir*, Dordrecht: Kluwer, 2001
Simons, Margaret A., "Beauvoir and Sartre: The Question of Influence," *Eros*, 8, 1 (1981): pp. 25–42
Simons, Margaret A. (editor), *Feminist Interpretations of Simone de Beauvoir*, University Park, Pennsylvania: Pennsylvania State University Press, 1995
Simons, Margaret A., *Beauvoir and The Second Sex: Feminism, Race, and the Origins of Existentialism*, Boston: Rowman and Littlefield, 1999
Singer, Linda, "Interpretation and Retrieval: Rereading Beauvoir," *Women's Studies International Forum*, 8, 3 (1985): pp. 231–8
Vintges, Karen, *Philosophy as Passion: The Thinking of Simone de Beauvoir*, Bloomington: Indiana University Press, 1996

BEGUIN, ALBERT
Literary Critic

Albert Béguin belonged to the generation of intellectuals who renewed literary criticism in the 1930s. His doctoral thesis on German Romanticism, which was published in 1937, *L'Âme romantique et le rêve* (Romantic Sensibility and Dreams), exerted an immediate influence on literary circles. The Surrealist movement found new material in this study that fed into its conception of dreams and surreality. But the main reason for the success of Béguin's first work lies in its affinities with the various existential philosophical strands of the 1930s. Dreams, myths, and poetry provided the basis for an ontological exploration in *L'Âme romantique et le rêve*. The analysis of works by Lichtenberg, Moritz, Herder, Hoelderlin, Novalis, Von Arnim, and Brentano did not only constitute a rich anthology of German Romantics, but also inaugurated a new critical approach to this area of study.

Béguin's methodology corresponds to the new critical paradigm of the Geneva School, which was initiated by Marcel Raymond, and which privileged the use of the first person singular discourse as part of textual analysis. The text itself was no longer considered as an object of analysis, but as a source of "presence." The commentator entered into an "existential" relationship with the author. The approach was governed by the intention of overcoming the historical and cultural differences of mentality in order to establish a communication with the "I" hidden behind the text. How can one define this critical method? First, the commentator's personal involvement in the interpretative discourse accounts for the fact that quotations no longer display their function of objective denotation but become re-appropriated by the critic's hermeneutical "I." From this perspective, the act of reading becomes linked to an act of reflection leading to self-knowledge. Thus, the famous introduction to *L'Âme romantique et le rêve* reads: "Is it myself who dreams of the night? Or is it rather that I have become the theatre in which someone else, something else is unfolding its performances, which are sometimes trivial, and sometimes full of inexplicable wisdom?" Second, as in Marcel Raymond's case, the biographical approach was established as part of a long-standing German hermeneutical tradition from Schleiermacher to Dilthey. The emphasis that Dilthey placed on *Erlebnis* (the inner, lived experience) in the process of creation as well as in the critical reception of art had already strongly influenced Marcel Raymond's conception of literary criticism. The relationship between the author and the commentator, which Albert Béguin calls "subjective interpretation," and which is similar to the vitalist philosophers' *Einfülhung*, refers to the work as to a world one can inhabit, and whose phenomenological dimensions one needs to share in the quest for a "living language (*parole*), man's spoken language (*parole*) to another man, running water capable of quenching our thirst." Thirdly, this active comprehension is often accompanied by mythical elements: the death of Novalis's young lover, Bettina Brentano's fantasies, Pascal's illness or Novalis's madness, guide and determine the process of interpretation. The act of reading becomes the site of a spiritual exercise through which the commentator confronts the questions raised by the work and, in particular, the ontological and religious questions.

What is the content of the work of art? The reading of the works leads to the classification of Romantic aspirations according to the myths of the Golden Age, of dreams, of knowledge, of the unconscious. At the center of these myths lies the idea that the genuine spiritual world belongs to the deep layers of the unconscious, which correspond to a cosmic or divine reality. The self can only regain this reality by freeing itself from any personal ties through poetic experience. However, Béguin does not fail to notice that, in granting poetry the status of "absolute reality," one elevates it beyond aesthetic pleasure to the level of "visionary" poet's art, on a par with knowledge and metaphysical or religious experience. "It will always be the greatest merit of Romanticism to have recognized and asserted the profound affinity between poetic states of mind and religious revelations, to have given credence to irrational powers, and to have devoted itself, body and soul, to the great nostalgia of exiled beings." Béguin emphasizes absolute idealism, as ultimate temptation of Romanticism, in his conclusion, while at the same time warning against the inherent risks of such myths: madness, Promethean excess, devaluation of the world, dissolution of the self. This is why the last passage of Béguin's study is an ode to the regained "presence of simple human beings," to the regained human intersubjectivity. This hoped-for spiritual communion actually ties in with Béguin's comprehensive method, which opens up to the reader's subjectivity through the reading process.

During the 1930s, Béguin's book had a significant impact on intellectual debates concerning the nature of poetry and its relationship with religious experience. Benjamin Fondane, J. Rivière, Rolland de Renéville, Jacques Maritain, and Marcel Raymond were among the most important writers and critics involved in this debate. Béguin continued to employ the same critical method during the 1940s and 1950s, when he wrote on Pascal, Léon Bloy (in *Léon Bloy, mystique de la douleur*—A Mystic of Suffering, 1948), Balzac (in *Balzac visionnaire*—The Visionary Balzac, 1946), and Ramuz (in *Patience de Ramuz*, Ramuz's Patience, 1950). However, it was especially Béguin's role as literary advisor and editor that enhanced his reputation, first when he launched the magazine *Cahiers du Rhône* (which was published between 1942 and 1945 in Switzerland, and gathered the poets of the Resistance, in opposition to the Vichy French government), and later, when he joined the team of *Esprit*, whose director he became in 1950. Having converted to Catholicism in 1940, Béguin participated in E. Mounier's personalist movement, although his belief in a "lived" rather than doctrinarian personalism marked his distance from Mounier's political commitments. Alongside his editorial work, Béguin initiated and maintained a dialogue between—on the one hand, the German Romantics, Balzac (whose writings he reprinted in 1962), Nerval, and—on the other hand, modern writers such as Charles Péguy, Bernanos, Ramuz, and P. Emmanuel in keeping with his personal interests and affinities. The religious aspiration came first in the list of such affinities: for example, in his analysis of Balzac's work (*Balzac visionnaire*), Béguin underlined the trangressive aspect, and sometimes the esoteric or visionary dimensions, within a sustained, if nonorthodox, interpretation of the redemptive character of Balzac's writing. This choice determined his emphasis on Balzac's "mystical" writings: *Louis Lambert, Sésaraphita, Melmoth réconcilié* (Melmoth Reconciled), and *Jésus Christ en Flandres* (Jesus Christ in Flandres). The second recurrent thematic concern can be observed in studies such as Béguin's *Patience de Ramuz* (1950), which highlights the dialectic of solitude and community, within a critical narrative penetrated by the tragedy of self-pride and of the human soul cut off from the divine grace. Thus, Béguin's participative criticism ultimately rejoined its genuine spiritual orientation, manifested in the author's religious interrogation.

OLIVIER SALAZAR-FERRER

See also **Georges Bernanos, Leon Bloy, Jacques Maritain, Marcel Raymond, Jacques Riviere**

Biography

Albert Beguin was born July 7, 1901 in Chaux-de-Fond. He studied in Geneva and Paris. His doctoral thesis on German Romanticism, *L'Âme romantique et le rêve* (Romantic Sensibility and Dreams), was published in 1937. He taught French literature in Geneva, and then in Basle. Beguin founded the journal *Les Cahiers du Rhône* in 1940. He quit teaching and returned to Paris in 1946, where he collaborated on a number of journals and reviews. He died May 3, 1957 of a heart attack in Rome.

Selected Writings

L'Âme romantique et le rêve, 1939
La Prière de Péguy, Les Cahiers du Rhône, edited by de la Baconnière, Neuchâtel, 1942
Léon Bloy l'impatient, 1944
Gérard de Nerval, 1945
Faiblesse de l'Allemagne, 1945
Léon Bloy, mystique de la douleur, 1948
Patience de Ramuz, 1950
Bernanos par lui-même, Ecrivains de toujours, edited by du Seuil, 1954
Poésie de la présence. De Chrétien de Troyes à Pierre Emmanuel, Les Cahiers du Rhône, de la Baconnière, Neuchâtel edited by du Seuil, 1957
Balzac lu et relu, Pierres vives, du Seuil de la Baconnière, 1965
Création et destinée. Essai de critique littéraire, Collection Pierres vives, edited by du Seuil and de la Baconnière, 1973
La Réalité du rêve. Création et destinée II, Collection Pierres vives, editors du Seuil and de la Baconnière, 1974

BENDA, JULIEN
Essayist, novelist, critic

Although during a career extending over thirty years Julien Benda wrote many books on a wide range of subjects, he is best known for a single work, a *Trahison des clercs* (*The Betrayal of Intellectuals*), which appeared in 1927. In challenging the role of the intellectual in France during the early decades of the twentieth century, it soon became a classic defense of enlightenment values in the face of what Benda saw as the rise of the irrational and the partisan in cultural and political life. Its main contention: "Les hommes dont la fonction est de défendre les valeurs éternelles et désintéressées, comme la justice et la raison, et que j'appelle les clercs, ont trahi cette fonction au profit d'intérêts pratiques" (Men whose role is to defend the eternal and disinterested values such as justice and reason, and whom I call intellectuals, have betrayed their role for the sake of more mundane interests).

This essay, together with his other main studies of literature and thought, *Belphégor* (1918) and *La France byzantine* (1945), delineates an attitude which runs against the grain of the then fashionable currents of thought led by Bergson, Alain, Valéry, and Gide on the center left of the political spectrum, and by Maurras and Barrès on the far right. For Benda, what these writers have in common is a total rejection of the critical inheritance of the enlightenment, and a tendency toward the comforts of irrationalism, intuition, or Catholic mysticism; politically, this often led to an almost mystical sense of nationalism, both left wing (Péguy) and ultra right wing (Barrès, Maurras).

Benda's analyses of French political and literary life during his career covered an extraordinary range: he read almost everything, from obscure Symbolists and musicologists to lesser-known philosophers, from Proust to the surrealists and Blanchot, from the then unknown Husserl, Levinas, and Jankélévitch to Bachelard. Ironically, the fame of *Trahison des clercs* has largely overshadowed his other works.

With hindsight, Benda may strike us as a lay prophet: his *Trahison des clercs* reads as an indictment of all the intellectuals who gave way to a lazy and superficial nationalism. Its most cogent remarks rebuff attempts to revitalize a French culture that was seen as having been decadent since the 1880s. By defining the intellectual as someone who uses reason to defend abstract values forged by Greek civilization and early Christian thinkers such as Aquinas and Augustine, Benda was not attempting to isolate thinking from its historical background. On the contrary, he wanted to re-establish a coherent and objective approach to history that eschews passionate involvement or "*engagement*." To Benda, the thinking process is abstract, independent, scientific, and, most of all, dispassionate; and he was convinced that this detachment was being sacrificed in the name of political involvement. From the 1920s onwards, the confusion between reason and action, however worthy the cause, alarmed Benda deeply.

His insights on nationalism and on the new powers of the State are penetrating. He viewed nationalism as a recent invention, born out of the German and Italian reunification in the 1870s, and put to use by Italy first, then by Germany. This rise of nationalism broke the long tradition, mainly "French" according to Benda, of moving from the particular to the universal: what is valid should also be valid for all, across national and cultural boundaries, and no nation should claim any kind of superiority to other nations. For Benda, "French nationalism" was an oxymoron: universal values were not French, but were simply brought to light in France in the eighteenth century.

The German sense of the supremacy of its own particular culture was, he insisted, alien to French thought. Blinded by his love for the eighteenth century, and pointedly ignoring Napoleon, Benda tells us, for example, that when Louis XIV invaded Alsace he did not impose the French language on its inhabitants. Any attempt to reclaim a past mythical grandeur revolted him, both for its lack of historical accuracy, and for its sheer romantic vagueness. Instead, Benda called for a return to what he thought of as the intellectual rigor and clear-sightedness of Goethe, Hegel, and Nietzsche (all German thinkers, in this case) in order to redefine the vague abstract categories amalgamated by the likes of Maurras, Barrès, and Bourget.

The worst danger Benda saw in the intellectuals who forego their independence is their tendency to think on behalf of the state and no longer for themselves, thereby helping to create an intellectual climate in which those in power are, in effect, able to justify the unjustifiable. Typical for Benda was the reclaiming of a "false" past in the name of an "assertion of the rights of *coutume*," which nations use as a divine right in order to expand and justify any atrocities. Benda pointed out that in such cases *coutume* (custom, tradi-

tion) is interpreted as a sacred truth, a moral justification for any national action; for Benda, the appropriate rights of *coutume* are subservient to the imperative claims of *raison*. For Benda, the "romantisme du positivisme" (Taine, Comte) and the "romantisme du pessimisme" (Barrès) were the two corrupting fashions that beset proper thinking during his day.

Benda's thesis is best summarized by Walter Benjamin in a article written in 1933, the year of fascism's triumph in Germany: "[Benda] is shocked by the slogans of an intelligentsia that defends the cause of nations against that of mankind, of parties against justice, and of power against the mind. The bitter necessities of reality were defended by the *clercs* of earlier times but not even Machiavelli tried to embellish them with the pathos of ethical precepts." Benjamin sees one main flaw: "The decline of the independent intelligentsia is determined crucially, if not exclusively, by economic factors." The utopian spirit summoned by Benda is dismissed by Benjamin as nothing more "than the manifestation of a figure of the past: the medieval cleric in his Benedictine cell" ("The Present Social Situation of the French Writer").

In his study of literature, Benda was the first thinker to establish clear links between the early twentieth-century French novels and the famous French school of psychologists and other scientists such as Ribot, Renouvier, Piaget, Janet, Poincaré, and Delacroix. Using their writings, Benda debunked the theories of art expounded by Valéry, Bergson, Gide, and Proust. Once again, Benda pits intellectual rigor and clarity against mystification, the clear separation of object-subject against the mystic fusion of the two, and the independence of reason against the anti-intellectualism of writers such as Proust and Gide. There is much to learn from his *France byzantine*, mainly from its numerous notes which comprise brilliant analyses of Gide, Valéry, Proust, and Mallarmé under titles that are now commonly found in modern criticism: purity, negativity, hermeticism, and the unconscious. Benda accuses Gide and Valéry of being irrational, grammatically incompetent, and of pandering to public taste. He views them as slaves of their own success, which owes nothing to talent but everything to their way of selling old ideas under new labels. Here Benda indulges in the same sort of irony employed by his *bêtes noires*, and in his study of Proust—in which he looks in particular at Proust's rejection of intelligence and his reliance on *mémoire involontaire*—he exposes the inner contradictions of Proustian rhetoric with a skill and subtlety worthy of Paul de Man. Benda's short study of Mallarmé is also revealing. By refusing to take Mallarmé's predilection for Wagner for granted, Benda successfully compares Mallarmé with Debussy, showing that the anti-Wagner feelings expressed by Debussy have more in common with Mallarmé than the poet himself was aware.

Paradoxically, if Benda has been ignored for the last fifty years, it is by the very same people who shared his own positivist, almost mathematical reasoning. The old debates between Classicism and Romanticism, rationality and irrationality, form versus content, positivist method versus intuition, in literature as well as in literary criticism and its avatars, continue, even though they cannot but supplement each other, and as much now as in Benda's day.

HUGO AZÉRAD

See also **Alain, Maurice Barres, Henri Bergson, Maurice Blanchot, Andre Gide, Emmanuel Levinas, Paul Valery**

Biography

Julien Benda was born in Paris on December 26, 1867 and educated at Louis-le-Grand. Both his parents were Jewish and middle-class. His favorite subjects were classics and mathematics. He attended the École Centrale to further his interests in mathematics but soon switched to history and graduated from the Sorbonne in 1894. His own life-long passion was for rationality, music, and literature. He started his career in the arts as a journalist for the *Revue Blanche* (1891–1903), where Léon Blum was the drama critic and Debussy covered music. Malarmé was one of their most famous contributors, and it comes as a surprise to see the advocator of rationalism making his debut among the chief proponents of Symbolism. His pro-Dreyfus articles are collected in *Dialogues*, but Benda saw himself as a thoroughly hellenized Jew, rejecting any form of Zionism, a fact which did not prevent the Nazis from destroying his papers and books, and he was made to wear the yellow star while writing *La France byzantine* in Carcassonne during the war. One of his novels, *L'Ordination*, was short-listed for the Goncourt, but his most famous works never sold very well. Writing for the *happy few* seems Benda's fate, but by the 1980s, *La Trahison des clercs* was translated in all major languages. Benda died in Fontenay-Aux-Roses, June 7, 1956.

Selected Writings

Belphégor: essai sur l'esthétique de la présente société française, 1918
Lettre à Mélisande pour son éducation philosophique, 1925
La Trahison des clercs, 1927
La Jeunesse d'un clerc, 1936
La France byzantine: ou, le triomphe de la littérature pure: Mallarmé, Gide, Proust, Valéry, Alain, Giraudoux, Suarès, les surrealistes, 1945
Exercice d'un enterré vif, 1946
Trois idoles romantiques: le dynamisme, l'existentialisme, la dialectique matérialiste, 1948
Songe d'Eleuthère, 1949

Further Reading

Benjamin, Walter, "The Present Situation of the French Writer," in *Selected Writings*, Vol.2, edited by Michael W. Jennings, Cambridge: Harvard University Press, 1999
Nichols, Ray, *Treason, Tradition, and the Intellectual: Julien Benda and Political Discourse*, Lawrence: Regents Press of Kansas, 1978
Niess, Robert J., *Julien Benda*, Ann Arbor: University of Michigan Press, 1956

ÉMILE BENVENISTE
Linguist

As an outstanding specialist in Iranian, Benveniste completed the Sogdian grammar left unfinished at R. Gauthiot's death, produced a complete revision of Meillet's classic *Grammaire du vieux-perse* (1931), and wrote an incisive *Les infinitifs avestiques* (1935) in which he eliminated 180 "formes douteuses" that had been unrealistically postulated for prehistoric Avestic. In *Études sur la langue ossète* (1959), devoted to a living trans-Causcasian variety of Iranian, he masterfully demonstrated the interplay between descent and adjustment, "*filiation iranienne*" and "*intégration caucasienne*."

From Iranian micro-comparatism, mostly confined to a palette of about fifteen ancient, medieval, and modern Iranian languages, Benveniste evolved into a consummate Indo-European macrocomparatist, juggling more than 100 languages and dialects of Celtic, Germanic, Slavic, Anatolian, or Indic stock. His doctoral dissertation on the origins of noun formation in Indo-European (1935) included a celebrated chapter on the structure of the Indo-European root. In the second part of the thesis, lost during World War II then rewritten and published in 1948 under the title *Noms d'agent et noms d'action en indo-européen*, Benveniste elegantly demonstrated that the two Indo-European agentive suffixes "-*ter* and -*tor*" (as in Latin *magister* vs. *auctor*) differed inasmuch as the first had a subjective value ("agent destined or apt to exercise a function") and the second had an objective value ("agent with respect to an accomplished action at a given moment in time"). In *Hittite et indo-européen: Études comparatives* (1962) Benveniste rejected the Yale School's hypothesis of a separate Indo-Hittite stage, recognizing in Anatolian an idiosyncratic, archaic, and isolated branch of Indo-European that was later influenced by unrelated ancient Near East languages such as Akkadian and Hurrian.

Benveniste's chef-d'oeuvre as an Indo-Europeanist is *Le vocabulaire des institutions indo-européennes* (1969). The task he assigned himself in this volume is to regress from scattered polyphonic designations toward past signification by relentlessly comparing forms, interrogating meanings, and rereading texts. Take for example Indo-European "*peku*," which survives in Indo-Iranian, Latin, and Germanic. Etymologists used to explain Latin *pecunia* "money, fortune" as deriving from Latin *pecus* "livestock." In fact, Benveniste showed, it is not the signification "property, riches" that was gradually evolved on the basis of the concrete designation but, on the contrary, an initial, larger signification "movable property" became the usual designation of the typical object of their activity among the insider group of "productors." To verify this hypothesis, Benveniste examined Greek, where he found the Homeric *próbasis*, with the more frequent equivalent *próbata* attesting a similar evolution. This development, Benveniste underlined, is not reversible. "Livestock" could not have evolved into "money, property"; it is always the general term that, by being displaced from insiders to outsiders, comes to be used as a designation for a specific element and not the reverse. Working on material mostly gathered from northwestern America, Marcel Mauss had shown that gifts are a primitive form of exchange. Benveniste brilliantly precised the institutions behind "giving," "taking," "buying," "selling," and "exchange" by interpreting the Indo-European vocabulary. He started from the remark that the same Indo-European root *do-* evolved into both "give" (in most Indo-European languages) and "take" (in Hittite). To explain this fact, shows Benveniste, one must first notice that the Indo-European root in question was used in the acceptation "to take hold of something," that could be equally involved in giving ("to take hold of in order to offer") and taking ("to take hold of in order to keep"). An analysis of Gothic *niman* "to take" and Greek *némo* "to give or to have legally as an allotment" (from an Indo-European *nem-*), as well as of their derivations, evidenced the missing link: "legal attribution as given or as received." Giving is then illuminated by the examination of a number of Greek synonyms for "gift" that reflect the opposition between the notions of "a present that does not impose the obligation of a gift in return" and "a gift in return or calling for a return." By extending the analysis to the Indo-European concept of "hospitality," Benveniste came to defining an attenuated, non-antagonistic form of Maussian *potlatch* (whereby a man is bound to another by the obligation to compensate a former prestation). Thus, in Latin, *hostis* first signified "a foreigner enjoying (as a guest) equal rights with the Roman citizens" via an institution of alliance and exchange with a particular Roman citizen and *hostire* had the signification "to compensate, counterbalance." Once the nation was constituted (as shown by the semantic evolution of *civis* and *civitas*), institutions ensuring reciprocity regulated by personal or family agreement was necessary no more and *hostis* came to the signification "foreigner," then "public enemy" which survives in *hostile, hostility*. In a similar way, Latin *daps* signified "banquet, magnificent feast," and the derived *damnum* came to mean, "damage inflicted, involuntary spending" and gave *condamnare* "to condemn." This shows that festive spending, frantically exhibiting and destroying riches during a feast, was perceived as unnecessary, "en pure perte" by later Romans. And the etymological feast continues with Latin *munus* (Indo-European *mei-*), signifying at some point both "a charge conferred as a distinction and donations imposed in return" and later giving "remuneration" or "community;" or the Greek word for value (*alfáno*) indicating at the beginning "the value of exchange that a human body possesses when it is delivered up for a certain price" and applicable either to slaves, or to a marriageable daughter.

Independently of Dumézil, who was developing the mythological paradigm of the tripartite ideology of the Indo-Europeans on the basis of an analysis of Scythian society, Roman religion, and Vedic India, Benveniste arrived at a parallel description of three social classes in ancient Iran. He also restored in Umbrian mythology a triple grouping equivalent to the Roman Jupiter–Mars–Quirinus triad by linking Vofionus to the Indo-European "*leudhyon-* "growth"; he read in the *suovet-aurilia* lustration rite of the old Roman religion a triple sacrifice involving the whole social structure, with the pig (*sus*) belonging to the Earth, the ovine (*ovis*) immolated to Jupiter, and the bull (*taurus*) dedicated to Mars; he saw in the Greek libation to the dead, the same tripartite organization symbolically expressed by the three liquid offerings: wine (corresponding to warriors), honey (corresponding to priests), and milk (corresponding to cultivators).

The extraordinary impact of Benveniste's vision for linguistics and semiotics became visible to the general public only after the publication of the two collections of articles entitled *Problèmes de linguistique générale* (1966 and 1974). Benveniste introduces the basic distinction between the "semiotic mode" and the "semantic mode" of language. In the semiotic mode we deal with an abstract system of signs and with *signification* (a property of *language*), from a *paradigmatic* point of view, inside language. In the semantic mode, we deal with *phrases* (the concrete manifestations of language when it is put to use), which are not signs, do not exhibit signification, are *syntagmatically* assembled, reach outside language, and ensure *communication* (a property of *discourse*).

Benveniste put in the center of his definition of *enunciation* the process through which a natural language (a particular *langue*) is converted into *discourse* by a speaker who appropriates it and thus becomes a *subject*. The enunciating subject produces her/himself by saying *I* ("Est 'Ego' qui dit 'ego' "). The various instances of the use of *I* (and correlative *you*) do not constitute a class of reference since there is no "object" definable as "I" to whom they can refer in identical fashion. Each *I* has its own reference and corresponds each time to a unique being that is set up as such in a discursive reality. *I* therefore signifies "the individual who utters the present instance of discourse containing the linguistic instance *I*" and *you* is "the individual spoken to in the present instance of discourse containing the linguistic instance *you*." They may have specific explicit forms in different languages or remain implicit. As "empty" signs, they serve to solve the problem of intersubjective communication.

To the dialogic correlation of "person" *I/you* are associated, via discursive agreement, (a) the demonstrative pronouns, adverbs, and adverbial locutions known as *deictics*, that is, as referring to the situation in which the utterance is produced by *I* as addressed to *you* (*this, that, now, then, today, yesterday*, etc.); (b) certain tenses/aspects to the exclusion of others (in French, for example, discourse necessarily appeals to present, perfect, and future, while excluding the *passé simple*), and what Benveniste calls "*indicateurs de subjectivité*," that is, verbs like *croire, supposer, présumer, conclure, jurer, promettre* in constructions such as: *Je crois que le temps va changer*; *Je suppose (je présume, je conclus) qu'il est parti*; *Je jure (je promets) de le faire*. Notice that the last construction, in which "*l'acte est accompli par l'instance d'énonciation de son 'nom' ('jurer), en même temps que le sujet est posé par l'instance d'énonciation de son indicateur ('je')*" exactly correspond to J. L. Austin's concept of performative act and was independently defined by Benveniste as early as 1958, in his article "*De la subjectivité dans le langage*."

According to Benveniste, the personal pronouns do not constitute a unitary class. They manifest in fact two basic correlations: the *correlation of personality* that opposes personal *I/you* to non-personal *s/he* and the *correlation of subjectivity* that opposes *I* to *you*. "I" is internal to the statement and external to "you" in a manner that does not suppress the human reality of dialogue; it is transcendent with respect to "you," who can be defined as the nonsubjective person, in contrast to the subjective person *I*. The ordinary distinction singular/plural (*I/we*, sing. *you*/pl. *you*) should be interpreted by a distinction *strict person/ amplified person*. Only the third person, being a nonperson, admits of a true plural.

Likewise, in verbal conjugation, the "third person" is the nonpersonal form of verbal inflection. In many languages (Semitic, Turkish, Fino-Ugric, and others), Benveniste showed, this is manifested by the fact that there is no specific ending for the verb at the "third person."

Historic utterances (which form a secondary type of enunciation) exclude all "autobiographical" linguistic forms (like *je, tu*, deictics), and are limited to the pronominal and verbal forms of the third person. In French, the tenses for historical enunciation are: aorist (*passé simple*, the tense of the event outside of the person of a narrator), imperfect and pluperfect, while present, perfect, future are excluded. Discursive enunciation, oral or written (in the form of correspondence, memoirs, theater, textbooks), can include narrative segments and, likewise, a *récit* can frame discursive segments. The discursive tenses par excellence are present, future, and perfect. In French, discourse does not tolerate aorist (*passé simple*). The present tense marks the coincidence of the event described with the instance of discourse in which it is described, "le temps où l'on parle," it is *sui-referential*. The perfect regroups the compound perfective forms of the corresponding simple tenses: perfect of the present (*il a écrit*), perfect of the imperfect (*il avait écrit*), perfect of the aorist (*il eut écrit*), and perfect of the future (*il aura écrit*); when inserted in a dependent clause, perfect also marks anteriority with respect to the correlative simple forms (*quand il a écrit une lettre, il l'envoie; quand il avait écrit une lettre, il l'envoyait . . .*). Notice that Benveniste's approach clarifies in the simplest way some of the difficulties of the "*concordance des temps*" in French.

Benveniste's volumes on general linguistics as well as those on Indo-European linguistics, are dominated by an elegant and sophisticated selectivity. None is a "*livre à thèse*." All of them are defined by an intentional looseness of configuration, brief prefatory notes, no formal conclusion, bibliographical apparatus trimmed to a minimum, and exotic scripts eliminated, thus enabling the reader to directly perceive their polished and daring scholarship, revisions of assumed meanings, of illusory paradigms, or of naively positivistic ideas. Benveniste has opened new ways not only in the linguistic and semiotic domains to which he mainly devoted his study, but also, and essentially so, in anthropology, sociology, history of religion, philosophy of language, pragmatics, psychoanalysis, poetics, and feminist studies (which benefited from his liberating definition of subject and intersubjectivity).

SANDA GOLOPENTIA

See also **Georges Dumezil, Marcel Mauss**

79

Biography

Émile Benveniste was born in Aleppo (now in Syria, then pertaining to the Ottoman Empire), on May 27, 1902. He was brought to Paris during his childhood, entered the Sorbonne at sixteen, and specialized in Near and Mid-Eastern languages and Indo-European linguistics under the mentoring of Antoine Meillet. Briefly involved in the surrealist movement, he signed the declaration *"La Révolution d'abord et toujours"* in 1925, together with Aragon, Breton, and Éluard. In 1927, at the age of twenty-five, he assumed Meillet's duties and responsabilities for Iranian Philology at the École Pratique des Hautes Études with a rank equivalent to that of a tenured professor and director of studies. Ten years later, after the death of Meillet, Benveniste became his successor at the Collège de France, where he taught general linguistics, Indo-European comparative grammar and Iranian for more than thirty years, with brief interruptions for study trips to Iran, Afganistan, and the United States. Beginning with 1945 he acted as secretary of the Société de Linguistique de Paris and as editor of the Society's *Bulletin*. In 1958 he succeeded J. Vendryès at the Académie des Inscriptions et Belles Lettres. In 1969, Benveniste survived a stroke but remained paralyzed and unable to speak for seven twilight years. He died on October 3, 1976, leaving a dense and extraordinary *oeuvre* comprising 18 book-length monographs, 291 articles, and up to 300 book reviews.

Selected Works

The Persian Religion, According to the Chief Greek Texts, 1929
Origines de la formation des noms en indo-européen, 1935
Les infinitifs avestiques, 1935
Les Mages dans l'ancien Iran, 1938
Codices Sogdiani, 1940
Textes sogdiens, 1940
Noms d'agent et noms d'action en indo-européen, 1948
Études sur la langue ossète, 1959
Hittite et indo-européen: Études comparatives, 1962
Titres et noms propres en iranien ancien, 1966
Problèmes du langage, by Émile Benveniste, Noam Chomsky, Roman Jakobson, et al, 1966 as *I problemi attuali della linguistica*, 1968
Problèmes de linguistique générale, Paris: Gallimard, 1966, as *Problems in General Linguistics*, translated by Mary Elizabeth Meek, 1971
Le vocabulaire des institutions indo-européennes . . ., 2 vols., 1969 as *Indo-European Language and Society*, translated by Elizabeth Palmer, 1973
Problèmes de linguistique générale II, 1974
Études sogdiennes, 1979

Further Reading

F. Bader, D. Cohen, et al, *Mélanges linguistiques offerts à Émile Benveniste*, Louvain: Peeters, 1975
Tristano Bolelli, *Émile Benveniste: discorso commemorativo*, Roma: Accademia Nazionale dei Lincei, 1978
Dany-Robert Dufour, *Le bégaiement des maîtres*, Paris: F. Bourin, 1988
Julia Kristeva, Jean-Claude Milner, Nicolas Ruwet (editors), *Langue, discours, société. Pour Émile Benveniste*, Paris: Seuil, 1975
Nicole Loraux, Gregory Nagy, and Laura Slatkin (editors), *Antiquities*, New York: New Press, 2001
S. Lotringer, Thomas Gora (editors), *Polyphonic Linguistics. The Many Voices of Emile Benveniste, Semiotica: Special Supplement*, The Hague: Mouton, 1981
Charles Malamoud, "L'oeuvre d'Émile Benveniste: Une analyse linguistique des institutions indo-européennes," *Annales Économies Sociétés Civilisations*, 3–4 (1971): p. 653–662.
Y. Malkiel, "Lexis and Grammar. Necrological Essay on Emile Benveniste (1902–1976)," *Romance Philology* 34 (1980), nr. 2, pp. 160–194.
A. Meillet (editor), *Étrennes de linguistique offertes par quelques amis à Émile Benveniste, Avant-propos* de A. Meillet, Paris: P. Geuthner, 1928
G. Serbat, et al. (editors), *Émile Benveniste aujourd'hui: Actes du colloque international du C.N.R.S.*, Université François Rabelais, Tours, 28–30 septembre 1983, 2 vols., Paris: Société pour l'information grammaticale; Louvain: Diffusion, Éditions Peeters, 1984

BERGSON, HENRI
Philosopher

Henri Bergson is known primarily as a philosopher of time. His investigations of the phenomena of time led him to be held at one point as the greatest living philosopher, and certainly he was the first modern philosopher to take time seriously. What was it about his ideas that made his philosophy so revolutionary? Near the beginning of his 1911 lecture, "Philosophical Intuition," Bergson says that in each philosophical system there is usually only one "infinitely simple" insight that is central to the philosophy (*The Creative Mind*). It is an insight that the philosopher must continuously reformulate in an effort to express it adequately. Yet this effort can only ever be an "approximation" to the thinker's original intuition. When we look then, for the defining insight of a Bergsonism, we are already embarking upon a problematic project. But if it has to be done, then we could do no better than return to the opening passage of this 1911 lecture and recall that Bergson states quite emphatically that *philosophy must be close to real life*. Both Bertrand Russell and Julien Benda labeled Bergson a "pragmatist" and it is certain that, no less than William James, Bergson's philosophy is anti-intellectualist, though without being anti-intellectual: in the place of abstraction, it posits concrete life as it is lived as paramount. Intellectual philosophies that are detached from this life are enabled thereby to conjure up such artificial and totalizing world-views as determinism, materialism, or idealism so long as they maintain a logical consistency within the terms of their own system. But because they make little recourse to the real world, they are deemed to be of no real philosophical value in Bergson's view. Does it matter to Idealism that plants exist? Is it significant to determinism that time moves forwards rather than backwards? Bergson's is a philosophy of *action, process,* and *movement,* and it is our lived experience alone that validates these as real truths. In various realms, physics, biology, psychology, and sociology, Bergson makes it his philosophical goal to argue for the irreducible reality of action, process, and movement, not only for themselves, but also as synonyms for consciousness and life.

Metaphysics

In many ways Bergson has been seen as an antithetical writer whose work consists in opposing the primary assumptions of the mechanistic and rationalistic philosophies of the post-enlightenment era. If such a characterization has any validity at all, it is in respect to his first work, *Essai sur les données immédiates de la conscience.* Its English title, *Time and Free Will,* is a better representation of the book's contents, for it attempts to validate the reality of human freedom by an analysis of real time or what Bergson calls "duration." It makes a detailed attack upon the "dogma of quantitative perception" whereby both "inner" and "outer" experience are deemed to consist of quantitative, homogeneous units. In contrast to this idea, Bergson attempts to recover the immediate experience of consciousnes duration. Central to *Time and Free Will* is the distinction between this inner duration and space. Duration is real time; it is the time of conscious experience. It is heterogeneous, qualitative, and dynamic. By contrast, science emphasizes the concept of "space," which is an abstract construct that is homogeneous, quantitative, and static. Its parts are identical and can be described mechanistically. Such a notion as this space is vital for the determinist, for it is the basis of a spatialized *time*—time stripped of its intrinsic heterogeneity—which represents the unfolding of a hidden destiny that exists predetermined in the present conditions of the world. Free creativity is outlawed in such a worldview. But duration, on the other hand, is a creativity whereby a new and unpredictable entity appears at each and every moment. The components of duration (our memories, perceptions, and affections) are all different, yet they also interpenetrate and cannot be sharply distinguished. In contrast, the artifice of spatialized time consists of segments that preserve nothing in themselves of any previous segment. They are all juxtaposed in an abstracted succession. This artificial time is created and thrown beneath real time for the practical purposes of action, of manipulating the world.

As such, duration cannot be measured and its progress is not predictable. For example, take the movement of your own arm. It passes in one indivisible act, one duration. But though it passes through space, the movement itself is not the space it passes over, for space is quantitative and immobile. Movement, like real time, is qualitative and processional. It cannot be analyzed into motionless parts that are sequenced together. Yet for the purposes of manipulation, we are forever throwing this diagrammatic space beneath movement and attempting to prove that the former truly describes the latter. But it is an attempt that is in vain, for it leads to the paradoxes of movement such as those posited by Zeno. These paradoxes are based on the illusion that space is prior to movement, that we move in a container called space. But it is the opposite view, movement as prior to space, that Bergson aims to champion.

It is in duration that we live, act, and are free. But in space we are "acted" upon mechanically and so our freedom appears to be a chimera. Associationist psychology unwittingly phrases the question of freedom in terms of space rather than in terms of duration. Psychological determinism can therefore appropriate the methods of theoretical physics and, utilizing a spatialized reality, portray a subject that is determined by its states, an entity which has forces acting upon it. The truth, however, is that the self is not determined by these states, it *is* these states. It does not make a predetermined choice between pre-existing alternatives rather, *it creates* these alternatives by its free action. It is only in reflection that it appears that the possible alternatives to what it actually enacted pre-existed and so were alternatives that it *could have chosen* but was determined not to. The real is prior to the possible; it creates the latter that is only seen as an existent in *retrospect.* Bergson's concept of freedom in *Time and Free Will* is grounded upon these distinctions between real action and possible choices, real and spatialized time. It is because the former in each of these oppositions is prior to the latter and is qualitative, heterogeneous, and irreversible, that the world is unpredictable and we are free.

However, if it is *enduring* consciousness alone that is real and spatialized time is an artificial construct, why is it that each of us has a spatial dimension to *our own* existence? Why do we possess a body? It was in his next work that Bergson would broach this question.

Philosophy of Mind

Matter and Memory, which appeared eight years later, was called for by the obvious Cartesian leaning that could be seen in *Time and Free Will* in its opposition of an inner duration and an outer spatial world. It attempts to overcome these difficulties while also retaining the previous work's major insights. In *Time and Free Will* memory was little discussed, but in *Matter and Memory* it becomes central. Duration is only possible, now, because of memory, in that by memory the past is accumulated in its entirety. In memory not one element is lost and every moment that it retains carries within itself the entire flow of the past and so is, as such, irreversible and unrepeatable. This is so despite the fact that the matter that constitutes the observable counterpart of these memories perishes and decays. From this Bergson speculates that memory is entirely independent of matter, that is, that it is in no way constituted by it. In thinking so, he opposes the reductionist point of view that considers memory, and with that all of consciousness, to be merely an epiphenomenon of the material brain. Consciousness, in this view, is seen as an unextended by-product of an extended material world, with memory differing from perception only by degree. However, for Bergson, this creates an irreconcilable and incomprehensible gap between mind and world and even more so between mind and body. In reply to this, he argues that the only way to understand the relationship between mind and body is through time (the past and the present) rather than through space (the extended and the unextended).

For Bergson, mind is primarily *memory* (a position shared with other philosophers such as Gilbert Ryle), but by memory, Bergson means the past in itself. The crucial point to be retained is the distinction between actual recollections and virtual memories: whereas a perceived recollection actualizes the past in the present, virtual memory *is* this past. The philosophical orthodoxy against which Bergson waged his own thesis held that memories were only copies of perception. Bergson wanted to argue, however, that perception and memory were qualitatively different and, as such, that our sensory mechanisms were connected only with the faculty of recollection, having nothing to do with the creation of memories. But without Bergson's crucial *ontological* distinction (between perception and memory), *and* identification (of pure memory with the past), it would be impossible to understand the emergence of novelty (we would only have repetition), and so the theory of duration. The body, on the other hand, understood as either the brain or our entire nervous system, cannot produce memories, thoughts, or representations: rather, belonging entirely to the material present, it can only serve to channel the actualization of our memories as they enter into and color our perceptions. Hence, there is covariance between mind and brain. There is clearly a correlation between the two: but it would be a metaphysical leap to add that the latter causes or produces the former entirely. The more complex our brains, the more choices we have in how to color our material present with the influence of our past, the more open to subjective variation we are in terms of our species-specific interpretations of our present perceptions, and, ultimately, the more are we free. Our body is the means through which our subjectivity is given a purchase on the material world: its greater complexity is our greater freedom.

Philosophy of Biology

Creative Evolution was by far the most widely read of Bergson's works. It is itself both a reflection upon, and a critique of, the Neo-Darwinian concepts of evolution that were established at the time of its writing in 1907. It has been said that *Creative Evolution* marks a shift in Bergson's thought from a philosophy of human consciousness toward a type of super-phenomenology for life itself. One might dispute this point—a pluralist ontology of process might seem a more appropriate label than simply an extension of the method of immediate data—but it is certainly true that this book is definitive in Bergson's own philosophical development, not only because of the early and ultimately destructive fame it brought to his work, but also because it does represent the most general extension of his philosophy of time. This last fact must be made clear from the outset: *Creative Evolution* posits a theory of time first and only second a philosophy of life. Even *Time and Free Will* suggested that the past was a reality for living bodies, and it is this temporal property of biological phenomena that draws Bergson toward this area in his third major work. Why it should be evolutionary biology in particular that Bergson tackles is self-evident: in any ordinary sense of the term, evolution means "change." That is all there essentially is to Bergson's theory of life: a theory of time generalized.

According to Bergson, mechanistic theories of evolution fail to account for the diverse creativity of nature. They explain the advent of life via the contingent conglomeration of material particles while also assuming a determinism or finalism that understands all future life forms to pre-exist in the material conditions of the present world. By contrast, Bergson believes that it is the virtual influence of the past that inclines (without determining) life to take certain directions. He often uses the term "organization" instead of life, which is quite appropriate as "organization" connotes the residual effect of past actions accumulated within the present. Organization is a type of movement rich with history. Bergson describes it as a continuous change of form linking the embryo with the adult organism, and aging itself is explained as the further development of the embryo. Life as such, on the other hand, when understood as a mode of organization, is a capacity prior to, or the condition of possibility of, any organic form.

In addition, life, according to Bergson, proceeds by dissociation and division. Bergson would take issue with the image of the tree of life prevalent in many contemporary versions of evolutionary theory. As the strong version of this thesis goes, there is a single tree of life with all species branching off from what was originally one common ancestor. This idea remains too Aristotelian and hierarchical for Bergson, for it pictures life as a successive linearity rather than as a network of coincident dissociations in every direction. Bergson's alternative image is of an explosion outward (with each exploded fragment itself generating a new explosion) rather than of growth upwards. It follows that there is no *"life in general"* (*Creative Evolution*) marching inexorably toward some goal, but simply sporadic currents of life with real creation ongoing at all points along them. Evolution does not operate gradually by slowly (and implausibly) accumulating minute changes mechanically until a new species is created. For Bergson, life is a continuum of heterogeneity, with each species being a sudden emergence of novelty and invention. This is not to claim that the constant creativity of evolution is harmonious or progressive (whatever that "progress" might entail): disparity, disharmony, and failure, Bergson writes, "seems to be the rule, success exceptional and always imperfect." What unity and coherence there is, is the product not of a movement toward unity, but the disintegration of one "implied in this movement itself."

The famous theory of the *élan vital*, therefore, is not arguing for a teleology so much as confirmation of some (strictly nontheological) anterior source of organization as against the accumulation of traits by pure chance being proposed by mechanistic theories at the time he was writing. Hence, it must be regarded as a type of complex movement rather than a mysterious power. Any specific point on its path, any organism in other words, represents a forced accommodation between the movement of the *élan* and that of another, inverse movement, that of matter. Bergson clearly shows what his so-called vitalism actually comprises: organic life simply consists of a mutual adaptation between two modes of movement, that is, nothing more substantial than time itself.

Ethics

The Two Sources of Morality and Religion is Bergson's attempt to produce a sociobiological explanation of the origin of ethics and religion. Naturally, then, Bergson's theory of time and life must always be kept in mind when discussing this examination. There are *two* sources of morality and religion and both are bio-

logical because there are two major facets to Bergson's theory of evolution, what he describes as a virtual type of organization on the one hand and the expression of that order in actual organic forms on the other: evolution itself and fragments of the evolved. Two facets of time, in other words, time flowing and time flown. In *The Two Sources of Morality and Religion*, these biological influences appear in morality as two types of motivation: moral obligation and moral aspiration, each corresponding to the evolved and the evolving, respectively. The first acts as a type of pressure, a centripetal movement of closure, fostering a closed model of society and a static, institutional form of religion. The second is an outward, dissociative, and centrifugal movement, bearing within it the seeds of open sociability and dynamic, nondogmatic spirituality. As neither source of the two is strictly and exclusively moral it would be foolish, Bergson writes, to try to explain either in terms of moral or religious theory. Our sociobiology must be biological.

Now it must be added that both these moralities, closed and open, are only extreme limits, and are never found in any actual society in their pure form. The forces of openness and closure are present in varying degrees in every society and are intermixed in actual morality. Such actual morality encompasses what Bergson describes as a "system of orders dictated by impersonal social requirements," as well as a "series of appeals made to the conscience of each of us by persons who represent the best there is in humanity" (*The Two Sources of Morality and Religion*). Nonetheless, the two remain distinct while being united in their difference, for they represent "two complementary manifestations of life." There never has been nor ever could be either a truly open society or a fully closed one. These are ideal limits. Where closed morality lies in obedience before the law, open morality lies in an appeal, attraction, or call. But the call does not come from just anyone: it requires a privileged personality. What is best in our society is bequeathed to us by individuals Bergson calls heroes, and each hero—living or dead—exerts a virtual attraction on us. The heroism Bergson describes is of a religious order, though one that is dynamic and wholly active rather than institutional and reified. Bergson also calls these heroes mystics, though again, the notion of some ascetic contemplative is far from what he has in mind. These mystics are creators, transgressing the boundaries of life, mind, and society in their inspirational morality. They are now the personal bearers of what also underpins all movement and change in thought, life, and society—the very stuff of time. Nonetheless, religious dynamism needs static religion for its expression and diffusion, and the two are not at all opposed in their common origin, which Bergson alludes to mysteriously as "some intermediate thing." The object of dynamic religion is also its source: the generative action of life, which Bergson periodically describes as "God," though this is clearly an immanent and suprapersonal divinity.

Methodology

In his 1903 essay "Introduction to Metaphysics," Bergson talks of the object of perception as a "metaphysical object." He goes on as follows: "a true empiricism is the one which purposes to keep as close to the original itself as possible, to probe more deeply into its life . . . and this true empiricism is the real metaphysics." (*The Creative Mind*). He argues that true, metaphysical empiricism is not a fall into the passivity of experience but an effort to create experience, to perceive what can only be perceived rather than what is a mixture of abstraction and everyday experience: as such, metaphysics becomes experience itself. This effort is its second, positive facet: radical empiricism is metaphysical to the extent that it focuses on the individual specificity of its object—the singularity of the individual that can only be sensed rather than imagined. Metaphysics is not the contemplation of an alternative reality but the perception of a heightened reality, a perception Bergson eventually calls "intuition."

Pinning down the meaning of this intuition requires a little detective work into the development of Bergson's thought. Intuition is described initially as a sympathy that seems to imply some type of immediate consciousness; yet intuition is clearly distinguished from immediate knowledge, being described elsewhere as a search requiring prodigious effort. It can also be "supra-intellectual"—Bergson might even have chosen to name this faculty "intelligence" instead of intuition (see *Mélanges*). By about the year 1911, though, there was a significant harmonization in Bergson's writing, its broad import being that "in order to reach intuition it is not necessary to transport ourselves outside the domain of the senses" (*The Creative Mind*). The superior intuition that Kant thought necessary to ground any would-be metaphysics, Bergson (unlike Kant) does hold to exist. But it exists, he says, as the perception of metaphysical reality. It is only because Kant pictured this intuition as radically different from consciousness as well as from the senses that he dismissed its likelihood so quickly. Bergson not only accepts its reality, he bases it on the primacy of perception. Rather than attempt to rise above perception as philosophers since Plato have wished, sensuous intuition must be promoted. He encourages us to "plunge" and "insert our will" into perception, "deepening," "widening," and "expanding" it as we do.

Bergson asserts that the other purpose of metaphysics is "to operate differentiations" (*The Creative Mind*). In this respect, intuition can be looked on, in part, as a method of multiplication. Put at its simplest, this is something of a reversal of Ockham's principle, "*entia non multiplicanda sunt praeter necessitatem.*" Instead of emphasizing the fact that the best solution is often the simplest one, the Bergsonian rule states that false problems most often ensue whenever we simplify too much in the face of a true, though unpalatable, multiplication of entities. Of course, our intelligence "loves simplicity": but, "while our motto is *Exactly what is necessary,*" Bergson claims that nature's motto is frequently "*more than is necessary*—too much of this, too much of that, too much of everything." Bergson's working hypothesis is one of disunity in the active sense of that term: a "dis-uniting" of the ego, of the present, and even of being. To escape from a false problematic we must multiply the number of variables at work within it. Indeed, the problems of philosophy, in Bergson's view, most often stem from a set of confusions about which version of an entity one is discussing. However, we would be wrong to view Bergson's alternative call for multiplicity as a gratuitous predilection for the baroque: the importation of wholly new entities in his method is not being endorsed. On the contrary, it is a sensitivity toward certain subtle differences pertaining to what is already within the ontological economy of the problematic which is at issue: variations on a theme, so to speak. Thus we have all the famous dualities and pluralities at work in Bergson's thought: types of time (duration and spatialized); types of memory (virtual and actual); and types of morality (open and closed).

Influence

For nearly two decades Bergsonism was at the forefront of European philosophy; for half of that time, from 1907 to 1917, Bergson was *the* philosopher of Europe with an influence spreading far beyond his own discipline and into the fine arts, sociology, psychology, history, and politics. The literature of Proust, Woolf, and Stein, the art of the Cubists, and the music of Debussy all bear the mark of Bergson's philosophy of change. It has also been recently written that French philosophy in the twentieth-century could well be read as "a series of footnotes to Bergson." Yet by the end of the Great War that influence was over. In a manner presaging our contemporary cult of change, Bergsonian thought departed from the scene almost as quickly as it had arrived. Among a later generation of philosophers he was attacked for what was seen as his residual naturalism by phenomenological thinkers (Heidegger, Sartre, and Bachelard) just as he was criticized by philosophical naturalists for his subjectivism. Yet most of the errors made in criticizing his work stem from confusions between the numerous levels at which Bergson's analyses operate. Both positions, (pure humanism and pure naturalism) distort Bergsonian philosophy and the richer possibilities contained within it. Just as his own philosophy asserts that there are levels to reality, space, and even being, so there are also levels to Bergsonism itself, some naturalist (in his methodological intercourse with science for instance), and some anti-naturalist (in his metaphysics of anti-reductionism).

Recent examinations of his work, moreover, have sought to re-establish the philosophical integrity of Bergsonism, one avenue of research being its status as a precursor to postmodernism. Part of this new enthusiasm must be put down to the influence of Gilles Deleuze and his postmodern appropriation of Bergson's thought. But this *actualité* of Bergson goes beyond an affinity with Deleuze alone. His critique of the spatialization of time, for example, has been described as foreshadowing Derrida's work. More broadly still, others think of Bergson's thought as an early attempt to articulate such various postmodern ideas as Ricoeur's narrative self or Lévinas' proto-ethics. One commentator has even gone so far as to point to the convergence between Bergson's treatment of the body and Foucault's account of power. A number of younger Continental philosophers, no longer so judgmental about the place of science and nature, are also returning to Bergson's texts as exemplary of a type of nonreductive naturalism, one that is also critical and metaphysical.

JOHN MULLARKEY

See also **Gaston Bachelard, Julien Benda, Giles Deleuze, Emmanuel Lévinas, Paul Ricoeur, Jean-Paul Sartre**

Biography

Henri Bergson was born in Paris in 1859. After graduation from the École Normale Supérieure in 1881, he was appointed professor of philosophy at a *lycée* in Angers and then, in 1883, in Clermont-Ferrand. He returned to Paris in 1888, teaching successively at three *lycées* for ten years. It was in 1889 that his doctoral thesis, *Time and Free Will*, was published along with his Latin thesis, *Quid Aristoteles de loco senserit*. Seven years later in 1896, *Matter and Memory* appeared. Bergson was given a chair in the Collège de France in 1900 and also in that year published his study of the phenomenon of humor, *Laughter: An Essay on the Meaning of the Comic*. In 1907 he published his most famous work, *Creative Evolution*, which has ever since defined Bergsonism as a vitalist or spiritualist philosopher, though not without controversy. It was this work that established his world reputation, Bergson being elected to the *Academie Française* in 1914 and receiving the Noble Prize for literature in 1927. However, from this point forward, due to ill health, his productivity was greatly reduced. In 1922 he published *Duration and Simultaneity*, which concerned the consequences of Einstein's theory of relativity for his own of duration as given in *Time and Free Will*, but his last major work, *The Two Sources of Morality and Religion*, did not appear until 1932. However, two collections of essays, one in 1919, *Mind-Energy*, the other in 1934, *The Creative Mind*, were also published, though the latter includes older essays such as his, "Introduction to Metaphysics," which dates back to 1903. Bergson died on January 3, 1941.

Selected Writings

Oeuvres, edited by André Robinet, 1959

Mélanges, edited by André Robinet, 1972

L'Energie Spirituelle: Essais et conferences, 1919, in *Oeuvres*, translated by H. Wildon Carr as *Mind-Energy: Lectures and Essays*, 1975

Les Deux sources de la morale et de la religion, 1932, in *Oeuvres*, translated by R. Ashley Audra and Cloudesley Brereton, with the assistance of W. Horsfall Carter, as *The Two Sources of Morality and Religion*, 1977

L'Evolution créatrice (1907), in *Oeuvres*, translated by Arthur Mitchell as *Creative Evolution*, 1983

Matière et mémoire: Essai sur la relation du corps avec l'esprit (1896), in *Oeuvres*, translated by Nancy Margaret Paul and W. Scott Palmer as *Matter and Memory*, 1991

Durée et simultanéité: A Propos de la Théorie D'Einstein, 1923, in *Mélanges*, translated by Leon Jacobsen, with an introduction by Robin Durie, as *Duration and Simultaneity, Bergson and the Einsteinian Universe*, 1999

Le Rire (1900), in *Oeuvres*, translated by Cloudesley Brereton and Fred Rothwell as *Laughter: An Essay on the Meaning of the Comic*, 1999

Essai sur les données immédiates de la conscience, 1889, in *Oeuvres*, translated by F. L. Pogson as *Time and Free Will: An Essay on the Immediate Data of Consciousness*, 2001

Key Writings, edited by Keith Ansell Pearson and John Mullarkey, 2002

La Pensée et le mouvant: Essais et conférences, 1934, in *Oeuvres*, translated by Mabelle L. Andison as *The Creative Mind: An Introduction to Metaphysics*, 2002

Further Reading

Ansell Pearson, Keith, *Germinal Life: The Difference and Repetition of Deleuze*, London: Routledge, 1999

The Time of Life: Bergson and the Adventure of the Virtual, London: Routledge, 2001

Antliff, Mark, *Inventing Bergson: Cultural Politics and the Parisian Avant-Garde*, Princeton, NJ: Princeton University Press, 1993

Bachelard, Gaston, *The Dialectic of Duration*, translated by M MacAllister Jones, Manchester: Clinamen Press, 1999

Burwick, F. and Douglass, P. (editors), *The Crisis in Modernism: Bergsonism and the Vitalist Controversy*, Cambridge: Cambridge University Press, 1992

Capek, M., *Bergson and Modern Physics*, Dordrecht: Nijhoff, 1971

Deleuze, Gilles, *Bergsonism*, translated by H. Tomlinson and B. Habberjam, New York: Zone Books, 1991

Gunter, P. A. Y. (editor), *Bergson and the Evolution of Physics*, Knoxville: University of Tennessee Press, 1969

Gunter, P. A. Y. (editor), *Henri Bergson: A Bibliography*, 2nd edition, Bowling Green, Ohio: Philosophy Documentation Centre, Bowling Green State University, 1986

Jankelevitch, V., *Henri Bergson*, Paris: Presses Universitaires de France, 1959

Kolakowski, Leszek, *Bergson*, Indiana: St. Augustine's Press, 2000

Lacey, A. R., *Bergson*, London: Routledge, 1989

de Lattre, Alain, *Bergson: Une Ontologie de la Perplexité*, Paris: Presses Universitaires de France, 1990

Lawlor, Len, *The Challenge of Bergsonism*, London: Continues Press, 2003

Matthews, Eric, *Twentieth-century French Philosophy*, Oxford: Oxford University Press, 1996

Miquel, Paul-Antoine, *Le Problème de la nouveauté dans l'évolution du vivant: Dialogue entre Bergson et la biologie contemporaine*, Lille: Presses Universitaires du Septentrion, 1997

Moore, F. C. T., *Bergson: Thinking Backwards*, Cambridge: Cambridge University Press, 1996

Mourélos, Georges, *Bergson et les Niveaux de Réalité*, Paris: Presses Universitaires de France, 1964

Mullarkey, John, *Bergson and Philosophy*, Edinburgh: Edinburgh University Press, 1999

Mullarkey, John (editor), *The New Bergson*, Manchester: Manchester University Press, 1999

Papanicolaou, A. C. and Gunter, P. A. Y. (editors), *Bergson and Modern Thought*, London: Harwood, 1987

Paradis, Bruno, "Indétermination et mouvements de birfurcation chez Bergson", in *Philosophie*, No. 32 (1991): pp. 11–40.

Worms, Frédéric, *Introduction à "Matière et mémoire' de Bergson*, Paris: Presses Universitaires de France, 1997

Worms, Frédéric, and Soulez, Philippe, *Bergson: Biographie*, Paris: Flammarion, 1997

Worms, Frédéric, *Le Vocabulaire de Bergson*, Paris: Ellipses, 2000

BERNANOS, GEORGES

Novelist and essayist

Georges Bernanos was one of the pre-eminent French novelists in the Catholic tradition and one of the most prolific polemicists of the first half of the twentieth century. Born into a Catholic and royalist family, Bernanos throughout his life had two great obsessions: the glory of God and the grandeur of France—ideals that shaped his Christian artistic vision and focused his political engagement. Coming relatively late in life to the profession of writing, he nonetheless produced an important body of fiction—eight novels and one drama—as well as voluminous and often controversial nonfiction—political essays, biographical essays, and compilations of articles, lectures, and broadcasts. His writing career was divided into two nearly equal periods. Between 1926 and 1937 he composed and published the majority of his fiction, and then devoted himself to his nonfiction from the mid-1930s to the end of his life.

As a novelist Bernanos was influenced notably by Barbey d'Aurevilly, Bloy, and Péguy—precursors of the Catholic revival—and he is frequently compared to Dostoyevski, whom he greatly admired. His novels, like the Catholic novel of the twentieth century in general, rooted in reaction to the rationalism of the Enlightenment and the ideologies of nineteenth century liberalism and materialism, depict the plight of modern man in a spiritually alienated world caught up in the drama of sin and salvation, torn between God and Satan. He portrays French society between the two world wars as being in a final stage of decay resulting from the loss of Christian virtues and chivalric honor dating back to France's distant past—a past embodied for him by heroic figures such as Jeanne d'Arc.

Bernanosian themes are centered on the heroism of innocence and suffering, the temptation of despair, poverty, honor, childhood, and purity, and revolve around two principal character types: the priest and the adolescent. The struggle of a country priest is the focus of Bernanos' first novel, *Sous Le Soleil de Satan* (1926, *Under Satan's Sun*), whose immediate success brought its author national prominence as a Catholic novelist. In Bernanos's view, the modern world's materialistic preoccupations had led to the "dis-incarnation" of Christianity, but for him Good and Evil were active agents in man's existence. Hence his young priest Donissan encounters Satan incarnate and must battle the demon for the soul of the parish. In his best-known and most successful novel, *Journal d'un curé de campagne* (1936, *The Diary of a Country Priest*), the impoverished and unnamed young priest struggles against another manifestation of Evil—ennui—that eats away at the soul of his parish like the cancer that causes his own death. Struggling to overcome self-doubt and failure, in the moment of his death he realizes: "Everything is grace."

The theme of the innocence and purity of the child overcoming Evil dominates *L'Imposture* (1927, *The Impostor*) and *La Joie* (1929, *Joy*), in contrast to the martyrdom of innocence that Bernanos portrays in *Nouvelle Histoire de Mouchette* (1937, *Mouchette*) wherein the young protagonist, raped and humiliated by the corrupt adult world, is driven to suicide. In *Monsieur Ouine* (1943, *Monsieur Ouine*), which Bernanos considered his "great novel," the adolescent Steeny emerges from the innocence of childhood and encounters Evil represented by the dying eponymous protagonist. In the powerful concluding chapter, the old professor of modern languages looks into his own soul but sees "nothing." This prophetic and complex work may perhaps best be read as an allegory of spiritual destitution at the demise of post-Renaissance civilization that had abandoned its Christian foundations—a demise that Bernanos associated with the fall of France in 1940. *Dialogues des Carmélites* (1949, *The Carmelites*) was Bernanos's last literary work written shortly before his death, and is generally considered to be his spiritual testament. Based on historical events, the play recounts the martyrdom of sixteen Carmelite nuns guillotined during the French Revolution. The work is a poignant portrayal of the power of Christian faith to conquer fear and, through sacrifice, attain redemption.

From Maurrasian activist to one of the inspirational voices of the French Resistance, Bernanos was witness to turbulent political events throughout his life. Over the years his thought evolved beyond any particular party line or political stance, and by the end of his life he was highly esteemed by both the left and the right. In his youth he greatly admired Édouard Drumont, one of France's foremost anti-Semites during the period of the Dreyfus Affair, who in his diatribes attacked Jewish power as a threat to France's centuries-old Christian values. Bernanos's own anti-Semitic tendency was the upshot of his anti-capitalist views. In his lengthy and controversial biographical essay on Drumont (*La Grande Peur des bien-pensants* [1931, The great fear of right-thinking people]), he argues that Drumont's anti-Semitism was aimed at money as a controlling force in the modern world, and fiercely attacks the political and religious complacency of the French bourgeoisie. During his university years Bernanos also enacted his monarchist idealism through adherence to *Action française* (French action)—a militant right-wing royalist movement headed by Charles Maurras—that vehemently attacked the Republic, Freemasons, Jews, and Protestants.

Bernanos's deep devotion to freedom, however, prevented him from fully embracing the rightist cause. Living in Majorca when the Spanish Civil War erupted in 1936, he witnessed firsthand the cruelty of Franco's repressive fascist "crusade," and thereafter until the end of his life he sacrificed his literary creation to devote his pen to essays and articles exposing injustice, decrying totalitarianism, criticizing bourgeois self-interest, bolstering French morale during the war years, and sounding the alarm about what he saw as the imminent disintegration of increasingly secular Western civilization.

His first and perhaps greatest political essay is *Les Grands Cimetières sous la lune* (1938, *A Diary of My Times*) wherein he describes his experience of the Spanish Civil War as "the major event" of his life. The work is a reflection upon the events of the war and French and European politics, but it also embodies Bernanos's prefigurative vision of the more universal tragedy of modern divisive society that eliminates bit by bit "*l'homme de bonne volonté*" (the man of good will). For Bernanos the union of mankind could only take place around ethical values such as honor, liberty, truth, and justice, and thus, while most French Catholic intellectuals viewed Franco's regime as a defense of Christianity against her enemies, Bernanos was among the few Catholic voices to criticize the abuses of the Spanish Catholic hierarchy and to speak out against the Church hierarchy and the financial opportunism of the conservative elements. The reaction to *Les Grands Cimetières sous la lune* was harsh. *Action française* accused Bernanos of abandoning the cause, the Jesuits condemned the book, and the Catholic press accused its author of vulgarity, anti-clericalism, and lack of respect for the spiritual hierarchy. Repudiated by the right, Bernanos drew attention from the left who were not then generally familiar with his work.

In the years immediately preceding the Second World War Bernanos broke off his friendship with Maurras, explaining in *Scandale de la vérité* (1939, The scandal of truth) that he felt Maurras had betrayed the ideals of France by sympathizing with Mussolini's invasion of Ethiopia in 1936 and the Munich Pact in 1938. With the world again engulfed in conflict, in *Les Enfants humiliés* (*The Humiliated Children*) completed in 1940, Bernanos reflected on the losses of World War I (in which he had fought) and Hitler's motives in the present war, and meditated on the theme of humiliated adolescence that is so central to his fiction. Revolted by Pétain's Vichy government, from Brazil where he was living at the time Bernanos responded to General de Gaulle's radio appeal of June 18, 1940 by taking up his pen and tirelessly supporting the Free French and the Resistance throughout the Occupation. The resulting articles and broadcasts written between 1940 and 1945 cover a variety of topics and give rich insight into Bernanos' thought during the war years. They were later published under the title *Le Chemin de la Croix-des-Âmes* (1948, *The Road of the Cross of Souls*). In *Lettre aux Anglais* (1942, *Plea for Liberty*) Bernanos addresses other nations to explain his idea of French honor and genius and his hope that his then defeated and humiliated nation might regain her historic mission as a leader of free men. In his last essay of the war years, *La France contre les robots* (*Tradition of Freedom*) completed in 1944, he rants against the culture of "imbeciles" and expresses his apprehensions about the dehumanizing effect of the machine age. After returning to France in 1945, Bernanos continued his journalist activity until his death, writing for a variety of newspapers. In these articles, compiled under the title *Français, si vous saviez* (1961, *Frenchmen, If You Only Knew*), he angrily decries the illusions besetting postwar France, appeals for vigilance against violence and imposture, and writes of his hopes for the France of tomorrow.

Bernanos has been called a visionary and prophetic writer. André Malraux called him "the greatest novelist of his time." But he himself always valued his independence and freedom over recognition and official honors; indeed, he declined the *Légion d'honneur* (Legion of honour) four times. Bernanos considered his mission as a writer to be a sacerdotal calling—"*vocatus*"—and true to his calling he never lost sight of the human dimension that he charted so compassionately throughout his fiction and nonfiction. He tells us in the preface to *Les Grands Cimetières sous la lune* that he liked to write in cafés, because he needed to be in the presence of human voices and faces and to speak nobly of them.

KENNETH S. McKELLAR

See also **Leon Bloy, Charles Maurras**

Biography

Georges Bernanos was born on February 20, 1888 in Paris, where he studied at the Collège jésuite from 1898 to 1901, and then at Collège Notre-Dame-des Champs until 1903. His finished his studies in provincial schools and completed the baccalauréat in 1906, then began university studies at the Sorbonne, completing a *licence* in literature and law by 1913. During his university years he was involved with the "camelots du roi" and Maurras's *Action française*. In 1913–14 he edited a small royalist weekly in Rouen, *L'Avant-Garde de la Normandie*. He served in the French army throughout World War I, was wounded and decorated. In 1917 he married Jeanne Talbert d'Arc, a descendent of the brother of Jeanne d'Arc, and by 1933 they had a family of six children. Between 1919 and 1927 Bernanos worked as an insurance inspector travelling in eastern France. In 1926 his first novel *Sous Le Soleil de Satan* was an immediate success, and he soon left his insurance job. His third novel *La Joie* received the *Prix Fémina* in 1929. From 1930 to 1932 he was a columnist for *Le Figaro*. As a result of a motorcycle accident in 1933, he would be crippled for the rest of his life. Because of financial difficulties, the family lived in Majorca (where the cost of living was cheaper) during 1934–37, and there Bernanos witnessed firsthand the Spanish Civil War. In 1936 his novel *Journal d'un curé de campagne* received the *Grand Prix du roman* awarded by the French Academy. During 1938–45 the family lived in Brazil, where Bernanos wrote numerous articles and broadcasts to support the Free French and the Resistance throughout World War II. At the end of the war General de Gaulle appealed to Bernanos to return to France, and the family moved back to Paris in 1945. In the period between 1945 and his death, Bernanos gave lectures in Switzerland, Belgium, and North Africa, and contributed to many newspapers, including *La Bataille, Carrefour, Combat, Le Figaro, L'Intransigeant*, and *Témoignage chrétien*. In 1946 he declined the *Légion d'honneur* for the fourth time. Disillusioned with postwar France, he moved to Tunisia in 1947, but suffering from liver disease he returned to Paris, where he died on July 5, 1948.

KENNETH S. McKELLAR

Selected Works

Sous Le Soleil de Satan, 1926; as *Under Satan's Sun*, translated by J. C. Whitehouse, 2001
L'Imposture, 1927; as *The Impostor*, translated by J.C. Whitehouse, 1999
La Joie, 1929; as *Joy*, translated by Louise Varèse, 1946
La Grande Peur des bien-pensants, 1931
Jeanne, relapse et sainte, 1934; as *Sanctity Will Out: An Essay on Saint Joan*, translated by R. Batchelor, 1947
Un Crime, 1935; as *The Crime*, translated by Anne Green, 1936
Journal d'un curé de campagne, 1936; as *The Diary of a Country Priest*, translated by Pamela Morris, 1937, 1965
Nouvelle Histoire de Mouchette, 1937; as *Mouchette*, translated by Colin Whitehouse, 1987
Les Grands Cimetières sous la lune, 1938; as *A Diary of My Times*, translated by Pamela Morris, 1938
Monsieur Ouine, 1943, 1946 (definitive edition 1955); as *Monsieur Ouine*, translated by William S. Bush, 2000
Scandale de la vérité, 1939
Lettre aux Anglais, 1942; as *Plea for Liberty: Letters to the English, the Americans, the Europeans*, translated by Harry Lorin Binsse, 1944
La France contre les robots, 1947; as *Tradition of Freedom*, anonymous translator, 1950
Le Chemin de la Croix-des-Âmes, 1948
Dialogues des Carmélites, 1949; as *The Carmelites*, translated by G. Hopkins, 1961
Les Enfants humiliés, 1949
Un Mauvais Rêve, 1950; as *Night is Darkest*, translated by W. J. Strachan, 1953
Français, si vous saviez, 1961

Collected Works

Oeuvres romanesques, 1961
Correspondance, 2 vols, 1971
Essais et écrits de combat, 2 vols, 1971–95
Romans, 1994

Bibliographies

Bush, William, "Georges Bernanos" in *A Critical Bibliography of French Literature*, vol. 6, part 1, edited by Douglas W. Alden and Richard A. Brooks, Syracuse, New York: Syracuse University Press, 1980
Jurt, Joseph, *Georges Bernanos: essai de bibliographie des études en langue française consacrées à Georges Bernanos durant sa vie*, 3 vols., Paris: Minard, 1972–75

Further Reading

Albouy, Serge, *Bernanos et la politique*, Paris: Privat, 1980

Béguin, Albert, *Bernanos par lui-même*, Paris: Seuil, 1954

Bernanos, Jean-Loup, *Georges Bernanos à la merci des passants*, Paris: Plon, 1986

Bothorel, Jean, *Bernanos le mal pensant: biographie*, Paris: Grasset, 1998

Bush, William, *Georges Bernanos*, New York: Twayne, 1969

Bush, William (editor), "George Bernanos in His Time and Ours: 1888–1988," special double issue of *Renascence: Essays on Values in Literature*, 41, nos 1–2 (Fall 1988/Winter 1989)

Clarke, Alan R., *La France dans l'histoire selon Bernanos*, Paris: Minard, 1983

Cooke, John E., *Georges Bernanos: A Study of Christian Commitment*, Amersham, England: Avebury, 1981

Halda, Bernard, *Bernanos ou la foi militante et déchirée*, Paris: Tequi, 1980

Le Touzé, Philippe, and Max Milner (editors), *Bernanos et l'interprétation*, Paris: Klincksieck, 1996

Milner, Max, *Georges Bernanos*, Paris: Desclée De Brouwer, 1967

Molnar, Thomas, *Bernanos: His Political Thought and Prophecy*, New York: Sheed and Ward, 1960

Renard, Pierrette (editor), *Georges Bernanos, témoin*, Toulouse: Presses Universitaires du Mirail, 1994

Speaight, Robert, *Georges Bernanos: A Study of the Man and the Writer*, London: Collins and Harvill, 1973

BEYALA, CALIXTHE

Novelist, Essayist

Calixteh Beyala is a controversial figure who has enjoyed almost overnight success (with *Le petit prince de Belleville* in 1992) while at the same time being repeatedly charged with allegations of plagiarism. These elements have contributed to make her one of the most visible African Francophone woman writers on the Parisian literary scene as well as outside France.

Her first three novels, *C'est le Soleil qui m'a brûlée* (1986), *Tu t'appelleras Tanga* (1988), and *Seul le Diable le savait* (1990), can be read as a search for new sexual ethics and social relations, through rethinking relationships among individuals, men and women, women, parents and children. In her use of vernacular, violent, sometimes crude and obscene language, Beyala has contributed to imposing a new visibility for women writers, demonstrating that political criticism and sexual or vulgar language are no longer men's prerogatives.

Le petit prince de Belleville (1992) and its sequel, *Maman a un amant* (1993), introduce the possibility of a dialogue—albeit limited—between men and women. They also mark a shift in the author's gaze, from the African continent to the African immigrants in Paris. Immigration is looked at in terms of its dynamics and the possibilities it may offer women (married, single, young, middle-aged) to become somebody new. The novel is often built around two female protagonists who are both antithetic and complementary. In that respect, they embody the two potential sides of the immigration experience for women, both in terms of opportunities and of risks and dangers. Men on the other hand are portrayed as vulnerable, unable to look toward the future.

All her novels since then —her Parisian novels as they are often called—have shown a decetering process pertaining to the author's progressive shift from Africa towards France. Beyala decenters language, writing, and identity. By humorously manipulating stereotypes and idiomatic expressions, which are an integral part of the French language, she both subverts the canonical language and literature and deconstructs the often-stereotypical representations of non-European immigrants. Although a certain folklorization is introduced in her representations, these images infuse new strength into her narratives. So does the inventiveness of her "*mots bâtons manioqués.*"

Likewise, that a Muslim Cameroonian protagonist (Saïda) in *Les honneurs perdus* calls herself "Me, the Arab" as she bakes Arab pastries points to a shift in her writing. The fact that Saïda becomes interchangeable with a Maghrebi woman in the Belleville neighborhood signals a loss of cultural identity. However, it also illustrates the similarities between the two experiences of immigration and suggests a phenomenon of globalization. The *métissage* of such representations may not be obvious to most readers; however, it represents a central point in the evolution of Beyala's writing. These linguistic and cultural shifts demonstrate successful negotiations between the writer and her environment and, undeniably, an interaction with the French reader.

Her essays show a similar shift and exemplify an interesting paradox in the readership. *Lettre d'une Africaine à ses soeurs occidentales* (1995) created a controversy and ambivalence. Several Africans, most notably women, objected to her portrayal of Africa, of the African woman, and of Africans in general. As suggested by the title, her choice of audience was Western women, and the author positioned herself as a representative of her African sisters. As such, she was perceived by the French as the representative *par excellence* of Africans, especially African women. In that sense, her second essay, *Lettre d'une Afro-Parisienne à ses compatriotes* (1999) is even clearer in her own positioning: she now identifies herself as a bicultural product, where Paris is her locus of cultural anchoring.

Like her protagonists, Beyala herself has become somebody new. She was initially disregarded by African readers and literary critics, because of, what appeared to be, a facile spectacle of sexual scenes, an environment of prostitution, and an overuse of vulgar language. She suddenly became an overnight success with the release of *Le petit prince de Belleville* by the major publishing house, Albin Michel. Very soon, it appeared in paperback, becoming available in all the supermarket aisles in France. Unlike most other Francophone writers, several of her novels were soon translated into English. Within a few years, Beyala became the African female voice heard on the airwaves, the recognized face featured in women's magazine articles, appearing in numerous shows on television. By then, her many literary awards had gained her acceptance within the academic circles and her texts were now routinely part of French and Francophone literature courses.

The years 1996 and 1997 were tumultuous for the author due to allegations of multiple instances of plagiarism (as can be found in *Le Monde*, the magazine *Lire*, and *Le Figaro*). Beyala did experience the effects of these charges even though it had no impact on the sales of her novels. In addition, French intellectual life seemed to regard the marks of plagiarism as "une écriture de la dissipation," as examined by Jean-Luc Hennig's *Eulogie du plagiat* (1997). She did continue to write and publish, but she has moved on to become a political figure, engaged in the struggle for a greater representation of minorities on television and in other media, through her Collectif Egalité Association, created in 1998. Most recently, she ran for Secretary-General of La Francophonie, a position that is voted by participating heads of state. Boutros Boutros-Ghali was the first to hold this important position of spokesperson for the Francophone world on the international scene. Beyala later withdrew her candidacy, but she had reached part of her objective: to take "la Francophonie" to the street, popularize it, make it less formal and more youthful, more energetic.

The different shifts occurring in Beyala's writing and persona indicate not only a change in the context of writing/reception within the framework of French-language African literature, but also emphasize a gap between the new African writings in France and the novel written from Africa. Her success with a greater public, which does not specialize in African literature, may signal a fascination with the author's flamboyance, but it also shows a new interest in the African diaspora in Paris and its literary imaginary. Indeed, Beyala has greatly contributed to shaking the establishment and to making Francophone literature much more visible on the French literary scene.

ODILE CAZENAVE

Biography

Born in Cameroon in a very modest milieu, raised by her sister, Calixthe Beyala has been living in France since the early 1980s. She is a prolific writer—eleven novels and two essays since the mid-1980s—and has received several literary awards, including the Grand Prix de l'Académie Française in 1996 for *Les honneurs perdus*.

Selected Writings

Tu t'appelleras Tanga, 1988
Le petit prince de Belleville, 1992
Maman a un amant, 1993
Lettre d'une Africaine à ses soeurs occidentales, 1995
Les Honneurs perdus, 1996
Amours sauvages, 1999
Comment cuisiner son mari à l'africaine, 2000

BLOCH, MARC
Historian

"What is the use of history?" Marc Bloch asks at the beginning of *Apologie pour l'histoire* (1949), and he answers, "to help human beings live better lives." Bloch's life and work are an eloquent and courageous testimony to his belief in the importance of his work. In his scholarship, Bloch insists that all of history is a single entity and that historians must understand periods and topics in relation to one another. His approach to his discipline combines economic and social history with the study of beliefs, rites, and customs. One of the founders of the history of *mentalités*, he demonstrates in his major study *La société féodale* (1939, 1940) how a social organization appears at a historical moment when people's worldviews make it possible. Bloch's is a total approach to history, supported by a vast array of documents of all types: maps, names of places, tools, aerial photographs, folklore, and the like.

Standing apart both from the triumphant scientific ideals of the earlier positivists and the lack of interpretive audacity of the pure historians' school, Bloch uses Einstein's relativity revolution as a model. For him, "each science is a fragment of the universal march toward knowledge," toward a better understanding of the working of each human society within its time frame. Bloch wants to see the fullness of human history, to understand permanence as well as change.

He stresses the need to recognize how slowly social constructs change. A society, Bloch writes, must find a balance between traditions and change, between immediate and long-term transmission of wisdom and knowledge. To effectively unearth documents, to use techniques and approaches capable of making sense of the past, historians must observe the reality in which they themselves live. For Bloch, "misunderstanding of the present comes from ignoring the past" (*Apologie*) and "without looking at the present, it is impossible to understand the past" (*L'étrange défaite*). In writing *L'étrange défaite* (1946), drawing on both his scholarly experiences and his direct participation in the events of his own time, he became a spiritual father of the field of the history of the present, notes Henry Rousso, the director of the Institut de l'Histoire du Temps Présent.

Bloch was open to many influences—Emile Durkheim's sociology, the geography of Paul Vidal de la Blache, François Simiand's interest in economic history, and the work of linguists Georges Dumézil and Emile Benveniste. His knowledge of English, German, and Italian, as well as French, gave him a broad vision of European scholarship, as did his stays in Germany and his contacts in many European capitals and universities.

In 1949, Bloch and Lucien Febvre, his Strasbourg colleague, introduced *Annales d'histoire économique et sociale*, an interdisciplinary journal dedicated to social and economic history. The project demanded enormous energy from Bloch in the interwar years.

Bloch is famous for three major works on the Middle Ages. *Les rois thaumaturges* (1924) explains the centuries-long belief in the healing value of the king's touch. It is a pioneering book in the history of *mentalités* marking a rebirth of historical anthropology. Bloch tells the story of a miracle, and of the belief in this miracle. His explanation covers duration and evolution, two major themes of the *Annales* school. By looking at the origins of the royal touch, Bloch explores the "sacred" character of the French/English kings and its political meaning.

La société féodale (1939–1940), Bloch's acclaimed two-volume masterpiece, a brilliant synthesis of his multiple skills and interdisciplinary approaches, is an illustration of the conception of "total society" he developed in his contributions to the *Annales*. He presents European feudalism as a geographically situated historical moment that brought to the West the idea of limiting the power of the ruler through a reciprocal binding contract, a concept essential in the quest for freedom.

Les caractères originaux de l'histoire rurale française (1931), a major contribution to rural history, stresses the diversity of French agrarian civilization and develops the concept of *longue durée*. Describing first the variety of field patterns in 1930s France, Bloch works back to the Middle Ages, seeking to understand the social and mental constructs such patterns embody.

Bloch's last work, *Apologie pour l'histoire*, was written during World War II, without his notes or library, and published after his death. It presents a summary of his insights and reflections on the value of history and on directions to explore. Bloch uses some

of his war experiences as illustrations of the persistence of human behavior, summarizing his long years of explorations and studies.

Marc Bloch is a "very French patriot," Emmanuel Le Roy Ladurie writes, a "republican citizen," Stanley Hoffmann adds. He has had a more lasting influence and represents a more powerful model than that of a medieval scholar and innovative historian. The most striking part of his legacy may well be his account of the tragic events of 1940. *L'étrange défaite* was written in the months that followed the collapse of France and is, as Febvre phrases it, "one of the two or three deepest and most truly thought-through books on those painful years." Hoffman emphasizes how exact and thorough Bloch's analysis of the debacle remains fifty years later. This short and angry book—written on the spot—in which Bloch lambastes the failure of the French intellectual spirit, is an illustration of his dedication to his craft, of the coherence of his life as a scholar, French citizen, patriot, and humanist. It is an expression of his decency and the fine quality of his moral and intellectual values.

There has been a Marc Bloch revival since the 1980s (as noted by Olivier Dumoulin), spurred by the republishing of all his major works and correspondence, with prefaces and introductions by the major scholars in the field (Jacques Le Goff, Emmanuel Le Roy Ladurie, Georges Duby, among others), by the constant reference to his name by specialists of social and contemporary history (Gérard Noiriel, for example), and by an increasing symbolic recognition expressed in publications and colloquiums and the naming of lycées and universities after him.

Bloch's life was difficult. From the interruption of his promising career by mobilization in 1914 to his removal from the Sorbonne after the adoption of the Statute of the Jews by the Vichy regime in October 1940 and his arrest and execution by the Gestapo in 1944 for acts of resistance, he had to confront opposition and misunderstanding. He was a first-hand observer of the spread of bolshevism, fascism, and militant anti-Semitism. Despite all this, Marc Bloch retained hope, serenity, and energy, along with a fidelity to his beliefs, his work, and his patriotic convictions.

"I am a Jew by birth, not by religion . . . [and] have neither pride nor shame about it," Bloch writes in *L'étrange défaite*. "I claim my origins only when confronted with anti-Semitism. . . . But my homeland is France. . . . I was born here, I drank from the spring of her culture, I made her past mine. I can breathe only under her sky, and I tried to fight for her as well as I could."

Marc Bloch's life borders on the tragic, but in no way did he submit to fate. He never relinquished his capacity to fight professionally, personally, and on the battlefields for his belief in France, universal values, and the future of humanity.

MONIQUE OYALLON

See also **Emile Benveniste, Georges Duby, Georges Dumezil, Emile Durkheim, Lucien Febvre, Emmanuel Le Roy Ladurie**

Biography

Marc Bloch was born in 1886 in Lyons to a family of Alsatian Jews with republican, liberal, and patriotic traditions. His father Gustave Bloch taught ancient history at the Ecole Normale Supérieure and the Sorbonne during the years of the Dreyfus affair, a major event in his son's youth. After studying at Louis-le-Grand, Marc Bloch entered the Ecole Normale Supérieure, placed second in the *agrégation* in history and geography in 1908, received a scholarship to study in Leipzig and Berlin the next year, then won a fellowship in the coveted Fondation Thiers from 1909 to 1912 to work on his doctoral thesis. In 1912 and 1913, he taught in lycées in Montpellier and Amiens. The war interrupted his work. Mobilized in 1914, Bloch spent over four years in active service. He was demobilized in 1919 with the grade of captain and assigned to teach medieval history at the University of Strasbourg, an institution set up to be a symbol of the reintegration of Alsace into France.

In 1919 Bloch married Simonne Vidal. In 1928, he traveled to Oslo to attend the Sixth International Congress of Historical Sciences. In 1936, Bloch was elected to a Sorbonne chair, after failing earlier to enter the College de France or the Ecole Pratique des Hautes Etudes. World War II interrupted his career a second time. Mobilized in 1939, Bloch was assigned to the First northern army, and declined to be excused from military duties, despite his age and his six young children. Unable to get back to the Sorbonne because of the German occupation, he joined the exiled University of Strasbourg in Clermont-Ferrand in 1940. First submitted to the vexations of Vichy's infamous Statute of Jews that prohibited him from holding public office, Bloch was exempted from the application of the statute in 1941. He then joined the university of Montpellier in 1942. Visa difficulties for some members of his family made it impossible to him to leave for the United States, despite an invitation from the New School in New York and financial backing from the Rockefeller Foundation. After the German invasion of the *zone libre* in November 1942, Bloch and his family fled Montpellier. The Vichy authorities again suspended him from his teaching duties. Bloch joined the Resistance movement in Lyons. Arrested by the Ge-

stapo in the spring of 1944, he was executed with seventeen other members of the Resistance in Saint-Didier-de-Fromans near Lyons on June 16, 1944.

Selected Works

Rois et serfs, un chapitre d'histoire capétienne, 1920
Les rois thaumaturges. Etude sur le caractère surnaturel attribué à la puissance royale particulièrement en France et en Angleterre, 1924; as *The Royal Touch; Sacred Monarchy and Scrofula in England and France*, 1973
Les caractères originaux de l'histoire rurale française, 1931; as *French Rural History: An Essay on its Basic Characteristics*, translated by Janet Sondheimer, 1966
La société féodale, tome 1 La formation des liens de dépendance, 1939; as *Feudal Society, Volume 1, The Growth of Ties of Dependence*, translated by L. A. Manyon, 1961
La société féodale, tome 2, Les classes et le gouvernement des hommes, 1940; as *Feudal Society, Volume 2, Social Classes and Political Organization*, translated by L. A. Manyon, 1961
L'étrange défaite, 1946; as *Strange Defeat*, translated by Gerard Hopkins, 1949
Apologie pour l'histoire ou Métier d'historien, 1949; as *The Historian's Craft*, translated by Peter Putnam, 1953
Mélanges historiques, 2 volumes, 1963
Souvenirs de guerre, 1914–1915, 1969; as *Memoirs of War, 1914–15*, translated and with an introduction by Carole Fink, 1980
La terre et le paysan. Agriculture et vie rurale aux 17e et 18e siècles, collated by Etienne Bloch, 1999

Further Reading

Atsma, Hartmut, and André Burguière, *Marc Bloch aujourd'-hui. Histoire comparée et sciences sociales*, Paris: Ecole des Hautes Etuoles en Sciences Sociales, 1990
Bloch, Etienne, *Marc Bloch, 1886–1944, une biographie impossible*, Limoges: Culture et patrimoine en Limousin, 1997
Burguière, André, entry on Marc Bloch in *Dictionnaire des Sciences historiques* edited by André Burguière, Paris: Presses Universitaires ole France, 1986
Dumoulin, Olivier, *Marc Bloch*, Paris: Presses de Sciences Politiques, 2000
Fink, Carole, *Marc Bloch: A Life in History*, Cambridge: Cambridge University Press, 1989
Friedman, Susan, Marc Bloch, *Sociology and Geography: Encountering Changing Disciplines*, Cambridge: Cambridge University Press, 1996
Geremek, Bronislaw, Préface in *Marc Bloch, Ecrire La Société féodale, Lettres à Henri Berr, 1924–1943*, Paris: Editions IMEC, 1992
Hoffmann, Stanley, Préface in *Marc Bloch, L'étrange défaite*, Paris: Gallimard, 1990
Le Goff, Jacques, Roger Chartier and Jacques Revel (editors), *La Nouvelle histoire*, Paris: Retz, 1978
Le Goff, Jacques, Préface in *Marc Bloch, Les rois thaumaturges*, Paris: Gallimard, 1983
Le Roy Ladurie, Emmanuel, Préface in *Marc Bloch, La terre et le paysan*, Paris: Armand Colin, 1999
Noiriel, Gérard, "En mémoire de Marc Bloch. Retour sur l'Apologie pour l'histoire," Genèses, 17 (1994): 122–139
Noiriel, Gérard, *Sur la "crise" de l'histoire*, Paris: Belin, 1996

Weber, Florence, "Métier d'historien, métier d'ethnographe," Cahiers Marc Bloch, 4 (1996): 6–24

BLONDEL, MAURICE
Writer

Born in Dijon in 1861, Maurice Blondel came to prominence as the author of a metaphysical work that aimed to prove that transcendence was a natural presupposition of human existence. His intended three-part demonstration (action, thought, and ontology) was to rely exclusively on philosophical reason. However, Blondel's first published volume, *The Action*, already pointed to the fact that philosophy alone could not provide the means to close his system of concepts, which therefore had to make recourse to religious spirituality for its grounding principles and ultimate goals. In situating action, or the conscious activity of the mind as a whole, between immanence and transcendence, Blondel stated that immanent phenomena necessarily related to a transcendent order of things. The analysis of discrete classes of phenomena (for instance, affectivity or political involvement) showed that no given level of activity was self-sufficient, but led to the assumption of something transcendent to it. This argument implied that autonomous reason, as outlined by the Kantian conception, had to make room for theological dogmatism in order to provide answers to the most important religious questions.

The methodology of Blondel's *Action* was modeled on the Kantian *a priori* analysis that established the transcendental conditions of thought and knowledge. The starting premise was that Christianity represented a way of life. Action constituted the "geometrical place" of the original dynamism of this way of life. In fact, the term "action" covered all the active manifestations of existence: sensation, perception, volition, wilful and moral action, artistic creation, and even divine action. However, Blondel's account of action, as situated between reason and religion, uncovered a virtually infinite distance between myself and I. The effort of the individual wills to bridge the distance between the subject and the self revealed an insufficiency, that in turn opened up the possibility of transcendence. The "willed will," which sought satisfaction in material, social, and cultural values, made room for the "willful will," the will that willed its own freedom. The third part of Blondel's study led to the idea of a subjective science of action, which would find its foundation in the very phenomenon of subjectivity. Following an analysis of the relationship between consciousness and the unconscious ("The unconscious is not down below only; it is also above and beyond deliberate resolutions"), Blondel arrives at the necessary postulate of the infinite through the very process that was supposed to integrate lived experience to consciousness, within action.

Initially, Blondel's *Action* became the object of severe criticism from contemporary academics and theologians. The latter considered Blondel's account of Christianity as exclusively guided by philosophical concerns. In academic circles, Blondel was perceived as a theologian rather than a philosopher, which accounted for his belated appointment to a position in Lille (two years after he defended his thesis at the Sorbonne). In 1895 he received a Professorship in Aix-en-Provence, where he spent the rest of his life, until his death in 1946.

The second part of Blondel's trilogy, *The Thought* (1934), employed the same integrative and regressive method as *The Action*. The term "thought" corresponded to the totality of psychological and synergetic processes. Individual thought represented only the first stage of a three-part process: the individual humanization of cosmic thought, the affirmation of a transcendent form of thought, and the aspiration of thought to become united with God. As a human achievement, this process presupposed language as well as the "thought of thought," that is to say, God. In relation to the material world, this process found support in a fundamental "disappointment" caused by the multiplicity, the instability, and the complexity of material phenomena. The observed insufficiency of thought, like the insufficiency of action, revealed a void that was to be filled in by transcendence. Therefore, thought was supposed to seek its grounding principle and the fundamental source of its knowledge, of its perception and of its blessedness. In order to be able to prove the existence of God, thought had first to be prepared to give, because only the act of giving could reveal transcendence. This spiritualist type of argument proposes to go beyond the classical Cartesian proofs of the existence of God through the infinity of the idea of God, as presented in the *Meditations*.

The third movement of Blondel's trilogy, *Being and beings* (1935), relied on the same methodology which had been used to deduce the idea of necessary Being through an exploration of contingent beings, in the Neo-Platonic tradition. The subjective experience of being was not limited to the contingent world, because it uncovered a longing that could only be satisfied by the absolute Being. Christian existence thus became integrated to the universal ontological history, which accounted for the participation of finite beings to divine ends. Under the influence of Leibniz's theory of the communication of substances in the *Monadology*, Blondel considered individual beings as progressive and distinct realizations of thought in the Universe. Hence, Christians were seen as mediators between the

Universe and God. They were supposed to accomplish a Christlike spiritualization of matter. Christ himself, who was attributed a comprehensible and rationalized function in this "panchristianism," provided the example of an active process of spiritual mediation in which all people could participate.

Ultimately, Blondel's work was defined by the refusal to set dogmatic theology apart from philosophical thought. The realm of Catholic supernatural phenomena was revealed in the natural realm of existence, and, more specifically, in every act of willing and thought, in as much as the essential determinations of these acts of existence are considered. The ascending movement of charity was disclosed neither through historical revelation, nor through dogmatic transmission, but through reflection. Nevertheless, Blondel attributed a religious vocation to pure philosophical reflection. He remained closely attached to the French Cartesian tradition of the autonomy of the spirit, although his system ultimately lead to the idea of a universe in which existence and transcendence were interdependent. Blondel's investigation into the legitimacy of the actual philosophical analysis of the concepts of grace, revelation, and faith gradually won recognition during the process of intellectual evolution within Roman Catholicism. From this point of view, one can say that Blondel's work made a significant contribution to widening the official doctrinal stand of the Catholic Church

OLIVIER SALAZAR-FERRER

Biography

Maurice Blondel was born in Dijon in 1861. He entered the École Normale Superieure in 1881. He published his dissertation, *L'Action: Essai d'une critique de la vie et d'une science de la pratique*, in 1893. In 1895, Blondel became a professor at the University of Lille. One year later, he took a professorship the University of Aix-en-Provence, where he stayed until 1927. He lived in Aix-en-Provence until his death in 1949.

Selected Writings

L'Action. Essai d'une critique de la vie et d'une science de la pratique, Thèse de doctorat, 1893; 1950
Le Procès de l'intelligence, with Archambault, Blond and Gay (editors), 1922 *Le problème de la philosophie catholique*, Blond and Gay (editors), 1932
La Pensée, *La genèse de la pensée et les paliers de son ascension spontanée, La responsabilité de la pensée et la possibilité de son achèvement* (editor) 1934
L'Être et les êtres. Essai d'ontologie concrète et intégrale. 1935
Lutte pour la civilisation et philosophie de la paix, 1939
La Philosophie et l'esprit chrétien, *Autonomie essentielle et connexion indéclinable*, 1944,: *Conditions de la symbiose seule normale et salutaire*, 1950
La lettre, histoire et dogme, etc, 1951.

BLOY, LÉON HENRI MARIE
Essayist, novelist, journalist

Léon Bloy occupies a marginal place in the history of French literature, among poets and writers such as Nouveau, Bertrand, Lautréamont, Hello, Barbey d'Aurevilly, and Villiers de l'Isle-Adam. Either coming from atheistic or Christian backgrounds, they exploded the corrupt values of bourgeois society from within and wished for nothing less than a total collapse of the Third Republic. Anarchy (of the right mainly) or Jesus were the two options left for the renewal of a society they perceived as being irrevocably decadent and moribund: in the hands of political usurers, as Bloy would put it. Such was the mentality of Bloy in particular, traumatized by the defeat of Sedan (1870, in which he fought as a *franc tireur* [crypto-guerrilla fighters] used by the army and later criticized for being mere bandits on the loose, by Zola in *La Débâcle*, 1892), the bloody repression of the Commune (vilified by Bloy, who sided with the Versaillais, led by Thiers), and the chaotic triumph of capitalism and its bourgeois ideology. The scandal of Panama in 1898 brought the entire economic and political system into disrepute, along with the Jewish community, which suffered even more from the surge of anti-Semitism with the "*affaire Dreyfus*" (January 13, 1898 was the day when "J'accuse" was published). Bloy was quick to find a divine punishment lying behind these catastrophes.

Contrary to Zola and the other Naturalists who all believed in scientific progress, Bloy was the most virulent proponent of Catholicism as an alternative to democracy and technical progress. It is in Bloy's historical and theological writings that can be found his Catholic vision, which runs counter not only to positivist thinking (Taine, Renan, Bernard) but also to the way the Church conducted itself toward the poor. As a historian, Bloy's main model was Thomas Carlyle, whose writings he encountered through Barbey d'Aurevilly and read throughout his life (*The History of the French Revolution* was translated into French in 1865). What links the Scottish Calvinist historian to the Catholic writer is their common conception of history. The role of the historian is to interpret the "hieroglyphs" of historical events as if they were signs of a higher divine design. Both claim that poetry and imagination can help revivify the rigid facts provided by events. The historian is an inspired prophet who decodes the visible text of history in order to find the transcendent and sacred text behind it. Carlyle casts a unifying eye on the fragmentary truths provided by events, guided by imagination, using a poetic and dynamic style, in hope of finding the divine plan. For Bloy, the divine plan is taken literally, for Carlyle it was perhaps more a metaphor without resolution ("the bible of universal history," with, one suspects, Carlyle as its main prophet and God). If transcendence manifests itself in historical reality, the real agents of history are its heroes, who take over in turn the task of guiding mankind. For Carlyle, heroes are privileged mediators between divinity and Man. For Bloy, saints like Joan of Arc, Christopher Columbus, even Marie-Antoinette are akin to Christ, as they partake in the redemption of mankind, in contrast to the more transitory actions of heroes like Napoleon. "history is the unfolding of the loom of eternity under temporal and transitory eyes" (Glaudes, 1992). Bloy's historical writings are more Christocentric than egocentric. Carlyle's history is grounded in a sacred and abstract book of revelation and is based on dynamic cycles of creation and destruction, whereas Bloy's is based on Parousia, an ever-postponed second coming: "history is the story of God's efforts to lead mankind toward eternal beatitude" (Glaudes, 1992). Bloy oscillates between an apocalyptic sense of history "a torrent of blood of the innocents slaughtered in ransom for the culprits," always streaming away for Christ, and a firm belief in the good that will come out of historical catastrophes: "God is behind it all. I am convinced that everything is for the better, even though it seems for the worse" (Glaudes, 1992).

Bloy's proclivity toward pessimism is perhaps a consequence of his hatred of the French Revolution and he saw in the Third Republic a regime that was entirely deprived of spiritual values and was symbolic of the nihilistic drive behind modern society. This helps us to understand his own apparent nihilism, which was directed only toward his time but which did not reflect his belief in redemption. It also explains his pro-Semitic stance in *Le salut par les Juifs*, which goes against the grain of the spate of anti-Semitism in France between 1890 and 1940. It is a complex demonstration based on the symbol on the Holy Cross. Instead of accusing the Jews of murdering Christ, he shows that they have a crucial role to play: somehow they hold the key to the second coming of Christ. For Bloy, to give in to the anti-Semitism of Drumont and his *Libre Parole* is to deny God's will, let alone the possible reconciliation of both Testaments. Bloy proved slightly less obscurantist than Drumont, but he remained a staunch anti-Dreyfusard, which can be explained by the fact that his enemies (Zola) were Dreyfusards, with all the anti-patriotic and pro-Republican connotations entailed.

As with Céline, thirty years later—his true disciple and follower in imprecation and self-abjection, Bloy makes it a principle to hate most of the other dinosaurs of French letters, Balzac, Stendhal, Zola, and Huysmans, not to forget the now-ignored Coppée, Bourget, and France. He described himself thus: "I write pamphlets because I am forced to do so as I live in a world famished for lack of absolute realities. A writer who writes without having anything to say is a prostitute, a scoundrel [. . .] my pamphlets were born out of my shame and in the name of love, and my shouts rise, in total despair, above the carcass of my ideal." (*Le Mendiantingrat*).

Bloy published two great autobiographical novels, *Le désespéré* (1886) and *La Femme Pauvre* (1897), featuring its hero Cain Marchenoir as the mystic beggar who vilifies society and marries a prostitute who becomes mad. These two novels clearly illustrate that Bloy sides with the underdogs: "the vanquished, the cursed, the crushed, those in despair, the starving . . ." His is a rhetoric of excess, which merges virulent mysticism with the sublime and grotesque as theorized by Hugo, who was perhaps the only author who did not incur Bloy's wrath. Béguin, in a perceptive study, uncovers the founding stone of Bloy's brand of political mysticism: "a wealth of coherent symbols, the idea of salvation *via* suffering which belongs to the realm of the invisible and revives the remembrance of the Garden of Eden" (Béguin, 1950, 20). Indeed, the intersection of the visible and the invisible is crucial to Bloy, as is his favorite idea expounded by Saint Paul that the world is an inverted mirror: His key sentence could be "We see everything as a riddle and as if in a mirror" (*Le Mendiantingrat*) Bloy's style aims at exploiting this idea in various fields such as love, social injustice, race relations, and faith.

To get the best glimpse of Bloy's variegated talent, one must look at his aphorisms—often inspired by his wife (Heppenstall, 1953)—interspersed throughout his writings, as they are worthy of Wilde or Baudelaire: "Since men have refused to obey life, they must obey death" (*Mon journal*); "I pray like a thief begging a farmer for alms, while intending to burn down his farm" (*Mendiant ingrat*); or his own untranslatable definition of his highly grammatical, style: "*Le réel, c'est de trouver des épithètes homicides [. . .] il faut inventer des catachrèses qui empalent, des metonymies qui grillent les pieds, des synecdoques qui arrachent les ongles, des litotes qui écorchent vif et des hyperboles de plomb fondu*" (in Le Figaro, 1884).

HUGO AZÉRAD

See also **Albert Beguin**

Biography

Léon Henri Marie Bloy, born in 1846, came from a family of artisans, farmers, and soldiers living near Périgueux. He was brought up brutally, between his father's republicanism and his mother's piety. He was expelled from school after a knife fight, and began an apprenticeship in industrial drawing. At eighteen, having read a good deal of poetry, Bloy moved to Paris to work for an architect. It was there that he met Barbey d'Aurevilly, who led him to convert to Catholicism in 1869. Barbey would mentor Bloy in his reading, and encouraged him to become a writer and a Catholic—an uncompromising one at that. He made friends with Bourget and Gobineau, who would become his archenemies ten years later. Incapable of keeping a stable job—he corrected proofs for Barbey, worked for Veuillot's *L'Univers*, for the railways—Bloy found himself in a state of psychological and financial crisis, of fragility and poverty which plagued him all of his life.

His encounter with Anne-Marie Roulet, a former prostitute-turned-mystic, drove him away from a strict religious life and led him instead to a life devoted to writing about his vision of pure Catholicism. Women always played a crucial role for Bloy, who acknowledged their influence in his writings. Until 1890, he ceaselessly wrote essays and fiction, but failed to gain any recognition. After his second mistress, Berthe Dumont, killed herself with a dirty needle, Bloy's life reached a nadir and he started living like a tramp, completely dependent on former friends. He had a child with another mistress, the child dying at the age of twelve. In 1890 he married a cultivated Dane, Jeanne Morbech. After a short self-imposed exile to Denmark, he wrote with increasing vehemence, while begging for money to help his family subsist, at the same time suffering intense bouts of depression. In 1905, Bloy converted Jacques and Raïssa Maritain (herself Jewish), who recognized him as one of the most important religious thinkers of the time and remained his friend until his death. However, his books were still not getting any success, and they have obtained the attention they deserve only in the last forty years. He died peacefully, on November 3, 1917, with his few true friends around him, after telling his wife that he was only curious about death. His writings have steadily become influential for writers and theologians of all faiths.

Selected Works

Le désespéré, 1887
Sueur de sang, 1893
Histoires désobligeantes, 1894
La Femme pauvre, 1897
Belluaires et porchers, 1905
Le Mendiant ingrat, 1898
Mon journal, 1904
L'invendable, 1909
Le pélerin de l'absolu, 1914
Le Prince noir, 1877
Le Révélateur du globe: Christophe Colomb et sa béatification future, 1884
Les Funérailles du naturalisme, 1891
Le Salut par les Juifs, 1892
Léon Bloy devant les cochons, 1894
Je m'accuse: notes sur Emile Zola, 1900
Le Fils de Louis XVI, 1900
L'Ame de Napoléon, 1912
Jeanne d'Arc et l'Allemagne, 1915

Further Reading

Aubry, Michel, *Léon Bloy*, Les dossiers H, Lausanne: L'Age d'homme, 1990
Bardèche, Maurice, *Léon Bloy*, Paris: Table Ronde, 1989
Barthes, Roland, "Bloy" in *Le Bruissement de la langue*, Paris: Seuil, 1984
Béguin, Albert, *Léon Bloy*, Lausanne: L'Age d'homme, 1950
Glaudes, Pierre, *Léon Bloy au tournant du siècle*, Toulouse: Presses Universitaires du Mirail, 1992
Glaudes, Pierre (editor), *Léon Bloy*, Cahiers de l'Herne, Paris: L'Herne, 1988
Hubert Juin, *Léon Bloy*, Paris: Obsidiane, 1990
Heppenstall, Rayner, *Léon Bloy*, Cambridge: Bowes and Bowes, 1953
Maritain, Jacques, *Pilgrim of the Absolute*, New York: Pantheon Books, 1944

BODY

Although it would seem that no object is more banal and familiar to the individual subject than his or her body, no reality more objective and transhistorical than the givens of anatomy, and no expression of freedom more self-evident and modern than liberation of the body, most of these assumptions have been called into question and subjected to a radical critique during the last forty years in France. This questioning and theoretical preoccupation with of the body has attracted great interest. In some sense, "the body" replaced "being," "structure," and the "sign" as the most important critical term in post-1968 French thought.

The author most responsible for this change, especially in the English-speaking world, was Michel Foucault. In his work on the history of madness and disciplinary institutions, the body emerges as an object of intense control and symbolic investments. In a memorable passage at the beginning of *Discipline and Punish*, Foucault describes the torture and execution of the eighteenth-century regicide Damiens. The terrible punishments inflicted on Damien's body were not gratuitous acts of cruelty but rather a systematic display of the king's vengeance on his would-be assassin. In this and many other instances, the body is a malleable substance, made to conform to specific tasks. "The body is directly involved in a political field; power relations have an immediate hold upon it; they invest it, mark it, train it, torture it, force it to carry out tasks, to perform ceremonies, to emit signs." Foucault's work reveals a body in flux, one that has taken strange and surprising forms throughout history. Instead of being an inert, neutral dwelling place for the soul, it has constantly been shaped and distorted by a host of discourses, disciplines, and physical practices. Although torture and other abuses of the body receded during the Enlightenment, the body remained the ultimate objective of power and signification. Prisons were more concerned with rehabilitating the criminal by appeal to his mind and soul; however, as Foucault insists, "The soul is the effect and instrument of a political anatomy; the soul is the prison of the body." Foucault's lesson is that in the political field, despite an ideology of kindness and humaneness, the body is still what matters most.

Foucault's *History of Sexuality* was a primordial text in the development of body studies. The first volume of this work, published in 1976, was an attack on the Freudian thesis that sexuality has been subjected to increasing repression from the mythical origins of society, through the Greeks to the Victorians. Foucault argues in this that, on the contrary, sexuality has been under increasing obligations to reveal its secrets, starting with the Christian obligation to confess, continuing into the present with psychoanalysis and other talking cures. One of discoveries of the *History of Sexuality* was that, before the "medicalization" of sexuality in the nineteenth century, the concept of "sexuality," as we understand it, did not exist; instead there was the Christian notion of "the flesh," which did not view particular sexual acts as conferring an identity. There was no heterosexual or homosexual identity; only a set of discreet acts that was all sinful, some considered more sinful than others. Thus, sodomy, in medieval legal texts, could mean sex between men or sex with animals. Foucault's history thus overturned a literal and conventional Freudian accounts of the sexual body. The physical and mental experiences of sexuality were not universal and transhistorical. Neither in historical terms nor in individual terms did sexuality develop according to inexorable evolutionary laws.

Such ideas were tremendously influential in the rewriting of gay and women's history. Sexuality was not a "nature." The female or homosexual body was no longer considered essentially castrated or perverted or regressive. The normative male body and its psychological correlatives were recent historical constructions. For each historical period or cultural milieu, the sexual body was fashioned out of a host of medical, legal, religious, and literary texts and practices. One observes in these different experiences of the sexual body fluctuating borders between maleness and femaleness, and very different descriptive schemes for describing bodily experiences. In the field of early modern anatomy, for example, according to the "single-sex model," the female genitalia are simply an internalized version of the male organs. According to

this vision of the body and its imaginary projections, the male and female bodies are perilously similar. Under extreme conditions of exertion, a woman could expel her interior body parts and become a man. During the early modern period, following the same single-sex mentality, medical theory believed that the female orgasm was necessary for successful procreation because the female needed to ejaculate in the same fashion as the male.

The two most influential ideas propounded by Foucault were thus that the body was not a transhistorical given and that discourse about the body, even "liberatory" discourse by individuals about their bodies, had a long pre-history of use in disciplinary institutions. Foucault was preceded in postulating the general idea that the body mattered most of all in political history, and that there might be alternative ways of talking about it, in philosophy, by Nietzsche and Merleau-Ponty.

The human body was central to Nietzsche's attempt to create new, life-affirming values in Western philosophy. Following the death of God, no order seemed apparent in the universe, and no hope or meaning available in individual lives. Nietzsche did not have faith that science could fill the theological gap and provide coherent and final explanations of nature. Anticipating the continual re-theorizing of the universe in modern physics, Nietzsche viewed the cosmos as fundamentally chaotic, "*Chaos sive natura*," "the beautiful chaos of existence." The human being can make an order of this chaos, but only through the work of the body. As Eric Blondel writes in his important work, "Chaos becomes a world only through the body. . . . Prior to the body, there is no order or relation or text, and the world is the greatest possible multiplicity. A text comes into existence only through (or for) drives, which reduce this 'absolute' multiplicity. But this reduction is not, like that of the intellect, the introduction of unity; if the body interprets, it does so as affect, and if affects *interpret*, they institute a certain simplicity only in order to pluralize it." Consciousness is only one of many "intelligences" in the human body, and a simplifying form of intelligence at that. The complex life of the body is a "miracle of miracles." Consciousness, enabled by language, is just one of the miracles, "an instrument, nothing more, in the same sense in which the stomach is an instrument of the same miracle."

Traditional philosophical language constantly obscures and distorts the relation between consciousness and the body, and the body to chaos. To correct this idealizing tendency, Nietzsche constantly used bodily metaphors to describe the thought process. Thinking is really a kind of "rumination"; perception is a kind of ingestion the expression of a "will to make external things resemble us." All of life is based on a general process of "nutrition" which includes "everything we call sensation, representation, and thought." Thus Nietzsche was fond of explaining moral and intellectual positions on the basis of digestion: "The wealthy class in England has need of its Christianity in order to endure its indigestion and headaches." Such ironic remarks, although not devoid of humor, are part of Nietzsche's desire to integrate physical and mental life, to establish a new monism in response to several centuries of mind-body dualism.

In his bodily approach to human thought, Nietzsche cut a middle path between idealism and mechanism. Human thought was neither a spiritual nor purely mechanical process. Human thought is *vital*, the product of multiple intelligences working together in one body. Each of these intelligences was guided by a drive, a will to power. As we have seen, Nietzsche used the metaphor of nutrition to describe all of the assimilating drives of the human body and mind. In a final suggestive metaphor, Nietzsche compared the assimilating process to *interpretation*: "It is our needs which interpret (*auslegen*) the universe . . . The organic process presupposes a continuous activity of interpretation." It is this overriding image of the body as an interpreting agency that links Nietzsche to Freud and has proven highly suggestive in cultural and literary studies.

For Merleau-Ponty (one of Foucault's teachers), all human knowledge remains embodied and subjective. All truth derives from perception, and this situated, embodied derivation of the truth can never be overcome—neither through the scientific, empirical project of sifting out the errors of human perception and describing objects in measurable terms, nor according to the idealist approach, which insists that the mind only grasps ideas, not the distorted data of perception. All perception and ideation occurs to and for the body. We see objects as situated in a perspectival field and not that of others; the pain that we feel from a pinprick is not objectively "in" the pin, yet it does prove that all awareness that we have of the pin derives from the body. Another example of the embodiment of all ideation is the case of pain experienced by amputees in phantom limbs no longer attached to their bodies. The reason why a man who has lost a limb still feels pain in the phantom limb is that he still operates in a world where things are within arms' reach, and this physical, habitual relation to the world carries with it the habit of feeling sensation in both arms. The pain in the phantom limb is purely subjective; there is no simple neurological explanation for this phenomenon. Although Merleau-Ponty's influence was cut short by his untimely early death, and the eclipse of phenomenology by structuralism in France, there is renewed interest in

his radical philosophy of the body, particularly in the area of visual studies.

For Freud, the bodily experiences of early childhood are determinate in the life of the adult, and the body remains the most important sign of the unconscious in mental life throughout life. The first successes of the "talking cure" involved correctly interpreting hysterical symptoms by making the affected body parts "join in the conversation." By listening to his patient's speech and their free associations, Freud was able to reconstruct original scenes, which had caused the symptoms. A case of paralysis, for example, was the recurrence of a woman's arm falling asleep while caring for her father in his final illness. In addition to the treatment of hysteria, all of Freud's major theories were grounded in the persistence and significance of bodily experiences. Sexual identity followed a pathway of erogenous zones, oral, anal, and genital. The ability to symbolize and use language was derived from encounters between the child and the maternal body. The mother's presence and absence gave rise to anxiety and vocal utterance in the "*fort . . . da*" language game. The traumatic discovery of anatomical difference lead to the designation of the phallus as the symbol of all sexual difference and the general law of the signifier. Under threat of castration, the male child renounces immediate sexual goals in favor of later fulfillment. Direct conflict with the Oedipal father is avoided by the acquisition of the name of the father. The body is thus the original symbolic repertory out of which the subject is constructed. In addition, although the medium of psychoanalytic practice is language, not physical therapy, the words spoken by the patients are often read as bodily symptoms. Psychoanalysis is thus directed at a signifying body. Its therapy is neither rational and cognitive nor simply somatic. Like Nietzsche, Freud believed that the most important part of mental life was spoken through the body and that the key to integrating the self was to listen carefully to this language and learn its strange rhetoric.

The work of the most influential philosophers of the body in France (Foucault and his predecessors) has been used beyond the political and historical arena that interested Foucault. Many correlations between the religious, juridical, and medical treatment of the body and the phenomena of the body in art and literature have been investigated. The school of criticism known as new historicism has focused attention on the body and its changing status from the early modern period to the present.

One of the most interesting arguments to be advanced from such perspectives is the idea that the birth of the novel can be traced to the disciplinary practices and preoccupation with the body during the Enlightenment. The novel emerges in the mid-eighteenth century, out of a culture increasingly concerned with privacy. Paradoxically, as the body becomes increasingly hidden from view and clothed, the novel seeks to violate and reveal this new space of intimacy. Mirroring disciplinary society's obsession with identity and control grounded in the body, the plot of novels often turns on revelatory marks inscribed on the body. In *Père Goriot*, for example, Vautrin is exposed as a criminal when his shirt is removed and a brand that he acquired in prison is revealed. Vautrin's shadowy criminal activities and his troubling sexuality are controlled and neutralized because the regime has marked his body with a readable sign that its agents are able to decipher at the opportune moment. In the case of Vautrin, an ambiguous and resistant body is successfully marked by disciplinary institutions.

The literature of this period also contains instances when the body evades society's attempts to mark and control it. In the *Confessions*, Jean-Jacques Rousseau recounts an experience that was foundational for his sexual life and his whole character. At the age of eleven, he received a spanking from Mlle Lambercier, his thirty-year-old governess. Instead of producing pain and shame, this chastisement provoked an erotic response, an erection. The young Rousseau is never disciplined again in this fashion and treated henceforth as a young man. In contrast to the arrest scene in Balzac, Rousseau's body resists and re-writes an attempt to control and typify it through punishment. The young Rousseau's body literally changes the meaning of the beating by *translating* a painful punishment into a pleasurable experience. The author of the *Confessions* is himself perplexed by the involuntary action of his body. His higher consciousness, which guides the writing of the *Confessions*, records the event as a chance occurrence that defined his erotic tastes for the rest of his life. Educators and psychiatrists can ponder this event and adjust their disciplinary practices to avoid such results in the future. In a sense, physical beating is a primitive attempt to control the body and harkens back to the scene of torture and execution described by Foucault. Child rearing and pedagogy adopted the same humane and subtle treatments of the body that succeeded the cruel treatments of the *ancien régime* in the centuries following Rousseau.

The *Confessions* and other similar texts designate an area of expertise for doctors, teachers, and psychiatrists; and one can see in Rousseau an exemplary modern subject who does the subtle work of discipline by himself, by recording his most intimate experiences and creating a mysterious divided self who does not understand the strange behavior of his body. The sum of these strange behaviors is, however, the core of Rousseau's personality and the key to his existence as a writer and a reader. He reads and writes to gratify his inclinations for masochistic scenarios. As opposed to the exposé of the sinful body in Augustine's *Confessions*, Rousseau's texts exhibit a mysterious and troubling body. The novel thus reflects the historical attempt to understand and control the body, but it is also the place where the body resists, escapes, and speaks its own language.

During the past century and a half, the body has been the object of considerable efforts to understand it and control it on the part of medicine, the human sciences, and a growing array of therapists, counselors, and experts. The body has been promoted as a human capital to be exploited; the individual's most precious source of freedom and pleasure. But if the modern body is no longer subject to gross forms of punishment and repression characteristic of the *ancien régime* (and it is far from certain that the modern treatment of the body has really decreased the physical suffering of bodies in third-world factories, prisons, and armies), it has become clear, following the work of Foucault and others, that the body is the objective of more refined techniques of investigation and control. In response to this, a micro-politics of struggle for the control of one's body and the right to live unsanctioned, "abnormal" lifestyles has evolved. The battle continues, as market forces and social institutions adapt quickly to investigate and exploit new forms of bodily expression.

An extreme form of resistance to the modern politics of the body is perhaps represented by the growing interest in cyber-bodies. In cyberspace, outside the exploitive domain of "meatspace," the human spirit can dream of escaping surveillance and control. Fleeting cyber-bodies can be created and inhabited that are more difficult to track and control by disciplinary agencies. This would seem an extreme and perhaps paranoid response to the dilemma of the body, a deliberate rejection of the utopia of the physical body promoted by modern liberal societies. Yet it is an understandable attempt to escape the normalizing agenda that goes along with the acceptance and exploitation of one's physical body.

MATTHEW SENIOR

See also **Michel Foucault, Maurice Merleau-Ponty**

Further Reading

Bynum, Carolyn. "Why All the Fuss about the Body? A Medievalist's Perspective," *Critical Inquiry*, 22 (Fall 1995): 1–33

Blakemore, C., Jennet, S. *The Oxford Companion to the Body*. Oxford University Press, 2001

Blondel, Eric. *Nietzsche: The Body and Culture*, translated by Sean Hand Stanford: Stanford University Press, 1991

Brooks, Peter, *Bodywork*, Cambridge: Harvard University Press, 1994

Butler, Judith, *Bodies that Matter: On the Discursive Limits of "Sex,"* New York: Routledge, 1993

Feyer, Michel, Ramona Haddoff, Nadi Tazi (editors), *Fragments for a History the Human Body*, 3 vols., New York: Zone Books, 1989

Foucault, Michel, The History of Sexuality: An Introduction, translated by Robert Hurley, New York: Vintage, 1990

Foucault, Michel, *Discipline and Punish: The Birth of the Prison*, translated by Alan Shericd, New York: Vintage, 1995

Greenberg, Mitchell, *Baroque Bodies: Psychoanalysis and the Culture of French Absolutism*, Cornell University Press, 2001

Jacquet, C., *Le Corps*, Paris: Presses Universitaires de France, 2002

Judovitz, Dahlia, *The Culture of the Body: Genealogies of Modernity*, Michigan University Press, 2001

Laqueur, Thomas, *Making Sex Body and Gender from the Greeks to Freud*, Cambridge: Harvard University Press, 1990

Merleau-Ponty, Maurice, *The Phenomenology of Perception*, translated by Colin Smith, Routledge, 1995

Michela, Maria and Parisoli, Marzano, *Penser Le Corps*, Paris: Presses Universitaires de France, 2002

BONNEFOY, YVES
Poet

Yves Bonnefoy, born in 1923, moved from his provincial town of Tours to Paris in 1945, where he came into close contact with the surrealist group and its founder, Andre Breton. Breton founded surrealism on the idea that reality—that is *surreality*—was in fact more than what society and tradition had so far defined as actual reality, and that it was better circumscribed by the alliance of the worlds of day and night, of wakening and sleep. However, only two years later, Bonnefoy split with the surrealists due to the fact that, because of their use of analogy, they missed the "evidence," the "simple"—that is, the *world*. Bonnefoy fully analyzed these years later in life (*Entretiens sur la poésie*, A la Baconnière, 1981). However, at heart, it was a matter of shifting conceptions because the understanding of reality for Bonnefoy and Breton came from different grounds, thus engendering in each a different concept of writing. In Bonnefoy's case, metaphors, which were so prominent in surrealism, are responsible for creating a counter-world in which man enjoys wonders that keep him away from accepting this world, the one we live in.

Why should poets and men alike escape the help of imagination and stick to harsh reality? For Bonnefoy, "peace" can only be made once we have faced our condition, and by this Bonnefoy explicitly meant our "finitude" [limits]. On the contrary, metaphors tend to give all power to desires and, above all, to that of immortality and infinity. From *Du mouvement et de l'immobilité de Douve* (1953) to *Débuts et fin de la neige* (1991), the author then disciplined himself to creating a language fully aware of its dangerous powers and, because of this very awareness, capable of keeping to the "simplicity" that best defines reality. His collections of poems and essays on poetry therefore revolve to a large extent around language. Child of his century, Bonnefoy formulated a critique of language that, paradoxically, only language can solve. In other words, if the "presence" of men *in* reality has vanished, it is because of language. But this presence is still at hand for those who are able to reach, through language itself, a preconceptual stage in which the once-natural link of words and things is restored (*La vérité de parole*, 1988). This stage has a name: poetry.

For these reasons, when *Du mouvement et de l'immobilité de Douve* was published, critics saw in Bonnefoy an important rejuvenator of French poetry. At this time, surrealism and "*poésie engagée*" had lost their initial influence and, together with Bonnefoy, significant new voices insisted on the importance of going back towards the sensitive world: Jacques Dupin, Philippe Jacotte, and André du Bouchet, for example. Jean-Michel Maulpoix, writer and contemporary French poetry, referred to this generation by the name of "*habiter*" (to live), because their aim was to live in the *real* world. In this respect, contrary to the city-orientated lives and books of surrealists (Louis Aragon, *Le paysan de Paris*; André Breton, *Nadja*; Paul Eluard, *Capitale de la douleur*; Marcel Raymond Queneau, *Zazie dans le métro*), Bonnefoy often spent time, and even lived, in the countryside, be it the Lot, Tourraine, or the Ardèche.

Bonnefoy has broken free from the immediate artistic past and has since tried to reach back to the "*vrai lieu*" (true place) where the infinite arises through the finite. This search has taken him across the entire scope of arts and ideas, from Italy and Holland to India, Japan, Iran, and Cambodia; from baroque and Renaissance to modern times; from Shakespeare and Yeats (he is a reknowned translator of both) to Celan, Balthus, Alechinski, and Giacometti. His varied interests, deep insights, and rich ideas convinced several famous universities to appoint him as a lecturer (Princeton, Harvard, Geneva) and, he was given the "*Chaire d'Etudes comparées de la Fonction poétique*" (Chair of comparative studies of the poetic function) at the Collège de France in 1981.

Bonnefoy never took part in the formalism that characterized French poetry from the start of the 1960s to the beginning of the 1980s. Once again, under the influence of structuralism (prominent in philosophy, science, and social sciences), the aim of poetry shifted, toward language itself this time. Radicalizing some of the logic positivists' assertions, poetry cut off its links with the outside world and became essentially interested in itself. This trend started with poets such as Michel Deguy, Denis Roche, the group Oulipo, the journal *Tel Quel*, and reached an extreme in the 1970s in the works of Jean Daive, Bernard Heidsieck, Anne-Marie Albiach, and Emmanuel Hocquard, who translated and introduced United States objectivist poets such as Oppen and Deznikoff to France. Along with the Italian *Trans-avanguardia* and the works of Jean-François Lyotard (*La condition postmoderne*, 1979), among others, on postmodernism, the 1980s witnessed the rise of "New lyricism" in French poetry. The expression describes a return to the individual, analogy, musicality, emotion, and a certain synthesis between tradition and modernity. Guy Goffette, André Velter, and James Sacré, for example, wished to produce a simpler kind of poetry and advocated the importance of everyday life. In this respect, these poets seem closer to the ideas of Bonnefoy, but in fact the world in his work, the "*lieu*" (place), is mainly essentialized, whereas it can be almost straightforward in the poems of the new generation.

Bonnefoy is constantly looking for the detail, in the painting or the poem, that shows that art is somehow able to meet with the "absolute," that is, the world. However, isolated in French twentieth-century poetry, he finds an expression of his unending search for a language freed from language in the plays of Shakespeare, the works of Giacometti, or the art-life of A.D. 1630 Rome. Besides, connections can be made between some of his claims and ideas linking modern and ancient philosophy: indeed, Bonnefoy's conceptions show various similarities with the work of Heidegger, Clément Rosset, or Marcel Conche, which all go back, for different reasons, to the pre-Socratics. Put otherwise, what seems to be at work here is a kind of ageless wisdom.

DENIS LEJEUNE

See also **Andre Breton, Jean-Francois Lyotard, Marcel Raymond**

Biography

Yves Bonnefoy was born in 1923. In 1945, he moved from his native town of Tours to Paris. In Paris, he associated with the surrealists, although he ultimately rejected them, disassociating himself from them two years later. He published his first book of poems, *Du mouvement et de l'immobilité de Douve*, in 1953. He edited *Mythologies*, a scholarly two-volume work with essays on myths from around the world, authored by approximately 100 French authors (an English translation was published in 1991). His *New and Selected Poems* was published in 1996.

Selected Writings

Poèmes, Mercure de France 1978
Ce qui fut sans lumière, Mercure de France 1987
Un rêve fait à Mantoue, Mercure de France 1967
Le Nuage rouge, Mercure de France 1977
L'Ordalie, Galerie Maeght 1975
Macbeth, Mercure de France 1983
L'Arrière-pays, Gallimard 1998

Further Reading

Finck Michèle, *Yves Bonnefoy, le simple et le sens*, José Corti, 1989 Paris
Gasarian Gérard, *Yves Bonnefoy: la poésie, la présence*, Champ Vallon, 1986 Senegal
Jackson John E., *Yves Bonnefoy*, Seghers, 1976 Paris
Ravaud Jacques (editor), *Yves Bonnefoy*, Le temps qu'il fait, 1998 Cognac
Richard Jean-Pierre, *Onze études sur la poésie contemporaine*, Seuil, 1981 Paris
www. maulpoix.net/diversite.html

BOURDIEU, PIERRE
Sociologist

In the course of a publishing career lasting just over thirty years, Pierre Bourdieu established himself as the most influential French sociologist of the postwar generation. His output was characterized by its impressive range, encompassing the sociology of education, theories of social class, socio-linguistics, the sociology of cultural production and reception, the sociology of intellectuals, and anthropological studies of the pre-capitalist society of Kabylia, Algeria. In the course of his empirical researches into all of these domains, Bourdieu forged a set of distinctive concepts—"habitus," "field," "practice," "symbolic capital," "symbolic violence"—that laid the foundations for an overarching social theory he once characterized as "a general theory of the economy of practices," but which is often simply referred to as "field theory." In the last decades of his life, Bourdieu increasingly sought to use the authority conferred upon him by his detailed sociological work as the basis for more directly political interventions, adopting the role of a public intellectual to speak out against the destructive social effects of neoliberal economic dogma. Such interventions were not always warmly received, with some critics claiming that Bourdieu's politics were as dogmatic and divorced from current realities as his social theory had become. Whatever the validity of such criticisms, their very vehemence paradoxically attested to the continuing influence of Bourdieu's thought, both within the "restricted field" of intellectual production and in the broader political and social fields that lay outside it.

At the core of Bourdieu's "general theory of the economy of practices" lies a series of fundamental principles, of assumptions about the social world. The first of these is that nearly all social practices involve the possibility for agents to accrue material profits or to suffer material losses. Furthermore, the profits and losses are not reducible to the workings of the cash economy proper. The social world is characterized by struggles for the conservation, and accumulation of specific forms of "capital," forms of "symbolic capital" whose nature and logic remains distinct from "economic capital," yet which can be "reconverted" into "economic capital" at a historically determined, and hence constantly shifting, "rate of exchange." Second, in advanced capitalist societies such struggles to accumulate and conserve these forms of "symbolic capital" are played out in any one of a series of "semi-autonomous fields"—the "intellectual field," the "political field," the "literary field," the "judicial field," the "religious field"—each of which generates its own specific form of capital—"intellectual capital," "literary capital," and so on. Indeed, Bourdieu's output might be read as a series of attempts to define these different forms of "symbolic capital," to trace the "structure and historical genesis" of the various "fields" in which such "capital" is on offer, to explain why different social classes and fractions possess such "capital" in differing forms and amounts, and how this contributes to the reproduction of class divisions in society. Finally, he examines how certain historical developments have led to changes in the relative value of each of those forms of "capital," changes in the "rate of exchange" between "cultural capital" and "economic capital," for example.

In his work in the sociology of education and culture of the 1960s and 1970s, Bourdieu was concerned with the role of "cultural" and "educational capital" in the reproduction of class divisions and distinctions. His empirical research into French higher education, in *Les Héritiers* (*The Inheritors*, 1964) and *La Reproduction* (*Reproduction in Education, Culture and Society*, 1970), and into European art galleries, in *L'Amour de l'art* (*The Love of Art*, 1966), attributed the strong statistical correlation between social class and either academic success, or the tendency to visit art galleries to the determining role of the "habitus." The "habitus" is a structure of incorporated dispositions, a set of anticipations and expectations, of tastes and aversions picked up from earliest childhood and hence heavily determined by social milieu. It was the "bourgeois habitus" that disposed bourgeois adolescents to consider university to be a natural or inevitable destination, while endowing them with the modes of speech, the categories of thought and action that the university recognized and rewarded as signs of inherent intellectual ability. Thus, Bourdieu argued that the primary function of education and high or "legitimate culture" was

to naturalize, legitimize, and reproduce class distinctions.

If his early work on education and culture had revealed the importance of "symbolic," rather than purely economic forms of capital in the reproduction of class divisions in the West, Bourdieu's anthropological studies of Kabylia offered the chance to examine a "pre-capitalist" society in which, in the absence of monetary exchange, only "symbolic capital" could be accumulated. In his two monographs on Kabylia, *Esquisse d'une théorie de la pratique* (*Outline of a Theory of Practice*, 1972) and *Le Sens pratique* (*The Logic of Practice*, 1980), Bourdieu could thus refine the conceptual tools he would subsequently use to elucidate the role and logic of "symbolic" forms of capital in the West. These anthropological studies also enabled Bourdieu to elaborate the concept of "habitus" into a fully-developed "theory of practice," an account of structure and agency which aimed to overcome the very opposition between object and subject, structure and agency by locating and working through the limitations of Sartre's subjectivist existential phenomenology and Lévi-Strauss's objectivist structural anthropology. According to this theory, Kabyles who accumulated "symbolic capital" through gift exchange or judicious "matrimonial strategies" were neither mutely submitting to the structural laws governing kinship and gift exchange nor were they making free rational choices as to the most profitable "strategy" to pursue. Rather, their "strategies" reflected their "pre-reflective" or "practical" investment in the stakes of the Kabyle social field, an almost intuitive "feel for the game," a "practical sense" of which moves would prove most profitable, which had been incorporated into their "habitus" at the level of embodied affect, "on the hither side of words or concepts."

Bourdieu argued that *Le Sens pratique* and his immense study of taste, class, and lifestyle in France, *La Distinction* (*Distinction*, 1979), should be seen as two complementary books. In *La Distinction*, he applied his "theory of practice" to an analysis of postwar French society, a society, that is, characterized by the existence of a range of differentiated semi-autonomous fields within which agents competed for specific forms of capital. Social classes, and the different fractions making up those classes, were defined not merely in terms of the amount of their economic capital but also of the amount and different forms of "symbolic capital" they possessed. Here Bourdieu rehearsed his earlier point about the role played by "linguistic" and "cultural capital" in the reproduction of class distinctions. However, the model of society contained in *La Distinction* was by no means static. In pursuing their various "strategies" in the particular "fields" they invested, in struggling to conserve or accumulate their stocks of, say, "cultural capital," agents and groups were also struggling to impose new definitions of just what would count as "legitimate culture." In particular, Bourdieu identified a struggle between two fractions of the "dominant class" over the dominant definition of "legitimate culture," a struggle between the intelligentsia, who were wedded to a *belle-lettriste* conception of culture, and a "progressive," cosmopolitan, commercially-minded fraction of the bourgeoisie, who were seeking to impose a kind of international business culture. In his later *La Noblesse d'état* (*The State Nobility*, 1989), Bourdieu traced the effects of this struggle into the field of French higher education, noting the relative decline of those *grandes écoles* that stood for a traditional humanist education in the face of the rise of more technocratic or commercially-oriented *écoles*. Moreover, in light of the role the *grandes écoles* play in training France's top civil servants, Bourdieu argued that the rise of these commercially-oriented *écoles* challenged the disinterested public-service ethos at the core of the civil service, threatening to bring the logic of the commercial world with its narrow and partial interests, into the heart of State institutions charged with working in the universal interest.

Both *La Distinction* and *La Noblesse d'état* had, therefore, begun to trace the rise of those social fractions and institutions that would promote the neo-liberal agenda against which Bourdieu's political interventions would be directed in the last decades of his life. Bourdieu's contributions to *La Misère du monde* (*The Weight of the World*, 1993), an extensive collaborative study of contemporary forms of social exclusion, examined the destructive effects of neo-liberal policy on some of France's most vulnerable social groups. Even *Les Règles de l'art* (*The Rules of Art*, 1992), a detailed study of the nineteenth-century French literary and artistic fields, formed part of this political agenda. An account of the struggles of Flaubert, Manet, and Baudelaire to achieve artistic autonomy, it was also an attempt to "rediscover the forgotten or repudiated principles of intellectual freedom," threatened by the increasing dominance of the "heteronomous" forces of media and market over the once relatively autonomous "field of intellectual and artistic production." This concern with the threat posed to intellectual autonomy by the power of the media and the market was to be echoed in the polemical pamphlet *Sur la télévision* (*On Television and Journalism*), which Bourdieu published in 1996. *Sur la télévision* was the first in a series of such pamphlets published in the "Liber-Raison d'agir" series, a series established by Bourdieu precisely to allow him and those researchers with whom he felt an intellectual and political affinity to communicate their ideas to the broadest possible audience. Bourdieu himself published two further books in the series, *Contre-feux* (*Acts of Resistance*, 1998) and *Contre-feux 2* (2001), collections of political speeches and articles that testify both to the energy of his interventions against neo-liberalism and, by the diversity of their locations, to the global influence of his ideas. When Bourdieu died in January 2002, he left behind him not only an immense body of work but also a model of detailed, engaged, and often collaborative sociological practice.

JEREMY F. LANE

See also **Clause Levi-Strauss, Jean-Paul Sartre**

Biography

Pierre Bordieu was born August 1, 1930 in the Béarn village of Lasseube. He attended, and excelled academically, at the École Normale Supérieure. He joined the military and was sent to Algeria in 1955. He stayed after his tour of duty to teach at the University of Algiers. He began teaching at the École des Hautes Études in 1964. In 1981, he was named chair of sociology at the Collège de France. He was featured in the award-winning film, *Sociology is a Marital Act,* in 2000. Bordieu died in January 2002.

Selected Works

Les Héritiers: les étudiants et la culture, with J. C. Passeron, 1964; as *The Inheritors: French Students and Their Relation to Culture,* translated by Richard Nice, 1979

L'Amour de l'art: les musées d'art européen et leur public, with A. Darbel, 1966; as *The Love of Art: European Art Museums and Their Public,* translated by C. Beattie and N. Merriman, 1991

La Reproduction: éléments pour une théorie du système d'enseignement, with J. C. Passeron, 1970; as *Reproduction in Education, Culture and Society,* translated by Richard Nice, 1977

Esquisse d'une théorie de la pratique, 1972; significantly modified, as *Outline of a Theory of Practice,* translated by Richard Nice, 1977

La Distinction: critique sociale du jugement, 1979; as *Distinction: A Social Critique of the Judgement of Taste,* translated by Richard Nice, 1984

Le Sens pratique, 1980; as *The Logic of Practice,* translated by Richard Nice, 1990

La Noblesse d'état: grandes écoles et esprit de corps, 1989; as *The State Nobility,* translated by L. C. Clough, 1996

Les Règles de l'art: génèse et structure du champ littéraire, 1992; as *The Rules of Art: The Genesis and Structure of the Literary Field,* translated by S. Emmanuel, 1996

La Misère du monde, 1993; as *The Weight of the World,* translated by P. P. Fergusson, 2000

Sur la television, 1996; as *On Television and Journalism,* translated by P. P. Fergusson, 1998

Contre-feux: propos pour servir à la résistance contre l'invasion né-olibérale, 1998; as *Acts of Resistance: Against the New Myths of Our Time,* translated by Richard Nice, 1998

Further Reading

Brown, Nicholas, Szeman, Imre (editors), *Pierre Bourdieu: Fieldwork in Culture*, New York and Oxford: Rowman and Littlefield, 2000

Jenkins, Richard, *Pierre Bourdieu*, London: Routledge, 1992

Lane, Jeremy F., *Pierre Bourdieu: A Critical Introduction*, London and Sterling, Virginia: Pluto Press, 2000

Swartz, David, *Culture and Power: The Sociology of Pierre Bourdieu*, London and Chicago: University of Chicago Press, 1997

BRETON, ANDRÉ
Poet

Although Breton was described by Leon Edel as the man "who more than any one in the world of art and literature sounded the depths of the twentieth-century imagination," his formal education in philosophy did not continue beyond his schooldays. His philosophy teacher was the positivist André Cresson, whom he recalls being particularly sarcastic about Hegel. The very eclectic range of reference in his writings, from Berkeley to Sade, from Raymond Lulle to Lenin, demonstrates, however, that he continued throughout his life to approach from different angles problems that have intrigued thinkers throughout the ages. His medical studies exposed him to the ideas of Freud, whose influence would prove crucial in his establishment of the theoretical basis of surrealism. Nonetheless he seems to have decided at a very early age that his true vocation was to be a poet, and he quickly realized that the crux of the problem was the nature of inspiration. His reading of Rimbaud and Lautréamont above all focused his attention on lyricism: one evening in 1919 he was struck by the nature of strange phrases that would come to him out of the blue as he was about to fall asleep. Rich in imagery and perfectly correct grammatically, their poetic potential was immediately apparent and they led Breton and Philippe Soupault to evolve a mode of automatic writing that resulted in their joint publication of *Les Champs magnétiques* (1919–20), which is widely regarded as the first surrealist text. The desire to access the subconscious led to experimentation with, for example, hypnosis and dream-narration. The *Manifeste du surréalisme* (1924) set out the movement's founding ideas, but perhaps inevitably it is by no means a complete or discursive presentation of his thought, which continued to evolve.

Its provocative starting-point was a profound skepticism about realism, logic, and the rationalism that had dominated Western philosophy since the Renaissance. He saw his stance as "absolute nonconformism." In such a climate Freud's discoveries opened up new possibilities, and Breton's response was to highlight the potential offered not only by dreams but also by the imagination and "*le merveilleux*" ("the supernatural" or "the magical," as well as "the marvelous"). In the domain of aesthetics, he pinned his hopes on the image, the more surprising and irrational the better. At the heart of the project was a fundamental re-examination of language, its origins, its nature, its function, its shortcomings (its inherent inadequacies as a tool of communication), and its achievements and potential (in poetry especially). This first *Manifeste* also contains Breton's famous epistemological "definitions" of surrealism: "Pure psychic automatism by which it is proposed to express, whether verbally or in writing or in any other manner, thought's true *modus operandi*; The dictation of thought, in the absence of any check exerted by reason, without any aesthetic or moral preoccupation.

ENCYCL. Philos. Surrealism is based on the belief in the higher reality of certain hitherto neglected forms of association, in the omnipotence of dream, in the disinterested play of thought. It tends to ruin definitively all other psychic mechanisms and to act as a substitute for them in the solution of life's main problems."

In the years that followed, his linguistic revolution went hand in hand with an awareness of the need for a social revolution. He began reading Marx (*The Holy Family, Poverty of Philosophy*, rather than *Capital*), Engels (*Anti-Dühring*), and Lenin (*Materialism and Empiric-criticism*), not to mention Hegel (*Phenomenology of Mind*) and Trotsky. When he joined the Communist Party in 1927, he was soon disillusioned by the nature of the tasks he was allotted (for example, compiling economic statistics rather than ideological matters proper) but a series of meetings with Trotsky while on a lecture tour of Mexico in 1938 were much more positive.

The philosophical background to his dealings with the Communists is one of the aspects of the *Second Manifeste du surréalisme* (1930), but this text is arguably more interesting for the way in which it steered surrealism in the direction of occultism. Breton's thinking began to take on many of the features of the subsequent New Age movements: in the *Second Manifeste* itself he discusses astrology, psychical research (including extrasensory perception), and alchemy. He proclaims "surrealist research and alchemical research are remarkably analogous as far as their goals are concerned" (*Manifestes*). He was later to spell out that the Great Work entailed an "inner revolution" (*Entretiens*).

Breton's study of alternative belief-systems lies behind his lifelong interest in tribal art, especially that of Oceania. His distrust of Western values led him to conclude his "*Introduction au discours sur le peu de réalité*" (1924) with a fervent invocation of the Orient;

his stay in the United States during the Second World War allowed him to study Hopi and Zuñi civilization at close hand and to develop an interest in Inuit art. This was to culminate in the writing (with Gérard Legrand) of *L'Art magique* (1957), an encyclopedic survey of the links between art and magic across the ages.

Ferdinand Alquié has claimed that surrealism represented in the history of humanism "the most daring, the most total project that has ever been conceived to restore to man all his right to happiness and the free deployment of his passions" (*Philosophie du surréalisme*). It involved *inter alia* a celebration of love, desire and revolt. Breton coined the concepts of *convulsive beauty* ("convulsive beauty will be erotic-veiled, exploding-fixed, magic-circumstantial, or it will not be") and *objective chance* ("the form of manifestation of exterior necessity working its way into man's subconscious"). The chance discovery in New York of the complete works of Fourier was the spur to a long poem, the *Ode à Charles Fourier* (1947), which combines reference and allusion to aspects of the nineteenth-century Utopian philosopher's system with reflections on the contemporary world, including the atomic bomb. *Arcane 17* (1945) too is a meditative response to the end of the war in which the difference between liberation and liberty is analyzed: the former is compared with struggle against sickness whereas the latter is presented in terms of health. A brighter future for women is envisaged in this text, even though Simone de Beauvoir would criticize its ongoing view of the "second sex" as the "Other" (*The Second Sex*, 1988).

Though it would be attacked by Camus in *L'Homme révolté*, Breton's almost Luciferian stance of revolt continued in the postwar period. His internationalism was demonstrated by his support for Garry Davis's Citizens of the World movement. He died two years too early to be able to witness his role as a guru for the Paris students in May 1968.

KEITH ASPLEY

See also **Simone de Beauvoir**

Biography

Born in Tinchebray in 1896, André Breton studied medicine in Paris, and during World War I worked in a military hospital. Breton became interested in Dadaism in 1919, but recognized its limitations by 1922. His studies of Freud, and his experiments with automatic writing influenced his formulation and development of surrealism. He helped found and edit the first surrealist periodical, *Littérature*. He published the first *Surrealist Manifesto* in 1924, joined the Communist Party in 1927, and published *Nadja* in 1928. (He helped found and edit the first surrealist periodical, *Littérature*.) He

published the second *Surrealist Manifesto* in 1930. With Trotsky and Diego Rivera, he founded the International Federation of Independent Revolutionary Art in 1938. The third *Surrealist Manifesto* appeared in 1942. Breton died in 1966.

Selected Works

Manifestes du surréalisme, 1962, 1985
Les Vases communicants, 1932, 1955
Arcane 17, 1945
Entretiens, 1952
Oeuvres complètes, 3 vols, 1988, 1992, 1999

Further Reading

Alquié, Ferdinand, *Philosophie du surréalisme*, Paris: Flammarion, 1955
Balakian, Anna, *André Breton, Magus of Surrealism*, New York: Oxford University Press, 1971
Fotiade, Ramona (editor), *André Breton—The Power of Language*, Exeter: Elm Bank Publications, 2000
Legrand, Gérard, "Un non-anti-philosophe," in *André Breton ou le surréalisme, même*, edited by Marc Saporta and Henri Béhar, Lausanne: Editions l'Age d'Homme, 1988

BREUIL, HENRI
Anthropologist

Henri Breuil dominated the study of Palaeolithic cave art in France for almost fifty years. "With his [Breuil's] death in 1961, the world lost the man who alone was responsible for more documentation of Palaeolithic art than all other workers put together" (Ucko and Rosenfeld 1967). Breuil's major work *Four hundred centuries of cave art* presented records made by Breuil and his contemporaries in over ninety caves in France and Spain. Breuil's copious drawings have profoundly influenced our image of the art.

Art is now considered one of the defining traits of anatomically modern humans, but at the start of the twentieth century it was considered more a mark of civilization. Most archaeologists refused to accept that the cave paintings at Altamira in northern Spain, discovered in 1879, could have been created by Stone Age hunter-gatherers. The paintings discovered in 1896 at La Mouthe, in the Dordogne, were met with equal skepticism. Breuil was among the first to accept that they were genuine. The year before Carthaillac famously apologized for having refused to accept the authenticity of Palaeolithic art, Capitan and Breuil had already published a preliminary report on the paintings and engravings of Les Combarelles and Font de Gaume (see Breuil 1952; Ucko and Rosenfeld 1967).

At the start of his career, Breuil was therefore faced with two problems. One was to date the art, and relate it to the sequence of material cultures found while excavating rock shelters. The other was to explain why supposedly primitive people (the first anatomically modern humans to enter Europe) had produced such sophisticated art. The idea of art for art's sake was soon rejected on the grounds that many paintings and engravings were difficult to reach, deep underground, and that hunter-gatherers would lack the time to paint purely for the sake of aesthetic contemplation. Breuil and others therefore turned to the available documentary evidence for art in small-scale societies and philosophical thinking on the evolution of human thought. By 1912, Breuil had defined the basic sequence of stone and bone tools in the Upper Palaeolithic. He identified three main stages, the Aurignacian, Solutrian, and Magdalenian, and later adopted Perony's argument that another stone tool tradition, the Perigordian, co-existed with the Aurignacian (Ucko and Rosenfeld 1967). This sequence is still broadly accepted.

Breuil approached the problem of dating from three angles. Carved portable objects and engraved fragments of rock wall were found in excavations, alongside stone tools diagnostic of particular stages in the Upper Palaeolithic. Breuil supplemented this evidence with a developmental model borrowed from art history. The Aurignacian/Perigordian cycle began with hand stencils, then developed into elementary animal figures and geometric "signs." "Barbarously" painted animals give way to sophisticated bichrome figures in red and black that reached a peak of sophistication at Lascaux. This first cycle was largely characterized by a twisted perspective, whereby horns and hoofs are depicted frontally, but the body of the animal from the side. In order to accommodate the evidence from excavations, Breuil had to propose a second cycle played out through the Solutrian and Magdalenian, which partially recapitulated the first but was distinguishable because artists had now mastered correct perspective. The second cycle culminated in the "very clever" black shaded paintings seen at Niaux (French Pyrenees), and the polychrome bison at Altamira (Breuil 1952).

Breuil ingeniously derived an absolute chronology by plotting the movement of Magdalenian sites into areas that became accessible with the retreat of glaciers, giving him a date of around 15,000 years before present for the final Upper Palaeolithic. Aurignacian deposits were contemporary with animals found in cold climates, implying the deposits were formed at the height of the last glaciation. "To attribute them 30- to 40,000 years" he concluded, "seems to be a very moderate average estimate" (Breuil 1952). Radiocarbon dating has since shown Breuil's absolute dating

to be broadly correct, but demolished his stylistic sequence. The youngest directly dated painting is a large horse from Le Portel, Ariège, at 11,600 plus or minus 150 years before present (see Chauvet et al. 1996). Niaux and Altamira prove (as Breuil anticipated) to be more or less contemporary, with at least some paintings created around 13,000 years ago. The earliest direct date so far obtained, 32,410 plus or minus 720 years before present, comes from a rhinoceros at Chauvet cave in the Ardèche. The paintings at Chauvet are, remarkably, as sophisticated as any found at later Upper Palaeolithic sites. The first radiocarbon date for excavated deposits at Lascaux (c. 15,000 B.P.) became available shortly before Breuil published *Four hundred centuries*, but he refused to accept it since the twisted perspective seen in numerous figures led him to attribute the art to the Aurignacian/Perigordian cycle.

At the start of the twentieth century, the best ethnographic work available on hunter-gatherers was that of Spencer and Gillen in central Australia. Spencer and Gillen were in correspondence with Durkheim in France, and Frazer in England. Following Frazer and Reinach, Breuil was impressed by the part that rock paintings in central Australia played in "increase ceremonies," designed to increase the numbers of a clan's totemic species such as "witchetty grub" or "red kangaroo" (Spencer and Gillen 1899). Influenced by Comte's philosophical notions about the evolution of human thought from magic through religion to science, Breuil regarded most paintings as magical in purpose. The production of paintings of game animals would have a direct effect on the success of the hunt. This explained the supposed presence of weapons placed against the bodies of animals, and the apparently random accumulation of figures over time. It could also explain why many figures were deep underground. Rectangular "signs" were interpreted as traps or huts, perhaps shrines to spirits. Breuil's assumptions about stylistic evolution led him to construe many ambiguous or obscure figures as primitive attempts at drawing animals, and stray lines tended to represent weapons symptomatic of homeopathic magic (Layton 1991).

By the 1950s, anthropology had advanced considerably. Shortly before Breuil's death, younger archaeologists proposed a radically different approach to the significance of Upper Palaeolithic cave art. Laming and Leroi-Gourhan argued that figures were not distributed at random through the caves and that the juxtaposition of different species expressed cognitive oppositions in Palaeolithic culture. Leroi-Gourhan claimed to have found the means to interpret these oppositions in the "signs" that Breuil construed as weapons or huts (Laming 1959, Leroi-Gourham 1958). Although these archaeologists' particular interpretations have since been rejected, there is no doubt that only a few of the possible pairings of species actually occur in Upper Palaeolithic caves (Sauvet and Wlodarczyk 2000–1). The currently most popular theory of Upper Palaeolithic art—that it is the product of shamanism—relies, however, on a method similar to Breuil's. A ubiquitous mode of cognition among hunter-gatherers (altered states of consciousness) is postulated by citing examples from contemporary cultures. The presence of art deep in the caves, the occurrence of composite human-animal forms, and simple "signs" resembling those experienced when entering trance are argued to show shamanic practices during the Upper Palaeolithic (Clottes and Lewis-Williams 1996).

ROBERT LAYTON

Biography

Henri Breuil, who was born in 1877, died in 1961. He was an Honorary Professor at the Collège de France.

Further Readings

Breuil, H., *Four hundred centuries of cave art*, translated by M. Boyle. Montignac: Centre d'Études et de Documentation Préhistoriques, 1952

Chauvet, J-M, E. B. Deschamps and C. Hillaire, *Chauvet cave: the discovery of the World's oldest paintings*, translated by P. Bahn. London: Thames and Hudson, 1996

Clottes, J. and D. Lewis-Williams, *Les chamanes de la préhistoire*, Paris: Seuil, 1996

Laming, A., *Lascaux*, Paris: Voici Science Information, 1959

Layton, R., "Figure, motif and symbol in the hunter-gatherer rock art of Europe and Australia," in *Rock art and prehistory*, edited by P. Bahn and A. Rosenfeld, Oxford: Oxbow, 1991

Leroi-Gourhan, A., "La fonction des signes dans les sanctuaires paléolithiques," *Bulletin de la Société Préhistorique Française*, 55: (1958): 307–321.

Leroi-Gourhan, A., "Le symbolisme des grands signes dans les sanctuaires paléolithiques," *Bulletin de la Société Préhistorique Française*, 55 (1958): 384–398.

Sauvet, G. and A. Wlodarczyk, "L'art pariétal, miroir des sociétés paléolithiques" *Zephyrus* (University of Salamanca) 53–53 (2000–1): 217–240.

Spencer, B. and F. J. Gillen, *The native tribes of central Australia*, London: Macmillan, 1899

Ucko, P. and A. Rosenfeld, *Palaeolithic cave art*, London: Weidenfeld and Nicolson, 1967

BRUNSCHVICG, LÉON
Philosopher

Léon Brunschvicg was *Maître de Conférences* and Professor of the History of Modern Philosophy at the University of Paris (Sorbonne), where he advanced the already prominent role of philosophy in the French educational system—notably as president of the jury supervising the *concours d'agrégation* (examinations for the degree required for a state-assigned teaching position). Well-known for his edition of Pascal and his studies of Descartes and Spinoza, he was respected for an idealist philosophy that placed science foremost in the history of ideas. Although Brunschvicg's *l'idéalisme critique* (critical idealism) recalls a Kantian critique of the necessary conditions of experience, he was more directly influenced by two nineteenth-century idealist traditions in France, one epistemological, the other metaphysical. Of the epistemologists, Charles Renouvier added finality, personality, and freedom of choice of Kant's categories of the understanding. The metaphysical group extolled a unified, purposive mind or self as freely creative, "an existence from which all other existence derive" (Félix Ravaisson).

Reflecting this complex background, Brunschvicg maintains that the interwoven histories of science and philosophy disclose the inventive vitality of mind as it immanently and progressively constitutes knowledge and moral self-awareness. *La Modalité du judgement* [1897; The Modality of Judgement], originally Brunschvicg's doctoral thesis, defines judgments as a unifying affirmation essential to thought. "The subject is he who judges, and to judges, and to judge is an act. The subject is activity." One judges that something is the case either by reflection on the relation between ideas (the "form the interiority") or in response to a "shock of reality," a self-imposed restraint through which a state of affairs is recognized as given (the "form of exteriority"). In *Les Étapes de la philosophie mathématique* [1912; Stages of Mathematical Philosophy], Brunschvicg interprets mathematical judgment as the highest expression of the form of interiority, yet inseparable from experience in its synthesizing task of assimilating being to the understanding. The Fichtean theme of limiting conditions the form of exteriority—is developed in *L'Expérience humaine et la causalité physique* [1922; Human Experience and Physical Causality], an historical analysis defending the continuous spontaneity of scientific invention against the claim that the nature of science can be determined from its present state. Le Progrès de la conscience dans la philosophie occidentable [1927; The Progress of Consciousness in Western Philosophy] is Brunschvicg's magnum opus, a history of philosophy (favoring Plato, Descartes, and Kant) intended to substantiate his thesis that in constituting intelligible order over the centuries, mind has also guided mankind's advance toward conscientious judgement and choice.

In adding a moral dimension to cognition, here and throughtout this work, Brunschvicg is aided by the double meaning of *la conscience*, which translates as both "consciousness" and "conscience," and by the fact that *l'esprit* means both "mind" and "spirit." Moreover, by distinguishing between *l'humanité idéale* (ideal humanity) and *l'humanité concrète* (concrete humanity), he is able to assert that the spiritual unity he envisions for mankind is not compromised by the actual beliefs and practices of a particular era. "The curve of human knowledge has an intrinsic significance," orienting mankind toward its ultimate goal as a community of rational beings. What remains problematic is not Brunschvicg's Socratic thesis of moral and epistemic parity, elaborated through immense erudition, but his evocation of mind—the term is never capitalized—as both individual and universal subject. The latter is said to be a vital force operating through but not to be identified with a succession of actual embodied minds. Why then refuse to call it transcendent? The answer seems to be that recognition of universal mind occurs or an entirely natural plane: "total knowledge" of the positive record allows one to recognize an immanent "rhythm of progress" operating throughout the history of intellectual achievement. Thus because the question is epistemological, not metaphysical, there is no reason to look toward a power superior to that of humanity at its best. Still, a critic may observe that Brunschvicg, who denies any encounter with the absolute, nevertheless employs a metaphysical vocabulary open to implications of a transcendent subject.

A related issue is bound to arise, once mind is defined as an activity apart from the particular choices of scientist and layman alike: are individuals free or determined? A possible inference, after all, is that the individual is merely the agent of universal mind. For Brunschvicg, however, the traditional opposition of freedom and determinism is mistaken; he writes that the "labor" of Western philosophy since Pythagoras and Socrates "is a question of understanding the affirmation of freedom, not as a thing which would be given to us, but as a work which is to be made." His distinction is between free will (*libre arbitre*) "given as a thing cut out of the discontinuity of becoming," that is, abstracted from natural and historical process, and freedom as a response to novel circumstance, unhindered by rigid methodology or (as in organized religion) fixed doctrine and ritual (*Le Progrès de la conscience*). Getting one's bearings within this idealist or spiritualist context is especially difficult because it is conceivable that Brunschvicg believed his reading of philosophical history to be reflexively disclosed and validated. Engaged in the progress of consciousness—not viewing it from the sidelines—he may have introduced his own understanding into the historical process.

In any case, a more concrete issue—science as the cornerstone of his thought—was of primary interest of his contemporaries. Dominique Parodi labeled Brunschvicg's philosophy of science a *positivisme idéa-*

liste (idealist positivism) and suggested that it has suppressed "every classical problem of interpretation" from "space and number" to "the nature of the real in its rapport with mathematics." Moreover, rejection of "a properly philosophical systematization of nature" opens the door to agnosticism, intuitionism, and mysticism (*La Philosophic contemporaine en France* [1919; Contemporary Philosophy in France]). Brunschvicg responded in an eighty-page essay reasserting many of the claims that Parodi questioned (reprinted in *Ecrits philosophiques* [1951; Philosophical Writings]). Although he and Parodi agreed that reason in science is not to be considered "a deductive system that closes on itself," Brunschvicg seemed to believe that even a "philosophical systematization" would misrepresent science's dynamic vitality. In fairness, it should be added that for Brunschvicg the future of science, however open to innovation, would be a rational future. Thus his philosophy, ambiguous as it may be, resists mysticism and intuitionism as strongly as it does logical methodology. (He was proud, however, to share his emphasis on creative spontaneity with the intuitionist Henri Bergson.)

Although it may seem that Brunschvicg's aversion to logical structure anticipates recent philosophical dissatisfaction with deductive models of scientific explanation, his emphasis on spiritual continuity gives us little reason to believe that he might have support such historical analyses as Gaston Bachelard's "epistemological break" or Thomas Kuhn's "paradigm shift." Still, Brunschvicg's defense of creative reason influenced a generation of his students, most notably Bachelard—see, for example *La Formation de l'esprit scientifique* [The Forming of the Scientific Mind]. Although only a few of his works are still likely to be found in the bookstores near the Sorbonne, Brunschvicg deserves to be remembered as an interpreter of the French philosophical tradition and as an exponent of the life of reason and the value of science.

BERNARD ELEVITCH

See also **Gaston Bachelard, Henri Bergson**

Biography

Leon Brunschvicg was born in Paris in 1869. In 1897 his doctoral dissertation, *La Modalité du jugement*, was published. He was granted a position as Professor of the History of Modern Philosophy at the Sorbonne in 1909. He published several works, including *Les Étapes de la philosophie mathématique* (1912), *Le Progrès de la conscience dans la philosophie occidentale* (2 vols., 1927), and *La Raison et la religion* (1939) during his life. He taught at the Sorbonne until his death in 1944.

Selected Works

Spinoza, 1894
La Modalité du jugement, 1897
Introduction a la vie de l'esprit, 1900
L'Idéalisme contemporaine, 1905
Les Etapes de la philosophie mathématique, 1912
Nature et liberté, 1921
Un Ministère de l'éducation nationale, 1922
L'Expérience humaine et la causalité physique, 1922
Spinoza et ses contemporains, 1923
La Génie de Pascal, 1924
Le Progrès de la conscience dans la philosophie occidentale, 1927
L'Orientation actuelle des sciences, 1930
De la connaissance de soi, 1931
Pascal, 1932
Les Âges de l'intelligence, 1934
La Physique du vingtième siècle et la philosophie, 1936
Le Role du pythagorisme dans l'évolution des idées, 1937
Descartes, 1937
L'Actualité des problèmes platoniciens, 1937
La Raison et la religion, 1939
Descartes et Pascal, lecteurs de Montaigne, 1942
Héritage de mots, héritage d'idées, 1945
Agenda retrouve, 1892–1942, 1948
La Philosophie de l'esprit, 1949
De la vraie et de la fausse conversion, 1950
Ecrits philosophiques, 3 vols, 1951–58
Blaise Pascal, 1953
L'Orientation du rationalisme, 1954
Pascal Pensées et opuscules, 1897
Pascal Oeuvres complètes de Blaise Pascal, with P. Boutroux and F. Gazier, 14 *vols*, 1904–14
Pascal, Pensées de Pascal, 1934
Reproduction en phototypie du manuscrit des *Pensées* de Pascal, 1905

Further Reading

Benrubi, *Les Sources et les courants de la philosophie contemporaine en France*, 2 vols, Paris: Alcan, 1933
Boirel Rene, *Brunschvicg, sa vie, son oeuvre avec un exposé de sa philosophie*, Paris: Presses Universitaires de France, 1964
Deschoux, Marcel, *La Philosophie de Léon Brunschvicg*, Paris: Presses Universitaires de France, 1949
Deschoux, Marcel, *Léon Brunschvicg ou l'idéalisme a hauteur d'homme*, Paris: Seghers, 1969
Gutting, Gary, *French Philosophy in the Twentieth Century*, Cambridge: Cambridge University Press, 2001
Messaut, O. P., *La Philosophie de Leon Brunschvicg*, Paris: Presses Universitaires de France, 1937
Parodi, D. *La Philosophie contemporaine en France*, Paris: Alcan, 1919
Revue de Métaphysique et de Morale, spécial issue, 1945
Yankélévitch, V., "Léon Brunschvicg," in *Sources*, Paris: Seuil, 1969

C

CAILLOIS, ROGER
Semiotician

Roger Caillois compared his life to the legendary river Alphée. It was believed that the Alphée flowed through the Mediterranean and kept going on the other side. Likewise, said Caillois in his late autobiography, he emerged from over thirty years of reading and passionate scientific writing (in the multiple domains of sociology, anthropology, history of religions, poetics, aesthetics, one could say general semiotics), which he called "*la parenthèse*," with a deeply-felt need to face and mystically describe "nontextual" stones, the taciturn archives of our world, and to author intriguing *récits fantastiques*, thus recapturing his initial "precultural" self during the last years of his life.

The first period of the "*parenthèse*" is an activist one. In the historical and sociopolitical context of the thirties, Caillois tensely looked for concrete action, for a "*révolte efficace*" that would go beyond "*l'équivoque surréaliste*," to reactivate the lost social dynamic. Such an action of "*sur-socialisation*" can be instrumented neither by literature (representation is alienating), nor by limiting political ideologies, doctrines, or programs; it requires, instead "*une activité unitaire de l'esprit*," that examines and convokes the affective energies, the powers of the imaginary, in order to infinitely enlarge the powers of reason. Affectivity is intelligible. A science of the irrational, a *hyperscience*, a *sacred sociology* would have as its object of study myths the sacred, the fantastic, power, and the like. Myth represents to conscience the image of a conduct that solicits it pressingly. The sacred opposes to the profane, that is, to the

rational occupations aiming at material security and the conservation of the subject; it is a category of sensibility in which the instinct for autoconservation and the freedom of action are absent. It is transcendent, unifies via affective communion, and reaffirms authentic social bonds. It is also ambivalent, basically oscillating between inducing respect and cohesion or bringing about transgression and a regenerating dissolution. The last is the case of the feast ("*la fête*") as well as that of war. The fantastic reveals the sensible points in the imaginary; their knowledge could provoke emotional states that, in being shared by a group of individuals, reinforce its cohesion. In Caillois's ethics of the moment, the *resacralization* of collective existence can be achieved only by an intransigent and methodically virulent "*élite*" that is able to go beyond the affective affinities of the individuals that compose society, by willfully mobilizing and disciplining them. The real power of such Luciferian elites paradoxically resides in their systematic refusal of power, in their capacity for a strictly controlled experience of the sacred, in their being permanent *producer*s and never *consumer*s of "*sur-socialisation*."

Caillois complements this post-Durkheimian "performative" sociology, visibly influenced by Mauss, Dumézil, and by Bachelard's *surrationalisme*, with a "*sociologie littéraire*" mainly devoted to illuminating the impact of literature on the collective sensibility of a given community. He will basically distinguish in this respect between three phases: a first phase, of sterile revolt, represented by the romantics and the surrealists (whose images have to be studied nevertheless in order to apprehend the mechanisms of empirical imagination); a second, pedagogical phase, exemplified by Balzac or Baudelaire, who offered models for "*sursocialisation*" (the secret societies and the dandy respectively); and the third phase, that of the rebellion against the real, represented by fantastic literature. Caillois situated the golden age of literary fantastic in the first half of the nineteenth century and viewed in it an essential reaction against positivism.

In Argentina (1939–45), during the war, Caillois reconsidered his approach. When exalted, strong social bonds can lead to violence and abuse of power. However, because the sacred exists and cannot be eradicated, one still has to learn to master it. Writing, which he now viewed as *the human instinct* par excellence, has such a civilizing force. Therefore literature is necessary and has an ethic value; it manifests the sacred in accordance with the rules of an aesthetic game, offering a symbolic feast, a "*fête du cerveau.*" It compensates the excess of utilitary action or of reason and allows one to "reprimitivize" oneself at the level of thought, while continuing to affirm one's anthropological reality. By proposing an abstract, internalized, mediated sacred, literature protects against the delirious externalization of the sacred. Fantastic literature, with its images of death, specters, vampires, and so on is a cathartic "*jeu avec la peur*" that helps purge its readers of their will to power and thus diminishes the risk of "*sursocialisation.*"

From then on, Caillois's approach steadily grew in extension and generality. He thus demonstrated that plastic arts in turn manifest the sacred via a specific aesthetics. In contradistinction to fantastic literature, which was contemporary with positivist strictness and countered it via representing supernatural beings, fantastic painting and engraving appeared during the Renaissance and were permeated by the infinite openness of young sciences and techniques. They therefore could remain figurative, presenting an "*insolite objectif,*" and resorting to "*idéogrammes objectifs,*" that is, to signs that materially realized in the external world lyrical and passional virtualities of conscience. A next move was the elaboration of the theory of natural fantastic. Nature becomes fantastic when it seems to refute its own laws. Natural anomaly induces fascination and anxiety inasmuch as it manifests "*des cohérences dérobées,*" "*des convergences dissimulées,*" "*des carrefours,*" "*des récurrences,*" "*des analogies aléatoires.*" Human, vegetal, and animal species, even minerals, dispose of a finite inventory of terrifying appearances to provoke the "*frisson fantastique,*" the desire to be scared or to scare is a universal law. Imagination is but "*un prolongement de la nature.*" Caillois chose "*le pari analogique*" and postulated a labyrinthine, unitary universe in which nature and human creation are regulated by a limited number of recurrent principles. Finally, Caillois examined the ways in which "diagonal sciences" can look for the manifestation of the same law, principle, element, by coalescing concrete and abstract, measurable or unmeasurable phenomena that would remain meaningless if kept in isolation. Thus, for example, the impeccable circle that one can find on some agates, the hypnotizing ocelli exhibited by peacocks and butterflies, the disposition of certain leaves around the stem, and the geometric circle are "diagonally" related fascinating forms that can be more fully understood if brought together. Likewise, the behavior of the praying mantis isomorphically echoes the myths of human destructive sexuality uncovered by psychologists, psychoanalysts, and anthropologists, and studying it together with them helps combine the self-interrogation of the knowing subject with the interrogation of her/his object of study. Caillois thus practiced what he called an "antropomorphisme à rebours": he detected features like imagination, intelligence, the capacity to dream, asymmetry, and so on that are common to humans and the nonhuman (animals, plants, minerals).

Coming out of the "*parenthèse,*" Caillois's fantastic stories complete the circle and mark his full reconciliation with literature. In *Ponce Pilate*, he ambivalently imagined the historical consequences of Jesus's acquittal by Pilate. Living in peace to reach an advanced age after a fruitful life, his fictional Jesus radically changes the course of history, because his death will not result in the emergence of Christianity. Likewise, in *Noé*, Noah comes to realize that the Deluge is an incongruous catastrophe, that in fact it benefits fish, and thus the feeling of revolt is born. Other *récits* play with the blurred limits between real life and dreams (*Mémoire interlope*) or with the authorial status (*Petit guide du XVE arrondissement à l'usage des fantômes* presents its author as a phantom).

SANDA GOLOPENTIA

See also **Gaston Bachelard, Georges Dumezil, Marcel Mauss**

Biography

Roger Caillois was born on March 3, 1913 in Reims. He was involved in the surrealist movement between 1932–35, animated the Collège de Sociologie together with Bataille and Leiris between 1937–39, and lived through the WW II years in Argentina, where he published the journal *Lettres françaises* and founded the Institut français of Buenos Aires. After the war, Caillois became a high officer at UNESCO, pursuing cultural missions all over the world. In 1952 he created the interdisciplinary journal *Diogène*. In 1971 he became a member of the French Academy. Caillois died on December 21, 1978.

Selected Works

Le mythe et l'Homme, Paris: Gallimard, 1938.

L'Homme et le sacré, Paris: Leroux, Presses universitaires de France, 1939; as *Man and the Sacred*, translated by Meyer Barash, Westport, Connecticut: Greenwood Press, 1959, 1980; Glencoe, Illinois: Free Press of Glencoe, 1959, 1960; and Urbana: University of Illinois Press, 2001

Le roman policier, ou Comment l'intelligence se retire du monde pour se consacrer à ses jeux et comment la société introduit ses problèmes dans ceux-ci, Buenos Aires: Lettres françaises/SUR, 1941; as *The Mystery Novel*, translated by Roberto Yahni and A. W. Sadler, Bronxville, New York: Laughing Buddha Press, 1984

Puissances du roman, Marseille: Sagittaire, 1942

Patagonie, Buenos Aires: Éditions de l'Aigle, 1942

La Communion des forts, Mexico, D.F.: Ediciones Quetzal, 1943; Marseille: Sagittaire, 1944

Les impostures de la poésie, Buenos Aires: Lettres françaises/SUR, 1944; Paris: Gallimard, 1945

Le rocher de Sisyphe, Paris: Gallimard, 1946

Circonstantielles, 1940–1945, Paris: Gallimard, 1946

Babel; orgueil, confusion et ruine de la littérature, Paris: Gallimard, 1948

Description du marxisme, Paris: Gallimard, 1950

Quatre essais de sociologie contemporaine: La représentation de la mort. L'usage des richesses. Le pouvoir charismatique. Le vertige de la guerre, Paris: O. Perrin, 1951

Poétique de Saint-John Perse, Paris: Gallimard, 1954.

L'incertitude qui vient des rêves, Paris: Gallimard, 1956

Art poétique, Paris: Gallimard, 1958

Les jeux et les hommes; le masque et le vertige, Paris: Gallimard, 1958

Méduse et Cie, Paris: Gallimard, 1960; as *The Mask of Medusa*, translated by George Ordish, New York: C. N. Potter, 1964 and London: V. Gollanoz, 1964

Ponce Pilate, récit, Paris: Gallimard, 1961; as *Pontius Pilate*, translated by Charles Lam Markmann, New York: Macmillan, 1963

Esthétique généralisée, Paris: Gallimard, 1962

Le mimétisme animal, Paris: Hachette, 1963

Bellone, ou La pente de la guerre, Bruxelles: Renaissance du Livre, 1963

Instincts et société, Paris: Gonthier, 1964

Au coeur du fantastique, Paris: Gallimard, 1965

Pierres, Paris: Gallimard, 1966

Images, images; essais sur le rôle et le pouvoir de l'imagination, Paris: J. Corti, 1966

Obliques, Paris: Montpellier: Fata Morgana, 1967

Cases d'un échiquier, Paris: Gallimard, 1970

L'écriture des pierres, Genève: Albert Skira, 1970; as *The Writing of Stones*, with an Introduction by Marguerite Yourcenar, translated by Barbara Bray, Charlottesville:

CAMUS, ALBERT
Writer

Albert Camus did not share the intellectual brilliance of some contemporaries such as Sartre, Beauvoir, Aron, Merleau-Ponty, or Lévi-Strauss; neither did he ever attain the radical chic of others such as Blanchot, Bataille, Klossowski, or Barthes. Even so, he occupied an important place in the French intellectual, artistic, and political scene as a nonpartisan voice of the Left. He emerged from the Second World War with more integrity than most, having edited the underground newspaper *Combat* through much of the Occupation. His friendship and subsequent rift with Sartre, his denunciation of Stalinism at a time when the brutality of the Gulags was still widely denied, and his reluctance to take sides over the Algerian War of Independence were all widely debated and helped establish his reputation as the tortured conscience of his age, deeply engaged with its most pressing issues and striving for clarity amid its murderous dilemmas and conflicts. His two long philosophical essays, *Le Mythe de Sisyphe* (1942) and *L'Homme révolté* (1951), analyzed the problems of the contemporary world through the lens of what would become defining terms of the mid-twentieth century: the Absurd and revolt.

The Absurd

Le Mythe de Sisyphe begins with a famous rhetorical flourish that brashly sweeps aside centuries of philosophical speculation: "There's only one truly serious philosophical problem: it's suicide" (*Le Mythe de Sisyphe*, Gallimard 1942, Idées edition, 15). Is life worth living or not? All other questions pale in significance when compared with this one. In a world without values, without God, without hope for an afterlife, without direction and meaning, why carry on living, why not simply kill oneself and put an end to the misery here and now? But Camus's aim is not to drive his readers to despair. He ends by describing Sisyphus, the hero of senseless endeavor who every day rolls his rock to the top of a hill only to see it roll down again; despite everything, we should not regard Sisyphus as a figure of despair, as Camus insists in a final sentence, which is no less famous than the first: "We must imagine Sisyphus to be happy" (166).

What robs life of hope and meaning is the awareness of the Absurd, the notion with which *Le Mythe de Sisyphe* is most notoriously associated. Although the term was in common use in the 1930s and 1940s, Camus gave it his own distinctive inflection, and one that must not be confused with the sense it would later acquire in the later Theatre of the Absurd, of which the best known representatives are Ionesco and Beckett. Camus's Absurd is not a quality of the world or of man; rather it is the nature of their relation or their nonrelation (in common with nearly all his contemporaries, Camus cheerfully uses the term *l'homme* to refer to all human beings). Man desires clarity, unity, and reason, but the world fails to comply with his desires:

> I said that the world is absurd and that was too rapid.
> This world in itself is not reasonable, that's all one can

say about it. But what is absurd is the confrontation of this irrationality and the hopeless desire for clarity that appeals to the deepest part of man. The Absurd depends as much on man as on the world. It is for the moment their only link. It binds them one to the other as only hatred can. (37)

The Absurd, then, lies in an essential mismatch between the world and human desire. No values are given; no knowledge is assured. Attempting to achieve something equivalent to a Cartesian *tabula rasa*, Camus dismissed all human thought and science as metaphor or simple error: "This world, I can touch it, and I judge that it exists. That's where my science ends, the rest is construction" (34). Man is a stranger to the world and to others; he is condemned to live in contradiction, paradox, and impotence. So why does he not kill himself? Camus's response was that we have the choice of evading the Absurd or confronting it. Suicide does not abolish it; it merely avoids it and robs us of the only value we can know: life itself. Camus also traced this evasion of the Absurd in the history of philosophy as he accused his intellectual precursors of what he called "philosophical suicide." Kierkegaard's leap of faith provides the best example of a philosophical renunciation that Camus also finds in Jaspers and in Husserlian phenomenology. The endeavor to fix the philosophical gaze unflinchingly on the Absurd falters when even the most able philosophers of existence glance aside to find transcendence, hope, and consolation. Camus's four heroes of the Absurd are Don Juan, the actor, the adventurer, and the creator, characters who have no illusions about the fixity of values and identity and who know that only failure and death await them.

The Absurd, then, appears as the stumbling of reason and knowledge. The world simply does not correspond to the faculties through which we apprehend it. However, this does not entail a thoroughgoing epistemological skepticism. It has frequently been observed that Camus's practice in *Le Mythe de Sisyphe* implicitly reaffirms the values of reason and clarity, just as he explicitly insists on logic, self-awareness, and lucidity. Moreover, Camus's prose is heavily laced with aphorisms that call for the reader's tacit assent: "Every healthy being aims to reproduce itself" (94), "A beautiful woman is always desirable" (95), "It's only in novels that people change state or become better" (96). The text does not pause over these provocative generalizations. Camus proffers them with breakneck rapidity, as if their self-evidence were too glaring to warrant justification. If the aphorisms do not amount to a coherent philosophical system, they nevertheless imply the pertinence of a stock of knowledge and authority for which Camus serves as privileged mouthpiece. The

Absurd may represent the limit of reason and the defeat of knowledge, but it does not invalidate all truths.

The preservation of some vestige of knowledge and intellectual authority is replicated in relation to ethics. For a work published during the Second World War, written by someone who had been a member of the Communist Party and who would be an active supporter of the Resistance, it is striking that *Le Mythe de Sisyphe* has virtually nothing to say about ethics or politics. Published a year later, Sartre's *L'Etre et le néant* also famously raised and then postponed the ethical question in its final lines. Neither thinker had yet found a means of deducing an ethics from the apparently bleak world picture of existentialism or the Absurd. Camus insisted, "There can be no question of writing a dissertation on ethics" (93), but he also stepped back from embracing ethical nihilism. There may be no rules, but this does not mean that all courses of action are of equal value. In a world without values and denied the tutelage of a moral God, it is hard to resist the appeal of Dostoyevsky's Karamazov as he declared, "Everything is permitted." But Camus countered that the absence of given values does not mean that there are no restraints on human action: "Everything is permitted does not mean that nothing is forbidden" (94). At this stage in his thinking, Camus did not get much further than this blunt paradox. He offered nothing that would explain what is forbidden, why, and by whom. He asserted rather tamely that "honesty doesn't need rules" (94). We may not know how to define values, but we all recognize them when we see them. So despite what might seem to be the ethically and epistemologically nihilistic thrust of the Absurd, Camus retained a sense that there is a core of value and knowledge that we neglect at our peril. His subsequent essay, *L'Homme révolté*, would be an attempt to develop this more fully.

Revolt

The theme of revolt is already present in *Le Mythe de Sisyphe*, where it is described as "a perpetual confrontation of man with his own obscurity" (76) and as a "demand for an impossible transparency" (77). Here, it is the individual's confrontation with his own condition as he comes to terms with the resistance of the world to his longing for clarity and unity. In *L'Homme révolté* Camus took the important step from the singular to the collective, a move reflected in his literary work by the shift from a focus on the individual in his first novel, *L'Etranger* (1942), to the depiction of a whole town in time of crisis in his second major fictional work, *La Peste* (1947). In this perspective murder replaces suicide as the most pressing question. Whereas *Le Mythe de Sisyphe* wrestled with the question of why man shouldn't kill himself, *L'Homme révolté* ponders why man shouldn't kill others in a century of totalitarianism, war, and revolution that had made murder commonplace. Camus observed that revolt is not only man's revolt against his own condition; it may also occur at the sight of another's mistreatment. Revolt, then, is not just for myself; it is also for the other, it is the discovery of solidarity and of a value that surpasses the individual. Provocatively using terms that definitively marked the distance between him and his existentialist contemporaries, Camus also insisted that revolt is the attempt to preserve something permanent, a value and a human nature that transcend history. On the basis of this, Camus proposed a new cogito, in which the certainties of the self ensure the existence of the collectivity: "I revolt, therefore we are [Je me révolte, donc nous sommes]" (*L'Homme révolté*, Gallimard 1952, Idées edition, 36).

It is difficult to know how seriously Camus wanted us to take this new cogito. Certainly he described his procedure as a version of Cartesian methodical doubt that discovers revolt as the first and only certainty that derives from the Absurd (21). It is unclear, though, whether Camus's cogito is intended as a provocative slogan or a genuine philosophical refounding of subjectivity. If the latter is the case, it lacks the intuitive appeal of its Cartesian precursor, and its influence on subsequent thinkers has been negligible. The logic underlying the shift from "I" to "we" in "I revolt, therefore we are" was not convincingly justified, and no sustained attempt was made to resolve the evident problems in demonstrating how my actions can found the existence of a community of others. Moreover, Camus equivocated over whether revolt is a historical phenomenon or an essential human trait, as it would need to be if it were to found a genuine new cogito. He claimed that it is "one of the essential dimensions of man" (34), but he also argued that the sense that he gave it applies only to a particular stage in the development of Western societies: "The problem of revolt only makes sense inside our Western society" (33).

Given these confusions, it is not surprising that Camus's contemporary critics had little trouble in belittling the philosophical seriousness of *L'Homme révolté*. Although Camus had had some training in philosophy in his student days, his academic studies had been curtailed by illness. He had neither the background nor the acumen to be a genuinely original philosopher. Where *L'Homme révolté* is more interesting is in its lengthy analysis of the artistic, political, and philosophical prehistory of the totalitarian régimes of the twentieth century. Camus's contention is that fascism and Stalinism are the culmination of a history of nihilism that can be traced back to European culture and thought from the eighteenth and nineteenth centu-

ries. To support this, Camus gave detailed readings of Sade, Romanticism, and Surrealism, and of Hegel, Nietzsche, and Marx. In particular, one aspect of Camus's work that would find an unexpectedly welcome reception in the 1970s among the so-called *nouveaux philosophes* (Bernard-Henri Lévy, André Glucksmann, and others) was his attempt to show how fascist and Stalinist totalitarianism could be seen as consequences of philosophical trends exemplified by Hegel, Nietzsche, and Marx. Nietzsche's world without meaning or God led to the release of irrational forces by fascism; Marx and Hegel's endeavor to find meaning in history led to Stalinist atrocities, which were justified by the need to expunge anything that did not conform to that meaning. Either way, the result is the same: "Those who rush into history in the name of the irrational, crying that it has no meaning, encounter servitude and terror and they emerge into the concentration-camp universe. Those who throw themselves into history preaching its absolute rationality encounter servitude and terror, and they emerge into the concentration-camp universe." (292)

As it sketches the philosophical roots of twentieth-century totalitarianism, *L'Homme révolté* develops into a diagnosis of a world in which murder is made legitimate and commonplace. This is the point at which Camus's notion of revolt comes into its own. Revolt is carefully and consistently distinguished from revolution. The latter is the attempt to overthrow the order of the world in order to make reality conform to an idea of what it should be. Far from being a first step on the way to revolution, revolt is in permanent opposition to it. Revolt has no overriding idea or goal to guide it; therefore it has no grounds on which to justify any crimes that might be committed in its name. It entails a rejection of the injustice of the world and also an affirmation and defense of values transcending the historical moment. Whereas the revolutionary sees man as infinitely malleable, to be formed in the image of his own ideals, revolt asserts the existence of a nature common to all. If only history counts, there can be no stable values that are separate from the process of historical change; but if values are sought outside history, then the misery and injustice that form our historical reality are neglected. So revolt rejects the belief that history is the sole reality, but equally it rejects any possibility of standing entirely outside history. Revolt, then, is a difficult position that attempts to maintain a balance between historical flux and stable values. It is an attitude of protest and affirmation, with no guiding idea to direct it, and no possibility of ultimate success. It is, as Camus concedes, an attitude to reality that is characterized by ignorance and risk.

Crucially, what distinguishes revolt from revolution is the notion of limits, which Camus retrieved from his youthful study of Greek thought. The revolutionary does not accept limits because the desire to fashion the world in the likeness of an ideal legitimizes any action that brings the ultimate goal closer. But revolt knows no ultimate goals; therefore it has no final ends that could justify its means. Revolt, then, is experienced as a permanent state of dilemma, in which choices must be made between competing imperatives without any assurance that we have got it right. Revolt poses the necessity of choice between violence and nonviolence, when the former justifies revolutionary murder but the latter tacitly perpetuates injustice; or between freedom and justice, when justice restrains freedom and the other's freedom may result in injustice. Violence and nonviolence, freedom and justice, find their limit in each other, although this limit is never stable and never given once and for all. Unlike revolution, revolt offers no picture of a better world to be created; it represents an intuition of values and of a human nature to be preserved, but it has no clear knowledge of what they might be. It must negotiate a difficult, constantly shifting limit between incompatible imperatives; its morality is founded neither in formal rules nor in future ends. Its limits are always to be drawn afresh, and its success is never guaranteed.

Revolt, then, is a state of mind that can never be fully identified with any particular political program. Because it has no clear goals, it refuses violence as a legitimate means to a desired end. Camus's essay displays distaste for violence, even in the most extreme situations. So, he suggests that the rebel who takes a life must be willing to give his own life in return. If there is no moral alternative to murder, at least the rebel should aspire to be what Camus calls an "innocent murderer." It is not surprising that Camus's desire to maintain some sort of moral purity in violent times attracted the derision of some contemporaries, and its political effectiveness may be limited in cases of the most extreme oppression. Camus was aware that there is a fine line between perpetuating injustice and sanctioning violence. To find a path between them is precisely the rebel's dilemma. Camus attempted to describe the sensibility of revolt, its consequences and risks, without denying his starting point in the perception of the Absurd. It is by no means certain, however, that he did not end by evading the Absurd in precisely the manner for which he criticized the philosophers of existence discussed in *Le Mythe de Sisyphe*. Solidarity, human nature, the intuition of values common to all: these emerge from man's nostalgia for unity, but they also entail in their way a leap of faith that turns away from the noncorrespondence of desire and reality that characterizes the Absurd. Camus's Absurd is the stumbling block of knowledge, but this is a harsh insight from which even he looked aside. This can also be

seen in his account of art, which is at once a privileged expression of the Absurd, a site of revolt, and a place where the Absurd is denied.

Creation and Revolt

Both *Le Mythe de Sisyphe* and *L'Homme révolté* contain lengthy discussions of artistic creation. In the earlier book, Camus described the creator as "the most absurd of characters" (124). The work of art is a phenomenon of the Absurd; it immerses the creator and the reader in the experience of the Absurd without trying to explain or to justify it. Rather than a refuge from unsavory realities, it is the place in which such realities can be honestly and lucidly confronted. While arguing this position, however, Camus's analysis of actual works suggests a rather different picture. Even important precursors such as Dostoyevsky and Kafka succumbed to the temptation of offering explanations and justifications. Art, it seems, is as much a refuge as a place of lucid confrontation. This ambivalence is reproduced in the more ambitious discussion of creation in *L'Homme révolté*.

In *L'Homme révolté* Camus described creation as an activity in which the sensibility of revolt can be observed in its purest form. Indeed, revolt is closely tied to art. Revolt is the demand for unity coupled with the knowledge that it cannot be achieved. It therefore attempts to fabricate a replacement universe that may supply the unity lacking in reality. In as far as this is precisely what art does, the fundamental impulse between art and revolt is identical, and revolt is revealed to be in part an aesthetic phenomenon. Art creates enclosed worlds in which "man can reign and know at last" (306). For Camus the novel in particular serves as a vehicle for revolt in its protest against the incompleteness of the world. The novel draws on the desire for a better world, but better here does not mean different in detail so much as unified. The novel remedies the incompleteness of the world by giving characters a destiny. Life acquires meaning and coherence; great emotions endure rather than fading away with the passing of time. Art, then, is the correction of experience through the lens of man's nostalgia for unity.

Camus was adamant that art should be related to the sensibility of revolt rather than to revolution because, in his account, the rejection of reality that it entails is not an absolute negation. The refusal of the world coexists with an acceptance of its beauty and of the nature of man. The artist's correction of reality is not a revolutionary destruction of it in the name of some abstract idea; it is rather a reconfiguration of experience in the light of the desire for unity. Creation is a revolt against the nonsense of the world, so that, as Camus put it, "there is no art of nonsense" (309), or more affirmatively still, "Literature of despair is a contradiction in terms" (314). Art both rejects the world and tries to save something of value in it from the pure flux of history. It is not difficult to see elements of Camus's own fiction in this uneasy balance between an awareness of meaninglessness, absurdity, exile, and alienation on the one hand and a perception of beauty, belonging, and the intensity of sensual experience on the other.

It might legitimately be asked, though, whether this conception of art and the theory of revolt to which it is related do not represent precisely the sort of evasion of absurdity that Camus uncompromisingly criticized in *Le Mythe de Sisyphe*. Moreover, it becomes clear that Camus's account of artistic creation is normative rather than descriptive when he castigates art that deviates from his account. Almost all of modern art is, Camus asserted, "an art of tyrants and slaves, not of creators" (323). It has succumbed to the nihilism that revolt combats. Camus's rhetoric implies quite simply that art that does not correspond to his principles is not true art at all. So the reason that he can assert that "there is no art of nonsense" is that in his account an art of nonsense would not deserve to be called art. And yet it might be thought that an art that reproduced the nonsense of the world rather than "correcting" it by supplying sense and unity to the fragmentation of experience would be more honest, more in tune with the Absurd, than Camus's art of revolt. Ultimately, although Camus castigated the evasion of the Absurd as a form of dishonesty, he was himself out of sympathy with the collapse of meaning and values that an uncompromising acceptance of the Absurd brings. Both his theory of revolt and his practice as a writer reaffirm the values of justice, decency, human nature, knowledge, and reason, even if these sometimes appear to be empty forms for which the content has still to be discovered. Camus's essays, like his fiction, are poised on the tension between a sense that no values are left and the need to affirm something, as yet unknown, in their place.

In the final section of *L'Homme révolté* Camus sketched what he calls "the thought of midday (la pensée de midi)." Gesturing back to Greek thought, he indicated that this would be a positive alternative to contemporary nihilism. It would be a philosophy of limits that refused the historical condition of man while maintaining a balance between nature and becoming, freedom and justice. It would be a philosophy of light to counter the dark forces that had overrun Europe in Camus's lifetime. This "thought of midday" remains ill defined, a poetic aspiration rather than a philosophical position. Camus was a solitary humanist voice on the left of the French political spectrum. His life and work can be read as the endeavor to maintain an ethical posi-

tion even when he could offer little by way of persuasive philosophical justification. His writing embodies nostalgia for unity, clarity, certainty, and knowledge, in conflict with his founding insight that the Absurd makes a mockery of our desire to know. The theory of Revolt can be read as the attempt to remystify the world, to restore to ethics and to politics a grounding in nature and values outside history. As a thinker, Camus is more interesting for what he illustrates than for what he says, for the struggle to preserve values against the odds, for the discrepancies between his most glib certainties and the skepticism of his founding insights. He can now be seen as a privileged witness to his century, sometimes lucid, sometimes overwrought, anxiously waving his arms in protest as he watched its most precious values and achievements being washed away on the tide of history.

COLIN DAVIS

See also **Roland Barthes, Georges Bataille, Simone de Beauvoir, Maurice Blanchot, André Glucksmann, Pierre Klossowski, Bernard-Henri Levy, Claude Lévi-Strauss, Maurice Merleau-Ponty, Jean-Paul Sartre**

Biography

Albert Camus was born in Algeria in 1913 into a working-class family. His father was killed in the First World War. Camus's sporting and academic ambitions were interrupted when he was seventeen by the onset of tuberculosis, from which he would suffer for the rest of his life. In the 1930s he was briefly a member of the Communist Party. He began to acquire a reputation as a writer and moved to France in 1938. During the Second World War he joined the Resistance and edited the newspaper *Combat*. He became an internationally known figure for his fiction, especially *L'Etranger* (1942), *La Peste* (1947), *La Chute* (1956), and *L'Exil et le royaume* (1957), and for his essays *Le Mythe de Sisyphe* (1942) and *L'Homme révolté* (1951). His position as one of the leading French writers of the twentieth century was affirmed by receiving the Nobel Prize for Literature in 1957. He died in 1960 in a car crash.

Selected Works

Fiction
L'Etranger (The Outsider), 1942
La Peste (The Plague), 1947
La Chute (The Fall), 1956
L'Exil et le royaume (Exile and Kingdom), 1957
Le Premier Homme (The First Man), 1994

Plays
Le Malentendu (The Misunderstanding), 1944
Caligula, 1945

L'Etat de siège (State of Siege), 1948
Les Justes (The Just), 1949

Essays

L'Envers et l'endroit (Betwixt and Between), 1937
Noces (Wedding), 1938
Le Mythe de Sisyphe (The Myth of Sisyphus), 1942
L'Homme révolté (The Rebel), 1951
L'Eté (Summer), 1959

Further Reading

Brée, Germaine (editor), *Camus: A Collection of Critical Essays*, Englewood Cliffs, New Jersey, Prentice Hall, 1962
Cruickshank, John, *Albert Camus and the Literature of Revolt*, Oxford and New York, Oxford University Press, 1959
Judt, Tony, *The Burden of Responsibility: Blum, Camus, Aron, and the French Twentieth Century*, Chicago and London, University of Chicago Press, 1998.
Todd, Olivier, *Albert Camus: Une vie*, Paris, Gallimard, 1996

CANGUILHEM, GEORGES
Philosopher

Although Georges Canguilhem's work has received little attention to date in the Anglo-American context, it played a crucial role in the French philosophical scene in the twentieth century. Indeed, Michel Foucault has claimed that Canguilhem was central to the development of a philosophy of rationality in opposition to the philosophy of experience offered by phenomenology and existentialism. Canguilhem's work rigorously denies the priority of the acting subject, instead emphasizing the formation of knowledge and the concept, which he grounds in the fundamental errancy and normativity of biological life. In this, his work stands as one of the most provocative contributions to the French tradition of philosophy of science.

Trained in both philosophy and medicine, Canguilhem's first major contribution to French thought was his doctoral thesis, later published under the title *The Normal and the Pathological*. In this work, he examined the concepts of the normal and pathological in the life sciences and developed the argument that life is fundamentally normative. He states that "life is polarity and thereby even an unconscious position of value; in short, life is in fact a normative activity" (*The Normal and the Pathological*, p. 126). The term *normative* should be understood to mean "that which establishes norms," or what can be considered "normal" in both the senses of habitual and ideal states. Canguilhem's definition of *normativity* understands the normal state of existence to derive from a complex interaction of an organism with its internal and external environment and rests on the conviction that there is no such thing as biological indifference. For Canguilhem, the notion that a biological organism might be indifferent to its environment is empirically false and would lead to a view of life as entropic, such that even the principle of natural selection would be disallowed. But, for him, even at the simplest level "living means preference and exclusion."

This means that the difference between normal and pathological states is qualitative rather than simply quantitative. Against the nineteenth-century medical doctrine that pathological states of the body are quantitative variations from the normal body, Canguilhem claims that pathological states are in fact qualitatively different, indicating new forms of life for the organism and, moreover, revealing the normal functioning of the body. He states that "diseases are new forms of life" and, further, "disease reveals normal functions to us at the precise moment when it deprives us of their exercise." As a correlate to this characterization of disease, he approvingly cites René Leriche's statement that "health is life lived in the silence of the organs."

Importantly, the qualitative distinction between normal and pathological states does not mean that norms only exist in a state of health. There are both healthy norms and pathological norms, though the latter will not be the same as the first. Hence, health and disease are consequences of the organism's relation to its environment: health is the state in which an organism is able to survive in a large range of environments by generating new norms for its existence and hence new forms of life. Disease indicates a diminution of the range of environments in which the organism can survive because it is less able to adapt to the new requirements the environment enforces on it. This also means that the pathological is not coextensive with anomalies or mutations because these express other possible norms of life. Their corresponding normality will depend on the interaction between those normative possibilities and the environment in which they are expressed.

One of the key characteristics of life as a normative activity is information. Life is an activity of assimilating and responding to information taken from both internal and external environments. Life requires the interpretation of "codes" or "messages" at a cellular level, a notion developed later in information theory and genetics. Canguilhem claims that this indicates the centrality of the concept for life: "There is a logos inscribed, preserved and transmitted in living things. Life has always done . . . what humans have sought to do with engraving, writing and printing, namely, to transmit messages" (*A Vital Rationalist*, p. 317).

In later reflections on *The Normal and the Pathological*, Canguilhem went on to argue that the centrality of information in life introduces the risk of error. He states that "there is no interpretation that does not involve a possible mistake," and it is precisely this error that gives rise to disease. Such mistakes or errors are not pathological in themselves, but may appear as pathological in the context of certain environments. Additionally, an error, a "false taken for a truth," might in certain circumstances be productive insofar as it precipitates certain choices of activities that allow the living being to live in relative health. This is particularly so for humans, whose activity in relation to an environment is much more amenable to choice than for other organisms. This is in fact confirmed by Canguilhem's examples of biochemical anomalies or lesions that confer an advantage on their bearers in certain contexts, and his timely claim of the project to eradicate genetic error in the name of cure: "to dream of absolute remedies is often to dream of remedies which are worse than the ill" (*The Normal and the Pathological*, p. 281).

In addition to this philosophy of life, Canguilhem developed a historical epistemology that drew on and modified Gaston Bachelard's views on the philosophy of physics and chemistry. The key distinguishing feature of Canguilhem's approach to the history of the life sciences is his isolation of "concepts," rather than terms or theories, as the relevant data of historical inquiry. Although theories seek to explain phenomena, concepts provide preliminary interpretations and provoke the formulation of questions that allow for the subsequent generation of explanatory theories. Concepts can operate within divergent theories, thus revealing a degree of continuity in the formulation of explanatory frameworks. Therefore, innovation in scientific understanding is properly understood as conceptual rather than theoretical. Hence, although Canguilhem can be seen as a historian of discontinuity, insofar as he opposed a progressivist view of the history of science, the discontinuities may not be as frequent or as radical as the epistemological breaks identified by Bachelard.

Influenced by his students Louis Althusser and Michel Foucault, Canguilhem also developed the notion of scientific ideology to help explain conceptual progression within the biological sciences. By scientific ideology, Canguilhem does not mean "false science," religion, or superstition, but rather "explanatory systems that stray beyond their borrowed norms of scientificity" (*Ideology and Rationality in the Life Sciences*, p. 38). This notion highlights the specific rationality of science as an axiological and veridical activity. Scientific discourse involves a search for truth, where truth is not absolute but emerges in relation to the internal norms of verification of scientific discourse. "A science," Canguilhem claims, "is a discourse governed by critical correction," and it is this that constitutes the historicity of the sciences (*A Vital Rationalist*, p. 32). Thus, the life sciences can be characterized as open

systems of knowledge, where progress in the search for truth occurs in relation to internal norms through conceptual shifts that can be generated or delayed by various errors, obstacles, and crises.

In bringing together his interest in a philosophy of life and the history of the life sciences, Canguilhem offers profound insight into the problem of a living being taking life as its object of knowledge. The importance of his work is evinced by its influence, most notably on Michel Foucault, Louis Althusser, and Pierre Bourdieu. Perhaps his work, particularly his philosophy of life, will soon receive the critical attention it deserves in the Anglo-American context, given the pressing importance of biotechnology, genetics, and the imbrication of biological life and politics in the contemporary world.

CATHERINE MILLS

See also **Louis Althusser, Gaston Bachelard, Michel Foucault**

Biography

Georges Canguilhem was born in the southwest of France in 1904. After completing his preparatory studies at the prestigious Lycée Henri IV under the philosopher Alain, he entered the École Normale Supérieure in 1924 along with Jean-Paul Sartre, Raymond Aron, and Paul Nizan. As was required of an École Normale *agrégé*, he taught in provincial schools from 1927 until 1940, when he resigned on the basis of refusing to teach the Vichy regime's doctrine of "Labor, Family, Fatherland." By this time, Canguilhem had begun medical training at the University of Strasbourg, at which he defended his medical thesis, "*Essais sur quelques problèmes concernant le normal et le pathologique,*" in 1943. During the war, Canguilhem took an active part in the French Resistance and was awarded both the Croix de Guerre and the Médaille de la Résistance for evacuating a field hospital under fire. After the war, he resumed his post at the University of Strasbourg, first taken in 1941 at the request of his friend Jean Cavailles, and remained there until 1948. Then he held the administrative post of inspecteur général de philosophie; in this position, he was responsible for overseeing the quality of teaching in the lycées and for grading professors. In 1955, he succeeded Gaston Bachelard as Chair of History and Philosophy of Science at the Sorbonne and director of the Institut d'histoire des sciences et des techniques. He retired from these positions in 1971 and died in 1995.

Selected Writings

Essai sur quelques problèmes concernant le normal et le pathologique, 1943

La Connaissance de la vie, 2nd ed., 1965

Le Normal et le pathologique, 1966; originally translated in English as *On the Normal and the Pathological*, translated by C. Fawcett, 1978; reprinted as *The Normal and the Pathological*, 1989

Etudes d'histoire et de philosophie des sciences, 1968

La Formation du concept de reflex aux XVIIe et XVIIIe siècle, 1977

Idéologie et rationalité dans l'histoire des sciences de la vie: Nouvelles études d'histoire et de philosophie des sciences, 1977; *Ideology and Rationality in the Life Sciences*, translated by A. Goldhammer, 1988

A Vital Rationalist: Selected Writings from Georges Canguilhem, edited by Francois Delaporte, translated by A. Goldhammer, 1994

Further Reading

Dews, Peter, *The Limits of Disenchantment: Essays on Contemporary European Philosophy*, London: Verso, 1995

Foucault, Michel, "Life: Experience and Science" [1985] in *Aesthetics, Method and Epistemology: The Essential Works of Michel Foucault, Volume 2*, edited by J. D. Faubion, translated by R. Hurley and others, New York: New Press, 1998

Gutting, Gary, *Michel Foucault's Archaeology of Scientific Reason*, Cambridge and New York: Cambridge University Press, 1989

Lecourt, Dominique, *Marxism and Epistemology: Bachelard, Canguilhem and Foucault*, translated by Ben Brewster, London: New Left Books, 1975

Macherey, Pierre, "From Canguilhem to Canguilhem by way of Foucault" and "Georges Canguilhem's Philosophy of Science: Epistemology and History of Science" in *In a Materialist Way: Selected Essays by Pierre Macherey*, edited by Warren Montag, London: Verso, 1998

Osborne, Thomas and Nikolas Rose (editors), Special Issue on Georges Canguilhem, *Economy and Society*, 27:2 and 3 (May 1998)

Rabinow, Paul, *Essays on the Anthropology of Reason*, Princeton, New Jersey: Princeton University Press, 1996

CASSIN, BARBARA
Philosopher

Barbara Cassin, philologist, philosopher, and researcher at the CNRS, is the creator of a meticulously researched and eloquently narrated sophist history of philosophy. Cassin's doctorate—a translation of and commentary on the anonymous treatise On Melissns, Xenophanes and Gorgias and its version of the *Treatise on Non-being or Nature* attributed to the sophist Gorgias—provides the incipit for this project. The fundamental claim that she makes apropos of the *Treatise* and its three famous propositions (that nothing is, that if something is, it is unknowable, that if something is and is unknowable, our knowledge of it is incommunicable) is that it can only be properly understood if the propositions are seen as having been derived directly from the position taken by Parmenides in his famous poem. Which is to say that if Parmenides's poem is rigorously consequential, it can only be a sophist text.

The title of the published version of her doctorate (*Si Parmenide . . .*) indicates what she calls the *logological* practice of sophistry: Gorgias takes seriously the diacritical operation of Parmenides when he distinguishes between the path of being and the path of nonbeing, but shows that in order to be able to make that distinction, nonbeing must already, in some sense, *be*. Furthermore: being (*l'être*), the supreme object of philosophy, is, like its nemesis (*le non-être*), a grammatical construct created through the use of the article. Cassin's analysis is important because the poem itself marks a key moment for both analytic and continental varieties of philosophizing. Either the first awakening of a form of critical reasoning (analytic view) or the beautiful moment of "aletheia" just prior to the inauthentic understanding of being as item for investigation (Heideggerian view).

The strength of this analysis derives, in part, from Cassin's way of treating the manuscripts she analyzes: the "Lille School" emphasizes a very strict editorial policy regarding the texts it analyzes—stick to the letter of the text as far as is possible (even if this sometimes results in texts that do not appear to be written in Greek). Such a precaution is of paramount importance in the case of the sophists because of the hostility the ulterior tradition shows toward sophistry: our understanding of ancient Greek texts is suffused by a doxography so imbued with the spirit of Platonic and Aristotelian philosophizing that it is almost certain any interpretation of the sophists relying uncritically on the doxa will yield a philosophically deformed account of what they were saying. The matter is flagrant in the case of Heidegger, whose own account of the sophists is thoroughly dependent on the account Sextus Empiricus leaves us of Gorgias. It is as if an attorney were allowed not only to present the case for the prosecution but also to decide what counts as admissible evidence.

For Cassin, the philosophical treatment of sophistry is not simply a polemical consequence of the position that philosophy takes with regard to arguments. It is an intrinsic component of philosophy's self-definition. Cassin develops the reading of Gorgias proposed in *Si Parmenide . . .* in *L'effet Sophistique*, which offers a more general account of the taming of sophistry in the history of philosophy. For the philosopher to be able to talk of the given or to make his or her arguments prevail, it is always necessary to exclude those who would mislead by using words in more than one sense or those who would claim that the entities of which one speaks are sophisticated (precisely!) verbal constructions. Philosophy is seduction—not just of the listener but also of sense and of reference. Indeed, the examples of Plato and Aristotle show that to counter sophistry, one must be more of a sophist than the sophist. More pointedly, the philosopher's attempt—whether qua fundamental ontologist or analyst of propositions—at creating a stable discourse from which to work occludes any understanding of the real import of sophistry: its connection with politics and the political.

It has been traditional to view the sophists either as dangerous demagogues or as eloquent orators, orthodox conservatives or subversives out to corrupt the young. For Cassin these very alternatives are signs of the persuasive and misleading force of the philosophical doxa. Cassin takes Antiphon as an example. If Antiphon has been considered in terms of the allegedly contradictory figures offered earlier, this is, she argues, because the sophist practice of language can and does have all these effects—but it is not reducible to any of them in particular. This becomes evident for Cassin in her examination of the extant fragments of his writings in which she shows that justice is the result of an ongoing discursive struggle (which Antiphon denotes by use of a neologism "to citizen"). As with "being" according to Gorgias, the truth which justice aims at is a secondary consequence of a prior discursive pretension to truth. "To citizen" is to maintain this pretension come what may and it requires the profession of a strict adherence to the institutions of the law while at the same time manipulating these values to other ends. The positive virtue that this makes hypocrisy suggests an alternative to the well-known reading of the Greek citizenry as free in public and tyrannized in private: with Antiphon one is free in private precisely to the extent that one citizens in public.

Cassin does not try to rehabilitate or propose a return to the sophists. The exclusion and downgrading of sophistry is an historical fact, but it is also the outcome of a struggle within philosophy in its earliest, defining moments. In L'effet sophistique and the earlier Décision du sens (with Michel Narcy), Cassin shows the extent to which major elements of the Platonic and Aristotelian corpus are directed against sophistry, including perhaps most importantly Aristotle's paradoxical "proof" of the principle of noncontradiction. The proof Aristotle ventures of this principle has long puzzled commentators because, following what Aristotle says of it, 1. Such a proof should be unnecessary and 2. To produce a proof of it is self-defeating, because to want to prove a principle of such importance and self-evidence would undercut any claim that principle might have to being foundational. To claim that something both is and isn't at the same time is an affront to the good sense of humanity.

Cassin's crucial insight here is to show that Aristotle's subsequent "proving" of this principle—which has as its aim the refutation of the sophists—is valid under that condition alone. It is sufficient for the adversary to say something for the principle to be proven: in speaking one means something, and one can only mean one thing at a time. Meaning gains an independence here from reference. That this is necessary to refute the sophists becomes clear on considering the second of the three propositions of Gorgias: if something is, it is unknowable. Parmenides had proclaimed the integral knowability of being by identifying being and thinking. For Gorgias, if this is the case then because nonbeing is just as much as is being, it is impossible to distinguish true from false. By separating sense from reference, Aristotle's performative demonstration of non-contradiction (which has attracted philosophers such as Karl Otto-Apel and Jurgen Habermas by reason of its ostensible universality), Cassin argues, permits nonbeing to be but only as fiction (like the unicorn or the squared circle). However, it comes at a cost: Aristotle relies on a normative understanding of humanity to ensure that when one speaks one only wants to say one thing at a time. To do otherwise is to be similar to a plant (that is, not human). With the Aristotelian "decision of meaning" in place, regulating sophistry amounts to a matter of disambiguation: Cassin shows how Aristotle's Sophist Refutations are organized around homonymy and a strategy of disambiguation.

If the Aristotelian "decision of meaning" accomplishes a decisive victory over sophistry, it does so at a cost: its ignorance of an "aesthetic" sensibility in language. The invention of rhetoric, by Plato, offers a margin of play in language permissible once the entities of philosophy are secured. However, the Platonic invention of rhetoric short-circuits: the dialogue Gorgias develops the equivalence sophistry = rhetoric, the dialogue Phaedrus (usually held up as the model for Aristotle's writings on the subject) develops the equivalence philosophy = rhetoric, such that rhetoric itself becomes a consummately ambivalent entity, with only the unstable appeal to an ethics of intentions to differentiate good and bad rhetoric. The difficulties stem from the problems that arise when one claims for rhetoric a self-sufficient status—it ends up becoming sophistry. Aristotle's own Rhetoric is shown to be organized almost entirely around the problem of homonymy, an indication of the policing operation philosophy has to undertake to discipline a practice of language recalcitrant in the face of the "one meaning at a time" principle of philosophy.

Historical posterity shows how, despite the relegation of the pre-Socratic sophists by philosophy, and despite its ambivalence, rhetoric experienced a blossoming. A sense of rhetoric thoroughly suffused by the pre-Socratic inheritance informs the Second Sophistic (in Imperial Rome), to the point that far from being a pale imitation of the first, it in fact inherits its most important lessons. Where the pre-Socratic Sophists developed the theme of ontology and its supreme referent nature as discursive effect, the Second Sophistic develops the theme of history and its artifacts as discursive effect: a second order mimesis or resemblance, language aping culture (that is, palimpsest). In this regard, Cassin suggests, figures such as Lucien, considered marginal and second-rate by the tradition, become crucial exemplars of this new practice and offer a new way of understanding the development of literature.

For Cassin literature is not the prose equivalent of poetry in its noble adherence to the blossoming of what is (this would be the philosopher's view, indicative of the sway of the Aristotelian naturalist aesthetic). Literature is the avowed shaggy dog story. Fiction told for no reason other than for the logic of its own unfolding is in some senses the supreme accomplishment of logology. Cassin's key contributions to modern thinking are, to summarize:

> The constructed, artefactual nature of ontology and philosophy's supreme hero, being,
>
> The consequent primacy of the political, understood as a hypocritical agonism inherent in our use of language,
>
> The irreversible but unstable taming of sophistry by philosophy through the invention of "signfication,"
>
> The emergence of literature as an historical consequence of the exclusion of sophistry.

ANDREW GOFFEY

Biography

Born in 1947, Barbara Cassin has been Directeur de Recherches at the Centre National de la Recherche Scientifique in Paris (Centre Léon Robin de Recherche sur la pensée Antique, Paris IV Sorbonne—CNRS), participant at Heidegger's seminar at Thor in 1969, and joint editor of the series "L'Ordre philosophique" and "Points-bilingues" at the Editions du Seuil.

Selected Writings

Si Parmenide, Lille, Presse universitaire de Lille, 1980
La decision du sens, Paris, Vrin, 1989, with Michel Narcy
Nos grecs, leurs modernes, Paris, Seuil, 1992
L'effet sophistique, Paris, Gallimard, 1995
Parmenide *Sur la nature ou sur l'étant*, Paris, Seuil, 1998
"Who's Afraid of the Sophists? Against Ethical Correctness" in *Hypatia*, 15, no. 4 (Fall 2000): 102–121
"Politiques de la mémoire. Des traitements de la haine" in *Multitudes*, 6 (Septembre 2001): 176–195

Further Readings

Cavell, Stanley, "Beginning to Read Barbara Cassin," *Hypatia*, 15, no. 4 (Fall 2000): 102–121
Donnard, Giselle, "A propos du texte de Barbara Cassin," *Multitudes*, 6 (Septembre 2001): 196–198
Goffey, Andrew, "If Ontology, Then Politics: The Sophist Effect," *Radical Philosophy*, 107 (2001): 11–20
Irwin, Terence, "Quelques apories de la science de l'être," in *Nos grecs et leurs modernes*, by Barbara Cassin, Paris, Seuil, 1992

CASTORIADIS, CORNELIUS
Philosopher, Psychoanalyst, Political Theorist

The thought of Cornelius Castoriadis defies easy classification. Traveling a path that passes by way of a critical interrogation of Marxism and structuralism, it would seem that his writings share an intellectual space with poststructuralism. This, however, is not the case. At a time when the political bearings of structuralism and poststructuralism appeared lost, and the primacy of the human subject was being challenged by the disciplines of philosophy, linguistics, politics, and psychoanalysis, Castoriadis claimed that the so-called death of man and the end of the subject were evasions of political responsibility. His own conception of reflective and deliberative subjectivity, shaped in the 1970s by a reformulation of Freudian psychoanalytic theory, rests on much stronger ontological claims regarding the subject and is tied to an emancipatory political project. This project of autonomy drew sustenance from classical Greek philosophy, and was expressed in the model of a radical participatory democracy in which subjects practice collective self-governance and continuously question the form and content of the law. A view of politics as the collective creation of new institutions thus characterizes Castoriadis's political thought and distinguishes it from the mass conformism of impoverished, heteronomous societies.

Castoriadis was first and foremost a critic of late-modern capitalist society. Many of his earliest writings were produced within the postwar Marxist group *Socialisme ou Barbarie*, which also contained within its membership Nicos Poulantzas, Claude Lefort, and Jean-Francois Lyotard and exerted a significant influence on the events of May 1968. It was here that Castoriadis began his trenchant critique of the rigid, bureaucratic nature of communist regimes with their totalization of economy and society. The project of social change, he argued, could no longer be conceived in terms of worker's self-management of production but must extend to the collective self-management of society. This interrogation was also to the ruin of what, for Castoriadis, encapsulated Marx's theory of history, namely a logic of determinism that tied creative *praxis* too closely to the material life of individuals. In "Marxism and Revolutionary Theory" (1984, Part I), Castoriadis developed his own account of history as the positing of new *eidos* or forms, be they practices, institutions, significations, or new modes of being. *Contra* functionalist and structuralist theories of history, what he called the *social–historical*, cannot be determined by natural or historical laws or be contained within a complex totality where its elements are identified through combination and opposition. No given law or structure can predetermine or account for the specific content of a particular society because there is a productive element of any structure that cannot be grasped by synchronic laws. The social–historical is this genuinely singular process of self-alteration and becoming that creates the mode of being of a society. Thus "what is given in history is not a determined sequence of the determined but the emergence of radical otherness, immanent creation, non-trivial novelty" (1984). Castoriadis located the *radical imagination* as the "capacity to posit that which is not, to see in something that which is not there" at the place of this temporal rupture with determination and repetition. As well as describing the collective and anonymous dimension of creative praxis, radical imagination also has a singular subjective mode of being pursued by Castoriadis through a psychoanalytic theory of the subject.

This dynamic ontology of radical imagination, set out principally in *The Imaginary Institution of Society* (1974), distinguishes Castoriadis from many of his contemporaries who deconstruct and resituate the subject in relation to language and power (Lacan, Derrida, Foucault). Just as Castoriadis was reluctant to attribute any model, rationale, teleology, or logic of final causes to history, so he claimed an ontology of being as indeterminancy underlies human—and indeed nonhuman—existence. Utilizing a distinct reformulation of Freudo-Lacanian psychoanalytic theory, Castoriadis described the presocial, natural stratum of subjectivity as a monadic core: "an indissociable unity of figure, meaning and pleasure" where self, object, and other are without distinction. The psyche has a primordial capacity to produce perpetually a flux of images, affects, and representations, which Freud called phantasy and Aristotle in *De Anima* called *phantasma* or *phantasia*. The singular mode of being of radical imagination is precisely this nonfunctional, creative aspect of phantasmatization; without it there could be no gathering together of thought or reflection. It is the reduction of this dynamic quality of the imaginary that is, for Castoriadis, occluded in Lacan's specular characterization of the imaginary in "The Mirror Stage," where the act of perceiving an imaginary object is taken as the source of the ontological status (*spaltung*) of the subject.

Rather like Althusser, Castoriadis provided an account of the construction of a social individual from this disparate psychic source. Although, for Althusser, ideology effectively seals the subject, rendering revolution without an apparent agent, Castoriadis offered a deeper account of the binding of the psyche that preserves the creative power of imagination and political *praxis*. As long as it satisfies the minimal requirements of the psyche by giving social meaning to separation, then the *magma* of social imaginary significations of society (that is, its horizon of organizable possibilities in the realm of language, norms, way of life, relation to death, and so on) can be organized in many different ways. By abandoning primary objects and investing in social ones, the emergent social individual is increasingly bound by institutions and significations that attempt to reproduce it. In this way social imaginary significations must lean on the natural substratum of the psyche, just as social–historical creations must be framed by inherited modes of thought and being. Indeed, if the intention of most societies has been to create cognitive closure and repress the radical imagination, producing heteronomous conformist individuals rather than autonomous, self-questioning ones, this is not an inevitable outcome. Castoriadis identified a profound crisis of contemporary society and culture. Social imaginary significations like those surrounding the family, work, and sexuality are no longer able to offer strong modes of identification for individuals. This crisis of values itself announces the opportunity to construct new forms of social and political existence. Castoriadis found precedents for such a break with instituted forms in the creation of the Soviets in 1917, the formation of workers councils in Hungary in 1956, as well as in the creation of Athenian democracy and the birth of an autonomous political realm in the eighteenth century.

Castoriadis's unswerving attention to the power of creation and the invention of the new invites comparisons with Hannah Arendt's notion of natality, whereas his account of the immanent productivity of imagination untied from perception recalls the later phenomenology of Merleau-Ponty. This resurrection and activation of the concept of imagination from its occultation in the history of philosophy is not an appeal to an original Being or social demiurge as Habermas and others have argued. Castoriadis remains a distinctive philosophical figure, resolutely opposed to postmodernism and Habermasian models of democracy. Indeed, as contemporary liberal democracies become more distant from the people and cloaked in an ideology of rights and duties, Castoriadis's sustained effort to revive the radical democratic project marks him as one of the more engaged philosophers and critics of our time, whereas his always cautious weaving together of psychoanalytic and political levels presents us with a novel conception of the subject.

CAROLINE WILLIAMS

See also **Louis Althusser, Jacques Derrida, Michel Foucault, Claude Lefort, Jean-Francois Lyotard, Maurice Merleau-Ponty, Nicos Poulantzas**

Biography

Cornelius Castoriadis was born in Greece in 1922, where he was a Trotskyist activist. After moving to France, he formed the activist group Socialism or Barbarism, which was also the name of the journal he edited from 1949 to 1967. Castoriadis was an economist at the Organization for Economic Cooperation and Development (OECD) until 1970. In 1974, he began practicing psychoanalysis. He was named Director of Studies at the École des Hautes Etudes en Sociales Sciences in 1979. Castoriadis died in 1997.

Selected Writings

Les Carrefours du Labyrinthe 1978; as *Crossroads in the Labyrinth*, trans. Martin Ryle and Kate Soper, 1984
L'Institution imaginaire de la societé 1975; as *The Imaginary Institution of Society*, trans. Karen Blamey, 1984
Domaines de l'homme. Les Carrefours du Labyrinthe II, 1986
Political and Social Writings (3 vols.), 1988
Philosophy, Politics, Autonomy: Essays in Political Philosophy, trans. David Curtis, 1991
Le Monde Morcelé, 1996; Parts of this and 1986 text above, as *World in Fragments*, trans. D. Curtis, 1997
The Castoriadis Reader, trans. David Curtis, 1997
Further Reading
Habermas, Jurgen, "Excursus on Cornelius Castoriadis: The Imaginary Institution" in *The Philosophical Discourse of Modernity*, trans. F. Lawrence, Cambridge, England: Polity, 1987
Honneth, Axel, "Rescuing the Revolution with an Ontology" in *The Fragmented World of the Social*, edited by Charles W. Wright, translated by G. Robinson, Albany: State University of New York Press, 1995
Kalyvas, Andreas "Norm and Critique in Castoriadis's theory of Autonomy," *Constellations*, 5, no. 2 (1998)
Revue européenne des sciences sociales, 37, no.86 (1989) (multilingual special issue)
Thesis Eleven, no. 49 (1997): (special issue)
Whitebrook, Joel, "Intersubjectivity and the Monadic Core of the Psyche: Habermas and Castoriadis on the Unconscious," *Praxis International*, 9, no. 4 (1990)

CATHOLICISM

In September 1996, John Paul II journeyed to France for the sixth time since becoming Pope in 1978. His purpose was to commemorate the fifteen-hundredth anniversary of the Catholic baptism of Clovis, King of the Franks. The event was destined to celebrate the French Catholic Church's special status as the elder daughter of Rome, but also served to accentuate the nation's long-standing Catholic heritage, openly and controversially recognized by Jacques Chirac, President of the Republic, in his official welcome speech. Nine months earlier, on December 9, 1995, ten thousand French had marched through Paris to mark the birth of the secular state exactly ninety years before, denouncing the Pope in Marxian terms as "l'assassin par opium du peuple" ("the assassin of the people by means of opium"). Events such as these illustrate that the question of the role and status of Catholicism in France continues to generate debate, arouse passions, and incite action, even at the end of an officially secular century.

Secularism has confirmed France as a pluralist nation in which no religion is either publicly recognized or subsidized by the state, but where freedom of religious conscience and expression are guaranteed provided that these are confined to the private domain. As the nation approaches the hundredth anniversary of secularism, statistics show that around half of all French now claim to be nonbelievers, and fewer than ten percent are categorized as actively practicing Catholics (*Le Monde: Dossiers et Documents*, September 2000, p. 5). Such figures indicate that Catholicism no longer represents a national focus, but it nonetheless still operates as a notable and complex component of French identity, and Catholic institutions and culture continue to have an impact on national life. The French Catholic Church is keen to reinforce this state of affairs. Catholicism sees and presents itself as the "senior" faith in France today, namely as the "first" religion according to the number of practicing faithful, and as the "eldest" faith in terms of its long-standing contribution to national history.

The turbulent twentieth century saw numerous political and social events, as well as a range of significant ideological developments, that challenged Church and faithful in terms of both their view of the world as well as of themselves and their institution. Every event and issue of consequence has tested Catholic hearts and minds. The struggle to articulate a response to the modern age has engendered crisis and division within the faith, and the institution, its hierarchy, clergy, intellectuals, and grassroots membership have often followed different pathways in the search for their way of being Catholic. Catholic responses to the events of the twentieth century bear witness not only to the continuing strength of the conservative mainstream, but also to the not insignificant impact of the intransigent, integrist current and to the growth of Catholicism's progressive and charismatic strands. By the dawn of the twenty-first century, the relationship of many Catholics to their Church had been altered beyond recognition. Being Catholic in France today no longer means the espousal of a particular political or social agenda, or regular and traditional religious practice, or even adherence to the dictates of the Church. Modern French Catholicism is truly a fragmented phenomenon.

The fragmentation of Catholic opinion was markedly less evident at the start of the twentieth century. Although a minority of Catholics accepted the 1905 Law of Separation of Churches and State, most felt victimized by a state that they believed wanted to erase their religion from the national framework. Rivalry and incompatibility were the principal watchwords, and the first signs of cooperation did not emerge until 1914, when the *Union sacrée* (Sacred Union) saw Catholics and Republicans join in government on the eve of the First World War. In the early years of the century, intransigence and social conservatism dominated French Catholic thought, and moderate, "modern" Catholics were few. One notable exception was Marc Sangnier, leader of the Sillon movement (founded in 1894). This promoted a form of Christianity that was democratic and socially aware in inspiration and is widely considered a forerunner of French Christian Democracy. The Sillon collapsed in 1910 following its condemnation by Pius X for advocating cooperation with non-Catholics and nonbelievers. However, former members would reemerge in later years to play a major role in Catholic social action via the specialized youth movements or in politics through parties of Christian Democratic flavor such as *Jeune république* or the *Mouvement républicain populaire*. Catholics of Sangnier's ilk were denounced in acutely forthright terms by right-wing intransigents such as Léon Bloy (an intellectual convert to Catholicism) and Paul Bourget. They were also trenchant critics of the "mediocrity" of their Church and desired to see Christianity afresh, rejecting the modern world in favor of an idealized Middle Ages that would restore power and influence to the Church. Right-wing Catholic intellectuals of the day—including Georges Bernanos and Jacques Maritain—also found much to attract them in *Action française* (AF), a political movement headed by Charles Maurras. This drew heavily on Catholic support and came to embody political Catholicism because many Catholics shared its authoritarian and traditionalist sentiments and identified their own and the movement's enemies as one and the same.

AF's condemnation by Pius XI in 1926 for subordinating religion to politics represents a crucial moment in the shift toward Catholic political pluralism because it diverted various right-wing Catholics away from their usual connections and toward an exploration of other political orientations. Many younger Catholics joined the youth action groups established from the later 1920s, including *Jeunesse ouvrière chrétienne* (to name but the original association), which sought to involve workers, students, agricultural employees, and other specific social groups in the spiritual renewal of France. At times, their activities highlighted tensions between clergy and laity, as sociopolitical concerns jostled with spiritual issues, but they had a major impact on national life well into the 1960s before slipping into a progressive decline.

The papal condemnation of AF also sparked a period of Catholic intellectual questioning on the functions of politics and faith, spearheaded by Maritain, who left AF following its censure. In *La Primauté du spirituel* (The Primacy of the Spiritual, 1927), he opposed AF's emphasis on the political first and foremost with the primacy of Catholic values in both political and social action. His thinking influenced intellectuals such as Emmanuel Mounier (founder and director of the review *Esprit*), Étienne Gilson, and Henri-Irénée Marrou who, in the 1930s, sought a fresh approach to the problems posed by the modern world. They treated both Left and Right with equal reserve and sought a "third" way or a "true" modernity, critical of the "false" modernity of capitalist democracy or Communist totalitarianism. Their aspiration matched the Catholic Church's goal, namely the foundation of a *nouvelle chrétienté* (new Christendom)—that is, a reconquest of the modern world and the establishment of a new culture and civilization of Christian inspiration. However, where the Church looked to the Middle Ages as halcyon days to be rediscovered, Maritain, Mounier, and their contemporaries preferred an "adapted" medieval model that would take into account modern circumstances and demands. Mounier and *Esprit* finally declared openly for the Left as the political climate of the decade became increasingly polarized. *Esprit* narrowly escaped the Index in 1936, in the face of official disapproval from a politically conservative Catholic hierarchy. Other intellectual reviews were less fortunate: both *Sept* and *Terre nouvelle* were banned by the Church, the first following its publication in 1937 of an interview with the socialist Léon Blum—leader of the Popular Front (1936–38)—and the second in 1936 for its audacious attempted synthesis of Marxism and Christianity.

The Catholic discovery of Communist Marxism represents one of the most significant developments of the 1930s, doubly important because it also shaped post-1945 Catholic approaches to Marxism. In line with their Church, most French Catholics were diehard anti-Communists. They identified the Popular Front with Communism and were wary of Communist efforts to court them with the 1936 offer of the *main tendue* (outstretched hand). Pius XI set the tone of the official Catholic response with his condemnatory encyclical *Divini redemptoris* (On Atheistic Communism, 1937) and categorically forbade Catholics from dealing with Communists. This demand was widely followed. Very few Catholics openly accepted the *main tendue*, with the exception of writers such as Robert Honnert or those Catholics associated with the revolutionary *Terre nouvelle*. But a minority of Catholic intellectuals (principally the Christian Democrats of the newspaper *L'Aube*, the Dominicans behind *Sept* and *La Vie intellectuelle*, and Catholic contributors to *Esprit*), articulated a "positive" anti-Communism, which meant they could condemn Communism as a political system, but nonetheless appreciate Communists as persons with fair social aspirations and objectives. These thinkers were interested by Communist Marxism as a potential stimulus to Catholic social thought, especially in its interpretation of capitalism, and their pursuit of such intellectual engagement and discovery stands as a significant new departure for French Catholic thought. This shift towards a Catholic–Marxist dialogue would receive fresh impetus after the Second World War, with many priests, theologians, and intellectuals increasingly convinced that Christians had much to learn from Marxist ideas.

During the Second World War, Vichy's program of National Revolution echoed the concerns of a Catholic conservatism. Many Church leaders were swift and enthusiastic in their backing for the regime, hoping for a reconversion of the nation to Catholicism. But, although Vichy seemed to value clerical support, no definitive agreement was ever reached. The experience of war and occupation revealed that—apart from a few notable exceptions such as Mgr. Saliège (Toulouse) and Mgr. Théas (Montauban)—the hierarchy failed to give a clear lead to the faithful, and Catholic activity in the Resistance or in defense of Jews was largely limited to lay Catholics and ordinary priests. Their efforts, alongside those of the worker–priests (who were sent to Germany to provide spiritual support to French workers on the enforced labor program), brought them into contact as never before with non-Catholics and nonbelievers, an experience that would prove significant for the evolution of Catholic involvement in postwar France.

Catholic intellectual life proved vibrant in the postwar years. An early stimulus came from within the Church in the shape of a document published in 1947 by Cardinal Suhard, Archbishop of Paris, and entitled *Essor ou déclin de l'Église?* (The Rise or Decline of the Church?). This made an important contribution to the revitalization of the Catholic Church in the postwar period. It raised the question of how the Church could and should respond to the modern world and called on the Catholic intelligentsia to play a major role in the debate on national reconstruction and regeneration and—significantly—to cooperate with believers and nonbelievers alike to that end. Its theoretical focus reconfirmed the primacy of the spiritual over the temporal, and it clearly sought to promote spiritual renewal, emphasizing the contribution Catholic values could make to the new, postwar France. A further related initiative came with the creation in 1948 of the *Centre catholique des intellectuels français* (Catholic Centre for French Intellectuals), which, for over twenty years, offered a formal structure for Catholic intellectual debate on social and other issues. Its robust public presence, sustained by well-attended and extensively reported annual conferences, also ensured that Catholic views found and enjoyed space for expression in the national forum. Intellectual activity was further nourished by the appearance of new and influential journals such as *Témoignage chrétien*, which joined the ranks of established, high-profile publications such as *Esprit*, *La Vie intellectuelle*, and *Études*.

The postwar period was a time when a sense of mission and a significant degree of social militancy was added to Catholicism. From the early days of the Fourth Republic, the espousal of a social agenda led a substantial number of Catholics to join a range of left-inspired groupings, including both the Socialist Party and, as demonstrated by intellectuals such as Maurice Caveing and Louis Althusser, the Communist Party (PCF). An investigation by *Esprit* in 1946 confirmed the spread of Catholic interest in Communism. Although the clergy generally continued to warn against Communism and most lay Catholics discouraged proximity, some militants, workers, and intellectuals chose to explore what connections were possible, finding common ground with Communists on matters of social, economic, moral, and cultural—if not ideological—interest. Specifically, intellectuals such as Maritain and Mounier, alongside Jean Daniélou and Marie-Dominique Chenu, pursued an investigation of the Left in their exploration of the theory of a Christian humanism that would supersede atheistic humanism. But the Cold War negatively affected the movement of Catholics into Communist organizations, as did the 1949 papal decree against cooperation with Communists. Just five years later, Pius XII halted the worker–priest movement, which had been revitalized after the war by a French Church keen to foster the idea of a Catholic mission that would re-Christianize the working class. Sent out to work alongside ordinary people, many worker–priests were deeply affected by the difficult conditions they experienced and elected to militate alongside the workers to help to improve their lot. Some priests even joined the PCF, which caused consternation among clerics and manifestly contributed to the Pope's decision. John XXIII maintained his predecessor's stance, but the worker-priest movement was finally reestablished in 1965 in agreement with the more tolerant Paul VI. And, by 1979, there were ten times as many worker-priests in France than in 1954, evidence of an evolving Catholic social militancy.

A new era of thinking about Catholicism emerged at Vatican II (1962–65)—begun during the papacy of John XXIII and continued by his successor—which was strongly influenced by French Catholics such as Daniélou and Henri de Lubac. The watchword of the council was *aggiornamento* (opening up), and it resulted in a large-scale reappraisal and review of the Church's systems, procedures, beliefs, and practices. Vatican II put Catholic life and teaching in the spotlight. Although initially set up to profile the Church's defensive attitude in the face of the modern world, Vatican II actually updated Catholic thinking beyond expectation. Henceforth, priests were no longer restricted to traditional garb, and in due course, apostolic nuns would also relax their dress code; religious music and the liturgy were modernized; the issue of religious freedom was accepted and Catholic views on interfaith relations were explored in a more tolerant and respectful climate; and of equal significance, the Church attempted to meet social and economic issues head-on.

Vatican II, followed in France by the events of May 1968, increased the flow of Catholic militants into left-wing groups and parties. Some found a niche in the Socialist Party, itself regenerated at Épinay in 1971 and now under the leadership of François Mitterrand, himself of middle-class Catholic origin. Others, however, opted for more radical solutions both within and outside politics. Keen to build on earlier connections and in the light of the *main tendue* policy (relaunched in 1970), the PCF's spokesman, Roger Garaudy, encouraged a fresh dialogue between left-wing Catholics and Communists in pursuit of a humanist synthesis that would focus on issues such as social injustice. Finally, in the early 1970s, the Catholic discovery of Communism culminated in the creation of a Christian–Marxist movement, unthinkable fifty years before.

At the same time, a strand of thinking known as Liberation Theology was gaining ground in the Catholic world, and nowhere more so than in France. Influenced by the spirit of Vatican II, as well as by the possibilities of combined action with other bodies, this represented an energetic albeit controversial force to underpin Catholic involvement and commitment on difficult social issues in the modern age. John Paul II's repeated action against supporters of Liberation Theology (as well as other bodies and individuals on the Catholic Left) since becoming Pope in 1978 has underscored his preference for conservative values. In France, the "modern" Jacques Gaillot, Bishop of

Evreux, was removed from office in 1995, in a move that was supported by Cardinal Lustiger, the conservative Archbishop of Paris. In an effort to reduce the influence of high-ranking supporters of Vatican II, the Pope also stacked the French Church, as well as the College of Cardinals in Rome, with conservative members. Such actions sit uncomfortably with the way many French feel today about being Catholic, and a good number have become indifferent toward their Church and institutional religious practice. Some now choose to express their faith privately, requiring no fixed external outlet to live as Catholics. Others have joined one of the many small but fervently committed progressive and charismatic groups that sprang up in France after Vatican II. But some, equally, have found even the conservatism of John Paul II to be insufficient for their needs, as witnessed by the minority breakaway integrist current, the *Fraternité Saint-Pie X* (The Fraternity of His Holiness Pius X), which enjoys the support of around 100,000 committed activists and 1,000,000 sympathizers in France. Founded by the late Marcel Lefebvre (1905–88) in reaction against the reforms of Vatican II, the group demands instead the restoration of a specifically Catholic order and a return to traditional Catholic doctrine.

Modern Catholic thought in France cannot be uniformly defined. The twentieth century proved to be an environment in which different and often divergent manifestations of that thought could develop and flourish, both in response to and in reaction against the modern world, its crises, and its conflicts. The century offered a climate propitious to new ways of thinking and new forms of expression, and although traditional, institutional Catholicism has declined, religious and spiritual preoccupations remain. The Catholic "ghetto" has long since been demolished, and today ordinary Catholics, activists, and intellectuals are to be found across the full range of the religious, political, and social spectrum.

KAY CHADWICK

See also **Louis Althusser, Georges Bernanos, Léon Bloy, Etienne Gilson, Henri Lefebvre, Jacques Maritain, Charles Maurras**

Further Reading

Atkin, Nicholas and Frank Tallett (editors), *Catholicism in Britain and France since 1789*, London: The Hambledon Press, 1996

Cholvy, Gérard and Hilaire, Yves-Marie, *Histoire religieuse de la France contemporaine*, A Religious History of Contemporary France 3 vols., Toulouse: Privat, 1986–88

Curtis, David, "True and False Modernity: Catholicism and Communist Marxism in 1930s France" in *Catholicism, Politics and Society in Twentieth-Century France*, edited by Kay Chadwick, Liverpool: Liverpool University Press, 2000

Fouilloux, Étienne, *Une Église en quête de liberté: la pensée catholique française entre modernisme et Vatican II (1914–1962)*, A Church in search of freedom: French Catholic Thought from Modernism to Vatican II (1914–1962) Paris: Desclée de Brouwer, 1998

Kelly, Michael, "Catholicism and the Left in Twentieth-Century France" in *Catholicism, Politics and Society in Twentieth-Century France*, edited by Kay Chadwick, Liverpool: Liverpool University Press, 2000

Laot, Laurent, *Catholicisme, politique, laïcité*, Catholicism, Politics, Secularism Paris: Éditions ouvrières, 1990

Leclerc, Gérard, *L'Église catholique, crise et renouveau 1962–1986*, The Catholic Church, Crisis and Renewal (1962–1986). Paris: Denoël, 1986

Maugenest, Denis (editor), *Le Mouvement social catholique en France au XXe siècle*, The Catholic Social Movement in Twentieth-Century France Paris: Cerf, 1990

Mayeur, Jean-Marie, *Catholicisme social et démocratie moderne: principes romains, expériences françaises*, Social Catholicism and Modern Democracy: Roman Catholic Principles, French Experiences Paris: Cerf, 1986

Nettelback, Colin, "Believers in the Republic: Catholics and French Intellectual Life since the Second World War" in *Forms of Commitment: Intellectuals in Contemporary France*, edited by Brian Nelson, Monash: Monash University, 1995

Nettelbeck, Colin, "The Eldest Daughter and the *Trente glorieuses*: Catholicism and National Identity in Postwar France," *Modern and Contemporary France*, 6/4 (1998): 445–62

Rémond, René, "La Fille aînée de l'Église" in *Les Lieux de mémoire*, "The Elder Daughter of the Church" in Sites of Memory, 3 vols., edited by Pierre Nora, Paris: Gallimard, 1992

Roberts, Colin, "Secularisation and the (Re)formulation of French Catholic Identity" in *Catholicism, Politics and Society in Twentieth-Century France*, edited by Kay Chadwick, Liverpool: Liverpool University Press, 2000

Tranvouez, Yvon, *Catholiques d'abord: approches du mouvement catholique en France (XIXe–XXe siècle)*, Catholics first and foremost: Approaches of the Catholic Movement in France (19th–20th centuries) Paris: Éditions ouvrières, 1988

Winock, Michel, "La République des catholiques" in *L'Histoire*. "Catholics and the Republic" 199 (1996): 40–45

CAVAILLÈS, JEAN
Philosopher

The work of Jean Cavaillès forms part of the tradition of French epistemology and philosophy of science that runs from Brunschvicg via Bachelard and Canguilhem to Foucault. Although his explicit interests lay in the philosophy of mathematics, the originality of his work on the historical dimension of formal and rational systems was influential well beyond that sphere alone.

Cavaillès addressed most of the problems within the philosophy of mathematics in the early part of the twentieth century. Central to all of his writing, however, remained a concern with the foundation of mathematics. Cavaillès was critical of the principal approaches to this issue, his reservations arising in the main from a concern that the provision of a foundation for mathematics should not rob mathematical thought of its capacity for generating wholly new ideas and conceptual objects. For Cavaillès, the status of mathematics as a deductive science was not to be secured at the expense of its scope for creativity. To resolve these apparently conflicting imperatives, he undertook a meticulous examination of the way deductive sciences had been established in post-Kantian philosophy. Ultimately departing from each of the possible avenues opened up by Kant, he denied a founding role either to transcendental consciousness or to the abstraction of rules of thought from physical reality. Instead, Cavaillès argued that mathematics should be treated as a wholly autonomous formal discipline. Moreover, it involves the creative transformation of its conceptual objects in a way that goes beyond what can be simply deduced at any given time and that equally owes nothing either to either cultural history or to an abstraction from the physical world. In this way, mathematics could be described as a deductive system that is both autonomous and distinctively historical.

Cavaillès took the view that mathematical activity should be experienced in its original development and that to engage with a concept is retrospectively to recognize the necessity of its emergence at a given moment in the history of mathematics. In his works, and in his teaching, he therefore engaged in a close dialogue with the recent history of mathematics, tracing the development of ideas through the work of contemporaries in an effort to elicit the changes required for the resolution of outstanding problems. He opposed the logicist attempt to ground mathematics in logic, finding a naive realism in its definition of a set of elementary signs and the rules governing their organization. The sign, he argued, is not a thing in the world. Even the most basic of mathematical objects is the outcome of antecedent acts and operations, and to trace the history of such acts is to discover a complex history with no simple origin. The definition of a sign as elementary reflects no more than an arbitrary decision to stop tracing such a history.

A concern over the nature of what mathematics thinks *about* was also at the bottom of Cavaillès's critique of intuitionism. Cavaillès agreed with intuitionists, such as Brouwer, that the objects of mathematical thought (and truths about them) were not simply there to be discovered, but were rather the results of an ongoing constructive process. However, in Cavaillès's view, because intuitionism regarded mathematical objects as essentially linked to intuitive acts, the development of mathematical concepts was drawn back into the temporal flow of consciousness, covering over the uniquely historical character of their construction.

To oppose this tendency, Cavaillès looked to the way Bolzano had broken the link between demonstration as a method and the residual intuition that had continued to underlie it in Kantian thought; an idea that was adopted by Hilbert in his attempt to place mathematics as a formal discipline on an axiomatic basis. The separation of demonstration from intuition made mathematics a purely conceptual matter divorced from the conditions of consciousness and had the added virtue of meaning that the foundation of mathematics did not lay outside it. Moreover, the Hilbertian conception of the sign as a constructed object in its own right without any further representative function underpinned the independence of mathematical activity from empirical reality (whatever its eventual application may be). All this was viewed positively by Cavaillès. However, the idea that one could establish a purely formal ground for the totality of all possible mathematical expressions foundered with Gödel's thesis that it is impossible to prove the completeness of any formal system. As a consequence, the formal grounds to any existent totality of statements must remain subject to revision and development.

Cavaillès died prematurely at the hands of the German army in 1944. He had been active in the French resistance and had taken on increasingly dangerous missions before being captured and held at Montpellier. During this period of imprisonment, remarkably, he wrote a long and closely argued essay setting out his views on mathematics and logic. He then escaped to London, before returning to fight in the resistance movement. Captured for a second time, he was executed. The essay, still partially incomplete, was edited by his friends and colleagues Canguilhem and Ehresmann and published posthumously under the title of *La logique et la théorie de la science* (The Logic and the Theory of Science). Arguably the most sustained and developed statement of his position, its third and final section is a critique of Husserl's *Formal and Transcendental Logic*.

Cavaillès's central objection to Husserl is that to aim at establishing a "theory of science"—the formal conditions for any possible theory and its objects—is to constrain in advance the possible development of the science of mathematics. That Husserl allowed for an ongoing revision of such formal grounds in the light of phenomenological evidence changed little for Cavaillès. In his view there should simply be no determination of the kind of concepts and objects belonging to mathematics prior to or in any way independently of the enterprise of mathematics itself. Mathematics, for Cavaillès, was not just an activity, it was a form of experience, an adventure (something reflected in his fondness for citing Rimbaud during his lectures). But if mathematics is a form of experience, where is this experience situated? Cavaillès saw that there could be no answer to this question as long as one continued to

work with a noncritical ontology divided between the sensible world and subjective thought. Cavaillès treated the mathematical object as neither abstracted from physical reality nor constituted by an act of the subject; rather, the mathematical object is the correlate of transformative operations performed by the mathematician on existing objects that are themselves historically constructed in a purely formal domain. If one is to speak of a foundation in this context, it is immanent to the movement of mathematical thought. Above all, it is not situated in the transcendental subject, as Husserl's phenomenology proposes. Cavaillès's essay ends with a call to replace the philosophy of the subject with a philosophy of the concept. Cavaillès's emphasis on the importance of an historical perspective was undoubtedly influenced by his own teacher, Léon Brunschvicg. One can also find in Cavaillès traces of Bachelard's conception of reason as a creative break with the natural world. His own work has exercised a significant influence on thinkers such as Canguilhem, Badiou, and especially Foucault. He was greatly admired for the way his own life bore witness to the union of abstract thought and the most concrete political action.

DAVID WEBB

See also **Gaston Bachelard, Alain Badiou, Leon Brunschvicg, George Canguilhem, Michel Foucault**

Biography

Jean Cavaillès was born in Saint-Maixent in 1903. He taught at the University of Strasbourg for one year, from 1938 to 1939. He was active in the resistance movement against the Nazis. Cavaillès was appointed to a professorship at the Sorbonne, teaching there from 1941 to 1943. In 1943, he was imprisoned for his anti-Nazi activities. Cavaillès was shot by the Nazis in Arras in 1944.

Selected Writings

Remarques sur la formation de la théorie abstraite des ensembles, étude historique et critique, 1938 [Notes on the formation of the theory of abstract wholes, on historical and critical study]
Méthode axiomatique et formalisme, Essi sur le problème du fondement des mathématiques, 1938 [Axiomatic Method and Formation: Essay on the problem of the Foundation of Mathematics]
"La pensée mathématique," 1939 [Mathematical Thought]
"Du collectif au pari," 1940 [From collective to wager]
Transfini et continu, 1947 [Transfinite and Continuous]
Sur la logique et la théorie de la science, 1947 [On the Logic and Theory of Science, in Joseph J. Kockelmans and Theodore J. Kisiel (eds) *Phenomenology and the Natural Sciences* (Evaston, Northwestern University Press, 1970)]

"Mathematiques et formalisme," 1949 [Mathematics and Formalism]

Further Reading

Campbell, R., "Essai sur la philosophie mathématique de J Cavaillès" I & II, *Critique* 67 (1952): 1058–1068 and 68 (1953): 48–66 [Essay on the Mathematical Philosophy of J Cavaillès]

Canguilhem, G., *Vie et mort de Jean Cavaillès* (1976), Paris: Allia, 1996. [The Life and Death of Jean Cavaillès]

Casson-Noguès, *De l'expérience mathematique: Essai sur la philosophic des sciences de J. Cavaillès* (2001), Paris, Librarie Philosophique J. [On Mathematical Experience: an essay on the Philosophy of Science of J. Cavaillès]

Dubarle, D., "Le dernier écrit de Jean Cavaillès," *Revue de métaphysique ed de morale*, LVIII (1948): 3, 225–247, and 4, 350–378 [The Last Writing of Jean Cavaillès]

Ferrieres, G., *Jean Cavailles; A Philosopher in Time of War, 1903–1944* (1982), translated by T. N. F. Murtagh, New York: Mellen Press, 2000

Granger, G.-G., "Jean Cavaillès ou la montée vers Spinoza," *Etudes philosophiques*, 2 (July-December 1947): 271–279 [Jean Cavaillès or the Ascent to Spinoza]

Imbert, C., *1938 point de non-retour*, Paris: Presses Universitaires de France, 2002 1938 [The Point of No Return]

Sinaceur, H., *Jean Cavaillès philosophie mathématique*, Paris: Presses Universitaires de France, 1994. [Jean Cavaillès Mathematical Philosophy]

"Structure et concept dans l'epistemologie mathématique de Jean Cavaillès," *Revue d'historire des sciences*, XL–1 (1987): 5–30. [Structure and Concept in the mathematical epistemology of Jean Cavaillès]

CERTEAU, MICHEL DE
Historian and Anthropologist

Michel de Certeau was an extraordinarily wide-ranging thinker whose ideas have exerted a major influence in fields as diverse as historiography, anthropology, sociology, theology, cultural studies, philosophy, and psychoanalysis. His work across these diverse fields is informed by a number of recurrent problematics, notably the question of alterity; the relations between representations and practices; the production of belief; and the relations between writing, reading, and orality.

Most commentators locate a key transitional period over the years 1968–71, when Certeau's intellectual activity started to reach beyond the relatively circumscribed network of publications associated with the Jesuit Order. It is important to stress, however, how his earlier work laid the foundations for his more influential writings. His extended archival research since the mid-1950s into the history of the Jesuits (focusing on Pierre Favre and, especially, the mystic Jean-Joseph Surin) would provide the seedbed both for *The Mystic*

Fable and the historiographical reflection in *The Writing of History*. His participation in the Jesuit review *Etudes* from 1966 would bring him to an ongoing engagement with general social and cultural issues. He would continue to reflect after this period on the status of Christian belief in contemporary society, but his affiliations with religious institutions would become less prominent and more problematic (see *Le Christianisme éclaté*, 1974).

Certeau's key texts on historiography can be found in *The Writing of History* (first French edition, 1975), to which should be added certain chapters of *Heterologies* (1986). He analyzes historiographical practice as a composite "operation" combining the institutional locus of the historian, specific techniques for the selection and ordering of archival material, and particular modes of staging this material through writing. The social particularity of these mediating instances ensures that the historian cannot master the past in a purely scientific representation. At the same time (and thanks to those same instances), this representation remains scientifically controlled and is not a pure fiction. Instead, it exerts a function of "falsification" (Popper) with regard to prevailing representations of the past. Certeau's reflection here has been taken up by leading thinkers on the practice of historiography, such as Roger Chartier and Paul Ricoeur.

Certeau's own historical research probes further the relation between representations and effective practices (both of the historian and of the historical agents under consideration). In his major study of "The Formality of Practices: From Religious Systems to the Ethics of the Enlightenment" (see part II of *The Writing of History*), he shows how the transition from a "religiously" to a "politically" ordered society over the early modern period can be traced not simply in overt challenges to religious authority, but also in the ways in which religious representations came to be "practiced" or "used" differently by different groups. In *Une Politique de la langue: La Révolution française et les patois* (1975) he challenges the representation of an emancipatory and unified Republic emerging through the French Revolution by showing how, at a linguistic level, this process also implied the suppression of the diversity of local spoken patois throughout France. His focus on what is repressed or absent in historical documentation and how elements of this return to destabilize established representations of alterity, constitutes a recurrent feature of his interpretative practice, and is a mark of his long familiarity with psychoanalysis (he was a founder member of Lacan's *Ecole Freudienne* in 1963). This can also be seen in studies like *The Possession of Loudun* (first French edition, 1970).

Certeau's account in 1968 of the May events of that year (in *The Capture of Speech*) shows how similar categories inform his analysis of the present. He explains the crisis in terms of a divorce between the effective beliefs and practices of society's members and the conceptual models and political institutions that putatively "represent" them. Partly as a result of this study, Certeau was subsequently drawn into various politico-cultural circles and think tanks (for example around Edgar Faure's university reforms, the Commission for Cultural Affairs of the Sixth National Plan, and the Council for Cultural Development). Much of his thinking issuing from such circumstances can be found in *Culture in the Plural* (first French edition, 1974). This considers notably how political and institutional resources can be redeployed in favor of the disseminated and "unrepresented" creativity of ordinary people and user-groups. In his most well known book, *The Practice of Everyday Life* (first French edition, 1980), Certeau presents a number of models designed to allow such anonymous creativity to be grasped more clearly. He sets the "strategies" of institutions that can map and control their terrain against the "tactics" of users who must "make do" with the resources they have to hand. He draws on Emile Benveniste's linguistics of "utterance": as speakers "appropriate" a preexisting linguistic system for their own ends, so inhabitants creatively appropriate an imposed urban system, and readers "poach" across texts they have not written. These analyses have been massively influential in anglophone cultural studies, as well as in sociological and ethnographic approaches to contemporary society.

The Mystic Fable (first French edition, 1982) combines the erudition on early modern religious history accumulated by Certeau since the mid-1950s with the theoretical instruments developed over *The Writing of History* and *The Practice of Everyday Life*. He rejects any transhistorical and fusional notion of mysticism and studies the transient "experiential science" of "*la mystique*" (as its contemporaries called it) as a historically circumscribed object. Faced with multiple political and epistemic crises affecting the capacity of both churches and Holy Scripture to represent divine presence, early modern mystics turned to their own bodily and intersubjective experience in attempts to devise what Certeau analyzed as tactics of "utterance" through which that absent presence might be called forth, represented, and communicated. In Certeau's account, this formation would not survive the disappearance of the traditional religious framework that it both required and corroded. However, he derived from this vestigial historical formation the model of a "mystic" subject that emerged from and is dependent on alterity and that, like the subject of psychoanalysis, can be opposed to the "economic" model of the self-sufficient individual that would characterize modernity. At the time of his death, Certeau was working on a second volume of *The Mystic Fable*.

JEREMY AHEARNE

See also **Emile Benveniste, Paul Ricoeur**

Biography

Michel de Certeau was born in 1925 and entered the Society in Jesus in 1950. He obtained a doctorate in religious science at the Sorbonne in 1960. Over the 1960s he worked notably for the Jesuit reviews *Christus* and *Etudes*. He also taught theology at the Catholic Institute of Paris (1964–78), psychoanalytic thought at the University of Paris-VIII Vincennes (1968–71), and religious and cultural anthropology at the University of Paris-VII Jussieu (1971–78). He was professor at the University of California (San Diego) from 1978–1984, and was a director of studies in the "historical anthropology of belief" at the Ecole des Hautes Etudes en Sciences Sociales in Paris from 1984 until his death in 1986.

Selected Writings

La Prise de parole, 1968; included in *The Capture of Speech and Other Political Writings*, translated by Tom Conley, 1997

La Possession de Loudun, 1970; as *The Possession of Loudun*, translated by Michael B. Smith, 2000

La Culture au pluriel, 1974; as *Culture in the Plural*, translated by Tom Conley, 1997

Le Christianisme éclaté (with Jean-Marie Domenach), 1974

L'Écriture de l'histoire, 1975; as *The Writing of History*, translated by Tom Conley, 1988

Une Politique de la langue. La Révolution française et les patois: l'enquête de Grégoire (with Dominique Julia and Jacques Revel), 1975

L'Invention du quotidien, vol. 1, *Arts de faire*, 1980; as *The Practice of Everyday Life*, translated by Steven Rendall, 1984

La Fable mystique, vol. 1: *XVIe-XVIIe siècle*, 1982; as *The Mystic Fable*, translated by Michael B. Smith, 1992

Heterologies: Discourse on the Other, translated by Brian Massumi, 1986 (a collection of essays of which a number appear in French in the volume edited by Giard)

Histoire et psychanalyse entre science et fiction, edited by Luce Giard, 1987 (augmented edition 2002)

The Certeau Reader, edited by Graham Ward, 2000

Further Reading

Ahearne, Jeremy, *Michel de Certeau: Interpretation and its Other*, Cambridge, England: Polity Press, 1995 and Stanford, California: Stanford University Press, 1996

Buchanan, Ian, *Michel de Certeau: Cultural Theorist*, London: Sage, 2000

Bogner, Daniel, *Gebrochene Gegenwart. Mystik und Politik bei Michel de Certeau*, Mainz: Matthias-Grünewald-Verlag, 2002

Delacroix, Christian, François Dosse, Patrick Garcia, and Michel Trebitsch (editors), *Michel de Certeau. Les chemins de l'histoire*, Paris: Complexe, 2002

Dosse, François, *Michel de Certeau: le marcheur blessé*, Paris: La Découverte, 2002

Geffré, Claude (editor), *Michel de Certeau ou la différence chrétienne*, Paris: Cerf, 1991

Giard, Luce (editor), *Michel de Certeau*, Paris: Centre Georges Pompidou, 1987

Giard, Luce (editor), *Le Voyage mystique. Michel de Certeau*, Paris: RSR/Cerf, 1988

Giard, Luce, Hervé Martin, and Jacques Revel, *Histoire, mystique et politique. Michel de Certeau*, Grenoble: Jérôme Millon, 1991

CÉSAIRE, AIMÉ

Poet, Playwright, Politician

It is for his role as cofounder, with Léopold Senghor, of the Negritude movement that Aimé Césaire is best known. Rejecting the oppression and cultural alienation that characterized the life of colonized peoples, poets and other writers from the various French colonies proclaimed their rebellion against colonialism, aiming to create through their works a new and authentic cultural identity. For Césaire, the defining moment in his discovery of Negritude came not in Martinique but as a student in Paris in the 1930s, when his interest in Africa was aroused by meeting Senghor and other African students, as well as by reading the works of Delafosse, Frobenius, and other European ethnologists on African civilization.

Frobenius's view that reason is European and emotion is African greatly influenced Césaire and Senghor, and this influence is evident in the *Cahier d'un retour au pays natal* (1939), Césaire's first and most famous poem, in which the term *Negritude* was coined and which forms the poetic expression of the ideology. According to Césaire, in contrast to a decadent Western civilization, those of African origin "s'abandonnent, saisis, à l'essence de toute chose." This line represents the epiphanic moment in the *Cahier* when the poet, accepting that the humiliation of slavery marks the past of his race, overcomes the alienation of his colonized identity and expresses his revolt against colonization. The *Cahier* is the best known of a significant number of literary works by Césaire, Senghor, and other African and Caribbean writers published in the 1930s and 1940s. Celebrated in Senghor's *Anthologie de la nouvelle poésie nègre et malgache* (1948), these works were hailed in the following decades as the birth of a new literature. The ideology of Negritude served as the cornerstone of this literary movement that, following in the footsteps of the writers of the Harlem Renaissance, gave a voice for the first time to writers and intellectuals from the French-speaking colonies and former colonies.

Although the theorization of Negritude was completed long after its initial expression in poetry, enabling Césaire to develop his views on the role of literary creation in the process of decolonization, early publications show that he has been consistent in his thinking from his student days onward. In an article in *L'Étudiant noir*, a review that he directed in Paris in 1935, one can see the first signs of his concept of the writer's ideological role, leading his people away from alienation and assimilation to discover an authentic cultural identity. He emphasized that "La Jeunesse noire" want their own poets and novelists, expressing their reality. These views are expounded in greater detail in the review *Tropiques*, founded by Césaire on his return to Martinique in 1939, in articles in the Paris-based journal, *Présence Africaine*, resulting from the debate with René Depestre on the concept of national poetry, and most notably, in two lectures on culture and colonization delivered at the first and second Congresses of Black Writers and Artists in Paris in 1956 and Rome in 1959.

The second of these, "L'homme de culture et ses responsabilités," forms the most complete statement of Césaire's ideological views on the writer's role in decolonization, clearly justifying his claim to a place among what Edward Said calls the great nationalist artists of decolonization and revolutionary nationalism, as well as in Said's category of theoreticians, militants, and insurgent analysts of imperialism. Because the relationship of colonizer and colonized is not only one of master and servant, but also of creator and consumer, Césaire sees literary creation as a means to reverse the historical process by restoring the initiative, which has been forcibly removed. Art is described as sacred, and the artist is presented as a prophetlike, demiurgic figure whose task is the creation or recreation of a culture destroyed by colonization. Later in the lecture these views are further developed, and the artist's role is seen as a unifying one, reestablishing the historical continuum, bringing together a precolonial past, present, and future. For Césaire, the writer has a crucial role to play in the cultural and historical realization of Negritude.

The initial acclaim of the *Cahier* and other literary works associated with Negritude, however, was soon to yield to controversy and then to criticism of their underlying ideology from varying perspectives. European intellectuals such as André Breton and Jean-Paul Sartre praised Césaire and his contemporaries as heroic founders of this new literature, presenting Césaire in particular as a source of renewal in European poetry. For Sartre, Negritude formed the antithetical moment in a dialectical progression, following the thesis represented by colonization and leading to the synthesis of a raceless society. This view was rejected by African and Afro-Caribbean writers who felt that, despite his praise of Césaire's ideas, Sartre's analysis of them once again denied their identity. In the light of later criticisms of the racist undertones of Negritude, Césaire stressed that his concept was cultural and historical, not biological, and Senghor later preferred the term "Africanité." However, this emphasis on the cultural and historical origins of Negritude failed to silence criticism, most notably by Wole Soyinka in *Myth, Literature and the African World* (1976). For Soyinka it was not the ideology underlying the concept that was problematic, but rather its development, in particular the fact that it took its reference points from European ideas and even accepted the dialectical structure of European ideological approaches to colonialism.

Later generations of Caribbean writers saw the harking back to a mythical African past as increasingly irrelevant to the ideological and cultural contexts of the present, coining terms that they perceived as more pertinent, such as "Antillanité." According to Maryse Condé's Marxist critique of Césaire's concept of Negritude, its return to a mythical African civilization represented a false process of self-discovery. Although accepting the *Cahier* as the most beautiful poem by a writer from a colonized country, she condemned it as having no relevance in the ongoing oppression of colonized peoples. From the 1980s onward, the emphasis on the African past has been replaced by a definition of cultural identity based on the Caribbean present in the context of "créolité" by writers such as Jean Bernabé, Patrick Chamoiseau, and Raphaël Confiant. In the strongly worded chapters of *Aimé Césaire: une traversée paradoxale du siècle* (1993), Confiant condemns both his ideological stance with its emphasis on the African past and, in the political sphere, his role in the change in status of Martinique to French department in 1946. Despite expressing his sympathy for these different approaches, Césaire continued to emphasize the importance of the link with Africa in the Caribbean intellectual and cultural context, for example, in an interview in *L'Express* in 2001. All the criticisms of this stance reveal not only the controversial nature of Negritude, but also how the movement and its main exponent, Césaire, dominated critical thinking on decolonization throughout the whole of the twentieth century to such an extent that, more than half a century after its inception, theorists were still obliged to take the movement as the starting point for working out their own ideological views.

In the light of these criticisms, it is not surprising that critical theorists in the latter part of the twentieth century should classify Césaire's ideological stance as nativist, finding its justification in the rediscovery of a native past, real or imagined, in marked contrast to the opposing concept of cultural hybridity, epitomized

in the works of Homi Bhabha and others, which accepts that cultural identity can be hybrid and syncretic in nature. It is undeniable that the ideology underlying the *Cahier*, and clearly expressed in numerous lectures, interviews, and other works, is based on the rediscovery of an Africa that Césaire had never visited at that time and that owed much to the views, accurate or otherwise, of European ethnologists. This raises the question of the continuing relevance of his works in a postcolonial context. It is important to note that, alongside the nativist ideology, which is evident in his fidelity to the African past as the fundamental characteristic in Caribbean cultural identity, one also finds in the poems a forceful expression of the fractured identity that is characteristic of critical models developed many decades after Negritude, based on hybridity and syncreticity. Indeed, his works share many essential characteristics with later postcolonial writers whom critics situate in the context of hybridity, such as difficulty in adapting to traditional Western literary genres (hence the title "*Cahier*" or "Notebook"), the appropriation of the language of the colonial master as a weapon rather than the use of an indigenous language or Creole, the use of imaginative language as a form of escape, and the importance of place. It is arguable that Césaire's poetry acquires its characteristic intensity from the inherent contradiction between the nativist ideology of Negritude and the explosive poetic expression of hybridity.

Although Césaire's inspiration for his first work emerged not from a specific desire to write poetry, but from a pressing need to find a means of self-expression, he discovered his poetic vocation while writing the *Cahier* and developed his aesthetic views in published lectures and articles, coinciding with his most prolific period as a poet in the 1940s. In his major article on poetry, "Poésie et connaissance," he acknowledges his debt to the French poetic lineage from Hugo to the Surrealists, influences that are evident in his poetry. The central theme of the article is the definition of poetry as "voyance et connaissance." Like Hugo and Rimbaud, Césaire sees the poet as a "voyant" or seer, a Promethean figure fulfilling a demiurgic function. Indeed, Prometheus and other mythological figures appear in the poems as *alter egos* of the poet. He sees the poem as the result of a primeval union of man and the universe, expressing the knowledge that the poet brings back from what Rimbaud terms "là-bas" and what Césaire, in more Jungian terms, describes as the "fond ancestral." This aesthetic clearly exerted a major influence in his developing ideological view of the poet's role in the process of decolonization.

The Surrealist poet and theoretician André Breton receives considerably more attention than any individual nineteenth-century poet in "Poésie et connaissance," corresponding to the obvious influence of Surrealism in *Les Armes miraculeuses* (1944) and the subsequent collections of poetry. Césaire accepts the surrealist theory of the supreme point ("point supreme") as the basis of his own poetic *credo*, quoting in full Breton's definition in the *Manifeste du surréalisme* (1924) of the point from which life and death, the real and imaginary, the past and future, the communicable and incommunicable, the heights and depths are no longer perceived as contradictions. In *Andre Breton et les données fondamentales du surréalisme* (1950) Michel Carrouges points out that the "point supreme" has its origin in the metaphysical context of the hermetic tradition, in particular the Cabbale and *Zohar*, where it is seen as the point of origin of creation. Ferdinand Alquié, however, notes in *Philosophie du surréalisme* (1955) that Breton has laicized the mystical concept of the supreme point, transferring it from the domain of cosmology to that of psychology. Césaire's views, like Breton's, can be situated at this meeting point of the religious, the secular and the psychological, with poetry replacing religion as the spiritual dimension in life, as well as providing an antidote to the mass psychological alienation resulting from colonialism. The poet's role thus combines and replaces those of priest and psychologist.

This heroic ideological and aesthetic vision was not, however, to be realized in the reality of decolonization, and many of Césaire's writings reflect this, as the confident assertions give way to a tone of despairing anguish when the reality of postcolonial Africa fails to live up to the poet's grandiose vision. In the collection of poems *Ferrements* (1960), the poet is at times presented as a tragic hero, which may explain why Césaire abandoned poetry at this time and concentrated on the theater. In an interview he describes poetry as an esoteric language inappropriate for a writer at a period in history as important as decolonization. The heroes of the plays, however, King Christophe of Haiti and Patrice Lumumba, also express this tragic vision.

Alongside the ideological and aesthetic writings, Césaire has also made a major contribution to more directly political analysis of the evils of colonialism and the process of decolonization, including numerous speeches in the French National Assembly and, in particular, the *Discours sur le colonialisme* (1950, revised 1955). In this impassioned attack, he compared colonial Europe with Hitler's Nazism, claiming that no one involved in the process of colonization can be innocent. Whether the involvement is political, commercial, economic, legal, religious, academic, philosophical, ethnological, or literary, it is all condemned as barbaric and indefensible. According to Thomas Hale, writing in *Les Écrits d'Aimé Césaire* (1978), this work

is recognized as the "modèle polémique" of the Third World's response to colonization.

Césaire's changing relationship with the French Communist Party and his views on their approach to colonialism have also given rise to a number of noteworthy publications. Hale reproduced Césaire's entry in a 1946 pamphlet entitled "Pourquoi je suis communiste," in which he justified his membership in the party on the basis of its aim to create a social order based on the dignity of all human beings regardless of origin, religion, or color. Better known is Césaire's sixteen-page *Lettre à Maurice Thorez* (1956), one of several documents in which he explains the reasons for his dramatic resignation from the party. In contrast to his earlier declaration, he now criticized their support for French policy in Algeria and, more fundamentally, their policy in relation to the Third World in general and Martinique in particular. Explaining that he is criticizing the current policies rather than the ideologies of Marxism and Communism per se, he condemned their policy in relation to Martinique, which he saw as distancing it from sub-Saharan Africa.

In addition to literary, ideological, and political writings, Césaire is the author of one important historical work, *Toussaint Louverture: la Révolution Française et le probème colonial* (1960). Rejecting what he considers the myth that the Haitian Revolution can be explained entirely in relation to the French Revolution, he rewrote the historical account, using contemporary documents to emphasize the important roles played by revolutionary leaders in Haiti itself.

In conclusion, Césaire's works can be read as a demythologizing process, replacing the Eurocentric account by one that restores the initiative that colonization removed from the colonized peoples. He has thus made a major contribution to twentieth-century literature and thought in the context of colonization and decolonization.

ANGELA CHAMBERS

See also **Andre Breton, Patrick Chamoiseau, Leopold Senghor**

Biography

Born in Basse-Pointe, Martinique, in 1913, Aime Césaire won a scholarship to study at the Lycée Schoelcher in Fort-de-France and a second to continue his literary studies in Paris in 1931 at the Lycée Louis-Le-Grand and the École Normale Supérieure, Rue d'Ulm. During this formative period in Paris he met Léopold Senghor and other Caribbean and African writers, forming with them the first major grouping of Afro-Caribbean writers in French and publishing in student reviews. Returning to Martinique in 1939 with his wife Suzanne after the publication of the *Cahier d'un retour au pays natal*, he taught at the Lycée Schoelcher from 1940 to 1945, numbering among his pupils Frantz Fanon and Édouard Glissant. During this period he founded the review *Tropiques* and continued to publish poetry. Elected as mayor of Fort de-France in 1945 and deputy in the French National Assembly a few months later, he embarked on a long, distinguished, and controversial political career, active at the local level, in the French context, and in the international context of decolonization. The greatest paradox, given his political and ideological views, is undoubtedly to be found in the active role that he played in the accession of Martinique to the status of French department in 1946. His resignation from the French Communist Party in 1956 also received considerable attention in the press in Martinique and in metropolitan France. He later founded the Parti Progressiste Martiniquais. Alongside an active political life Césaire published several collections of poems and four plays, although the largest volume of his complete works consists of historical, political, ideological, and aesthetic writings. He continued as deputy until 1993 and as mayor until 2001.

Selected Writings

Poetry
Cahier d'un retour au pays natal, 1939
Les Armes miraculeuses, 1946
Soleil cou coupé, 1948
Corps perdu, 1950
Ferrements, 1960

Theatre
La Tragédie du roi Christophe, 1963
Une Saison au Congo, 1966
Une Tempête, 1968

Historical, Political, Ideological, and Literary Works
"Poésie et connaissance," *Cahiers d'Haïti* (December 1944): 14–19. Reprinted in Kesteloot, Lilyan and Barthélémy Kotchy, *Aimé Césaire, l'homme et l'oeuvre*, Paris: Présence Africaine, 1973, 112–126
Discours sur le colonialisme, 1950
Sur la poésie nationale," *Présence Africaine*, 4 (October–November 1955): 39–41
Lettre à Maurice Thorez, 1956
"Culture et colonization," *Présence Africaine*, 8–10 (June–November 1956): 190–205
"L'homme de culture et ses responsabilités," *Présence Africaine*, 24–25 (February–May 1959): 116–122
Toussaint Louverture: la Révolution Française et le probème colonial, 1960

Further Reading

Arnold, A. James, *Modernism and Negritude: The Poetry and Poetics of Aimé Césaire*, Cambridge, Massachusetts: Harvard University Press, 1981

Condé, Maryse, "Négritude césairienne, Négritude senghorienne," *Revue de Littérature Comparée* (1974): 409–419
Confiant, Raphaël, *Aimé Césaire: une traversée paradoxale du siècle*, Paris: Éditions Stock, 1993
Hale, Thomas A., *Les Écrits d'Aimé Césaire. Bibliographie commentée*, Études Françaises, Numéro spécial, 14/3–4 (October 1978), Montréal: Les Presses de l'Université de Montréal
Kesteloot, Lilyan, *Les Écrivains noirs de langue française: naissance d'une literature*, Brussels: Éditions de l'Institut de Sociologie, Université Libre de Bruxelles, 1963
Kesteloot, Lilyan and Barthélémy Kotchy, *Aimé Césaire, l'homme et l'oeuvre*, Paris: Présence Africaine, 1973
Leiner, Jacqueline (editor), *Tropiques*. Paris: Éditions Jean-Michel Place, 1978
Ngal, Mwabil a Mpang, *Aimé Césaire: un homme à la recherche d'une patrie*, Dakar: Nouvelles Éditions Africaines, 1975
Ngal, Mwabil a Mpang and Martin Steins (editors), *Césaire 70*, Paris: Éditions Silex, 1984
Sartre, Jean-Paul, "Orphée noir," Introduction to L. S. Senghor, *Anthologie de la nouvelle poésie nègre et malgache*, Paris: P.U.F., 1948. Also in *Situations III*, Paris: Gallimard, 1949

CHAMOISEAU, PATRICK
Novelist, Essayist

The acclaimed Martiniquan novelist and essayist Patrick Chamoiseau is a Caribbean writer, a Francophone writer, a French writer from a French overseas department (Martinique), and a Creole writer (Creole by virtue of birth in a former colony of the Americas). As a francophone writer, he was awarded one of the most important French literary prizes for his novel *Texaco*. Discussing Chamoiseau's contribution and influence in modern French thought is not unproblematic because his relation to the mother country is itself complex and might appear to be paradoxical to some. Indeed, Chamoiseau's support for the independence of Martinique is no secret to those who know his affiliation to political movements for independence, and his essays question the present political status, identity, and culture of the French overseas departments. His birthplace and political stance unquestionably complicate the issue of his contribution to the social, historical, and cultural life of modern France. In one of his essays, *Écrire Dans Un pays Dominé*, Chamoiseau denounces the domination exercised by France and spells out his position as a dominated writer. His work, which is produced within the French or francophone canon, challenges the canon from within—the national seems to always intermix and collide with the vernacular. Although writing on the margins and constantly reaffirming his regional identity, he is a writer who is part of the French canon.

French critics have reveled in his contribution to a quasi "rejuvenation" of the French language and modern French fiction. Chamoiseau's literary works, which reveal the cultural dynamics of language, have been compared to the works Rushdie, Rabelais, or Joyce. His challenge of established linguistic laws, creation of new literary norms, and constant hybridization of his *parole* have become his trademarks. His enrichment and expansion of French literary expressions are obvious in his application of processes of transculturation. He is a postmodern writer because he writes at the crossroads of cultures in which imaginaries intermingle (Asian, European, African, Indian) with various genres (his work stands as an interface between oral and literary tradition) and multiple narrative voices. His fictional writing cannot be dissociated from his essay writing in which he formulates new theories and questions existing conceptualizations and theorizations of critical issues, such as the way we read and interpret culture and history and the way language and identity contribute to self-assertion.

As a postmodern thinker and postmodern writer, Chamoiseau has brought new approaches to the concept of cultural memory in the France/overseas departments binary. In the postmodernist style he challenged conceptions of "the grand History" to concentrate on a system of histories composed of individual stories, multiple imaginaries, and world events. He has been working on a reassessment of the legacy of French colonialism. He also addressed the loss that marginalized memories have suffered as well as the assimilation of those memories into the dominant collective memory of France. This questioning of colonial legacy and memory underlines his commitment to recover histories that were submerged under the grand History written by dominant voices. There is a deliberate attempt at reclaiming the past, rewriting history from a local perspective: rediscovering the Martiniquan past through individual and collective stories. Some question whether the regional can ever be reconciled with the national because the vernacular seems to constantly oppose the national. France's sociocultural and political life has been marked by various movements both on the continent (Brittany) and in the overseas departments (Corsica, Martinique) that have gradually shaped and reshaped French identity in the recent decades. Successive laws for regionalization (1970s) and decentralization (decentralization law of March 1982) implemented by the French government have increased demands for vernacular cultures and languages to be recognized within the French Republic. The European Charter on Regional Languages has strengthened support for those claims, especially in the French overseas departments.

Rather like other contemporary postcolonial writers, Chamoiseau has revived questions of how regional identity relates to national and global identity, preferring a nonconformist approach relying on the concept of creolization (sociohistorical and cultural formation of Creole societies from the Americas that started during colonization). He proceeds to debunk definitions of monolithic identity, preferring a pluralistic interpretation of identity rather than a single-rooted one. Chamoiseau's conceptualization of identity draws on the Martiniquan essayist and writer Edouard Glissant's poetic of rhizomic identity, which in turn is a reappropriation of the metaphorical use of rhizome by two French theorists, Gilles Deleuze and Félix Guattari—the rhizome, a subterranean stem with many ramifications, stands as a metaphor for the multiplicity, infinitude, and interconnectedness of culture and language (Deleuze & Guattari, 1987, 6–7).

Although most French critics have studied the characteristics of francophone countries along binaries such as center/periphery, dominant/dominated, Chamoiseau proposes a new theorization of francophone identities that give increased prominence to sociocultural elements, forms, and languages specific to societies from the French overseas departments. Patrick Chamoiseau shares with modern French thinkers and other thinkers in general the importance of language and culture in processes of self-definition and economic development. He works at relocating theories of culture and identity drawn by French critics in new sites that are more appropriate to his regional identity, demonstrating the significance of cross-culturalism, of interactions between oral and textual traditions.

An active member of the Creole cause, he collaborated on the manifesto *Éloge de la Créolité* (*In Praise of Creoleness*) with two other Martiniquan scholars (the writer Raphaël Confiant and the linguist Jean Bernabé) promoting a new cultural identity, which they called "Créolité" (creoleness). The major conceptual points of the Créolité thesis are about the reinvesting of Creole cultural practices, unearthing of orality, and creation of a new literary language. One of the crucial aspects of Chamoiseau's ideas, reflected notably in the *Éloge*, is the expression of the nonethnicity of nationalism and the spelling out of a new Creole aesthetic, which both looks inward at the culturally specific and reaches out to other cultures and peoples. He contends that the complexity of contemporary societies can only be fully understood when issues of multiculturalism, multilingualism, and transculturation (how cultures interact and react to each other within the same space) are integrated into discourses of self-definition. He insists that old conceptualizations of identity, culture and history, and nationalist ideologies centered on purity should integrate the complex relations that have emerged out of the development of a new world order. Indeed, the increasing globalization of the world economy and culture has provoked noticeable changes in the relations between peoples and cultures that are irremediable. Identity is being redefined; cultures are being reshaped (France is going through a period of intensified regionalism).

Creolization, a multicultural exchange and dynamic interpenetration, is not about the juxtaposition of cultures but about true relations between peoples. The writers of the créolité movement spoke about the progressive creolization of the world. If this is to be believed, Patrick Chamoiseau's work constitutes an asset to French modern thought because it defines concepts that are not only characteristic of the region from which they emerged but also concepts that are becoming characteristics of contemporary world communities transformed by globalization. His conceptualization of identity as routes rather than roots illuminates and influences concepts of identity and culture previously established by French theorists from the metropolis. His work is an acclamation of the pluralistic and polyphonic nature of communities that compose the French Republic. His appropriation of creolization as a mode of definition is an attempt at establishing discourses that would facilitate mediations between the region and the nation, the nation and the world. Finally, his acknowledgment that modes of relating to language, culture, and identity have to embrace new ways of understanding the interconnectedness of phenomena (ethnicity, nationalism, language, culture) is pertinent to all communities that hope to survive or transcend globalization.

KATIA MÉRINE

See also **Gilles Deleuze, Eduoard Glissant, Felix Guattari**

Biography

Patrick Chamoiseau was born in 1953 in Fort de France, Martinique (a French overseas department) where he lives as of this writing. He studied law in Paris. He is the author of numerous novels, *Chronique des sept misères*, Prix Kléber Haedens, Prix de l'île Maurice (1986), that have been translated into several major European languages. He published a theater piece, *Manman Dlo contre la fée Carabosse* (1982), memoirs of his childhood, and essays, *Éloge de la créolité* (1989). His work received national and international recognition (the latter more than the former) after the publication of his novel *Texaco*, which was awarded the Prix Goncourt in 1992.

Selected Writings

Manman Dlo contre la fée Carabosse, 1982
Chronique des sept misères, 1986; as *Chronicle of the Seven Sorrows*, translated by Linda Coverdale, 1999
Solibo le magnifique, 1988; as *Solibo Magnificent*, translated by Rose-Myriam Réjouis and Val Vinokurov, 1999

Au temps de l'antan, 1988
Éloge de la créolité/In Praise of Creoleness, 1989
Lettres créoles, tracées antillaises et continentales de la littérature, 1991
Texaco, 1992; as *Texaco*, translated by Rose-Myriam Réjouis and Val Vinokurov, 1998
Antan d'enfance: Une enfance créole, I, 1993; as *Childhood*, translated by Carol Volk, 1999
Chemin d'école; Une enfance créole, II, 1994; as *School Days*, translated by Linda Coverdale, 1998
Écrire la parole de nuit, la nouvelle littérature antillaise, 1994
L'esclave vieil homme et le molosse, 1997
Écrire en pays dominé, 1997
Biblique des derniers gestes, 2003

Further Reading

Akai, Joanne, "Creole . . . English: West Indian Writing as Translation," *TTR*, X, no. 2 (1997): 165–196
Arnold, James (editor), *A History of Caribbean Literature: Hispanic and Francophone Regions*, Vol.1, Amsterdam, Philadelphia: J. Benjamins, 1994
Ashcroft, Bill, Gareth Griffith, and Helen Tiffin (editors), *The Empire Writes Back: Theory And Practice in Post-Colonial Literatures*, London: Routledge, 1989
Balutansky Kathleen and Marie Agnes Sourieau (editors), *Caribbean Creolization: Reflections on the Cultural Dynamics of Language, Literature, and Identity*, Gainesville and Kingston: University Press of Florida and The Press University of the West Indies, 1998
Condé, Maryse and Madeleine Cottenet-Hage (editors), *Penser la Créolité*, Paris, Karthala, 1995
Gilles Deleuze and Guattari, Félix, *Mille Plateaux*, Les Éditions de Minuit, 1980; as *A Thousand Plateaus: Capitalism and Schizophrenia*, translated by Brian Massumi, 1987
Édouard, Glissant, *Poétique de la Relation* (Poétique III), Paris: Gallimard, 1990
Moudileno, Lydie, *L'écrivain Antillais au Miroir de sa Littérature*, Paris: Éditions Karthala, 1997
Perret, Delphine. *La Créolité: Espace de Création*, Martinique: Ibis Rouge Éditions, 2001

CIORAN, EMIL MICHEL
Philosopher, Essayist

References to nothingness, to despair, and to anguish recur throughout the writings of Emil Cioran, a philosopher who rejects all systems and exorcises his fears by means of incisive aphorisms. At the age of twenty-three, as soon as his studies in philosophy were over, he published a first collection in Romanian, *Pe culmile disperari*, in which he was already broaching the question of the meaning of existence and the relationship between man and God and asking questions about the problem of death. Here he comes across as a thinker who is convinced of the futility of philosophy and is immersed in tedium, in an agonizing emptiness, even, all of which consumes him to the point of insomnia and takes him to the gates of madness. The titles of the opening sections, "Unable to live any longer" and

"The passion for the absurd," give an indication of the work to come, which is an apologia for skepticism, but one that still measures itself against the divine, as does *Lacrimi si Sfinti*. He wishes, then, to be the equal of Schopenhauer or to be nothing.

After writing several collections in Romanian, the essayist settled in France and chose to write in the French language, "the ideal idiom for delicately translating elusive feelings," in order to express an increasingly dark pessimism, as is voiced in uncompromising titles from the *Précis de décomposition*, *De l'inconvénient d'être né*, or *La tentation d'exister* up until *Aveux et anathèmes*. Changing languages also provided an opportunity to make a complete break with a Romanian past he wanted to forget. "Writing in a foreign language is a form of emancipation. You are liberated from your own past," he declared in an interview in 1984.

His brevity, here more than elsewhere, is closely implicated with paradox and irony. It made it possible to escape the overweening presumption of philosophy, yet still to write rigorously. Cioran has a place in a line of descent from Heraclitus, for his sense of conciseness, and Mallarmé, for the attention he gives to the language. The lover of aphorisms has henceforth chosen the humility of the essayist. "How is it possible to be a philosopher? To have the audacity to attack the time, beauty, God, and the rest? The mind puffs up and struts shamelessly. Metaphysics, poetry—the impertinences of a louse. . ." (*Syllogismes de l'amertume*).

In fact, the philosopher speaks about ideas and constructs a system of abstracts, whereas the essayist speaks about his own existence: "The aphorism is cultivated only by those who have known fear *amidst* words, that fear of collapsing *with all the words*." This existential quest always goes hand in hand with the work of writing, Cioran's tone being particularly easy to locate in the succinctness of his pessimistic sentences, written in a very classic French, and in his taste for paradoxical statements, sarcasm, and derision. This derision led him, in his early beginnings in Romania, to some reactionary statements and to virulent anti-Semitic positions, but positions that he was to repudiate after the war in a new awareness of the suffering inflicted on European Judaism. Side by side with these aphorisms, a few books were made up of longer pieces, such as *Histoire et utopie*, in which he attempted to denounce all ideologies because no political undertaking could make good the loss of the vanished paradise of one's origins. He therefore followed a course that ran parallel to that of his compatriot Ionesco, choosing French, the better to tell of the absurdity of life, but, being more radical than Ionesco in his opinions, on the model of Joseph de Maistre whom he admired, and

in the same line as that other foreigners who chose the French language, the Irishman Samuel Beckett, but also Maurice Blanchot or Henri Michaux, other figures of literature who were haunted by suicide. Because the irreparable had been committed from birth ("Not to have been born, just to think of it—what happiness, what freedom, what space !"), he was left to live like Job on his dung-heap, torn between lamentations and fatalism. Cioran had an increasing mistrust of God, or any other form of the absolute, and a cynicism that held at a distance the new idols we might be tempted to set up for ourselves. Only lucidity had any importance: we must therefore be mistrustful of ourselves and resist the desire of organizing philosophy like "a coherent vision of chaos." There is no outcome to be hoped for because "the tragedy of detachment is that we cannot measure its progress. We move forward in a wilderness, and never know where we are." Man, for Cioran, emerged from the Apocalypse to end in disaster. There is little but music that finds favor with him, principally that of J. S. Bach "to whom God owes everything," and a few writers such as Samuel Beckett, Paul Valéry, his compatriot Mircea Eliade, or Henri Michaux, to whom he was to dedicate his "exercises in admiration."

Nevertheless, this pessimism only represents one aspect of his view of the world—one that is exacerbated because he only writes at times of anguish in an attempt to free himself from them. In 1984, he confided: "I don't believe in literature, I only believe in books that reflect the spiritual state of the writer, the profound need to rid oneself of something. Each of my books is a victory over discouragement." For Cioran, publishing a book meant projecting his anguish outside himself, providing a form of temporary liberation. Writing and publishing were therefore needed to help him survive, torn as he was between the mystical allure of the absolute and the sense of an irremediable emptiness.

It is his lucidity that explains the constant success of an author who had never wished to be modern, long after existentialism and the writers of the absurd ceased to occupy center stage. The man who dreamed of writing "a light and irrespirable book, which would be at the edge of everything, and would be addressed to no one," who declared, "a book, which, after demolishing everything, did not demolish itself, will have infuriated us in vain," keeps an important audience of admirers, as much for his uncompromising ethics as for his incisive style. The last words of his last book of aphorisms, *Aveux et anathèmes*, put forward an ultimate paradox: "After all, I have not wasted my time, I, too, have been flung up and down, just like anybody else, in this aberrant universe." This is the final evasion of a moralist who refused to take up a position on morality, of a philosopher who did not offer any transcendental explanation of the world, of a writer who did not believe in literature, of a misanthropist who wanted to publish and hence to have readers, of a suicide whose work will assure his survival.

MARC LITS

See also **Maurice Blanchot, Paul Valery**

Biography

Born in Rasinari near Sibiu in Romania in 1911, Emil Cioran showed brilliance in his philosophical studies in Bucharest, but he never completed his doctorate. He published his first books there in Romanian. He frequented the profascist circles of the "Iron Guard" until 1940, something he came to regret later. Cioran traveled to Paris in 1937 on a scholarship, to write a thesis about Bergson at the Sorbonne, and settled there permanently. From 1947 onward, he wrote in French. He already suffered from insomnia, an affliction that was to remain with him throughout his life. It was during these sleepless nights that he had his encounters with nothingness and wrote his books. He knew Ionesco, Eliade, and Beckett, but his books achieved hardly any kind of critical or public acclaim until the 1970s. He lived in a modest garret, earning his living through his translations, although he became more successful in the 1980s and 1990s. He died in 1995 at the age of 84, leaving behind large numbers of unpublished notebooks.

Selected Writings

Pe Culmile disperari, 1934; as *On the Heights of Despair*, translated by Ilinca Zarifopol-Johnston, 1992

Lacrimi si Sfiti, 1937; as *Tears and Saints*, translated by Ilinca Zarifopol-Johnston, 1996

Amurgul Gândurilor, 1940; as *Le crépuscule des pensées*, translated in French by Mirella Patureau-Nedelco, 1991 [The twilight of the thoughts]

Précis de décomposition, 1949; as *A Short History of Decay*, translated by Richard Howard, 1975

Syllogismes de l'amertume, 1952; as *All Gall is Divided: Gnomes and Apothegms*, translated by Richard Howard, 1999

La tentation d'exister, 1956; as *The Temptation to Exist*, translated by Richard Howard, 1968

Histoire et utopie, 1960; as *History and Utopia*, translated by Richard Howard, 1987

La chute dans le temps, 1964; as *The Fall into Time*, translated by Richard Howard, 1970

Le mauvais démiurge, 1969; as *The New Gods*, translated by Richard Howard, 1974

De l'inconvénient d'être né, 1973; as *The Trouble with Being Born*, translated by Richard Howard, 1976

Ecartèlements, 1979; as *Drawn and Quartered*, translated by Richard Howard, 1983

Exercices d'admiration, 1986 [Exercises of admiration]

Aveux et anathèmes, 1986; as *Anathemas and Admirations*, translated by Richard Howard, 1991

Œuvres (collected works edition), 1995

Entretiens, 1995 [Interviews]

Cahiers 1957–1972, 1997; as *Notebooks*, translated by Richard Howard, 2002

Further Reading

Bollon, Patrice, *Cioran l'hérétique*, Paris: Gallimard, 1997 [Cioran the heretic]

Calinescu, Matei, "Reading Cioran," *Salmagundi*, 112 (1996): 192–215

Dodille, Norbert, and Gabriel Liiceanu (editors), *Lectures de Cioran*, Paris, L'Harmattan, 1997 [Lectures of Cioran]

Gopnik, Adam, "The Critics. Five Books by E. M. Cioran," *The New Yorker*, 1906 (2000): 172–180

Gruzinska, Aleksandra, "Emile Michel Cioran," *Miorita: A Journal of Romanian Studies*, 10 (1986): 27–53

Jaudeau, Sylvie, *Cioran ou le dernier homme*, Paris: J. Corti, 1990 [Cioran or the last man]

Kimball, Roger, "The Anguishes of E. M. Cioran," *New Criterion*, 6, no. 7 (1988): 37–44

Kluback, William, and Michael Finkenthal (editors), *The Temptations of Emile Cioran*, New York: Peter Lang, 1997

Liiceanu, Gabriel, *Itinéraire d'une vie: E. M. Cioran*, Paris: Michalon, 1995 [Itineraries of a life]

Parfait, Nicole, *Cioran ou le défi de l'être*, Paris: Desjonquères, 2001 [Cioran on the challenge of being]

Sontag, Susan, "Thinking against Oneself," in her *Styles of Radical Will*, New York: Bantam Doubleday Dell, 1969

Sora, Mariana, *Cioran jadis et naguère*, Paris: L'Herne, 1988 [Cioran formerly and not long ago]

Tiffreau, Philippe, *Cioran ou la dissection du gouffre*, Paris: H. Veyrier, 1991 [Cioran or the dissection of the abyss]

CIXOUS, HÉLÈNE
Philosopher, Literary Critic, Novelist, and Playwright

The work of Hélène Cixous defies easy categorization. Although she is perhaps best known in the English-speaking world for her theoretical writings on feminism and literary criticism, her numerous experiments in fiction and drama are also significant. Indeed, she declines to see herself as a theorist and has asserted her conviction that poetic expression contains the greatest truth. The fact that her œuvre refuses to be confined to one discipline or genre is an important indicator of her interest in boundaries, limits, and frontiers, wherever she encounters them. Her many and varied texts are marked by a common desire to explore the ways in which writing can work against such boundaries or limits and free the self for new possibilities of relationship with others.

For Cixous, the writing that has the greatest liberatory potential is instantiated in what she calls *écriture féminine*, a practice that seeks to subvert the power of language to construct certain limited kinds of subjectivity. *Écriture féminine*, which originates from a feminine subject position (although it is not, in her view, limited to women), undermines what Cixous terms the masculine economy, the dominant mode of intersubjective exchange within the Western tradition. In such an economy, "giving" is always quid pro quo; that is, the subject gives only in order to get something—generally an increase in prestige, wealth, or power—and thus is never truly open to otherness. Conventional modes of writing, bound by disciplinary and generic conventions, are inscribed within and reinforce such a masculine economy, and thus must be refused. Cixous's wager that an *other* mode of writing—*écriture féminine*—exists, or can be brought into existence, informs all her writing, from her novels and plays to her theoretical work in feminism, philosophy, and literary criticism.

Although she resists the label of "feminist," seeing the term as allied with a certain politics of equality that she rejects on theoretical grounds, Cixous is typically identified by her anglophone readers as one of the so-called French feminists (along with, most notably, Julia Kristeva and Luce Irigaray). This identification is valid in some important respects; for example, Cixous shares with Kristeva and Irigaray a methodological debt to Jacques Derrida and Jacques Lacan. Indeed, Cixous has been friends with Derrida since the early 1960s, and their common methods and shared interests are clearly apparent in their recent collaboration, *Voiles* (1998), an extended meditation on the interrelationships between vision and knowledge. It should be noted, however, that Cixous, unlike Lacan or Derrida, Kristeva or Irigaray, views herself primarily as an artist, not a theorist. She finds her highest truth in poetry, in the imagination, and argues in *Hélène Cixous, photo de racines* (1994) that concepts are less true than poetic forms of expression by virtue of their power to subject life to the grasp of a limited rationality.

In spite of her reservations about theory, however, Cixous is probably best known in the English-speaking world for her theoretical feminist writings of the middle 1970s. In these texts—which include *Prénoms de personne* (1974); *La Jeune née* (1975), cowritten with Catherine Clément; and "Le Rire de la Méduse" (1975)—Cixous explores ways that the symbolic expressions of Western philosophy, psychoanalysis, and literature work to oppress women. Turning to the work of Freud, Kleist, and Joyce, among others, she maps an imaginal association of women with death and argues that such an association in fact reveals the death drive underlying the masculine economy, which is characterized by a fear of otherness in all its guises. In contrast, Cixous offers her view of a *feminine* economy, an economy marked by mobility, receptivity, and

the creation and sustenance of difference-in-itself. Here, as in the "general economy" of Georges Bataille, the self gives of itself endlessly, refusing the fear that would imprison it in a risk-free solitude. For Cixous, this economy is feminine by virtue of its affinity for establishing relations with otherness (because the feminine is, in her view, always already multiple and relational). It operates in and through a feminine mode of writing that opens up a passage between the self and its others—including the other selves that make up the self—and in so doing helps to overcome death. By emphasizing the relational quality of the feminine economy, Cixous is able to substitute *alterity*, genuine difference or otherness, for the *opposition* between the self and others that marks the masculine economy. In an exchange based on the affirmation of alterity, the self approaches the other asymptotically, but without ever merging with the other in a fusion that would destroy the self or the other. Thus both self and other are able fully to *live*.

The insistence that *écriture féminine* is on the side of life is apparent in many of Cixous's writings, but especially in the autobiographical musings scattered throughout both her literary and her theoretical texts. Indeed, the link between writing and memory is crucial for Cixous. She sees the practice of writing as rooted in an experience of loss, of death, of having been banished to the *outside* of life. Remembering loss, writing (beyond) death, allows the subject to rediscover what was lost, to reenter the living world from which she was exiled.

Thus her first "novel," *Dedans* (1969), which tests the limits of its genre to the extent that it seems to have no plot, characters, or chronology, explores her childhood experience of the death of her father in order to show how writing can vanquish death by giving expression to love. Here, as in the work of Lacan, the father's death thrusts the subject into language. However, the subject of *Dedans* is feminine, and the language into which "she" is initiated is not the death-driven language of the masculine economy but *écriture féminine*. In *La Venue à l'écriture* (1977), Cixous returns to the death of her father in order to link writing, in its power to overcome death and time, to the unconscious and God. Her father here becomes the Father; the death of her personal father embodies a Nietzschean death of the Father-God; and writing emerges as a figuration of a divinity aligned with life, and feminine by virtue of its identification with *écriture féminine*.

Cixous's particular interest in the work of Brazilian novelist Clarice Lispector, too, is understandable in the context of Cixous's claim that *écriture féminine* is on the side of life. Although Cixous has often been criticized for relying mostly on male authors as examples (Joyce, Kleist, Blanchot, Kafka, to name a few), it is Lispector who serves for Cixous as a privileged model of the practice of feminine writing. In the many readings of Lispector found throughout her œuvre, Cixous emphasizes the life-enhancing qualities of Lispector's work and allows Lispector's writing to transform her own. The results, then, are not so much applications of a formalized feminist literary theory as they are expressions of a relational mode of reading/writing that affirms sensual experience, freedom, transformation, and life.

For Cixous, the power of a feminine practice of writing goes beyond mere affirmation of life; *écriture féminine* can also help the exile (re)establish ties with the world from which she has been cast out. This is apparent in Cixous's representation of herself as "Jewoman," a figuration that condenses the multiple senses of exile, foreignness, and alterity that have marked her intercourse with the dominant cultural tradition of the West and that are expressed in her ongoing concern for boundaries, limits, and frontiers. The many autobiographical references in her texts make it clear that she experiences herself as a perennial outsider, owing to her Sephardic Jewish background, her childhood in French colonial Algeria, and—certainly not least significantly—her femaleness. However, the "Jewoman" is not merely an exile. Although as "Jewoman" Cixous lacks the authority to write, nevertheless she writes, and it is writing itself, for Cixous, that demands that she write, that she find ways to break out of the prison of otherness in which she finds herself.

The desire to overcome exile, estrangement, and alienation also figures prominently in Cixous's dramatic works, where—perhaps more than in any of her other writings—content and form combine to express her faith in the life-affirming power of *écriture féminine*. In her plays, Cixous gives voice to her concern with the ethical and political questions posed by contemporary history, especially as seen in the effects of colonialism and racism. In *L'Histoire terrible mais inachevée de Norodom Sihanouk, roi du Camboge*, for example, Cixous is primarily concerned with the status of the individual subject who is subjected to the multiple domains of power and knowledge that constitute states and nations, structures that she sees as allied with the death-driven masculine economy. *History*, with a capital *H*, represents for Cixous the process whereby otherness is suppressed for the sake of the construction of a necessarily oppressive collective "identity." Against this, Cixous once again asserts the importance of a feminine economy that remains open to the Other, that relies on "re-membering" as a way of creating multiple alternate *histories* and that facilitates the construction of an intersubjectivity based on compassion and responsibility to otherness. *L'Histoire* emerges as

a passionate insistence on the need for remembering—and thus, for Cixous, writing—as a means for recovering what was lost. Drama itself—being essentially processual, always susceptible to transformation as it is performed over and over again—offers Cixous a tangible example of the feminine economy she seeks to invoke.

All of Cixous's œuvre, then, reveals her strong commitment to a politics of personal and social transformation and liberation. Her celebration of *écriture féminine* in the works of other authors and her ongoing attempts to allow a life-enhancing feminine economy to speak through her own writings point to her desire to participate in the birth of a practice of writing that allows the Other to live. *Écriture féminine* is her primary tool in the struggle against the repression and social injustice that mark the masculine, death driven economy she wants to overturn. For Cixous, the practice of writing, across any generic or disciplinary boundaries, is directed at creating a language that recognizes and supports the value of all life.

JUDITH POXON

See also **Georges Bataille, Maurice Blanchot, Jacques Derrida, Luce Irigaray, Julia Kristeva, Jacques Lacan**

Biography

Hélène Cixous was born in Oran, Algeria, in 1937 and pursued an early career as an academic. She successfully completed her *agrégation* in English in 1959 and subsequently taught at the Université de Bordeaux and the Sorbonne in Paris. Following the Parisian riots of May 1968, she was authorized to found the Université de Paris VIII—Vincennes, an experimental and nonhierarchical alternative to the traditional French academy. She has been Professor of English literature at Paris VIII since 1968. In 1969, her first experimental novel, *Dedans*, won the prestigious Prix Médicis, and she is perhaps best known in France as a literary artist. However, she has attracted more attention in the English-speaking world for her works of feminist theory, notably *La Jeune née* (1975), and her commitment to women's issues is evident in her 1974 founding of the Centre de Recherches en Etudes Féminines. Throughout her prolific writing career, she has been profoundly affected by her early experience of colonialism, and—whether in fiction, plays, criticism, or theory—she has attempted to give voice to the "Other" who is silenced by the dominant discourses of the Western literary, psychoanalytic, and philosophical traditions.

Selected Works

Le Prénom de Dieu, 1967 [*The First Name of God*]
Dedans, 1969; as *Inside*, translated by Carol Barko, 1986

Le Troisième corps, 1970; as *The Third Body*, translated by Keith Cohen, 1999
Un Vrai jardin, 1971 [*A True Garden*]
Neutre, 1972 [*Neuter*]
Prénoms de personne, 1974 [*First Names of Anyone/No one*]
La Jeune née, with Catherine Clément, 1975; as *The Newly Born Woman*, translated by Betsy Wing, 1986
Portrait de Dora, 1976; as *Portrait of Dora*, translated by Anita Barrows, 1976
Angst, 1977
La Venue à l'écriture, 1977; republished in *Entre l'écriture*, 1986; as *"Coming to Writing" and Other Essays*, edited and translated by Deborah Jenson et al., 1991
Nom d'Oedipe, 1978; as *The Name of Oedipus*, translated by Christiane Makward and Judith Miller, 1991
Vivre l'orange/To Live the Orange, 1979
Le Livre de Promethea, 1983; as *The Book of Promethea*, translated by Betsy Wing, 1991
L'Histoire terrible ais inachevée de Norodom Sihanouk, roi du Camboge, 1985; as *The Terrible but Unfinished Story of Norodom Sihanouk, King of Cambodia*, translated by Juliet Flower MacCannell et al., 1994
L'Indiade ou l'Inde de leurs rêves, 1987
Manne: aux Mandelstams aux Mandelas, 1988; as *Manna, for the Mandelstams for the Mandelas*, translated by Catherine A. F. MacGillivray, 1994
Writing Differences: Readings from the Seminar of Hélène Cixous, edited by Susan Sellers, 1988
Readings: The Poetics of Blanchot, Joyce, Kafka, Kleist, Lispector, and Tsvetayeva, translated and edited by Verena Andermatt Conley, 1991
Three Steps on the Ladder of Writing, translated and edited by Sarah Cornell and Susan Sellers, 1993
Hélène Cixous, photo de racines, with Mireille Calle-Gruber, 1994; as *Hélène Cixous, Rootprints: Memory and Life Writings*, translated by Eric Prenowitz, 1997
The Firstdays of the Year, translated by Catherine A. F. MacGillivray, 1998
Stigmata: Escaping Texts, translated by Eric Prenowitz, 1998
Voiles, with Jacques Derrida, 1998; as *Veils*, translated by Geoffrey Bennington, 2001
Les rêveries de la femme sauvage, 2000 [*The Dreams of a Wild Woman*]
Benjamin à Montaigne, 2001 [*Benjamin to Montaigne*]

Further Reading

Barreca, Regina, and Lee A. Jacobus (editors), *Hélène Cixous: Critical Impressions*, Florence: Gordon & Breach, 1999
Conley, Verena Andermatt, *Hélène Cixous: Writing the Feminine*, Toronto: University of Toronto Press, 1992
Dobson, Julia, *Hélène Cixous and the Theatre: The Scene of Writing*, New York: Peter Lang, 2001
Jardine, Alice, and Ann Menke (editors), "Hélène Cixous," in *Shifting Scenes: Interviews on Women, Writing, and Politics in Post-68 France*, New York: Columbia University Press, 1991
O'Grady, Kathleen, "Guardian of Language: An Interview with Hélène Cixous," *Women's education des femmes*, 12 (1996–1997): 6–10
Penrod, Lynn Kettler, *Hélène Cixous*, London: Prentice Hall International, 1996
Sellers, Susan, *Hélène Cixous: Authorship, Autobiography, and Love*, Oxford: Polity Press, 1996
Shiach, Morag, *Hélène Cixous: A Politics of Writing*, London: Routledge, 1991
Wilcox, Helen (editor), *The Body and the Text: Hélène Cixous, Reading and Teaching*, New York, St. Martin's Press, 1990

CLASSICS

In his recently published memoirs, the leading French Hellenist Pierre Vidal-Naquet characterized the postwar French classical scene in the following way: "I am accustomed to saying that at the end of the sixties Greek studies in France were marked by the domination of a Church, the Sorbonne, against which certain sects were formed who resisted its dominance as best they could: a Marxist sect at Besançon with Pierre Léveque at its head, a philological sect at Lille with Jean Bollack and his disciples and an anthropological sect at the École [Pratique des Hautes Études] with Jean-Pierre Vernant and his friends" (Vidal-Naquet, Pierre *Mémoires: Le trouble et la lumière 1955–1998*, 209). Although Vidal-Naquet is talking exclusively about the institutional demarcation of Greek studies in postwar France, his comments are highly instructive for a discussion of the interrelations between the discipline of classics and modern French thought.

There are three main points that arise from Vidal-Naquet's characterization. The first is precisely the question of why Vidal-Naquet isolates Greek studies rather than talking about a unified discipline of classics. In fact, one of the main difficulties of tracing the development of the discipline of classics in postwar France is that such a discipline does not, in fact, exist. The English term *classics* has no equivalent in French—a difficulty well known to French scholars of the ancient world. Thus the incommensurability of the Anglo-American term *classics* to the study of the classical period in France raises serious problems of definition that are anything but incidental to an attempt to provide an overview of the discipline. In particular, although Latinists and Hellenists may not coexist in perfect harmony in English and American classics departments, from an institutional perspective, at least, most Anglo-Saxon Hellenists and Latinists share a common disciplinary formation. This is not as obvious in France. French Latinists rarely belong to the same academic department as their Hellenist counterparts. There are, of course, exceptions, and this configuration differs substantially from institution to institution. The prestigious École Normale Supérieure, for instance, does have a center dedicated to *études anciennes* that combines the study of Latin and Greek. At other institutions scholars known to Anglo-Americans as classicists are found in departments as varied as history, anthropology, *lettres*, philosophy, art history/archaeology, history of religion, and so on. Some French classicists defy such institutional categorization altogether: Jean-Pierre Vernant is often described as Hellenist but also as a philosopher, a historian of religion, a psychologist, or simply a theorist, an intellectual, not to mention a resistance fighter.

So despite some exceptions, it is fair to say that the term *French classics* is, generally speaking, a convenient Anglo-Saxon construct. This is not just a pedantic point about taxonomy. As will be seen, the different institutional contextualization of the postwar French study of the ancient world has had a very significant effect on the developments and the debates within the discipline over the past fifty years. It is also fair to note from the outset that although there are numerous Latinists who have had a very significant influence on their individual fields (Claude Nicolet, Roman republican politics; Paul Veyne, Roman elegy and Roman arena; John Scheid, Roman religion; and Florence Dupont, Latin literature, to name just a few) it is generally true that Greek studies in France have developed a much more distinctive approach to the ancient world. Their influence has consequently been far more extensive both within the international classical academy and more widely across other disciplines in France and beyond.

The second area of note is the political context of postwar French studies of antiquity. The contrast that Vidal-Naquet established between an orthodox church and various dissident sects has a strong ideological dimension. Not only have Greek/Latin studies often been seen as falling along a Left/Right divide, but the institutional map of classical studies also corresponds to an ideological map of the French academy. As Vidal-Naquet indicates, the ancient Greek historian Pierre Lévêque was a committed Marxist, and it was firmly within this tradition that new approaches to the study of the ancient city were pioneered at Besançon. Jean-Pierre Vernant, a former resistance fighter, was equally an active member of the French Communist Party (Parti Communiste Français) for twenty-five years, and his innovative readings of Athenian democracy are intimately connected to his own experience of the battles of the postwar left in France. Vidal-Naquet himself has led several alternative careers, most notably as a historian of the Algerian War and a campaigner against Holocaust denial. The École Pratique des Hautes Études, where both Vernant and Vidal-Naquet held chairs, has strong left-wing credentials. Vernant's archrival, the French academician Jacqueline de Romilly, can, on the other hand, be identified with all things conservative. At the Sorbonne, de Romilly came to represent the orthodoxy of French Greek studies, and her known hostility to the Vernantian circle gave rise to numerous debates about the role of the classical past in the modern French academy. It is not just the case

that French classicists have been actively involved in French postwar political debates but rather that this ideological perspective is integral to their engagement in debates about the ancient world.

The third point relates to the interconnection of French classical studies to the wider currents of postwar French thought. In modern France the study of the ancient world has gone hand in hand with a questioning of the various methodological positions that emerged on the postwar intellectual scene. Scholars of the ancient world adopted, in addition to Marxism, a plurality of different theoretical positions. Vernant, Vidal-Naquet, and their associates were often identified with the projects of structuralism. Their interest in myth shows the influence of Claude Lévi-Strauss, and their particular emphasis on the mediation of binary oppositions in the analysis of ritual aligned them unambiguously with structural anthropology. But Vernant and his colleagues by no means blindly followed an orthodox structuralist position; instead their focus on the historical and political aspects of the ancient city posed a challenge to Lévi-Straussian anthropology. The Lille Hellenist Jean Bollack has explicitly placed his work within a tradition of German hermeneutics. Bollack combines a highly traditional interest in philology and textual transmission with the insights of hermeneutics to deliver innovative readings of ancient texts. The Roman historian Paul Veyne brought his interest in historicism to bear on his readings of ancient culture and literature. Veyne's particular take on historicism and new historicism was defined and redefined in a famous debate with his close friend Michel Foucault.

Three scholars whose work exemplifies French postwar classics at its most distinctive are the Roman historian Paul Veyne, the anthropologically-inclined Hellenist Jean-Pierre Vernant, and the Greek philologist Jean Bollack. Although they offer only a partial account of the general state of French classics, these scholars are paradigmatic in their willingness to engage in intellectual debates beyond the confines of their discipline.

Paul Veyne and the Problems of Historiography

Paul Veyne was elected to a chair in Roman history at the prestigious College de France in 1975. When Veyne took up this position his reputation had been established as much in the field of historiography as in Roman history. Two complementary books had made his name in seventies: the historiographical essay *Writing History* and the learned tome *Bread and Circuses*. His polemical essay, *Writing History*, set out to repudiate all theories of history that were based on grand generalization and social laws. Reacting in part against the dominance of a Marxist tradition of historiography, Veyne insisted that there was "neither progress nor reason in history, neither dialectic nor human nature which once disbanded has returned to haunt us, nor is there a kind of Weberian or pseudo-Weberian rationalism. History cannot be understood through some great cause such as the class struggle. The real causes are small ones in the sense that they have no epic grandeur. 'Origins are rarely grand' so spoke Nietzsche . . . and Maurras" (Veyne, 1995, 33). History is for Veyne an account of the "sublunary" world of the particular rather than the revelation of some great universal truth. But Veyne does not only put into question the grand narratives of historiography, he also challenges the very notion that there are such categories as political history, social history, economic history, and cultural history. These modern constructs, Veyne insists, are superimposed onto the quite different societies of the past that have their own internal structures. Instead, Veyne advocates a model of history in which the task of the historian is to make an inventory of the differences among social forms. He returned to many of the themes of *Writing History* in a later essay, "Foucault révolutionne l'histoire," in which he reflects on the interconnections between his nihilist vision of history and Foucault's development of a theory of "discourse."

Bread and Circuses is in many ways the application of the paradigm of history developed in these theoretical works. An 800-page volume, it explores the development of a theme over more than one thousand years of history. In his attempt to trace the development of "euergetism" over its many transformations, Veyne tries to free himself of any theoretical viewpoint that would obscure the particularity of the practice he set out to elucidate. The first 200 pages of the book continue the polemic of his earlier historiographical writing by insisting on the autonomy of historical periods from the universalist theories we use to make sense of them. *Bread and Circuses* brings to fruition Veyne's meditation on history as "the inventory of differences." In many ways, Veyne's book functions as a rejection of orthodox economic histories of the ancient world. Instead of castigating the Greeks and Romans for having failed to produce a "rational economic system," Veyne sets in place an alternative model that is more sensitive to the historical specificity of ancient culture. To this end he borrows from the gift theory developed by the French anthropologist Marcel Mauss to create a new way of understanding the "archaic form of exchange" practiced in classical times. Veyne does not force the ancient material into this foreign framework, but rather aims to show how his analysis of a range of phenomena in all their complexity can correspond to the alternative theory that he sets in place. In its

rejection of traditional economic history, *Bread and Circuses* pioneered a new form of history, an *histoire des moeurs*, which remains highly influential for ancient historians today.

Veyne's role in the development of a new understanding of historicism had a further dimension in his well-known intellectual comradeship with Michel Foucault in the last years of his life. Indeed, Foucault's renewed interest in antiquity in his final writings has been attributed to his association with Veyne. Together they studied stoic philosophy, and Veyne provided a crucial historical and philological background for Foucault's venture into the ancient world in the final two volumes of the *History of Sexuality*. Foucault's influence can in turn be seen not only in Veyne's own work on stoicism but also in *Do the Greeks Believe in their Myths?* in which Veyne used Foucault's analysis of discourse to explain the role of the "divine" in the Greco-Roman conception of the world order.

Jean-Pierre Vernant and the Anthropology of Ancient Greece

If Veyne's dialogue with Foucault gave rise to a new practice of historiography within the field of Roman history, Vernant's dialogue with Lévi-Strauss was behind the development of a groundbreaking reinterpretation of the ancient Greek city. When Vernant founded the Centre de Recherches Comparées sur les Sociétés Anciennes (later renamed the Centre Louis Gernet after Vernant's mentor) at the heart of the École Pratique des Hautes Études, he brought together an extremely diverse group of researchers who shared a commitment to the insights of structural anthropology. Indianists, sinologists, sumerologists, and ethonologists met every week with classicists for ten years to explore in their seminars such themes as war, land, sacrifice, oracles, hunting, and polytheism in a cross-cultural perspective. But despite this emphasis on a comparative methodology, it was paradoxically the specificity of Greek culture that emerged from this encounter with other ancient societies. Indeed, what is most distinctive about Vernant and his associates of the so-called Paris School (most notably Pierre Vidal-Naquet, Marcel Detienne, and Nicole Loraux, but also the director of the Centre, Gernet François Hartog, François Lissarague, Alain Schnapp, and many others) is their combination of the insights gained from structural anthropology with a strong emphasis on the historical and political dimension of Greek society.

Nowhere is this dual perspective more apparent than in Vernant's seminal readings of Greek tragedy in *Myth and Tragedy*. In two of his most famous essays he sets out to deliver a radical new interpretation of Sophocles' *Oedipus Tyrannus*. "Oedipus without the complex" sets out to discredit Freudian and Freudian-influenced readings of Greek tragedy. Vernant starts by asking: "In what respect is it possible that a literary work belonging to the culture of fifth-century Athens, itself a very free transposition of a much more ancient Theban legend dating from before the institution of the city-state, should confirm the observations of a doctor on the patients who thronged his consulting rooms at the beginning of the twentieth century?"(Vernant/Vidal-Naquet *Myth and Tragedy*, 85). For Vernant "this demonstration has all the semblance of rigor of an argument based on a vicious circle," and he uses this negative comparison to define his own model of "historical psychology" against the Freudian methodology: "Here we seize upon the difference in method between the Freudian approach on the one hand and historical psychology on the other. Freud's point of departure is an intimate experience undergone by the public, which is historically unlocated. The meaning attributed to this experience is then projected onto the work in question regardless of its own socio-cultural context. Historical psychology proceeds in the opposite manner" (*Myth and Tragedy*, 87).

His attack on the Freudian reading is, then, framed by an explicit promotion of his own alternative methodology. Indeed, "Oedipus without the complex" cannot be read in isolation from its companion essay that appears alongside it in *Myth and Tragedy*, "Ambiguity and Reversal: On the Enigmatic Structure of *Oedipus Rex.*" "Ambiguity and Reversal" is precisely the application of Vernant's notion of "historical psychology," which he expounds in his critique of the Freudian reading. By shifting the focus of interest away from incest and parricide, Vernant's Oedipus emerges as a paradigm for the competing structures of political power. For Vernant, Oedipus's fate is structured by an irreconcilable opposition between the *pharmakos* (the scapegoat) and the *tyrannos* (the tyrant): "*Divine king* and *pharmakos*: these are the two sides to Oedipus that make a riddle of him by combining within him two figures, the one the reverse of the other, as in a formula with a double meaning"(*Myth and Tragedy*, 122). But this anthropological binary opposition is immediately mapped onto the sociopolitical landscape of the ancient city. "This mythical image of the hero," he writes, "exposed and saved, rejected and returning in triumph, is continued in the fifth century in a transposed form, in one particular representation of the *turannos*" (*Myth and Tragedy*, 116). In "Ambiguity and Reversal," then, Oedipus is a figure trapped between the incompatible social institutions of tyranny and democracy. Vernant substitutes the Freudian Oedipus as sexual subject with the Vernantian Oedipus as political subject.

Jean Bollack and the Priority of the Text

If Vernant's reading of the Sophoclean text is marked by an emphasis on the historical and political dimension of Greek culture, Jean Bollack's reading of Sophocles represents a radical withdrawal from such socio-cultural contextualization. Bollack established the Centre de Recherche Philologique in Lille and hailed a new return to the classical text. His rejection of the Vernantian approach could not have been more marked. Where Vernant's readings stressed the collective values of the audience of ancient literature, Bollack's interpretations are preoccupied with genres, texts, and authors—all categories that maintain the autonomy of artistic creation from their social and historical reception. It is the unique quality of the Sophoclean literary mind rather than tragedy's meditation on the problems of society that is the object of the philologists' analysis. Bollack explains his opposition to the Vernantian method: "It is the function of philological analysis in its reading of texts to highlight the principle itself of univocity and establish the singular sense of a text, this is the real essence of my practice. Vernant's research, on the other hand, which has its roots in structuralism, links up with postmodernism in its emphasis on indeterminacy"(Bollack, 2000, 70).

So Bollack's denunciation of historicist readings is not just a form of aestheticism. For Bollack, the rejection of context implies the possibility of the discovery of a singular meaning of any given text. The arduous task of the philologist is to recover this essential meaning by abstracting from all forms of extraneous evidence. Moreover, Bollack's theory of reading has a further dimension in its assertion of the necessity of reconstructing the original meaning of an ancient text. Although many classicists have not only accepted, but have indeed made a virtue of the impossibility of a return to a singular authentic meaning, Bollack insists that no philology worth its name can fail to strive to achieve a direct access to the "meaning" of classical literature. Rather than seeing the history of reading as forming an integral part of this "meaning," Bollack and his associates set out to remove the obstructing accretions that have multiplied over the centuries since the Renaissance to reveal the naked ancient text in all its original glory. Bollack's contribution to French classics is not only distinctive in the extremism of his commitment to a dialogue between modern scholar and ancient text but also in his combination of the very traditional classical skills of philology and textual criticism with the insights of a German nineteenth-century tradition of hermeneutics.

Conclusion

The French postwar classical academy, then, is marked by a plurality of different interests and methodologies.

But unlike its Anglo-American counterpart, it could be argued that French classics have been conspicuous in the desire to conduct a genuinely interdisciplinary dialogue across the humanities. Moreover, many French classicists have found themselves at the forefront of the theoretical and political debates that have dominated French intellectual life in the postwar era. It is this interconnection to the wider intellectual scene that accounts for the presence of the ancient world in so many of the writings of modern French thought: in addition to Foucault and Lévi-Strauss, who showed an active interest in the ancient world, a return to antiquity can be traced further afield in many of the central texts of Lacan, Derrida, Deleuze, Girard, Cixous, Irigaray, and Kristeva.

MIRIAM LEONARD

See also **Helene Cixous, Gilles Deleuze, Jacques Derrida, Michel Foucault, Luce Irigaray, Julia Kristeva, Jacques Lacan, Claude Lévi-Strauss, Nicole Loraux, Charles Maurras, Marcel Mauss, Jean-Pierre Vernant**

Further Reading

Bollack, Jean, *La Grèce de personne: Les mots sous le mythe*, Paris: Seuil, 1997
Bollack, Jean, *Sens contre sens: Comment lit-on?* Paris: La passe du vent, 2000
Cassin, Barbara (editor), *Nos Grecs et leurs modernes: Les stratégies contemporaines d'appropriation de l'antiquité*, Paris: Seuil, 1992
Derrida, Jacques, "Nous autres Grecs" in Les stratégies contemporaines d'appropriation de l'antiquité, edited by Barbara Cassin, Paris: Seuil, 1992
Droit, Roger-Pol (editor), *Greeks and Romans in the Modern World*, New York: Columbia University Press, 1998
Knox, Bernard, *Essays Ancient and Modern*, Baltimore, Maryland: Johns Hopkins University Press, 1988
Loraux, Nicole, "Back to the Greeks?: Chronique d'une expédition lointaine en terre connue" in *Une école pour les sciences sociales*, edited by Jacques Revel and Nathan Wachtel, Paris: CERF, 1996
Loraux, Nicole, Gregory Nagy, and Laura Slatkin (editors), *Antiquities: Postwar French Thought*, New York: New Press, 2001
Sissa, Giulia, "Philology, Anthropology, Comparison: The French Experience" *Classical Philology* 92 (1997):167–171
Vernant, Jean-Pierre, *Entre Mythe et Politique*, Paris: Seuil, 1996
Vernant, Jean-Pierre, *La volonté de comprendre; Entreteins avec J. P. Vernant*, Paris: L'aube, 1999
Vernant, Jean-Pierre and Pierre Vidal-Naquet, *Tragedy and Myth in Ancient Greece*, translated by Janet Lloyd, New York: Zone Books, 1988
Veyne, Paul, *Comment on écrit l'histoire?; suivi de Foucault révolutionne l'histoire*, Paris: Seuil, 1979
Veyne, Paul, *Writing History: Essay on Epistemology*, translated by Mina Moore-Rinvolucri, Manchester, England: Manchester University Press, 1984
Veyne, Paul, *Did the Greeks Believe in their Myths: An Essay on the Constitutive Imagination*, translated by Paula Wissig, Chicago: Chicago University Press, 1988
Veyne, Paul, *Bread and Circuses: History, Sociology and Political Pluaralism*, edited with an introduction by Oswynn Murray, translated by Brian Pearce, London and Frome: Allen Lane, 1990
Veyne, Paul, *Le quotidien et L'intéressant: Entreteins avec Catherine Dorbo Peschanski*, Paris: Les Belles Lettres, 1995
Vidal-Naquet, Pierre, *Mémoires—Le trouble et la lumière 1955–1998*, Paris: Seuil, 1998

COLONIAL AND POSTCOLONIAL EXPERIENCE

Recovering evidence of the colonial experience undergone by indigenous subjects in France's overseas empire is a process fraught with practical difficulties. Not only is there a risk of conflating radically different regional experiences (and perpetuating the homogenization that is a characteristic of colonial discourse itself), but also it was not until the early to mid-twentieth century that distinctively indigenous voices would find fora and media in which they could express themselves with any clarity. Earlier traces are often restricted to imperial archives (in which colonial subjects are invariably treated as an indistinguishable mass or simply reduced to statistics) or to the narratives of metropolitan travelers and exoticist novels (in both of which the colonies and their inhabitants are often little more than the backcloth against which French identities are projected and Western ideas explored).

Even Haiti (the former French colony of Saint-Domingue), whose independence was won in 1804 after a decade of slave rebellion led by Toussaint Louverture, remained heavily dependent on France in intellectual and cultural matters well into the nineteenth century. Chronologically postcolonial, its authors and thinkers were often guided by metropolitan movements (such as romanticism), just as the emerging state's attitudes to ethnicity continued to be dictated by the strict divisions of French colonial pigmentocracy. The years following independence were nevertheless marked by a fiercely nationalistic search for identity, and traces of the early twentieth-century *indigénisme* movement, which rejected European values and celebrated local culture, are to be found in the work of earlier authors such as Oswald Durand (whose *Choucoune* is one of the first examples of poetry written in Haitian Creole). Other later nineteenth-century essayists (especially Anténor Firmin) were to begin to explore the African roots of Haitian culture, often inspired to do so by contemporary French racial thinking such as Gobineau's *Essai sur l'inégalité des races humaines* (1853–1855).

Although regularly ignored in studies of francophone postcolonial experience, the Haitian example foreshadows the more recent struggles of other former French colonies (in North Africa, sub-Saharan Africa, Indochina, the Caribbean, and the Indian Ocean) to produce a distinctive intellectual or literary culture once independence (or a greater degree of autonomy) had been won. The constant threat of neocolonialism is a reminder that apparent freedom from colonial domination is often followed by a sustained effort by the former colonizer to maintain sovereignty. This political struggle is mirrored in the striving for intellectual self-determination that becomes a characteristic of postcolonial states: initial adoption of Western norms leads to a rapid desire for their adaptation to specific national circumstances. In the colonial period, such independence of thought was resisted by the networks of metropolitan power. An imaginary geography of center and periphery placed Paris as the focus of culture, civilization, and thought. The colonies were accordingly relegated to marginal positions, seen in relation to this benchmark as inherently inferior and denied coevality with metropolitan France as a result of their primitivism (for example, sub-Saharan Africa) or terminal decay (for example, Indochina). In addition, the French *mission civilisatrice* (civilizing mission) trumpeted the developmental aspects of French-language schools and relied on education as one of the mainstays of procolonial propaganda (in order, in particular, to signal the supposedly ethical bases of French expansionism). School manuals were used to disseminate Eurocentric accounts of culture and history, and an emphasis on French-language teaching led to the denigration of indigenous languages and often also to the erosion of heterogeneous elements within colonized cultures. Social advancement—and elevation to the status of *évolué*—depended, however, on mastery of the French language and an adoption of a French mind-set, and education often entailed a geographical distancing from a pupil's point of origin: the itinerary of the protagonist of Camara Laye's novel *L'Enfant noir* (1953) is emblematic of such a journey, from the Koranic school of his village to the exile of a French technical college, via the *lycée* in the capital Conakry.

Although by the 1930s the French had instituted a rapid expansion of French schooling in the colonies and increasing numbers of colonial students were traveling to France to complete their studies, it was military service in France during the First World War (as well as the experience of workers in France in the period immediately following the conflict) that led to the initial growth in awareness of the iniquities of the colonial system and of the flaws of the propaganda on which it depended. The interwar years witnessed a rapidly growing consciousness of the realities of colonial experience and a consolidation of indigenous anticolonial thought. The 600,000 colonial troops (or *tirailleurs indigènes*) shipped to the front during the 1914–18 conflict and used as shock troops in some of the most brutal engagements in the war were faced with images of European civilization far removed from those disseminated in French colonial propaganda. The dissatisfaction voiced on their return was part of a more general questioning of the colonial situation, and the idea of *la dette de sang* (blood debt)—that is, that France owed greater recognition to the colonies who had sacrificed so many of their inhabitants' lives—became central to the rhetoric both of those demanding greater parity with metropolitan France and of more radical anticolonial activists.

Added to this experience was that of a number of colonial subjects who worked in France in the immediate postwar period. Their intellectual and literary production has often been ignored in favor of those more easily identifiable intellectuals whose meeting in 1930s France led to the emergence of Negritude, but the previous decade itself witnessed radical activity, with the launch of papers such as *Le Paria, La Race nègre,* and *La Voix des nègres* and the publication by the Senegalese author Lamine Senghor of one of the first explicitly anticolonial novels by a French colonial subject, *La Violation d'un pays* (1927). In Paris at the same period, the emergence of Indochinese anticolonial thought was epitomized by the activities and publications of the Vietnamese immigrant Nguyên Aí Quôc (better known as Hô Chí Minh), whose stay in France lasted for six years from 1917 (although his *Procès de la colonisation française* appeared two years after his departure in 1925). Both Senghor and Hô Chí Minh were influenced in their thinking by dealing with the French Communist Party, with which they each had a volatile relationship. French colonial subjects were beginning to travel to France, but refusing to learn the lessons that such a journey was supposed to teach. The situation was accentuated in the following decade when, instead of becoming obedient servants of Empire (i.e., future teachers and administrators), colonial students in Paris began an intellectual movement that would serve as one of the central foundations of postwar decolonization.

Despite the political commitment of certain activists, the few francophone texts produced by colonial subjects in the 1920s, such as Bakary Diallo's semiautobiographical account of a *tirailleur, Force-Bonté* (1926), tend to reflect the structures of French colonial ideology. Even René Maran's *Batouala, véritable roman nègre,* the controversial winner of the Prix Goncourt in 1921, despite its acerbic attack on the conditions of French colonialism, relies on the devices of metropolitan exoticism for its portrayal of West Africa.

It was the proliferation of published literature by French speakers from Africa and the Caribbean in the 1930s that transformed poetry and the novel into sites of more subversive reflection on colonial experience and of increasing anticolonial resistance. Many historians view 1931, the year of the Exposition Coloniale, as the apogee of the French Empire, the point at which colonial expansion was consolidated by a large-scale propaganda campaign. Although the Exposition at Vincennes is regularly (and rightly) seen as central to the metropolitan experience of Empire, with its slogan—"le tour du monde en un jour" (around the world in a day)—allowing the French to reduce their colonial possessions to a domesticated scale, it was nevertheless also part of colonial experience because many indigenous subjects were transported to France to work in living dioramas—or "human zoos." The Senegalese author Ousmane Socé, in his novel *Mirages de Paris* (1937), describes the experience of a protagonist exiled in France for the duration of the exhibition, underlining the dehumanization and institutionalized racism on which such a stage management of empire depended. Although Socé's novel represents an early reflection on the intercultural contact in which colonialism results and can even be read as an apology for *métissage*, its ambiguous conclusions focus on the fate of the colonial subject exiled in France and alienated from both cultures of origin and arrival.

It is the same anxiety over point of origin and fear over its assimilation that led to the emergence of Negritude. This cultural movement developed in a climate of international dialogue among African, American, and Caribbean intellectuals (such as Césaire, Damas, Ménil, and Senghor) in 1930s Paris, but was heavily influenced by both Communism and surrealism while also drawing on the work of a number of French authors, such as Delafosse and Delavignette, whose attitude toward Africa was marked by a new cultural relativism. The intellectual debates of the movement were conducted in a series of periodical publications, such as *La Revue du monde noir* and the more radical *Légitime défense*. Negritude is a theory of the distinctive nature of Black African culture and psychology. It attempts to recover the dignity of a complex African heritage (rooted in Africa, but also diffused through diaspora) that has been obscured by colonialism, and to transform this into a trigger for political action. One of the major statements of Negritude is the Martinican Aimé Césaire's long poem *Cahier d'un retour au pays natal* (1939), but the principal force behind the movement was the Senegalese poet (and future statesman) Léopold Sédar Senghor, whose thought emerged from the coexistence of his African heritage with a close knowledge of French and classical culture. Although Negritude had both cultural and political associations and

was central to the reemergence of political consciousness in the francophone Black Atlantic, its influence on anticolonial thought declined after the 1940s. Césaire's *Discours sur le colonialisme* (1955), comparing French colonial ideology with that of Fascism and criticizing a number of metropolitan intellectuals (such as Jules Romains) whose work was implicitly procolonial, underlined the pressing need for an increasingly active struggle against political oppression.

After the Second World War, during which colonial troops were once again involved in the French war effort, interwar anticolonial sentiment developed rapidly into a movement toward decolonization. At Sétif in Algeria, a pronationalist demonstration on VE Day (May 8, 1945) was brutally repressed by the French army, signaling the start of an increasingly violent struggle that would culminate in the granting of the country's independence in 1962. The period is marked by a sudden proliferation of publications by committed intellectuals and writers from the colonies, of whom the most prominent include Camara Laye, Mongo Beti, Sembène Ousmane, and Ferdinand Oyono (from sub-Saharan Africa); Driss Chraïbi Mohammed Dib, Albert Memmi, and Kateb Yacine (from North Africa); and Joseph Zobel, Léopold Sainville, and Édouard Glissant (from the Caribbean). *Présence africaine* was founded in 1947 by Alioune Diop with the support of progressive French intellectuals such as André Gide, Jean-Paul Sartre, and Théodore Monod. The 1950s also saw the publication of a series of important essays, such as the Tunisian Albert Memmi's *Portrait du colonisé* (1957) and Octave Mannoni's *Psychologie de la colonisation* (1950), both of which explored the psychological, cultural, and political context of colonialism and the binary relationship between the colonizer and the colonized. From the perspective of postcolonial criticism, however, the most prominent colonial intellectual of the period immediately preceding decolonization was the Martinican-born psychiatrist Frantz Fanon. As the principal French-language theorist of anti-imperial revolution, Fanon's early work was heavily influenced by Western intellectuals such as Sartre and Freud. His *Peau noire, masques blancs* (1952) is a study of imperial domination and the psychology of racism; *Les Damnés de la terre* (published, with a preface by Sartre, in 1961) argued that anticolonial sentiment must be channeled into violent struggle to achieve true liberation. Although Fanon's later texts are rooted in his experiences of the Algerian War, they also represent a major projective reflection on the nature of the future postcolonial nation state, underlining the need for the indigenous intelligentsia to reject the structures of the white colonial elite and rebuild society according to the needs and values of the people. His aim was to avoid a nostalgic return to an imaginary precolonial society, while resisting the neocolonial persistence of the hegemonic structures of colonial society.

The empire built over centuries was dismantled in a matter of years, largely between the defeat of Dien Bien Phu in 1954 and the end of the Algerian War in 1962. Despite the efforts of many national historians to suggest that in the aftermath of empire the interdependence of France and its former colonies came to a rapid and tidy end, the shift from colonial to postcolonial experience remains a troubled and as yet incomplete one. Bernard Dadié's pseudoethnographic account of an African's journey to Paris, *Un Nègre à Paris* (1959), not only signals the changing status of the postcolonial traveler but also reveals people's increasing mobility after the end of Empire. France's rapid economic expansion in the thirty years following the Liberation was, for instance, heavily dependent on the importation of immigrant labor. The former colonies retained ties to France through such economic and political dependence, but cultural links were at the same time perpetuated through the organizations of *la Francophonie*. Moreover, the status of DOM-TOM accorded to other colonies (especially in the Caribbean and the Indian Ocean) led to the more explicit continuation of colonial dependency. As a result of this situation, the last four decades of the twentieth century witnessed a range of intellectual responses to the complexities of the postcolonial situation.

In the immediate period following independence, a series of literary works were published that explored the watershed between colonialism and independence, either highlighting the chaotic state of a suddenly postcolonial culture (e.g., Ferdinand Oyono's *Chemin d'Europe*, 1960) or the dilemma faced by the postcolonial subject forced to choose between two civilizations (e.g., Hamidou Kane's *L'Aventure ambiguë*, 1961). Pragmatic observation of the postcolonial condition led quickly, however, to a number of intellectual and creative responses to continuing French influence, with certain authors (such as Ahmadou Kourouma and Sony Labou Tansi) subjecting the French language to the often violent demands of indigenous reality and others (notably Yambo Ouologuem) pillaging European sources to create distinctively postindependence literatures. In North Africa, the ultimately outlawed Moroccan journal *Souffles* (1966–1972; edited by Abdellatif Laâbi) was similarly devoted to radical interventions in the postcolonial use of the French language, while exploring the pitfalls of adherence to traditional Arabic cultures. In texts such as *Maghreb pluriel* (1983), one of the contributors to the journal, Abdelkebir Khatibi, was instrumental in moving beyond the binary dilemmas of the period following independence and outlining a further decolonization of the epistemological foundations of the West's attitudes and approaches to its former colonies. Focusing on bilingualism and biculturalism, Khatibi elaborated a "double-critique," a method that undermines both the reductive processes of imperial thought and the totalizing metaphysical foundations of indigenous systems. It is also in this period following independence that the colonial and postcolonial experience of women, hitherto largely ignored, was given the consideration it deserves, especially in the work of a number of prominent postcolonial women writers and thinkers (such as Assia Djebar, Maryse Condé, and Mariama Ba). The Algerian-born novelist, historian, and filmmaker Djebar has, for instance, been instrumental in salvaging and foregrounding the colonial and postcolonial experience of North African women, looking in particular at their social identity in relation to predominantly masculine spaces.

The later twentieth-century experience of the francophone Caribbean cannot strictly be described as postcolonial because such a term is prematurely celebratory in the light of the region's continuing dependence on metropolitan France. Francophone Caribbean thinkers have nevertheless made a major contribution to more general reflections on postcolonial experience, often as a result of this ambiguous historical position. Although the Guadeloupean-born writer and scholar Maryse Condé has criticized the exclusion of women's experience from contemporary Caribbean intellectual movements, Francophone Caribbean thought remains dominated by a group of male thinkers. Most prominent among these is Édouard Glissant, the Martinican author and intellectual, whose work explores the complexities of Caribbean cultural identity and the risks of continued neocolonial dependency. One of Glissant's principal contributions to postcolonial thought is the concept of "la Relation," an understanding of identity that eschews monocultural essentialism to assert a more fluid, rhizomatic (the idea is borrowed from Deleuze and Guattari) understanding of cultures. From Glissant's thinking has emerged a separate theory of *Créolité*—stated most clearly in *Éloge de la créolité* (1989)—that rejects residual notions of Negritude to celebrate the composite and inherently heterogeneous nature of Caribbean cultures (combining African, European, Amerindian, and Asian elements). Although not so well known, Indian Ocean intellectuals explore similar issues in their work, and Axel Gauvin's *Du Créole opprimé au créole libéré* (1977) is an apology for bilingualism (French and Creole) and a call for recognition of hybrid cultural identities.

The Caribbean and Indian Ocean contributions to postcolonial thought are not restricted to regional dimensions and have more general applications to a variety of contemporary situations, including that of France itself. The postcolonial experience of immigrants and those of immigrant origin living in the old imperial center received little attention until the last decade of the twentieth century, and Pierre Nora's groundbreaking *Les Lieux de mémoire* has been criticized for presenting France as a self-sufficient nation state whose "sites of memory" fail to reflect the porous, interdependent nature of French identity. The increasing demographic mobility of the postcolonial era has transformed France into a country that, despite its republican desire for homogeneity, can no longer deny its multiethnic character. From the 1980s onward, a group of French novelists of North African immigrant origin (such as Mehdi Charef, Azouz Begag, and Mounsi) have described the experience of belonging to ethnic minorities dwelling on the margins of French society. Authors from other former colonies—such as the Cameroonian novelist Calixthe Beyala—have also described the problematic nature of integration into a French society often unwilling to accept its own postcolonial status.

French resistance to postcolonialism is in fact a common phenomenon, and the concept is often perceived as solely Anglo-Saxon, not relevant to considerations of twentieth-century French-speaking cultures and excluded accordingly from the French academy. This is despite the reliance of early postcolonial theory on French-speaking thinkers as diverse as Césaire, Sartre, Fanon, Lacan, Derrida, and Memmi, and also despite the more recent discovery by English-language postcolonial critics of such influential contemporary figures as Glissant and Khatibi. There is, however, a pressing need to consider French society itself in postcolonial terms. The former colonies' continued dependence on metropolitan thought risks neocolonial perpetuation of the former center-periphery model, whereby the metropolitan capital dictated thought on the colonial periphery—especially through the mechanisms of publication and intellectual recognition, both of which remain centered on France itself. However, whereas the role of French authors and thinkers in contemporary francophone postcolonial thought remains persistent, it is becoming increasingly ambiguous. For example, the early twentieth-century French theorist of the exotic, Victor Segalen, is a point of reference for a number of authors (such as Khatibi and Glissant), but emerges from Patrick Chamoiseau's work in a more ambiguous, anthropophagic relationship. In addition, a number of intellectuals previously seen as part of a French tradition, such as the Algerian-born Jacques Derrida and Hélène Cixous, have begun to explore their own colonial backgrounds and the relationship of their own thought to childhood experiences of Empire. Such complex questions of identity are central to the intellectual issues characterizing Francophone postcolonial experience. The binary structures and strict hierarchies on which colonial experience depended—and by whose consolidation and perpetuation the French Empire was long protected—have been replaced by more complex relationships, still tainted by historical experience yet reflecting nevertheless the shifting nature of a postcolonial world.

CHARLES FORSDICK

See also **Aime Cesaire, Patrick Chamoiseau, Hélène Cixous, Gilles Deleuze, Jacques Derrida, Fritz Fanon, Andre Gide, Eduoard Glissant, Felix Guattari, Abdelkebir Khatibi, Jacques Lacan, Jean-Paul Sartre, Leopold Senghor**

Further Reading

Bancel, Nicolas (editor), *Les Zoos humains*, Paris: La Découverte, 2002

Bernabé, Jean, Patrick Chamoiseau, and Raphaël Confiant, *Éloge de la créolité*, Paris: Gallimard, 1989

Britton, Celia, *Édouard Glissant and Postcolonial Theory: Strategies of Language and Resistance*, Charlottesville and London: University Press of Virginia, 1999

Burton, Richard D. E. and Fred Reno (editors), *French and West Indian: Martinique, Guadeloupe and French Guiana Today*, London and Basingstoke: Macmillan, 1995

Cooper, Nicola, *France in Indochina: Colonial Encounters*, Oxford and New York: Berg, 2001

Donadey, Anne, *Recasting Postcolonialism: Women Writing Between Worlds*, Portsmouth, New Hampshire: Heinemann, 2001

Forsdick, Charles and David Murphy (editors), *Francophone Postcolonial Studies*, London: Arnold, 2003

Glissant, Édouard, *Le Discours antillais*, Paris: Seuil, 1981

Haddour, Azzedine, *Colonialism and the Ethics of Difference: From Sartre to Said*, London: Pluto, 2000.

Hargreaves, Alec G., *Immigration and Identity in Beur Fiction: Voices from the North African Immigrant Community in France*, Oxford and New York: Berg, 1991

Hargreaves, Alec G., *Immigration, "Race" and Ethnicity in Contemporary France*, London and New York: Routledge, 1995

Hargreaves, Alec G. and Mark McKinney (editors), *Post-Colonial Cultures in France*, London: Routledge, 1997

Hennessy, Alistair (editor), *Intellectuals in the Twentieth-Century Caribbean—Unity in Variety: The Hispanic and Francophone Caribbean*, London and Basingstoke: Macmillan, 1992

Jack, Belinda, *Francophone Literatures: An Introductory Survey*, Oxford: Oxford University Press, 1996

Lionnet, Françoise and Ronnie Scharfman (editors), *Post/Colonial Conditions: Exiles, Migrations, and Nomadisms*, 2 vols., New Haven, Connecticut: Yale University Press, 1993 [*Yale French Studies* 82/83]

Lionnet, Françoise, *Postcolonial Representations: Women, Literature, Identity*, Ithaca, New York and London: Cornell University Press, 1995

Majumdar, Margaret (editor), *Francophone Studies*, London: Arnold, 2002

Miller, Christopher L., *Nationalists and Nomads: Essays on Francophone Literature and Culture*, Chicago and London: University of Chicago Press, 1998

Mudimbe, V. Y. (editor), *The Surreptitious Speech: "Présence Africaine" and the Politics of Otherness 1947–1987*, Chicago and London: University of Chicago Press, 1992

Murdoch, H. Adlai, *Creole Identity in the French Caribbean Novel*, Gainsville, University Press of Florida, 2001

Trang-Gaspard, Tru, *Hồ Chí Minh à Paris (1917–1923)*, Paris: L'Harmattan, 1992

Walker, Keith L., *Countermodernism and Francophone Literary Culture: The Game of Slipknot*, Durham, North Carolina and London: Duke University Press, 1999

Woodhull, Winifred, *Transfigurations of the Maghreb: Feminism, Decolonization, and Literatures*, Minneapolis and London: University of Minnesota Press, 1993

Young, Robert J. C., *Postcolonialism: An Historical Introduction*, Oxford: Blackwell, 2001

CULTURE

At the beginning of the twentieth century, French culture was perceived as essentially high, Parisian, white, bourgeois, male, and, overtly at least, firmly heterosexual. In terms of its content and means of expression and diffusion, culture was equated automatically with high culture, embodied in a canon of accepted historical classics, and replicated in new works. This dominant canonic body of cultural production was preserved and propagated through a network of powerful institutions including museums, libraries, theaters, and concert halls, together with specialist journals, publishing houses, and bodies such as learned societies, academies, and the education system. In the heyday of the Third Republic, not least through the propagation of a ruling élite deriving from the same educational system and institutions, the exercise and cultivation of high culture were synonymous with both political power, as evidenced by the privileged state role of the Académie Française, and a unified concept of national identity. At the same time, however, that monolithic concept of a powerful high culture was beginning to come under threat from a new awareness of popular culture with new means of production and distribution in the form of cinema, recorded music, and mass publication. Whereas in the past these activities had often been confined to circumscribed localities, rural or urban, and were rarely in a form that guaranteed either durability or wide diffusion, new technologies in film, recordings, and the print media enabled popular culture to attain a mass audience, often the product of urbanization, and to be replicated and preserved. In other words, this new mass audience together with its new objects of cultural consumption came to constitute what was perceived as a serious threat to the dominance and immutability of previously accepted definitions of high culture.

These definitions had been essentially exclusive, designed to reinforce a national culture. As Eugen Weber has persuasively demonstrated, the educational reforms enacted by Jules Ferry in the early 1880s were the culmination of a process throughout the nineteenth century, including urban growth and mass conscription, designed to turn "peasants into Frenchmen," to weld the French population into a cohesive nation–state with one culture and one set of political and social aims. This entailed the rejection, marginalization, and suppression of ethnic cultures from France's colonial communities and overseas francophone populations. This Eurocentricity was accompanied by a similar suppression of regional cultures, particularly through the education system. Regional languages were banned from the education system, as were local dialects, and regional culture itself, when not eradicated through conscription and population movements, was corralled, like that of the colonial communities, into the unchallenging concept of "folklore." This process, in its turn, built on and confirmed the traditional dominance of Paris, the seat of government, the center of executive and administrative power, and the holder of a virtual monopoly of high-cultural production and consumption, itself the preserve of the bourgeoisie. Thus became enshrined a connection between culture and power, which tended to orient cultural debates to the issue of access. At the same time, this essentially bourgeois culture, to which access was to be either regulated or demanded as a right, depending on the political perspective, excluded manifestations of popular culture, women's culture, and gay culture. French culture at the turn of the century, therefore, was designed and used to propound what de Gaulle would later term a "certain idea of France" defining and maintaining a strong national identity, both within and in terms of foreign relations. In this context, culture was conceived of as a powerful and indispensable weapon against the threat of German "barbarism." Similarly, the image of the essentially civilized nature and heritage of France was used to express severe reservations regarding France's relations with the Anglo-Saxon world, in particular the American "threat" that surfaced as early as the 1880s.

It is no coincidence, however, that this process took place against the background of profound cultural changes in France. The Parisian cultural community, that focal point of national cultural activity, had, in the early years of the century, become genuinely cosmopolitan with the establishment in the field of the plastic arts of the "Ecole de Paris," including figures from all over Europe, Japan, and the Americas. The potential challenge that this posed was replicated on a theoretical level by the attractions of cultural relativism, embodied particularly in the work of Nietzsche, and taken up by Gide, that questioned the supremacy of a Eurocentric Christian civilization.

The beginning of the interwar years explored these theories of cultural relativism further. In "La Crise de l'esprit" (1919), Paul Valéry adopted a Spenglerian perspective on cultural permanency, proposing that Western civilization, like its predecessors, was no more immune than they from a finite cycle of birth, growth, and decline. More specifically, André Malraux, in *La Tentation de l'Occident* (1926), borrowing on a tradition going back to Montaigne and Montesquieu, contrasted unfavorably the achievements of Western and Eastern civilizations and, in his later novel, *Les Noyers de l'Altenberg* (1943), used the work of the German anthropologist Leo Frobenius on African cultures to reflect on the incoherence and meaninglessness of the term *civilization* altogether. The 1920s saw the emergence of Black poets from France's colonies, such as Léopold Senghor and Aimé Césaire, propounding an authentic Black culture, totally independent of its French counterpart, in the concept of "négritude." This emergence was soon followed by the surrealists' campaign against the Colonial Exhibition of 1931. None of this went without provoking a backlash from the extreme right, in particular from a disciple of Barrès, Henri Massis, who, in his essay *Défense de l'Occident* (1927), argued for the preservation of Western values as a bastion of authority and order.

It was on the Left, however, that the most sustained reflection on culture took place. Continuing the iconoclasm of the prewar avant-garde, the surrealists launched a wholesale attack on the coherence, lucidity, professionalism, and above all, respectability of bourgeois culture with the aim of forging new forms of cultural activity into a genuinely revolutionary movement. Their hopes of uniting with international communism were frustrated by the triumph in the Soviet Union of Stalin and the ensuing imposition of a rigid cultural orthodoxy, but other cultural theorists were more temperamentally equipped to formulate a critique of bourgeois culture and cultural hegemony from a Marxist perspective. The battle lines were drawn at their clearest in the polemic between Julien Benda and Paul Nizan. Benda, a liberal intellectual, denounced in *La Trahison des clercs* (1927) the abandonment by French intellectuals of their sacred mission of neutrality and objectivity in becoming politically partisan. Nizan's essay of 1932, *Les Chiens de garde*, derided this position, claiming that it was the very pretense of objectivity of bourgeois culture that rendered it so politically dangerous in that it constituted a covert defense of the status quo of the capitalist state.

Nizan was a member of the Communist Party (PCF), and his denunciation of the politically reactionary nature of all bourgeois culture, even of its progressive manifestations, was part of a generalized attempt on the Left to create a genuine Socialist or Communist culture, heavily influenced by the Soviet Union and its cultural theorists, notably Andrei Zhdanov, the proponent of Socialist Realism. In this vein, a number of loosely organized movements came into being in the 1920s and early 1930s aimed at forging a cultural weapon to combat fascism and defining prescriptions for a revolutionary culture. This raised once again the vexing question of access, present either implicitly or explicitly, since the turn of the century. Although there was genuine enthusiasm on the left for a new revolutionary parallel culture that would operate beyond the ambiguities and inherent conservatism of bourgeois culture, there remained nonetheless a powerful nostalgia and respect for the prestige of the canon, that "cultural capital" in Bourdieu's term, that was the moral right of all citizens and their indispensable currency in the prerevolutionary status quo. It was this paradox that dominated debates on culture at the time of the Front Populaire, whose government from 1936 to 1937 presided over the most coherent and sustained attempt to rewrite the cultural rules that had pertained up to that time. Alongside its championing of "agitprop" revolutionary art and theater and the festivities and street carnivals that accompanied its election, the Front Populaire remained dominated by an obsession with access to high culture and highly distrustful of popular and consumer culture, regarded as both economic exploitation and a deliberate attempt to distract from political consciousness. Thus, in their attempts to give extra leisure time to the workers, Front Populaire theoreticians and politicians were also exercised to make sure that this newly won leisure should be used productively. In the field of leisure, emphasis was placed on healthy activities away from the urban cafés. Inevitably, the same prescriptions emerged in the field of culture, with group activities such as drama groups or choral societies being privileged, along with access to forms of high culture hitherto the preserve of the bourgeoisie. The same government, however, that opened the Louvre in the evenings and provided cheap tickets for the state theaters was less sanguine about popular cinema, popular music, and the new phenomenon of radio. In other words, the Front Populaire and its theoreticians, in prioritizing access to an unchallenged concept of high culture, failed to seize the significance and the opportunity offered by mass culture itself and the new cultural technologies, preferring to see them in a uniformly negative light. This blindness, however, continued a division among theory, doctrine, and popular taste that would last well into the postwar era.

The cultural impact of France's defeat in 1940 and the subsequent four-year occupation was many-faceted and produced some unexpected results. As with the previous conflicts with Germany, in 1870 and 1914, the occupation provoked a renewed assertion of national cultural identity, this time overlaid with a powerful anti-Fascist ideology. In fact, the occupation and France's reduction to virtual noncombatant status had the effect of according to cultural activity, its diffusion, and its institutions, a primacy that they rarely held in peacetime. The German occupants were keen to maintain a sense of social and cultural normality, which entailed the fostering of acceptable non-Jewish forms of cultural production, and strove to control some of its more prestigious outlets such as publishing houses, film studios, and journals like the *Nouvelle Revue Française*, in addition to forms of the mass-media, notably radio and the press. The Resistance also quickly adopted culture as its favored battleground through clandestine publishers like Editions de Minuit and a plethora of cultural periodicals, such as Pierre Seghers' *Poésie* and the voice of the Comité National des Ecrivains *Las Lettres Françaises*. More ambiguous was the cultural policy of Vichy that, despite its distaste for the Front Populaire, nevertheless directed that government's distrust of mass culture and urban leisure pursuits into similar celebrations of the healthy traditions of rural France. At the same time, the German occupation, although concentrating its grip on the capital, also had the effect of decentralizing the nation culturally to an extent that had not been seen since 1870. Cities such as Lyon, the center of the resistance; the southern capital Marseille; and Nice, the focal point for many Parisian émigrés; assumed a national and international cultural vibrancy that they had not known previously. Similarly, suppressed regional autonomist movements harbored hopes of securing political, linguistic, and cultural independence within the frontiers of the new Europe.

The Liberation put a rapid stop to such secessionist aspirations, and it did have the effect of establishing a cultural orthodoxy that lasted into the early 1950s and that was essentially based on the values of the victorious Resistance. The vogue for "Existentialism" in the mid- and late 1940s, with its emphasis on choice, action, and, above all, commitment, derived clearly from the ethics of the resistance struggle. Culturally, however, its insistence on authenticity as being dependent on the politically utilitarian in the concept of "engagement" also marked a continuity with the politically committed cultural theories of Communist writers of the 1930s. The late 1940s and early 1950s were dominated culturally by the policies of the Communist Party and its continuing commitment to Zhdanov's Socialist Realism.

The Communist position, essentially high cultural in its emphasis, was reinforced by a postliberation resurgence of the debates on popular and mass culture and, particularly, by the perceived threat to French culture presented by the United States. The Blum-Byrnes trade agreement of 1946 was very controversial in France because of its clauses relating to import quotas for U.S. films. This was not merely perceived as an outright assault on the French film industry, more broadly it signaled a major threat to French cultural identity and the nation's way of life, just as it did nearly fifty years later with France's resistance to the GATT Treaty of 1994. The Coca-Cola Company's proposals to open a bottling plant in France in the late 1940s provoked a wave of protest against American "Coca-colonization," which later dovetailed into generalized opposition to the Korean War as a symbol of an imperialist process begun with the Truman Doctrine of 1947. In the same way, Etiemble's best-seller *Parlez-vous franglais?* (1964) gave voice to French concerns about their linguistic vulnerability in the face of a global threat posed by the English language.

Independently of these external factors, French society changed on an unprecedented scale in the thirty years between the liberation and world oil crisis of 1974, the "trente glorieuses." With an accelerating exodus from the countryside to the cities, particularly Paris, the generalization of mass production in industry, and the creation of a consumer culture available to all, the aspirations, both material and cultural, of the French people were transformed, as the sociologist Edgar Morin charted in his 1962 study of the Breton village of Plodémet. It was precisely these social changes and the creation of a mass society in France that prompted the growth or development of methodologies, academic disciplines, and their university institutions in order to analyze them: in particular sociology, linguistics, and anthropology, which often combined into structuralism, notably in the work of Barthes and Lévi-Strauss.

Cultural policy, however, reinforced by the continuing dominance of theories of high culture, remained slow to respond to the implications of this newly created mass society. Under de Gaulle's presidency, and especially under his Minister of Culture André Malraux, culture was deployed as a vital tool in the assertion of national prestige. Yet the author of the postwar work of art and philosophy *Les Voix du silence* was ill-adapted to deal with contemporary phenomena of mass culture such as television, and Malraux's creation of the regional Maisons de la Culture, a concept derived from the Front Populaire era, was conceived of in terms of disseminating the high-cultural riches of the nation, in particular of the capital, to the provinces, rather than encouraging local cultural expression. Once again, access rather than expression was the dominant theme.

It is no coincidence, therefore, that the Maisons de la Culture should have become one of the privileged areas of conflict in May 1968. The events were an explosion of discontent at government inability to meet the challenges of a rapidly urbanizing economy and society. Politically, the triggers were both the entrenched autocratic nature of the Gaullist regime and the resurgence of perceived American imperialism in Vietnam. In cultural terms, the causes of opposition were more complex. On one level, the events of May 1968 were an essentially consumerist revolt on the part of students, the product of the postwar baby boom, whose heavily commercialized youth culture was paid scant recognition in the government-controlled mass media and the education system. More profoundly, however, the May events posed a direct challenge to the political and social structures of 1960s France and to its cultural apparatus and theory. It is not insignificant that the movement began in the sociology faculty at Nanterre, nor that its political impetus came from a Maoist concept of cultural revolution, in which existing cultural orthodoxies, along with the political parties who perpetuated them, were implacably rejected. The situationists, arguably the most influential force in the cultural debates in May 1968, attacked consumerist culture in the form of television and film and also derided high culture, enshrined in the Ministry of Culture and its flagship the Avignon theater festival, as essentially being part of that same consumerism, designed to perpetuate bourgeois power. In this respect, their concept of a new revolutionary culture broke down the dichotomy between high and popular culture, which had dominated cultural theory and policy throughout the century and also sidestepped the traditional alignment of political forces.

The new Left's ambitions for permanent revolutionary political and social change were never realized, but the cultural landscape of France changed irremediably. The broader francophone world was recognized as an essential component of French culture, both through a recognition of the cultural importance of France's former colonies and overseas Departments and through the interrelated presence in metropolitan France of ethnic communities with their own means of cultural expression, distinct from their original societies and increasingly influential in the new France of the 1980s and 1990s. At the same time, the formal administrative devolution of power to the regions under the Loi Deferre of 1982 recognized the increasing significance of local cultures. Late twentieth-century France may well have seen the explosion and domination of the means of mass cultural production so feared and castigated by cultural theorists throughout the century, but those cultural forms often served, alongside more insidious commercial and overseas influences, to give an authentic expression to groups that had hitherto remained voiceless. Similarly, postmodern theorists such as Lyotard challenged the post-Enlightenment tradition of a unilinear cultural project imposed by single actors within an exclusively high-cultural frame of reference.

However, in spite of postmodernism and the efforts of Mitterrand's Minister of Culture, Jack Lang, to broaden the definition of culture and despite the discovery and reevaluation of the culture of daily life, in particular as regards women, the privileged position of high culture remained and remains unassailable and an essential component of Bourdieu's "capital," indissoluble from real power. In its concerns and its priorities, French cultural discourse and theory remain inextricably close to the preoccupations of the 1900s.

NICHOLAS HEWITT

See also **Maurice Barrès, Roland Barthes, Julien Benda, Aimé Césaire, Claude Lévi-Strauss, Jean-Francois Lyotard, Henri Massis, Léopold Senghor, Paul Valéry**

Further Reading

Cook, Malcolm, *French Culture since 1945*, Harlow: Longman, 1993

Hewitt, Nicholas, *The Cambridge Companion to Modern French Culture*, Cambridge: Cambridge University Press, 2003

Hughes, H. Stuart, *The Obstructed Path. French Social Thought in the Years of Desperation 1930–1960*, New York: Evanston and London: Harper and Row, 1966

Rigby, Brian, *Popular Culture in Modern France. A Study of Cultural Discourse*, London: Routledge, 1991

Sowerwine, Charles, *France since 1870. Culture, Politics and Society*, Basingstoke: Palgrave, 2001

Weber, Eugen, *Peasants into Frenchmen. The Modernization of Rural France 1870–1914*, London: Chatto and Windus, 1977

D

DEBORD, GUY
Writer, Philosopher, and Filmmaker

Few French thinkers have been as detached from French public life as Debord was his whole life. To the degree that both his life and thinking were characterized by detachment and distance, Debord remained unaffected by contemporary philosophical and artistic fashions, whether they were the libidinal philosophy of Lyotard, Deleuze, and Guattari; the theoretical antihumanist Marxism of Althusser; or the films of the New Wave. Debord nourished a deep distrust for academia, journalism, publishing, politics, and media. All of these were part of the spectacle, the alienation of late capitalism. More like Rousseau or Burke than Garaudy or Debray, Debord practiced philosophy no matter the costs and stayed away from any contact with the cultural establishment. He refused to be contained within the pacifying representation of the spectacle that reduced people to stale identities: artist, politician, revolutionary, writer, filmmaker, and so on. These identities, he thought, now prevented people from doing the activities once prescribed by these terms.

The key concept in Debord's theory and practice was that of the spectacle. With its connotations of separation, passive contemplation, and estrangement, the concept of the spectacle characterized all the things wrong with modern capitalist society. The notion of the spectacle was a continuation of the theory of alienation found in the young Marx and Georg Lukács, in which the incomprehensible mechanism of capitalism separates the worker from the objects that s/he produces. The salary-, value-, and money-form distort the rela-

tionship between wo/man and his/her products, so that the products of his/her endeavor confront the worker as alien, independent objects. As Debord wrote in his major work *La Société du Spectacle* (1967): "With the generalised separation of the worker and his products, every unitary view of accomplished activity and all direct personal communication among producers are lost" (Debord, 1967, thesis 26). The entire world is transformed into a world separate from the worker, now no longer at home in the world.

According to Debord, capitalism had undergone a decisive change from an older laissez-faire model to a planned capitalism, or what he called the society of the spectacle. Unlike industrial capitalism, which was mainly concerned with production, the society of the spectacle is primarily centered on consumption, with the commodity acquiring paramount significance. The commodity becomes the motor of socioeconomic reproduction, as well as the locus of social control. Given its importance for the reproduction of capitalism, consumption is judged to be too central to be left to the autonomous judgment of individual consumers. Consumption must be thoroughly managed and regulated, with nothing left to chance. This monitoring is effected through control of the very communicativity and linguistic being of humans. Capitalism, according to Debord, not only expropriated the productive activity of man, it alienated language itself; in the society of the spectacle, language not only constitutes itself as an autonomous sphere, it no longer reveals anything at all.

Like Henri Lefebvre and Kostas Axelos from *Arguments*, Debord contested orthodox Marxist attempts to reduce all forms of alienation to economic alienation, concluding that the primary mutilation of men occurred no longer at work, but in leisure activities. A new era was already in advanced stages of development, an era that witnessed new contradictions very different from Marx's nineteenth-century English model. The new contradictions were located in the confrontation of a world of material security, comfort, and abundance with a strange symbolic lack. Western societies were caught in a kind of self-simulation, where capitalism fabricated pseudoneeds by means of advertising, news, culture, the mass media, and other mechanisms of conditioning and suggestion. People were freed from material poverty only to be increasingly trapped in a qualitative poverty. The society of the spectacle was a society exposed to nothing but itself. The abundance of commodities and images was evidence of a symbolic lack, a lack Debord interpreted as problematic. Beyond the lack, hidden beneath the profusion of images, an authentic presence was realizable. All of Debord's theoretical and artistic activities were attempts to expose this lack, criticize alienation, and point toward real lived experience, toward other worlds.

Debord's work was therefore primarily an analysis of how, in modern capitalism, the accumulation of images—the spectacle—had become more important than the accumulation of commodities themselves. According to him, the role of mediation in social relationships was central to any understanding of life in the society of the spectacle. What was once a lived experience now existed as a spectacle unfolding at a distance. The spectacle was the concrete inversion of life, the autonomous movement of nonliving.

Drawing on the work of not only the young Marx, Lukács, Karl Korsch, and council communists like Anton Pannekoek, but also surrealism and the artistic avant-garde, Debord posed a vision of the sort of society that could be created on the basis of the existing material forces. He described this future society both in terms of the negative accomplishments—the abolition of money, wage labor, the state and commodity production, and the like—and in terms of the positive accomplishments—freedom and community. If capitalist society was a world totally beyond the control of its creators, Debord's vision of communism was of a society in which each and every individual would actively participate in the conscious and deliberate transformation of each moment of life. Communism would be the prerequisite for the life of an unabashed humanity: play and cognition, aesthetic practice and reflection fused into a higher unity.

In a period in which it was fashionable to deny the proletariat's revolutionary potentials, Debord insisted on the revolutionary capacities of the working class while at the same time refraining from joining any political-revolutionary organization or trend. He felt he was carrying on the heritage of council communism during the bleak times of the counterrevolution. Debord's theoretical output was marked by on the one hand the widespread feeling that one could no longer speak of the existence of the working class, and on the other hand by the hegemonic role of the French Communist Party advocating the corrupted nationalist state-capitalism of the so-called socialist regimes. This led him to a total refusal of any Leninist, Trotskyist, Maoist, or Third-World position. Debord defined the working class as all those with no possibility of altering the social space-time that society allots for their consumption. Following this definition, the working class encompassed almost everybody, and its demands were not simply for higher wages, but for a totally different society in which boredom, passivity, and isolation would be overcome.

It is impossible to separate Debord from the work and destiny of the Situationist International, the artistic and revolutionary group Debord led from 1957 to 1972. The Situationist International was in many respects the stage on which Debord's life and activity took place. The group is best characterized as an attempt to unite the antiartistic practice of the dada and surrealist movements with both the political theory of the council communists movements of the 1920s and the neo-Trotskyist group Socialisme ou Barbarie headed by Cornelius Castoriadis. The situationists were convinced that the whole world should be torn down and rebuilt under the sign not of the economy but of a generalized creativity.

Debord wrote relatively little and for years remained a somewhat mysterious figure, often invoked in leftist debates, but rarely taking center stage. A number of philosophers nevertheless owe a great deal to Debord's thought, among them Jean Baudrillard, Jean-Francois Lyotard, and Jean-Luc Nancy. Since Debord took his own life in 1994, he has received a great deal of attention, and a veritable fight over his legacy is being fought in the early years of the twenty-first century. The influence of Debord's thought seems to be growing, but considering his own relentless skepticism toward the massive recuperation of radical critique—the spectacle can incorporate even its own subversion—he just might deserve to remain in the shadows.

MIKKEL BOLT RASMUSSEN

See also **Louis Althusser; Jean Baudrillard; Cornelius Castoriadis; Regis Debray; Gilles Deleuze; Felix Guattari; Henri Lefebvre; Jean-Francois Lyotard; Jean-Luc Nancy**

Biography

Guy Debord was born in Paris in 1931. He grew up in Paris, Nice, and Cannes and went to lycée Carnot in Cannes. Debord joined the Paris-based Letterist movement led by Isidore Isou in 1951 and made the film *Hurlements en faveur de Sade* in 1952. He broke off from the Letterist movement the same year and founded *Internationale lettriste*. In 1957 he played a significant role in the foundation of *Internationale situationniste*, the antiartistic and antipolitical group he headed until 1972. During the existence of the organization he wrote several articles for the journal *International situationniste*, produced two films, *Sur le passage de quelques personnes à travers une assez courte unité de temps* (1959) and *Critique de la separation* (1961), and wrote his most important book, *La Société du Spectacle* (1967). After the involvement of the situationists in May 1968, Debord and Gianfranco Sanguinetti dissolved the group in 1972. During the 1970s Debord lived in Paris and Florence in Italy and made the film version of *La Société du Spectacle* (1973), as well as the films *Réfutations de tous les jugements, tant élogieux qu'hostiles, qui ont été jusqu'ici portés sur le film "La Société de Spectacle"* (1975) and *In girum imus nocte et consumimur igni* (1978). In the 1980s—especially after the assassination of his publisher and friend Gérard Lebovici in 1984—and the 1990s he withdrew first to Arles then later to Champot in the Auvergne. He wrote several small books in this period, among them *Commentaires sur la société du spectacle* (1988), *Considérations sur l'assassinat de Gérard Lebovici* (1985), and *Panégyrique* (1989). In December of 1994 he killed himself.

Selected Writings

La Société du Spectacle, 1967; as *The Society of the Spectacle*, translated by Donald Nicholson-Smith, 1994

La Véritable Scission dans l'Internationale (with Gianfranco Sanguinetti), 1972; as *The Veritable Split in the International*, translated by Lucy Forsyth and others, 1990

Considérations sur l'assassinat de Gérard Lebovici, 1985; as *Considerations on the Assassination of Gérard Lebovici*, translated by Robert Greene, 2001

Commentaires sur la société de spectacle, 1988; as *Comments on the Society of the Spectacle*, translated by Malcolm Imrie, 1990

Panégyrique, vol. I, 1989; as *Panegyric*, translated by James Brook, 1991

Panégyrique, vol. II, 1997

Further Reading

Apostolidès, Jean-Marie, *Les Tombeaux de Guy Debord*, [The Tombs of Guy Debord], Paris: Exils, 1999.

Blissett, Luther, *Guy Debord e'morto davvero*, [Guy Debord is really dead], Feltre: Crash Edizione, 1994.

Bourseiller, Christophe, *Vie et mort de Guy Debord*, [Life and Death of Guy Debord] Paris: Plon, 1999.

Edwards, Phil, *Guy Debord*, London: Pluto, 2003.

Gonzalves, Shigenobu, *Guy Debord ou la beauté du negatif*, [Guy Debord and the Beauty of the Negative] Paris: Mille et Une Nuits, 1998.

Jappe, Anselm, *Guy Debord*, Pescara: Edizioni Tracce, 1993; as *Guy Debord*, translated by Donald Nicholson-Smith.

Kaufmann, Vincent, *Guy Debord. La revolution au service de la poésie*, [Guy Debord: The Revolution in the Service of Poetry] Paris: Fayard, 2001.

DEBRAY, RÉGIS
Philosopher, Political Writer, and Essayist

Since his days as a young Marxist militant and his return from a highly publicized imprisonment in Bolivia in 1967, Régis Debray has become a prolific author and a major intellectual figure in France. A talented writer who excels in all genres, ranging from autobiographical accounts to political essays and philosophy, Debray joins a long line of multifaceted intellectuals in France.

Debray is mainly associated with the emergence of mediology (*la médiologie*), a term he coined in *Le Pouvoir intellectuel en France* (*Teachers, Writers, Celebrities: The Intellectuals of Modern France*). This new critical discipline is a form of cultural investigation that has attained considerable visibility in France. Mediology devotes itself to the task of exploring the ways and means of symbolic efficacy in the transmission of culture and ideas. It thus reconciles culture and technique, message and mediation, as well as politics and means of transmission. In other words, the purpose of mediology is to develop a theory of the transmission of ideas through history in order to understand how ideas become action or institutions. On its most ambitious level, the mediological method investigates how abstract ideas can end up as world-changing ideologies, as, for instance, Marxism. The methodology of mediology consists of focusing simultaneously on the nature of symbols (ideas, signs) and the role of the medium (whether a person or material support) in transmitting them materially within culture. Therefore, the originality of the mediological approach is to incorporate the technical element, the technical support, or medium in the analysis of culture. In particular, mediology is concerned with how the different technologies of transmission have modified the ways of understanding and organizing our cultural environment and human organization. Mediology, thus, goes beyond the contemporary field of communication studies by studying the agents, processes, and vectors of all symbolic transmission.

Debray's practice of mediology often attempts wide-ranging, sweeping analyses, although many academic disciplines and practitioners are increasingly working in specialized fields. Mediologists have a predilection for studying great apparatuses of mediation, such as church and state, but also architecture, and even more prosaic material objects like railroad systems or paper. Mediology is interdisciplinary by nature and, therefore, unstable and constantly defining new avenues of inquiry that reveal the mechanisms of history itself. Mediology pretends not to be a discipline, or a science, but merely a tool, a method or a rearrangement of preexisting and compartmentalized bodies of knowledge. One may see a contradiction between the modesty of these claims and the kind of critical "super-tool" mediology appears to be. By presenting itself as an all-encompassing method reminiscent of a master narrative (without being one), mediology opens itself to the question of whether the reconciliation of the technical and the epistemological (tekhnè/epistémê) help produce a different understanding of history. If so, mediology can be viewed as a major theoretical development in the reading of culture and history. Or does mediology overstate the limits of traditional disciplines such as philosophy, sociology, or history, as well as the unique quality of the practice of mediology, which Debray himself seems to see as the first ever to undertake questions of signification and communication from a materialist perspective?

Evidently, Debray strives to avoid making mediology into a variant of media studies, that is to say, wedded to presentism and the latest technological advances, arguing further that it is philosophical historiography. Mediology indeed gives preference to diachrony rather than synchrony, to the medium as well as the message, and to civilization rather than the representation and identity politics of particular groups or subcultures. In fact, the tripartition of mediated practices in history offered by Debray proposes a movement from logosphere (writing prior to Gutenberg) to graphosphere (printing) and finally to videosphere (video-based culture since around 1968). These three mediaspheres can actually be conceived of as cultural ecosystems or medio-systems. In the end, mediology may very well become to cultural production what ecology is to biology: a medio-ethics. However, Debray is quick to mention that mediology should limit itself to a descriptive and explicative analysis of cultural transmission and contribute to the undoing of walls erected between technical and symbolic spheres, but not become a prescriptive and moralistic discourse on the media. Thus mediology should chiefly be considered as an attempt to create a new materialist philosophy rather than be part of a field of media criticism. Sociologists of the media, whose works are more focused on the socioeconomic-political use of the media, have raised concerns about mediology's apparent lack of engagement in modern media criticism.

The questioning of mediation began with, and has to be considered in light of, the role of the intellectual in France as mediator of ideas in the public sphere. With *Le Pouvoir intellectuel en France (Teachers, Writers, Celebrities: The Intellectuals of Modern France)*, Debray was the first in a long series of commentators to deplore the slippage of traditional intellectual power. The "French intellectual" is consubstantial with a print culture and part of a collective system that defines the conditions of his or her emergence. According to Debray, an image-based culture can only usher in the demise of the traditional intellectual that emerged around the Dreyfus affair with Émile Zola's famous *J'accuse* and incite the emergence of a new media-savvy personality who is more attuned to videospheric modes of communication.

DELEUZE, GILLES
Philosopher

In spite of the notorious complexity and variety of Gilles Deleuze's work, its essential principles are both broadly consistent and relatively easy to explain. Three such principles stand out, and they govern many of the more startling implications of this, the most fertile and provocative of recent French philosophies.

First and foremost Deleuze presumed the equation of philosophy with ontology, the identity of thought and being, such that all that is (or all that can be thought) *is* in the same way. All that is, be it material or ideal, organic or inorganic, perceived or imagined, expresses its being in one and the same sense. Deleuze's work begins with a recognition that "there has only ever been one ontological proposition: Being is univocal. There has only ever been one ontology, that of Duns Scotus, which gave being a single voice [. . .]. From Parmenides to Heidegger it is the same voice which is taken up, in an echo which itself forms the whole deployment of the univocal" (*Différence et répétition*, 52/35). It is because he saw in Spinoza's work the most uncompromising assertion of ontological univocity that Deleuze considered him to be the veritable "prince of philosophers," "philosophy incarnate" (*Qu'est-ce que la philosophie?*, 59/59–60). Deleuze's own project was in large part an attempt to renew, on virtually every imaginable front, the broadly cosmological orientation of the "new naturalism" he attributed to Spinoza and Leibniz against the proto-Kantian methodological orientation of Descartes: rather than seek to elaborate rational rules for the consistent *representation* of reality, Deleuze saw the fundamental task of philosophy as conditioned by our immediate *partici-*

pation in this reality. And for exactly the same reason, before he declared his well-known antipathy to Hegel Deleuze sought to confirm Bergson's break with the broadly neo-Kantian configuration of French philosophy in the latter part of the nineteenth century. In this sense it is Kant who figures as the real enemy of Deleuze's philosophy; Hegel is better conceived as its most dangerous *rival*.

Second, Deleuze presumed that this univocal order of being or reality is essentially creative. Univocity in no sense implies uniformity; on the contrary, being *is* nothing other than unlimited creativity. Creativity, expressed as an innumerable multiplicity of creative events or individuations, is all there is; being is the deployment, in every conceivable medium and dimension, of an infinitely varied sequence of *creatings*. Every psychological or social configuration is a creating, so to speak, and so is every language, every linguistic articulation, every utterance, every impression, every perception or hallucination. These creatings *are* creative in themselves, immediately, and not merely on account of their interactions with other things. In other words, the merely relative differences that exist or arise between things themselves stem from a deeper, more fundamental power of creative difference, a sort of creative *differing*. Deleuze's philosophy everywhere relies on the point of departure he adapted from Nietzsche and Bergson against Hegel: whereas according to Hegel "the thing differs with itself because it differs first with all that it is not," Bergson affirmed that a "thing differs with itself first, immediately," on account of the "internal explosive force" it carries within itself ("La conception de la différence chez Bergson," 96/53, 93/51). A univocal philosophy must show difference actively differing before it considers what is differed, let alone how the results of such difference might be represented, classified, or controlled. This is the principle that underlies the most rigorous and demanding of Deleuze's own philosophical works, *Différence et répétition* (1968), which set out to free the concept of difference from any external mediation, any subjection to the normalizing channels of identity, opposition, analogy, and resemblance.

What is eliminated along the way is "simply all value that can be assigned to the terms of a relation [*un rapport*], for the gain of its inner reason, which precisely constitutes difference." Difference no longer exists primarily *between* the polygon and the circle, for instance, but rather "in the pure variability of the sides of the polygon" (*Le Pli*, 88/65). In this sense at least, creative difference is neither a fundamentally relational nor derivative force. No more than Bergson's conception of a purely spiritual movement or thought, the assertion of a creative intensity is not itself a principle that can be deduced from some more primi-

tive assumption. Whether Deleuze's point of departure can in turn be conceived in *ultimately* relational terms—on the model, for instance, of the differential logic whereby he claims in *Différence et répétition* to derive the "singular points" that serve to individuate the trajectory of any particular differing or creating—is one of the more far-reaching controversies in current Deleuze scholarship (Smith makes a compelling case for a relational approach in his *Deleuze*; Badiou's *Deleuze* and Hallward's *Creationism* defend broadly antirelational readings).

Third, Deleuze assumes that only pure thought can achieve *absolute* creativity or unlimited differing power. All being is indeed creative, but unequally so. "Equal, univocal being is immediately present in everything, without mediation or intermediary [. . . but] things reside unequally in this equal being" (*Différence et répétition*, 55/37). This inequality is determined by the proximity of any particular creating to the unmeasurable maximum of pure intensity, that is, the degree to which its creative velocity, so to speak, approaches the limit of a literally infinite or absolute speed. And whereas material beings or creatings must naturally work through the medium of materiality or extension—even light travels at a specified speed—Deleuze maintains, again after Spinoza and Leibniz, that purely spiritual creatings take place at absolute speed, through exclusively intensive processes that create their own medium of existence. Material creatings proceed *through* a territory, society, organism, or perception; spiritual creatings generate itinerary, territory, and map in one and the same movement, in the singular element of a radical *conception*. "From Epicurus to Spinoza (the incredible book 5) and from Spinoza to Michaux the problem of thought is infinite speed. But this speed requires a milieu that moves infinitely in itself—the plane, the void, the horizon" (*Qu'est-ce que la philosophie?*, 38/36). According to Deleuze, every concept is an invention and in the end only conceptual invention can be unlimited, precisely because it relates to nothing outside itself: every "concept posits itself and its object at the same time as it is created" (*Qu'est-ce que la philosophie?*, 27/22).

The peculiar quantitative orientation of Deleuze's work follows from this presumption of a primordial ontological inequality. Conceived in its creative univocity, "quality is nothing other than contracted quantity" (*Le Bergsonisme*, 73/74), "quality is nothing but difference in quantity" (*Nietzsche et la philosophie*, 50/44), and the true "transcendental field is, however close two sensations may be, the passage from one to the other as a becoming, as increase or decrease of power (virtual quantity)" ("L'Immanence: une vie," 3). Deleuze can thus follow both Nietzsche in his insistence upon an original "hierarchy [. . .], hierarchy as the originary fact, the identity of difference and origin" (*Nietzsche et la philosophie*, 8–9/8), and Leibniz in the affirmation of "the two principles of principles [. . .]: Everything is always the same thing, there is only one and same Basis; and: Everything is distinguished by degree." Or in short: "everything can be said to be the same at all times and places except in degrees of perfection" (*Le Pli*, 78/58; *Différence et répétition*, 114/84).

Against Mediation

From these three affirmative principles the broad orientation of Deleuze's main critical priorities follows more or less as a matter of course.

In the first place, the presumed univocity of being precludes any constituent distinction between (representing) subject and (represented) object, along with an long list of related distinctions: the distinctions between desire and the object it supposedly "lacks," between language and the world to which it supposedly "refers," between a figural expression and the supposedly "proper" meaning it manipulates, and so on. All these distinctions are part of the "long error" Deleuze associates with that roughly neo-Kantian program of thought that, having admitted that things in themselves are inaccessible, concerns itself with the supervision of the rules whereby we might represent how such things appear to us (as if such appearances had a different kind of reality from that of the things themselves). By contrast, Deleuze's ontological univocity simply prescribes one single order of reality, one exclusive order of being, or production, or desire, or expression. "There is only one kind of production, the production of the real" (*L'Anti-Oedipe*, 40/32), and neo-Lacanian distinctions among real, symbolic, and imaginary, for instance, are themselves more apparent than real. Rather than supervise the measured representation of appearances, then, Deleuze orients his philosophy in line with that immediate, overwhelming participation in reality which in *Anti-Oedipus* he attributes, with Guattari, to the figure of the schizophrenic—a participation that "brings the schizo as close as possible to matter, to an intense [*intense*], living centre of matter," "closest to the beating heart of reality, to an intense point identical with the production of the real" (*L'Anti-Oedipe*, 26/19tm, 104/87).

It is precisely such participation that Deleuze applauds, for instance, in the writing of authors like Kafka and Artaud, writings that proceed "on the same level as the real of an unformed matter" such that "writing now functions on the same level as the real, and the real materially writes" (*Mille plateaux*, 638/512, 177/141). The essays collected in Deleuze's *Critique et clinique* presume, in keeping with his general conception of literature and art, that language does not represent the impressions or sensations of the world but is made up of the same "stuff" as the world itself. An appropriately creative or literary use of language will, therefore, tend to paralyze, estrange, or desacralize its representational ambitions, so as to bring out those aspects of language that allow it directly to convey the vitality of sensation and experience, always at levels of intensity that are serenely (or cruelly) indifferent to the limitations of the individual subject or author. In this as in every case, a genuine creating is in no sense limited by the specified characteristics of a particular creature: both writer and critic should look, either by excessive inflation and excess (à la Joyce) or through sobriety and subtraction (à la Beckett), for ways of conveying intensities that remain properly pre- or postindividual and asignificant. What matters, then, is not what such a text might *mean* but what it can be made to produce or accomplish. Conventional interpretation is to be replaced with an appreciation for the mechanical and diagnostic potential of literary texts, as so many clinical experiments for investigating "what a reader can do," for exploring how we might stretch or overcome the limits of our experience, for discovering how we might live as intensely and as inventively as possible.

Becoming Imperceptible

In the second place, the essentially creative orientation of being underlies the main dualism in Deleuze's work, which in honor of his scholastic predecessors we might term the distinction between originary creatings and derivative creatures. In Deleuzian terminology the former are "virtual," the latter are "actual"; the former are differentiated on a plane of pure potentiality (for the scholastics: the plane of an exclusively divine or intensive creativity), whereas the latter are distributed as so many existent actualizations of the former (for the scholastics: the domain of a creaturely or material extension). The one real problem of philosophy is simply this: although all there *are* are creatings, nevertheless some of these creatings give rise to the understandable, persistent but unwarranted illusion of a creaturely difference or independence. Again Bergson anticipates the problem: "everything is obscure in the idea of creation if we think of things which are created and a thing which creates, as we habitually do." The truth is rather that "there *are* no things, there are only actions," and absolutely creative force (or God) "has nothing of the already made, He is unceasing life, action, freedom," a freedom in which "we ourselves participate insofar as we act creatively" (Bergson, *L'Evolution créatrice*, 249). Nevertheless, the fact remains that unlimited creation cannot avoid the risk of such obscurity: unlimited creation must include the creation of creatures capable of denying or at least misunderstanding their ultimately creative orientation. As Deleuze, reader of Bergson, recognizes, though life is essentially movement, still "life as movement alienates itself in the material form that it creates; by actualising itself, by differentiation itself, it loses 'contact with the rest of itself' " (*Le Bergsonisme*, 108/104). Again, although "the whole creates itself," nevertheless its creative intensity is "explicated in systems in which it tends to be cancelled" (*Différence et répétition*, 293/228). *Our* problem is that specifically human beings take on their initial shape from within this cancellation: whereas creative "becoming, change, and mutation affect composing forces, not composed forms" (*Foucault*, 91/87tm), nevertheless we ourselves must begin as composed forms, as mere creatures, in what Spinoza calls "impotence and slavery," in ignorance of our genuine nature as expressions of a divine creativity (*L'Idée d'expression*, 241/263; 268/289–90).

The primary task of philosophy is thus always a variant of the same essential re-orientation, the shift from a creaturely ignorance to an active participation in creative reality. Every creative actualization, every "explication" of virtual intensity, is "always an auto-explication" (*Spinoza*, 103/68tm). For the same reason, every creative description "*replaces* its own object" after first "erasing or destroying" its merely apparent existence (*Cinéma 2*, 18/7). Our main task is in every situation to develop mechanisms "that liberate man from the plane or level that is proper to him [as a creature], in order to make him a creator, adequate to the whole movement of creation" (*Le Bergsonisme*, 117/111). Such liberation remains broadly consistent with Bergson's conception of mysticism, namely "the establishment of a contact, consequently of a partial coincidence, with the creative effort which life itself manifests. This effort is of God, if it is not God himself. The great mystic is to be conceived as an individual being, capable of transcending the limitations imposed on the species by its material nature, thus continuing and extending the divine action" (Bergson, *Deux sources*, 233). Or in less obviously Bergsonian terms: our "problem is therefore one of knowing how the individual would be able to transcend his form and his syntactical link with a world" (*Logique du sens*, 176), so as to "attain once more *the world before man*, before our own dawn, the position where movement was under the regime of universal variation" or absolute creativity, and thereby to express "the non-organic life of things which burns us [. . .,] which no longer belongs either to nature or to our organic individuality, which is the divine part in us, the spiritual relationship in which we are alone with God as light" (*Cinéma 1*, 68, 57).

How are we to pursue this task? "How can we rid ourselves of ourselves?" (*Cinéma 1*, 97/66). The answer lies above all in the promise of "imperceptibility, indiscernibility, and impersonality—the three virtues: To reduce oneself to an abstract line, a trait, in order to find one's zone of indiscernibility with other traits, and in this way enter the haecceity and impersonality of the creator. One is then like grass: one has made the whole world into a becoming because one has suppressed in oneself everything that prevents us from slipping between things and growing in the midst of things . . . ." Only a creating freed from the mediation of any creaturely opacity can attain an unlimited power of inventive self transformation or "becoming-other." This is why "the imperceptible is the immanent end of becoming, its cosmic formula" (*Mille plateaux*, 342–343/279–280).

Tendential Disembodiment

The great question is then: as the actually existent or creaturely aspect of a creating becomes imperceptible, what remains to individuate a particular creating? Is the cosmic formula of becoming a process of radical dissolution or extinction on something like the Buddhist model? Or is it rather the *becoming* itself that is carried into the absolute, a process that requires the material evacuation (though not necessarily the full annihilation) of its creaturely support?

Along with the implications of ontological univocity, this has become one of the most acutely contested questions in the reception of Deleuze's work. Simplifying things considerably, we might say that Badiou's reading of Deleuze as a profoundly "ascetic" metaphysician of the One-All encourages the first, extinguishing, alternative. "It is in renouncing their form and by dissolving themselves within their own (virtual) depth," Badiou writes, "that beings are finally disposed, thought, imaged, according to the univocity of the One"—hence his controversial interpretation of Deleuzian vitalism as driven, in the end, by a power of "death," by the ultimate "identity of thinking and dying" (Badiou, *Deleuze*, 94/63; 24/13–14). Many of Deleuze's more enthusiastic readers, by contrast, continue to present him as the freewheeling apostle of transgression and dissonance, the engineer of unsettling machinic assemblages and eccentric bodily encounters: Rosi Braidotti, for instance, goes so far as to align Deleuze's work alongside that of Luce Irigaray, conceived as parallel contributions to a essentially embodied or "fleshy" materialism.

Now it's certainly true that the ascetic reading underestimates the importance of Deleuze's allegiance to a neo-Nietzschean investment in the (pre- or postpersonal) mechanics of active or affirmative individuation against Schopenhauer's pessimistic assessment that we are "at best beings who suppress themselves" (*Nietzsche et la philosophie*, 94–95/83–84) and downplays the flamboyantly experimental emphasis of so much of Deleuze's work. Precisely because we *begin* in ignorance and impotence, precisely because all finite creatures begin in ignorance of their degree of creative power, so then the process of actively becoming creative is irreducible: abstract knowledge of our creativity will never suffice. We only learn what we can do by testing how we enter into composition with other beings, other bodies, other doings, other affects or ways of being affected. The bulk of Deleuze's work is undeniably preoccupied with the invention of various techniques of such becoming active. He sees Francis Bacon's painting, for instance, as more powerful than that of Rothko precisely because it avoids the painterly equivalent of nirvana: Bacon's work preserves just enough of the figural domain so as to allow art to "act directly upon the nervous system" and thus to "extract directly the presences beneath and beyond representation" (*Francis Bacon*, 37).

It is equally undeniable, however, that all such becoming involves the tendential evacuation or disembodiment of the creatures concerned. In each case, Deleuze's general effort remains that of tearing the process of creation away from any mediation through the organic, semantic, or psychological mediation of the creaturely as such. If art can be conceived as a process of "co-creation" with life itself, this is because, by "recreat[ing] everywhere the primitive swamps of life" (*Qu'est-ce que la philosophie?*, 164/173–174), it taps into the inhuman intensities of properly anorganic sensation. The simple coordination of sensations and reactions through the sensorimotor mechanism that defines an organism already serves to subordinate the perception of movement to the interests of that organism, but "as soon as it stops being related to an interval as sensory-motor center, movement finds its absolute quality again, and every image reacts with every other one, on all their sides and in all their parts. This is the regime of universal variation, which goes beyond the human limits of the sensory-motor schema towards a nonhuman world where movement equals matter, or else in the direction of that super-human world which speaks for a new spirit . . ." (*Cinéma 2*, 57–58/40). Such is precisely the governing sequence at work in Deleuze's work on cinema: setting out from the coordinated movements registered in the "action-image" of classical Hollywood cinema, cinema attains its "truth" in the works of Italian neorealism and the French *nouvelle vague* when, through "paralysis of the sensory-motor schema" in the face of situations to which it is impossible to react, it reaches an eventually immediate intuition of "time in its pure state"—and with it partici-

pation in the ultimate creative identity, grasped in "pure thought," of "Brain and Universe" (*Cinéma 2*, 197/151, 268–269/206–207).

In other words, though Deleuze's work is certainly preoccupied with the invention of transformative machines and assemblages, what such things enable is not the consolidation of identities, bodies, or relations but their tendential evacuation in favor of *becoming as such*, that is, becoming carried to the limit of absolute or immediate creativity, with no other norm than that of a creating that moves at infinite speed. In the end "nothing other than the Event subsists, the Event alone, *Eventum tantum* for all contraries . . ." (*Logique du sens*, 207/176). Witness the disjunctive affirmative power of the schizophrenic in *L'Anti-Oedipe*, who is "not simply bisexual, or between the two, or intersexual," but "transsexual": "he does not abolish disjunction by identifying the contradictory elements by means of elaboration; instead, he affirms it through a continuous overflight spanning an indivisible distance," activating within himself "this distance that transforms him into a woman," into a child, and so on (*L'Anti-Oedipe*, 91/76–77). Deleuze's Proust pursues a comparable task, insofar as he makes "from every finite thing a being of sensation that is constantly preserved, but by vanishing on a plane of composition of Being: 'beings of flight' "(*Qu'est-ce que la philosophie?*, 179/189). Such again is the power of the nomad in *Mille plateaux*: "if the nomad can be called the Deterritorialized par excellence, it is precisely because there is no reterritorialisation *afterward* as with the migrant, or *upon something else* as with the sedentary (the sedentary's relation with the earth is mediatized by something else, a property regime, a State apparatus). With the nomad, on the contrary, it is deterritorialization that constitutes the relation to the earth, to such a degree that the nomad reterritorializes on deterritorialization itself." Nomad and schizo both testify, in short, and without passing either through the relative stability of a global system or toward the definitive collapse of all individuation, to the absolute power of *a* creating; they operate precisely as "a *local absolute*, an absolute that is manifested locally" (*Mille plateaux*, 473/381–382). In the end there is no better description of Deleuze's philosophy than this: it inspires and maps, from every imaginable locality, absolutely creative trajectories.

PETER HALLWARD

See also **Alain Badiou; Henri Bergson; Felix Guattari; Jacques Lacan**

Biography

Gilles Deleuze was born in 1925 and studied philosophy at the Sorbonne, passing the aggrégation exam in

1949. He spent most of his academic career teaching at the University of Paris VIII at Vincennes/Saint-Denis, where he enjoyed an almost legendary fame as an exceptionally inspiring teacher. After an early exposition of Hume (1953), his work took on its distinctive shape through a series of enthusiastic studies of thinkers he saw as external to the established (rationalist or neo-Hegelian) history of philosophy—Nietzsche (1962), Bergson (1966), and Spinoza (1968)—before acquiring what was to remain its most rigorous and comprehensive formulation in the treatise *Différence et répétition* (1968). Quickly associated with the ideas of transgressive liberation that proliferated during and after the rebellions of 1968, his later works include both the exuberant collaborative projects with Félix Guattari that secured his international reputation (the two volumes of *Capitalisme et schizophrénie: L'Anti-Oedipe* [1972] and *Mille plateaux* [1980], along with *Kafka: Pour une littérature mineure* and the more programmatic *Qu'est-ce que la philosophie?* [1991]) and several highly original monographs on cinema, Leibniz, and Foucault. Though his work bears some limited comparison with the early works of Derrida and (especially) Lyotard, Deleuze always opposed any vaguely poststructuralist declarations of an end to philosophy or the closure of metaphysics. After suffering for years from a painful respiratory illness, he eventually committed suicide at the age of seventy.

Selected Works

Nietzsche et la philosophie, 1962; as *Nietzsche and Philosophy*, translated by Hugh Tomlinson, 1983

Proust et les signes, 1964; as *Proust and Signs*, translated by Richard Howard, 1972

Le Bergsonisme, 1966; as *Bergsonism*, translated by Hugh Tomlinson and Barbara Habberjam

Différence et répétition, 1968; as *Difference and Repetition*, translated by Paul Patton, 1994

L'Idée d'expression dans la philosophie de Spinoza, 1968; as *Expressionism in Philosophy: Spinoza*, translated by Martin Joughin, 1990

Logique du sens, 1969; as *The Logic of Sense*, translated by Mark Lester with Charles Stivale, 1990

Spinoza: philosophie pratique, 1970; as *Spinoza: Practical Philosophy*, translated by Robert Hurley, 1988

Francis Bacon: Logique de la sensation, 1981

Cinéma 1: L'Image-mouvement, 1983; as *Cinema 1: The Movement-Image*, translated by Hugh Tomlinson and Barbara Habberjam, 1986

Cinéma 2: L'Image-temps, 1985; as *Cinema 2: The Time-Image*, translated by Hugh Tomlinson and Barbara Habberjam, 1989

Foucault, 1986; as *Foucault*, translated by Seán Hand, 1988

Le Pli: Leibniz et le baroque, 1988; as *The Fold: Leibniz and the Baroque*, translated by Tom Conley, 1993

Pourparlers, 1990; as *Negotiations*, translated by Martin Joughin, 1995

With Félix Guattari

L'Anti-Oedipe, 1972; as *Anti-Oedipus*, translated by Robert Hurley, Mark Seem, and Helen R. Lane, 1977

Kafka: pour une littérature mineure, 1975; as *Kafka: For a Minor Literature*, translated by Dana Polan, 1986

Mille plateaux, 1980; as *A Thousand Plateaus*, translated by Brian Massumi, 1986

Qu'est-ce que la philosophie?, 1991; as *What is Philosophy?*, translated by Hugh Tomlinson and Graham Burchell, 1994

Further Reading

Ansell-Pearson, Keith, *Germinal Life: The Difference and Repetition of Deleuze*, London: Routledge, 1999

Ansell-Pearson, Keith (editor), *Deleuze and Philosophy: The Difference Engineer*, London: Routledge, 1997

Badiou, Alain, *Deleuze: La clameur de l'être*, Paris: Hachette, 1997

Bogue, Ronald, *Deleuze and Guattari*, London: Routledge, 1989

Boundas, Constantin, and Dorothea Olkowski (editors), *Gilles Deleuze and the Theatre of Philosophy*, New York: Routledge, 1994

Colebrook, Claire, *Gilles Deleuze*, London: Routledge, 2001

Hallward, Peter, "Deleuze and Redemption from Interest," *Radical Philosophy* 81 (1997): 6–21

Hallward, Peter, *Deleuze: Creationism in Philosophy*, forthcoming

Hardt, Michael, *Gilles Deleuze: An Apprenticeship in Philosophy*, Minneapolis: University of Minnesota Press, 1993

Marks, John, *Gilles Deleuze: Vitalism and Multiplicity*, London: Pluto Press, 1998

Mengue, Philippe, *Deleuze: Le système du multiple*, "The System of the Multiple" Paris: Kimé, 1995

Patton, Paul, *Deleuze and the Political*, London: Routledge, 2000

Patton, Paul (editor), *Deleuze: A Critical Reader*, Oxford: Blackwell, 1996

Smith, Daniel, *Deleuze*, forthcoming

Stivale, Charlie, *The Two-Fold Thought of Deleuze and Guattari: Intersections and Animations*, New York: Guilford Press, 1998

Zourabichvili, François, *Deleuze: Une philosophie de l'événement*, "A philosophy of the event." Paris: PUF, 1995

Other Works Cited

Bergson, Henri, *L'Evolution créatrice* [1907], Paris: PUF, 1941

Bergson, Henri, *Les Deux sources de la morale et de la religion* [1932], Paris: PUF, 1997

DEPESTRE, RENÉ
Poet

Depestre has been criticized for adhering all too easily to most of the major movements that have shaped the great postwar explosion of Caribbean thought and culture: Négritude, surrealism, Marxism, and most recently, Créolité. In truth, however, Depestre has worn these various influences fairly lightly and has consequently been able to shed them more freely than those with more rigid ideological or philosophical standpoints. Négritude is a case in point. Depestre was naturally drawn to Césaire and to Négritude's bold affirmation of "black" identity. He never, however, became part of the movement. This nonengagement was essentially because Césaire and Martinique were out of sync with Depestre and Haiti. During and following the American occupation of 1915–1934, Haitian culture had undergone a prolonged indigenist phase, which had the effect of valorizing the previously neglected peasant, or "Africanized," aspects of national culture. A fundamental aspect of the indigenist project was an overt challenge to racist views of black inferiority, and a realignment of Haiti's ongoing anti-imperialist struggle with that of the colonized African nations. In other words, Haitian indigenism shared much of Négritude's concerns, but had predated Césaire by at least fifteen years. Racial identity, therefore, was a relatively well-established and uncontested aspect of Haitianity for Depestre and his generation of intellectuals, and whereas Césaire has largely remained fixed in his belief in the importance of race and Africanity, Depestre's work has absorbed many other influences and followed a quite idiosyncratic path.

The longest phase in Depestre's intellectual life was his Marxist period, which only ended when he left Cuba. Depestre was drawn to Marxism for two essential reasons: first, like his great Haitian predecessor Jacques Roumain, Depestre believed in the commonality of struggle of the international proletariat and that social change was a cross-national preoccupation; and second, he felt that Marxism held the key to demystifying the idea of race in colonial and postcolonial societies. Depestre has made his arguments on race most persuasively in a 1980 essay, tellingly entitled *Bonjour et adieu à la négritude* (Hello and Farewell to Négritude). This is Depestre's most influential and cohesive contribution to ideas of race to date, and it bases its thesis on the essential arbitrariness of the very concept of race. Depestre argues that modern conceptions of race were (de)formed by the entirely "unnatural" processes of the Atlantic slave trade and the particular set of polarized social relationships that slavery instigated. Therefore, he argues, to perpetuate racial identity, be it "black" or "white," is to adhere to this initial, foundational myth. As he sees it, the great error in colonial societies, and in Haiti in particular, has been to privilege race as the primary site of social conflict. The unnatural, misleading concept of race has obscured the true divisions in colonial societies which he says, are class based. In this essay, Depestre is also sensitive to the cultural aspects of race, to the ways in which conceptions of "black" cultures have been essentialized as part of the wider imperialist project. Ultimately, Depestre calls for a deracialization of cultural anthropology and of literary criticism, as these, he argues, are inextricably linked to "conceptual imperialism," and he proposes a true, nonhierarchical intercultur-

alism, a syncretic "common Americanity" among New World cultures.

These ideas are important because they prefigure central elements of Édouard Glissant's extended theorizations of "Antillanité," in particular Glissant's promotion of relational, nonreductive intercultural contact. However, although Glissant has, since the publication of *Le Discours antillais* (Caribbean Discourse) in 1981, risen to prominence as the Caribbean's most profound and influential thinker, Depestre has largely not engaged in theoretical work, preferring to work on poetry and to establish himself as a prose fiction writer. Moreover, in a way that mirrors wider movements in Caribbean literature and thought, Depestre's concern with collective issues has largely been superseded by his growing preoccupation with the personal and the particular. That said, Depestre's *Le Métier à métisser* (1998) offers some innovative, original ideas on culture and society, notably in his theorization of exile. Having returned to Haiti only once in almost sixty years and having wandered incessantly for much of that time, Depestre has a unique perspective on the experience of displacement and migration. Whereas his early work represents exile as a source of trauma, he has more recently come to celebrate his multirooted identity and now makes a connection between his own experience and the wider, global movement toward postnational, fluid, and idiosyncratic subjectivity. Depestre sees postmodern migration in largely positive terms, as a movement toward cultural and identitary multiplicity, to a point where traditional, national, and racial frontiers and classifications become ever more obsolete. The self-proclaimed "nomade enraciné," in his own particular way, is an embodiment of Glissant's theorization of Caribbeanized rhizomatic identity, an experiment in exilic being who has given up the nostalgic notion of an original unity. Indeed, if there is one thread that cuts across every phase of Depestre's thinking, it is this mistrust of oneness of roots, whether it is framed in terms of race, nation, or culture.

MARTIN MUNRO

See also **Aime Cesaire; Edouard Glissant**

Biography

Born in Jacmel, Haiti, in 1926, René Depestre first came to prominence as one of the young militants of the *La Ruche* group in the immediate postwar period. Since then, he has proved to be an enduring and influential presence in Haitian and Caribbean literature and thought. A prodigious poet, Depestre's published his first collection, *Étincelles*, in 1945, and the following year the surrealist-influenced *Gerbe de sang* was published. 1946 also marked his departure from Haiti to study in Paris. During his time at the Sorbonne, he came into contact with many of the metropole's foremost literary and cultural figures, and also with the nascent Négritude group that was taking shape around Césaire, Senghor, and Damas. The French authorities expelled him in 1951 due to his left-wing political activities, and he then spent brief periods in Prague, Havana, Vienna, Chile, Argentina, and Brazil before going back to Paris in 1956. Depestre returned to Haiti in 1957, but after refusing to work with Duvalier, had no choice but to leave. Enthused by the early developments in revolutionary Cuba, Depestre accepted Guevara's invitation to go to Havana, where he lived, and worked in various cultural and political posts until his disenchantment with the restrictions of Castro's regime led him to leave in 1978. A period of eight years working with UNESCO in Paris followed, before his retirement in 1986. In 1991, he, his wife, and two sons obtained French citizenship. At this writing, he lives in Lézignan-Corbières in the Aude region of France.

Selected Works

Bonjour et adieu à la négritude, Paris: Robert Laffont, 1980
Le Métier à métisser. Paris: Stock, 1998

Further Reading

Coutton, Claude, *René Depestre*, Paris: Seghers, 1986
Dash, J. Michael, *Literature and Ideology in Haiti, 1915–1961*, London and Basingstoke: Macmillan, 1981
Munro, Martin, *Shaping and Reshaping the Caribbean: The Work of Aimé Césaire and René Depestre*, Leeds: Maney Publishing for the Modern Humanities Research Association, 2000

DERRIDA, JACQUES
Philosopher

Risking oversimplification, one sentence might define Jacques Derrida's effort: In order to open thought (and so ethical and political action) to the arrival of singular others, to events of alterity, Derrida questions philosophical tradition's decision that being is merely presence. Philosophy's inaugural decision reducing being to presence results in a "metaphysics of presence" that defines presence as the foundation and goal of all thought. Acting as philosophical tradition's constitutive reading of itself, this metaphysics insists that if presence does not center one's thinking, one is not thinking. Irreducible to being as presence, alterity is unthinkable for the metaphysics of presence. Yet an irreplaceable resource for thinking alterity is the philosophical tradition. That tradition, argues Derrida, harbors a thinking unheard of by the metaphysics of presence. Through examinations of Plato, Augustine, Descartes, Rousseau, Kant, Hegel, Nietzsche, Husserl, and many other thinkers, Derrida meticulously details how the philosophical tradition opens to another reading that allows for a thinking that displaces presence and its privilege. This reading's merit is not merely and not even primarily that it yields a better understanding of philosophy's resources and limits. Derrida certainly does put much effort into arguing that although philosophical tradition has handed itself down in terms of the metaphysics of presence, philosophical tradition also entails virtually unheard-of chances for thought that dismantle philosophy's predominant self-understanding. But the urgency of the claims Derrida makes on readers is ethical and political, even if those claims are inextricable from Derrida's intricate engagement with tradition. In order for Derrida's ethical and political claims to touch one, one must confront the difficulties of Derrida's work. This essay can and should be only an invitation to read Derrida with persistence and care. Perhaps one of the less difficult entry points for such reading is Derrida's argument about the binary oppositions that the metaphysics of presence tends to elaborate.

Dismantling Binary Oppositions

Working on philosophy's margins, neither simply within nor without tradition, Derrida specifies how defining oppositions of philosophical thought are only possible because of infrastructures that render such oppositions both possible and impossible. These oppositions (presence/absence, form/content, intelligible/sensible, soul/body, man/woman, human/animal, and so on) tend to be asymmetrical, establishing distinctions between terms by exclusionary acts privileging one term over the other. For example, in defining the soul and the body as opposites, Platonic–Christian tradition privileges the soul as ethically superior to the body. When this tradition associates "man" with the soul and "woman" with the body, it privileges man over woman. If having a soul and so the capacity for reason defines the human, and if tradition associates woman with the body more than man, then the representative human tends to be male, to the exclusion of women.

The only recently and partially overcome tendency of Western civilization to exclude women from official institutional political life is symptomatic of the exclusions characterizing the Platonic–Christian tradition's network of oppositions. Such exclusions enact the value judgments informing the systems of thought that specific hierarchical oppositions underpin. The coherence of philosophy's arguments is inextricable from philosophy's desire for what it judges should be. An opposition's abjected term often links to traits that a philosophy desires to exclude from the privileged term. Derrida musters abjected terms strategically. "Writing" is an example. One of philosophy's most traditional gestures, Derrida finds, is to oppose speech to writing. For the metaphysics of presence, the philosophical *logos* is a presence transparently present to itself, a voice of reason and truth immediately hearing itself, uninhabited by the absence, mediation, and opacity philosophical tradition associates with writing. For Derrida, "writing" refers to the traits specified in philosophy's speech/writing opposition but also to traits allowing for and dismantling that opposition. The voice of the *logos* turns out to rely on the writing that it would exclude. When speech turns out to be inhabited by and to require a writing that displaces the trait of self-presence valorizing speech over writing, "writing" refers to an "arche-writing." This arche-writing is an infrastructure of the speech/writing opposition and so of the philosophical systems relying on that and related oppositions. Tied to arche-writing, a condition of (im)-possibility, writing threatens to destabilize such a system's founding oppositions.

For example, the concepts that Plato had Socrates elaborate, and the ethical and political conclusions Socrates endorsed, depend on the opposition between the intelligible and the sensible. Not only do the particular concepts depend on this opposition; more importantly, the Platonic concept of what a concept in general is depends on the intelligible being cleanly distinguished from the sensible. In *Dissemination*, Plato's texts emerge as complex attempts to secure the intelligible/sensible opposition by denigrating and excluding what troubles yet allows for that distinction: writing, which Plato designated a "*pharmakon*," a word referring both to cure and to poison. Derrida shows how Platonic conceptuality turns out to depend on the very writing that dismantles it. Writing is at once Platonic philosophy's cure and its poison. In addition, Derrida points out, the word *pharmakon* relates to the word *pharmakos*, which refers to the persons in ancient Greece ritually put to death as sacrifices to purify the city when calamities indicate the need for atonement. The fate of Socrates enacts the sacrifice of the *pharmakos*.

Derrida's interest in the connection between this explicit sacrificial violence and the subtler violence of Plato's abjection of writing characterizes Derrida's concern to underscore how philosophy's desire for conceptual closure informs the exclusions defining various institutional borders. Conceptual oppositions rely on borders demarcating insides from outsides. To found a coherent system of distinctions, the opposition between nature and culture requires a border demarcating an inside as entirely distinct from an outside. At least in one founding instance, a border must distinguish culture from nature, one as an inside and the other as an outside nowhere in that inside. Derrida attests how such borders divide themselves and so dismantle the oppositions they attempt to establish. An opposition's deconstruction does not simply erase the opposed terms or move directly from the privileged to the abjected term. Rather, by way of a transformative reversal that strategically privileges the abjected term in displacing both terms from their metaphysical hierarchy, deconstruction reinscribes them in a relation of *différance* their opposition assumes but would preclude.

Différance

In relying on hierarchies valuing one term over the other, the metaphysics of presence characterizes difference as opposition. If opposites, Y and Z are different: where and when Y is present, Z is absent, and vice versa. Difference so defined assumes presence and absence to be opposites between which one can draw a strict dividing line. But if absence occurs only as the presence of absence, and presence only in reference to absence, then their difference as opposites assumes (but would arrest and erase) their *différance* by which each is marked by the other's trace, displacing and deferring the final purity or full presence of either. Presence and absence's *différance* is their opposition's condition of (im)possibility. Instead of disappearing, the line dividing presence and absence divides interminably so that the question of whether one is on one side of the line or the other becomes undecidable. The various oppositions the metaphysics of presence entails rely on but are rendered undecidable by *différance*. With the undecidable, the hierarchies these oppositions posit tremble, perhaps even ruin, and thought reaches an aporia or impasse. Rather than going away, questions of intelligible *versus* sensible, soul *versus* body, man *versus* woman, human *versus* animal, and so on, go into suspense, allowing for previously unheard of questions and thoughts, including questions asking whether thought finally reduces to questioning. This is one way Derrida's texts are affirmative: They give thought fresh chances.

The Signified/Signifier Opposition

The deconstruction of the speech/writing and signified/signifier oppositions concerns Derrida because the metaphysical determination of being as presence uncontaminated by absence relies on them and they in turn rely on this determination. The opposition presence/absence privileges presence as being while abjecting absence as a lack of being to be overcome in a return to full presence. The speech/writing and signified/signifier oppositions assume the presence/representation opposition. Metaphysics relegates the sign to secondary status in defining it as a representation: Presence precedes any sign representing presence in presence's absence. The sign would originate in, refer to, and hail the return of presence. Representation suggests absence's recuperation in and the other's consignment to presence. In assuming that reference finally refers only to presence, the concept "sign" enacts a violent reduction of otherness to presence.

For the metaphysics of presence as representation is secondary to presence, so the written sign is secondary to the spoken word. The determination of being as presence has been inextricable, Derrida argues, from the definition of presence as a spoken signified uncontaminated by any writing, representation, or signifier. Metaphysics is logocentric: Truth and meaning should center in the *logos* from which writing remains strictly external. The voice of the *logos* would be present to itself, uninhabited by the absence associated with the written mark. The logocentric understanding of writing restricts writing to being the representation of a presence: speech. The speech/writing inside/outside opposition has a moralistic valence: Speech associates with breath and spirit, whereas writing associates with the fallen body and inscription.

Requiring the distinction between signified and signifier, the concept "sign" carries defining oppositions of metaphysics. In positing at least one signified, the transcendental signified, as a presence uncontaminated by any signifier, the concept "sign" assumes the opposition between presence and representation. But if the signifier always contaminates the signified and representation presence, then the concepts "sign" and "representation" begin to deconstruct. Although the sign would bring all reference back to presence, the deconstruction of the signified/signifier opposition renders any transcendental signified presence also another signifier, or rather, when the signifier contaminates any signified, the sign gives way to the "trace." Presence becomes a trace referring to the trace of alterity. Rather than the referent all reference refers to, presence as trace refers to otherness in a generalized movement of reference presence neither anchors nor controls. The trace refers to alterity without simply reducing the other to presence.

In academia, the pedagogy and research now called "cultural studies" suggest the import of the deconstruction of the sign and of representation. Works published as cultural studies occasionally have the subtitle *Representations of——*, the blank containing a word designating an ethnic, national, religious, or cultural group. But if such cultural studies fail to engage representation's deconstruction, especially the deconstruction of specific notions of representation that the metaphysics of presence hands down to the modern university and so to the "humanities," these studies risk reinforcing the very abjection of diverse others cultural studies would contest. For example, a pedagogue might try to combat racism by denouncing or praising particular representations while leaving the relevant concepts, structures, and institutions of representation unexamined. Many academics pursuing cultural studies realize that representation, the template of both "negative" and "positive" representations of others, must be questioned. Cultural studies that track the representational sign's deconstruction to register the trace of the other will more effectively contribute to the dismantling of hierarchies between dominant and subordinate groups. However, as Derrida's engagement with Lévinas suggests, deconstruction involves no simple rejection of representation and the sign.

Two Examples: Derrida's Engagement with Lévinas and Austin

The majority of Derrida's writings are readings of philosophical but also literary, psychoanalytic, and other texts. Derrida's thought interweaves with the texts it reads. Derrida proceeds by engaging with the thinking of predecessors. Two examples of this engagement are Derrida's encounters with the work of Emmanuel Lévinas and J. L. Austin.

Lévinas's effort to think alterity otherwise than being, to release thought from ontology's primacy, and to retrieve ethics as first philosophy intrigues Derrida; following Lévinas, Derrida also seeks to displace ontology. Finding ontology to attempt a violent reduction of the other to a being present within the totality of beings, Lévinas claims one may welcome the other as other by way of an infinity that breaches totality. The other's ethical call constitutes the "I" as hostage. So burdened, the "I" quests for autonomy's mirage, an "I" without a relation to alterity. Lévinas quotes the phrase "Here I am," uttered by Abraham, Isaiah, and Moses in response to God's call, as encapsulating the "I's" relation to the other: the responsibility of the "I" to the other constitutes the "I." Others affect the "I" in excess of any initiative on the part of the "I." Lévinas finds welcoming others, whether hospitably or inhospitably, to be the condition of but irreducible to any ethical or political significance profiling others. Reducing others to profiles or themes assimilates others to the same.

Although very close to Lévinas, Derrida, in *Writing and Difference*'s "Violence and Metaphysics," brings several questions to bear. The face-to-face encounter that for Lévinas characterizes ethics, a matter of presence Lévinas links to voice, comports with the privilege of speech Derrida questions. And although Lévinas claims that no rhetorical figures contaminate the face-to-face, figures that profile and so reduce the other, the logic of the interhuman face-to-face, Derrida notes, relies on at least one figure, the analogy with humanity's face-to-face relation with God. Derrida also points out that although, on the one hand, Lévinas retrieves a relation to alterity that philosophy tends to erase because ontology reduces the other to being as presence, on the other hand Lévinas can only describe that relation with concepts borrowed from philosophy. Derrida makes this argument not to criticize Lévinas. Neither simply inside nor outside philosophy, deconstruction is distinct from critique. If Derrida's questions about Lévinas's entanglement with the philosophical tradition were a critique, this would assume that Derrida occupies a position merely beyond philosophy. Rather, Derrida wants to demonstrate how Lévinas's work is important precisely in that it hovers on the border of philosophy's reduction of the other.

This reduction, Derrida agrees, entails violence. But Derrida claims that one will never be able simply to leave behind the violence that Lévinas associates with the profiling of the other. The confrontation with the face of the other eschews all violence, Lévinas argues, because this confrontation involves an approach to the other disengaged from thematization and so from any rhetorical figures on a theme. Rather than a phenomenon or a figure of a phenomenon, the face of the other is a trace. But the trace, although irreducible to the sign, is also inseparable from the sign. One reads the other's trace, Derrida stresses, only as signification dissembles or erases it. Being significant threatens to reduce the other to a profile. Racial profiling in police work is an example, yet so is the profiling of singular others as praiseworthy representatives of diverse cultural or ethnic groups. The analogy of the human face-to-face with the human–God face-to-face involves signification. An example of the trace's inseparability from signification, this analogy is but one example of how respect for the other supposes the profiling Lévinas rejects. Rather than opposites that are simply different, the trace and the representational sign contaminate each other. The trace of the other is only readable by way of its erasure in the representation that the trace allows for, exceeds, and dismantles.

Welcoming the other in reading the trace entails an unavoidable violence also because, in Derrida's phrase from *The Gift of Death, tout autre est tout autre.* As a trace of the other, any face is no less other than any other face. Every other is as completely other as any other, and one is as obliged to each other as other as to the remaining others. In this situation, to respond at all, one must respond selectively to compelling yet unreservedly singular ethical calls. Any response calculates among incommensurable, incalculable obligations. The choice will inescapably require the violence of preferring another to the other others, and this violence is irreducible: No knowledge yields an alibi that finally exonerates one's choice. By way of the trace, the other calls one to promise to meet an obligation, but no program can guide one to take this call but not that one. And any response always runs the risk that its necessary disavowal of knowledge entails: In welcoming the other, one never finally knows who or what one welcomes.

The notion that alterity exceeds thought but solicits a promise informs Derrida's reading of speech act theory in *Limited Inc.* The twentieth-century British philosopher J. L. Austin's speech act theory distinguishes between language that describes things and language that does things. Austin calls language that describes constative and language that acts performative. In describing a person as guilty, a jury produces constative language. In sentencing that person to death, the judge commits performative language. One evaluates constative language, Austin states, as true or false. Performative language is felicitous or infelicitous. Felicitous speech acts occur in conjunction with precise conditions defining a specific context dominated by the intention of the speech act's enunciator. For Austin, a felicitous speech act must be intended seriously. Promises made in novels, poems, and plays are infelicitous because fictitious, not to be taken seriously. Speech acts made in literature are parasitical on serious speech acts. Austin claims that speech acts in literature may be excluded from serious consideration by speech act theory. Austin's arguments rely on an exclusionary opposition (serious/nonserious) that is also a moralistic judgment.

Why is Austin so anxious to distinguish speech acts from stage acts, speech actors from stage actors? Pursuing such questions, Derrida loosens the hold that a version of the metaphysics of presence has on speech act theory. Rather than dismissing or simply criticizing speech act theory, Derrida underscores how Austin's attempt to exclude literature retreats from speech act theory's own most remarkable implications. Articulating these implications, Derrida pursues speech act theory to affirm and complicate it in ways prompting a new question: How are speech acts inventions of the other?

The constative/performative opposition suggests the limits of the definition of communication as the conveyance of meaning. This definition assumes that a unified meaning precedes language and that language, merely a dispensable vehicle, delivers such meaning to auditors or readers. Relying on the preexisting meaning, one can judge communication as true or false. This definition of communication as the delivery of meaning roughly corresponds to Austin's notion of constative statements. However, argues Derrida, what Austin calls the performative communicates in a way other than the delivery of meaning. More than meaning, performatives communicate force. A constative delivers a message about things, but a performative delivers a force that does things. Yet Austin defines this delivery of force as controlled by the intention and the institutional felicity conditions defining any given speech act. The conditions and the intention centering them form what Austin calls a speech act's total context. For Austin, constative statements can define this totality of conditions and the intention that centers it. When one attempts to reduce performative force to the force the speaker or writer intends to convey guided by felicity conditions, the constative reins in the performative, returning it to the definition of communication as merely the conveyance of meaning. Derrida questions such a limitation on performative force, not to deny intention or context, but to deconstruct the constative/performative opposition and to demonstrate how the factors that allow for infelicity also decenter intention and disallow the saturation of context intention as controlling center assumes.

Derrida examines the infelicitous speech acts Austin wishes to exclude from his investigation. Austin tends to consider infelicity an accident befalling a speech act from the outside, but he also emphasizes that all speech acts are equally subject to infelicity. If infelicity is a necessary possibility of any speech act, then that possibility cannot simply be external to the speech act. Rather, the possibility of infelicity characterizes the structure of any speech act. This structural possibility of infelicity suggests that the lack of full intention Austin attributes to the fictions he wants to exclude as not serious also necessarily haunts the speech acts he includes as serious. Derrida establishes how the exclusion of fiction constitutes Austin's speech act theory and betrays its limited capture by metaphysical presuppositions. Like any spoken or written language, Derrida notes, any speech act may be iterated in the absence of its speaker or author; even after the speaker's or the author's death, the speech act is still iterable. One can quote or cite any speech act in virtually innumerable contexts that depart from the context of its production. Never simply without a context, any speech act is always already iterable and so extricable from any given context and repeatable in other contexts. A speech act is even irreducible to its "first" context because iterability disallows intention from ever absolutely "saturating" the contexts and consequences of a speech act's performance. For example, a judge's intention to do justice never fully or necessarily determines what the judge may or may not be doing

in uttering the performative, "I sentence you to death." To contest death sentences more effectively, one can always iterate them in contexts other than the judicial system.

Austin defines the performative as the act of an autonomous "I" whose intention is or, more specifically, should be that act's master. Questioning this mastery, Derrida suggests that speech acts respond to an unmasterable alterity. The speech act assumes an "I can," but the performative's solicitation involves an event, the other's arrival, beyond any possibility of the "I." The other's coming is the performative's (im)possibility. As responses to others, speech acts are inventions of the other. A singular other invents and is invented by the speech act. On the one hand, another solicits one, prompting a reply, often an "I promise." On the other hand, that reply inevitably attempts to figure, posit, or define, that is, to invent the other that the speech act addresses. To keep a promise to another, one must remember that other above all others. In promising, one promises fidelity to another, and so, because fidelity requires a target, one must invent or determine that other, as if the other were definable by a set of constative statements. Any other, as other, however, is just that which cannot be invented in this second sense. Alterity marks thought yet exceeds any thought one might have. No set of constative statements, however copious, can define the other without reducing the other to the same, canceling the other's arrival. Any singular other "as such" exceeds any constative "as such" speech acts invent. The speech act invented in response to the other will always risk inventing, and so dissembling or even erasing, the other. So the speech actor who promises, both making a promise to another and promising to manifest, determine, or define that other, always stands in need of responding again.

Politics

Derrida has long been politically active in ways recognizably "on the left." His participation in campaigns to dismantle South African apartheid, for the rights of immigrants in France, and against the death penalty is well known. Although Derrida's earlier texts engage political issues, Derrida's more recent texts often address such issues more explicitly. Dealing with, among other topics, Marx's legacy, political friendship's determination as fraternity, and the university's fate, Derrida welcomes a democracy to come in interrogating the limits of what the political has been and continues to be.

Dissenting from the choruses praising neoliberal globalization as ending history in a capitalist utopia, choruses that want also to sing Marx and the hope of communism to their graves, Derrida asserts that Marx's specters, including the specter of communism, continue to haunt political thought and action. (Of course, given the constative/performative opposition's deconstruction, political thought also commits actions.) Marx's legacies are irreducibly plural. Marx haunts diverse political situations diversely. The predominant tendency to disavow Marx, an attempt to exorcise his specters, teaches us, claims Derrida's *Specters of Marx*, just how pervasive and unavoidable Marx's legacies are. Any contemporary political actor inherits from Marx in terms of one legacy or another. In the name of a certain messianic legacy of Marx, to contest capitalism's dominance of globalization, Derrida calls for new international political activism and organizations, for a new "international."

Yet, while affirming deconstruction's affiliation with Marx, Derrida also examines how Marx's thought might stall or compromise the legacy of Marx with which Derrida allies. Derrida points out that, on the one hand, Marx identifies religion as ideology's defining instance, but, on the other hand, a messianic promise of justice to come informs Marx's work. This promise shares the structure of promise common to the Abrahamic messianisms. Marx's critique of ideology relies on a political-economic ontology allergic to the alterity Marx's messianic promise presupposes. In defining politics by way of ontology, Marx may help to chase away the specter of communism his messianic promise would conjure.

Derrida leagues with Marx for a democracy to come. This democracy departs from fraternity. The concepts of democracy hitherto thought and institutionalized tend to assume a community defined by friendship conceived of as a relation among brothers. The friendship of democratic citizens has been fraternal. As a fraternity, democracy has a hard time thinking or institutionalizing equality except in terms of homogeneity. To solicit a democracy to come, Derrida, in *Politics of Friendship*, deconstructs the fraternal schema to invent a notion of friendship, and so a politics, more welcoming of diversity and heterogeneity.

In soliciting a democracy to come, Derrida welcomes a democracy in excess of any political order that does or will exist and that either is or could be known. The "to come" is only a future if it happens as a surprise that never completely arrives and that society cannot finally institutionalize. The democracy to come opens societies (including those now called "democratic") to futures they cannot anticipate but must welcome in justice's name. In politics, justice, always in excess of existing law, must be done but, Derrida suggests, can never be finished.

One institutional site where the democracy to come may happen is the university. The speech act's irreducibility to context has political implications for the university. One usually assumes, Derrida notes, that the university's primary concern is with constative statements that convey established knowledge to students. Even when universities pursue performative statements, say in rhetoric departments, one commonly supposes that the goal is not to generate but to study performatives. The study of rhetoric only establishes knowledge, a set of constative statements. But Derrida remarks that such assumptions ignore a feature distinguishing the profession of professor: A professor of chemistry, for example, does not merely establish constative statements about chemicals; he or she also professes chemistry, professes a commitment to chemistry limited by nothing describable in constative terms. One can know a great deal about chemistry without being its professor, but one cannot be a professor of chemistry without performing a speech act (professing) irreducible to any knowledge.

This speech act would distinguish the professor who professes chemistry to students from the employee who works on chemicals as a participant in the global economy. But, Derrida suggests, as capital's influence on the university augments, pressuring education to become just one more profit-maximizing enterprise, that professor and that employee are increasingly likely to be the "same" person. The university's professed commitment to professing assumes a sovereign freedom of inquiry that is increasingly in doubt. In this situation, to profess chemistry or any other topic in the name of a democracy of the university to come is to act politically for the reinvention of the university's sovereignty. Derrida conjoins such acts with a deconstruction of the notions of sovereignty still appealed to by the nation–states that are ceding more sovereignty to the transnational organizations capital dominates.

Religion

A concern with religion informs Derrida's earlier publications if only because the privileging of speech over writing is inextricable from theologies defining God as the Supreme Being. If one can legitimately refer to Derrida as a kind of atheist, one can especially do so in relation to any Supreme Being. In focusing ontology on a highest and best being, the Platonic tradition is also theological in that it characterizes God as that founding being. For this "ontotheology," God is the being founding all lesser beings. Ontotheology thinks of the God of the Abrahamic traditions (Judaism, Christianity, and Islam) in terms of Platonic notions of being, especially the idea of the good that Plato's Socrates hyperbolically places beyond being. The figure of hyperbole suggests not only "beyond" but also "exceedingly." The good is hyperbolically beyond being not only in being beyond the beings it founds, but also by exceeding all other beings in the excellence of its being. So in the Christian negative theologies that have appropriated the Platonic good to think of God, the good renders God a hyperbeing, a superessential being beyond being. In 1968, during the postlecture discussion of Derrida's "Différance," one auditor suggested that Derrida's thought of *différance* is a negative theology. Deconstruction certainly shares negative theology's concern with the irreducibly other. But, however uncannily Derrida's thought might resemble a negative theology, it departs from negative theology in that such theology, at least in its dominant tendency, perpetuates a metaphysics of being as presence.

Dismantling ontotheological determinations of religion, Derrida reopens the (im)possibility of the messianic promises defining the Abrahamic religions. A speech act, the messianic promise of justice to come informs yet is distinguishable from the particular messianisms. Judaism, Christianity, Islam, and their messianic promises associate with deserts. Derrida describes the structures of promise and hospitality these religions presuppose as a desert within the Abrahamic desert. Vacant of idols determining the other as some presence, the desert within the desert is a place where one wanders without knowledge, a calculable program, or any horizon of expectation. Wandering in this desert, one cannot foresee with certainty whether one will welcome there the other or radical evil. Perpetually risky, the messianic promise assumed by but irreducible to the particular messianisms, a promise of justice, allows for a relation to and a respect for the singularity of others that might inform an enlightened culture to come.

But to engage a messianic promise, to act in religion's name, runs the risk of what Derrida calls "autoimmunity" in *Acts of Religion*'s "Faith and Knowledge." To keep the holy unscathed and safe, the Abrahamic religions immunize themselves from their others. In promising, each religion promises to keep faith with that promise, to be accountable, to count on itself, and so must be one, countable, uncontaminated by any other. Any religion's immunity from other religions is also an autoimmunity from that religion as other. Acting out the logic of immunity, a religion, in promising, promises to cleanse itself, to exclude its others, and so, via autoimmunity, to do violence to itself so as to become one. The logic of autoimmunity, most spectacular in "fundamentalism," is at work generally in Abrahamic religion. There is no simple alternative to autoimmunity. Again violence is irreducible. Derrida stipulates that his thought of religion runs the risks of autoimmunity, so the question he poses is this: How, in relation to religion, should one strategize for a lesser violence?

Contemporary violence in religion's name often occurs in reaction to technology. Religions are both entangled with and reacting to technology's abstracting, delocalizing effects. On the one hand, some, in religion's name, would act against the ways in which television, the Internet, and the global economic forces that work these and additional technologies threaten to deracinate and so potentially to dissolve religious traditions, cultures, and ways of life. On the other hand, many of these same actors use these very technologies in campaigns to save and preserve "religious roots." The religious leaders who denounce the spread of a "modernity" unthinkable without television frequently do so precisely on television. The terrorist Osama Bin Laden using video in Islam's name to denounce a globalizing "modernity" inseparable from video is a recent case among many. And religion's effort to oppose itself to technology entails aporias more intimate than those suggested by ironic media appearances. In attempting to refine a religion as "one," the autoimmunity of that religion tries to outbid and so participates in the very abstracting technological dynamic against which contemporary religions react. Even more problematic, the Abrahamic promise, a speech act, is structurally iterable, indomitable by intention, so constitutively open to "heresy," to extrication from any context (including "religious roots"), and thus to hooking up promiscuously with technology. In short, Abrahamic religion's most intimate feature, the messianic promise, provokes and is a target of autoimmunity. Caught up in autoimmunity, Derrida warns, religion can become quite unpromising.

Evident in the political culture of the United States, global televangelism, and the increasing militancy of Jewish, Christian, and Islamic "fundamentalisms," the "return" of religion is inseparable from globalization. A "globalatinization" of the earth is occurring in which any particular religion's appropriation of technology resonates with but reacts autoimmunely to a technicity, the promise's iterability, characteristic of Abrahamic religion in general. Yet the Latin-derived word *religion* suggests that contemporary general ideas about religion comport with a specific religious tradition. Derrida writes of "globalatinization" because religion's resurgence is happening, he argues, more through dynamics linked to the Roman and Latin heritage than the Judaic and Hebrew or Islamic and Arabic heritages. These dynamics are displacing Islam, Judaism, and Christianity into a global and capitalistic cyberspace of religious manifestation. When Judaism and Islam manifest tele-technically, they tend to assimilate or to accommodate themselves to the notion of manifestation, faith's miracles made visible, that, especially via Roman and Latin tradition, characterize Christianity.

Conflicts waged today in a particular religion's name, Derrida suggests, are inevitably conducted in relation to this more general logic of religion. Contemporary "wars of religion," sometimes declared as such, occur also where and when no overt declaration of war in religion's name has been made. Terrorism in the name of religion characterizes overtly declared "wars of religion." But military action insuring economic globalization's profitable installation and smooth perpetuation cannot avoid also being an undeclared "war of religion" in that globalization's hegemonic proselytizers invoke notions of law and human right carrying traits of irreducibly religious, specifically Christian, provenance.

Conclusion

Through lectures given across the globe and texts translated into many languages, Derrida has had and continues to have various impacts. In France, texts by the playwright and feminist thinker Hélène Cixous, the theologian Jean-Luc Marion, and the philosopher Jean-Luc Nancy testify to Derrida's influence. In the United States, Derrida's reception initially occurred most noticeably in university literature departments. At Yale, working with Derrida, Paul de Man and J. Hillis Miller promulgated literary criticism extending deconstruction. Derrida's visits to New York's Cardozo School of Law and writings on law have contributed to legal theory's engagement with deconstruction. John D. Caputo's and Mark C. Taylor's work registers Derrida's contribution to religion's study. Derrida has collaborated on architectural projects. Mark Wigley examines deconstruction and architecture's mutual implications. Besides vigorously distinguishing Derrida's work from postmodernism, Christopher Norris elaborates the implications Derrida's texts have for the epistemology of the sciences, especially quantum mechanics, implications Arkady Plotnitsky also pursues. In England, Simon Critchley pioneered the study of the relations of Derrida's work to Lévinas's, and Simon Glendinning has undertaken a careful renegotiation of analytical philosophy's somewhat dismissive response to deconstruction. Also in England, the study of Derrida's work in relation to politics and philosophy (Geoffrey Bennington), feminism (Diane Elam), literature (Nicholas Royle), and additional topics proceeds intensively.

ROBERT S. OVENTILE

See also **Hélène Cixous; Emmanuel Lévinas; Jean-Luc Nancy**

Biography

Jacques Derrida was born in El-Biar, Algeria, on July 15, 1930. Derrida and other Jewish students began to confront official anti-Semitism in 1940 with the "Pétainization" of Algerian educational institutions. In 1942, anti-Semitism's institutionalization resulted in Derrida's expulsion from the Lycée de Ben Aknoun. In 1949 Derrida traveled to France and in 1952 gained admittance to the École Normale Supérieure, where he studied under Louis Althusser and Michel Foucault. In 1964 Derrida accepted a position at the École Normale Supérieure. Derrida participated in the 1966 Johns Hopkins University International Colloquium on Critical Languages and the Sciences of Man, at which he met the literary critic Paul de Man, who would become Derrida's friend and colleague. Other important friendships include Maurice Blanchot, Jean-Luc Nancy, and J. Hillis Miller. Derrida began to teach at Yale University in 1975. In France during the 1970s, Derrida participated in struggles to defend the philosophy curriculum from threatened cutbacks. In 1983 Derrida was elected to the École des Hautes Études en Sciences Sociales and became the first president of the Collège International de Philosophie. Derrida accepted a professorship at the University of California at Irvine in 1986. As of the early years of the twenty-first century, Derrida continues to publish frequently and to teach at several institutions.

Selected Works

L'écriture et la différence, 1967; as *Writing and Difference*, translated by Alan Bass, 1978

De la Grammatologie, 1967; as *Of Grammatology*, translated by Gayatri Spivak, 1976

La Voix et le phénomène: Introduction au problème du signe dans la phénoménologie de Husserl, 1967; as *Speech and Phenomena and Other Essays on Husserl's Theory of Signs*, translated by David B. Allison, 1973

La Dissémination, 1972; as *Dissemination*, translated by Barbara Johnson, 1981

Marges de la philosophie, 1972; as *Margins of Philosophy*, translated by Alan Bass, 1982

Glas, 1974; as *Glas*, translated by John P. Leavey, Jr., and Richard Rand, 1986

La Vérité en peinture, 1978; as *The Truth in Painting*, translated by Geoff Bennington and Ian McLeod, 1987

La Carte postale: De Socrate à Freud et au-delà, 1980; as *The Post Card: From Socrates to Freud and Beyond*, translated by Alan Bass, 1987

De l'esprit: Heidegger et la question, 1987; as *Of Spirit: Heidegger and the Question*, translated Geoffrey Bennington and Rachael Bowlby, 1989

Psyché: Inventions de l'autre, 1987 [Psyche: Inventions of the Other]

Mémoires pour Paul de Man, 1988; as *Memoires: For Paul de Man*, revised edition, translated by Cecile Lindsay, Jonathan Culler, Eduardo Cadava, and Peggy Kamuf, 1989

Du droit à la philosophie, 1990 [Right to Philosophy]

Limited Inc, 1990; as *Limited Inc*, translated by Samuel Weber and Jeffrey Mehlman, 1988

Memoires d'aveugle: L'atuoportrait et autres ruines, 1990, as *Memoirs of the Blind: The Self-Portrait and Other Ruins*, translated by Pascale-Anne Brault and Michael Naas, 1993

Donner la mort, 1992, 1999; as *The Gift of Death*, translated by David Wills, 1995

Spectres de Marx, 1993; as *Specters of Marx*, translated by Peggy Kamuf, 1994

Politiques de l'amitié, 1994; as *Politics of Friendship*, translated by George Collins, 1997

Adieu à Emmanuel Lévinas, 1997; as *Adieu, To Emmanuel Levinas*, translated by Pascale-Anne Brault and Michael Naas, 1999

Le toucher, Jean-Luc Nancy, 2000 [Touch: Jean-Luc Nancy]

Acts of Religion, Gil Anidjar (editor), 2002

Further Reading

Beardsworth, Richard, *Derrida and the Political*, London: Routledge, 1996

Bennington, Geoffrey and Jacques Derrida, *Jacques Derrida*, Paris: Seuil, 1991; as *Jacques Derrida*, translated by Geoffrey Bennington, Chicago: University of Chicago Press, 1993; 2nd edition, 1999

Caputo, John D., *The Prayers and Tears of Jacques Derrida: Religion without Religion*, Bloomington: Indiana University Press, 1997

Cixous, Hélène, *Portrait de Jacques Derrida en jeune saint juif*, Paris: Galilée, 2001 [Portrait of Jacques Derrida as a Young Jewish Saint]

Cohen, Tom (editor), *Jacques Derrida and the Humanities: A Critical Reader*, Cambridge and New York: Cambridge University Press, 2001

Cornell, Drucilla, *The Philosophy of the Limit*, London: Routledge, 1992

Critchley, Simon, *The Ethics of Deconstruction: Derrida and Levinas*, Oxford and Cambridge, Massachusetts: Blackwell, 1992; 2nd edition, 1999

Critchley, Simon, *Ethics–Politics–Subjectivity: Essays on Derrida, Levinas, and Contemporary French Thought*, London: Verso, 1999

Elam, Diane, *Feminism and Deconstruction: Ms. en Abyme*, London: Routledge, 1994

Gasché, Rodolphe, *The Tain of the Mirror: Derrida and the Philosophy of Reflection*, Cambridge, Massachusetts: Harvard University Press, 1986

Glendinning, Simon, *On Being with Others: Heidegger–Derrida–Wittgenstein*, London: Routledge, 1998

Glendinning, Simon (editor), *Arguing with Derrida*, Oxford and Malden, Massachusetts: Blackwell, 2001

Hobson, Marian, *Jacques Derrida: Opening Lines*, London: Routledge, 1998

Howells, Christina, *Derrida: Deconstruction from Phenomenology to Ethics*, Oxford and Malden, Massachusetts: Polity, 1999

Krell, David Farrell, *The Purest of Bastards: Works of Mourning, Art, and Affirmation in the Thought of Jacques Derrida*, University Park: Pennsylvania State University Press, 2000

Lawlor, Leonard, *Derrida and Husserl: The Basic Problem of Phenomenology*, Bloomington: Indiana University Press, 2002

Miller, J. Hillis, "Jacques Derrida," in *Speech Acts in Literature*, Stanford, California: Stanford University Press, 2001

Norris, Christopher, *Against Relativism: Philosophy of Science, Deconstruction, and Critical Theory*, Oxford and Malden, Massachusetts: Blackwell, 1997

Plotnitsky, Arkady, *Complementarity: Anti-Epistemology after Bohr and Derrida*, Durham, North Carolina: Duke University Press, 1994

Royle, Nicholas, *After Derrida*, Manchester, England: Manchester University Press, 1995

Taylor, Mark C., *Erring: A Postmodern A/Theology*, Chicago: University of Chicago Press, 1984

Trifonas, Peter Pericles, *The Ethics of Writing: Derrida, Deconstruction, and Pedagogy*, Lanham, Maryland: Rowman and Littlefield, 2000

Wigley, Mark, *The Architecture of Deconstruction: Derrida's Haunt*, Cambridge, Massachusetts: MIT Press, 1993

DIDI-HUBERMAN, GEORGES
Art Historian, Philosopher

Georges Didi-Huberman's work as an art historian encompasses the ancient, the medieval, the modern, and the contemporary and embraces the visual arts, the historiography of art, psychoanalysis, the human sciences, and philosophy. Three strands may be detected in his work: a critical reading of the tradition of art history, the location of an alternative philosophy of images in the work of Freud and Warburg, and studies in the poetics of contemporary art. To sum up Didi-Huberman's work to date, one could say that he investigates the implications of psychoanalysis for the study of images, especially through the concept of the symptom.

A good introduction to the ideas, methods, and sensibilities of Didi-Huberman may be found in the essay "Question de détail, question de pan," published as an appendix to *Devant L'Image* (1990). The essay examines the status of pictorial details in relation to the whole of a painting. The interpretation of significant details is a crucial part of the approach of traditional art history because the details provide the key to determining which figure and which story are being represented. Didi-Huberman is more interested in how a section of a painting can defy explanation and integration into a coherent whole. In his view the idea of the detail makes painting too dependent on its referent in reality, because it assumes the mimetic transparency of the iconic sign. Inspired by Proust's *petit pan de mur jaune*, which refers to a section of Vermeer's *View of Delft* that greatly affected the novelist Bergotte in *La Prisonnière* (1923), he adopts the term *pan*, meaning a section or part, to restore attention to the parts of a painting where the referent is not dominant and where the material of paint and its visual intensity are equally important, so that in fact they disrupt mimetic coherence. In the case of Fra Angelico, discussed in *Devant L'Image* and explored at length in *Fra Angelico: Dis-*

semblance et figuration (1990), Didi-Huberman turns his attention to the abstract use of paint dripping and other nonmimetic patches of color in the frescoes at St. Mark's convent in Florence.

Didi-Huberman is looking at these inexplicable parts of a painting in different ways, both as pictorial phenomena and as elements in a structure. He turns to the idea of the symptom to provide him with a model for understanding the structure of these disruptive parts of a painting. The *pan* not only spills over onto the whole of which it is a part but also signals a hidden structure at work. Didi-Huberman here combines Freud's ideas about the surface-depth relationship in symptoms and the convergence of figures in a dream. The instability ascribed to the *pan* involves a fertile combination of temporal and spatial fluidity; to evoke its parameters Didi-Huberman cites passages from later in *La Prisonnière* where the narrator reconsiders his view of Vinteuil's septet in a lecture-conversation with Albertine and insists on art's singular and real beauty. For his part Didi-Huberman argues that to engage with an image's logic of contradictory indications and dissimulation the spectator needs to adopt the free-floating attention of the analyst.

Devant l'Image constitutes Didi-Huberman's first major engagement with the discourse of art history. For Didi-Huberman the dominant discourse of the discipline has emerged from a lineage that can be traced back from Panofsky through Kant to Vasari. In *Devant l'Image* this triumvirate is discussed with the aid of Freud, Lacan, and the subversive spectacles of Poe's occasional detective, Dupin. Didi-Huberman's methodical analysis sets out how the discourse of originality and immortality in Vasari is later given a theory of knowledge by Kant and a humanistic turn by Panofsky. These foundations are challenged, in Didi-Huberman's view, if we recognize our ignorance about images, their overdetermined content, and their status as disarming signs of our interpretative fallibility. The twin poles of the visible (imitation) and the readable (iconology) should cover everything in a painting but the poststructuralist Didi-Huberman argues that they instead obscure our investigation into the visual and the figurative. In a critically strategic reading of Panofsky's accounts of the Renaissance, Didi-Huberman also questions the privileged position given to that period.

In *Devant l'Image* Didi-Huberman proposes a series of working concepts or approximations for an alternative interpretation of images: the tear or rupture, the screen, the symptom and incarnation. The choice of the word *approximations* suggests the desire to hold back from the certainties of art history and to recognize the distance between the spectator and the image. The tear (*déchirure*) refers to the need to open up the study of the image, acknowledging its withheld or potential power. Didi-Huberman treats the image like the screen of a dream, highlighting the merging of powerful and contradictory desires, the dislocation and displacement of the order of representation and the decentering of the subject. In his investigation into the configuration of a particular "screen" Didi-Huberman looks for the symptoms or marks of this state of creative tension, as seen in the investigation into the *pan*. These symptoms signal a challenge to Panofsky's iconology, which claims to deduce the nature of represented objects from an established symbolic order. In the case of the medieval and renaissance art he discusses during his critical reading of Vasari and Panofsky, Didi-Huberman signals his preoccupations by examining the pictorial mediation of the theological concept of incarnation as the enigmatic and unexplored combination of surface (color) and depth (the body) in painting, a topic treated fully in his study of Fra Angelico.

Didi-Huberman's critique of the discourse of art history has been driven by an interest in an alternative approach to art, which he has explored in studies of Bataille and *Documents* (1929–30), and Giacometti's *Cube* (1934). He has devoted much of the last decade to the study of a neglected cultural historian, Aby Warburg (1866–1929). In his attempt to retrieve the full complexity of Warburg's projects, Didi-Huberman has harnessed his own interest in aligning psychoanalysis with a revised history of art. In *L'Image survivante* (2002), arguably his major work to date, Didi-Huberman is first interested in the complex time of images through Warburg's concept of *Nachleben*, translated into French as *survivance* and English as "afterlife." *Nachleben* defies chronology and refers to the process whereby images incorporate cultural memory, comprising elements that tenaciously return in different places and under different guises.

It is a matter of debate as to what extent Warburg has led Didi-Huberman to adopt a more cultural approach to images. Certainly there is a move from the study of "art" to the study of "images." More specifically, Didi-Huberman has extrapolated a cultural theory of the symptom from Warburg. From 1921 to 1924 Warburg was treated for psychosis by Ludwig Binswanger at his clinic in Kreuzlingen on the shores of Lake Constance. This period is crucial for Didi-Huberman because it was only by working through his mental illness of the early 1920s, partly brought on by the trauma of World War I, that Warburg was able to reconstruct and refine his overview of the life of images. He rethought the notion of the symptom in cultural and anthropological terms and posited that every image comes from the body and returns to it. Rather than interpretation through judgment or aesthetic feeling, Didi-Huberman therefore emphasizes in Warburg a dual mechanism of seeing and looking, with spectators engaged with the forces of release and blockage at work in images and engaged themselves as sentient forms.

It is the "pathos" of images that Warburg sees being channeled by their anachronistic time and symptomatic structure. The term *Pathosformel* (pathos seen as a principle or theory) conveys the crucial convergence of feeling and gesture in art and ritual. Time, structure, and pathos are all set to work in the experimental final project of Warburg, the Mnemosyne Atlas (1927–1929). This project is a montage of black and white photographs arranged by topic or motif on large black boards in ninety sections. Without any textual accompaniment at all, these montages assemble images (including "details") of sculptures and low-reliefs from Greece and Rome, as well as sculptures and paintings from Renaissance Florence, juxtaposed with Babylonian terra-cotta, Etruscan bronzes, Ptolemaic miniatures, Egyptian reliefs, and photographs of Native American sacred dances. The agile spectator has to look for the link between the images, according to the "rules" of *Nachleben* and *Pathosformel*. The project eschews synthesis and seeks to mobilize the images displayed, allowing, according to Didi-Huberman, "the unconscious of time" to be tracked across and between the images.

Modern and contemporary visual poetics are at the heart of Didi-Huberman's ongoing projects, as can be seen in his books on an international quintet of artists, Simon Hantaï, Pascal Convert, Giuseppe Penone, Claudio Parmiggiani, and James Turrell. These artists are all featured in the 1997 exhibition he cocurated, "L'Empreint" (Paris, Centre Pompidou). The five individual volumes resulted in a further collaboration at Le Fresnoy in Tourcoing in 2001. This exhibition, "Fables du lieu," investigated the sorts of place created by the artists through the use of memory, imprints, and traces. Didi-Huberman considers the works as fables, a term invoked to refer both to the combination of reality and fiction—produced by the forging of individual and collective memory in the works—and the strange spur to writing that they generate.

NIGEL SAINT

Biography

Born in Saint-Étienne in 1953, Georges Didi-Huberman did his doctoral research at the École des Hautes Études en Sciences Sociales in Paris under the supervision of Louis Marin. Didi-Huberman has taught there since 1985; his well-attended seminar is currently entitled "Anthropologie du visuel" and is devoted to Warburgian interpretations of the Renaissance. He is also part of the wide-ranging research cluster "Images"

at the EHESS. He has lectured frequently in the United States, Italy, Germany, and England. In the last decade Didi-Huberman has organized large exhibitions at the Centre Pompidou ("L'Empreinte," 1997, cocurated with Didier Semin) and at the Centre d'art contemporain in Tourcoing ("Fables du lieu," 2001). Few books by Didi-Huberman have been translated into English so far, but this will probably not be the case for long.

Selected Works

Invention de l'hystérie. Charcot et l'iconographie photographique de la Salpêtrière, 1982; *Invention of Hysteria: Charcot and Photographic Iconography at Salpêtrière*, translated by Alisa Hartz, 2003
Mémorandum de la peste. Le fléau d'imaginer, 1983
La Peinture incarnée, 1985
Devant l'Image. Question posée aux fins d'une histoire de l'art, 1990
Fra Angelico: Dissemblance et figuration, 1990, *Fra Angelico: Dissemblance and figuration*, translated by Jane Marie Todd, 1995
Ce que nous voyons, ce qui nous regarde, 1992
Le Cube et le visage. Autour d'une sculpture d'Alberto Giacometti, 1993
La Ressemblance informe, ou le gai savoir visuel selon Georges Bataille, 1995
L'Empreinte, 1997
Phasmes: Essais sur l'apparition, 1998
L'Étoilement: Conversation avec Hantaï, 1998
La Demeure, la souche: Apparentements de l'artiste, 1999
Ouvrir Vénus: Nudité, rêve, cruauté (L'Image ouvrante, 1), 1999
Être Crâne: Lieu, contact, pensée, sculpture, 2000
Devant le Temps: Histoire de l'art et anachronisme des images, 2000 (see "Molding Image: Genealogy and the Truth of Resemblance in Pliny's *Natural History*, book 35, 1–7," in *Law and the Image: The Authority of Art and the Aesthetics of Law*, edited by Costas Douzinas and Lynda Nead, Chicago: University of Chicago Press, 1999; and "The Supposition of the Aura: The Now, the Then, and Modernity," in *Negotiating Rapture: The Power of Art to Transform Lives*, edited by Richard Francis, Chicago: Museum of Contemporary Art, 1996
L'Homme qui marchait dans la couleur, 2001 (see "The Fable of the Place," in *James Turrell: The Other Horizon*, edited by Peter Noever, Ostfildern-Ruit: Hatje Cantz, 1999
Génie du non-lieu: Air, poussière, empreinte, hantise, Paris: Minuit, 2001
Ninfa moderna: Essai sur le drapé tombé, Paris: Gallimard, 2002
L'Image survivante. Histoire de l'art et temps des fantômes selon Aby Warburg, Paris: Minuit, 2002
"Before the Image, Before Time: The Sovereignty of Anachronism," in *Compelling Visuality: The Work of Art in and out of History*, edited by Claire Farago and Robert Zwijnenberg, 2003
"Foreword," in *Aby Warburg and the Image in Motion*, edited by Philippe-Alain Michaud, 2003

Further Reading

Antoine, Jean-Philippe, "Warburg Terminator?" *Critique*, 58. no. 667 (December 2002): 939–956

During, Elie, "Georges Didi-Huberman: Aby Warburg, Art History and Its Ghosts," *Art Press*, 277 (2002): 18–24

Hersant, Yves, "Inquiètes nudités," *Critique*, 58. no. 667 (December 2002): 957–967

Nagel, Alexander, "Fra Angelico," *Art Bulletin*, 78 (September 1996) 559–565

DIOP, CHEIKH ANTA
Historian

The pioneering legacy of Cheikh Anta Diop is one of liberation and unprecedented innovation, one that seeks wisdom in a true understanding of Africa's origins. The idea put forward by colonial historiography that Africa is empty of history, culture, and humanity has largely been left behind. As the first historian of the African renaissance, Diop led a moving effort to help Africa free itself from the claws of cultural alienation, which had gripped the continent for far too long, and enable Africans to regain a history that they had not lost until colonialism. At the beginning of the 1920s, Africa found itself subject to the domination of the European colonial powers, who had taken over from the trade in Black slaves that began in the sixteenth century. The violence to which Africa was subjected was not solely political, military, and economic in nature. Thinkers such as Hegel, Voltaire, Gobineau, Hume, and Bruhl, as well as European institutions such as, for example, the Institut d'Ethnologie de France established in 1925 by Lucien Lévy Bruhl, provided moral and philosophical legitimation for the attribution of intellectual inferiority to Black people. The vision of an ahistorical, atemporal Africa, the inhabitants of which had never been responsible for a single civilized achievement, was imposed in writings and anchored in people's minds. Furthermore, Egypt was arbitrarily associated with the Orient and the Mediterranean world in geographical, anthropological, and cultural terms.

Diop set out the context for the vehement ideological struggle in which the most enlightened of the African elites found themselves in opposition to the remains of colonial order, witnessing their collapse when they proved to be less solid than expected. His work associated the idea of well-being with the umbilical cord that links Black Ancient Egypt to the rest of the African continent. Similarly, the irresolvable contradiction that pharaonic Egypt, the mother of civilizations, was accorded no place in a continent thought to be primitive and savage finally found a rational solution. Cheikh Anta Diop's revolutionary ideas and his attacks on the mystifications of colonial historiography undermined the generally held idea that Africa was not part of the historic world because the continent had remained immobile and hardly developed. In addition

to this often-expressed accusation of immobility, there was a belief that the Asian and European worlds originated in the north. If this were true, Carthage would be an important transitional phenomenon most closely linked to Asia as a Phoenician colony, and Egypt would be examined in terms of the passage of human civilization from the east to the west, but would not depend on the African mind. This kind of historical falsification, which had been idealized for some time, has contributed to the myth of the African continent's antihistoricity. As Diop showed, Africa was the cradle of all civilizations. Reacting against "fascist" and "racist" claims that Africans are not capable of creating viable political institutions, Diop produced his major work, *Nations nègres et culture: De l'Antiquité nègre égyptienne aux problèmes culturels de l'Afrique d'aujourd'hui* (1954). His unusual learning and his liberating inspiration have inspired many African intellectuals. Théophile Obenga is one of his contemporaries who often invokes Diop's belief that history should not be defined as the study of humanity's past, but as the construction of the future in the name of life. At the time when Cheikh Anta Diop undertook his first research during the 1940s, Black Africa did not constitute a coherent field of history. *Nations nègres et culture*, is the founding book of the corpus of academic writing about African history. The critical reconstruction of Africa's past became possible thanks to the introduction of the concepts of "historical time" and "cultural unity." The restoration of historical awareness then also became possible.

All the knowledge of African and European cultures Diop accumulated and assimilated is presented in a coherent, significant œuvre that demonstrates his standing as a scholar and a humanist. He was not only a Francophone intellectual, but also had a past as a man committed to political militancy when necessary, as exemplified in his caustic leading articles for *La voix d'Afrique*, a student journal of the Rassemblement Démocratique Africain. In the 1930s, when African parliamentarians chose a policy of compromise, his articles raised the question of independence and the federation of France's former colonies. Diop's political ideas provided the cultural foundations for attempts to realize this ideal. Their touchstone was the notion of unity within a federal or confederal structure. In his eyes, the imperatives of economic independence, the uncertain political entities issuing from colonialism, industrial development, and the cultural unity of the Black world came together to render political unity indispensable. The European Africanist schools were unanimous in rejecting, usually without examination, Diop's fundamental theses relating to the "cultural unity" of Africa, the migrations that started in the original Neolithic basin and provided the continent's present population, and the continuity of African national history. In Diop's works, this becomes a critical precedent with the capacity to inspire new directions of thought. His deconstruction of the fundamental assumptions of European Africanist discourse is apparent in his work, *Nations nègres et culture*, in which he identifies blatant contradictions in the erroneous attribution of values from an Egyptian civilization designated as white to a Greece that was equally white. Diop compares this to evidence of Egyptian civilization's Black origins.

In this context, Diop's œuvre is intended to challenge, by means of investigation using scientific method, the accepted accounts of the very foundations of Western civilization and the genesis of humanity and civilization. In his *L'Afrique noire précoloniale*, for example, he compared the sociopolitical systems of Europe and Black Africa from antiquity to the constitution of modern states. This work highlights the importance of a scientific understanding of precolonial societies in Africa, Europe, and the Mediterranean. He regarded the African renaissance, which involves the restoration of historical awareness, as an inescapable task, a task to which he dedicated his life. In consequence, his work often emphasized the links between those precolonial societies and the earliest genesis of human development. Although his analysis of the similarities between the West and Black Africa could be controversial, his original theories are remarkably striking on the differences between them as well. His ideas followed the path first mapped out in *Les origines Africaines de la civilisation*, which has had a significant impact on the American scholarship on Africa: "Those who read this book seriously are in for a shock and a rewarding experience in learning. This is a major work by a major Black historian. At last, the renaissance of African historiography from an African point of view has begun" (J. H. Clarke, 1987).

Cheikh Anta Diop's ideas may be categorized in several fields relating to the origins of man and his migrations as well as the origin of civilization. His ideas are manifested through his treatment of the process of the biological differentiation of humanity, the process of semitization, the ancient presence of man in Africa, the identification of major currents of migration, the emergence of the Berbers in history, and the formation of African ethnic groups. On the evolution of societies, Diop explored the developments that led to the genesis of the ancient forms of social organization found in the south (Africa) and the north (Europe). His meticulous investigations uncovered the foundations for the birth of the state, starting from the example of the formation and organization of African states following the decline of Egypt. His analysis was given greater breadth by his consideration of European and African social and political structures before the colonial period, their respective evolutions and modes of production, and the social-historical and cultural conditions that presided over the European Renaissance. If the cultural, economic, scientific, and institutional development of Africa plays an important role in Diop's hypotheses, this is because these are major questions with which anyone seeking to build a modern Africa is confronted. His theories take into account that the mastery of political, educational, and civic systems can also be achieved by using national languages at all levels of public life. Diop's establishment of the radiocarbon dating laboratory that he led until his death was symbolic of the great importance he accorded to "the entrenchment of the sciences in Africa." This interest did indeed contribute to the development of fundamental research on the continent and the development of energy infrastructure there, which formed a paradigm applicable to the building of a "planetary civilization."

Diop's work expresses a belief that humanity should break away from racism and the various forms of slavery and genocide in order to defeat an unnatural civilization. As expressed in *Civilisation ou barbarie* (1981), this would bring the advent of an era that would see all the nations of the world holding out their hands to each other "to build the planetary civilization instead of sinking into barbarism." This wish is explained later in the article "L'unité d'origine de l'espèce humaine" (1982) as the reaffirmation of the biological unity of the human species. This unity provides the basis for a new form of education that would challenge all racial inequality and racial hierarchies. In other words, the goal would be to reeducate people's perception of what it means to be human so that this perception is detached from "racial appearance and focuses on the human released from all ethnic coordinates." Black people lost their historical memory due to the influence of false history books, so the rule of oppression could be ended by correcting world history. Diop constantly placed emphasis on the modern forgery of history, which he denounced energetically but objectively in *Antériorité des civilisations nègres; mythe ou vérité historique*:

The consciousness of modern man cannot really progress unless there is a determination to explicitly recognize the errors in scientific interpretations, even in the very delicate field of History, to return to its falsifications and to denounce the way people have been deprive of their inheritance. It deludes itself by wishing to establish its moral constructions on the most monstrous falsification of which humanity has ever been guilty while demanding of its victims that they forget so they can better go into the future.

Diop has shown that African history is the foundation of world history, even if the question remains of how it is possible to combine "through meaningful research, all the fragments of the past into a single ancient epoch, a common origin that will reestablish African continuity" (*Nations nègres et culture*). His convincing conclusion that Africa flowed into the Mediterranean world through Greece demonstrates that history does not recognize cultural, national, or ethnic borders. Roman history, for example, is Greek as well as Roman, and both the Roman and the Greek historical narratives are Egyptian because the Mediterranean was civilized by Egypt, to which parts of Africa, Ethiopia in particular, had contributed. Diop's works have challenged the place given to African people in history by academic researchers worldwide.

His great influence on his contemporaries and younger scholars was strengthened even further at several major international events, such as the First and Second Congresses of Black Artists and Writers held in Paris in 1956 and Rome in 1959, The World Festival of Arts held in Dakar in 1966, The UNESCO-sponsored Symposium on Ancient Egypt in Cairo in 1974, The Ninth Conference of The International Union for Prehistoric and Protohistoric Sciences in 1976, and the Congress of the Association of Researchers of the Black World in 1980, which he chaired. Paradoxically, non-African historians claim that Egypt is problematic in their historiography, although the problem is actually created by their scholarship, which has posited the foundation of what is known as Western civilization on the assumption that the ancient Egyptians were White. In fact, these scholars have disregarded White scholarship that did not advocate this view, such as the works of Count Volney, *The Ruins of Empires* (1787), A. H. L. Heeren, *Politics, Intercourse, and Trade of the Carthaginians, Ethiopians, Egyptians* (1833), and Gerald Massey, *Ancient Egypt, The Light of the World* (1907).

More recently, this situation has led to the gradual development of an African school of Egyptology, which seeks to address the subjects mapped out by Diop as well as the recommendations of the Symposium on Ancient Egypt in Cairo. The most recent results of the various research projects on Egyptian civilization, combined with the results of archaeological work, illustrate the academic relevance and great fertility of the work done by Black Africans. The publication *ANKH* (*Revue d'égyptologie et des civilisations africaines*), which was founded in 1992 and is edited by Théophile Obenga, concentrates on the publication of work of this kind. The contributors to *ANKH* come from many different countries, demonstrating its international prestige. *ANKH* is dedicated to studies of ancient Egypto-Nubian civilization using philosophical, linguistic, archaeological, anthropological, religious, and cultural approaches. It also seeks to synthesize research on Africa in general with a section on the exact sciences, including physics, computer science, and mathematics and a bibliographic section. This publication is part of the francophone legacy of Cheikh Anta Diop. In parallel, *ANKH* has expanded its activities to include books presenting the richness of Egyptological research. This high level of intellectual production is enriched each year by new studies and constitutes the necessary basis for strong teaching on ancient Africa and the relationships among Africa, Europe, and the West. As a committed researcher and militant in the African student movements, Diop constantly demanded the independence of France's colonial possessions. He believed that the barriers erected by French colonialism could be erased only by a reexamination of African culture aimed at restoring it to its proper place in world history.

KAMAL SALHI

See also **Gaston Bachelard; Lucien Levy-Bruhl**

Biography

Cheikh Anta Diop was born in Diourbel, Senegal, on December 29, 1923. He died on February 7, 1986 in Dakar and was buried in Thaiyatou, his native village in the region of Diourbel. He went to a traditional Qur'anic school at the age of four and then attended the French school in Diourbel. His secondary education at the lycées of Dakar and Saint-Louis led to two successful French baccalaureates in philosophy and mathematics. At the age of twenty-two, he traveled to Paris to study physical sciences, although he soon abandoned them for humanities and philosophy, which he was taught by Gaston Bachelard. In 1948, he published two articles, "Quand pourra-t-on parler d'une renaissance africaine?" in *Le musée vivant* and "Etude linguistique ouolove: Origine de la langue et de la race valaf" in *Présence Africaine*. In winter 1950, he visited Dakar and Saint-Louis briefly, lecturing on the foundations of modern African civilization and the teaching of mother tongues in Africa. Between 1951 and 1954, he was the Secretary General of the Association des Etudiants du Rassemblement Démocratique Africain. He organized the first postwar pan-African student congress in 1951 and later, in 1952, published articles in the association's monthly bulletin, *La Voix de l'Afrique Noire*. In 1951, he submitted a doctoral thesis on Ancient Egypt to the University of Sorbonne in Paris but was rejected because a jury could not be constituted. In 1954, Éditions Présence Africaine published this dissertation as *Nations nègres et culture. De l'Antiquité nègre égyptienne aux problèmes culturels de l'Afrique d'aujourd'hui*. It was not until 1960 that he successfully defended his doctoral thesis before a jury of historians, sociologists, and anthropologists. This work was published in the same year by Éditions Présence Africaine as *L'Afrique noire précoloniale* and *L'Unité culturelle de l'Afrique noire. Les fondements économiques et culturels d'un état fédéral d'Afrique noire* also appeared in the same year. When he returned permanently to Senegal in 1960, he established a radiocarbon dating laboratory in Dakar. In 1966, he received, jointly with W. F. B. DuBois, the Prix du Premier Festival des Arts Nègres, which had been established to honor writers who had influenced African thought. In 1967, his book *Antériorité des civilisations nègres: mythe ou vérité historique* was published by Éditions Présence Africaine, followed the year after by *Le Laboratoire du radiocarbone* (Dakar: IFAN). In the early 1970s, he won further recognition from UNESCO, which sponsored the international conference on Egyptology he initiated in Cairo and published its proceedings in 1974. In the same year, Diop published *Physique nucléaire et chronologie absolue*. On April 4, 1975, he received a medal from the American-based African Heritage Studies Association. Another prominent work, *L'Antiquité africaine par l'image*, was published by Edition NEA-IFKN in Dakar. Two years later, he published *Parenté génétique de l'égyptien pharaonique et des langues négro-africaines* (NEA-IFAN). His other academic activities won him the Médaille d'Or de la Recherche Scientifique and the Grand Prix du Mérite Scientifique Africain awarded by the National University of Zaire in 1980, and he became a professor in the Arts Faculty of the University of Dakar. In 1981, his *Civilisation ou barbarie* was published by Présence Africaine. The following year a symposium was held in his honor under the aegis of Professor Pathé Diagne of the University of Dakar, and he received the Grand Prix Scientifique ICA from the Institut Culturel Africain. April 4, 1985, the day of his visit to Atlanta in the United States, where he was welcomed by Mayor Andrew Young and the Martin Luther King Association, was proclaimed Dr. Cheikh Anta Diop Day. He gave his last lecture, "Nubie, l'Egypte et l'Afrique noire" at the Palais des Congrès in Cameroon a month before he died in 1986. His posthumous book, *Nouvelles recherches sur l'égyptien ancien et les langues négro-africaines modernes*, was published by Présence Africaine in 1988 with an introduction by Professor Théophile Obenga. Diop's works have been translated into English, and his bibliography includes more than thirty articles.

Selected Works

Nations nègres et culture, 1954, 1964, 1979
L'unité culturelle de l'Afrique noire, 1959, 1982; translated as *The Cultural Unity of Black Africa, The Domains of Matriarchy and of Patriarchy on Classical Antiquity*, 1962, 1989

L'Afrique noire précoloniale, 1960, 1987; *Precolonial Black Africa*, translated by Harold Salemson, 1986
Les fondements économiques et culturels d'un etat fédéral d'Afrique noire, 1960, 1974; *Black Africa, the Economic and Cultural Basis for a Federated State*, translated by Harold Salemson, 1978, 1987
Antériorité des civilisations nègres: mythe ou vérité historique? 1967
The African Origin of Civilization: Myth or Reality? Translation of sections of *Antériorité des civilisations nègres, mythe ou vérité historique?* and *Nations nègres et culture* by Mercer Cook, 1974
Parenté génétique de l'égyptien pharaonique et des langues négro-africaines, 1977
Civilisation ou barbarie. 1981, 1988
Nouvelles recherches sur l'égyptien ancien et les langues négro-africaines modernes, 1988

Further Readings

Anselin, Alain, "Pour une morphologie élémentaire du Négro-africain—Essai sur l'ouvrage de Cheikh Anta Diop, Nouvelles recherches sur l'Égyptien ancien et les langues négro-africaines modernes," *Revue CARBET, Revue Martiniquaise de Sciences Humaines et de Littérature*, 8, (1989): 163–174
Bilolo, Mubabinge, "Les tâches laissées par Cheikh Anta Diop. Hommage au père de l'égyptologie / africanologie africaine," *Les Nouvelles Rationalités Africaines*, I, 3 (1986): 429–460
Bilolo, Mubabinge, "La civilisation pharaonique était-elle Kame-Kmt-Nègre? L'état de la question avant et après *Nations nègres et Culture*," *Hommage à Cheikh Anta Diop, Présence Africaine* (1989): 68–100
Gomez, Jean-Charles Coovi, "L'oeuvre de Cheikh Anta Diop et la Renaissance de l'Afrique au seuil du troisième millénaire," *Racines & Couleurs*, 126 (Fall, 1997): 193–206
Obenga, Théophile, "Méthode et conception historique de Cheikh Anta Diop," *Présence Africaine*, 74 (1970): 3–28
Obenga, Théophile, "L'univers puissant et multiple de Cheikh Anta Diop," *Éthiopiques*, 4, no, 1–2 (1987): 9–b16
Obenga, Théophile. *Cheikh Anta Diop, Volney et le Sphinx—Contribution de Cheikh Anta Diop à l'historiographie mondiale*, Paris: Éditons Présence Africaine, 1996.
Sall, Babacar, "Histoire et conscience historique: De la philosophie de l'histoire dans l'œuvre de Cheikh Anta Diop," *Présence Africaine*, 149–150 (1989): 283–291

DJEBAR, ASSIA
Novelist, Essayist, Filmmaker, University Professor

Assia Djebar (the pen name of Fatima-Zohra Imalyen) is the most prominent Algerian woman writer and intellectual of her generation and one of the major figures writing in French in the late twentieth/early twenty-first centuries. As a Muslim intellectual of Arabo-Berber origin educated within the French school system set up under the colonial system in Algeria and as one who witnessed the struggle for independence and its aftermath, Djebar's work encompasses personal and collective experiences of the colonial and postcolonial cultures of North Africa. She pays particular attention to the position of women in colonial and post-colonial situations, and the issues she raises extend beyond the field of francophone literary and cultural studies.

Her early novels, published in the decade 1957 to 1967, focused on the experience of women, the body, and the couple, all themes that would be developed in her later work. Although Djebar attracted some criticism in Algeria for not paying sufficient attention to the country's political situation during and in the immediate aftermath of the War of Independence, another shared theme in her work is the experience of the young generation marked by the struggle for liberation.

Her relationship to the written word is made more complex not only because she is a Muslim woman, but also because of the conflict between her oral "maternal" Berber language and the written "paternal" language, which for Djebar is not Modern Standard Arabic but French. Although she has famously called French her "Stepmother tongue," it is increasingly identified in her work with her father, who himself was a teacher in a French primary school in Algeria and thanks to whom she received her schooling. The conflict between oral and written modes of experience and the struggle to reappropriate the written word for herself and other women remains at the heart of her identity as a writer and her writing strategies. Assia Djebar remains ambiguous about her relationship to French both in her writing and in interviews. Her stance, which is unafraid of the contradiction that the French language offered liberation while at the same time posing a threat to her identity and exiling her from her maternal culture, makes an essential contribution to debates concerning bi/multilingualism and issues of individual and collective identity. In Djebar's project, the schism between her oral and written languages provides a space in which "representation" in both meanings of the word can take place.

Finding that her work became increasingly autobiographical, as she explains it, Djebar retreated from novel writing during the 1970s. During this period she continued to work creatively, making two acclaimed films that allowed a return to her maternal oral language (*La Nouba des femmes du Mont Chenoua*, 1978, winner of the Critic's Prize at the Venice Bienalle, 1979; and *La Zerda ou les chants de l'oubli*, 1982). This film work, which involved collecting the testimonies of women from her native region during the Algerian War, is essential for an understanding of her creative journey, giving her writing "a vision," as she has said.

Djebar returned to prose writing with a new, more experimental style, melding together a single individual narrative voice with the voices of the multitude of Algerian women, past and present, denied the opportunity to express themselves in the public space. *Femmes d'Alger dans leur appartement* (1980; *Women of Algiers in Their Apartment*) takes as its title the key Orientalist Delacroix painting and contains a complex theoretical essay in the form of a postface entitled "*Regard interdit, son coupé*" that offers a meditation on the politics of the gaze and female representation.

Yet rather than refusing what seemed an inescapable urge toward autobiographical expression, Assia Djebar was able in the 1980s, nearly thirty years after her first novel, to take this "dangerous enterprise," as she has termed it, further to encompass a reflection on personal memory and on a wider cultural memory, on the writing and rewriting of individual and collective history and on the analysis of the nature of selfhood in language necessitating the development of a number of writing strategies, and culminating in a politics and a poetics of identity. The "Quatuor," of which three volumes have been published to date, *L'Amour, la fantasia* (1985; *Fantasia. An Algerian Cavalcade*), *Ombre sultane* (1987; *A Sister to Scheherazade*), and *Vaste est la prison* (1995; *So Vast the Prison*), continues the themes explored in the short stories of *Femmes d'Alger* to build a vast panorama of Algerian female experience. Using historical research, Djebar rewrites not only the history of the colonization of Algeria by the French, but also rereads other histories of the region, its legends, and its symbolic figures. The metaphor of the palimpsest is often used by critics to describe this vast work of uncovering and rewriting.

In between the second and third volumes of this project, several other texts, both fictional and more theoretical, were published; for example *Loin de Médine* (1991; *Far from Madina*), a rewriting of the lives of the wives of the Prophet; and *Le Blanc de l'Algérie* (1995; *Algerian White*), a book of mourning for the dead of Algeria, mostly writers but also including those journalists and schoolteachers executed in the violence that erupted there in the early 1990s in the continuing struggle for power when both the fundamentalist FIS (*Front Islamique du Salut*) and the military government posed threats to the intellectual elite and to women.

Through her excavation and exploration of history, Assia Djebar's writing suggests another space that secures a place for the exiled of history within the postcolonial situation. A new way of being is created through a reinvented relationship to language, to history, to other, and to self. The return from exile and liberation must certainly be constantly renegotiated, but it is given a potential form in a writing project that bestows an ethic as well as an aesthetics on the work of literature and on autobiographical discourse.

DEBRA KELLY

Biography

Fatima-Zohra Imalayen was born in 1936 in Cherchell, Algeria. She chose the pen name Assia Djebar for the publication of her first novel, *La Soif* (1957; *The Mischief*). After her own education in Algiers and Paris, she was the first Algerian woman to be accepted at the Ecole Normale Supérieure de Sèvres in 1955, but ended her studies the following year after participating in the strike by Algerian students. During the Algerian War of Independence, she wrote for the newspaper of the FLN (Front National de la Libération), *Moudjahid*, by publishing interviews with Algerian refugees in Morocco and Tunisia. After continuing studies in history, she lectured in history at the universities of Rabat, Morocco (1959) and Algiers (1962), where she was also involved in journalism and broadcasting. She had a prolific early career as a writer, publishing four novels by the age of thirty-one. She holds a doctorate from the Université Paul Valéry-Montpellier III. In the 1980s she divided her time for a number of years between France and Algeria, although she has more recently worked increasingly within academic centers in the United States, at Louisiana State University, Baton Rouge (1997–2001) and as Silver Professor (French and Francophone Studies) at New York University since 2001. In 1999 she was elected to the Belgian Royal Academy of French Language and Literature, and in 2001 was made Commandeur des Arts et des Lettres en France.

Selected Writings

La Soif, 1957 (*The Mischief*, 1958; 1980)
Les Impatients, 1958 (The Impatient Ones)
Les Enfants du Nouveau Monde, 1962 (The Children of the New World)
Les Alouettes naïves, 1967 (The Naïve Larks)
Femmes d'Alger dans leur appartement (augmented edition), 1980, 2002 (*Women of Algiers in their Apartment*, 1992; 1999)
L'Amour, la fantasia, 1985 (*Fantasia. An Algerian Cavalcade*, 1989; 1992)
Ombre Sultane, 1987 (*A Sister to Scheherazade*, 1988; 1993)
Loin de Médine, 1991 (*Far from Madina*, 1994)
Le Blanc d'Algérie, 1995 (*Algerian White*, 2001)
Vaste est la prison, 1995 (*So Vast the Prison*, 1999)
Oran, langue morte, 1997 (Oran, dead language)
Les nuits de Strasbourg, 1997 (Strasbourg Nights)
Ces voix qui m'assiègent: en marge de ma francophonie, 1999 (These voices that beseige me)
La Femme sans sépulture, 2002 (The Woman without a Grave)

Further Reading

Calle-Gruber, Mireille, *Assia Djebar ou la résistance de l'écriture—regards d'un écrivain d'Algérie*, Paris: Maisonneuve et Larose, 2001
Chikhi, Beida, *Les Romans d'Assia Djebar*, Algiers: SNED, 1990
Clerc, Jeanne-Marie, *Assia Djebar. Ecrire, Transgresser, Résister*, Paris: Harmattan, 1997
Donadey, Anne, "The Multilingual Strategies of Postcolonial Literature: Assia Djebar's Algerian Palimpsest," *World Literature Today* 74.1 (Winter 2000): 27–36
Erickson, John, *Islam and the Postcolonial Narrative*, New York: Cambridge University Press, 1998
Geesey, Patricia, "Collective Autobiography: Algerian Woman and History in Assia Djebar's *L'Amour, la fantasia*," *Dalhousie French Studies*, 35 (1996): 153–167
Orlando, Valerie, *Nomadic Voices of Exile. Feminine Identity in Francophone Literature of the Maghreb*, Athens: Ohio University Press, 1999
Ruhe, Ernstpeter and A. Hornug, *Postcolonialisme et Autobiographie*, Amsterdam: Rodopi, 1998 (important section on Assia Djebar)
Woodhull, Winifred, *Transfiguration of the Maghreb. Feminism, Decolonisation and Interaction*, Minneapolis: University of Minnesota Press, 1993
World Literature Today (Autumn 1996): issue devoted to Assia Djebar

DUBY, GEORGES
Historian

The career of Georges Duby spanned nearly five decades. As one of the most brilliant students of the *Ecole des Annales*, he was instrumental in changing how medieval society, and most particularly, French medieval society, was viewed. He helped dispel the romanticized image of knights, lords, ladies, and peasants that had long held sway in both popular imagination and scholarly studies of the Middle Ages. Although the majority of Duby's work concentrated on the period from the tenth to the thirteenth century, it is the focus on structures, mentalities, and social environment that allows his works to transcend their chronological and geographical settings and become models for other historians. If Duby's works were able to reach beyond the confines of academia to guarantee him a privileged place among the "new historians," it was because he infused them with his passion, and combined erudition and clarity with imagination and style. Duby followed the model of Jules Michelet in that he thought that history must be written as though it were a work of literature. Duby recognized, too, that historians always expressed a personal opinion, that the writing of history did not carry with it a key to truth.

Duby also undertook the challenge of creating a bridge between the academic elite and the wider public. He understood the power of less traditional media, film, and television, to communicate. He consulted on a film based on his *Dimanche de Bouvines*, saw his *Temps des Cathédrales* become a model of historical programming on television, and took over the directorship of *La Sept*, later to become *Arte*. This ability to blend the scholarly and the popular without sacrificing historical accuracy allowed his vision of medieval life to permeate contemporary French culture. Moreover, as contributor, as editor or co-editor of several general studies—*Histoire de la Civilisation française* (1958), *Histoire de la France* (1970), *Histoire de la France rurale* (1975–76), *Histoire de la France urbaine* (1985), *L'Histoire de femmes en Occident* (1990), *Histoire artistique de l'Europe* (1999), among others—Duby's perspective guided and shaped some of the most important historical works produced in Europe during the second half of the twentieth century.

The theoretical basis for Duby's work grew out of the Annales School, founded in 1929 by Marc Bloch and Lucien Febvre, and continued by Fernand Braudel, whom Duby considered his greatest influence. The rejection of factual history organized around the study of important political figures and events, the study of economic and social structures, in medieval western Europe, the incorporation of other humanities into the study of the past provided the framework for modern historiography that Duby would follow in his work.

Duby's earliest study explored the fundamental relationships of feudal society and established him as a master of this new historiography. The publication of his thesis on *La Société aux XIe et XIIe siècles dans la région mâconnaise* (1953) illustrated how knighthood was a military attribute within the noble class of Mâcon society and thus revised Bloch's analysis of the status of knights. However, it was in the 1970s that his ability to reveal the complex structures that created and defined medieval society was definitively established. *Guerriers et paysans* (1973) foregrounded both the gift and plunder economy and the work of simple peasants to demonstrate how these forces interacted to spur the first major wave of economic growth in Western Europe. He delineated the interplay of church and society and, at the same time, he showed the importance of art to social history in his *Temps des Cathédrales* (1976). He further explored the hierarchical system articulated through the Catholic church that structured nearly every aspect of feudal society in *Trois ordres ou l'imaginaire du féodalisme* (1978). Duby was keenly cognizant of the fact that the texts upon which historians rely were often the products of the Church or the courts and as such reveal little about groups other than the aristocracy. These same texts reflect those groups' prejudices when they treat members of the other classes. Thus, Duby brought to his readings of these documents a critical, questioning component in his studies of sexuality, marriage, and kinship in feudal society.

Social structures in relation to marriage provided a fruitful field of enquiry in Duby's work. He recognized that the history of women under feudal society had been given little scholarly attention. His *Le Chevalier, la femme et le prêtre* (1981) examined the structures of married life and attempted to fill in some of the gaps. Yet Duby would later comment on that work, "Between [the knight and the priest], the woman. What do we know of women?" He began to answer this question in one of his last works, *Les Femmes au XII siecle* (1995). The three-volume study examines the ideological underpinnings of the representation of women under the medieval patriarchal system. Duby's innovation was to reveal the linkages among courtly love, genealogies, lineage, and power structures and to expose how the multiple roles of wives, mothers, concubines, and widows intersect in the ecclesiastic discourse on women as the embodiment of sin.

Nonetheless Duby's most significant contribution to new history may well be his reconceptualization of "old" history. In *Dimanche de Bouvines* (1973), Duby showed how an event could become important, that is, through the invention and the transmission of the event that meaning is produced after the fact. On the Sunday in question, the battle in which Philip Augustus defeated Otto IV took place. Duby's study, however, focused as much on the ideas (*mentalités*) of those involved—their concepts of honor, loyalty, bravery—as on the event that only later was seen as a major turning point in the shift of power in Europe. His use of the present tense and the inclusion of a contemporary account of the battle create immediacy in this text, pulling it from the past into a recognizable present. In a similar way, Duby relegitimized biography in his 1984 study, *Guillaume le Maréchal, le meilleur chevalier du monde*. Where the Annales School rejected biography as an outmoded way of conceiving of the study of the past, he reformulated the historical biography to integrate the study of the individual into a study of one of the three orders. Thus, the social structures of the twelfth century are exposed and analyzed through the life of one of its members.

Although Duby classified himself as an artisan rather than a theoretician, his *L'histoire continue* (1991) may be read as his personal philosophy of history. Part intellectual autobiography, part memoir, this text offers insights into Duby's varied career and provides a history of the French school—including Bloch, Febvre, and Braudel since the mid-twentieth century. Perhaps more importantly, an integral part of this chronicle of a historian deals with how Duby gathered archival data, how he chose his subjects, how he developed his theses and structured his arguments. Although the intellectual impact of his work is not neglected, Duby's text is also a practical introduction to the métier of historian. This work reveals, perhaps more than his historical studies, the workings of the mind of a thinker who will remain one of the most influential historians of the twentieth century.

EDITH J. BENKOV

See also **Marc Bloch; Lucien Febvre**

Biography

Georges Duby was born October 7, 1919 in Paris. He attended high school in Mâcon. He studied history and geography at the University of Lyons and received his aggregation there in 1942. Appointed assistant professor of medieval history at the University of Besançon, 1951, Duby followed this with a position at the University of Aix-en-Provence. He defended his thesis at the Sorbonne in 1953. Appointed to the chair of medieval history in Aix, in 1953, Duby was promoted to professor, holding the chair of history of mediaeval societies at the College de France, 1974. He was invited to head the European Society for Television Programs (SEPT) in 1986 and elected to the Académie Française in 1987. Duby died on December 3, 1996, at Aix-en-Provence from cancer.

Selected Works

Dimache des Bouvines, 1973; as *The Legend of Bouvines*, translated by Catherine Tihanyi, 1990

Guerriers et paysans, 1973; as *The Early Growth of European Economy: Warriors and Peasants from the Seventh to the Twelfth Centuries*, translated by Howard B. Clarke, 1978

Temps des Cathédrales, 1976; as *The Age of Cathedrals: Art and Society, 980–1420*, translated by Barbara Thompson and Eleanor Levieux, 1981

Trois ordres ou l'imaginaire du féodalisme, 1978; as *The Three Orders: Feudal Society Imagined*, translated by Arthur Goldhammer, 1982

Le Chevalier, la femme et le prêtre, 1981; as *The Knight, the Lady, and the Priest: the Making of Modern Marriage in Medieval France*, translated by Barbara Bray, 1983

Guillaume le Maréchal, le meilleur chevalier du monde, as *William Marshal: The Flower of Chivalry*, translated by Richard Howard, 1987

L'histoire continue, 1991; as *History Continues*, translated by Arthur Goldhammer, 1994

Les Femmes au XII siècle, 1995; as *Women of the Twelfth Century*, translated by Jean Birrell, 1997–98

Qu'est-ce que la société féodale?, 2002

Further Reading

Georges Duby, Aix-en-Provence: L'Arc, 1978

Axel, Ruth and Jocelyn Holland, "The Battle of Bouvines: Event History vs. Problem History," *MLN* 116: 4, French Issue (Sept, 2001): 816–843

Bleton-Ruget, Annie, Marcel Pacaut and Michel Rubellin, *Regards croisés sur l'oeuvre de Georges Duby*, Lyon: Presses Universitaires de Lyon, 2000

Constable, Giles, "Georges Duby (7 October 1919–3 December 1996)," *Proceedings of the American Philosophical Society*, 143:2 (1999): 299–309

Duhamel-Amado, Claudie and Guy Lobrichon (editors), *Georges Duby: l'écriture de l'histoire*, Bibliothèque du Moyen Age 6, Bruxelles: De Boeck Université, 1996

Evergates, Theodore, "The Feudal Imaginary of Georges Duby," *Journal of Medieval and Early Modern Studies*, 27: 3 (1997): 641–660.

Klapisch-Zuber, Christiane and Michelle Zancarini-Fournel (editors), "Georges Duby et l'histoire des femmes." *Clio, histoire, femmes et sociétés*, no 8 (1998)

Romagnolied, Daniela, *Medioevo e oltre: Georges Duby e la storiografia del nostro tempo di Itinerari medievali*, Bologna: CLUEB, 1999

Tsikounas, Myriam. "L'historien en amateur d'art: Georges Duby et les images," *Revue d'Histoire Moderne et Contemporaine* 48: *Supplément 4* (2001): 69–74.

Velcic-Canivez, Mirna, "Histoire et intertextualité: l'écriture de Georges Duby," *Revue Historique*, 302; 1 (2000): 187–206

DUFRENNE, MIKEL
Philosopher, Aesthetician

Mikel Dufrenne belongs to an important generation of postwar thinkers who through phenomenology revitalized French philosophy. The phenomenological receptivity allowed Dufrenne to assimilate the experiences of modern art and literature into the otherwise traditional discipline of philosophical aesthetics. Through an analysis of the relation between what is given prelinguistically and what is actualized in language, Dufrenne saw art as elucidating our interaction with the world as such. Despite their aesthetic focus, Dufrenne's major works thus all revolve around the classically philosophical occupation of describing Man's relation to the world.

Dufrenne's rigorous and theoretical approach parallels the 1960s move in the French humanities toward the development of a "science de l'homme." In opposition to the emerging structuralism, however, Dufrenne never lost sight of the aspect "homme" in the excitement caused by the prospect of "science." Art is clearly an object of systematic thought, but to Dufrenne it could never constitute a system whose structures can be studied in isolation of its agents. The antihumanist tendencies of modern French thought are therefore repeatedly rejected, for instance in *Pour l'homme* of 1968, which was particularly aimed at the Althusserian school of thought. Dufrenne's contemporaries who proclaimed the "death of Man" simply failed to see that they rather express Man. This detriment of Man in French thought at the time also provides the context for Dufrenne's interest in the American sociologists Kardiner and Linton. In *La Personnalité de base* of 1953 and 1966, Dufrenne ventured outside the confinement of aesthetics to establish a theory of Man in the light of their cultural anthropology.

Dufrenne's humanist instinct is intimately related to his early recognition of the limits of any philosophical inquiry. His early reflections were shaped by existentialist thought that indicated that the wreckage of philosophy might precisely be a manifestation of life. Although World War II and years of captivity by the Germans interrupted his traditional, French academic itinerary as "normalien" and "agrégé," good fortune placed Dufrenne in the same prisoner camp as Paul Ricoeur. Upon their liberation, they wrote a book on one of their main topics of discussion, Karl Jaspers's existential thinking. Ricoeur was to remain a lifelong interlocutor, critic, and friend, and they eventually became colleagues when they both took part in the foundation of the University of Nanterre outside Paris.

If thus always founded on an ethical and existential keystone, philosophical inquiry is bound to hold its own limitations. Man is not essentially defined by his self-reflection. Thinking about thinking is a dubious activity, and philosophy is its own worst enemy, as it constantly fails to capture Man's relation to the world. Metaphysical inquiry must therefore pass indirectly through another domain, and because art—through its expressivity—becomes the manifestation of the world in Man, aesthetic insight hence becomes the most effective mode of inquiry into the ontology of the world.

When Dufrenne therefore opened the aesthetic field to phenomenology, in the landmark thesis *Phénoménologie de l'expérience esthétique* of 1953, he retained the anthropocentric perspective of existentialism, significantly evading both the dualism between naturalism and idealism and the discrepancy between Man and the Other. Although producing Man, the world only becomes what it is through Man's presence. As in Merleau-Ponty's philosophy, Man thus "fulfills" the world, and this perfect complementarity allowed Dufrenne to dissociate himself from the somewhat solipsistic tendencies of contemporary French thought. Unlike Sartre, Dufrenne did not hold the world to constitute an unsurpassable Other; one is one with the Other as a given, as an "*a priori*."

If philosophy cannot capture Man's relation to the world and must pass through art, this is to a large extent due to the transcendental nature of language. Two ostensibly different works from 1963, *Language and Philosophy* and *Le Poétique*, jointly demonstrate that the complex status of language obliges us to work with poetry as an epistemological tool. In the former book, Dufrenne exhibits the fundamental phenomenological presupposition that the human being who speaks is not the one who initiated the language. Establishing a phenomenology of speech will therefore serve to reveal the metaphysics of language. Where philosophy gives up, poetry then sets in. Significantly, to Dufrenne, poetry is not an artifact constructed from words, but is the closest we can get to a natural language. As such it provides the key to a deeper understanding of our otherwise unknown relation to the world, to Nature. Poetry lies prior to our concepts, constituting the original communication between Man and the world. Thus occupying a place between Nature and the articulated, poetry does what philosophy can only think, allowing *a priori* communication between the object and the subject, further underpinning the complementarity between Man and world.

If the fundamental accord between Man and the world is revealed through poetry and art only, Dufrenne's conception of philosophy, however, encounters certain problems. Ostensibly, one must leave "the final word to poetry" (Introduction to *Language and Philosophy*), but philosophy can still establish a discourse that adds to the poetical: "Philosophy is still able to meditate on poetry" (Conclusion of *Language and Philosophy*). Philosophy therefore seems bound up in a dilemma between hesitation and pure meditation. Ricoeur picked up on this exact dilemma when pointing out that not only is the role of philosophy ambiguous; Dufrenne's radical separation between the *expression* of poetry and the supposed *knowledge* of philosophy may not be epistemologically desirable. Other commentators such as Lyotard have accused Dufrenne of ignoring, in his division between language and Nature, the powers of psychoanalytic explanation. Such observations, however, mainly serve to accentuate the classic, philosophical outlook of Dufrenne, who as a modern aesthetician did not refrain from facing ontology and essences at a time when metaphysical inquiry otherwise fell into disregard.

NIELS BUCH-JEPSEN

See also **Louis Althusser; Jean-Francois Lyotard; Maurice Merleau-Ponty; Paul Ricoeur; Jean-Paul Sartre**

Biography

Born in 1910, Mikel Dufrenne, a former student of the *École Normale Supérieure*, finished the *agrégation* in philosophy in 1932. After years in the same prisoner camp as Paul Ricoeur during World War II, he submitted his doctoral thesis in 1953 and became professor at the University of Poitiers. He subsequently participated in the foundation of the University of Paris–X in Nanterre, where he taught until his retirement in 1974. Dufrenne died in 1995.

Selected Works

Karl Jaspers et la philosophie de l'existence (with Paul Ricoeur), 1947
Phénoménologie de l'expérience esthétique, 2 vols., 1953; as *The Phenomenology of Aesthetic Experience*, translated by Edward S. Casey et al., 1973
La Personnalité de base—Un concept sociologique, 1st ed. 1953, 2nd ed. 1966
La Notion d' "a priori," 1959; as *The Notion of the A Priori*, translated by Edward S. Casey, 1966
Le Poétique, 1st ed. 1963, 2nd ed. 1973
Language and Philosophy, translated by Henry B. Veatch, 1963

"The Aesthetic Object and the Technical Object," 1964
Jalons, 1966
Esthétique et philosophie I, 1967
Pour l'homme—Essai, 1968
"Pour une philosophie non théologique," 1973
Art et politique, 1974
Esthétique et philosophie II, 1976
Subversion, perversion, 1977
"Esthétique et sciences de l'art" in *Tendances principales de la recherche dans les sciences sociales et humaines II*, 1978, as *Main Trends in Aesthetics and the Sciences of Art*, 1979
"Intentionality and Aesthetics," 1978
Esthétique et philosophie III, 1981
L'Inventaire des "a priori," 1981
"Eye and Mind," in *Merleau-Ponty: Perception, Structure, Language*, 1981
"Phenomenology and Literary Criticism," in *Continental Philosophy and the Arts*, 1984
In the Presence of the Sensuous: Essays in Aesthetics, edited and translated by Mark S. Roberts and Dennis Gallagher, 1987
L'Œil et l'oreille, 1987

Further Reading

Charles, Daniel, "Le Dernier mot," *Revue d'esthétique* 30 (1996): 25–33.
Feezell, Randolph, "Mikel Dufrenne and the World of the Aesthetic Object," *Philosophy Today*, 24 (1980): 20–32
Lascault, Gilbert (editor), *Vers une esthétique sans entrave. Mélanges Mikel Dufrenne*, Paris: U.G.E., 1975
Lyotard, Jean-François, "Langage et nature," *Revue d'esthétique*, 30 (1996): 45–49.
Mouloud, Noël, "Analyse du *Poétique* de Mikel Dufrenne," *Revue d'esthétique*, 17, no. III-IV (1964): 319–322.
Ricoeur, Paul, "Mikel Dufrenne," in *Lectures II. La Contrée des Philosophes*, Paris: Seuil, 1992.
Silverman, Hugh, "Dufrenne's Phenomenology of Poetry," *Philosophy Today*, 20 (1976): 20–24
Special issues of *Revue d'esthétique*, 21 (1992), 30 (1996)
Special issues of *Philosophy Today*, 14 (1970), 20 (1976), 24 (1980)

DUHEM, PIERRE
Philosopher, Historian of Science

Pierre Duhem was a French physicist and mathematician by training whose interests subsequently turned to the philosophy and history of science. Nevertheless, it was a cause of great annoyance to Duhem that his work was known chiefly for its contribution to these latter (as he thought them) inferior and secondary disciplines, rather than acknowledged as having made an important contribution to the advancement of physics and mathematics. Yet, ironically enough, his work pointed the way toward later developments that pressed much further in a strongly historicist direction. Indeed, it has often been construed as lending support to a form of Kuhnian paradigm-relativism that Duhem would scarcely have endorsed, even though it can plausibly claim warrant in certain aspects of his thinking.

His earliest publications (during the 1880s) were devoted to his conception of thermodynamics as the best prospect for a unifying general theory that would elucidate the basic laws of physics and chemistry. At this stage his thought already manifested some of the features that would characterize Duhem's later "philosophical" turn, among them a disdain for ontological commitments (such as atomism) that went beyond the empirical evidence and—concordant with this—a fixed aversion to any form of "metaphysical" realism that claimed to reveal the ultimate nature of things or the underlying causal powers that explained phenomenal appearances. That is to say, Duhem inclined very strongly toward a Machian (positivist) view of scientific method as best devoted to "saving the phenomena" (that is, the empirical/observational data), and not yielding hostages to skeptical fortune by advancing realist hypotheses that could not be established by reference to those same data. This is one reason why Duhem's philosophy of science has met with a receptive response among thinkers such as W.V. Quine, who likewise adopt an empiricist approach that eschews any surplus ontological commitment beyond that entailed by our acceptance of a certain, pragmatically efficacious conceptual scheme. On this view there is no making sense of the idea that a physical theory might be verified or falsified through an *experimentum crucis* that tested it directly against the evidence. On the contrary: we can always save some attractive theory in the face of discrepant empirical results by adducing the limits of precise observation, by invoking alternative "auxiliary hypotheses," or by redistributing truth-values and predicates across the entire "fabric" of currently held scientific beliefs. Then again, we can always conserve some anomalous empirical result by abandoning a hitherto well-entrenched physical theory or—at the limit—suspending certain classical axioms of logic such as bivalence or excluded middle.

Hence the "Duhem-Quine thesis" according to which observation-statements (even the most basic) are ineluctably "theory-laden" and theories themselves "underdetermined" by the best empirical evidence. This thesis has been subject to widespread debate and a good deal of criticism, the latter chiefly on the grounds that it appears to undermine the rationality of theory-choice and to deprive science of any normative standard by which to adjudicate rival truth-claims or hypotheses. Also it comes rather sharply into conflict with certain of Duhem's working principles as a physicist, among them his theory of thermodynamics as providing a unitary framework—or grounding rationale—for the entirety of physics and chemistry. Thus some commentators have put the case for decoupling Duhem's from Quine's contribution to the thesis that routinely conjoins their names and thereby rescuing

Duhem from any imputation of wholesale paradigm-relativism or ontological relativity. On the other hand, this tends to play down the very marked leaning in just that direction evinced by some of Duhem's later work. The issue is further complicated by his book *German Science*, published during the First World War, where Duhem indulged in a bout of patriotically motivated (at times crudely chauvinistic) cultural polemics. Here he championed the "typical" French preference for a fine-tuned combination of common sense, intuitive, and rational procedure as against the "typical" Germanic style of rigorous axiomatic-deductive thought. In support of this claim, Duhem called Pascal to witness on the two supposedly distinct mentalities—"*l'esprit de finesse*" and "*l'esprit géometrique*"—which he (Duhem) took to characterize the French and German approaches to science. That this account produces some passages of near-caricature on both sides must no doubt be put down to the pressures of historical and political circumstance. All the same it exhibits, once again, the curious tension between Duhem's convictions as a working physicist and his thinking about issues in the history and philosophy of science. Thus it is hard to square his attack on those supposed Teutonic excesses with his elsewhere fiercely maintained commitment to the "Gallic" (Cartesian) ideals of mathematical exactitude and logico-conceptual rigor.

These problems are raised in their sharpest form by Duhem's strong-revisionist account of early modern science and, in particular, its supposed radical break with previous, medieval, or scholastic modes of thought. This had much to do with his Catholic faith and with Duhem's desire to push back the intellectual origins of scientific modernity so as to establish its dependence on—and continuity with—those earlier developments. Central to his argument was the claim that Renaissance philosopher—scientists such as Leonardo da Vinci were drawing on a rich heritage of thought handed down by hitherto marginalized thinkers, among them Jean Buridan, Nicole Oresme, and Albert of Saxony. Most scholars identify a marked change in his thinking around the years 1904–1905, when he converted from something like the then orthodox "clean break" (progressivist and antischolastic) view to a conviction that this was merely the result of deep-laid secularist prejudice, an outlook typified for Duhem by the French Third Republic and its anticlericalist campaigns. Just how far his subsequent work was motivated by theological as opposed to strictly scientific or historiographic concerns is a matter of widespread debate among Duhem's commentators. According to some—those of a broadly kindred persuasion—it enabled him not only to reconcile the claims of scientific knowledge and religious belief but also to achieve a more balanced, less partisan cultural–historical approach. Others have seen it as a product of deep-laid doctrinal adherence that led him to espouse an outlook resembling that of Paul Feyerabend, for whom the issue between the Church authorities and astronomers such as Copernicus and Galileo was one that could not—cannot even now—be settled on "purely" scientific terms.

This interpretation is doubtless wide of the mark, given both the depth of Duhem's historical scholarship and his meticulous respect for the methods and procedures of scientific thought. Indeed, his revisionism works most often to opposite effect by finding those methods and procedures strikingly anticipated among thinkers who had hitherto been consigned to the prehistory of modern science. Still there is a conflict in Duhem's work between, on the one hand, his commitment to the values of rigor, objectivity, and truth and, on the other, his attraction to an instrumentalist doctrine that has at least something in common with the ruse whereby Galileo was required to affirm not the truth but merely the "empirical adequacy" of the heliocentric hypothesis. Thus a chief characteristic of Duhem's "uneasy genius"—to cite the title of a shrewd study by one of his coreligionist admirers—was the constant striving to maintain a balance between these disparate elements in his thought. So likewise with his effort to reconcile the claims of philosophy and history of science, the former conceived as having to do with the long-run scientific "context of justification," while the latter is taken to concern itself solely with conditions obtaining in the original "context of discovery." Here again it would be wrong to think of Duhem the physicist–philosopher as in any way committed—like the present-day "strong" sociologists of knowledge—to collapsing that distinction and, along with it, the very idea that scientific truth-claims are subject to assessment by standards quite distinct from those deployed by social or cultural historians.

Nevertheless, his work has sometimes been put to the service of arguments like these on account of its textbook association with Quine's radically holistic approach and hence—although Quine would just as strongly disown the idea—with Kuhn-derived doctrines of thoroughgoing paradigm-relativism. Thus Duhem is a figure of particular interest for anyone seeking to unravel the tangled history of "analytic" and "continental" developments over the past half century and more. Still there are signs of an emergent revaluation by scholars less concerned with Duhem's role in these latter-day contexts of debate and better equipped to assess his contribution both to physics and philosophy of science.

CHRISTOPHER NORRIS

Biography

Pierre Duhem was born in Paris in 1861 and received his higher education at the École Normale Supèrieure and then at the Sorbonne, where his doctorate (in the field of electro-magnetism) was awarded in 1888. Despite a career of outstanding achievements in mathematics, physics, and philosophy and history of science, he never obtained a teaching post at any Parisian institution and took up a series of provincial appointments in Lille, Rennes, and Bordeaux. When offered a chair in history of science at the Collège de France (in 1893) Duhem indignantly declined it on the grounds that he was first and foremost a working physicist—one who had made important contributions to the field—and no mere historian of the subject. His resentment on this score was offset to some extent by his 1913 election as a member of the Académie des Sciences. His status as a relative outsider no doubt had much to do with this somewhat cantankerous side to Duhem's temperament. However, it can also be explained in terms of his staunchly traditional Catholic faith—which stood out against the secularist and anticlericalist ethos of the time—and by the fact that his major scientific as well as philosophico-historical claims were such as to provoke sharp opposition from those with the power to make or break academic careers. Yet, despite these setbacks and frustrations, Duhem managed to produce a quite extraordinary range of published work, first in mathematics and physics, then in philosophy of science, and lastly—with his ten-volume *Le système du monde*—on the history of scientific thought. His theological standpoint (that is, his adherence to certain tenets of Catholic doctrine) is very often apparent in Duhem's later, more philosophically oriented thinking. Again this made his work highly controversial during his lifetime and continues to divide opinion among commentators. Duhem died in 1916.

Selected Works

Le potential thermodynamique et ses applications à la méchanique et à l'étude des phénomènes électriques, 1886 [The Thermodynamic Potential and its Applications to Mechanics and the Study of Electrical Phenomena]
Le mixte et la combinaison chimique: essai sur l'évolution d'une idée, 1902. [Chemical Mixture and Combination: Essay on the Evolution of an Idea]
L' évolution de la mécanique, 1903 [The Evolution of Mechanics]
Les origines de la statique: les sources des théories physiques, 2 vols., 1905–1906 [The Origins of Statics: The Source of Physical Theories]
La théorie physique: son objet et sa structure, 1906; as *The Aim and Structure of Physical Theory*, translated by Philip P. Wiener, 1954
Recherches sur l'élasticité, 1906 [Researches on Elasticity]

Etudes sur Léonard de Vinci, ceux qu'il a lu et ceux qui l'ont lu, 3 vols., 1906–1913 ΣΩZEIN TA ΨAINOMENA: *Essai sur la notion de théorie physique, de Platon à Galilée*, 1908; as *To Save the Phenomena: an essay on the idea of physical theory from Plato to Galileo*, translated by E. Dolan and C. Maschler
Traité d'énergétique ou de thermodynamique générale, 1911 [Treatise on Energetics on General Thermodynamics]
Le système du monde: histoire des doctrines cosmologiques de Platon à Copernic, 1913–1959 [The World System: A History of Cosmological Doctrines from Photo to Copernicus]
Medieval Cosmology: Theories of Infinity, Place, Time, Void, and the Plurality of Worlds, edited and translated by Roger Ariew, 1985 (selections from *Le système du monde*)
La science allemande, 1915; as *German Science*, translated by John Lyon, 1991.
"Logical Examination of Scientific Theory," translated by P. Barker and R. Ariew, *Synthèse*, 83 (1990): 183–88
"Research on the History of Physical Theories," translated by P. Barker and R. Ariew, *Synthèse*, 83 (1990): 189–200
Essays in the History and Philosophy of Science, translated by R. Ariew and P. Barker, 1996
"Atomic Notation and Atomistic Hypotheses," *Foundations of Chemistry*, 2000

Further Reading

Artigas, Mariano, "Pierre Duhem: The Philosophical Meaning of Two Historical Theses," *Epistemologia*, 10 (1987): 89–97
Brenner, A, *Duhem: science, réalité et apparence. La relation entre philosophie et histoire dans l'oeuvre de Pierre Duhem*, Paris: Vrin, 1990 [Duhem: Science, Reality and Appearance. The Relation between Philosophy and History in the work of Pierre Duhem]
Brouzeng, P., *Duhem, 1861–1916: science et providence*, Paris: Belin, 1987 [Science and Providence]
Crowe, Michael J., "Duhem and the History and Philosophy of Mathematics," *Synthèse*, 83 (1990): 431–447
Duhem, Hélène, *Un savant français: Pierre Duhem*, Paris: Libraire Plon, 1936 [A French *Savant*: Pierre Duham]
Goddu, André, "The Realism that Duhem Rejected in Copernicus", *Synthèse*, 83 (1990): 301–315
Harding, Sandra G. (editor), *Can Theories Be Refuted? Essays on the Duhem-Quine Thesis*, Dordrecht & Boston: D. Reidel, 1976
Howard, Don, "Pierre Duhem," in *The Routledge Encyclopedia of Philosophy*, London & New York: Routledge 1991 (I am indebted to this article and to Jaki's book [reference following] for numerous points of factual information and bibliographical data.)
Jaki, Stanley L., *Uneasy Genius: The Life and Work of Pierre Duhem*, Dordrecht: Martinus Nijhoff, 1987
Jaki, Stanley L., "The Physicist and the Mathematician," *New Scholasticism*, 63 (1989): 183–205
Joy, Glenn C., "Pierre Duhem on the Testing of Hypotheses," *Philosophy Research Archives*, 5, no. 1336 (1979):
Lowinger, A., *The Methodology of Pierre Duhem*, New York: Columbia University Press, 1941
Martin, R. N. D., *Pierre Duhem: Philosophy and History in the Work of a Believing Physicist*, La Salle, Illinois: Open Court, 1991
Picard, E., *La vie et l'oeuvre de Pierre Duhem*, Paris: Gauthier-Villars [The Life and Work oif Pierre Duhem]

Poirier, René, "L'epistémologie de Pierre Duhem et sa valeur actuelle," *Les études philosophiques*, 4 (1967): 399–419 ["The Epistemology of Pierre Duhem and its Contemporary Value"]

DUMAZEDIER, JOFFRE
Sociologist

Joffre Dumazedier is recognized as the pioneer of the sociology of leisure in France. Upon entering Henri Wallon's laboratory in 1947, he was influenced by Georges Friedmann, attending his seminar along with Roland Barthes, Michel Crozier, and Alain Touraine. In 1953 he created his own research unit on the sociology of leisure and cultural models. He was to direct it until 1984. He also created the International Sociology Association's research committee on leisure in 1956.

Dumazedier introduced France to leading American theorists on leisure, arranging, for instance, for the first French translation of David Riesman's *The Lonely Crowd* (Paris: Artaud, 1964). His historicist approach to the study of leisure, based on an experimental sociology describing its various aspects, paralleled the work of Max Kaplan and foreshadowed the work of Jeremy Rifkin. According to Dumazedier, scholarly discourse on leisure as an area of study is often characterized by semantic confusion either inherited from past social situations or owing to ideal situations in which leisure is denied and dismembered. He tended to place leisure in the context of a secular evolution in which work time has dramatically receded. He often repeated, for instance, that the 4,000 customary hours of work a year in the middle of the nineteenth century were reduced to 1,600 in the second half of the twentieth century.

As founder and president of the *Peuple et culture* (People and Culture) association, Dumazedier was engaged as a militant of popular education, always eager to explore the borders between elite and popular culture. A militant in youth organizations (he was twenty when the Popular Front came to power), he developed early on a method of mental training and began his career researching sport and most particularly the Olympic games. In 1966, he founded the *International Review of Sport Sociology*. He consistently dealt with the problem of a larger access to education and culture among the mass public. He believed, as did Paul Lafargue, that the majority of leisure should be devoted to education. As a member of numerous state committees such as *Groupe 85*, he advocated a constructive sociology in which thought was conducive to action. Rather than discuss the nineteenth-century concepts from which sociology was derived, he foresaw a prospective sociology based on the experience of contemporary "lived" culture.

In perhaps his most well-known work, *Vers une civilisation du loisir?* (1962; translated as *Toward a Society of Leisure*, 1967), Dumazedier demonstrated how the dynamics of leisure shape social transformations, thereby creating new sociocultural practices. Defining leisure dialectically by opposing it to various forms of work, he distinguished it from the vast majority of family oriented, religious, and political activities. He recognized three overall functions of leisure: relaxation, entertainment, and personal development. The second is an obstacle for the third. Dumazedier's insistence on the third function is revelatory both of his continuous preoccupation with education and the existential underpinnings of his thought. Balance (between these functions, and other factors) is a key concept of a book, which is centered on the idea of personal development, a notion that is not at odds with the old and classical notion of leisure as contemplation developed in Aristotle's *Politics*.

Dumazedier coauthored the initial volume of *Le Loisir et la ville, Loisir et culture* [1966; Leisure and the City, Leisure and Culture] with Aline Ripert. The work is based on data relating to cultural practices collected between 1954 and 1962 in the town of Annecy and modeled after Robert and Helen Lynd's seminal anthropological study of Middletown. In this work leisure is characterized as emancipative, free, hedonistic, and personal. Dumazedier goes on to oppose spontaneous and organized sociability (as in the case of cultural associations and local networks of public servants specialized in organizing cultural events) and also introduces the controversial idea of semileisure. In volume two, *Société éducative et pouvoir culturel* [1976; Educative Society and Cultural Power], coauthored with Nicole Samuel, he analyzes leisure and sociocultural action in terms of autonomy and dependency vis-à-vis work, family, education, or spirituality, while insisting on the increasing role played by sociocultural workers.

Dumazedier's method is exposed in *Sociologie empirique du loisir. Critique et contre-critique de la civilisation du loisir* (1974; translated as *Sociology of Leisure*, 1974), originally his doctoral thesis (presiding the jury was Raymond Aron). The post-1968 rise of the consumer society, as well as the fact that sociology at the time was heavily dependent on philosophy and critical theory in French universities, where leisure was often deemed too unclear a concept and too uncertain a field, contributed to its relative marginalization in the 1970s and 1980s. In the wake of the May 1968 movement, he studied the rise of cultural power and forwarded the cause of cultural development, a concept introduced by Karl Mannheim in *Freedom, Power and Democratic Planning*. Influenced by André Gorz's and Ivan Illich's writings, he studied new processes of knowledge acquisition based on autobiographical reflection and experience, which he termed *autodidaxie*. He also analyzed, in terms of the creation of new values, the potential effects that the forty-hour week and retirement at sixty would have on society, developing the concept of a new social agency based on a sociology of interactions rather than on the psychology-derived sociology of the subject.

La Révolution culturelle du temps libre: 1968–88 [The Cultural Revolution of Free Time], although giving many explanations of Dumazedier's intellectual itinerary, takes into consideration the changes in French society since 1968—symbolized by the brief appearance of a *ministre du temps libre* (Secretary to Free Time) in 1981—and continues the analysis of the effects of leisure on social change in ethical terms. Chapter 2 introduces (pp. 47–48) the notion of so-called ipsative social time (*temps social ipsatif*), in which "ipsative" refers to Theodore D. Kemper's 1968 definition in "Reference Groups, Socialization and Achievement." It is a liberated time appropriated by the subject and used for his self-development as an individual. In sum, the explosion of leisure is for Dumazedier the essential event of modernity, an event that he analyzes within a post-Marxist theory of social time. In his perspective—and his distance vis-à-vis Friedmann is clearly marked here—the silent cultural revolution of free or liberated time that brings about leisured society is based on the relativization of the factors that determine work

CHRISTOPHE IPPOLITO

See also **Raymond Aron; Roland Barthes; Andre Gorz**

Biography

Born in 1915 in Taverny (Northern France), Joffre Dumazedier first studied linguistics but soon chose sociology. He was selected to train at the national school for executives in Uriage during World War II and later became an active member of the French Resistance. In 1946, he founded the popular education organization *Peuple et Culture* [People and Culture]. He soon became head of a CNRS (*Centre National de la Recherche Scientifique*) research unit on leisure and an internationally renowned scholar. He is the author of several books on the subject of leisure, including *Vers une civilisation du loisir?* (1962), *Le Loisir et la ville* (1966 and 1976), *Sociologie empririque du loisir. Critique et contre-critique de la civilisation du loisir* (1974), and *La Révolution culturelle du temps libre: 1968–1988* (1988). He also taught sociopedagogy and adult formation at the University of Paris V.

Selected Works

Regards neufs sur les Jeux Olympiques (with Jeanine Dumazedier), 1952

Vers une civilisation du loisir?, 1962; reedited in 1971 with new preface and annexes as *Toward a Society of Leisure*, 1967, translated by Stewart E. McClure, preface by David Riesman, 1967

Le Loisir et la ville, vol. I. *Loisir et culture* (with Aline Ripert), 1966

Sociologie empirique du loisir. Critique et contre critique de la civilisation du loisir, 1974, translated as *Sociology of Leisure*, 1974

Le Loisir et la ville, vol. II. *Société éducative et pouvoir culturel* (with Nicole Samuel), 1976

La Révolution culturelle du temps libre: 1968–1988, 1988

Further Reading

Friedmann, Georges, *Où va le travail humain?* Paris: Éditions Gallimard (collection Idées), 1963

Green, Anne-Marie (editor), *Les Métamorphoses du travail et la nouvelle société du temps libre. Autour de Joffre Dumazedier*, Paris: Éditions L'Harmattan (collection Logiques sociales), 2000

Kaplan, Max, *Leisure: Theory and Policy*, New York: Wiley, 1975

Lipovetsky, Gilles, *Le Déclin du devoir*, Paris: Éditions Gallimard, 1993

Lynd, Robert and Helen Lynd, *Middletown: A Study in Contemporary American Culture*, New York: Harcourt, Brace and World, 1929

Méda, Dominique, *Le Travail, une valeur en voie de disparition*, Paris: Éditions Aubier, 1995

Pronovost, Gilles. *Loisir et société. Traité de sociologie empirique*, Sainte-Foy: Éditions des Presses de l'Université de Québec, 1993

Pronovost, Gilles, Claudine Attias-Donfut, and Nicole Samuel (editors), *Temps libre et modernité. Mélanges en l'honneur de Joffre Dumazedier*, Paris: Éditions L'Harmattan, Sainte-Foy (Québec): Presses de l'Université de Québec, 1993

Riesman, David, with Nathan Glazer and Reuel Denney, *The Lonely Crowd: A Study of the Changing American Character*, New Haven: Yale University Press, 1950

Rifkin, Jeremy, *The End of Work. The Decline of the Global Labor Force and the Dawn of the Post-Market Era*, New York: Tarcher-Putnam, 1995

Rojek, Chris, *Decentring Leisure. Rethinking Leisure Theory*, London: Sage, 1995

Sue, Roger, *Temps et ordre social*, Paris: Presses Universitaires de France, 1996

Sue, Roger, *Vers une société du temps libre*, Paris: Presses Universitaires de France, 1982

DUMÉZIL, GEORGES

Author

Georges Dumézil is one of the most important French thinkers of the twentieth century. Yet, he is all but completely unknown in the anglophone world. A prolific author and a scholar of more than thirty languages, ranging from Old Norse to Sanskrit, Dumézil had a profound influence on the theories and intellectual development of figures as diverse as the linguist Émile Benveniste, the anthropologist Claude Lévi-Strauss, the scholar of comparative religion Mircea Eliade, and the philosopher Michel Foucault. The latter explicitly acknowledged the importance of Dumézil to his own intellectual formation in his inaugural address at the *Collège de France*. "It is he who taught me to analyze the internal economy of a discourse in a fashion completely different from the methods of traditional exegesis; it is he who taught me to move from one discourse to another, through the play of comparisons, the system of functional correlations; it is he who taught me how to describe the transformations of a discourse and its relations to the institution" (*L'ordre du discours*, 1971). From this tribute, one might well think that Dumézil was a philosopher. In the anglophone community, however, Dumézil is known almost exclusively to scholars of ancient languages and primarily to those interested in comparative Indo-European mythology, his major area of disciplinary expertise.

How could a scholar of such recondite materials, the author of articles arguing that Quechua and Turkish are related languages and therefore that the Inca came from central Asia, have had such a profound influence on many of the most important figures of twentieth-century French thought? The answers are several. First, it must be remembered that the Parisian intellectual community is a very small world. All the established figures know one another. Second, until very recently French students studied both Latin and Greek. Knowledge of the ancient world and its cultural importance is presumed in intellectual circles to a degree that is simply not the case in the anglophone world. Third, Dumézil's depth and breadth of learning, his tremendous productivity, in a culture that still values sheer erudition and in the highly competitive world of French intellectual life were bound to be noticed.

These reasons are important, but they are contingent rather than essential. They explain why Dumézil was important in France in a way that one could never imagine an Indo-Europeanist being so in the United States, Canada, or the United Kingdom. Nonetheless, they do not explain the true nature of his intellectual contribution. To understand that we must return to the words of Foucault. Dumézil's most revolutionary work is not to be found in his empirical discoveries, although he made important contributions to our understanding of Roman religion, Vedic cosmology, and Celtic theories of kingship. His most important contribution has been to the elaboration of a theory of reading that can be applied to vast cultural ensembles in terms of a "system of functional correlations" between different discursive formations. This methodological insight was the most widely generalizable aspect of his work.

Traditional Indo-Europeanists would look at a set of myths such as those surrounding the rape of the Sabine women and the foundation of Rome and would attempt to reduce them to some preexisting meaning: Frazier's fertility cults, Müller's solar mythology, or philology's unvarnished historical truth lying behind various mythical and literary embellishments. Dumézil's first rule of procedure, however, was to never treat facts in isolation. His first step was to analyze the story into its component parts, establish their function within the narrative, and then look at cognate traditions to validate and clarify his findings. Thus, in our example, he noted that Romulus, founder of Rome, was the king and his men were portrayed as rough warriors. The Sabines, on the other hand, had two principle associations: fertility and wealth. Thus, according to Livy, it was their women that were kidnapped to become the Roman's brides, and when the Sabine army came to avenge them, their wealth was contrasted with that of the Romans.

Dumézil then noted the presence of a series of other stories concerning the foundation of cities that involved a coming together of two peoples representing the same three functions: kingship, warfare, and material prosperity. These stories are found in the Scandinavian oral tradition, the lore of the Ossetian tribes in Russia, and the tales of Vedic India. Inasmuch as ancient India and prehistoric Rome had no cultural or trading relations, nor did early Scandinavia and Ossetia, then the most economical hypothesis is to assume that these stories derive from a common source. If we note that all of these cultures speak Indo-European languages possessing a common vocabulary of legal, ritual, and familial institutions, then it is logical to assume that the common source would be an Indo-European ideology of communal functions dividing the population into three orders: rulers, warriors, and economic producers (pastoral, agricultural, and mercantile). This thesis is then confirmed by finding these three functions repeated at a variety of levels (gods, social orders, cosmology) in various cultural materials stretching from Ireland to India.

The great advantage of Dumézil's theory of three functions is that it assumes no defined content beyond a basic division of social roles. The functions are placeholders in a structure, not intrinsically meaningful elements. They can ultimately assume a variety of discrete contents and underwrite vastly different political, ideological, and religious systems. Thus, in his *Archaic Roman Religion* (1970), Dumézil wrote, "As my work proceeded, I gained a clearer awareness of the possibilities, but also of the limits, of the comparative method, in particular of what should be its Golden Rule, namely that it permits one to explore and clarify structures of thought, but not to reconstruct events, to 'fabricate history,' or even prehistory." What Dumézil has discovered is a set of inherited structures that, although not determining the political or intellectual content of any given intellectual production, nonetheless create formal limits. Like Foucault's story of how the leper colonies of the sixteenth century became the insane asylums of the Enlightenment (*Madness and Civilization*, 1965), these comparative Indo-European structures created possibilities for organizing thought in ancient society. Thus, Dumézil, who first began to publish the results of his research on "trifunctionality" in Indo-European ideology in 1938, before Lévi-Strauss's fateful encounter with Roman Jakobson, may be called the father of the structural study of myth.

PAUL ALLEN MILLER

See also **Emile Benveniste; Michel Foucault; Claude Lévi-Strauss**

Biography

Georges Dumézil was born March 4, 1898, in Paris. In 1916, he entered the École Normal Supérieure. After he received the aggregation in letters, he served for some time as lecturer in French at the University of Warsaw. Upon returning to France he defended his dissertation, *Le festin d'immortalité*. This was an essay in the traditional comparative mythology that he would later renounce. In 1925 he again left France to teach history of religion at the University of Istanbul. He stayed there for six years before moving to Upsala, where he lectured in French. In 1948 he was elected to the Collège de France. He is the author of countless books. Georges Dumézil passed away October 11, 1986.

Selected Works

Mythes et dieux des Germains, essai d'interpretation comparative, 1939
Servius et la fortune, essai sur la fonction social de louange et de blâme et sur les éléments Indo-Européens du cens romain, 1943
Tarpeia, Essais de philologie comparative Indo-Européene, 1947
La Religion romaine archaïque suivi d'un appendice sur la religion des Etrusques, 1966; as *Archaic Roman Religion*, translated by Philip Krapp, 1970
Mythe et épopée, tome I, L'Idéologie des trois fonctions dans les épopées des peuples Indo-Européens, 1968
Idées romaines, 1969
Mythe et épopée, tome II, Types épiques indo-européens: Un héros, un sorcier, un roi, 1971
Mythe et épopée, tome III, Histoires Romaines, 1973
Mariages Indo-Européens, 1979
Apollon sonore et autres essais: Esquisses de mythologie, 1982

Further Reading

Coutau-Bégarie, Hervé, *L'Oeuvre de Georges Dumézil: catalogue raisonné. Suivi de textes de Georges Dumézil*, Paris: Economica, 1998
Dubuisson, Daniel, *Mythologies du XXe siècle: Dumézil, Lévi Strauss, Eliade*, Villeneuve d'Ascq: Presses universitaires de Lille, 1993
Dumézil, Georges, *Entretiens avec Didier Eribon*, Paris: Gallimard, 1987
Eribon, Didier, *Faut-il brûler Dumézil?: mythologie, science et politique*, Paris: Flammarion, 1992
Hommages à Georges Dumézil, Bruxelles: Revue d'études latines, 1960
Littleton, C. Scott, *The New Comparative Mythology: An Anthropological Assessment of the Theories of Georges Dumézil*, rev. ed., Berkeley: University of California Press, 1973
Magazine littéraire, 229 (1986), dossier spécial Georges Dumézil
Polomé, Edgar C. (editor), *Indo-European Religion after Dumézil*, Washington D.C.: Institute for the Study of Man, 1996
Segal, Robert A. (editor), *Structuralism in Myth: Lévi-Strauss, Barthes, Dumézil, and Propp*, New York: Garland, 1996

DURKHEIM, ÉMILE DAVID
Sociologist

Émile Durkheim is one of the main philosophers of the early twentieth century and one of the most eminent representatives of the generation of intellectuals who were actively engaged in building and supporting the political works of the Third Republic. Two facts are indeed at the source of the Durkheimian enterprise: first, the crisis of the integration of the social body, second, the fragility of the individualist ideals of revolutionary modernity, that is, those ideals born of the Enlightenment. While industrialization and the rise of social movements threatened social cohesiveness, the values of the individual were still being ridiculed. How then to reconcile order and progress, society and individual, authority and freedom? The founder of a "school" of sociology that would call itself the founder of modern sociology, Durkheim, with his academic status, strove unflaggingly to build an ideology and a morality. In line with the Comtean process, he tried to create the theoretical and methodological tools needed to produce a positivistic knowledge of the social world, which, he thought, might construct a morality and inspire political activism.

Durkheim was nominated to the *Faculté des Lettres* in Bordeaux in 1887 due to the support of Liard, who was then the director of higher education at the Ministry of Public Education. In charge of a course on "pedagogics and social science," he displayed throughout his fifteen-year stay formidable scientific and academic activity that led him to create about a dozen courses, publish three works: *De la division du travail social*, (The Division of Labor in Society) 1893; *Les Règles de la méthode sociologique* (The Rules of the Sociological Method), 1895; *Le Suicide* (Suicide: A Study in Sociology), 1897; and contribute about 300 articles.

He also founded and edited a journal, *L'Année Sociologique* (The Sociological Year) in 1896.

This Bordeaux period was not free of painful events. The Dreyfus affair, which broke out in 1894, affected him on three levels: as a Jewish citizen, as a rational intellectual, and, most importantly, as a fervent republican. The Affair mobilized him as soon as Zola became involved in 1898. To an already exhausting scientific activity, he added a tireless activism. To obtain a revision of the trial, he gathered signatures in an academic milieu that was either hostile or reluctant to get involved. He took part in Trarieux' national foundation of the *Ligue pour la Défense des Droits de l'Homme* (League for the Defense of Human Rights) and presided over several of its Bordeaux branches. He also replied to the pro-Dreyfus and Catholic Brunetière in an article that became famous, *"L'individualisme et les intellectuals"* (Individualism and Intellectuals). This civic activity would be carried on with the foundation, with Hamelin, of the local branch of the *Fédération de la Jeunesse Laïque* (Federation of Secular Youth)—an association for the defense and promotion of popular education, where he gave several lectures.

In 1902, Durkheim was nominated to the Sorbonne, first as a substitute, then as Buisson's successor to a chair whose title he would fight to have renamed "of sociology" until he succeeded in 1913. This Parisian period, as active as the one that preceded it, was devoted to the institutional promotion of his discipline, to the publication of his journal *L'Année Sociologique*, and to the writing of the *Formes élémentaires de la vie religieuse* (The Elementary Forms of Religious Life, 1912). In spite of his friendship with Jaurès, Durkheim rejected political militancy. He was, however, deeply involved in Republican and secular reforming fights, especially that of the "new Sorbonne" that aimed to renew higher education and that would bring him solid and at times odious adversaries.

The Basis of the Durkheimian Paradigm

As with any sociology, at the base of the Durkheimian paradigm lay an anthropology, according to which human needs and desires are, in opposition to those of other living things, indefinitely expandable: there is no "natural" limit to what human beings may want. Only external rules that is social rules—can put a limit on these needs by defining an object for them. By being interiorized, these rules govern and discipline these yearnings while simultaneously making a feeling of satisfaction possible. Human needs and desires had therefore a *de facto* social nature as well as, in essence, the human behaviors they engender (*Le Suicide*). Hence this definition of the social fact as "any manner of action, fixed or not, that might exert an external constraint on the individual" (*The Rules*). The only possible salvation for the individual comes through his integration to society by means of highly cohesive social groups in which he will find the social norms that will free him from his natural demons, which are "egoism" (that is, individualism) and "anomy" (that, is the fundamental indetermination of the goals and the means).

In *Le Suicide*, this paradigm and these two concepts were extensively exposed and showed their full potential because it could be demonstrated that the evolution of suicide rates was in direct correlation with collective states either of social disorder (the "anomic suicide," observed during the most serious social crisis) or of insufficient integration of social groups (the "egoist suicide" of bachelors, for example). If society must be "sufficiently present to the individuals" by its norms and solidarity ties, it can not be too present either because this would lead to the "altruistic" suicide of societies that crushed the person or the "fatalistic" suicide of societies that imposed unbearable norms.

Because of the accelerated growth of the division of labor and functions and, in effect, of the multiplication and disjunction of social segments, modern societies are permanently threatened with anomy (*De la division du travail social*). The "solidarity" that automatically grew between individuals sharing the prescriptions and representations of the same "collective conscience" now strains to find an "organic" form in which social cohesion no longer comes from similarity but rather from the functional *complementarity* of the social segments, especially professional ones. It is therefore in the reform of the political and social organization done by the "reattachment of all economic functions, or some of them that are diffuse, to the directing and conscious centers of society" (*Le Socialisme*, 1928) and by the freedom granted to individuals (in a culture that only legitimizes personal achievements) to reach their potential and receive what they deserve, that industrial and democratic societies will reach their equilibrium and that individuals will attain their "happiness." Therefore, the State plays a key role in maintaining civil peace as well as in controlling social life and economic activity. The State must not dictate these regulations authoritatively; it needs only make sure that society be appropriately controlled, that is that it has rules that correspond to its developmental level.

Durkheim had hoped that education—which is for society "the means by which it prepares in the heart of children the vital conditions of its own existence" (*Éducation et sociologie*, 1922)—would have the most beneficial social effects. He saw education as the best tool that would allow the individual to freely consent to abide by social rules without which he could not live, and that would also allow society to enforce, without violence, the rules it needed to function depending on its developmental level and, consequently, its collective consciousness (*L'Éducation morale*, 1925). For this ardent proponent of the educational mission of the Third Republic, school was obviously the best place and mean to educate: first because it was more apt to socialize the child to the culture of the global society than parents, second because only a social in*stitution* could have the necessary authority for the act of teaching (*L'Évolution pédagogique en France*, 1938).

A General Sociological Theory

With *The Rules of the Sociological Method*, Durkheim sought to impose a general sociological theory and to give his discipline the foundation of its empirical process. A true manifesto, the work was in line with Comtean positivism for which acts can and must be enlightened by science when it succeeds to elaborate inductive "laws" from which explanations and deductions can be drawn.

"To consider social acts as things" was no doubt the most basic rule of all: because social acts really exist (their existence is manifested through their external and constraining characteristics), they must be approached with the observation and analysis methods usual to any science. The comparative method (or indirect experimentation) is therefore the method most apt to explain these acts. The ties between the subject and the object, however, (the sociologist being a social agent, too), make the scientific approach of social acts difficult. One must "systematically put aside all prenotions" that agents may have of reality and that hide it to them. Likewise, the specificity of the social acts, their autonomy from other realms of reality, forbid using any explanation that does not belong to the social world and, especially, to psychological or biological agents. In short, one must, as the saying goes, "explain the social with the social." Lastly, "to show why a fact is useful is not to explain how it came to be nor how it is what it is." This targeted Spencerian finalism: the social cannot be analyzed as the expected result of intentional individual behaviors, but rather as a spontaneous product (*sui generis*) of a mysterious alchemy (the "association") in which the parts contribute to a whole in which they dissolve to become a single dimension.

Thus the complete autonomy of sociology as a "natural" science of the social dimension of reality was solemnly stated. No matter that it may have digested the worst digressions of hypostasis, holism, determinism, and even solipsism (the accusation of "sociologism" from its detractors), this epistemology probably allowed the discipline to obtain the status of, if not a

science "as any other," at least a science that could aim to become so and, as such, one that might know an institutionalization to which the Durkheimian school greatly contributed. The dogmatism of the *Rules*, moreover, was transgressed by its own author, who did not hesitate in more relevant works (especially in the *Suicide*) and therein lies the value—to reach within the social agents to relate their behaviors and, consequently, the resulting macroscopic phenomena.

The Role of the Religious in the Social

With *Les Formes élémentaires de la vie religieuse*, his last work, Durkheim clearly went beyond the limits of his own *doxa* to deliver, as if a last message, his final vision of social reality. The thesis of the religious as a functional transfiguration of the social by its own actors (society does have "all it needs to arouse in the minds, through the sole action it has on them, the feeling of the divine; because it is to its members what a god is to his faithful.") is well-known: through religion, human beings revere their own society, without which they are nothing, and to which they therefore grant an authority they make sacred.

Today, if it still may be as difficult as it was then to see the work as an established fact of religious anthropology, it still holds, for the sociologist of knowledge, a "freshness" whose scientific virtues were detailed by Boudon (1999). These virtues, both methodological and theoretical, are many: they essentially are part of the capacity of the last Durkheimian program to allow a scientific knowledge of collective beliefs. Thus Durkheim would have won his wager to give a sociological answer to Kant's project and even beyond it because he extended Kantian problematic to all the categories through which we grasp reality. The category of "cause," however fuzzy it may be even in the most pointed sciences, has universally become a necessity because of its indispensable characteristic in any human activity.

For Boudon, the "continuist" hypothesis that was formulated and tested in the work is the most remarkable: continuity of the individual and the social, of religion and science, of human thought over time—whether that of the "primitive" or of the modern scientist. It is this hypothesis alone that allowed the sociologist to explain beliefs that he did not himself share. Inasmuch as he accepted that he could access the believer's reasons, no matter his social milieu, if he could reason with the same empirical data as the believer; the sociologist could indeed as Durkheim did in the *Forms*—give an account of beliefs in magic rites, the existence of the soul, ascetic practices, or the feeling of the sacred.

Durkheim's School

Durkheim worked tirelessly to impose his idea of sociology. His main tool was the journal *L'Année Sociologique*, which he founded with a core of carefully selected faithful (Mauss, Fauconnet, Hubert, Simiand, and Bouglé). The point was to move away from the superficial essays then in fashion in the field and to create a specialized and empirical body of knowledge, as well as to record and review the entire contemporary sociological literature. The school that was thus founded never stopped fighting against institutionalized French trends—such as the "inter-psychology" of Tarde, who was famous for his *Lois de l'Imitation* (Laws of Imitation, 1890), the collective psychology of Le Bon (*Psychologie des Foules*, [Psychology of Crowds] 1895), or the organicism of Worms, the founder of the *Revue internationale de sociologie*.

Durkheim's hegemonic intent radicalized the break with psychology (which moved toward biology) and the other social disciplines, which became subordinate to sociology. The incredible silence that followed the German works of Weber and, to a lesser degree, Simmel, would deprive French sociology of especially fecund theoretical and epistemological resources. French sociology would pay a dear price for this after the death of its leader, and it would have a hard time to renew its concepts and methods and, most of all, to reach beyond its national borders. Only by transgressing some of Durkheim's most formal interdicts would his successors (Halbwachs, Simiand, or Bouglé) help preserve the intellectual ideals and the school of the master between the two world wars. Still, it is quite remarkable that Durkheimianism remained ignored across the Atlantic—where it actually met its first and greatest success—in spite of some attempts at theoretical synthesizing that involved Durkheim thanks to Parsons (*The Structure of Social Action*, 1937) and the methodological reading of *Suicide* by the Columbia school.

Today, in spite of its role in the growth and institutionalization of the discipline, Durkheim's work follows an odd destiny: a key element in the academic baggage of any sociologist, cited and recited *ad nauseam*, it remains disparaged by the very same people it helped, especially in France, to gain recognition as scientists. In this respect, if sociology must blame itself and its own limitations and, most of all, the dogmatic manner in which it drew them, one must also deplore that the knowledge we have of it is often reduced to an outdated version.

CHARLES-HENRY CUIN

See also **Henri Bergson; Maurice Halbwachs; Jean Jaures; Marcel Mauss; Sociology**

Biography

Born in 1858 into a fully assimilated family of rabbis in Épinal in the Vosges region of France, Émile David Durkheim attended the *École normale supérieure* (School of Higher Education for Teaching) where he was taught by Fustel de Coulange, Boutroux, and Renouvier, and where he met Jaurès, Bergson, and Janet. After the philosophy agrégation (1882) and a few years spent teaching in various province high schools, he left to study in Germany, from where he brought back a dissertation on the state of philosophy and social sciences. On the faculty at Bourdeux, became a member of the agrégation jury as soon as 1891 and a tenured Professor of social science in 1896. He had great success with his students and was highly esteemed by his peers. He quickly attracted, beyond his own students, a learned audience whose members came from Bordeaux as well as from Paris, and among whom he would find his first disciples. In academia, the jurist Duguit and the historian Jullian were seduced by his scientific doctrine. Durkheim's local circle of friends seemed to have consisted mostly of his two philosopher colleagues, Hamelin and Rodier, who would always remain by his side The end of his life, during World War I, would be marked by painful personal attacks of an anti-Semitic nature and by the death of his son on the Serbian front. Durkheim died on November 15, 1917 in Paris.

Selected Works

De la division du travail social, 1893
Les Règles de la méthode sociologique, 1895
Le Suicide. Étude de sociologie, 1897
Les Formes élémentaires de la vie religieuse, 1912
Sociologie et philosophie, 1924
L'Éducation morale, 1925
Le Socialisme : sa définition, ses débuts, la doctrine saint-simonienne, 1928
L'Évolution pédagogique en France, 1938
Leçons de sociologie. Physique des mœurs et du droi, 1950
Textes, 2 vols., edited by V. Karady 1975

Further Reading

Alexander, Jeffrey (editor), *Durkheimian sociology: cultural studies*, Cambridge: Cambridge University Press, 1988

Aron, Raymond, *Les Étapes de la pensée sociologique*, Paris: Gallimard, 1968

Berthelot, Jean-Michel, *1895, Durkheim, l'avènement de la sociologie scientifique*, Toulouse: PUM, 1995

Besnard, Philippe (editor), *The sociological domain. The Durkheimians and the founding of French sociology*, Cambridge: Cambridge University Press, 1983

Borlandi, Massimo and Cherkaoui, Mohamed (editors), *Le Suicide. Un siècle après Durkheim*, Paris: PUF, 2000

Boudon, Raymond, "Les formes élémentaires de la vie religieuse," *L'Année sociologique*, vol. 49–1, (1999) p. 149–198

Cuin, Charles-Henry (editor), *Durkheim d'un siècle à l'autre. Lectures actuelles des 'Règles de la méthode sociologique,'* Paris: PUF, 1997

Lukes, Steven, *Emile Durkheim. His Life and Work. A Historical and Critical Study*, London: Penguin Press, 1973

Marcel, Jean-Christophe, *Le Durkheimisme dans l'entre-deux-guerres*, Paris: PUF, 2001

Pickering, William S. F., Martins, H. (editors), *Debating Durkheim*, London: Routledge, 1994

Steiner, Philippe, *La Sociologie de Durkheim*, Paris: La Découverte, 1994

DUVERT, TONY
Novelist

Tony Duvert first entered the public domain with the novel *Récidive* in 1967, attracted notoriety for his fifth, overtly pederastic, novel *Paysage de fantaisie*, which won the Prix Médicis in 1974, published his last novel (his eighth), the relatively light-hearted but equally pederastic *Un anneau d'argent à l'oreille* in 1982, and then fell silent, breaking that silence only once, in 1989. His three works of explicit theory are *Le bon sexe illustré* (1974), *L'enfant au masculin* (1980), and his *Abécédaire malveillant* (1989), but it is arguable that these texts need to be read against his novelistic practice because the forms of narration and the attitude to language that the latter reveal are reflections of the same value system that the theoretical works expound, in that they challenge traditional concepts of form and language and oblige the reader to undertake an active role in interpretation. Indeed, even the changing forms of the theoretical works themselves have a role in this exploration of the interplay of idea and expression, representing, as the three works do respectively, (1) a sexual manifesto ostensibly couched as an illustrated critique of the multi-volume Hachette 1973 *Encyclopédie de la vie sexuelle*, (2) an even more challenging critique of contemporary attitudes to gender and sexuality posing as a set of brief essays—"modest, humble, fragile things, raw expressions of opinion" as the authorial liminal note puts it, and (3) a final set of critical observations provocatively shaped as an alphabet book.

Duvert's work should be seen in the context of the progress of the movement for sexual liberation, which formed part of the political agenda of antiestablishment thinkers in the post–May 1968 period. The timing of the appearance of *Le bon sexe illustré* in 1974 was conditioned not only by the date of publication of the encyclopedia which it superficially targets but also by the growing profamily rhetoric of the Pompidou administration (seen as a sinister echo of Pétainiste values by the Left). Equally important was the fact that, under the influence of Guy Hocquenghem (who as a schoolboy had been the younger partner in a pederastic relationship with his teacher, the philosopher René Schérer), the manifestos of the militant *Front homosexuel d'action révolutionnaire* (1971–1974) included statements in favor of the sexual rights of minors and the recognition of the validity of intergenerational sexual relations, a position that commanded growing support from the liberal French intellectual community for the rest of the decade: the most notable examples appeared in 1971 in the periodical *Tout*, no. 12, a Maoist publication directed by Sartre, and the special March 1973 edition, entitled "Grande encyclopédie des homosexualités," of the review *Recherches*, edited by Felix Guattari. At the heart of this support, and of Duvert's texts, too, lies a view of sexual freedom as a prerequisite for, and symbol of, social liberation. Duvert's arguments in *Le bon sexe illustré* are coherent with Foucault's view that the sexual repression of minors was, like the hystericization of female sexuality, part of a strategy of social control: "Man is only exploitable if he produces something; the golden rule of a society based on exploitation will therefore be: everything should be productive. Sexual expenditure is the first form of expenditure to be restricted, because it is unproductive." (The aptness of the expenditure metaphor is easier to see if you remember the Victorian use of the verb "to spend" as a euphemism for having an orgasm.) Sex is only "productive" if it is *repro*ductive, that is, designed to produce more workers. Sex education therefore must be designed not to serve the desire of the student, but to limit and channel it, to insist on the submission of desire to one model, in the interests of a particular form of social order. Duvert uses the analysis of the principles concealed in the Hachette encyclopedia as a vehicle for attacking the family and marriage as institutions, parental power, and what he sees as the abusive and hypocritical way in which contemporary sex education actually seeks to deprive people of their natural sexual development and consequent potential pleasure. In basing himself on a specific text in this way, he emphasizes, as Foucault does, the role played by conventional discourses in constructing a thought-prison.

L'enfant au masculin, which develops the positions established in *Le bon sexe illustré*, deals more specifically with homosexuality in general and pedophilia in particular. If the channeling of desire into a single reproductive model is a central tenet of capitalist ideology designed to ensure the maintenance of order in all its forms, this by definition excludes nonreproductive sex, and in particular those forms of nonreproductive sex that also subvert other accepted hierarchies, such as generation and class. By 1980, when the book appeared, pederasty had been the subject of a series of high-profile nonfiction texts: notably, in 1974 René Schérer had published *Emile perverti*, in which he denounced the hypocrisy of the desexualized education that prevails in France and argued for the liberation of children's bodies, and in 1978 he published a further essay, entitled *Une érotique puérile*, in which he attacked the stupidity of laws that set up barriers between adults and children.

What distinguishes Duvert's work from these apologias for pederasty is that there is nothing apologetic about it. It is pure polemic. Starting from the statistic that fewer than twenty percent of French families were prepared to accept a homosexual child, and emphasizing the psychological and physical pressures to which the young male homosexual is exposed, Duvert explored, in a number of brief reflections on such key topics as the abuses of parenthood and the arbitrary limitations put on physical pleasure, what he sees as the central distorting force of contemporary society: heterocracy, that is, the compulsory imposition by society of a particular model of relationships on the natural and ungendered flux of desire. Although openly admitting his own status as a lover of prepubic boys (which places him outside the tacitly accepted French tradition of adult-adolescent male relationships in literature, as represented by André Gide), his plea is against the formulation of any one model of relations: "The aim of sexual liberation is not that everybody should or should not make love with everyone else: but that the State, its structures and its laws should refrain from any interference in private lives, regardless of age, gender or one's individual tastes. Sexualities do not fall into the sphere of public morality: that is the only principle that needs to be adduced."

The content of Duvert's third theoretical work, *Abécédaire malveillant*, adds nothing new to the range of his ideas as such, but its form adds a new set of implications to his position. Presented as an alphabet book and formulated as a series of maxims on the seventeenth-century French model (in itself an ironic swipe at the tradition of the *moralistes* and their pronouncements on ethical issues), Duvert stresses the rejection of system, the refusal to impose a particular model of thought or representation. For him, as for Barthes, the fragment is essentially a provisional form, adapted to preserving the individual response and more easily harnessed in eluding the temptations of conventional language than the longer essay. Hence, too, the many attacks in the volume on the limits of freedom of expression manifested in contemporary literature. Here, as in his novels, it is his aim to unmask both the immunity from criticism enjoyed by the "rules" to which the collectivity submits and the discourse that justifies that immunity, and in doing the latter he separates himself deliberately from the forms and language of the society that he attacks.

CHRISTOPHER ROBINSON

See also **Roland Barthes; André Gide; Felix Guattari; Guy Hocquenghem**

Biography

It is difficult to construct even the briefest outline of Tony Duvert's life because all evidence for it has been carefully concealed by Duvert himself. By his own account he was born in 1945. Between 1967 and 1982, he published eight novels. Since then, he published only one more, in 1989.

Selected Works

Paysage de fantaisie, 1974
Le bon sexe illustré, 1974
L'enfant au masculin, 1980
Abécédaire malveillant, 1989
Quand mourut Jonathan, 1978

Further Reading

Pinon, Laurent, "Tony Duvert, la persistance du lieu," in *La Parole vaine*, 7 accessible at www.atol.fr/lldemars/lestextes/pinon/pinduvert.htm
Robinson, Christopher, *Scandal in the Ink: Male and female homosexuality in 20th-century French literature*, London and New York: Cassell, 1995
Woods, Gregory, *A History of Gay Literature: The Male Tradition*, New Haven, Connecticut: Yale University Press, 1998

DUVIGNAUD, JEAN
Sociologist, Anthropologist, Essayist, Novelist, Playwright, Drama Critic, Theater Theoretician

A retired professor of sociology and a well-known chronicler in the left-leaning *Nouvel-Observateur*, Jean Duvignaud is renowned for his critique of structuralism. Like a number of important postwar French theorists (Roland Barthes, Jean Paris, Bernard Dort, Emile Copfermann), Duvignaud began his career as an enthusiast for popular theater as it took France's population by storm in the ten years following the Liberation. He was an important participant in the May 1968 social explosion, apparently the originator of the slogan: "Let's be realistic, and demand the impossible," and announcing (perhaps prematurely) the death of structuralism. However, his own theater writing was criticized for being about revolt and not revolution (Barthes 1956/1993), a distinction that characterizes much of his later sociological work.

Duvignaud is best known as sociologist, whose prolific publishing record has produced important work on Durkheim (1965, 1969), Gurvitch (1969), and sociological method (1966, 1972). His methodology is characterized by a strong belief in "sociological imagination," in which literature and the literary play an important role, although he avoids the excesses of structuralism in favor of a more pluralistic approach to society.

Appointed to a Lectureship in Sociology in 1960 at the University of Tunis, Duvignaud became fascinated with nomadism (real and intellectual). In 1962 he visited a tiny village in Southwest Tunisia, Chebika, where he carried out (what is now regarded as) a classic sociological study of change. Over four years he tested structuralist anthropological method and concluded that Lévi-Strauss's "parenté" model did not fit. His evidence in Chebika was that of wandering and expectation in the psyche of the local population, characteristics that undid any determinist or reductionist models of society. The results of his research (1968) display his use of interview and free expression by his subjects and betray his Maussian search for a "total" sociology. His overall conclusion is that decentralization, political and psychological, is the only future for a village trying to hold onto its traditions in the new independent Tunisia. This conclusion drew on his experience of the decentralization of popular theater that took place in France in the early 1950s, in which the encouragement of imagination and autonomy was meant to counteract the demotivation and passivity characteristic of cultural paternalism.

Indeed, Duvignaud's work was constantly linked to theater. Trying to avoid the distinction between "acteur" and "comédien," his historical sociology of the actor (1965), alongside his sociology of theater (1965)—his doctoral thesis, in fact—were to be a defining perspective in his future career, as they both illustrate his culturalist approach to social phenomena.

Having put forward a theatrical view of mass society as a stage (confirmed by the events of May 1968) and having rejected Lévi-Strauss's structuralist view of society (1973), Duvignaud produced a classic text of libertarian individualism, on the anomic as heresy and subversion (1973). In this post-1968 France of rupture and upheaval, the anomic is threatened, he argued, by the normalization brought about by generalization and/or reduction, evident, he claimed, even within Marxist thought. The study aims to find out where creativity comes from and how society always tends to neutralize all anomic features. Duvignaud's analysis works on the basis that not only is the subversive, the anomic, often a product of a particular moment in history when a society changes radically or fundamentally, but also it is an anticipation of a utopia. Duvignaud takes writers as actants (by definition anomic) who use their writing as a way of dealing with their anomic status. As examples, he takes nineteenth-century French literary characters—in Stendhal and Balzac—as well as German romantic playwrights—

Büchner, Kleist— relating their compositions to historical instabilities and ruptures. He theorizes the fates of the various individual characters within a Proudhonian, Babeuvian, and Nietzschean constellation, deploying of a critique of centralization. His analysis culminates in praise of the anomic personality of Louise Michel in the Paris Commune and in the libertarianism of a Durruti during the Spanish Revolution. Though not using the word *recuperation*, Duvignaud concludes by suggesting that society deals with its "anomies" today (such as Bataille and Artaud) by teaching them in University curricula.

At the same time his *Fêtes et civilisations* appeared, which places the carnivalesque in its global and historical dimensions (South America, the French Revolution, Nazi Germany, the Eastern Bloc, May 68, Nepal) and within an anthropological framework, considering the festival as a sublimation of death and sex. Then, as professor of sociology at Paris-VII (Denis Diderot), he moved in the midseventies into collaborative projects on mainstream sociological phenomena, working on youth (1975), dreams (1979), and France's taboos (1981).

A good example of Duvignaud's application of theater to sociology is his work on dreams and daydreams (1979). He takes those dreamers not covered by Freud (that is, workers and peasants) to find out how dreaming operates in different social strata (managers, office workers, manual workers, and so on, but also with young and old people), collected in free conversations and letters. The effects of the mass media on dream contents are also traced. Methodologically the aim in the study is not to normalize and structure our understanding of dreams, but to see how the dreamer deals with the big themes of life (hunger, sexuality, death, work) in the dream work. Then, more influenced by Winnicott than Freud, he looks at what society wants via people's dreams. The study comes to conclusions about the link between "jeu"—acting, game and play—and the content of people's dreams, and suggests that dreaming—both gratuitous and necessary—is a way of completing incomplete real lives, a way of escaping the determinisms and ideologies of daily life. This is typical of much of his work, which, in an anarchist libertarian fashion, celebrates and refuses to narrow the individual's creativity and acts of revolt in the face of strong social controls and determinants.

ANDY STAFFORD

See also **Roland Barthes; Georges Bataille; Emile Durkheim; Georges Gurvitch; Claude Lévi-Strauss; Marcel Mauss**

Biography

Born in 1921 Paris in modest circumstances, Jean Duvignaud came out of the Second World War as a cultural activist fascinated by theater. He was drama critic for the *Nouvelle Revue Française* and editorial board member of *Théâtre populaire* (writing monographs on Georg Büchner and Roger Planchon). A novelist and playwright, his *Marée basse* (1956) was produced by Roger Blin at the Noctambules. Influenced in the immediate postwar period by alternative forms of communism and the burgeoning area of French sociology as defined by Gurvitch, Friedmann, and Lévi-Strauss, he was also involved in left-wing movements and journals, especially around anticolonialism (Georges Balandier being a major influence here). He was a founding member, with Morin and Barthes, of the dissident New Left journal *Arguments* in 1956. His anthropological work on Chebika (Tunisia) in the 1960s was hailed as a new model of research (1968). His prolific sociological investigations in the 1970s made him an important, if overlooked, sociologist of modern culture. More recently he has turned his attention to notions of solidarity (1984, Dijon Academy prize 1989), laughter and the comic (1985 and 1999), and to memory (1995), all in tune with his original passion for theater. He has also republished and prefaced classics of anthropology (Bastide, 2000, and Freyre, 1992), and regularly published novels.

Selected Works

Durkheim, 1965
Sociologie du théâtre. Essai sur les ombres collectives, 1965, 1973
L'Acteur, esquisse d'une sociologie du comédien, 1965, 1973
Introduction à la sociologie, 1966
Sociologie de l'art, 1967, 1972, 1984; as *The Sociology of Art*, translated by Timothy Wilson, 1972
Chebika. Mutations dans un village du Maghreb, 1968, 1973 (new augmented edition 1990); as *Change at Chebika*, translated by Frances Frenaye, 1970

Gurvitch, 1969
E. Durkheim, *Journal sociologique*, preface by J. Duvignaud, 1969
Itinéraire de Roger Planchon, 1953–1964, 1970
Spectacle et société, 1971
Le Théâtre et après, 1971
La sociologie (dir.), 1972
Le Langage perdu. Essai sur la différence anthropologique, 1973
L'Anomie, hérésie et subversion, 1973
Fêtes et civilisations, 1974, 1984 (augmented edition, 1991)
La Planète des jeunes, 1975
Le Ça perché, 1976
Le Don du rien. Essai d'anthropologie de la fête, 1977
La Banque des rêves: essai d'anthropologie du rêveur contemporain (with F. Duvignaud and J.–P. Corbeau), 1979
Le Jeu du jeu, 1980
Les Tabous des Français (with F. Duvignaud and J.–P. Corbeau), 1981
Le Propre de l'homme. Histoires du comique et de la dérision, 1985
La Solidarité. Liens de sang et de raison, 1986
La Genèse des passions dans la vie sociale, 1990
L'Almanach de l'hypocrite. Le théâtre en miettes, 1991
G. Freyre, *Terres du sucre: Nordeste*, preface by J. Duvignaud, 1992
L'Oubli ou la chute des corps, 1995
Rire et après. Essai sur le comique, 1999
R. Bastide, *Le Candomblé de Bahia: rite Nagô*, introduced by J. Duvignaud, 2000

Further Reading

Arguments, 1956–1962, 2 vols., Toulouse: Privat, 1983
Barthes, Roland, "Sur *Marée basse* de Jean Duvignaud," in *Œuvres complètes*, 1, 1942–1965, Paris: Seuil, 1993, First published 1956
Consolini, Marco, *Théâtre populaire, 1953–1964. Histoire d'une revue engagée*, Paris: Editions de l'IMEC, 1998
Dosse, François, *Histoire du Structuralisme*, 2 vols., Paris: La Découverte, 1991
Stafford, Andy, "Dégel, Hegel and the Launch of *Arguments*," *French Cultural Studies* (October 1997): 283–294

E

EDUCATIONAL THEORY

A number of factors make understanding educational thought in France a challenge, especially when one is not familiar with the French system of education or with the politics of its institutions. Highly centralized by tradition, the French educational system has striven to remain "an encyclopaedic heartland" (McLean, 1990). In addition, there persists a serious lack of consensus on a terminology that would be common to all education specialists. A close examination of the field of education in France, its publications, and its institutions reveals five current domains of reflection: *science(s) de l'éducation*, *philosophie de l'éducation*, *pédagogie*, *didactique(s)*, and, more recently, *curriculum*. A description of these fields and a look at their genealogy reveal how they intersect, blend, and compete, each vying to develop its own identity and define its own specificity, while scholars work in more than one of these domains under more than one title.

Educational Science(s)

Ambiguity marked the beginnings of a search for a "science of education." From its onset, educational science was closely linked with philosophy, pedagogy, and psychology. In 1902, Durkheim distinguished himself by bringing a sociological approach to education. Under his influence, the Sorbonne position took the title of Sociology and Educational Science. After his death in 1917, the department changed it again to Social Economy, and Bouglé, a follower of Durkheim's, found himself in a position that no longer made

any reference to education. Those newly established university departments and courses would not survive World War I. Their specificity disappeared as they were either renamed or terminated.

These first efforts to develop a discipline identified as educational science had not included the creation of specific degrees. It was with a concern for institutional recognition that, in 1962, several projects were elaborated under the direction of Château, Debesse, and Mialaret. Although these projects did not materialize, they helped establish new certificates for philosophy and psychology undergraduate degrees. In 1966, following an increase in student population and discipline diversity, a different context was created by the "Fouchet reform." New projects were elaborated, and a title had to be agreed on, preferably under the label of "psycho-pedagogy" to give the notion of pedagogy an appearance of scientific legitimacy. A summary of these debates written by Debesse was published in 1966, titled *Projet de création d'une licence et d'une maîtrise de sciences de l'éducation*. It soon became the document of reference. For the first time, the term "educational sciences" was introduced in an official document and explained in great detail. A mandate from the Ministry of Education (February 11, 1967) finalized the creation of two programs: one leading to an undergraduate degree (*licence de sciences de l'éducation*), the other to a graduate degree (*maîtrise de sciences de l'éducation*). These degrees marked a definite break from the content of general pedagogy and its public. Applied linguistics and social and political economy were added to the fields of educational sociology, educational law, and comparative education mentioned in the 1966 project.

These changes indicated a concern with affirming not only the necessity of a plural scientific approach to education but also the need to broaden the notion of pedagogy toward a public of adults and beyond problems of educational practices.

Philosophy of Education

Many scholars believe that philosophical reflection is "more than ever necessary" in education. Most consider Reboul a leading figure in philosophy of education in France, notwithstanding his engagement with educational sciences. He created a program of philosophy of education in Montreal (1969–1975) and then at the University of Strasbourg (after 1975), where he also participated in the creation of the Unité de Formation et de Recherche (UFR) in educational sciences and became director of the educational sciences doctoral program. According to him, what philosophy brings is a method or, rather, a number of methods created by philosophers or borrowed or adapted from the scholars who preceded them, this choice itself philosophical. He described five methods he used: reliance on traditional doctrines, reflection on sciences, logical analysis, argument "a contrario," and dialectics.

Fabre believed that only the first type of approach, based on the history of philosophy, "come under a specific professional knowledge," with philosophy's three cardinal functions of epistemology, elucidation, and axiology guiding this reflection. However, the development of educational sciences brought into question the status and functions of a philosophy of education. Avanzini wondered whether philosophy of education and educational sciences are competitive or complementary, whereas Fabre believed that, "[t]he very fact of assigning a space [to philosophy in education] (Above? Next to it? In the margins?) must be questioned." Hadji argued that this philosophical questioning bears on legitimacy, and its criteria on values and the value of our values, in search of a fulcrum conceived as objective principle (Plato), reason (Kant), origin (Nieztsche), or originary (Husserl, Heidegger). According to Fabre, philosophy of education does not question the inadequacy of sciences or the imperfection of practices but, rather, the self-satisfaction or certainty of either when they believe they have found the solution or the answer. Such questions include What do we mean when we say we intend to form someone? (Fabre); What do we claim we do when we evaluate? (Hadji); To educate, what for? (Hocquard); On what do we pretend to found our authority as educators? (Houssaye); and What is worth teaching? (Reboul)

In the early 1880s, philosophers were at the origin of educational science (singular then): Although attempting to work pedagogy through applied psychology to create a science of education, they did so within philosophy. Based on such blurring of definitions, responsibilities, and domains, it is professors of philosophy who became professors of psycho-pedagogy in 1947, teaching general pedagogy, philosophy of education, child psychology, and social anthropology to future teachers. Again, in 1969, two years after the creation of the first departments of educational sciences, philosophers were asked to teach general pedagogy and the history of the doctrines of education. According to Houssaye, this is how philosophy of education became "the specialist of generalities" and how the role of philosophers in the programs of initial teacher education continues to be justified. As a consequence, unlike other traditional philosophical disciplines, philosophy of education has had some identity problems as to its place and the place of philosophers of education in French universities, exasperated by institutional constraints. This is evident in the lack of philosophy of education tenured positions in departments of philosophy, or even in departments of educational sciences, and in its restriction to teacher education. Therefore, in France, philosophy of education has not been very visible and has appeared to be treated, in Fabre's words, as "a minor occupation."

However, in 1998, philosophy of education found itself in the limelight when a new department was opened at the Institut National de Recherche Pédagogique (INRP) in Paris, immediately after the nomination of Philippe Meirieu as the new director of the INRP: the department of *Philosophie de l'éducation et pédagogie* (distinct from the department of *Sciences de l'éducation*), under the direction of François Jacquet-Francillon. When, after the demise of Claude Allègre, Minister of Education, Meirieu resigned from his position as director of the INRP in May 2000, a fierce debate had already been raging for several months through the daily *Le Monde* (e.g., September 8, 1999, and April 8, May 12, May 19, and June 22, 2000), the monthly magazine *Le Monde de l'éducation* (e.g., May, July–August, and October 2000), as well as in a number of books by Finkielkraut, Kambouchner, and Meirieu. Guibert discussed how it reawakened the ancient antagonism between "owners of knowledge" (i.e., university professors and researchers, working essentially in philosophy and the humanities) and "pedagogues" (i.e., researchers in sciences of education, historians, sociologists, and teachers).

Pedagogy

Pedagogy has always been the underdog in the field of education. In the introduction to a 1997 special issue of the *Revue Française de Pédagogie*, Forquin wrote, "pedagogy as thinking, as a mode and posture of thinking, seems to have recently come to being devalued." Pedagogy has a long history of being caught and torn between practical theory and empirical practice, and it is characterized in French by a highly inconsistent use of the term. Reboul pointed out that, from the beginning, an opposition has existed between "the content of education and its form, the matter to be taught and the manner to teach it." At times, the debate currently raging has taken a vicious turn as evidenced in books especially by Finkielkraut and Meirieu, and in articles published in the media by Blanchard, Dupuis, Finkielkraut, Guibert, Le Bars, Meirieu, and Prost.

Didactics

The term "didactics" came into common use relatively recently, especially in connection with specific disciplines, projecting a more modern image than does pedagogy, perceived as more traditional. The definition of didactics as "the art of teaching" found its way into dictionaries after 1955, but pedagogy had already been defined in those terms by, among others, Marion. Develay preferred to situate the emergence of the current brand of didactics (*la didactique*) in the 1970s as a reaction against educational sciences. In this perspective didactics viewed educational sciences as too disconnected from practical issues. In a 1990 article on the theory of conceptual fields, Vergnaud defined didactics as "the study of the teaching and learning processes pertaining to a particular domain of knowledge. . . . It rests on pedagogy, psychology, [epistemology] and of course the discipline studied. But," he added, "it cannot be reduced to that." Relying on psychology, pedagogy, and epistemology, didactics as a field is still striving to develop its own concepts and theoretical frameworks. The emergence of this brand of didactics had an effect on two levels: on institutions and programs in the *écoles normales*, and on professional development and career advancement of university professors and teacher educators.

In the 1970s, two main currents of thought developed out of the resurgence of didactics. Authoritative references to established scholars were sought, and two names were prominent: Bachelard, bringing the notions of epistemological obstacle and school epistemology to the field of didactics even before those terms were actually coined, and Piaget, toward whom didacticians turned for psychological references, his work on experience and exchange, and his notion of *conflit socio-cognitif*. Develay pointed to a paradox of some consequence in the didacticians' use of Piaget in as much as it enabled them to leave out the ethical aspect of educational thought and to introduce a positivist approach to their field of study. The second current of thought emerged at the intersection of social and cognitive psychologies, and it took two directions. In some didactics (e.g., sciences), the notion of representation or conception played a central role supported by social psychology. In other didactics (e.g., mathematics), the notion of representation was less important than the notions of didactic situation, didactic transposition, didactic contract, and the learning processes of diverse concepts (Vergnaud's work on subtraction and Richard's on mental activities). Within each discipline, discipline-specific didactics developed their own constructs. Yet one can identify a common trend: in all cases, focus is on learning and teaching contexts within the respective disciplines. Dissention, divergence, misunderstanding, or differences appear when addressing the functions of didactics, their objects, and the trends in research. Develay identified three different "attitudes": didactics of elucidation, didactics of injunction, and didactics of suggestion.

In addition, two schools of didacticians emerged in respect to the objects of their reflection. Some believe that, to create learning situations, there is no need to investigate content epistemology; only theories generally from the field of psychology are relevant (akin to psycho pedagogy as in Aebli and the psychological didactics based on Piaget's theories). Opponents of this approach believe that it is not possible to suggest learning situations without considering the epistemology of the content to be taught or learned. Using didactic transposition, didactic reconstruction, notions of paradigms, or disciplinary matrices, this kind of didactics no longer relies on psychology only. Develay underscored that these two positions are but the extremes of a continuum. He further noted that the borders of didactics are still not clear. Didacticians consider that the specificity of the contents is determinant to explain success or failure, whereas pedagogues focus on the relations in the classroom among students and between students and teachers. The controversy played out between these two positions, brought to caricature-like extremes, is at the heart of one of the most virulent debates as reported by Guibert in *Le Monde*.

Didactics are said to offer a new approach to thinking education precisely through their relations to contents and through identifying themselves as discipline specific, but not everyone agrees. A clarification of the question of didactics' relation to knowledge was attempted from four standpoints: psychoanalysis, sociology, epistemology of school learning, and the anthropological dimension of the relation to knowledge. Develay believes that scholars in the field of didactics still need to resolve some serious problems. They claimed to be not merely designing methods to teach some given content with a maximum of efficiency but also aiming to understand the relation of the student to knowledge and to establish ethical precepts issued from that comprehension. Develay emphasized that, to achieve these goals, they still have a lot of research to do, especially on questions of anthropology, epistemology, logic, and ethics.

Curriculum

Recently, educational thought has further developed around the concept of curriculum. However, in France, this work takes place mostly outside education. In fact, curriculum issues have been addressed mostly indirectly and essentially by sociologists and historians. Forquin stressed the semantic problems around the word *curriculum* in a French context where the terms *programme d'études* or *plan d'études* are more frequently used, though with different meanings. Following the English common use of the word *curriculum*, he posited that it "implies taking into consideration the whole course of studies and not just one aspect or one stage considered separately." In this context, he considered that it raises two major questions: "the issue of educational coherence between the various forms of content, the various subjects taught, and the different learning experiences included in a course of study"; and "the issue of educational progression . . . over a given period of time." In the study of curriculum, he also suggested including "what students are actually taught," which may be different from the prescribed syllabus; "the underlying content of teaching or of school environment," acquired—albeit unwittingly—in a school context, and "the cognitive and cultural dimension of education." On the basis of these aspects of educational thought, Forquin "deem[s] that the curriculum issue should be at the center of any thinking and any theory of education." Furthermore, the question of curriculum coherence and relevancy, raised by Durkheim earlier in the century, is, according to Forquin, "one of the main strands of present thinking about curriculum in France." A report presented to the French Ministry of Education in 1989 by Bourdieu and Gros supports this point and indicates that it has been a constant problem through the years—one that continues, Forquin notes, to feed current debates if not conflicts between the proponents of "an encyclopaedic ideal aiming at rationality, universality, and fairness and [the proponents of] the new requirements for flexibility, individuality, and usefulness."

Another important line of investigation in curriculum comes from French-speaking Switzerland. In 1984, Perrenoud suggested a distinction between the intention to instruct, as laid out in programs, study plans, and formal curricula, and the actual experiences of the learners, the actual curriculum. In a more recent analysis, in 1993, he revisited his constructs of formal and actual curricula and added a third concept, the

hidden curriculum, well known in Anglophone literature. In France, Isambert-Jamati and Grospiron followed up on Perrenoud's line of inquiry with some empirical research, and other scholars carried out similar investigations on formal and actual curricula, but at different levels (e.g., Dannepond and Plaisance in preschool, and Demailly in middle school). The relationship between students and the curriculum has also been an object of research as reported by Charlot, Bautier, and Rochex. Linked to the concept of curriculum, some current concerns are specifically analyzed, such as evaluation (Mitterand, Thélot), and the notion of proficiency (Ropé and Tanguy). Ropé and Tanguy showed that these factors all contribute to putting pressure for a greater focus on behavioral objectives and measurable outcomes, thereby calling for a restructuring of curricula.

Forquin saw the emergence of didactics and some work done in this field as "a major breakthrough in French thinking about curriculum." The concept of didactic transposition formulated by Chevallard in 1985 is useful to understand some major issues in curriculum, in particular the gap between original knowledge (learned or acquired by future teachers in university courses) and school knowledge (what teachers are able to teach in their classrooms). Forquin discussed constraints on "the morphological and stylistic features of the discourse" in textbooks and classrooms and at the "epistemological level." In France, he saw "a whole trend of research" trying to identify "the route taken by knowledge" "from laboratory to classroom" (Grosbois, Ricco, and Sirota) or the specific elements of "school epistemology" (Astolfi and Develay).

Forquin declared that "[n]ew prospects are now open for a sociological research more directly centered on curriculum issues and more cogently linked to other research fields such as the history of education, cognitive psychology, or didactics." If in France there is indeed a reflection on curriculum, it is still, in Forquin's words, "very scattered," and as of this writing it is still a long way from being anywhere close to organizing itself into a "unified and structured field of study."

Current Debates and Contemporary Issues

Throughout the years, neither the ambiguity among terms and the concepts they carry nor the antagonism among their respective proponents have abated, as evidenced by controversies aired in the media, especially *Le Monde* and *Le Monde de l'éducation*, and argued by Avanzini, Barthelmé, Beillerot, Finkielkraut, Froment, Caillot, Roger, Houssaye, Kambouchner, and Meirieu. In this web of meanings, educational sciences, philosophy of education, pedagogy, didactics, and curriculum all contribute to thinking and understanding education, and pedagogy appears as a common link, although all other educational areas have repeatedly tried to deny it, reject it, or devalue it while trying to appropriate it.

The field of educational sciences seems, in turn, to present itself as containing all other areas of educational studies, where pedagogy, philosophy of education, didactics, and now curriculum would be subsets. Because the complexity of the phenomenon (i.e., education) to be analyzed cannot be reduced to a simple and unidimensional explanation, some scholars, such as Plaisance and Vergnaud, believe that an internal pluridisciplinarity would be the key to gaining this unity; however, this approach does not satisfy all researchers. Despite the enduring vocabulary and semantic "ambiguities, uncertainties, epistemological metissage" Charlot denounced, most French scholars agree that any reflection on education rooted in, and enriched by, research from the sciences would remain insufficient if not misleading if it did not engage in a specific analysis of the ends and values of education.

The same factors that make understanding education in France a challenge—a highly centralized system, traditional encyclopedic approach to knowledge, and lack of consensus on terminology—explain why it is also closely linked to French political life and vulnerable to political upheavals and why its debates and controversies can arouse passions that play out in the public forum through popular media before unfolding in books. In an article published in the daily *Le Monde*, Prost summarized the recent developments in the debates around some current issues in education. Especially virulent following the demise of Claude Allègre, articles were published by a panel of over 100 teachers, researchers, and writers; by Bourdieu and Christophe; and by Finkielkraut. Prost strongly emphasized that such a debate would be better served by a work of research and analysis characteristic of academic scholarship, rather than by "diatribes" and "rhetoric, empty of meaning."

Beillerot acknowledged that "the expressions educational sciences and pedagogy"—and one may add philosophy of education, didactics, and curriculum—are not interchangeable as one would believe when reading certain texts; they are not "univocal, because they cover different realities, and have different uses." However, whether the names of educational specialists, departments, or degrees are changed within the institutions, the questions remain fundamentally the same. When considering the same issues, each different perspective throws a different light on the given problem, and each contributes different elements to a better knowledge and understanding, each substantially enriching the others. Each lights up a different facet of the possible approaches to thinking education.

DENISE EGÉA-KUEHNE

See also **Gaston Bachelard; Pierre Bourdieu; Emile Durkheim**

Further Reading

Ardoino, J., and G. Vigarello, "Identité des sciences de l'éducation," in *L'état des sciences sociales en France*, edited by M. Guillaume, Paris: La Découverte, 1986

Avanzini, G., *Introduction aux sciences de l'éducation*, Toulouse: Privat, 1987

Avanzini, G., "Les déboires de la notion de pédagogie," in *Penser la pédagogie*, special issue edited by J.-C. Forquin, *Revue Française de Pédagogie*, 120 (1997). 17–24

Barthelmé, B., *Une philosophie de l'éducation pour l'école d'aujourd'hui*, Paris: L'Harmattan, 1999

Beillerot, J., "Sciences de l'éducation et pédagogie: un étrange manège," in *Penser la pédagogie*, special issue edited by J.-C. Forquin, *Revue Française de Pédagogie*, 120 (1997): 75–82

Bertrand, Y., "Expérience et éducation," in *Éducation et philosophie. Approches contemporaines*, edited by J. Houssaye, Paris: Éditions Sociales Françaises, 1999

Bouveresse, R., ed., *Éducation et philosophie: Écrits en l'honneur de Olivier Reboul*, Paris: Presses Universitaires de France, 1993

Charlot, B., ed., *Les sciences de l'éducation: un enjeu, un défi (Rapport CORESE)*, Paris: Éditions Sociales Françaises, 1995

Debesse, M., and G. Mialaret, *Traité des sciences pédagogiques*, 1st edition, 6 volumes, Paris: Presses Universitaires de France, 1969

Develay, M., ed., *Savoirs scolaires et didactiques des disciplines*, Paris: Éditions Sociales Françaises, 1995

Develay, M., "Origines, malentendus et spécificités de la didactique," in *Penser la pédagogie*, special issue edited by J.-C. Forquin, *Revue Française de Pédagogie*, 120 (1997): 59–66

Égéa-Kuehne, D., "Understanding Education in France: A Multifaceted Approach to Thinking Education," in *Handbook of International Curriculum Research*, edited by W. F. Pinar, Mahwah, New Jersey: Lawrence Erlbaum Associates, 2003

Fabre, M., "Conclusion. Qu'est-ce que la philosophie de l'éducation?" in *Éducation et philosophie*, edited by J. Houssaye, Paris: Éditions Sociales Françaises, 1999

Finkielkraut, A., *Une voix qui vient de l'autre rive*, Paris: Gallimard, 2000

Forquin, J.-C., "The curriculum and current educational thinking in France," *The Curriculum Journal*, 6,2 (1995): 199–209

Forquin, J.-C., "Argument," in *Penser la pédagogie*, special issue edited by J.-C. Forquin, *Revue Française de Pédagogie*, 120 (1997): 5–6

Gautherin, J., "La science de l'éducation, discipline singulière," in *Les sciences de l'éducation: un enjeu, un défi*, edited by B. Charlot, Paris: Éditions Sociales Françaises, 1995

Gautherin, J., *Une discipline pour la république*, Berne: Peter Lang, 2001

Hadji, C., "La philosophie de l'éducation, un luxe inutile," in *Pour une philosophie de l'éducation*, edited by H. Hannoun and A.-M. Drouin-Hans, Dijon: CNDP-CRDP de Bourgogne, 1994

Hocquard, A., *Éduquer, à quoi bon?* Paris: Presses Universitaires de France, 1996

Houssaye, J., *Autorité ou éducation?* Paris: Éditions Sociales Françaises, 1996

Houssaye, J., "Spécificité et dénégation de la pédagogie," in *Penser la pédagogie*, special issue edited by J.-C. Forquin, *Revue Française de Pédagogie*, 120 (1997): 83–97

Houssaye, J., ed., *Éducation et philosophie: Approches contemporaines*, Paris: Éditions Sociales Françaises, 1999

Kambouchner, D., *Une école contre l'autre* Paris: Presses Universitaires de France, 2000

Marion, H., "Pédagogie," in *Dictionnaire de pédagogie*, edited by F. Buisson, Paris: Hachette, 1911

Marmoz, L., *Les Sciences de l'éducation en France, histoire et réalités*, Issy-les-Moulineaux: Éditions EAP, 1988

McLean, M., *Britain and a Single Market Europe: Prospects for a Common School Curriculum*, London: Kogan Page, 1990

Meirieu, P., *La pédagogie entre le dire et le faire* Paris: Presses Universitaires de France, 1995

Meirieu, P., *Lettres à quelques amis politiques sur la République et l'état de son école* Paris: Plon, 1998

Mialaret, G., "La création des sciences de l'éducation," in *30 ans de Sciences de l'Éducation à Paris V*, edited by M. Froment, M. Caillot, and M. Roger, Paris: Presses Universitaires de France, 2000

Morandi, F., *Philosophie de l'éducation*, Paris: Nathan, 2000

Perrenoud, P., "Curriculum: le formel, le réel, le caché," in *La pédagogie: une encyclopédie pour aujourd'hui*, edited by J. Houssaye, Paris: Éditions Sociales Françaises, 1993

Plaisance, É., and G. Vergnaud, *Les sciences de l'éducation*, Paris: Éditions La Découverte, 1999

Reboul, O., *La philosophie de l'éducation* Paris: Presses Universitaires de France, 1989a

Reboul, O., *Les valeurs de l'éducation*, Paris: Presses Universitaires de France, 1989b

Vergnaud, G., "La théorie des champs conceptuels," *Recherches en Didactique des Mathématiques*, 10,2.3 (1990): 133–170

ELLUL, JACQUES
Sociologist, Theologian

Jacques Ellul was an eccentric and thoroughly dialectical thinker: A thoroughgoing iconoclast, Ellul always emphasized "the positivity of the negative" (Hegel). He was a sociologist, legal scholar, and historian of institutions; at once an anarchist writer and a lay theologian in the French Reformed tradition. He made contributions to a wide variety of fields including communication theory, legal history, political science, theology, biblical studies, and Christian ethics.

Ellul is perhaps best known for his book *La technique, ou, l'enjeu du siécle* (1954, *The Technological Society*). This book is much less about technology than about technique, "the totality of methods rationally arrived at and having absolute efficiency in every field of human activity" (p. xxv). Although rational methods are not new in the twentieth century, Ellul argued that the relationship between technique and society has changed such that technique (of which "technology" is but one element) becomes the governing principle of society, especially since the Second World War. Technique has progressively enveloped all spheres of society from the state, economy, education, and science to religion, sex, and life itself. In the technological society, the primary environment for human beings is no longer nature, or even history, but the artificial and rational world made by and for technique. All the problems that human beings now face are technical problems: not only are they the result of technical "advances" (such as environmental degradation, nuclear war, and state administration of human life) but the only discourses that are permitted as responses are technical. In this world of Technique, the means and ends are indistinguishable, and efficiency becomes the sole criteria.

For Ellul, the Modern State (enveloped by Technique) is both more powerful than ever and totally impotent. As Ellul argued in *L'illusion politique* (1965, *The Political Illusion*), it is more powerful because of the efficiency of modern administrative State techniques (taxation, regulation of education, vaccination, and weapons of minor and mass destruction) and fortified by the technical capabilities of propaganda (*Propagandes*, 1967). It is at the same time totally impotent to make any substantive change of direction, which is to say anything that is not facilitated and mandated by the dictates of technique. Thus, when François Mitterand was elected in 1981, Ellul wrote an article in which he claimed that nothing had changed. Although Ellul shared many of Mitterand's socialist values, he had always been deeply skeptical that anything revolutionary (i.e., any significant change of direction) can be accomplished through the mechanisms (democratic or not) of the State.

A change (revolution or conversion) is desperately needed, and yet, as Ellul argued, violent revolutions typically simply replace the functionaries of the state without really changing the direction of the society (*Histoires des institutions*, 1955–1956). Although sympathetic to those who commit violence against the state (he himself admitted that he once contemplated placing a bomb under the Paris *Bourse*), he was totally opposed to violence on moral and pragmatic grounds. The revolution that Ellul espoused entails consistently saying "No" to power, a refusal of power dedicated to forming alternate grassroots communities of resistance and mutual aid. Although Ellul was an anarchist, it is the anarchist project that he espouses, rather than the anarchist *telos* (of the good society without a State), which he did not believe could ultimately be achieved (*Anarchie et Christianisme*, 1988 [*Anarchy and Christianity*]).

Similar to his sociological writings, Ellul's theology is thoroughly dialectical, again with an emphasis on the negative. He was committed to the Church, but he often found himself saying "No" to the Church for its complicity with power. He believed in a theology of "confrontation" whereby he opposed the Word of God to the Church and argued that the Church should be in confrontation with the World. Because of its experience of the "Wholly Other," the Church must say "No" to power and live as a symbol that a radically different life can be lived, a life characterized by freedom rather than by servitude. Christians are citizens of the Other Kingdom, which does not mean abandoning "the world" but, rather, participating actively in it as ambassadors, with the freedom of those whose citizenship lies elsewhere (*Présence au monde moderne*, 1948 [*Presence of the Kingdom*]).

Ellul never claimed to be a philosopher (of religion, or of anything else). He was reticent to engage in speculations about God—the "Wholly Other"—because these tend to treat God as if God were merely another object to be submitted to the technical probing of a technological society. Ellul argued that although we cannot know anything about God, God reveals Godself to humans—not in power, but in nonpower: in the poor, the marginalized, the suffering, and especially in the Word of God (Jesus) and in the testament to the Word (the Bible). This is why Ellul devoted so much of his intellectual energy reading the Bible and provoking a confrontation between the Bible and the Church. Ellul was no fundamentalist, and he felt no need to read scripture literally, but he typically provided what he sometimes called "naive" readings, rather than delving into the methods of "higher criticism" (to which he was nonetheless not opposed). He was always preoccupied with the big picture, preferring to speak of the Bible as a complex and diverse message rather than as a series of smaller messages. For Ellul, this message was that of "God for me," although not to the exclusion of anyone else. The Word of radical grace is inconsistent with anything but a hope in universal salvation, and he often quoted Karl Barth, saying, "You have to be crazy to teach universal salvation but you are impious if you do not believe it" (*What I Believe, Entretiens*).

Ellul's relation to the French intellectual scene was often distant, and he drew his primary sociological and theological inspiration from German-speaking thinkers (Karl Marx and Karl Barth). As a student, however, Ellul became committed to the Personalist movement, (best known through the writings of Emmanuel Mounier, whom Ellul knew). Ellul began to develop a local variant of this movement before he ultimately broke with the movement, criticizing Mounier for being too exclusively Roman Catholic. One can nonetheless see a continuing Personalist influence on Ellul's thought, as well as on his mode of personal and political involvements right up until the end of his life.

Although Ellul does have a following in France, his work has proved much more influential among North American dissidents. His sociological writings on the technological society, although often seen as overly "determinist," have been influential for a diverse set of scholars and critics, including Ivan Illich, Lewis Mumford, and Christopher Lasch. Anarchist (or anarchist leaning) activists often find in Ellul's work a source of inspiration and analysis; the most infamous of these is the "Unibomber" (Theodore Kaczynski), whose "Industrial Society and Its Future" (*Washington Post*, Sept. 19, 1995) shows a misplaced debt to *The Technological Society* (1967). Ellul's theological writings have left their mark on a number of neo-evangelical intellectuals (such as Vernard Eller and David Gill), as well as on Christian peace and justice activists, including William Stringfellow, Jim Wallace, and Daniel and Phillip Berrigan. A number of friends and admirers have formed the International Jacques Ellul Society/Association Internationale Jacques Ellul and have published a journal, *Ellul Forum*, twice a year since 1988.

ANDREW M. MCKINNON

Biography

Jacques Ellul was born in 1912 and raised in Bordeaux, where he was to spend most of his life. His family was poor but deeply committed to aristocratic values. Although he wanted to join the navy, his father urged him to study law, and he earned his doctorate with a dissertation on "The History and Legal Nature of the *Mancipium*" (the right of fathers to sell their children). Until 1940, he taught law at Montpellier, Strasbourg, and then Clermont-Ferrand, when he was dismissed from his post by the Vichy government because his father was a "foreigner" (his father was from Trieste and had Austrian and British Citizenship). Ellul then moved to the village of Martres, where he farmed potatoes and participated in the Resistance, transporting Jews to safer locations.

Refusing to take advantage of his social capital as a member of the Resistance, Ellul did not pursue a more prestigious academic position in Paris after the war, largely because he remained deeply committed to the city of Bordeaux and its people. After a brief stint as Deputy Mayor of Bordeaux, he returned to academic life, teaching law and politics at the University of Bordeaux until he retired in 1980. A prolific writer, he was also an inspiring teacher and always engaged as a public intellectual. He participated actively in the ecological movement and the Committee for the Defense of the Aquitaine Coastline; he organized a club for "maladjusted" youth (which in fact worked on the premise that it was society, not the youth, that was maladjusted). He was active for more than half a century in the Reformed Church in France. Ellul died in 1994.

Selected Writings

Le fondement théologique du droit, 1945; as *The Theological Foundation of Law*, translated by Marguerite Wieser, 1969

Présence au monde moderne: problèmes de la civilisation post-chrétienne, 1948; as *Presence of the Kingdom*, translated by Olive Wyon, 1951

La technique, ou, l'enjeu du siècle, 1954; as *The Technological Society*, translated by John Wilkinson, introduction by Robert K. Merton, 1967

Histoire des institutions, 5 volumes, 1955–1956

Propagandes, 1967; as *Propaganda: The Formation of Men's Attitudes*, translated by Konrad Kellen and Jean Lerner, 1965

Contre les violents, 1972; as *Violence: Reflections from a Christian Perspective*, translated by Cecelia Gaul Kings, 1978

L'illusion politique, 1965; as *The Political Illusion*, translated by Konrad Kellen, 1967

Sans feu ni lieu: Signification biblique de la Grande Ville, 1975; as *The Meaning of the City*, translated by Denis Pardee, 1970

L'Apocalypse: Architecture en mouvement, 1975; as *Apocalypse: The Book of Revelation*, translated by George W. Schreiner, 1977

With William H. Vanderburg, *Perspectives on Our Age: Jacques Ellul Speaks on his Life and Work*, translated by Joachim Neugroschel, 1981

Ce que je crois, 1987; as *What I Believe*, translated by Geoffery W. Bromiley

Anarchie et Christianisme, 1988; as *Anarchy and Christianity*, translated by Geoffery W. Bromiley

With Patrick Chastanet, *Entretiens avec Jacques Ellul*, 1994

With Patrick Didier Nordon, *L'homme à lui même: correspondance*, 1992

Further Reading

Chastenet, Patrick, *Lire Ellul: Introduction à l'oeuvre socio-politique de Jacques Ellul* Bordeaux: Presses Universitaires de Bordeaux, 1991

Clendenin, Daniel B., *Theological Method in Jacques Ellul*, Landham: University Press of America, 1987

Christians, Clifford G., and Jay M. Van Hook, eds., *Jacques Ellul: Interpretive Essays*, Urbana: University of Illinois Press, 1980

Gill, David, *The word of God in the ethics of Jacques Ellul*, Metuchen, New Jersey: ATLA and The Scarecrow Press, 1984

Hanks, Joyce Main, *Jacques Ellul: A Comprehensive Bibliography*, Greenwich, Connecticu: JAI Press, 1984

Hanks, Joyce Main, *Jacques Ellul: an annotated bibliography of primary works*, Stamford, Connecticut: JAI Press, 2000

Holloway, James, *Introducing Jacques Ellul*, Grand Rapids, Michigan: Wm. B. Eerdmans, 1970

Lovekin, David, *Technique, Discourse and Consciousness: An Introduction to the Philosophy of Jacques Ellul*, Bethlehem, Pennsylvania: Lehigh University Press, 1991

Vanderberg, William H., *The Growth of Minds and Cultures*, Toronto: University of Toronto Press, 1985

EXISTENTIALISM

Although the intellectual sensibility to which it refers already had a long and distinguished pedigree, it was only in post–World War II France that existentialism transcended philosophical and literary circles to become a full-blown cultural movement. The reason for this phenomenon is not difficult to discern. During the Nazi occupation of France, which was facilitated by the collaboration of many of France's leading citizens, even the most seemingly innocuous actions could have life-and-death consequences. Under these highly pressurized conditions, France became a kind of social laboratory within which, it seemed, the basic structures underlying human existence—crudely, what Heidegger called "existentials"—were more starkly revealed in everyday life. The public mood that these conditions fostered, moreover, did not dissipate in the war's aftermath, but was reinforced by virtue of a painful national self-examination, the use of the atomic bomb, and the burgeoning cold war. Existential themes—even though grasped only intuitively by many who spent a fair bit of their time at the café talking about "the meaning of life"—were the cultural fare of the day.

It was in this context, appropriately enough, that the term "existentialism" itself was first coined by Jean-Paul Sartre, who was, nevertheless, leery of it. And although, in addition to Sartre, such French thinkers as Gabriel Marcel, Maurice Merleau-Ponty, Simone de Beauvoir, and Albert Camus were also deemed existentialists, all of them sought, in varying degrees, to distance themselves from the label. Still, because all of these thinkers were motivated by a concern for the individual's plight in the modern age, which is the conventional hallmark of the longstanding intellectual sensibility to which the term "existentialism" came to refer, it is not unreasonable to speak of them as existentialists. And, because the distinctive intellectual commitments that they shared were motivated by the particulars of both the French philosophical tradition and the sociohistorical conditions through which they were living, it is not unreasonable to speak of French existentialism as a unique philosophical phenomenon.

Although, perhaps, to a somewhat lesser degree, French existentialism, like its non-French antecedents, is a rejoinder to Western rationalism, which, historically, has expressed itself in the dominance of the scientific paradigm, or, more pejoratively, scientism. Thus, although science's experimental style sharply contrasted with Church dogma, in supplanting Christianity as an all-encompassing worldview, science itself became the reigning dogma. The substantial benefits conferred by science's objectifying, universalizing, systematizing methodology were not without substantial costs, however. Objectification engendered a crisis of meaning. Dispossessed of an underlying telos, the world and all that is in it (including, ultimately, human beings) came to be seen in stripped down material terms, as mere objects to be manipulated. So, too, universalization, which is reflected in science's drive to find fewer laws to encompass more diverse phenomena, found its social expression in mass society and the bureaucratic state. Paradoxically, then, although Western rationality is theoretically in the service of "the individual," it tends, practically, to give the individual short shrift.

This phenomenon finds philosophical expression in René Descartes's "First Philosophy," in which the *cogito* is set over and against a now alien world. The immediate impetus for existentialism, however, was G. W. F. Hegel's "systematic philosophy," which animated the concerns of Soren Kierkegaard and (via Arthur Schopenhauer) Friedrich Nietzsche, the putative fathers of existentialism. In response to Hegel's "science of experience," which culminates in "Absolute Knowing," Kierkegaard and Nietzsche emphasized the irreducibility of personal experience. In response to Hegel's emphasis on the ethical community, which culminates in "the State," Kierkegaard and Nietzsche attacked what they called "herd mentality" and "slave morality," respectively. Finally, most generally, in response to Hegel's emphasis on Spirit (crudely, the human collective), Kierkegaard and Nietzsche emphasized "the individual." The strongest influences on French existentialism, however, were not Kierkegaard and Nietzsche, but rather Edmund Husserl and Martin Heidegger. Indeed, in some sense, French existentialism represents the attempt to synthesize the most prominent features of their respective philosophies, many of which are at odds. Siding with Husserl against Heidegger, the French existentialists (in varying degrees) continued to believe in the primacy of consciousness, which resonated with their deeply ingrained Cartesian commitments. Conversely, siding with Heidegger against Husserl, they rejected the wholly immanent, disembodied nature of the transcendental ego, which hearkens back to the *cogito*, as well as the classical epistemological orientation of Husserl's Cartesian-inspired phenomenology, in favor of seeing all philosophical inquiries as always already enmeshed within the horizon of our worldly concerns.

The French existentialists' preoccupation with Cartesianism, which had found its most recent expression in Husserl's philosophy, belies the commonly held belief that existentialism—at least in its French manifestation—was merely a reaction against Western rationalism. To the contrary, although they rejected the substantialist metaphysics that underlies Cartesianism, as well as Husserl's account of consciousness comprehending the objects of experience in their ideality through a transcendental reduction, the French existentialists more or less accepted the Cartesian duality of consciousness and world. However, with the exception of Marcel, who embraced a "theistic existentialism,"

they either refused recourse to God or argued, at least implicitly, that such recourse could not obviate the crises of meaning and knowledge that Descartes's dualistic metaphysics had engendered, but that his proof of God's existence had supposedly repaired.

This problematic is reflected in Camus's essay *The Myth of Sisyphus*, in which he reconstitutes Kierkegaard's notion of "the absurd." On the one hand, Camus argues that "the absurd" results from our rationality, which leads us to demand a coherent explanation from a universe that is indifferent to our plight. This is in sharp contrast to Kierkegaard's rendition of "the absurd," which refers to the paradoxes that arise for the understanding in connection with a being that is both human and divine. Indeed, for Camus, recourse to God, who plays such a pivotal role for Kierkegaard and Descartes because He mediates the relation between consciousness and the world (even if only negatively), is nothing less than philosophical suicide. On the other hand, by contending that Sisyphus's plight is emblematic of the absurdity of the human condition, Camus is implicitly suggesting that even if questions concerning God and, for that matter, our mortality are bracketed, "the absurd" would not be mitigated. Sisyphus, it will be recalled, had been condemned by the gods to eternally roll a boulder up a mountain, for the gods believed that futile, repetitive labor was among the worst forms of punishment. On this account, "the absurd" arises from a Schopenhauerian awareness that our labors and concerns, that the *Sturm und Drang* of life, all add up to nothing. For Camus, there are two possible responses: to scorn and defy our fate, which smacks of the sort of life-denying *ressentiment* that Nietzsche and Kierkegaard had criticized, or to throw yourself into your life's projects, to live in the moment. This second, more life affirming, option belies the outside or "objective" perspective that Descartes's duality breeds. It repairs the breach, though arguably at the cost of reflection.

There is, accordingly, a line of thought within the existentialist tradition that suggests that reflection and *ressentiment* are closely aligned, if not inextricably intertwined, and that they are so to the detriment of life itself. In *The Present Age*, Kierkegaard asserts that envy is the "unifying principle" of reflection, and that it gives rise to "moral *ressentiment*," which "hinders and stifles all action." And, in *Twilight of the Idols*, Nietzsche draws parallels between ancient Greek reflection and the Socratic diagnosis that life (even if it is examined) is not worth living, as is reflected in Socrates's dying declaration that "to live . . . means to be sick a long time: I owe Asclepius a rooster." Less pejoratively, the main character in Sartre's first novel, *Nausea*, declares, "you have to choose: live or tell." Certain recent interpretations concerning the nature and scope of reflection notwithstanding, this "either/or" is too simplistic and is arguably directed only at the pretenses of a certain kind of reflection. The claim that experience is infinitely rich and that reflection impoverishes, falsifies, or even precludes it is no more justified than the claim that experience is infinitely poor and that it is only reflection that enriches it.

In two of Camus's novels, *The Stranger* and *The Fall*, the logic of these extremes is played out. The chief protagonist in *The Stranger*, Meursault, is, in the first half of the book, an extraordinary example of a nonreflective consciousness. Written in a sparse style designed to mirror the sparseness of Meursault's consciousness, it is a phenomenological account of a nonreflective consciousness that lives in the moment. However, what Meursault's example teaches is that without reflection, experience is as impoverished as his atomized, emotionless account of it suggests, and that the alleged innocence of a nonreflective consciousness, of Rousseau's noble savage, as it were, is a fundamentally misguided piece of nostalgia. Without deliberation, and under conditions that at best only raise the specter of self-defense, Meursault kills an Arab in French colonial Algeria, and is put on trial. At this point, which is when he becomes reflective, and thereby self-conscious, he comes to realize, much like Joseph K. in Kafka's *The Trial*, that we are all guilty—not in a juridical or even moral sense, but in an existential one. As Heidegger would say, Meursault comes to realize, as he develops self-consciousness, that by virtue of being human, he is "fallen." The chief protagonist in *The Fall*, Jean-Baptiste Clamence, in contrast, is nothing but the self-consciousness of this "fallenness." Formerly a celebrated lawyer living the high life in Paris, Clamence, who had no apparent flaws, was wholly undermined by innocuous events, thus suggesting our own susceptibility. Indeed, the novel, set in a grimy bar in the dreary Red Light district of Amsterdam (suggesting the inner circle in Dante's *Inferno*), involves Clamence's cynical attempt to seduce the reader into recognizing his own existential guilt. Trapped in the prison house of his own reflection, and without any life to speak of, Clamence's *ressentiment* plays out in an all-consuming desire to judge. Subverting the biblical injunction not to judge so as to avoid judgment, Clamence, a self-styled "judge-penitent," judges himself in the harshest possible terms to give himself an unimpeachable standpoint from which to judge.

Sartre gives a more systematic expression to many of these concerns in his philosophical works. Given the absence of God, he argues in "Existentialism is a Humanism," there is no human essence; or, as he famously puts it, "existence precedes essence." Sartre's notion, simply put, is that there is nothing "essential" about us, and that we make ourselves through our choices. However, given the ungrounded nature of these choices, which results from our ultimate inability to found ourselves, he states in *Being and Nothingness* that "man is a useless passion." This twist on the theme of "the absurd" plays out in what Sartre calls the "fundamental" project of human beings, namely, the unobtainable desire to be (as we conceive of) God. This abstract, universal desire, which finds its concrete expression in every individual, refers to the desire to be both essential, that is, self-identical, and absolutely free. Crucially, however, although for Camus "the absurd" is a psychological sensibility, for Sartre it is merely an ontological given. Camus's sensibility is but one way that we might freely choose to comport ourselves in the world, given that we cannot avoid positing values despite the fact that we can found neither ourselves nor absolute values toward which we should strive.

Our inability to found ourselves or to be self-identical, Sartre contends, is the result of the fact that consciousness is always already beyond "the self." Extending and transforming Husserl's notion of "intentionality," namely, that all conscious states are about some object, Sartre argues that consciousness itself is insubstantial (or, as he puts it, "nothing"), and that "the self" is an object for it. We are thus estranged from ourselves. What's more, "the self" is contested terrain insofar as it is not in consciousness, but rather is out in the world, where it is constituted not only by consciousness but also by the limiting "facts" and other people. To use the Hegelian categories that he appropriates and reconfigures, "the self" is a construction of the interaction between being-for-itself, being-in-itself, and being-for-others, respectively. With his notion of being-for-others, Sartre expresses philosophically what Camus implicitly conveys in *The Fall*, namely, that human beings seek in various ways to dominate one another in the attempt to bolster their own self-conceptions. This portrayal of selfhood draws on Hegel's master–slave parable in the *Phenomenology of Spirit*, but with one key difference: although, for Hegel, the battle for recognition is ultimately overcome, as human beings increasingly come to recognize themselves in one another, for Sartre there are no higher-order syntheses. Because of his conception of consciousness, namely, his Cartesian position that consciousness is always beyond the facts and others, not to mention its very own "self," ultimate reconciliations with others are impossible. This also sharply contrasts with Heidegger's view of social relations as a "being-with," which, Sartre claims, is facilitated by Heidegger's unnuanced rejection of the Cartesian *cogito*.

Because consciousness or being-for-itself is always beyond both the facts (being-in-itself) and what other people try to make of it (being-for-others), as well as "the self" that it constructs in conjunction with these other two aspects of being, we are free. Indeed, given Sartre's ontological commitments, we are, as he graphically puts it, "condemned to be free." With this freedom, which, he argues, is "absolute," comes an absolute responsibility for not only everything that we do but also for the world itself. Sartre's point, although hyperbolic, is that it is only through our projects that we constitute a world, as our most basic choice of ourselves, which is free and gives rise to our projects, is what orients us within the world as an initial matter. Without such an orientation, indeed, the world would be a blooming, buzzing confusion. This absolute freedom to choose the way in which we comport ourselves within the world, which should not be confused with practical freedom, that is, the freedom to obtain what we desire, is something that we usually hide from ourselves. Drawing on Kierkegaard and (to a lesser extent) Heidegger, Sartre argues that acknowledging this freedom to comport ourselves in the world as we choose induces anxiety, and that we almost always flee this uncomfortable insight in bad faith: it is only though a "purifying" reflection that we can come to grasp the exigencies of our irreducible freedom. However, what induces this type of reflection (unlike its counterpart, an all but ubiquitous instrumental or "accessory" reflection), and how it relates to the seeming necessity of having an initial orienting project (which seems to ineluctably lead to bad faith), are questions that Sartre does not answer.

This emphasis on the inextricable relation between freedom and responsibility, which, in Sartre's case, is engendered by a neo-Cartesian conception of consciousness, as well as the experience of the German occupation (when even mundane choices could have deeply negative consequences), is, perhaps, the distinctive feature of French existentialism. As Camus's Clamence declares in *The Fall*, "freedom is not a reward or decoration . . . [but] a long distance race, quite solitary and very exhausting." Similarly, in *The Rebel*, Camus asserts that one who rebels in the name of freedom must do so in a responsible spirit of self-sacrifice. This reflects the recognition of a prior commitment to others in terms of understanding our freedom, and it is a recognition that Merleau-Ponty shares. Although he endorses many of Sartre's commitments with respect to freedom, as his references to Sartre's account of freedom in his own magnum opus *Phenomenology of Perception* attest, Merleau-Ponty saw Sartre's notion of freedom, and indeed his overall philosophy, as a bit too Cartesian. In his own account of freedom, Merleau-Ponty emphasizes its embeddedness in a network of human relations: "We are involved in the world and with others in an inextricable tangle [that]

rules out absolute freedom at the source of our commitments, and, equally, indeed, at their terminus." Freedom here is at least as much a matter of identification as it is transcendence.

Like Sartre, Merleau-Ponty worked out his thought in the interregnum between Husserl's and Heidegger's philosophies. More than Sartre, however, Merleau-Ponty is concerned with working out the implications of Husserl's phenomenology in terms of classical epistemological questions concerning perception. However, in addition, as indicated, he is, more than Sartre, concerned with moving away from a Cartesian-cum-Husserlian conception of consciousness as standing over and against the world of its experience. This had also been Heidegger's chief concern: it had induced him to refer to human beings as *Dasein* (being-there) and to describe human existence as a being-in-the-world. What mediates these two commitments for Merleau-Ponty, and, indeed, leads him to go beyond both Husserl and Heidegger, is "the body." Sartre, too, had contended in *Being and Nothingness* that the body is one with consciousness, and that it is our point of departure on the world, but it is Merleau-Ponty who explores the insight. In particular, according to Merleau-Ponty, prereflective bodily perception is the ground on which all subsequent knowledge arises.

The French existentialists, in contrast to their predecessors in the existentialist tradition, were also unique in terms of the richness of their ethical and, especially, political commitments. After *Being and Nothingness*, Sartre attempted to work out an existentialist ethics, but deemed his efforts a failure and therefore chose not to publish his work in this area. De Beauvoir, however, sought to make good the project. In *The Ethics of Ambiguity*, she attempts to show that Sartrean freedom presupposes a commitment to the freedom of others, and, furthermore, that to speak of "freedom" abstractly—that is, without giving it content through our actions—is, invariably, to falsify it. (Along similar lines, in *The Second Sex*, one of the seminal works in feminist thought, de Beauvoir argues that there is no abstract, eternal "feminine," but rather a sociohistorically produced femininity that must be understood within its concrete situation.) Accordingly, it is on the plane of the concrete that de Beauvoir considers the ethical failures of certain archetypal subjectivities, which she juxtaposes with the tensions inherent in an existentialist ethics. Distancing herself from both Camus's notion of "the absurd," which suggests that existence cannot be given a meaning, and the hypostatized meanings of historical materialism, de Beauvoir argues that an existentialist ethics is one of ambiguity. In response to the antinomies intrinsic to both action (using violence against violence) and inaction (leaving the existing violence in place to avoid doing violence), it counsels a thoroughgoing consideration of how the dialectical relation between means and ends will play out within the concrete situation in which action is being contemplated.

Pointing to the French resistance (in which the French existentialists all participated), de Beauvoir suggests in *The Ethics of Ambiguity* that, from a theoretico-political standpoint, the negative attitude of resistance is easy compared with the attempt to posit substantive ends. This insight was borne out as to the French existentialists themselves. Camus and Sartre split over Camus's book *The Rebel*, in which Camus attacks not only the Soviet Union under Stalin but also the pretenses of Hegelian-Marxist philosophy itself, which, he asserts, can be used to justify any heinous action. So, too, although an erstwhile communist who had mentored Sartre on political issues, Merleau-Ponty and Sartre split over Merleau-Ponty's positions in such books as *Humanism and Terror* and *The Adventures of the Dialectic*, in which he not only attacks communism's "objectivistic" conception of history and Sartre's "subjectivistic" philosophy but also sees convergences between the two. In response, Sartre produced *Search for a Method* and his mammoth *Critique of Dialectical Reason*, in which he attempts to break up the ossified structures of the materialistic dialectic with existentialism. Rejecting historical materialism's reliance on both an ontological macrosubject and an ultimate totalization, Sartre tries to show how human beings freely aggregate in an attempt to remake the history that has made them.

DAVID SHERMAN

See also **Simone de Beauvoir; Albert Camus; Gabriel Marcel; Maurice Merleau-Ponty; Jean-Paul Sartre**

Selected Writings

Camus
The Fall, translated by Justin O'Brien, 1991
The Myth of Sisyphus, translated by Justin O'Brien, 1991
The Plague, translated by Stuart Gilbert, 1991
The Rebel, translated by Anthony Bower, 1991
The Stranger, translated by Matthew Ward, 1989

De Beauvoir
Memoirs of a Dutiful Daughter, translated by James Kirkup, 1959
The Ethics of Ambiguity, translated by Bernard Frechtman, 1994
The Mandarins, translated by Leonard M. Friedman, 1991
The Second Sex, translated by H. M. Parshley, 1989

Merleau-Ponty
The Adventures of the Dialectic, translated by Joseph Bien, 1973
Humanism and Terror, translated by John O'Neill, 2000
Phenomenology of Perception, translated by Colin Smith, 1962

The Visible and the Invisible, translated by Alphonso Lingis, 1968

Sartre
Anti-Semite and Jew, translated by George J. Becker, 1974
Being and Nothingness: An Essay in Phenomenological Ontology, translated by Hazel E. Barnes, 1956
Critique of Dialectical Reason, Volume I, translated by Alan Sheridan-Smith, and *Volume II*, translated by Quintin Hoare, 1991
"Existentialism is a Humanism," translated by P. Mairetin *Existentialism*, Robert C. Solomon (ed) 1974
Nausea, translated by Lloyd Alexander 1964
Search for a Method, translated by Hazel E. Barnes, 1968
The Emotions: Outline of a Theory, translated by Bernard Frechtman, 1975
The Transcendence of the Ego, translated by Forest Williams and Robert Kirkpatrick, 1990

Further Reading

Works on Camus
McBride, Joseph, *Albert Camus: Philosopher and Littérateur*, St. Martin's Press, 1992 New York
McCarthy, Patrick, *Camus*, Random House, 1982 New York
O'Brien, Conor Cruise, *Camus*, Fontana, 1970 London
Sprintzen, David, *Camus: A Critical Examination*, Temple University, 1988 Philadelphia

Works on de Beauvoir
Bergoffen, Debra, *Gendered Phenomenologies, Erotic Generosities: The Philosophy of Simone de Beauvoir*, SUNY Press, 1996 Albany, NY
Lundgren-Gothlin, Eva, *Sex and Existence: Simone de Beauvoir's* The Second Sex, Athlone, 1996 London
Simons, Margaret A., ed., *New Feminist Essays on Simone de Beauvoir*, Pennsylvania State University Press, 1995 University Park, PA

Works on Merleau-Ponty
Edie, J. M., *Merleau-Ponty's Philosophy of Language, Structuralism and Dialectics*, University Press of America, 1987 Lanham, MD
Madison, G. B., *The Phenomenology of Merleau-Ponty: Search for the Limits of Consciousness*, Ohio University Press, 1982 Athens, OH

Works on Sartre
Aronson, Ronald, *Jean-Paul Sartre: Philosophy in the World*, New Left Books, 1980 London
Barnes, Hazel, *Sartre*, J. B. Lippincott, 1973 London
Caws, Peter, *Sartre*, Routledge & Kegan Paul, 1979 London
Danto, Arthur C, *Sartre*, Fontana Press, 1991 London
Flynn, Thomas, *Sartre and Marxist Existentialism*, University of Chicago Press, 1984 Chicago
Howells, Christina, ed., *The Cambridge Companion to Sartre*, Cambridge University Press, 1992 Cambridge
Jeanson, Francis, *Sartre and the Problem of Morality*, translated by Robert V. Stone, Indiana University Press, 1980 Bloomingham

McCulloch, Gregory, *Using Sartre*, Routledge, 1994 London

Schilpp, Paul Arthur, ed., *The Philosophy of Jean-Paul Sartre*, Open Court Publishing Co., 1981 La Salle, Ill.

Generally

Descartes, René, *Meditations on First Philosophy*, translated by Donald A. Cress (Indianapolis: Hackett Publishing Co. 1993)

Hegel, G. W. F. *Phenomenology of Spirit*, translated by A. V. Miller (Oxford: Oxford University Press 1977)

Kierkegaard, Søren. *The Present Age and two minor ethico-religious treatises*, translated by Alexander Dru and Walter Lowrie (London: Oxford University Press 1962)

Nietzsche, Friedrich. *Twilight of the Idols*, translated by Walter Kaufmann in *The Portable Nietzsche*, Walter Kaufmann (ed) (New York: Viking Press 1954)

F

FANON, FRANTZ
Psychiatrist, Writer, Ambassador

What is remarkable about Frantz Fanon is that his life and career stand at the crossroads of many intense and engaging challenges. He served as a psychiatrist in French colonial hospitals, was a writer, and ended up an ambassador in the Provisional Algerian Government during the war of liberation. He was born a Frenchman from Martinique and died in Washington, D.C., as an Algerian citizen. Nevertheless, it is in his writings that Fanon has had a profound influence as both a political figure and an intellectual in the field of social sciences. Although he did not leave a major opus, his three main works, *Peau noire, masques blancs* (1952), *L'An V de la révolution algérienne* (1959), and *Les Damnés de la terre* (1961), mark a fundamental shift in the analyses of colonial systems and the way they were founded, perceived, and eventually questioned.

After he volunteered for World War II, for which he was awarded the Croix de Guerre, Fanon enrolled in medical school at the University of Lyons. Then, in 1951, he earned his doctorate in psychiatry. The essential question that was to initiate his quest and subsequent fight against France's colonial system can be summed up as: What does racism do to people? Going beyond Césaire, for whom racism was instrumental in the reification of the subject, Fanon developed his own argument with the notion of "objectification" (*Peau noire*). He debunked Western humanism and its values by suggesting that colonialism aims at dehumanizing the native. Fanon's attack on racism and colonialism became a case he witnessed firsthand in his daily work as a physician to Algerians, as well as in the political atmosphere of the post–World War II anticolonial movements. He identified several degrees in the process of dehumanization of the colonized: infantilization, denigration, distrust, ridicule, exclusion, rendering invisible, scapegoating, and violence. However, the most thorough form of oppression according to Fanon was to force the native to accept his or her own objectification. It is against such positions and trends that he advocated social-therapy in the Blida psychiatric hospital, where the current doctrine was that Algerians were too intellectually and emotionally immature to grasp the benefits of European civilization (*Manuel alphabétique de psychiatrie* [1952], authored by Fanon's own work colleagues: Aubin, Bardenat, Porot, and Sutter). Fanon's discourse was not just revolutionary, it was new altogether.

Unlike many French intellectuals of the time—Lévi-Strauss, Althusser, and above all Sartre—Fanon's vision and program of decolonization rested on what he called a "complete disorder" (*Les Damnés*). Although Western Marxist thinkers found many reasons to dispute the values of the Enlightenment, Fanon carried out the consequences of the anticolonial discourse against the essential and hegemonic features of Western culture as such. The dialectical emphasis on social, economic, and psychological forms of alienation was not historically conditioned along the means of production but was exposed in the principles of both racial and cultural inequalities. It is such a contention that Fanon tried to transcend. Although France pushed for a universal Western model for all humanity in its colonies, he opposed resistance as violent as it was urgent while the Algerian war of liberation was unfolding (*L'An V de la révolution algérienne*). That was a major break from the stance of the intellectuals of the *négritude* movement (Césaire, Damas, and Senghor), who invited the working classes of Europe to join in the struggle of the black people. In 1956, Fanon resigned from his position of *médecin-chef* at the Blida hospital. He became a steady contributor to the underground newspaper, *El Moudjahid*, though he never signed any article with his name. The *je* pronoun he used in *Peau noire* was transformed into an inclusive *nous*, as if to secure a new humanism that would only be fulfilled through revolution by the oppressed peoples.

In the summer of 1961, while he was terminally ill, Fanon met with Sartre in Rome. The former had denounced the French intellectual star of the time for failing to consider the psycho-existential effects of racism on the Black subject (*Peau noire*). Yet in his own reflections, all along his works and years of political commitment, Fanon reached the same positions as Sartre's: *négritude* was irrelevant in its search for the past (African cultures, roots, and so on), and actions and demands needed to be oriented toward the future. Both Sartre and Fanon agreed that Western culture and its humanism formed an ideology divided against itself and that the colonized were paying the price for it. In less than three months, Fanon wrote his most militant book (*Les Damnés*) and naturally asked Sartre to preface it. Fanon's strong political positions were probing in two main respects: nationalism and revolution. Yet the supporting claim was that of a theory of liberation with its own praxis, as Fanon had become an active member of the FLN. From a regressive state, the "wretched" were to turn the table on their tragedy and take hold of progress. In the objective reality of violence (physical, cultural, and economic), Fanon refused to equalize matters. For the colonizer, violence was a threat; for the colonized, it was a situation in which he or she had been living for too long.

Fanon's concept of political denomination was naturally to reject the idea of a Third World to espouse the notion of a third way, refuting both capitalism and Marxism. However, his intellectual choice rested on socialist principles (*Les Damnés*). The trouble with Fanon's formulations of revolution and socialism was that they arose from the conflict itself, not from a program for a postcolonial society. In *Les Damnés*, he underscored his own misgivings with the idea of a single party leading the newly liberated people. Yet the end of colonial oppression meant first of all the destruction of the system and then the constitution of a national entity. Violence was positive so long as it was that of the colonized against the colonizer. Achieving

freedom or a "new humanity" (*Les Damnés*) not only invoked the possibility for a new order but also came with an ethical counterpart about the legitimacy of violence. Fanon believed that violence was coextensive to the concept of national identity. Only struggle and ultimate victory could lead to the advent of new values because it put an end to the cultural separatism fostered by the colonial system. The revealing input of violence was its unifying power.

Fanon's account of a struggle purported to provide a new understanding of man free of overdeterminations. That was also a reason he criticized any longing for precolonial traditions. These were antithetical to the trends of history (*Les Damnés* and *L'An V de la révolution*). His concept of a national identity was thus conditioned by the idea of universal opening and international cooperation. Whereas Sartre sought to leap beyond the vindication of history in terms of race and class, Fanon refused the communist plan for a bourgeois transitory society before the recently independent people could implement socialist principles. Based on the experiences of young nations (Congo, Ghana, Tunisia), he sensed that any bourgeois settlement brought about a degradation of national unity, economic regression, and finally, antidemocratic regimes (*Les Damnés*). No wonder that Fanon enthusiastically agreed with the resolutions of African liberals (Cotonou, 1958) who called for the creation of an African Community of Socialist States. In this juncture nationalism coincided with the idea of national identity as such but also presupposed an ideological frame for the control of all national means of production and distribution. With an almost Hegelian flourish, Fanon oversimplified Marxian levels of meanings of history and its materialism. He underlined the dangers of neo-colonialism by, for instance, keeping at the head of state a bourgeois class educated and trained by the former colonial power, but his socialist models were too entrenched in a normative consciousness of confrontation.

What Fanon called "an atmosphere of battlefield" (*Les Damnés*) was in fact the state of independence of the new nation. Its underlying implications posit the negation of a negation of what colonialism meant. Moreover, to come out of that condition, the party of the revolution had to take the lead not as a supreme authority but, rather, as an instrument in the hands of the free people. That is where, according to Marxist thinkers, Fanon erred because he advocated pure and simple decentralization of power. He contended that socialism as such (i.e., from the Soviet bloc) could not apply to the situation of new and underdeveloped countries. In his conclusion of *Les Damnés*, when Fanon calls on his brothers from colonized nations to leave Europe, he does not underscore any particular difference between capitalist Europe and the communist one. Another basis for Fanon's disillusionment was that European working classes had been too often complicit or silent in the face of the aggravating system that was colonialism. Although Fanon debunked the so-called universal laws of the market on the one hand and Marxist science on the other, he strove to find a solution within the nonaligned movement. The basis for his reflection was that if national social structures were different, the revolutionary process had to be as well, although the inevitability of the revolution was never put into question. Thirty years later, the breakdown of communism and several nationalistic conflicts have proved Fanon right. To succeed, socialism has to respect identities and the people's free will.

Fanon can be considered the key thinker of what could be dubbed the colonial situation. He was also an actor in that historical moment known as decolonization. It is from this unique context that Fanon's work takes its power and originality. Following suit on his reflection, revolution, nationalism, and socialism become obsolete because colonialism can only be solved when two nations come to terms with their own national identities. The trick would be to eliminate ethnocentric presuppositions that put the West in opposition to the rest of the world and also that keep the two concepts of nationalism and socialism inside the fold of Europe. Yet Fanon's great inspiration lies in the foundation of a new humanism. It soars above the temptation of national fundamentalism and the belief in an all-powerful state. One may question his idealistic positions on harmonious class relations—especially with working class and peasants—on the power of the revolution, or on his trust of a single-party regime. In the same regard, Fanon's distrust for traditions and culture, as well as his support for an all-out violence in times of national liberation, entail the notion that his theories needed perhaps to get past intuition and anger. Sadly enough, the situation of Algeria (for which he fought) since its independence shows that aspirations for peace, social equality, economic well being, and justice have been burdened by something too well known: repression and corruption. However, Fanon only promoted a new humanism, not a new man, and he therefore cannot be blamed for the failures of postcolonial nations. As his writings are still very popular in Western academe as well as among the Third World country elite, they prove that Fanon is topical, if not entirely right.

FARID LAROUSSI

See also **Louis Althusser; Aime Cesaire; Claude Levi-Strauss; Jean-Paul Sartre; Leopold Senghor**

Biography

Frantz Fanon was born July 20, 1925, in Fort-de-France, Martinique. In 1939–1940 he studied at the Lycée Schoelcher, working under Aimé Césaire during his last year. He joined the Free French Forces in 1943–1945. In 1945, Fanon was awarded the Croix de Guerre for outstanding courage in action. In summer of 1946, he worked for Césaire's election campaign. During 1946–1951, he attended medical school in Lyons, and in 1951, he earned a doctorate in psychiatry. He published *Peau noire, masques blancs* in 1952. In 1953, he became médecin chef at the Blida-Joinville hospital, Algeria, and in 1956, he resigned his post. In 1957, he was expelled from Algeria and joined the FLN. In 1959, he narrowly escaped assassination and published *L'An V de la révolution algérienne*. In 1960, Fanon became permanent Ambassador to Ghana for the Provisional Algerian Government. In 1961, he published *Les Damnés de la terre*, prefaced by Sartre. Fanon died of leukemia on December 6, 1961, in Washington, D.C., and was buried in Algeria.

Further Reading

Cherki, Alice, *Frantz Fanon, portrait*, Paris: Le Seuil, 2000
Dacy, Elo, ed., *L'Actualite de Frantz Fanon: Actes du colloque de Brazzaville*, Paris: Editions Karthala, 1986
Gibson, Nigel, ed., *Rethinking Fanon: The Continuing Dialogue*. Amherst, New York: Humanity Books, 1999
Gordon, Lewis, *Fanon and the Crisis of European Man*, New York: Routledge, 1995
Macey, David, *Frantz Fanon: A Biography*, New York: Picador, 2001
Sekyi-Otu, Ato, *Fanon's Dialectics of Experience*, Cambridge, Massachusetts: Harvard University Press, 1996

FEBVRE, LUCIEN PAUL VICTOR
Historian

Although he did not himself produce any great work of history, Lucien Febvre changed the course of historical writing in France. His achievement was in the realm of historical method, rather than in that of historical writing. His books were inclined to be brief, his chapters to be self-contained essays (and sometimes straight reprints or adaptations of already published review articles), and his broader conclusions to be vulnerable.

Febvre's achievement was to show that the social sciences were all fundamentally historical and inseparable from one another. It was an approach to history that was long overdue, and he enunciated it with such skill and verve, and with such a wide-ranging selection of examples, that it immediately attracted a large a group of adherents among professional historians. Its promotion was institutionalized in what became in 1929 the *Annales: économies, sociétés, civilisations*. Among the most important fruits of Fevre's historiographical insights are the works of Fernand Braudel and the enduring influence of the *Annales*.

The paradox is that he demolished forever the possibility of segregation between different historical disciplines, and between historical investigation and other disciplines, whether in humane studies or in the social sciences, but that his own greatest successes as a historian were achieved through the minutiae of conventional historical analysis. Febvre did not really prove, for example, that rationalist atheism could not have existed in France in the age of Rabelais (*Le Problème de l'incroyance au XVIe siècle: la religion de Rabelais*, 1942), although he was right that it did not, but he did prove that an important confusion in the dating of the second edition of Marguerite de Navarre's *Miroir de l'âme péchéresse* resulted from a failure to distinguish "new style" dating, which starts the year from 1 January as it still does today, and "old style," which had not completely disappeared by the mid-sixteenth century and that dated the start of the year from Easter.

Febvre's methodology has its own antecedents, notably in Dilthey's concept of *Geistesgeschichte* (*Einleitung in die Geisteswissenchaften*, 1883), itself coined from Friedrich von Schlegel, as put into practice by cultural historians like Burckhardt and Wölfflin. However, successful practitioners remained rare, primarily on account of the vast amounts of evidence cultural history demands from what are still for practical reasons a vast range of disparate and traditionally segregated academic disciplines. Burckhardt and Wölfflin, however immense their historical importance and stimulating their insights, each wrote, similar to the literary critic H. A. Korff, a form of history dominated by philosophies that have had to be abandoned. Febvre himself, who for preference defined his positions under the stimulus of points of view expressed by other scholars that he could not himself wholly accept (*Au cœur religieux du XVIe siècle*, 1957), despite prodigious amounts of intelligent reading and an engagingly conversational dialogue tone, came for lack of specialist forms of knowledge to important historical conclusions that are not sustainable.

It is not, for instance, true that the successes of the French reform movement in the sixteenth century depended solely, or even chiefly, for its defining characteristics on the vernacular Bible and on justification by faith ("Les origines de la réforme française et le problème des causes de la réforme," *Revue historique*, 1929). Later studies, inspired by Febvre's own methodological thinking, have shown that, however important these elements were, the successes and failures of the reform movement in France depended also, and more, on other constraints, including a still-perceived need for a national religion and the possibility that the spirituality and even the creed of the reformed church in France was doctrinally compatible, certainly until 1535, with communion with Rome.

Febvre's work on Rabelais is, perhaps inevitably, spiritually sensitive, perceptive to literary nuance, and deeply knowledgeable about the cultural background. However, he fails to observe how an obtusely reactionary Roman curia, at the crucial moment dominated by Eck, virtually showed Luther how the wedge he was quite slowly driving between the order of grace and a hierarchically dependent sacramental order led to the necessary repudiation of the divine institution of Rome as the primatial see of the Christian church. The bestowal of indulgences, which Luther was at first easily able to countenance and justify, did in fact rest on the papal presumption that it might at its discretion dispense a pool of merit, the *thesaurus ecclesiae*, made available to it by virtue of the direct bestowal by divine institution of primatial status on the Roman see. However invaluable in detail Febvre's own work on the French reformation undoubtedly was, the historical synthesis that emerged has wrong notes and false harmonies.

The methodological breakthrough does not depend on its application by Febvre himself, even in his chosen *locus* for its justification, a refutation of the accusation that Rabelais was a religious scoffer rather than a thoroughgoing Erasmian. It remains intact. Its weakness, not wholly overcome even by Braudel, is that the true object of historical research, the *mentalités*, has to be limited, because the evidence on which it depends is so immense and so diverse. Febvre's own publications show how the integration of the disciplines into a unified study of cultures proceeded. Step by step, starting with contributions to Henri Berr's *Revue de Synthèse* and the 1911 study of the "Political, Religious, and Social History" of Franche-Comté and Philip II, an ambitious but still relatively manageable topic. After World War I, in which he served in the army, Febvre was appointed first to a lecturership at Strasbourg, where with Marcel Bloch he founded what was at first known as the *Annales d'histoire économique et sociale*, and then in 1933 to a chair at the Collège de France. By then he had published in 1922 the more programmatic *La Terre et l'évolution humaine: introduction géographique à l'histoire* and the 1928 *Martin Luther: un destin*.

Febvre's major work on *Le Problème de l'incroyance au XVIe siècle* and his essays on Marguerite de Navarre, *Autour de l'Heptaméron*, were published during World War II, after which he was himself to found the sixth section of the *Ecole Pratique des Hautes Etudes* and to publish the two volumes of essays, *Combats pour l'Histoire* and the posthumous *Au cœur religieux . . .*, collected by Fernand Braudel. Throughout Febvre's career, his historical insights are remarkable, no doubt partly because of the attention he paid to human psychology and, especially, mass psychology and to the cultural ambiance in which human individuals and societies were formed and within and on which they operated, so difficult to seize and define, but nonetheless so powerful a force acting on them. It is primarily for the systematic definition of his methodological aims, however, that Febvre deserves a major place among great modern French thinkers.

ANTHONY LEVI

See also **Marc Bloch**

Biography

Lucien Paul Victor Febvre was born in Nancy in 1878. He fought in World War I. After returning from the war in 1920, he took a teaching post at the University of Strasbourg. In 1929, he cofounded the influential journal *Annales: économies, sociétés, civilisations* with Marc Bloch. Febvre died in 1956.

FEMINISM

A form of identity politics, feminism in twentieth-century French thought is, in a general sense, an examination of the concept "woman" in an effort to understand, reveal, or subvert sexist practices. Similar to other branches of political thought based on an identifiable group, for which it is an early model—for example, Gay Studies, African-American Studies, and the like—feminism immediately poses the problem of essentialism and calls for an understanding of "woman" that is not specific: How to discuss "woman" in all her contradictions and complexities without fixing sexual identity in overly rigid definitions. Often hostile to feminist ideas, as examples from texts, the law, and institutions make clear from the Middle Ages to the twentieth century, French society has frequently viewed "woman" in essentializing, oppressive ways and systematically discriminated against her. Although a discussion of the hostile environment seems to emphasize the male, this focus is necessary for an understanding of the ways in which most French feminists have attempted to subvert patriarchy from within. Able both to see more than one point of view from their marginalized position as women and to use the resources provided by their class, relatively wealthy educated women have been among the most influential feminists. They have written theoretical texts (cultural, religious, philosophical, and scientific), along with novels, memoirs, and correspondence. Their writing is often interdisciplinary with a dialogic structure highlighting woman's ability to cross boundaries. French feminists frequently demonstrate the relevance of sexual difference to an understanding of contemporary

life. They have, for instance, recently revealed how the seemingly "objective" discourse of biology describing woman's "nature" is, in fact, gender-inflected.

For the medieval psyche that still forms part of the history of current ideas and practices in France, authority derived from one God reigning over the "great chain of being" and resided in the king governing both church and state. Although patriarchal society is virtually universal, the French monarchy until 1789 imposed a legal system and an ideology arguably among the most resistant to sharing governance and economic resources with women. France's sexist heritage includes the Frankish legal system, especially the notion of primogeniture in Salic law, which prevented women from inheriting resources. The centralization of state power and the rationalist tradition emerging in the seventeenth century are also part of this heritage. René Descartes's *Discours de la méthode* (Discourse on Method, 1637) elaborated an influential, rationalist world view that was patriarchal, built on the notion of a male thinker/writer able to remove himself from the "distortions" of physical experience, the emotions, and the female with whom they are associated, at least as far back as the biblical story of Adam and Eve. French rationalism provided philosophical justification for patriarchal practices begun in the Middle Ages. It equated writing with the masculine, thus excluding women from one of the most significant and influential forms of public, political life.

As early as the Middle Ages, certain feminist texts opposed the orthodox, patriarchal view of "woman" and, in doing so, implicitly combated essentialism (e.g., *Aucassin et Nicolette* [Aucassin and Nicolette]). The French-Bulgarian theorist, critic, and novelist, Julia Kristeva—arguably one of the most thought-provoking feminists now writing—draws attention to another such text, the relatively unknown Antoine De La Sale's *Le Petit Jehan de Saintré* (1456). A linguistic examination of symbol and sign, Kristeva's first book, *Le Texte du roman* (1970), along with a later article, "The Bounded Text" (Kristeva, 1980) focuses on the narrative, *Jehan de Saintré*, showing that although the Lady in the work appears to be the idealized, inaccessible woman of courtly love, she is an ambiguous cipher, both pure and lascivious. According to Kristeva, as a landmark text providing roots for the realist novel — and, implicitly, for feminism as well—*Jehan de Saintré* rethinks the woman's role in a society moving toward a capitalist mentality, using women as various kinds of exchange objects. Kristeva's analysis is an example of French feminism's contributions, recovering knowledge about history, society, and sexuality that would otherwise be lost.

Kristeva has rejected the term "feminist" because of the narrow perspective of some feminists. In her newest work, *Colette*, she states that the totalizing analysis of contemporary feminism, growing out of Enlightenment philosophy, is no longer useful or flexible enough to bring about sociopolitical or intellectual change. Her recent trilogy on woman intellectuals can be seen as an attempt to move beyond overly rigid forms of identity politics and the impasses they face. However, because of the ways in which Kristeva illuminates French thinking on the category "woman," her writing is feminist in the sense used throughout this entry.

The fifteenth-century Christine de Pizan is often recognized as an early example of a feminist thinker and the first French woman known to have earned a living by writing, as Nathalie Zemon Davis, the American feminist historian, states. In the forward to Pizan's *Book of the City of Ladies*, Davis highlights her contributions to feminism, including the late scholastic's interdisciplinary breadth, which is characteristic of many of the strongest feminist thinkers. Pizan also demanded that more education be provided for women, a belief held by virtually all feminists. She contributed early versions of both the equality/universalist and difference/gynocentric arguments, stating that women are equal to men and that, where they are different, women are stronger; for instance, intellectually and morally (see Davis's "Forward").

Activist women, along with women writing oppositional, marginalized bodies of thought (Madame De La Fayette's and Jeanne Guyonne's Quietism, for instance), alter the concept of "woman" by subverting the sexism of many institutions even as they accept limited participation in them. They have won the poetry prize awarded by the Académie Française, for example, after being excluded from membership in the prestigious, government-supported association until 1980. Although the Catholic Church, like the State, continues to be rigidly patriarchal—as late as the twentieth century, when it condemned contraception as well as Simone de Beauvoir's *The Second Sex*, not to speak of its stand on abortion, divorce, and the ordination of women—nuns have begun to provide instruction for wealthy women in the newly formed teaching orders.

The historian Dena Goodman stated that equality between the sexes and a female-centered sociality in the eighteenth century lead to the development of the republic in France, positing a link between the Feminine and the democratic or universal (see her *Republic of Letters*; Olympe De Gouges had also envisioned such a link in 1791 in her *Declaration of the Rights of Woman*). Laws and public policy nevertheless remained repressive in the nineteenth century. Napoleon's *Code Civil* relegated females to the status of a minor and a madman under the control of their fathers or husbands. It is remarkable that women in this period managed to make substantial contributions as writers and as political activists. Working-class women played a vital role, for example, in initiating the short-lived, influential revolution known as the Commune in 1871, a broad-based attack on repressive government prefiguring the events of May 1968. Nineteenth- and twentieth-century French women were also able to create a public space for themselves in theater.

By its very nature, the stage provided a place in Paris for women to acquire an audience, as illustrated by the case of Sarah Bernhardt (see Gilman, 1993). The notorious actress analyzed her status as woman on the French, British, and American stage in the second half of the nineteenth and the early years of the twentieth century in her autobiography, *Ma Double Vie* (My Double Life, 1907). Questioning, for example, why actors resent her success although other actresses do not, she discovers a link between acting and the Feminine: putting on makeup; displaying emotions different from "your own"; and aiming to please and attract others, often using physical and emotional means, are common to each. Acting, similar to being a woman—at least, as Western cultures conceive of the Feminine—demands that one recognize and assume the role of another, often of the disempowered or Other in a master-slave relationship, described by the German philosopher Friedrich Hegel. Existentialism and especially psychoanalysis will employ the concept of the Other in ways that become useful to feminism's examination of sexual difference (see below). Bernhardt's discovery transforms what had been a source of oppression into an advantage, enabling her to confront the stereotypes of woman (and Jew) that create psychological and institutional restrictions and conflicts for an actress (*Ma Double Vie*, Vol. 2, p. 133). A "good mother," for instance, does not leave her child to perform in the United States. Bernhardt indicates that sometimes she does, although not without anguish and risk (*Ma Double Vie*, Vol. 2, p. 248), suggesting that at times, woman assumes the role of Other or "bad mother." *Ma Double Vie* demonstrates Bernhardt's versatility as a woman and as an actress, creating a fluid identity that combines the strengths of each.

As Bernhardt did on the stage, Colette took what had been the mark of woman's weakness under patriarchy—affect, or her sensations and emotions—and mobilizes them in a creative way on the page. She achieves a degree of autonomy as an individual, for instance, in *Les Vrilles de la vigne* (Tendrils of the Vine, 1908), a collection of short, pungent essays that represents Colette's contribution to an erotic literature invented by women with, as Kristeva points out, roots in the Sulamite female narrator of the Biblical Song of Songs (see Kristeva's *Colette*, p. 328). In *Les Vrilles de la vigne*, a nightingale/artist sings the suffering and fear aroused by a lesbian love. Colette expresses such a love, as Kristeva indicates, at the very time that Freud described women's psyche as more frequently bisexual than man's (see Colette and Freud's Female Sexuality).

Homosexual love unfolds in essays describing friends, especially Valentine, and pets, cats and dogs, for whom the narrator feels affection to the point of identifying with the animals she describes. A replaying of the Mother's role along with an analysis of male psychology emerge as themes in the various short pieces. Although Colette, the narrator, is at various times melancholy, fearful, lyrical, cynical, or masochistic, the overall tone and content of the collection is reflective and constructive. The focus on the Mother in this and later work marks Colette as one of the few writers, female or male, to explore the experience of motherhood, not as a primarily biological process but, rather, as a socio-psychic formation supporting relationships between lovers as well as between parent and child (writing a few years later, Virginia Woolf is another important exception). Similar to other Modernist texts, the work has a structure that breaks with the rational order of linear time and realistic narrative—in this case, a cyclical pattern emerges, appropriate in essays centered on the Mother.

Women's liberation in France in the twentieth and twenty-first centuries has taken significant strides through three phases: activism and the struggle for political rights, the ontological demonstration of woman's equality, and most recently, the identification of woman's difference and creativity, as Colette's writing indicates (see Kristeva, *Colette*, p. 540). Laws have steadily improved: married women gained their majority status in 1938, with the right to bank accounts and to work outside the home in 1946. French women obtained the right to vote in 1944. The Women's Liberation Movement (*le Mouvement de la libération des femmes*, or *MLF*), the feminist organization emerging from the events of May 1968, helped to win abortion rights in 1974. Women won the right to parity in having females on the ballot for public office in 2001. Feminists write new versions of existentialist and psychoanalytic thought, shaping attitudes and providing a philosophical foundation for intellectuals in many disciplines.

Beauvoir achieved international recognition as a feminist in 1949 with her influential work *Le Deuxième Sexe* (The Second Sex). She documented patriarchal structures through time and place in the context of an existential philosophy showing how woman can be trapped into playing the role of the Other, allowing herself to be made into an "object" in a difficult relationship with man. Her much quoted "One is not born

a woman, one becomes one" succinctly states that gender and sexuality are primarily social constructions and indirectly argues that the concept of "woman" is fluid. Beauvoir has also written compelling novels and memoirs, including *L'Invitée* (She Came to Stay, 1943). In this narrative, the female protagonist is a playwright struggling to create and strengthen intimate friendships with two men and a woman. Although Françoise fails, conveying the pain of Beauvoir's own struggles, as her memoirs make clear, the playwright's example resonates for women today in their effort to integrate work and relationships. Françoise's fight to combine a private voice with a public one denied by a patriarchal society and to thereby unite alienated segments of her psyche is more than the story of an individual woman. Despite her criticism of Freudian psychology, Beauvoir's analysis of Françoise in *L'Invitée* recognizes the psychological and sexual dynamics underlying French intellectual life.

Psychoanalysis is arguably the most fertile discourse for the contemporary women's movement in France today—a fact often surprising to some feminists in England, France, and the United States, who, similar to Beauvoir, view Sigmund Freud's work more negatively. Although these feminists raise the legitimate question of essentialism, they condemn a body of work that is nevertheless substantial and influential (e.g., see Drucilla Cornell and Adam Thurschwell's "Feminism, Negativity, Intersubjectivity," p. 161). Psychoanalytic writing in France, taken as a whole, has breadth and depth, drawing on Modernist, Surrealist, and Existential thinkers—Marcel Proust, for instance—who are both philosophical and political. Problematic to the extent that it risks essentialism, that is, uses the bipolar categories of gender identity, male and female, psychoanalysis nevertheless need not, and in its strongest forms does not, reify these categories. Instead, it provides a useful framework and foundation for French feminist thought.

As many French feminists read him, Freud discovered that sexuality is arguably the most significant component of contemporary life, shaping the individual psyche and the dynamics of groups and institutions. Three feminist writers in particular, Julia Kristeva, Algerian-born Hélène Cixous, and the Belgian Luce Irigaray, have each written several books bringing creative psychoanalytic theories to bear on questions of sexuality and focusing on sexual difference rather than the male, often the prominent figure in Freud's work.

Cixous's psychoanalytic examination of the Feminine appears, for example, in her book; in her essays on James Joyce, the Irish novelist; and in her autobiographical writings. *Rootprints* (1997) and a videotaped interview (*Hélène Cixous*, 1998) document the sexism palpable in French academia on her arrival in Paris from Oran, Algeria, in 1955. In *Rootprints*, she discusses her cultivation of a "literary nationality," made up of Algerian, French, German, and Jewish components, to counter sexual discrimination. She is French via her German maternal grandmother, who acquired French citizenship when Alsace became French; Cixous's Spanish-born father and Algerian-born mother are both Jewish. She develops a "literary nationality" by using the French language for her work, constructing an identity for herself in writing. Creating texts in which she transforms national/racial and gendered elements, she acquires unique qualities through her writing, which give her semi-autonomy at the same time that she remained an Algerian Jewess.

Similar to Joyce, on whom she wrote her doctoral dissertation (1968), she aligns herself, through and beyond literature, with the Feminine in a way that combines gender, nationality/race, and writing. She analyzes Joyce's life and work in *L'Exil de James Joyce ou l'Art du remplacement* without needing to say that in doing so, she retells her own story of estrangement growing up in Oran and working in Paris (in *Rootprints*, she writes, "All biographies like all autobiographies like all narratives tell one story in place of another story"). Her book describes the reciprocal shaping of institutions and individual as Joyce becomes a writer surrounded by family, the Catholic Church, and Ireland. She sees the Other, the rebel, doubt, and the death instinct, no less than the seemingly contradictory impulse to live, as the presence of the Feminine in Joyce's writing. Cixous reveals the maternal reasserting herself in the psyche as a body opposing authority or the paternal when she states that in Joyce, the body is "the only place in which one can still be aware of one's own integrity." She examines "Joyce's insistence on Bloom's various bodily functions" as a "defensive narcissism" with links to the Mother. Bloom is "attached to his body as to a place from which he cannot be dispossessed," and lingers near a female "the other one, jar on her head, getting the supper: fruit, olives, lovely cool water out of the well stonecold like the hole in the wall at Ashtown. . . . She listens with big dark soft eyes" (*L'Exil de James Joyce ou l'Art du remplacement*, p. 728; *Ulysses*, pp. 77–78). The form itself of her essay on the Circe episode in *Ulysses*, "At Circe's, or the Self-Opener," typical of a variety of Cixous's writing for which she is well-known, can be read as a kind of Feminine writing, or *écriture féminine*, a Joycean or stream-of-consciousness narrative replete with puns.

The Feminine reemerges in the image of the Mother in her autobiographical essay, "My Algeriance: In Other Words to Depart Not to Arrive from Algeria" (1997). This essay focuses on her problematic connection to Algeria, especially during the time it struggled to achieve independence from France. Her understanding of Algeria, the Mother ("with women's arms . . . something stronger than wars . . . something gentler, more immediate, more fleshy") brings about a sense of renewal in herself. She is able to embrace an Algeriance that is a dream for the future and to reject an Algeria with racial and sexual oppression, just as in the past she has been able to submit to the hate of certain Algerians for herself as French. Her psychoanalytic feminist reading of Joyce and of the world enables her to develop a point of view that is both complex and politically informed. In this way, French feminism opens new lines of critical reflection and expands the reading even of important male authors.

"Le Sujet de la science est-il sexué?" ("Is the Subject of Science Sexed?" 1982) demonstrates how Irigaray's version of psychoanalytic theory, no less than Cixous's and Kristeva's, contributes to feminist thought by identifying influential gender-inflected discourses. Irigaray focuses on science's rhetoric as a form of sexist social practice shaped by French philosophical and psychological traditions, a form symptomatic of sexual politics in France. Not primarily a utopian feminist, Irigaray acknowledges the power exerted by the male and the presence of the phallus in social practice, including language and capitalist economic mechanisms, which language has helped to put in place as elaborated in Jacques Lacan's influential work. Irigaray is engaged in a seemingly impossible goal: to argue convincingly about what is repressed and to confront sexism at the root of psychoanalysis in both Freud's and Lacan's focus on the male. She demonstrates the unconscious sexual dynamics and, in particular, the union with and murder of the Mother at the origins of Western psychic formations. Fundamental to her feminism and to her understanding of the concept "woman" is the matricide enacted by the psyche as the infant grows, at least in Western cultures ("Is the Subject of Science Sexed?" p. 84). Originally dependent on the Mother in a symbiotic relation, the infant separates from her, retaining the memory of both this union and of the painful separation and murder demanded to acquire language and to accept the social contract with male authority as its core. In the social practice that dominates, woman, a subaltern figure historically deprived of power, is relegated to the place of the Other, which, in psychoanalytic theory, often designates the silenced or repressed.

Along with Freud and Lacan, other significant writers provide a context for Irigaray's work, documenting unconscious structures that shape the psyche and political behavior. Paul Ricoeur has stated that banishment under repressive governments is the political equivalent of repression in the psyche ("The Question of Proof in Freud's Psychoanalytic Writings," in *Paul Ri-*

coeur: An Anthology of His Works). Theodor Adorno and Max Horkheimer have discussed scientific language as both a psychological and political practice that silences the disempowered (*Dialectic of Enlightenment*), examining this practice in Western cultures beginning in ancient Greece, with some emphasis on the condition of women.

"Is the Subject of Science Sexed?" analyzes the psychological formation existing in the language of scientific journals: ostensibly "objective," science is not focused on an "object of inquiry" but, rather, attempts to construct an object/text whose rhetoric closes or removes the subjectivity of everywoman/man. Recognizing the difficulty of initiating a dialogue with scientists given the impersonal character of their language, she decides to ask questions, as in the questionnaires appearing in women's magazines. In doing so, Irigaray chooses a mode frequently used in the social sciences—the questionnaire or public-opinion poll—suggesting, as she does earlier in the essay, that the human sciences (*les sciences humaines*, the term used in French to designate the social sciences and literature), despite the scorn the "hard" sciences often heap upon them, are better suited for a dialogue among individuals, a "common inquiry" (66). Her questions thus introduce the very world that the physical sciences seek to suppress and immediately confront sexuality and especially the "nature of woman" in ways that are alternately absurd and reasonable by scientific standards: "Two eggs can produce a new being?" and "Is masculine contraception hormonally possible?" The first question, for example, pokes fun at biology's exclusive focus on the physical and its sexist view of the egg as unproductive without the sperm. Two eggs can, after all, produce a new being and often do in the sense that two women can raise a child. Irigaray explains that scientific language takes pains to eliminate the world of the everyday, including sense perceptions, and especially gender-inflected experience. Such language posits a closed, isolated space constructed like a mirror facing the spectator, a space based on a previously existing model defined by the scientist. Mathematics, for example, often part of the "scientific" language of physics, is frequently circular and very much a "closed system." Fearing the openness needed to bring about change, scientific language, according to Irigaray, often corrects imbalances using a rhetoric of mastery over nature and the Mother with whom it is associated, at least in Western cultures. Elsewhere, she states that such imperialist language has led to deadly problems including war and pollution, leaving little hope for recovery (*Sexes and Genealogies: Each Sex Must Have Its Own Rights*).

Irigaray's rhetoric is strikingly different from that of science. Straightforward, everyday vocabulary and syntax appear in French and English versions of the text printed side by side. Questions dominate, some seeming both reasonable and foolish in the different contexts created as she moves among disciplines and groups of disciplines ("hard" science: biology, mathematics, and the like; "human" sciences: religion, philosophy, psychology, economics, linguistics, etc.). In this way, she engages in an interdisciplinary dialogue with readers in many fields, playing the role of "Other" (what science represses: subjectivity, the everyday, etc.) and providing them an opportunity to share a public venue having a political and ethical function, the subversion of sexist practices.

Clear examples of the relevance of Irigaray's theory of scientific language appear in the recent feminist critique of the biological rhetoric describing reproduction, including Nancy Tuana's in the volume *Feminism and Science*, where Irigaray's essay is published. Emily Martin, for instance, explains that the sex-inflected metaphor of masculine heroism including the adjectives "active," "vigorous," "autonomous," "penetrating," "transmitting," and "activating" describe sperm (Martin, 1991). A metaphor of feminine passivity characterizes the egg: "transported," "taken away," "slipping," "penetrated," and "fertilized." Bruce Alberts, a biologist aware of how beliefs and cultural practices influence biology, emphasizes the egg's active functioning. Eggs produce the proteins and molecules needed for them to unite with sperm, for instance (see Alberts et al., *Molecular Biology of the Cell*; see also Keller, 2000). Although she does not discuss Martin or Alberts, Irigaray provides the philosophical, psychological, and political context for their critique of biology's gender-inflected language.

Exemplifying feminist oppositional writing, Irigaray's texts reveal the masculist psychological formations underlying the rhetoric of Western rationalism, especially in its French versions. French feminists show how conceptions of sexual difference structure contemporary life, including the story of human creation. Taken as a whole, they confirm Irigaray's insight that "sexual difference [is] the most fundamental, irreducible characteristic of lived human existence and subjectivity." Interdisciplinary and dialogic, this oppositional writing indicates that the nature of "woman" is constantly in flux and that the place for feminist scholarship is secure.

CAROL MASTRANGELO BOVÉ

See also **Simone de Beauvoir; Helene Cixous; Luce Irigaray; Julia Kristeva; Jacques Lacan; Paul Ricoeur; Psychoanalytic Theory**

Further Reading

Bernhardt, Sarah, *Ma Double Vie: Mémoirs de Sarah Bernhardt*, 1907, Paris: Charpentier, 1923; as *My Double Life:*

The Memoirs of Sarah Bernhardt, translated by Victoria Tietze Larson, Albany: SUNY Press, 1999

de Beauvoir, Simone, *Le Deuxième Sexe*, Paris: Gallimard, 1949; as *The Second Sex*, edited and translated by H.M. Parshley, Harmondsworth: Penguin, 1984

de Beauvoir, Simone, *L'Invitée*, Paris: Gallimard, 1943; as *She Came to Stay*, translated by Y. Moyse and R. Senhaouse, London: Fontana, 1987

de Pizan, Christine, *Le Livre de la cité des dames*, 1404 Paris: Stock, 1986; as *Book of the City of Ladies*, translated by E. Richards, 1982, New York: Persea, 1988

Cixous, Hélène, "At Circe's, or the Self-Opener," translated by Carol Bové, *boundary* 2, 2.3 (1975): 387–397

Cixous, Hélène, *L'Exil de James Joyce ou l'Art du remplacement*, Paris: B. Grasset, 1968; as *The Exile of James Joyce*, New York: David Lewis, 1972

Cixous, Hélène, "Mon Algériance," as "My Algeriance, in other words to depart not to arrive from Algeria," translated by Eric Prenowitz, *Triquarterly* 100 (1997): 259–279

Cixous, Hélène, *Rootprints: Memory and Life Writing*, London: Routledge, 1997

Colette, *Les Vrilles de la vigne*, 1908, *Oeuvres*, Paris: Gallimard, 1984, pp. 959–1063

Cornell, D., and A. Thurschwell, "Feminism, Negativity, Intersubjectivity," in *Feminism as Critique*, edited by S. Benhabib and D. Cornell, Minneapolis, Minnesota, 1987, pp. 143–162

Gilman, Sander L., "Salome, Syphilis, Sarah Bernhardt and the Modern Jewess," *The German Quarterly* 66.2 (1993): 195–211

Goodman, Dena, *The Republic of Letters: A Cultural History of the French Enlightenment*, Ithaca, New York: Cornell University Press, 1994

Hollier, Denis, *A New History of French Literature*, Cambridge, Massachusetts: Harvard University Press, 1989

Irigaray, Luce, "Le Sujet de la science est-il sexué?" in *Parler n'est jamais neutre*, Paris: Editions de Minuit, 1985; as "Is the Subject of Language Sexed?" translated by Carol Mastrangelo Bové, *Hypatia: A Journal of Feminist Philosophy* 2.3 (1987): 65–87

Keller, Evelyn Fox, "Langage scientifique (sexuation du)," in *Dictionnaire critique du féminisme*, edited by H. Hirata, et al. Paris: Presses universitaires de France, 2000, pp. 91–95

Kristeva, Julia, *Le Génie féminin: Colette*, Vol. 3, Paris: Fayard, 2002

Kristeva, Julia, "The Bounded Text," in *Desire in Language: A Semiotic Approach to Literature and Art*, translated by Leon S. Roudiez, New York: Columbia University Press, 1980

Kristeva, Julia, *Histoires d'amour*, Paris: Denoël, 1983; as *Tales of Love*, translated by Leon S. Roudiez, New York: Columbia University Press, 1987

Martin, Emily, "The Egg and the Sperm: How Science Has Constructed a Romance Based on Stereotypical Male-Female Roles," *Signs* 16,3 (1991): 485–501

Oliver, Kelly, ed. *French Feminism Reader*, Lanham, Maryland: Rowman & Littlefield Publishers, 2000

Sartori, E., ed. *The Feminist Encyclopedia of French Literature*, Westport, Connecticut: Greenwood, 1999

Sartori, E., and D.W. Zimmerman, eds. *French Women Writers: A Bio-Bibliographical Source Book*, New York: Greenwood, 1991

FOCILLON, HENRI-JOSEPH
Art Historian

Methodologically, the writings of Henri Focillon differ substantially from those of Émile Mâle, another art historian important to modern French thought. Whereas Mâle's scholarly interest in art was principally iconographic, Focillon concentrated on the subject of artistic form. As a consequence, he devoted much more attention to architecture, the art in which form imposes itself on the viewer most directly, than did his senior colleague Mâle. Because style, composition, and technique occupy a larger role in his core writings than subject matter, his approach is identified as "intrinsic" as opposed to "extrinsic" (and interdisciplinary), which is to say that it deals with the internal structure of works rather than their place in a broader sociohistorical spectrum. His limited concern with extrinsic meaning is most striking in the area of medieval art and architecture, in which he developed a major interest after succeeding Mâle in the chair of medieval archaeology and history of art at the Sorbonne in 1924. This interest culminated in his *Art d'Occident* (1938), probably the most widely read of his many works. Both here and in other studies, he denied the genesis of Romanesque and Gothic art and architecture in religion, locating it rather in technical and stylistic experiment and formal development. This denial is largely implicit, but no less forceful thereby, when set against the success of Mâle's theories and contemporary methodological developments in Germany, which paid minute attention to subject matter in the pictorial arts.

Focillon's scholarly interests and intellectual resources were remarkably diverse. His political and pedagogical concerns, and the intense feeling for art with which his upbringing (in a professional engraver's household) imbued him, all bear closely on his writing. Much of his scholarship assumes and even requires, for thorough comprehension, an understanding of and commitment to art in its readers. He published prodigiously (his bibliography lists 378 items) and expressed himself imaginatively. These factors have sealed his popularity with historiographers of art history, among whom he is generally esteemed more highly than Mâle. He did not, however, elaborate an original theory of art. His main theoretical work, *La Vie des formes* (1934), is in certain important respects derivative. Its original argument is, moreover, obscure in places—Focillon admits that his terminology is "inexact" and "provisional"—and laced with romantic and (in the spirit of Baudelaire's art criticism) irrational propositions. Indeed, readers are instructed to eschew logic and scientific reasoning if they wish fully to understand form as it relates to art. The book is nevertheless considered an important contribution to art historical discourse and constitutes the best ground for assessing Focillon as a thinker.

La Vie des formes is an investigation of the nature of form as it exists in art. In modern art historical writing, the concept of form is not associated with Platonic metaphysics but, rather, broadly speaking, with that of shape (which gives rise to style, thus permitting the classification of works, schools, periods, and the like according to intrinsic criteria). Like other formalist scholars (e.g., Alois Riegl [1858–1905] and Heinrich Wölfflin [1864–1945]), Focillon assumes this identification, but he embellishes it greatly. Without attempting a concise definition of form (Focillon seems to consider this impossible, and certainly his understanding of form's ontological status is never clear), *La Vie des formes* presents its subject in various guises as association, emotion, line, matter, time, vocation, structure, touch, and so on. Above all, however, form is interpreted as a life force. Obviously this life is not biological, but rather a self-generating and perpetual "energy," contingent on and referring to nothing but itself. It finds its most enduring, vital expression in art and architecture, with which it shares a special relationship. ("Art" and "form" are not interchangeable terms, however, for although all works of art are essentially form, form embraces more than art.) Artistic form is never abstract, although it is said to exist in the minds of artists before its realization in stone, paint, canvas, glass, metal, and so on. It is not, however, psychological in any recognized sense but, rather, a particular type of epiphenomenon whose relationship to mental life generally is "inconstant" and "indefinite." It is superior to mind and does not share mind's weaknesses (e.g., mortality). Form rather "visits" the artist (the term derives from Sartre's aesthetics, but the idea is Focillon's), eliciting manufacture of a work in which it finds phenomenal expression.

The life force of artistic forms is conceived in terms of movement. For Focillon, a work of art or architecture is never still. This movement is not construed as perceptible but, rather, as a process of perpetual internal metamorphosis, the momentum for which is supplied by form's angles, curves, and lines and the effects that the dynamic established by their combination has on the space they occupy (not three dimensional space, but the special type of space that form creates around itself). In more accessible terms, formal metamorphosis is elsewhere explained with reference to the phases through which all artistic styles are said to pass. A style, for example, the Gothic, is defined as "a coherent grouping of forms united by a reciprocal fitness"; thus, style organizes form and makes it intelligible. Every artistic style, no matter where or when it arises, goes through four distinct "ages": the experimental, the classic (its zenith), the age of refinement, and the baroque (a formulation deriving from Wölfflin's prior classification of styles into early, classic, and baroque phases). As the baroque age of one style ends, so the experimental age of another begins. Artistic form thus turns in great and perpetual cycles, not according to historical circumstances, but obeying "rules that are inherent in the forms themselves." Thus, although a given work may appear static, its location in the stylistic cycle endows it with movement.

In fact, the extreme formal autonomy proposed by Focillon—form is said to occupy a "fourth realm," a parallel universe "distinctly not our own . . . with its own laws, material and development"—renders his subject very difficult to understand with reference to the human experience and endeavor of which art is generally reckoned a product. It has the dual effect of exulting art (and artists, who belong to an elite "spiritual group") and estranging it, placing it substantially outside the command of the viewing consciousness. The extrinsic meaning and historical context of works, which for many constitute art and architecture's most significant aspects, are set aside as trivial and irrelevant—something criticized by iconographers, who complain of Focillon's "disqualification" of art from semantic interpretation. Ultimately, however, his concern with the intrinsic nature of art and architecture may be seen to lend critical support to the discipline of art history, which has always struggled to define itself on its own terms. For this reason, as much as for the breadth, quality, and acuity of his scholarly writing, Focillon will always be considered one of the twentieth century's most important art historians.

JULIAN M. LUXFORD

See also **Emile Mâle**

Biography

Henri Joseph Focillon was born at Dijon in 1881, the son of Victor-Louis Focillon, a successful engraver. He was educated in Paris at the Lycée Charlemagne, Lycée Henri IV, and the École Normale Supérieure (1901–1905). Between 1908 and 1913, he taught philology at secondary institutions before being appointed professor of Modern History at the University of Lyon and (a concurrent appointment) director of the Musée des Beaux-Arts, Lyon. In 1924, he succeeded Émile Mâle as professor of Medieval Archaeology at the Sorbonne. From 1933, Focillon taught regularly at Yale. In 1934, he published *La vie des formes*. He took up a professorship at Yale in 1938 and remained there after World War II broke out, writing strongly against the German occupation of France in the press. He died at Yale in 1943, aged sixty two.

Selected Writings

Giovanni-Battista Piranesi, 1918
Les Pierres de France, 1919
La Peinture aux XIXe et XXe siècles, 2 volumes, 1927–1928
Maîtres de l'estampe: peintres graveurs, 1930
L'Art des sculpteurs romans: récherches sur l'histoire des formes, 1931
La Vie des formes, 1934; as *The Life of Forms in Art*, edited and translated by Charles Beecher Hogan and George Kubler, 1992
Art d'Occident: Le moyen âge roman et gothique, 1938; as *The Art of the West in the Middle Ages*, 2 volumes, edited by Jean Bony, translated by Donald King, 1963
Rembrandt, 1936; as *Rembrandt: Paintings, Drawings and Etchings*, edited and translated by Ludwig Goldscheider, 1960
Moyen Âge: survivances et réveils: études d'art et d'histoire, 1943
L'An mil: avec 20 planches hors texte, 1952; as *The Year 1000*, edited and translated by Fred Wieck, 1969

Further Reading

Bony, Jean, Henri Focillon (1881–1943), in *The Art of the West in the Middle Ages*, vol. 1, Oxford: Phaidon, 1963, ix–xxi
Cahn, Walter, Focillon's *Jongleur, Art History*, 18, 1995, 345–362
Cahn, Walter, Henri Focillon (1881–1943), in *Medieval Scholarship: Biographical Studies in the Formation of a Discipline: Volume 3: Philosophy and the Arts*, edited by Helen Damico, New York: Garland, 2000, 259–271
Fernie, Eric, *Art History and Its Methods: A Critical Anthology*, London: Phaidon, 1995, 168–178
Grodecki, Louis, *Bibliographie Henri Focillon*, New Haven, Connecticut: Yale University Press, 1963
Chastel, André, ed., *Henri Focillon*, Paris: Éditions du Centre Georges Pompidou, 1986
Mélanges Henri Focillon—Gazette des Beaux-Arts, 6th series, 26, 1944 (volume dedicated to Focillon, incorporating a number of articles in English)
Molino, Jean, Introduction, translated by Elisabeth Ladenson, in *Focillon, Henri, The Life of Forms in Art*, New York: Zone Books, 1992, pp. 9–30
Relire Focillon: cycle de conférences organisé au musée du Louvre par le Service culturel du 27 novembre au 18 décembre 1995 sous la direction de Matthias Waschek, Paris: Ecole nationale supérieure des beaux-arts, 1998
Turner, Jane, ed., Focillon, Henri(-Joseph), in *The Grove Dictionary of Art*, vol. 11, London: Macmillan, 1996, p. 233

FOUCAULT, MICHEL
Philosopher

A former pupil of the Ecole Normal Supérieure, like Sartre and Merleau Ponty, Michel Foucault is one of the major figures of postwar French philosophy. His oeuvre is remarkable for its scope (from Greek antiq-uity to the Modern period), its methodological innovations (such as "archaeology" or his revival of Nietzschean genealogy), and the originality of its main concepts ("historical *a priori*," "élistimé *episteme*," "power/knowledge," and "subjectivization," just to mention a few). Beyond its philosophical interest, Foucault's work was also very influential on other disciplines, such as history, sociology, and gender studies. Although he had already written two books, Foucault achieved sudden notoriety with the publication in 1966 of *Les Mots et les Choses*, which unexpectedly became a bestseller. Taking up Kant's concerns in the *Critique of Pure Reason*, the book was concerned with finding *a priori* (i.e., universal, necessary, and nonempirical) conditions of possibility for knowledge (*savoir*); however, unlike Kant, Foucault deemed these conditions to be historical, both in the sense of being given in history and of changing within history—hence their name, taken up from Hussel's *Origin of Geometry*: the historical *a priori*, or *épistémès*. In writing his "archaeology of knowledge" in the West, Foucault thus identified four *épistémès*, each corresponding to a well-circumscribed historical period: the Renaissance, the Classical age, Modernity, and Post—modernity. The common feature of all these historical *a priori* is that they refer to an ontological connection between language (words) and being (things), a connection presupposed by all the discourses of each epoch and that governed the form and content of what could count as knowledge at that time. Thus, for the encyclopedic man of the Renaissance, words were things, with natural characteristics identified by grammar; conversely, the world itself was a cypher, and to know meant to spell out the infinite network of similarities, analogies, antipathies, and sympathies linking together the things of the world, a spelling out itself connected to its objects by similarity relationships (because the properties of words echoed those of things). Knowledge was a *mise en abyme* of the world and of itself based on the identification of resemblances that could never be fully clarified, and thus called for endless commentary. However, the next *épistémè* that of the Classical age, dismissed this underlying notion of a fundamental opacity of words and things reflected *ad infinitum* by discourse and started from the reverse premise; that is, from the idea that being can be fully and adequately captured by representation. Thus, Descartes's *Discourse of Method* replaced the search for resemblances with the systematic analysis of differences as the correct method for the formation of knowledge. Correlatively, the *Meditations* grounded knowledge in the transparency of the relationship between being and being thought provided by the *cogito*. To know something, then, meant to have a clear representation of it; that is, a representation that could be decomposed into its primary elements and logically connected to other representations to form a table in which further representations would find their place.

The third *épistémè*, that of Modernity, began with Kant's questioning of the conditions of possibility of representation and the discovery that these lie outside of representation, in the transcendental subject. For Foucault, the former reversibility of being and being represented thus collapsed in two directions: on the one hand, unknowable things in themselves, that is, things as they are independent of human perceptual conditions (such as the need for a spatio-temporal framework, or for conceptual identification), and on the other hand, phenomena that can be known, but only from an analysis of their conditions of possibility, that is, from the perspective of transcendental idealism. Things and words, identical in the Renaissance and transparent to one another during the Classical age, became irreconcilable in principle. To know, then, took on two opposite meanings: either to try and recapture the direct access to being forbidden by Kant's *Critique of Pure Reason* (post-Kantian metaphysics such as Hegel's or Schopenhauer's, or conversely positivism) or to focus on phenomena and deepen our understanding of the transcendental conditions of representation (Fichte, and then phenomenology).

According to Foucault, these two trends, although they appear antithetical, are thus rooted in the same historical *a priori* (opened by the Copernican turn) and have shaped the development of philosophy from the end of the eighteenth century to the rise of structuralism. However, as shown by Foucault's "analytic of Finitude," both are doomed: the first, because the refusal to consider transcendental conditions leads to either to precritical metaphysical dogmatism or to the naïve belief in "facts" (the myth of the given); the second because spelling out these conditions turns out to be an infinite task in which the boundary between the transcendental and the empirical become thinner and thinner and philosophy runs the risk of being identified with psychology or anthropology. Indeed, according to transcendental phenomenology, to know phenomena, one has to consider the conditions according to which they are given to us; that is, the structures of intentionality. These structures, however, are not disembodied but rooted in the ambiguity of "man" as an empirico-transcendental doublet; that is, as a being who lives in the world but is also the only being through which the world can be constituted and make sense as a world. Man thus occupies a unique position in the Modern *épistémè*: he is both an object of knowledge (like any other entity) and the condition of possibility of that knowledge. From this circularity between the empirical and the transcendental stem both what Foucault calls the "anthropological sleep" and the im-

possibility for knowledge of having a stable foundation. So the final *épistémè*, that of the "return of language," reacts to this aporia by generating another ontological shift in which the primacy given to man by the phenomenological tradition analyzed by Foucault is displaced. From the perspective of structuralism, language can be analyzed independent of intentionality. This search for nonsubjective foundational structures can in turn be extended to other sectors of human activity (such as the analysis of myths by anthropology or that of social structures by ethnology, and so on), a move whose benefit would be to free knowledge from the analytic of finitude. Thus, *Les mots et les choses* closed with Foucault's much-criticized heralding of the "end of man" and his hope in the rise of the new *épistémè* of language.

The success, and more important the theoretical claims, of the book generated a heated debate with some of the most prominent French intellectuals, especially Sartre, who led the attack against Foucault on the grounds of antihumanism, whereas others (such as Canguilhem or Dumézil) defended him. These attacks caused Foucault to try and clarify his method and aims in his most abstract book, *L'archéologie du savoir* (1969), in which he tried to redefine the historical *a priori* independent of the ontological claims underlying *Les Mots et les choses*. Foucault adopted a resolutely nominalist position by rejecting the idea of any referent for words ("things" becoming dependent on the conceptual tools used to identify and analyze them) and attempted to define *épistémès* at the level of discourse by introducing new notions such as the "discursive formation" (*formation discursive*), the "statement" (*énoncé*), or the "archive" (*archive*). Not all sentences are statements: as Foucault says, the proposition "green thoughts sleep furiously," although grammatically correct, is not a statement unless put in a specific context, such as a coded exchange during wartime. What makes a proposition a statement is thus the way it fits within a specific discursive formation (e.g., a sentence such as "it will rain tomorrow" has a different meaning and value depending on whether it is said by me or features in the weather forecast, backed by scientific evidence). Each *épistémè* spells out the requirements that a statement must obey to be part of a specific discursive formation, whereas the archive describes the way in which the various *épistémès* fit together. Archaeology must proceed in a holistic way because statements can only be identified through their belonging to a discursive formation that in turn is clarified by the analysis of the statements that it governs. The general horizon of such an enterprise was to lay out explicitly the conditions of possibility of discourse at a given time without having recourse to any metaphysical or ontological assumptions—hence Foucault's new definition of himself as a "happy positivist."

However, it quickly became apparent that his positivism was not so happy and that archaeology as a new method was fraught with difficulties. For one thing, as pointed out by Dreyfus and Rabinow, the status of the "laws of discourse" was very ambiguous: Did discourses actively conform to these laws, or were the latter a common feature retrospectively observable? Did the *épistémès* have real regulative power, or were they a descriptive term only? Furthermore, Foucault himself quickly became dissatisfied with the claim that the requirements that propositions must satisfy to be considered as statements can be identified solely at the level of discourse. Not only did it not accord with his own methodological approach in such books as *Madness and Civilisation* or, more important, *The Birth of the Clinic* (which was supposed to be an "*archaeology of medical perception*") but it also worked on an artificial premise; that is, the idea that the conditions of possibility of discourse can be understood at a purely theoretical level, as if they had no connection with the social, political, and institutional practices of their time. The consequence of this approach was the inability of Foucault to account for change, more precisely, for the transition from one *épistémè* to the next: Each *a priori* appeared as a closed totality whose historical character was made contradictory by its isolation from nondiscursive practices. For example, as shown by the *Birth of the Clinic*, the rise of anatomo-pathology as a new discursive formation was only made possible by the many changes in institutional practices generated by the French Revolution: the development of population control, the instauration of a national policy of hygiene, and the grouping of patients in hospitals (as opposed to visits by the family doctor), which made it possible for the medical profession to exchange observations (whereas previously notes would get lost when the doctors died), to compare cases, and to evolve better treatments. Thus, Foucault himself was only able to account for historical change by referring discourses to their institutional and political conditions of emergence.

Foucault's explicit move from archaeology to genealogy was thus motivated by the realization that discourses can only be analyzed from the perspective of their insertion within what he called "nondiscursive" practices: The conditions of possibility of knowledge were not only epistemological but also political. Correlatively, in his inaugural lecture at the Collège de France, *The Order of Discourse* (1970), Foucault refined his account of the relationships between discourse and truth by making a crucial distinction between the truth value of a proposition, which cannot be determined by archaeology or by genealogy, and

what he called its "acceptability," the conditions of which are the real object of his investigations. Although truth itself may be definable independently of context, what counts as true is fully dependent on historical conditions, which are both discursive and nondiscursive (being rooted in institutional and political practices). Thus, a discourse like Mendel's, although true, was rejected by his contemporaries because it was not acceptable; that is, because it did not conform to the requirements of biology as a discursive formation. Conversely, Schleiden's theses, although retrospectively shown to be false, were accepted because they worked from the premises that formed the horizon of acceptability at that time. In Foucault's own words (borrowed from Canguilhem), being true and being "in the truth" are not identical. Moreover, the possibility of something being said to be true is dependent not on its objective truth value, but on its being "in the truth" of an epoch: Acceptability preempts truth predication. The consequence for Foucault of this major discovery was thus the need to refocus the search for the conditions of possibility of knowledge on acceptability and to assess the relationships between the latter and nondiscursive practices.

However, the main models of political thinking available turned out to be inadequate for carrying out this project. What Foucault criticized as the "juridico-repressive hypothesis" (*La volonté de savoir*, 1976) was a top-down model that viewed power as intentionally exerted by a monarch and the discourse of rights as both a tool of, and a limit imposed on, the exercise of sovereignty. However, Foucault's analysis of the birth of the prisons (*Surveiller et Punir*, 1975) had demonstrated the impossibility of this model accounting for the rise of the new horizontal forms of power linked to the progressive institutionalization of the state, a power that could not be referred to the conscious decisions of any particular subject and in which the production of discourses often seemed independent of any design. The other main model, derived from Althusser's "scientific" Marxism, understood the generation of discourses in terms of the supra/infrastructure distinction and thus saw knowledge as ideological and its conditions of possibility as ultimately determined by economical constraints. Foucault criticized this conception on two accounts: first, because the Marxist model, although apparently opposed to the juridico-repressive hypothesis, is in fact also based on the naïve notion of a sovereign consciousness, as shown by the part granted to the rise of class awareness of social struggles in the fight against capitalism. Second, because understanding the production of discourses as solely dependent on economics was far too unidirectional insofar as it did not take into account the retro-effects of discourse on economic determinations.

Foucault concluded that although the juridico-repressive hypothesis was outdated, the model of ideology was both naïve and overly restrictive.

Foucault thus had to evolve his own theoretical tools to account for the conditions of possibility of discourses and their relationships to the political. This was done via the introduction, in *Surveiller et punir* and in the 1976 Lectures at the Collège de France, of a new concept—"power/knowledge" with its associated notions of "objectification" and "subjugation." In answer to the conceptions examined above, Foucault defined power/knowledge as a "nexus" animated by a circular, non-subject-centered dynamics according to which the development of new mechanisms of power generates new objects and forms of knowledge; but conversely, this knowledge allows for the refinement and expansion of power relationships in ways that are neither intentional nor fully predictable. Foucault's favorite example of this complex dynamic is the relationship between disciplinary power and the rise of the human sciences examined in his study of imprisonment. Thus, the reformation of the prisons at the end of the eighteenth century generated new practices of power, which Foucault called "disciplines": disciplines are ways of transforming and controlling individuals via the organization of the space they live in (hence the new designs for prisons, colleges, barracks, and the like, with the ultimate example of innovative spatial control being Bentham's famous Panopticon), the management of their time through strict schedules, and the constant breakdown and monitoring of their occupations. The trademark of disciplines is that they do not operate on consciousnesses but, rather, directly on bodies, imposing on individuals new modes of being and of acting from which stem an increase in economic efficiency (the prisoners become better workers) and a decrease in political awareness (which in turn reinforces efficiency by fostering docility).

However, the development of the disciplinary apparatus (*dispositif*) created the conditions for the apparition of new objects (the process referred to by Foucault as "objectification") and of associated theoretical fields. For example, the need to standardize and maximize the efficiency of bodily movements in military formations led to a new understanding of the body, seen neither as the Cartesian body-machine nor as the organic body of physiology but, rather, in terms of its possibilities for useful action; it thus gave rise to a new science, ergonomy, which in turn helped to maximize further the disciplining of bodies. In the same way, the need to make punishment proportionate to the crime led to the development of criminology as the science capable of comparing and classifying crimes, and the "criminal" mind emerged as the object of a new discipline, penal psychiatry, concerned with the assessment of motivation and responsibility. Conversely, the findings of criminology and psychiatry helped to refine penal procedures and sentences as well as imprisonment practices, thus furthering the implementation of disciplines and the normalization of social behavior.

For Foucault, the point of these analyses was to show the failures of the previous models to explain the actual workings of power and the subsequent impossibility of considering the relationships between discourse and power either as instrumental or as unilaterally determined. The discovery of the power/knowledge model also allowed him to refine his former analysis of the conditions of possibility of discourse, now identified as "regimes of truth" (*régimes de vérité*). Following up the distinction between truth predication and acceptability, Foucault was now able to expand on his former criticism of the human sciences by showing that in their case, the conditions of acceptability (to which statements had to conform to count as true) were not determined by detached, epistemological concerns but, rather, by the requirements of disciplinary power. In his course at the College de France of 1976, Foucault presented an analysis of early psychoanalytic practices based on the claim that curative efficiency, itself understood as the normalization of the patient, was the real criterion on the basis of which the truth value of a statement was decided. In Foucault's ironical terms, "truth heals": To be cured, the hysterical subject had to recognize the practitioner's diagnosis as the truth of her condition. By means of this process of internalization and belief, her symptoms were progressively alleviated, a success that "confirmed" the original diagnosis and from which it retrospectively derived its truth-value. For Foucault, the so-called scientificity of the human sciences thus rests on a question-begging process (because a statement has to count as true in the first place to work, which in turn is meant to establish it as true), a process itself governed by the expansion of normalization practices in capitalist societies. As Foucault puts it, truth is not the "child of solitude" but a "commodity," like wealth, the value of which depends on a regime that itself must be understood from a political standpoint.

Foucault's analysis of the relationships between power and truth has been both praised for its originality and heavily criticized: Habermas charged him with generating a "metaphysics of power," and others claimed that his model of power rests on the undue generalization of observations that are more limited in scope and time (the development during the nineteenth century of specific institutions, such as prisons, colleges, or barracks). Even from Foucault's own perspective, however, there was a heavy theoretical price to pay for his claims: the circularity of the relationships between power and knowledge was such that it made the identification of a specific level for the conditions of possibility for discourse impossible. So the main discovery of genealogy, the power/knowledge nexus, ironically turned out to be the undoing of the old archaelogical project as it undermined the very idea of an *épistémè* or historical *a priori* for knowledge. Foucault's awareness of this problem is shown by his unsuccessful attempts to distinguish a more specific "discursive regime" from the more general regime of truth, but perhaps also, more indirectly, by his long silence and sudden turning away from the study of power and discourse to focus on the question of subjectivity.

Between 1976 and 1982, Foucault did not publish any major work. The series of five books announced on the back cover of the *Volonté de savoir* (*The Flesh and the Body, The Children's Crusade, The Wife, the Mother and the Hysteric*, and *The Perverse and Populations and Races*) was never completed. In his long introduction to the second volume of the *History of Sexuality, L'usage des plaisirs* Foucault justified his change of plans by saying—surprisingly enough, given his early antihumanism—that "his problem had always been the question of the subject," and that to fully understand the genesis of the Modern subject, it was necessary to go backward, beyond the study of the rise of disciplinary power, beyond the analysis of confessional practices and of their associated discourses, to see how the very notion of a "subject of desire" was constituted in the early days of Christianity. By contrast, this entailed a study of what it meant to be a subject for the ancients, both during the Classical Greek period and under the Roman Empire. In a massive retrospective shift, Foucault thus refocused his whole oeuvre on the idea of a "history of subjectivity," or which his former examination of the conditions of possibility of truth and their relationships to power, as well as his previous "history of sexuality," covered only the most recent stages.

The idea of a constitution of subjectivity brought the later Foucault unexpectedly close to a philosophical trend he had vigorously rejected in the 1960s; that is, phenomenology, especially in its Sartrean version. Just like existentialism, the idea of a history of subjectivity rests on the rejection of any essentialist definition of the subject (e.g., the Enlightenment idea of a universal "human nature"). Like Sartre, Foucault put a heavy emphasis on the part played by freedom and reflection in the constitution of the self: the subject is a conscious "form" that individuals voluntarily impose on themselves and that is susceptible to almost infinite historical variations. Although the historical contents of this form may change (see below), its structure remains the same: It involves the free and conscious projection of an understanding of the self, which is recognized as true by the individual and appropriated by the use of

specific practices (the "techniques of the self"). "Subjectivization" is the generic name Foucault gives to this process, and "problematizations" refer to its most active part. Thus, being a subject means to "problematize oneself and the world"; that is, to form an understanding of one's identity and position within the wider context of relationships with nature, society, and other subjects.

Such a problematization is a reflective and theoretical process by means of which individuals gain the ability to articulate an understanding of self and also to use this articulation to shape their lives accordingly. For example, the study of philosophy and the contemplation of ideas allow the Platonic Guardian to understand his soul as a tripartite composite (reason, spirit, and desire), of which the rational part is the best. This understanding can then be used to discipline the lower parts of his soul and, thus, to reinforce the preeminence of reason. However, Foucault insists that conjointly with their reflective aspect, problematizations also entail various practices by which a specific understanding of the self can be furthered: thus, the same Guardian will have recourse to various ascetic techniques (such as those used by Socrates according to Xenophon; i.e., fasting, sleeping in the snow, spending nights with the object of one's desire without having sexual intercourse, and so on) that will further the control exerted by the rational part of his soul. The general aim of problematizations is thus the shaping of what Foucault calls the subject's "ethical substance," a shaping that involves the awareness of a specific *telos* and the adoption of etho-poetical techniques. At the end of the subjectivization process, the subject's conscious representations of himself and his deeds will be perfectly harmonized: he will have become a "parrhesiast"; that is, someone whose *logos* and *bios* reflect each other to the extent that he can ground the truth of his discourse in his behavior (in the way the truth of Socrates's apology for the laws of the city, which must be obeyed no matter how unjust a particular decision may be, is grounded in his refusal to flee with Crito and his willingness to drink hemlock).

Foucault's new interest in the constitution of subjectivity is very closely linked to his former analysis of the conditions of possibility of truth and power by the central part played by truth in subjectivization. As suggested above, to constitute oneself as a subject means to consciously recognize and practically appropriate one's own truth. This truth, however, is not formed by the subject in isolation, nor does it pertain to the individual in his singularity—in the example given earlier, Plato's claim that the rational element of the soul is its best part was meant to be recognized as true by all individuals in fourth-century B.C. Greece, regardless of class (be they Guardians, Auxiliaries, or Producers) or personal idiosyncrasies. Foucault is clear that the truths used in subjectivization, although they may entail an element of personal interpretation, are "patterns" or "models" that are already present in one's culture. According to the epoch, these patterns find their expression in particular philosophical, cosmological, theological, or scientific theses to use early Foucault's words, in the various discursive formations that were the object of archaeology. Being subject to historical change, they depend on complex relationships between economic determinations, political decisions, social modifications—in genealogical terms, on the diverse historical forms taken by the power/knowledge nexus. Thus, the later Foucault's "history of subjectivity" is not such a departure from archaeological and genealogical concerns as it seems at first sight: on the contrary, it brings together the themes and methods he had previously evolved to retrace the complex connections between the constitution of subjectivity and the history of the conditions of possibility of truth and of its relationships to power.

According to him, this history unfolds in five main steps. It begins with the Platonic subordination of the *epimeleia heautou* (the care of the self, i.e., the most original form of problemation in the West) to the Socratic *gnōthi seauton* ("know thy own self"): to care for oneself now meant to seek the truth about oneself and, ultimately, to become the embodiment of that truth according to the logic of *parrhesia*. As suggested by the examples above, the main source of such a truth was philosophy; because relationships of power were fluid and worked on a small scale (the city), the Greek constitution of the self was seen as fully conscious and active, the prerogative of free male individuals. The second step of the history of subjectivity resides in the Stoic moment: although the structure of problematization (as the recognition/appropriation of truth) remains identical, the truths used for subjectivization are now provided by a rational cosmology according to which the individual is a small part of the great *logos* of the cosmos. Because of the progressive expansion and institutionalization of the Roman empire, social pressures exerted on individuals increased and the constitution of the self, although still viewed as a free activity, became more rigid and systematic. The third stage of the history of subjectivity, early Christianity, however, saw a radical change in the apparition of a very different understanding of the self: the hermeneutics of desire. The truth central to the constitution of the self became the idea that the subject is fundamentally untrue to himself, having impure and opaque thoughts and desires, which he consequently must constantly seek to eradicate to reveal his true self. Although many ascetic practices remained nominally identical, their meaning was deeply changed: For example, in "The Battle for Chastity" the Stoic self-examination was a factual recapitulation of the deeds of the day, meant to help the practitioner become aware of his mistakes and how to avoid them in the future and, thus was designed to reinforce his confidence in his rational judgment.

However, the Christian form of self-examination was not so much interested in the facts of daily life as in the motivations of the doer: What mattered was less the exactitude of representations than their origin, their relationship to the secret and guilty desires of the believer. Instead of reasserting rational self-control, the Christian self-examination thus opened up subjective interiority as a new, dangerous, and obscure field in need of infinite analysis and redress. Subjectivization became an endless process of guilty self-doubt, requiring the constant and methodical mediation of another, more advanced subject—the confessor. This deeply affected the meaning of the constitution of the self, although the Platonic or Stoic relationship between the apprentice and the master of truth was meant to be temporary and had as its horizon the emancipation of the disciple (via his becoming a parrhesiast), the Christian expurgation of secret desires was a lifelong process during which the sinner must remain subordinated to the authority of his confessor. The constitution of the self, instead of being a "practice of freedom," started to become a process of domination by means of which the individual had to recognize the authority of the Church and its institutions. Whereas the Greek subjectivization was designed to maximize autonomy, its Christian counterpart thus paved the way for the disciplines, both by laying out an infrastructure of specific practices (such as the tight regulation of space, work, and time in monasteries) and by fostering a culture of submission.

The fourth stage of the history of subjectivity, that is, the birth of the disciplines, emphasized this new trend by bringing about two major changes: first, the nascent disciplinary power took advantage of the Christian turn and generalized to the whole of society practices that originally were much more limited in space and time, such as confession. It also increased the passive aspect of the constitution of the self by applying disciplines directly to bodies, consequently diminishing the part played by reflection and judgment in the process. The second change comes from the objectification processes that accompanied the rise of the disciplines: The newly generated discursive formations (the human sciences) progressively replaced religious dogma as the source of the truths used for subjectivization. Subjects were incited to recognize themselves, not as sinners or penitents anymore, but as healthy, nondeviant, noncriminal individuals, according to the newly formed standards of psychology, psychiatry, criminology, and the like. Correlatively, the new dominant paradigm for acceptability became scientificity (as opposed to conformity to the revealed canon). This combination of the growing institutionalization of the various sectors of human life (as seen, e.g., in the development of governmental educational and heath policies in the nineteenth century) with the rapidly expanding new sciences (such as pedagogy or sociology) accelerated the transformation of subjectivization from a private and largely autonomous practice into the institutionalized modes of subjugation (such as the examination) formerly criticized by genealogy as producing a "subject of obedience." Finally, the more recent transformation of disciplinary power into biopower, that is, a power that focuses on the management and development of life, only increased this trend.

The fifth stage of the history of subjectivity, the twentieth century, looks therefore rather bleak to Foucault in the sense that it shows an ever-growing tendency to what he calls "normalization"; that is, the standardization and extension of subjugation practices backed up by the alleged scientificity of the human sciences. Most of Foucault's very last interviews were thus dedicated to a search for means of resistance to normalization, among which was his redefinition of freedom and the "aesthetics of existence" he advocated during the last years of his life.

BÉATRICE HAN

See also **Louis Althusser; George Canguilhem; Georges Dumezil; Michel Foucault; Maurice Merleau-Ponty; Jean-Paul Sartre**

Biography

Michel Foucault was born in Poitiers, France, in 1926. A former pupil of the Ecole Normale Supérieure (like Sartre and Merleau-Ponty), he studied psychology and philosophy. Having passed the Agrégation, he took the post of "Attaché Culturel" in Uppsala, where he found the material from which *Madness and Civilisation*, his doctoral thesis, was to emerge. After publication of the book in 1961, Foucault became a Lecturer in Psychology at the University of Clermont-Ferrand. The huge editorial success of *The Order of Things* (1966) propelled him to the front of the philosophical scene, where he remained until his death in June 1984. By then, he was holding a chair in France's most prestigious institution, the Collège de France (to which he was elected in 1970). As well as being a thinker of international status, Foucault took an active and public part in French political life, frequently writing for newspapers and taking positions on the main issues of his time. He is the author of nine books and more than 3,500

pages of collected articles (gathered in the four volumes of the *Dits et Ecrits*).

Selected Works

Histoire de la folie à l'Age classique (Madness and Civilization), 1961
Naissance de la clinique (The Birth of the Clinic), 1963
Les mots et les choses (The Order of Things), 1966
L'archéologie du savoir (The Archaeology of Knowledge), 1969
L'ordre du discours (The Order of Discourse), 1970
Surveiller et punir (Discipline and Punish), 1975
La volonté de savoir (History of Sexuality, vol. 1), 1976
L'usage des plaisirs (The Use of Pleasures, History of Sexuality, vol. 2), 1982
Le souci de soi (The Care for the Self, History of Sexuality, vol. 3), 1984
Dits et écrits, 4 vols., 1995.
L'herméneutique du sujet (Cours au Collège de France, 1982) 2001

Further Reading

Dreyfus, Hubert, and Paul Rabinow, *Michel Foucault: Beyond Structuralism and Hermeneutics*, Brighton: Harvester Press, 1982
Gutting, Gary, *Michel Foucault's Archaeology of Scientific Reason*, Cambridge: Cambridge University Press, 1989
Gutting, Gary, ed., *The Cambridge Companion to Foucault*, Cambridge: Cambridge University Press, 1994
Han, Béatrice, *Foucault's Critical Project: Between the Transcendental and the Historical*, Stanford, California: Stanford University Press, 2002
Kant, Immanuel, *Grifth of Pure Mafia*, trans N. Kemp-Smith, MacMillan, 1929.
Major-Poetzl, Pamela, *Michel Foucault's Archaeology of Western culture: Toward a New Science of History*, Chapel Hill: University of North Carolina Press, 1983

FRANCOPHONIE, LA

La Francophonie is a term that has many different applications. It can be used as a purely descriptive category for the French-speaking peoples and areas of the world, although it often serves as a marker of difference between metropolitan France and the non-metropolitan "Other." It is also the term used for the institutional apparatus that has been set up to manage the relations between the various constituent parts of the Francophone world. Equally important, however, it serves to denote a body of thought that evolved in the aftermath of the decolonization of the French Empire to articulate the vision of a new relationship between France and its former colonies and to constitute a characteristic worldview. This has not been a static set of ideas. Indeed, the multifaceted nature of the term is matched by major shifts in the content of the Francophone discourse since its inception in the early 1960s to the present day.

It was as an intellectual movement that *La Francophonie* was first born. Its birth is generally located in the collection of articles published as a special issue of *Esprit* in 1962. This contained contributions by some of the leading figures of the newly independent former colonies or protectorates, among them, Léopold Sédar Senghor of Senegal, Habib Bourguiba of Tunisia, and Norodom Sihanouk of Cambodia. The significance of the circumstances of its birth needs to be emphasized. On the one hand, the importance of ideas and the intellectual dimension to the subsequent development of *La Francophonie* was paramount. On the other hand, the initiative to bring it into being came not from France but from the formerly colonized themselves. Indeed, France showed a marked disinclination to get involved at the beginning and adopted a very low profile in the movement from its inception until the 1980s. On both these counts, *La Francophonie* needs to be differentiated from the British Commonwealth, with which it has often been compared.

The vision of *La Francophonie* that was set out in the initial stages was one of a community that would henceforth be united by the common language and culture inherited from the French colonial experience. The term *Francophonie* had indeed been coined by the French geographer Onésime Reclus to denote the community of French speakers throughout the world (in his *France, Algérie et Colonies*, 1880). It had not been widely used however, until taken up by Senghor in 1962, when he defined it as "an intellectual or spiritual community whose national, official, or working language is French." (Deniau, 1983) Moreover, in borrowing this term, the founding fathers were to imbue it with their own very special content.

Most important, *Francophonie* was not seen as the product of the particular historical circumstances and relations associated with French imperialism but, on the contrary, took its inspiration from the universalism, characteristic of French Enlightenment, and, indeed, from Republican values. This was a universalism that did not simply found itself on the notion of a single human race, with the same fundamental human qualities, but that was largely based on the notion of universal human natural and political rights, in which the rights to liberty, equality, and fraternity were paramount.

The idealism of the notion was striking. Senghor, for instance, described it as "this integral humanism which is weaving its threads around the globe, this symbiosis of dormant sources of energy arising from all the continents, all the races which are awakening to their shared warmth" (Deniau, 1983).

Moreover, it took on a virtual, almost abstract quality, in which the actual historic and geographic circumstances of its birth were occluded. This was made very explicit by Habib Bourguiba, who claimed that "this community is situated beyond politics or geography—its criteria are above all philosophical, involving the great ideals of 1789 and the aspirations of humanity to freedom, dialogue and mutual support" (Deniau, 1983).

However, this universalist philosophy did not remain on the plane of abstract political idealism but was conditioned in practice by its specific association with the French body politic, and particularly the French colonial state apparatus. For the early proponents of *Francophonie*, this association was not seen as problematic. Indeed, it would seem that the decolonization process had finally removed the barriers to the effective realization of the ideal universal political project, to which lip service had been paid through the colonial doctrine of (eventual) assimilationism.

Moreover, it was a universalism further tempered by its close linkage with the particular French language and culture, which were themselves elevated to universal status. For Bourguiba, addressing the National Assembly of Niger in 1965, it was "the French language which contributed to our cultural heritage . . . and to forging our intellectual destiny and making of us complete human beings, belonging to the community of free nations." (Deniau, 1983) Yet not only was this association not seen as problematic but, indeed, the supposed universalism of French culture and, particularly, the French language was made the key tenet of the *Francophone* worldview.

The significance attached to the role of the French language was fully in line with the policy of the French State at this time, which gave considerable importance to the promotion or *rayonnement* of French language and culture throughout the globe, through its own cultural agencies as well as through the Alliance française. Leading political figures took every opportunity to extol the virtues of the "universal" language. Charles de Gaulle, for instance, claimed that "France has always ploughed the furrow of intelligence with passion and offered the entire earth a rich harvest; it is also true that she has given the world a language which is perfectly well-suited to express the universal character of thought." (Deniau, 1983) Georges Pompidou also highlighted the important role of the French language; indeed, for him, "it was because of the French language that France stood out in the world and was not a country like any other." (Deniau, 1983)

This was entirely linked to the belief in the mission of France to bring about a universal humanism on earth. De Gaulle, in his New Year's message for 1968, confidently opined that "the objectives of our action are related to each other and, because they are French, correspond to the interests of humanity." (Le Monde, January 1, 1968) This was still a potent message at the time of François Mitterrand's presidential inauguration speech of May 21, 1981, when he spoke of "a France standing for justice and solidarity, governed by the desire to live in peace with everyone, (which) may act as a beacon for the progress of the human race." (www.elysee.fr/instit/invests.htm)

However, in spite of the universalist discourse characteristic of the French political leadership, there was no real commitment to the burgeoning institutional developments of *La Francophonie* in the 1960s and 1970s by the French States which continued to see bilateral ties between the former colonies and the *Métropole* as the main way forward. Indeed, the initiative to set up the first major *Francophone* institution was largely undertaken by Canadians, with the establishment of the AUPELF (Association des Universités partiellement ou entièrement de langue française—now known as AUF, or Agence Universitaire de la Francophonie) in Montreal in 1961, with the aim of fostering academic cooperation. Serious rivalry and disputes between France and Canada marked the early years of the first intergovernmental *Francophone* institution, the ACCT (Agence de cooperation culturelle et technique—now known as the Agence intergouvernmentale de la Francophonie), which was set up in 1969 and went on to become the main operating agency to coordinate the activities of *La Francophonie*. Nonetheless, in spite of these reservations and reluctance on the part of France, the institutional development went on apace, with a multiplicity of bodies coming into being to promote cooperation across specific sectors of the Francophone world, such as the AIPLF (Association Internationale des Parlementaires de Langue Française—now known as APF) founded in 1967, CONFEJES (Conférence des Ministres de la Jeunesse et des Sports de la Francophonie) founded in 1969, and AFAL (Association Francophone d'Amitié et de Liaison) founded in 1974, to name just a few.

Developments were also taking place within the *Francophone* discourse. The predominance given to the French language as the key unifying factor and *raison d'être* of *La Francophonie* was inherently problematic, given the fact that in many of the supposed *Francophone* countries, French remained a minority language, used mainly by elites and for certain specific purposes, such as government and administration. Moreover, on the global plane, the French language was perceived as coming under increasing threat from the onward progress of English as the truly universal language.

In response to this menace, a certain polarization came to characterize *Francophone* discourse in a second stage of development. Increasingly, *Francophonie* was presented as the alternative to the global domination of the English language and Anglo-Saxon culture, characterized by its appeal to the lowest common denominator. There was a shift away from a celebration of the universal qualities of the French language and culture to their promotion as bastions of resistance to the homogenizing onslaught of the English language and American mass consumerist culture—the worldwide use of English, the consumption of Coca Cola, McDonald's and other standardized fast food, the purchase of branded clothing by a global mass market, and the vogue for American leisure and cultural products such as Hollywood films, television series, and Disney cartoons. Against this homogeneity, the French language and culture came to be increasingly characterized by their difference, even though this had traditionally been a concept quite alien to the universalist ideal. In the uneasy balance between universalism and French exceptionalism, it was the latter that began to tilt the scales.

However, in this turning of the tables, it was not only the uniformity spreading across the planet that was to be resisted, it was also the infantilization, the dumbing-down that was an inherent part of this process. Here again, *Francophonie* could play a role, and for its more discerning supporters who realized that French could not compete as a world language against English, it was increasingly portrayed as the vehicle for a more high-minded, intellectually elevated culture, perhaps not suitable for mass consumption but certainly of value to the elites.

While these developments were taking place, the potential value and importance of the *Francophone* movement as a useful adjunct to the global policy interests of France herself became increasingly evident. The presence of the French language "on all five continents" was celebrated as evidence of the continuing importance of France as a world power. However, it was really only with the advent of François Mitterrand to the presidency in 1981 that the full possibilities of *La Francophonie* were seized and France began to assume a leading role.

The initiative taken by the French State to establish TV5 in 1984 as an international collaborative channel for the promotion of French language and culture in all its diversity was significant in this respect. Even more important, when Mitterrand called the first Francophone Summit at Versailles in 1986, he set in motion a process of organized institutional development that would lead to the establishment of overarching bodies covering all aspects of *La Francophonie* and that would ultimately replace the mainly piecemeal, developments that previously had been taking place.

The General Agreement on Tariffs and Trade negotiations of 1993 and the growing importance of the cultural battleground in the struggle against Anglo-Saxon global hegemony were also to provide a significant impetus to the development of the *Francophone* dimension of French policy. This led to further shifts in the *Francophone* discourse. Not only was the role of *Francophonie* as a champion of difference and diversity promoted as its prime quality in the face of the American juggernaut, it became apparent that, given the need for allies in this confrontation, the appeal needed to be broadened. Hence, the shift came about from the defense of the right to French linguistic and cultural difference to the defense of the right to diversity *per se*, not just for French culture, but for all cultures. This first became apparent at the time of the General Agreement on Tariffs and Trade negotiations, in the extension of the argument for French cultural exceptionalism to all cultures, particularly those European cultures that were perceived as equally under threat from the American audiovisual industry in particular.

This theme was taken up at the Francophone Summit held in Mauritius in 1993, under the heading "Unity in Diversity." The Minister for Culture and *Francophonie* at the time, Jacques Toubon, made this explicit in his declaration that "the use of the French language which our peoples have in common provides us with the means to refuse the increasing uniformity of the planet which is being accomplished in accordance with the Anglo-Saxon model under the cover of economic liberalism . . . . There can be no true liberty without a respect for cultural and linguistic identities, the kind of respect which exists within *La Francophonie*." (Le Monde, October 15, 1993)

In a further development, this defense of the merits of linguistic and cultural pluralism was extended to *Francophonie* itself, which, through its spokespersons, increasingly came to express itself as a vehicle for the expression and promotion of a philosophy based not on the communality of the French language but on a broader belief in the values of plurilingualism and cultural diversity. Since that time, the importance of the French language as the common element has been decreasing. Indeed, the most recent version of the *Charte de la Francophonie* does not require any language qualification from its members. This has coincided with the broadening of membership of *La Francophonie* to include countries, many from Eastern Europe, without significant French-speaking populations.

This further significant development was initiated at the Hanoi Francophone Summit held in 1997 and entailed a major thrust to develop the political dimension of *Francophonie* with the decision to set up a permanent political organizational apparatus under the umbrella of the OIF (Organisation Internationale de la Francophonie) and the appointment of a Secretary-General. The choice of Boutros Boutros-Ghali, an Egyptian and former Secretary-General of the United Nations, as the first to fill this post (he has now been replaced by Abdou Diouf of Senegal) was significant in terms both of broadening the appeal of the organization as well as defining its mission as a major international body with a political focus. There have certainly been moves to broaden its focus to include a wider political agenda through the monitoring of elections, the organization of peace missions, and the promotion of human rights. Economic initiatives in the field of cooperation and development have also been prioritized, although cultural and linguistic issues still figure prominently in the matters covered. In some ways, the organization has come closer to the Commonwealth in the scope of its activities.

However, it is also true that the body retains a highly ideological flavor. Ideas and their expression remain to a very large extent the lifeblood of the grouping, taking the form of the promotion of a radical idealism. Certainly one of the most curious aspects of the developments is the mantle of subversion with which *La Francophonie* has come to be cloaked over the last decade of the twentieth century. The official French government Web site for the 1995 Cotonou Francophone Summit contained the following slogan: "*Francophonie* will be subversive and imaginative or will not survive!" (www.france.diplomatie.fr/francophonie)

For the most recent summit, held in Beirut in October 2002, the idea of *Francophonie* was officially designated as "a postcolonial concept" (on the summit Web site at http://www.sommet2001.org). This is entirely in line with the continuing evolution of the discourse of *La Francophonie* as a counterdiscourse, setting out an alternative to attract countries seeking some form of counterweight to offset the global hegemonic balance of power. Given the links with French global strategy and interests, which are necessarily intertwined with this ideological role, it remains to be seen whether the ideas of *La Francophonie* will be able to command the support of future generations of intellectuals of the stature of the founding fathers. Whatever the case, these ideas seem certain to continue their process of evolution into new forms in accordance with the dynamics of the shifting relations between the various components of *La Francophonie*, as well as in the interaction with wider global forces.

MARGARET MAJUMDAR

See also **Leopold Senghor**

Further Readings

Ager, Dennis, *Francophonie in the 1990's: Problems and Opportunities*, Clevedon: UK Multilingual Matters, 1996

Deniau, Xavier, La Francophonie, PARIS: PUF, 1983
Majumdar, Margaret A., ed., *Francophone Studies: The Essentials*, London: Arnold and New York: Oxford University Press, 2002
Salhi, Kamal, ed., *Francophone Post-colonial Cultures: Critical Essays*, Lanham/Boulder/New York/Oxford Lexington Academic Books, Rowman and Littlefield, 2003
www.france.diplomatie.fr/francophonie, official french government Web site
www.francophonie.org, official Web site of OIF

FRENCH COLONIAL THOUGHT

At its apogee in the 1920s and 1930s, France and its overseas possessions, *la plus grande France*, second only to the British Empire in scale, encompassed over 11 million square kilometers. French possessions included a vast North African empire (Algeria, Tunisia, and Morocco), great swathes of Africa (French Equatorial Africa, French West Africa, Togo, and the French Indian Ocean colonies), and the nations of Cambodia, Vietnam, and Laos, united under the name *Indochine française*. The French empire also included longstanding island possessions in the Caribbean and toeholds in India, South America, and the Pacific. French international expansion has a long history. Charlemagne, crowned Holy Roman Emperor in 800 A.D., created an extensive European Empire; in the eleventh century, the Normans occupied Britain and were in Sicily; the Crusades took the French to the Holy Lands; and brief periods of French rule were established in Cyprus and the Canary Islands between the twelfth and the fourteenth centuries. In the early 1500s, France made its first excursions into the New World, but it was the seventeenth century that witnessed substantial French expansion in Canada and the Antilles. The French presence in Africa and the islands of the Indian Ocean grew out of the plantation businesses of the Caribbean possessions, and rivalry between France and Britain led to their long struggle for domination of the Indian subcontinent from the 1600s onward. In these early episodes of expansion, various imperatives were at work that were to propel France in its drive to create a colonial empire in the nineteenth century: the search for power and prestige, often driven by international rivalries; the desire to establish trade routes and outposts and to further French economic interests; and the cultural and religious evangelism that lay behind many later justifications of empire.

However, it would be difficult to argue that France ever truly established a coherent and concerted plan of imperial expansion or that the nation had in place a consolidated colonial policy once the Empire had been acquired. The renewed French conquest of overseas territories that the nineteenth century witnessed was often the result of autonomous actions on the part of explorers and merchants with little, if any, direction from Paris. The wealthy activists and sponsors of the Société de géographie de Paris (founded 1821), who financed and promoted voyages of exploration, were probably more influential in the acquisition of new territories than were the politicians of France. Similarly, the growth in missionary congregations frequently opened up pathways for subsequent colonial involvement, and the correlation between evangelical zeal and what was later to become colonialism's ideal of a civilizing mission provided both a pretext and a justification for French intervention overseas. Territorial acquisitions thus often owed more to *la force des choses* than to a defined imperial vision and purpose.

Although the conquest of Algeria was begun in 1830, the acquisition of what was later to become France's colonial nemesis was viewed not as an important step in a concerted plan of colonial expansion but, rather, as a means through which Charles X hoped to prop up a failing regime. The conquest of Algeria instigated a limited amount of colonial debate: Toqueville viewed the conquest of Algeria as disastrous for Algerian civilization yet crucial to the glory of the French nation (*Oeuvres complètes* "Travail sur l'Algérie," Vol. 1, 1847). At this juncture, nationalist arguments tended to hold sway over the racialized and ethnocentric standpoints espoused by thinkers such as Gobineau (*Essai sur l'inégalité des races humaines*, 1853–1855), and Toqueville's insistence on the necessity of colonies to fortify a sense of French *grandeur* exercised a tenacious hold over attitudes toward empire in French for many years to come ("L'Émancipation des esclaves," 1843).

Three axes of colonial thought gradually began to emerge in the mid-nineteenth century, even if of limited political influence at the time. Certain key thinkers published colonial apologia that, although receiving little attention at the time of publication, later came to inform the ideals and policies expounded by politicians who favored colonial expansion. Jules Duval's work (*Les Colonies et la politique coloniale de la France*), inspired by Saint-Simon and Fourier, promoted the notion that colonization was a means through which to achieve social harmony and unity across the globe: Through the organized application of the values of progress and development, the transformative action of colonization would improve wealth and happiness through the exploitation of the earth's natural resources. Paul Leroy-Beaulieu (*De la Colonisation chez les peuples modernes*, Paris: Guillaumin, 1874) judged settlement colonies to be of limited use in the modern world and preferred trading establishments, which he perceived to be vital to the success of contemporary economic interests in France. Jules Ferry famously noted that "la politique coloniale est fille de la politique industrielle" (Robiquet, 1897). Nevertheless, economic arguments appear far less of a concern than political, and later, humanitarian ones. The second axis of thought was espoused by Lucien-Anatole Prévost-Panadol (*La France nouvelle*), who saw in colonization a way in which to stem and offset what he perceived to be the decadence of France as well as its growing insignificance on the global stage. Panadol maintained that colonial expansion was a crucial method by which to renew and rejuvenate a stagnating France and to increase the nation's declining prestige and grandeur. A similar stance was adopted by Jules Ferry in the wake of France's crushing and humiliating defeat at the hands of Prussia in 1870. A further strand of thought, which was later to inform debates on colonialism, was put forward in the writings of Prosper Chasseloup-Laubat (president of the Société de géographie from the mid-1860s, and briefly Minister for Algeria and the Colonies) and Francis Garnier (an explorer). Respectively, they promoted what were perceived as humanitarian arguments in favor of colonization, whereby it was the responsibility of France to export overseas the universal value of French civilization and of a France "porteuse de lumière." Under Chasseloup-Laubat's presidency in the mid-1860s, the Société de géographie transformed itself into an influential lobby group whose membership (Ferry, Brazza, and de Lesseps) actively advocated colonial expansion under the twin imperatives of exploration and civilization.

Although the piecemeal acquisition of a French colonial empire continued apace, there was a distinct lack of unanimity within France as to the course to follow in expansion and whether or not it suited France to acquire and preserve far-flung imperial domains. In the 1870s and 1880s, when a vanquished France was looking inward for national renewal, external events in far-flung corners of the world became for many a distracting irritation or, worse, a shameful waste of French blood and French gold. The well-documented polemic that divided France's politicians was one that pitched colonial expansion against an inward-looking stagnation born of the defeat of 1870 and a *revanchardiste* vision of France's status and prestige. As early as 1872, Gambetta articulated the procolonial view, stating that "pour reprendre le rang qui lui appartient dans le monde, la France se doit de ne pas accepter le repliement sur elle-même," although Déroulède found no compensation for the loss of "two sisters" (Alsace and Lorraine) in the acquisition of "20 domestic servants" (the colonies). Parliamentary debate over the colonies raged intermittently between 1880 and 1885, and the clash of these opposing views came to a crisis point over affairs in Tonkin (Indochina). In the aftermath of *l'Affaire tonkinoise*, Jules Ferry's speech to the Chamber of July 28, 1885, drew a sense and logic from events in Indochina and set the terms for a colonial policy specific to France. What had essentially amounted to the piecemeal acquisition of empire was represented as a veritable demonstration of imperial policy. Distinguishing between a "politique qui consiste à aller au hazard" and "une entreprise coloniale . . . poursuivie à l'origine d'un plan concerté, d'un dessein arrêté à l'avance," Ferry sought to provide his (mis)management of events with an order and purpose, a weight and import. Ferry constructed a conception of colonial expansion that sought to coincide with Republicanism and humanitarianism, while simultaneously emphasizing the renewal of French grandeur and prestige. Ferry's vision was to exercise a tenacious hold over French ideas of colonialism for decades: "[la France] ne peut pas être seulement un pays libre; . . . elle doit aussi être un grand pays, exerçant sur les destinées de l'Europe toute l'influence qui lui appartient, . . . elle répandre cette influence sur le monde, et porter partout où elle le peut sa langue, ses moeurs, son drapeau, ses armes, son genie." These ideas were popularized by the *groupe colonial* (founded in the Chamber of deputies in 1892) under the presidency of Eugène Étienne and disseminated through periodicals such as *La Dépêche coloniale* and *La Quinzaine coloniale*.

By the turn of the century, once pacification of France's newly acquired empire had largely been accomplished, most commentators and politicians in France rallied to the idea of Empire. However, if the nineteenth century had been dominated by concerns to demonstrate economic and military prowess through the acquisition of a colonial empire, then the early twentieth century was marked by a desire to legitimize that acquisition and to express national prestige through the beneficial contribution of French rule to colonized territories. This shift became all the more evident in a chastened post–World War European climate, where France, as did many of its imperial counterparts, distanced itself from the violent and acquisitive origins of empire to concentrate instead on the humanitarian value of French colonialism. Albert Sarraut (Governor of French Indochina and Minister for Colonies) retrospectively conceded that colonialism had originally been a primitive act of force, but asserted that this initially violent confrontation could be transformed into a collective triumph of solidarity (Sarraut, 1931). This evolution in colonial thought was often formulated in the field and expressed primarily by military chiefs, colonial administrators, and governors. Galliéni, and Lyautey in his stead, popularized the "tache d'huile" method of consolidating French rule abroad: once forward posts had been established, military force was to be used in a limited way and emphasis placed instead on the creation of institutions that would be beneficial to native peoples; the "spot of oil" was thus to spread forward gradually, creating schools, hospitals, and markets, giving native populations time to get used to the perceived advantages of a French presence (Galliéni, *Rapports d'emsemble sur la pacification, organisation et la colonisation de Madagascar*; Lyautey, 1920). This less bellicose approach to colonial pacification was accompanied by a shift in colonial policy from assimilation to association, a move that epitomized the way in which the nation attempted to distance itself from the violence of conquest and to establish a new legitimacy of empire. In keeping with the Jacobin tradition of mainland France, the policy of assimilation had universalist principles and a centralizing effect. It entailed the forcible imposition of French administrative, judicial, fiscal, and social models on the colonies, creating "copies" of France abroad, thereby ensuring the eradication of differences between the various colonies and indigenous peoples.

The ultimate goal of assimilation was also to erase differences between mainland French and indigenous peoples, to create a greater French polity—*la plus grande France*—a vast empire of French men and women all enjoying the same civil rights. However, given that colonialism is premised on the maintenance of difference and boundaries between colonized and colonizer, most colonial commentators acknowledged that this objective remained a distant goal. The policy of association, however, acknowledged the disparities inherent between the component parts of the French empire and allowed for greater flexibility in the administration of the colonies. The ideological shift toward association reflected the growing desire to demonstrate respect and "tolerance" toward indigenous peoples, their customs, and their institutions. The doctrine of association was officially endorsed in 1905 by Minister for Colonies Etienne Clémentel, and the policy was finally given sanction in a resolution of the Chamber of Deputies in 1917.

From this period on, there was something of a consensus established over Empire, and few anticolonial voices were to emerge in France until the post–World War II period. Most writing on the French empire was concerned with the management of the colonies and with the just application of colonial policies. Albert Sarraut (Minister for Colonies and Governor-General of Indochina; *La Mise en valeur des colonies françaises* and *Grandeur et servitudes coloniales*) emerged as one of the foremost commentators on the French empire and theorized much of France's colonial practice and more ethical approach to empire during the interwar years. A major corner stone in French practice was *mise en valeur*. It is a term that connotes not only economic development of the kind pursued by other capitalist imperial nations but also the moral and cultural improvement to be wrought in the colonies. This emphasis on the moral and cultural dimension stemmed from French belief in the universal value of its civilization, which in turn found its roots in the nation's revolutionary legacy.

Both an ideology underpinning the French colonial doctrine and a set of policies, *mise en valeur* is a polyfunctional concept that was much cited and invoked in the defense of French colonialism. Through the careful application of a policy or set of policies of *mise en valeur*, France sought to bring the component parts of the empire into the era of progress. The principle was pursued through a variety of means: the construction of schools and hospitals, the industrialization of the colonies, the construction of vast transport networks, and the implementation of educational policies intended to "enlighten" the native peoples of the empire. This more ethical version of colonial intervention reposed on what might be conceived as a trinity of values and principles that came to embody the French nation's vision of its colonial role—generosity, benevolence, and protection. *Mise en valeur* could be put forward as an example of the beneficial value of French colonial action, and thus served as a form of autolegitimation for imperial France. *Mise en valeur* came to be one of the pillars of French colonial ideology—a touchstone and a means through which to measure and display the beneficial effect of the French enterprise abroad. It was the policy through which France quite literally constructed the empire.

Once colonialism had been drawn onto the international stage following World War I (and particularly in the light of the creation of the *Société des Nations*), the developmental aspects of French colonial policy became a vital factor in the defense and promotion of French colonial action. As a response to the scrutiny of the international community, the focus of procolonial ideology and propaganda in France changed. The desire to distance France from the bloody legacy of conquest and pacification and to represent colonialism as a more ethically based project required France's colonial apologists to find worthy points of emphasis that would epitomize the humanitarian and developmental aspects of French action abroad. The notion of *mise en valeur* lent itself readily as an example of an ethically based colonial goal with a beneficial outcome. In colonial texts from the turn of the century onward, but most particularly in the post–World War I period, there is an increasing emphasis on *mise en valeur* as a defining figure of successful and ethical French colonialism.

It is a measure of the nation's belief in the beneficial value of its colonial action, and of the tenacity of

France's colonial "ideal," that France held onto its empire so tenaciously in spite of growing international distaste for Empire and the global climate of decolonization. It was not until 1962 that France finally retreated from Algeria, and many would argue that France's *doctrine coloniale* lives on in its policies of *francophonie* and in its relationship with the former colonial possessions that form its DOM-TOM (Départements d'outre-mer, Territoires d'outre-mer).

NICOLA COOPER

Further Reading

Betts, R., *Tricouleur: The French Overseas Empire*, London: Gordon & Cremonesi, 1978

Brunschwig, H., *Mythes et réalités de l'impérialisme colonial français 1871–1914*, Paris: Armand Colin, 1960

Duval, Jules, *Les Colonies et la politique coloniale de la France*, Paris: Bertrand, 1864

Galliéni, *Rapports d'emsemble sur la pacification, organisation et la colonisation de Madagascar*, Paris: Charles-Lavauzelle, [s.d]

Giarardet, R., *L'Idée coloniale en France de 1871 à 1962*, Paris: La Table Ronde, 1972

Prévost-Panadol, Lucien-Anatole, *La France nouvelle*, Paris: Michel Lévy, 1869

Lyautey, *Lettres du Tonkin et de Madagascar*, Paris: Colin, 1920

Robiquet, P., *Discours et opinions de Jules Ferry tome 5: Discours sur la politique extérieure et coloniale*, Paris: Armand Colin, 1897

Ruscio, A., *Le Crédo de l'homme blanc*, Brussels: Editions complexe, 2002

Sarraut, Albert, *La Mise en valeur des colonies françaises*, Paris: Payot, 1923

Sarraut, Albert, *Grandeur et servitudes coloniales*, Paris: Sagittaire, 1931

Todorov, T., *Nous et les autres: la réflexion française sur la diversité humaine* Paris: Seuil, 1989

FRENCH THOUGHT IN THE UNITED STATES

In their introduction to *French Theory in America*, Sylvère Lotringer and Sande Cohen make the bold claim that French theory is "an American invention," the ingenious conversion of what the French call "thought" (*pensée*) into a concept that is probably as foreign to the French as it is to the lay American public. Although in American English *theory* carries by now a general, expansive meaning analogous, but by no means equivalent, to the word *thought*, theory (*théorie*) in French has an odd resonance, unless it is related to a specialized field of inquiry (that is, theory of literature, theory of genres, and so on). But as Lotringer and Cohen persuasively argue, the somewhat arcane term of "theory" allowed French "thought" to enter into American discourse, under cover so to speak, and steer

clear of the two pillars of American wisdom, which the writers call "utopianism" and "legalism." According to the writers, the former includes the many versions of "American exceptionalism" (or "Manifest Destiny"), by which the discourse of freedom and the right to enforce it translate into action, and the latter relates to the American passion for facts and legal arbitration.

It is fair to say, however, that not all forms of modern French thought require such precautionary measures. One cannot forget that in the eighteenth century, French thought was a crucial influence on the founding fathers, and that the ideas of the *philosophes* were vital in the process of drafting the American Constitution. French positivism in the nineteenth century, represented most notably by Auguste Comte, was certainly congenial to the American academy. In effect, in many ways, the methods promoted by the positivist doctrine, such as quantitative analysis, and the derivative doctrines of behaviorism and operationalism still hold sway today in many areas of the social sciences.

In philosophy, the influence of twentieth-century French thought is marginal, however, outranked by far by the pragmatist tradition initiated by the American philosophers, C. S. Peirce, William James, and John Dewey. In the wake of logical positivism, which had its heyday in 1930s, analytical philosophy became the prevalent form of philosophical thought in America, after 1945. Its main task has been a preeminently pragmatic one: to determine the meaning of complex systems through "linguistic analysis." In its more recent versions, the emphasis on logic and reductive methods prescribed by Bertrand Russell, and the German schools (including such names as Rudolf Carnap, Kurt Gödel, Carl Hempel, Ludwig Wittgenstein, and Karl Popper), was supplemented by a more comprehensive outlook, which takes into account the general structures of language and thought, as well as cultural context and use, in the case of pragmatics.

In most American departments of philosophy today, the dominant philosophical trends in twentieth-century French thought—phenomenology and existentialism—have been relegated to an auxiliary status, under the label of "continental philosophy," which could hardly survive without an alliance with "literature" and "French theory." The International Association of Philosophy and Literature, chaired for many years by Hugh Silverman, is perhaps the single most faithful advocate of modern French thought (that is, philosophy) in America. More recent forms of French thought represented by structuralist and poststructuralist thinkers had to take cover under the rubric of "theory," and are usually taught in literature departments. The names of Louis Althusser, Claude Lévi-Strauss, Jacques Lacan, Pierre Bourdieu, Gilles Deleuze, Jacques Derrida, Michel Foucault, Jean Baudrillard, and Jean-

François Lyotard may now make unexpected appearances in disciplines such as history, social studies, and political science, which have until recently been impervious to the lure of French theory, and to philosophy in general.

The initial reluctance on the part of the American academe, not to mention the general public, to accept contemporary French thought in its midst, has been lucidly explained by Lotringer and Cohen in their Introduction to *French Theory in America*. This reluctance, which can sometimes take the form of downright rejection, is attributable to the very nature of structuralist and especially poststructuralist French thought. The radical critique of language and values proposed by contemporary French thinkers is essentially incompatible with the staunch belief in "clear and distinct" notions that underlies American epistemology and ethics. For a philosophical tradition dominated by the two opposite, but not necessarily incompatible, principles of empiricism and moral idealism, the French position (ultimately derived from Nietzsche), according to which truth and value are provisional constructs, has a definite heretical resonance. Ironically, perhaps, America's aversion to contemporary French thought is partly due to its anachronistic attachment to the eighteenth-century ideals of the *philosophes*, and their belief in the essential, universal nature of truth and value.

The thinkers associated with French theory may have ideological or methodological differences, but they all share the belief in the importance of language in determining the nature and forms of social interaction, and the consequent assumption that, given its constitutive status, language inevitably plays an important, often unacknowledged, political role in the conduct of human affairs. Contrary to traditional philosophical views, which embrace the idea of language as a passive medium or tool, contemporary French thinkers have argued in favor of a productive role of language, which serves to construct, rather than simply express, social reality. Foucault's notion of *discourse*, and discursive practices, which link various forms of representation and usage to power structures, is perhaps the most cogent expression of the linguistic emphasis that characterizes contemporary French thought. Equally disturbing, this time for traditional psychology, and even for some American practitioners of psychoanalysis (ego psychologists), is Lacan's idea that the unconscious is structured like a language, and can hence be interpreted through linguistic analysis (not to be confused with the linguistic analysis practiced by analytical philosophers for which meaning is a given).

The rediscovery in France, in the late 1960s, of Ferdinand de Saussure, the "father" of structural linguistics, was an essential element in the general revamping of French thought during that period. The idea, implicit in Saussure's *Course in General Linguistics*, (according to which language is a combinatorial system, and linguistic signs, variable elements in a fluctuating puzzle,) served to inspire and rejuvenate a good number of areas in the human sciences, some of which had already benefited from a structuralist or formalist influence: anthropology with Lévy-Strauss, cultural theory and history with Barthes and Foucault, sociology with Bourdieu, political theory with Althusser, and psychoanalysis with Lacan.

Equally important was Saussure's idea that meaning is a function of difference, and is generated through the very movement of signifiers. The method of deconstruction (that is, of traditional metaphysical notions, and binary oppositions set in a hierarchical order) was partly modeled on Saussure's understanding of language, in the vein already opened by philosophers like Nietzsche and Heidegger. For Deleuze and Derrida, the main representatives of deconstruction in France, difference and repetition replace the fundamental notions of the "one and the same", which are at the core of the Western philosophical tradition. For Deleuze, the resulting de-centered type of thought proliferates on a horizontal line, and is often represented by the figure of the rhizome, an arborescence that defies any totalizing attempt. In Derrida's case, difference is expressed by the untranslatable term *différance*, which connotes both difference and deferral. According to Derrida, meaning is endlessly fleeing, and is endlessly postponed in the unstoppable dissemination of signs.

An important ingredient in the transformation of recent French thought were the events of May 1968, in which intellectuals and students took an active part in challenging the traditional authority of the state (embodied at the time by the venerable figure of the General De Gaulle). In spite of its failure, the revolt of May 1968 created the illusion, one might say in retrospect, of the inherent frailty of social institutions, and the optimistic (not to say naïve) belief that discourse can play a performative role in changing social conditions, in other words, the belief that language can both make and undo a power structure. Many of the young intellectual Marxists, Trotskyites, or Maoists of the day retreated in their later years into calmer philosophical waters, but this does not mean that their major works, published for the most part in 1960s and 1970s, do not bear the imprint of these youthful ideological allegiances.

This aspect may also explain why contemporary French thinkers pose a particular challenge to the American public. In addition to their radical philosophical message and difficult, artful style (even more difficult to render into clear syntactic English forms), contemporary French thought also carries the miasma of subversion and revolutionary passion, even if limited for the most part to the domain of language, as Julia Kristeva's title, *Revolution in Poetic Language*, clearly suggests, or to the rambunctious power of desire, as Deleuze and Guattari argue in their *Anti-Oedipus*. Going against the grain of Freudian psychoanalysis, the authors contend that in capitalist societies, the Oedipus complex, whose successful resolution grounds, according to Freud, the subject in society, is nothing but a tool of domination. In Deleuze and Guattari's view, the resulting frustration of the libidinal subject is complicit with the repression exerted by the system, and the only escape, according to the writers' proposed method of "schizoanalysis," lies in the liberating energies of the libido, which can "deterritorialize," and thus defy the limits and constraints imposed by bourgeois society.

Since it entered the American academic arena with the controversial 1966 colloquium held at Johns Hopkins University where Derrida delivered his famous speech, asserting the preeminence of language and repetition over the subject, the influence of French theory in the American academe has waxed and waned. From its clamorous debut at Johns Hopkins, French theory settled at Yale, under the auspices of Paul de Man, and spread to other universities, where it took hold primarily in French departments, and in comparative literature departments, already used to welcoming a certain amount of foreignness in their midst. This was particularly true of comparative literature, which had already an affinity for theory, (in the sense of *Literaturwissenschaft*), due to the role played by René Wellek and Austin Warren's *Theory of Literature* in shaping its curriculum, in the 1950s. English departments resisted for a long time the foreign import of French theory, which disturbed their traditional methods of interpretation, inspired in large measure by New Criticism, but gradually relented under the combined pressures of students and faculty, and competition from French and comparative literature departments.

Reaction against French theory outside literary departments proper has been strong among conservative political thinkers, analytical philosophers like John Searle, and new pragmatists like Richard Rorty. It is of interest that, although Rorty dismisses Foucault for his "cynical detachment," he rescues Derrida, whom he views, perhaps not without some justice, as a "sentimental, hopeful, romantically idealistic writer." Besides the fact that, as Rorty argues, Nietzsche's suspicion for metaphysical values is shared by some pragmatists, Derrida's critique of the humanist tradition represented by philosophers like Plato, Descartes, and Kant in no way implies a wholesale rejection of humanist values. According to Rorty when Derrida talks about deconstruction as the anticipation of "the democracy that is to come," he joins the band of uto-

pian dreamers to which Rorty himself belongs. There are, however, limits to Derrida's possible admission into the pragmatist fold, as he resists the promises of empiricism and naturalism.

Following the climactic 1970s and 1980s, French theory no longer holds a controversial sway on literature departments. The Paul de Man affair has soured the debate; the end of the cold war has made radical gestures, in philosophy as well as in life, seem out of sync with reality; the French thinkers themselves have mellowed, and moved in other directions; most of the famous figures are no longer living presences, able to make a surprise guest appearance on an American academic stage, and bring down the house. The academic world itself has moved forward. The landscape seems more eclectic, and tolerant of difference, to use one of the key terms "disseminated" by French theory. Globalization has, paradoxically it seems, stimulated the interest in the local, and led to the proliferation of cultural research and area studies. French thinkers, like Henri Lefebvre, Michel Serres, and Bruno Latour have brought an idiosyncratic approach to the understanding of culture and science, and an intriguing view of modernity as such, and have, in this respect, influenced the development of cultural studies in this country. French theory is now part of the curriculum, a chapter in the history of literary studies in America, in a sequence that includes, more recently, besides cultural studies, postcolonial theory, queer theory, and other particular forms of knowledge (for example, trauma studies, disability studies). French theory has gained, with time, a certain respectability and acceptance, and lost in the process its initial rough edge.

The debates surrounding "postmodernity," opened by Fredric Jameson's classical text, *Postmodernism or the Cultural Logic of Late Capitalism*, (1984) have been fueled by arguments derived from poststructuralism, and by the seminal works of Jean-François Lyotard and Jean Baudrillard. In *The Postmodern Condition*, Lyotard announced the end of the Enlightenment, through the demise of "grand narratives" founded on the ideals of human progress and social justice. Baudrillard, on his part, has criticized contemporary consumer societies for their pervasive use of media images, which undermine the very principle of originality, and substitute a shimmering world of simulations for a meaningful order of representations. The universal degradation of representation is matched by the decline or end of ideologies (a notion reinforced by the fall of communism), and subsumed in a general crisis of legitimacy. In this sense, deconstruction may have indeed announced "the shape of things to come" (in Orwell's phrase), rather than the utopian democracy envisaged by Rorty in his reading of Derrida.

Finally, as is the case with many controversial forms of thought, such as Freudian psychoanalysis for instance, French theory has seeped not only into many academic fields, but also into liberal public discourse, and even into popular culture (Baudrillard's *Simulacra and Simulation* is quoted in *The Matrix*). Its most lasting effect can be seen, however, in the works of American feminists, in the development of gay and lesbian studies, in certain forms of postcolonial theory, in film studies, and theories of popular culture. Here, Derrida's concept of *différance*, Deleuze and Guattari's notion of the "minor," Foucault's use of discourse, Lacan's theory of sexual difference and the Other, all play an important role in questioning traditional assumptions concerning the subject, and its position in a certain field of action or in a particular historical/geographical context. In effect, it is perhaps in its contribution to radical views of subjectivity in American thought, that French theory still exerts a fertilizing role, and asserts its political function.

French feminism, represented by Hélène Cixous, Luce Irigaray, and Julia Kristeva, laid the emphasis on femininity and the *jouissance* of the female body, expressed in the notion of *écriture féminine*. Although this direction has had a limited audience among American feminists, the basic critique of the patriarchal order is common to both schools of thought. French feminism was facilitated in its approach to sexual politics by Derrida's critique of traditional metaphysics as a "logocentric" order, and by Lacan's equation between the Phallus (the transcendental male signifier), and the "Name of the Father", an identity that defines the symbolic order in both Western and non-Western societies. Short of revolutionizing the social system, French feminists advocate a linguistic subversion of the "phallogocentric" order, which can provide at least a measure of imaginary satisfaction.

American feminists, especially in the early stages of the movement, were more in tune with reality and political action than their French counterparts, and found inspiration for their theoretical reflections in the civil rights movement, and he protest actions against the war in Vietnam. Many, like Kate Millett and Juliet Mitchell, combined a Marxist view of social oppression, with a critical understanding of Freudian psychoanalysis. With the advent of French theory, American feminists became receptive to poststructuralist notions of the subject, viewed as unstable construct, a "split" entity traversed by language. Although Lacan could be criticized for his endorsement of the Phallus as the transcendental signifier, he could also be used as an ally in deconstructing binary notions of sexual difference and desire.

One of the best examples of a synthetic philosophical approach to the question of sexual identity inspired by French theory is Judith Butler's *Gender Trouble* (1990). Challenging the essentialist view of sexual difference, Butler asserts that it is "compulsory heterosexuality" that dictates gender roles. These cultural formations "congeal over time to produce the appearance of substance, of a natural sort of being" (and sexuality). In Butler's approach the subversion of the patriarchal order takes the form of "trouble," a disturbance of the normative coherence of the social sphere through role-playing ("performativity") or overt homosexual behavior of the kind adopted by butch lesbians or drag queens. Butler's understanding of gender has had a considerable influence on the development of queer theory, which in its practical consequences, is another token of the political implications of French theory.

Postcolonial theories have also benefited from the influence of poststructuralist thought. Edward Said's deconstruction of Orientalism as the negative Other of the rational West, Gayatri Spivak's critique of the Western intellectual who vows to speak for the subaltern Other, Homi Bhabha's notion of "hybridity" which emphasizes the radical dislocation of the subject situated between discourses, in a "liminal" space, all bear the evidence of the impact left on American theory by contemporary French thought. The same analysis could be extended to film studies and popular culture, in which the Lacanian notions of the gaze, image, and desire are put to interpretive, critical use.

Although contemporary French thought has left an indelible mark on American discourses in the academe, few would recognize its presence in the "outside" world. Returning to Lotringer and Cohen's insightful introduction to *French Theory in America*, it is no doubt true that contemporary French thought has provided "new senses of art, philosophy, and science 'outside' reigning American ideas and writing," but its critical, destabilizing function has not extended far beyond the academic sphere. Ideally, French theory could "counter" the two philosophical foundations represented by law and utopia, but few beside the initiated would understand its language, which is, one must say, programmatically untranslatable. Even if terms such as "the Other" or "the Gaze" may circulate in public discourse, it is often in a reductive form, and Baudrillard's unexpected appearance in the *Matrix* was no doubt an imperceptible event for most spectators in the audience. America is still waiting for its own home-grown critical philosophy to move into a different paradigm of thought.

ALINA CLEJ

See also **entries on individuals mentioned in this article**

Further Reading

Althusser, Louis, Balibar, Etienne, *Reading Capital* (1968), translated by Ben Brewster, London: New Left Books, 1975

Barthes, Roland, *The Pleasure of the Text* (1973), translated by Richard Miller, New York: Hill and Wang, 1975

Baudrillard, Jean, *Simulacra and Simulation* (1981), translated by Sheila Faria Glaser, Ann Arbor, MI: University of Michigan Press, 1994

Bourdieu, Pierre, *An Outline of a Theory of Practice* (1972), translated by Richard Nice, Cambridge University Press, 1977

Bourdieu, Pierre, *Distinction* (1979), translated by Richard Nice, London and New York: Routledge 1986

Debord, Guy, *The Society of Spectacle*, Detroit; Black and Red, 1970

Debord, Guy, *Dissemination*, translated by Barbara Johnson, Chicago; University Press, 1981

Deleuze, Gilles, *Difference and Repetition* (1969), translated by Paul Patton, London: Athlone Press, 1994

Deleuze, Gilles, Guattari, Felix, *Anti-Oedipus: Capital and Schizophrenia* (1972), translated by Robert Hurley, M. Seem H. R. Lane, New York: Viking Press, 1977

Deleuze, Gilles, Guattari, Felix, *Kafka: Toward a Minor Literature* (1975), translated by Dana Polan, Minneapolis: University of Minnesota Press, 1986

Derrida, Jacques, *Of Grammatology*, translated by Gayatri Spivak, Baltimore and London: Johns Hopkins University Press, 1976

Derrida, Jacques, *Writing and Difference* (1967), translated by Alan Bass, Chicago: Chicago University Press, 1978

Foucault, Michel, *The Archeology of Knowledge* (1969), translated by A. M. Sheridan-Smith, London: Travistock, 1974

Irigaray, Luce, *Speculum of the Other Woman* (1974), translated by Gillian C. Gill, Ithaca, NY: Cornell University Press, 1985

Kristeva, Julia, *Revolution in Poetic Language* (1974), translated by Margaret Waller, New York: Columbia University Press, 1984

Lacan, Jacques, *Écrits* (1966), *A Selection*, translated by Alan Sheridan, London: Travistock, 1977

Latour, Bruno, *We Have Never Been Modern*, translated by Catherine Porter, Cambridge, MA: Harvard University Press, 1993

Le Doeuff, Michèle, *The Philosophical Imaginary* (1980), translated by Colin Gordon, Stanford, Stanford University Press, 1989

Lefebvre, Henri, *Introduction to Modernity* (1962), translated by John Moore, London: Verso, 1995

Levinas, Emmanuel, *Otherwise than Being, or Beyond Essence* (1974), translated by Alphonso Lingis, Kluwer Academic Publishers, 1981

Lévi-Strauss, Claude, *Structural Anthropology* (1958), translated by Claire Jacobson and Brooke Grundfest Schoepf, New York: Basic Books, 1963

Lyotard, Jean-François, *The Postmodern Condition* (1979), translated by Geoffrey Bennington and Brian Massumi, Minneapolis, Minnesota University Press, 1984

Serres, Michel, *The Parasite* (1980), translated by Lawrence R. Schehr, Baltimore: Johns Hopkins University Press, 1982

Selected Works

Barrett, Michèle, *The Politics of Truth: From Marx to Foucault*, Cambridge: Polity Press, 1991

Cohen, Paul (editor), *Jacques Derrida and the Humanities, A Critical Reader*, Cambridge: Cambridge University Press, 2001

Culler, Jonathan, *On Deconstruction: Theory and Criticism After Structuralism*, Ithaca, NY: Cornell University Press, 1982

Docherty, Thomas, *After Theory: Postmodernism/Postmarxism*, Edinburgh University Press, 1990

Eagleton, Terry, *The Illusions of Postmodernism*, Oxford: Blackwell, 1996

Featherstone, Mike, *Consumer Culture and Postmodernism*, London: Sage, 1991

Harari, Josué, *Textual Strategies, Perspectives in Post-Structuralist Criticism*, Ithaca, NY: Cornell University Press, 1979

Hutcheon, Linda, *The Politics of Postmodernism*, London: Routledge, 1989

Jameson, Fredric, *Postmodernism or, the Cultural Logic of Late Capitalism*, Durham, NC: Duke University Press, 1991

Kaplan, Ann, (editor), *Postmodernism and Its Discontents*, London: Verso, 1988

Megill, Allan, *Prophets of Extremity, Nietzsche, Heidegger, Foucault, Derrida*, Berkeley: University of California Press, 1985

Moi, Toril, *Sexual/Textual Politics, Feminist Literary Theory*, London and New York: Routledge, 1985

Mouffe, Chantal (editor), *Deconstruction and Pragmatism, Simon Critchley, Jacques Derrida, Ernesto Laclau, and Richard Rorty*, London and New York: Routledge, 1996

Mukerji, Chandra and Michel Schudson, eds, *Rethinking Popular Culture*, Berkeley: University of California Press, 1991

Norris, Christopher, *Deconstruction: Theory and Practice*, London: Routledge, 1982

Sarup, Madan, *The Sexual Subject. A* Screen *Reader in Sexuality*, London and New York: Routledge, 1992

Sarup, Madan, *An Introductory Guide to Post-Structuralism and Postmodernism*, Harvester Hemel Hempstead, 1993

Sim, Stuart, *Beyond Aesthetics. Confrontations with Poststructuralism and Postmodernism*, Toronto: University of Toronto Press, 1992

Williams, Patrick and Chrisman, Laura (editors), *Colonial Discourse and Postcolonial Theory: A Reader*, Harvester Hemel Hempstead, 1993

FRENCH-JEWISH INTELLECTUALS

The social role of the modern French intellectual was defined during the Dreyfus Affair and intertwined with "the Jewish Question" from the outset. Although the term *intellectuel* was first given popular currency in the wake of Émile Zola's famous intervention in the Affair when his "J'Accuse!" appeared on January 13, 1898, and was supported the following day by the signatories of the "Manifesto of the Intellectuals," the cultural image of the intellectual was constructed by the anti-Dreyfusard response. Maurice Barrès's "La protestation des intellectuels" published in *Le Journal* on February 1, 1898, was exemplary in this regard, picking up on the new noun to brand intellectuals as a decadent, avant-garde group on the margins of society, who used the esoteric, urbane, universal, "Kantian" language of philosophy. For Barrès, intellectuals were thus severed from the rootedness of the true French language and the culture of *la patrie* and, similar to

Jews, are only "pretenders," "half-cultured . . . poisoned spirits" who have destroyed French instinct and substituted consciousness for it because they are "ashamed to think like the simple French." The image of the intellectual was thus fused with the discourse from "the Jewish Question" even as the collective engagement against injustice in the name of the universal ideals of the French Revolution using the means of the modern media to publicize their support of the oppressed henceforward defined the social role of the intelligensia.

The differing responses by French-Jewish intellectuals to this fusion defined their twentieth-century role. Émile Durkheim, Marcel Proust, Julien Benda, and Léon Blum embraced the republican, Revolutionary credo as a means to escape their social marginalization, reconciling their Jewish heritage with the universal values associated with the modern intellectual. In so doing, as Jews they were often caught in the double binds of the republican social contract. Durkheim (1858–1917), an integrated Frenchman but the son of a rabbi, one of the founders of modern academic sociology and a defender of Dreyfus in the name of the ideals of 1789, was vilified by the nationalist and anti-Semitic right. Like many assimilated Jews (*Israëlites*), he was therefore haunted by the fear that he would be too closely associated with his Jewishness. Marcel Proust (1871–1922), the son a Jewish mother, but who was raised in his father's Catholic faith, whose Jewish consciousness was awakened by the Dreyfus case (it was Proust who convinced Anatole France to intervene), but whose Jewish characters reflect a basic insecurity about their Jewish backgrounds is another example of this dilemma. Like Proust's Jewish characters, writer and philosopher Julien Benda (1867–1956) was burdened by his Jewish origins. He established his reputation in a series of essays that were critical of intellectuals who emphasized class, racial, or national differences rather than espousing universal, humanist values, most famously in *La trahison des clercs* (The Treason of the Intellectuals, 1927). He was forced to seek refuge in southern France during World War II, but believed that "the Jewish Question" was only a minor facet of the war.

A key figure in French interwar politics was Léon Blum. Like all those of his generation, the Dreyfus Affair was also decisive for Blum, who approached his idol Barrès, the prince of youth and leading voice for the literary avant-garde, to align with the Dreyfusards at the end of 1897, only to be rejected. After the rupture and guided by the librarian at the École Normale Superieure, Lucien Herr, Blum would wind his way to his tutelage under Jean Jaurès and to eventual leadership in the socialist party. In his memoirs of the Affair, he heroized the courage of Jews like Mathieu Dreyfus and Bernard Lazare while vilifying the passivity of wealthy Jews and the leaders in the Consistory who were bystanders. Like Durkheim, Blum as the first socialist and first Jewish premier would become a symbol for the extreme right in the 1930s, that insisted in the words of Laurent Viguier that, "The Jew Blum did everything to bring about the war, and war under the harshest conditions for France." When war did come in May 1940, its harshest conditions were clearly reserved for Jews, and Blum would be arrested by the Vichy government and put on trial as a traitor in February 1942 and then handed over to the Germans, who held him prisoner until 1945.

Lazare would emerge from the Dreyfus Affair advocating an auto-emancipationist, Zionist solution to "the Jewish Question," but this was an unusual response for the leading French-Jewish intellectuals until the Jewish revival after World War I. With 200,000 Jews immigrating to France in the wake of pogroms in the East, a transformed Jewish community led to a reawakening of Jewish culture in France, with Zionism as a significant influence, especially for intellectuals like Gustave Kahn (1859–1936), the art critic, novelist, and symbolist poet, and Henri Franck, the great-grandson of the chief rabbi of Strasbourg, whose poetry tried to balance his Jewish nationalism with the French Cartesian tradition. Edmond Fleg (1874–1963) devoted himself to deepening the understanding of Jewish history and culture, presenting French readers with the multifaceted dimensions of Judaism through his translations of Shalom Aleichem, Maimonides, the Zohar, and the Passover *Haggadah* and in works like his *Anthologie juive des origines à nos jours* (The Jewish Anthology, 1925), as well as in his writings on the Zionist pioneers. In his religious poetry and biographical and autobiographical works, he emphasized the Jewish mission and messianic yearnings, connecting them to a faith in humanity, and thus refusing to bifurcate particularism and universalism, Jewishness and Frenchness. Perhaps the most active Zionist intellectual of the interwar period was André Spire (1868–1966), who was roused from assimilation by the Dreyfus Affair to become a passionate defender of Jewish national revival. He personally dueled with the anti-Semite Drumont, supported self-defense groups for Russian Jews during the pogroms, and helped organize those who came to France. He founded the Ligue des Amis du Sionisme (League of the Friends of Zionism) in 1918 and was the French Zionist representative at the Paris Peace Conference in 1919. As a critic and poet, Spire was also the leader of the rebirth of Jewish literature in the interwar period that included Albert Cohen and Jean-Richard Bloch.

After the dark years of Vichy, the postwar generation of French-Jewish intellectuals built on the foundations of this renaissance in Jewish thought and culture. Inaugurated by the *École de pensée juive de Paris*, named by Emmanuel Levinas after the renowned "Paris school" of Jewish painters that included Marc Chagall, Chaim Soutine, and Amadeo Modigliani, its most outstanding exponents included André Neher, Albert Memmi, Éliane Amado Lévy-Valensi, Vladimir Jankélévitch, and Wladimir Rabinovitch (Rabi). This ensemble represents the remarkable fusion that characterizes postwar French-Jewish thought: Sephardim and Ashkenazim, Zionism and Franco-Judaism, religious existentialism and humanism. The École juive de Paris reevaluated Jewish identity, Jewish religion, and Jewish Gentile relations in light of the challenges to Jewish emancipation from scientific racism and Nazism, Zionism and the foundation of the State of Israel, and the revitalization of the Jewish community in France created by decolonization. With upward of 600,000 Jews, France witnessed the building of synagogues, community centers, schools, kosher restaurants and butcher shops, new umbrella organizations that represented the community, and a new interest in Jewish intellectual concerns.

The École juive launched their rebirth of Judaism from two institutional bases: the *École des Cadres d'Orsay* and, in the forum of an annual meeting of French-Jewish intellectuals, the *Colloques des intellectuels juifs de langue française* (Colloquia of Francophone Jewish Intellectuals). Established in 1946 (and remaining open until 1965) by Robert Gamzon, a leader of the Resistance who saved Jewish children from deportation as director of the Jewish boy scouts, the *École d'Orsay* was formed during the Nazi Occupation to produce a new "school of prophets" to preserve Jewish learning and values for the Liberation. Its charismatic teachers, especially Jacob Gordin and Léon Askenazi, brought together unique components characteristic of the new Jewish thought in France. Gordin (1896–1947), influenced by Hermann Cohen, was a disciple of the Neo-Kantian Marburg School and steeped in Kabbalah (Jewish mysticism) and medieval Jewish philosophy, especially Maimonides. After Gordin's premature death in 1947, Askenazi, the son of the head rabbi of Oran, continued Gordin's legacy, making the *École d'Orsay* the most creative institution of Jewish learning for Jewish youth for twenty years after the war.

Incorporating but transcending the Franco-Jewish synthesis of prewar intellectuals like Spire and Fleg, who would give the opening address of the *Colloque* on the meaning of Jewish history, the first colloquium met in Versailles in May 1957 with about thirty in attendance and subsequently moved to Paris for annual meetings as interest in the group grew. The *Colloque* was convoked around broad themes that would be in-

terrogated in new ways, including the role of Israel in relation to the Occident, the interconnections of memory and history, politics and religion, the unique and the universal, Jewish conscience/consciousness, the body, the idea of money, idolatry, humanity, the state, and justice. Each intellectual would respond to the year's theme from his domain of expertise: Neher, the bible; Askénazi, the Kabbalah; Lévi-Valensi, psychoanalysis; Jankélévitch, general philosophy; and Rabi, politics. The highlight was the Talmudic lectures that Levinas delivered each year. The *Colloque* thus gathered the threads of Jewish thought around modern preoccupations and became the principal matrix of the intellectual reformulation of French Judaism. Animated today by the 1968 generation of Jews, the *Colloque* now draws nearly a thousand people and is divided into many sessions, symbolic of the intellectual effervescence of the contemporary generation, as well as its diversity.

If the generation of the École juive de Paris was defined by the Shoah, the foundation of Israel, and the decolonization of the Maghreb, then the second generation of postwar French intellectuals was marked by the Six Day War, General de Gaulle's response to it, and the events of May–June 1968. At the height of the Arab-Israeli conflict, Jews in France and around the world feared an *Étatcide* (genocide of the people of the state of Israel) and joyously celebrated the rapid victory of the Israelis and the unification of Jerusalem effected in June 1967. In the jubilation, several prominent Jewish intellectuals of the first postwar generation left France for Israel, thus sapping the French community not only by their absence, but also by the divisions over the centrality and legitimacy of Israel culturally and politically.

In response to the Six Day War, on November 27, 1967, in a press conference from the Elysée Palace, which some term his "sermon to the Hebrews," President Charles de Gaulle condemned Israel, severed France's alliance, and legitimated an arms embargo as the beginning of a major shift in France's foreign policy in the Middle East. In castigating Israel's policy, de Gaulle also defamed the character of the Jewish people as a whole, calling them "a self-assured, domineering, elite people," and thus echoing anti-Semitic myths. The distinguished philosopher and sociologist Raymond Aron led a chorus of voices that charged that when de Gaulle, the symbol of the Resistance, the intransigent fighter for liberty and national autonomy, invoked the images of Jewish arrogance, superiority, power, and domination, he removed the protective shield that he represented and authorized "a new anti-semitism."

With the taboo on public anti-Semitism that had persisted since the Holocaust undermined, public acts of anti-Semitism—from graffiti to terror attacks and the desecration of cemeteries to assaults on Jewish establishments and synagogues—became an important influence on French Jewish intellectuals after 1967. Pierre Goldman, the son of Polish resistance fighters and author of *Dim Memories of a Polish Jewish Born in France*, represented many Jewish radicals of his generation when he insisted that "to be Jewish is not what I have, but my condition . . . . It's a space that I fill existentially with this and that . . . . And why is this so important? Because of antisemitism. Because of the hatred. The only answer to the question of what it means to be a Jew is Auschwitz." As if to underscore this point, Goldman was assassinated by a neo-Nazi group.

Goldman was one example of a wide gamut of French-Jewish extreme leftists for whom the May–June events of 1968 would centrally shape their entire generation. Inspired by movements of decolonization and anti-Stalinist revolts in Eastern Europe, May 1968 began as a series of sporadic student protests against the bureaucracy of the university, sexual prescriptions in the student dorms, and the constraints of consumer society. In alliance with workers, by the middle of May, a general wildcat strike had spread across France, shutting down the country and threatening to topple de Gaulle's regime. Many young Jews—including Daniel Cohn-Bendit, Benny Lévy, and Alain Geismar—made up the leadership and membership of the plethora of small groups on the extreme left that animated the events.

Daniel Cohn-Bendit, known as "Red Danny" both because of his hair and his political views, was the most famous of the student revolutionaries and the quintessential example of the radical Jew. Today a member of the European Parliament from the Green Party, Cohn-Bendit was born in France in 1945 to a family of German Jews who fled Nazi persecution in 1933. After passing his matriculation exam in Germany, he returned to France in 1965, attending the Nanterre campus in the suburbs of Paris, emerging as the infamous instigator of the "Mouvement du 22 mars," named after the date that the coterie of anarchists, Maoists, communists, and Situationists occupied the administration building, beginning the student uprisings. At the height of the events, Cohn-Bendit was prevented from returning to France by the government after a short trip to speak at other student revolutionary gatherings in Europe. A huge protest on May 24 had as its rallying cry the slogan, "We are all German Jews!" In their support of Cohn-Bendit, the rebels of 1968 thus identified with German Jews, with undesirables, outsiders, and foreigners and simultaneously associated the Gaullist government with the Vichy regime. This was only one moment of several where the

Vichy past would loom large in the conscience of this generation.

Benny Lévy's trajectory "from Mao to Moses" represents the shift from Jewish radicals to radical Jews that constitutes one vector of the contemporary generation's trajectory. Lévy was only one of a number of important Jewish intellectuals for whom Levinas was a central influence. These include Catherine Chalier, Marc-Alain Ouaknin, Bernard-Henri Lévy (often referred to by his initials, BHL), and Alain Finkielkraut, all of whom are united by Levinas's rethinking of the priority of ethics for every dimension of human existence. Ouaknin, a rabbi and son of the chief rabbi of Metz, is from Morocco but was trained in the Litvak yeshiva tradition. He has a doctorate in philosophy and works with psychoanalysts, and he combines these influences as an extraordinarily prolific writer, who, along with the influence of Levinas, incorporates a wide coterie of French philosophers and writers as well as the Hassidic masters in the way he opens the Talmud and Jewish tradition to new interpretations and contemporary relevance.

Both BHL and Alain Finkielkraut are largely secular intellectuals, influenced by Levinas's reevaluation of humanism, which they stress in perennial interventions in contemporary cultural and political debates and in their wide influence in the media. BHL, the darling of French television because of his charisma and good looks, achieved notoriety as the leader of the "Nouveaux Philosophes" (New Philosophers). At the height of the media frenzy that focused on them as the new stars of the French intellectual scene, in no small measure because they emphasized anti-totalitarianism and a critique of the Marxist tradition as the leitmotif of their work, BHL published books like *L'idéologie française*, suggesting that a fascist impulse lay at the core of French national identity, and *Le Testament de Dieu*, which explored the meaning of monotheism for the modern world.

In search of a secular Jewish culture in France, Finkielkraut, who has emerged as perhaps the most visible secular Jewish intellectual in France, was initially attracted to Le Cercle Gaston Crémieux, named for an adept of Saint-Simon and leader of the Marseille Communards who revolted in the aftermath of the Franco-Prussian war. The Cercle was founded by Richard Marienstras—a Polish Jew who moved to France as a child and who fought in the Resistance as a boy—an editor of *Kadimah* (the journal of the Union d'Etudiants Juifs) who taught English at the Ecole Maïmonide (a Jewish lycée that helped cultivate several of the contemporary generation of Jewish intellectuals) before he became a professor of English literature at the University of Paris. Marienstras's vision is for a diaspora Jewish community modeled on the Bund: a socialist

Jewish workers union founded in 1897 with strongholds in Lithuania, Poland, and Russia that advocated Jewish minority nationalism concomitantly with its socialist politics. Marienstras's version of Jewishness is critical of the state of Israel and institutionalized Judaism in France, as well as of the assimilationist social contract that characterizes the French Republican tradition. The Cercle was thus an important milieu for cultivating secular Jewish activists.

Before breaking with the Cercle, Finkielkraut first presented his brilliant analysis of the dilemmas of contemporary Jewish identity, *The Imaginary Jew*, to this group. In this and subsequent works, he negotiates the fragile precipice between a critique of anti-Semitism and assimilation that still supports the ideals of Jewish emancipation and advocacy for the state of Israel and for Diaspora Jewish life. He thus espouses ethnic particularism rooted in history that nevertheless aspires to universal ideals. Finkielkraut's critical stance is characteristic of many of the social scientists, historians, philosophers, and other academics who work on Jewish topics and who represent another important constellation of Jewish intellectuals, including Robert and Elisabeth Badinter, Pierre Birnbaum, Elizabeth de Fontenay, Chantal Benayoun, Catherine Kintzler, Doris Bensimon, Freddy Raphaël, Pierre Vidal-Nacquet, Maurice-Ruben Hayoun, Annie Kriegel, Daniel Lindenberg, and Dominique Schnapper (Aron's daughter).

Several of the prominent French Jewish intellectuals today were direct products of the École d'Orsay, including Gérard Israël, Armand Abécassis, Henri Atlan, and Jean Zacklad. Israël, born in Algeria, is the author of numerous books and the editor-in-chief of *Les Nouveaux cahiers*, one of several major Jewish journals that include *Combat pour la Diaspora, Revue des études juives, Yod, Traces, L'Arche* and *Pardès*. Abécassis, from Strasbourg like his teacher André Neher, continues the work of the great biblical scholar by exploring the contemporary relevance of the Pentateuch and the Prophets and engages in open dialogue with Christianity. Atlan is a doctor and biologist and a philosopher and Talmudic scholar. He investigates the scientific field conscious of its limits, working to open the dead ends of modern rationalism by exploring alternative truths in aesthetics, morality, and science from the purview of the Talmud.

Jean Zacklad represents yet another milieu in which contemporary Jewish intellectuals are reinvestigating the significance of the Jewish tradition. Zacklad has held a weekly study group for years in his home on the aptly named rue de Dieu. In this intimate setting attended by the likes of Benny Lévy and Charles Mopsik, Zacklad would read and translate a passage from the Tenach and then analyze the text on the basis of

the teachings of Léon Askenazi and his university professors André Neher and the influential philosopher Paul Ricouer, along with his Moroccan *rav* (rabbinic master). This confluence of influences has reached fruition in a number of books that explore the vitality of Jewish ethical approaches for the problems of the present age (e.g., his analysis of how Judaism considers femininity).

From the perspective of Jewish thought, the vanguard of the contemporary generation is represented by those who have returned to traditional Jewish texts to rethink Jewish identity and who seek simultaneously to transform the Jewish community and French society on the basis of a reexamination of Jewish values. In addition to those already discussed, these include Raphaël Draï, who comments on the Torah in light of political theory and political theory in light of the Torah, and Charles Mopsik, an ultra-orthodox Jew who writes on Jewish mysticism and directs the venerated series of Jewish books published by Verdier, a publishing collective started by former Maoists.

Two of the most intriguing figures in this constellation are Gilles Bernheim and Shmuel Trigano, who together recently formed GESHER, which is committed to bridging the various groups within the Jewish community under the rainbow of a heterogeneous but normative Judaism. Bernheim is both an ordained rabbi and an accredited philosopher associated with the Centre Nationale de Recherche Scientifique. His dynamic teaching style has energized those who attend his classes at cultural centers (Centre Universitaire Edmond Fleg and the Centre d'Art et de Culture Espace Rachi), the Beit Hamidrach of the Alliance Israélite Universelle, or at his sermons at the synagogue on Rue de la Victoire and the Jewish student center. In his classes, interviews, articles, and books, Bernheim deftly balances Jewish particularism and universality, tying together ritual, reflection, and textual praxis by insisting that Jewish election is not a privilege but bears the burden of responsibility for the Other, embodied in *mitsvot* (religious commandment) that demands that we change our patterns of thought, speech, and action and provides the model for doing so.

Trigano expands on this vision in his many books by developing a theory of Jewish politics critical of diaspora emancipation, revolutionary anti-Judaism, culturally autonomous diaspora Judaism, and political Zionism, claiming these all lead to (Jewish) self-alienation. Instead, he calls for a return to the Jewish community structured by its relation to Jewish law and the critical reading of Jewish texts, while denouncing radical separation. He thus discerns the distinguishing facets of a revived Judaism in France that can become a new model beyond Enlightenment paradigms.

The stars of the postwar French-Jewish intellectual community represent a multifarious constellation that constitutes at once a remnant and a renaissance of European-Jewish culture. They serve to illuminate a galaxy of concepts, publications, and institutions that have not only revitalized French Jewry but that might yet serve the Jewish mission of *tikkun olam* (redeeming the world).

JONATHAN JUDAKEN

See also **Maurice Barres; Julien Benda; Emile Durkheim; Vladimir Jankelevitch; Jean Jaures; Emmanuel Levinas; Bernard-Henri Levy; Paul Ricoeur**

Further Reading

Astro, Alan, ed., *Discourses of Jewish Identity in Twentieth-Century France: Yale French Studies*, no. 85, New Haven, Connecticut: Yale University Press, 1994

Birnbaum, Pierre, *Jewish Destinies: Citizenship, State, and Community in Modern France*, New York: Hill and Wang, 2000

Datta, Venita, *Birth of a National Icon: The Literary Avant-Garde and the Origins of the Intellectual in France*, Albany, New Yorks: SUNY Press, 1999

Finkielkraut, Alain, *The Imaginary Jew*, translated by Kevin O'Neill and David Suchoff, Lincoln: University of Nebraska Press, 1980

Friedlander, Judith, *Vilna on the Seine: Jewish Intellectuals in France Since 1968*, New Haven, Connecticut: Yale University Press, 1990

Hyman, Paula, *From Dreyfus to Vichy: The Remaking of French Jewry, 1906–1939*, New York: Columbia University Press, 1979

Hyman, Paula, *The Jews of Modern France*, Berkeley: University of California Press, 1998

Judaken, Jonathan, " 'To be or not to be French' ": *Soixante-huitard* Reflections on '*la question juive*,' "*Journal of Modern Jewish Studies*, 1, 1 (2002): 3–21

Kritzman, Lawrence, ed., *After Auschwitz: Race, Culture and "the Jewish Question" in France*, New York: Routledge, 1995

Lehrmann, Charles, *The Jewish Element in French Literature*, translated by George Klin, Rutherford: Fairleigh Dickinson University Press, 1971

Levinas, Emmanuel, *Difficult Freedom: Essays on Judaism*, translated by Seán Hand, Baltimore, Maryland: Johns Hopkins University Press, 1990

Malino, Frances, and Bernard Wasserstein, eds., *The Jew in Modern France*, Hanover, New Hampshire: University Press of New England, 1985

Marks, Elaine, *Marrano as Metaphor: The Jewish Presence in French Writing*, New York: Columbia University Press, 1996

Marrus, Michael, *The Politics of Assimilation: The Jewish Community in France at the Time of the Dreyfus Affair*, Oxford: Oxford University Press, 1971

Schnapper, Moninique, *Jewish Identities in France: An Analysis of Contemporary French Jewry*, translated by Arthur Goldhammer, Chicago: University of Chicago Press, 1983

G

GARAUDY, ROGER
Political and Religious Thinker

Roger Garaudy started his meandering intellectual life in the postwar period as a cultural *apparatchik* of the French Communist Party (PCF). At the time that he was the director of the main communist research institute in France, the *Centre d'Etudes et de Recherches Marxistes*, he became recognized as a specialist in Hegelian philosophy. A prolific author, during this period he published more than fifty monographs and essays, and also numerous reviews and papers, frequently defending the Party's Stalinist line on most subjects and revealing himself a hagiographer of Stalin and the French long-serving General Secretary, Maurice Thorez.

An important role played by Garaudy within the PCF inner circle was to act as a critical analyst of the arts, denouncing noncommunist writers as bourgeois, for instance, in *Literature of the Graveyard* (1948), where he summed up his approach as follows: "Every class has the literature it deserves. The upper bourgeoisie in decay delights in the erotic obsessions of a Henry Miller or the intellectual fornications of Jean-Paul Sartre." However, from the early 1960s, more receptive to other forms of thinking, he became the PCF envoy toward the broader intellectual community. For instance, his writings on art (such as *Realism without Walls*, 1962) show that although apparently supporting the classic socialist-realism point of view, he gave full autonomy to art as a creative field. During this period, he opened dialogues with existentialism, structuralism, and even modern Christian thinking (*Perspectives de l'homme*, 1959; *Le Communisme est un humanisme*, 1960), thereby shedding his Stalinist image to become a humanist Marxist.

From the mid-1960s he became increasingly disenchanted with Soviet communism, and closer to Togliatti, which inspired Eurocommunism, the less totalitarian form of Marxist politics favored for instance by Italian communists in the late 1960s and 1970s. Although he still engaged in ideological clashes within the PCF (for instance, clashing with the philosopher Louis Althusser about his book *For Marx* in 1969, against whom he defends a humanist Marxist position), he also began to distance himself, supporting the student revolt of May 1968 and condemning the Soviet invasion of Czechoslovakia in terms that were not acceptable to the hard-line of the PCF led by Georges Marchais. He lost his seat in the politburo and was then expelled from the Party in 1970.

He continued to teach philosophy, and to write studies of the arts, for instance on dance (*Dancer sa vie*, 1973). He became more and more interested in religion, of which he wrote in 1966 that it is "transcending the given" and "anticipating the real, whether by justifying the existing order or by protesting against it and attempting to transform it." In mid-1975 he converted to Roman Catholicism in a *parcours* analyzed in several works (notably *Parole d'homme*, 1975). However, his intellectual and spiritual evolution was not yet complete. In 1984 he converted to Islam, continuing to examine religious experiences including the most extreme, as in *Integrismes* (1990).

In 1996 he published *The Founding Myths of the State of Israel*, in which he criticized the sociopolitical basis of Israel, including, according to him, the use that is made of the Holocaust. In part, he sought to reassess the extent of the "final solution": though he does not deny it completely, he claims, using arguments of revisionists and "negationists," that the scale of the Holocaust has been exaggerated. In 1998 he was brought to court for denying crime against humanity, and heavily fined. The whole episode became a front-page scandal when a well-known and charismatic Roman Catholic figure and charity founder, the popular Abbé Pierre, gave Garaudy his support (then retracted it under pressure from the church hierarchy). The situation was made more complex when it became known that Garaudy had numerous contacts with extreme-right intellectual groups in the 1990s, such as the GRECE. As a result, Garaudy is, as of this writing, a popular figure in many Moslem countries, notably Morocco and Lebanon, and among "negationists" on the internet.

FRANÇOIS NECTOUX

See also **Louis Althusser; Jean-Paul Sartre**

Biography

Born into a Marseilles protestant family in 1913, Roger Garaudy was educated at the prestigious École Normale Supérieure. He was influenced by the modernist theologian Teilhard de Chardin and by Kierkegaard before discovering Marxism. During the Second World War, after briefly serving in the French army, he joined the Resistance and was interned in a French camp in Algeria's Sahara Desert by the Vichy authorities. At the end of the war, having joined the French Communist Party, he began a career as a politician and a leader of the Party in which he became a member of the Central Committee (1945) and later of the Politburo (1956). As early as 1945 he was elected as a *député* to the National Assembly, where he served until 1958 (including a period when he was Deputy President of the National Assembly), and was later a Senator for the Seine department (1959–1962).

Selected Works

From Anathema to Dialogue, 1970
Marxism in the Twentieth Century, 1970
Turning Point of Socialism, 1970
Whole Truth, 1971
The Alternative Future: a Vision of Christian Marxism, 1976
The Founding Myths of Modern Israel, 1997

GENETTE, GÉRARD
Literary Theorist

Gérard Genette is the major figure in the collective effort begun in the 1960s to adapt and extend to literary studies the structuralist theories developed for linguistics by Ferdinand de Saussure and for anthropology by Claude Lévi-Strauss. In a dozen important books, Genette has developed a model for describing and analyzing the structures and figures that compose literary texts, establishing a foundation for the study of literary art on its own terms. His work adds up to a rational and consistent poetics that aspires to the clarity and rigor of a scientific discipline without sacrificing the ability to focus on the uniqueness and subtlety of individual texts, writers, and readers.

Genette's reputation and influence are grounded primarily upon his classic structuralist study of narrative, *Discours du récit* (*Narrative Discourse*), which lays out the most comprehensive and self-consistent framework yet proposed for the analysis of narrative texts. By analogy with the discipline of linguistics, which plays a role in describing language parallel to the role Genette envisions his poetics playing for literary texts, he organizes his analysis according to categories borrowed from the grammar of verbs. The major divisions are tense, which considers temporal relations in narrative, subdivided into relations of order, duration, and frequency (this last a highly original concept in narrative analysis); mood, under which Genette revolutionizes the traditional study of narrative point of view; and voice, which addresses narrators, audiences, and narrative levels in new and fruitful ways.

Genette blends theory with practice in *Narrative Discourse* by illustrating and testing his theories against one of the monuments of French fiction, Marcel Proust's *À la recherche du temps perdu* (*Remembrance of Things Past*), making his book a watershed for both narrative theory and Proust criticism. All of his work is characterized by this movement back and forth between general hypotheses and the data of specific texts, a combining of theory and criticism that has helped make his work much more user-friendly than that of such contemporary structuralists as Michel Foucault and Jacques Lacan, whose interests parallel Genette's in some ways. Although the volume and diversity of response to Genette's theory was so great as to compel him to reply in a second book, *Nouveau Discours du récit* (*Narrative Discourse Revisited*), his original model has weathered the test of time largely intact, and remains the foundation upon which virtually every subsequent discussion of narrative theory is based. Genette has also contributed to narratology as an editor. He edited the special number of the journal *Communications* that brought structuralist literary theory to the forefront of critical attention in 1966, and in 1970 Genette, Tzvetan Todorov, and Julia Kristeva founded *Poétique*, still the flagship of French journals devoted to poetics. Genette and Todorov also founded the influential *Poétique* monograph series, which Genette still directs as of this writing.

Although Genette's major works on narrative theory have reached a broad international audience, the bulk of his subsequent (and increasingly broad and ambitious) work in the 1970s and 1980s was not translated into English until the 1990s. Among anglophone critics, who made up the largest audience for his early work, those later works thus remain relatively unknown and untried. These innovative and comprehensive studies break ground in a number of important fields, including a few which must be considered as his discoveries. Genette surveys the historical foundations of the study of language and linguistics in *Mimologiques* (*Mimologics*), and rediscovers for modern criticism the long and, until his book, almost entirely ignored tradition of mimetic theories of language origin and development. Genette's next three works identify and analyze three types of what he terms "transtextuality," a term that includes virtually everything that puts a given text into relation with other texts. He offers an analysis of "architextuality," which considers the question of the relations of texts to their genres, in *Introduction à l'architexte* (*The Architext: An Introduction*). Despite the relatively familiar field he addresses, it should be noted that his conclusions about genres differ from all previous divisions. His next two long books develop what amount to new areas for research and discussion. The relations that Genette includes under the label of "hypertextuality" are classified and explored in *Palimpsestes* (*Palimpsests*). His theory states that hypertextuality covers any relations between a text B (hypertext) and an anterior text A (hypotext) that are not citations of A by B ("intertexts") or commentaries by B on A ("metatexts"), but stylistic transformations of A in B, such as in parody or pastiche. For the subject of *Seuils* (*Paratexts*), Genette coins the term "paratextuality," which designates the myriad relations of texts to their own surrounding apparatus of titles, prefaces, advertisements, epigraphs, authorial interviews and correspondence, and so on. As usual, Genette does not simply offer a list of such possible relations, but instead offers a comprehensive analysis of the range of significant functions performed by these elements.

The four essays of his *Fiction et diction* (*Fiction and Diction*) attempt to define an aggregate of terms fundamental to the study of narrative, among them "literature," "fiction," and "style." Genette offers analyses of the factors that make some written works of art "literature" although others are not, maps out the factors that constitute the fundamental differences between fictional and nonfictional writing, and develops a semiotic approach to style and its role in creating meaning. Genette's most recent works are perhaps his most ambitious to date. In the two volumes of *L'Oeuvre de l'art* (*The Work of Art*) he considers the two aspects of art implied by the double sense of the title, proposing a theory both of the nature of the artwork and of the aesthetic work performed by art. As Genette concedes, his concerns in these volumes have extended far beyond the traditional confines of literary criticism and theory and into areas formerly reserved for philosophers of aesthetics. His examples are as sweeping as his topic, drawn from virtually every field of art, including architecture, music, painting, and sculpture, not just from literature. Genette's argument, though not discounting the importance of such factors as genre and artistic intention, leads to a highly subjective and relativistic view of art, in which there are no agreed-upon criteria that can outweigh the interpretations and judgments of the subject who experiences the work of art. Although no treatment of such vast issues can hope to be considered definitive, Genette's work remains consistently provocative and challenging.

WILLIAM NELLES

See also **Michel Foucault; Julia Kristeva; Jacques Lacan; Claude Levi-Strauss; Ferdinand de Saussure; Tzvetan Todorov**

Biography

Genette was born in Paris, France, in 1930. He graduated from the *École Normale Supérieure* in 1955 and taught secondary school from 1958 to 1963 before taking a position as a lecturer in French literature at the Sorbonne. In 1967, he became an assistant professor at the interdisciplinary *École des Hautes Études en Sciences Sociales*, where he later became the director of studies. Genette's reputation became international after his first two books, and he has been highly sought after as a visiting professor, teaching as a visiting scholar at such American universities as Yale, Johns Hopkins, the University of Wisconsin, the University of California at Berkeley, and New York University. When not working abroad, Genette lives in Paris.

Selected Works

Figures, 1966

Figures II, 1969

Figures III, 1972; "Discours du récit: essai de méthode," pages 65–282, translated by Jane E. Lewin as *Narrative Discourse: An Essay in Method*, 1980

Mimologiques: Voyage en Cratylie, 1976; as *Mimologics*, translated by Thaïs Morgan, 1995

Introduction à l'architexte, 1979; as *The Architext: An Introduction*, translated by Jane E. Lewin, 1992

Palimpsestes: La littérature au second degré, 1982; as *Palimpsests: Literature in the Second Degree*, translated by Channa Newman and Claude Doubinsky, 1997

Figures of Literary Discourse, selections from *Figures, Figures II, and Figures III*, translated by Alan Sheridan, 1982

Nouveau Discours du récit, 1983; as *Narrative Discourse Revisited*, translated by Jane E. Lewin, 1988

Seuils, 1987; as *Paratexts: Thresholds of Interpretation*, translated by Jane E. Lewin, 1997

Fiction et diction, 1991; as *Fiction and Diction*, translated by Catherine Porter, 1993

L'Oeuvre de l'art [1]: Immanence et transcendence, 1994; as *The Work of Art: Immanence and Transcendence*, translated by G. M. Goshgarian, 1997

L'Oeuvre de l'art [2]: La Relation esthéthique, 1997; as *The Aesthetic Relation*, translated by G. M. Goshgarian, 1999

Figures IV, 1999

Further Reading

After Genette: Current Directions in Narrative Analysis and Theory, Special number of *Studies in the Literary Imagination*, 25.1 (1992): 1–112

Booth, Wayne, "Rhetorical Critics Old and New: The Case of Gérard Genette," in *Reconstructing Literature*, edited by Lerner-Lawrence, Totawa, NJ: Barnes and Noble, 1983

Chatman, Seymour, *Story and Discourse: Narrative Structure in Fiction and Film*, Ithaca: Cornell University Press, 1978

Diengott, Nilli, "The Implied Author Once Again," *Journal of Literary Semantics*, 22.1 (1993): 68–75

Fludernik, Monika, "New Wine in Old Bottles? Voice, Focalization, and New Writing," *New Literary History*, 32.3 (2001): 619–38

Gorman, David, "Gérard Genette: An Anglo-French Checklist to 1996," *Style*, 30.4 (1996): 539–50

Keskinen, Mikko, "Reading on the Threshold: Gérard Genette's Peritexts as Interpretive Commentary," in *Reading Reading: Essays on the Theory and Practice of Reading*, edited by Andrew Bennett, Tampere, Finland: University of Tampere, 1993

Lanser, Susan Sniader, *The Narrative Act: Point of View in Narrative Fiction*, Princeton: Princeton University Press, 1981

Mosher, Harold F., Jr, "The Structuralism of Gérard Genette," *Poetics*, 5 (1976): 75–86

Mosher, Harold F., Jr, revues of *The Work of Art* and *The Aesthetic Relation, Style*, 33.2 (1999): 336–46

Nelles, William, *Frameworks: Narrative Levels and Embedded Narrative*, New York: Peter Lang, 1997

Rimmon-Kenan, *Narrative Fiction: Contemporary Poetics*, London: Methuen, 1983

VAN GENNEP, ARNOLD
Anthropologist

Arnold van Gennep was a pioneer of the anthropological school of thought known as structuralism. The structuralists reacted against earlier writers who had interpreted customs reported in non-Western societies as survivals from what were supposed to be earlier stages in human social evolution. Structuralism contends that the cultural significance of objects and actions derives from their place in a cognitive system. The earliest structural analysis, Durkheim and Mauss's *Primitive classification* (1963), was published in 1903. Van Gennep's *The rites of passage* appeared two years later, in 1905. Anthropologists associated with Durk-

heim argued that the internal logic of a culture's belief system gave meaning to ritual actions. As van Gennep wrote, "The primary purpose of this book is precisely to react against the procedure which consists of extracting various rites from a set of ceremonies and considering them in isolation, thus removing them from a context which gives them meaning and reveals their position in a dynamic whole." Van Gennep contended that there is a general tendency among human societies to conceive of a change in status on the model of a journey from one town or country to another or, as he expressed it, a "territorial passage." Territorial passage had three aspects: separation from the place of origin, transition (*la marge*), and incorporation into the destination. Territorial passage could stand for any change of status in society. "marriage by capture," where the groom and his brothers ride to the bride's house, snatch her and carry her back to the wedding is not a survival from some fancied early epoch in human evolution when cave men clubbed women and dragged them home, but a symbolic enactment of the separation of the bride from her status as an unmarried girl in her parents' house, and her incorporation into the groom's household as a married woman. Through a series of case studies, van Gennep demonstrated that rituals of birth, entry into adulthood, and death might all have the same structure. Van Gennep's contemporary Robert Hertz later applied this approach to the study of "double funerals," in which one ritual takes place immediately after death, and a second ritual some months later. Hertz argued the first ceremony copes with relatives' immediate grief by disposing of the corpse. Mourners remain in a marginal state until the second funeral consigns the dead to the afterlife, and reintegrates relatives into the community of the living.

Van Gennep did not join the group of scholars that worked with Durkheim (*L'Année Sociologique*). Instead, he went on to hold the first chair in ethnography at the University of Neuchâtel. In 1920 van Gennep published a devastating critique of Durkheim's structural theory of totemism, arguing that totemism is not a unitary phenomenon and cannot therefore be treated as the prototypical religion. The structural anthropologist Lévi-Strauss, reformulating Durkheim's theory, acknowledged the force of van Gennep's critique. During the 1930s and 1940s, van Gennep worked on a massive compilation of French folklore, dealing on a region-by-region basis with rituals surrounding life crises and seasonal transitions.

The first monograph in the Anglo-American tradition of anthropology to use van Gennep's ideas was Warner's *A Black Civilization* (1937). Warner conducted extensive fieldwork among the "Murngin" (Yolngu) of northern Australia. Although he does not mention van Gennep by name, he was familiar with van Gennep's work, and uses the French phrase *rites de passage* to describe Yolngu initiation ceremonies. Warner belonged to the functionalist school of thought, which paralleled structuralism is emphasizing the need to study customs in their contemporary context, but argued that the function of a custom was its contribution to sustaining the social structure. For Warner, the function of *rites de passage* was to regulate social behaviour appropriate to age and gender. His description of the rites, however, makes it clear they conform to van Gennep's three stages. The initiates are snatched from the camp, secluded while they are taught the correct patterns of behavior, and then reintroduced as adults. In one ceremony, women and children are told that the initiates have been swallowed by the "Rainbow Serpent," only to be reborn.

The Rites of Passage was translated into English in 1960, and contributed to the rise of structuralism in British anthropology. Mary Douglas used van Gennep's ideas in her book *Purity and Danger* (1966). Douglas argued that concepts of "dirt" are not based on hygiene, but on matter out of place. Animals that do not fall neatly into categories (such as the pangolin, a mammal with reptile-like scales) are considered dangerous and polluting. The phase of transition is the most dangerous stage in an initiation rite because it takes people out of their stable social roles. "The whole cultural repertoire of ideas concerning pollution and purification are used to mark the gravity of the event." Victor Turner saluted van Gennep as "the father of formal processual analysis." In his discussion of central African initiation rituals, Turner highlighted the suspension of normal social regulations while initiates are secluded. People in a liminal state elude or slip through the networks of classifications that normally locate states and positions in cultural space, existing in a state of "communitas." Turner later developed this insight into a more general argument that the most creative ideas occur not during daily routines but in liminal moments, such as play and joking, that facilitate fresh perceptions of social life. More recently still, the historian Robert Darnton has drawn on van Gennep in his analysis of "the Great Cat Massacre." Not only does Darnton rely, in part, on van Gennep's compilation of French folklore to elucidate the customs he discusses. He also argues the journeymen responsible for the alleged massacre hold marginal status in their profession, awaiting full admission. This helps to explain the license they sense, to act in riotous or grotesque ways.

ROBERT LAYTON

See also Emile Durkheim; Claude Levi-Strauss; Marcel Mauss

Biography

Arnold van Gennep was born in Holland in 1873. In his youth he studied in Nice. He went on to study at L'École Pratique des Hautes Etudes in Paris. He was the first Professor of Ethnography at the University of Neuchâtel. Van Gennep died in 1957.

Selected Works

L'État actuel du problème totémique, 1920
Maneul de folklore français contemporain, 1937–58.
The rites of passage, translated by M. B. Vizedom and G. L. Caffee, 1960

Further Reading

Darnton, R., *The Great Cat Massacre and Other Episodes in French Cultural History* New York: Basic Books 1999
Douglas, M., *Purity and Danger*. London: Routledge, 1966
Durkheim, E., Mauss, M., *Primitive Classification*, translated by R. Needham. London: Cohen and West, 1963
Hertz, R., "A contribution to the study of the collective representation of death," in R. Hertz, *Death and the Right Hand*, translated by R. and C. Needham, London: Cohen and West 1960
Kimball, S.T., "Introduction," in A. van Gennep, *The Rites of Passage*, translated by M. B. Vizedom and G. L. Caffee, London: Routledge, 1960
Layton, R., *Anthropology and History in Franche-Comté: A Critique of Social Theory*, Oxford: Oxford University Press, 2000
Lévi-Strauss, C., *Totemism*, translated by R. Needham, London: Merlin, 1960
Turner, V.W., *The Ritual Process: Structure and Anti-structure*, London: Routledge, 1969
Turner, V.W., "Are there any universals of performance in myth, ritual and drama?" in *By Means of Performance: Intercultural Studies of Theatre and Ritual*, edited by R. Schechner and W. Appel, Cambridge: Cambridge University Press, 1990
Warner, W.L., *A Black Civilisation; A Study of an Australian Tribe*, New York: Harper and Row 1937

GÉNY, FRANÇOIS
Jurist

François Gény undertook a thorough reappraisal of the sources and the process of decision in law. He outlined the methodology that would make jurisprudence into a "science of action," putting it "among the scientific hierarchy of our times." (*Méthode*, 1899) But philosophy, according to Gény, offered but a "meager harvest" to law (*Science et technique*, 1914–24). His philosophizing centered on the notion of "irreducible natural law." He led a trend of questioning and rethinking the civil law tradition. His first is probably his most important work: *Méthode d'intérpretation* is a classic. It was followed by a work on a different tack, *Science et technique*. These two, together, stand as his contribution to jurisprudence.

Méthode d'intérpretation was published first in 1899 and substantially expanded in 1919 by footnotes and by an epilogue of almost two hundred pages. The expressed purpose of the *Méthode* was to inquire into "the nature, function, and hierarchy of formal sources of law" and "the means to supplement them by a free objective search, the processes and proper value of which must be determined." (*Méthode*, 1899)

Gény's thesis is that judges under the codes, such as in France dominated in culture and tradition by the Napoleonic/Revolutionary codes, have "always and perforce" done more than apply legislation with the use of the processes of formal logic. His argument rests on the following grounds. First, that positive law is more than legislated law. Human and social relations cannot be satisfactorily regulated by "several verbal formulae" that could not encompass the whole situation even at the time they were promulgated. (Here Gény voices Portalis, the chief draftsman of the Napoleonic codes.) Second, the contrary thesis—that of the nineteenth-century exegetic positivism—is based on fictions that legislation is necessarily complete (the hermeneutic nature of legislation), that statutes are isolated from their drafters (the independence of statutes), and that presumed legislative intent can fill any gaps in statutes. The existence of a gap to be filled by analogy indicates that there was no such intent. Third, the constitutional position of the modern legislature requires that its laws be always fully applied. But "justice and social utility" dictate that the judge use all legitimate resources when he makes a decision. In the absence of applicable legislated law, he must first refer to the other formal source, customary law. Fourth, when no "appropriate" (that is, clearly and directly applicable) formal norm is available, the judge must seek guidance from doctrine and decisional law as persuasive though not binding, authorities. Fifth, if all these sources fail him, the judge must freely search for a rule on which to base his decision. This search is discretionary, but it must not be arbitrary. It must be objective, which means based on the social realities, needs, and values; on the nature of things; in short, on "science" as Gény uses the word. This means that in his exercise of the pretorian power the judge must act as a model legislator would. But his rule is limited to the specific case (*Méthode*, 1899). Sixth, because "the only justified principle of interpretation is to determine the scope of the text with reference to the time of its enactment" (*Méthode*, 1899), the so-called interpretation by analogy is in reality not an interpretation, but a response to the absence of any formal norm to be interpreted.

Thus it is a legitimate use of judicial discretion, one form of the free search. And therefore, seventh, only if we discard the fictions and frankly admit the need for the creative method of free search and the existence of its sociological sources will it be possible "to get positive law back on the track." "Our conclusion tends to affirm," Gény wrote in the last-but one paragraph of the original edition of the *Méthode*, "that the purely formal and logical elements . . . are insufficient to satisfy the desiderata of law in action. . . . The judicial process must look . . . outside of, and beyond, these elements."

Despite impressions Gény's main purpose was not philosophical. He sought a practical work, with critical focus on the positivist myth that legislation is exclusive and self-sufficient. The complement of this myth, the exegetic method, was an adjunct focus. That is to say, the method of erecting upon the legislative text a system of concepts handled in closed circuit by means of formal logic, independent to the changing world of facts, was a target, predating a kind of legal postmodernism. The German word for this method, *Begriffsjurisprudenz*, appears repeatedly in Gény's footnotes, which are full of citations that illustrate and criticize "conceptual jurisprudence." Gény proposed, as an alternative, a conception inspired by his idol Jhering and summarized in the famous aphorism "through the civil code, but beyond it." In this perspective, the legislated law is the alpha but not the omega. It is the structural frame and the principal matter, but not the limiting contour.

By Gény's own appraisal, the *Méthode* was essentially a negative exercise. The "cracks in the edifice" were "disclosed;" the problems were "raised and tackled." (*Méthode*, 1899) But the "positive conclusions" suffered a "radical infirmity." Although the need for the method of free search was established, the concrete elaboration was "vague, incomplete, wrong, sometimes contradictory," and "obviously insufficient to provide a firm and comprehensive framework." The outstanding task was to close the "gaping hole," to outline as clearly as possible the positive direction for the "free search." (*Science et technique*, 1914–24) The result was *Science et technique en droit privé positif*, in four volumes, 1,423 pages in all, published between 1914 and 1924.

He explained, following the focus on method, now the focus was on practice: Questions are seldom raised, and always only incidentally. We are told that such theoretical problems are without influence on the actual development of law, that method is a matter of *pouvoir* (power) rather than *savoir* (knowledge).

"The point is not to sacrifice practice to theory, or even to contest the pragmatic superiority of the former over the latter. The question is simply whether enlightened practice does not achieve its goals with greater assurance and more fully than blind practice. . . . Either we must take refuge in pure empiricism . . . [or we must] develop a rational theory for law. The task is similar to that in all [contemporaneous] scientific disciplines. . . . Decisive experience indicates that the intimate secret of the life of law cannot be glimpsed from the elevated observation point of abstract speculation, but only in close touch with its concrete processes. . . . Consequently only the jurist provided with the necessary minimum of a philosophical mind has any chance of discovering the innermost mechanism of law that he is to administer. . . . The better research perspective places decisional law, customary and legislative law . . . [in a] comprehensive perspective . . . which shows their relative position in the whole, of which they are only particular functions. . . . This is the spirit of the present study . . . which places law in the midst of other social disciplines. . . . Methodologically it is today no more a question—as Taine postulated—of soldering social sciences onto natural sciences. We must treat all science as a whole and in this complex find the proper place for law, while confessing that the sources that nourish law as a scientific discipline remain weak and insufficient." (*Science et technique*, 1914–24)

Méthode was warmly received, *Science et technique* less so. In identifying the scope of legislation and the corollaries of any doctrine other than absolute "logically necessary completeness of the legislated [code] system," Gény recognized the freedom of the judge to fill gaps, that is, to make law. His theme was that the source of the decision that must then be made was outside the existing normative apparatus. Despite his efforts, a failing remains. Gény made little progress toward making explicit his theory of justice.

With some extrapolation and translated into simple language, Gény seems to say nothing else than that law consists of policy and norm, in that order. "Policy" corresponds to Gény's "science" and includes the data, the nature of things, and the value judgement, which determines the selection of the specific principle of justice. "Norm" corresponds to "technique," the articulation, on the basis of "science," of the legislative or decisional rule.

But the need to infuse social interests and values into the application of law has been one of the most worked over topics since Gény. Since Gény, the term *sociologie de droit* has been somewhat vulgarized to mean everything beyond law in the narrowest sense of positive rules. But the American realists drew on Gény in their "sociological" dimension. And further, Gény's gestaltlike conception of the process, whereby data is transformed into a rule, has been developed not only by the American realists but also by a number of European writers. The recognition of decisional case law as a formal source of law in continental Europe and by some Latin American writers owes much to Gény.

Gény was then one of the first contributors to the sweeping trend that sought to modernize the law. This direction, not some overarching dogmatic theory, explains the universal nature of Gény's doctrine. What would be, in the last analysis, the principal features of Gény's doctrinal signature? First, he was the most articulate and comprehensive of the writers who assigned the judge the central place in the life of law: "There must be some intermediary between the complex, varied, and evasive needs [of the life of law] and the rigid formula of the statute. . . . This intermediary . . . is the judge" (*Méthode*, 1899). Second, Gény "indicated the foremost problem of the legal order: accurate delimitation of . . . the exercise of judicial discretion" (Morrow), but recognized that "no matter how broad discretionary power we give to the judge, its exercise cannot constitute any interference in the legislative sphere as long as the authority of the judicial decision remains limited to the particular case" (*Méthode*, 1899). Third, he conceptualized the task of finding the "ought to be" when the "is"—the applicable positive rule of law—is lacking; and he found in "sociology . . . the practical tool," the policy source for the rule of decision, as well as a source of "higher principles that [positive law] cannot violate . . . a more complex system, which, on the one hand, tries to enlarge the formal sources and assign each a place according to its nature; and, on the other hand, recognizes that outside the sphere of these sources, clearly delimited, there is a need for free interpretation [or search] that is subject only to the fact it is supposed to govern and to the requirements of any scientific investigation." (*Science et technique*, 1914–24)

None of the preceding points of criticism, as even as they may be, can reduce the stature of these achievements. It is the essence of a seminal thinker that he does not travel the whole road but that he makes a decisive turn onto it, and that the hypotheses stir the imagination of others. Gény started civil law on the road to an interdisciplinary questioning and understanding of the concept of a rule. His work linked legal thought and method with advanced contemporary currents in science and philosophy, and his impact was extensive. Gény led a reconsideration of the role of the judge in civil law systems, a role that in France was still largely defined exclusively by revolutionary precedent and prejudice. But Gény's impact was not restricted to France; his ideas played a key role in the development of the Swiss legal system and he remains well regarded among the American-French academics of Louisiana.

MATTHEW HUMPHREYS

Biography

Geny was born December 17, 1861 in Baccarat (Meurthe-et-Moseles department, Lorraine). He studied at Nancy and was awarded his doctorate in 1885. He moved to Dijon in 1889. In 1899 jis "Méthode d'interprétation et sources en droit privé positif: Essai critique" was published. In 1901 he was made chair of civil law at Nancy (he kept the position until his retirement in 1931 (apart from spending World War I, 1914–1918 in Dijon). Between 1919 and 1925 he was dean of the faculty of law at Nancy. It was during his tenure at Nancy that the bulk of his scholarship appeared as part of course from the *Méthode*. Geny died December 16, 1959.

Selected Works

Méthode d'interprétation et sources en droit privé positif Essai critique, 1899
Méthode d'interprétation et sources en droit privé positif; critical essay, translated by Jaro Mayda, 1954
Science et technique en droit privé positif: nouvelle contribution à la critique de la Méthode juridique, 1914–1924

Further Reading

Dewey, *Logical Method and Law*, 1925
du Pasquier C, *Introduction à la théorie générale et à la philosophie du droit*, 3rd ed. Neuchatel: 1948
Jhering R, *Der Zweck im Recht*, Leipzig: Breitkopf und Härtel, 1877
Morrow CJ, "Louisiana blueprint," *Tulane* Law Revue, XVII (1943): 351, 556
O'Toole TJ, "Jurisprudence of François Gény," *Villanova Law Revue* III (1958): 455
Pound R, "Fifty years of jurisprudence," *Harvard Law Review*, (1937): 557
Recueil d'études sur les sources du droit en honneur de François Gény, Lambert. Paris: 1935
University of Nancy, Faculté de droit et des sciences économiques, *Le centenaire du doyen François Gény : recueil des conférences prononcées les 26 et 27 octobre 1962* Paris: Dalloz, 1963

GIDE, ANDRÉ PAUL GUILLAUME
Writer

Gide was a major French literary figure. He was at the outset a follower of Mallarmé and a member of a group of young symbolist writers who maintained the idealist aesthetic position that art should make manifest the truth behind the veil of appearance. Such a stance distanced him from taking issue with contemporary politics in his creative writings. However, his early works also include burlesque "soties" written in reaction to the contemporary artificial artistic world (*Paludes* [*Marshlands*, 1895]), lyrical evocations of sensuous temptations enhanced by a symbolic thirst born of abnegation (*Les Nourritures terrestres* [*Fruits of the Earth*, 1897]), and autobiographical and confessional writings (notably his *Journal* [*Diary*, from 1887 onwards, first extracts published 1909]). *La Porte Étroite* (*Straight is the Gate*, 1909) uses personal material in fictionalized form to describe a love rendered impossible by the heroine Alissa's devotion to an absolute religious ideal. He later brought to its final expression his theory of what a novel should be: namely, a replication by its complex form of the kaleidoscopic and arbitrary sequence of events and moral concerns that are characteristic of life itself. Among his plays, *Le Roi Candaule* (*King Candaules*, 1901) and *Œdipe* (*Oedipus*, 1931) examine the role of self-knowledge in the pursuit of happiness.

Gide's attitudes towards social and political commitment changed during his life, being individualistic at the outset and becoming more generally humanitarian as a result of a combination of circumstances before, during, and after World War I. Although he criticized Maurice Barrès's promotion of the values of nationalism, which was much in vogue, he himself had not in fact been a fervent supporter of Dreyfus, placing the interests of France before those of an individual. But then, together with many French intellectuals of the period, he also saw in Nietzsche's philosophy a call for healthy individualism and moral truth. During 1914–15 he worked with Belgian refugees at the Foyer Franco-Belge in Paris; in 1916 he discovered that spiritual love as well as sensual excitement could be found with a younger person of his own sex—hitherto he had identified the former with his chaste love for his wife (his cousin Madeleine Rondeaux), the latter with his erotic encounters with youths in public baths, on the boulevards, and in North Africa. In 1925–26 he visited the Congo and Chad, publishing on his return a travelogue, which included a denunciation of the activities of the concessionary companies and the injustices of the colonial system. In the 1930s he was attracted to communism, but rejected it after visiting the USSR in 1936 as an honored guest of the régime. His political stance was sometimes inconsistent and never orthodox. In an age when commitment was of paramount importance, he tended rather to question the validity of any form of authority, be it state, political party, or church. He was in consequence reviled both by Catholics (Jacques Maritain) and Communists (Aragon). He was valued by those who found independence of mind and spirit in his writings as well as by those who sought sexual and emotional freedom. This liberating influence was experienced, for example, by André Malraux and Albert Camus. Recent critics (such as Derrida) have seen as exemplary the importance that his imaginative works accord to the theory of inconsequentiality.

His significant achievement was to create with a group of friends the influential literary periodical *La Nouvelle Revue Française*, which provided a focus for new literary talent. This, together with the associated publishing house of Gallimard, introduced the French public to important contemporary works by American, British and other European writers.

Brought up by his mother in a strict French Protestant environment (his father died in 1880), he was acutely aware of a dualism within himself between desire and asceticism. His moral education was enlarged by the writings of Goethe, the German idealists (notably Fichte), Schopenhauer, Carlyle, and Nietzsche. He was overwhelmed on first meeting Oscar Wilde in 1891 and again in 1895. At the root of his sympathy with the marginalized members of society was undoubtedly his own sexual nonconformity. He published an autobiography, *Si le grain ne meurt . . . (If it die,*1920), which covers his childhood and the years up to his marriage. Although honest in detail, it is constructed to show the evolving conflict between the two sides of his nature: heaven, as exemplified in his love for Madeleine, and hell, as witnessed by his eroticism. This work is conceived as parallel to the public defense of pederasty, *Corydon* (1924), in which the Interlocutor ironically takes a hostile role. Gide was furthermore fascinated by criminal and deviant behavior, especially in the context of what he judged to be complacent bourgeois conformity. In this he was unlike many of his contemporaries, who saw in such manifestations simply a sign of moral, social, and physical degeneracy. Characters of this type occur in several of his major works. *L'Immoraliste* (*The Immoralist*, 1902) features the Arab boy thief Moktir, young Normandy poachers, and Sicilian ruffians toward all of whom the hero Michel is strongly attracted as he engages in a conflict between culture and nature. In *Les Caves du Vatican* (*The Vatican Cellars*, 1914), the young hero Lafcadio is a nihilist of sorts whose actions are arbitrary, often criminal, but nearly always charming. The reason for the lack of a moral directive on the part of the author/narrator can be found in the central position occupied by the concept of *l'acte gratuit* (an arbitrary action with no discernable motive of profit or benefit) in Gide's thought. The idea had been used as early as *Le Traité du Narcisse* (*The Treatise of the Narcissus*, 1891) as a symbol of the chance nature of existence, then in a burlesque form in *Le Prométhée mal enchaîné* (*Prometheus Mismatched*, 1899) to characterize the arbitrariness of conscience. Gide found a clear example of the theme in the opening chapters of Dostoievsky's *Crime and Punishment*, which he greatly admired. In *Les Faux-Monnayeurs*

(*The Counterfeiters*, 1926), the notion of crime and the conflict of true and false values is again extensively present: the plot, subplots, characterization, and implied moral values turn essentially on whether what seems can reasonably be thought to be what is. And this enables Gide to raise again the question of whether it is possible for a work of fiction to be a truthful representation of life. In addition to his renewal of the form of the novel, Gide has earned a place among modern literary theorists for his invention of *"mise en abîme"* (specular narration, or the mirroring of a text within itself). He originally defined this device as the "retroaction of the text on the author in the process of writing," but it has come to mean the placing of an episode or discourse within a text in such a way that it reflects the main narrative.

Complex and multifaceted, Gide valued the imperatives of truth, independence of mind and spirit, curiosity, and a refusal to remain within the straightjacket of social norms and received opinions. Although never declaring himself an atheist, he moved from the strict Protestantism of his early years, which was doubtless at the root of his notion of self as a constant driving force, toward a more libertarian stance, but he would probably now be seen as retaining a rather severe sense of moral rectitude. From the interwar period onward, he espoused a form of humanitarianism that had no need of doctrinal or institutional support.

PATRICK POLLARD

See also **Maurice Barres; Albert Camus; Jacques Derrida; Jacques Maritain**

Biography

Born November 22, 1869 in Paris, Andre Gide enrolled briefly at the École Alsacienne, Paris in 1877, but was expelled for "bad habits." His education was disrupted and he returned to the École Alsacienne in 1887 (Rhétorique). Gide's first substantial publication was *Les Cahiers d'André Walter*. In 1891 he first met Oscar Wilde in Paris. He was rejected for military service on grounds of health (tuberculosis) in 1892. In 1893–94, he first visited North Africa, and had his first sexual encounters. In 1895, during a second visit to North Africa, he met Wilde and Lord Alfred Douglas. In 1895, Gide married his cousin Madeleine Rondeaux. In 1916, Gide faced a significant religious crisis (*Numquid et tu . . . ?*) and the beginning of his love for Marc Allégret, the son of a Protestant minister, close friend of the family. The first public edition of *Corydon* was published in 1924. During 1925–26, Gide traveled with Marc to the Congo and Chad, publishing his notes on his return. In 1926, *Les Faux-Monnayeurs* was published. In 1932, Gide became increasingly involved in

Communist activity, culminating in his visit to the USSR (1936), his travelogue and critique (*Retour* de *l'URSS* [*Back from the USSR*, 1936]), and further criticisms (*Retouches . . .* [*Further Relections . . .*, 1937]). In 1940, Gide declared himself in favor of Pétain, but broke with the collaborators in 1941. During 1942–45, Gide lived in Tunis and Algiers. Gide was awarded an honorary doctorate at Oxford University on June 5, 1947, and on November 13 the Nobel Prize for Literature. On February 19, 1951, Gide died in Paris and was buried at Cuverville, his home in Normandy; his friends objected that a Protestant Minister had conducted a religious service over him. On May 24, 1952 his complete works were placed on the *Index librorum prohibitorum* by the Catholic church.

Selected Works

Essais critiques, edited by P. Masson, 1999
Journal 1887–1950, edited by E. Marty and M. Sagaert, 1996–7
Romans, Récits et Soties. Œuvres lyriques, edited by Y. Davet and J. J.Thierry, 1961
Souvenirs et Voyages, edited by Pierrre Masson, 2001
Fruits of the Earth, 1897, translated by Dorothy Bussy, 1949
The Immoralist, 1902, translated by Dorothy Bussy. 1930
Pretexts, 1903, Reflections on Literature and Morality . . . selected by Justin O'Brien, 1949
Straight is the Gate, 1909, translated by Dorothy Bussy, 1924
The Vatican Swindle, 1914, translated by Dorothy Bussy, 1927
Two Symphonies, 1919, translated by Dorothy Bussy, 1931
If it dies . . ., 1920–21, translated by Dorothy Bussy, 1935
Dostoievsky, 1923, translated anon, 1925
Corydon, 1924, translated by Richard Howard, 1983
The Counterfeiters, 1926, translated by Dorothy Bussy, 1927
Travels in the Congo, 1927, translated by Dorothy Bussy, 1929
Two Legends, Theseus and Oedipus, 1931, translated by John Russell, 1950
The Journals, 1932–54, translated by Justin O'Brien, 1947–51
Back from the USSR, 1936, translated by Dorothy Bussy, 1937
So Be It; or, The Chips are Down, 1952, translated by Justin O'Brien, 1960

Further Reading

Brée, Germaine, *Gide (revised edition)*. New Brunswick: 1963
Claude, Jean, *André Gide et le théâtre*. Paris: 1992
Delay, Jean, *La Jeunesse d'André Gide (1869–95)*. Paris: 1956–57
Goulet, Alain, *Fiction et vie sociale dans l'œuvre d'André Gide*. Paris: 1986
Martin, Claude, *Bibliographie des livres consacrés à André Gide 1918–1995*. Lyon: 1995
Martin, Claude, *La Maturité d'André Gide*. Paris: 1977
Masson, Pierre, *André Gide. Voyage et Écriture*. Lyon: 1983
Moutote, Daniel, *Le Journal de Gide et les problèmes du moi (1889–1925)*. Paris: 1968
Pollard, Patrick, *André Gide: Homosexual Moralist*. New Haven: 1991
Savage, Catharine, *André Gide. L'Évolution de sa pensée religieuse*. Paris: 1962

Savage-Brosman, Catharine, *An Annotated Bibliography of Criticism on André Gide 1973–1988*. New York: 1990
Sheridan, Alan, *André Gide. A Life in the Present*. London, 1998.
Walker, David, *André Gide*. London, 1990.

GILSON, ETIENNE HENRY
Catholic Philosopher

The place of Etienne Gilson in modern French intellectual life rests on his rejection of previous models of medieval thought to insist that the major interest of the scholastic thinkers was theology, and that their thought was primarily shaped by theological concerns. Largely for apologetic reasons, their texts had been plundered for whatever they yielded to support modern Catholic rebuttals of Kantian idealism, using nineteenth-century philosophical categories. The result was that, trapped within the historical model constructed by Joseph Kleutgen (1811–83) and Albert Stöckl (1823–95), the history of scholastic thought was evaluated and its thinkers rated according to their ability to respond to the philosophic agenda and categories imposed by the German idealists. Gilson's achievement was to strike a decisive blow at the nineteenth-century view of the history of scholasticism, and to redraw its map.

Schooled at the Sorbonne, Gilson's teachers included Bergson for philosophy, Brunschvicg for general philosophy, and Durkheim for sociology, and Mauss for French philosophy and sociology. His dissertation, supervised by Lévy-Bruhl, was published as the *Index scolastico-cartésian* and as the 1913 *La Liberté chez Descartes et la théologie*. Nine of a series of twenty-five public lectures he gave at his first university post at Lille were published in the *Revue des cours et des conférences*.

Gilson was appointed to the chair of the history of philosophy at Strasburg in 1919. He was to leave in 1921, but in the meanwhile reorganized the philosophy department, which still bore the imprint of the German academic tradition of its foundation, adapting it to the needs of the French system, where philosophy was taught in the highest school classes. The later resituation of medieval scholars within their theological context and institutional loyalties was the result of prolonged discussions on the problems at Strasburg with the founders of the *Annales* school, Lucien Febvre and Marc Bloch.

From 1921 to 1932 Gilson taught the history of medieval philosophy at the Sorbonne, moving thereafter to the Collège de France. Meanwhile in April 1926 Gilson, representing the rector of the University of Paris, attended a congress on education in Montreal, read a paper on Aquinas and another to commemorate the 700th anniversary of the death of Saint Francis.

This was significant because Gilson was later, although still under his thralldom to Aquinas, to draw attention to the relatively neglected Franciscan theological tradition to which belonged Bonaventure, Scotus, and Ockham.

Gilson lectured at a number of eastern seaboard universities, of which Ottawa and Toronto, wanted to celebrate the fiftieth anniversary of Leo XIII's *Aeterni patris* in 1929 by responding to its call to foster the study of medieval philosophy. The Dominican initiative at Ottawa led to the foundation of what became the *Institut d'Etudes Médiévales* at Montreal, and Gilson agreed with the Basilians to create Toronto's Institute of Medieval Studies in 1929. He was to remain its director until his death in 1978, although he never returned to it after his departure for France in 1972. From 1939 granted the title "pontifical," the Toronto institute also nurtured a series of new journals, of which the most important, *Medieval Studies*, was directed by Gilson himself.

John Inglis (*Spheres of Philosophical Inquiry and the Historiography of Medieval Philosophy*, 1988) cogently argued that, since the formation of the Kleutgen-Stöckl model of the history of medieval philosophy, differences of interpretation of individual scholastic thinkers have been contained within it. Two distinct views have been distinguished, both safely within the model. Maurice de Wulf in his 1900 *History of Medieval Philosophy*, with six editions to 1946, bolstered by the outstanding researches of Martin Grabmann, especially in his early two-volume *Die Geschichte der scholastischen Methode* (1909–11), held that the scholastics from the twelfth to the fourteenth centuries shared a common philosophical patrimony. That view continued to be held against Gilson by Wulf's pupil, Fernand van Steenberghen, as late as his 1955 *The Philosophical Movement in the 13th Century*.

Although Grabmann is undoubtedly the greatest historian of scholasticism of the twentieth century, he unfortunately never published his projected third volume to have been devoted to Aquinas, and his view has been largely superseded by that of Gilson, who, while continuing to honor Aquinas's writings as constituting the apex of medieval philosophy, nonetheless distinguishes a plurality of fundamentally different philosophies in the Middle Ages.

In 1974, two years after Gilson had left Toronto for the last time, but while he was still the Institute's director of studies, the Institute held a commemoration of the seventh centenary of the death of Aquinas and published the papers. Gilson wrote the forward explaining the philosophical importance of Aquinas, which he saw in Aquinas's theory of knowledge. Unlike Descartes, who strove to establish the unity of all nonem-

pirical knowledge and, at least initially, regarded the principles of medicine and mechanics as deducible from apodictic metaphysical principles, Aquinas had upheld that knowledge consisted in the conformity of the mind to its objects, with each science grounded in the objects it studies.

The views of both Aquinas and Descartes are products of the periods and problems in which they were formulated, as indeed was Gilson's view of the history of medieval philosophy itself. What is of interest in the present context is that, at the end of long life, in his ninetieth year, Gilson should have looked back and still found in Aquinas's epistemological realism the core of the philosophy of the author whom he regarded as the greatest of the medieval philosophers. He was reaffirming the view he had taken in the two-volume 1922 *La philosophie au moyen âge: de Scot Erigène à G. d'Occam* (*History of Christian Philosophy in the Middle Ages*, 1955), which remains the outstanding general history of medieval philosophy.

Aquinas, in Gilson's *History*, is remarkable for his achievement in reconciling the spheres of faith and reason, but his defense of the plurality of philosophies in the middle ages means that any move away from Aquinas as constituting the apex of medieval thought must be seen as a decline, and in the decades since Gilson's death institutionally loyal defenders of Scotus and Ockham have been trying to rectify this view, defending the increased emphasis on revelation and on the transcendent divine will of these authors, and paying growing attention to the theological constraints behind their thinking. In their efforts, however, virtually all historians of medieval thought have profited from Gilson's own investigation into the roots of what has been regarded as the Franciscan "tradition," in his 1924 *La Philosophie de saint Bonaventure*.

Bonaventure had been seen as a rival to Aquinas even during their lifetimes. Bonaventure was four years older than Aquinas, but both were given chairs at the young University of Paris at the same time, and both died in 1274. In the *History* Gilson scarcely distinguishes between their achievements. He calls the second half of the thirteenth century "the classical period in the development of medieval scholasticism" and regards both Bonaventure and Aquinas as confident that "if properly understood, philosophy was on the side of theology and reason in fundamental harmony with revelation." Elsewhere, however, he clearly attaches more importance to the achievement of Aquinas, and, given that he thought it lay in establishing the rationality of revelation, his view is undoubtedly correct. On the use of reason in the pursuit of truth and on the metaphysics of knowledge Aquinas's reliance on Aristotle makes his position look stronger than that of Bonaventure, whose reliance on Augustinian illuminism is greater, but whose metaphysics of knowledge is for theological reasons much weaker.

The adoption of what was in fact a very corrupt form of "Aristotelianism" in the early thirteenth century, especially prominent in the work of Albert the Great and Aquinas, is what in the end enables Gilson to situate Aquinas at the apex of medieval philosophy. Anselm is less satisfactory than Aquinas only because so little Greek thought was available in the eleventh century. Aquinas had used Aristotle as Augustine had used Plato, to provide the basis for a new Christian philosophy. Both used powerfully innovative approaches, on each occasion boosted by an infusion of the Greek rationality which Aquinas was so completely to incorporate into his theology, but which nevertheless retained its own philosophical integrity within it.

The chief interest of Gilson's analysis is to point to the reasons for his conclusions about the nature of philosophical achievement in the scholastic period. His historical achievement in a field little regarded in the academic world of France between the wars is indeed considerable. He put the study of medieval thought firmly back on the map in France, and insisted on its theological context. His achievement inevitably remains dated notably by the semi-autonomy he still grants to the philosophical content of scholastic thought and by the still timid approach to the plurality of philosophical concerns, especially in later scholastics whom he saw as nibbling away at the roots of Aquinas's thought, until Ockham, he thought, finally brought down the whole tree.

Gilson's views on social and political philosophy, also and not surprisingly, can claim to derive from Aquinas's principles, which come from Aristotle. The moral good of every rational being is to act so that its nature realizes its full potential. The moral good of individuals is to choose that which human nature comprehends to be its true good, so that "the natural law is nothing else than the rational creature's participation of the eternal law."

Leo XIII had thought that Aquinas's texts could produce the intellectual basis for social justice, and Gilson does indeed draw from them a doctrine of the natural equality of human beings, particularly in the 1960 *Elements of Christian Philosophy*, in which he states rather than argues that every society that disregards the fundamental laws of human nature and the order established by God brings about its own destruction. Leo XIII had argued in the 1891 encyclical *Rerum novarum* that human beings are not naturally equal in wealth, strength, or power, and the social order dependent on divine principles actually respects natural inequalities in these domains. The argument against Marxism is that it fails to take natural inequalities into account.

Gilson's instincts on problems of equity and social justice are stronger than his arguments, heavily tinged with reminiscences of the effects of revolution and war. In the *Elements of Christian Philosophy*, acceptance of personal deprivation is necessary when the alternative involves the use of force. Violence is always to be avoided. In 1954 Gilson published an edition of the social encyclicals of Leo XIII, insisting that the pope's advocacy of a return to Aquinas was linked in his mind with the social principles of his encyclicals that had caused some perturbation in Catholic aristocratic circles in France.

Gilson's achievement therefore lay primarily in the rehabilitation in French academic life of the study of the high medieval theologians. Within that study he initiated, by his insistence that the major scholastics were all theologians, the breakup of the model, to which he himself continued to adhere, of the supremacy of epistemology in philosophy. He ensured eventual victory for the view that there was no common fund of methods or doctrines shared by all scholastic theologians, but instead a vigorous plurality of viewpoints, which made their study more rewarding than their common recruitment to the fight against Kant and the German idealists had allowed to become apparent.

ANTHONY LEVI

See also **Henri Bergson; Marc Bloch; Leon Brunschvicg; Emile Durkheim; Lucien Febvre; Maurice Merleau-Ponty; Marcel Mauss**

Biography

Gilson was born in Paris in 1884. He studied at the Sorbonne and, after completing his studies, was made a professor at the Sorbonne. He taught there from 1921 to 1932. In 1929, he founded the Pontifical Institute of Mediaeval Studies at Toronto University. He taught at the Collège de France from 1932 to 1951; during this period, he split his time between the two institutions. From 1951 to 1968, he worked exclusively at Toronto. Gilson died in 1978.

Selected Works

La liberté chez Descartes et la théologie, 1913
Le Thomisme, 1919; translated by Edward Bullough as *The Philosophy of Saint Thomas Aquinas*, 1924
La Philosophie de saint Bonaventure, 1924; translated by Illtyd Trethowan and Frank Sheed, 1938
Introduction à l'étude de saint Augustin, 1931; translated by L. E. M. Lynch as *The Christian Philosophy of Saint Augustine*, 1960
L'Esprit de la philosophie médiévale, 2 vols., 1932; translated by A. H. C. Downes as *The Spirit of Medieval Philosophy*, 1936
The Unity of Philosophic Experience, 1937

Further Reading

A Gilson Reader, edited by Q. Anton C. Pegis, New York: Hanover House, 1957

Etienne Gilson Anniversary Studies, Toronto: Institute of Medieval Studies, 1958

Inglis, John, *Spheres of Philosophical Inquiry and the Historiography of Medieval Philosophy*, London/Boston/Cologne:Brill, 1998

McGrath, Marguerite, *Etienne Gilson, a Bibliography*, Toronto: Institute of Medieval Studies, 1982

Owens J., *Towards a Philosophy of Medieval Studies*, Toronto: Institute of Medieval Studies, 1986

Shook, Lawrence K., *Etienne Gilson*, Toronto: Institute of Medieval Studies, 1984

GIRARD, RENÉ
Cultural Theorist

Every so often, a thinker comes along with a great idea, a singularly powerful understanding that changes the way we think about the world and ourselves within it. Freud's discovery of the unconscious is an example, Nietzsche's will-to-power another. René Girard's "mimetic hypothesis" is in this category.

Girard has elaborated his theory in three successive stages. His first claim is that desire is mimetic. Hegel is credited with having introduced the theme of desire into Western philosophic discussion in his *Phenomenology*. But in Hegel, desire has a goal, namely, "recognition." For Girard, desire is purely appropriative, nonobjective. We desire what others desire; we desire the desire of the other. Counter to romantic writers who would claim desire is rooted either in the uniqueness of the subject or the uniqueness of the object (Rousseau is the "classic" example), Girard argues that desire is purely imitative.

As a consequence, it is also inevitably conflictual. We reach for the object of the other's desire and another does the same, perhaps even the very individual whose desire we are modeling. Girard first discovers "mimetic hypothesis" within a literary context, in his study of the great European novel (Cervantes, Stendhal, Flaubert, Dostoyevsky, and Proust), where all its manifestations are in evidence. In fact, becoming the great writer that we recognize is, for Girard, precisely a matter of breaking away from the destructive potential of mimetic desire, of owning and overcoming its deleterious effects.

The publication in 1961 of *Mensonge romantique et vérité romanesque*—in which all these ideas are first laid out in full—leads Girard to new considerations. All culture, Lévi-Strauss had been arguing (on the model of Sausurrean structural linguistics), is founded upon difference. But our greatest literary writers (Greek tragedy, Shakespeare, Dostoyevsky), Girard notes, instruct us in the collapse of differences, the transformation of differences into "undifferentiation" or violence, the spread of mimetic rivalry throughout the community. What if culture itself, the very possibility of community, is founded upon the effective management of such runaway "mimetic" crises?

The result of this questioning is the second stage of Girard's elaboration—the idea that all culture is founded upon collective lynching. Accepting the anthropological commonplace that all cultures distinguish between the sacred and the profane, Girard suggests that violence and the sacred are one and the same. The sacred and violence are not substantives but categories. The sacred is violence that is effectively removed from the community, and violence nothing other than the sacred come down from its divine sequestration and now wreaking havoc upon the city.

The difference between the two is maintained through sacrifice. In *La violence et le sacré* in 1972, Girard argues that cultures ethnologists designate as "primitive" maintain the difference between the sacred and violence through a process of sacrificial substitution, a process that is not necessarily manifest as such, but that originates in the collective removal from the community of an enemy twin, a communal double. Girard combines here Lévi-Strauss's purely structural logic with Freud's logic (in *Totem and Taboo*, for example) for a fuller understanding of the sacrificial origins of culture. In a "sacrificial crisis," where differences breakdown, where distinctions between the sacred and the violent are no longer efficacious, the removal from the community of a surrogate victim turns the Hobbesian "war of all against all" into a more manageable war of all against one and difference is reestablished. The traditional wisdom that one "fights fire with fire" has, in this context, ancient communal roots. How is it that we can know about this process and not be destroyed by it? In the primitive religious community, the sacrificial logic remains hidden, obscured behind its beneficial effects. Even cultures in which the sacrificial act becomes explicit deflect its understanding in some fashion. It becomes manifest only at the price of the renewed propagation of the crisis itself. There is no such thing as conscious scapegoating. How therefore has the modern world become possible?

The answer—and here is the third and final stage of Girard's elaboration of the mimetic hypothesis—is Judeo-Christian scripture. In *Des choses cachées depuis la fondation du monde* in 1977, for example, Girard argues that the exposition of the mimetic and sacrificial origins of our culture is the central concern first of the Hebrew and later of the Christian Bible. The Old Testament begins to demystify myth and the process of sacralization, and Christian scripture pursues this demystification process to the end. Jesus is the last victim in the primitive sense of sacrificial expulsion, the one whose death uniquely exposes the victim's innocence of the communal charges brought against him (and therefore the arbitrariness of those charges), who shows us where our violence is leading us in order that we may give it up, that we might take responsibility for that violence and refuse it.

The exposure of this truth of violence does not immediately stop it, of course, and historical Christianity for Girard (at least in this first book of the third stage) is the record of the struggle of its adherents with exposing the truth of mimetic violence on the one hand and reenacting its primitive sacrificial mechanisms on the other. *Le bouc émmisaire* (1982) examines the ways this struggle informs the famous medieval "texts of persecution" in which Jews are denounced as child killers and poisoners of the wells, and women are denounced as witches, and *La route antique des hommes pervers* (1985) suggests ways in which this same struggle is already at work within Hebrew scripture, in a text like the "Book of Job." *Quand ces choses commenceront* (1994) is a book-length conversation with Michel Treguer in which Girard relates this theory to more secular and contemporary approaches to social change, and in *Je vois Satan tomber comme l'éclair* (1999), Girard argues that the satanic is the persistence of the bad sacrificial in the life of the Christian, that the imitation of Jesus offers us a model of the good mimesis, and that anti-Semitism, far from one sacrificial error among others for the believing Christian, repudiates Christian revelation itself.

Where do René Girard's ideas stand in context of poststructuralism? Girard shares the assumptions of other deconstructive French writers of his generation who would identify textual and differential foundations for anthropology, psychoanalysis, language, and philosophy (among them Lévi-Strauss, Lacan, Barthes, and Derrida) in place of older more essentialist conceptions, and of still others who would trace the origins of that textually in power or seek alternatives to its platonic representational construction (Foucault, Deleuze, and Guattari, for example). But he goes further than they do, globalizing the question of difference and of power or governmentalizing as the problem of the sacred, and, in general, posing at large a theory of order and disorder in the primitive and modern universe. Is Girard practicing theology? Not unless we deem it a species of anthropological theology—comparable to that of Karl Rahner or Bernard Lonergin. Moreover, neither is it an ethics, even a descriptive ethics of the kind Emmanuel Levinas describes, for example, although it could be argued Girardian thinking leads us to the door of such Levinasian ethical analyses. Rather he offers us a critical analysis, a descriptive account of the origins of culture in its management of mimetic violence and appropriation and

the implications of the exposure of that mechanism in the modern world. Girardian thinking locates itself just after Greek tragedy's prophetic reading of myth and just "before" the Platonic-Aristotelian philosophic matrix suppresses such tragic prophetic critical discoveries. Is it specifically Christian? How other "revealed" religious traditions deal with the same sacrificial crises—Buddhism, Hinduism, Islam, and Judaism, for example—is also a separate matter. Furthermore, whatever the personal beliefs of René Girard the individual (or of many of the individuals attracted to his thinking especially within the group formed around his work—the Colloquium on Violence and Religion), Girardian thinking is not a species of Christian (or of any other kind of) supersession or triumphalism but a critical account of the origins of culture in the logic of sacrifice, in its management of runaway violence and mimetic desire, and in the exposure of its mechanisms in the most powerful scriptural texts of our tradition.

SANDOR GOODHART

See also **Roland Barthes; Gilles Deleuze; Jacques Derrida; Michel Foucault; Felix Guattari; Jacques Lacan; Emmanuel Levinas; Claude Levi-Strauss; Ferdinand de Sausure**

Biography

René Noel Girard was born in Avignon, France on December 25, 1923. The son of the local curator in Avignon, he trained to enter his father's profession and attained the status of *archiviste-paléographe* at the prestigious École de Chartes in Paris in 1947 with a thesis entitled "*La vie privée à Avignon dans la seconde moitié du XVe siècle.*" Availing himself of an opportunity to study in the United States in the same year, he pursued a degree in medieval French history, literature, and culture at Indiana University completing a Ph.D. in 1950 with a dissertation entitled "American Opinion of France, 1940–1943." He taught French at Indiana University (1947–1952), at Duke University (1952–1953), at Bryn Mawr College (1953–1957), and at Johns Hopkins University (1957–1968), where he chaired the department of modern languages and organized, with Richard Macksey and Eugenio Donato, the 1966 colloquium on the "Languages of Criticism and the Sciences of Man" that introduced the work of thinkers such as Lévi-Strauss, Barthes, Lacan, Foucault, and Derrida to America. In 1969, he came to SUNY at Buffalo as a distinguished professor where he remained until 1976, when he returned to Hopkins as a chaired professor of French. In 1981, he accepted the Andrew B. Hammond professorship of French at Stanford University, from which position he retired in

1995. He has lectured at every major university in the United States. His more than fourteen books (and hundreds of articles) have appeared worldwide and won him all the prestigious awards academia has to offer—in America and France. His ideas and his presence provide the central focus of the yearly Colloquium on Violence and Religion (formed in the 1980s by admirers in Great Britain, Europe, and America), a group that has conducted international conferences on the "mimetic hypothesis" since its inception. As of this writing, René Girard lives in California, where he continues to work.

Selected Works

Mensonge romantique et vérité romanesque, 1961; as *Deceit, Desire, and the Novel: Self and Other in Literary Structure* translated by Yvonne Freccero, 1966

Dostoïevski: du double à l'unité, 1963; as *Resurrection from the Underground: Feodor Dostoevsky*, translated by James G. Williams, 1997

La violence et le sacré, 1972; as *Violence and the Sacred*, translated by Patrick Gregory, 1977

Critique dans un souterrain, 1976

"To Double Business Bound," in *Essays on Literature, Mimesis, and Anthropology*, 1978

Des Choses cachées depuis la fondation du monde, 1978; as *Things Hidden Since the Foundation of the World*, translated by Stephen Bann and Mochael Metteer, 1987

Le Bouc émissaire, 1982; as *The Scapegoat*, translated by Yvonne Freccero, 1986

La Route antique des hommes pervers, 1985; as *Job: The Victim of his People*, translated by Yvonne Freccero, 1987

A Theater of Envy: William Shakespeare, 1991; translated into French as *Shakespeare: Les Feux de l'envie*, 1990

Quands ces choses commenceront: Entretiens avec Michel Treguer, 1994

The Girard Reader, edited by James G. Williams, 1996

Je vois Satan tomber comme l'éclair, 1999; as *I See Satan Fall Like Lightning*, translated by James G. Williams, 2001

Celui par qui le scadale arrive, 2001

La Voix méconnu du réel, translated from the English by Bee Formentelli, 2002

Further Readings

Anspach, Mark Rogin, *À charge de revanche: Figures élémentaires de la réciprocité*, Paris: Seuil, 2002

Barberi, Maria-Stella (editor), *La spirale mimétique, dix-huit leçons sur René Girard*, Paris: Desclée de Brouwer, 2001

DeGuy, Michel and Jean-Pierre Depuy (editors), *René Girard et le problème du mal*, Grasset, 1982

Dumouchel Paul, et Dupuy Jean-Pierre, *L'enfer des choses, René Girard et la logique de l'économie*, Paris: Seuil 1979

Gans, Eric L., *The End of Culture: Toward a Generative Anthropology*, Berkeley: University of California Press, 1985

Gans, Eric L., *Originary Thinking: Elements of Generative Anthropology*, Stanford: Stanford University Press, 1993

Golsan, Richard J., *René Girard and Myth: An Introduction*, New York: Routledge, 2001

Goodhart, Sandor, *Sacrificing Commentary: Reading the End of Literature*, Baltimore: Johns Hopkins University Press, 1996

Hamerton-Kelly, Robert G. (editors), "Violent Origins: Ritual Killing and Cultural Formation," in *Violent origins/Walter Burkert, René Girard and Jonathan Z. Smith on Ritual Killing and Cultural Formation*, Stanford: Stanford University Press, 1987

Juilland, Alphonse, (editor) "To Honor René Girard," *Stanford French Review* 10/1–3 (1986)

Livingston, Paisley, *Models of Desire: René Girard and the Psychology of Mimesis*, Baltimore: Johns Hopkins University Press, 1992

McKenna, Andrew J., *Violence and Difference: Girard, Derrida, and Deconstruction*, Urbana: University of Illinois Press, 1992

McKenna, Andrew J, (editor), "René Girard and Biblical Studies," *Semeia: an experimental journal for biblical criticism*, 33 (1985)

Schwager, Raymund, S. J., *Brauchen wir einen Sündenbock?* Munich: Kösel, 1987; translated as *Must There Be Scapegoats? Violence and Redemption in the Bible* by Maria L. Assad, New York: Harper and Row, 1989

Siebers, Tobin, *The Mirror of Medusa*, Berkeley: University of California Press, 1983

Swartley, Williard M., (editor), *Violence Denounced: René Girard, Biblical Studies, and Peacemaking*, Pennsylvania: Pandora Press US, 2000

Webb, Eugene, *The Self Between: From Freud to the New Social Psychology of France*, Seattle and London: University of Washington Press, 1993

Williams, James G., *The Bible, Violence, and the Sacred*, San Francisco: Harper Collins, 1991

GLISSANT, ÉDOUARD
Novelist, Essayist, Poet, Playwright

Martinican novelist and essayist, poet and playwright Édouard Glissant has been a key participant in the francophone intellectual scene since the 1950s. The central thread running through all of Glissant's work, from his early writings in the 1950s right up until his 2003 publication of the novel *Ormerod*, is the urgent need to locate the Caribbean islands in time and space and thereby to construct a uniquely Caribbean identity. Glissant's insights are inextricably linked with the history of Martinique and its complex and often troubled relationship to metropolitan France. Colonized by the French in 1635, Martinique and the neighboring island of Guadeloupe were subject to slavery from the time of colonization until the abolition of the plantation system in 1848. Despite their newly found political freedom, the two islands remained heavily dependent upon French subsidization, a state that culminated in their complete assimilation as overseas departments in 1946.

These dramatic historical events form a constant backdrop to Glissant's theoretical and fictional explorations and are linked to his conviction that the past is the key to understanding and mastering the present and is a central factor in the process of taking root in one's land. His work is thus characterized by the passionate desire to overcome Martinique's absence from a tangible historical and cultural continuum.

In his celebrated 1981 publication, *Le Discours antillais* (*Caribbean Discourse*), Glissant paints an exhaustive portrait of the island's "missed opportunities" in regard to independence from France and the possibility of creating a uniquely Caribbean identity. The driving force behind this book is Glissant's fundamental belief that Martinicans need to carve a place within the specific geographical and historical context of the Caribbean and not simply to be a forgotten appendix to the history of metropolitan France. In his eyes the only way for the French Caribbean to move from a place of nonhistory to history is to consolidate all that is uniquely Caribbean in contrast to and in defiance of the alienating gaze of metropolitan France. Building upon Aimé Césaire's groundbreaking theory of *négritude*, or the claiming of a black identity, Glissant developed the concept of *antillanité* that shifts the focus of Caribbean identity back from its origins in Africa to the specific context of the Caribbean. *Le Discours antillais* remains the central theoretical reference point of *antillanité*, enhanced by his later book, *Poétique de la relation* (*Poetics of Relation*), published in 1990. Perceiving the role of the writer or intellectual as instrumental in bringing a consciousness to the people, Glissant and his work have come to be celebrated as "the militant foundation of a specifically *situated* literature" (Peter Hallward, 1998).

Although the tree with its roots firmly in Africa is an effective symbol to conceptualize *négritude*, Glissant employs the image of a rhizome (a thick root whose buds form new plants), borrowed from Gilles Deleuze and Felix Guattari's *Mille plateaux*, as a useful way to consider *antillanité*. "Submarine roots: that is floating free, not fixed in one position in some primordial spot, but extending in all directions in our world through its network of branches" (*Caribbean Discourse,* 1989). In Glissant's view of Caribbean identity, French–Caribbean people are not a simple derivation from Africa, but, rather, a complex cultural creation. Further developed in *Poétique de la relation*, the image of the rhizome emphasizes the notion that identity is rooted in a particular historical, cultural, and geographical context, but underlines the fact that identity is not dominated by a single totalitarian root. "Rhizomic thought is the principle behind what I call the poetics of relation, in which each and every identity is extended through a relationship with the other" (*Poetics of Relation,* 1997). In the case of the French Caribbean, Glissant maintains that while the nucleus of the Caribbean identity may be African, there are nonetheless important grafting of European, Indian, and Caribbean influences that result in a distinct cultural entity. Glissant thereby calls attention to the process of *métissage* and creolization in Martinique and Guadeloupe and argues that the mixing of color, country, and culture produces an identity that is uniquely Caribbean. Moreover, in a symbolic resonance of Glissant's thought, the physical composition of the Caribbean archipelago, with its geographical proximity to the Americas and its cultural link to Europe, embodies the openness and fluidity of this conception of Caribbean identity.

An important tool in Glissant's assertion of a distinct Caribbean identity is the entwining of his political message with his aesthetic style as he consistently draws on the complexities of language to subvert Martinique's cultural domination by France. One of the central ways in which he manipulates this influential mode of communication is through his proposal for a writing of opacity. According to Glissant, writing has traditionally been linked to transparency and clarity and therefore with a reductive levelling and universalism. He draws attention to the contrast between writing and orality, the former linked with France and the latter with Martinique, which remains a highly contested debate in the Caribbean context and one that carries important implications for the place of Creole in this society. Reacting to the universal models and denial of difference that are embedded in a writing of clarity, Glissant produces a literary *oeuvre* grounded instead in opacity. Although one critic describes his works as labyrinthine and enigmatic, Glissant sees obscurity as a function of the absence of history and of the linguistic conflicts between French and Creole in the Caribbean. A fundamental component of this creative strategy is Glissant's desire to celebrate diversity and thus his literary works frequently feature an explosion of narrative points of view, which subverts the notion of a single truth. The sense of multiplicity that Glissant achieves through an opaque approach to his subject matter and a variety of perspectives is a dominant characteristic of his thought.

Although Glissant continues to be significant in his own right, publishing and teaching to the date of this writing, his influence can also be measured by the reception of his work among younger writers. The flourishing intellectual movement of *créolité*, developed by the dynamic Martinican trio of Patrick Chamoiseau, Raphaël Confiant, and Jean Bernabé (who is from Guadeloupe although he works in Martinique) retains a direct link with the ideas of Glissant's *antillanité*. Indeed, Glissant is quoted at the beginning of the theoretical tract that accompanies this body of thought, *Éloge de la Créolité*, as well as featuring in the dedication of Chamoiseau's 1992 *Prix Goncourt* winning novel, *Texaco*. To a large extent, then, *créolité* and the *créoliste* writers represent Glissant's literary heirs, expanding and overturning the ideas he established on Caribbean identity.

Glissant's significance to the world of ideas is further evident in the wide readership his works attract—he has been translated into languages as diverse as English, German, Portuguese, and Italian and his readers can be traced as far away as Australia. He is the subject of countless theses, scholarly articles, critical works, special issues of magazines or journals, and book chapters, and he has also been the recipient of a number of international conferences organized in his honor. In 1993 Alain Baudot published an exhaustive annotated bibliography of Glissant's work containing 1,347 pages and covering all aspects of his literary *oeuvre* (*Bibliographie annotée d'Édouard Glissant*). Due to the wide-ranging possibilities of his insights into the postcolonial condition, Glissant has come to be known as one of the most "*éminents éveilleurs de conscience*" ("eminent awakeners of consciousness") (Jacques Chevrier, 1999) and, according to Jack Corzani, one of the three great writers produced by Martinique along with Saint-John Perse and Aimé Césaire (*L'Information littéraire*, 1977).

BONNIE THOMAS

See also **Aime Cesaire; Patrick Chamoiseau; Gilles Deleuze; Felix Guattari**

Biography

Édouard Glissant was born on September 21, 1928 in Sainte-Marie, Martinique. He was educated at the Lycée Schoelcher in Fort-de-France before pursuing tertiary studies in philosophy at the Sorbonne in Paris and ethnology at the Musée de l'Homme. He published his first collection of poetry, *Un champ d'îles*, in Paris in 1953 and went on to publish two more poetic collections and a book of essays, *Soleil de la conscience*, in the years up until 1956. In 1958 he published his first novel, *La Lézarde*, which won him the prestigious French literary prize, the Prix Renaudot. Glissant was also active politically at this time, participating in the *Société Africaine de Culture* and other Caribbean political groups as well as co-founding the *Front antillo-guyanais* with Paul Niger. These militant activities resulted in travel restrictions placed on Glissant by the French government, preventing his return to Martinique and forcing him to take up residence in France.

Following his return to Martinique in 1965, Glissant founded *the Institut martiniquais d'études*, which fostered educational and cultural activities in the island and provided the *baccalauréat* curriculum with a Caribbean context. He also launched a new journal entitled *Acoma*. Glissant continued to write prolifically in this period, publishing fictional works such as *Malemort* (1975), *La Case du commandeur* (1981), and *Mahagony* (1987); poetry anthologies including *Boises*

(1977) and *Pays rêvé, pays réel* (1985); and his groundbreaking books of theory, *Le Discours antillais* (1981) and *Poétique de la relation* (1990). In 2003 he published the novel *Ormerod*. From 1980 Glissant worked for UNESCO in Paris and in 1989 accepted a distinguished lectureship position at Louisiana State University. Since 1995 Glissant has been distinguished professor of French at the City University of New York.

Selected Works

Essays
Soleil de la conscience, 1956
Le Discours antillais, 1981
Poétique de la relation, 1990
Faulkner, Mississippi, 1996
Traité du Tout-Monde, 1997

Poetry
Le Sel noir, 1960
Les Indes, Un champ d'îles, La Terre inquiète, 1965
L'Intention poétique, 1969
Boises, 1979
Le Sel noir; Le Sang rivé; 1983
Pays rêvé, pays réel, 1985
Fastes, 1991
Le Monde incrée, 2000

Novels
La Lézarde, 1958
Le Quatrième Siècle, 1964
Malemort, 1975
La Case du commandeur, 1981
Mahagony, 1987
Tout-Monde, 1995
Sartorius, 1999
Ormerod, 2003

Theatre
Monsieur Toussaint, 1961

Further Reading

Anderson, Debra L., *Decolonizing the Text: Glissantian Readings in Caribbean and African-American Literatures*, New York: Peter Lang, 1995

Baudot, Alain, *Bibliographie annotée d'Édouard Glissant*, Toronto: Éditions du GREF, 1993

Britton, Celia, *Édouard Glissant and Postcolonial Theory: Strategies of Language and Resistance*, Charlottesville: University Press of Virginia, 1999

Burton, Richard D.E., *Le Roman marron: études sur la littérature martiniquaise contemporaine*, Paris: L'Harmattan, 1997.

Cailler, Bernadette, *Conquérants de la nuit nue: Édouard Glissant et l'Histoire antillaise*, Tübingen: Gunter Narr Verlag, 1988

Crosta, Suzanne, *Le Marronnage créateur: dynamique textuelle chez Édouard Glissant*, Fort-de-France: GRELCA, 1991

Dash, J. Michael, *Édouard Glissant*, Cambridge: Cambridge University Press, 1995

Hallward, Peter, "Édouard Glissant Between the Singular and the Specific", The Yale Journal of Criticism, 11 (2), 1998

World Literature Today, 63 (4), (1989): special issue on Édouard Glissant. (Ed. Ivar Ivask)

GLUCKSMANN, ANDRÉ
Philosopher, Human Rights Activist

Alongside Bernard-Henri Lévy, André Glucksmann is a minor *enfant terrible* of French political, philosophical, and intellectual life. A philosophy student of Raymond Aron, Glucksmann was officially a CNRS researcher at the time of the May 1968 events, working on television and violence on the screen (1966). Deeply inspired by the growing social revolt, he published *Stratégie de la révolution en France* (1968) in the wake of the May events. It is a polemical account of the possibilities for revolutionary change in France. Drawing on the Marx of 1848 (and especially the *18th Brumaire*), Glucksmann calls for France to rediscover its revolutionary past. He is highly sceptical of the need for a Leninist vanguard party in France, rejecting the Bolshevik model in favor of a more spontaneous, Europe-wide revolt, reminiscent of the 1848 revolutions.

He joined the ill-fated University of Vincennes, created in the wake of May 1968, helping to found the Grassroots Committee for the Abolition of Wage-labor and the Destruction of University. Along with Sartre he then became a member of the editorial board of the Maoist newspaper *La Cause du peuple*, denouncing Pompidou's France as "fascist," and proclaiming in 1972 the Maoists' victory in weaning the "pleb" from fascism (something, he claimed, the Left had never managed to do). But he was soon, along with many others, to become disaffected by the Maoists' populist moralism. And leaving Maoism and Marxism behind, he maintained from this period only an attachment to peripheral social activists, proclaiming in 1977 that the "rabble"—homosexuals, hippies, the marginalized—were the basis of anti-Soviet dissidence.

His first recanting of his *gauchiste* past, *La Cuisinière et le mangeur d'hommes* (1975), has been linked to Foucault's *Surveiller et punir*, for it analyzed the Soviet gulag using Foucauldian terminology. The thesis was that, not only did Leninism lead to Stalinism, but also Marx is the philosopher of the Gulag, and, just as outrageously, that the Gulag mentality could be traced back as far as Plato. At a time in France when the Left was playing down revelations about Soviet oppression of its dissidents (the 1972 *Union de la Gauche* was uniting the Communists and the socialists for the first time), Glucksmann's book caused a storm. Here began his long and painstaking critique of totalitarianism, whether East and West, Brezhnev or Pino-

chet, which predates Revel's book on totalitarianism (1976). Glucksmann's work was a libertarian critique of state oppression, offering no concrete solutions, except that of "not being oppressed." The state in modern society is for Glucksmann a "disciplining machine," a "panoptical apparatus," and its intellectuals are nothing more than "experts of the disciplining society."

Concomitantly, his philosophy tended more and more now towards anti-totalizing paradigms: the singular, the exception, the individual, a development not dissimilar to that of other intellectual groupings at the time, such as *Tel Quel* (Marx-Scouras 1996). And, as one of the *nouveaux philosophes*, he began to practice what they preached by being the keenest to appear in every media-friendly place (especially the television programme *Apostrophe*), and became an exponent of what Aubral and Delcourt (1977) called "la pub-philosophie." This was worse than its English appearance. Sitting in a public house discussing philosophy would have been music to the ears of Aubral and Delcourt. Instead, the "new philosophy" was an "ad-philosophy," a media-led exercise in self-promotion, which seemed to confirm Debray's view (1981) that the third age of the modern intellectual (that is, 1968 onwards) was one in which the intellectual became a media figure.

The summer of 1977 saw the *nouveaux philosophes* reach the height of their media fame, as they protested against Soviet President Leonid Brezhnev's visit to Paris. The same year Glucksmann's philosophical *magnum opus*, *Les maîtres penseurs* (1977), was published. It is a wide-ranging critique of the classics of modern German philosophy, from Fichte through Hegel and Marx, and as far as Nietzsche. The master thinkers of German philosophy, he argued, have helped to create and legitimate new "master-thinkers," who, as "master-purgers," have the job of normalizing and assimilating the population. In a manner not dissimilar from the Frankfurt school, Glucksmann's philosophical critique centered on reason, the rational human drive of contemporary society. But strangely, and rather outrageously, Marx is placed at the center of the firing line. And somewhat surprisingly to us now perhaps, Foucault lent his full support to *Les maîtres penseurs*, seeing Glucksmann as prophet to Solzhenitsyn's Dante. Ten years later, Glucksmann would consider Descartes as the antithesis to the "master thinkers" of Hegel, Marx, and Nietzsche, when he described (1987) how Descartes dodged any claims to truth.

Against the perceived drive in humans to seek out tragedy, Glucksmann moved in the 1980s to posit humanity's tendency towards cynicism and passion as the antidote, praising Montaigne, Aeschylus, and Bodin for their individuality, pathos, and personal sovereignty (1981). Addressing himself in 1981 to the incoming President Mitterrand, he now also praised universal suffrage as the key to destroying totalitarianism; and more recently, he appeared as a true Gaullist (1995). The work on universal suffrage led to his most "realist" of studies, in which reactions to humanity's crises, especially that of pacifism, are analyzed (1983). His philosophical essayism now knew no bounds, and "stupidity"—the great Flaubertian theme—became his next target (1985), against the background of a failing socialist Presidency in France. But his study of stupidity did not stop him from defending "the spiritually uplifting qualities of the nuclear deterrent" (Reader, 1993).

The fall of the Berlin Wall in 1989 seemed to confirm his anti-totalitarian stance. His work with Vaclav Havel in theorizing the liberation of Czechoslovakia, "Sortir du communisme, c'est rentrer dans l'histoire" ("To Come Out of Communism is to Get Back into History"), certainly did not replicate Francis Fukuyama's "end of history" thesis, as his later work has shown. Glucksmann has consistently tried to intervene in politics and history. His work on AIDS (1994), and in Bosnia, annoyed some, amused others, but it is undeniable that his political philosophy, libertarian and pacifist anti-totalitarianism, has had a practical application.

ANDY STAFFORD

See also **Raymond Aron; Regis Debray; Michel Foucault; Bernard-Henri Levy**

Biography

Born in 1937, an *agrégé* in philosophy from the Ecole Normale Supérieure, Andre Glucksmann was, in the early 1960s, a member of the (Communist-led) *Union des Etudiants Communistes* (UEC). Having written a thesis on General von Clausewitz, the nineteenth-century Prussian theorist of war strategies, he published a study of the language of war (1967), using a perspective that informs his (now classic) study of the May 1968 events (1968). His trajectory is perhaps that of the classic *soixante-huitard*: a belligerent and terroristic *gauchiste* in his early career and important figure in the May 1968 *événements*, omnipresent alongside Jean-Paul Sartre, he became in the mid-1970s a key member of the (so-called) *nouveaux philosophes*. Recanting their militant left-wing past, in the light of Solzhenitsyn's revelations about the camps in the Soviet Union, and of the bankruptcy of Maoism in China, they denounced Marxism and flipped over to an anti-totalitarian, liberal Western philosophy and political practice (1975, 1977). He then became an important agitator and activist in favor of human rights—supporting the Vietnamese boat people in 1978, alongside

Bernard Kouchner, Solidarnosc in Poland in 1980–1981, the end of Communism in Czechoslovakia (1989), the Bosnians of Sarajevo in 1994, and most recently the Chechens against Russia (2002). He is also an essayist of political and social philosophy (1981, 1983, 1985, 1987, 1994).

Selected Works

"Violence à l'écran", 1966; as *Violence on the Screen*, translated by Susan Bennett, 1971
Le Discours de la guerre, 1967
Stratégie de la révolution en France, 1968; translated (in part) as "Strategy and Revolution," in *New Left Review* I:52 (Nov/Dec 1968)
"Nouveau fascisme, nouvelle démocratie," in *Les Temps Modernes*, 1972
La Cuisinière et le mangeur d'hommes, 1975
Les maîtres penseurs, 1977; as *Master Thinkers*, translated by Brian Pierce, 1980
Cynisme et passion, 1981
La force du vertige, 1983
La Bêtise, 1985
Descartes c'est la France, 1987
(with Vaclav Havel) *Quelques mots sur la parole*, 1989
Le Onzième commandement, 1991
La fêlure du monde: éthique et sida, 1994
De Gaulle, où es-tu?, 1995
Le bien et le mal: lettres immorales d'Allemagne et de France, 1997
La Troisième mort de Dieu, 2000

Further Reading

Aubral, François and Delcourt, Xavier, *Contre la nouvelle philosophie*, Paris: Gallimard, 1977
Debray, Régis, *Teachers, Writers, Celebrities: The Intellectuals of Modern France*, translated by David Macey, London: NLB and Verso, 1981
Foucault, Michel, "La grande colère des faits," in *Nouvel Observateur*, 1977
Hamon, Hervé and Rotman, Patrick, *Génération. 2. Les années de poudre*, Paris: Seuil, 1998
Le Goff, Jean-Pierre, *Mai 68. L'héritage impossible*, Paris: Seuil, 1998
Lévy, Bernard-Henri, *La barbarie à visage humain*, Paris: Grasset, 1977
Marx-Scouras, Danielle, *The Cultural Politics of Tel Quel. Literature and the Left in the Wake of Engagement*, Pennsylvania: Pennsylvania University Press, 1996
Reader, Keith, *Intellectuals and the Left in France since 1968*, London: Macmillan, 1987
Reader, Keith (with K. Wadia), *The May 1968 Events in France. Reproductions and Interpretations*, London: Macmillan, 1993
Revel, Jean-François, *La Tentation totalitaire*, Paris: Laffont, 1976
Sirinelli, Jean-François, *Intellectuels et passions françaises*, Paris: Fayard, 1990

GODARD, JEAN-LUC
Film Theorist, Critic, Director

A veritable culture machine whose own production is as motley as its sources of inspiration, Jean-Luc Godard has left an indelible mark on twentieth-century history, if by nothing else then by his refusal to confine his work to any of the historical categories situated within it. He brazenly participated in the constellation known as the French New Wave as well as in certain forms of postwar Marxism. However, his critical investigation of the history of aesthetics, his persistent study of the role of moving pictures in the constitution of the twentieth century, and his preoccupation with the conjunction of art, politics, technology, and civilization testify to the uniqueness of Godard's cultural machine: it has simultaneously participated in the "factory of the century" (film) and created an *effet de distanciation* (distancing effect) by constantly questioning its modes of operation.

Godard's early work as a film critic was, for him, already part of his cinematic corpus: "to write was to make films." An avid member of the emerging postwar *ciné-clubs* and an early participant in some of the burgeoning film journals, he made an important contribution to the *politique des auteurs* advocated by the "Schérer Gang" (Rohmer, Truffaut, Chabrol, Rivette, among others). Based on a critique of the Cinema of Quality and its tendency to reduce directors to servants of script writers and the studio system, the *politique des auteurs* promoted the original cinematic contributions of those directors who refused this secondary role: Bresson, Cocteau, Hawks, Hitchcock, and many others. The first edition of Godard's writings and interviews appeared with much critical acclaim in March of 1968, testifying to his persistent belief in the importance of both producing and commenting on art.

Georges de Beauregard, the producer of Godard's first feature-length film, *A Bout de souffle*, expressed the well-founded fear that Godard's encyclopedic inclinations and fervent cinéphilia might lead him to "fill the film full of citations." Already present in one of his most important shorts, *Tous les garçons s'appellent Patrick*, Godard's propensity for cinematic citation was soon to become one of the signature features of his films. In conjunction with the innumerable pictorial, sonic, and scripto-visual allusions to film history, Godard's work is saturated with an endless proliferation of cultural references, ranging from Charlotte's copy of Hegel's *Aesthetics* in *Tous les garçons* to the names that Guillaume erases from a chalkboard in *La Chinoise* (from Sartre to Brecht). This preoccupation with the historical heritage informing film-making is also visible in the elaboration of aesthetic forms that broke with a certain tradition of artistic production. Valorizing experimentation, improvisation, site-specific filming, and the need to "film free people," Godard systematically contravened the imposed laws of filmic representation by employing the following subversive techniques: jump-cuts, unconventional angles and framing, unanticipated long takes, hand-held cameras, elliptical montage, discontinuous sonority, the liberation of the off-screen and off-mike, the use of word play in filmed text, and the parody of genres such as the interview, documentary, news reporting, and film noir.

Most critics agree that Godard's work took on a new militancy after the events of May 1968. Influenced by both Leninist and Maoist forms of Marxism popular in France at the time through the work of Sartre, Althusser, and many others, Godard rejected his status as a star director and sought to establish artistic communities. His friendship with the militant Leninist Jean-Pierre Gorin in the 1970s was to prove decisive in this regard. Advocating the Maoist principle according to which education and revolution go hand in hand, Godard recognized the need for a form of cinema that truly participated in revolutionary practice. A dialectic of opposites can be discerned in his work from this time period which aims at dismantling established aesthetic and political value systems by valorizing the second term in classical oppositions such as distribution and production, image and sound, actor and spectator, or man and woman.

Even before his supposed return to more traditional cinematic concerns in 1979 with his "second first film" *Sauve qui peut (la vie)*, Godard's long-standing critique of Hollywood production had extended to the very concepts of presentation and representation. Rejecting the Platonic thesis regarding the derivative status of imagery, he maintained that the image is not simply a copy that unfaithfully replicates an original. On the contrary, it is precisely the montage of images that is capable of revealing the invisible by disclosing rare and unobserved forms of the real. This reversal of Plato, typified by the famous caption from *Vent d'Est* ("it's not a just image, it's just an image"), became increasingly important for Godard's confrontation with television and video in the mid to late 1970s. Characteristic of this reversal was his 1976 televisual assault, *Six fois deux*, in which Deleuze recognized a cinema of intervals that rejected the dominant "cinema of the One." Godard's method of the *between*—what Deleuze refers to as the serial *and* of creative stammering—aimed at displacing the obsolete paradigm of image and referent by focusing on "*comment ça va* (how it's going)?" from image to image.

This preoccupation with the philosophical denigration of imagery came to full fruition in the late 1970s and later reached its apex at the end of the 1990s with the eventual completion of his *Histoire(s) du cinema* in 1998. As Jacques Rancière has since pointed out, cinematic history is interpreted in Godard's *Histoire(s)* in terms of a missed rendezvous between film and the history of its century. This is due to the fact that the cinema has misrecognized its own historicity and the power of its images, which have been obsequiously subordinated to *histoires* (stories in the form of scenarios). Taking advantage of all of the artifices of video editing, Godard sought to reveal the invisible: the virtual history of pure images inherent in a century of cinematic production.

This concern with the ambiguous nature of *histoires* (stories/histories) and the presentation of the unpresentable has continued to guide his work through the end of the 1980s and up to the present. The multiple facets of his recent projects testify to his ongoing negotiations with twentieth-century art. They might briefly be summarized as follows: a preoccupation with the historical relationship between film and the other arts, a valorization of seeing over naming ("the cinema must show things before we name them"), an ongoing debate with the history of aesthetics over the nature of the sublime and the possibility of presenting what is unrepresentable (most notably in the Sublime Trilogy: *Passion, Prénom Carmen, Je vous salue Marie*), a confrontation with the religious interdiction of iconography, and an increased role played by his own autobiography. "Me, I am an image," he claimed in perhaps the most significant twentieth-century reappropriation of Rimbaud's *voyant* (visionary), "I am the other, I am the other you, I am the other myself . . ."

GABRIEL ROCKHILL

See also **Louis Althusser; Gilles Deleuze; Jacques Rancière; Jean-Paul Sartre**

Biography

Born in 1930, Jean-Luc Godard spent his primary and part of his secondary school years in Switzerland. A French National by birth, Godard was naturalized as a Swiss citizen during World War II and kept his Swiss passport throughout his long sojourn in Paris, which began when he enrolled at the *Lycée Buffon*. At the age of nineteen, he began studying for a degree in ethnology at the *Sorbonne*. The very same year (1949), he became one of the regulars at the *Cinémathèque* on *rue Messine* and at the *Cinéclub* in the Latin Quarter. After his parental financing was discontinued, he returned to Switzerland to work odd jobs and began making his first short films. In 1959, Godard moved back to Paris to direct his first feature-length film and, following its commercial and critical success, continued to work there as a director and writer. After years of artistic production and two consecutive marriages (to Anna Karina in 1960 and to Anne Wiazemsky in 1967), he returned with his associate and partner, Anne-Marie Miéville, to Grenoble in order to establish the *Sonimage* film and video production studio. Since

1979 he has been living and working in Switzerland. Among his most well-known and noteworthy films are: *A Bout de souffle* (1959), *Vivre sa vie* (1962), *Le Mépris* (1963), *Pierrot le fou* (1965), *Numéro deux* (1975), *Sauve qui peut (la vie)* (1979), *Je vous salue Marie* (1983), *Histoire(s) du cinéma* (1998), and *Éloge de l'amour* (2001).

Selected Works

Films

A Bout de souffle (Breathless), 1959
Une Femme est une femme (A Woman Is a Woman), 1961
Vivre sa vie (My Life to Live), 1962
Le Mépris (Contempt), 1963
Pierrot le fou, 1965
Deux ou trois choses que je sais d'elle (Two or Three Things I Know about Her), 1966
La Chinoise, 1967
Numéro deux, 1975
Sauve qui peut (la vie), 1979
Passion, 1981
Je vous salue Marie (Hail Mary), 1983
Histoire(s) du cinéma, 1998
Éloge de l'amour (In Praise of Love), 2001

Writings

Introduction à une (véritable) histoire du cinéma, 1980
Jean-Luc Godard par Jean-Luc Godard, 1985; as *Godard on Godard: Critical Writings by Jean-Luc Godard*, edited by Jean Narboni and Tom Milne, 1988
Histoire(s) du cinéma, 1998
Jean-Luc Godard: Interviews (Interviews With Filmmakers Series), edited by David Sterritt, 1998
Archéologie du cinéma et mémoire du siècle (with Youssef Ishaghpour), 2000

Further Reading

Bergala, Alain, *Nul mieux que Godard*, Paris: Cahiers du cinéma, 1999
Cerisuelo, Marc, *Jean-Luc Godard*, Paris: Lherminier, 1989
Deleuze, Gilles, *Cinema II: The Time-Image*, translated by Hugh Tomlin and Robert Galeta, Minneapolis: University of Minnesota Press, 1989
Deleuze, Gilles, "*Trois Questions sur* six fois deux," in his *Pourparlers*, Paris: Les Éditions de Minuit, 1990
Lesage, Julia, *Jean-Luc Godard: A Guide to References and Resources*, Boston: G. K. Hall, 1979
MacCabe, Colin, *Jean-Luc Godard, Images, Sounds, Politics*, Bloomington: Indiana University Press, 1980
Rancière, Jacques, "*Le Rouge de La Chinoise: politique de Godard*," and "*Une Fable sans morale: Godard, le cinéma, les histoires*," in his *La Fable cinématographique*, Paris: Éditions du Seuil, 2001
Sterritt, David, *The Films of Jean-Luc Godard: Seeing the Invisible*, Cambridge: Cambridge University Press, 1999

Collective Publications

Art press 4 (1984), articles by Juliet Berto, Raoul Coutard, Alexandre Delay, Jean Douchet, Jacques Drillon, Bernard Dufour, Jean-Paul Fargier, Hal Foster, Pierre Guislain, Jacques Hanric, Julia Kristeva, Rachel Laurent, Robert Longo, Britt Nini, Dominique Paini, Jackie Raynal, Myriem Roussel, Guy Scarpetta, and Paul Virilio

Études cinématoraphiques, "*Jean-Luc Godard, au-delà du récit*," 57–61 (1967), articles by Michel Estève, Guido Aristarco, Pio Baldelli, Jacques Belmans, Guy Braucourt, Christian Jacotey, Mireille Latil-Le Dantec, Vincent Pinel, and Marie-Claire Ropars-Wuillemier

See also: *Revue belge du cinéma* 16 (1986) and *Cinémaction* 52 (1989)

GOLDMANN, LUCIEN
Philosopher

The question concerning the meaning and significance of cultural creations, primarily works of art and philosophy, constituted the focal point of Lucien Goldmann's interests. To answer it, he argued that one must go beyond the analysis of isolated works. All that is done, made, or created by human beings have a meaning to be understood. Meanings, however, are never intrinsic properties of that to which they are attributed. They are constituted by the function the given human phenomenon fulfils within a more encompassing whole, a historically specific environment, itself a meaningful structure for its participants and, in turn, again part of a larger unity, ultimately of "totality."

It was Lukács, in his *History and Class-Consciousness* whose importance for his own thought Goldmann always underlined, who disclosed the significance of the principle of "totality" for dialectical thought. Totality as the integrated and self-reproducing social whole incessantly changing in the very process of its reproduction is the genuine concrete; isolated facts or works are actually its "abstract" constituents. As a methodological principle of cultural analysis this demands the unification of hermeneutical understanding and sociological explanation, or rather a constant "oscillation" between the two. It is its meaning-constituting structure that makes a cultural creation historically significant. This latter, however, can only be disclosed by relating the work to that social situation in which it originated, more concretely to that collective, *transindividual* subject whose comprehension of, and attitude to, this situation it articulates. According to Goldmann's "genetic structuralism," only the disclosure of social genesis allows the understanding of the meaning conferring, structuring principles of the work. But once it is done, it throws a new light upon this objective situation because works of culture are among the most important documents that render possible the understanding of our collective past, and thus our own place in history, with its open, future possibilities.

This is connected to the fact that the notion of "totality" was for Goldmann not only a methodological presupposition, but also a practical value-concept. Its idea implies a striving for authentic human community, in which social integration is not imposed upon the individuals by force or by uncontrollable, impersonal mechanisms, but is the outcome of their autonomous decisions. Because humans are social beings, such conscious choices can only be meaningfully undertaken in those smaller communalities within which they live their life. "Totality" as the rational and harmonious unification of many self-managing social units was for Goldmann the ultimate value ideal, and the faith that it was realizable, his own "wager" informing his activity.

Goldmann always situated his work within the Marxist tradition. His cultural analyses, however, significantly differed from the usual practice of ideology critique. The notion of ideology established the connection between works of culture and their social bearer, usually a class, through the concept of "objective interest." For Goldmann this necessarily involved the danger of economic reductionism. He replaced it by the idea of the "vision of the world." It designates a relatively stable mental structure, an ensemble of interrelated aspirations, sentiments, and ideas that members of a social group share owing to the similarity of their practical life-situation and thus of the problems with which they must cope. It is this largely unconscious commonality in the way they comprehend their environing world and conceive—cognitively as well as emotively—their place and possibilities within it that confers a unity upon a group, making it a *transindividual* subject. And although Goldmann in general—at least in respect of the past—underlined the determining role of class-belonging in the formation of group identities, in his analyses he usually dealt with smaller units, fractions of a class, whose members possess similar cultural resources and are often connected with each other by a loose network of communications.

The relation of cultural creations to the vision of the world of their *transindividual* subject is neither that of passive reflection, nor of simple expression. The actual consciousnesses of individuals belonging to the same social group are neither homogeneous, nor consistent, already owing to the fact that concrete persons usually participate in a number of such groups. Significant cultural creations bring the unconscious and vague similarities underlying the empirical reality of a shared world-vision to a maximum of internal coherence and unity. They are the realizations of what Lukács has called the "imputed" consciousness of a class. Their relation to the empirical consciousness of their collective subject is—in Goldmann's later terminology—that of an "idealizing" (in the above sense) homology because the assumed correspondence holds not in respect of particular contents. A work of culture, to be socially and historically significant, does not need to address itself to the concrete concerns that may preoccupy the related empirical consciousness. What it brings to awareness is the categorical structure, the structuring principle of a system of feelings and beliefs that make possible a shared comprehension of, and attitude to, the world as such, to draw out consistently its consequences.

At the same time in his analyses Goldmann operates also with another type of homology. This concerns the structural correspondence among works pertaining to different cultural forms but genetically related to the same *transindividual* subject. Thus, in his most significant and influential book, *The Hidden God*, he disclosed the underlying identity of the way problems of human existence have been articulated in the theology of Jansenism, the philosophy of Pascal, and the dramas of Racine. They all provided a coherent expression of the vision of the world of the same subject, the *noblesse de robe* in seventeenth-century France. Each of them did it with its own particular means—philosophy through conceptual abstraction, drama through imaginary presentation—using their specific, partly inherited from their own traditions, means of representation because particular cultural forms possess a relative autonomy. They shared, however, as their ultimate meaning, a common perspective upon the contradictions of human life.

Genetic structuralism presupposes, however, a third type of homology. In spite of his strong historicism, Goldmann accepted the existence of some transhistorical correspondences. Transposing some of the ideas of Piaget's psychology concerning the development of mental structures in the individual into a social-historical plane, he argued that there are only a few basic types of world vision capable to articulate coherently a balanced relation between human beings and the environing reality, an always partial identity of the subject and the object. At different times, in different historical circumstances particular social groups can find themselves in analogous situations as far as the principal possibilities of their social action are concerned. Then cultural creations that succeed to present their life attitudes will manifest essential structural similarities; they will belong to the same type of world vision.

In opposition to Dilthey and Jaspers, Goldmann never presented a closed typological system of the possible worldviews. The openness of history condemns such an enterprise to failure. He was, however, particularly interested in the historical recurrence of a particular vision: the tragic vision of the world. It was the subject of his early book on Kant, *The Hidden God*,

and he returned to it in his last, unfinished work on Lukács and Heidegger. A tragic vision originates in situations when a social group—like the *noblesse de robe* in seventeenth-century France or German liberal bourgeoisie in the eighteenth century—finds its aspirations systematically thwarted or denied by that power on which its very existence depends and from which it cannot dissociate itself. In works of tragic vision this social crisis appears as the unresolvable contradiction between a fallen world and the absolute values demanding realization in a true, harmonious community. At the heart of such a vision is the paradox of an unconditionally obligating striving for "totality" accompanied by the recognition of its inevitable failure, of the inadmissibility of any compromise with a world that cannot be practically transcended. Cultural creations embodying such a form of consciousness—with their enhanced sensitivity toward the contradictions of reality and with their intention directed at totality—are the necessary precursors of dialectical thinking capable of solving their antinomies.

The openness of history, however, demands that the method of its understanding was also open, able to adapt to the changes of its object. In his later writings, first of all in his *Towards a Sociology of the Novel*, Goldmann significantly reformulated genetic structuralism. In present-day Western societies commodity relations permeated and subordinated all spheres of life. The autonomy of a technocratically organized society now undermines the autonomy of the individuals. The ensuing process of reification transforms consciousness into a mere reflex of exchange relations. Reification today encompasses the members of all the main classes of society, integrating them into this whole and simultaneously rendering them incapable of developing communal forms of social awareness. Representative works of culture thus no more can be related to mental structures specific to a particular class or its fraction. They became homogenized. Cultural creations of significance—like some fictions of nouveau Roman—now directly, without mediation disclose a homology with the fetishistic structure of this social whole in which objects determine the destinies of faceless individuals.

This methodological reorientation was accompanied also by a change in Goldmann's political views. In the sixties he came to reject, as no more valid, the traditional Marxist idea of the proletariat as the revolutionary agent of human emancipation. He now put his "wager" on the emerging "new working class" of well-educated white-collar employees, dissatisfied by the mindless character of their labor and striving for a "revolutionary reform" of the system from below, through the democratization of the workplace.

These political ideas (which he largely shared with Andre Gorz and Serge Mallet) brought Goldmann into conflict with the "structuralist" Marxism of Louis Althusser and his school, which was becoming ever more influential in the French left from the late 1950s. He sharply criticized Althusser for his theoretical antihumanism, the elimination of the concept of the subject, for the ahistorical transformation of the idea of totality—always in the historical becoming in the result of conscious human actions—into a pregiven closed structure with irresistible immanent laws.

From the early 1950s on, Goldmann had been a major figure in French intellectual life and an internationally influential thinker of the cultural Left. After his untimely death, although his legacy has been actively carried on by a number of former students and followers (Annie Goldmann, Michael Löwy, Jacques Leenhardt, Sami Naïr, Robert Sayre), his influence rather waned as first structuralism then varieties of post-structuralism acquired a dominant position in France. But in a world that conspicuously lacks the idea of utopia and the hope of transcendence, Goldmann's "wager" on the possibility to overcome the tragic vision may well again become realized.

GYORGY MARKUS

See also **Louis Althusser; Andre Gorz**

Biography

Born in 1913 in Bucharest, Romania into a Jewish family, Lucien Goldmann studied law at the University of Bucharest, actively participating in Communist student circles. In late 1934 he emigrated to France. In 1938 he completed a license at the *Faculté des Lettres* of the Sorbonne. After the fall of Paris to the Nazis, Goldmann first fled to Toulouse, then to Switzerland, where he met and befriended Jean Piaget. He completed his doctoral work in philosophy on Kant in 1944 at the University of Zürich. In 1945 he returned to Paris and joined the *Centre Nationale de Recherches Scientifique*. He obtained his doctorate with "The Hidden God" in 1956 at the Sorbonne. In 1959 Goldmann became the director of studies and the chair for sociology of literature at the *École des Hautes Études*. While holding this position he founded in 1961 the Centre for the Sociology of Literature at the Free University of Brussels. He died at the age of fifty-seven in 1970.

Selected Works

Mensch, Gemeinschaft und Welt in der philosophie Immanuel Kants: Studien zur Geschichte der Dialektik, 1945; as *Immanuel Kant*, translated by R. Black, 1971
Sciences humaines et philosophie, 1952; as *The Human Sciences and Philosophy*, translated by B. V. White and R. Anchor, 1969
Le Dieu caché: Étude sur la vision tragique dans les Pensées de Pascal et dans le théâtre de Racine, 1955; as *The Hidden God: A Study of Tragic Vision in the Pensées of Pascal and the Tragedies of Racine*, translated by P. Thody, 1964
Jean Racine, dramaturge, 1956; as *Racine*, translated by A. Hamilton, 1969
Recherches dialectiques, 1959
Pour une sociologie du roman, 1965; as *Towards a Sociology of the Novel*, translated by A. Sheridan, 1975
Structures mentales et création culturelle, 1970
Marxisme et sciences humaines. 1970
La Création culturelle dans la société moderne, 1971; as *Cultural Creation in Modern Society*, translated by B. Grahl, 1976
Lukács et Heidegger. Fragments posthumes établis et présentés par Youssef Ishaghpour, 1973; as *Lukács and Heidegger*, translated by W. Q. Boelhower, 1977

Further Reading

Bader, Wolfgang, *Grundprobleme der Literaturtheorie Lucien Goldmanns*, Frankfurt: Lang, 1979
Baum, Hermann, *Lucien Goldmann. Marxismus contra Vision Tragique*, Stuttgart: Frommann, 1974
Cohen, Mitchell, *The Wager of Lucien Goldmann: Tragedy, Dialectics, and the Hidden God*, Princeton: Princeton University Press, 1994
Cohen, Mitchell (editor), *Lucien Goldmann: Tragedy and Dialectics. Special double issue of The Philosophical Forum*, (1991–1992): Vol. 23, nos. 1–2.
Crispini, Franco, *Lo Structuralismo dialettico di Lucien Goldmann*, Naples: Libreria Scientifica, 1970
Evans, Mary, *Lucien Goldmann: An Introduction*, Sussex: Harvester, 1981
Goldmann, Annie–Sami Naïr–Michael Löwy (editors), *Le Structuralisme génétique: L'Oeuvre et l'influence de Lucien Goldmann*, Paris: Denoël, 1977
Goldmann, Annie–Sami Naïr–Michael Löwy (editors), *Hommage à Lucien Goldmann: Lucien Goldmann et la sociologie de la littérature*, Brussels: Éditions de l'Université de Bruxelles, 1975
Naïr, Sami and Michael Löwi, *Lucien Goldmann ou la dialectique de la totalité*, Paris: Seghers, 1973
Zima, Pierre, *Goldmann, dialectique de l'immanence*, Paris: Éditions Universitaires, 1973

GORZ, ANDRE
Writer

One of the major figures of the post-1968 Left in France, André Gorz has presented, in a significant body of works, a vision of struggles for a postindustrial ecological socialist order in which increased amounts of time are taken from waged work and freed up for creative, self-determined activities. Gorz is among the group of authors whose works find audiences in academia and social movements, and his body of work has had a profound influence on social and political debates within those spheres.

Influenced early on by Sartre's *Being and Nothingness* and its emphasis on radical contingency, Gorz came to find Sartrean ethics to be wanting. Sartre's work offered only unsatisfactory answers to questions of how one might make judgments or choices or achieve authenticity. In writings since the late 1960s Gorz has turned his attention toward developing a libertarian critique of capitalist political economy influenced greatly by the works of Ivan Illich.

Within modern capitalist societies, Gorz explains, there has developed a separation of a sphere of heteronomy and a sphere of autonomy. In Gorz's definition the sphere of heteronomy includes economically rational activity and productive labor. This "social production" is founded on a social division of labor and large-scale production driven by market processes or central planning. It is the realm in which free cooperation and reciprocity have ceased. The realm of heteronomy must be circumscribed as much as possible to allow for the opening and extension of realms of autonomy and mutuality.

In contrast to economic rationality, Gorz identifies two main forms of noncommodity production. The first he terms "autonomous activity," which includes actions that are ends in themselves, performed freely rather than being dictated by necessity or use value. These activities affirm personal self-development and sovereignty. Here Gorz includes all activities that are experienced as fulfilling and enriching sources of meaning and happiness such as art, philosophy, science, and education. These are, in his words, "mutual aid activities" or "activities of auto-production." The meaning of this type of work lies as much in its performance as in its product.

The second noncommodity activity Gorz terms "work for oneself." This refers to the production of use values of which the creators are "both the originators and sole beneficiaries." With the commodification of domestic work, what remains of these tasks are tasks of self-management including child rearing, leisure, and bodily care. Work for oneself is the means by which people come to belong to themselves and their communities. Many of these activities have been encroached upon by the market. Gorz argues that this shift of work for oneself to commercial services must be resisted and the realms of work for oneself expanded to open up common spaces where people can determine collective needs and the means for securing them. These "micro-social activities" provide a ground for the critique of capitalist consumption and of social relations dominated by commodity exchange.

In his view, however, a wholesale return to craft production and village economies is undesirable because, he maintains, a developed division of labor is necessary for mobilizing the enormous stores of knowledge embodied in machines and industrial systems. Thus, Gorz does not seek a re-integration of the system and realms of autonomy, of work and life. In his view such a re-integration would mean a return to the conditions of precapitalist societies. Eliminating the relative autonomy of different realms of activity or social subsystems might overcome the rift between working and living, but this would come at the cost of social development. Gorz remains a defender of modernity and especially the structural differentiation between the system and realms of autonomy.

In recent works, especially *Capitalism, Socialism, Ecology* (1994), Gorz argues against the socialist goal of doing away with the system because this would only impede society's potential for development by limiting the complexity that drives modern creativity. The goal for socialists should now be to limit the system to its indispensable aspects. Postindustrial socialism must shift the economy and technology away from profit maximization and toward addressing those needs that have been arrived at democratically. Thus Gorz's socialism is really an updated variant of social democracy. He does not aim to eliminate capital, the logic of which he views as economically rational, but rather the elevation of capital in the hierarchy of everyday life, values, and politics. He does not wish to see capital's economic and administrative systems abolished, only limited and integrated into the world where they might be put to noneconomic ends. Gorz argues for the democratization of economic decision-making and increased political participation.

Indeed, Gorz argues that the spheres of noncommodity activity can only flourish when the state safeguards them against the intrusion of economic rationality. The state has a crucial part to play in regulating markets and ensuring that economic rationality applies only in the sphere of waged work. Even more than this, the state can assist in reducing the amount of waged work that individuals need to do, thereby releasing time for autonomous pursuits. In Gorz's postindustrial socialism the state will administer a social wage which will not be linked to an individual's expenditure of productive labor.

Political ecology and the defense of nature, by placing limits on the system, offer a defense of autonomy. Socialism and ecology together are the crucial elements in the subordination of heteronomy. Socialism is not the establishment of an alternative system but rather an ongoing practical project of abolishing everything that makes society into a system. Ecology is an indispensable part of the struggle against capitalism. Ecological concerns must be a fundamental part of socialism and they cannot be compromised, postponed, or subordinated to other political objectives.

In earlier ecological writings, such as *Ecology as Politics* (1980), Gorz offers a limited vision of ecology restricted to a focus on nature as the "material prerequisites of the economic system," or the limits of economics. In more recent writings, however, Gorz clearly differentiates environmentalism, which only seeks constraints on the development of capitalist economic rationality without altering the system's tendencies, and ecology, which aims to shrink the sphere of economic rationality and subordinate it to nonquantifiable social and cultural goals.

Environmentalism focuses on resources depletion and ecological destruction in relation to industrialization, but fails to situate industrialization within the historically specific development of capitalism. By failing to relate industrial growth to the specific forces of capitalist accumulation, environmentalism has limited its political activity to appeals to states to place regulations on production and consumption.

Political ecology, on the other hand, situates ecological crisis within the specific practices of capitalist accumulation. In this view ecological crisis can only be overcome by replacing the capitalist logic of production for exchange and profit with a system of production for use. Political ecology must work to challenge economic rationalization and to limit its sphere of application. To aid this task, Gorz attempts to demonstrate the ontological and existential limits of economic rationality.

Loss of autonomy has a number of consequences that contribute to ecological destruction. The expansion of waged work reduces people's capacities, in available time and energy, to meet their needs through their own individual and collective efforts. This, then, fuels the expansion of commodified consumption, which, in turn, increases the need to undertake waged work. Current struggles for socialism must be based on "qualitative" demands for autonomy, decreased waged work, and healthy environments, demands that correspond to new social movements, rather than traditional union demands for increased wages or full employment.

Gorz argues that green movements cannot limit their efforts to an exclusive focus on the regulation of production because capital can take on these concerns, through development of new forces of production, without changing anything. The crucial problem that remains is the capitalist pressure to extend commodification into ever-increasing spheres of life, which impels increased production and consumption.

If the preservation of nature is not achieved through an expansion of work-for-ourselves and the limitation of spheres of economic rationality by autonomous spheres of self-determination, then ecology will succumb to techno-bureaucratic power or "technofascist" central regulation.

In that case the regeneration of nature will be separated from people's subjective intentions and directed by the imperatives of capital and administrative regulation.

JEFFREY SHANTZ

See also **Jean-Paul Sartre**

Biography

André Gorz was born in Austria in 1924 and exiled to Switzerland with his family during the *anschluss*. He settled in Paris in 1948 and in 1961 joined Sartre on *Les Temps Modernes*. In 1964 he helped to found the socialist weekly *Le Nouvel Observateur,* to which he contributed for more than twenty years. During the late 1960s until the early 1980s, through writings such as *Strategy for Labor* and *Farewell to the Working Class*, Gorz established himself as a main theoretician of the "new working class" or the postindustrial working class. In influential writings since the 1980s he has developed an ecological postindustrial socialism based on the liberation from work and economic rationality.

Selected Works

Strategy for Labor, 1967
Capitalism in Crisis and Everyday Life, 1977
Ecology as Politics 1980
Farewell to the Working Class, 1982
Paths to Paradise: On the Liberation from Work, 1985
Critique of Economic Reason, 1989
Political Ecology: Expertocracy versus Self-Limitation, 1993
Capitalism, Socialism, Ecology, 1994
Reclaiming Work: Beyond the Wage-Based Society, 1999

Further Reading

Bowring, Finn, "André Gorz: Ecology, System and Lifeworld." *Capitalism, Nature, Socialism.* 6,4 (24)(1995): 65–84
Bowring, Finn, "Post-Fordism and the End of Work," *Futures.* 34 (2)(2002): 159–72
Byrne, David, "A Rejection of André Gorz's Farewell to the Working Class," *Capital and Class, (1984–85)*
Giddens, Anthony, "The Perils of Punditry: Gorz and the End of the Working Class," in *Social Theory and Modern Sociology*, Cambridge: Polity, 1987
Hirsch, Arthur, *The French New Left*, Montréal: Black Rose Books, 1982
Howard, Dick, "New Situation, New Strategy: Serge Mallet and André Gorz," in *The Unknown Dimension*, edited by Dick Howard and Karl E. Klare, New York: Basic Books, 1972
Hyman, Richard "André Gorz and his Disappearing Proletariat," in The *Socialist Register*, edited by R. Miliband and J. Saville, London: Merlin Press, 1983
Livesay, Jeff, "Post-Marxist Theories of Civil Society," *Current Perspectives in Social Theory* 14 (1994): 101–134
Sayers, Sean, "The Need to Work," *Radical Philosophy.* 87 (1987):
Sayers, Sean, "Gorz on Work and Liberation," *Radical Philosophy*, 58 (1991): 16–19

Strange, G, "Which Path to Paradise?: André Gorz, Political Ecology and the Green Movement," *Capital and Class*, 59 (1996): 81–102

Strange, G, "Capitalism, Valorization and the Political Economy of Ecological Crisis," *Capital and Class*, 72 (2000): 55–80

Whitbread, Chris, "Gorz, Nove, Hodgson: The Economics of Socialism," *Capital and Class*, 26(1985): 125–145

Whiteside, Kerry, "French Ecosocialism: From Utopia to Contract," *Environmental Politics*, 6 (3)(1997): 99–124

GREIMAS, ALGIRDAS JULIEN
Semiotician, Linguist

Algirdas Julien Greimas was the initiator of a dynamic semiotic theory of meaning. Having begun his career pursuing research in lexicology, Greimas became dissatisfied with analysis that remained on the level of the word. He turned to a textual semiotics, which he conceived as a scientific endeavor, at the juncture of linguistics, anthropology, and formal logic. In contrast with other semiotic systems that focus on signs, Greimassian semiotics, also known as the Paris school of semiotics, examines signification more broadly defined.

Guiding all of Greimas's work is the attempt to account for signification in light of the human world and its social context. Following the Danish linguist Louis Hjelmslev, Greimas was concerned with describing the general conditions necessary for the emergence of meaning. Like Ferdinand de Saussure, he makes no claim to get to the root things that generate meaning, but rather attempts to account for "meaning-effects."

Influenced by basic structuralist tenets such as the concept of structure as difference and the principle of binary oppositions, Greimas proposed a new, generative semiotic model of the constitution of meaning in discourse. According to this model, discourse production unfolds in various stages, beginning with fundamental elementary structures and moving toward surface manifestations. Greimas's theory incorporates different levels of analysis: an immanent level, or a sort of deep structure, and a manifest level, that which we perceive in a given semiotic object, such as a written text. Fittingly, Greimassian semiotics can be best described in narrative terms. Just as the theory was founded upon the analysis of narrative, its history is a tale of adventure demonstrating Greimas's zest for innovation, which sometimes took the theory in surprising directions. Following study of the work of thinkers including not only Saussure and Hjelmslev but also Georges Dumézil and Claude Lévi-Strauss, Greimas discovered Vladimir Propp's *Morphology of the Folktale*, a narrative study of Lithuanian tales. Building upon these sources, Greimas wrote *Sémantique structurale* (1966), in which he developed an ac-

tantial, or action-based model to describe the various actants, or roles in narrative, such as those of hero, sought-after person, helper, and villain. In Voltaire's *Candide*, for example, Candide is the hero, Cunégonde is the sought-after object of Candide's quest, Dr. Pangloss is a helper, and pirates number among the villains.

Working to uncover narrative structures postulated as universal, Greimas developed a theory of the elementary structure of signification, constructed around four basic terms located along two semantic axes (*Du sens*). This elementary structure is represented graphically by the innovation for which Greimas is probably best known: the semiotic square. Useful for distilling fundamental constituents of meaning in any system, the semiotic square both builds upon and moves beyond basic binary structuralist distinctions. It functions as a visual map of interactions of meaning, represented in a less cumbersome manner than would be possible in ordinary prose writing. Let us take, for example, the semiotic square of "veridiction"(*Du sens II*): falsehood.

Any semiotic square represents three types of relations: contradiction (between a1 and non-a1, and between a2 and non-a2), contrariness (between a1 and a2, and between non-a1 and non-a2) and implication (between a1 and non-a2, and between a2 and non-a1). Truth (the combination of being and seeming), falsehood (non-seeming and non-being), secret (being and non-seeming) and deception (non-being and seeming) in this example are known as second-generation terms. For Greimas, meaning can only be grasped in its transformations; no semiotic object is as static as the semiotic square may at first seem to suggest. However, it is possible to align various actors and events with terms in the square. To return to the example of *Candide*, Candide himself is a naive and truthful young man who combines being and seeming. As for being and non-seeming, in Constantinople Candide dines with six fellow travelers whose secret turns out to be that they are dethroned kings. The hanging death of Pangloss is a deception, as he later reappears very much alive. Turning to non-seeming and non-being, the pessimistic character Martin denounces Candide's eternal optimism, which, in a world full of human violence and natural disasters, is borne out neither by appearance nor by reality.

Having developed the model, Greimas and his collaborators came to realize that every action presupposes an ability to act. To account for the competence underlying any utterance, that is, the preconditions of signification, Greimas and his colleagues decided that the narrative grammar they were developing needed also to be a modal grammar. This realization led to the development, beginning in the 1970s, of a semiotic theory of modalities, using common modal verbs such as knowing (*savoir*), being-able-to (*pouvoir*), wanting-to (*vouloir*), and having-to (*devoir*). Because it can characterize, for example, various "actants'" ability or lack of ability to fulfill a certain task or have it fulfilled by another, this facet of the theory has been termed a semiotics of manipulation.

Following the development of this narrative syntax of modalities, a major innovation in Greimassian semiotics involved a discursive syntax of "aspectualities." Aspect, which deals with modulations of process, applies to both time and space. For example, aspect treats questions of beginning, lasting, and ending. Significantly, "aspectualities" disturb neat semiotic categories. As the theory of aspect demonstrates, many differences in meaning are less accurately characterized as strict oppositions and more usefully described as involving degrees of a quality. Paris semiotics underwent a progressive shift away from structures and toward operations or acts, away from discrete oppositions and toward gradual differences.

For anyone familiar with Greimassian semiotics in its earliest formulations, one of the most surprising innovations is the semiotics of the passions, articulated in Greimas and Fontanille's *Sémiotique des passions: des états de choses aux états d'âme* (1991). Going beyond traditional philosophical approaches to the passions, which focus on individual words such as "anger" or "jealousy," Greimas and Fontanille describe passions as a mood that permeates an entire discourse, whose presence is signaled by ruptures and marks of emotion. The theory of aspect is closely related to the passions. As the subtitle of Greimas and Fontanille's book suggests, the development of the semiotic theory of passions marked a shift away from the study of object-centered states of affairs toward subject-centered states of feelings. If modalities subtend action, the passions underlie both modalities and actions. Although the model described subjects solely in terms of actions, the semiotics of passions characterizes subjects as endowed with an interior dimension. This evolution beyond a structural paradigm has been described as a turn away from a semiotics of the discontinuous, where meaning is conceived as a set of discrete units, toward a semiotics of the continuous, where meaning is understood as a whole that is marked by modulations.

In addition to the passions, later Greimassian semiotics attends to perception and its role in signification. In this sense, it shares strong links with phenomenology, demonstrating the influence of thinkers such as Edmund Husserl and Maurice Merleau-Ponty. This phenomenological tendency includes attention to the act of enunciation, including the role of the subject of enunciation.

Greimassian semiotics has continued to expand thanks to a diverse group of theorists who study signification in fields ranging from the humanities and social sciences to the fine arts. The continuing vibrancy of Greimas's project is reflected in the variety of work his former colleagues and students have undertaken, such as analyses of architecture and space, law, advertising, communication theory, visual media, music, and sacred texts. Narrative literary texts, however, remain the subject of most work inspired by the theory.

A symbol of the collaborative nature of the Greimassian semiotic project, the second volume of *Sémiotique: dictionnaire raisonné de la théorie du langage* (1986) includes entries written by some forty contributors. These articles, many of which contain several sections by various authors, extend, modify, or even contest earlier facets of the theory. One of Greimas's most admirable qualities as a theorist was his unflinching embrace of potentially disruptive challenges to his theory. Thanks in part to his openness to growth, which has been carried on by Greimas's students, Paris semiotics continues to provide powerful analytic tools for the study of meaning.

HEIDI BOSTIC

See also **Georges Dumezil; Claude Levi-Strauss; Maurice Merleau-Ponty; Ferdinand de Saussure**

Biography

Born in 1917 in Russia, of Lithuanian origins, Algirdas Julien Greimas immigrated to France where he earned a *Doctorat d'État ès lettres* at the Sorbonne in 1948. Greimas taught in Egypt and Turkey before earning a university post in Poitiers, France, and finally at the *École Pratique des Hautes Études* in Paris in 1965. In addition to directing a lively seminar, whose participants have become the leaders of the next generation of the Paris school of semiotics, Greimas authored many articles and books, the best known of which are *Sémantique structurale* (1966), *Du sens* (1970), *Sémiotique et sciences sociales* (1976), *Du sens II* (1983) and *Sémiotique des passions* (1991, coauthored with Jacques Fontanille). He also co-edited, with Joseph Courtés, *Sémiotique: dictionnaire raisonné de la théorie du langage*, the two volumes of which appeared in 1979 and 1986, respectively. Greimas died in Paris in 1992.

Selected Works

La Mode en 1830: Essai de description du vocabulaire vestimentaire d'après les journaux de modes de l'époque, 1948
Sémantique structurale: Recherche de méthode, 1966; as *Structural Semantics: An Attempt at a Method*, translated by Daniele McDowell et al., 1983
Dictionnaire de l'ancien français, 1968

Du sens: Essais sémiotiques, 1970

Maupassant: La sémiotique du texte, 1976; as *Maupassant: The Semiotics of the Text*, translated by Paul Perron, 1988

Sémiotique et sciences sociales, 1976.

Greimas, A. J., and Joseph Courtés, eds. *Sémiotique: dictionnaire raisonné de la théorie du langage*, Vol 1, 1979; as *Semiotics and Language: An Analytical Dictionary*, translated by Larry Crist et al, 1982.

Du sens II: Essais sémiotiques, 1983.

Sémiotique: dictionnaire raisonné de la théorie du langage, Vol. 2, 1986

De l'imperfection, 1987

On Meaning: Selected Writings in Semiotic Theory, translated by Paul Perron and Frank Collins, 1987

The Social Sciences: A Semiotic View, translated by Paul Perron and Frank Collins, 1990

Dictionnaire du moyen français, 1991

Sémiotique des passions: des états de choses aux états d'âme, 1991; as *The Semiotics of Passions: From States of Affairs to States of Feelings*, translated by Paul Perron and Frank Collins, 1993.

Further Reading

Broden, Thomas F., "A.J. Greimas (1917–1992): Commemorative Essay," *Semiotica* 105/3–4 (1995): 207–242.

Budniakiewicz, Therese, *Fundamentals of Story Logic: Introduction to Greimassian Semiotics*, 1992

Coquet, Jean-Jacques (editor), *Sémiotique: L'École de Paris*, Paris: Hachette, 1982

Fontanille, Jacques (editor), *Le discours aspectualisé* (Proceedings of the First Linguistics and Semiotics Colloquium, University of Limoges, France, February 1989), Amsterdam: Benjamins; Limoges: PULIM, 1991

Fontanille, Jacques (editor), *Hommages à A. J. Greimas*, special issue of *Nouveaux Actes Sémiotiques* 25, (1993)

Hénault, Anne, *Histoire de la sémiotique*, collection Que sais-je?, Paris: PUF, 1992

Perron, Paul and Frank Collins, (editors), *Greimassian Semiotics*, special issue of *New Literary History* 20/3 (1989)

Perron, Paul and Frank Collins, (editors and translators), *Paris School Semiotics*, 2 vols., Philadelphia: Benjamins, 1989

Schleifer, Ronald, *A.J. Greimas and the Nature of Meaning: Linguistics, Semiotics and Discourse Theory*, Lincoln: University of Nebraska Press, 1987

GRENIER, JEAN

Philosopher, Essayist, Man of Letters, Art Critic

Jean Grenier's professional career was spent almost entirely within the school and university system, as a philosophy teacher. His published work ranged well outside the confines of European academic philosophy, however, extending to Indian and Chinese traditions (*L'Esprit du Tao*, 1957); and it was as an essayist and regular contributor to Paulhan's *Nouvelle Revue Française* that he made his mark in the 1930s, later becoming a noted interpreter of modern art. He is often thought of primarily as the influential mentor of Albert Camus, but such an assessment is unduly limiting.

Rather like Alain, Grenier was a philosopher-essayist in the tradition of Montaigne, opening up multiple perspectives rather than developing a system. Indeed, it was his insistence on the intellectual untenability of orthodox belief-systems that kept him apart from many of the philosophical and political movements of the period. His *Essai sur l'esprit d'orthodoxie* (1938), which infuriated Marxists at the time (though neo-Thomists are not spared either), was widely read, and was to influence Camus's *L'Homme révolté*. It expounded the principle enunciated in an article published in the *Nouvelle Revue Française* in 1935: "*se décider non d'après les mouvements de la foule mais d'après la plus profonde exigence*" ("make up your mind not according to the movements of the crowd but according to the highest [intellectual] demands").

Grenier's main philosophical interests were metaphysics and aesthetics. The problem of evil was his earliest and most constant concern. He discovered Schopenhauer at an early age, and his 1920 thesis for the *Diplôme d'Études Supérieures* highlighted the centrality of evil in the neocriticist system of Renouvier. Renouvier's emphasis on the connection between evil and the right use of freedom led Grenier to devote his doctoral thesis to Renouvier's friend Jules Lequier (1814–62). Lequier's grand project was to base a complete Christian philosophy on the idea of freedom as a "*première vérité*" (his maxim "*Faire, et en faisant, se faire*" was later taken up by Sartre, though Sartre dropped the complementary notion of God as "*faire faire*"). Grenier's interest was less in the system than in the ambitious attempt to reconcile irreconcilable truths, and in what he calls the heuristic approach that Lequier adopted, and that he himself was to follow in his own sensitive, exploratory writing.

Grenier's best-known work remains *Les Îles* (1933), a collection of essays that was originally conceived as an introspective novel. In their brevity, suggestiveness, and lyricism (in which they are indebted to Barrès), these texts combine a celebration of life and an acute awareness of its impermanence. They express an existential-metaphysical solitude in which the individual subject (whose status is always in question) is aware of the absolute as the only true value, but also as unattainable. A key concept is that of the instant, a moment at which time is suspended and there is a simultaneous loss of individuality and finding of identity. Indian metaphysical concepts underlie some of the essays: Grenier had originally planned to write his doctoral thesis on the influence of Indian thought on Europe, particularly in relation to Schopenhauer, and one of his early essays (published by Daniel Halévy alongside texts by Malraux and others) had compared Indian and Greek sculpture. *Inspirations méditerranéennes* (1941, the title borrowed from Valéry) develops the fragmentary, aphoristic, and poetic potential of the essay form, establishing Grenier as one of its leading exponents. This potential is perhaps most fully realized in the series of teasing *Lexiques* (1949–73), which he referred to as involuntary self-portraits. The close link between essay and autobiography is also seen in Grenier's two novels, *Les Grèves* (1955) and *Voir Naples* (1973), which are extended self-explorations, as is the more overtly autobiographical *Mémoires intimes de X.* (1971).

Le Choix (1941) is an important statement of pure idealism, in which the intellectual conviction of absolute value is affirmed despite its incompatibility with the relative categories of belief and action. Camus was one of the first to recognize the importance of this work, calling his own *Le Mythe de Sisyphe* "*grossier*" (crude) in comparison. Grenier unsurprisingly went on to tax the existentialism of Sartre with tricking the intellect into betraying its own *raison d'être*, and thus paradoxically crushing the freedom it set out to assert. On the other hand, like his friend Jean Wahl, he welcomed the emphasis on existence, freedom, and choice, and he himself made major contributions to the postwar debate by publishing *L'Existence* (1945), a collection of essays by himself, Camus, Fondane, Gilson, Lavelle, Le Senne, Parain and others, and his own *Entretiens sur le bon usage de la liberté* (1948) (which concludes with a study of Taoist *wou-wei* or indifference) and *L'Existence malheureuse* (1957). *A propos de l'humain* (1955) and *La Vie quotidienne* (1968) show Grenier as a philosopher of the everyday.

His importance for Camus was considerable. He was not only his teacher for several years, and the joint supervisor of his *Diplôme d'Études Supérieures* thesis *Métaphysique chrétienne et néo-platonisme*, but he lent him books, encouraged him to write, commented extensively on his drafts, and facilitated publication, as well as encouraging him to join the Communist party in 1935. The early lyrical essays of Camus were inspired by Grenier's in both content and form, but he soon found his own voice. Camus's preface to the 1959 edition of *Les Îles* is a fine tribute to Grenier, who returned the compliment in his prefaces to the two collected editions of Camus's works (Monaco: Sauret, 1962; Paris: Gallimard, 1962) and in his *Albert Camus (souvenirs)* (1968). Their *Correspondance* (1981) is richly rewarding.

By asking him to write on art for *Combat* in 1944–45, Camus gave Grenier the opportunity to become a major critic. Having worked on Greek sculpture and then Rembrandt in the 1920s, Grenier now made a point of visiting contemporary artists in their studios and using their own words to interpret their work. A book on Braque (1948) was followed by collections of articles explaining the basis of nonrepresentational painting (*L'Esprit de la peinture contemporaine*, 1951, including studies of Lhote as both painter and critic) and exploring the work of a wide range of artists (*Essais sur la peinture contemporaine*, 1959; *Entretiens avec dix-sept peintres non-figuratifs*, 1963). Short monographs were devoted to Lanskoy, Borès, Musič, and others. *L'Art et ses problèmes* (1970) brings together some of his Sorbonne lecture-courses.

Grenier was associated at various times with the individualist philosopher Georges Palante, the poet Max Jacob, the review *Philosophies* in its pre-Marxist days, the *Fondation de Lourmarin* (but not its right-wing ideology), moderate left-wingers such as Louis Guilloux (his closest friend) and Jean Guéhenno, the Pontigny *décades*, and the postwar *Société Européenne de Culture*. His spiritual home was somewhere between the NRF and Mounier's *Esprit*, but he preserved his own freedom, and in exploring his personal intellectual archipelago (the metaphor of travel is frequent in his work) he stimulated others to realize their own potential. He gave encouragement and practical assistance to many aspiring literary figures, helping his pupil Edmond Charlot to set up his publishing house, providing copy for new reviews, and making detailed and sensitive comments on manuscripts. His own output, though very considerable, is disparate, and has not yet attracted the attention it deserves. A growing critical appreciation of the importance of the essay and associated genres in the twentieth century may help to give him his rightful place.

TOBY GARFITT

See also **Maurice Barres; Albert Camus; Etienne Gilson; Daniel Halevy; Louis Lavelle; Rene Le Senne**

Biography

Camille Jean Charles Grenier was born February 6, 1898 in Paris. He studied at (private) École Saint-Charles in Saint-Brieuc, Brittany, then in Paris at *Lycée Louis-le-Grand*, 1915–18; Sorbonne, 1915–22, achieving agrégation in philosophy, 1922. He taught at lycées in Avignon, 1923, Algiers, 1923–24; Institut Français, Naples, 1924–26; worked for *Éditions de la Nouvelle Revue Française*, Paris, 1927–28; taught at lycées in Cherbourg, 1928, Vendôme, 1929, Albi, 1929–30, Algiers, 1930–38 (where he taught Albert Camus); Lycée Michelet, Vanves, 1938–39; served as military nurse in Draguignan, 1939; taught at lycée in Montpellier, 1940–41 (where he made friends with Gabriel Marcel). Grenier was professor of philosophy, University of Lille, 1942–62, with periods of secondment to Universities of Alexandria, 1945–48, and Cairo, 1948–50; professor of aesthetics and science of art, Sorbonne, Paris, 1962–68. He received the *Grand*

Prix National des Lettres in 1968. Grenier died in Dreux on March 5, 1971.

Selected Works

Les Îles, 1933 (new edition 1959, with a preface by Albert Camus)

La Philosophie de Jules Lequier, 1936

Essai sur l'esprit d'orthodoxie, 1938; as *Conversations on the Good Uses of Freedom*, translated by Alexander Coleman, 1967

Le Choix, 1941

Inspirations méditerranéennes, 1941

L'Existence, 1945

Entretiens sur le bon usage de la liberté, 1948

L'Esprit de la peinture contemporaine, 1951

Jules Lequier, Œuvres complètes, 1952

A propos de l'humain, 1955

Les Grèves, 1955

L'Esprit du Tao, 1957

L'Existence malheureuse, 1957

Sur la mort d'un chien, 1957

Essais sur la peinture contemporaine, 1959

Lettres d'Égypte 1950, suivies d'Un Été au Liban, 1962

Entretiens avec dix-sept peintres non-figuratifs, 1963

Célébration du miroir, 1965

Albert Camus (souvenirs), 1968

La Vie quotidienne, 1968

Entretiens avec Louis Foucher, 1969

L'Art et ses problèmes, 1970

Music, 1970

Mémoires intimes de X., 1971

Réflexions sur quelques écrivains, 1973

Voir Naples, 1973

Jacques, 1979

Jean Grenier—Georges Perros: Correspondance 1950–1971, 1980

Lexique, 1981 (incorporating the earlier *Lexique, Nouveau Lexique*, etc.)

Albert Camus—Jean Grenier: Correspondance 1932–1960, 1981

Prières, 1983 (incorporating the earlier *Prières* and *Quatre Prières*)

Jean Paulhan—Jean Grenier: Correspondance 1925–1968, 1984

Carnets 1944–1971, 1991

Sous l'Occupation, 1997

Further Reading

André, Jacques (editor), *Jean Grenier*, Romillé: Folle Avoine, 1990

André, Jacques (editor), *Les Instants privilégiés: Jean Grenier*, Bédée: Folle Avoine, 1992

Campbell, Robert, "L'Indifférence selon Jean Grenier," *Nouvelle Revue Française*, 64 and 65 (1958), 691–701 and 879–90

Les Chemins de l'Absolu (Actes du colloque Jean Grenier 1998), Saint-Brieuc: Ville de Saint-Brieuc, 1999

Garfitt. J. S. T., *The Work and Thought of Jean Grenier (1989–1971)*, London: Modern Humanities Research Association, 1983

"Jean Grenier", special number of *Nouvelle Revue Française*, 221 (1971)

Yadel, Martina, *Jean Grenier—Les Îles, eine Untersuchung zu werkkonstituerenden Themen und Motiven*, Frankfurt: Peter Lang, 1995

GUATTARI, FÉLIX
Psychoanalyst, Philosopher, Social Ecologist

Félix Guattari's philosophical contributions and activist engagements ranged across the practical domains of psychotherapy, Marxist revolutionary politics, cultural criticism, and social ecology. His critical thought was grounded in the practical analysis of the diverse institutional arrangements and groups in which he participated. His theoretical work ultimately aimed to articulate an analytic method that could traverse these multiple fields of engagement, aligning them within a common "ethico-aesthetic paradigm," which he identified variously as "schizoanalysis," "transversality," or "chaosmosis." This paradigm connects the "three ecologies"—the subjective, the social, and the natural—in terms of the creative process of their production, and in terms of their inherent potential for transformation.

From his psychotherapeutic work at the experimental clinic La Borde, Guattari developed a constructivist understanding of identity as a process of "subjectivation," involving individuals, their social relations, and the multiple institutional structures circumscribing their existential practices and modes of sociability. The aim of La Borde was to provide an environment where psychotic patients could be actively involved in the processes of their treatment, particularly by redefining themselves in terms of their participation in dynamic, interactive groups that functioned as centers for collective subjectivization.

In line with Freudian/Lacanian psychoanalytic theories, Guattari conceived of subjectivization as a process and a task: the construction and production of the self through the determining forces of unconscious desire. However, he countered the traditional psychoanalytic association between unconscious desire and castration/lack with a purely positive concept of desire as connectivity and productivity. This enabled him to present a concept of selfhood neither restricted by a (Western bourgeois) mythology of familial relations, nor structurally predetermined in response to a primary ontological lack or loss. To this end, his first collaborative work with Gilles Deleuze, *Anti-Oedipus*, described the unconscious as composed of "desiring-machines" that perpetually combine and disassemble in synthetic and disjunctive relations. Reworking Melanie Klein's theory of partial-object relations, Guattari redefined subjectivization as the creative assemblage of elements into a coherent unity, according to underlying synthetic forces of "desiring-production." These forces combine according to contingent, socially inscribed rules of connective relation. The subject's primary determining structure is therefore the social field in which he/she is situated, and in which the family is included, but only as a mediating part.

Accordingly, for Guattari, as for Foucault and Deleuze, a subject is produced by the relations into which he/she enters. In aligning desire and the Unconscious with sociability and productive relations, Guattari argued that the individual is always already a "group subject," thereby denying a polarization of individual and society. An alternative distinction is made between two types of "group subject," closely paralleling Sartre's earlier distinction between the modes of action of the "serial group" and the "group-in-fusion." For Guattari, the "subjected-group" has its identity and its coherence imposed from an external source, which unifies the component elements by homogenizing them. This represses and eradicates their heterogeneity, and arrests their creativity by imposing a fixed, standard identity upon them. In this case, self-consciousness is a phenomenon of external domination. By contrast, the "subject-group" has an internal source of unity because its elements identify in terms of their commitment towards a common project. Because each element identifies with multiple projects in various and overlapping organizations, this kind of group-subjectivity in no way compromises the heterogeneity of the composing elements. The subject-group is dynamic, an identity in process, which adapts itself as its defining project develops and changes.

In advocating the organization of dynamic subject-groups, Guattari was not only concerned with the process of subject-formation, but also with the post-structuralist destabilization and transformation of subjectivity, which indeed became a defining facet of his "schizoanalytic" therapeutic strategy at La Borde. An experimental, rather than interpretive strategy, schizoanalysis aimed to interrupt the personal impasses experienced by patients, releasing them to create new subjective possibilities. Guattari proposed that significant events in the treatment process signalled moments when the subjects' "desiring-machines" were in the process of breaking down, creating disjunctive ruptures in the productive flows of desire. Guattari suggested that this might facilitate an opening on to a virtual and indeterminate state of identity, making tangible the permanent potential for creative renewal. Patients were encouraged to engage in unfamiliar activities and form novel alliances with different groups. When successful, this strategy worked to initiate a pragmatic decomposition of the "blocked" self, and an invention of new synthetic relations of desire, resulting in a new actualization of subjectivity.

Guattari's theory of transformative subjectivization opens onto an analysis of institutional repression, resulting in a theory of practical social revolution underscored by a trenchant critique of capitalism. For Guattari, social relations and their supporting institutions, including language and discourse, are the apparatuses of subjectivization. Social structures impose a regular organization upon the underlying forces of desire by constraining the desiring-machines, imposing rules upon them to regulate the connections and combinations they can form. This delimits the kinds of group interactions individuals are likely to enter into, and so constrains creativity within the group processes of subject-formation. The political significance of Guattari's work lay in his insistence that societies must analyze the way their institutions codify desire and repress it, with the aim of developing subject-groups that abandon the organizing principles of serialization and domination, and become capable of fostering the capacity for critical and creative transformation.

Accordingly, he conducts a critique of the structural repression of desire inherent in capitalist institutions, social relations, and subjective forms, where "repression is first and foremost the eradication and perversion of the singular" (*Communists Like Us*). Guattari's critique of "integrated world capitalism" centers upon its tendency to erode specific, or "singular," value systems, subsuming and equalizing them under the universal dominance of the capitalist economy. For example, he questions the capitalist logic of equivalence, which reduces natural, cultural, and intellectual entities to an economic resource value, denying or suppressing the various, singular and noneconomic ways in which they are valuable. Similarly, he criticizes the tendency towards economic and political globalization, which erodes specific, local economies, political forms, and cultural difference. Guattari's contention is that capitalism involves the forceful repression of alternative economies of desiring-production and heterogenous modes of valorization, production, and subjectivization, which nevertheless persist and so threaten to undermine the capitalist system. Furthermore, capitalism has a conflicting tendency to "decode" and release flows of desire in order to establish equivalence, which potentially challenges the repressive functions that secure the stability of the system.

Corresponding with this account of repression is a critique of representation and of the "despotism" of the Signifier, which "silences the infinite virtualities of minor languages and partial expressions" (*Chaosmosis*). Guattari departed from Saussurian structuralist linguistics to develop a semiotic theory that displaces the primacy of signification in favor of an a-signifying regime. His aim was to reveal the unconscious social and political determinations of signification, the collective agency of enunciation that precedes and produces representation. Drawing from Hjelmslev, Guattari proposed that signs are produced from an unformed thought-mass ("purport") common to all languages, by a process of semiotic capture, organization, and discipline, in which consistency of expression materializes content. Representation is neither the organizing principle nor the totality of significance, but is itself an emergent structure, an imposition of semiotic order upon a primary and chaotic a-signifying field. The permanent presence of this a-signifying semiotic within signification destabilizes representation from within, suggesting the permanent possibility of transforming the dominant order of meaning.

Guattari argued against certain postmodern visions of narrative collapse and social fragmentation, such as Lyotard and Baudrillard's, which have accompanied such critiques of representation. He asserted that our continued survival depends upon the collective development of mental and social ecologies capable of sustaining human social forms and the natural environment upon which they depend. Particularly in his collaborative works with the philosopher Gilles Deleuze and with the militant social theorist Toni Negri, Guattari outlined the communitarian conditions and aims of "micropolitical revolution."

The primary task of the micro-political revolutionary is to "constitute an organization which continually remakes itself" (Communists Like Us). This involves a rejection of fixed, molar forms of revolutionary subjectivity and organization, such as the traditional binary antagonism between proletariat and bourgeoisie. What is required is a "functional multicentrism" capable of articulating different dimensions of social criticism and transformative action across the "three ecological registers" of self, society, and nature. Within this multicentric revolutionary system, the common goal is the strategic organization of institutional settings, enabling the formation of revolutionary subject-groups that express and reinforce their singularity as a practical resistance to forces of repression.

As described in his final published work, "chaosmosis" is the conceptual apparatus framing the micropolitical practices of subjective and social transformation. Chaosmosis describes the process of complex organization as an imposition of form upon a primary network of forces, arresting their chaotic movement into a stable regularity of actual relations. Repressive orders claim to represent the only possible actuality, resisting the possibility of their transformation. Guattari aims to show how the foregrounding of creative process makes possible the transformation of existing subjective and social orders, through a reconfiguration of the elements and practices that combine

to produce the domain of the actual. The overall aim of "chaosmosis" is therefore "to develop possible openings onto the virtual and onto creative processuality" (Chaosmosis). Intrinsic to Guattari's "chaosmotic" paradigm is an ethical perspective and an aesthetic practice, consisting of a striving to counter repression, to develop community relations supportive of creative individuality, and to cultivate a critical awareness of one's own processes and practices of subjectivization, desire and sociability.

SIMONE BIGNALL

See also **Jean Baudrillard; Gilles Deleuze; Jacques Lacan; Jean-Francois Lyotard; Ferdinand de Saussure**

Biography

Born in Paris on April 30, 1930, Felix Guattari grew up in the working class district of Villeneuve-les-Sablons. In 1953, after studying pharmacology and philosophy, he helped to establish La Borde, an experimental psychiatric clinic directed by the Lacanian analyst, Jean Oury. In 1962, Guattari began training analysis with Lacan, and in 1969 he became an analyst at the École Freudienne, while continuing his clinical work at La Borde. While his own theoretical developments definitively departed from the primary assumptions of Lacanian psychoanalysis, he remained associated with the École Freudienne until it ceased operation in 1982.

While still in his youth, Guattari became active in social and political movements and joined the Union des Jeunesses Républicaines de France (JRP), the youth wing of the Communist party. He worked on the publication of the newspaper of the Parti Communiste Français (PCF) until 1958, when he began editing and contributing to the dissident newspaper La Voie Communiste. In the 1960's Guattari helped to set up the Groupe de travail de psychologie et de sociologie institutionelle (GTPSI). In 1965, he founded the Societé de psychothérapie institutionelle (SPI), and the Fédération des groupes d'études et de recherches institutionelles (FGERI), which occupied the Théâtre de l'Odeon in the revolt of May 1968. This organization became focused around the Centre d'étude de recherches et de formation institutionelles (CERFI), responsible for producing the interdisciplinary journal Recherches, founded by Guattari in 1966. He also became active in the Opposition de Gauche (OG), a non-party, Leftist alliance.

Throughout the 1970s Guattari remained committed to diverse micro-political practices. In 1973, he was tried and fined for publishing an issue of Recherches on homosexuality. In 1975, he contributed to the founding of the international association *Réseau International d'Alternative à la Psychiatrie*. Guattari publicly supported Toni Negri upon his arrest for alleged terrorist involvement against the Italian government's suppression of the Red Brigade. In 1979, Guattari founded the *Centre d'initiatives pour de nouveaux espaces de liberté* (CINEL), and began collaborating with Negri in writing *Nouvelles espaces de liberté* (1985).

Guattari published a number of philosophical, political, and psychoanalytic works reflecting and expressing his overriding concern with the question of institutional repression. His most significant early solo works are *Psychanalyse et transversalité* (1972) and *La revolution moléculaire* (1977). In addition, Guattari's celebrated collaboration with the philosopher Gilles Deleuze produced the enormously influential *L'anti-Oedipe: capitalisme et schizophrénie I* (1972), followed by *Kafka: pour un littérature mineure* (1975), *Mille Plateaux: capitalisme et schizophrénie II* (1980), and *Qu'est-ce que la philosophie?* (1991). They also jointly founded the journal *Chiméres* in 1987.

In the final decade of his life, Guattari's attention focused more closely on questions of social ecology and on developing and articulating the conceptual framework within which his diverse concerns, activities and ideas achieved a practical coherence. *Les trois écologies* (1989), *Cartographies schizoanalytiques* (1989) and *Chaosmose* (1992) each reflect this focus. Guattari died at La Borde in August 1992.

Selected Works

Psychanalyse et transversalité: essays d'analyse institutionelle, 1972
With Gilles Deleuze, *L'anti-Oedipe: capitalisme et schizophrénie I*, 1972; as *Anti-Oedipus: Capitalism and Schizophrenia I*, translated by Robert Hurley, Mark Seem and Helen Lane, 1984
With Gilles Deleuze, *Kafka: pour une literature mineure*, 1975; as *Kafka: Toward a Minor Literature*, translated by Dana Polan, 1986
La revolution moléculaire, 1977; as *Molecular Revolution: Psychiatry and Politics*, translated by Rosemary Sheed, 1984
L'inconscient machinique: essays de schizo-analyse, 1979
With Gilles Deleuze, *Mille Plateaux: capitalisme et schizophrénie II*, 1980; as *A Thousand Plateaus: Capitalism and Schizophrenia II*, translated by Brian Massumi, 1987
With Toni Negri, *Nouvelles espaces de liberté*, 1985; as *Communists Like Us: New spaces of liberty, new lines of alliance*, translated by Michael Ryan, 1990
Les années d'hiver 1980–1985, 1986
Les trois ecologies, 1989; as *The Three Ecologies*, translated by Ian Pindar and Paul Sutton, 2000
Cartographies schizoanalytiques, 1989
With Gilles Deleuze, *Qu'est-ce que la philosophie?*, 1991; as *What is Philosophy?*, translated by Graham Burchell and Hugh Tomlinson, 1994

Chaosmose, 1992; as *Chaosmosis: an ethico-aesthetic paradigm*, translated by Paul Bains and Julian Pefanis, 1995
The Guattari Reader, edited by Gary Genosko, 1996

Further Reading

Attias, B. A., "To Each Its Own Sexes? Towards a Rhetorical Understanding of *Molecular Revolution*," in Kaufman and Heller (editors) *Deleuze and Guattari: New Mappings in Politics, Philosophy and Culture*, Minneapolis: University of Minnesota, 1998
Bogue, R. *Deleuze and Guattari*, London and New York: Routledge, 1989
Genosko, G., "The Life and Work of Félix Guattari: From Transversality to Ecosophy," in Felix Guattari *The Three Ecologies*, translated by Ian Pindar and Paul Sutton, London and New Jersey: Athlone Press, 2000
Genosko, G., (editor), *Deleuze and Guattari: Critical Assessments of Leading Philosophers*, Volume II (on Guattari), London and New York: Routledge, 2001
Goodchild, P., *Deleuze and Guattari: An Introduction to the Politics of Desire*, London: Sage, 1996
Massumi, B. *A User's Guide to Capitalism and Schizophrenia*, Cambridge; MIT Press, 1992

GUÉRIN, DANIEL
Historian, Revolutionary Activist

A major figure on the French left for over fifty years, both as a militant and as a writer, Daniel Guérin was active as a syndicalist, a socialist, a Trotskyist, an antiracist and anticolonialist, a campaigner for homosexual liberation, an anarchist, an antimilitarist, and a libertarian communist. Although, at first sight, Guérin may appear to have been somewhat protean—indeed, problems of identity recur in his autobiographical writings—what in fact emerges from an analysis of his ideological and political trajectory is a certain consistency. It is probably fair to say that, throughout his life, Guérin was a historical materialist and a libertarian Marxist with an increasingly strong belief in the importance of a "total revolution" that would attach equal importance to issues of race, gender, and sexuality as well as to workplace-based conflict.

A socialist from an early age, Guérin discovered Marx thanks to Elie Halévy's lectures at the Paris *Ecole des Sciences Politiques*, and he soon came to see himself as belonging to the "Marxist extreme Left" in the sharpening conflict with the Right: "*Marx contre Maurras*," as he put it. His early readings were eclectic—Marx, Lenin, Trotsky, Kautsky, Proudhon, Pelloutier, Sorel, Jaurès, and Gandhi—but the influence of Marx was predominant, and from the mid-1930s on Guérin would also be heavily influenced by Trotsky. The two publications that were most innovative methodologically were *Fascisme et grand capital* (first published in 1936) and *La lutte de classes sous la Première*

République, 1793–1797 (1946). Not uncontroversial, both are still regarded by many as classics in their respective fields. Influenced by Leon Trotsky, Andrès Nin, and Ignazio Silone, *Fascisme* was a pioneering work in several respects, though it has been criticized for its arguably instrumentalist view of the state. Based on a class analysis of fascism and Nazism, it also analyzed the reasons for the failure of European antifascist movements, concluding that the latter must not ally with the bourgeoisie and that the only sure strategy for defeating fascism was working-class revolution. Similar political conclusions were drawn by Guérin from his reinterpretation of the French Revolution, considered by Sartre to be "one of the only contributions by contemporary Marxists to have *enriched* historical studies" (*Critique de la raison dialectique*). Applying the concepts of permanent revolution and combined and uneven development (a method used by Trotsky in his *History of the Russian Revolution*), Guérin argued that the beginnings of a conflict of class interest could already be detected within the revolutionary camp between an "embryonic" proletariat (the *bras nus*, represented by the *Enragés*) and the bourgeoisie (represented by Robespierre and Jacobinism). For Guérin, the French Revolution thus represented not only the birth of bourgeois parliamentary democracy, but also of "a new type of democracy," a form of working-class direct democracy as seen, however imperfectly, in the *sections*, precursors of the Commune of 1871 and of the *soviets* of 1905/17—and in a later edition of the work he would add "the Commune of May 1968" to the genealogy. Guérin wrote to Marceau Pivert that the book was "an introduction to a synthesis of anarchism and Marxism-Leninism I would like to write one day": the possible sources of this "synthesis" and the precise form it might take are what Guérin would work on for the next thirty years or so. In "La Révolution déjacobinisée" (1959), Guérin went on to argue (on the basis of extensive readings of Marx and Engels in the original German) that the "Jacobin" traits in Marxism and particularly in Leninism were the result of an incomplete understanding on Marx and Engels's part of the class nature of Jacobinism and the Jacobin dictatorship (to be distinguished from the democratically controlled "*contrainte révolutionnaire*" exercised by the working-class *sections*). Thus by applying a historical materialist analysis to the experiences of the French revolutionary movement, Guérin came to argue, essentially, that "authentic" socialism arose spontaneously out of working-class struggle (*contra* Blanqui or Lenin) and that it was fundamentally libertarian: authoritarian conceptions of party organization and revolutionary strategy had their origins in bourgeois modes of thought. Indeed in Lenin, Guérin thought, the "seeds of authoritarian and statist tendencies" that would bloom under Stalin were already present. Guérin was far more attracted to Rosa Luxemburg and what he saw as her critique of Leninist centralism and authoritarianism, and her emphasis on spontaneity and "socialism from below." Guérin rediscovered Bakunin and Luxemburg around the time of the Hungarian uprising of 1956, and would play an important rôle in the revival of interest in Luxemburgism, anarchism, and "council communism" in the 1960s and 1970s. Guérin had contact for the first time with the libertarian communist wing of the anarchist movement (largely because he shared their support for the Algerian nationalist movement) about the same time, and in the 1960s he went through what he called a "classic anarchist" phase, being interested especially in Proudhon (in whom he admired the first theorist of *autogestion*), Bakunin (seen by Guérin as being very close to Marx and as a representative of a revolutionary, working-class anarchism) and Max Stirner (admired as a "precursor of 1968" because of his concern with sexual liberation and his determination to attack bourgeois prejudice and Puritanism). Guérin's "libertarian turn" coincided with his writing more and more about sexuality and ultimately with his coming out as bisexual in 1965: he would come to be seen as the "grandfather" of the gay liberation movement. He was particularly interested in and influenced by Fourier, Kinsey, and Reich, and was keen to theorize sexuality in historical materialist terms.

DAVID BERRY

See also **Jean Jaures; Charles Maurras; Georges Sorel**

Biography

Born in Paris in 1904 of a wealthy but *Dreyfusard* family, Daniel Guérin was heir to the Hachette empire. He was educated at the *Lycée Louis-le-Grand* and the *Ecole des Sciences Politiques*. Visits to the Lebanon and Syria (1927), Djibouti (1928), and French Indochina (1929) made of Guérin a lifelong anticolonialist. In 1930, he cut his ties with his family and abandoned literary work. Involved with the syndicalists around Pierre Monatte and the campaign for the reunification of the *Confédération générale du travail* (CGT), he joined the Belleville group of the Socialist party, but resigned because of its electoralism and anti-communism. He joined the *Syndicat des Correcteurs* in 1932. He was co-founder of the *Centre Laïque des Auberges de la Jeunesse* in 1933. He visited Germany in 1932 and 1933. In October 1935, he rejoined the Socialist Party, becoming a leading member of Marceau Pivert's *Gauche Révolutionnaire* tendency, clashing both with the Communists over their attempts to dominate trade union activities, and with the SFIO leadership over the colonial question. He worked as a local CGT organizer during the 1936 strikes. When the *Gauche Révolutionnaire* was expelled from the SFIO (Royan Congress, 1938), and the *Parti Socialiste Ouvrier et Paysan* created, Guérin joined the new party, remaining firmly attached to the principles of revolutionary defeatism and proletarian internationalism. Guérin had close links with Trotsky, who would remain a major lifelong influence, although Guérin disagreed with the creation of a Fourth International and was critical of what he saw as the French Trotskyists' dogmatism and lack of realism. Delegated by the *Front Ouvrier International* to establish an international secretariat in Oslo in the event of war, Guérin produced a monthly bulletin from October 1939 to April 1940. Arrested by the German army, he returned to Paris in 1942 and worked with the Trotskyist resistance. At the liberation, he was appointed secretary general of the *Office professionnel du Livre*, the reincarnation of the *Comité d'organisation du Livre* for which he had worked during the war. In 1946–49, Guérin toured the United States. Throughout the 1950s Guérin was heavily involved in anticolonial agitation, and helped initiate the "*Manifeste des 121*" against the Algerian war in 1960. In 1963 he presented a report to President Ben Bella on self-management. After the *coup* of 1965, he helped found the committee, which supported Ben Bella and opposed political repression in Algeria. He was also behind the creation of a committee to establish the truth about the disappearance of Moroccan leader Ben Barka in 1965. Active in the *Nouvelle Gauche* in 1955–57, he would later be attracted to the libertarian communist movement. From the 1950s, he was a leading campaigner for sexual liberation, coming out in 1965. In 1968, he was invited to lead open debates on self-management in the Sorbonne and in an occupied factory. The following year he joined Georges Fontenis's *Mouvement Communiste Libertaire*, later to become the *Organisation Communiste Libertaire*, and was responsible for its organ, *Guerre de Classes*. In 1973 he joined the *Organisation Révolutionnaire Anarchiste*. He joined the *Union des Travailleurs Communistes Libertaires* in 1980 and remained a member until his death in 1988.

Selected Works

La Peste brune, 1933
Fascisme et grand capital, Italie, Allemagne, 1936, 1945, 1965, 1969, 1971, 1999
La lutte de classes sous la Pemière République, 1793–1797, 1946, 1968
Où va le peuple américain?, 1950–1951
Quand le fascisme nous devançait. Souvenirs et leçons de dix ans, 1930–1940, 1955
Les Antilles décolonisées, 1956, 1986
Jeunesse du socialisme libertaire, 1959
Front populaire, révolution manquée? Témoignage militant, 1963, 1970, 1976, 1997
L'Algérie qui se cherche, 1964, 1979
L'Anarchisme, de la doctrine à la pratique, 1965, 1968, 1976, 1981, 1987
Ni dieu ni maître, anthologie de l'anarchisme, 1965, 1970, 1973, 1974, 1976, 1999
Pour un marxisme libertaire, 1969
Essai sur la révolution sexuelle après Reich et Kinsey, 1969
La Révolution française et nous, 1969, 1976
Rosa Luxemburg et la spontanéité révolutionnaire, 1971, 1982
Autobiographie de jeunesse, d'une dissidence sexuelle au socialisme, 1972
Ci-gît le colonialisme: Algérie, Inde, Indochine, Madagascar, Maroc, Palestine, Polynésie, Tunisie. Témoignage militant, 1973
Editor and introduction to Léon Trotski, *Sur la Deuxième Guerre mondiale*, 1974
Les assassins de Ben Barka, dix ans d'enquête, 1975
Proudhon oui et non, 1978
Le Feu du sang, autobiographie politique et charnelle, 1979
Son testament, 1979
Quand l'Algérie s'insurgeait, 1954–1962: Un anticolonialiste témoigne, 1979
Homosexualité et révolution, 1983
A la recherche d'un communisme libertaire, 1984

Further Reading

Bechir Ben Barka, Denis Berger, et al, *Daniel Guérin, Alternative Libertaire*, Paris: Agora, 2000.
Berger, Denis, "La révolution plurielle (pour Daniel Guérin)," in E. Balibar, J. S. Beek, D. Bensaïd, et al: *Permanences de la Révolution. Pour un autre bicentenaire*, Paris: La Brèche, 1989
Birchall, Ian, "Sartre's Encounter with Daniel Guérin" in *Sartre Studies International*, vol.2, Issue 1 (1996): pp.41–56
Carlin, Norah, "Daniel Guérin and the working class in the French Revolution," in *International Socialism* no.47 (1990): pp.197–223
Chaperon, Sylvie, "Le fonds Daniel Guérin et l'histoire de la sexualité," in *Journal de la BDIC* no.5 (Juin 2002): p. 10
Copley, Anthony, *Sexual Moralities in France, 1780–1980. New ideas on the family, divorce and homosexuality. An essay on moral change*, London: Routledge, 1989
Lequenne, Michel, "Daniel Guérin, l'homme de 93 et le problème de Robespierre," in *Critique communiste* no.130–131 special issue, "1793–(1993): Révolution, République, Radicalité", pp.31–34.
Maitron, Jean, "Daniel Guérin," in, *Dictionnaire Biographique du Mouvement Ouvrier Français*, edited by Jean Maitron, Paris: Edns. ouvrières), 1988
Marshall, Bill,"The Autobiographies of Daniel Guérin and Yves Navarre," in *The Modern Language Review* vol.90, no.3 (July 1995): pp. 622–31.
Sedgwick, Peter, "Out of hiding: the Comradeships of Daniel Guérin," in *Salmagundi: A quarterly journal of the humanities and social sciences*, 58–9, special issue on homosexualism (June 1982),:pp. 197–220.

GURVITCH, GEORGES
Sociologist

Georges Gurvitch was one of the last great systematizers in sociological theory. In his more than thirty books he sought to develop and apply his "hyper-empirical" system to all major aspects of social reality. Unfortunately, his works have remained relatively neglected, especially in the English-speaking world. Gurvitch, like Marcel Mauss, sought to study the "total social phenomenon." Thus, he believed that all previous theories that emphasized one specific aspect of social reality were unnecessarily reductionist. This opposition to single predominant factors led Gurvitch to embrace a typological approach that attempted to bracket out theoretical preconceptions and avoid value judgments.

Any typology that encompasses the "total social phenomena" must include the historical dimension as well as the vertical and horizontal aspects of society. The vertical dimension of society was made up of many layers (the number of layers varied depending on the subject matter) with the deeper layers being more difficult to study empirically or scientifically. Representative vertical layers include the demographic level, symbols, organization, unorganized collective behavior, spontaneous collective behavior, values and ideals, and the collective mind. The horizontal level includes global societies, groups, classes, and forms of interaction, and each of these can be broken down by different criteria (for examples, the groups of society could be classified by fifteen criteria, while Gurvitch listed thirteen types of global societies). Each aspect of society, be it law, economics, politics, knowledge, could be analyzed using the historical, vertical, and horizontal dimensions. However, each field should not be understood in isolation. For instance, law needs to be studied sociologically, and sociology must grapple with questions of law.

For Gurvitch, the dialectic was extremely important for understanding social reality. Such dyads as the individual and the society and freedom and determinism were bound by a dialectical tension. Further, there is a dialectic progression through history, but Gurvitch did not claim that this progression would lead to an ultimate synthesis. As he wrote, "the dialectic cannot be domesticated."

Because of his emphasis on empiricism and dialectic, Gurvitch denies the possibility of sociology discovering causal laws that will govern human behavior. Causation can only be understood in specific intersections of the vertical and horizontal sphere, and these laws would only apply to that particular case. Any attempt to abstract from the individual instance to more comprehensive laws would be movements away from social reality.

In his many works, he applied his typological system to the sociology of time, the sociology of law, the sociology of knowledge, ethics, and freedom. For example in *Les Cadres Sociaus de la Connaissance*, Gurvitch argues that the sociology of knowledge and

the philosophy of knowledge should exist in a dialectical tension where both fields feed off of each other, but remain separate disciplines. The sociology of knowledge must account for four horizontal groups (microsociology, groups, classes, global societies), and each group takes part in seven types of knowledge (perceptual knowledge of the external world, knowledge of the Other, we, classes, etc., common sense knowledge, technical knowledge, political knowledge, scientific knowledge, and philosophical knowledge), and each of the seven types of knowledge can be understood along five dimensions that are in a dialectical tension, mystical-rational, empirical-conceptual, positive, speculative, symbolic-concrete, and collective-individual knowledge.

Gurvitch then used the most current anthropological and sociological evidence to describe the predominant types of knowledge for each intersection of the vertical and horizontal dimensions as well as each historical period. For example, Gurvitch looked at eleven different types of global societies from archaic societies and "theocratico-charismatic" societies up through organized capitalism, fascist, and centralized state collectivism, and even included a possible future global society that he called decentralized, pluralist collectivism. He divided archaic societies into four types from those with mainly a clan basis to those with some type of monarchic state. In clan-based systems he ranked perceptual knowledge of the external world as predominant, followed by technical knowledge, political knowledge, knowledge of the other and the we, and common-sense knowledge. In monarchic states, on the other hand, the most important type of knowledge was a combination of mythological knowledge, political knowledge, and technical knowledge.

In democratic-liberal societies in the wake of the American and French revolutions, there is a striking "decline of philosophical knowledge" as technical and political knowledge increase. In contemporary societies, technical and political knowledge predominate, thus "knowledge of the other, the perceptual knowledge of the external world, scientific and even philosophical knowledge are strongly technicalized and politicized" which will include the application of technical knowledge to the manipulation of men, partisan groups, and sometimes large masses.

It is perhaps in his study of knowledge that Gurvitch's theoretical relativism is most apparent. The sociologist of knowledge as opposed to the epistemologist should never test the validity of any type of knowledge; "he must only ascertain the effect of their presence, combination, and effective function." Despite the distinction between facts and values in his writings, Gurvitch remained active in politics throughout his life, helping form workers' soviets in 1917, joining the French underground in the 1940s, writing against the French occupation of Algeria, and arguing in favor of third world development in the 1960s.

It could be claimed that Gurvitch's typology of knowledge could have predicted the end of his type of thinking. The grandiose, totalizing, systematizing philosophies that marked the early twentieth century have been replaced by an era where complexity, uncertainty, and technical knowledge predominate.

WILLIAM PAUL SIMMONS

See also **Marcel Mauss**

Biography

Georges Gurvitch was born in Novorossisk, Russia, in 1894. After taking part in the Russian Revolution of 1917, he fled to Czechoslovakia, and then settled in France in 1928. He was appointed director of the *Institut de Sociologie* at the *Ecole Libre des Haute Etudes*. Gurvitch died in Paris in 1965.

Selected Works

Les tendances de la philosophie allemande, 1930
Twentieth Century Sociology, edited by Georges Gurvitch and Wilbert E. Moore, 1945.
Sociolgia Juridica, 1947 as Sociology of Law, 1974
Le Concept de Classes. Sociales de Marx à Nos Jours, 1954
Déterminismes sociaux et liberté humaine, 1955
La Vocation Actuelle de la Sociologie. Vers une Sociologie Différentielle, 1957

"Mon Itinéraire Intellectuel." *Lettres Nouvelles* Juilet-Août 1958: 65–83.
La crise de l'explication en sociologie' in *Cahiers Internationaux de Sociologie*, XXI 1956
Dialectique et sociologie, 1962
The Spectrum of Social Time, translated by M. Korenbaum and P. Bosserman, 1964
Études sur les classes sociales, 1966
Les Cadres Sociaus de la Connaissance, 1966; as *The Social Frameworks of Knowledge*, translated by Margaret A. Thompson and Kenneth A. Thompson, 1971
"My Intellectual Itinerary, or 'Excluded from the Horde.'" in *Sociological Abstracts* 17 1969

Further Reading

Balandier, Georges, *Gurvitch*, as *Gurvitch*, translated by Margaret A. Thompson and Kenneth A. Thompson, Oxford: Blackwell, 1975
Bosserman, Phillip, *Dialectical Sociology: An Analysis of the Sociology of Georges Gurvitch*. Boston: Porter Sargent, 1968
Bosserman, Phillip, "The Twentieth Century's Saint-Simon: George Gurvitch's Dialectical Sociology and the New Physics," *Sociological Theory* 13 (1), (March 1995): 48–57
McDonald, Pauline, "The Legal Sociology of Georges Gurvitch," *British Journal of Law and Society*, 6 (1979): 24–52
Sorokin, Pitirim, *Sociological Theories of Today*, New York: Harper and Row, 1966
Swedberg, Richard, *Sociology as Disenchantment: The Evolution of the Work of Georges Gurvitch*, New Jersey: Humanities Press, 1982
Toulemont, R, *Sociologie et pluralism dialectique, introduction à l'oeuvre de Georges Gurvitch*, Louvain: Editions Nauwelaerts, 1955

H

HALBWACHS, MAURICE
Sociologist

In addition to France, where his writings have always remained important and influential, Halbwachs's distinguished legacy continues to be a source of inspiration for many German social scientists. In anglophone settings, particularly North America, interest has come only posthumously, and more recently, alongside the translations of some of his many notable achievements. This current and almost sudden interest in Halbwachs in the United States is due, for the most part, to a central theme that, arguably, connects his most important writings: the analysis of the social processes of memory.

Halbwachs's interest in memory began early in his student days, in the 1890s, at the *Lycée Henry IV* in Paris, where he studied with the philosopher Henri Bergson. Bergson had, at this point in his career, already elaborated the difference between time as conceptualized in the sciences—where it was considered as a homogeneous, mechanical medium marked by divisions such as minutes and hours—and time as a more fluid, active, and continually changing stream of events; a pure time which we experience in the immediate and subjective sense. Halbwachs came to disagree with Bergson on this point, arguing instead that time is a social construction which is real only when it has content, when events take on a material form which can then be grasped by thought.

Following his years at the Lycée with Bergson, Halbwachs studied philosophy at the *Ecole normale supérieure* in addition to teaching at various provincial lycées. At this time he also made a research trip to Hanover to study the works of Gottfried Wilhelm Leibniz as well as participating in the preparation of the *Catalogue des manuscripts leibniziens*. The outcome of his research was a short book titled, simply, *Leibniz* (1907). In it he took up Leibniz's attack on intuition to show the relevance of Leibniz's thought on the seemingly insurmountable problem of mind versus matter. Halbwachs aligned himself with Leibniz, arguing that the Cartesians and the empiricists had failed to account for the more gradual transitions in this distinction. Innate ideas and intuitions should not be attributed only to our nature, where it can be awakened by experience, nor on the other hand should the mind be thought of as a blank slate completely devoid of experience until learned. For Halbwachs, innate ideas never arose fully developed, nor should intuition be thought of as a potential state of becoming. This was more clearly demonstrated by Halbwachs where he invoked Leibniz's view on forgetting and remembering. As Halbwachs interpreted Leibniz, complete forgetting never occurs; rather, all our thoughts and impressions leave their trace in us as conscious memories and vague impressions. Even though our perceptions and experiences lose their original lucidity, partial remembering of past events takes place under certain external stimuli, like seeing a friend. Thus, unlike Bergson, who held that forgetting takes place in the face of an obstruction, and remembering is the removal of obstructions, Halbwachs, with Leibniz, took the view that forgetting is the result of vague recollections, and remembrance is their coming together again due to external forces.

Although his shift from philosophy to Durkheimian sociology around 1905 resulted in a number of forays into economic and statistically related topics such as his important study on working-class living standards (1913), Halbwachs never lost interest in the indispensability of collective memories for the functioning of social groups, especially families, social classes, and religious communities. With the notion of collective memory Halbwachs was able to fill in the missing piece of Durkheim's argument about the forces that maintain group solidarity and the group's commitment to its values and purposes. For example, in the study just mentioned as well in two later studies, *Analyse des mobiles qui orient l'activité des individus dans la vie sociales* (1928) [(1952; republished as *Esquisse d'une psychologie des classes sociales {The Psychology of Social Class}*] and *L'evolution des besoins dans les classes ouvriéres* (1933), Halbwachs utilized the principle known as Engels's law to analyze workers' expenditures. In relation to *needs*, Halbwachs opposed the individualistic physiological based theories, arguing instead that social class was a more accurate determinant of needs, where class was defined in the more Weberian sense as a status group with shared values.

Contained in this corrective was the implied idea of how social structuring might offer a better explanation of pressured consumption patterns among lower earning classes than that offered up by purely utilitarian theories of demand. Thus, consumption patterns, participation in social life, class characteristics, and beliefs and sentiments played a crucial part in Halbwachs's program of how groups come to form collective representations of themselves. It is ultimately through membership in a social group that individuals acquire, recollect, and pass on their memories. For example, in the collective mentality of workers, they create their group memory by taking into account memories that uphold and sustain their feeling of not participating in the general collective life of the community and, in fact, of resolving to remain some distance from it. At work, in the factories and mines, the worker executes but does not order and instruct. The worker supplies labor power but does not participate in the decision-making of the company's future.

His commitment to demonstrating how specific groups create and maintain a sense of cohesion and identity, or in this case where it is lacking, is nowhere more evident than in *Les causes du suicide* (1930; *The Causes of Suicide*). This study should be approached as an example of the loss of group cohesiveness and the concomitant crisis of the *conscience collective*. Furthering Durkheim's well-known work on the same topic, Halbwachs sought to extend it, particularly the category of anomic suicide and its relation to modern industrial societies. Halbwachs advanced the argument that there is a reciprocal relationship between anomie and neurosis; that is, upheaval in the sphere of values and disequilibrium in moral codes create anomie as a social condition, but to that should also be added the effect of depression, lack of self-esteem, and other pathological features that are usually present as well. Thus a social catastrophe like the death of a loved one, cultural and social displacement, poverty, and disgrace produces *déclassés* as the individual is discriminated against by the *conscience collective* and is forced to the margins where the possibility of suicide increases. By extension, as Halbwachs made clear, no neurotic can be considered as having adapted to his or her environment fully; every mental illness is an element, in other words, of social instability which can only be explained by the combinatory arrangement of social and organic causes.

Although the aforementioned works established Halbwachs's reputation as a first-rate sociologist during his life, it is his three pioneering studies of memory, *Les cadres sociaux de la mémoire* (1925), *La topographie légendaire des évangeles en terre sainte* (1941), and the incomplete *La mémoire collective* (1950), that set the parameters for much of what has subsequently been written on this topic. In all three works Halbwachs considered the linkage between personal and collective dimensions of recollection. Conceding the existence of introspective accounts of memory as developed by psychologists, Halbwachs went on to show that quite often, individual recollections showed a direct relationship to collective representations. Memory for the individual is possible only by the fact that the individual is a member of a social group; that is, it is individuals, as group members, who remember. Against the racial determinist approaches of his day, Halbwachs noted the important influences of social groups as constituting factors by and in which we create our memories. As opposed to history, which he considered as manipulative, disruptive, and political, collective memory was a natural, unitary creation of a group, creating a seamless bond between past and present.

Collective memories also contain a strong spatial dimension and are grounded to certain places in the landscape. In his *La Topographie légendaire des évangiles en terre sainte, étude de mémoire collective*, (1941), a study of the topography of the Holy Land, Halbwachs showed the ways in which many locations of events described in the Bible became sacred places of the collective memory of religious groups, even though the exact places were often later invented rather than accurately remembered. Here he showed how Christian religious beliefs are based on a history whose essential events are materially situated in very particular places such as the Sea of Galilee and Mount Zion.

In this study Halbwachs pointed out the basic irrelevance of historical authenticity by arguing that the accurate reconstruction of the past is only of minor importance when compared to the spiritual needs of the present. Thus, the various transformations of the Holy Land coincide with the how particular religious groups have imagined or constructed it. Given that there is no one authentic trace in the whole of Palestine to mark the historical existence of Jesus, all that remains are collective representations of it.

In the end, what is most important about Halbwachs is that he was the first sociologist to show how conceptions of the past are directly linked to the past such that collective memory is a reconstituting of the past in light of present conditions.

DENIS WALL

See also **Henri Bergson; Emile Durkheim**

Biography

Maurice Halbwachs was born in Rheims on March 11, 1877 into a family of Catholic and Alsatian origin. When he was two years old the family moved to Paris, where, later, the young Halbwachs was enrolled in the prestigious *Lycée Henri IV*. Following the lycée, he entered the *Ecole normale supérieure* (1898–1901) to continue his studies in philosophy. In 1904 he was lecturer at the University of Göttingen while working on the unpublished manuscripts of Leibniz, which he completed in 1907. With the completion of Leibniz, Halbwachs had made the move from philosophy to sociology and subsequently went on to acquire a doctoral degree in law in addition to, at the age of thirty-seven, a *doctorat és lettres*. At this time he also became a major contributing member to the Durkheimian influenced *Année sociologique* group as well as being involved with *the Société de Statistique de Paris*. In 1910 he took a fellowship in Berlin to collect material for his thesis. While there he acted as correspondent for the socialist journal *l'Humanité*, publishing an article in its pages denouncing the brutality of the Berlin police at a mass demonstration. Given a week to leave Prussia, Halbwachs was forced to complete his fellowship term in Vienna. In 1913 his primary doctoral dissertation on the working class and its living standards as well as his secondary dissertation on the Belgian statistician François Quételet were published. As a result of his myopia he was not drafted into the army during World War I, working instead in the Ministry of Armaments. In 1919 he moved from Caen, where he had recently become a *chargé de cours* in philosophy, to the new university in Strasbourg. He remained in Strasbourg for sixteen years, first as professor of sociology and pedagogy, and then, from March 1922,

as France's first professor of sociology. He visited the University of Chicago in 1930, which resulted in his study *L'evolution de besoins dans les classes ouvrières* (1933), an analysis of a large number of budget surveys covering American as well European households. In 1935 he moved to the Sorbonne, where he occupied positions in the history of social economics (1935–1937), the methodology and logic of the sciences (1937–1939), and sociology (1939–1944). He was appointed to a chair of collective psychology at the prestigious Collége de France in 1944. In July 1944 he was arrested by the Gestapo in Paris and sent to Buchenwald concentration camp, where he joined his previously arrested son. While in Buchenwald, Maurice Halbwachs died of dysentery on March 16, 1945, having just reached his sixty-eighth birthday.

Selected Works

Leibniz, 1907

Les expropriations et le prix des terrains à Paris, 1909

La classe ouvriére et les niveaux de vie. Recherches sur la hiérarchie des besoins dans les sociétés undustrielles contemporaines, 1913

La théorie de l'homme moyen. Essai sur Quetlet et la statistique morale, 1913

Les origines du sentiment religieux, 1925; as *Sources of Religious Sentiment*, translated by John A. Spaulding, 1962

Les Cadres sociaux de la mémoire, 1925; as *The Social Frameworks of Memory*, in Maurice Halbwachs

On Collective Memory, translated by Lewis Coser, 1992

Les causes du suicide, 1930; as *The Causes of Suicide*, translated by Harold Goldblatt, 1978

L'evolution des besoins dans les classes ouvrières, 1933

Analyse des mobiles dominants qui Orientent l'activité des individus dans la vie sociale, 1938; republished, as *Esquisse d'une psychologie des classes sociales*, 1952; as *The Psychology of Social Class*, translated by Claire Delavenay, 1958

Morphologie sociale, 1938; as *Population and Society: Introduction to Social Morphology*, translated by Otis Dudley Duncan and Harold W. Pfautz, 1960

"Individual and Collective Consciousness", in *American Journal of Sociology* 44, 1939

Sociologie économique et démographie, 1940

La Topographie légendaire des évangiles en terre sainte, étude de mémoire collective, 1941; as *The Legendary Topography of the Gospels in the Holy Land*, in Maurice Halbwachs *On Collective Memory*, translated by Lewis Coser, 1992

La mémoir collective, 1950; as *The Collective Memory*, translated by Francis J. Ditter, Jr. and Vida Yazdi Ditter, 1980

Further Reading

Assmann, Jan, "Collective Memory and Cultural Identity," translated by John Czaplicka, *New German Critique* 65 (1995): 125–133

Canguilhem, Georges, "Maurice Halbwachs (1877–1945)," in his *Faculté de Lettres de l'Université de Strasbourg: Mémorial des années 1939–1945*, Paris: Les Belles Lettres, 1947

Coser, Lewis A., "Introduction: Maurice Halbwachs 1877–1945," in *Maurice Halbwachs Collective Memory*, Chicago and London: University of Chicago Press, 1992

Craig, John E., "Maurice Halbwachs à Strasbourg," *Revue français de sociologie*, 20 (1979): 273–292

Craig, John E., "Sociology and Related Disciplines between the Wars: Maurce Halbwachs and the Imperialism of the Durkheimians," in *The Sociological Domain: The Durkheimians and the Founding of French Sociology*, edited by Philippe Besnard, London and Paris: Cambridge University Press and Editions de la Maison des Sciences de l'Homme, 1983

Douglas, Mary, "Maurice Halbwachs, 1877–1945," in her *In the Active Voice*, London, Boston and Henley: Routledge and Keagan Paul, 1982

Hutton, Patrick, "Sigmund Freud and Maurice Halbwachs: The Problem of Memory in Historical Psychology," *Historical Reflections/Reflexions Historiques*, 19, 1 (1993): 1–16

Llobra, Joseph R., "Halbwachs, Nora and 'History' Versus 'Collective Memory': A Research Note," *Durkheimian Studies/Etudes Durkheimiennes* 1 (1995): 35–44

Montlibert, Christian de, *Maurice Halbwachs 1877–1945: Colloque de la Faculté des Sciences Sociales de Strasbourg* (mars 1995)/textes réunis par Christina de Montlibert, Strasbourg: Presses Universitaires de Strasbourg, 1997

Mucchielli, Laurent, "Pour une psychologie collective: l'héritage durkheimien d'Halbwachs et sa rivalité avec Blondel durant l'entre-deux-guerres," *Revue d'histoire des sciences humaines*, 1 (1999): 101–138

Travis, Robert, "Halbwachs and Durkheim: A Test of Two Theories of Suicide," *British Journal of Sociology* 41, 2 (1990): 225–243

Vromen, Suzanne, *The Sociology of Maurice Halbwachs*, doctoral dissertation, New York University, 1975

HALÉVY, DANIEL

Socialist

Daniel Halévy's political commitments, as for many of his generation, were forged during the years of the Dreyfus affair. Like contemporaries such as Zola, Péguy, and Sorel, Halévy emerged from the Affair with contempt for the values of the bourgeoisie, which appeared as a dissipated force in need of replacement. The experience of the Affair also led to the conclusion that parliamentary democracy was a failed arrangement.

The victory of the Dreyfusards gave impetus to a burst of socialist ideas, which held out the promise of a complete regeneration of French society. Great effort was expended to preserve the links that had been forged between the intellectuals and the proletariat during the struggles over Dreyfus and extend them in a regenerative pursuit of social and economic reforms.

Eventually many young socialists, including Halévy, lost interest in the platforms of opportunistic politicians seeking their place in a political system that was discredited. In his *Apologie*, written years after the Affair, Halévy expressed remorse over the disparity between the ideals of the early Dreyfusards and the manner in which, in his view, those ideals were corrupted in a battle between competing political interests. What began as a "generous impulse" for justice had been corrupted by the politicians, especially, in Halévy's view, by Jaurès.

Halévy moved from the republican socialism of Jaurès, which sought the integration of the proletariat within the Republican institutions, to a workers' vision of socialism. Through decades of writing Halévy developed and gave voice to a unique socialist perspective that upheld libertarianism as the most enduring tradition in French socialism.

Halévy expressed great sympathies with libertarian socialism that saw the task of social transformation as based in the self-determined efforts of the workers themselves rather than any political party. Proudhon's vision of a vast federation of autonomous institutions, or mutualism, suggested to Halévy the most probable basis for a truly free society. Avoiding the threats of centralization and mass culture and holding no illusions in the deficient system of parliamentary democracy, mutualism, for Halévy, held out the possibility of a unification of all people. The mutual relations of a freely entered federation of voluntary associations protected the liberties of each individual and collectivity.

This mutualism was the only system that could ensure human freedom and dignity while maintaining social order. Committed to working class autonomy and direct action, rather than political machinations, this libertarian socialism suggested to Halévy the strongest expression of an authentic popular ethic. This tradition, which became a minority position after the crushing of the Commune, remained in Halévy's day as a vital dissenting voice in French socialism especially in the actions and ideas of the syndicalist movement and its main spokespeople such as Pelloutier.

The syndicalist movement suggested, to Halévy, the transformation of Proudhon's mutualism into a practical social system. Halévy shared with Pelloutier a belief that the bourses, as amalgams of the traditional and the revolutionary, could serve as the catalyst for a new revolutionary project based upon the autonomous moral development of the working classes.

The freedom of the individual was impossible so long as the worker remained the object of an external discipline. Individual freedom could only be experienced in autonomous workers' organizations such as the syndicates. As the self-created institutions of the working class, the syndicates allowed for the revolutionary spirit that could oppose the bourgeoisie and its institutions, the state system of parties.

The task of emancipation was, of course, the task of the workers themselves and would necessarily be carried out through direct action. Direct action, more than a means to fulfill immediate aims, served to keep the revolutionary spirit alive in the working class and to channel the impulses of liberty. Syndicalism, by developing working class self-confidence in its own activities and in the realization of a heroic future, held the promise of a new free society. Syndicalism held out a humanitarian promise beyond the needs of the working class. Halévy, like Sorel, saw in syndicalism the source of moral improvement, of social regeneration.

Syndicalism also stood opposed to the authoritarian aspects of Marxist socialism that Halévy deplored. Marxism, in his view, offered only another version of the growing centralized state. This would greatly threaten the independent workers' associations and along with them the possibilities for individual and collective freedoms. Marxism, by perpetuating coercion and tyranny, stood to impede the development of real social progress. Again Halévy favored the libertarian pluralism of the syndicates to the authoritarian collectivism of Marxism. Indeed, Halévy's great contribution was to be among the first socialists to appreciate that the true divide in socialism was not the contrived contrast between utopian and scientific but the distinction between authoritarian and libertarian.

His preference for a libertarian variant of socialism became apparent as early as 1901 in early published studies on the range of proletarian activity that emerged after the Affair.

Halévy clearly favored the *bourses du travail*, or labor exchanges that developed from the immediacy of workers' own needs. Commenting on the impressive growth of Pelloutier's federation, Halévy exuberantly referred to the militant craftspeople of the *bourses* as "the true representatives of the people." As the cauldron in which working class self-consciousness was brewing, the *bourses* presented to Halévy that place in which "the syndicalist movement reaches out beyond itself and holds out the hope of the new world to come."

Halévy's socialist views were also greatly shaped by his decade-long involvement in the *Universités Populaires*. These lively institutions brought together working class militants and Dreyfusard intellectuals. Halévy even formed his own *Université Populaire* on the Rue Saint-Martin, which he eventually affiliated with the local *bourse du travail*. This allowed Halévy to recruit for the syndicalists while bringing more people to his school. Together the workers and intellectuals would create a new socialist culture that would replace the decayed culture of the bourgeoisie. This put Halévy in opposition with Sorel, who warned that such reconciliation between the classes would dissipate the workers' revolutionary fervor. The end of the

movement in disillusionment seemed to uphold Sorel's view.

Along with Charles Guieysse, Halévy began the fortnightly syndicalist review *Pages Libres*, which began as the unofficial paper of the *Universités Populaires* but went on to outlive the movement itself. The paper was an experiment in a new kind of social reporting with attention to working class life. The paper championed independence, providing space for wide varieties of socialist ideas, reports on cooperative projects, and proletarian efforts. Readers were always encouraged to contribute to its pages. In keeping with Halévy's distaste for organized authority, parties, or doctrines, *Pages Libres* provided a forum for the obscure and neglected working class projects and the unorthodox, and libertarian, perspectives/versions/visions of socialism.

Halévy became an important chronicler of working class life. In the activities of workers and peasants, Halévy, like others of his era, thought he had found the source of moral progress. Popular regional cultures supposedly held the source of social transformation and should be preserved against the intrusions of political parties and centralizing bureaucracies.

Halévy took a conservative approach to the question of workers and peasants in industrializing France. His solution to the turmoil of laborers torn from the land and from their craft was to preserve past traditions that rooted them to the soil and to their craft. Halévy sought to unite the populism of the worker and peasant masses with past traditions. In doing so he sketched the outlines of a tradition of dissent in French thought that reached from Proudhon to Sorel.

JEFFREY SHANTZ

See also **Jean Jaures; Georges Sorel**

Biography

Born in 1872, Daniel Halévy was the son of Ludovic Halévy, the celebrated author and librettist, and the brother of the historian Elie Halévy. A perceptive chronicler of the mood and movements of turn-of-the-century France, his work engaged all of the key debates of the era. His varied work, as critic, essayist, journalist, editor, and teacher, which engaged all of the key debates of the time, was especially relevant in the decades between the Dreyfus affair and World War I. Like many of his generation, he emerged from the Affair with a strong contempt for bourgeois values and institutions. A meeting with Charles Péguy in 1900 led Halévy to a lengthy collaboration on the *Cahiers de la Quinzaine*. Through his association with Péguy, he was brought to the influence of Jaurès and social reformism. Halévy joined the Socialist party and took part in the founding of *L'Humanité*, the great party newspaper, but soon moved to a heterodox socialism drawing on libertarian traditions from Proudhon and syndicalism. His libertarian socialist views were also shaped by his decade-long involvement in the working-class *Universitês Populaires*, of which he was a founder. Between the wars he devoted thirteen years to the publication of the *Cahiers Verts*. While at the Grasset publishing house he oversaw the publication of works by Maurois, Malraux, and Benda, among others. During this period his growing sense of regret over the failed promise of the early Dreyfusards pushed him politically to the Maurrasian right. Halévy's dissatisfaction with the Third Republic led him into collaboration with the Vichy regime during the Nazi occupation of France. He later spoke on behalf of Maurras and Pétain at their trials. These acts led many to regard him as an apologist for fascism, a view that persisted through the last years of his life. Halévy died in 1962 after failing in his second attempt to enter the *Académie Française*.

Selected Works

"Un Entretien sur la démocratie," *Pages libres*, 1908
Apologie pour notre passé, 1910
The Life of Friedrich Nietzsche, 1911
La jeunesse de Proudhon (1809–1847), 1913
Quelques nouveaux maitres, 1914
Visites aux paysans du centre, 1921
Vauban, 1923
Jules Michelet, 1928
Pays Parisiens, 1932
La République des comité, 1934
La République des ducs, 1937
Pour l'étude de la troisième république, 1937
Trois epreuves: 1814, 1871, 1940, 1942
Proudhon d'après ses Carnest inédits 1843–1847, 1944
Péguy and Les Cahiers de la quinzane, translated by Ruth Bethell, 1946
La vie de Proudhon II. Le mariage de Proudhon, 1955
Quatre précurseurs. Proudhon, Sorel, Péguy, Dandieu, 1958
[1930–37]. *La Fin des notables*, 1972
The End of the Notables, translated by Alain Silvera and June Guicharnaud, 1974
Regards sur l'affaire Dreyfus. Paris: Éd. de Fallois

Further Reading

Fidus, "Daniel Halévy, un notable de Paris," *La Revue des Deux Mondes* (1936)
Guth, Paul, "Daniel Halévy," *La Revue de Paris*, (1954)
Guy-Grand, Georges, 1931. "M. Daniel Halévy et la démocratie," *La Grand Revue* (1931)
Laurent, Sebastien, *Daniel Halévy*. Paris: B. Grasset, 2001
Pourrat, Henri, "Daniel Halévy," *Nouvelle Revue français* (1932)
Silvera, Alain. 1966. *Daniel Halévy and his Times: A Gentleman-Commoner in the Third Republic*. Ithaca: Cornell University Press
Rousseaux, André, "Un Quart d'Heure avec M. Daniel Halévy," *Candide* (1930)
Thibaudet, Albert, "D'Alexis de Tocqueville à Daniel Halévy," *Nouvelle Revue française* (1931)

HAZARD, PAUL
Historian

Paul Hazard's final aim was to write the cultural history of Western Europe at one of its defining moments through an investigation of the history of its literature. The aim itself is dated, as are the results, but for the half-century after its appearance in 1935 the three-volume *La Crise de la conscience européenne (1680–1715)* dominated the study of central European culture in the eighteenth century. An English translation appeared in 1953.

La Crise de la conscience was followed and complemented by the posthumous three-volume *La Pensée européenne au XVIIIe siècle, de Montesquieu à Lessing*, which appeared in 1946 immediately after the war, and was published in English translation in 1954. The agents of change operating the move towards what Leibniz called "the new order" were grouped around Leibniz himself, Spinoza, Malebranche, Bayle, Fontenelle, Locke, Bossuet, and Fénelon. That list of names comes from the preface. In the conclusion, the list loses Malebranche and Fontenelle, but adds the name of Newton.

Outwardly Hazard's career was conventional enough for a brilliant academic. Born in 1878, the son of a schoolteacher, Hazard was conventionally educated until acceptance in 1900 by the *Ecole Normale Supérieure*, leading to the *agrégation* in letters in 1903. His doctorate on the influence of the French Revolution on Italian letters 1789–1815 was awarded in 1910 after a three-year stay in Rome, and was followed by a first teaching appointment in 1910 at the University of Lyons.

Then in 1913 came the call to a chair at the Sorbonne, war service, return to Paris, and in 1925 elevation to the chair of modern and comparative literature at the Collège de France. Elected to the French academy on January 11, 1940, the war prevented him from taking his chair, and he died, an *Officier de la Légion d'Honneur*, in 1944, having from 1932 until 1940 spent alternate years at Columbia University.

The publications began in 1906 with a book on foreign perceptions of France, followed by publication of the doctoral dissertation in 1910, several works on Italian topics, a pseudonymous novel of 1918, *Maman*, studies on Lamartine, Stendhal, and *Manon Lescaut*, to join those already published on Leopardi and Petrarch and soon to be followed by works on Michelangelo and Don Quixote. Thereafter came *Les livres, les enfants et les hommes* (1932) and, jointly with Bédarida, a book of 1934 on French influence on Italy in the eighteenth century. There finally followed the two major three-volume works mentioned above.

Although what can be called the Hazard vision lingers on in dusty books and increasingly remote corners of the academic world, his work now presents a view of intellectual history that is more nearly simply wrong than merely inadequate, and as a guide to cultural history it is frankly risible. But there is little point is writing a belated review of *La Crise de la conscience*, which starts from the premise that between about 1680 and about 1715 there was a little-known pivotal period, which Hazard sets out to investigate. This, he supposed, was the era of transition from a period characterized by a love of hierarchy, discipline, order, and dogma to a new order in which constraint, authority, and dogma were detested, from a Christian culture to an anti-Christian one.

What is of much greater absolute importance, and is alone relevant in the context of the present volume, is Hazard's own position in the tradition of intellectual history in twentieth-century France. He was intellectually and spiritually formed very early in the century, at the height of the battle being won by the secularizing forces of the anticlerical academic establishment against the beleaguered reaction of outdated clerical opposition to scientific advance and a church demanding continued cultural domination. The ministry of Combes came to power in 1902. France's representative at the Vatican was withdrawn in 1904, and the possessions of religious congregations were sequestered. Members of religious orders were forbidden to teach, and the church's failure to accept the law separating church and state resulted in the further confiscations of religious property in 1907 and 1908.

At the beginning of Hazard's career, the eighteenth century was still the century of enlightenment. He was to publish his major work in 1935, just in time to miss all but the very first of the series of reinterpretations of major authors, including Shakespeare, Montaigne, Erasmus, Rabelais, and Goethe, showing that, despite the assumptions inherited by Hazard, Europe's greatest authors had not achieved their stature through the secularizing power of their work. Hence the start from a discontinuity, which never existed, between two opposed cultural homogeneities in seventeenth- and eighteenth-century France, whose existence has also now long been discredited.

Yet if Hazard's vision was fundamentally flawed, it would still be difficult to quarrel with his choice of significant thinkers within the period he has chosen, and even today his analysis of detail is often powerfully perceptive. What has become unsustainable has inevitably to do with the excessive polarizations of

attitude fathered on to his subjects, as in the ferocity of Fénelon's repudiation of the values for which Louis XIV is taken to stand, the insensitivity to literary registers betraying views much more tentative or exploratory than Hazard allows them to appear, as in the consideration of Bayle, and a whole succession of discontinuities invented to suit the historical schema, as between the "rationalistes" and the precursors of Rousseau, Richardson, and *Sturm und Drang*.

The other great work, *La Pensée européenne*, takes up where its predecessor stops, in 1715, and is more programmatically comparative. There is also, unsurprisingly given its later date, more nuances in the attitude to natural religion, the anti-atheistic deism of d'Alembert and Voltaire. Yet the eulogy of Montesquieu, truly a great man but for reasons quite other than those alleged by Hazard, is almost embarrassingly wrong in its attribution of virtue, industriousness, and devotion to mankind.

Hazard is not to be criticized for not having realized all that we have subsequently uncovered about Montesquieu's career and *De l'Esprit des lois*, but his treatment of Montesquieu, coming after all that was contained in *La Crise de la conscience*, makes clear that he was a sensitive, intelligent, widely-read historian of intellectual attitudes whose positions were only ever very slightly in advance of the cultural constraints of his own era. He was effectively blinded by the perspectives of his age and milieu to the nature of Montesquieu's achievement. In consequence, he quite overlooked the need Montesquieu felt to rehabilitate himself, to head off the revolution of which he himself was a harbinger, the significance of Montesquieu's opening sentence, which announced an ethic without divine origins. He missed the late addition of the ill-fitting first two books of *De l'Esprit des lois*, and even the meaning of the title, which has to be translated not as "The Spirit of the Laws," as Hazard's interpretation demands, but as "The Spirit of Laws."

ANTHONY LEVI

Biography

Hazard was born in 1878. In 1900 he entered the *Ecole Normale Supérieure*. In 1910 he was awarded a doctorate based on his dissertation on the influence of the French Revolution on Italian letters from 1789 to 1815. In 1910 he took a teaching post at the University of Lyons. In 1913 he was appointed to a chair at the Sorbonne. After serving during the war, he returned to Paris, and in 1925 he was appointed chair of modern and comparative literature at the Collège de France. From 1932 until 1940, he spent alternate years at the Collège de France and Columbia University. Although he was elected to the French Academy in 1940, the war prevented him from being able to take his chair. Hazard died in 1944.

Selected Works

Histoire illustrée de la littérature française, 1923–4
Les livres, les enfants et les hommes, 1932; as *Books, Children, and Men*, translated by Marguerite Mitchell, 1960
La Crise de la conscience européenne, 1680–1715, 1935; as *The European Mind 1680–1715*, translated by J. Lewis May, 1964
La pensée européenne au XVIIIe siècle, de Montesquieu à Lessing, 3 vols. 1946; as *European Thought in the Eighteenth Century from Montesquieu to Lessing*, translated by J. Lewis May, 1954

HERVÉ, GÉRALD
Philosopher, Novelist

The history of thought contains new worlds whose discovery is inevitable. The works of Gérald Hervé represent one of these worlds. Yet the near silence that surrounds them suggests that their fate and meaning should be questioned. His influence stands in inverse proportion to the extent and range of his thought, which is mainly developed in the philosophical and fictional texts. The background to his thinking is the result of an event that had a decisive effect on his life: in 1955, the young Navy Administrator was dismissed from the Navy for homosexuality. From humanist and liberal beginnings, this "inner exile" conquered a singular independence of thought ("*pensée libre*") in relation to contemporary trends and he pursued a broad meditation on the sources of oppression and the essence of freedom. From this there are two possible axes to his thinking: first, a historical-cultural approach to the search for intelligibility, enabling him to elaborate a genealogy of morals and philosophy; and second, the preeminence of liberty as the essence of mankind and his presence in the world, which is inseparable from the question of sexuality and writing.

Gérald Hervé is a thinker of the ontological, historical, personal cut. Homosexuality, as "hidden social drama" (*Orphée interdit*, 1960) forms the object of bimillennial neurotic Christian condemnation, but also structures it as "ontological incest." Adopting phenomenological developments and the premises of existentialism (Kierkegaard, Heidegger, Sartre), he exploits psychoanalytic theory in order to create a Weberian, ideal type of homosexual, opposed to the accepted values of society, developed from an analysis of "totalities" (church, army, stadium) as collective forms of sublimated desire. In other words, social action, which is essentially repressive, destines the gay man to alienation: man is "a humiliated entity." Because sexuality is an instrument of knowledge, experiencing desire as immediate pleasure is not enough, it is also necessary to be aware of condemnation. Dealienation implies critical awareness, and the exercising of distanced intelligence. The primacy of this concept, based on a definition of homosexuality as "the drama of the impossible incarnation of the spirit," precedes minority rights claims. Tolerance is not equal to liberty. The 1960 text thus proposes the first conceptualization of dealienation that goes beyond a state of (self) justification (Gide, *Corydon*, 1925). Homosexuality enters French philosophical thought not with Sartre or Foucault but with Gérald Hervé.

The ideal of antiquity (Eros), which is neither regressive nor utopian, takes on the role of a critical model, as an ontological totality repressed by a "universe naked on the surface of being." The historicity of sexual prohibition plays an important role because it reveals the permanence of the lie as interiorized fault within the individual and within modern rationality. This analysis is the basis of a critical essay on the confrontation between the Greek and Jewish ideals, from which the author subsequently distances himself (*Le Mensonge de Socrate*, 1984).

Demands for justice and the anchoring of philosophical revolt in the current affairs of the 1990s thrived on a militant concept of liberated reason (*La Nuit des Olympica*, 1999). American philosophical resources, notably the pragmatism of Charles S. Peirce, radicalized the anti-spiritualistic position. The adoption of the "thought-sign" and the revival of the category of the corporeal within the space carved out from Western philosophy helps to define the challenge of the "cosmic problematic of the third millennium" and of essential liberty, always threatened by "neolithic thought" and the fear of reaching existential limits (death). Here, also, the problem of sexuality reveals the true intentions of all philosophy (the values of existence: "How ought we to live?"). The deconstruction of so-called Cartesian rationality, including Descartes's hypothesis of homosexuality (which, in reply to unanswered or conventionally treated questions, is supported by indications from the "masked philosopher's" biography, psychology, and sociological background) forms part of the task of clarifying the phenomena of belief and the criticism of the *Aufklärung* and its disciples. A positive philosophy of existence is therefore affirmed, which represents the synthesis of contemporary nonreligious thought (Adorno, Wittgenstein, Derrida, Deleuze, among others) with objective rationality, due to an "alternative education" in *matters of fact* and the democratic values of an open society, freed from obscure mental archaisms and totalitarian temptations.

Like philosophy, art "is not a game" but an essential form of compensation and engagement. However, works of fiction do not demonstrate but realize (hence the "voluntary outsiders," the transnational doubles of the author). In a cerebral existence, the other side of the conceptual is the imaginary. This is why the themes advanced since 1960—(original homothetics, paternity, childhood, time, memory and origins, love, alterity otherness) are developed in the novels (notably in *Les Hérésies imaginaires*, 1989). The image, which is the expression and celebration of conceptual sensibility and the source of "pleasure," is fully realized in literary creation. Obsessed with achieving absolute truth, it is the fruit of a culture developed to "exhaustion" and of the poetic and phantasmic process of the transposition of the real. Liberty submits the demand for beauty to the expression of a radical truth, "impossible to say or intolerable," like that expressed by Anselm the metaphysician of sodomy (*Les Aventures de Romain Saint-Sulpice, 2004*). The singular liberty of the poetic reaches the writer as a *causa sui* (Jamblin, in *Marseilles*, 2003). Thus thought, writing, and the (sexualized) body, united in the need for ethical coherence, accomplish the existential project. "Thinking things out is the greatest excellence and wisdom: to act and speak what is true, perceiving things according to their nature." (Heraclitus about 540–480 bc)

HERVE BAUDRY

See also **Gilles Deleuze; Jacques Derrida; Michel Foucault; Andre Gide; Jean-Paul Sartre**

Biography

Gérald Hervé (pseudonym Yves Kerruel) was born in Marseille in 1928. He studied law and political science in Paris, was awarded a post in the Navy administration and was initially drafted near to Saigon in September 1954. In May 1955, the victim of anti-gay purges, he was dismissed from the Navy (the affair is retold in *Des Pavois et des fers*). He worked in Paris in insurance until he moved to Brittany in 1970 to teach economic sciences. In 1993 he retired to Nice. He died in Miami in June 1998 from injuries caused by a motorboat accident in Nassau, Bahamas. One third of his work was published during his lifetime; the remaining works are being published at Talus d'approche Editions in 2003–2004.

Selected Works

Using the pseudonym Yves Kerruel:
Des Pavois et des fers, 1971
Les Soldat nu, 1974
Les Hérésies imaginaires, 1989
La Nuit des Olympica. Essai sur le national-cartésianisme, 1999
Marseilles, 2003
Orphée interdit, 2004

Further Readings

Baudry, Hervé, *Fin d'empire et mac carthysme sexuel: «Des Pavois et des fers» par Yves Kerruel*, Amsterdam: Homodok, 2001
Baudry-Kruger, Hervé, *Ni Oubli ni pardon*, Soignies: Talus d'approche, 2001
Bonnaud, Robert, *L'Histoire, le progrès, le communisme*, Paris: Kimé, 1997
Guérin, Daniel, *Shakespeare et Gide en correctionnelle?*, Paris: Scorpion, 1959
Vidal-Naquet, Pierre, *Mémoires. I*, Paris: Seuil/La Découverte, 1995

HISTORICAL SURVEY: 1870–1918

Like other western nations, the watchword for France between 1870 and 1918 was *change*: sudden, drastic change, occurring at what appeared to contemporaries as breakneck speed. The worlds-apart character of the Franco-Prussian War and World War I that bookend the period punctuate the magnitude of this transformation. Economically, socially, and politically, France of 1870 still bore much resemblance to the Old Regime. But by 1918, it had already acquired most of the traits we would recognize in today's society. This was the period when the modern French nation truly became modern and a nation.

The impact on thought of this transformation was to produce conflict, precisely over what the change meant and how to grapple with it. The forces that forged the nation were both centripetal and strikingly divisive. But unlike how contemporaries framed the conflict—as one between revolution and reaction, science and religion, modernity and tradition—it was not simply a question of being for or against the changes before them. Rather, one sees wildly different theories about how to comprehend and navigate a modern society that seemed increasingly to shift under the feet of its members. From positivism to the philosophy of Henri Bergson; impressionism, expressionism, and cubism in the arts; naturalism, realism, and symbolism in literature; and the formal emergence of academic disciplines like history, psychiatry, sociology, criminology, and anthropology, the sudden mutation gave rise to a dizzying array of new ideas, comprising a uniquely dynamic culture that became the hub of modernism. Although the Great Depression of the nineteenth century (1873–1896) would cede way to *la belle époque* of relative prosperity during the decade or two before World War I, its *crise d'adaptation*—the pangs of adjustment to the new industrial economy—would translate into the cultural arena for decades to come. It was a heterogeneous culture that both embraced and balked at the social, political, and economic developments that generated it.

The changes of the early Third Republic were themselves the product of prior developments, especially those in the economic realm during the Second Empire that preceded it. Although French economic history is conspicuous for its lack of a *décollage*—a "take-off" period properly so called— developments in the 1850s were decisive. From 1850 to 1870, France experienced double-digit annual percentage growth in leading economic sectors such as fuel, chemicals, and engineering, a tripling of coal production (with imports growing at an even quicker pace) and in total capitalization of stocks, a sevenfold extension of railroads, and an eightfold increase in steel production. By 1870, the structural shift that would assure the dominance of industry over artisanal production and agriculture was complete, and the 1867–68 economic crisis was France's last crisis to be caused by harvest failure. The shift procured a society that appeared already in the 1860s to some contemporaries as on the verge of something entirely new and different. It was a society about to become modern.

But the majority of the population remained unaware or unaffected by these developments. The change that affected all people living in all parts of France— and indeed linking them to one another—occurred during the period at hand. By the end of World War I, France was an industrial, urban nation with all the markers of modernity. Although the general population barely grew in size, the urban population doubled—with a full one tenth living in the capital and its suburbs—to become the majority by 1914. Measured by the yardstick of coal production, French industry also doubled in size and it was the world's largest exporter of iron ore. It boasted the world's second largest automobile industry, great advances in aviation, a burgeoning film industry, and with Paris—the City of Lights—and the now thirteen other cities with a population over 100,000 electrified. Therefore, while structural change preceded the Third Republic, the actual growth, spread, and eventual triumph of urban, industrial capitalism occurred between 1870 and 1918.

France's longest-lasting constitutional regime to date was born in part by a fluke. Faced with the news of Napoleon III's capture at Sedan two days earlier, the "men of September 4"—notably including Léon Gambetta (1838–1882), the defining figure of the Republic's first decade—seized the moment and proclaimed France a republic. Like its economic transformation, the early Republic was shaped, however, by a generation that came of political age during opposition to the imploding Empire and sought to put into practice the political vision they formulated then. In part because Gambetta vied to continue the war, monarchists, suing for peace, garnered a majority of the universal male votes, and it was not until 1879 that republicans

under Gambetta's stewardship ousted the sitting president MacMahon and took hold of all branches of government.

The 1870s were therefore spent reeling from the economically recoupable but psychologically damaging defeat—of which the scar of the dismembered Alsace-Lorraine region would serve as a painful reminder—and building a political framework viable enough to save the still-fragile Republic. After the bloody crush of the Paris Commune in 1871 by Adolphe Thiers, the Republic's first executive, the defining moment was the precarious task of writing a republican constitution with monarchists still in parliamentary majority. When it finally passed in 1875, it did not reestablish the unicameral National Assembly of 1792—the First Republic—favored at heart by all republicans. Instead, based on the constitutional charter of 1814, it added an upper-house Senate elected by indirect suffrage and designed as a *chambre de résistance* to rein in the Chamber of Deputies—the senate would block women's suffrage in 1919—and a president elected to a seven-year term by the Chamber. The seat of government was located at Versailles and designed for a ready restoration of the monarchy. The split among republicans whether to support this constitution generated the ensuing division between Opportunists (among them the former *irréconciliables* Gambetta and Jules Ferry [1832–1893]) who were in favor, and Radicals (Georges Clemenceau [1841–1929] and others) who opposed it. Until 1898, Opportunists—a coalition between Gambetta's Union républicaine (Republican Union) and Ferry's Gauche républicaine (Republican Left)—would govern the Republic.

Once in power, republicans set out to entrench their principles in the course of a decade of aggressive reforms. The 1879 Freycinet Plan paved the way by pouring an unprecedented nine billion francs into the nation's infrastructure. Half went toward 16,000 kilometers of railroad, and the remainder to build or renovate roads, canals, ports, and navigable rivers. The regime also set out to remake France's intellectual infrastructure. It moved the seat of government back to Paris, adopted the Marseillaise as the national anthem, and began officially to commemorate July 14 as the *fête nationale*. It decreed the construction of city halls and monuments and the renaming of streets, all with the aim of cementing the Republic and its values. Most important were the school reforms during Jules Ferry's tenure as minister of public instruction, which not only made primary education obligatory, gratis, and secular, but also geared the content of the curriculum toward the "principles of '89," with a heavy emphasis on civics and patriotic inculcation. Ferry was also the architect of a program of colonization, which extended an existing colonial presence in North Africa and in the Senegambian basin of West Africa eventually to make up the supercolonies of *Afrique Occidentale Française* (French West Africa, 1895) and *Afrique Equatoriale Française* (French Equatorial Africa, 1910), together occupying virtually the continent's entire northwestern quadrant. By further adding to footholds in the South Pacific, Indochina (1883–85), and Madagascar (1894), the Third Republic would end up creating an empire of almost 4 million square miles and 50 million subjects, ten times what it was in 1871. In the colonial area, too, purportedly universal republican values were both the content of and rationale for their ensconcement.

This crucial decade put France far along the way of building, consolidating, and expanding the nation along republican principles. With republicans of this generation devotees of positivism, optimistic that science alone could improve society, Gambetta declared clericalism the enemy par excellence. It was a powerful *Kulturkampf* of sorts, with a regime determined to convert the hearts and minds of new and old compatriots alike, sweeping away what they considered past and retrograde: a Catholic, backward France of cloddish village priests. In colonial matters, however, anticlericalism would not be a matter of export, declared Paul Bert (1833–86)—who revealingly served terms both as Gambetta's education minister and later as a colonial governor-general in Indochina—merging church interests with secular republicanism in a colonial policy with the revealing tag "the civilizing mission." The decade ended with fitting fanfare with the centennial celebration of the French Revolution during the Universal Exposition with its Gallery of Machines and erection of the Eiffel Tower—that towering, steely ode to modern science and industry—as its crowning achievement, the tricolor flying on top. With the exception of the Vichy regime (1940–44), the principles inherited from 1789 would from the 1880s on define the ideology of the French state, officially *La République française*.

If the 1880s were triumphant, the fin de siècle 1890s were characterized by anxiety and doubt about the fruits of industry, modernity, and the Republic. What historians have come to call to the Franco-French Wars over the nation's true identity were raised to a whole new pitch. Drawing strength from an expanding urban working class, amnestied communards, and the bourgeois Republic's reticence to engage in any meaningful social reform, the left began organizing in unions and socialist parties. Although not united until 1905, socialists consistently gained seats in parliament in the 1880s and were a major political force by the 1890s. Social Catholics and other traditional critics of modernity also reasserted themselves. For them, the Revolution was at fault, the skidding off course in an entire *Syllabus of Errors*, as in the encyclical screed issued by Pope Pius IX to enumerate the evils of progress, liberalism, and modernity. Their rallying point became the construction of the Sacré-Cœur basilica on the hills of Montmartre: a stake through the heart of the Paris Commune and a kind of anti-Eiffel Tower named after the central symbol of nineteenth-century royalist opposition to the revolutionary cause—a site for pilgrimage, penance, and salvation from the Republic's sins.

But a new type of criticism also emerged, one that did not correspond either to the conventional lines of the Franco-French War or to a simple left–right split. Although life got measurably better for most of the population in material terms—real wages increased by fifty percent in the period, the average factory workday was shortened by two hours to ten, and food, leisure, plumbing, and consumer goods became more readily available—elites agreed on the deleterious effect of modernity, and that it was of biological proportion. Fearing a simian working class and a bourgeoisie turned soft, they settled on a diagnosis of "degeneration." Although divided over its antidote—regeneration—politicians, journalists, academics, doctors, and businessmen raised alarm about the health of the individual body, the social body, and the body politic. Concerns about French decline—especially compared to its looming neighbor across the Rhine—became a veritable obsession. Historians point to the Boulanger Affair (1887–89) as the inaugural moment for the demagogic right. But although the specter of this Minister of War as a possible new Caesar threatened the foundation of the republic, Boulanger (1837–91) was supported by a melange of royalists, workers, Bonapartists, and radical republicans, all malcontent in some way with modernity and the drab, centrist Republic. The responses to the diagnosis also included natality—the project of diagnosing and redressing France's falling birthrates—and an attendant focus on determining the normal female and male body. And it included an array of artists and intellectuals who were critical either of what was becoming of the world or of existing intellectual tools with which to describe it. Where realism and naturalism had made use of the scientific model, new poets and artists—self-proclaimed "decadents" and symbolists—set out to capture what eluded it in a flurry of experimentation in thought and in the arts, one that would set out to reject—or at least to "shock"—bourgeois society in a development that would continue well beyond the period at hand.

Accentuating these themes of a flaccid and effete Republic, a new Right added outright racism and anti-Semitism to the degeneration/regeneration stew. It is important not to confuse mainstream Catholic misgivings about anticlericalism with those opposed to parliamentary democracy and basic civil rights, virtually all of whom nevertheless invoked Catholicism as the basis for their reactionary, xenophobic, and anti-Semitic image of the nation. While themselves very much the products of mass society and of what Gambetta had termed "the new social layers," members of the new Right would rail against the inanity, mediocrity, and anonymity of the modern world. They pointed to scandals such the Panama Affair and to the collapse of the Union Générale Bank as proof of the corruption of the entire republican project. Edouard Drumont's (1844–1917) *La France juive*—"Jewish France," 1886—fused anti-Semitism old and new, religious and secular, scientific and folk. With 100,000 copies sold in its first year and 200 editions by 1900, it warned that Catholic France was becoming Jewish and foreign. In making this bizarre argument—there were 68,000 Jews in a total French population of 38 million in 1886—Drumont exemplified how critics of modernity were nevertheless scurrying about for scientific-sounding explanations to France's perceived fin-de-siècle national malaise. Maurice Barrès (1862–1923) stated his opposition to *Les Déracinés* (The Uprooted), an 1897 novel that pitted the traditional permanence of his native Lorraine against the fluid, "Jewish" modern world. Charles Maurras (1868–1952), whose ultraconservative theory of civilization continues to define the extreme Right in France, espoused a radical, royalist, antiparliamentarian, and anti-Semitic "integral nationalism" that targeted the "anti-France"—Jews, Freemasons, Protestants, and generic *métèques*, or "foreigners"—that he argued threatened the French race.

The case of the Jewish army captain Alfred Dreyfus, falsely convicted of treason by a military tribunal in 1894, magnified these attacks on modernity and the Republic to an extreme, and in turn rallied defenders to their cause. Proponents and critics alike latched on to Dreyfus to put the nation on trial. At first, the press and public opinion supported the verdict. The case exploded into an "Affair" in early 1898 when Émile Zola published an open letter on the front page of Clemenceau's paper the *Aurore*, accusing the army and war ministry of framing Dreyfus and shielding the real culprit, one Commandant Esterhazy. 200,000 copies of the *Aurore* issue were sold that day. Anti-Semitic riots ensued, and Zola was found guilty of libel, fined, and sentenced to one year in prison. France's high court ordered a new court-martial in 1899, which again found Dreyfus guilty.

Dreyfus became a lightning rod for a thundering opposition to the Republic, organized in the anti-Dreyfus *Ligue de la patrie française* (League for the French Fatherland), which would plot a coup against it. Maurras defended Colonel Henry, the forger of the document that implicated Dreyfus. Drumont's paper *La Libre parole*—founded with the profits from *La France juive*, with "France for the French" on its masthead—followed suit, and *La Croix*, a reactionary weekly established by the assumptionist order, sold over two million copies per issue during the height of the Affair. The specter of the new right—variegated but unified in their opposition to the Republic and to the modern society over which it had presided—was no longer limited to the nobility. In the Affair it came out of the châteaux and flooded the streets, joining and helping to shape the mass society it opposed.

But Dreyfus's cause also became a rallying point to consolidate the Republic's backers. Some 3,000 persons, including a host of intellectuals, signed a petition demanding revision of the trial. In 1898, Dreyfusards would form the *Ligue des droits de l'homme et du citoyen* (the League of the Rights of Man); in 1899 René Waldeck-Rousseau formed a "government of republican defense," including Alexandre Millerand—the first socialist to hold a ministerial post—and a pardon by President Émile Loubet finally freed Dreyfus. In 1901, Radicals—who had been a smattering of politicians, journalists, and writers—formed France's first organized political party, the Radical and Radical-Socialist Party, under the leadership of Léon Bourgeois and under the theme of "solidarism." The 1902 elections brought back the great socialist leader Jean Jaurès, an avid defender of the captain's, who organized further cooperation through the *Délégation des Gauches* committee of the left. In 1905 Jaurès unified socialists in the *Section française de l'internationale ouvrière*, the French section of the Workers' International (SFIO). Other direct outcomes of the Affair were the 1901 Law of Association, which required both chambers to authorize organizations, including religious orders (resulting in the dissolution of more than 100 of them, including the Assumptionist Order); a 1904 law expelling priests and nuns from state schools; and finally a complete separation of church and state in 1905. In 1906, the Court of Appeals finally annulled the verdict, and Dreyfus was reinstated, promoted, and decorated with the Legion of Honor.

The Affair, then, cut like a swath through the early Third Republic. It brought out, entrenched, and radicalized those opposed to the Republic. The Right, which had comprised squabbling Bonapartists, legitimists and Orléanists—the latter two advocating the royal lines contending for the throne they hoped once again would be filled—mutated into a mass phenomenon with a vociferous press and ominous racial overtones. But with Radical republicans replacing Opportunists in power, supported by a strengthened and unified socialist party with a commitment to the regime, the Affair also won over those who had expressed doubts about the Republic and hardened the solidarity of its supporters.

The decade between the Affair and World War I appears calm in contrast, and therefore subsequently earned the moniker of *la belle époque*, "the good old days." In truth, neither the center-left political cooperation nor the temporary social tranquility imposed by aggressive anticlerical legislation would last. Already in 1905, the SFIO withdrew from the left bloc, and the *Confédération Générale du Travail*, the General Confederation of Workers (CGT), created in 1902 to comprise all worker's organizations in the nation, veered toward syndicalism and rejected parliamentary cooperation in favor of a policy of "direct action." Between 1906 and 1911, strikes crippled the nation. The harsh republican policies also served further to swell the ranks of the political right. Only the uncompromising ministry of Georges Clemenceau between 1906 and 1909 was able to resist these challenges, and after that escalating international tension leading up to World War I tempered and finally temporarily superseded the internal strife.

Although the regaining of Alsace and Lorraine had remained a sore point since 1870—the statues symbolizing the regions on the Champs-Elysées in Paris were still draped in black veil—and there was a nationalist resurgence during the events leading up to 1914, the French were not eager to go to war. Having saved Paris from the German assault at the "Miracle of the Marne," the French army pitted its defense together with British troops in a system of trenches stretching from the Atlantic to the Alps. The war of attrition that ensued struck the French more than any other nation psychologically, economically, and in terms of infrastructure and proportional manpower, but not even the ten-month German siege of the fortress town of Verdun in 1916 moved the lines of battle. French men and women rallied in trenches and factories to what the leaders Raymond Poincaré and Clemenceau called a *union sacrée*—a holy union—of the nation. Tested to the breaking point by a four-year slaughter of millions of soldiers—1.3 million French men, or twenty percent of those between twenty and forty-four years of age died—the union held up with the help of propaganda, tight censorship, centralized economic management on the home front, and the rotation of troops by General Philippe Pétain on the battlefield. With the assistance of tanks and fresh American soldiers, French and British armies under the unified command of Ferdinand Foch at last brought the German invader to its knees in November 1918.

The radical change and subsequent conflict that postwar observers attributed to the war were, however, already present before it. The forging of and the suspicion toward a modern nation; the belief in technology and science as solutions to all social ills and the awareness of their destructive potential; economic centralization, government planning, a technocratic state, and syndicalism and anarchism; trade unions, strikes, and the emergence of large, Taylorist factories; racial thinking and the demand for human rights; mass society and the critique of consumerism: all were key features of the prewar period. The essentialist image of women as mothers evident in the postwar nostalgia for a prewar world was of course at least as prevalent before the war as well, but in reality forty percent of women were gainfully employed before 1914 and the stable gender roles supposedly part of the *belle époque* had long been in question. In fact, the sudden and drastic change that was perceived as resulting from the war was the principal characteristic of the entire half-century that preceded it. And above all, the rethinking of the modern world that the war seemed to have engendered was indeed the most prominent feature of thought from 1870 to 1918. Criticism of the present society, the desire to improve upon it, the quest to begin anew, and even the will to destroy it, defined modernity. The impact on modern French thought by these historical developments is therefore something of a paradox: thought was characterized by ambivalence about the world it helped bring about. This paradox would continue to organize ideas in the century ahead.

TORBJÖRN WANDEL

See also **Maurice Barres; Jean Jaures; Charles Maurras**

Further Reading

Agulhon, Maurice, *The French Republic 1879–1992*, translated by Antonia Nevill, Oxford, United Kingdom and Cambridge: Blackwell, 1993

Andrew, Christopher, and A. S. Kanya-Forster, *France Overseas: The Great War and the Climax of French Imperial Expansion*, London: Thames and Hudson 1981

Auspitz, Katherine, *The Radical Bourgeoisie: The Ligue de l'enseignement and the Origins of the French Third Republic, 1866–1885*, New York: Cambridge University Press, 1982

Barrows, Susanna, *Distorting Mirrors: Visions of the Crowd in Late Nineteenth-Century France*, New Haven, Conn.: Yale University Press, 1981

Becker, Jean-Jacques, *The Great War and the French People*, New York: Berg, 1993

Berenson, Edward, *The Trial of Madame Caillaux*, Berkeley: University of California Press, 1993

Bury, J. P. T., *Gambetta and the Making of the Third Republic*, London: Longman, 1973

Bury, J. P. T., *Gambetta's Final Years: "The Era of Difficulties," 1877–1882*, London and New York: Longman, 1982

Charle, Christophe, *A Social History of France in the Nineteenth Century*, translated by Miriam Kochan, Oxford: Berg, 1994

Conklin, Alice, *The Mission to Civilize*: The Republican Idea of Empire in France and West Africa, 1895–1930, Stanford: Stanford University Press, 1997

Datta, Venita, *Birth of a National Icon: The Literary Avant-Garde and the Origins of the Intellectual in France*, Albany: State University of New York Press, 1999

Earle, Edward Mead (editor), *Modern France: Problems of the Third and Fourth Republics*, New York: Russell and Russell, 1964

Eksteins, Modris, *Rites of Spring: The Great War and the Birth of the Modern Age*, Boston: Houghton-Mifflin, 1989

Elwitt, Sanford, *The Making of the Third Republic: Class and Politics in France, 1868–1884*, Baton Rouge: Louisiana State University Press, 1975

Gibson, Ralph, *A Social History of French Catholicism, 1789–1914*, London: Routledge, 1989

Gildea, Robert, *Education in Provincial France: A Study of Three Departments, 1800–1914*, Oxford: Clarendon Press, 1983

Goldstein, Jan., "The Hysteria Diagnoses and the Politics of Anti-Clericalism in Late Nineteenth-Century France," *Journal of Modern History* 54 (1982): 209–239

Hazareesingh, Sudhir, *From Subject to Citizen: The Second Empire and the Emergence of Modern French Democracy*, Princeton: Princeton University Press, 1998

Hoffman, Stanley (editor), *In Search of France*, New York: Harper and Row, 1965

Hyman, Paula, *The Jews of Modern France*, Berkeley: University of California Press, 1998

Jonas, Raymond, *France and the Cult of the Sacred Heart: An Epic Tale for Modern Times*, Berkeley: University of California Press, 2000

Kale, Steven, *Legitimism and the Reconstruction of French Society, 1852–1883*, Baton Rouge: Louisiana State University Press, 1992

Lebovics, Herman, *True France: The Wars over Cultural Identity, 1900–1945*, Ithaca: Cornell University Press, 1992

Lehning, James, *To Be a Citizen: The Political Culture of the Early French Third Republic*, Ithaca: Cornell University Press, 2001

Irvine, William, *The Boulanger Affair Reconsidered: Royalism, Boulangism and the Origins of the Radical Right in France*, New York: Oxford University Press, 1988

Kern, Stephen. *The Culture of Time and Space, 1880–1918*, Cambridge: Harvard University Press, 1983

Matsuda, Matt, *The Memory of the Modern*, New York: Oxford University Press, 1996

Mayeur, Jean-Marie and Madeleine Reberioux, *The Third Republic from its Origins to the Great War, 1871–1914*. Cambridge: Cambridge University Press and Paris: Éditions de la Maison des Sciences de l'Homme, 1984

Nora, Pierre (editor), *Realms of Memory: Rethinking the French Past*, New York: Columbia University Press 1996

Nord, Philip, *The Republican Moment: Struggles for Democracy in Nineteenth-Century France*, Cambridge: Harvard University Press, 1995

Nord, Philip, *Impressionists and Politics: Art and Democracy in the Nineteenth Century*, London: Routledge, 2000

Nye, Robert, *Crime, Madness, and Politics in Modern France: The Medical Concept of National Decline*, Princeton: Princeton University Press, 1984

Nye, Robert, *Masculinity and Male Codes of Honor in Modern France*, New York: Oxford University Press, 1993

Offen, Karen, "Depopulation, Nationalism and Feminism in Fin de Siècle France," *American Historical Review* (1984): 648–676

Perrot, Michelle, "On the Formation of the French Working Class," in *Working-Class Formation: Nineteenth-Century Patterns in Western Europe and the United States*, edited by Ira Katzelson and A. R. Zolberg, Princeton: Princeton University Press, 1986

Perrot, Michelle, "Women, Power, and History: The Case of Nineteenth-Century France," in *Women, State, and Revolution: Essays in Power and Gender in Europe since 1789*, edited by Sian Reynolds, Amherst: University of Massachusetts Press, 1987

Perrot, Michelle, *Workers on Strike: France, 1871–1890*, New Haven: Yale University Press, 1987

Pick, Daniel, *Faces of Degeneration: A European Disorder, c. 1848–1918*, Cambridge: Cambridge University Press, 1989

Price, Roger, *An Economic History of France, 1730–1914*, New York: St. Martin's Press, 1981

Prochaska, David, *Making Algeria French: Colonialism in Bône, 1870–1920*, Cambridge: Cambridge University Press, 1990

Rémond, René, *The Right Wing in France from 1815 to de Gaulle*, Philadelphia: University of Pennsylvania Press, 1969

Roberts, Mary Louise, *Civilization without Sexes: Reconstructing Gender in Postwar France, 1917–1927*, Chicago: Chicago University Press, 1994

Rothney, John, *Bonapartism after Sedan*, Ithaca: Cornell University Press, 1969

Schwartz, Vanessa, *Spectacular Realities: Early Mass Culture in Fin-de-Siècle Paris*, Berkeley: University of California Press, 1998

Sedgwick, Alexander, *The Third French Republic, 1870–1914*, New York: Crowell, 1968

Silverman, Debora, *Art Nouveau in Fin-de-Siècle France: Politics, Psychology, and Style*, Berkeley: University of California Press, 1989

Soucy, Robert, *Fascism in France: The Case of Maurice Barrès*, Berkeley: University of California Press, 1972

Taithe, Bertrand, *Citizenship and Wars: France in Turmoil, 1870–1871*, London: Routledge, 2001

Thomson, David, *Democracy in France since 1870*, fourth edition, New York: Oxford University Press, 1964

Tombs, Robert, *The War Against Paris, 1871*, Cambridge: Cambridge University Press, 1981

Tombs, Robert, *France 1815–1914*, London: Longman, 1996

Weber, Eugen, *The Action Française: Royalism and Reaction in Twentieth-Century France*, Stanford: Stanford University Press, 1962

Weber, Eugen, *Peasants into Frenchmen*, Stanford: Stanford University Press, 1976

Weber, Eugen, *France, Fin de Siècle*, Cambridge: The Belknap Press of Harvard University Press, 1986

Wilson, Stephen, *Ideology and Experience: Antisemitism in France at the Time of the Dreyfus Affair*, London: Farleigh Dickinson University Press, 1982

HISTORICAL SURVEY: 1918–1939

The two decades that separate the two World Wars are now often presented as a parenthesis in the history of French culture and thought, an exhausted lull in the half-century-long storm that blew through the country. These years are seen either as a prolongation of the *Belle Époque* that saw an explosion of the Arts and Science and anchored Paris in the firmament of intellectually creative cities, or a twilight era before running into the abyss of World War II. The 1930s especially, this decade resounding of tremors and rage of crisis in France and in the world at large, have been denounced as "hollow years" by no less an historian than Eugen Weber, or, more charitably, as having produced an "autumnal culture," according to René Rémond.

There may be indeed some grounds for such dismissive views of the interwar period; at the same time, there are equally strong arguments for viewing intellectual, artistic, and social life at that time as being as productive as ever, and preparing the future in some remarkable ways. But a characteristic of the whole period, which may explain why it is seen in contradictory ways by so many analysts, is to be pulled apart between different worlds. On one hand, it was a time of wistful hankering back to mythical pasts (a leitmotiv and theme of the time, especially on the right and conservative circles, is that of decadence: decadence of the West, of France, of civilization). At the same time, French society worked furiously at accelerating modernity, often in contradictory ways—for instance, themes such as planism, which would be an intrinsic part of the French model in the postwar period, were adopted in the early 1930s by trade unions as well as neofascists. At the level of ideologies, similar oppositions occurred, with French society deeply divided and active and large minorities occupying the two extremes of the spectrum; for intellectuals the stakes were so high that it became difficult not to engage in the political and ideological debate, and in practical politics. This was a reflection of the deep social tensions, political conflicts, and economic crises that occurred then and that mostly were unresolved, as if they could only be so through some form of catharsis. However, with hindsight, it is clear that the explosion of debates and ideas that occurred then can be seen as preparing the future.

It is interesting too that in this period a number of themes were simply not discussed. A first issue concerns the Empire—a vast array of colonies, mostly in Africa and southeast Asia, constituting the main economic backyard of France and allowing France to ride through economic crises because these colonies were by and large its main trade outlet. A feature of the colonial adventure at this time was the conservatism of management, as if it would continue forever: very few (Gide is an exception) questioned the long-term prospects of the Empire. Another theme accepted by many across society was the view of France as a society in crisis, especially because it was getting old demographically and socially. The demographic deficit created by the low birthrate, a recurrent theme since the 1880s, associated with the huge losses of human life in World War I, contributed to a genuinely askew

population structure, which worked as a political background to much of all policy framework at the time, but also as a metaphor for the uneasiness and doubt about the prospects of France as a society as well as its place in Europe.

Usually two periods are distinguished in the interwar decades—1929 being the cutting point, with the start of the Great Depression signaling the beginning of the slow slide down toward World War II. In the case of France, 1929 is not that relevant as a marker, nor is the carving of the era in two periods sufficient. Four periods can be identified and delineated. The first one is obviously the immediate after-war period, the so-called crazy years (Années Folles, the Roaring Twenties) that range from the 1918 armistice to the mid-1920s. Behind the apparent jolliness and excitement, these were difficult years. The victory celebrations soon turned into a time of questioning and, behind the apparent festive and carefree atmosphere propagated by the world of art and fashion, a darker mood prevailed, with social difficulties and the burden of economic reconstruction compounded with political dissent and widely differing interpretations and disputes of the recent trauma of war.

However, this was followed by a brief respite, which looks retrospectively as an epiphany. The second half of the 1920s and the very early 1930s were a time when it could appear that, once the dust was settled, the road to modernity was once again opened. Years of high artistic and intellectual productivity, as well as socio-economic progress, were accompanied by the effects of social reforms in terms of pension, working conditions, and social insurance. The financial crisis appeared to be resolved. Social issues seemed to settle and the inventiveness of the immediate postwar period started to produce fruits. This relatively positive time did not last. The years from 1931 to 1936 (1931 was the year during which the Great Depression really started in France) were a period during which the social divisions, economic foes, and political crises within France as well as Europe crystallized in a series of dramatic crises, some of which appeared briefly like the death knell of republican democracy. Then the post-1936 period, after the brief and strange period of the Front-Popu, full of hopes for a part of population and of fears for another, became a slow drowning toward World War II. The reverberation of world crises such as the Spanish Civil War, the invasion of Abyssinia, the reoccupation of the Ruhr by Hitler, and others then spurred intellectual life to engage further into social debates—bringing to the fore new approaches to thinking.

Coming back to the immediate aftermath of the World War I, the Armistice in November 1918, once past the immediate relief, sorrow, and joy, soon engendered ambivalent feelings in France, and it soon proved very difficult to bring a closure to the whole tragic episode. Indeed, if the country had won the war, it had been at a horrendous human cost. Some 1.4 million soldiers were dead, 1.1 million were seriously injured: a quarter of four classes of age of young men, plus a demographic "baby deficit" of some 1.3 million birth. All these factors did not improve the long-term prospects of a France in which demographic trends were already quite negative. The sacrifice of a generation of embittered or dead young men was for little apparent purpose, apart from the recovery of Alsace-Lorraine, and France was left exhausted, an old country to continue its course into modernity.

The postwar attitudes, once the celebrations and the grieving were over, were of three types, often intermingled. A first one was based on the exhilaration to be alive and the need to forget: many wanted to start again where things had been left in 1914, enjoy life to the hilt, helped by the marvelous new mass communication tools that technology now offered, such as the cinema, higher quality music recordings, or the wireless (Radio-Tour Eiffel started to broadcast in 1921). This, coupled with new forms of entertainment—American films and music such as early jazz, dance from the Charleston to Djaghilev's Ballets Russes and other classical ballets, the speed of oceanliners and cars, and so on—allowed an explosion of popular entertainment in the early 1920s that spread faster and wider than ever before across the whole country. Art forms such as Art Deco, with its gratuitous luxuriousness and modernity, and the new liberating fashion exemplified by Coco Chanel were other elements contributing to this atmosphere.

The end of the war also signaled the eruption of triumphalism and revenge politics, exalting France and national unity, the so-called sacred union that culminated in the election of the "blue horizon" parliamentary majority of the conservative Bloc National in 1919. Each little village in France started to build its "monument to the dead"—and there were more than 36,000 of them: an architectural and cultural program of quasi-Pharaonic dimensions. Overall, the whole of France was at this time still mostly conservative, rural, provincial, and deeply protectionist. The traditionalism of the Catholic church that dominated most provinces except part of the south and east stifled social change. The return of soldiers from war was in the heart of France an opportunity for opening its culture to foreign influences (including more penetration of the French language), but also for bitterness that the "system" did not take their sufferings more into account. The *Anciens Combattants* (veterans) organizations became very important in the political and social life of the nation—especially in the early 1930s. Indeed, not only

the parliamentary right but also the extra- and anti-parliamentary right became intellectual forces, fighting against the perceived decadence and corruption of the Republic, signaled by the growth of Maurras's radical, anti-Semitic, royalist *Action Française* movement, which again will be one of the driving forces behind the anti-republicanism of the early 1930s. The popularity of Maurice Barrès, the prolific novelist and essayist who promoted an emotional nationalism since the early 1900s, was exemplified by the enormous crowd that followed his funeral in 1923, comparable to that of Victor Hugo's. It should be noted that the nationalist fervor crossed over the political chasm, and if Barrès was definitely marked on the right, and was part of the anti-Dreyfusard family (the Dreyfus affair was still very potent as an ideological marker), there was also a republican, populist nationalism, admiring Peguy. Patriotism, the acceptable face of jingoistic nationalism, found its way even in more rarified circles of literary reviews such as the *Nouvelle Revue Française*, home of Gide, Claudel, and others.

A third reaction, which was particularly productive although largely limited at first to the Paris of the avant-garde movements, was one of total rejection of the old. This was the expression of a revolutionary will to demolish the bourgeois world that had allowed such wanton destruction, and to negate all the old values that had proved useless in the hell of war. It manifested itself in the world of politics as well as in literature and arts. A radical Communist party emerged after the scission from the socialists at the Congress of Tours in 1922, and called for a total social revolution based on class war, influencing a number of intellectuals. On the cultural side, the creation of the surrealist movement led by André Breton (the first surrealist manifesto was published in 1922) was also a watershed. Partly originating from the Dada nihilist literary movement of Tristan Tzara, which advocated the destruction and subversion of language itself, the surrealist movement was itself not adverse to provocation, to say the least. Although very Parisian in its development, surrealism illustrated the opening of France to outside influences, and a significant number of its members had recently arrived in the country. It was interested in Freud's ideas, African arts, a refusal of French classicism, and in espousing late-1900s avant-gardes. Playing on the language and on the forces of unconscious in order to subvert all forms of expression and explore what is behind the apparent reality of the senses, it influenced a wide circle of artists in arts as different as painting, poetry, cinema, theater, and the like. Another point to note is that the rejection of the "old" ways was not limited in the early 1920s to avant-garde artistic groups, nor to political extremes. It can also be found in mainstream thinking about, say, management, or economics because the war effort forced a rethinking of social organization: Bertrand de Jouvenel proposed *L'Economie Administrée*, and Fayol wrote on industrial administration in terms comparable to Taylor in the United States, whereas a whole new generation of technicians (often trained at Ecole Polytechnique) developed new ideas on the role of the state.

The early 1920s however can be seen as a failed period insofar as the inventive minority that worked in Paris, many from foreign shores, and many having started to produce before the war, could not seek to resolve the deep social and ideological divisions, fed by the sheer exhaustion of the aftermath of war, that tore the French population apart. This brought a feeling of protectionism and provincialism of a France entrenched into its colonial Empire—the political impotence of alternating right-wing governments and center-left ones (especially the 1924–26 Cartel of the Lefts lead by the so-called radicals of Herriot, more interested in managing their power) was signaled for instance by the failure of the occupation of the Ruhr by the French from 1923 to 1930 to resolve the German war reparation issue, or by the inability of the various governments to resolve economic woes and modernize society. The period was also marked by numerous strikes and social movements, as economic reconstruction stumbled through a series of financial and monetary difficulties that deepened towards the middle of the decade.

It was only toward the end of the 1920s that for a few years there was a sense of respite in the continued crisis. The conservative governments of "national union," from 1926 to 1929, first led by Poincaré, briefly gave impetus to the economy by strengthening the Franc and restoring investors' confidence at a time when the reconstruction efforts began to bear fruits. Investments rose throughout the economy, and France became at this time the third industrial power in the world, equaling the United Kingdom for steel production, for instance, in 1929. At the same time some important reforms finally modernized social relations, especially the development of a generalized social insurance system and social retirement pension schemes. In the same positive line, new art expression such as surrealism and modernism (design and architecture progressed rapidly at the end of the 1920s, with new names acquiring popularity such as Le Corbusier) started to have a wider impact. If surrealism signaled the critical rejection of prewar rationalism in the arts, parallel changes also affected the rest of the intellectual life. This period was particularly productive in terms of scientific and philosophical developments. In sciences such as physics and chemistry, French scientists participated in the world revolution in the study of matter, with the works of the Joliot-Curies and Langevin on

radioactivity and de Broglie on quantum mechanics. In philosophical and epistemological terms, similar moves are made. Indeed, here too the old positivist rationalism is rejected (following Bergson's work) with the work of philosophers such as Jankelevich; Freud finally translated in 1926, and phenomenology recognized at the end of the 1920s. Anthropology also takes wing, for instance, with the recognition of the work of Marcel Mauss. New historical research receives a considerable impetus with the launch in 1929 of the *Ecole des Annales* of Braudel, Febvre, and Bloch. History went beyond factual description and ideological frameworks and, through the use of new historiography methods, reintroduced ordinary people and societies in their long-term environment.

However, even in this period, the ambivalence of French intellectual life continued, stuck between its retrenchment in national, traditional debates and the explosion of modernity. A typical example is literature. Most of the great novelists of the interwar period, from the older generation such as Martin du Gard to the emerging generation such as Bernanos, Malraux, or Gide were not modernist form experimenters, of which there were very few (Céline is an example, with the first of his great works, *Voyage au bout de la nuit*, published in 1932), contrary to other art forms revolutionized by surrealism, abstraction, and modernism, such as poetry, painting, architecture, or music (with *Les Six*: the group of six, including Honegger, Milhaud, Poulenc, and Auric, who revolutionize modern music in an anti-Wagnerian move); however, most of these novelists involved themselves with social and political issues.

Then the 1930s cut short the prospects of a more settled society. The Great Depression was a watershed in France as in the rest of the world—however, its impact only started to be felt in France in 1931, which saw a deep recession, a fall of living standards, and mass unemployment in industrial areas, with its dole corteges and *soupes populaires*. However, the crisis was not only social and economic. The political impotence of this period is particularly noticeable, and there was a growing lack of confidence into the institutions and the politicians of the Third Republic. After the retirement of Poincaré in 1929, the successive center-right governments of national union, none of them lasting for long, are only remarkable for lack of ambition and their immobility facing the economic crisis. In 1932, the various political clans constituting the left-of-center radicals won the parliamentary elections, under the direction of the old radical chief Herriot, and formed governments noticeable for their application of deflationary economic policies and restrictive public budgets (adding to the day-to-day difficulties of the population). These governments were also particularly unstable. In 1933, not less than four successive governments were constituted. Within this growing sense of crisis, unease was added by a succession of scandals that culminated in the Stavisky scandal in 1934, which discredited the whole political class in the eyes of many. All this gave a good pretext to the extreme-right organized *ligues*, the backbone of which consisted of World War I veterans (including the most important of them, with some two million members, the "*Croix-de-Feu*"), and to *Action Française* to march on the National Assembly in February 1934, intending a coup.

These events show how polarized French society had become. Indeed, it was becoming increasingly difficult not to choose on what ideological and political side to be and act. The political engagement of a majority of intellectuals, scientists, and artists in France in the 1930s is indeed one of the main characteristics of the period. The Catholic church itself, this cornerstone of French society, at the time appeared to be torn between a traditional rejection of modernity and various attempts at humanist and social approaches to the same modernity. This is clearly illustrated by the trajectory of two central figures—Jacques Maritain, the Thomist theologian, and Emmanuel Mounier, the essayist and creator of personalism, a Christian humanist social philosophy that was very influential from the 1930s to the 1960s. Maritain, who came from Bergsonism, came close to social Catholicism in the early 1930s, but from a position defending Thomas Aquinas's natural law, thus rejecting most aspects of modernism. Mounier, on the contrary, embraced modernism and defined personalism as a social philosophy engaged with the world, that seeks to steer clear of pure capitalism as well as communism, in a humanist attempt to see the individual and society as inextricably linked.

A large proportion of intellectuals in the early 1930s saw fascism and Nazism as the prime menace to democracy and freedom in Europe—a broad alliance was constituted in 1934 to counter the rise of such movements. The *Comité de Vigilance des Intellectuels Antifascistes (CVIA)* was a very broad church, the manifesto of which, first published in the NRF, was signed by people as different as Gide, Barbusse, Giono, Breton, Febvre, Malraux, Joliot-Curie, Langevin, Martin du Gard, Rolland, and so on. The presence of a large number of sympathizers (*compagnons de route*) and members of the Communist party had the committee accused of being a stooge for the Comintern and Stalin. There is evidence that these were intending to use the Committee for their own purpose, but at the time, it was a genuine broad church expressing a widespread worry that the Hitler and Mussolini regimes were bringing the whole of Europe closer to the abyss. It was also a reaction against the recent anti-

parliamentarian demonstrations of February 1934. And, in a way, it was a prefiguration of the alliance of the political forces on the left, from the radicals to the communists, with the socialists of the SFIO constituting the most important force, in the popular front coalition constituted in 1935, and which won the election in 1936. However, the CVIA would soon explode in multiple tendencies, with divisions between pacifists (such as Giono, Weil, and Alain, or extreme-left people such as Marceau-Pivert) and confrontationists, between communists and all the others, between partisans of intervention in Spain and those who opposed it, and so on. These divisions again surfaced at the time of the Munich Agreement in 1938.

The importance of the CVIA should not hide the fact that, on the other side were many intellectuals and thinkers such as Brasillach, Drieu la Rochelle, and the ex-communist Deat going towards the extreme right, fascinated by Nazism and Hitler; others tempted but not engaging fully (Montherlant, Léautaud); and still others engaging because of anti-Semitism (Rebatet and his popular weekly *Je Suis Partout*). Indeed, a "Manifesto of Intellectuals for Peace in Europe and the Defense of the Western World" for the support of Mussolini and his colonial conquest was created when he invaded Abyssinia in 1935, with expected signatories such as future collaborationists Bonnard, Drieux la Rochelle, and Brasillach; extreme-right intellectuals such as Maurras, Maulnier, and Daudet; but also many such as Marcel Aymé, Pierre Mac Orlan, or André Suarès. Maurras was then calling for a "national revolution" that would be nationalist, anti-democratic, and totalitarian insofar as it would recreate society along traditional casts and hierarchies in a more radical approach than the "national revolution" of Vichy.

French people were then pitted more and more into two camps, with the left (including the Communists) regrouped into a popular front and winning the parliamentary elections in May 1936. This brought a vast movement of occupations and strikes around the country, with the new Left government of Léon Blum (supported by, but not including the Communists) negotiating with *patronat* (business associations) and implementing a number of basic social and labor reforms such as paid holidays, limitation of the working week, union rights, and the like. Extreme-right leagues were dissolved. At the same time the hatred of a large proportion of anti-Semitic, conservative traditionalists concentrated on Blum, as anti-Semitism and xenophobia continued to be a major issue in the second half of the 1930s, with many press organs devoted to its promotion. Maurras and Rebatet became wild in their denunciation of "the Jew Blum."

The Blum government introduced a number of reforms modernizing French society and its economy that prefigure many aspects of the general transformation of the after war period. This is also true at social level, which saw reforms such as the forty-hour week, widespread paid annual leave, and so on, resulting in the generalization of a new modern lifestyle. Modernization also happened in economic terms, with a number of nationalizations and elements of economic planning put in place by the administration, including a number of policies at the cultural level, with a growing role given to public administrations and the State for the promotion and development of *culture populaire* that would become a feature of the 1950s and 1960s (especially in the subvention of associations, youth cultural groups, and theater). The second half of the 1930s, indeed, despite (and in many circumstances because of) political engagement, saw an explosion in many forms of expression. The historian Serge Berstein wrote about the 1930s being "a pivotal period" that "is the time of an immense intellectual bustling." An iconic example is, obviously, Picasso's *Guernica*, a visceral reaction to the Spanish Civil War tragedy. In other arts, similar explosions occurred, for instance the proliferation of now classic films of a new generation of directors such as Renoir, Clair, and so on. Cinema, as a mass art, also participated to social movements through these authors, although others (such as Duvivier or Gremillon) carefully avoided direct engagement in their films.

However, the failure of the *Front Populaire* was soon to become apparent, domestically as well as on the international scene. Domestically, the economic crisis was not to be fully resolved and unemployment would persist up to the war. Politically the alliance would be weakened at the parliamentary level, with new coalitions and new governments coming in (mostly under Prime Minister Daladier). At the international level, the Blum government found itself in great difficulties over the Spanish Civil War, which started in July 1936. It was thought that the government would have helped the legal, democratically elected republican government. At the end it bowed to British pressure and agreed to nonintervention despite German support of Franco. The international weakness of the French governments (already signaled by the lack of reaction to the re-armament of the Ruhr by Hitler in March 1936) then would become a feature of international French involvement, and this would culminate in the Munich Agreement in September 1938. Although the governments since 1936 had started to reinforce French armament industries (especially the air force), there was little doubt that France was quite unprepared for a new war with the Axis. This was the case militarily, but also socially. The French, deeply divided ideologically, intellectually, and politically, were not prepared to fight for a system that was op-

posed by so many, for so many diverse reasons. When, finally, Poland was invaded in September 1939 and France and the United Kingdom declared war on Germany, starting the tragic comedy of the *Drôle de guerre*, it was as if all the fears and doubts of the French suddenly were revealed. The only ray of hope, in this final descent to hell, was that in the multiple intellectual revolutions of the two interwar decades, tools for the distant postwar peace regeneration had been forged.

FRANCOIS NECTOUX

See also **Alain; Maurice Barres; Henri Bergson; Georges Bernanos; Marc Bloch; Andre Breton; Lucien Febvre; Andre Gide; Drieu La Rochelle; Jacques Maritain; Charles Maurras; Marcel Mauss; Andre Suares; Simone Weil**

Further Reading

Berstein, Serge, *La France des années 30*, Paris: Armand Colin, 1988

Hughes, Stuart H., *The Obstructed Path: French Social Thought in the Years of Desperation 1930–1960*, Transaction, 2001

Jackson, Julian, *The Politics of Depression in France 1932–1936*, Cambridge: Cambridge University Press, 2002

Nadeau, Maurice, *The History of Surrealism*, London: Penguin Books, 1973

Prost, Antoine, *In the Wake of War: "Les Anciens Combattants" and French Society 1914–1939*, London: Berg, 1992

Rémond, René, Paris: Notre Siècle, Fayard, 1988

Sirinelli, Jean-François, *Intellectuels et passions françaises*, Paris: Fayard, 1990

Weber, Eugen, *The Hollow Years: France in the 1930's*, Sinclair Stevenson, 1995

HISTORICAL SURVEY: 1939–1968

There can be few periods in French history when the country experienced such contrasts in fortune as during the period 1939–1968. France underwent a series of crises beginning with World War II, extending through a period of decolonization, and leading to a decline in her world status. Political instability was a constant backdrop prior to the late 1950s. Despite all these problems, the country benefited from a period of unparalleled economic growth and engaged in a process of modernization. French identity was in mutation. Urbanization, Europeanization, and immigration offered both advantages and challenges. Not everyone accepted these challenges, and France remained a country prone to political disturbances. In their different ways the Poujadists and the students of May 1968 each challenged the changing nature of French society.

It is difficult to view World War II as anything other than a disaster for the French. It was on September

3, 1939 that the Allies reluctantly declared war on a bellicose Nazi Germany. Throughout the 1930s Hitler had shown his ruthless determination to avenge the Versailles settlement and to expand Germany eastwards. When Poland was threatened it was realized that Hitler's continued attacks on neighboring countries threatened the security of the whole of Europe. But the Allied ultimatum securing Poland's frontiers was left unanswered by the Nazis, who marched into the country. War had become inevitable. At the time war was declared the French army was viewed by many as the best in the world. Once the Germans launched an attack in the west in May 1940, this army collapsed within six weeks, incurring casualties of around 100,000 men in the process. The defeat was inspired largely by the outdated tactics of France's aged military leadership. They underestimated the importance of tanks and aircraft to modern warfare and were under the mistaken belief that the enemy would not be able to penetrate the poorly guarded Ardennes forest.

The humiliation was only just beginning. The country was carved up into zones by the Axis powers. The North was directly occupied, or in the case of Alsace-Moselle annexed, by the Germans. A southern zone retained an autonomous status until it was in turn occupied by the Axis as a response to the Allied landings in French North Africa in November 1942. The World War I hero, Marshall Henri-Philippe Pétain, who had obtained mythical status because of his defense of Verdun in 1917, became head of a government based in the spa town of Vichy. Pétain was granted full powers by the National Assembly, meeting on July 10, 1940, and used his position to ensure the abolition of parliament. His Vichy government attempted to introduce a reactionary and authoritarian political program, known as the *Révolution Nationale*, which turned its back on Republican and democratic tradition and included the persecution of certain social or political categories. Jews, foreigners, Freemasons, Communists, trade unionists, and Socialists all experienced varying degrees of persecution. Pétain, together with his prime ministers, naval officer François Darlan and the scheming politician Pierre Laval, actively sought out collaboration with the Axis powers. The occupiers were determined to milk France by demanding massive payments to cover the cost of occupation, but they were undoubtedly surprised at the degree of cooperation offered. Vichy helped to organize the deportation of 76,000 Jews, the round-up of workers to be sent to Germany, and the arrest of resisters. Acting in place of the Nazis was supposed to assure administrative sovereignty, but it undoubtedly facilitated the occupier's designs.

Against this negative backdrop there were some more positive aspects of the occupation. Although the population continued to worship Pétain personally, Vichy's divisive policies rapidly earned it widespread public contempt. Indeed, hostility was so strong that in August 1941, one of the Marshall's radio broadcasts was used to try to combat what Pétain referred to as the "ill wind" of discontent that was sweeping over France.

More active opposition came from resistance movements and networks. Debate has raged as to how effective they were. Most of the attention has focused on military questions. Some local liberation did take place without direct Allied intervention. Indeed, much of the southwest was freed before the Allies arrived. But this was often because the Germans had withdrawn. It is certainly true that the Resistance could not have liberated France without allied help. Despite their enthusiasm, they did not have sufficient weaponry to finish the job. In Paris, for instance, they got the Germans to the point of accepting a temporary truce in August 1944, but had to plea with the Allies to send in the heavy artillery to finally oust their occupier. Lack of equipment also limited the sabotage efforts of the Resistance. They did manage to blow up some German military installations and equipment and they certainly did slow down German convoys when they headed for the war zone after D-Day. But the feeling remains that if they had had more arms and explosives they could have done this job even more effectively. However, the military contribution of the resistance should not be restricted to just their role in fighting or sabotage. Probably their most important military role was in the form of espionage. Military and political intelligence is vital to any would-be invader keen to limit their own losses. Knowing where the enemy is and how well armed is of crucial importance and this sort of information is best collected from behind enemy lines. Volunteers had begun plying the Allies with political and military intelligence from 1940 and this was slowly integrated into Allied planning of future operations.

The true significance of the Resistance was probably more social and political than it was military. Movements disseminated patriotic and/or anti-fascist propaganda that provided alternative sources of information to those featured in heavily censored official outlets. Help offered to victims of persecution was vital if France was to be able to reaffirm its claim to being a country of refuge and one of the cradles of human rights. The fact that France had one of the lowest rates of Jewish deportation of any occupied country, despite its own government's involvement in the persecution, is generally attributed in part to shelter offered by the population. Providing refuge and assistance was even more in evidence with regard to French people to be sent off to work in Germany. This seriously undermined the *Service du Travail Obligatoire* imposed by the Germans in February 1943. The Resistance was creating a society in opposition to Vichy and the Nazis. It also ensured that political structures were ready to fill the vacuum once Vichy had been removed.

Vichy compromises left a terrible legacy of hatred. Those who had not shared France's suffering or had enriched themselves under the occupation were singled out for public criticism and in some cases hunted down. Between 1943 and 1946, about 20,000 women were humiliated by having their heads shaved in the public square. For the most part they were being punished for "horizontal collaboration" but in other cases their crime was having provided the Germans with information or black market goods or simply having lived or worked in proximity to the occupiers. The necessary emphasis placed by historians in recent years on this question of shaved women should not allow one to forget that men were also subject to brutal reprisals at the liberation. Lynching could turn very nasty. Beatings of those suspected of collaboration or profiteering were commonplace and there were many examples of nameless bodies being left in ditches. An estimated 9,000 men and women were killed without due recourse to the legal process between 1944 and 1945. The majority of these abuses occurred either before the liberation or in its immediate aftermath. Isolated incidents of this kind continued into 1946 but slowed down as legal procedures were put in place to deal with those who had "betrayed" the country.

Re-establishing Republican order was a priority for the liberation authorities from the outset. At a national level an *Haute Cour de Justice* was set up to try 100 Vichy ministers and senior administrators. These trials led to three executions: former Vichy premier Pierre Laval, the head of the *Milice* Joseph Darnand, and the Vichy ambassador to the occupied territories, Fernand de Brinon. A further fifteen death sentences were handed out by this court but not put into effect. In five cases this was because the sentence was subsequently commuted (including Pétain's), and in a further ten because the trial had taken place in absentia. At a regional level "*cours de justice, chambres civiques*" and "*tribunaux militaires*" tried those further down the social ladder. This led to a further 1,500 executions and a large number of prison sentences. In addition to the purge carried out by the courts an *épuration administrative* removed suspect individuals from state administrations. The publicity surrounding the recent trials of the former Vichy administrator Maurice Papon, the *Milicien* Paul Touvier, and the proceedings against the former police chief René Bousquet (assassinated in 1993 before he could stand trial) have led some to believe that the purge of the immediate post-war was incomplete. It should be noted, however, that the accusation of excessive zeal has also been leveled against

the liberation purges both by those sympathetic to Vichy and by some resisters (for example, the writer Jean Paulhan).

Inequality of treatment is a frequent recrimination. There has always been a suspicion that those lower down the ladder were more likely to called to account. With regard to the *épuration administrative* this is certainly untrue. The proportion of senior administrators removed from their posts was far greater than that of their subordinates. However, when it came to court proceedings those in more senior positions certainly had an advantage. Often they were able to call on powerful contacts. They had more money to ensure the best lawyers. The simple fact that they had been in a position of greater influence usually meant that their cases were more complicated. This meant that they generally came to trial later and it is accepted that the justice meted out by the courts was much harsher in 1944 than in subsequent years. Having money and influence allowed some individuals to hide in the crucial early months after the Liberation. A wartime record of anti-communism was also more likely to be perceived harshly in the early trials than in those that took place in 1947 and 1948, when the onset of the cold war led to a reassessment. It is generally recognized today that the post-liberation trials did not give sufficient weight to the question of anti-Semitism. The full enormity of the Nazi crimes in this respect had yet to sink in. Many French Jews, for their part, were reluctant to put too much emphasis on this question because after four years of being discriminated against they were often keen for a return to the status of "normal" citizen. A lot of the foreign Jews, who were the principle victims of the extermination program, were unable to testify either because they had returned to their country of origin or because they had been gassed to death in the horrific Nazi camps. Overall, it was inevitable that the purge procedures were imperfect. They took place against the backdrop of contradictory pressures. On the one hand, there was a desire to punish those who had transgressed accepted behavior and to prevent vigilante justice. On the other hand was the need to use the expertise of many of these individuals in the rebuilding process and to see a return to normality as quickly as possible.

Political rebuilding meant not just eradicating Vichy but also creating new structures to fill the power vacuum. With regard to creating a new constitution, there was a broad consensus on two points. First, the new regime should be democratic and republican. Second, there should be no return to the Third Republic whose credibility had been left in tatters by the corruption of the 1930s and even more so by its inability to ward off defeat in 1940. Looking beyond the consensus on these two issues, it was not difficult to detect important divergences on the shape of the new system. Fundamentally there were three constitutional viewpoints represented within the provisional government that assured the interim between 1944 and 1946. The position of General de Gaulle was that the new regime should be based on a strong executive able to act as arbiter by standing above party politics. There was deep suspicion about such a position. Republicans traditionally viewed strong government as one step away from dictatorship. In 1940s France, they did not have to look back to the mid-nineteenth century example of Bonaparte to justify this fear: they had had recent personal experience of it. De Gaulle was so frustrated at not finding a wider audience for his viewpoint that he resigned from his post of President of the Provisional Government in January 1946. The second viewpoint was that of the left-wing parties: the socialists and communists. They were pressing for an all-powerful parliament with the scrapping of the second chamber (the Senate) because it was traditionally dominated by rural conservatives. But the Left failed to get their proposals adopted by popular referendum. The path was clear for a third constitutional position. This rejected a strong executive but maintained the Senate. It was this compromise that was finally adopted by referendum in 1946.

The general elections of 1946 were the first in which women could vote. The new assembly showed some differences with prewar parliaments. Having sufficient resistance credentials became a prerequisite for those wishing to enter the political arena at the Liberation. The notion of scrapping the old political formations in favor of new structures born directly from the Resistance was briefly considered. The idea quickly fell out of favor and the former resisters were left to join the re-emerging traditional parties if they wished to participate in the political process. There was, however, a shift in the balance of power among these parties. The Right was largely discredited by association with the collaborating Vichy governments. The right, which now emerged was significantly altered because the Catholics, who made up its traditional backbone, were broadly reconciled to the Republic for the first time since 1789. A new right wing force, the MRP, was born to represent these new views. On the left the socialist re-emerged, but the communists were the real winners. Forgotten were the shameful compromises of the 1939–41 period, when the PCF had endorsed the Nazi-Soviet nonaggression pact much to the embarrassment of many of its militants. Instead the focus fell on the undoubted bravery and heroic sacrifice of the period 1941–44. The party adopted the slogan of the *parti des 75,000 fusillés* (party of the 75,000 executed). That such a figure clearly exaggerated the real communist losses did not prevent the communists from emerging as the biggest single force in French politics.

Despite these changes, the Fourth Republic quickly came to be seen as too close a relation of the prewar regime. Its governments were ineffectual, short-lived, and seemed incapable of imposing their authority on parliament. The initial period of three party rule (communists, socialists, MRP) ran into trouble with the onset of the cold war. In 1947, the communists were expelled from the government under American pressure. Corruption was a negative aspect of the Fourth Republic, as was its failure to deal decisively with the major crises of the period—most notably that of decolonization. In 1958 de Gaulle agreed to return to power but he made his return conditional on the adoption of a new constitution. The Fifth Republic thus came into effect on January 8, 1959. In keeping with de Gaulle's wish that the President should not be limited to a role of "inaugurating chrysanthemums," significant power was henceforth invested in the resident of the Elysées Palace.

With the creation of this Republic France had a stable political system. However, she was also still looking for ways to halt her diplomatic decline and to play a real role in international affairs. Hopes were pinned on three possible sources of regaining her status: the Empire, closer European cooperation, and the regeneration of the French economy.

During World War II the Empire had once again showed its importance. Colonial troops had made a significant contribution in the fighting of 1939–40 as they would in the French army of 1944–45. The struggle between Vichy and de Gaulle's free French to take over the colonies underlined the symbolic importance of these territories. Once the Americans had wrestled control of North Africa from Vichy, de Gaulle rapidly left his British exile for the "French" soil of Algiers. For most Gaullists, and for many other French people, hopes of re-establishing great power and status rested on drawing on the resources and diplomatic value of the colonies.

However, the situation within the colonies had been profoundly modified by the war. From the rapidity of France's defeat in 1940 nationalists drew the conclusion that the colonizer was vulnerable. Even after the armistices of 1940 anti-French sentiment was stirred up in the colonies by propaganda disseminated by the Italians, Spanish, and Germans, who either coveted these colonies or were simply keen to keep the French weak and divided. After the allied landing in North Africa the Americans sent round tracts in Arabic stressing the advantages of self-determination. The fallacy of white supremacy had been underlined by Japanese gains in the East.

The inability of French leaders to accurately assess the sentiments in the colonies was shown at the Brazzaville conference of January 1944. The assembled governors of France's West African colonies discussed the possibility of a degree of administrative decentralization. This was a far cry from what nationalists were demanding and any assertion of their rights to independence was fiercely repressed. A nationalist revolt in the Sétif area of Algeria in May 1945 was crushed by the colonial authorities, resulting in thousands of deaths. Worse was to follow in Madagascar in 1947. Here the French made use of a tactic of colonial divide and rule. When Madagascans protested for greater independence, French-led Senegalese troops were sent in to put down the uprising. Almost 90,000 Madagascans were slaughtered. To this day relations between the two former colonies are strained. In 1997, the Madagascan singing group Tarika issued an album entitled "*Son égal*"—a deliberate play on words to show that this was the first tentative step at reconciliation. But it was Indochina (Laos, Cambodia, and Vietnam) that first managed to break off the shackles of French imperialism. Indochina had been occupied by Japanese troops in July 1941. It was local nationalists who managed to liberate the area in 1945. Their leader, Ho Chi Minh, then declared independence from France. French attempts to reassert control by gunboat diplomacy were not appreciated and a bitter battle ensued. It only ended when the French were defeated militarily at Dien Bien Phu in 1954.

The loss of Indochina was a military humiliation, but in mainland France it was not felt as keenly as subsequent events in Algeria. Initially the campaign to keep Algérie Française, even if this meant using force, was popular in France. This North African colony held a special place in French affections. It was the oldest and most assimilated of French colonies. It was also geographically very close. Indeed, Marseille is as close to Algiers as it is to Paris. There were about one million European settlers in Algeria and this encouraged a sense of attachment. It also encouraged intransigence. Once the War of liberation began in November 1954 the French settlers and army leaders in Algeria would resist all attempts at imposing moderate reform from Paris. Such intransigence merely hardened the resolve of the nationalists, who became even more radical.

The fighting between 1954 and 1962 resulted in the deaths of up to a million Algerians. The "events in Algeria" (the French government refused to acknowledge a state of war) became increasingly violent. It should not be imagined that all the brutality was on the French side. The main group of Algerian nationalists, the *Front de Libération Nationale* (FLN), used brutal methods both against the colonizers and compatriots willing to appease the French. But the practices of torture and summary executions engaged in by the settlers and units of the French army were the most

subject to criticism. Their intransigence appeared as a failure to acknowledge the wider process of decolonization since the war. Their use of torture came less than twenty years after the French had been complaining of similar methods being used on them by the Nazi occupier. Their behavior also highlighted a paradox of French colonial policy. France, the country of universal human rights, the professor of the values of liberty, equality, and fraternity, had utterly failed to apply these noble principles to its own colonies. Such hypocrisy is rarely appreciated. It was not only international opinion that turned against the colonial army. As the war became bloodier support in France began to dwindle. French intellectuals as diverse as Sartre and Mauriac felt it their historic role to speak openly of their disgust. Behind French disenchantment with the war was also the unpopularity of the conscription of three million soldiers to the front line. The failure to find and impose a resolution to the Algerian crisis led to the collapse of the unstable Fourth Republic. France held true to its tradition of calling in strong personalities at moments of crisis and it was at this juncture that de Gaulle was lured out of his self-imposed political exile.

De Gaulle's return to power was not necessarily programmed to put an end to colonial presence in Algeria. But it was hoped it would provide more resolute direction and a clear set of answers to the dilemma. In fact the General himself seemed initially unsure of the direction to be taken. However, he came to the realization that France must withdraw from the colony if a favorable postcolonial settlement was to be reached that would allow the former colonizer a continued influence in the area. The first public step toward this new strategy was his speech of September 16, 1959 in which he declared himself favorable to self-determination in Algeria. Negotiations with the FLN dragged on until a ceasefire was agreed on March 19, 1962. By the terms of the Evian agreements France was to be allowed continued use of some Algerian ports and military installations and preferential access to the country's oil and gas. In return Algeria gained independence. De Gaulle's progressive withdrawal from the colony angered the settlers and some parts of the army. The President had to repel an army putsch in Algeria in April 1961 and to survive a series of subsequent assassination attempts. His personal prestige and the strengthened position accorded to the President by the new constitution allowed him to weather the storm and to successfully impose a settlement. Similar withdrawals were also agreed for other parts of the French empire in the early 1960s such as Senegal and Madagascar.

Running parallel to this decolonization was the creation of European structures. France was a key player in the shift toward European integration. She was one of the six signatories of the Treaty of Rome in 1957, which established the Common Market (EEC). There were three essential underlying reasons for French keenness to participate in a European superstructure. Successive Franco-German conflicts since 1870 encouraged French leaders to examine other ways of guaranteeing her security. Greater cooperation with Germany would surely remove the threat of these recurrent and devastating wars. The common market also seemed to offer massive advantages in the economic sphere both by opening up new markets for French produce and by offering protection to her farmers through the common agricultural policy. Finally, if European countries could cooperate sincerely within the context of a French led structure this would fulfill France's aim of securing her diplomatic strength as a counterweight to the two emerging superpowers. De Gaulle was therefore keen to maintain his country's dominance within this structure and that meant being very careful about admitting new members. His rejection of Britain's applications to join the EEC in 1961 and 1967 was as much about maintaining this dominance as it was about keeping out a country seen as "America's Trojan horse" and whose commonwealth ties were also likely to complicate inter-European trading relations. France's European policy was successful in its main objectives. It encouraged reconciliation with Germany, it improved French standing in the world, and it served as a backdrop to economic recovery.

Rebuilding the country economically had appeared extremely difficult in the immediate postwar. In 1945 the economic situation was dire. The country was only producing forty percent of what she had in 1938. Much of her infrastructure had been devastated during the occupation or the liberation. The Nazis' retreat was accompanied by destruction. Some parts of France had been badly and clumsily bombed by the Allies. Much of the population was without shelter and there were extreme shortages. Agricultural production was low and four years of depravations had exhausted the country's reserves.

It was from these unlikely beginnings that France made an impressive recovery. It is certainly true that the world economic climate was favorable. Most countries experienced growth during this time as they attempted to rebuild after years of destruction. At the same time rapidly improving technological progress fueled consumer demand everywhere. Western Europe also benefited from massive American investment. The United States had been criticized for its isolation from world politics in the 1930s. Now it would be criticized for its more hands-on approach. The Marshall Plan was designed to kick-start European econo-

mies to discourage them from falling into the communism, which now engulfed Eastern Europe. The French resented that aid was often accompanied by interference as the United States brought pressure to remove communist ministers from the French government in 1947 and financed the *Force Ouvrière* trade union movement as an anti-communist counterweight to the *Confédération Générale du Travail* (CGT). But the $15 billion aid itself was a vital component in economic resurrection.

Although French economic prosperity can be put in a wider context, it should also be noted that the country's growth rates in the 1950s and 1960s far outshone those of competitor nations, with the exception of Japan. This was due to two things. First, the French economy had more potential for growth because its structures were more backward. Second, she now embarked on an intelligent program of economic planning. The *Commissariat Général du Plan* was set up with just this purpose in mind in January 1946. Henceforth priority in the allocation of raw materials was given to those who accepted the planning schemes. France also embarked on a nationalization project, which encouraged nationalization. Some industries were nationalized because they had shamed themselves through collaboration. This was the case with the car factories of Louis Renault that had produced military vehicles for the Germans. The explanation for most nationalization, however, was that the industry was in a strategically important position: energy, transport, or finance. These newly nationalized industries were in the vanguard of economic recovery.

So successful was the French economy that the years 1945 to 1975 were christened *Les Trente Glorieuses*. By the 1960s annual growth rates of six percent a year were recorded. Exports grew from ten percent of production in 1958 to seventeen percent in 1970. As real wages shot up, living standards increased significantly. By the end of the 1960s most houses were equipped with televisions and refrigerators and the ownership of cars had increased dramatically. As the Citroen and the Renault 4 became symbols of the consumer society, the superhighway network was developed making rapid transportation of people and products a possibility. The country had become a consumer society.

Economic prosperity was accompanied by changing social structures. France had traditionally prided itself on being a rural country. The antiquated farming structures were modernized through cheap finances made available by the *Crédit Agricole*. Subsidies provided through the European common agricultural policy also encouraged investment for modernization. Modernized farming was less labor intensive. An unprecedented exodus from the countryside to the cities almost halved the rural workforce between the beginning of the 1960s and the mid 1970s. This was necessary too because the rapid economic growth had caused an urban labor shortage. Growth was not the only reason for a lack of workers in the cities. Despite the political rights gained by women at the liberation, women were increasingly withdrawing form the workplace. Beginning in 1943 and reaching its peak in 1946 an important increase in the birthrate meant that women were often reverting to their traditional childcare role. After 1946 the growth of the population continued at a slower rate and did not begin to fall off again until the mid-1960s. But the baby boom children would not begin to be available to the work force until the early 1960s. France's desperate need for workers encouraged a change in French immigration policy. A decline in immigration in the 1940s was followed by the beginnings of a rise from the mid-1950s. Foreigners represented 4.38 per cent of the French population in 1946 and 5.28 per cent in 1968. The nature of the immigration was changing too. There were proportionately fewer Europeans. Of European immigrants only the number of Portuguese increased significantly. The proportion of North Africans increased, in particular as concerns the influx from Algeria. Overall the population in France grew from 40.5 million in 1946, to 52.75 million in 1975.

Since the increases were in the urban not the rural areas, this meant the urgent question of accommodation needed to be addressed. About a quarter of the housing stock had been damaged or destroyed during the war. The state encouraged a massive investment in new housing. Whole towns such as Le Havre were virtually rebuilt. Elsewhere social housing programs were introduced as a way of reducing the pressure on inner-city slums and removing the eyesore of the shantytowns. France underwent a concrete revolution. Drab grey housing estates sprawled out from the cities like concrete acne. Their high-rises offered cheap mass housing. These constructions were perhaps an improvement on what went before, but they were soulless and had few amenities. The Parisian suburb of Sarcelles gave its name to a new illness "Sarcellite" referring to the psychological effects of living in these housing estates.

The ongoing changes in French society were contested from different sides. In the 1950s Pierre Poujade had led a movement of farmers to protest against the decline of the rural community in France. For entirely different reasons students and trade unions would take to the streets in May 1968 in a series of protests of unprecedented proportions.

Daniel Cohn-Bendit and the other leaders of the 1968 movement were drawn from what came to be known as the gauchistes. This was the non-Stalinist revolutionary left: anarchists, Maoists, and Trotsky-ites. They were campaigning for a radical restructuring of society along more libertarian and egalitarian lines. If their appeal went beyond the usual audience for these views this was because they tapped into a number of concerns of the moment regarding authoritarian politics, crises in the University system and a feeling of alienation from the consumer society.

Of course protests in the late 1960s were by no means just restricted to France. Countries as diverse as Czechoslovakia, Spain, and the United States all experienced similar phenomena. What was exceptional about the French case was both the violence of the protests and the fact that they were accompanied by a general strike that almost brought down the government, if not the regime.

Vietnam was the common denominator of international protest. Since the early 1960s America had progressively implicated itself in a war to prevent this former French colony from spreading communism throughout Southeast Asia. It was the American use of chemical weapons on the civilian population that so appalled the civilized world. This was the age of mass media and images of children burnt by napalm bombs were quickly disseminated. American foreign policy caused outrage. Not only was the policy brutal but it also seemed to fly in the face of political trends. Decolonization was the order of the day but here was the United States behaving like a colonizing power. The war was portrayed as a David and Goliath struggle: a superpower trying to dictate internal policy to a Third World minnow. Vietnam was a particularly sensitive subject in France because they had only just given up their colonial interests in the area.

The student leaders were not just opposed to the Americans but also to their superpower rivals in the Soviet Union. Stalinist communism was also seen as a form of oppression, as had so recently been seen in the crushing of demonstrations in Prague. In fact it was traditional authority in all its manifestations that they sought to combat. In France, de Gaulle had then been in power for eight years and much of the younger generation saw him as out of touch and authoritarian. In their eyes the proof of this was further given by the reaction of the authorities to the early stages of the student movement. The university authorities at Nanterre in the Paris suburbs were so infuriated at the disruption organized by a committee set up by Cohn-Bendit in March that they closed the campus. As a consequence the protest movement relocated to the Sorbonne in the center of the capital. The police were sent in to remove the protesters. As a result unrest spread to the student district (*Quartier Latin*). Baton-wielding police officers charged the protesters with gusto.

That the student movement had spread to such an extent was not just the result of student leaders seeking radical social change. Not all of those who joined the demonstrators wanted to opt out of the consumer society. Many were actually worried that the expansion of the university system as a result of the baby-boom generation would undermine the value of their diplomas when they entered the job market. Pressures on the university system were considerable. There had been 150,000 students in France in 1956–57. The intake had more than tripled in 1967–68 to reach the figure of 483,000. There had not been a similar increase in the number of teachers or the facilities available. Most campuses were chronically underfunded and under-equipped. Nanterre where the 1968 movement began was situated in the middle of a shantytown and did not even have a library.

The condition of university campuses was of little concern for the workers who decided to go on strike in the middle of May. Initially their unions did express some sympathy with respect to the fact that the students had been subjected to brutal police methods. They also shared the belief that de Gaulle had been in power too long. But the concerns of the unions were actually largely materialistic. They felt that the economic richness of the decade had not been shared equally and indeed these deficiencies in redistribution of wealth had furthered existing inequalities. They also saw an opportunity. The reaction of the government when faced with the student movement had oscillated between repression and conciliation. Ministers had not spoken with one voice and had displayed hesitancy. Governmental inability to come to grips with this student protest led the workers' unions to believe that the time was right to raise their demands for better pay and a greater say in the running of factories. As up to 10 million blue- and white-collar workers put down their tools, student leaders hoped to be able to reach out to them in a gesture of solidarity. The workers' unions were unresponsive. For them the students were basically middle class and likely to be the future generation of industry leaders. What's more is that the student leaders, with their "gauchist," positions, had been overtly critical of the communist party to which the biggest workers' biggest confederation, the CGT, was affiliated. Politically and socially, reconciliation between the two groups of protesters bordered on the impossible and the two movements remained quite separate.

While the students dominated the protests, the authorities had seemed unsure how to put an end to it. Student protest on this scale was uncharted territory. Ironically once the workers entered the fray the government seemed more sure of its footing. It had more experience of trying to resolve industrial disputes and hoped to be able to take advantage of the divisions between students and workers. Prime Minister Georges Pompidou convened a meeting of trade union leaders and representatives of the employers. This took place in the rue de Grenelle in Paris between May 25 and 27 and offered important concessions. These would actually be rejected by the workers, but by that stage events had moved onto a different political level. The center-left political parties had begun to try to hijack events. Two of the leaders, Pierre Mendès-France and François Mitterrand, publicly discussed at the Charléty stadium in Paris the possibility of a left-wing government to replace de Gaulle, who seemed to have lost his touch. On May 29, two days after the Charléty rally, de Gaulle shocked everyone by vanishing for several hours without informing even the Prime Minister of his whereabouts. He had flown to Germany to meet with one of his senior Generals, General Massu. The discussion was probably designed to make sure he had the loyalty of the army. His disappearance caused a psychological shock. His return was triumphant. He came back more resolute and immediately dissolved the National Assembly. The resultant general elections were a massive success for the Gaullists, who were returned to power with a huge majority. Undoubtedly the fear of disorder had triumphed but any thought that the result was a long-term victory for de Gaulle was dispelled the following year when the results of a referendum forced de Gaulle out of office.

May 1968 was probably not the ultimate cause of de Gaulle's demise. After all, the nation had shown signs of weariness with his overlong tenure of power in 1965 when, against all expectation, François Mitterrand had forced the Presidential election into a second round. But no one could claim that May 1968 did not leave a lasting legacy. It is sometimes claimed that May 1968 was the starting point for views such as feminism or concern for the environment. This is of course untrue. Feminist movements had been active even before World War II and despite setbacks in women's position since the heady days of 1945, writers such as Simone de Beauvoir had kept a feminist tradition alive. Ecological concern for the environment also predated 1968. For example, in 1963 France had finally created a national park (at Vanoise near Chambéry), eighty-nine years after the Americans had invented the concept at Yellowstone. But May 1968 undoubtedly became a symbol of a wider period of substantial change. It also served as a catalyst for accelerating these changes and therefore radicalized many of the existing ideas. Those who participated in the May 1968 events were convinced they had participated in events of significant historical importance. Although their revolution failed in the immediate it certainly had a long-lasting effect on attitudes and identity in France.

The questions raised in May 1968 would have validity beyond the France of the 1960s because they are fundamental interrogations about the structure of human society in an industrialized world.

SIMON KITSON

See also **Simone de Beauvoir; Jean Paulhan; Jean-Paul Sartre**

Further Reading

Berstein, Serge, *The Republic of De Gaulle, 1958–69*, Cambridge: Cambridge University Press, 1993

Cole, Alistair, *French Politics and Society*, London: Longman, 1997

Forbes, Jill and Michael Kelly (editors), *French Cultural Studies: an Introduction*, Oxford: Oxford University Press, 1995

Gildea, Robert, *France since 1945*, Oxford: Oxford University Press, 1997

Jackson, Julian, *France: the Dark Years*, Oxford: Oxford University Press, 2001

Kedward, H. R., *Occupied France*, Oxford: Blackwell, 1985

Larkin, Maurice, *France since the Popular Front, Government and People, 1936–1996*, Oxford: Oxford University Press, 1997

McMillan, James F., *Twentieth Century France: Politics and Society, 1898–1991* Arnold, 1992

Reynolds, Sian and William Kidd (editors), *Contemporary French Cultural Studies*, Arnold, 2000

Rioux, Jean-Pierre, *The Fourth Republic, 1944–58*, Cambridge: Cambridge University Press, 1987

Stovall, Tyler, *France since the Second World War*, London: Pearson, 2002

Vinen, Richard, *France, 1934–1970*, Palgrave, 1996

HISTORICAL SURVEY: 1968–PRESENT

A difficulty in tracing the relation of French thought to social and political events over the past thirty or so years is evidently the proximity of this near history but more significantly the complexity of the relation between thought and the event. Thought does not respond directly to the event; neither does it have any directly causative role. The dimension in which thought exists is as much related to its present moment as it is to a historical dimension in which trajectories may be plotted over a far longer time-scale. The past thirty years in French thought are as much characterized by this tension between the actual and the inactual hypothetical as any other period, although, to an extent, the fact that this period is a time of relative peace as opposed to war makes a difference. If, however, the period immediately preceding 1968 is for some the arena of an epistemological or paradigmatic shift, we can ask of the period since 1968: is there any evidence of such a shift in the shape of French thought as such, in the role of the intellectual, in the claims made or the horizons evoked in and by French thought? Are there specific events that radically alter the context and induce difference in thought? A historical survey of French thought since 1968 must address these questions, which concern the relation of thought to its time and to the event as such, as opposed to being locked on to transient moments in the fashion of thought.

This said, a salient characteristic of French thought in this period is the tendency toward the spectacularization, sensationalism, and "mediatization" of thought, a factor noted by Régis Debray and Pierre Bourdieu among others, which has more to do with the social use of thought than it does with thought itself. The ongoing meditations of writers such as Blanchot and Levinas, for example, are to be distinguished by their wider historical trajectory from the work of a writer like Bernard-Henri Lévy, whose work is significant for the larger context only at a particular moment in the mid-seventies.

A number of European countries witnessed student revolts in 1968, but in France the events took on a wider significance, leading to national strikes and a profound crisis in the country as a whole. The events of that May have given rise to a proliferation of interpretations, but a common emphasis is on the radical unexpectedness of what happened. This is to say that the spirit, which drove the students was not in any sense prepared for or informed by the critical and theoretical work, which in hindsight was pushing at epistemological boundaries. 1968 was not a symptom of the critique of the metaphysics of presence, of the death of man, or the dissolution of the subject. The references of the students were more likely to be figures such as Marcuse, Che, or Mao than Derrida, Foucault, or Lacan. More precisely, among the various different principles of contestation which informed the students, one could identify as significant the nonaffiliated leftist tradition of late 1950s groups such as *Arguments* or *Socialisme ou barbarie*, and specifically the *Internationale situationniste*, which critically combined their rigorous critique of bureaucratic capitalism with the contestatory oppositional spirit of surrealism. What was unexpected about 1968 was that, in a context of increased and increasing technologizing and bureaucratization of everyday life, and in the context of relative decline of faith in Soviet Communism, French society as a whole could be shaken by a moment of communal revolt that was not directed against specific issues but was a manifestation of contestation and community as such (this is Blanchot's interpretation). This gives rise to one thesis about 1968, which is that it was a kind of trauma, the trauma of "the event" which ruptured the structures of society and the structures of thought proposed for their analysis and critique. From this perspective, the "event" of 1968 does not take place for French thought when it takes place, but inscribes a long-term effect such that French thought attempts over the ensuing period to come to terms with *the event as such*, as a form of rupture or transcendence. This is consistent with a second thesis on the effects of 1968, which emphasizes its mobilizing effect; the events would from this perspective have induced a sense of possibility, the possibility of chance, to which one is enjoined to remain faithful. If the student revolt was eventually absorbed into the national strike and resolved through wage increases and short-term measures, the more generalized possibility of critical contestation, the vision it enabled, would inform the generation of intellectuals and writers in the next decade. A third thesis is expressed by Lacan in the "impromptu" lectures he gave at the University of Vincennes, post-1968, according to which what the students wanted was a master. If a graffiti in 1968 called upon its readers to "take their desires for reality," Lacanian psychoanalysis, although recognizing the cultural shock of the event, insists on the contingent but deep-rooted inscription of desire in structures of authority; this sets the agenda for the exploration of the relations between desire and power in the next decade, and after.

A significant emphasis of currents of thought in the 1970s is thus on the critique of the rigidity of structures as modes of authority, with an affirmation of the effects of rupture of something unaccountable from within a structural perspective. The late 1960s and early 1970s work of Jean-François Lyotard on libidinal economy, on the figural as opposed to the discursive, partakes thus in the critique of structuralism, and is informed by the effect of 1968. The publication of *Anti-Oedipe* by Gilles Deleuze and Felix Guattari in 1972 is a major event in French thought, in its affirmation of the possibility for the expression of intensities outside the structure of language and (against orthodox Freudianism) outside the family, and in its parallel emphasis on the capacity of power to (re-) inscribe intensity within fixed structures. From this perspective, power *is* structure, and structural thought complicit with power. But just to what extent does power infiltrate the structures of life? Michel Foucault, to whom is attributed the statement that the next century would be Deleuzian, for his part is led from the analysis of the structures, the archeology of knowledge, to the question of power and in *Surveiller et punir* (1975) and *La volonté de savoir* (1976) emphasizes the *productive* nature of power, its insidious seepage into and subtle management of "life," particularly the (sexual) life of the body. The next question, logically resulting, will be: given the ubiquity of power, what possibilities are there for thinking otherwise, and for living otherwise. To this extent Foucault's thought is indirectly affected by the moment of 1968.

The disconnection between the French Communist Party (PCF) and the students of May was both symptom and cause of the decline of faith in Soviet Communism as the horizon and reference point for Marxism. The intellectual wing of the Party underwent as a result a profound crisis, post-1968. Althusser's Marxist philosophy, already veering away from the insistence on determination by the economic infrastructure, is held in a difficult tension between its Maoist tendency (to affirm the role of the superstructure and the importance of cultural revolution) and the debatable necessity of remaining within the party. A generation of Althusserian Marxists is thus split, after 1968, between those who remain in the PCF and those who opt for various Maoist groupuscules. This is already a symptom of the fracturing of Marxism as a theoretical framework, and definitively of Soviet Communism as *the* intellectual reference point (an effect which can be traced over a longer term). Thus the revelations about the gulags of Solzenitzyn's *The Gulag Archipelago*, in 1974, were as disruptive as the slightly later emergence of the totalitarian realities of Maoist China on the occasion of Mao's death. The effect of this is evident in the paths taken by the review *Tel Quel* since 1968; from a strategic alliance with the PCF, preventing any direct support of the students, it opted in 1971 for a militant Maoism, which dominated its intellectual and theoretical positions in the first half of the 1970s and led to a visit to China by its principal adherents (including Barthes and Kristeva); then in 1976 almost overnight it dropped the reference to Mao, affirming thereafter the transcendence of the literary and theological exception. Rather than purely as a volte-face, this emphasis on transcendence can be seen as consistent with the previous faith in Maoism or more specifically in China, as the radically heterogenous alterability which will disrupt the status quo, and in this light *Tel Quel* is affected, *après-coup*, by the events of 1968, and Philippe Sollers (ostensibly the director of the journal) continued to affirm 1968 as a crucial and critical moment, whose consequences have not yet been reaped. A further symptom of the loss of faith in Marxism is the more short-lived but influential movement known as the *Nouvelle philosophie*; in the mid-1970s writers such as André Glucksmann and Bernard-Henri Lévy pronounced the complicity of Marxism with totalitarianism, signaling what would later be named by Lyotard in a different context as a loss of faith in "grand narratives," and a critical account of the (arguably) inevitable totalitarian consequences of these teleologies. The figure of the intellectual undergoes a significant shift in relation to the definitive decline of Soviet Communism as a reference point. Less linked to overarching philosophies of social revolution, the intellectual's role becomes far more punctual, as one can see in the social and political interventions of writers like Foucault and Deleuze in the 1970s over penal institutions (the *Groupe d'Information sur les Prisons*), or in relation to state policy regarding the events in Poland, or Derrida's involvement in *Groupe de Recherche sur l'enseignement de la philosophie* (GREPH) in relation to Giscard's policy of minimizing the status of philosophy in the curriculum.

These developments took place in a political context in which, under the presidency of Giscard d'Estaing, France took a proactive role in the promotion of the free market economy, but also in which the Socialist party under Mitterand became increasingly popular while moving steadily towards the center. The Socialist and Communist parties had in 1973 formed the "Union of the Left" and established a common program which, although it was to be abandoned at successive moments over the next eight years, was revived for the legislative elections of 1981, resulting in the triumph of the Left under the presidency of Mitterand from 1981 until 1995. The emphasis of the Socialist party under Mitterand eschewed the Marxist rhetoric of class and of work, and emphasized the ethos of individual freedom—with concomitant stress on ethnicity, the rights of women, the spirit of self-management ("autogestion") inherited too, in a sense, from 1968. Immediately after its election, whether as symbolic gesture or as the real engagement of a left politics, the government introduced measures that went against the majority views in the country: the abolition of the death penalty, an end to nuclear testing, major nationalization programs and reform of working conditions. The departure of the Communist deputies from the government in 1984, and the policies of economic constraint introduced from that point made it evident, however, that the Socialists were a party of social democracy rather than of radical change. 1968 seems thus to have given rise to two opposing legacies, that of individual freedom and reform, and that of an "enlargement of the field of the possible" (Sartre). The intermittent periods of "cohabitation" from 1986 signal to what extent party politics ha become increasingly centralized, the ethos of democratic individualism dominant, and political philosophies of radicalism marginalized.

If among certain writers thought continued, after the mid-1970s, to address the possibilities of critique and difference, in simpler terms of change in the conditions of subjection, among others the demise of frameworks or programs for social change or revolution leaves only a melancholic, ironic analysis of the sovereignty of technology and of the spectacle, and the dominance of individualism. The analysis of "postmodern" society through the 1980s and since, among writers such as Baudrillard, Lipovetsky, and Virilio, offers an arguably pessimistic account of our contemporaneity. The former group of thinkers, whose work continues to explore the possible, rather than the actual, may be characterized as turning towards different forms of ethics, rather than politics. Either as a concern with one's "hospitality" to the other or the social inclusion of specific others (in the work of Derrida, Levinas, Kristeva, Ricoeur, Cixous, and Todorov), or as an exploration of different modes of subjectivization and becoming (in Deleuze or Foucault), or as a militant emphasis on the universalizing potential of the radically incommensurate "event" (in Badiou), the critical role of the intellectual to explore ways of thinking differently continued and continues, but not in relation nor with reference to constraining teleological frameworks.

If one of the paths followed post-1968 in the policies of successive governments has been an apparent emphasis on individual freedom, self-management, and the rights of different social groups (whether or not this has been translated into the real), and to the extent that these were some of the affirmative emphases of the students in 1968, the events inform the development of feminism and of gay rights in France. The *Mouvement de libération des femmes* (MLF) was founded in 1971, as was the *Front homosexuel d'action révolutionnaire* (FHAR). But the same distinction, effectively between reform and revolution, remains in force here. In 1977 the Socialist Party produced a Bill of the rights of women, abortion was legalized under Giscard's presidency in 1975, but in writers such as Cixous, Irigaray, Kristeva, and particularly Monique Wittig, whose works rise in prominence throughout the 1970s and 1980s, there remains a tension between the demands of immediate social reform of the position of women and those of a wider reconfiguration of social and sexual relations. One of the more recent incidences of intervention in the social field on the part of French thinkers has been around the complex issue of social inclusion. Although Derrida, in *Spectres de Marx* and related texts, has argued for a hospitality to the other which does not sacrifice the horizon of a "democracy to come," Kristeva's work has consistently stressed the value of "foreignness." In a context of the rise in popularity of the Front National, the crisis in the immigration policies of the French State, the *affaire du foulard*, French thought has become increasingly dominated by issues of social inclusion and exclusion. The opening of the Berlin Wall in 1989 and the collapse of Soviet Communism in the USSR and in its satellites in the same year signaled the definitive demise of the model, however flawed, of social communism and the triumph of capitalism and individualism. French thought has been concerned as a result both with the violence and the politics of ethnicity that have resulted, and with rethinking the possibility of community beyond atomistic individualism and the dominance of technique.

The legacy of 1968 has thus informed developments in French through over the last thirty years. Moreover, French thought has been concerned with the issue of the legacy in different ways: the deaths of Barthes (in 1980), of Lacan (in 1981, following his dissolution of the *Ecole Freudienne de Paris* in 1980), of Foucault (in 1985), of Sartre (in 1980) and the internment of Althusser in 1980 have induced a reflection on the process of mourning and on the question of the legacy in thought, most significantly with regard to psychoanalysis of a Lacanian color. A legacy is both a gift and an obligation, and much of what has been written since the early 1980s is an attempt to fulfill the demands imposed by these deaths. In a wider sense French thought over the past two decades has been concerned with the issue of memory, the memorial and the immemorial, particularly in the work of Derrida, Lyotard, Jean-Luc Nancy, and Philippe Lacoue-Labarthe and particularly in relation to the Holocaust and collaboration (the extradition and trial of Klaus Barbie took place in the 1980s, and that of Papon in 1997). The past and its effects on the present was also at issue around the publication of Farias's book *Heidegger et le nazisme* in 1987, the most public symptom of the suspicion that one of the key philosophical texts that informed existentialist and deconstructionist philosophy, in different ways, was, at its core, complicit with the ideology of Nazism.

Over a long-term perspective it is evident that one of the salient concerns of French thought in the period under consideration is that of community, and the most significant event the withdrawal of Soviet Communism as the unique reference point. This has induced at the same time a thought that is concerned with the legacy of the past and at the same time with what is to come, while confronted with the issues that arise in a situation of unequally globalized capitalist individualism. This period is thus to be contrasted with the postwar era of the Cold War, characterized by the Manichean divide between United States' dominated individualism and the "Socialism in one state" of the USSR, and with the prewar era of political crisis around the rise of the ideologies of totalitarianism, on both sides.

PATRICK FFRENCH

See also **articles on the individuals mentioned herein**

Further Reading

Blanchot, Maurice, *La communauté inavouable*, Paris: Minuit, 1983 as *The Unavowable Community*, translated by Pierre Joris, Barrytown, New York: Station Hill Press, 1988

Bourdieu, Pierre, *Homo academicus*, Paris: Minuit, 1984, as *Homo academicus*, translated by Peter Collier, Cambridge: Polity Press, 1990

Coudray, Jean-Marc, Lefort, Claude and Morin, Edgar, *Mai '68: La Brèche*, Paris: Fayard, 1968

Debord, Guy, *La société du spectacle*, Paris: Buchet-Chastel, 1967, translated as *The Society of the Spectacle*, New York: Zone Books, 1994

Debord, Guy, *Considérations sur la société du* spectacle, Paris: Editions Gérard Lebovici, 1988, as *Comments on the Society of the Spectacle*, translated by Malcolm Imrie, London: Verso, 1990

Debray, Régis, *Le pouvoir intellectuel en France*, Paris: Editions Ramsay, 1979 as *Teachers, Writers, Celebrities. The Intellectuals of Modern France*, translated by David Macey, London: New Left Books, 1981

Dosse, François, *Histoire du Structuralisme*, vol. 2, Paris: La Découverte, 1991–2, as *History of Structuralism*, translated by Deborah Glassman, Minneapolis, London: University of Minnesota Press, 1997

Ferry, Luc, and Renaut, Alain, *La pensée '68*, Paris: Gallimard, 1985, as *French Philosophy of the Sixties. An Essay on Antihumanism*, translated by Mary Schnackenberg Cattani, Amherst, Mass, London: University of Massachusetts Press, 1990

Ffrench, Patrick, *The Time of Theory: A History of Tel Quel*, Oxford: Oxford University Press, 1996

Hamon, H. and Rotman, P., *Les intellocrates*, Paris: Ramsay, 1981

Lacan, Jacques, *L'envers de la psychanalyse*, Paris: Seuil, 1991

Lavers, Annette, *Roland Barthes: Structuralism and After*, London: Methuen, 1982

Nancy, Jean-Luc, *La communauté désœuvrée*, Paris: Christian Bourgeois, 1986, as *The Inoperative Community*, edited and translated by Peter Connor, translated by Peter Connor, Lisa Garbus, Michael Holland, and Simona Sawhney, Minneapolis, : University of Minnesota Press, 1991

Reader, Keith, *Intellectuals and the Left in France since 1968*, Basingstoke: Macmillan, 1987

Roudinesco, Elizabeth, *La bataille de cent ans: Histoire de la psychanalyse en France*, 2 vols., Paris: Seuil, 1986, vol. 2 as *Jacques Lacan and Co.: a history of psychoanalysis in France, 1925–1985*, translated by Jeffrey Mehlman, London: Free Association, 1990

Sartre, Jean-Paul, *Situations X: Autour de* mai, Paris: Gallimard, 1976

Turkle, Sherry, *Pyschoanalytic Politics*, London: Burnett Books, 1979

HISTORIOGRAPHY

Historians of modern French history—meaning the scholarly discipline of historical research and writing in France—locate its origins at the end of the nineteenth century. In the wake of France's defeat by Germany in 1870, the study of the nation's past and its traditions became an essential part of rebuilding national pride and unity. Prominent historians, such as Alfred Croiset, Ernest Lavisse, and Gabriel Monod, were influential in the sweeping reform of French schools and universities that was a vital element of national regeneration. History thus became the flagship that guided innovations in auxiliary disciplines such as literature, philosophy, and the nascent social sciences.

French historians, inspired by the research methods and erudition of the German universities where many of them had studied before 1870, sought to reinvigorate French historiography along the lines of the German model. They looked especially to the techniques of Leopold von Ranke and his disciples. Ranke's method of careful analysis of primary documents in order to reconstruct the past "as it really was" (*wie es eigentlich gewesen*) appealed to the French historians eager to invest their discipline with an objective, scientific rigor comparable to that found in the exact sciences. Thus, the new history—known as positivist history—bore the mark of the nineteenth-century "cult of science." Positivist historians minimized the influence of the historian's own subjective perspective. They insisted, instead, on his ability to allow the primary sources to speak for themselves. Through the exhaustive accumulation of these sources—for the most part official written documents submitted to meticulous paleographical and philological analysis—the positivist historians claimed to arrive at an objective, Rankean understanding of past reality.

One sign of the "professionalization" of the discipline at the turn of the century was the considerable increase in the number of university professorships and students of history. Another was the creation of numerous specialized historical journals, the most important of which was *La Revue Historique*, founded by Gabriel Monod in 1876 for the express purpose of circulating among the growing community of historians examples of positivist historiography. In 1898, Charles Victor Langlois and Charles Seignobos published their *Introduction aux études historiques*, the first manual of historiographical method. The influence of this "classic of the trade," every history student's guidebook for decades after its publication, is a testament to the firm institutional establishment of positivist history in France at the start of the twentieth century.

As the prevailing historical school of thought in the French university, positivist history was also the primary target of those who had an alternative vision of the discipline. Founded in 1900 by Henri Berr, *La Revue de Synthèse Historique* became a leading journal for opponents of the established academic historiography of Langlois and Seignobos. Berr denounced the excessive analysis and narrow specialization promoted by the positivist historians and promoted greater cooperation between historians and researchers in social sciences such as geography, economics, psychology, and sociology. It was in this journal that François Simiand, an economist and student of the sociologist Émile Durkheim, published his famous 1903 article, "*Méthode historique et science sociale*," an incisive critique

of the positivist school's most basic assumptions concerning historical events and the individual's role in shaping them. Attacking, for example, Seignobos's explanation of the Franco-Prussian War in terms of the individual efforts of Bismarck or Napoleon III, Simiand argued that the actions of these political and military leaders could not be explained in isolation from the social, institutional, and cultural contexts from which they emerged. Arguing that society itself was a legitimate object of historical study, Simiand called for more rigorous application of sociological method to the practice of history. Social phenomena such as religious belief, superstition, custom, moral values, forms of ownership, modes of commercial exchange, divisions of labor, and habits of fashion, said Simiand, were observable as objective fact. The study of "social facts," however, would require a different use of evidence. The predominant positivist analysis of written documents (decrees, letters, official reports) for insight into the author's intention would no longer suffice in the study of collective social phenomena whose meaning was most often embedded in linguistic codes and systems of representation of which the individual, historical actor was typically unaware. Simiand, moreover, doubted the scientific validity of the positivists' view of historical causality. The positivist's explanation of one event by locating its causes in an earlier event was, he argued, more a product of the historian's imagination than a result of objective observation.

It would be hard to overstate the significance of Simiand's article for the subsequent developments in French historiography. His criticism of the reigning historical practice of analyzing official written documents to produce narratives of political and diplomatic events would be invoked repeatedly by the historians of the *Annales* school, the most innovative and influential French historical movement of the twentieth century. Indeed, there is a clear influence of Simiand's thought on the work of Marc Bloch and Lucien Febvre, the founders of the *Annales* movement. In fact, Bloch and Febvre were frequent contributors to *La Revue de Synthèse Historique* before founding their own journal in 1929, *Annales d'histoire économique et sociale*, from which the movement takes its name. The interdisciplinary spirit promoted by Berr and Simiand was also characteristic of the intellectual environment at the University of Strasbourg in the 1920s, where Bloch and Febvre met and where they developed their conception of history in collaboration with social scientists such as the psychologist Charles Blondel and the sociologist Maurice Halbwachs.

In addition to their emphasis on interdisciplinary collaboration, in particular with the social sciences, the *Annales* founders eschewed "event-based history" or *histoire événementielle*. The term, used derisively by

Annales historians, referred to the common historical practice of taking ephemeral events as the primary object of study. In this regard, the *Annales* historians clearly maintained the line of criticism begun by Simiand. Instead of *histoire événementielle*, they proposed "problem-oriented history," a type of inquiry in which the scope and method of research would be determined by the kind of problems the historian sought to elucidate. An example of a problem-oriented investigation is Marc Bloch's *Les Rois thaumaturges* (1924), a study of the popular belief in medieval England and France that the king possessed supernatural powers to cure the disease of scrofula. To understand better how subjects believed in such miracles, Bloch examined the continuation of these beliefs well beyond the medieval period into the seventeenth century. In other words, the nature of the historian's question (or "problem") required an extension of the scope of his research beyond the customary bounds of a chronological period, or historical unit, called "the Middle Ages."

Today, Bloch and Febvre are often remembered as pioneers in the history of "mentalities" (*mentalités*), the study of a past society's attitudes and beliefs as observed through everyday customs, rituals, linguistic codes, and other forms of representation. Lucien Febvre's 1942 study, *Le Problème de l'incroyance au XVIe siècle, la religion de Rabelais*, is perhaps his most important contribution to the history of mentalities. He there debunks the prevalent claim that Rabelais's literary work was evidence of his atheism and anticlericalism. Through an examination of the "collective mentality" of the period, Febvre shows that atheism was not an available concept to people in the sixteenth century and argues that it is anachronistic to think of Rabelais as an unbeliever despite his criticism of the late Medieval Church. Even this cursory look at two works by Bloch and Febvre makes clear an abiding priority of *Annales* historians, namely an interest in a wide range of socio-cultural questions as opposed to the narrow focus on political events to which, they claimed, positivist historians typically hewed.

Bloch and Febvre's interest in the history of mentalities notwithstanding, much important scholarship by practitioners of the new history was in the field of economic history. For example, a landmark study in economic history, owing much to François Simiand's earlier research on price movements, was Ernest Labrousse's *Esquisse du mouvement des prix et des revenus en France au XVIIIe siècle* (1933). By examining fluctuations in commodity prices such as grains and wine and their affect on revenues, Labrousse was able to distinguish long-term economic trends from short-term cycles and intercycles. A sequel to this work was Labrousse's 1944 study of *La Crise de l'économie française à la fin de l'ancien régime*, in which he iden-

tified a recession in the 1780s as a contributing factor in the French Revolution. These two monographs stand out as early studies in "*conjoncture*," a uniquely French term that can be roughly understood as changing economic and social conditions measured over time. In the 1950s and 1960s this concept proved paramount for historians intent on moving beyond the enduring practice of viewing the past as a narrative of chronologically ordered individual events and periods. One must use the term *Annales* "school" with caution because it gives a misleading impression of a doctrinal coherence that the *Annales* luminaries tried to avoid. The historians who published in *Annales* used eclectic approaches to a wide range of subjects; they did not adhere to anything resembling the methodological prescription one finds in Langlois and Seignobos's *Introduction*. Nevertheless, Marc Bloch's *Apologie pour l'histoire, ou, Métier d'historien* (1941), while not a programmatic pronouncement, does provide an eloquent explanation of the major "unifying" themes of what has been called a "revolution" in French historiography (Burke, *The French Historical Revolution: The Annales School 1929–89*, 1990). Furthermore, with Lucien Febvre's founding of the Sixth Section of the *École Pratique des Hautes Études* in 1946, the historians' permanent institutional home, the *Annales* "movement" completed its transformation from a fringe group of unorthodox scholars in Strasbourg to an established and influential "school" of historical thought in Paris.

Fernand Braudel took over the direction of the *Annales* in 1956 following Lucien Febvre's death (Marc Bloch, who joined the French resistance during the war, was executed by a German firing squad in 1944). It is perhaps under Braudel's dynamic leadership that the *Annales* school and French historiography in general reached the height of its influence both in France and around the world. Like his intellectual forebears, Braudel saw *histoire événementielle* as inadequate for understanding collective experience and advocated studying the slow, almost imperceptibly changing structures that underlie human activity.

In Braudel's monumental study of *La Méditerranée et le monde méditeranéen à l'époque de Philippe II* (1949), one sees most clearly his effort to explore what he considered to be the most "profound" structures of history. The work is divided into three sections corresponding to Braudel's conception of the different "layers" of historical time: the almost unchanging environment, the slowly changing cycles of the economy and societal evolution, and finally the ephemeral realm of events. Braudel sees the first of these, the geographical region of the sea and the countries surrounding it, as most important, and he describes in great detail the area's topography, climate, and major trade routes.

Braudel's purpose is to show that this "geo-structure" has its own history that cannot be ignored if one is to understand the region's civilizations and economic cycles, which in turn provide the context for understanding the "superficial" political and military events of late sixteenth-century Spain. By taking into account all "three speeds" of history, Braudel believed one could arrive at what he called "total history," a comprehensive understanding of the way human activity has been shaped by underlying "medium-term cyclical changes" (*conjonctures*) and long-term, millennial, almost timeless structures, "*la longue durée*." Braudel presented a more theoretical development of the *longue durée* in a celebrated article published in the *Annales Economies Sociétés Civilisations* in 1958 (this was the new postwar title for the journal founded by Bloch and Febvre in 1929). Appearing in the same year that Claude Lévi-Strauss published his influential *Anthropologie structurale*, Braudel's article, an apologia of the importance of long-term structures to the historian's task, reveals the challenge felt by the *Annales* school from the growing influence of structuralist and explicitly anti-historical social sciences.

A work particularly noteworthy for its use of quantitative data in order to produce a "total history" is *à la Braudel*, is *Les Paysans de Languedoc* (1966) by Emmanuel Le Roy Ladurie. Through a sweeping study (replete with extensive appendices, tables, and sources) of tax records, wage and price trends, and demographic statistics in Languedoc from 1500 to 1700, Le Roy Ladurie establishes a correlation between agricultural output and population changes. Le Roy Ladurie connects economic and social *conjonctures* to changes in peasant consciousness or *mentalité*, suggesting that particular episodes of rebellion, fanaticism, and hysteria observed among the population were related to underlying economic conditions. Pierre Goubert's *Beauvais et le Beauvaisis de 1600 à 1730*, an outstanding example of demographic history and a major achievement in the use of quantitative evidence, centers even more dramatically on questions of population. In this statistical analysis of life expectancy, birth, death, and fertility rates combined with price and wage data, Goubert applies the lens of the demographer to the ancien régime and identifies moments of "demographic crises" resulting from bad harvests and elevated food prices.

The 1970s opens a new phase in French history. In institutional terms, a younger generation of historians, lead by figures such as Jacques Le Goff and François Furet, replaced Fernand Braudel at the head of *Annales*, and the Sixth Section of the *École Pratique des Hautes Études* was reorganized to become the prestigious degree-granting research center known as the *École des Hautes Études en Sciences Sociales* (EHESS). In terms of the practice of history itself, the 1970s saw a relative decline in the monolithic influence of the *Annales* "paradigm." This is witnessed by the move away from studies of economic *conjonctures* and long-term *structures* that were ubiquitous in the 1950s and 1960s toward a wide variety of new research areas such as childhood, death, the history of the book, the body, film, the unconscious, restaurant menus, and public opinion. Many of these new directions were presented in 1974 in *Faire de l'histoire*, a collection of articles edited by Jacques Le Goff and Pierre Nora.

Of particular interest is Pierre Nora's contribution to the collection, "The Return of the Event," an article that reclaims the event as a valuable object or unit of historical inquiry and thus represents a bold departure from the longtime taboo against *histoire événementielle*. Nora makes the case that the event in the late twentieth-century age of mass media is not the same as the event examined by the positivist historians at the end of the previous century. The positivists' study of events, *Annales* historians had argued, provided information limited to the decisions of political and military leaders. But the media age, according to Nora, democratizes "the event"; through television, news media, and radio, everyone is aware of, reacts to, and to some extent participates in events. Modern events thus become "sites" for observing "deep-seated social phenomena" and collective attitudes, precisely and paradoxically, notes Nora, what the *Annales* patriarchs—Bloch, Febvre, and Braudel—had endeavored to apprehend. The 1970s also marked a renewed interest in the history of "mentalities," sometimes called "historical anthropology." One of the most important figures to emerge in this area of research was Philippe Ariès, an *Annales* outsider. His most famous work, *L'Enfant et la vie familiale sous l'Ancien Régime*, though published in 1960, did not receive much attention until the 1970s. In this study, Ariès explains that the concept of childhood as a developmental stage in the life of an individual did not exist for the medieval mind. By examining changing habits with respect to the treatment of childhood in clothing styles and as depicted in paintings, Ariès shows that the "modern" notion of childhood begins in the early-modern period. Until then, children had been regarded as subhuman until the age of seven, at which point they passed directly to being treated as full adults. Ariès extends his study of the awareness of child development to general ideas of development and the progress of civilization in the West. Related to this study of attitudes toward childhood was Ariès's *Homme devant la mort* (1977), an influential study of Western attitudes toward death that had an important influence on Michel Vovelle's *La Mort et l'occident* (1983), a long term study of attitudes toward death using quantitatively rigorous methods influenced by Labrousse.

The philosopher of history, Michel Foucault, whose historical research is considered specious by more than a few practicing historians, has nevertheless made a profound contribution to recent historical debate. His work may be compared to that of other historians of mentalities. Foucault's interest in "discursive practices" or thought systems through which human beings unwittingly perceive and order their world bears a certain resemblance to the mental attitudes studied by Ariès (as Patrick Hutton observes in "The History of Mentalities, The New Map of Cultural History," 1981). In *Surveiller et punir: naissance de la prison* (1975) for example, Foucault explores the way attitudes toward sequestration and imprisonment reappear in other disciplinary practices implemented in schools and the military.

Important challenges to the orthodoxies of the 1950s and 1960s came from historians questioning the epistemological claims of historical research. Key figures in these debates were Paul Veyne and Michel de Certeau, both of whom examined historians' use of literary techniques and rhetorical strategies in even the most seemingly objective studies. In *Comment on écrit l'histoire* (1971), Veyne exposed the scientism at the heart of the structuralist movement. Because historians would never be able to establish laws like those of the natural sciences and thus would never provide a totally truthful account of the past, Veyne treated history as a fundamentally literary exercise. It followed the rules of narrative: organizing and prioritizing information and using figurative language in order to create coherent stories about the past. The Braudelian notion of "total history" was impossible, said Veyne, because of the infinite diversity of human experience, and he recast Braudel's tripartite view of historical time as a powerful "metaphor" for gaining historical perspective. Although critical of a certain positivist and pseudo-scientific idea of history, Veyne did not criticize history *per se*. He defended the value of historical inquiry not because it could lead to the discovery of an objective, "real" past, but because something that escapes scientific understanding may nevertheless be a worthy object of study. In *L'Écriture de l'histoire* (1975), Michel de Certeau analyzed the rhetorical maneuvers that historians use to give a semblance of objectivity to their work. He showed in particular how the discourse of quantitative history hides the historian's own subjectivity and creates the illusion that the object of the study "speaks for itself." He also revealed how the apparatus of bibliography, sources, and references lends authority to the historian's voice and serves to persuade the reader. A point dear to Certeau was the way in which the historian's situation in the present

motivates his interest in the past; it is no accident, he wrote in 1974 (in Le Goff and Nora's *Faire de l'histoire*), if the historian turns from "social history" to "economic history" precisely at the time of the great economic crisis of 1929. Another important study of the narrative aspects of historical writing is Paul Ricoeur's *Temps et récit* (1983–85), a three-volume philosophical exploration of the ways in which both fictional narratives and historical narratives are concerned with a representation of man's relationship to time. Just as Pierre Nora cast a new light on event-oriented history, other historians in the 1970s and 1980s returned, but from a new angle, to the old nineteenth-century staples of military and political history. Steering clear of the classic military history focus on generals, strategists, and diplomats, Jean-Jacques Becker's *1914, Comment les Français sont entrés dans la guerre* (1977) studies World War I "from below," from the perspective of the ordinary soldier in the trench. Becker attacks the myth that soldiers went off to war enthusiastically and presents a darker, more cynical picture of French public opinion on the eve of war. Another important revisionist history of the war experience is Antoine Prost's *Les Anciens combattants et la société française, 1919–1939* (1977), a study of interwar veteran movements that exposes the myth of camaraderie in the trenches as a postwar invention.

René Rémond, François Furet, and Maurice Agulhon stand out as historians who have resuscitated political history. In ways that recall Pierre Nora's reclaiming of the event as an object of study, Rémond, in his edited collection, *Pour une histoire politique* (1988), defends politics as a privileged site for observing the interaction of other spheres of human activity. In *Penser la Revolution Française* (1979), François Furet examines the "discourse" or "semiology" used by the revolutionaries to garner support and wield political power. Furet shows how the history of the Revolution was determined by representations of politics that took hold over the popular imagination (*l'imaginaire*). In his *Marianne au combat* (1979) and his *Marianne au pouvoir* (1989), Maurice Agulhon studies nineteenth-century iconography of the Republican symbol of Marianne as it appeared on statues, money, stamps, and in paintings and shows how political conflict was filtered through public debates over "civic art."

The relationship between history and memory has been, arguably, the most vigorous field of historical inquiry in recent years. Much of this research builds on earlier work by the sociologist Maurice Halbwachs, whose theory of collective memory attempted to explain how social groups do not actually remember their past but rather recreate or reimagine it based on their contact in the present with remnants of material objects, rituals, and traditions. Henry Rousso's *Le syn-*

drome de Vichy (1987) stands out as a particularly innovative look at the construction of national memory and commemorative practices. Rather than directly studying German-occupied France during World War II, Rousso examines the successive postwar phases through which France as a nation has collectively mourned, repressed, confronted and, most recently, debated the wartime experience of collaboration and the Vichy régime.

The most celebrated treatment of memory, however, is found in *Les Lieux de mémoire* (1984–1992), the encyclopedic seven-volume collection of articles by France's most distinguished historians and edited by Pierre Nora. The articles cover the gamut of topics related to the French Republic, the French nation, and French culture such as monuments, song, pedagogy, iconography, heroes, legends, religious debates, class conflict, commemoration ceremonies, literature, and so on. What unifies these sundry articles is that they all attempt to present a specific topic in terms of the symbolic value that it holds for some collective notion of French identity. In theory, all of the article topics— for example, "Joan of Arc," "The Eiffel Tower," "La Marseillaise," "Bastille Day"—constitute "places" (*lieux*) that over time have come to crystallize key aspects of what it means to be "French" and share a common history. It is significant, as Steven Englund has noted (in "The Ghost of Nation Past," 1992) that this project should appear at a moment when it has become a commonplace to speak of a "crisis" of French identity—a crisis stemming, it is said, from the end of the economic prosperity of the *trentes glorieuses*, from the demographic and cultural changes resulting from massive immigration, and from uncertainty about the role of France in the new supranational European Union. The exploration of the national patrimony in *Les Lieux de mémoire* seems to be more than a project of pure scholarly inquiry. It seems to be an effort to find unity around a common (albeit contested) heritage and culture. In this respect, the undertaking of Nora and others, resembles that of the late nineteenth-century historians with which this survey began (Englund, 1992). They too, it should be recalled, put their discipline in the service of the national interest. The history of French history, one might say, repeats itself.

LEON SACHS

See also **Philippe Aries; Marc Bloch; Michel de Certeau; Emile Durkheim; Lucien Febvre; Michel Foucault; Maurice Halbwachs; Emmanuel Le Roy Ladurie; Claude Levi-Strauss; Paul Ricoeur**

Further Reading

Bloch, Marc, Léopold Benjamin. *The Historian's Craft*, translated by Peter Putnam, New York: Alfred Knopf, 1953

Bourdé, Guy, and Hervé Martin, *Les écoles historiques*, Paris: Seuil, 1983
Braudel, Fernand, *On history*, translated by Sarah Matthews, Chicago: University of Chicago Press, 1980
Burke, Peter, *The French Historical Revolution: The Annales School 1929–89*, Stanford: Stanford University Press, 1990
Certeau, Michel de, *The writing of history*, translated by Tom Conley, New York: Columbia University Press, 1988
Iggers, Georg, *New Directions in European Historiography*, Connecticut: Wesleyan University Press, 1975
Keylor, William R, *Academy and Community. The Foundations of the French Historical Profession*, Cambridge: Harvard University Press, 1975
Le Goff, Jacques, and Pierre Nora, (editors) *Constructing the Past: Essays in Historical Methodology*, Cambridge: Cambridge University Press, 1985
Noiriel, Gérard, *Qu'est-ce que l'histoire contemporaine ?* Paris: Hachette, 1998
Nora, Pierre, and Lawrence D. Kritzman, (editors), *Realms of Memory: Rethinking the French Past*, translated by Arthur Goldhammer, New York: Columbia University Press, 1996–1998
Pomian, Krysztof, *Sur l'histoire*, Paris: Gallimard, 1999
Revel, Jacques, Introduction, in *Histories: French Constructions of the Past*, translated by Arthur, et al., edited by Lynn Hunt and Jacques Revel, New York: The New Press, 1995
Stoianovich, Troian, *French Historical Method: The Annales Paradigm*, Ithaca: Cornell University Press, 1976

HOCQUENGHEM, GUY
Writer

Guy Hocquenghem was one of the founders of the modern gay movement in France, and the author of the first work of what might be termed gay theory, *Le Désir homosexuel* (*Homosexual Desire*), published in 1972. In the late 1970s, he began to distance himself from the more commercial and identity-centered orthodoxy of the contemporary gay scene, and became preoccupied with interrogating the concept of modernity. Lambasting the politics and culture of the Mitterrand presidency of the 1980s, he turned especially to novel-writing in order to explore his philosophical ideas. Like Foucault, his AIDS-related illness was kept secret, but is explored in fictional form and in a posthumously published fictional memoir, *L'Amphithéâtre des morts* (*The Amphitheatre of the Dead*).

Le Désir homosexuel is determined by the historical event of May 1968 and the intellectual influence of Gilles Deleuze and Félix Guattari, whose *Anti-Oedipe* (*Anti-Oedipus*) was also published in 1972. May 1968, the high-water mark of Marxist and other leftist thinking in postwar France, had generated both radical social questioning (including direct action) and in the early 1970s a reaction, partly influenced by American counterculture, against the movement's sexism and heterosexism. Results had included the feminist and gay movements, the latter in 1971 taking the form of the *Front homosexuel d'action révolutionnaire*,

(FHAR), whose *Rapport contre la normalité* located homophobia as systematic, part of the wider gender oppression within capitalism. Deleuze and Guattari had developed a liberationist theory in which the miserable individuals produced by capitalist modernity and its sidekick, Freudian psychoanalysis, are replaced by an ontology of particles and flows, the famous "desiring machines." *Le Désir homosexuel* is therefore not about object-choice or gay identity, but is rather an attempt to reconnect with the polymorphous perversity of the human infant that Freud evokes but then insists on channeling into the Oedipal trajectory founded on difference and lack. For Hocquenghem, homosexual desire is about "the self-production of desire" because it represents a crack in this Freudian system, which insists that such desire can be lived only as sublimation or neurosis/abjection. Hocquenghem thus rehabilitates "promiscuous" gay cruising, "the system in which polyvocal desire is plugged in on a nonexclusive basis." Moreover, in the famous section on "capitalism, the family and the anus," Hocquenghem argues for the deprivatization of the anus. In modernity the anus is the noncodified and abject other to the supremely socially symbolic organ that is the phallus. Desiring use of the anus (which he concedes is just one form of homosexual activity) would have the advantage of re-socializing that most private and "personal" (as generating "personhood") of orifices, get us away from anxiety surrounding lack (no one ever threatens to take away your anus, and sexual difference has nothing to do with the view from behind) and thus from capitalism's masculinist "jealousy-competition" system.

Even this first work showed Hocquenghem's distinctiveness within the early French gay movement, in the distance he took from notions of "rights" and "identity," the "1789 of sex" which he saw as full of risks. By the latter half of the decade, under again the twin impulsions of historical change (the more visible, commercial gay scene) and theoretical developments (most notably Foucault's *History of Sexuality*), Hocquenghem's intellectual interests had turned to the historical constructions of homosexuality, and a longer-term, "civilizational" critique of modernity. *La Dérive homosexuelle* (*Homosexual Drift*) of 1977 approaches the new epoch in very Foucauldian terms, seeing it as a redistribution of sexual categories and interdictions rather than a straightforward liberation or desublimation. *Race d'Ep! Un Siècle d'images de l'homosexualité*, the book and film he made with Lionel Soukaz in 1979 ("rasdep" is "backslang" for *pédéraste*) is a chronicle of images and identities of homosexuality that succeeds in deconstructing its subject as a very provisional solution to the dilemmas of modernity. With another—prescient—text from 1979, *La Beauté du métis: réflexions d'un francophobe* (*The Beauty of Mixed Blood: Reflections of a Francophobe*), he engages in a savage critique of the nation-state and its most coherent avatar, "the france system" (sic).

Hocquenghem's most sustained theoretical works of this later period are those written with his former philosophy teacher, the Fourier specialist René Schérer, or in the form of novels which resemble eighteenth-century *contes philosophiques*. Already in *Co-ire: album systematique de l'enfance/Co-ire: a systematic album of childhood*, Hocquenghem and Schérer had continued Fourier's critique of the consequences for children in particular of the society ushered in by the events of the 1790s, and produced a Foucauldian history of childhood and its representations in that period. They argue that the child is caught in panoptic and disciplinary fields, always localized and observed in the institutions of school and family, the result of which is an oppressive "personhood." The liberation of the child will imply the undermining of the adult/child distinction so central to modern instrumentalism. Their *magnum opus* is, however, *L'Âme atomique/The Atomic Soul* of 1986, the theoretical counterpart to Hocquenghem's savaging that same year of ex-*soixante-huitard* Mitterrand fellow-travellers and nuclear apologists, *Lettre ouverte à ceux qui sont passés du col Mao au Rotary/Open Letter to those who have gone from the Mao Collar to the Rotary Club*. The oxymoronic formulation of *L'Âme atomique*, along with the subtitle, "For an Aesthetics of the Nuclear Age," represents an attempt to reinvigorate the critical value of the aesthetic without falling back on the kind of totalization found in, for example, the Frankfurt school. Combining Lucretius with quantum theory (and not a little influenced by Deleuze and Guattari's *Mille plateaux/A Thousand Plateaus* of 1980), Hocquenghem and Schérer argue for an open, decentered universe in which the aesthetic priority is given to those intermittences between humanity and machine, nature and artifice, real and illusion, and they thus emphasize processes of dilation, expansion, and dispersion. The hunt is on for those aesthetic forms that permit the cultivation of discontinuities in the forward march of modernity and rational progress: Benjaminian constellations, auras and allegories; the child and color perception; melancholy; and especially the baroque. Hocquenghem explored ways of confronting same-sex desire, historical breaks and transformations, the modern city, and contemporary globalization in fictional works such as the short story *Oiseau de la nuit/Nightbird* of 1977 (a reworking of Diderot's *Le Neveu de Rameau/Rameau's Nephew*), *L'Amour en relief/Love in Relief* of 1982 (about a blind Tunisian and whose philosophical ideas owe much to Diderot's *Lettre sur les aveugles/Letter on the Blind* of 1749, as well as to Foucault and Deleuze), and *La Colère de*

l'agneau/The Wrath of the Lamb of 1985, an epic portrait of the first century A.D.

Hocquenghem is in some ways typical of the critiques of Enlightenment totality and identity that characterize much of contemporary French thought. He is
firmly in the social constructionist vein of sexual theory. However, he is difficult to pigeon-hole in terms
of gay politics, enjoying the very inconsistency of the
terms "gay" or "homosexual," which appear and disappear according to historical context. It is this play of
visibility and invisibility that leads him to argue, in a
late theoretical text from 1987, for a "musicalization"
of homosexuality, existing "only in its rhythm, its intervals and its pauses." "Being oneself" is thus not for
him a liberating concept. The republication in the
1990s of *Le Désir homosexuel* in both English and
French resulted in greater attention to his work, and a
partial appropriation of him by 1990s "queer theory."
Despite the slightly dandyish or aristocratic aspect of
his later works, the lack of any specific engagement
with different social positions such as those of women,
and a partial failure to recognize the risks of denying
personhood and consent to children while simultaneously re-sexualizing them, he provides a useful utopian—and irreverent—critical take on contemporary
orthodoxy while reminding his readers of their historicity. For Hocquenghem, supremely universalizing in
his reach, "gay" or "queer" are to be located on the
same heterogenous continuum as multifarious other
manifestations of history and culture.

BILL MARSHALL

See also **Gilles Deleuze; Michel Foucault; Félix Guattari**

Biography

Guy Hocquenghem was born in the suburbs of Paris
in 1944. He attended *L'Ecole Normale Supérieure*, and
participated in the 1968 Paris uprising. One of the first
men to join the Front *Homosexuel d'Action Révolutionnaire*, he published *Le Désir homosexuel* (*Homosexual Desire*) in 1972. He began writing experimental
fiction in the 1980s. Hocquenghem died of an AIDS-
related illness in 1988.

Selected Works

Le Désir homosexuel, 1972, as *Homosexual Desire*, translated
by D. Dangoor, 1978 and 1993
La Dérive homosexuelle, 1977, as "Towards an Irrecuperable
Pederasty," translated by C. Fox, in *Reclaiming Sodom*, ed-
ited by Jonathan Goldberg
La Beauté du métis: réflexions d'un francophobe, 1979
Race d'Ep! Un Siècle d'images de l'homosexualité, 1979
L'Amour en relief, 1982; as *Love in Relief*, translated by M.
Whisler, 1986

La Colère de l'agneau, 1985
Lettre ouverte à ceux qui sont passés du col Mao au Rotary,
1986
"L'homosexualité est-elle un vice guérissable?" as "On Homo-
Sex", translated by B. Marshall 1999–2000
L'Amphithéâtre des morts: mémoires anticipées, 1994
with René Schérer
Co-ire: album systématique de l'enfance, 1976
L'Âme atomique, 1986

Further Reading

Marshall, Bill, *Guy Hocquenghem*, London and Durham: Pluto
Press, and Duke University Press, 1996 and 1997.
Marshall, Bill, "Reconsidering 'Gay': Hocquenghem, Identity
Politics and the Baroque," in *Gay Signatures: Gay and Les-
bian Theory, Fiction and Film in France, 1945–1995*, edited
by Owen Heathcote et al., Oxford: Berg Publishers, 1998
Marshall, Bill, "Commentary on 'On Homo-Sex," *New Forma-
tions*, 39 (Winter 1999 2000): 75–9.
Moon, Michael, introduction to *Homosexual Desire*, Durham:
Duke University Press, 1993
Weeks, Jeffrey, preface to *Homosexual Desire*, Durham: Duke
University Press, 1993

HOLOCAUST IN FRANCE

The war against the Jews was central to Nazi ideology,
as Adolf Hitler made clear in *Mein Kampf* and made
evident soon after the Nazi assumption of power on
January 30, 1933. The segregation of Jews in Germany
was facilitated by the Nuremberg Laws in 1935, and
the mass slaughter of Jews with the onset of war in
Poland in September 1939. Freed from the need to
fight on two fronts due to the Nazi-Soviet nonaggression pact of August 1939, the Germans prepared their
offensive on the western front for nine months, launching their attack against Norway and Denmark in April
1940 and against the Netherlands, Belgium, and France
on May 10. By the middle of June, the German army
marched triumphantly through the Arc d'Triomphe,
and on July 10 the World War I hero Marshal Philippe
Pétain was made head of state of a new government
established in the resort city of Vichy and given power
to seek an armistice with Germany that laid the groundwork for collaboration.

According to the armistice, France was divided into
two main zones, with a demarcation line dividing the
south from the occupied zone in the north. Occupied
France was subject to direct administration by military
headquarters (*Militarbefehlhaber* in Frankreich) on security matters and by negotiations between the German
embassy and the Vichy government in political affairs,
with the German security and intelligence apparatus
(SiPo-SD) and the State Secret Police (Gestapo) serving to prod and enforce policy. Theodor Dannecker, a
subordinate of Adolf Eichmann, headed the Gestapo's

Jewish Affairs Department (*Judenreferat*), the most active in the planning of Jewish policy. The *Einsatzstab* Rosenberg was a competing authority authorized to plunder archives and art collections of Jews. Still, the Vichy government defined the law of the land in both zones, so long as it collaborated and did not contradict the German regulations in the occupied zone.

The Vichy policies toward the Jews, based upon indigenous French anti-Semitism and instituted before any direct Nazi prompting, made clear very early that state anti-Semitism aimed at reducing the presence of Jews in the public realm and would be a key lever of Vichy's "national revolution." From July 1940, the naturalization of foreign-born Jews could be revoked and in August, the *loi Marchandeau*—the April 1939 law that had banned racist press attacks—was repealed, thus legalizing anti-Semitic propaganda. On October 3, 1940, Vichy's version of the Nuremberg Laws, the first *Statut des juifs*, was passed, defining as a Jew "any person descended from three grandparents of Jewish race or from two grandparents of the same race if his spouse is also a Jew." It then excluded Jews from top positions in the public service, in the officer corps and from positions that influenced public opinion: teaching, the press, radio, film, and theater. This was reinforced the next day when it became legal for the police to arrest arbitrarily "any foreigner of the Jewish race."

To house these newly criminalized "stateless Jews," an existing network of internment camps was transformed into a concentration camp system manned by French police. The camps had been set up by the French government to intern refugees and republican soldiers fleeing the Franco regime, and on the eve of war thousands were interned as "enemy aliens," mostly Jews fleeing Nazi Germany.

But the assault on the Jews intensified as a result of Nazi pressure. Pushed by Dannecker, French officials conducted a census of Jews in the occupied territories in late 1940 and established a *Commissariat General aux Questions Juives* (CGQJ), a ministry of Jewish affairs, in March 1941. A second *Statut* was passed in June 1941 that broadened the definition of a Jew and placed further restrictions on Jews, followed a month later by an Aryanization law that enabled the seizure of Jewish property. A Jewish council (*Union Générale des Israelites de France*) was also established to coordinate the Jewish response.

With these legal and institutional preparations in place in France, and Hitler's war of annihilation in full force in the east, the summer of 1942 was the turning point for the *Shoah* in France. Already in the middle of 1941, the first mass arrests of Jews had begun. In January 1942 at the Wannsee Conference in Berlin, state, party, and SS leaders began to coordinate the bureaucracy of murder. The first deportation of Jews from France to Auschwitz took place March 27, 1942. In April, with a zealous new head of the CGQJ, the fanatical anti-Semite Louis Darquier de Pellepoix, and the secretary general of national police, René Bousquet, anxious to assert control by the French police in the occupied zone, French authorities agreed to aggressive new efforts to pursue the mutual enemies of the Reich and Vichy—Jews, Communists, and Gaullists. Although the French government objected to arresting Jews who were still legally French citizens, on July 16 and 17, 1942 the Paris police were organized into 888 arrest teams and aided by about 4,000 blue-shirted fascist youth from the *Parti Populaire Française*. They hunted down 12,884 Jews, including approximately 4,000 children, moving them in city buses to the *Vélodrome d'Hiver*, an indoor sports and bicycling stadium, before transporting them to Drancy, from whence they were sent in cargo cars to Auschwitz. Before the end of 1942, nearly 42,000 Jews had already been deported, with 17,000 more in 1943 and an additional 15,000 in 1944.

Depending on a range of factors—including geographic region, class, religious sensibilities, politics, and moment in time—the reaction of the French to Jewish persecution was mixed. Many French people were horrified by the spectacle of their own police, soldiers, and even firemen hunting down Jews, and there were some protests, including by leading clergymen. Most were too concerned with their own existence, however, and a sizable portion of the population supported the measures. It was only when the Allied victory looked more certain that the French police became more reluctant to participate in the roundups of Jews. Then, the notorious *Milice Française* (French militia), founded in 1942 by Joseph Darnand, picked up the slack. By 1943, more and more ordinary French people helped to save Jews and to support escape routes, best represented by the Protestant community of *Le Chambon-sur-Lignon*, where the 5,000 Christians rescued about an equal number of Jews. Along with the distinction made by the authorities between French and foreign Jews, these factors enabled seventy-five percent of Jews in France to survive the war. Nonetheless, including the Jews who died of malnutrition and disease in French concentration camps, there were nearly 80,000 from France among the six million victims of the final solution.

The impact of Vichy France and the Holocaust within French culture is a seismic event, but one that did not always register on the cultural seismograph. Henry Rousso has famously called the process of memorializing and forgetting World War II in various cultural contexts—public commemorations, radio broadcasts, newsreels, public speeches, novels, and film—"the Vichy syndrome," which profoundly impacted politics in four phases: (1) repression from 1944–1954 in the interest of reconstruction, the purging of collaborators and ending with the granting of amnesty; (2) the construction of the Gaullist myth of the occupation from 1954–1971 that involved minimizing the role of French collaboration and identifying the French nation with the Resistance; (3) the "return of the repressed" when the myth was shattered between 1971 and 1974; (4) and the present moment that Rousso characterizes as one of "obsession."

Reinforcing Rousso's analysis, Charlotte Wardi has shown that from 1945–1970 among non-Jewish novelists, there is not one major work that explicitly addresses the subject of the genocide of the Jews. Nor did it have a significant impact on the forms of literature and its images, including representations of "the Jew," that were largely extensions of depictions in the interwar period. Although Sartre's *Réflexions sur la question juive* (*Anti-Semite and Jew,* 1946) was a major existentialist analysis of anti-Semitism, he almost exclusively targets pre-genocidal judeophobia, with scant mention of the extermination centers in the East, and does not radically challenge the antisemitic conception of "the Jew," instead interrogating how this projection masks the *mauvaise foi* (self-deception) of the anti-Semite. Albert Camus's *La Peste* (*The Plague,* 1947), conceived and begun in Le Chambon, depicts a raging epidemic and those who attempt to alleviate the suffering. It is often read as an allegory of resistance to Nazism, but there are few details that connect the work directly to a concern with the plight of the Jews, including in Camus's meticulous *Notebooks* from 1938–1947. Although Catholic writers like Julien Green and Jacques Maritain express profound sadness about the Christian roots of anti-Semitism, there is largely a silence on the *Shoah* and a continuation of imagining "the Jew" through the prism of their eschatological preconceptions. François Mauriac, for example, heroizes the convert Simone Weil, and the beatified nun Edith Stein. No important surrealist or Marxist broached the Holocaust in literature. Although militant anti-Semites were silenced by the defeat of Hitler, antipathetic images do reappear in the works of among others Philippe Hériat, Marcel Aymé, and Jean Dutourd.

Compounding this silence has been what Pierre-Vidal Nacquet calls "the assassins of memory," or the nefarious effort to deny the Holocaust, claiming in Robert Faurisson's words that "the alleged Hitlerian gas chambers and the alleged genocide of the Jews form one and the same historical lie, which permitted a gigantic financial swindle whose chief beneficiaries have been the state of Israel and international Zionism, and whose main victims have been the German people

and the Palestinian people." Faurisson is the most famous "paper Eichmann," and has advanced the tradition of Holocaust denial started in France by the self-proclaimed fascist Maurice Bardèche. While Bardèche's opinions were sullied because of his fascism, Paul Rassinier, a former Communist and member of the French resistance who was himself interned in the Buchenwald concentration camp, began to publish books in 1948 that attacked the testimonies of survivors and in time formulated the basic outline of Holocaust denial filled in by others. Faurisson's books were published and sold by *La Veille Taupe,* an ultra-leftist organization, and echoed by Jean-Marie Le Pen, the leader of the ultra-right *Front nationale,* who contended in 1987 that the death of six million Jews was "a minute detail of the war" adding that "there are historians debating those issues." The work to advance the Holocaust by exterminating its memory thus stands at the crossroads of several contradictory ideological currents: ultra-left Marxism, far-right nationalism, anti-Zionism, and anti-Semitism.

If much of French culture remained silent on the Holocaust until the 1970s, it was film that would first capture the inexpressible horror of the concentration camps for most French people, in newsreels and later in the acclaimed documentary by Alain Resnais, *Nuit et Brouillard* (*Night and Fog,* 1955). Resnais' evocation of the death factories, however, sacrifices all particularities, especially about the extermination of the Jews, to the universal existential thematic of guilt and responsibility, and humanity's capacity for inhumanity. There is only one mention of the word "*Juif*" in Jean Cayrol's narration, the *Vel d'Hiv* sequence recalled in the film is silent about the 9,000 Frenchmen who engaged in the roundup, and the one sequence that clearly showed a French gendarme's *kepi,* identifying him as a guard at the Pithiviers assembly camp, was cut from the film in order to get it released, thereby leaving it mute about the Holocaust in France.

The turning point was the events of May 1968, where the memory of the German occupation was often broached, with students defining themselves against fascism, shouting "CRS equals SS" (*Compagnies Républicaines de Sécurité,* the riot police, equal the Nazi SS) or "*Nous sommes tous des juifs allemands*" ("We are all German Jews"). The myths at the heart of the Vichy syndrome were ultimately exploded by Marcel Ophul's *Le Chagrin et la pitié* (*The Sorrow and the Pity,* 1971). Originally made for French television, it was so provocative it was banned for ten years, deemed dangerous to the common good, but appeared in cinemas where it found a large audience. Set in the southern town of Clermont-Ferrand, near Vichy, the documentary foregrounded French domestic issues, making clear the politics of collaboration and the amnesia about French anti-Semitism, balanced by the struggle of the Resistance, encapsulating the various ideological tendencies of the period by juxtaposing contemporary newsreel, film, and radio clips with eyewitness testimony.

Ophul's film ushered in a new era in film and literature called "*le mode rétro*" where "looking backward" at the Vichy past and some its most insidious aspects became a major preoccupation, with attention to the "the Jewish question" most successfully accomplished in films like François Truffaut's *Le Dernier Métro* (1981) and Louis Malle's *Au revoir les enfants* (1987) and *Lacombe Lucien* (1973), written by Patrick Modiano, whose novels remarkably captured the spirit of the period in all its complexity and ambivalence. Perhaps no work encapsulated the impact of the Holocaust more forcefully than Claude Lanzmann's 586-minute documentary *Shoah* (1985) that resists all efforts to represent what happened and why, focusing entirely on the personal testimony of what perpetrators, victims, and bystanders did and felt.

Shoah was shown on television during the last nights of the trial for crimes against humanity of Klaus Barbie, known as the "butcher of Lyon" while head of the Gestapo in France's second largest city, whose life and trial was interrogated in Ophul's documentary *Hôtel Terminus* (1988). Along with the trials of René Bousquet, *milicien* Paul Touvier, and Vichy officials Jean Leguay and Maurice Papon, these French versions of the Nuremberg trials have gone a long way toward bringing the question of French responsibility home.

Although the *Shoah* was largely repressed by French collective memory until 1968, this was not the case for Jews, for whom it became constitutive of their identity. Elaine Marks usefully distinguishes between the Jews writing in French "after Auschwitz." There are those who write about the Holocaust, memorializing, documenting, and historicizing the events and combating their denial, like Nadine Fresco, Marek Halter, André Kaspi, Serge Klarsfeld, Annie Kriegel, Léon Poliakov, Renée Poznanski, André Schwarz-Bart, Pierre Vidal-Naquet, Georges Wellers, Elie Wiesel, Annette Wieviorka, and the postwar generation of French-Jewish intellectuals who re-examined "the Jewish question." There are also those who write about how to write about the Holocaust, including Robert Bober, Hélène Cixous, Jacques Derrida, Serge Doubrovsky, Jean-Pierre Faye, Alain Finkielkraut, Edmond Jabès, Sarah Kofman, and Georges Perec. These Jewish writers are contextualized by a new generation of Jewish and non-Jewish historians of Vichy France including Jean-Pierre Azéma, Yves Durand, Pierre Laborie, Pascal Ory, Denis Peschanski, Jean-Pierre Rioux, Henry Rousso, and Dominique Veillon. The

result is that today, the memory and history of Vichy France and the Holocaust is broached collectively and individually with greater self-consciousness and self-questioning, precluding any monolithic synthesis and thus more attentive to the gray zones during France's dark years.

JONATHON JUDAKEN

See also **Maurice Bardeche; Albert Camus; Helene Cixous; Jacques Derrida; Jacques Maritain; Simone Weil**

Further Reading

Burrin, Philippe, *France Under the Germans: Collaboration and Compromise*, translated by Janet Lloyd, New York: New Press, 1996

Cone, Michèle, *Artists Under Vichy: A Case of Prejudice and Persecution*, Princeton: Princeton University Press, 1992

Diamond, Hanna and Claire Gorrara (editors), *Modern and Contemporary France*, v. 7, 1999

Finkielkraut, Alain, *The Imaginary Jew*, translated by Kevin O'Neill and David Suchoff, Lincoln and London: University of Nebraska Press, 1980

Finkielkraut, Alain, *The Future of a Negation: Reflections on the Question of Genocide*, translated by Mary Byrd Kelly, Lincoln and London: University of Nebraska Press, 1988

Finkielkraut, Alain, *Remembering in Vain: The Klaus Barbie Trial and Crimes Against Humanity*, translated by Roxanne Lapidus with Sima Godfrey, New York: Columbia University Press, 1992

Fishman, Sarah, Laura Lee Downs, Ioannis Sinanoglou, et al: *France at War: Vichy and the Historians*, Oxford and New York: Berg, 2000

Flood, Christopher and Richard Golsan (editors), *Journal of European Studies*, vol. 23, 1993

Golsan, Richard (editor), *memory, the Holocaust, and French Justice: The Bousquet and Touvier Affairs*, translated by Lucy Golsan and Richard Golsan, New Hampshire and London: University Press of New England, 1996

Golsan, Richard and Jean-Franois Fourny, (editors), *L'Ésprit créateur*, vol. 33, no. 1 1993

Gordon, Bertram *Collaborationism in France During the Second World War*, Ithaca: Cornell University Press, 1980

Hallie, Philip, *Lest Innocent Blood be Shed: The Story of the Village of Le Chambon and How Goodness Happened There*, New York: Harper and Row, 1979

Hirschfeld, Gerhardt and Patrick Marsh (editors), *Collaboration in France: Politics and Culture during the Nazi Occupation 1940–1944*, Oxford: Berg, 1989

Kedward, H. R. *Occupied France: Collaboration and Resistance, 1940–1944*, Oxford and Cambridge: Blackwell, 1985

Kedward, H. R. and Roger Austin (editors), *Vichy France and the Resistance: Culture and Ideology*, London: Croom Helm, 1985

Kedward, H. R. and Nancy Wood, (editors), *The Liberation of France: Image and Event*, Oxford: Berg Publishers, 1995

Klarsfeld, Serge, *The Children of Izieu: A Human Tragedy*, New York: H. Abrams, 1985

Klarsfeld, Serge, *French Children of the Holocaust*, translated by Glorianne Depondt and Howard Epstein, New York and London: New York University Press, 1996

Kritzman, Lawrence (editor), *Auschwitz and After, Race, Culture and "the Jewish Question" in France*, New York: Routledge, 1995

Marrus, Michael and Robert Paxton, *Vichy France and the Jews*, Stanford: Stanford University Press, 1995

Marks, Elaine, *Marrano as Metaphor: The Jewish Presence in French Writing*, New York: Columbia University Press, 1996

Nochlin Linda and Tamar Garb (editors), *The Jew in the Text: Modernity and the Construction of Identity*, London: Thames and Hudson, 1995

Ory, Pascal *Les Collaborateurs 1940–45*, Paris: Éditions du Seuil, 1976

Poznanski, Renée, *Jews in France during World War II*, translated by Nathan Bracher, New Hampshire: University Press of New England for Brandeis University Press in association with the United States Holocaust Memorial Museum, 2001

Paxton, Robert, *Vichy France: Old Guard and New Order*, New York: Columbia University Press, 1972

Rousso, Henry, *The Vichy Syndrome: History and Memory in France since 1944*, translated by Arthur Goldhammer, Cambridge: Harvard, 1991

Rousso, Henry and Eric Conan, *Vichy An Ever-present Past*, Hanover: University Press of New England, 1998

Ryan, Donna, *The Holocaust and the Jews of Marseille*, Urbana and Chicago: University of Illinois Press, 1996

Sweets, John F. *Choices in Vichy France: The French Under Nazi Occupation*, New York: Oxford University Press, 1986

Sweets, John, "Hold that Pendulum!: Redefining Fascism, Collaborationism and Resistance in France," *French Historical Studies*, v. 15, no. 4 (Fall 1988): 731–758

Weisberg, Richard, *The Law and the Holocaust in France*, Amsterdam: Harwood Academic Publishers, 1996

Zucotti, Susan, *The Holocaust, the French, and the Jews*, New York: Basic Books, 1993

HOMOSEXUALITY

French thought in the first half of the twentieth century, often taking the form of literary discourse, provides what we might term a rich prehistory of self-conscious focus on male same-sex relationships and even gay identity. The strands may be summarized via those two interrelated pairings of André Gide and Marcel Proust, Jean Cocteau and Jean Genet. In the *Sodome et Gomorrhe* (*Cities of the Plain*) volume of *A La Recherche du temps perdu* (*Remembrance of Things Past*), Proust traced in novelistic and comic detail a Parisian gay *demi-monde*, prefaced by a discursive piece on "the race of men-women" which largely buys into prevailing third-sex theory while constructing an ambiguous and ironic mythology of a kind of gay diaspora characterized by subtle games of recognition and secrecy. (Eve Sedgwick of course used this as a point of departure for her *Epistemology of the Closet*; Julia Kristeva took the novel's central discourse of "*en être*"/"being one of them" to explore questions of identity and belonging in *Le Temps sensible*/*Proust and the Sense of Time*). In contrast, the slippery and contradictory figure of Gide, in his early life imbued with the influences of French Protestantism, Nietzsche, and Wilde, had sketched out pagan temptations in his early works, the explicitly and joyfully homosexual side of which emerged fully in his autobiography, *Si le grain ne meurt*/*If It Die*. In the 1924 work *Corydon*, which in late journal entries Gide considered the most important of his books, he takes the defense of homosexuality, via "socratic dialogues," on to the very ground of homophobia's condemnation of it, appropriating it as "natural" and "normal" (all the time seeking to distinguish among the [valorized] pederast who is a man who loves boys, the sodomite who desires mature men, and the invert who assumes the woman's role). Jacques Lacan devoted an essay to Gide in his *Ecrits*, "*Jeunesse d'André Gide ou la lettre et le désir*" (otherwise the French Freudo-Lacanian tradition is not rich in specific focuses on male homosexuality, but see *La Clinique lacanienne* on "*Les Homosexualités*", 2000).

The interwar gay literary scene in Paris was also marked by Cocteau, whose *Livre blanc*/*White Book*, published in a limited edition in 1928, is an autobiographical apologia for homosexuality. Cocteau was responsible for discovering Genet, whose *Journal du voleur*/*Thief's Journal* was written in prison in the early 1940s. Genet followed the aesthetic strand of Cocteau, but combined it with the post-Romantic tradition of the *poète maudit* or outcast poet, juxtaposing homosexuality and criminality in a rejection of bourgeois society and of France itself. Although he left no nonfictional work on homosexuality, and indeed took no interest in the gay liberation movement of the 1970s, preferring to concentrate on the struggles of African Americans and Palestinians, Genet is an important figure in the dominant intellectual movement of the mid century, namely Existentialism. Jean-Paul Sartre's monumental "existential psychoanalysis" of Genet, *Saint Genet comédien et martyr*/*Saint Genet Actor and Martyr* of 1952, typically sees his homosexuality in terms of choice, analogous to the choices of being a thief or a genius, as a way of dealing with his "situation."

Sartre (and indeed de Beauvoir) at the time shared many of society's (and the Left's) prejudices against homosexuality. The interwar European gay scenes and movements would take a generation to recover from the devastation wrought by Nazism and Stalinism (it should be recalled that Gide's condemnation of the USSR in 1936 was partly based on its anti-gay laws.) When that recovery came, it took on distinctive forms from those of the older Left, which when it had addressed gay issues had tended to identify a functional fit between capitalism and sexual oppression, and relied for amelioration on legislative change and the socialization of the economy. May 1968, a product of the social contradictions thrown up by French modernization, was both the high-water mark of those traditions and the point of departure for new developments, in terms of the renewal of the French parliamentary left, the further modernization of French capitalism, and the further waning of the Sartrean/Hegelian-Marxist strand in French thought in favor of those trends that had already emerged in the 1960s, which paid attention to language, difference, and the construction of subjectivities. An intriguing transitional figure here was Daniel Guérin, who had been a left socialist militant in the 1930s but who, recognizing for example the importance of the Kinsey report in the early 1950s (his *Kinsey et la sexualité* was first published in 1955), became more open about his homosexuality and sought to integrate it into his critique of capitalism and colonialism (essays on the topic were collected in a volume entitled *Homosexualité et révolution* and published in 1983). Like Gide, he also took the autobiographical route: his *Autobiographie de jeunesse/Autobiography of My Youth* accompanies its narrative with a psychoanalytic commentary.

The new gay and feminist movements of the early 1970s adopted the direct action of May 1968 and echoed its defiance of mainstream politics, but were also a reaction to its sexism and heterosexism. The *Front d'action révolutionnaire* (FHAR) thus had as its main interlocutors the revolutionary leftists. The collective text which emerged, the *Rapport contre la normalité/Report against Normality* of 1971, continued the Marxist critique of the family but also of the couple, adding the direct personal action of "coming out," which spoke to the counter-cultural priority of revolt and personal liberation, as well as being reminiscent of the personal authenticity demanded by Existentialism. Indeed, Sartre as director of the journal *Tout* (*All* or *Everything*) published the FHAR's reflections in a special issue. The moment of the FHAR unraveled fairly quickly, partly due to divisions between the men and the women, who by and large have gone their different theoretical ways ever since. Two members of the FHAR were the philosopher Gilles Deleuze and radical psychoanalyst Félix Guattari, who in 1973 had been fined for publishing the special issue of *Recherches*, the *Grande Encyclopédie des Homosexualités*. Deleuze and Guattari's *Anti-Oedipus* of 1972 sought to analyze the workings of capitalist society via an ontology of flows and codes inspired by Lucretius, Spinoza, Nietzsche, and Bergson as well as by 1960s alternative psychiatry. In this perspective, identity and personhood are seen to be oppressive coding of desire to which are preferred "desiring machines." These are to be distinguished from the mechanical, and are simply a model of connections and flows that organize recurring states of intensity out of potentialities. These molecular "becomings" are to be distinguished from the molar processes, which attempt to create unity and wholeness (or images of such). In a move away from classical Marxism, "social production and relations of production" are seen to be "an institution of desire, and (...) affects and drives form part of the infrastructure itself." The latest manifestation of "reterritorialization" is Oedipus, for the psychoanalytic institution assigns us to fixed and docile units governed by the phallus' distribution of codes according to the either/or of gender, forcing us either to integrate and conform or become neurotic. A new politics is therefore possible. Homosexuals are a "subject group" partaking of "the unconscious libidinal investment of desire" as opposed to a "subjected group," partaking of "the preconscious investment of class or interest." Thus they have the potential for "schizophrenically" destabilizing the capitalist axiomatic. (These formulations are a source of Deleuze and Guattari's more sustained reflections on "major" and "minor" cultures to be found in their work on Kafka, and in *Mille plateaux/A Thousand Plateaux* of 1980.)

Anti-Oedipus was immensely influential on one of the founders of the FHAR, Guy Hocquenghem, whose *Le Désir homosexuel/Homosexual Desire* was also published in 1972. The emphasis is on desire and the way that "homosexual desire" speaks to a wider troubling of the Oedipal codification that characterizes social oppression. Hocquenghem attempts to reconnect with the polymorphous perversity of the human infant that Freud evokes but then insists on channeling into the Oedipal trajectory founded on difference and lack. For Hocquenghem, homosexual desire is about "the self-production of desire" because it represents a crack in this Freudian system, which insists that such desire can be lived only as sublimation or neurosis/abjection. Hocquenghem thus rehabilitates "promiscuous" gay cruising, "the system in which polyvocal desire is plugged in on a non-exclusive basis." Moreover, in the famous section on "Capitalism, the Family and the Anus," Hocquenghem argues for the deprivatization of the anus. In modernity the anus is the noncodified and abject Other to the supremely socially symbolic organ that is the phallus. A desiring use of the anus (which he concedes is just one form of homosexual activity) would have the advantage of resocializing that most private and "personal" (as generating "personhood") of orifices, get us away from anxiety about lack (no one ever threatens to take away your anus, and sexual difference has nothing to do with the view from behind) and thus from capitalism's masculine "jealousy-competition" system.

This first example of the encounter between modern French thought and gay politics both asserts the centrality of homosexuality for any reflection on sex and society, and at the same time undermines any fixed position that centrality might otherwise invite. As Deleuze wrote in 1973, "no gay (*pédé*) can ever say with certainty 'I am gay'," and he continues this "transversal" attitude towards homosexuality in his preface to Hocquenghem's 1974 collection of essays, *L'Après-mai des faunes/The After-May of the Fawns*: "there are homosexual utterances, but there is no such thing as homosexuality, it's just a word, and yet let us take the word seriously, let us pass through it and make it give up everything else it contains (*tout ce qu'il contient d'autre*)." Hocquenghem himself would later distance himself further from the orthodoxy of the contemporary commercial and hyper-visible gay scene, and although hostile to notions of gay identity, he became interested in the contrasting historical constructions of same-sex activity present in the contemporary world, (*La Dérive homosexuelle/Homosexual Drift*), in modernity (*Race d'Ep! Un siècle d'images de l'homosexualité/Race d'Ep! A Century of Images of Homosexuality*), and, in his fiction, in antiquity. In the 1980s his interests included a turn to the baroque, evident in his 1987 essay "*L'Homosexualité est-elle un vice guérissable?*"/"Is Homosexuality a Curable Vice?", in which, influenced by Kierkegaard and Leibniz, he argues for the creative play of visibility and invisibility, rather than the pursuit of confession and visibility as ends in themselves.

This turn to history was of course also the major contribution in this period of Michel Foucault. Emerging from the school of discourse analysis in the *sciences humaines* of the 1960s and in turn influenced by American counterculture, Foucault's post-Enlightenment project had been to dislodge central, unifying categories such as "man" in favor of the analysis of different ways in which institutions such as the prison or medicine had mapped out in modernity the heterogeneous possibilities of the "self" and body. His 1961 work, *Histoire de la folie à l'âge classique/A History of Madness*, was already preoccupied with the delineation of boundaries between "normal" and "abnormal," locating a "Great Confinement" in the seventeenth century, when the "mad" and other categories, including homosexuals (although this section did not figure in the first English edition), were segregated from society. The originality of the first volume of the *History of Sexuality* in 1976 was to break with the Freudo Marxist orthodoxy of the sexual "repression" imposed by, and functional within, capitalism. In this "repressive hypothesis," there is supposedly something "natural" or at least beyond discourse which the apparatuses of authority and society then negate, distort, damage, or seek to suppress. But for Foucault, power—the regulation and struggle that characterize social relations—is not unidirectional or even simply "top-down." Rather, it is discourse that in a positive sense gives rise to our sexual

categories and our understanding of ourselves as sexual beings. Thus, for example, from the role of the Catholic confession onwards, even and especially at the height of the Victorian era, sex is constantly talked about rather than passed over in silence. In the modern era, this results in the crucial change from discourse about acts to discourse about identity. Whereas the principle category for mapping out same-sex desire before the mid-nineteenth century was that of "sodomy" (an act which theoretically anyone could indulge in, and one which could extend to any kind of non-reproductive sex), from the 1860s the "scientific-rational" term "homosexual" came to refer to a *species* of person. One result of this was that many interpolated by such a designation appropriated that identity both politically and culturally. This "reverse discourse" enabled the modern gay rights movements to exist. In modern liberal societies, social order is achieved not by external coercion but through internalized processes of "free" citizens. Foucault's complex take on the workings of power is not, however, a template for political quietism, but rather a call to attentiveness to that central paradox of there being no one-way street of liberation, progress, more and more "freedom." There is always a "complex and unstable process whereby discourse can be both an instrument and an effect of power, but also a hindrance, a stumbling-block, a point of resistance and a starting-point for an opposing strategy." The last two volumes of the *History of Sexuality*, *L'Usage du plaisir/The Use of Pleasure* and *Le Souci de soi/The Care of the Self* mark a turn to ethics, in which the discursive grids of ancient Greek and Roman understanding of sexuality not only relativize our own, but form the basis of an exploration of the creation of an "aesthetics of existence," an active self-fashioning or "style of life" very different from the obedience to a code of rules and interdictions, which in any case is fast disappearing from late twentieth-century society. Foucault's premature death in 1984 prevented the full elaboration of his further analyses of the history of sexuality in the early Christian era, and of his then central preoccupation with male friendship.

Although Roland Barthes wrote no specific work on homosexuality and was reluctant to write publicly about his own until the posthumously published *Incidents*, his theorizing in the 1970s of the practice and erotics of reading has important implications for gay cultural politics. The opposition set up in *Le Plaisir du texte/The Pleasure of the Text* of 1973 between the text of pleasure ("that contents . . . that comes from culture and does not break with it") and the text of bliss or *jouissance* ("the text that discomforts . . . unsettles the reader's historical, cultural, psychological assumptions") is in fact one that is very conscious of the interdependency of the two terms, not least because the attainment of the blissful noncultural state of being is impossible. Rather, the reader returns from the process in a better position to challenge and resist the culturally given. Barthes challenges not only a normative sexuality, but the very notion of a stable norm, and this represents an "atopic" strategy that disturbs binary categories: "Utopia (à la Fourier): that of a world in which there would no longer be anything but differences, so that to be differentiated would no longer mean to be excluded" (*Roland Barthes*). This is consistent with his fondness for the fragment, whose eroticism on several occasions he likens to "cruising" or *la drague*. His posthumous preface for Renaud Camus's *Tricks* emphasizes the text's inauguration of an ethic of dialogue.

The most prominent French theorists of homosexuality, Foucault and Hocquenghem, at their best exemplify a tension between a proliferating and polymorphous utopian sexual possibility, if not future, and the concrete political dilemmas and identifications, however provisional and problematic, with which it is necessary to engage. In the 1980s and 1990s, the specifically French context of these engagements was apparent: a progressive legislative environment, beginning with the equalization of the age of consent in 1982, and culminating in the adoption of the *Pacte civil de solidarité PACS* law on same-sex couple recognition in 2000; the persistence in civil society of patriarchal and homophobic discourse; the AIDS crisis and the higher infection rate in France than in many of its European neighbors; the mobilization of ACT-UP; the continuous debate in the 1990s and beyond, faced with the pluralization of society and for example the large Muslim minority, about the French republican model of centralization, assimilation, and abstract universal citizenship, and the alternative of "communitarianism." This is in part the context in which Foucault and Hocquenghem refused to "come out" about their illness, to the extent that their relationship to it has to be discerned obliquely: in Hocquenghem's case, the posthumous memoirs, *L'Amphithéâtre des morts*, which fictionalize a "self" surviving with his illness into the twenty-first century; and the figure of Muzil (Foucault) enduring and succumbing to the illness that is bound to engulf the narrator of Hervé Guibert's "autofictions," *A l'ami qui ne m'a pas sauvé la vie/To the Friend Who Did not Save My Life* and *Le Protocole Compassionnel/The Compassionate Protocol*. In fact the most sustained nonfictional account of living with HIV/AIDS comes from the resolutely "antitheoretical" Jean-Paul Aron, whose *Mon Sida/My AIDS* was published in 1988.

One fertile strand has been in the domains of sociology and history, with the work of Michaël Pollack and Florence Tamagne. To a certain extent, the intervention of France's star sociologist Pierre Bourdieu in these debates is determined by specifically French dilemmas around the particular and the universal. In an appendix to his 1998 work on *La Domination masculine/Masculine Domination*, "Some Questions on the Gay and Lesbian Movement," Bourdieu sketches an application to gay issues of his key concepts of symbolic violence or domination, and cultural capital, following on from his analysis of the fundamental relation of domination in patriarchal societies of the active, penetrating masculine principle over the passive, penetrated feminine. Bourdieu argues that the analysis of homosexuality can lead to a politics or even utopia of sexuality precisely because it acutely recalls the link between sexuality and power that this "mythology" inscribes in bodies and behaviors. The fundamental dilemma, however, for a gay and lesbian movement is how to bypass "hypocritical universalism without universalizing a particularism." The challenge is to wed a strongly subversive disposition, linked to a stigmatized status, to a highly developed cultural capital characteristic of the members of that movement.

Didier Eribon's *Réflexions sur la question gay*, published in 1999, offers a provisional balance sheet of French gay theory in the ideologically disorientating context of the end of century. A biographer of Foucault, Eribon devotes a third of his work to an analysis of his output, with a final emphasis on the capacity for building and re-inventing new subjectivities that it promises. This is prefaced by sections on homophobia ("A World of Insults," taking up the implications of Althusser and Bourdieu on the damaged subjectivities of homosexuals) and gay history ("*Spectres of Wilde*"). Both critical and benevolent towards a transatlantic theoretical world with which he is unusually fluent, Eribon addresses a very French intellectual context that is profoundly troubled by the "communitarianism" that gay activism purportedly demands. (It is this which forms the main obstacle to the development of a distinct lesbian and gay studies there, although Eribon himself has contributed to its development with a colloquium on "gay and lesbian cultures" at the Pompidou Centre in 1997 and a seminar he directed with Françoise Gaspard on "the sociology of homosexualities" at the *Ecole des Hautes Etudes en Sciences Sociales*.) In the end, Eribon recuperates Jean-Paul Sartre and Hannah Arendt for gay politics, primarily for the way in which they use the example of the Jewish experience, which for Eribon illuminates the necessity for lesbians and gays to assume creatively, without the illusion of a given essence or identity, the stigmatized status that society gives them, and then to intervene in a common public space to defend both political and legal equality, and also the idea of difference or cultural differentiation. The intensity with which these debates are posed in contemporary France promises more theoretical richness to come in debates about sexuality, identity, and modernity.

BILL MARSHALL

See also **Louis Althusser; Simone de Beauvoir; Henri Bergson; Pierre Bourdieu; Gilles Deleuze; Michel Foucault; André Gide; Félix Guattari; Daniel Guérin; Guy Hocquenghem; Julia Kristeva; Jacques Lacan; Marcel Proust; Jean-Paul Sartre**

Further Reading

"Les Homosexualités", *La Clinique lacanienne*, 4 (2000)

Aron, Jean-Paul, *Mon Sida*, Paris: Christian Bourgois, 1988

Barthes, Roland, *Le Plaisir du texte*, 1973; as *The Pleasure of the Text*, London: Jonathan Cape, 1976

Barthes, Roland, *Roland Barthes*, 1975; translated by R. Howard, London: Macmillan, 1977

Bourdieu, Pierre, *La Domination masculine*, 1998; as *Masculine Domination*, translated by R. Nice, Cambridge: Polity, 2001

Cocteau, Jean, *Le Livre blanc*, 1928, translated by M. Crosland, London: Peter Owen, 1969.

Deleuze, Gilles, and Felix Guattari, *L'Anti-Oedipe: capitalisme et schizophrénie*, 1972; as *Anti-Oedipus: Capitalism and Schizophrenia*, translated by R. Hurley, M. Seem, and H. Lane, London: Athlone Press, 1984

Deleuze, Gilles, "Lettre à un critique sévère", in *Pourparlers*, 1990; as *Negotiations*, translated by M. Joughin, NewYork: Columbia University Press, 1995

Eribon, Didier, *Réflexions sur la question gay*, Paris: Fayard, 1999

Eribon, Didier, *Papiers d'identité: interventions sur la question gay*, Paris: Fayard, 2000

Rapport contre la normalité, Paris: Champ libre, 1971

Foucault, Michel, *Histoire de la folie à l'âge classique*, 1961; as *Madness and Civilization: a History of Insanity in the Age of Reason*, translated by R. Howard, London: Routledge, 1965

Foucault, Michel, *Histoire de la sexualité, I. La Volonté de savoir*, 1976; as *The History of Sexuality, vol.1. The Will to Knowledge*, translated by R. Hurley, London: Allen Lane, 1979

Foucault, Michel, *Histoire de la sexualité, II. L'Usage des plaisirs*, 1984; as *The History of Sexuality, vol. 2. The Use of Pleasure*, translated by Robert Hurley, Harmondsworth: Viking, 1986

Foucault, Michel, *Histoire de la sexualité, III. Le Souci de soi*, 1984; as *The History of Sexuality, vol. 3. The Care of the Self*, translated by Robert Hurley, London: Allen Lane, 1986

Foucault, Michel, *Dits et écrits 1954–1988, 4 vols.*, 1994; as *Ethics, Subjectivity and Truth, vol. 1*, edited by Paul Rabinow, translated by Robert Hurley, et al, London: Allen Lane, 1997

Gide, André, *Corydon*, 1925; as *Corydon*, translated by P.B., New York: Farrar, Straus 1950

Guattari, Félix, (editor), "Trois Milliards de pervers: Grande Encyclopédie des Homosexualités", *Recherches*, 12 (1973)

Guérin, Daniel, *Kinsey et la sexualité*, Paris: Julliard, 1955

Guérin, Daniel, *Autobiographie de jeunesse, d'une dissidence sexuelle au socialisme*, Paris: Belfond, 1972

Guérin, Daniel, *Homosexualité et révolution*, Paris: Vent du Ch'min, 1983

Hocquenghem, Guy, *Le Désir homosexuel*, 1972; as *Homosexual Desire*, translated by D. Dangoor, Durham: Duke University Press, 1993

Hocquenghem, Guy, *L'Après-mai des faunes*, Paris: Grasset, 1974.

Hocquenghem, Guy, *La Dérive homosexuelle*, 1977; as "Towards an Irrecuperable Pederasty", translated by C. Fox, in *Reclaiming Sodom*, edited by Jonathan Goldberg, London: Routledge, 1994

Hocquenghem, Guy "L'homosexualité est-elle un vice guérissable?" 1987; as "On Homo-Sex", translated by B. Marshall, *New Formations*, 39 (Winter 1999–2000): 70–74

Hocquenghem, Guy, *L'Amphithéâtre des morts: mémoires anticipées*, Paris: Gallimard, 1994

Kristeva, Julia, *Le Temps sensible: Proust et l'expérience littéraire*, 1994; as *Proust and the Sense of Time*, translated by S. Bann, New York: Columbia University Press, 1993

Lacan, Jacques, "Jeunesse d'André Gide ou la lettre et le désir," in *Écrits*, (1966): 739–764

Pollack, Michaël, *Les Homosexuels et le sida: sociologie d'une épidémie*, Paris: Métailié, 1988

Sartre, Jean-Paul, *Saint Genet, comédien et martyr*, 1952; as *Saint Genet: Actor and Martyr*, translated by B. Frechtman, London: W.H. Allen, 1964

Tamagne, Florence, *Histoire de l'homosexualité en Europe: Berlin, Londres, Paris, 1919–1939*, Paris: Seuil, 2000

Tamagne, Florence, *Mauvais genre? Une histoire des représentations de l'homosexualité*, Paris: La Martinière, 2001.

HOUELLEBECQ, MICHEL
Novelist

Michel Houellebecq is one of contemporary France's most controversial novelists and thinkers. Possibly the Balzac, Camus, and Aldous Huxely of the late twentieth century, Houellebecq is a lucid chronicler, existential philosopher, and virulent critic of the world of consumerism, sexual liberation, and technology. Educated as an agricultural engineer, but also publishing poetry since the age of twenty, Houllebecq incorporates into his novels challenging discussions of quantum mechanics, cloning, poststructuralist philosophy, and psychoanalysis. His heroes are deeply flawed bourgeois males, toiling away in government bureaucracies and laboratories, eating TV dinners in their apartments, flipping through *Les Trois Suisses* catalogues, and smoking, drinking, and masturbating excessively. The tone is brutally frank. Uncensored sexual fantasies and acts, misogynist and racist remarks, wrenching self doubt and thoughts of suicide and despair spill onto the page, intermingled with serious discussions of philosophical and scientific issues and poetic evocations of French, Irish, and Tai landscapes. With the publication of several volumes of poetry; a group of critical essays; and three major works, *Extension du domaine de la lutte* (1994), *Les Particules élémentaires* (1998), and *Plateforme* (2000), Houellebecq has become the most important philosophical novelist in France, a polemicist and *provocateur*, a widely read social critic in the tradition of the existentialists, Roland Barthes, and Jean Baudrillard.

A central idea in all of Houellebecq's work is that an epistemological break occurred in the early twentieth century that promises to carry our civilization beyond the era of materialism, individualism, and positivism. The work of Nils Bohr and the Copenhagen physicists destroyed the notion of an ultimate reality of discrete objects and accurate scientific measurement. At the subatomic level, matter behaves in a strange, almost intersubjective, way. At a wedding, the phrase "The two shall become one flesh" strikes the microbiologist Michel Djerzinski, in *Les Particules élémentaires*, as an apt way to describe the bonding of elementary particles, even if the sentence has become a mockery in most marriages. The classical notion of the atom, and its corollary the individual ego, has collapsed. Out of this ruin of classical physics and psychology, Houllebecq hopes and speculates that more generous and fraternal social forms may be forged.

Extension du domaine de la lutte (1994), meaning "extension of the domain of struggle" but given the title *Whatever* in English (1998), is the chronicle of an unnamed, thirty-year-old computer engineer who works in a stultifying office complex in Paris, loathes his job and most of his colleagues, and lives a life of utter solitude and sexual frustration. The narrator has attained professional success but considers himself a failure, sexually. "Deprived of beauty and charm, subject to frequent bouts of depression, I do not correspond at all to what women are looking for. And so I have always sensed, on the part of women who opened their organs to me, a certain reticence; in fact, for them, I was always a consolation prize." Professional and private lives have become "domains of struggle" under late capitalism. The free market has created conditions in which the well-educated mercilessly enforce their advantages and grow richer and richer, while the poor grow poorer. Sexuality follows these same laws of monopoly and pauperization. The young and beautiful accumulate pleasure after pleasure while the unattractive and the old wither away in jealousy and frustration.

What sustains belief and enthusiasm for this brutally competitive and fragmentary system is an ideology of freedom and information. These ideas are formulated and defended by J. H. Fréhaut a minor character in the book, a talented programmer and an enthusiast of "the society of total information." Fréhaut believes that maximum freedom will be attained when each individual has access to a maximum of information and choices, like a neuron in the brain with its multiple connections. For Houellebecq, this saturation of information and "freedom" is precisely what has created the contemporary dystopia. Professionally and sexually, we are increasingly free, but totally unmoored from any social base and incapable of meaningful human relations. Fréhaut and others like him have ac-

celerated the process of *reification*, which consists, as Marx said, of conceiving of human beings as machines and creating workplaces and social relations that reduce them to machines. Houellebecq's writing reflects this vision of professional and sexual life as a series of mechanical processes. He describes all of human life as an accumulation of electromagnetic force, with a great discharge at puberty followed by a slow decline. "Little by little, the oscillations slow down and slowly resolve themselves into melancholy waves, from this point on, it's all over, and life is nothing but a preparation for death."

In this dark landscape, in a world of isolated and selfish egos, there are glimpses of another kind of life. From the depths of the psychiatric hospital where he is confined at the end of the novel, the narrator pens a beautiful description of human love, figured as two mirrors facing each other, drawing two people out of themselves toward "the absolutely inaccessible." Another path away from the hell of competing egos occurs in the form of citations from Buddhist wisdom literature exhorting the believer to transcend the self. "There is a path to follow and one must follow it, but there is no traveler. Acts are accomplished, but there is no actor."

In *Les Particules Elémentaires* (1998), Houellebecq continues his critique of the "*âge matérialiste*" and raises it to new theoretical heights, using as protagonists two half brothers, Michel Djerzinski, a molecular biologist, and Bruno Clément, a professor of literature. Emotionally, the two men suffer from a tumultuous upbringing brought about by self-indulgent, libertarian parents from the sixties. Their mother has married, in succession, a plastic surgeon, a filmmaker, and a New Age psychologist from California; she now lives on a commune and sleeps with almost any young hippie passing through. In addition to absent parents, Bruno is traumatized by severe hazing in the lycée of Meaux (which Houellebecq attended). Bruno's neglect as a child and his mistreatment both occur under the sign of an unfettered sexuality. His mother's debauchery and his peer's brutality are both instances of a totally free, animal expression of sexuality. The cruel schoolboys behave like Alpha male dogs or baboons enforcing a sexual hierarchy. Houellebecq's extreme and despairing thesis is that, emotionally and biologically, human sexuality has become a source of pain and chaos. Bruno and Michel bear this out in their personal lives. Michel is betrayed by his fiancée, Annabelle, who has sex with a rock musician. He never recovers from this incident. Bruno is obsessed with sex, spending his money on prostitutes, ruining his marriage and his career by harassing his female students. He does finally meet a woman as libidinous as himself, but this ends tragically as well. She is stricken with paralysis while engaged in group sex. In scientific terms, Michel's research attempts to prove that sexual reproduction is an inefficient and destructive process. Cellular division weakens the gametes, predisposing them to mutations and death. The scientific and sociological solution to this impasse is not a nostalgic return to the past but a bold step forward. Michel perfects a method of cloning that will make sexual reproduction unnecessary. There are hints that human sexual organs, freed from the necessity of reproduction, can be redesigned for greater pleasure. Michel's ideas seem a bitter irony. They read like Swift's *A Modest Proposal* or Huxley's *Brave New World*, just as Houellebecq's latest novel, *Plateforme* advances another false and parodic solution to a contemporary injustice: the idea that sexual tourism would be the perfect solution to faltering third-world economies.

The last scenes of *Les Particules Elémentaires* take place in western Ireland, where Houellebecq now lives, at the farthest edge of Europe. This would seem to conform to the place of his imagination as well, at the extreme end of one historical period, barely able to see into the future.

MATTHEW SENIOR

See also **Roland Barthes; Jean Baudrillard**

Biography

Born Michel Thomas, in 1958, and raised by his paternal grandmother whose name, Houellebecq, he adopted as a writer. As of this writing he lives in western Ireland.

Selected Works

Extension du domaine de la lutte, 1994; as *Whatever*, translated by Paul Hammond 1998
Les Particules élémentaires, 1998; as *The Elementary Particles*, translated by Frank Wynne 2001
Plateforme, 2001; as *Platform*, translated by Frank Wynne, 2003
H. P. Lovecraft: Contre le monde, contre la vie, 1991
Interventions 1998
Le Sens du combat, 1996
Rester vivant 1997

Further Readings

Noguez, Dominique. *Houellebecq, eu fait* Paris, Fayard, 2003
Abbecassis, Jack. "The Eclipse of Desire: L'Affaire Houellebecq" *Modern Language Notes* 115 (2000) 801–26.
Crowley, Martin. "Houellebecq: The Wreckage of Liberation" *Romance Studies* 20(1), 2002, 17–28.

HUMANISM AND ANTIHUMANISM

The critique of humanism in postwar French thought derives from a complex set of debates within philosophy, structural anthropology, political theory, psychoanalysis, and feminism. These debates are complicated by the tendency of the interlocutors to caricature their opponent's position. Thus antihumanists frequently criticize a conception of liberal humanism that has been systematically interrogated by humanists themselves. Broadly, the critique of humanism centered on two related issues: essentialism and morality. The first concerns the idea that there is an essential or universal essence of "man" and that this essence is the attribute of all individuals. This is what we generally refer to as "human nature." The second concern follows on from this and suggests that we can form the basis for our moral actions on this universal conception of human nature.

Hegelian Antihumanism

Contemporary antihumanism within French philosophy derives from Alexandre Kojève's influential course on Hegel delivered between 1933 and 1939. Kojève presented a reading of Hegel's master/slave dialectic as a dialectic of desire and struggle for recognition through which subjects fought to death. As Vincent Descombes describes it, Kojève "bequeathed to his listeners a *terrorist conception of history*" in which men fought to the death over ludicrous stakes. Kojève's reading of Hegel was humanist in the sense that human history provides the space within which conflicts are fought out and resolved and it is through action or *praxis* that something becomes true. Through this *anthropological* reading, however, Hegel's "end of history" thus comes to be interpreted as "the end of man" and humanism passes over into antihumanism. Kojève's humanism sought to reclaim for the human subject what the theologians attributed to the divine, and it is in this sense that Sartre was to defend humanism.

Existential Humanism

In 1946 Jean-Paul Sartre delivered a defense of existentialism in a lecture entitled "Existentialism is a Humanism." Sartre argued that there is no such thing as human nature in the sense of a universal essence of man; "man" is what he makes of himself, there is nothing before or after that. For Sartre, there is no other universality except the universality of human subjectivity, and it is the basis of subjectivity to be self-surpassing. In other words, the foundation of human subjectivity is self-transcendence, which Sartre sums up in his slogan "existence precedes essence." Like Sartre, the existential-phenomenologist Maurice Merleau-Ponty also espoused a form of humanism in the 1940s and 50s that was based on a critique of traditional notions of liberal humanism. Merleau-Ponty's "critical humanism" rejected the idea of an inner essence or fixed and universal human nature. For Merleau-Ponty the values of humanism are not timeless and immutable but are themselves human creations and therefore open to modification and change. Although liberal humanism promotes a notion of the rational autonomous individual, for Merleau-Ponty all subjectivity is "situated" and our autonomy, rationality, and freedom are the result of human praxis. As with Sartre, Merleau-Ponty argues "we are what we do." Where they diverge is that while Sartre stresses the creative self-transcending nature of human subjectivity, Merleau-Ponty places greater emphasis on the historical situation and the constraints that this places on the subject.

For existential humanism there remains one absolute truth that overrides the maxim "existence precedes essence" and that is the Cartesian *cogito*. For Sartre "I think therefore I am" is the absolute truth of consciousness and the only philosophy compatible with the dignity of man. It was precisely this point, however, that drew the most criticism of Sartre, not only from structuralists and Marxists, but also from humanists. In his "Letter on Humanism" Heidegger disclaimed any affiliation between his own philosophy and existentialism and criticized Sartre's absolute affirmation of the *cogito*. Existence, he argues, is that which lies beyond Cartesian subjectivism and all humanisms as they have so far been conceived. Humanism is the concern for man's freedom and potential humanity, but as humanism has only ever thought of this humanity within an established understanding of nature, history, and the world, it has been unable to really address the essence of man and his relationship to what Heidegger calls "Being." In short, humanism has only been able to show what differentiates us from animals rather than our essential humanity. Contrary to Sartre, existentialism does not think the humanity of man high enough. The essence of man consists precisely in being more than human, or merely a subject in relation to others.

Structuralist Antihumanism

Heidegger's "humanist" critique of Sartre therefore mirrors the antihumanist structural anthropology of Claude Lévi-Strauss. In *The Savage Mind* Lévi-Strauss similarly criticized existential historicism for its prioritization of the *cogito*. Existential historicism, he argued, presupposes that historical facts are given and capable of being experienced or known in their own

right by the individual perceiving subject. This turns history into essentially an aesthetic experience, whereby the subject tries to understand the historical process by placing themselves in the position of the subjects who lived that history. For Lévi-Strauss, historical facts are no more given than any other, they are constituted by the historian, and in this sense history can be seen to be tied to neither the perceiving subject nor the objective fact but is defined solely by its method. By prioritizing the *cogito* as the primary site for understanding history, Sartre was practicing a form of cultural imperialism through which a European consciousness and subjectivity imposes its own structure and understanding upon a disparate and heterogeneous past. In this context, Lévi-Strauss made the scandalous claim that that the ultimate goal of the human sciences was not to constitute "man" but to dissolve him.

Lévi-Strauss's important distinction between history itself and our knowledge of history informed probably the most influential antihumanism to emerge in the 1960s, that of the Marxist philosopher Louis Althusser. Althusser's antihumanism was also based on a critique of Sartre's existential or humanist Marxism. Sartre had sought to bridge the gap between the collective and the individual subject through a renewed theory of praxis and in the process to humanize Marxism. According to Althusser, humanism is an ideology that presupposes "empiricism of the subject" and "idealism of the essence." By this he meant that humanism rests on a notion of the subject that is given and of human nature or essence as transparent to itself. Marx's epistemological break was to replace the notion of the individual subject and human essence with new concepts of historical understanding (mode of production, forces and relations of production, and so on) and a new understanding of the subject as ideologically constituted. As with Levi-Strauss, therefore, the precondition for any scientific understanding of history and subjectivity was that the philosophical myth of man is reduced to ashes. The rigorously scientific critique of humanism presented by Althusser is often taken by critics as symptomatic of his "Stalinism," although, just as Sartre's existential (humanist) Marxism was formulated as a critique of Stalinism and orthodoxy within the French Communist party, so too was Althusser's antihumanist Marxism. In short, we cannot simplistically read off progressive and reactionary politics in relation to the humanist and antihumanist debates of this period.

Post-Structuralist Antihumanism

Within the Anglophone world structuralism was strongly criticized for its antihumanist polemics, but within France itself it was criticized for not being antihumanist enough. In *"The Violence of the Letter"* Jacques Derrida accused Lévi-Strauss of "phonologism," that is, of privileging speech over writing and thus bestowing authority on the sciences of "man." Although structuralism had set out to displace the myth of man, it had in fact reconfirmed it by persistently contrasting the contemporary myth with a primitive other that served as a model of natural goodness. Unintentionally, Lévi-Strauss's structuralism displays a Rousseauesque nostalgia for small communities where everyone knows and speaks with everyone else and the workings of the community are transparent to all. In this sense it represents a view of archaic and natural innocence, a world of self-presence in speech that contrasts with the present and posits a residual humanism.

The problem with structuralism, argued Derrida, was that while it denounced the limitations of the human sciences it retained and used its concepts, thus it did not fully interrogate the historicity of the concept of "man." Derrida argued that the problem with both humanism and antihumanism in postwar France was that it derived from a mistaken and overly anthropological reading of Hegel, Husserl, and Heidegger. Both positions start as if the concept of man has no origin, as if the concept has not been historically, culturally, and linguistically constructed. If we are to deconstruct the concept of "man" then we must begin with the way the concept has been constituted and constructed.

Derrida's essay "The Ends of Man," was delivered in 1968, the year students joined striking workers and barricades went up in the streets of Paris; in the heady days that followed, revolution seemed to be at hand. As order was quickly restored, political despondency and disillusionment with traditional forms of politics and organization set in. Within the academy the theoretical positions articulated by humanists, structuralists, and Marxists were seen to be complicit with the forces that had betrayed the spirit of May 1968. For many radical theorists the question was not simply how the forces of the State defeated a potential revolution but why so many who had advocated revolutionary change for so long did not seize the moment. Rejecting the scientism underlying both structuralism and Marxism and drawing on alternative traditions of libertarian anarchism, new forms of autonomous political organization and praxis were developed. In conjunction with these movements an antihumanist irrationalism emerged valorizing desire and the necessity for libidinal liberation. Jean-François Lyotard's *Libidinal Economy* and Gilles Deleuze and Felix Guattari's *Anti-Oedipus: Capitalism and Schizophrenia* sought to analyze the intricate ways through which external structures of power were internalized in the psyche to create subjects who were not only complicit but actively desired their own subjection. Michel Foucault is a key figure in this shift from the analysis of "man" as a concept constituted through external structures and discourses to the ways in which subjectification itself takes place.

In his initial "archaeological" phase Foucault was essentially an orthodox structuralist, interested in uncovering the "unconscious" rules that formed knowledge in the human sciences as manifested through their effects, rather than empirically given. At the center of the human sciences is the category of "man," but according to Foucault not as a universal, autonomous, knowing, subject, but rather as a product of "discursive practice." Moreover, this is a rather recent category and one whose time has passed. Through his microhistories of madness, criminality, and sexuality Foucault looked at the ways in which modern forms of subjectivity had been "discursively" constructed rather than being universal attributes or biologically innate. Foucault's later work on the "ethics of care" and "technologies of the self" changed focus from the analysis of scientific discourses to the processes of subjectification itself, that is, to how subjects take up discourses to constitute themselves as specific kinds of subjects. A persistent criticism of Foucault is that he does not actually have a theory of the subject prior to its discursive constitution and therefore presupposes a "humanist" subject that can be subjectivized; it is only with the work of Jacques Lacan that we find a fully theorized antihumanist subject.

As with Foucault, Lacan's theory of the subject developed over his career, and his philosophical and linguistic re-reading of Freud proposes a split or divided subject that is in opposition to all theories emanating from the *cogito*. For Lacan, the subject is not a unified or unique individual; indeed, the subject does not exist as such but is an assumption on our part, it "is" the split between consciousness and the unconscious. In the 1950s Lacan equated the unconscious and the subject with the symbolic order, as opposed to the imaginary function of the ego. As such the subject was seen to be an effect of language, although more precisely it "is" the relation to the symbolic order, the stance one adopts to language and the law. From the mid-1960s onwards, however, Lacan placed much greater emphasis on the real order and the notion of *jouissance* (painful pleasure). In this sense the subject is that which is in excess of structure and language, the subject functions as a "precipitate" or link between one signifier and another but also as a "breach" within the signifying chain which forges a link between the symbolic and the real. The subject exists in this gap between the symbolic and real orders as essentially a metaphor, or that which comes to fill the void around which the Symbolic is structured.

Anti-Essentialism

An important outcome of Lacanian psychoanalysis was to de-essentialize the subject and thus facilitate an antihumanist feminism. For Lacan, masculinity and femininity are not biologically given but are symbolic positions that can be occupied by either men or women. Subjectivity depends on which of these positions one assumes and in this sense "man" and "woman" are signifiers that stand for two sexed positions. This provides the starting point for Hélène Cixous, Luce Irigaray, and Julia Kristeva to advance a critique of the gender bias of liberal humanism and also the "phallocentrism" of contemporary psychoanalytic and philosophical discourse. While Cixous has prioritized *ecriture féminine*, Irigaray has provided a sustained critique of Western philosophy and psychoanalysis, seeking ways in which women can be represented in the symbolic rather than as "lack" in the Lacanian schema. Kristeva on the other hand has formulated a number of innovative psychoanalytic concepts: the pre-Oedipal semiotic and chora, the subject in process and psychic abjection.

The Ethical Turn

The legacy of antihumanism in France persists today through the work of ex-Althusserian Marxists: Alain Badiou, Étienne Balibar, and Jacques Rancière. These figures continue the critique of liberal humanism and remain committed to the radicalism of May '68 and the emancipatory project, but they eschew the ideological positiontaking of Althusserianism as well as the irrationalism of post-1968 antihumanism. Their work presents a more ethical, engaged antihumanism through their concerns with Truth, equality, and universality respectively.

SEAN HOMER

See also **Louis Althusser; Alain Badiou; Étienne Balibar; Helene Cixous; Gilles Deleuze; Jacques Derrida; Michel Foucault; Felix Guattari; Luce Irigaray; Alexandre Kojeve; Julia Kristeva; Jacques Lacan; Claude Levi-Strauss; Jean-Francois Lyotard; Maurice Merleau-Ponty; Jacques Ranciere; Jean-Paul Sartre**

Further Reading

Althusser, Louis, "Marxism and Humanism," in *Pour Marx*, 1965; as *For Marx*, translated by Ben Brewster, Harmondsworth: Penguin, 1969

Deleuze, Gilles and Guattari, Felix, *L'Anti-Oedipe*, 1972; as *Anti-Oedipus:Capitalism and Schizophrenia, vol. 1*, translated by Robert Hurley et al: London: Athlone Press, 1984

Derrida, Jacques, "The Violence of the Letter: From Lévi-Strauss to Rousseau," in *De la Grammatologie*, 1967; as *Of Grammatology*, translated by Gayatri Chakravorty Spivak, Baltimore: John Hopkins University Press, 1976

Derrida, Jacques, "The Ends of Man," in *Margins of Philosophy*, Brighton, Sussex: Harvester Press, 1982

Descombes, Vincent, *Le Même et L'Autre*, 1979; as *Modern French Philosophy*, translated by L. Scott-Fox and J. M. Harding, Cambridge : Cambridge University Press, 1980.

Fink, Bruce, *The Lacanian Subject: Between Language and Jouissance*, Princeton: Princeton University Press, 1995

Foucault, Michel, *Les Mots et les choses*, 1966; as *The Order of Things: An Archaeology of the Human Sciences*, London: Tavistock/Routledge, 1970

Foucault, Michel, *The Care of the Self*, London: Allen Lane, 1988

Heiddegger, Martin, "Letter on Humanism," in *Basic Writings*, edited by David Farrell Krell, London and Boston: Routledge and Kegan Paul, 1978

Kojève, Alexander, *Introduction à la lecture de Hegel*, 1947; as *Introduction to the Reading of Hegel*, translated by James H. Nicholls Jr., New York: Basic Books, 1969

Lévi-Strauss, Claude, "History and Dialectic," in *La Pensée Sauvage*, 1962; as *The Savage Mind*, London: Weidenfeld and Nicholson, 1996

Lyotard, Jean-François, *Économie Libidinale*, 1974; as *Libidinal Economy*, London: Athlone Press, 1993

Merleau-Ponty, Maurice, *Humanism and Terror*, Boston: Beacon, 1969

Moi, Toril, (editor), *The Kristeva Reader*, Oxford; Blackwell, 1986

Sartre, Jean-Paul, "Existentialism is a Humanism," in *Existentialism from Dostoevsky to Sartre*, edited by Walter Kaufmann, New York: Meridan, 1975.

Shiach, Morag, *Hélène Cixous: A Politics of Writing*, London: Routledge, 1991

Soper, Kate, *Humanism and Antihumanism*, London: Hutchinson, 1986

Whitford, Margaret (editor), *The Irigaray Reader*, Oxford: Blackwell, 1991

Žižek, Slavoj, "The Split Universality," in *The Ticklish Subject: the absent center of political ontology*, London: Verso, 1999

HUYGUE, RENÉ
Art Historian

Art historian and critic, member of the *Académie française*, and chief curator of the Louvre drawings collection, René Huyghe has held the chair of visual arts psychology at the *Collège de France*. He is known for his general investigation into the arts through works such as *The Dialogue with the Visible* (1956), *Art and the Soul* (1960), *Meaning and Destiny of Art* (1967), *Forms and Forces* (1971), *The Turn of the Real* (*La relève du réel*, 1974) and *The Turn of the Imaginary* (*La relève de l'imaginaire*, 1976), which pertain to Elie Faure and Focillon's classical tradition. René Huyghe's art criticism is informed by *Gestalttheorie* and the writings of Riegl, Semper, and Wölfflin. His contribution to the field has not been limited to the mere popularization of art history, and can be said to reflect an attempt at setting art on Bergsonian foundations, while at the same time endeavoring to assimilate the data of the most advanced sciences of the time.

The great philosophical synthesis which Huygue set out to accomplish in *Forms and Forces* showed that the theoretical basis of his approach drew on Bergsonian and vitalist ideas of the beginning of the century and, more generally, on the romantic conception of art (in particular that of August Wilhelm Schlegel). To a certain extent, Huygue's understanding of art criticism is analogous to the organic and comprehensive approach to literary studies promoted by the Geneva critical theory school. The idea of a discourse on the synthesis of visual arts, spurred by the new iconographic possibilities opened up during the 1950s and 1960s, echoed André Malraux's conception of the *Musée imaginaire*. Vitalism, which makes the transition from nature to art, ensures the unity of the notion of creation, which is thought to introduce new forms both in nature and the arts. This parallel goes on to justify the idea of a manifest homogeneity between artistic creation and the various fields of the applied sciences (for example, geology, physics, biology).

In true Bergsonian fashion, Huygue argued that the universe is made up of forms and forces, of quantity and quality, of space and duration. Art, therefore, appears as a dialectics of forms and forces that evolve throughout art history. The work of art represents the "appeased drama" of the struggle between the acting forces of subjectivity and the forms of a particular style. However, the finality of artistic creation points to the humanistic project of self-knowledge. In the dialectical relationship between form and content, the form is identical to the work, and has a limiting aspect, whereas the content relates to the totality of one's past life: feelings, impulses, and ideas. In *Art and the Soul* (1960), Huygue's main concern was to add a social, and further on, a cosmic dimension to his psychological investigation of art. From this point of view, art "from the atom to Rembrandt" can be said to defy entropy and determinism. Like consciousness, art affirms the creative power expressed by duration, according to Bergson's theses in *The Creative Evolution* (*L'Evolution créatrice*). Obviously, one cannot simply proceed to classify artists as organizers of forms and of space: on the one hand Della Francesca, Raphael, and the classics who conform to Greek thought, and on the other the rebels who brought about movement: Tintoretto, Rubens, Turner, and the baroque artists. The dialectics of forms and forces manifests itself through each creator. Nevertheless, given his Bergsonian background, Huygue finds it difficult to articulate his condemnation of the materialistic aspects of contemporary art. According to Huyghes, phenomena of regression, dissolution, and mechanization were sapping the transgressive and anticlassical movements of the 1970s, which were unlikely to generate new fertile forms.

In *Forms and Forces* (1971), the distinctive iconographic context of the work of art is sometimes unduly neglected in favor of Huygue's hyperbolic digressions, which explore the possible links between the forms of artistic creation and those pertaining to natural sciences, to biology, zoology, astro-physics, or mathematics. However, in *The Turn of the Real* (*La Relève du réel*, 1976), Huygue came back to detailed studies of impressionism, expressionism, and symbolism as movements situated in their historical context. This time, his affinity for Bergsonian theories accounted for the minute reconstruction of the profile of artists such as Degas, Monet, Renoir, and Cézanne, in keeping with Huygue's idea that "every great artist adopts a human attitude which becomes the driving spirit of his creation." As in previous studies, the law of the "alternate and compensating predominance of form and force" governed Huygue's analysis of nineteenth-century art in *The Turn of the Imaginary* (1976). The alternation between classical and baroque tendencies stood out as the cornerstone of his conception of art. From this perspective, the nineteenth century displayed the "releasing of the tension" that had been contained since the Renaissance. However, the tensions between forms and forces, or, more specifically, between neoclassicism and romanticism, would re-emerge, before long, within the boundaries of nineteenth-century art. The artist was at the heart of the confrontation between individual rights and society. As a historian, Huygue has been aware of the distance that separates the main theoretical concerns of his discourse from the irreducible personality of artists whose work he has explored.

The study of Géricault provided Huygue with the opportunity of deploying his argument of the synthesis between the cult of the form and the dynamism of energy with reference to a specific case. Delacroix thus seemed to manifest "burning passion," Ingres "bourgeois integrity," and Corot "purity." The choice of title reflected the author's intention of capturing the essence of an artist, which proved undoubtedly beneficial to the popularization aims of his study. As Huygue argued, following the escapist aesthetics of two successive periods, one dominated by the imaginary (Ingres, Delacroix), the other by solitude (Corot), nineteenth-century art resolutely led to the "turn of the real" (*la relève du réel*), which corresponded to an orientation toward social objectivity (Courbet, Caillebotte, Millet). Overall, the analysis of these great personalities involved the vastly erudite investigation of both the literary and the socio-historical context pertaining to each individual artist. Delacroix made the object of a particularly compelling study. According to Huygue, Delacroix introduced the power of imagination in art, by transfiguring Orientalism as well as contemporary themes such as the war between the Greeks and the Turks. In his detailed interpretation of Delacroix's *Massacre of Scio*, Huygue highlights the manner in which the painter used the historical motif in order to render his own obsession with violence, death, and inevitability. Building on his previous writings (*Delacroix*, 1963), Huygue carefully retraced the evolution of the painter's work, through a close study of his *Diary*. This example eloquently proves that Huygue belongs to the German tradition of the psychology of artistic creation.

OLIVIER SALAZAR-FERRER

See also **Henri Bergson; Henri-Joseph Focillon**

Biography

Rene Huygue was born in Arras, May 3, 1906. He studied philosophy and esthetics at the Sorbonne. He became assistant curator at the Louvre in 1930, and head curator in 1937. That same year he became a professor in the school of the Louvre. He was asked to join Jean Mistler's (Undersecretary d'État aux Beaux-Arts) cabinet in 1932. Huygue was named professor at the Collège de France in 1950. He was elected to the French Academy in 1960, formally accepted the honor in 1961. Huygue died February 5, 1997.

Selected Works

Dialogue avec le visible, 1955
L'Art et l'homme, 3 vol., 1957, 1958, 1961
L'art et l'âme, 1960
Delacroix, 1963
Les Puissances de l'image, 1965
Sens et destin de l'art, 2 vols., 1967
Formes et forces, 1971
La relève du réel, 1974
La Relève de l'imaginaire, 1976

HYVRARD, JEANNE
Writer

Jeanne Hyvrard claims to have come to writing by accident or fate: after spending two years teaching in the French Antilles, she wrote her first work with the intention of producing an objective social report on the living conditions of natives—especially women—that she had witnessed there, in the hope of raising awareness of the appalling conditions under which natives of the Caribbean were forced to live after colonization. However, in spite of her intentions, in the resultant text (*Les Prunes de Cythère*, 1975), Hyvrard's lyric, literary language and powerful inscription of the first

person into the text rendered the intended objectivity impossible. Fact blended with fiction, imagination with experience, setting the precedent for much of Hyvrard's later writing and making of *Les Prunes de Cythère*, her first novel: "*J'ai fait sans le savoir œuvre de littérature, je dirais presque malgré moi. Ainsi s'est écrit et non pas j'ai écrit 'Les Prunes de Cythère'. J'accédais à la littérature en parfaite sauvage.*" (Verthuy-Williams, et al, 1988). Despite her use of different genres and apparently diverse subjects, there is a similarity evident in all of Hyvrard's texts, and each individual work forms part of a broad philosophy and testimony of the world as she has seen it and recorded it in a substantial opus of novels, poetry, plays, and social reports.

As well as a writer, Hyvrard is also an important theorist, and her relevance in contemporary theory is by no means restricted to feminist thought/concerns, despite a tendency to categorize her within French feminist theory and literature because of the context in which she came to writing and her involvement in the events of May 1968. Hyvrard's writing brings together many different areas of contemporary study, such as gender and identity (including notions of maternity and female genealogy), as well as language and the symbolic. Hyvrard's writing is more than "*écriture féminine*"—a term she in fact rejects, claiming that it implies that men do "writing" and women "écriture féminine." Hyvrard writes for the world rather than simply for women, and her concerns are global rather than purely feminine. However, Hyvrard's texts are unquestionably female-focused, and all draw on her own experience without being entirely autobiographical: *Les Prunes de Cythère* (1975) draws a parallel between the oppression of women and that of colonized natives/territories, *Le Cercan* (1987) cites cancer of the female sexual organs as the physical manifestation of society's oppression of women, and *La Jeune morte en robe de dentelle* (1990) is a harrowing psychological analysis of the abject relationship between a mother and her daughter. Thus, Hyvrard's texts generally posit the female body as the locus of social disease, with the emancipation/redemption of the feminine subject used as metaphor for that of all marginalized or silenced groups. This reflects the way in which all of Hyvrard's writing comes out of her own experience, as she turns her writing outwards toward more global issues in order to find the social or political equivalent of her experience of being a woman. It is for this reason that Hyvrard is also discussed in works on ecofeminism, as she establishes a connection between the abuse of the planet through pollution, economic exploitation, or scientific advances and the abuse of the female subject position in contemporary society.

Like many French women writers in the latter half of the twentieth century, Hyvrard rejects a linear writing style, favoring circular, centerless texts that spiral outwards and fall back in on themselves, often through the repetition of fragments of the narrative that echo like a refrain. Reading Hyvrard has been likened to listening to music or to studying water flow (Waelti-Walters, 1996), both of these analogies attesting to the fluidity and mutability of Hyvrard's work. Nonetheless, the lack of linearity in Hyvrard is not to say that she does not apply a certain structure to her writing. She claims that her texts are works of "literary constructivism": applying a scientific method to works of literature, she describes writing as *"un acte volontaire de pousser la langue au maximum de ce qu'elle peut fournir, comme on pousse les mathématiques, comme on pousse la physique, [. . .] Donc, j'ai l'impression de faire une espèce de démarche scientifique. [. . .] [T]oute mon œuvre est une œuvre scientifique. Et que c'est se servir, comment dire, de la langue, comme un outil scientifique."* ("a voluntary act of pushing language to the limit of what it can yield, as one pushes mathematics or physics [. . .] Thus, I have the impression of undertaking a kind of scientific exercise. [. . .] All of my work is scientific work. And it implies using language, so to speak, as a scientific tool." (Vassallo, 2002). Thus, although Hyvrard rejects logic or rational thought and indeed rejects many advances in science, suggesting that these lead to a dehumanization of the species, she nonetheless implements her own kind of scientific theory to her work, resulting in what she calls "chaorganisation" (the organization of the world rather than its ordering, through a system that prioritizes chaos as opposed to logos). Hyvrard's philosophy is a result of what she sees as the inadequacy of contemporary culture faced with the reality of the world. This is evident in her opposition of linearity and *pensée ronde* (round thought), as she questions repeatedly *"comment l'homme peut-il naviguer droit sur un monde ronde?"* ("How can Man navigate a round world in a straight line?") (*Canal de la Toussaint*).

In order to express her philosophy, Hyvrard invents a series of neologisms to define her "encepts" (itself an Hyvrardian neologism—arguing that concepts are closed, and therefore cannot adequately express an evolving thought, Hyvrard believes that we *enceive* open thoughts). As Hyvrard's thought spiralled and grew, so her invented terminology expanded, to the point at which, in 1989, she created a dictionary of her neologisms, *La Pensée corps* (*Body Thought*). This text is crucial to an understanding of Hyvrard's work because in it she sets out her ideas for a new world ("the Tierce Culture or Third Culture") to counteract the problems that she identifies in the existing structures of contemporary society.

The principal metaphor around which Hyvrard's work revolves is drawn from the book of Genesis: the chaos that existed before separation and the naming of things. This is also when reason became recognized as the only acceptable way of viewing the world—a view that Hyvrard rejects emphatically and energetically. Hyvrard views the pre-Genesis state as a fusional one in which man and woman were the same substance, but this substance has since been separated and divided into increasingly precise categories. Therefore, Hyvard considers that when the male and female body join together in an act of love, we come closer to regaining this fusional, chaotic state. A pre-Genesis time is presented as a period when totality and unity existed, and Hyvrard describes this as a pre-rational utopia that we should strive to regain, citing this as the third culture and positing a return to the archaic as a blueprint for the future.

HELEN VASSALLO

Biography

Born in Paris in 1945, Jeanne Hyvrard trained as an economist and lawyer and, as of this writing, still holds her long-term job as a teacher at a Parisian technical college. Hyvrard spent two years teaching in the French Caribbean (1969–1971), and her experiences there prompted her to begin writing as a testimony to what she saw as the destruction of the world through Western society and values. Very private, Jeanne Hyvrard is a pseudonym, and the author refrains from engaging with the Parisian literary scene, preferring to keep her work and her private life separate.

Selected Works

Les Prunes de Cythère, 1975
Mère la Mort, 1976
La Meurtritude, 1977
État de veille au commencement de la nuit, 1981–1982
La baisure suivi de *que se partagent encore les eaux*, 1984
Auditions musicales certains soirs d'été, 1984
Paroles de suicidaires: cette vie passée à la sauver, 1985
Canal de la Toussaint, 1985
Le cercan, 1987
La pensée corps, 1989
La jeune morte en robe de dentelle, 1990
Au Présage de la mienne, 1997
Resserres à louer, 1997
Ton nom de végétal, 1998
Grand choix de couteaux à l'intérieur, 1998
Cella: essai sur le représentement à l'encre de Chine et aux sels d'argent, 1998
Minotaure en habit d'Arlequin suivi de *Le marchoir*, 1998
La formosité: inventaire de la beauté et de toutes les formes de formes, 2000
Ranger le monde: essai sur l'emballement, 2001

Further Reading

Atack, Margaret and Phil Powrie, (editors), *Contemporary French Fiction by women: feminist perspectives,* Manchester and New York: Manchester University Press, 1990

Bishop, Michael (editor), *Thirty Voices in the Feminine,* Amsterdam/Atlanta: Rodopi, 1996

Cauville, Joëlle and Metka Zupancic, (editors), *Réécriture des myths: l'utopie au feminine,* Amsterdam/Atlanta: Rodopi, 1997

Fallaize, Elizabeth, *French Women's Writing,* London: MacMillan Press, 1993

Heathcote, Owen, "Reinventing gendered violence? The autobiographical writings of Hyvrard, Jeanne, Hélène Cixous and Marguerite Duras," *Modern and Contemporary France,* 8 (2) (2000): 203–214

Kramarae, Cheris, Muriel Schulz and William O'Barr, *Language and Power,* California, London, and New Delhi: Sage, 1994

Lourie, Margaret A., Donna C. Stanton and Martha Vicinus (editors), *Women and Memory,* Michigan: Michigan Quarterly Review, 1987

Saigal, Monique, *L'écriture: lien de mere à fille chez Jeanne Hyvrard, Chantal Chawaf et Annie Ernaux,* Amsterdam/Atlanta: Rodopi, 2000

Sorrell, Martin, *Elles: A Bilingual Anthology of Modern French Poetry by Women,* Exeter: University of Exeter Press, 1995

Verthuy-Williams, Maïr and Jennifer Waelti-Walters, *Jeanne Hyvrard,* Amsterdam: Rodopi, 1988

Waelti-Walters, Jennifer, "La pensée fusionnelle et la pensée séparatrice chez Jeanne Hyvrard," *Mosaic,* xix, 4

Waelti-Walters, Jennifer, *Fairytales and the female imagination,* Montreal: Eden Press, 1982

Waelti-Walters, Jennifer, *Jeanne Hyvrard: Theorist of the Modern World,* Edinburgh: Edinburgh University Press, 1996

Waelti-Walters, Jennifer (editor), *Jeanne Hyvrard: la langue d'avenir,* Canada: APFUCC, 1998

Ward Jouve, Nicole, *White Woman Speaks with Forked Tongue,* London: Routledge, 1991

Worton, Michael and Judith Still (editors), *Intertextuality: theories and practices,* Manchester and New York: Manchester University Press, 1990

I

THE INFLUENCE OF GERMAN THOUGHT

Since the 1920s, French thinkers have used often unorthodox interpretations of German thought to move beyond the narrow concerns that had rendered French academic philosophy almost entirely irrelevant outside of France, and to engage with contemporary problems of history, politics, and ethics in a way that gave French philosophy worldwide importance. In the 1920s and 1930s, French philosophers were drawn to German thinkers such as G. W. F. Hegel, Karl Marx, the phenomenologist Edmund Husserl, and Martin Heidegger, who was often linked in early French commentaries to the "philosopher of existence," Karl Jaspers. The heady mixture of Hegelian dialectics, phenomenology, existentialism, and Marxism would hold sway over French philosophy until the 1950s, when it would be displaced first by a nonexistentialist interpretation of Hegel and Heidegger, and then in the 1960s by new interpretations of Marx, Sigmund Freud, and Friedrich Nietzsche. Besides these dominant currents, there was also considerable French interest in the philosophy of history of Wilhelm Dilthey and Max Weber, and with the critical idealism of Immanuel Kant. Modern French philosophy's involvement with German thought produced some of its richest works, and encompassed its most important thinkers, including Emmanuel Levinas, Jean-Paul Sartre, Maurice Merleau-Ponty, Jacques Lacan, Louis Althusser, Gilles Deleuze, Michel Foucault, Jean-François Lyotard, and Jacques Derrida.

Hegel was an anathema to French academic philosophy in the 1920s and 1930s when his philosophy gave new impetus to French thought by being interpreted in terms of his unfaithful descendants, Marx and Kierkegaard. In the interwar period of political upheaval and modernization, when the future of society and the place of the individual were both very much in question, interpreters looked to Hegel for a philosophy of history and action that would address problems of alienation, class division, and divisions within the self. In articles in 1923–24, Bernard Groethuysen linked Hegel to Marx, and to contemporary Marxists, such as the Hungarian Georg Lukács, whose *History and Class Consciousness* (1922) argued for a Hegelian Marxism in which the central problem was human alienation, or self-estrangement under capitalism. Alienation was also the central problem for the surrealist André Breton, who in his *Second Manifesto of Surrealism* (*Second manifeste du surréalisme*, 1930) thought Hegel's dialectic of negation and "the negation of the negation," whereby a category (such is waking life) gives rise to its opposite (dreaming), and then is negated and overcome in a category that combines both together (surreality), pointed the way to the overcoming of the psychic divisions plaguing the human mind, such as the opposition between unconscious desires and rational conscious awareness, as well as the class divisions within society. Hegel's revolutionary dialectic of destruction was the link between Freud and Marx. A number of intellectuals within the French Communist party in the 1930s, such as Jean Baby, René Maublanc, and Georges Friedmann, likewise seized on the revolutionary nature of Hegel's dialectic, even though they derided Hegel's "idealism," arguing that Marx's dialectical materialism, with its emphasis on productive and revolutionary activity, placed negation in reality rather than mere thought. The most remarkable Communist philosopher of the period, Henri Lefebvre, based his philosophy of *praxis* (human practical activity) on Hegel's analysis of work in the "Master and Slave" chapter of the *Phenomenology of Spirit* (1807). For Hegel, work negates matter in its natural form by giving it a form determined by human needs and purposes; as such, work is a synthesis of mind and matter, and human labor is the engine of human progress, negating nature, or things as they are, to create a new and more human order of things. Lefebvre likewise sees *praxis* as the creative destruction of what exists for the sake of "total man," the individual living in harmony with nature and with others under a social order that expresses her own needs and desires. This philosophy of *praxis* greatly influenced Sartre's *Critique of Dialectical Reason* (*Critique de la raison dialectique*, 1960).

Hegel's "master-slave dialectic" was also crucial for the influential lectures on Hegel given in Paris at the *École Pratique des Hautes Études* from 1933–39 by Alexandre Kojève (*Introduction à la lecture de Hegel*, 1947), and attended by Breton, Lacan, Merleau-Ponty, Georges Bataille, and Pierre Klossowski, among others. For Kojève, the desire that makes us human is not our physical needs, but our desire to have another human being recognize and validate our choices and point of view, or our freedom. The master is willing to sacrifice his life to compel others to recognize his freedom; the slave surrenders because he values life more than freedom, and is then compelled to work to satisfy the master's needs. However, the slave's labor transforms the world, and so the slave's deferral of the satisfaction of his own desires is a more creative and significant form of negation than the master's satisfaction through consumption. Ultimately, humans are satisfied in the full sense only when the universal laws of the state recognize and guarantee their individual rights as citizen-workers, at which point the creative negation definitive of humanity becomes useless, history is at an end, and "man is dead." This thesis of the "end of history" would profoundly mark Merleau-Ponty's Hegelian-Marxist philosophy of history in *Humanism and Terror* (*Humanisme et Terreur*, 1947), a defense of Soviet communism, and Georges Bataille's works are preoccupied with the question of what becomes of human negativity at the end of history, after the desire for recognition has been satisfied. With the postwar loss of faith in the imminence of a revolution that would usher in Kojève's "universal homogeneous state," the "death of man" was taken up in a different way by Michel Foucault in *The Order of Things* (*Les mots et les choses*, 1966) and by Jacques Derrida in "The Ends of Man" ("Les fins de l'homme," 1968). For both, it signifies a move beyond the humanist metaphysics of Sartre and others, who had made human existence the measure of all things. In Kojève's interpretation, however, there are very strong existentialist elements, especially Kojève's thesis that work is a way of avoiding the anxiety before death, which the master fearlessly confronts, an idea that owes much to Heidegger's notion of "freedom for death" in *Being and Time* (1927).

The existentialist interpretation of Hegel began earlier, with Jean Wahl's *The Unhappiness of Consciousness in Hegel's Philosophy* (*Le Malheur de la conscience dans la philosophie de Hegel*, 1929). Wahl argued that the struggle between self and other of the master-slave dialectic was merely the outward expression of a deeper struggle within the self, between the being of the self and its nothingness as a negating power. The theme of a self divided and opposed to itself, which is continually negating itself, Wahl took from Hegel's "Unhappy Consciousness" section of the *Phenomenology*, and would greatly influence Sartre's *Being and Nothingness* (*L'Être et le néant*, 1943) and Jean Hyppolite's *Genesis and Structure of Hegel's Phenomenology of Spirit* (*Genèse et structure de la Phénoménologie de l'esprit de Hegel*, 1946) and his French translation of the *Phenomenology* (1939–41). In a similar vein, Benjamin Fondane's *The Unhappy Consciousness* (*La conscience malheureuse*, 1936) argued that the Marxist and surrealist attempts to overcome alienation would necessarily fail, as the condition of society is the repression of instinctive desires. From this existentialist standpoint, the "end of history" was an impossible ideal, a "beyond" longed for but never realized, because the divisions within the self were intractable—a view also shared by Wahl, the early Sartre, and Alexandre Koyré ("Hegel à Iéna," 1934–35).

Existentialism was introduced to France simultaneously with phenomenology, such that Husserl and Heidegger were often mentioned together. Like Hegelianism, existentialism in the 1930s was seen as a philosophy that could deal with the concrete problems of human existence in a way that academic philosophy could not. It is not surprising, then, that although some, such as Georges Gurvitch (*Tendances actuelles de la philosophie allemande*, 1930) saw in Husserl and Heidegger a way of resisting Hegel's "idealism," many others—such as Kojève, Koyré, Sartre, and Bernard Groethuysen (*Introduction à la philosophie allemande depuis Nietzsche*, 1926), combined "the three Hs," sometimes adding Marx to the mix as well. Husserl gave lectures at the Sorbonne in 1929, soon translated by Levinas and Gabrielle Peiffer as *Cartesian Meditations* (*Méditations cartésiennes: Introduction à la phénoménologie*, 1931). In the meantime, Levinas's important monograph on Husserl, *The Theory of Intuition in Husserl's Phenomenology* (*La théorie de l'intuition dans la phénoménologie de Husserl*, 1930) examined phenomenology from the standpoint of Heidegger's ontology, emphasizing the theme of understanding being through the finitude of human existence (*Dasein*). Much later, in *Totality and the Infinite* (*Totalité et l'infini*, 1961), Levinas would criticize Heidegger and Hegel for giving primacy to ontology over ethics.

Heidegger in 1930s France was universally regarded as an existentialist, and became known through Henri Corbin's translation of *What is Metaphysics?* (*Qu'est-ce que la métaphysique?*, 1931), and a translation of *The Essence of Grounds* (De la nature de la cause) in *Recherches Philosophiques* in 1931–32. *Recherches Philosophiques* also published numerous reviews (usually by Kojève) of books on Heidegger, as well as Wahl's essay on Heidegger and Kierkegaard (1932–33) and Sartre's early study of Husserl, *The Transcendence of the Ego* (1936–37), and from 1931 to 1937 provided a forum for the discussion of German thought, and for the work of German emigrés such as Karl Löwith (who had studied with Heidegger) and Eric Weil. A number of Wahl's books in this period explored existential themes in Heidegger, notably *Toward the Concrete* (*Vers le concret*, 1932) and *Kierkegaardian Studies* (*Études kierkegaardiennes*, 1938). The existentialist reading of Heidegger was cemented by the publication of Corbin's *Qu'est-ce que la métaphysique?* (1938), which included translations of sections 46–53 (on anxiety before "the Nothing," death, and finitude) and 72–76 (on history, historicity, and resolute decision) of *Being and Time*, and the sections of *Kant and the Problem of Metaphysics* dealing with "fundamental ontology" in light of *Dasein*'s finitude, "thrownness" and care: precisely the most dramatic and existential portions of these books. The excitement aroused by this reading of Heidegger was matched by the enthusiasm for Husserl, who, like Heidegger, seemed to take philosophy beyond the French neo-Kantian idealism in which consciousness encountered only its own products, and "toward the concrete." As Sartre breathlessly explained in his 1939 article in *La Nouvelle Revue française*, "Intentionality: A Fundamental Idea of Husserl's phenomenology" ("*Une idée fondamentale de la phénoménologie de Husserl: l'intentionnalité*"), Husserl's doctrine of intentionality, according to which consciousness is always directed toward objects other than and beyond itself, tells us that "everything is outside, even ourselves . . . outside, in the world, among others . . . in the city, amidst the crowd, a thing among things, a man among men." Existential phenomenology, combining Husserl and Heidegger, and sometimes also Hegel, Marx or Jaspers, became the order of the day.

"The concrete" in Merleau-Ponty's important *Phenomenology of Perception* (*Phénoménologie de la perception*, 1945) was interpreted as the embodied existence revealed in Gestalt psychology, interpreted

through the later Husserl's idea of a "life-world" that forms the preconscious basis for conscious choices. Together with Karl Jasper's idea of "understanding" others by attempting to see their situation in terms of their goals, Merleau-Ponty's phenomenology inspired Mikel Dufrenne's *Phenomenology of Aesthetic Experience* (*Phénoménologie de l'expérience esthétique*, 1953), Paul Ricoeur's early works, such as *Freedom and Nature: The Voluntary and the Involuntary* (*Philosophie de la volonté. I. Le volontaire et l'involontaire*, 1950), and even Sartre's *Search for a Method* (*Questions de méthode*, 1960), works that mark the end-point of existential phenomenology's ascendancy. In perhaps the most ambitious synthesis of all, Simone de Beauvoir's *The Second Sex* (*Le Deuxième sexe*, 1949) combined existential phenomenology, Hegel, Marx, sociology, and anthropology in her pioneering analysis of sexual difference and the oppression of women, raising an issue later taken up by Luce Irigaray in the 1970s, albeit using very different methods from de Beauvoir's.

The grand synthesis of Hegel, Husserl, and Heidegger was undone by Heidegger himself, whose 1946 letter to the French philosopher Jean Beaufret, "Letter on Humanism" ("Lettre sur l'humanisme," 1947, 1953) denounced Sartre's humanist reading of *Being and Time*, and argued that rather than understanding Being through human existence, human existence should be understood through its relation to Being. This "turning" in Heidegger's thought, toward Being and away from human existence, influenced later works by Merleau-Ponty, such as *The Visible and the Invisible* (*Le visible et l'invisible*, 1964), and by Hyppolite, such as *Logic and Existence* (*Logique et existence*, 1953). More significantly, it influenced their students, such as Althusser, Deleuze, Foucault, and Derrida. "Humanism" was off the agenda. For Althusser, Deleuze, and Foucault, this meant a move away from Hegel and phenomenology; for Derrida and those influenced by him (Jean-Luc Nancy, Philippe Lacoue-Labarthe, Sarah Kofman, Irigaray), it meant seeking a nonanthropological reading of Husserl (see Derrida's *Husserl's Origin of Geometry; L'origine de la géométrie*, 1962), Heidegger, and sometimes Hegel. The move to Being was a move away from human agency, motivated in part by the disappointment of revolutionary hopes in postwar France, and the consequent feeling that the existentialist-Hegelian view of history and human agency had aroused inflated and hubristic expectations. Merleau-Ponty played a key role in the deflation of these expectations in his *Adventures of the Dialectic* (*Les aventures de la dialectique*, 1955). Directed primarily against Sartre, it also applied to his own earlier synthesis of Hegel and Marx, and was prompted by his disillusionment with Soviet communism after the Korean War. Now profoundly skeptical of any "end of history," Merleau-Ponty criticized the entire tradition of "Western Marxism," from Lukács to Sartre, using the liberalism of Max Weber, also based on understanding an event by situating the actions of historical agents within their historical horizon, as in Jaspers or Dilthey, but which is "a politics of understanding [*compréhension*] that has learned to doubt itself." Rather than a speculative dialectic of history, in which the present foreshadows the future and historical development unfolds according to a kind of logic, there can only be an understanding of the past that helps situate the present, and which leaves the future open. In using Weber against Hegel and Marx, Merleau-Ponty takes up a strand of German thought that had been introduced to France in the 1930s by Raymond Aron, in his *Contemporary German Sociology* (*La sociologie allemande contemporaine*, 1935), which contains an important chapter on Weber on contingency in history, as does his *Critical Philosophy of History* (*La philosophie critique de l'histoire*, 1935), which also deals with Dilthey and Georg Simmel on the limits of historical understanding, and begins with the ringing declaration, "The traditional philosophy of history reaches its fulfillment in Hegel's system. Modern philosophy of history begins with the refusal of Hegelianism." In his *Introduction to the Philosophy of History* (*Introduction à la philosophie de l'histoire*, 1938), Aron succinctly explains that the truth of the past, attainable from the point of view of Hegel's absolute, is lost to us if we accept that we are historically determined and limited. Modesty in historical interpretation, and an awareness of limits, is the byword of the "Critical" approach to history, and implies a nonutopian and modest politics. By the 1950s, skepticism concerning historical progress and the possibilities of human action took hold in France, as the politically unstable Fourth Republic found itself embroiled in conflicts in Viet Nam and Algeria.

As uncertainty changed to stasis with De Gaulle's consolidation of power under the Fifth Republic, French thought turned away from dynamism and agency toward an analysis of the structures of power. Louis Althusser would abandon Hegel's historical dialectic in order to save Marx, not to criticize him. In essays collected in *For Marx* (*Pour Marx*, 1965) and the collaborative work undertaken with Pierre Macherey, Etienne Balibar, and others, *Reading Capital* (*Lire le Capital*, 1965), Althusser not only tries to separate the "mature" Marx from the Hegelian "young" Marx, but reads Marx in light of what Ricoeur calls the "hermeneutics of suspicion" of Freud and Nietzsche (and Marx himself), according to which a text is not to be interpreted through the supposed intentions of its author, but through "symptoms" manifesting the underlying (and unconscious) forces and structures that produced it. Society was not to be understood through conscious intentions, but through structural relations governing economic and productive forces, and the relations among intellectual practices that, although "relatively autonomous," nevertheless reflected the economic relations. The task of Marxism, said Althusser, was to bring to light the structures that govern *praxis* without individuals being aware of them, rather than to uncover a truth in *praxis* as consciously experienced.

The importance of a productive and structured unconscious had been argued for by Lacan in a number of papers since the 1940s, finally collected and published as *Writings* (*Écrits*, 1966). This thesis was taken up by Julia Kristeva in *Revolution in Poetic Language* (*La révolution du langage poétique*, 1974), as well as by Gilles Deleuze, with particular reference to Nietzsche's concept of the "will to power," in *Nietzsche and Philosophy* (*Nietzsche et la philosophie*, 1962) and *Difference and Repetition* (*Différence et répétition*, 1968), and later, with Félix Guattari, in *Anti-Oedipus* (*L'Anti-Oedipe*, 1972) and *A Thousand Plateaus* (*Milles plateaux*, 1980). Marx, Nietzsche, and Freud were all used to argue that since consciousness was unaware of the sources of its own thoughts, existential phenomenology was based on an illusion, with Deleuze also arguing that Hegel's dialectic of the negation of the negation was an expression the slavish resentment Nietzsche had diagnosed as "nihilism."

The anti-Hegelian use of Nietzsche was also evident in Pierre Klossowski's *Nietzsche and the Vicious Circle* (*Nietzsche et le cercle vicieux*, 1969) and in Foucault, who, like Althusser and Deleuze, saw consciousness more as a repository of delusions and errors than as providing access to reality. Foucault's essay "Nietzsche, Genealogy, History" (1971) argues that history must be freed from teleology, continuity, and notions of progress; his studies of the prison (*Discipline and Punish; Surveiller et punir*, 1975) and of the history of sexuality (*Histoire de la sexualité*, 1976–1984) use Nietzsche's "genealogical" method to examine how these social products produce effects on the body and on behavior. Paradoxically, the emphasis on unconscious forces seemed to potentially open up greater and more radical possibilities of changes in social relations than had the phenomenology of consciousness, although more in post-structuralist Nietzscheans such as Deleuze and Foucault than in structuralists like Althusser or Lacan. In the 1960s and 70s, when Marx-Nietzsche-Freud became the new triumvirate of German thinkers, Derrida and Irigaray nevertheless continued to use Hegel's dialectic as a way of subverting traditional oppositions, but they denied the possibility of any synthesis emerging from negations, and displaced the dialectic from consciousness to language (see Derrida, *Glas*, 1974; Irigaray, *Ce sexe qui n'est pas un*; *This Sex Which is Not One*, 1977).

As the twentieth century neared its end, French philosophy once again turned to German thought, but this time to free itself from the apparent inability of the new consensus to generate an adequate set of ethical norms. Formerly a Marxist, Jean-François Lyotard turns in his later works to the leading German thinker in French philosophy at the beginning of the century, Immanuel Kant. Lyotard wants to use Kant's critique of the limits of human knowledge, but without the teleological view of history as progress that Kant shared with Hegel. In *The Post-Modern Condition* (*La condition post moderne*, 1979), he argues that because different fields of knowledge operate according to different norms and parameters, and so are incommensurable with one another; an overarching synthesis can only result from the forcible imposition of one particular norm to the exclusion of all others, which is a form of terror. The experience of the sublime also humbles the understanding by revealing its limits, showing the folly of trying to overstep those limits or to reduce other points of view to our own (*Lessons on the "Analytic of the Sublime," Kant, Critique of Judgment*; *Leçons sur l'"Analyitique du sublime", Kant, Critique de la faculté de juger*, 1991). Foucault, in one of his last essays, also relied on Kant, much as Aron and Merleau-Ponty relied on Weber and Dilthey, to argue for the impossibility of a total critique that would take a point of view outside of one's historically and socially determined situation. All criticism could only be, in the final analysis, self-criticism, the basis for an ethics of remaking the self (*What is Enlightenment?*, 1984). A similar concern for an ethics of the self, and indeed of the subject, is evident in the works of Luc Ferry and Alain Renaut, who argue that Heidegger's insistence on the finitude and openness of *ek-sistence* is fully compatible with a Kantian philosophy of a limited but autonomous subject, not fully conditioned by its environment, but capable of taking a critical distance from itself through its capacity for reflecting on itself and its situation (*French Philosophy of the Sixties*; 1985). A return to Kant is the surest method of avoiding the extravagances of Hegel, Marx, and existentialism, and the foundation of a politics and ethics of individual human rights (*From the Rights of Man to the Republican Idea; Des droits de l'homme à l'idée républicaine*, 1985). After the debacles of Communism, and the fall of communism in the Soviet bloc, it is not surprising that French thought should return to the emphasis on limits and on individual rights in Kant's critical philosophy.

At each stage, then, French philosophy has made use of those German thinkers who best met the needs of their own situation, especially when the need was to overcome the overwhelming dominance of a previous German thinker. In the tumultuous 1920s and 1930s, Hegel, Husserl, and Heidegger liberated French thought from conservative neo-Kantian idealism; in the 1950s, Heidegger's *Letter on Humanism* broke up the existential-phenomenological synthesis and Merleau-Ponty's rediscovery of Weber overturned Hegelian Marxism during a time of political and social retrenchment; in the renewed upheaval of the late 1960s, new readings of Marx, Nietzsche, and Freud seemed to offer an infinity of social possibilities even as the "subject" was eclipsed; and finally, the return to Kant was an attempt to establish limits and to reassert the importance of the individual subject, now disabused of its existentialist illusions.

BRUCE BAUGH

Further Reading

Althusser, Louis, *Pour Marx*, Paris: F. Maspero, 1965.

Althusser, Louis, et al., *Lire le Capital* Paris: F. Maspero, 1965

Aron, Raymond *La sociologie allemande contemporaine*, Paris: Presses Universitaires de France, 1935.

Aron, Raymond, *La philosophie critique de l'histoire* Paris: Vrin, 1938

Aron, Raymond, *Introduction à la philosophie de l'histoire* Paris: Gallimard, 1938.

Baby, Jean, Marcel Cohen, Georges Friedmann, René Maublanc, *A la lumière du marxisme*, Paris: Editions Sociates Internationales, 1935.

Bataille, Georges, *L'expérience intérieure* Paris: Gallimard, 1943

Bataille, Georges *Le coupable* Paris: Gallimard, 1944

Bataille, Georges. *Sur Nietzsche* Paris: Gallimard, 1945.

Breton, André. *Second manifeste du surréalisme*, Paris: Editions Kra, 1930

Cornu, Auguste, *Karl Marx: l'homme et l'oeuvre. De l'hégélienisme au matérialisme historique (1818–1845)*, Paris: Alcan, 1934.

De Beauvoir, Simone. *Le deuxième sexe* Paris: Gallimard, 1949.

Deleuze, Gilles, *Nietzsche et la philosophie* Paris: Presses Universitaires de France, 1962

Deleuze, Gilles. *Différence et répétition* Paris: Presses Universitaires de France, 1968

Deleuze, Gilles and Félix Guattari, *L'Anti-oedipe* Paris: Minuit, 1972

Derrida, Jacques, *L'origine de la géométrie de Husserl*, Paris: Presses Universitaires de France, 1962

Derrida, Jacques, *L'écriture et la différence*; Paris: Seuil, 1967

Derrida, Jacques, *La Voix et le phénomène*, Paris: Presses Universitaires de France, 1967.

Derrida, Jacques, *Marges de la philosophie*, Paris: Minuit, 1972

Derrida, Jacques, *Glas*, Paris: Galilée, 1974

De Waehlens, Alphonse, *La Philosophie de Martin Heidegger* Louvain: Nauwelaerts, 1942

Dufrenne, Mikel, *Phénoménologie de l'expérience esthétique*, Paris: Presses Universitaires de France, 1953

Ferry, Luc and Alain Renaut, *La pensée 68. Essai sur l'anithumanisme contemporain*; Paris: Gallimard, 1985.

Ferry, Luc and Alain Renavit, *Desdroits de l'homme à l'idée, republicaine*, Paris: Presses Universitaires de France, 1985

Fondane, Benjamin, *La conscience malheureuse*, Paris: Denoël et Steele, 1936

Foucault, Michel, "Nietzsche, la généalogie, l'histoire", in Suzanne Bachelard et al., *Hommage à Jean Hyppolite*. Paris: Presses Universitaires de France, 1971.

Foucault, Michel, *Surveiller et punir*, Paris: Gallimard, 1975.

Foucault, Michel, *L'histoire de la sexualité I: La volonté de savoir* Paris: Gallimard, 1976

Foucault, Michel, "What is Enlightenment?", in *The Foucault Reader*, ed. Paul Rabinow. New York: Random House, 1984, 32–50.

Groethuysen, Bernard, "Les Jeunes Hégéliens et les origines du socialisme contemporainen Allemagne," *Revue philosophique de la France et de l'étranger* 95 (1923): 379–402

Groethuysen, Bernard, *Introduction à la philosophie allemande depuis Nietzsche*, Paris: Stock, 1926.

Gurvitch, Georges, *Tendances actuelles da la philosophie allemande*, paris: Vrin, 1930

Hegel, G.W.F, *La phénoménologie de l'esprit*, 2 vols., translated by Jean Hyppolite, Paris: Aubier-Montaigue, 1939–41.

Hegel, G. W. F., *Principes de la philosophie du droit*, translated by André Kaan, Paris: Gallimard, 1940.

Heidegger, Martin, "Qu'est-ce que la métaphysique?" translated by Henri Corbin, *Bifur* no. 8 (June 1931):

Heidegger, Martin, "De la nature de la cause," translated by A. Bessy in *Recherches philosophiques* (1931–32): 83–124.

Heidegger, Martin. *Qu'est-ce que la métaphysique?*, translated by Henri Corbin, Paris: Gallimard, 1938.

Heidegger, Martin, "Lettre sur l'humanisme," Cahiess du Sud, nos. 319–320 (1953)

Husserl, Edmund. *Méditations cartésiennes; Introduction à la phénoménologie*, translated by Gabrielle Peiffer and Emmanuel Levinas, Paris: A. Colin, 1931.

Husserl, Edmund. *Idées directrices pour une phénoménologie*, translated by Paul Ricoeur, Paris: Gallimard, 1950.

Hyppolite, Jean, "Les travaux de jeunesse de Hegel d'après des ouvrages récents," *Revue de métaphysique et de morale* 42 (1935): 399–426, 547–77.

Hyppolite, Jean, "Vie et prise de conscience de la vie dans la philosophie hégélienne," *Revue de métaphysique et de morale* 45 (1938): 45–61

Hyppolite, Jean. *Genèse et structure de la Phénoménologie de l'esprit de Hegel*, Paris: Aubier, 1946

Hyppolite, Jean, *Logique et existence*, Paris: Presses Universitaires de France, 1953

Irigaray, Luce, *Ce sexe qui n'est pas un*; Paris: Minuit, 1977

Irigaray, Luce *Speculum de l'autre femme*, Paris: Minuit, 1974.

Klossowski, Pierre, *Nietzsche et le cercle vicieux*, Paris: Mercure de France, 1969

Kojève, Alexandre (translator), "Autonomy and Dependence of Self-Consciousness:Mastery and Servitude" in *Phenomenology of Spirit, Mesures* (14 January 1939)

Kojève, Alexandre. *Introduction à la lecture de Hegel*, Paris: Gallimard, 1947

Koyré, Alexandre. "Rapport sur les etudes hégéliennes en France, QcF Verhandlungen des Ersten Hegel Kongress. Tübingen, 1931.

Koyré, Alexandre. "Hegel à Iéna" [Hegel in Jena]. *Revue philosophique de la France et de l'étranger* 118 (1934): 274–83

Kristeva, Julia, *La révolution du langage poétique* Paris: Seuil, 1974

Lacan, Jacques, *Écrits*, Paris: Sevil, 1966

Lefebvre, Henri and Norbert Guterman, *Morceaux choisis de Marx*, Paris: Gallimard, 1934

Lefebvre, Henri and Norbert Gutermann. *La conscience mystifiée*, Paris: Gallimard, 1936

Lefebvre, Henri and Norbert Guterman, "Introduction" to V. I. Lenin, *Cahiers sur la dialectique de Hegel*, Paris: Gallimard, 1938.

Lefebvre, Henri and Norbert Guterman, *Morceaux choisis de Hegel*, Paris: Gallimard, 1939

Lefebvre, Henri, *Le matérialisme dialectique*, Paris: Alcan, 1939.

Levinas, Emmanuel, *Totalité et l'infini*, The Hague: Martinus Nijhoff, 1961

Levinas, Emmanuel, *Théorie de l'intuition dans la phénoménologie de Husserl*, Paris: Alcan, 1930

Löwith, Karl, "L'achèvement de la philosophie classique par Hegel et sa dissolution chez Marx et Kierkegaard," *Recherches Philosophiques* 4 (1934–35): 232–67

Lyotard, Jean-François. *Leçons sur l'"Analyitique du sublime", Kant, Critique de la faculté de juger, paragraphes 23–29* Paris: Galilée, 1991

Lyotard, Jean-François. *La condition postmoderne*, Paris: Minuit, 1979.

Merleau-Ponty, Maurice. *La Phénoménologie de la perception*, Paris: Gallimard, 1945

Merleau-Ponty, *Humanisme et Terreur: Essai sur le problème communiste*, Paris: Gallimard, 1947.

Merleau-Ponty, Maurice. *Les aventures de la dialectique*, Paris: Gallimard, 1955.

Merleau-Ponty, Maurice, *Le Visible et l'invisible*, Paris: Gallimard, 1964

Renaut, Alain, *L'ère de l'individu: contribution à une histoire de la subjectivité*, Paris: Gallimard, 1989

Ricoeur, Paul. *Le volontaire et l'involontaire*, Paris: Aubier-Montaigne, 1950

Sartre, Jean-Paul, "La transcendance de l'ego. Esquisse d'une description phénoménologique," *Recherches Philosophiques* 6 (1936–37): 85–123

Sartre, Jean-Paul, "Une idée fondamentale de la phénoménologie de Husserl: l'intentionnalité," *La Nouvelle Revue française* 304 (January 1939): 129–31.

Sartre, Jean-Paul, *L'Imaginaire, psychogie phénoménologique de l'imagination*, Paris: Gallimard, 1940.

Sartre, Jean-Paul, *L'être et le néant*, Paris: Gallimard, 1943.

Sartre, Jean-Paul, *Critique de la raison dialectique, précédé de Questions de méthode*, Paris: Gallimard: 1960

Tchijewsky, D, "Hegel et Nietzsche," *Revue d'histoire de la philosophie* 3 (1929): 321–47

Wahl, Jean, *Le malheur de la conscience dans la philosophie de Hegel*, Paris: Rieder, 1929.

Wahl, Jean. *Vers le concret*, Paris: Vrin, 1932.

Wahl, Jean, "Hegel et Kierkegaard," *Recherches Philosophiques* 2 (1932–33): 347–70.

Wahl, Jean, *Études kierkegaardiennes*, Paris: Aubier, 1938

Special Hegel issue of the *Revue de métaphysique et de morale*, 1931

Further Reading

Baugh, Bruce, *French Hegel*. New York and London: Routledge, 2003

Descombes, Vincent, *Modern French Philosophy*, Translated by L. Scott-Fax and J. M. Harding. Cambridge: Cambridge University Press, 1980

Gutting, Gary *French Philosophy in the Twentieth Century*, Cambridge: Cambridge University Press, 2001

Poster, Mark, *Existential Marxism in Postwar France*, Princeton: Princeton University Press, 1975.

Roudinesco, Elisabeth, *Jacques Lacan and Company: A History of Psychoanalysis in France, 1925–1985*, Chicago: University of Chicago Press, 1990

Zévaès, Alexandre, *De l'introduction du marxisme en France*, Paris: M. Rivière, 1947.

INTELLECTUALS

Since the eighteenth century, the public sphere in France has given rise to a type of cultural producer who exerts considerable symbolic power over various fields, such as art, literature, humanities, science, and politics. Since the Dreyfus affair, the judiciary scandal that shook the Third Republic around 1900, such a cultural producer has been called an "intellectual." The intellectual is an engaged cultural producer—a professional who integrates a political and moral orientation with a scientific or high cultural project. The intellectual's political engagement may consist in articulating the legitimate interests of the people, in reclaiming the democratic and universal values of the republic, or in denouncing forms of social injustice.

A survey about French intellectuals in the twentieth century has to take into account the relationship between intellectual ideas and their political and social contexts. It also has to consider the historical configurations without which the richness of French intellectual history can hardly be grasped. Thus, in order to understand the cultural significance of the period from 1898 (outbreak of the Dreyfus affair) to 1984 (Foucault's death), it is necessary to put this short golden age of the modernist French intellectual in historical perspective. The other golden age was, of course, the era of the Enlightenment (*l'âge des lumières*), when the modern intellectual was born. However, if during the eighteenth century a distinct public sphere emerged against the absolutist state and the clerical system, what was the situation of the intellectuals who entered the scene over a hundred years after the French Revolution? Before we turn to French intellectuals in the twentieth century, let us dwell on the immediate prehistory of the modernist intellectual whose model was given by Zola.

Certainly the view that France's intellectual life in the nineteenth century was less intense as compared to its own immediate past and to other European countries needs in many ways correction. During this time, there was a significant group of autonomous literary producers, such as Victor Hugo, who were both eminent literary stars and political activists. Yet although the major republican narratives and the founding myths in national politics reached back to the French Revolution, the achievements of the more academic and scholarly producers were in a certain sense still dwarfed by the success of their German competitors. During the nineteenth century and despite the nationalist tendencies in Europe, a broad import of German academic works and academic standards set in, from idealist philosophy over sophisticated methods in philology to rigorous and specialized scientific research based on a high degree of division of labor. This trend continued until after World War II, when Hegel, Marx, Nietzsche, Husserl, Freud, Heidegger were greeted enthusiastically by many French intellectuals.

The main reason for the relative weakness of French academic life in the nineteenth and the first half of the twentieth century was the absence of strong, autonomous institutions of higher education, which were not created until 1968, when the traditional faculties (*facultés*) were finally transformed into full-fledged universities. Although in the nineteenth century German bourgeois academics and intellectuals (*Bildungsbürger*) had a prestigious and well funded institution at their avail, that is, Humboldt's University, French faculties and schools (*écoles*) were an extension of the primary system of high or grammar schools (*lycées*) rather than an autonomous system of rigorous research, graduate education, and pure scholarship. As late as during the first half of the twentieth century, the faculties, whose roots mostly reached back before the Revolution, served primarily as the purveyors of academic degrees (for example, *licence, maîtrise*), but they did not offer comprehensive programs of advanced academic education, let alone independent research. The schools (*écoles*), by contrast, were products of the French Revolution. Although set up by the republican state in order to produce highly qualified state bureaucrats and teachers, they could not make up for the lack of prestigious academic work and rigorous research in the faculties either. Despite the high prestige and the splendid careers they promised (and continue to promise) to their graduates, these schools' primary purpose was to fulfill the state's needs and to produce future civil servants. Even the most "intellectual" of all elite schools, the *École Normale Supérieure (Rue d'Ulm)*, focused more on the reproductive drilling of philosophy teachers than on the productive creation of autonomous academic work.

Therefore it is important to note that during the nineteenth century and the first half of the twentieth century an important number of symbolic producers existed outside of the institutions of higher education and of the centers of traditional academic learning (like the *Sorbonne* and the *Académie française*). The modernist conjuncture of symbolic production that originated with the establishment of the modernist field of vanguard art in the last third of the nineteenth century would have been hardly conceivable without this growing group of independent high cultural producers both from the French province, where the secondary system absorbed only a marginal number of their graduates, and from abroad. As a consequence of the continuing influx of new ambitious producers into the capital, the market of symbolic production expanded to a degree that an autonomous subsector of restrained production emerged. According to Bourdieu, restrained production is geared toward the exclusive demands of other symbolic producers, and the modernist conjuncture can be seen as a spin-off of the differentiation of cultural production. It is against the background of a well developed, both centralized and highly differentiated market of symbolic production that the modernist producers and intellectuals could gain such an important role in France. The concentration of cultural producers in Paris and the differentiated structure of the intellectual field did not only lead to a rapid succession of new trends and fads, but also promised high symbolic profits to those intellectual leaders able to assert themselves in the various fields of high cultural production, of academic excellence, and of national politics.

During the Dreyfus affair the modernist intellectual subjectivity and discourse were articulated for the first time. Alfred Dreyfus was a captain on the French general staff convicted for espionage in 1894, although it soon became clear that his transgression consisted rather in his Jewish religion than in actual treason. From 1897 on, a growing number of literary and academic producers, among them Charles Péguy, André Gide, Marcel Proust, Lucien Herr, and Émile Zola, rallied in order to plea for a retrial, and Zola's famous article "I accuse" ("*J'accuse*", 1898) became the manifesto of the newly formed group of intellectuals. Rapidly, the affair became much more than a simple judiciary scandal and led to the explosion of a long and fierce conflict between the clerical conservative forces and the liberal democratic adherents of the Third Republic, who were represented by the intellectuals.

The activation of intellectual engagement that ensued thereafter has been characterized by rapid shifts and upheavals that can be broadly rubricated under five symbolic conjunctures represented by five major intellectual "pontificates": the first high modernist conjuncture of the historical avant-garde during World War I (for example, Marcel Proust), the second high modernist conjuncture of the *front populaire* and surrealism (for example, André Gide, André Breton), the first late modernist conjuncture or existentialism (led by Jean-Paul Sartre), the second late modernist conjuncture and the astounding success of the *sciences humaines* and the psycho-Marxo-structuralist discourse (whose politically most visible representative was Michel Foucault), and the postmodernist conjuncture (the return of liberal political theory and the "left of the left" intellectual Pierre Bourdieu). These symbolic conjunctures were supported by specific groups and networks that in most cases had an intellectual journal at their disposal, for example, *La Nouvelle revue française* (founded in 1908 by Gide), *Les Temps modernes* (founded in 1945 by Sartre), *Tel Quel* (founded in 1960 by the avant-garde theorist and writer Philippe Sollers), *Actes de la recherche en sciences sociales* (founded in 1975 by Bourdieu), *Le Débat* (founded in 1980 by the liberal historian Pierre Nora).

The complex and contradictory tendencies of the intellectual history of the twentieth century notwithstanding, a constant factor in the transition from the high modernist to the late modernist conjunctures was the increasing role of academic producers, finally culminating in Bourdieu's social scientific pontificate. Although the two high modernist conjunctures were predominantly led by artists and writers, the late modernist period witnessed the rise of more academic intellectuals. Jean-Paul Sartre, for instance, the first star intellectual earning both literary and academic recognition, became the exemplar of the French intellectual: A graduate from *École Normale*, he started out as a philosophy teacher at high school (*lycée*) and then became an independent writer who was politicized in the French *résistance*. His impact on French intellectual life was so decisive that his skillful shifting between hitherto separated fields of symbolic production (such as philosophy, literature, theater, print and radio journalism, compare Boschetti) left a durable imprint on the field of symbolic production (such as the French newspaper *Libération*, which began under his auspices in 1973). Sartre personifies the engaged intellectual who employs his consecration as a literary and scholarly producer in the service of political action.

In order to explain the receding dominance of nonacademic high cultural producers, three important developments that occurred after World War II should be considered: 1) After the Sputnik shock and toward the end of the Algerian War (1954–1962), an unprecedented explosion of academic positions occurred under de Gaulle's ministry of Culture (1958–1969) and ex-leftist intellectual André Malraux. In no other Western country did academic research and higher education expand so powerfully from such a low level in such a short period of time. As a consequence, freelance intellectuals, *hommes de lettres*, and autodidacts like Roland Barthes were rapidly absorbed by an academic system in full expansion. 2) The increasing standing of the more technocratic branches of higher education gradually undermined and devalued the prestige of the more intellectual schools, perhaps best exemplified by the success of the *Ecole Nationale d'Administration* (ENA), founded in 1945, over the *Ecole Normale Supérieure* (ENS), Rue d'Ulm, founded in 1794. Up until after World War II, the philosophical, humanistic training of the ENS was considered sufficiently prestigious to lead their graduates to the highest positions in French politics, economy, or culture (compare Jean Jaurès, Léon Blum, and Georges Pompidou's splendid political careers). From the early 1960s on, however, the most brilliant students began to turn away from philosophy and the traditional humanistic canon. These students, still heavily imbued with French philosophical culture, either tried to adapt their cultural capital to the new demands of the fledgling *sciences humaines* and its *science pilote*, linguistics, or they switched directly over to ENA, which promised more successful careers in French politics, administration, and economy. 3) With the advent of the society of the spectacle (Debord), the print media increasingly gave way to television. Television is not only much more prone to the diffusion of images and iconic representations; television journalists in France have also come to exert a far-reaching influence on political issues (Debray). Television offers a vast audience and rapid careers to symbolic producers who no longer have to be consecrated as legitimate high cultural or academic producers in order to gain an important voice in national politics. So even though intellectual journals and newspapers continue to thrive (*Le Nouvel Observateur, Le Monde*), the crisis of the modernist hegemony of nonacademic high cultural production could not help but sharpen.

In the first half of the 1980s, the era of the modernist intellectual, who mediated between academic and non-academic symbolic production, ended and the post-modernist or, to be more precise, an antimodernist period was heralded. A great many of the intellectual stars of the preceding period passed away or disappeared from the public (Sartre, Lacan, Barthes, Foucault; Althusser was interned after murdering his wife, and Sollers terminated *Tel Quel*) and a new generation of liberal intellectuals entered the scene. This crisis of modernist ideology and subjectivity set in soon after the French publication of Solzhenitsyn's *The Gulag Archipelago* (1976), which ushered in a period not only of de-Marxification of French intellectual life, but also of the disenchantment with the major intellectual prophets of the past, be they Marxists, existentialists, psychoanalysts, or structuralists (Hourmant). Thus this postmodernist period—which should not be confounded with the Anglo-American phenomenon of postmodernism or poststructuralism, a term not familiar in the French context—has led to a rehabilitation of liberal and antitotalitarian thinkers of the past (compare Raymond Aron or the anti-Stalinist circle *Socialisme ou Barbarie* of Claude Lefort and Cornélius Castoriadis) and to a resurgence of liberal and neo-liberal ideas (compare Ferry/Renaut's assault on the "*pensée 68*"). The so-called new philosophers (*nouveaux philosophes*) were the first to get wide attention by articulating the crisis of the left project that was also a crisis of intellectual prophethood. As late modernist intellectuals (compare Deleuze) have pointed out, the success of this group of young *normalien* philosophers and ex-Maoists who gathered around the illustrious Bernard-Henri Lévy demonstrates the increasing influence of national television on intellectual strategies and careers.

With the demise of the modernist intellectual, French intellectual life entered a period of redifferentiation and recompartmentalization. No longer did intellectuals bridge the various subfields of symbolic production as they did until the mid-1970s; academics, journalists, and artists increasingly opted for a return to their respective disciplinary, journalistic, or artistic origins. When in 1981 the Left under François Mitterand finally came to power, the major intellectual newspaper *Le Monde* announced the curious disengagement of intellectual production (publicized under the slogan of *le silence des intellectuels*). The intellectuals who now became politically dominant no longer climbed trash cans to arouse the revolutionary spirit of the people (as Sartre did). Instead, in becoming a political counselor, commentator, and analyst, the successor of the modernist intellectual prefers American-style engagement, for example, the sociologist Alain Touraine, whose political analyses have gained wide diffusion both with the media networks and with political think tanks (like the *Fondation Saint-Simon*), or the aforementioned Luc Ferry, who became Minister of Culture after Chirac's electoral triumph in 2002.

Thus for French intellectuals the early 1980s marked a caesura in both theoretical and political terms: The structuralist critique of the free autonomous subject was abandoned in favor of a renewed interest in human rights, ethics, and morality. Philosophers reclaimed the liberal heritage of the Republic and pleaded against the "irresponsible" politico-philosophical projects of the 1960s and 1970s represented by German philosophers like Nietzsche and Heidegger (compare Victor Farias, *Heidegger et le nazisme*, 1987, or Luc Ferry and Alain Renaut, *Heidegger et les modernes*, 1988). The period since 1980 has also been a period of a sharpening crisis of journals and publishing houses. Intellectual works and products, it seems, are no longer as controversial and influential as they used to be. Although France's major publishing firms pull back from the market of intellectual production (compare the financial difficulties of *Presses Universitaires de France*), the massive export of certain French intellectual brands—Derridian deconstruction, Lacanian psychoanalysis, Foucauldian discourse analysis, Sartrean existentialism, which, it is true, never represented more than a fraction of French intellectual life—to humanities departments in North America and Great Britain has diminished.

But even though there is evidence that intellectual power in France is on the decline, the 1990s have seen a growing movement of political contestation whose undisputed intellectual leader became the sociologist Pierre Bourdieu. Adopting in a certain sense the radical political rhetoric of his late modernist predecessors, Bourdieu insisted on a clear demarcation from the "non-scientific," that is, philosophical and aesthetic preoccupation of the modernist producers. Ironically enough, it is the anti-Sartrean social scientist Pierre Bourdieu who turned out to be the most faithful adherent of the Sartrean model of an engaged intellectual combining sophisticated scholarly capacities with a strong political perspective. But through his emphasis on rigorous academic work and scientific methodology, Bourdieu epitomizes the overarching success of the certified academic worker over the independent *homme de lettres* and avant-garde artist. Bourdieu's success as both a sociologist and political activist testifies that French intellectuals continue to play an important role vis-à-vis the current political challenges, such as racial and social discrimination (*exclusion*), neoliberalism, and globalization.

JOHANNES ANGERMÜLLER

See also **Louis Althusser; Raymond Aron; Roland Barthes; Pierre Bourdieu; Andre Breton; Cornelius Castoriadis; Guy Debord; Regis Debray; Gilles Deleuze; Jacques Derrida; Michel Foucault; Andre Gide; Jean Jaures; Jacques Lacan; Claude Lefort; Bernard-Henri Levy; Jean-Paul Sartre**

Further Reading

Bodin, Louis, *Les Intellectuels*, Paris: PUF, 1964

Boschetti, Anna, *L'Impresa intellettuale. Sartre e "Les Temps modernes"*, Bari: Edizioni Dedalo, 1984

Boudon, Raymond, "L'intellectuel et ses publics: les singularités françaises," in *Français–qui êtes vous?*, edited by Jean-Daniel Reynaud and Yves Grefmeyer, Paris: La documentation française, 1971

Bourdieu, Pierre, "Champ intellectuel et projet créateur," *Les Temps modernes* 246 (1966): 865–906

Bourdieu, Pierre, *Homo Academicus*, Paris: Minuit, 1984

Bourgin, Hubert, *De Jaurès à Léon Blum. L'Ecole Normale et la politique*, Paris: Arthème Fayard, 1938

Charle, Christophe, *Naissance des "intellectuels,"* Paris: Minuit, 1990

Le Débat, special number (50): *Notre histoire. Matériaux pour servir à l'histoire intellectuelle de la France, 1953–1987*, 1988

Debray, Régis, *Le Pouvoir intellectuel en France*, Paris: Ramsay, 1979

Deleuze, Gilles, *A propos des "nouveaux philosophes" et d'un problème plus général.* Supplément au no 24, mai 1977, Paris: Minuit, 1977

Domenach, Jean-Marie, "Le monde des intellectuels," in *Société et culture de la France contemporaine*, edited by G. Santoni, Albany: State University of New York Press, 1981

Ferry, Luc and Alain Renaut, *La Pensée 68. L'essai sur l'anti-humanisme contemporain*, Paris: Gallimard, 1985

Foucault, Michel and Gilles Deleuze, "Les intellectuels et le pouvoir," *L'Arc* 49 1972: 3–10

Furet, François, "Les Intellectuels français et le structuralisme," *Preuves* 192 (1967): 3–12

Hamon, Hervé and Patrick Rotman, *Les Intellocrates: Expédition en haute intelligentsia*, Paris: Ramsay, 1981

Hirsh, Arthur, *The French New Left. An Intellectual History from Sartre to Gorz*, Boston: South End Press, 1981

Hourmant, François, *Le Désenchantement des clercs. Figures de l'intellectuel dans l'après-Mai 68*, Rennes: Presses universitaires de Rennes, 1997

Julliard, Jacques and Michel Winock, *Dictionnaire des intellectuels français*, Paris: Seuil, 1996

Kauppi, Niilo, *French Intellectual Nobility. Institutional and Symbolic Transformations in the Post-Sartrean Era*, Albany, New York: State University of New York Press, 1996

Le Goff, Jacques, *Les Intellectuels au Moyen Age*, Paris: Le Seuil, 1985

Lévy, Bernard-Henri, *Éloge des intellectuels*, Paris: Grasset, 1987

Lourau, René, *Le Lapsus des intellectuels*, Paris: Privat, 1981

Morin, Edgar, "Ce qui a changé dans la vie intellectuelle française," *Le Débat* 40 (1986): 72–84

Nora, Pierre, "Que peuvent les intellectuels?" *Le Débat* 1 (1980): 3–19

Ory, Pascal and Jean-François Sirinelli, *Les Intellectuels en France, de l'affaire Dreyfus à nos jours*, Paris: Armand Collin, 1992

Reader, Keith, *Intellectuals and the Left in France since 1968*, Basingstoke: Macmillan, 1987

Revue française de science politique, special number: *Les intellectuels dans la société française contemporaine*, 1959

Rieffel, Rémy, *La Tribu des clercs. Les intellectuels sous la Ve République, 1958–1990*, Paris: Calmann Lévy, 1993

Rieffel, Rémy, "Les normaliens dans la société intellectuelle française depuis 1945," in *Ecole Normale Supérieure. Le livre du biencentenaire*, edited by Jean-François Sirinelli, Paris: PUF, 1994

Ringer, Fritz, *Fields of Knowledge. French Academic Culture in Comparative Perspective, 1890–1920*, Cambridge: Cambridge University Press, 1992

Rioux, Jean-Pierre and Jean-François Sirinelli (editors), *La Guerre d'Algérie et les intellectuels français*, Paris: Complexe, 1991

Sirinelli, Jean-François, "Le hasard ou la nécessité? Une histoire en chantier : l'histoire des intellectuals," *Vingtième Siècle. Revue d'histoire* janvier-mars (1986): 97–108

Sirinelli, Jean-François, *Génération intellectuelle. Khâgneux et normaliens dans l'entre-deux-guerres*, Paris: Fayard, 1988

Sirinelli, Jean-François, "Les intellectuels," in *Pour une histoire politique*, edited by René Rémond, Paris: Le Seuil, 1988

Sirinelli, Jean-François, *Intellectuels et passions françaises. Manifestes et pétitions au XXe siècle*, Paris: Fayard, 1990

Starr, Peter, *Logics of Failed Revolt. French Theory after May '68*, Stanford: Stanford University Press, 1995

Verdès-Leroux, Jeannine, *Au Service du parti. Le parti communiste, les intellectuels et la culture (1944–1956)*, Paris: Fayard/Minuit, 1983

Winock, Michel, "L'âge d'or des intellectuels," *L'Histoire* 83 (1985): 20–34

Winock, Michel, *ꝙoF Esprit ꝙcF. Des intellectuels dans la cité. 1930–1950*, Paris: Le Seuil, 1996

IRIGARAY, LUCE
Philosopher, Psychoanalyst, Linguist, Feminist, Theorist

The considerable influence of Luce Irigaray's work, including some nineteen books to date, extends across the humanistic disciplines, informing such fields as philosophy, literary theory, film studies, art criticism, and religious studies. Her texts have been translated into many languages, attracting a particularly large audience of anglophone readers, most notably in North America, England, and Australia. Although Irigaray is best known as a major figure in the field of feminist thought, she has declared herself allergic to labels such as "feminist" and "feminism" that, according to her, suggest formal and dogmatic adherence to some code. Instead, she describes her efforts on behalf of women in a more general way as part of a striving toward human liberation.

Irigaray has described the path of her thought as divisible into three closely related phases. The first of these, which gave rise to *Speculum de l'autre femme* and *Ce sexe qui n'en est pas un*, focused on a critique of the Western philosophical tradition for its privileging of the male subject. Although this phase ended in the early 1980s, Irigaray is still most often identified with it. The second, of which *Éthique de la différence sexuelle* signaled the beginning, emphasized creating a new understanding of female subjectivity. The current phase, starting with *J'aime à toi*, examines ways to cultivate relations between men and women that are founded upon a real respect for sexual difference. For Irigaray, such relations could provide the basis for a new social order.

Throughout these phases, Irigaray's thought has always centered on the basic question of sexual difference. In light of this sustained focus, Irigaray takes exception to critics who would identify dramatic shifts in her work. Although the different phases of her thought have addressed issues as varied as the history of philosophy, the family, gender difference in language use, spirituality, Eastern thought, and the need for gender-specific legal rights, they represent moments in the progressive unfolding of her theory of sexual difference.

Rather than settling for a neuter equality, which too often has meant that women aspire to imitate men, according to Irigaray we should strive for a true formulation and recognition of distinct feminine and masculine identities. Although this attention to sexual difference has provoked charges of essentialism, the overtly socio-historical and political aspects of Irigaray's recent work have made it clear that she does not subscribe to any notion of a gender's predetermined, fixed essence across time and cultural differences. According to Irigaray, Western thought relies upon pretensions to universality that are actually male-biased. Man has been constituted as the Subject and woman as the object, the unknown, at the same time sexless (lacking a penis) and available as a sexual object or tool for men. Women have been trapped by the only archetypal roles available to them: virgin, whore, mother, or some combination of these. Against this schema, Irigaray

argues that the universal is in fact two, male and female, and that any theory of the human subject must take account of this double universal.

Although some critics have cast her work solely in the light of psychoanalytic theory, making much of her debt to Freud and her eventual break with Lacan, Irigaray emphasizes that she is first and foremost a philosopher. Her project is part of a long philosophical tradition critically engaging the work of other philosophers from the pre-Socratics to Derrida. In addition to the philosophical content and references in Irigaray's texts, her at times dense, allusive style presents a daunting challenge to translators. These obstacles help to explain some of the misunderstandings of her work.

The richness of Irigaray's texts has given rise to a diversity of interpretations. For example, she has been variously described as advocating lesbian separatism (following her work of the late 1970s) and exclusive heterosexism (in her more recent work). In response, Irigaray maintains that neither of these interpretations testifies to a careful attentiveness to her thought. Her most sustained inquiries into relations among women, in fact, deal with mother-daughter relations (*Le Corps-à-corps avec la mère, Sexes et parentés*). As for the more recent interpretation, Irigaray might suggest that critics' difficulty in conceiving of relationships between men and women outside of a sexual context is further evidence of heterosexism in the society in which we live.

Two major themes in Irigaray's thought that have provoked significant critical interest are language and intersubjectivity. As far back as *Le langage des déments* (1973), the production and use of language has been a central concern in her work. Irigaray's understanding of the speaking subject as a sexed being has led her to carry out linguistic studies on language production by both sexes in different countries. The data yielded in these inquiries demonstrate an emphasis on intersubjective relations in girls' speech and a focus on relations with objects on the part of boys. The speech of both sexes attests to the erasure of the feminine subject, an effacement easily carried out in languages such as French whose grammar often masks the feminine, as in the combination of the pronouns "she" and "he" to form a "they" marked as masculine. For Irigaray, this repression of the feminine is, in fact, a constitutive element of our male-dominated social order.

Much of Irigaray's recent thought on intersubjectivity relates directly to language, including by examining the conditions for the possibility of dialogue between two human subjects. The curious title of *J'aime à toi* points to several of Irigaray's most pressing theoretical concerns, from the grammatical to the sociopolitical. The insertion of the "à" in the title challenges the way in which syntax, with its treatment of the other as a transitive object, suggests the other's capture by the subject. Irigaray's project involves theorizing a relation between two human subjects without the domination of one by the other. For her, topics like dialogue, love, and the relation between men and women are not simply personal issues, but rather are of vital importance for the public sphere. A politically active thinker since her involvement with women's movements of the 1970s, Irigaray has worked with students and youth organizations with a view toward creating civil identities that respect difference. The more accessible style of some of her recent books suggests that she aims to reach an increasingly wide audience. Her concern for the transformation of civil society is especially evident in books such as *J'aime à toi* and *La democrazia comincia a due*. Society as Irigaray envisions it would no longer be a homo-social arena where men are the only subjects in interaction while women are simply objects of exchange. Instead, laws and practices that respect the identity of each gender would allow for the real coexistence of sexual difference and the flourishing of humanity. In Irigaray's ambitious project to found an ethical social order, what is at stake is no less than achieving spiritual enlightenment, acceding to a new epoch of history, and even saving the human species as well as the natural world.

HEIDI BOSTIC

See also **Jacques Derrida; Jacques Lacan**

Biography

Born in Belgium in 1932, Luce Irigaray studied philosophy and literature at the University of Louvain. In the early 1960s, she moved to Paris, where she earned graduate degrees in linguistics, philosophy, and psychoanalysis. Following the publication of *Speculum*, she was rejected by members of the Freudian school of psychoanalysis. Although marginalized by most French academic institutions since that time, she maintains a position at the distinguished *Centre National de la Recherche Scientifique* in Paris. A prolific writer, Irigaray frequently gives seminars in France and abroad. She is the author of many articles and books, of which the best known are *Speculum de l'autre femme* (1974), *Ce sexe qui n'en est pas un* (1977), *Éthique de la différence sexuelle* (1984), *Sexes et parentés* (1987) and *J'aime à toi* (1992).

Selected Works

Le langage des déments, 1973
Speculum de l'autre femme, 1974; as *Speculum of the Other Woman*, translated by Gillian C. Gill, 1985
Ce sexe qui n'en est pas un, 1977; as *This Sex Which is Not One*, translated by Catherine Porter, 1985
Et l'une ne bouge pas sans l'autre, 1979
Amante marine: De Friedrich Nietzsche, 1980; as *Marine Lover of Friedrich Nietzsche*, translated by Gillian C. Gill, 1991
Le Corps-à-corps avec la mère, 1981
Passions élémentaires, 1982; as *Elemental Passions*, translated by Joanne Collie and Judith Still, 1992
L'Oubli de l'air chez Martin Heidegger, 1983; as *The Forgetting of Air in Martin Heidegger*, translated by Mary Beth Mader, 1999
Éthique de la différence sexuelle, 1984; as *An Ethics of Sexual Difference*, translated by Carolyn Burke and Gillian C. Gill, 1993
Parler n'est jamais neutre, 1985; as *To Speak is Never Neutral*, 2002
Sexes et parentés, 1987; as *Sexes and Genealogies*, translated by Gillian C. Gill, 1993
Le Temps de la différence: Pour une révolution pacifique, 1989; as *Thinking the Difference: For a Peaceful Revolution*, translated by Karin Montin, 1994
Je, tu, nous: Pour une culture de la différence, 1990; as *Je, Tu, Nous: Toward a Culture of Difference*, translated by Alison Martin, 1993
Sexes et genres à travers les langues: éléments de communication sexuée, 1990
J'aime à toi: esquisse d'une félicité dans l'histoire, 1992; as *I Love to You: Sketch for a Felicity within History*, translated by Alison Martin, 1996
La democrazia comincia a due, 1994; as *Democracy Begins Between Two*, translated by Kirsteen Anderson, 2000
Essere due, 1994; as *To Be Two*, translated by Monique M. Rhodes and Marco F. Cocito Monoc, 2000
Entre Orient et Occident: De la singularité à la communauté, 1999; as *Between East and West: From Singularity to Community*, translated by Stephen Pluhacek, 2002
The Way of Love, or This Nothingness That Separates Us, translated by Heidi Bostic and Stephen Pluhacek,

Further Reading

Burke, Carolyn, Naomi Schor and Margaret Whitford (editors), *Engaging with Irigaray*, New York: Columbia University Press, 1994
Chanter, Tina, *Ethics of Eros: Irigaray's Rewriting of the Philosophers*, New York: Routledge, 1995
Huntington, Patricia, *Ecstatic Subjects, Utopia and Recognition: Kristeva, Heidegger, Irigaray*, Albany, New York: State University of New York Press, 1998
Whitford, Margaret (editor and introduction), *The Irigaray Reader*, Oxford: Basil Blackwell, 1991
Whitford, Margaret, *Luce Irigaray: Philosophy in the Feminine*, London and New York: Routledge, 1991

J

JANKÉLÉVITCH, VLADIMIR
Philosopher

A French philosopher born at Bourges in a family of Russian origin, Vladimir Jankélévitch became known during the 1920s through his books on Georg Simmel. Two of his early studies had a decisive impact on his further orientation towards metaphysics, moral philosophy, and musicology: *Georg Simmel, Philosopher of Life*, published in the *Revue de métaphysique et de morale* in 1925, and *Bergson*, published in 1931. The intuition of duration, with its original modes of apprehension of different continuities, fluctuations, speeds, and qualities of inner life, which Bergson had contrasted to the spatial deployment of geometrical thought, determined the originality of moral life, according to Jankélévitch. Moreover, the temporal movement of consciousness in Bergson opened up a creative form of freedom, which Jankélévitch sought to apply to the analysis of moral consciousness.

Starting from these premises, Jankélévitch devoted his work to the attempt at defining notions such as melancholy, regret, the moral intention, good will, innocence and guilt, charm—which he related to the permanent duplicity of moral consciousness, constantly torn between spontaneity and reflection. In *The Alternative* (1938) he dealt with this duality of consciousness for the first time, and focused on the manner in which one's initial intention is taken over, justified, and muddled by the chattering eloquence of the reflective discourse. This orientation led him to specialize in the paradoxes of consciousness, which he explored in studies such as *Irony* (1936), *Treatise of Virtues*

(1949), *The Pure and the Impure* (1960), and *Death* (1966). Jankélévitch opposed moral reflection, with its countless nuances, to abstract intellectual thought and conceptualization, which empty the living person of its reality and temporal character, thus ignoring the "here" and "now" of moral action. The seriousness of the good intention always finds expression in its immediacy. This phenomenology of immediacy implies a rejection of sociological, psychoanalytical, or philosophical relativism. Ultimately, even the reference back to the antinomies and paradoxes of freedom cannot help one circumvent the idea of the good. The question of death, as well as the question of freedom or that of the goodness of the moral intention, belong to what Jankélévitch designates as the "next-to-nothing" (*le presque rien*) that conceptual thought fails to capture, given its conformity to geometrical and motionless entities. The paradoxes of the infinitely small, of "being" (*l'être*) in relation to motion, and of reflectivity led Jankélévitch to a conception of moral life as an extremely delicate balance, which is constantly threatened by the conceptual search for certainty. The question of death, and its paradoxes, prompted a particularly extravagant proliferation of metaphors in Jankélévitch's writing. Nevertheless, his metaphorical style can be said to find justification in the light of his critique of reflection. According to Jankélévitch, any reflection freezes, petrifies, and renders dull what by definition are movement, action, and plenitude. For example, every time that irony, generosity, innocence, or charm are thought or aspire to become part of a theoretical discourse, they lose their spontaneity in the very act of self-reflection.

To a large extent, Jankélévitch tried to capture the *je ne sais quoi* and the "next-to-nothing" (*le presque rien*) of moral qualities. This is the reason why irony and humor play such a major part in his enterprise. Reflective, yet mobile, these two attitudes, through their corresponding "games of love and laughter" (*jeux de l'amour et de l'humour*), prevent the dogmatic petrifaction of thought and introduce the actual movement of life into the psyche. The philosopher therefore becomes attached to the uncertain or nocturnal areas of consciousness where the essential moments of one's moral life reside. He strives to focus on the reverse side of diurnal and demonstrative thought, in order to highlight phenomena such as silence, ineffability, and incompleteness (*l'inachevé*). It is precisely in these territories, which Jankélévitch does not hesitate to describe as "enchanted," that one can find innocence and inspiration, as long as they are not corrupted by self-reflection and thus suddenly transformed into presumption and vanity. The constant threat posed by reflectivity accounts for the alternation between philosophical discourse and what could be described as musical and poetic phenomenology in Jankélévitch's writing. This alternation fully comes into view in the series of interviews entitled *Midway to Infinity* (*Quelque part dans l'inachevé*, 1978), which brings together the main orientations of Jankélévitch's work. His philosophical discourse turns into poetry, and draws on musical terminology in order to find the right metaphors to express the qualitative and "melodic" aspects of moral life (*Gabriel Fauré and His Melodies*, 1938). This is why one cannot really dissociate Jankélévitch's musical work from his philosophical writing. Music and philosophy find support and illustration in each other, as for example, in Jankélévitch's *The Nocturnal* or in his *Music and the Ineffable*.

Having been a member of the French resistance during the war, he went on to reject German culture on ideological grounds after 1940. The German people's responsibility for the genocide of the Jews could not be treated in isolation because it actually formed an integral part of German culture. Jankélévitch, who had written a thesis on Schelling, never returned to German philosophy, and concentrated instead on French and Spanish moral philosophy. This willful denial was also going to affect his philosophical musicology. Jankélévitch's postwar work would find inspiration mainly in the moralists of the Enlightment, the philosophers of the Renaissance, such as Baltasar Gracian, and the Greek authors. One can describe Jankélévitch as the French philosopher of the nuance and the impossible innocence par excellence. His praise of decency and humor provides an accurate definition of his approach to philosophical questions: "Decency is an expression of the most delicate part of our inner civilization," he argued. According to Jankélévitch, decency of the soul (*la pudeur de l'âme*) is what saves the mystery of essential values, which we only catch a glimpse of at privileged moments. Jankélévitch's distinctive "paradoxology" finally brings into play the mysteries of temporality, of love, goodness, or freedom, in an occasionally self-conscious manner. His critique of ideality finds support in humor because humor, far from being a power strategy, involves affinity. "The smile of reason," humor is not fully accepted unless it takes the form of "humorous irony," which plays with the ideality of love only to acknowledge the imperfection of finitude with compassion. Humor is essentially "wandering humor," similar to Plato's Greek Eros, both rich and poor, symbol of a perpetually dynamic synthesis, which never closes up.

OLIVIER SALAZAR-FERRER

See also **Henri Bergson**

Biography

Vladimir Jankélévitch was born in Bourges in 1903. He held the chair in moral philosophy and politics at the Sorbonne for almost thirty years, where he was an immensely popular teacher, as attested to by the large numbers of students who attended his courses. He died in Paris in 1985.

Selected Works

Gabriel Fauré, ses mélodies, son esthétique, 1938
Maurice Ravel, 1988
Debussy et le mystère, 30 ex. musicaux, 1949
La Vie et la Mort dans la musique de Debussy, 1968
Le Nocturne, 1943
La rhapsodie, verve et improvisation musicale,
La Musique et l'ineffable, 1961
De la musique au silence, 3 vols. (I—*Fauré et l'inesprimable*; II—*Debussy et le mystère de l'instant*; III—*Liszt et la rhapsodie*), 1989
La Présence lointaine, Albeniz, Severac, Mompou, 1983
La musique et les heures, 1988

Philosophy

L'Odyssée de la conscience dans la dernière philosophie de Schelling, 1933
Henri Bergson, 2e éd, 1959
La Mauvaise conscience, 2e éd, 1951
L'Ironie, 2e éd, 1964
L'Alternative, 1938
Philosophie première, 1954
Le mal, 1947
L'Austérité et la Vie morale 1, 1956
Le Pur et l'Impur, 1960
L'Aventure, l'Ennui et le Sérieux, 1963
la Mort, 1966
Le Pardon, 1967
Traité des vertus, 2e éd, 1968–1972

L'irréversible et la nostalgie, 1974
Quelque part dans l'inachevé (with B. Berlowitz), 1978
Le Je ne sais quoi et le Presque rien, 2e éd, 1981
Sources, 1984
Le Paradoxe de la morale, 1981
L'Imprescriptible, 2e éd, 1986
Premières et dernières pages, 1994

JAURÈS, JEAN
Socialist Theoretician

As primary theoretician of the Socialist party, Jean Jaurès developed a non-Marxist perspective on socialism. He put forward a democratic and evolutionary socialist vision. An opponent of centralization and bureaucracy, he rejected Marx's notion of revolutionary dictatorship. In place of the "dictatorship" of the proletariat, Jaurès emphasized the ethical aspects of socialism and its relationship to democracy. Socialism, for Jaurès, was not a revolutionary break with society but rather a fulfillment of already existing democratic tendencies.

In *Studies in Socialism* Jaurè put forward an evolutionist view of the transition to socialism. He saw attempts to bring about socialism through revolutionary means as the desperation of a weak an unprepared class. Socialism would not be brought about through revolutionary upheaval but by the pragmatic and legal organization of the working class in the rule of law and extension of suffrage. For Jaurès, socialism would grow out of the Republic as the Republic grew out of the Revolution. It would represent a continuation of democratic government. Socialism would result not from the violent efforts of a social fraction but as a national movement. This was the impulse behind Jaurès's patriotism. Workers, in his view, must uphold the nation as the basis of its improvement through reforms and the gradual replacement of the bourgeoisie by the proletariat. War above all else threatened orderly social evolution. Only peace and international security could provide the context for a transition from bourgeois society to socialism that would be free from violence, bloodshed, and economic destruction.

Jaurès developed the Socialist party's majority position on antimilitarism and drafted the resolution relating to war at the International Congress of Stuttgart in 1907. He affirmed the solidarity of the workers of all countries and argued that every effort, from parliamentary participation to the general strike and insurrection, must be made to avoid all wars. Out of consideration for the German socialists, who would have faced repression as a result, Jaurès replaced an explicit commitment to the general strike with references to actual solidarity work undertaken against war by socialists in a variety of countries. In later years Jaurès maintained that war could be avoided prior to the end of capitalism through international arbitration and treaties. He argued that increased economic relations between nations would allow for easier resolution of conflict.

Jaurès argued for a federation of free nations that have given up military force as the basis for a future human unity. He did not argue for the destruction of nations but for an international context in which they could coexist peacefully. He did not want to see the dissolution of nations into a general humanity, and argued for federated nations instead of governance in a centralized international bureaucracy. At the same time he argued for a "league of nations," a federation of autonomous nations that might pressure governments to moderate chauvinistic sentiments.

As a "patriotic socialist" Jaurès's antimilitarism was divorced from any call to abolish the state. His opposition to war ended up in a contradictory position of arguing against militarism while upholding the state that was constituted by wars and pursued wars as its vocation.

As foremost socialist leader he delivered a message of defending France, which encouraged socialists to view Germany with suspicion, to privilege French imperialism, accept the severance of Alsace-Lorraine as an unpunished crime, and view international affairs from a national rather than an international perpective. This meant that his appeals to national security played into the hands of the militarists as war with Germany approached.

Jaurès's major contributions to socialist theory included the notion of the citizen army, which would replace standing conscript armies. His 1910 publication, *L'Armeé nouvelle* remains one of the most unique documents in socialist history. In his view, the military authorities relied too heavily on the conscript army that served two years in the barracks. His solution came in the form of the citizen army that held its own weapons at the ready to carry out national defense and that carried on civil life as usual and was not separated from the population in barracks or camps. This would contribute to the organization of a true "nation in arms," which Jaurès had long advocated. This militia of the people would represent a truly popular defensive army. Jaurès called for a thorough reform of the French army and its reconstruction along democratic lines. Rather than serve two years in barracks, he argued that soldiers serve no more than six months in barracks. That period would be spread over two periods in the same year and would be served at the nearest local barracks.

Members of the proletariat should not only form the army but should lead it as well. A democratic army could never be possible as long as officers formed a separate caste appointed from wealthier sections of society. The officers formed the permanent part of the army, isolated from civilian life and out of touch with citizens' concerns. This made them unsympathetic to arguments against war that were offered by the public. In Jaurès' system only 1/3 of officers would be professional military people, and they would serve only as a permanent teaching corp. They would be chosen by competition. The remaining 2/3 of officers, civil officers, would be chosen from among those who had taken special military courses or from the noncommissioned officers.

All French males should serve in the military from twenty-one to forty-five years of age. Children were to be prepared for military life through physical training in school. Military teaching would be taken from the military colleges and placed within the universities. Soldiers would share classes with other students in a range of subjects of common interest. Jaurès went so far as suggest that anyone who resisted service be denied full rights of citizenship. In Jaurès's view this new army would greatly contribute to the preservation of peace. Members of the militia, living with their families and rooted in home communities, would refuse to leave the country to fight an aggressive war. If the government attempted to mobilize for an aggressive war the militia would be more likely to revolt. In the case of invasion, however, the militia members would fight to defend their homes.

The vision put forward in *L'Armée nouvelle* was in part directed at the internationalist minority that rejected all manifestations of national loyalty, including any national defense, and put forward a policy of internationalist insurrection that paid no regard to national borders.

Jaurès's other major contribution to French socialist policy concerned his writings on the peasantry. He rejected orthodox social democracy, which followed Marx in viewing the peasantry as a class destined to disappear in the face of industrialization and bourgeois farms. Jaurès also opposed orthodox socialist opinion that saw the peasantry as a primarily reactionary class who posed only an obstacle to the development of socialism. Against this view Jaurès argued that the peasants must be protected against any forced dispossession. He further argued that the state should play an active part in reducing agricultural rents. He proposed a plan to bring agriculture under public control. This would be accomplished by assuming ownership of land controlled by large landholders and using reduced rents to provide a capital fund for agricultural improvement. Large-scale farming would be organized on a cooperative basis under public ownership.

Despite the Revolution's affirmation of the "right of property," Jaurès argued that socialism was the logical outcome of the French Revolution and the only way to realize the promise of justice, liberty, and equality. Socialism, in making ownership collective, would restore property to the masses, breaking the concentration of property that existed under capitalism.

According to Jaurès, the Socialist party would show its capacity for serving the collective good through a program of legislative reform. Socialism also required that workers gain education to prepare themselves for the many tasks of transforming the social system. Experience in economic development would come through the cooperative movement, and Jaurès personally supported a number of cooperative industrial projects.

In opposition to Guesde, who maintained that cooperatives only had value for propaganda and financial support of the Party, Jaurès argued that cooperatives would play an important part in the evolution toward socialism by introducing socialized property. Jaurès's vision was the one adopted by the Socialist party in 1910.

Jaurès rejected Marx's notion that socialism would develop from an "immiseration of the proletariat." Absolute destitution would not give rise to absolute liberation. Workers at the beginning of the twentieth century were enjoying immense gains through their collective efforts. Shorter hours, better pay, access to education, and the right to vote were tangible gains that spoke against the immiseration hypothesis. The evolution toward socialism was advanced by the economic, political, and intellectual advances made by the working class.

Jaurès advocated an idealistic socialism that emphasized reciprocity rather than class struggle. It was in contradictions between economic conditions and this sentiment of reciprocity, part of human development itself, that one could find the basis for social change. Socialism was the historical development of this ideal of reciprocity. His great preoccupation was the search for unity and he worked to overcome the division of the socialist movement in France into competing factions.

JEFFREY SHANTZ

Biography

Born in Castres in 1859, Jean Jaurès graduated from the *École Normale Supérieure* in the early 1880s and went on to teach philosophy at the University of Toulouse, where he later gained his doctorate. From 1885–1889 he served his first term as a delegate to the Chamber of Deputies, where he sat as an independent. His involvement in the miners' strike in Carmaux in 1892 brought him forcefully into the socialist movement and between 1893 and 1898, and 1902 and 1914, he served in the chamber of deputies as a socialist. His eloquent and passionate speeches made him a respected champion of socialism, even among opponents. During the Dreyfus affair he became one of the most outspoken and active Dreyfusards. Jaurès's approval of the socialist Millerand's participation in the Waldeck–Rousseau ministry led to a split within the Socialist party in 1900 when the more radical wing, led by Jules Guesde, left. Jaurès assumed leadership of the French Socialist party and in 1904, he co-founded the Party newspaper, *L'Humanité*, as an organ of democratic socialism, anti-militarism, and socialist unity. That same year, eager for socialist reunification, Jaurès abandoned the argument for ministerial participation and was instrumental in the formation of the Unified French Socialist party (*Section Française de l'Internationale Ouvrière*) (*SFIO*) in 1905. As war threatened in 1914, Jaurès advocated peace through arbitration and reconciliation between France and Germany. His positions enraged nationalists and he was assassinated by a fanatical patriot in July 1914 on the eve of the war.

Selected Works

Journal officiel de la Chambre de Députés, 1886–89, 1893–98, 1902–14.

Action socialiste. Le socialisme et l'enseignement; le socialisme et les peuples, 1899

L'Art et le socialisme, 1900

L'Histoire socialiste de la Révolution française: La Constituante. Histoire Socialiste (1789–1900), Vol. 1 1901

L'Histoire socialiste de la Révolution française: La Législative. Histoire Socialiste (1789–1900), Vol. II, 1901

L'Histoire socialiste de la Révolution française: La Convention. Histoire Socialiste (1789–1900), Vols. III and IV, 1902

Etudes socialistes, 1902

Discours parlementaires, edited by Edmond Claris, 1904

"Socialisme et radicalisme in 1885," *Discours parlementaires* edited by Edmond Claris, 1904

Studies in Socialism, 1906

La Guerre franco-allemande (1870–71), Histoire Socialiste (1789–1900), Vol. XI, 1908

Les Idées politique et sociales de Jean Jacques Rousseau, 1912

L'Organisation socialiste de la France. L'Armée nouvelle, 1915

Histoire socialiste de la Révolution française. 8 Vols., 1922–24

Oeuvres de Jean Jaurès. Texte rassemblés, présentes at annotés par Max Bonnafous. 9 Vols 1931–1939

Anthologie de Jean Jaurès Edited by Louis Lévy, 1946

"La Question religieuse et le socialisme," *La Question religieuse et le socialisme*, edited by Michel Launay 1959

Textes choisis. Tome 1er. Contre la Guerre et la politique coloniale, edited by Madeleine Rebérioux, 1959

Les Origines du socialisme allemand, 1960

Further Reading

Auclair, Marcelle, *La Vie de Jaurès, ou la France d'avant 1914*, Paris: Editions du Seuil, 1954

Auriol, Vincent, *Souvenirs sur Jean Jaurès*. Paris: Editions de la Liberté, 1945

Boitel, Maurice, *Les Idées libérales dans le socialisme de Jaurés*, Paris: L'Emancipatrice, 1921

Coombes, J.E., "Jean Jaurès: Education, Class and Culture." *Journal of European Studies* XX (1990): 23–58

Desanges, Paul and Luc Mériga, *Vie de Jaurès*, Paris: G. Crès, 1924

Field, Frank, "Jaurès, Péguy, and the Crisis of 1914," *Journal of European Studies* XVI (1986): 45–57

Goldberg, Harvey, *The Life of Jean Jaurès*, Madison: University of Wisconsin, 1962

Lévy-Bruhl, L., *Jean Jaurès: esquisse biographique*, Paris: Ricder, 1924

Rappoport, Charles, *Jean Jaurès. L'homme, le penseur, le socialiste*, Paris: L'Emancipatrice 1915

Rebérioux, Madeleine, "Party Practice and the Jaurèsian Vision: The SFIO (1905–1914)" in *Socialism in France: From Jaurès to Mitterand* edited by Stuart Williams, New York: St. Martin's, 1983

Tétard, Georges, *Essais sur Jean Jaurès*, Colombes: Centre d'apprentissage d'imprimerie, 1959

Weinstein, Harold, *Jean Jaurès: A Study of Patriotism in the French Socialist Movement*, New York: Columbia University Press, 1936

Zévaès, Alexandre, *Le Socialisme en France depuis 1871*, Paris, 1908

Zévaès, Alexandre, *Jean Jaurès*, Paris: La Clé d'Or, 1951

THE JEWISH QUESTION

The catch-phrase "*la question juive*" emerged in the 1840s from the German *die Judenfrage* as the crystallization of a series of eighteenth-century questions: Should Jews be granted civil and political rights equal to Christian subjects and citizens? Would civic education make them more like gentiles? Can they be loyal soldiers? Are the Jews a distinctive people, race, or nation? Is there a contradiction between Judaism and modernity?

In the aftermath of the defeat in the Franco-Prussian war in 1870 and the establishment of the Third Republic on the principles of 1789, "the Jewish question" became linked to a critique of the Republic that would cohere around integral nationalism and racial anti-Semitism. The prominent role Jews played within the Third Republic was identified as a symptom of its decadence. This new, racial anti-Semitism fused two older strains. The first was a counterrevolutionary, conservative, Catholic tradition for whom Jews were the spirit and corrupting force of modernity and revolution, whose carriers were also republicans, Free-Masons, and Protestants, who advanced the destruction of the family and true France, the organic France of the peasant and provinces. The second was a socialist anti-Semitism that argued that capitalism created a new aristocracy of money, whose most visible symbol was the Rothschilds, a sign of everything nascent socialism opposed.

The "pop" of the new anti-Semitism was the journalist Eduoard Drumont, who rose to prominence with the publication of *La France juive* (1886), a 1,200-page synthesis of socialist and counterrevolutionary "Judeo-phobia" that combined folk stereotypes, anecdotes, and pseudo-science in a historical narrative to produce a powerful mix of political, economic, religious, and racial anti-Semitism. With more than 200 editions by 1900, it was the best-selling political work of the century. The fertile ground for its reception was laid by the 1882 crash of the Union Générale bank, established four years earlier with the support of Church institutions and thousands of small investors ostensibly to provide an alternative to Protestant and Jewish banking houses. Although failing due to mismanagement, the Catholic press, especially the mass daily *La Croix* of the assumptionist religious order, charged that Jewish bankers had orchestrated its fall. Drumont generalized this Jewish plot into a widespread conspiracy theory.

La France juive was lucrative enough to launch *La Libre parole* (1892), a newspaper whose masthead "*La France aux français*" (France for the French) summarized its position as a propaganda spearhead for the new anti-Semitic leagues agitating for extraparliamentary solutions to what they perceived as France's decay: the *Union Nationale* (1893), *Jeunesse Antisémite et Nationaliste* (1894), Jules Guérin's *Ligue Antisémitique Française* (1897), the revival of Paul Déroulède's *Ligue des Patriotes* (1898), and the *Ligue de la Patrie Française* (1899). These *ligues*, their leaders, and the news organs that fostered their interpretation of French modernity were the bridge between the Boulanger affair (1886–1889) and the formation of the new revolutionary right-wing royalism of the Action Française, formed in 1899 during the Dreyfus Affair.

The Boulanger affair transformed anti-Semitism into a populist political code that cohered those opposed the Republican state (Blanquists, socialists, workers, radicals, Bonapartists, and royalists). Boulangism was nationalist and authoritarian, uniting left and right antiparliamentarianism in a movement focused on a popular general who was heroically to save France from its perceived decadence. After the Affair passed, the organized movement by his followers continued with anti-Semitism as a key lexical refrain.

A crucial adherent was Maurice Barrès, who, as one of the great writers of his generation and a deputy from Nancy, provided intellectual credibility and doctrinal coherence to the new revolutionary right. Barrès infused nationalism with a mystical dimension incarnated in French traditions and *la terre et les morts* ("the earth and the dead"). The martyrs for France (the dead) served as progenitors for a resurrection promised when France returned to her roots (the earth). Moving from his early volumes in his *culte de moi* trilogy that advocated self-glorification and ego worship, Barrès's later trilogy *Le Roman de l'énergie nationale* (1897–1902) with *Les Déracinés* (the uprooted: individualistic, cosmopolitan, urbane, abstract, universalist, in short, Judaized) criticized in the first novel, collectivized and nationalized the subject, insisting that community and nation were constitutive of individual identity. For Barrès, the purity and stability of the civilized nation were threatened by "barbarian" foreigners with "the Jew" as the quintessential outsider.

The Dreyfus affair (1894–1906) fused the mass political movements of the right. What started as a case about Captain Alfred Dreyfus, a Jew on the general staff falsely accused and found guilty of treason for selling military secrets to the Germans, had by 1898 become a veritable civil war. Far more than merely an anti-Semitic incident, the Affair was a national, religious, political and cultural *guerre franco-française*, a war among the French between Republicans versus monarchists and Bonapartists, modernists versus traditionalists, liberals and socialists versus conservatives, secularists versus clericalists, progressives versus reactionaries. It was an affair fought over the identity of modern France where the struggle was a palimpsest over "the Jew" Dreyfus. Anti-Semitism had become a political weapon employed by the opponents of liberalism and the Republican state that anti-Dreyfusards identified as *la France juive*.

The Dreyfus affair had three outcomes that affected the Jewish question. First, with Waldeck-Rousseau's government of "republican defense" that came to power in 1899 and the radicals consolidating the republican victory, anticlericalism and republicanism triumphed. Jews felt more certain than ever that Franco-Judaism was safe and reaffirmed the emancipation contract of the French Revolution. Second, the Action Française with Maurras its central figure emerged as the major group on the extreme right. The theorist of "integral nationalism," Maurras was one of the founders of the *École Romane*, which called for a return of French letters to the classicism of the seventeenth century and its imagined roots in Greco-Roman culture. He came to prominence with his defense of Colonel Henry, the forger of the evidence that indicted Dreyfus. At the height of the Affair, the Action Française was formed around a journal, shortly followed by the cultivation of activist student groups, the creation of an institute as an alternative to the university, and then the launching of the newspaper *L'Action Française* in 1908, sold by the *Camelots du Roi* (Hawkers of the King) who also served as the group's shock troops. The Action Française was defined by antirepublicanism, exclusionary nationalism, monarchism, clericalism, traditionalism, and anti-Semitism. Maurras's integral xenophobia was even more coherent than Barrès's in delineating what he termed "anti-

France"—the Jews, Protestants, Freemasons, and *métèques* (foreigners), "four confederated states" inherently discordant with the French nation. The doctrines of the Action Française were key to defining the opposition to the Republic in the early twentieth century, and Maurras along with Drumont and Barrès formed the trinity of founding fathers of the French extreme right.

The third result of the Dreyfus affair was that it would become mythologized as the origin of Zionism, especially as a result of the acclaim accorded Bernard Lazare (1865–1903) at the Second Zionist Congress in 1898. Lazare, an assimilated Sephardic Jew with anarchist and socialist leanings, was a contributor to the symbolist movement and the first Dreyfusard, writing to demonstrate Dreyfus's innocence several years before Émile Zola and others entered the fray. His *L'Antisemitisme, son histoire et ses causes* (*Antisemitism: Its History and Causes*, 1894), one of the first systematic analyses of anti-Semitism, reflects how the Dreyfus affair transformed Lazare's perception of the problem. Even though Lazare's history reiterated a slew of anti-Semitic representations of Jews, he thought that anti-Semitism was an anachronism of modernity and would disappear. The Dreyfus affair led him to forge an auto-emancipationist national solution to "the Jewish question" and steered him to defend Eastern European, especially Romanian, Jews, before his untimely death. While Zionism goes back much further, Theodor Herzl (whose book *Judenstaat* [*The Jewish State*, 1896] was subtitled *Attempt at a Modern Solution to the Jewish Question*), Max Nordau, Ahad Ha'am, and other major Zionists were convinced that if an anti-Semitic backlash could happen in France then Jewish emancipation within Europe was doomed. The Zionist Federation of France was founded in 1901 but had a hard time gaining a foothold among French Jews. It was successful primarily among the influx of Eastern-European immigrants—200,000 over the next thirty years—who transformed the Jewish community in France between the Dreyfus affair and Vichy. They transfigured French Jewry demographically (making Paris the third largest Jewish city in the world on the eve of World War II); challenged the synthesis of Franco-Judaism through the public expression of their ethnic difference; and asserted socialist and Zionist ideals that came out of their working-class background.

Although the established Jews of France and their institutions generally rejected Zionism, the 1920s witnessed a renaissance of Jewish culture and Zionism exerted a significant influence, especially on intellectuals (Gustave Kahn, André Spire, Henri Franck, Edmond Fleg) and the youth movements established in this period. Zionist organizations sponsored a variety of publications, and Yiddish language and French-Jewish periodicals treated extensively the questions of Jewish identity and history raised by Zionism.

The period after World War I was also characterized by a change in the depiction of Jewish characters in French literature that through the nineteenth century had been bankers, art dealers, outsiders, cosmopolitan financiers, parasites, unscrupulous *parvenus*, and other stereotypes, or depicted as crude, immoral, cowardly, treacherous, and dishonest. These images of "the Jew" littered the work of George Sand, Honoré de Balzac, Paul Bourget, Edmond de Goncourt, Alphonse Daudet, and even Zola's *L'Argent*. In the *crise de civilisation* of interwar France, however, for some like Romain Rolland, Judaism was perceived as a repository of cultural and spiritual values that could contribute to revitalizing civilization. But often the Jewish protagonist in interwar novels was depicted as estranged from both the Jewish and French traditions, a figure of the social alienation of the period. This problem would be taken up by Jewish writers, including members of the Philosophies Circle, Albert Cohen, and the communist Jean-Richard Bloch, for whom "the Jew" served the role of revolutionary ferment.

The economic depression, political polarization, and xenophobic nativism in a period of high Jewish immigration fostered the fascist anti-Semitism of the 1930s. Inheriting the tradition of extra-parliamentary agitation from the fin-de-siècle *ligues*, a profusion of heterogeneous fascist groups like the *Francistes, Jeunesses Patriotes, Cagoule, Solidarité Française, Croix de Feu*, and the *Parti Populaire Française* arose in the 1920s and 1930s with newspaper allies (*Action Française, Gringoire, Candide, Je suis partout*) decrying decadence, demographic decline, parliamentary disorder, the specter of communism, socialism, and the Jewish republic. The symbol of their hatred was Léon Blum, who came to power as head of the Popular Front government in 1936 as France's first Jewish and socialist prime minister.

This grim state would take a turn for the tragic under the Vichy regime. When the Third Republic was finally smashed in June 1940 by the Nazi *Blitzkrieg*, an armistice agreement was signed by Marshal Pétain, hero of Verdun and self-proclaimed savior, who was given full powers on July 10 as head of the new government located in the spa town of Vichy. Pétain's regime promptly launched a "national Revolution" whose values were the obverse of the Third Republic's, replacing the Republican demand for liberty, equality, and fraternity with the trinity "work, family, fatherland" and banning the *Declaration of the Rights of Man and Citizen* and the "abstract" principles of the French Revolution. The exaltation of work organized through imposed corporate structures that bound employers and laborers together in obligatory occupational associations was coupled with a "back to the land" policy of peasant pieties. Nativism was joined to a cult of the family organized through the creation of the Secretariat of State for the Family in November 1940 that outlawed abortion, dissuaded contraception, and reified gender roles with femininity construed solely in reproductive terms.

The Fatherland was to be purified of the sources of contamination beginning with the first *Statut des Juifs* passed on October 3, 1940 and shored up by a second statute in June 1941. Based upon autonomous measures and an indigenous anti-Semitic tradition, the *Statuts* defined who was a Jew, and excluded Jews from important positions in the public sector, including the military and civil service and all posts influencing public opinion (including teaching, the press, radio, film, and theater), and placed quotas on Jews in most other professions and educational institutions. The second statute was followed a month later by an Aryanization law that enabled the government to seize Jewish property. Vichy established concentration camps (where Jews died of disease and malnutrition) manned by French police officers, who also assisted in round-ups based upon the census of the *Commissariat Général aux Questions Juives*, established in March 1941 as the French ministry responsible for Jewish affairs.

Although the legislative procedures denying Jewish citizenship were met with no opposition, visible anti-Semitic measures like the branding of Jews with the yellow star in 1942 resulted in the first open protests to Jewish persecution. Though lacking general approval, the mass round-ups of Jews were met with no collective resistance. The most notorious was the Vel d'Hiv *raffles* on July 16–17, 1942 when 12,884 Jews, including approximately 4,000 children, were assembled in a bicycle stadium and transported to Drancy, an internment camp that was the antechamber to Auschwitz. The majority of French people were bystanders while 75,721 Jews in France (approximately twenty-five percent) were deported to the extermination centers in the east. However, due to the distinctions made between French and foreign Jews, the establishment of escape routes and organizations, and the assistance of non-Jews, seventy-five percent survived, more than in Holland and Belgium.

Amid the general silence about the Holocaust in the Gaullist myth that represented the Vichy regime as a shield against the worst excesses of Nazism and the Resistance as the sword, thus depicting France as an entire nation in revolt, Jean-Paul Sartre published *Réflexions sur la question juive* (*Anti-Semite and Jew*, 1946). Insisting that the French take responsibility for their part in the final solution, Sartre's innovative analysis influenced the entire postwar intellectual debate

about Jewish identity, its relation to anti-Semitism, and the politics of (Jewish) emancipation. Sartre maintained that anti-Semitism did not rest upon economic, historical, religious, or political foundations, but demanded an existential analysis of the self-identity of the anti-Semite and "the Jew." The anti-Semite defines himself as superior in opposition to his image of "the Jew," a figure of depravity, corruption, pollution, the urbane or the foreign; in short for what threatens his essential Frenchness. As such, he is a man of self-deception who fears the human condition where "existence precedes essence" and people must be responsible for the choices they make with no resort to absolute values. Radically, Sartre also castigated the "politics of assimilation"—the Enlightenment and liberal tradition that defined Franco-Judaism—contending that it ultimately eliminated Jewishness through its universal and abstract principles that did not recognize Jewish difference. Sartre then described the inherent dilemmas of the Jewish struggle for authenticity based upon the anti-essentialist and anti-foundation premise that "the Jew is a man that other men consider a Jew," thus posing the question of Jewish identity in terms of the anti-Semite's gaze. Seeking to solve the problem of anti-Semitism, the contradictions of liberalism and the antinomies of Jewish existence in one fell swoop, he offered a socialist revolution as the only viable solution to "the Jewish question."

The postwar French-Jewish community was in turn itself revolutionized by three events: the *Shoah* (which lacerated Franco-Judaism by ripping apart the belief that Jews would be protected by the state that they supported), the creation of the state of Israel, and the migration of Jews returning from the decolonized Maghreb. North African Jewish immigrants made France the largest and most vibrant Jewish community in western and central Europe. Upwards of 600,000 Jews throughout the hexagon built synagogues, community centers, schools, kosher restaurants, and butcher shops, with new umbrella organizations created to represent the community, and a new interest in Jewish intellectual concerns.

In this new context, leading lights of this intellectual efflorescence—Emmanuel Levinas, André Neher, Albert Memmi, Vladimir Jankélévitch, and Wladimir Rabinovitch (Rabi)—would rethink the terms of "the Jewish question" through the creative fusion that characterizes postwar French-Jewish thought: a remnant of Eastern European Jewry and Jews from North Africa, Zionism and Franco-Judaism, religious existentialism and humanism. They would be followed by the contemporary generation of French-Jewish intellectuals who came of age with the Six Day War, General de Gaulle's reversal of French policy in the Middle East in its aftermath, and his castigation of Israelis as "a self-assured, domineering, elite people" thus tacitly legitimating a new era of anti-Zionism fused to anti-Semitism, and the events of May and June 1968 that were largely led by young Jewish militants like Daniel Cohn-Bendit, Alain Geismar, Alain Krivine, and Benny Lévy.

Lévy, leader of the *Gauche prolétarienne*, the most important post-1968 new left movement, became a symbol of one trajectory followed by some Jewish *soixante-huitards* (sixty-eighters) who moved from adherence to Mao and Marx to devotion to Moses and orthodox Judaism, immersing themselves in the Jewish tradition. This was a trend followed by one section of the Jewish community that was very different from the path of prewar Jews. Others remained secularists, like the members of the *Nouveaux Philosophes* (New Philosophers), whose leading figures were young Jews who created a media sensation in the late 1970s, when they were heralded as the forefront of a new intellectual movement, coming to prominence by trading in their militant past and decrying Marxist and totalitarian ideologies. *Le Cercle Gaston Crémieux*, led by Richard Marienstras, was another venue of secular Jewish activists, advocating a critique of the homogenizing tendencies of French Jacobin nationalism, the Jewish establishment, and Zionism, in the interest of defending minority nationalism and "the right to be different" that become a slogan of post-1968 tendencies.

Alain Finkielkraut, today perhaps the most visible French-Jewish intellectual whose concerns almost invariably return to "the Jewish question," first presented his brilliant analysis of the post-Holocaust Jewish situation *Le Juif imaginaire* (*The Imaginary Jew*, 1980) to the *Cercle Gaston Crémieux*. Excluded from the horrors of Jewish persecution and denied a Jewish heritage through the silence of his parents, Finkielkraut applies his critique to his whole generation, suggesting that most Jews today, from orthodox to secular, activists to Zionists, are "imaginary Jews" in a postmodern world without access to a primordial authenticity. In subsequent books, Finkielkraut attacked the Holocaust deniers, whom Pierre Vidal-Naquet famously called *Assassins of Memory*, analyzed anti-Zionism, celebrated the work of Emmanuel Levinas, evaluated the memory of Vichy France, and ultimately become an eloquent defender of human rights and the Enlightenment and humanist tradition.

This tradition has been deconstructed by postmodern thinkers who have rethought the Western tradition from the margins, including from the perspective of Jews and Judaism. Some postmodernists are Jews (Jacques Derrida and Hélène Cixous), and several have developed and criticized Sartre's analysis of the relation between self and other, identity and difference, through ruminations on "the Jewish question," which

runs like *Theseus'* golden thread through the labyrinth of much postmodern theory. Reconceptualizing human subjectivity as multiple, decentered, and defined in relation to others, postmodernists have drawn upon the thematics so eloquently expressed in the poetry of Edmond Jabès, an Egyptian Jew educated in Paris, whose work weaves images of nomadism and exile, resulting in the postmodern celebration of that peripatetic figure, "the wandering Jew"—perhaps the archetype of postmodern subjectivity—as the rootless outsider without a national home whose destiny is to bear witness to a future messianic moment. For the followers of Jacques Lacan, including Julia Kristeva and Slavoj Zizek, "the Jew" is a figure of the unconscious of the Western tradition, the repressed, abject other who is a symptom of totalitarian ideology's desire to master alterity. Jean François Lyotard's *Heidegger and "the jews"* explores "the Jew" as a trope of the forgotten debt that the West owes to the unrepresentable and excluded other.

Lyotard's text was a contribution to "The Heidegger affair," which involved both the deconstructive thinkers influenced by Martin Heidegger and their opponents. It erupted after the publication of Victor Farias's *Heidegger and Nazism* (1987) charged that the relationship between Heidegger's thought and his politics, specifically his turn toward National Socialism in 1933–1934, was far from momentary or a mere deviation. The same year it was discovered that Paul de Man, another major thinker associated with deconstruction, had contributed 180 book reviews and short articles to collaborationist journals from 1940–1942, including one, "*Les Juifs dans la littérature actuelle*" ("The Jews in Current Literature"), rife with anti-Semitic slurs about the Jewish contribution to culture.

This was disturbing precisely because the Jewish contribution to culture (Levinas, Walter Benjamin, Franz Rosenzweig, Karl Marx, Sigmund Freud, Hannah Arendt, the Frankfurt school, Franz Kafka) has profoundly influenced postmodern theory, as well as the approach to interpretation in postmodernism, which invariably involves reading not only the literal work, but its rhetorical dimensions and the history of its interpretation, which is a "Talmudic" approach to hermeneutics. Like the inherent deferral of signification in postmodernism, "the Jewish question" therefore remains an unresolved but fecund site for exploring the critical modern questions concerning citizenship, civic duty, education, (national) identity, civilization, and the meaning of modernity itself.

JONATHAN JUDAKEN

See also **Maurice Basses; Helene Cixous; Jacques Derrida; Vladimir Jankelevitch; Julia Kristeva; Jacques**

Lacan; Emmanuel Levinas; Jean-Francois Lyotard; Charles Maurras

Further Reading

Astro, Alan (editor), *Discourses of Jewish Identity in Twentieth-Century France: Yale French Studies*, no. 85, New Haven: Yale University Press, 1994

Benbassa, Esther, *The Jews of France: A History from Antiquity to the Present*, translated by M. B. DeBevoise, Princeton: Princeton University Press, 1999.

Berkovitz, Jay, *The Shaping of Jewish Identity in Nineteenth-century France*, Detroit: Wayne State University Press, 1989

Birnbaum, Pierre, *Anti-Semitism in France: A Political History from Léon Blum to the Present*, Oxford and Cambridge: Basil Blackwell, 1992

Birnbaum, Pierre, *The Jews of the Republic: A Political History of State Jews in France from Gambetta to Vichy*, Stanford: Stanford University Press, 1996

Birnbaum, Pierre, *Jewish Destinies: Citizenship, State, and Community in Modern France*, New York: Hill and Wang, 2000

Bredin, Jean-Denis, *The Affair: The Case of Alfred Dreyfus*, translated by Jeffrey Mehlman, New York: Georges Braziller, 1986

Burns, Michael, *Rural Society and French Politics: Boulangism and the Dreyfus Affair*, Princeton: Princeton University Press, 1984

Burns, Michael, *France and the Dreyfus Affair: A Documentary History*, Boston and New York: Bedford/St. Martins, 1999

Byrnes, Robert, *Antisemitism in Modern France, vol. 1: The Prologue to the Dreyfus Affair*, New Jersey: Rutgers University Press, 1950

Caron, Vicki, "The 'Jewish question' from Dreyfus to Vichy" in *French History Since Napoleon*, edited by Martin Alexander, London, Sydney, and Auckland: Arnold, 1999

Carroll, David, *French Literary Fascism: Nationalism, Anti-Semitism and the Ideology of Culture*, Princeton: Princeton University Press, 1995

Datta, Venita, *Birth of a National Icon: The Literary Avant-Garde and the Origins of the Intellectual in France*, Albany: SUNY Press, 1999

Davies, Peter, *The Extreme Right in France, 1789 to the Present*, London and New York: Routledge, 2002

Finkielkraut, Alain, *The Imaginary Jew*, translated by Kevin O'Neill and David Suchoff, Lincoln and London: University of Nebraska Press, 1980

Finkielkraut, Alain, *The Future of a Negation: Reflections on the Question of Genocide*, translated by Mary Byrd Kelly, Lincoln and London: University of Nebraska Press, 1988

Finkielkraut, Alain, *Remembering in Vain: The Klaus Barbie Trial and Crimes Against Humanity*, translated by Roxanne Lapidus with Sima Godfrey, New York: Columbia University Press, 1992

Friedlander, Judith, *Vilna on the Seine: Jewish Intellectuals in France Since 1968*, New Haven and London: Yale University Press, 1990

Griffiths, Richard, *The Use of Abuse: The Polemics of the Dreyfus Affair and its Aftermath*, Oxford: Berg, 1991

Hertzberg, Arthur, *The French Enlightenment and the Jews*, New York: Columbia University Press, 1968

Hyman, Paula, *From Dreyfus to Vichy: The Remaking of French Jewry, 1906–1939*, New York: Columbia University Press, 1979

Hyman, Paula, *The Jews of Modern France*, Berkeley and Los Angeles: University of California Press, 1998

Irvine, William, *The Boulanger Affair Reconsidered: Royalism, Boulangism and the Origins of the Radical Right in France*, New York: 1988

Judaken, Jonathan, "Bearing Witness to the *Différend*: Jean-François Lyotard, The Postmodern Intellectual and 'the jews,' " in *Studies in Contemporary Jewry: An Annual*, v. 16, *Jews and Gender: The Challenge to Hierarchy*, edited by Jonathan Frankel, New York: Oxford University Press, 2000

Judaken, Jonathan, "To be or not to be French,": *Soixante-huitard* Reflections on "la question juive," in *Journal of Modern Jewish Studies*, vol. 1, no. 1 (April 2002): 3–21

Judaken, Jonathan, "Reflections on the 'the Jewish Question' in Postwar France: Céline, Bataille, Levinas, Lanzmann" in *Dynamics of Antisemitism*, Harwood Academic Publishers, 2003

Katz, Jacob, *From Prejudice to Destruction: Anti-Semitism, 1700–1933*, Cambridge: Harvard University Press, 1980

Kleeblatt, Norman, *The Dreyfus Affair: Art, Turth and Justice*, Berkeley and Los Angeles: University of California Press, 1987

Lehrmann, Charles, *The Jewish Element in French Literature*, translated by George Klin, New Jersey: Fairleigh Dickinson University Press, 1971

Lichtheim, George, "Socialism and the Jews", *Dissent* (July-August 1968): 314–342

Malino, Frances and Bernard Wasserstein (editors), *The Jew in Modern France*, New Hampshire: University Press of New England, 1985

Marks, Elaine, *Marrano as Metaphor: The Jewish Presence in French Writing*, New York: Columbia University Press, 1996

Marrus, Michael, *The Politics of Assimilation: The Jewish Community in France at the Time of the Dreyfus Affair*, Oxford: Oxford University Press, 1971

Marrus, Michael and Robert Paxton, *Vichy France and the Jews*, Stanford: Stanford University Press, 1995

Mehlman, Jeffrey, *Legacies of Anti-Semitism in France*, Minneapolis: University of Minnesota Press, 1983

Poliakov, Léon, *The History of Anti-Semitism*, vol. 3 and vol. 4, New York: Vanguard Press, 1965–1985

Rémond, René, *The Right Wing in France from 1815 to de Gaulle*, Philadelphia: University of Pennsylvania Press, 1969

Sartre, Jean-Paul, *Anti-Semite and Jew*, translated by George Becker, New York: Schocken Books, 1948

Schnapper, Moninque, *Jewish Identities in France: An Analysis of Contemporary French Jewry*, translated by Arthur Goldhammer, Chicago and London: University of Chicago Press, 1983

Soucy, Robert, *Fascism in France: The Case of Maurice Barrès*, Berkeley and Los Angeles: University of California Press, 1972

Soucy, Robert, *French Fascism: The First Wave, 1924–1933*, New Haven and London: Yale University Press, 1986

Soucy, Robert, *French Fascism: The Second Wave, 1933–1939*, New Haven and London: Yale University Press, 1995

Sternhell, Zeev, *Neither Right nor Left: Fascist Ideology in France*, Berkeley and Los Angeles: University of California Press, 1986

Sternhell, Zeev, *Antisemitism and the Right in France*, Jerusalem: Shazar Library, Institute of Contemporary Jewry, Vidal Sassoon International Center for the Study of Anti-Semitism, 1988

Sternhell, Zeev, *The Birth of Fascist Ideology: From Cultural Rebellion to Political Revolution*, Princeton: Princeton University Press, 1994

Toury, Jacob, " 'The Jewish Question': A Semantic Approach," *Yearbook of the Leo Baeck Institute*, vol. II, London: Horvitz Publishing, (1969): 85–106

Vidal-Naquet, Pierre, *Assassins of Memory: Essays on the Denial of the Holocaust*, New York: Columbia University Press, 1992

Weber, Eugen, *The Action Française: Royalism and Reaction in Twentieth-Century France*, Stanford: Stanford University Press, 1962

Weinberg, Henry, *The Myth of the Jew in France, 1967–1982*, Oakville, New York, and London: Mosaic Press, 1987

Wilson, Nelly, *Bernard-Lazare: Anti-Semitism and the Problem of Jewish Identity in Late Nineteenth-Century France*, Cambridge: Cambridge University Press, 1978

Wilson, Stephen, *Ideology and Experience: Anti-Semitism in France at the Time of the Dreyfus Affair*, London: Farleigh Dickinson University Press, 1982

Winock, Michel, *Nationalism, Anti-Semitism, and Fascism in France*, translated by June Marie Todd, Stanford: Stanford University Press, 1998

Wistrich, Robert, "France: From Dreyfus to Le Pen," in *Antisemitism: The Longest Hatred*, New York: Schocken Books, 1991

Zola, Emile, *The Dreyfus Affair: "J'accuse" and Other Writings*, edited by Alain Pagès, New Haven: Yale University Press, 1996

JOURNALS AND PERIODICALS

Until relatively recently the journal was the major site for any intervention on the part of French intellectuals into their present moment. A salient characteristic of journals and periodicals in French intellectual life is their proliferation, a proliferation that reflects as a defining characteristic of this life an almost automatic imperative to intervene, a commitment (in the broad sense) to public dissemination beyond institutional or disciplinary constraints. Any account of the role of journals and periodicals in French thought of the twentieth century is thus forced to sacrifice some detail. Certain key journals have indeed played a determinative role in shaping and constituting the context for French thought, and are seen in hindsight as indistinguishable from the philosophical or aesthetic movement that informed them. But, even if the following account privileges those landmarks, what should also be stressed is that the journal is arguably the defining characteristic of French thought, and its importance and proliferation are evidence of the peculiar commitment of French intellectuals to intervention. The manner in which the journal differs from the book is significant: the journal is both punctual and serial (or intends to be so; there are many examples of journals which last for only a few issues or a single issue, or of projected journals which do not appear at all). While the book is monumental and singular, intervention in a journal is a response to the wider context and an addition to it, a distinct event in a periodic continuity which itself has a form of coherence. Though the intensity of the commitment of each journal to any *particular* ideology or movement is different, intervention through publication in the journal always commits the individual writer to a movement that has a temporality beyond that specific publication. The significance of the journal in French intellectual life indicates to what extent modern French thought is not the unique province of the isolated thinker producing the work, but consists of punctual interventions in specific contexts, polemical or critical responses within a community, albeit not a cohesive one. The thinker, in this light, is engaged with shifting groups and tendencies constituting a network of relations. Journals are more often than not associated with particular explicit or implicit tendencies or affiliations, linked to groups or movements. The history of the French journal over the twentieth century can thus offer a picture of this network of relationships, which will parallel and supplement the individual itineraries of key thinkers, or the broader trajectory of currents categorized under various movements or ideologies.

In *Le pouvoir intellectuel en France* Régis Debray argues that the defining site of French intellectual activity, and its locus of power, shifted in the 1920s from the university to the publishing house, with the journal playing the major role. The 1960s, for Debray, saw a further shift from the publishing house to the media as the dynamic locus of intellectual power in France. Debray's argument is accurate in identifying the journal as playing the major role in shaping the context for French intellectual life of the twentieth century, but overemphasizes the relationship of journals to publishing houses, and cuts short the period of the dominance of the journal by at least ten years. Although certain journals are closely tied to publishers (as the *Nouvelle revue française* is almost indistinguishable from Gallimard), the major reviews of the postwar period are independent of them, and cannot be accounted for solely in terms of intellectual capital. Although the intellectual interventions of Foucault (to take a telling example) outside his books, tend from the 1970s onwards to take place in newspapers and magazines such as *Libération* or *Le Nouvel observateur*, and the radio and television play an increasingly determining role, the journal continues to play a decisive role in the dissemination of French thought, and still, to an extent, shapes the field in which it is articulated.

The journal is the space in which literature becomes articulated associated with politics; in which transhistorical, or (for some) essential, concerns address themselves to the moment, to actuality. An account of the role of the journal in French thought of the twentieth century is thus to an extent an account of the manner in which aesthetic or philosophical thought becomes embroiled, or in a more positive sense, engaged, in the complexity of its time; "its time" referring not to broad historical periods but to precise conjunctures. The journal is in other words the place where the intellectual gets his or her "hands dirty." The journal is also the forum in which the individual writer or thinker is engaged with another defining characteristic of French intellectual life: the group. Although journals and groups are often polarized around particular figures; intellectual figureheads, heroes, or saints (for example, Peguy and the *Cahiers de la quinzaine*, Gide and the *Nouvelle revue française*, Breton and *La révolution surréaliste*, Mounier and *Esprit*, Rolland and *Europe*, Sartre and *Les temps modernes*, Bataille and *Critique*) the journal is necessarily the space of a plurality that will have varying degrees of cohesion. Through its punctuality and its serialization, the journal is a space in which any intervention enters into relation service with community. This community consists of different and shifting constituencies: the group, the party (in some instances), the Left, and so on. It is rare that journals are so polarized around their figureheads as to be indistinguishable from them. However, it remains true that certain journals sanctify their founding fathers and thereby perpetuate their communality. *Esprit* (1932–), for example, dedicates its masthead to its founder Emmanuel Mounier. *Europe* founded by a group supporting Romain Rolland in 1923, indicates as much on its title page and continues to promote Rolland's universalist pacifism through special issues on writers, artists, and philosophers. The case of *Cahiers de la quinzaine* (1900–1914), founded and directed by Charles Peguy until his death, stands out as an example of almost complete diminution of a group to the presence of the director, the review increasingly monopolized as a space for his mystical, polemical, and satirical thrusts. Ironically the review *Acéphale* (1936–39), founded by Georges Bataille, by its fifth and final issue featured only Bataille as author; the "headless" community whose virulence it sought to express having abandoned its principal instigator. These exceptions aside, the most significant journals are those, which while they may be associated with a tutelary figure, mobilize not only an immediate group, but also a wider constituency, and thus change the context in which they appear. The *Nouvelle revue française, Les temps modernes, Critique* and *Tel Quel* do tend to be associated with individual thinkers (Gide, Sartre, Bataille, Sollers), but these associations are misleading if overemphasized, and obscure the reality of a more complex and mobile network of relations. These reviews, which differ significantly from each other in the way that they function in relation to the intellectual communities whose thought they articulate, offer spaces for the experimentation and dissemination of thought outside particular institutional ties; they are spaces of theoretical and polemical intervention that constitute the nevalgic points of French thought in the twentieth century.

These landmark journals each articulate different ideological positions, but are distinct in not being affiliated to any particular institution (publisher, academy, school, or party). The group in this sense must be distinguished from the more defined locus of the institutional constituency. The journal that is linked to a particular constituency certainly plays a role, but this role is one constrained by the limits of that institution. The journals *La nouvelle critique* (1948–), *Lettres françaises* (1945–), or *La pensée* (1939–), affiliated to the French Communist Party (PCF), constitute solid points of reference both for the literary and philosophical development of the PCF, and outside it, but in their affiliation do not appear as spaces of independent thought, spaces, that is, in which thought is experimented and articulated without explicit determination by a predefined agenda. The *NRF, Les temps modernes, Critique*, and *Tel Quel* attain an independence from their publisher and do not represent their publishing houses in such a way as to render their status susceptible to an analysis of the marketplace. They constitute states within states. The relation of the landmark journal to the university is also a complex one. Within the field of philosophy certain journals (such as *Recherches philosophiques, Deucalion, La revue de métaphysique et de morale, Cahiers pour l'analyse*) have played a significant and acute role that can be seen in hindsight as formative of the present context of French thought. Within other disciplines, journals have often played definitive and dynamic roles within and outside those contexts: *Annales* for history (the journal which gives its name to the school), *L'année sociologique* (polarized around Durkheim) and *Actes de la recherche en sciences sociales* (around Bourdieu) for sociology, *Nouvelle revue de psychanalyse*, and the various journals of the *Ecole freudienne* (*Scilicet, Ornicar?* around Lacan) for psychoanalysis, *Poétique* for literary theory, and *Communications* for semiology. But a distinctive factor of the landmark journal is the impetus to totality, to thought as considered in the broad sense, where literary criticism, literature, or other aesthetic practices are not considered as separate, supplementary, or parallel to philosophical thought, and thought is not considered the domain of the specialist. The commitment of the landmark journal involves a commitment to thought that engages beyond the boundaries of disciplines or institutions, to thought conceived as totalizing.

An account of the role of the journal in shaping the context of modern French thought must thus consider these landmark journals as determinative of the broad context of French thought, while also emphasizing the importance of particular journals within the narrower field of French philosophy. At stake in the former aspect of the account is the way each journal figures the relation between specific forms of thought, address, or enquiry (literature, philosophy, science, and so on) and the totality of thought to which it commits itself. Also at stake are the degree to which this commitment is explicit, and the degree to which it signals a commitment to explicitly political intervention in the present.

La nouvelle revue française, founded in 1909 by a group of writers around Gide, is thus to be contrasted with *Les temps modernes*, founded by a group around Sartre in 1945. Both journals, as of this writing, are still extant. From the outset the *NRF* signaled its commitment to a pure creativity, in literature and in thought. Its editorial statements present the intention to provide a space for creativity disengaged from the present, disinterested and impartial, in the absence of political preferences. This intention is reiterated when the journal, interrupted by both World Wars, relaunched itself. The journal thus continues to represent the imperative of a pure creativity, the aesthetic considered as an essential and transhistorical value over and above the political. This is not so much an absence of commitment as a commitment to creativity in thought and in writing—fictional, poetic, or other—in the pure sense. "Literature is literature, and art is art," wrote Jean Schlumberger in the first issue after World War I. The ascendancy of the *NRF* and of this ideology was severely put to the test in the 1920s by the more radical and explicitly subversive notion of the aesthetic theorized and practiced in the surrealist journals (Littérature, *La Révolution surréaliste* and *Le Surréalisme au service de la révolution*, as well as in the many and varied proto-surrealist journals of which *Le grand jeu* is a striking example), and again in the 1930s by the urgency and tension of the political situation. But it crumbled, and revealed its intellectual bankruptcy during the Occupation, when the review, directed by Drieu la Rochelle, became the symbol of apathy and complicity. The purity of literary creativity showed itself incapable of remaining uncorrupted. The emphasis on the literary and the aesthetic of the *NRF* meant that it was not a space in which French thought, in the narrower sense of French philosophy, had a particular prominence, though it did publish significant material such as, for example, Valéry's *La crise de l'esprit* (1919), and regular essays by Blanchot from 1953. The incidence of Blanchot's work in the *NRF* suggests to what extent the journal's commitment to the purity of literature was susceptible of producing a rigorous commit-

ment to the demand of thought, rather than an indulgence in *belles lettres*. In this light one might propose that the *NRF* set itself an impossible ideal, and, in the context, that it symbolized this ideal of the impossible essence of literature.

At its foundation in 1945 *Les temps modernes* occupied the vacuum left by the suspension and moral corruption of the *Nouvelle revue française*, which ceased publication in 1943, to recommence in 1953. The explicit intention of the team around Sartre, which initially included de Beauvoir, Merleau-Ponty, Jean Paulhan, Raymond Aron, and Michel Leiris among others (Merleau-Ponty, Aron, and Paulhan would soon leave the journal), was to "*fournir à l'après-guerre une idéologie.*" (to supply the postwar period with an ideology). This ideology was explicitly opposed to the notion of the disinterestedness of the writer, and sought to mobilize both philosophy and literature toward engagement in history. Marxism was thus, inevitably, the political and to some extent philosophical horizon for *Les temps modernes*. The ideology articulated in the journal, and which informed it, was also synthetic, construing literature and political intervention and analysis as interdependent activities within the context of a wider imperative. *Les temps modernes*, whose title rather obviously signaled its commitment to intervention in the present, represents perhaps the model of the journal, since it most explicitly formulated itself as a space for self-reflective analysis of and intervention in actuality in view of a commitment to a totalizing ideology. It may appear, however, as such a model because it effectively formed the paradigm for other postwar journals, dynamically shifting the context— so that, as here, the *NRF* was judged by its standard rather than the alternative view. The period from 1945 to 1960 was dominated by *Les temps modernes*, and by the shifting forms of Marxism it articulated.

The principal rivals to *Les temps modernes* in the immediate postwar period are *Critique* and *Esprit*, both journals, like *Les temps modernes*, not constrained by any institutional affiliation. *Esprit* is, however, particular in representing a strand of leftist-Catholic thought that originated in the personalism of Emmanuel Mounier, founder of the review and director from 1932 to 1950. During the prewar period *Esprit* was an important forum for a non-Marxist revolutionary agenda and for analyses of fascism. After 1945 (publication of the review was suspended from 1941 to 1944), however, the spiritualist humanism of *Esprit* must have seemed less powerful than the existentialist Marxism of *Les temps modernes*. *Esprit* was and continues to be a proving ground from which new voices emerge, or find expression (Paul Ricoeur, for example).

Critique, founded in 1946 by a fairly disparate group of intellectuals around Georges Bataille, is perhaps as important as *Les temps modernes* for the post-war context for French thought, both in the wider and more specific sense. The format of *Critique*, as its name suggests, was such that it consisted entirely of critical accounts and analyses of recently published books and articles taken from diverse fields such as philosophy, anthropology, economics, sociology, psychology, psychoanalysis, and literature. Editorial statements were absent. Since inception it has consistently presented a relatively exhaustive picture of French thought through review and critique. It is also significant that from its foundation *Critique* reviewed books in other languages before their translation, thus functioning as a conduit for the introduction of thought from outside France. The format in effect prevents the journal from being associated with any particular movement or from adopting a position in relation to any polemical issue that engages the journal as a whole rather than the author of an article, and to that extent it is possible to say that *Critique* does not espouse any distinct ideology. The reviews in *Critique*, however, are seldom merely informative or summary, and often act as polemical positions in relation to doctrines or theories, or as articulations of new thought, in cases where the review attains an importance over and above its object. Moreover, from the outset the perspective of the review is as totalizing as that of *Les temps modernes*, this imperative drawing on the principles of the tradition of French sociology espoused in the 1930s by Bataille, Caillois, and Leiris for the *Collège de Sociologie*, to offer an analysis of "*le fait total humaine.*" *Critique* was also specifically and rigorously critical of the existentialism articulated by Sartre and in *Les temps modernes*, publishing from 1946 to the late 1950s work by Bataille and others that either explicitly analyses and critiques Sartre's work, or addresses issues that are also those of *Les temps modernes*. The aim of *Critique* in this period was also to provide a synthetic picture and an analysis of the knowledge and thought of the time. In its early days, moreover, *Critique* featured contributions for figures that precisely do not belong to the camp of *Les temps modernes* (although Leiris, a friend and long-term associate of Bataille, was on the editorial committee of *Les temps modernes*, and Blanchot was connected to both), writers such as Alexandre Kojève and Jean Wahl. As a forum distinct from and critical of *Les temps modernes*, *Critique* will represent the alternative which will be drawn upon when the ascendancy of *Les temps modernes* is contested. Its crucial importance for the development of French thought is explained by its opposition and distinction from *Les temps modernes* because it offers a forum for thought without the necessity of reference either to Sartrean existentialism or to Marxism as authorities. If *Les temps modernes*

occupies a hegemonic position, other seams of French thought developed and passed through *Critique*, so that in the early 1960s when a different disposition began to emerge, *Critique*, then under the editorship of Jean Piel, was publishing important articles by the figures who will achieve prominence from 1967 onwards. Partly due to the importance of Bataille as a reserved but exemplary thinker, but also to the intellectual pedigree of *Critique* and its links to figures such as Blanchot, Wahl, and Kojève, in the late 1950s and early 1960s, *Critique* was the principal forum for writers such as Barthes, Foucault, and Derrida, who at one moment were all members of an advisory committee. *Critique*, for example, published Ricoeur's "De l'interprétation," the review articles from which Derrida's book *De la grammatologie* originates, Lacan's "Kant avec Sade," Foucault's text on Blanchot, "La pensée du dehors," and work by Kristeva, Lyotard, Deleuze, Virilio, and Serres. The opening of the review to currents from abroad has also more recently enabled it to act as a significant conduit for Anglo-American analytic philosophy in France.

Tel Quel (1960–1982) brought together the synthetic commitment of *Les temps modernes* and *Critique* with the commitment to literature of the *NRF*, but significantly articulates these through an avant-gardism that echoes the examples of the Surrealist journals, the prewar journals, and groups around Bataille (*Documents, Acéphale*, the Collège de Sociologie) and its part contemporary *L'international situationniste* (1958–1969). Literature, art, philosophy, science (which includes psychoanalysis and linguistics), and politics (at one point the subtitle that appeared on the review) are mobilized in the review toward a rethinking of writing and textuality that is conceived as conducive to cultural and social revolution. This affirmation of new currents in philosophy, in linguistics, and in psychoanalysis, with the emphasis on the practice of writing, meant that for a key period between about 1965 and 1975 *Tel Quel* functioned as a site of intersection among these different discourses, constituting a theoretical power base where Althusserian Marxism, Lacanian psychoanalysis, and Derridean critique of the metaphysics of presence could be inflected toward a reformulation of the notion of writing and of subjectivity. The avant-gardism of *Tel Quel* was, however, a strategic one. The editorial committee, which suffered the usual series of departures and exclusions, effected a strategy of constant displacement in relation to the context. Emerging currents or movements in thought were affirmed insofar as they represented newness or transformation, but the review would distance itself from these currents as soon as they became established or retentive. The journal functioned in relation to a highly reflective strategy and practiced, in the words of its primary animator, Philippe Sollers, the "permanent dissolution of itself." The dissolution of avant-gardism that the history of *Tel Quel* put into practice may also have meant the dissolution of the committed journal on the model of *Les temps modernes*; commitment overleaps the form of the present and is projected onto the utopia either of inscrutable alterity (China, for *Tel Quel*, in its Maoist phase) or of the transcendent exception (in the review's late emphasis on theology). *Tel Quel* dissolved the model of the commitment of the journal into an infinity (*Tel Quel* changed publisher and name to *L'Infini* in 1982, and Philippe Sollers assumed the review's directorship). Nevertheless, over the course of its twenty-two-year history, the mobile strategy of *Tel Quel* was enormously influential as a channel for the affirmation and launching of individual thinkers, and for the *post hoc* identification of broad tendencies. *Tel Quel* (as other reviews) also gave its name to a book series, and at one time or another the journal and series were the platform for the work of Genette, Todorov, Eco, Irigaray, Cixous, Girard, Foucault, Derrida, Jean-Joseph Goux, and most conspicuously, Roland Barthes, most of whose work was published by *Tel Quel* in essay or book form. A salient characteristic of *Tel Quel*'s role was pointed out by Barthes when he said that he could only aspire to the example of militancy that the journal and its committee provide. *Tel Quel* also theorized and practiced a critical reformulation of the history of literature and thought, emphasizing and affirming writers dissident to or marginalized by the major currents of surrealism or existentialism, such as Artaud and Bataille, but also Sade, Lautréamont, Mallarmé, Joyce, Céline. It thus contributed significantly to a reformulation of the canon to which the present is indebted. The overall strategy of *Tel Quel*, its insistence on the transgressive potential of poetic language, significantly informed the development by its major theorist, Julia Kristeva, of a powerful theory of subjectivity, informed by psychoanalysis.

If an account of these four journals, (*Nouvelle revue française, Les temps modernes, Critique,* and *Tel Quel*) maps out the landscape of French thought of the twentieth century, they do not monopolize it. The identification of these landmarks sacrifices the detail of the terrain. A more detailed account would consider, in detail, the roles of journals such as *Mercure de France*; the short lived *Philosophie*; the Resistance journal *Combat*, Rolland's *Europe; La pensée*, whose subtitle "Revue du rationalisme moderne," (Review of modern rationalism) suggests its orientation; the conservative journals *La table ronde* and *Preuve*, the eclectic *Bifur*; discreet literary journals such as *Mesures, Commerce,* and *Fontaine*; the leftist journals *Arguments* and *Socialisme ou barbarie*; the role of weekly papers like Drieu la Rochelle's *Je suis partout*; or newspapers such as

Libération and *L'humanité*. However, it is worth considering in more detail the role of certain journals within the narrower field of French philosophy, which with hindsight can be seen to have been crucial moments of intersection. The obvious danger is to overemphasize in the past those moments that are illuminated by a perspective in the present informed by what may only contingently and temporarily be its major concerns. Other acute moments could no doubt be identified; the following may offer a sense of the extent to which the journal is the primary locus for the expression of independent and critical thought.

The first of three such instances is the review *La critique sociale*, which was published between 1931 and 1933 and directed by the significant dissident Marxist Boris Souvarine. Its principal agenda was to propose a critical analysis of Marxist philosophy and of the state of Communism. As a nonaffiliated journal it was one of the first sites where a left-wing critique of Stalinism was articulated. The aim to propose a critique of Marxism within a commitment to social revolution also meant that the review was open to other intellectual currents, and through the work of Jean Bernier, Georges Bataille, Michel Leiris, and others the review effected a more considered analysis of Freudian psychoanalysis than had been proposed by the Surrealist reviews. The aim to critically analyze the state of Communism also meant a focus on the philosophy of Marxism. The contributors to *La critique sociale*, aside from Souvarine, included dissident surrealists grouped around Bataille; Simone Weil, involved in syndicalist movements and in another dissident Marxist journal *Le bulletin communiste*; and writers such as Pierre Kaan and Lucien Laurat, significant critics of Communism attempting to develop a different Marxist vision.

A second example is the prewar annual journal *Recherches philosophiques* founded in 1931 by the historian of philosophy Alexandre Koyré, the historian of religion Henri-Charles Puech, and the logician and mathematician Albert Spaier. In its five issues, until 1937, it published formative early work by Levinas, Sartre's "La transcendance de l'ego," a translation of Heidegger's *Von Wesem des Grundes*, Bataille's "Le labyrinthe," (part of *L'expérience intérieure*), articles by Bachelard, Caillois, Dumézil, Gabriel Marcel, the early work of Klossowski, and a short text by Lacan. It is significant in the exploration it enabled of phenomenology, and in the attention it gave to the philosophy of Hegel, which would be the focus of important work in the journal by Jean Wahl. The review *Deucalion*, founded by Wahl in 1946, continued the itinerary of *Recherches philosophiques*, offering like *Critique*, but in a way more focused on philosophy as such, an analytic critique of Sartrean existentialism and an alternative to it through Wahl's own work and those of associates like Levinas and Bataille.

The third instance is the review of the "*Cercle d'epistemologie of the Ecole Normale Supérieure,*" *Cahiers pour l'analyse.* Its participants included Jacques-Alain Miller, who would edit Lacan's seminars and be closely associated with Lacan from the early 1970s and Alain Badiou. Its ten issues appeared between 1966 and 1970, and among those who contributed to it were significant figures such as Foucault, Derrida, Irigaray, Althusser, and Lacan. The founders and animators of the reviews were pupils of Althusser at the Ecole Normale Supérieore (ENS), whose focus in the *Cahiers* was the epistemological foundations for science and philosophy. Their interests led them to explore Lacan's psychoanalytic theory, not as a clinical practice but in relation to philosophy and to logic. It is the association with *Cahiers* that led Lacan to consider the epistemological and philosophical dimensions and consequences of his thought, and particularly to explore the fields of logic and topology. The epistemological dimensions of Lacanian theory explored by current writers such as Badiou or Zizek are arguably indebted to *Cahiers pour l'analyse* (Badiou for obvious reasons) for its early insistence on them. Lacan's "La science et la vérité," and Miller's crucial article on "La suture," (an important text for the exportation of French theory into British film theory in the 1970s) appeared in the first issue of the journal. *Cahiers pour l'analyse* has an underestimated significance in the attention it gave to logic and epistemology. It featured articles on Frege and Russell as well as translations of mathematicians Boole and Cantor. The work of Alain Badiou in the review, particularly on the theory of infinity, would be drawn on by the theorists of *Tel Quel.* But these more abstruse concerns, nevertheless crucial for later developments in philosophy, were accompanied by important work in psychoanalysis, such as a republication of Schreber's *Mémoires d'un névropathe,* and a special number on Rousseau, to which Derrida contributed a piece. The review also paid homage to the tutelary figure of Georges Canguilhem. The reference to Canguilhem in the review suggests something of the importance of *Cahiers,* even though at the time, despite Lacan's mention of it in his seminars, it had a fairly limited presence. Its focus lay in an investigation and of the foundation of knowledge, of its conditions of possibility and the consequences for

these of the work of Althusser, Lacan, Foucault, and Derrida. If it has been given some attention here it is because it is an example of how a fairly minor review can seem to define as if secretly an intellectual moment.

These arguably contingent identifications of discrete but key journals within the narrow field of social, political, and philosophical thought, and the larger scope of the account of the landmark journals, give a limited picture of the role of the journal in defining the context for twentieth-century French thought. The punctual and serial nature of journal publication means that much is sacrificed in generalization. It is certain, however, that the independent critical journal is a specific attribute of the French intellectual milieu.

PATRICK FFRENCH

See also **the entries on individuals mentioned in this article**

Further Reading

Anglès, Auguste, *André Gide et le premier groupe de la Nouvelle Revue Française,* 3 vols., Paris: Gallimard, 1978

Boschetti, Anna, *Sartre et Les Temps modernes: une entreprise intellectuelle,* Paris: Editions de Minuit, 1985

Cornick. Martyn, *Intellectuals in History. the Nouvelle Revue Française under Jean Paulhan, 1925–1940,* Amsterdam: Rodopi, 1995

Davies, Howard, *Sartre and Les temps modernes,* Cambridge: Cambridge University Press, 1987

Debray, Régis, *Le pouvoir intellectuel en France,* 1979 as *Teachers, Writers, Celebrities. The Intellectuals of Modern France,* translated by David Macey, London: New Left Books, 1981

ffrench, Patrick, *The Time of Theory: a History of Tel Quel,* Oxford: OUP, 1996

Gombin, Richard, *Origines du gauchisme,* 1971, as *The Origins of Modern Leftism,* Harmondsworth: Penguin, 1975

Halévy, Daniel, *Peguy et les Cahiers de la Quinzaine,* 1979, as *Peguy and the Cahiers de la Quinzaine,* translated by R. Bethell, London: Dennis Dobson, 1946

Richman, Michèle, "Bataille Moralist? *Critique* and the Postwar writings," in *Yale French Studies 78: On Bataille* (1990): 143–168

Roche, Anna, *Boris Souvarine et La critique sociale,* Paris: La Découverte, 1990

Roudinesco, Elizabeth, *La bataille de cent ans: Histoire de la psychanalyse en France,* 2 vols., 1986, vol. 2 as *Jacques Lacan & Co.: A History of Psychoanalysis in France, 1925–1985,* translated by Jeffrey Mehlman, London: Free Association, 1990

Winock, Michael, *Histoire politique de la revue Esprit,* Paris: Editions du Seuil, 1975

K

KHATIBI, ABDELKEBIR
Philosopher

One of the foremost Franco-Moroccan thinkers of the postcolonial period, Khatibi's work is diverse and eclectic, incorporating strands of philosophy, literature, criticism, and sociology. At the center of this wideranging thought, however, is a preoccupation with decolonization and with the confrontation or interaction between French and Arabic cultures. Exploring in both his novels and his theory the status of the colonial language and its logocentric pretensions, Khatibi uses deconstruction to critique the conceptual structures of colonialism and invokes in their stead a more openended and plural *pensée autre*. This alternative mode of thought undermines notions of linguistic and cultural hegemony, "deterritorializing" language and celebrating the interpenetration of diverse signs, echoes, and nuances within a multifaceted and dynamic poetic system.

One of his most noted early works is the autobiography *La Mémoire tatouée*, a curious and subtle mixture of memory and fiction that traces the contradictory influences of the author's intellectual trajectory while also expressing a sense of anxiety regarding the French language in which he writes. Educated in French, Khatibi is compelled to write in the colonial language yet suggests that it struggles to encapsulate the nuances of the Moroccan, Islamic culture that simultaneously shaped his upbringing. The text begins with a reflection on his own name, derived from *Aïd-El-Kebir*, the commemoration of Abraham's sacrifice of his son Isaac, and he asserts that this original rupture or "déchirement" characterizes his (non)identity. Torn between French and Moroccan cultures, he is at home in neither community and describes the text as an "autobiography without foundation." Traveling from Morocco to Paris, Berlin, London, Stockholm, and Cordoba, he conveys in his writing a sense of exile and rootlessness both in his relations with the places he visits and in his use of language itself. Fractured and unstable, the memories he reconstructs are *"tatouées,"* grafted with fragments of foreign signs that remain detached from the hybrid experiences they set out to translate. Khatibi's text engages with the political question of the fight for independence, and with racism on the part of the Parisians, while forming a highly poetic and sophisticated study of linguistic alienation.

Such notions both of exile and of linguistic hybridization occupy a central position in *Maghreb pluriel*, perhaps Khatibi's most significant and widely read theoretical intervention. It is here that he associates decolonization with the deconstruction of ethnocentrism and logocentrism in the West, using Derridean philosophy and Foucault's discourse analysis to criticize the colonial exclusion of otherness, and privileging instead cultural and linguistic *métissage*. Recognizing Fanon's contribution to theories of decolonization, he moves beyond the earlier thinker's Manichean vision and advocates an ongoing process of *différance*. The *pensée autre* or *pensée en langues* evokes the dynamic circulation and interaction of signs, celebrating the transfer of nuances across cultural frontiers. Denouncing at the same time the neocolonial undertones of the francophone movement, Khatibi displaces French culture from its centralized position and explores its interpenetration with traces from other sources such as Arabic. This critique is also evolved through a reading of Berque, whose work on North African culture is revealed to have essentialist or Orientalist undertones.

Disconcertingly, however, Khatibi's attitude to this *pensée autre* fluctuates between celebration and anxiety. If on the one hand he seeks actively to "deconstruct" colonial or neocolonial thinking by exploring the enriching potential of linguistic *métissage*, on the other hand he laments the continued influence of ethnocentrism and conceives his position in terms of exile and uncertainty. The bilingual confrontations he upholds are at times perceived as a form of subversive creativity while at others they risk disorienting the postcolonial writer, leaving Khatibi irrevocably divided between two cultures that themselves remain self-same and intact. This contradiction is explored in the form of a poetic meditation in *Amour bilingue*, where the Moroccan narrator describes his relationship with a French lover in terms of fusion and separation by turns. A celebration of the exchange of associations between French and Arabic languages is juxtaposed with a lamentation on incommunicability and loss. The figure of the androgyne, explored also in *Le Livre de sang*, incorporates this uncertain duality.

Analyses of bilingualism and translation recur in texts such as *Par-dessus l'épaule* and *Un Eté à Stockholm*, and the essays printed in *Figures de l'étranger dans la littérature française* examine the varying depictions of cultural alienation in works by writers such as Segalen, Genet, and Barthes. Khatibi is keen to explore both the specific cultural experiences of the colonized people in Morocco and, more broadly, notions of marginality and migration in texts by writers perceived to belong less problematically to the *métropole*. Despite this cross-cultural interest, however, Khatibi's work also includes precise and rigorous discussion of Islamic and Arabic cultures, and *L'Art calligraphique arabe* is an exposition both of the Islamic philosophy of writing and of the practice of calligraphic art. Explaining the theory of *tawqif*, which states that the language of the *Qu'ran* is sacred or "uncreated," Khatibi traces the evolution of calligraphy as an exploration of this miraculous origin. Calligraphy also opens the space between the referent and the realization of the work of art, incorporating both signification and pure musicality or form. The multiple suggestions and forms of calligraphic art, examined further in *La Blessure du nom propre*, also challenge the widespread belief that Islamic culture is rigid or monolithic. This in turn works against recent nationalist and Islamist movements that freeze the dynamism of Arab culture.

Now perceived as one of the most theoretically sophisticated writers of francophone North Africa, Khat-ibi's work is nevertheless difficult to categorize. His thinking is genuinely interdisciplinary, researching cultural, literary, political and sociological perspectives on a set of central concerns. The richness of his diverse engagements are increasingly recognized both in Morocco and by French philosophers. Roland Barthes's *Ce que je dois à Khatibi*, for example, venerates the latter's invention of a "heterological language" and suggests that French thought should learn from this decentering of the Western subject. Despite its enthusiasm it should nevertheless be noted that Barthes's approach is itself Orientalist in that it omits to consider the specific implications of colonialism in Morocco in favor of an unequivocal celebration of Eastern culture. More recently, Khatibi has been incorporated into the center of French philosophical debate; his edited collection *Du bilinguisme* institutes discussion between himself and thinkers such as Todorov and Jacques Hassoun, and Derrida's *Le Monolinguisme de l'autre* includes a direct engagement with his conception of Franco-Maghrebian relations. Esteemed also outside the Moroccan and postcolonial spheres, Khatibi's influence now transcends the specific context upon which it was initially based.

JANE HIDDLESTON

See also **Roland Barthes; Jacques Derrida; Frantz Fanon; Michel Foucault; Tzvetan Todorov**

Biography

Khatibi was born in El-Jadida in 1938, and was educated in both Koranic and Franco-Moroccan schools. Having been exposed to French culture and civilization through his adolescence, he then went on to study sociology at the Sorbonne in Paris, and he completed his thesis on the Moroccan novel in 1969. He published *La Mémoire tatouée* in 1971, following up with *Le Livre du sang* in 1979, *Amour bilingue* in 1983, and *Maghreb pluriel* in the same year. His successful *L'Art calligraphique arabe* was also completed during this period, first appearing in 1976, reedited in 1980 and 1996. He was a member of *Souffles*, the bilingual literary review founded in 1966, until it was banned in 1972. More recently Khatibi has returned to sociology, topically updating his thinking on Israel and Palestine in 1990 and also publishing *L'Alternance et les partis politiques* in 1999, where he comments on the position of the Moroccan people in relation to broader currents of globalization and *délocalisation*. He continues to teach literature in Rabat, and is director of the journal *Signes du présent*, formerly *Bulletin économique et social du Maroc*. The breadth and scope of his work means that he can safely be perceived as one of Morocco's leading intellectual commentators.

Selected Works

La Mémoire tatouée, 1971
La Blessure du nom propre, 1974
L'Art calligraphique arabe, 1976
Le Livre de sang, 1979
Maghreb pluriel, 1983
Amour bilingue, 1983
Du bilinguisme (ed.), 1985
Le Même livre (with Jacques Hassoun), 1985
Dédicace à l'année qui vient, 1986
Figures de l'étranger dans la littérature française, 1987
Par-dessus l'épaule, 1988
Paradoxes du sionisme, 1990
Un Été à Stockholm, 1990
Triptyque de Rabat, 1993
Du signe à l'image, le tapis marocain, 1996
L'Alternance et les partis politiques, 1999
Pélerinage d'un artiste amoureux, 2002

Further Reading

Barthes, Roland, "Ce que je dois à Khatibi," In *La Mémoire tatouée*, Paris: UGE, 1979
Cheng, François, et al, *Abdelkebir Khatibi*, Rabat: Okad, 1990
Derrida, Jacques, *Le Monolinguisme de l'autre*, Paris: Galilée, 1996
Erickson, John, *Islam and Postcolonial Narrative*, Cambridge: Cambridge University Press, 1998
Gontard, Marc, *La Violence du texte: la littérature marocaine de langue française*, Paris: L'Harmattan, 1981
Khatibi, Abdelkebir, Christine Buci-Glucksmann, et al., *Imaginaires de l'autre: Khatibi et la mémoire littéraire*, Paris: L'Harmattan, 1987
Mcguire, James, "Forked Tongues, Marginal Bodies: Writing as Translation in Khatibi, Abdelkebir," *Research in African Literatures* 23.1 (1992): 107–116.
McNecce, Lucy Stone, "Decolonizing the Sign: Language and Identity in Abdelkebir Khatibi's *La Mémoire tatouée*," *Yale French Studies* 83.2 (1993): 12–29
Memmes, Abdallah, *Abdelkebir Khatibi: l'écriture de la dualité*, Paris: L'Harmattan, 1994
Wahbi, Hassan, *Les Mots du monde: Khatibi et le récit*, Agadir: Publications de la faculté des lettres et des sciences humaines, 1995
Wolf, Mary Ellen, "Rethinking the Radical West: Khatibi and Deconstruction," *Espritcréateur* 34.2 (1994): 58–68
Woodhull, Winifred, *Transfigurations of the Maghreb: Feminism, Decolonisation and Literatures*, Minneapolis: University of Minnesota Press, 1993

KLOSSOWSKI, PIERRE
Novelist, Essayist, Painter, Translator

Pierre Klossowski, a novelist, essayist, painter and translator, was one of the most singular intellectual figures in twentieth-century French thought and writing. Brother of the painter Balthus and a close associate of Georges Bataille, Klossowski wrote novels and philosophical essays that made a decisive contribution to the development of thought and aesthetics in France from the 1950s onward. Klossowski began writing in the 1930s, publishing articles in a number of journals that varied from the psychoanalytic (*La Revue Française de la Psychanalyse*) to the philosophical (*Recherches Philosophiques*), and included the religious and political *Esprit* as well as Bataille's *Acéphale*. Throughout this early period he began to read and comment upon the works of two figures which would come to dominate his writing in the following decades: Sade and Nietzsche. His major works include a highly influential literary-philosophical study of Sade's writing, *Sade mon Prochain* (1947 [2nd edition 1967]), and important commentaries on Nietzsche's thought published in the collected volume of essays *Un si funeste désir* (1963) and in his extended study of the posthumous fragments, *Nietzsche et le cercle vicieux* (1969). Klossowski was the author of five novels published between 1950 and 1965, and throughout his career he also worked as a translator, producing translations of, among others, Virgil, Suetonius, Kafka, Nietzsche, Heidegger, and Wittgenstein. From 1972 he dedicated himself to drawing in pencil and exhibited widely.

Klossowski's commentaries on Sade were extremely influential in setting the terms of debate for the French reception of the libertine writer in the decades that followed the Second World War. Alongside Bataille and Blanchot, he was one of the first to see Sade's work as philosophically important and relevant to an understanding of the transgressive potential of literary texts. Klossowski's Sade is not just the author of pornographic or shocking novels. His readings seek to engage with a complex logic of transgression, which underpins the discourse of the Sadeian libertine. The transgressive force of Sade's texts, Klossowski argues, involves a paradoxical play with limits, with the limits set by moral categories and interdictions but also with those of language thought and meaning. Central to his account is the relation of the Sadeian libertine to his victims. Klossowski unites a structure (borrowing heavily from Kojève's account of the Hegelian master/slave dialectic) whereby the destruction or annihilation of the Sadeian victim also entails a loss of subjectivity or identity on the part of the libertine. It is in this context that the self is reliant on others for its existence and any attempt to negate their value in order to affirm mastery over others is also, paradoxically, a form of self-negation. This structure of affirmation and negation stands as a figure in Klossowski's thinking for the impossibility that strikes any attempt to firmly ground a self-identical subject (and the impossibility of absolute subjectivity in the Kojèvian/Hegelian sense). Such a structure of affirmation and negation also underpins the logic of Sade's writing itself. The attempt to give voice or reason to extreme forms of perverted desire that outstrip reason marks the limit point of rational conceptuality in the same way that the relation between libertine and victim marks the limit point of subjectivity. In Klossowski's account of Sade's writing, writing itself emerges as that which is always in excess of any dialectic of subjectivity or reason. It operates as a residue or remainder that cannot be accounted for by thought or representation.

Klossowski's commentaries on Nietzsche also engage with the limits of rational or discursive thought and were highly influential throughout the 1950s, 1960s, and 1970s. His reading of the doctrine of eternal return and the emphasis he places on the motifs of repetition, parody, and simulacrum exert a significant influence in particular on the interpretations of Nietzsche by both Gilles Deleuze and Michel Foucault in texts such as Deleuze's *Différence et répétition* and *Logique du sens* and Foucault's important essay, "Nietzsche, la généalogie, l'histoire." More generally, from the late 1930s onward Klossowski's interpretation of the doctrine of eternal return marks a shift in the focus of French readings of Nietzsche away from the doctrine of the will to power. As Deleuze points out on a number of occasions, Klossowski's reading of eternal return is decisive for the critique of representation and identity that occurs in France during the postwar years. For Klossowski, this doctrine follows through a mode of thought that occurs in the wake of the Nietzschean "death of God." A universe without God is necessarily a universe devoid of moral, conceptual, or teleological explanation. The doctrine of return is read by Klossowski as a radical apprehension of human finitude. Within this perspective, any moment of human existence is affirmed as both entirely fortuitous and at the same time, so utterly singular that it cannot be subordinated to, or determined in terms of, any principle outside, above, or beyond itself. Without teleological movement or rational purpose, existence, according to Klossowski's reading, is only ever a repetition of fortuitous instances that necessarily escape or are in excess of the determinations of linear history, representational categories, and rational conceptuality. In the movement of eternal return what is repeated is never a stable identity or moment of presence but rather the nonidentity of fortuitous instances, which repeat their difference from each other but also crucially from their difference from themselves.

It is in this perspective that the motifs of parody and of simulacrum come to dominate Klossowski's thought and fictional writing. According to Klossowski, what the thought of eternal return tells us is that existence is in excess of thought; it thinks an existence as an impossible object of thought and so exists only as a parody or simulacrum of a doctrine. In Klossowski's writing parody and simulacrum move beyond their platonic determination, which implies the relation of a bad copy to an original or ideal moment endowed with a certain integrity or plenitude. Figures of thought or writing, the difference between them here being indeterminate, emerge in Klossowski's work as parodies or simulacra, singular instances or points of intensity that are never posed as stable points of origin, but which are infinitely caught up in a play of repetition and nonidentity. Klossowski's commentaries on mythical images (for example, Diana and Acteaon in *Le Bain de Diane* [1956]), on Sade's libertines, and on Nietzsche's doctrines all exist as simulacra, as do the obsessively repeated tableaux of his fictional writing. In all cases writing is placed in an infinitely parodic relation to an impersonal and indecipherable exterior (such as is marked by Blanchot's terms the "dehors" and the "neutre") in a way that displaces the traditional lines of demarcation that might separate the literary from the philosophical.

Klossowski's insistence on returning thought and writing to the singular and anonymous points of intensity, which constitute human existence in the groundlessness of a radical finitude, make of him at once a highly idiosyncratic but at the same time a highly influential writer. His writing prefigures some of the most important and preeminent thinkers of postwar France while at the same time asserting its own unique marginality. For all his idiosyncrasy, Klossowski deserves recognition as a major figure in the development of postmodern thought.

IAN JAMES

See also **Georges Bataille; Maurice Blanchot; Gilles Deleuze; Michel Foucault; Alexandre Kojeve**

Biography

Born in 1905, the eldest son of Polish émigrés, Pierre Klossowski spent his first ten years in Paris in an artistic milieu, heavily influenced by the neo-impressionism of figures such as Bonnard and Derain. At eighteen he became Gide's secretary and helped him work on the drafts of his famous novel *Les Faux-monnayeurs*. It was not until 1930, though, that Klossowski began his career proper, translating with Jean-Pierre Jouve a collection of poems by Friedrich Hölderlin. Throughout his life Klossowski was a prolific and influential translator into French from both German and Latin, translating among others Nietzsche, Kafka, Heidegger, and Wittgenstein from the German, and Suetonius, Virgil, Augustine, and Tertullian from the Latin. In the 1930s he made a number of key friendships and acquaintances, most importantly with Georges Bataille, but also many others including Walter Benjamin, André Masson, Jean Wahl, and Maurice Heine. During this period he published a number of articles and collaborated with Bataille on the review *Acéphale* and in the avant-garde experiment of the *Collège de Sociologie* (where, it is said, he would attend meetings dressed in a *soutane*). During the war years Klossowski trained in a number of Catholic seminaries, a vocation that ultimately failed and led to the writing of his first novel *La Vocation suspendue*, published in 1950. In the postwar period he married a war-widow, Denise Morin Sinclair, who had been interned in Ravensbrück for her activities in the Resistance and who became the model for Roberte, a key figure in much of Klossowski's fiction and painting. After the war Klossowski also began publishing the influential works for which he will be remembered; literary philosophical essays on Sade and Nietzsche, but also six important novels written between 1950 and 1965. Klossowski died in 2001.

Selected Works

Sade mon prochain, 1947, revised edition 1967
La Vocation suspendue, 1950
Roberte ce soir, 1954
La Révocation de l'Édit de Nantes, 1959
Le Souffleur ou le Théâtre de société, 1960
Un Si Funeste Désir, 1963
Les Lois de l'hospitalité, 1965
Le Baphomet, 1965
Le Bain de Diane, 1980
Nietzsche et le cercle vicieux, 1990
La Monnaie vivante, Joëlle Losfeld, 1994

Further Reading

Alain Arnaud, *Pierre Klossowski*, Paris: Seuil/Les Contemporains, 1990
Butor, Michel, and Maxime Godard, *Une visite chez Pierre Klossowski le samedi 25 avril 1987*, Paris: Éd. de la Différence, 1987
Dardigna, Anne-Marie, *Les Châteaux d'Éros ou les infortunes du sexe des femmes*, Paris: Maspero, 1980
Decottignies, Jean, *Klossowski, notre prochain*, Paris: Veyrier, 1985
Henric, Jacques, *Klossowski*, Paris: Éd. Adam Biro, 1989
Hill, Leslie, *Bataille, Blanchot, Klossowski: Writing on the Limit*, Oxford: Oxford University Press, 2001
James, Ian, *Pierre Klossowski: The Persistence of a Name*, Oxford: Legenda, 2000
Kaufman, Eleanor, *The Delirium of Praise: Bataille, Blanchot, Deleuze, Foucault, Klossowski*, Baltimore: Johns Hopkins University Press, 2001
Lugan-Dardigna, Anne-Marie, *Klossowski, l'homme aux simulacres*, Paris: Navarin, 1986
Madou, Jean-Pol, *Démons et simulacres dans l'œuvre de Pierre Klossowski*, Paris: Klincksieck, 1987
Orfali, Ingrid, *La Fiction érogène à partir de Klossowski*, Lund: Institute of Romance Languages of Lund University, CWK Gleerup, 1983
Wilhem, Daniel, *Pierre Klossowski: le corps impie*, Paris: 10/18, 1979

KNOWLEDGE AND TRUTH

The relation between knowledge and truth is a fundamental problematic underlying French thinking and writing since the mid-nineteenth century. Its origins may be found in the "modernist turn," when Baudelaire, associating poetry with an unknowable secret language, sent literature into a difficult, indeed an impossible, quest for an unspeakable truth. Baudelaire thus established a disjunction between knowledge and truth that was to become a distinctive feature of modern French thought as it was elaborated first in the 1930s, then through the structuralism of the 1960s and into what is now called poststructuralism—our most recent past.

By diverting romanticism away from its German origins and its more purely emotional or psychological content, Baudelaire turned it into a more philosophical, abstract matter. As he lifted language out of its "natural" roots and therefore its capacity to represent the world, he construed poetic language as something problematic that can never fully be known. Yet what the poet does know is that he must express an ideal truth that forever eludes him, and that poetry has no other aim. That is how the disjunctive relation between knowledge and truth is established: ever more desire to know, ever less truth.

At the same time as the language of poetry was becoming increasingly involved in this paradoxical bind, in the social sciences, a new positivism was being invented. There could be, it was thought, sciences of man, or human sciences, as knowable as the sciences of nature. However, in the case of these sciences of man, the knowledge/truth relation would soon show itself to be complicated by the fact that the object of knowledge and the knowing subject were one and the same. Two such sciences that were invented at the turn of the century, psychoanalysis and linguistics, were to become particularly important for the knowledge/truth relation, as it would be formulated later in France. In both cases, the positive knowledge in which they were founded would soon be confronted with the problematic truth of their object. Indeed, Freud's unconscious supposes a relation of the subject to its own truth for which it would soon be clear that there was no objective knowledge, and basing linguistics on his now famous oppositional distinctions, Saussure in fact immediately revealed the impossibility of a simple, objective definition for his new science.

In the 1930s, Jacques Lacan, a French psychoanalyst associated with the surrealists, read the work of Freud focusing on the relation between knowledge and truth and its ambiguities in Freud. In *Le stade du miroir* (*The Mirror Stage*) of 1936, Lacan showed, in the narcissistic relation and the drive toward death, the fundamental "*méconnaissance*" that characterizes the subject's desire to know its own truth. Life itself was a long journey of this impossibility, and the end of analysis was the knowing that no one knows this truth, not oneself, not even one's analyst. Lacan would turn the Father-analyst that was Freud into the "subject-supposed-to-know"; it is on the mere supposition of this knowledge that transference, which makes the work of analysis possible, depends. As Lacan would show, even Freud was obliged to question the certainty of his findings when the case of the hysteric named Dora revealed to him the disturbing truth of his own counter-transference.

With this notion of an impossible truth, Lacan rejoins the work of his contemporary, Georges Bataille, who would refer to thinking as a *non-savoir* also of the order of the impossible. God is dead: the law becomes an empty truth for which there is no knowledge. Eroticism, in its endless "*dépense*," would ever push toward that truth, without ever reaching it.

In these same years, two French historians of science, Gaston Bachelard and Georges Canguilhem, invented a historical epistemology that would question the continuity and certainty of scientific knowledge with the idea of epistemological breaks. Such discontinuities in knowledge would undo the presupposition that a unified truth in science could be given once and for all, allowing instead for the idea of different "problematics" of knowledge that establish what counts as true or false at any given time rather than what is, in any absolute sense, true or false. Knowledge is thus not a method (in the tradition of Descartes or Kant), and central to knowledge is what counts as an object, which, in turn, is irreducible to any knowing subject.

Throughout the 1920s and 1930s, Saussure's linguistics was taken up and developed outside of France, mainly in Eastern Europe, through the creation of new "scientific" fields of inquiry, such as phonology, poetics, and the like, that were to profoundly alter not only the study of language, but of literature as well. The side of linguistics that made it problematic in the epistemological sense was temporarily abandoned.

It was not until the 1960s that the French anthropologist Claude Lévi-Strauss turned what was by now called structuralism into a systematic mode of inquiry that was to radically change France's philosophical landscape that had been steeped so pervasively in phenomenology and existentialism after the war. Following the earlier work that had been done by Eastern Europeans such as Roman Jakobson (whom Lévi-Strauss met in New York in the 1940s and who had a transformative influence on his work), he proposed that a set of rather precise operations performed on new objects of knowledge, in his case, anthropological ones such as "myth," would lead to "deep" universal truths.

In the wake of Lévi-Strauss, literary critics such as Roland Barthes, along with Julia Kristeva and Tzvetan Todorov (who themselves had come to Paris from Bulgaria in the mid 1960s equipped with their "formalist" linguistic and literary baggage) applied this structuralist method to the study of literature. Under the influence also of the "scientistic" nouveau-Roman of the time, even literature was now thought to contain hidden but accessible truths that could be revealed through the careful categorizations by linguists and literary critics alike.

The structuralism of the 1960s in its strong positivistic sense lasted barely a decade, but its influence was felt everywhere: no object was thought impenetrable to its method. And yet, even then, it contained a tension within it (inherited from the sense of a problematic of the linguistics on which it was based) that would eventually lead to the undoing of this positivity and to the turn to poststructuralism after 1968.

It is indeed only after 1968 that the problem of the subject (which, earlier, had been "evacuated" to allow for structuralist "objectivity") makes its return in its full, problematic, "negative" sense that had been developed much earlier by Lacan. It is then that thinking in France is tied up once again with the strong sense of a disjunction between knowledge and truth; it is then that the "impossible" side of linguistics, psychoanalysis, and literature (now, under the influence of the group *Tel Quel*, thought of as "*écriture*") all come together to define, perhaps most characteristically, contemporary French thought.

It is perhaps interesting to now look at the work of two French thinkers whose work initiated in the structuralism of the 1960s, but who each found a way of "re-problematizing" the relation between knowledge and truth in ways that still influence us today: Jacques Derrida and Michel Foucault.

Derrida approaches the question from the standpoint of the "deconstruction" of the metaphysics of presence. What he criticizes in the traditional conception of truth is that it presupposed stable entities that are shown or uncovered. But once these entities are themselves shown to be "disseminated," the traditional notion of truth has to be rethought. Central to this way of posing the problem is the question of writing and its relation to the truth. In this respect he rejoins the French poetic tradition of Baudelaire, and also Bataille and Lacan. But in each case he wants to show that the truth is in even a more radical position of absence than is supposed; there is always still an assumption of presence that can be challenged. Thus when Lacan in "*Le séminaire sur la lettre volée*" (*The Purloined Letter*) used Poe to show the analytic conception of the absence of truth as a place from which the truth of desire speaks, Derrida finds in it still too much place: "*le manque a sa place*," he will say, the lack has its place, there is still too much truth.

Derrida, unlike Foucault, was not directly involved in the epistemological debate that descends from Bachelard and Canguilhem. Although he then radicalized the notion of truth, he dealt implicitly, but not directly, with its relation to knowledge. Foucault, on the other hand, who was directly influenced by Bachelard and Canguilhem, would rethink the relation between knowledge and truth, and indeed the very activity of "truth-saying," through his new method of analyzing "discourse."

Foucault would say that the discourse that makes knowledge possible has a regularity, but that this regularity changes; there are therefore discontinuities (or breaks) in knowledge; and thus knowledge can't be reduced to a single, unalterable truth. Each historical period constitutes its own positivities in knowledge; Foucault then tried to analyze the kinds of power, which such positivities suppose and help to establish. Foucault's particular "will to truth" thus starts with a loss of certainty about knowledge. The problem then becomes not so much what is true, but the cost of saying it, the risks, the consequences: "What does it cost for reason to tell the truth?" he would ask. In so doing, he found a connection with the ancient activity of "truth saying" in which a speaker would express his relation to the truth, even at the risk of his own life. Thus, for Foucault, knowledge and truth are linked, though in this peculiar new way: knowledge is never given once and for all, and it costs to tell even this truth.

Following 1968, the problem of women took a central place in French thinking and writing, much influenced by the teachings of Lacan. "Femininity" was to be given the place of the impossible truth in the conceptual scheme that had been put in place since the mid-nineteenth century. "*Ecriture féminine*," as it was called and called for by Hélène Cixous, was to be the expression of this place, not, this time, in the negative mode of an absence, but in an affirmation of the body and the desire of women. Could the truth, this "other" of the male, phallocentric, symbolic be said? If so, this truth was, after all, speakable, knowable; its long held secret could after all be revealed. The answer to this question might depend on what one thinks of "*écriture féminine*" (and possibly of *écriture* in general), but it can certainly be said that this attempt at a positive expression of what for over a century had been postulated as void, absence, and even death put some kind of end, at least until further notice, to what we may think of as the characteristically French tension in the relation between knowledge and truth.

ANNE BOYMAN

See also **Gaston Bachelard; Roland Barthes; Georges Bataille; Georges Canguilhem; Helene Cixous; Jacques Derrida; Michel Foucault; Julia Kristeva; Jacques Lacan; Claude Levi-Strauss; Ferdinand de Saussure; Tzvetan Todorov**

Further Reading

Bachelard, Gaston, *Le nouvel esprit scientifique*, 1934
Bachelard, Gaston, *Le rationalisme applique*, 1949
Bataille, Georges, *La notion de depense*, 1933
Baudelaire, Charles, "Les fleurs du mal," and "Le peintre de la vie Moderne," (The Flowers of Evil" and "The Painter of Modern Life")
Canguilhem, Georges, *Etudes d'histoire et de philosohie des sciences*, 1968
Cixous, Helene, "The laughter of the medusa"
Derrida, Jacques, *Writing and Difference*, University of Chicago Press, 1978
Derrida, Jacques, *Dissemination*, University of Chicago Press, 1981
Foucault, Michel, *The Archaeology of Knowledge*, 1969
"Fearless Speech," *Semiotexte*, (2000).
Freud, Sigmund, "The Dora Case," *Case Histories*, Penguin Books, 1977
Freud, Sigmund, *Metapsychological Essays*
Jakobson, Roman, *Essais de linguistique generale*
Kristeva, Julia, *Revolution in Poetic Language*, Columbia University Press, 1984
Lacan, Jacques, *Encore*, Seminaire XI
Lacan, Jacques, Ecrits I and II
Levi-Strauss, Claude, *Structural Anthropology*, Basic Books, 1963
Rajchman, John, *Truth and Eros*, New York: Routledge, 1990
Todorov, Tzvetan, *The Potics of Prose*, Cornell Univerisity Press, 1977

KOJÈVE, ALEXANDRE
Philosopher

The lectures on Hegel that Alexandre Kojève presented in Paris between 1933 and 1939 opened a new chapter in the history of Hegel interpretation in France. This renaissance of Hegelian thought was to go hand in hand with a new beginning or change of orientation within modern French philosophy altogether, as Vincent Descombes was to describe in detail in *Le même et l'autre* (1979). Kojève's approach to Hegel from the perspective of Marxist-existentialist anthropology paved the way for a new history of political, phenomenological, and structuralist thinking in France. It was not until 1947 that the famous lectures on "Hegel's philosophy of religion" that Kojève held as a successor of Alexandre Koyré at the *École Pratique des Hautes-Études* were published as a collection by Raymond Queneau under the title *Introduction à la lecture de Hegel, Leçons sur la phénoménologie de l'esprit* (published in English as *Introduction to the Reading of*

Hegel [1969]). Yet these lectures certainly had a direct and immediate impact on French intellectual life, which becomes clear when one considers the impressive names that were part of the audience: Lacan, Merleau-Ponty, Klossowski, Bataille, Aron, Breton, Lévinas, Althusser, Fessard, Eric Weil, and many others.

Kojeve wrote his doctoral thesis, *The religious philosophy of Wladimir Solowjew* (1926), under Karl Jaspers in Heidelberg. In this book Kojève began to tackle the problems of Hegel's philosophy of history. He attacked the theological conditions on which Solowjew's interpretation of history was based, criticizing Solowjew for conceiving the process of history from the ahistorical perspective of a knowledge of revelation, for defining future ideals without regard for history, and for speculating instead on the complete appropriation of history through human practice. Kojève secularizes human history, seeing it as the product of man's self-production. Of fundamental importance for his interpretation of Hegel's philosophy is the idea that God must be denounced, in the sense described by Feuerbach and Marx, as a self-alienating figure and regarded as an ideological hindrance that must be overcome for humans to be free.

Kojève's interpretation of Hegel's philosophy is not conceived as an ordinary exegesis of classical texts; it attempts rather to realize the political consequences of his thought. The idea that Hegel's philosophy is fundamentally atheist gives rise to particularly heated discussion. Kojève connects Hegel's criticism of Christianity, according to which religious conceptions are to be overcome by philosophical thought, with a criticism of the idealistic figure of thought and claims that the finality of human existence cannot be overcome toward infinity—either by imagination or concepts. Kojève considers the *Phenomenology of Spirit* to be Hegel's philosophical autobiography as it were, the text in which Hegel's progress toward perfect wisdom is portrayed. The revolutionary element of Hegel's philosophy resides in the human deification it implies, whereby man is seen to expect historical progress as a consequence of his worldly labor and not by the mere intervention of a heavenly lord.

Kojève's Hegel lectures (seen as a whole) provide an anthropological version of the *Phenomenology of Spirit*. He proposes to conceive the phenomenology of Spirit as a systematic and complete phenomenological description (in Husserl's sense of the word) of man's existential attitude. This interpretation draws on Marx—on the so-called "1848 manuscripts" in particular—as well as on Heidegger's ontology of *Dasein*. Kojève translates Hegel's concept of desire (*Begierde*) into the French *désir*, thus connecting the Marxist issue of needs being satisfied with an existential interpretation of longing in terms of ontological negativity.

Kojève analyzes the relations between Marx and Heidegger in his commentary in *The Phenomenology of Spirit*. The section on the "freedom and dependency of self-consciousness" deals with the dialectic between domination and slavery that Kojève considers of central significance not only for an understanding of *The Phenomenology of Spirit*, but for Hegel's philosophy in general. Kojève sees this as the first articulation of a characteristic tension that defines the historical dynamic of the spirit as such. This explains why the French edition of Hegel's *Phenomenology* uses Kojève's commentary of this section as an introduction to the whole book.

Unlike the first three chapters of the *Phenomenology*, the fourth chapter concerns the problem of self-consciousness such that for the first time not a natural object but a different desire becomes the object of longing. Kojève explains this distinction with his concept of a dualistic ontology, which Jean-Paul Sartre picks up later in another form in *L'être et le néant* (1943). The reflectivity of desire is what constitutes the intersubjective structure of recognition as a model of human communalization. Kojève considers desire as characteristic of a conception of human being in terms of finality—Lacan later radicalizes this point—and goes beyond Hegel in understanding the figure of the slave as the source of all human, social, and historical progress. In Kojève's thinking, man's struggle is to exercise the freedom of negativity in order to produce a world in which his desires are satisfied, and in the course of which he may come to accept his own freedom, ridding himself of the illusions of religion and claiming his own mortality.

The desire for recognition is the most significant moment of movement in the process of history. History moves across a certain number of stages on the way to its "end," which stands for a state of complete humanism, based on reciprocal recognition between free and equal citizens. Kojève refers to Hegel's master-slave dialectic in order to show how political inequality must necessarily be overcome. According to this dialectic, the relation between a master and his slave is unstable because the master is dependent on the slave working for him and recognizing him as master. Furthermore, the slave cannot exist as an equal for he is forced to recognize his master, which strips away the value of his recognition. The subordination of the slave means that his recognition of the master is not voluntary and free but merely due to his secondary position. Successful recognition requires therefore that asymmetrical relations between humans be abolished.

With clear reference to Marx, Kojève declares the slave to be the main figure in the progress of history.

It is the slave who labors and thus embodies the power of negativity that is needed in order to change the world, that is, to satisfy human needs. As Kojève writes in his 1946 review of Henri Nicl's *De la médiation dans la philosophie de Hegel* (1945), "the slave cannot be content forever with the imaginary satisfactions procured by art and the religious beyond. He struggles for his master to recognize him; that is, he attempts to do away with his master. And this explains why states in which there are slaves (which means 'classes') are the stage of bloody battles whose purpose is to establish social homogeneity." The figure of the slave manifests a desire and longing to overcome the state of imprisonment: a longing that can only be fulfilled when the desire for recognition is satisfied. In Kojève's eyes, all the revolutions and struggles of the previous 150 years created the conditions for the completion of history, that is, for the realization of the highest human ideals.

Kojève's statements regarding the end of history diverge: for a time he regarded Stalinism to be the contemporary counterpart to the Napoleonic empire in which Hegel saw redemption. In later years he considered economic development to have culminated in capitalism and rejected the Marxist thesis of immanent contractions as the conditions for its collapse and overcoming. From 1948 Kojève saw the United States as an economic model for the posthistorical world: capitalism, he thought, did not engender exploitation and impoverishment of the working classes but enabled prosperity for a larger number of people than ever. The development of man's productive capacities and his ability to master nature in order to satisfy his needs were bound to result in affluence and freedom.

Globalization and cultural homogenization are what characterize the era of *posthistoire*. Seen in this way, Hegel was right to announce the end of history because since then nothing essentially new has occurred and the dynamic of the spirit is being erased in the universal world state comprising mutually recognizing state citizens. Revolutions are over; the hopes that fed them have been satisfied—at least as far as it was possible for them to be satisfied: to expect any more is but outdated romanticism and bound to be deceived by the plain and sober truth of human finality. It is in this sense that in *The end of history and the last man* (1992) Fukuyama vindicates Kojève's thesis that history has found its end in the global triumph of capitalism and liberal democracy.

MARC RÖLLI

See also **Louis Althusser; Raymond Aron; Georges Bataille; Andre Breton; Pierre Klossowski; Alexandre Koyre; Jacques Lacan; Emmanuel Levinas; Maurice Merleau-Ponty; Jean-Paul Sartre**

Biography

Alexandre Kojève (1902–1968) was born as Aleksandr Vladimirovich Kozhevnikov in Russia and educated in Berlin. He studied philosophy in Heidelberg, Germany and completed under the supervision of Karl Jaspers a thesis about the religious philosophy of Vladimir Solov'ev (1931). He later settled in Paris where he gave his influential lectures on Hegel's *Phenomenology of Spirit* at the *Ecole Pratique des Hautes Etudes* from 1933 till 1939. His lectures on Hegel were collected and edited by Raymond Queneau under the title *Introduction à la lecture de Hegel* (1947) and appeared in English translation as *Introduction to the Reading of Hegel* (1969). After World War II Kojève worked in the French Ministry of Economic Affairs as one of the chief ministers until his death 1968. He exercised a great influence over French policy and was one of the leading architects of the European Economic Community (EEC) and General Agreement on Tariffs and Trade (GATT). He continued to write philosophical books about different problems such as the concept of right, the development of capitalism, Kantian philosophy, atheism, and Christianity in the modern world.

Selected Works

Hegel, Marx et le Christianisme, 1946
Hegel, Marx, *Introduction à la lecture de Hegel*, 1947 (*Introduction to the Reading of Hegel*), translated by James H. Nichols
Hegel, Marx, *Kant*, 1973
Hegel, Marx, *Le concept, le temps et le discours*. Paris, Gallimard 1990
Hegel, Marx, *Essai d'une histoire de la philosophie paienne* (vols. 1–3), 1997
Hegel, Marx, *L'athéisme*, 1998
Hegel, Marx, *Outline of a Phenomenology of Right*, 2000
Hegel, Marx, *Peintures concretes de Kandinsky*, 2002

Further Reading

Auffret, Dominique, *La philosophie, l'état, la fin de l'histoire*, Paris: Librairie Générale Française 2002
Butler, Judith, *Subjects of Desire: Hegelian Reflections in Twentieth Century France*, New York: Columbia University Press, 1999
Cooper, Barry, *The End of History. An Essay on Modern Hegelianism*, Toronto: Toronto University Press 1984
Descombes, Vincent, *Modern French Philosophy*, Cambridge: Cambridge University Press, 1980
Drury, Shadia B., *Alexandre Kojève. The Roots of Postmodern Politics*, Basingstoke: Macmillan, 1994
Goldford, D. J., "Kojève's reading of Hegel," *International Philosophical Quarterly* 22 (1982)
Goldman, Steven L,: "Alexandre Kojève on the Origin of Modern Science," *Studies in the History and Philosophy of Science* 6 (1975): 113–124.
Hyppolite, Jean, *Figures de la pensée philosophique* (2 vols), Paris: Quadrige/Presses Universitaires de France 1971.

Jarczyk, G., Labarrière, P. J., *De Kojève à Hegel: 150 ans de pensée hégélienne*, Paris: Albin Michael, 1996

Jubara, Annett, "Vom Reich des Antichristen zum homogenen Weltstaat. Das 'Ende der Geschichte' bei Vladimir Solov'ev und Alexandre Kojève," in: *Dialektik und Differenz. Festschrift für Milan Prucha*, Wiesbaden: Harrassowitz, 2001

Poster, M., Existential Marxism in Postwar France; Princeton, Princeton University Press, 1975

Riley, P., "Introduction to the reading of Alexandre Kojève," in: *Political Theory 9: 1* (1981)

Roth, Michael S., "A problem of recognition: Alexandre Kojève and the end of history," in: *History and Theory* 24 (1985)

Roth, Michael S., *Knowing and History. Appropriations of Hegel in Twentieth Century France*, Ithaca and London: Cornell University Press, 1988

Strauss, Leo, *De la tyranny. Correspondance avec A. Kojève 1932–1965*, Paris: 1997 (*On Tyranny*, expanded edition, 1991)

ALEXANDRE KOYRÉ
Philosopher, Historian of Science

Koyré is a thinker who defiantly resists classification according to any standard academic division of intellectual labor. He is best known as a philosopher-historian of early modern science, although one whose intense speculative bent and vast range of interests (in mathematics, physics, cosmology, philosophy, theology, and various traditions of neo-Platonic and mystical thought) place his work far apart from mainstream approaches to the subject. All the same his writings have exerted a powerful influence, not least through their incisive originality of mind and their expansive vision of philosophy of science as a quest for universal yet historically emergent and culturally salient truths. *Etudes galiléennes* (1939) is the foremost example of Koyré's capacity to provide the most detailed and exacting analysis of scientific theories—in this case theories of movement, stasis, and inertial force—while drawing out the kinds of problem and paradox that have preoccupied philosophers from Zeno to the present. It is also typical of Koyré's work in the way that it treats these issues within a larger metaphysical framework that takes them to involve fundamental questions such as those first broached by the conflicting claims of Platonic and Aristotelian ontologies. His preference for Plato is everywhere apparent, above all in Koyré's realist philosophy of mathematics and his antipathy toward empiricist conceptions of scientific method.

This heterodox approach also emerges very clearly in his historiographic researches. Like Pierre Duhem, Koyré rejected the conventional view that genuine scientific knowledge only made a start with the passage from Medieval to Renaissance modes of thought, that is to say, through a decisive break with the kinds of scholastic thinking which had characterized that earlier period. Thus he made no sharp distinction between the sorts of theological issue (such as realism *versus* nominalism) that had so preoccupied medieval thinkers and the sorts of metaphysical issue that continued to emerge with undiminished force when science took its turn toward a broadly secularized worldview. This also had to do with Koyré's attraction toward approaches like that of the anthropologist Lévy-Bruhl, who posited the existence of certain collective mind-sets (*mentalités*) or dominant modes of thought, knowledge, and perception. It was further reinforced by his reading in nineteenth century hermeneutic philosophy and his consequent sense of the problems involved in negotiating differences of cultural outlook or deep-laid metaphysical commitment. Yet he never went as far in a skeptical-nominalist direction as later thinkers—notably Michel Foucault—who treated all knowledge and the objects thereof (in particular those of the life-sciences) as discursive constructs that had their place only within this or that period-specific *episteme*. Nor was he by any means a paradigm-relativist in the Kuhnian sense, at least if one interprets Kuhn at face value when he claims that "the world changes" for scientists working before and after some major revolution in thought. Such notions go against Koyré's belief that science is indeed a continuing venture of discovery and that differences of mind-set—however profound—can none the less be rendered intelligible from a sufficiently informed historical-philosophical viewpoint. Indeed, it was Koyré's enduring realist conviction—no doubt influenced by his studies in scholastic philosophy—that scientific knowledge was properly aimed toward discovering the essence of things rather than contenting itself with merely nominal definitions. Once again this brought him out very much at odds with the then prevalent mode of positivist thinking in Anglophone philosophy of science that confined itself strictly to the analysis of statements in terms of their verifiability-conditions and which steadfastly eschewed any recourse to such otiose "essentialist" talk.

Thus Koyré was uncommonly receptive to certain previously marginalized intellectual currents—among them Renaissance hermetic philosophies (Paracelsus), Romantic mysticism (Boehme), and various nineteenth-century Russian "proto-existentialist" ideas—all of which he sought to bring within the compass of a unified history of thought. At the same time—and despite this seemingly hybrid and unfocused range of enquiries—his chief motive was to vindicate the claims of mathematics and the physical sciences as aimed toward a truth that transcended the socio-cultural vicissitudes of time and place. One indicator here is the fact that, during his early years, Koyré pursued intensive courses of study with thinkers as diverse as Henri Bergson (in Paris) and the mathematician David Hilbert (in Göttingen), as well as with Etienne Gilson, the great scholar of medieval philosophy and theology. This clearly impressed him with the need to go beyond existing (academically defined) areas of special expertise while nonetheless respecting those essential standards—of truth, objectivity, and conceptual rigor—that characterized mathematics and the physical sciences. Another great influence was Edmund Husserl's project of transcendental phenomenology, which Koyré first encountered while still living in his native Russia and with which he continued to engage—even if (very often) from a sharply dissenting viewpoint—throughout his subsequent sojourns in France and the United States. From Husserl he took the idea of philosophy as a rigorous, reflective, self-critical activity of thought which suspended (or bracketed) our commonsense beliefs and thereby sought to reveal the underlying, *a priori*, and hence universally valid structures of knowledge and experience. Nevertheless Koyré—like Husserl himself—tended to oscillate between this austere conception of philosophy's task and an approach that acknowledged its ultimate grounding in modes of intuitive self-evidence that had more to do with our being-in-the-world as historically and culturally situated agents.

For all these reasons Koyré's work made a great impact during that period of prewar French intellectual debate when thinkers like Sartre were attempting a synthesis of Husserlian transcendental with Heideggerian existentialist phenomenology, and these in turn with an understanding of Hegel mediated by Kojève's strong revisionist reading. What Koyré most strikingly brought to this debate was a grasp of its sources much further back in the history of thought. Thus he criticized certain elements in Husserl's work, among them the strain of transcendental idealism that emerged most clearly in the *Cartesian Meditations* and which struck him as a falling-away from the vocation of rigorous, scientifically disciplined enquiry. In making this argument Koyré had recourse not only to the evidence of modern (post-Galilean) scientific thought but also to the Thomist theological tradition that likewise—albeit for different reasons—rejected any notion of human knowledge (even at the limit of idealized rational acceptability) as the ultimate arbiter of truth. Here again one can see how the productive tensions in Koyré's thought were also a source of its greatest strength at a time when philosophy was torn among various competing and (on their own terms) irreconcilable tendencies. Koyré was a realist insofar as he maintained—in company with some medieval thinkers—that science could deliver objective knowledge of a mind-independent physical reality. Moreover—and to this extent at least he agreed with Aristotle—that reality consisted of objects, properties, and causal powers whose essential nature was such as to determine whether or not scientific enquiry was on the right track.

Thus Koyré's philosophy of science was squarely opposed to any form of instrumentalist thinking—like that of Duhem—which relativized truth to the powers and capacities of humanly attainable knowledge. That is to say, he shared Duhem's great aim of reawakening philosophers to the range and vitality of medieval thought, while stressing just the opposite (realist) aspects of what he took to constitute its chief and enduring legacy. Still Koyré never ceased to emphasize that scientific knowledge always had recourse to a far greater range of sources, analogues, and modes of comprehension than could ever be explained by a doctrinaire adherence to the precepts of scientific positivism. Hence his attraction to hermeneutic approaches, among them Wilhelm Dilthey's idea of those different world views or *Weltanschauungen* that at the deepest level shaped our conception of physical reality. Along with this went his claim that modern science had by no means shed its metaphysical commitments—as argued by hard-line positivists—but on the contrary continued to enlist such resources so as to render its truth-claims and theories intelligible. At the same time Koyré held out firmly against the kind of instrumentalist approach that resulted not only from Duhem's strain of theologico-metaphysical thinking but also—strangely enough—from the outlook of radical empiricism adopted by a hard-line physicalist such as W. V. Quine, with whom his name is routinely conjoined in discussions of the "Duhem-Quine" thesis concerning the underdetermination of theory by empirical evidence and the theory-laden character of empirical observation-statements. What enabled Koyré to avoid this paradigm-relativist upshot was his espousal of a basically Platonist outlook that aspired to transcend the epistemic contingencies of scientific knowledge at this or that stage in its advancement to date.

No philosopher in recent times has done more to uphold the claims of scientific rationality and truth while taking on board such a range of arguments from (seemingly) opposed viewpoints. Thus his critique of positivism for its antimetaphysical prejudice went along with his equally trenchant critique of those idealist—metaphysical—currents of thought that paid insufficient regard to the manifest achievements of physical science. By the same token Koyré can now be seen as a thinker who did much to bridge the gulf among various emergent orthodoxies, among them the postures adopted by adversary parties to successive rounds in the so-called "science wars" or "culture wars" debate. These have typically pitched adherents to an outlook of hard-line scientific realism against proponents of a wholesale cultural-relativist or social-constructivist doctrine that would treat all scientific truth-claims as nothing more than a product of this or that short-term ideological *parti pris*. What Koyré held out was the prospect of achieving a perspective atop these particular kinds of academic or interdisciplinary dispute. Just how far he succeeded in that enterprise is a question that can scarcely be settled so long as the debate is conducted in terms that reproduce the same professionally motivated conflicts of interest. At very least it may be said—on the evidence of his copiously detailed and rigorous enquiries—that Koyré's work points a way forward from some of the more sterile or deadlocked disputes in recent philosophy, history, and sociology of science.

CHRISTOPHER NORRIS

See also **Henri Bergson; Pierre Duhem; Michel Foucault; Etienne Gilson; Alexandre Kojève; Lucien Levy-Bruhl**

Biography

A Russian native, Koyré was caught up in the abortive revolution of 1905 and as a result arrested and imprisoned, during which time he first conceived an interest in philosophy and the history of ideas. After a period of intensive studies (1908–1914) in Paris and Göttingen—when he laid the basis for much of his subsequent life's work—Koyré enlisted with the Foreign Legion, saw service on the Russian front, and fought in the 1917 October Revolution. Thereafter he returned to Paris and embarked upon a highly successful (if academically unconventional) career as a teacher of the history and philosophy of science along with the history of religion and various aspects of medieval scholastic thought. He was also much involved—not least through collaborative work on the journal *Recherches philosophiques*—with the great interwar ferment of ideas brought about by the French reception of German philosophers, among them Hegel (*via* Kojève's revisionist reading), Husserl, and Heidegger. After the outbreak of World War II, Koyré established another home base in the United States, working first in New York (where, together with Jacques Maritain, he set up the *Ecole Libre des Hautes Etudes*) and then at Princeton, where he was elected to membership of the Institute for Advanced Study. Until his death in 1962 Koyré divided his time between the United States and Paris. Although his work was too wide-ranging and idiosyncratic to generate a movement or school of disciples, it can nonetheless be seen to have exerted a powerful influence on French thinkers from Sartre and Merleau-Ponty to Lévi-Strauss and Foucault.

Selected Works

Essai sur l'idée de Dieu et les preuves de son existence chez Descartes, 1922

L'idée de Dieu dans la philosophie de Saint Anselme, 1923
La philosophie de Jacob Boehme, 1929
La philosophie et le problème national en Russie au début du XIXe siècle, 1929
Trois leçons sur Descartes, 1938
Etudes galiléennes, 1939; as *Galileo Studies*, translated by J. Mepham, 1978
"Galileo and Plato," *Journal of the History of Ideas*, 1943
Discovering Plato, 1945
"Manifold and Category," *Philosophy and Phenomenological Research*, 1948
"Condorcet," *Journal of the History of Ideas*, 1948
Descartes After Three Hundred Years, 1951
"The Origins of Modern Science: a new interpretation," *Diogenes*, 1956
From the Closed World to the Infinite Universe, 1957
Newtonian Studies, 1957
La révolution astronomique, 1961
Etudes d'histoire de la pensée philosophique, 1961
Metaphysics and Measurement: essays on the scientific revolution, 1968
De la mystique à la science: cours, conférences et documents, 1986
(with Paola Zambelli) "Present Trends in French Philosophical Thought," *Journal of the History of Ideas*, 1998 (posthumous publication)

Further Reading

Clagett, M. and Cohen, I., "Alexandre Koyré", *Isis* 57 (1966): 157–66.
"Koyré", in *Dictionary of Scientific Biography*, New York: Charles Scribners vol. 7 (1973):
Kuhn, Thomas, "Alexandre Koyré and the History of Science," *Encounter* 34 (1970): 67–9
Redondi, Pietro (editor), "Science: The Renaissance of a History, Proceedings of the International Conference Alexandre Koyré," *History and Technology* 4 (1987)
Redondi, Pietro, "Alexandre Koyré," *The Routledge Encyclopedia of Philosophy*, London: Routledge, 1999
Speilberg, H., *The Phenomenological Movement: a historical introduction*, 2 vols., The Hague: Martinus Nijhoff, 1960
Vinti, Carlo (editor), *Alexandre Koyré: l'avventura intellettuale*, Naples: ESI, 1994
Wahl, Jean, "Le rôle d'Alexandre Koyré dans le développement des études hégéliennes en France," *Archives de philosophie* 23 (1965): 323–36.
Zambelli, P., "Alexandre Koyré *versus* Lucien Lévy-Bruhl: from collective representations to paradigms of scientific thought," *Science in Context* 13 (1995): 531–55.

KRISTEVA, JULIA
Semiotician, Philosopher, Psychoanalyst

Julia Kristeva's oeuvre, which at his writing spans over thirty-five years, positions her variously within the fields of semiotics, philosophy, psychoanalysis, and literary theory. In addition to the theoretical side of her work, she is also a practicing psychoanalyst, a teacher at the University of Paris VII, and a literary writer. Although she has written in French from the outset of her career and has become one of the most important of contemporary French thinkers, she was actually born in Bulgaria and came to France at the age of twenty-five. As she herself has acknowledged, her status as an outsider to the French system has had a fundamental influence on her thinking. Her belief that some form of exile is necessary to be able to write is borne out by the formative effect that her own personal experience has had on her intellectual concerns.

Although Kristeva's work is frequently discussed in association with that of Luce Irigaray and Hélène Cixous, and all three are labeled French feminists, Kristeva does not fit comfortably into this category. She has problems with feminism as a political project and would refuse to accept the label "feminist" for her own work. According to Kristeva, "woman" is that which cannot be represented. She gives this position of excess a positive value, understanding woman's status as outsider to lend her subversive power. This places Kristeva in a contrasting relation to a large number of feminists because she hereby questions the possibility of recognizing "woman" or "women" respectively as identity categories marking a transgressive political position or group within society. Yet her work on the maternal and the feminine has been of importance to feminists nonetheless.

Kristeva follows Freudian and Lacanian psychoanalysis in a less overtly critical way than Cixous or Irigaray. And this is evident in the important theoretical positions fleshed out within her early work. Accepting the Lacanian paternal prohibition that marks entry into the symbolic order of social representations, she does, however, mark out an important difference between herself and her male psychoanalytic forebears, namely by placing emphasis on the maternal function in the Oedipal relation and beyond. Her focus on the mother-child bond works in line with Melanie Klein's research on the infant's preverbal expression of bodily drives. These preverbal sounds of early infancy are what constitute the Kristevan semiotic; they are repressed when the child enters into the symbolic, converted, as they have to be, into linguistic signifiers. These psychic/biological drives erupt within the symbolic, serving as a remainder and reminder of the earliest bond with the mother. Kristeva's lengthiest discussion of the semiotic occurs in her published doctoral thesis *La Révolution du langage poétique* (1974), in which she traces the eruption of these drives within the language of two French avant-garde poets. The poets are male but the disruptive effects of the semiotic that she perceives in their work are feminine on the basis of the bond to the mother. Wholesale refusal of the symbolic is impossible because we fail to signify if we step outside of this social order of representation, so the temporary challenges to this system are deemed

to reintroduce what the symbolic requires we forget. Although entry into the symbolic depends on our accepting the law of the father, then, Kristeva's work testifies to the impossibility of ever completely severing our original connection to the mother. We never quite get over her, even though we must. Kristeva's subsequent thinking continues to bear witness to this difficult but necessary task of breaking the maternal bond.

In *Soleil noir* (1987) Kristeva discusses depression and melancholia, dealing with the painful states caused by a failure to accept the necessary loss of a tie to the mother in the early stages of a child's life. She focuses on the child's founding separation, marking the necessary but traumatic step the child must take in order to accede to its own sense of identity in the symbolic order. Separation from the mother is a prerequisite for entering the symbolic and the acquisition of language bridges the gap left by this loss of an original tie. The cases of depression and melancholy to which Kristeva refers reveal an estranged relation to language in which the subject indicates a failure of the linguistic signifier to provide an escape route for the state of inactivity s/he has lapsed into. *Soleil noir* is a text in which Kristeva explores the depressive and melancholic responses to separation in most detail, but these states recur in her other texts, especially in those that deal with exile.

The initial separation from the mother is re-enacted by the "exilé" or "étranger" who moves away from his or her country of origin. *Étrangers à nous-mêmes* (1988) traces the history of the Western notion of l'étranger from antiquity through to the twentieth century. The matricide that Kristeva speaks of in *Soleil noir* returns in the form of a distant memory in *Étrangers à nous-mêmes* that serves as a reminder to the exile of his/her move away from the maternal terrain. This move is accompanied by a sense of nostalgic longing to return to a state that will, however, remain forever inaccessible. The exile, according to Kristeva, lives in a state of indifference and detachment as an incurable melancholic because the compensatory gesture that language performs to assure entry into the symbolic when we start out in life appears here to offer nothing quite so reassuring. The melancholic state results from an inability to sever the link to the lost paradise of the maternal relation. The exile is estranged from his/her mother tongue and the new language does not appear to offer any compensation for the lost connection. The longing for a past paradise in this sense becomes the enactment of the melancholia that characterizes the depressive's relation to his/her mother tongue. The exile and the melancholic are conflated in their failure to feel at home in any language and both testify to an inability to overcome separation and loss on the basis of their alienated relation to language. The figure of the melancholic exile is an important theoretical construct in Kristeva's work, and given the focus of some of her more autobiographical writings, her theory ties in with her own sense of never being fully assimilated into France.

There is an incontestable ethical and political thrust to Kristeva's writings, pertaining specifically to French society but also stretching beyond. Her explorations of the problems associated with French nationalism in *Étrangers à nous-mêmes* cause her to examine how the connotations of *étrangeté* have altered through the ages to produce French legal definitions of how one can be classified as foreign to the French system. Her study culminates in a reading of Freud's work, and, referring specifically to his writings on the uncanny, she suggests that it is only by accepting that we are strangers to ourselves that we will have any hope of living alongside others. She focuses on the possibility of finding new forms of community that no overarching organizing principle can fully embrace. This paradoxical notion of (anti)community is linked specifically to a rethinking of how we define national identity and attempt to combat xenophobia. The psychoanalytic element of her work thus dovetails with her wider socio-political concerns and also provides a starting point from which to explore her ethics.

In her psychoanalytic work (especially in *Histoires d'amour* [1983] and *Étrangers à nous-mêmes*) she focuses on the psychological mechanism of identification, celebrating it as the capacity to slide into the other's place in order better to understand him or her. This is one of the ways in which the ethical thrust of her work emerges in relation to the politics of interpersonal relations, drawing out from the narrower analytical encounter. Apart from brief references to Spinoza in her work, Kristeva is more concerned with dissociating her use of "ethics" from established understandings of this term. She aims to free the term from its association with the constrained repetition of a given code of conduct. She challenges a normative ethics founded on a belief in the reliability of consciousness such that the question of ethics is brought about by the eruption of unconscious processes within consciousness. The unconscious forces that subvert the social code also disrupt any theory of ethics that would try to harness them and keep them under control. Kristeva's rethinking of the ethical dimension not only takes the unconscious into account, but also suggests that the transgressive force of the unconscious plays a formative role in forging relations between self and other. The ethical capacity to appreciate otherness within the self is not only associated with the identification mechanisms of the transference in the psychoanalytic situation. Kristeva also works within poetic language and within mater-

nity in order to question discrete identity and suggest a rethinking of human relationships.

In a somewhat different manner, her work on abjection also questions the stability of identity, troubling the limits of the body and the contours of the subject. The abject, strictly speaking, is neither subject nor object; it questions identity since it challenges the boundaries between inside and outside, designating the product of the drive to expel from the body that which was once so familiar to it. The reaction that one might equate with experiencing the abject has to be traced back to the initial connection to the mother, for it is associated with fear and horror of separation; the experience of abjection involves revolt against specificity and identity. Abjection serves to combine revolt against the boundaries society imposes on separation from the mother and a reminder of forbidden fusion. One of Kristeva's most concrete illustrations of the psychical and bodily response to the abject in *Pouvoirs de l'horreur* (1980) is that of one's lips coming into contact with the skin of milk. The revulsion of touching the skin is akin to what occurs in the psyche in experiencing abjection—a feeling of disgust that is at once symbolic and somatic. Being bound to the difficulty of establishing distinctions between subjects and objects, abjection is also traced by Kristeva to broader cultural and religious phenomena that depend upon demarcating the pure from the impure and defining the sacred. Religious and cultural rituals are thus understood to re-enact symbolic separation from the mother's body in their effort to establish clear boundaries between coherent identities. In *Pouvoirs de l'horreur* Kristeva is interested in how art, and in particular literature, is able to speak the abject and *Céline* is emblematic for her in this respect. Her work on abjection has been highly influential to theorists such as Iris Marion Young who seek to understand sexism, racism, homophobia, and other kinds of prejudice that demarcate identities in order to create hierarchical systems of subordination between them.

Kristeva's more recent work marks a continued interest in the revolution and revolt that have characterized her thinking from the outset. Asking, in *Sens et non-sens de la révolte*, whether revolt is still possible, she focuses on the uprising fundamental to Freud's work in *Totem and Taboo*: that of the murder of the father by the primal horde. The necessary matricide that launches the individual into the symbolic order might be seen as Kristeva's specific addition to this Freudian account of patricide. The revolution in poetic language that she explored in the early stages of her research revealed that fantasy could subvert the symbolic code but that this latter was necessary to keep the imagination from taking over fully. But revolution and revolt represent the possibility of stirring up the social code and productively questioning what it strives to keep in place. *Sens et non-sens de la révolte* and *La Révolte intime* focus on Barthes, Sartre, and Aragon, all of whom are gathered together because they grew up without a father figure; their Oedipal revolt is therefore displaced and takes the form of a creative revolt in the literary realm. In her most recent work in this series of psychoanalytically inspired readings she focuses on the specifically female contribution to twentieth-century culture, psychoanalysis and the social sciences, devoting individual studies to Hannah Arendt, Melanie Klein, and Colette to date.

In its phenomenal diversity but sustained strength of focus, Kristeva's work has a secure and prominent place in contemporary French thought.

SARAH COOPER

See also **Helene Cixous; Luce Irigaray; Jacques Lacan**

Biography

Julia Kristeva was born in Bulgaria in 1941. At the age of twenty-five, she moved to Paris on a doctoral research fellowship. In the mid-1960s her articles began to appear in the journal *Tel Quel*; she subsequently became associated with the *Tel Quel* group of structuralist thinkers. At this writing, she teaches at the University of Paris. She is also a practicing psychoanalyst.

Selected Works

Séméiotikè: recherches pour une sémanalyse, 1969
La Révolution du langage poétique: l'avant-garde à la fin du XIXe siècle: Lautréamont et Mallarmé, 1974
Polylogue, 1977
Pouvoirs de l'horreur, 1980
Histoires d'amour, 1983
Au commencement était l'amour: psychanalyse et foi, 1985
Soleil Noir: dépression et mélancolie, 1987
Étrangers à nous-mêmes, 1988
Les Nouvelles Maladies de l'âme, 1993
Le Temps sensible: Proust et l'expérience littéraire, 1994
Sens et non-sens de la révolte: Pouvoirs et limites de la psychanalyse I, 1996
La Révolte intime: Pouvoirs et limites de la psychanalyse II, 1997
Hannah Arendt: Le Génie féminin I, 1999
"Melanie Klein" *Le Génie féminin II*, 2000
"Colette" *Le Génie féminin III*, 2002

Further Reading

Guberman, Ross Mitchell, *Julia Kristeva: Interviews*, New York: Columbia University Press, 1996
Lechte, John, *Julia Kristeva*, London: Routledge, 1990
Oliver, Kelly, *Reading Kristeva: Unraveling the Double-Bind*, Bloomington and Indianapolis: Indiana University Press, 1990
Oliver, Kelly, (editor), *Ethics, Politics, and Difference in Julia Kristeva's Writing*, New York: Routledge, 1993
Smith, Anna, *Julia Kristeva: Readings of Exile and Estrangement*, Basingstoke: Macmillan, 1996
Smith, Anne-Marie, *Julia Kristeva: Speaking the Unspeakable*, London: Pluto Press, 1998

L

LA ROCHELLE, PIERRE-EUGÈNE DRIEU

Poet, Novelist and Essayist

Though he dallied with a range of political ideologies and movements, Pierre Drieu La Rochelle attained his enduring reputation and influence as one of the foremost exponents of French literary fascism. His writing career was framed by both world wars. His first published work, *Interrogation* (1917), was a collection of poems inspired by his experience in the trenches and lauding the virile virtues of the frontline soldier. The last work published during his lifetime, *Le Français d'Europe* (1944), reflected his waning faith in fascism and the growing personal and political despair that would presage his suicide in March 1945.

Between these two points in time, Drieu's itinerary was one of progressive disillusionment. As an *ancien combattant* imbued with both the horror and the exhilaration of war, he deplored the petty, emasculating mores of civilian life. Translating personal disgust into political terms, he rejected parliamentary democracy and liberal capitalism, castigating in his early works the small-minded, tired, complacent France of his youth (*État civil* [1921], *Mesure de la France* [1922], *Plainte contre inconnu* [1924]). His revolt against prevailing values found an echo for a time in the Dadaist and Surrealist movements. Early influences such as Nietzsche, Barrès, Maurras, and Péguy, together with friends such as Aragon and Malraux, exposed Drieu to diverse political sensibilities. He flirted with communist, radical, and integral-nationalist ideas before espousing fascism as the ideology most apt to rescue France, and Europe, from decadence.

In the late 1920s and early 1930s, Drieu's writings expressed his mounting political anxiety. In *Le Jeune Européen* (1927), *Genève ou Moscou* (1928) and *L'Europe contre les patries* (1931), he argued against narrow nationalism and in favor of a strong federal Europe as a third force, both economic and political, between the United States and the Soviet Union. Without such a federation, he urged, Europe would either consume itself in a further war or be consumed by American or Russian expansionism. He denounced the materialism that he associated with industrialization, city life, and a loss of spiritual bearings, arguing that Ford and Lenin were two sides of the same pernicious, machine-dominated, homogenizing modernity. His anti-Semitism derived its essence from this source, projecting Jews as the incarnation of a mercantile, hedonistic world obsessed with consumption and comfort. Contrasting the salutary privations of the soldier, his collection of short stories, *La Comédie de Charleroi* (1934), reflected on battle as a rite of passage to manhood, though he lamented the dehumanizing effects of mechanized warfare and its undermining of personal heroism. Intensely confessional, his fictional writings of the period (*L'Homme couvert de femmes* [1925], *Blèche* [1928], *Une femme à sa fenêtre* [1929], *Le Feu follet* (1931), and *Drôle de voyage* [1933]) developed psychological portraits of the individual within a degenerate society embarked on the futile search for self-fulfillment. They flowed from the pen of a man who recalled a bayonet charge at Charleroi as the most regenerative of human experiences.

Following the antiparliamentary riots of February 6, 1934 (proof, for Drieu, that the French still had some political energy in them), he proclaimed his adherence to fascism in *Socialisme fasciste* (1934). He advocated an authoritarian regime, fusing left- and right-wing elements, to re-instill moral fiber among the French, to create a "new man" in body and soul. His hope of a political revolution, however, was quickly dashed. Having visited both Nuremberg and Moscow, he translated his desire for charismatic leadership into support for the communist-turned-fascist Jacques Doriot and his Parti Populaire Français (PPF). This was arguably the closest France came to an indigenous fascist party, and the closest Drieu came to a definite political engagement, writing regularly for the party's newspaper, *L'Émancipation Nationale*, helping to fashion its doctrine, and exalting its leader in his book *Avec Doriot* (1937).

Doriot turned out to be no more the providential savior of France than Hitler was that of Europe. Despite disenchantment with both, Drieu became after the defeat of 1940 a strong advocate of collaboration with Nazi Germany, convinced now that European unification had to be imposed by force. On the eve of war, he had published the novel—*Gilles* (1939)—for which he is best known. Here he narrates the story of a First World War veteran struggling to adjust to civilian life in a morally bankrupt France. With the successive failures in his private life culminating in the abortive political events of February 1934, the protagonist seeks fulfillment fighting for Franco in the Spanish Civil War, where he rediscovers the self-affirmation and comradeship that he had known in the trenches allied to a new political sense of purpose.

The semiautobiographical *Gilles* is a distillation of the personal and political development of its author. For Drieu, however, there would be no redemptive denouement. Instead, he was charged with editorship in Nazi-occupied Paris of France's most prestigious literary journal, the *Nouvelle Revue Française* (NRF), which he used largely as a forum for intellectual collaborationism. He contributed to more overtly collaborationist periodicals such as *Je suis partout* and *La Gerbe*, wrote a number of profascist works (*Ne plus attendre* [1941], *Notes pour comprendre le siècle* [1941], *Chronique politique* [1943]), and dismissed Pétain's Vichy as a regime of reactionary conservatives rather than fascists. Contemplating the failure of collaboration, he abandoned the NRF in summer 1943, grew increasingly pessimistic about the political outlook, and took his own life at the Liberation rather than confront a hostile justice.

An urbane intellectual who wished himself a heroic man of action, Drieu promoted in his writings a cult of physical health, instinct, and will that recalled an earlier generation of French radical right-wing thinkers (notably Barrès) and resonated with the language of fascism. Going beyond his French mentors, however, he was one of the earliest and most forceful advocates of a pan-European fascism to replace the outmoded nationalism of Barrès and Maurras. This would be his most important legacy to Maurice Bardèche and other postwar exponents of European neofascism. He has served as a reference point for ideologues on the French and European radical right, for intellectuals across the political spectrum, and for extreme-right movements in France from Europe-Action and Occident to the *Nouvelle Droite* and the Front National.

Drieu's writings, like his life, were marked by an irresolvable tension between the lure of facile pleasure and a strong ascetic principle, between nihilism and a highly aestheticized desire for order, between narcissism and self-disgust. At one level, they read as the product of a mind that never outgrew some of its juvenile dispositions; at another level, they offer telling insights into the engagement of certain French intellectuals with fascism. Drieu was one among a number of voices decrying the feebleness of the French and calling for a new aristocracy of virility and force. War and death were ever the fixed points around which his creative imagination turned, whereas his fascism (like that of his kindred spirit in so many respects, Robert Brasillach) remained intensely subjective, utopian, and ultimately remote from practical politics: the *beau idéal* of an elite rather than an ideology for the masses. His posthumously published memoirs (*Récit secret* [1951], and *Journal 1939–1945* [1992]) recount a journey of moral, philosophical, and political questioning in which Drieu articulates, in exacerbated form, some of the most pressing anxieties of his generation.

J. G. SHIELDS

See also **Louis Aragon; Maurice Bardeche; Maurice Barres; Charles Maurras**

Biography

Born January 3, 1893, in Paris, Drieu attended Collège de Sainte-Marie-de-Monceau and École des Sciences Politiques in Paris; he failed his final examinations in 1913. Mobilized in 1914, La Rochelle saw action at Charleroi, Champagne, the Dardanelles, and Verdun; he was three times wounded. He traveled and wrote extensively: poetry, novels, short stories, and political essays, plus literary and political journalism. He declined Légion d'Honneur (1931), then won Prix de la Renaissance for *La Comédie de Charleroi* (1934). Drieu declared support for fascism in *Socialisme fasciste* (1934). He joined Doriot's Parti Populaire Français (PPF) in 1936 and was a member of PPF's central committee and editorialist for its newspaper, *L'Émancipation Nationale* (1936–1938). Under Occupation, he joined Alphonse de Chateaubriant's Groupe Collaboration and edited *Nouvelle Revue Française* (1940–1943). After two attempts in summer 1944, he committed suicide on March 15, 1945, as a summons was being served on him.

Selected Works

Interrogation, 1917
Fond de cantine, 1920
État civil, 1921
Mesure de la France, 1922
Plainte contre inconnu, 1924
L'Homme couvert de femmes, 1925
La Suite dans les idées, 1927
Le Jeune Européen, 1927
Blèche, 1928
Genève ou Moscou, 1928
Une femme à sa fenêtre, 1929
L'Europe contre les patries, 1931
Le Feu follet, 1931
L'Eau fraîche, 1931
Drôle de voyage, 1933
Journal d'un homme trompé, 1934
Socialisme fasciste, 1934
La Comédie de Charleroi, 1934
Beloukia, 1936
Doriot ou la vie d'un ouvrier français, 1936
Avec Doriot, 1937
Rêveuse bourgeoisie, 1937
Gilles, 1939 (censored), 1942
Ne plus attendre, 1941
Notes pour comprendre le siècle, 1941
Chronique politique 1934–1942, 1943
L'Homme à cheval, 1943
Charlotte Corday, Le Chef, 1944
Les Chiens de paille, 1944 (suppressed), 1964
Le Français d'Europe, 1944 (suppressed)
Récit secret, (posthumous) 1951, 1961
Histoires déplaisantes, (posthumous) 1963
Sur les écrivains, (posthumous) 1964
Mémoires de Dirk Raspe, (posthumous) 1966
Journal 1939–1945, (posthumous) 1992

Further Reading

Andreu, Pierre, and Grover, Frédéric, *Drieu La Rochelle*, Paris: Hachette, 1979.
Balvet, Marie, *Itinéraire d'un intellectuel vers le fascisme: Drieu La Rochelle*, Paris: Presses Universitaires de France, 2000.
Dambre, Marc, *Drieu La Rochelle: écrivain et intellectuel*, Paris: Presses de la Sorbonne-Nouvelle, 1995
Desanti, Dominique, *Drieu La Rochelle: le séducteur mystifié*, Paris: Flammarion, 1978.
Grover, Frédéric, *Drieu La Rochelle and the Fiction of Testimony*, Berkeley: University of California Press, 1958.
Grover, Frédéric, *Drieu La Rochelle*, Paris: Gallimard, 1962.
Hervier, Julien, *Deux individus contre l'histoire: Pierre Drieu La Rochelle, Ernst Jünger*, Paris: Klincksieck, 1978.
Kunnas, Tarmo, *Drieu La Rochelle, Céline, Brasillach et la tentation fasciste*, Paris: Les Sept Couleurs, 1972.
Mabire, Jean, *Drieu parmi nous*, Paris: La Table Ronde, 1963.
Soucy, Robert, "The Nature of Fascism in France," *Journal of Contemporary History*, 1,1 (1966), 27–55.
Soucy, Robert, "Romanticism and Realism in the Fascism of Drieu La Rochelle," *Journal of the History of Ideas*, 31,1 (1970), 69–90.
Soucy, Robert, *Fascist Intellectual: Drieu La Rochelle*, Berkeley: University of California Press, 1979.
Tucker, William R., "Fascism and Individualism: The Political Thought of Pierre Drieu La Rochelle," *Journal of Politics*, 27,1 (1965): 153–177.
Winock, Michel, *Une parabole fasciste: Gilles* de Drieu La Rochelle, in his *Nationalisme, antisémitisme et fascisme en France*, Paris: Seuil, 1990.

LACAN, JACQUES
Psychoanalyst

The psychoanalyst Jacques Lacan is arguably the most important psychoanalyst following Freud. His work has transformed the world of psychoanalysis institutionally, theoretically, and as a clinical practice. Lacanian analysts now constitute over fifty percent of the world's analysts, and schools of psychoanalysis deriving from his work are the predominant trends in South America and southern Europe. At the same time, Lacan's influence on a wide range of academic disciplines beyond the narrow confines of the consulting room and analyst's couch is unsurpassed among modern psychoanalytic thinkers. Lacanianism now pervades the disciplines of literary and film studies, women's studies, and social theory and has been applied to such diverse fields as education, legal studies, and international relations. Through his "return to Freud" in the 1950s, Lacan elaborated a rereading of psychoanalysis mediated by contemporary philosophy, linguistics, and toward the end of his career, mathematics. First and foremost, he articulated a theory of the human subject and unconscious desire, not as universal essences or biologically determined but as socially and culturally situated.

The Imaginary

Lacan's first important innovation in the field of psychoanalysis took place in 1936 at the fourteenth congress of the International Psychoanalytic Association, held at Marienbad. Lacan presented a paper entitled *Le stade du miroir* (later translated into English as "The Mirror Stage"). Through the mirror stage, Lacan provided an account of the infant's emergent sense of self in relation to an Other. Crucially, the ego that develops at this stage is not the site of a stable identity but of neurosis and aggressivity. The mirror phase occurs roughly between the ages of six and eighteen months and corresponds to Freud's stage of primary narcissism. At this time, the infant begins to recognize his or her image in the mirror (this does not mean a literal mirror but rather any reflective surface; for example, the mother's face), and this recognition is usually accompanied by pleasure. The child is fascinated with its image and tries to control and play with it and for the first time becomes aware that his or her body forms a totality. Although initially the child confuses its image with reality, he or she soon recognizes that the image has its own properties, finally realizing that the likeness is their own image, a reflection of themselves.

The illustration holds together, and through the mastery of this image, in the sense that the infant can govern its movements through the movements of its own body, the infant experiences pleasure. This sense of completeness and mastery, however, is in contrast to the child's experience of their own body as something that is fragmented and over which it does not yet have full control. Thus, the image anticipates the infant's mastery of its own body and provides the infant with a sense of unification and wholeness. The infant identifies with the image at the same time that the child finds it alienating, in the sense that the image is confused with the self. The image actually comes to take the place of the self. The sense of a unified self is acquired at the price of this self being an Other; that is, our mirror image.

For Lacan, the ego emerges at this moment of alienation and fascination with one's own image. The ego is the effect of images, or as Lacan terms it, an imaginary function. The ego, based on the image of wholeness and mastery, carries the illusion of coherence and autonomy. The function of the ego is to maintain this illusion, to perpetuate the feelings of wholeness and mastery—in other words, a process of misrecognition (*méconnaissance*), the refusal to accept the truth of fragmentation and alienation.

For Lacan, from the moment the image of unity is posited in opposition to the experience of fragmentation, the subject is established as a rival to itself. This is the first moment of alienation for the subject. A conflict is produced between the infant's fragmented sense of self and the imaginary autonomy out of which the ego is born. The same rivalry established between the subject and him or herself is also established in future relations between subject and Other, and this dialectic of identification and rivalry forms the basis of the relationship between the ego and social institutions.

The Symbolic

Lacan's paper on "The Mirror Stage" remained firmly within the categories and language of psychoanalysis.

From the mid 1950s, however, Lacan instigated a rereading of Freud through the structural anthropology of Claude Lévi-Strauss and the structural linguistics of Ferdinand de Saussure and Roman Jakobson. From Lévi-Strauss, Lacan derived the notion that a single elementary structure underlies all kinship and social relations and, more important, that this structure remains unconscious to social agents. Second, what takes place within kinship systems is not the giving and taking of real persons but a process of symbolic exchange. In other words, what characterizes the human world is the "symbolic function," a function that mediates all aspects of our lives and experience. Finally, Lévi-Strauss also provided Lacan with the initial idea that the unconscious is merely an empty space in which the symbolic function achieves autonomy; that is, a space where symbols are more real than what they symbolize and where the signifier precedes the signified (see Roudinesco, 1999, p. 211).

Lacan combined this conception of the symbolic function with a radical rereading of Saussurean linguistics. For Saussure, the linguistic sign consists of the inseparable bond between the signifier and the signified, the concept and its meaning. Lacan, however, interpreted Saussure's "bar" binding the two halves of the sign together as the bar of Freudian repression, the boundary between consciousness and the unconscious. The bar between signifier and signified represents the separation between signification and meaning: One can never attain the ultimate meaning of the signifier because all we are presented with is another signifier and another in an almost continuous chain of signification. In short, Lacan prioritized the now capitalized Signifier over the unobtainable signified. Finally, from Jakobson Lacan borrowed the reformulation of the rhetorical tropes of metaphor and metonymy as functions of substitution and contiguity, respectively, and mapped these onto Freud's unconscious processes of condensation and displacement in the dream work. In this sense, Lacan was to declare that the unconscious is structured like a language. He did not mean by this that the unconscious simply is language or is reducible to language, but that it functions like a language according to its own rules and grammar and that we can read the unconscious just as Freud taught us how to read dreams. Moreover, as we only have access to unconscious desire through the Symbolic order of Signifiers, therefore, the Signifier structures that desire and our subjectivity.

These ideas were crystallized in a paper delivered in Rome in 1953, entitled *Fonction et champ de la parole et du langage en psychanalyse* (translated as "The function and field of speech and language in Psychoanalysis"). There had been growing tensions between Lacan and the International Psychoanalytic Association (IPA) for a number of years over Lacan's refusal to follow IPA rules over questions of technique and training and especially over his use of the variable session. These tensions came to a head in 1953, when Lacan and a group of prominent Parisian psychoanalysts broke with the officially recognized Paris Psychoanalytic Society (SPP) to form the Société française de psychanalyse (SFP). The Rome Discourse, as it subsequently became known, was seen as the founding text of the new society and announced Lacan's "return to Freud." This return was to mark a break with all the revisionist developments within psychoanalysis since Freud—in essence, those traditions that had developed from Anna Freud and that focused on the ego and defense mechanisms—and a return to the centrality of the unconscious and the constitutive role of language. The radicalism of psychoanalysis, Lacan told his audience in 1953, was its recognition, although Freud lacked the terminology to articulate it, of the decentering of the human subject through the Symbolic.

Psychoanalysis—theoretically, institutionally, and clinically—is embedded within language, and it is to the function of speech and language that it should direct its attention.

The Subject of the Signifier

For the next ten years, Lacan would devote his fortnightly seminar to a systematic reading of Freud's major texts. According to Lacan, Freud's radical discovery was a theory of subjectivity that was distinct from previous theories of the individual or the ego. Traditionally, the ego has been associated with consciousness and with the notion of a unique, individual, and irreducible experience. The individual was seen as the sum of his or her own uniquely personal experiences. Following Kojève's extraordinarily influential reading of Hegel's master/slave dialectic as a dialectic of desire and struggle for recognition fought between subjects to death, Lacan claimed that Freud's "Copernican revolution" was to recognize the ex-centric nature of the human subject, that man is not entirely in man. Psychoanalysis reveals an experience of the subject and the formation of the "I" in opposition to all philosophies issuing from the *cogito*. The subject, suggests Lacan, is not a unified coherent being, a unique individual, but rather our subjectivity refracted through the desires of others. The subject, as a series of events within language, is distinct from the ego, and neither subject nor ego are entities in themselves, objects that can be filled with qualities or properties; they are, rather, functions. Psychoanalysis teaches us that there is always something beyond the individual, something that eludes the certainties by which "man" recognizes himself; that is, the unconscious.

The ego is an "imaginary function" in the sense that it is formed through the infant's imaginary relationship with its own body; the subject, however, is constituted in the Symbolic realm of language. Lacan also draws a distinction between the subject and the "I" in speech. "I" is a phenomenon of speech and does not correspond to either the subject or the ego. There is always a disjunction between the subject of enunciation and the subject of the utterance; that is, the subject that speaks and the subject in speech. This disjunction derives from the linguist Emile Benveniste's conception of the "I" as a shifter, as having no specific referent but in the act of speech designating the person who says "I." Lacan was to take this one step further and insisted that the "I" does not refer to anything stable at all but, rather, that as a site within speech, it could be occupied by a number of different phenomena, the subject, the ego, or the unconscious. For example, in what Lacan called "empty speech," the "I" would correspond to the ego, whereas in "full speech," it would correspond to the subject, and at other times, it would correspond to neither. Lacan de-essentializes the "I." The subject emerges at the point at which it is able to symbolize itself as an "I" in the Symbolic Order; that is, the point at which it can separate the "me" as ego from the "I" as subject in relation to others. This distinction corresponds to a further distinction in Lacan's theory between the "ideal ego" and the "ego ideal." The ideal ego originates in the imaginary and is the image to which one aspires; the ideal ego is a symbolic position. The ideal ego always accompanies the ego as the promise of future unity and cohesiveness to which the ego aspires. The ego ideal is based on the Signifier operating as ideal or a point within the symbolic order that guarantees one's position and anticipates secondary (Oedipal) identification. The subject, therefore, is "split" and decentered in relation to the ego or individual—it is not self-identical with itself or, as Lacan puts it, "I is an other" (1988b, p. 7).

In 1955, Lacan gave his famous seminar on Edgar Allan Poe's short story *The Purloined Letter* to illustrate his conception of the subject as the Subject of the Signifier or, in a slightly different formulation, as that which one Signifier represents to another Signifier. Lacan's interpretation of Poe's story focuses on two main themes: first, the anomalous nature of the letter, which for Lacan serves as the "true subject" of the story, and second, the pattern of intersubjective relationships that is repeated in the two halves of the story. The story concerns the open theft of a letter from the Queen by one of ministers and the retrieval of the letter in a similar way by the detective Dupin. The reader knows very little about the letter, except that it will compromise the Queen if the King knows of its contents; therefore, it bestows a great deal of power on its possessor.

We also know nothing about the sender except that the original script was in a male hand. According to Lacan, the letter is a "symbol of a pact," it situates the Queen in relation to the symbolic chain regardless of her own intentions. As the letter passes from hand to hand—from Queen to Minister, Minister to Dupin, Dupin to Prefect of Police, Prefect of Police back to Queen—the letter forms a similar pact with each person who possesses it. As the content remains unknown throughout this process of symbolic exchange, we can say that the letter is a signifier without a signified.

The seminar clearly illustrates Lacan's thesis of the insistence of the signifying chain and the determination of the subject by the Signifier. The term "insistence" has a number of different connotations here. It refers to the bar separating the Signifier and the signified and, hence, Lacan's contention that meaning no longer "consists" in the signifying chain but is excluded and continually "insists" on expression. It also emphasizes the idea that the subject of the unconscious is continually "pressing" or "insisting" on manifesting itself in the Symbolic. In relation to Poe's tale, therefore, we can see how the subjects are continually unconsciously displaced during intersubjective repetition. This displacement is determined by the place occupied by the letter within the trio. The letter is a floating signifier that passes along the signifying chain, with each person unconscious of the full import of what is taking place and how it subjectivizes them. This early "structuralist" Lacan provides us with one definition of the subject, the subject as precipitate or the sedimentation of meanings determined by the retroactive effect of one signifier on another. This corresponds to Lacan's "definition" of the subject as the Subject of the Signifier or, "that which one signifier represents to another signifier." (1977b, p. 207) In later Lacan, however, there is another definition of the subject as a breach within the signifying chain, and this corresponds to the growing importance and reformulation of the Real within his theory from the mid-1960s onward. For Lacan in the early 1950s (the Structuralist Lacan), the Signifier always interpellates the subject successfully, and he concludes with the assertion that, "the letter always arrives at its destination." (1988b, p. 205) This final assertion provoked the philosopher Jacques Derrida to formulate a highly influential critique of Lacanianism and claim that, the letter "never truly arrives" at its destination (1987, p. 489).

The Real

The Real is one of the most difficult concepts within Lacanianism to grasp. This is partly because of the fact that the Real is not a "thing" that can be defined but also because the notion developed considerably over

Lacan's career. Initially, the notion of the Real was opposed to the notion of the Imaginary in the sense that it was beyond the realm of appearance and images. In the Poe seminar, Lacan had elevated the concept to one of his three orders, and it was now opposed to both the Imaginary and the Symbolic; the Real is "that which remains in its place" (Muller and Richardson, 1988, p. 40); it is indivisible and carries with it connotations of brute materiality before symbolization. From the mid-1950s to the mid-1960s, Lacan was concerned with elaborating his concept of the Symbolic and the subject as the Subject of the Signifier. During this period, the Real took on the status of that which is unable to be symbolized. This is what Freud called in *The Interpretation of Dreams* the navel of the dream, that hard, impenetrable kernel of the dream that remains uninterpretable. The Real is that which is beyond the Symbolic and the Imaginary and that acts as a limit to both. The concept, however, remained a fairly undertheorized notion at this point. Whereas the Imaginary is a realm of images, identification, and an illusory unity, and the Symbolic is the order of the Signifier and the subject and moreover is structured around something that is always absent and exceeds it—according to the binary logic of presence and absence—the Real is simply that which resists symbolization absolutely, and in this sense, the concept increasingly became associated in Lacan's later work with the idea of "impossibility."

In 1963, almost a decade of negotiations between the SFP and the IPA concluded with the SFP being refused recognition by the IPA and with Lacan, to use his own terminology, "excommunicated" from the international psychoanalytic community. This precipitated a split with the SFP, and Lacan formed a new school, the École freudienne de Paris (EFP). This split was to prove decisive for the development of Lacanianism. Lacan was forced to move his seminar from the Hôpital St. Anne—where he had delivered it for the past eleven years—to, at the invitation of Louis Althusser, the École normale supérieure. The move provided Lacan with a completely new audience of nonclinicians, philosophers, and political militants and marked the break in the seminar between the close reading of Freudian texts and the elaboration of what we might call a properly Lacanian psychoanalysis. From the 1964 seminar, *The Four Fundamental Concepts of Psychoanalysis*, onward, the Real became the central category of Lacanian theory because psychoanalysis, he suggested, is essentially an encounter with the Real that eludes us. The term Lacan used to describe this encounter is *tuché*. The *tuché* presents itself in the form of trauma or that which is impossible for the subject to bear and to assimilate. For Freud, the notion of trauma is linked to the primal scene whereby a child has either a real or imaginary experience that it cannot comprehend. This inassimilable memory is forgotten and repressed until some later, perhaps insignificant, event brings it back to consciousness. What Lacan added to this Freudian conception of trauma is the notion that the trauma is Real so far as it remains unable to be symbolized—it is a permanent dislocation at the very heart of the subject. In his later work, this conception of the Real will also become associated with the death drive and *jouissance*.

One figure who has done more than any other to elevate the concept of the Real to the primary organizing category of Lacanian psychoanalysis is the Slovenian social theorist and philosopher Slavoj Žižek. For Žižek, the true radicalism of Lacanian theory is not so much the theory of split (barred) subject but rather the barred Other. For late Lacan, the big Other, the social or Symbolic order, is inherently riven with conflict and antagonism, and it is the function of the Symbolic to cover over this traumatic fact. Just as with the split subject, the social is structured around a traumatic impossible kernel, the Real, which continually threatens to erupt in the form of psychosis or violence and disrupt our Symbolic world. There is, in other words, an inherent paradoxicality to the Real: As the limit of the Imaginary and the Symbolic, it is a necessary support for the other two orders, but as trauma, it is also that which threatens to undermine them. The lesson of Lacanian psychoanalysis, for Žižek, is how we as subjects can live with this inherently impossible encounter.

The Gaze and the *objet petit a*

In *The Four Fundamental Concepts of Psychoanalysis* (1977), Lacan also once again returned to challenge the primacy of the Cartesian *cogito* to elucidate two concepts that became central for the adoption of Lacanianism in cultural and film studies: the notion of the gaze and the *objet petit a*. Drawing on the posthumous publication of Merleau-Ponty's *The Visible and the Invisible*, Lacan criticized the idealizing presumption whereby the subject assumes it can see itself seeing itself and sought to develop the idea of a gaze that preexists the subject and stares at us as if by the outside world itself. Although Merleau-Ponty posits a Platonic conception of an absolute all-seeing subject from which this gaze emanates, Lacan suggests that there is not an all-seeing subject as such but a "given-to-be-seen" (1977b, p. 74). Contrary to phenomenology, before there can be a seen or a seeing subject, there must be a "given-to-be-seen." We are not primarily discrete consciousnesses viewing the world, but rather, we are always already "beings that are looked at" (1977b, p. 75). Lacan insisted that there was a separation between

the eye and the gaze; although "I" see from only one point, "I" am looked at from all sides. There is a gaze that preexists my subjective view, what Lacan calls a "seeing," to which the "I" is subjected in an original way. Lacan is proposing a reversal of the relationship set up in the Mirror Stage, whereby the subject sets itself up as a subject and the other as an object. In relation to the gaze, the subject is constituted as the object of the Other. The gaze therefore positions us as an object and at the same time is excluded from our field of vision. The gaze is in a sense the underside of consciousness; it is that which is elided in the illusion of consciousness seeing itself seeing itself.

This separation of the eye and gaze must also be understood in relation to the reformulation of the Imaginary and the Real. The visible world, the world of our perceptions, is a world of images; in other words, what is shown to us and what we see belong to the imaginary order. The preexistence of the gaze, in contrast, is correlated with the "given-to-be-seen" of the subject and the Real. As mentioned above, Lacan gradually came to associate the Real with Freud's concept of the drive and especially the death drive; the gaze thus can be seen as the manifestation of the drive in the scopic order. As with his earlier notion of the Symbolic order and insofar as our relations to things are constituted in the visual field, in representation, there is always something that escapes or is elided in the act of the subject "seeing itself." The gaze is not something that can be seen because by its very nature it is that which escapes the field of vision, but it is something that can be represented in the form of the *objet petit a*. The *objet a* is the object-cause of desire, it belongs to neither the subject nor the Other but falls between subject and Other. Desire in Lacanian theory is always inextricably bound up with the desire of the Other in the sense that we perceive ourselves as that which can satisfy the desire of the other and the Other as that which can satisfy our desire. As Bruce Fink (1995, p. 59) formulated it, "In the child's attempt to grasp what remains essentially indecipherable in the Other's desire—what Lacan calls the X, the variable, or (better) the unknown—the child's own desire is founded; the Other's desire begins to function as the cause of the child's desire." Although the desire of the Other always escapes the subject, there nevertheless always remains something that the subject can recover and thus sustain him or herself in being, as a being of desire or desiring subject. That remainder is the *objet petit a*, the object-cause of desire. This notion was first elaborated in Lacan's 1959 seminar, *The Ethics of Psychoanalysis, as das Ding* (the Thing). The Thing of desire is "objectively" speaking nothing: It does not exist as a thing-in-itself, it only exists in relation to the desire that brings it about. The object of desire therefore is always an unattainable object, and it is the function of fantasy to enable a subject to bear this "impossible" relation to the *objet a*. Just as much as the subject is divided, the Lacanian ethics of alienation and separation insist on the irreducible division of the Other as lacking Other. The Other, the Symbolic order, can no more satisfy the desire of the subject that the subject can fulfill the demands of the Other. It is through fantasy that the subject attempts to reconcile this impossible situation.

Sexual Difference

Lacan's speculations on fantasy and the object of desire as always already unattainable eventually lead in his final seminars to some of his most controversial statements on women and feminine sexuality, especially the notion that "the woman does not exist" (1998, p. 7) and "there is no such thing as a sexual relation" (1998, p. 59). Freud's theorization of sexual difference through the Oedipus complex, castration anxiety, and penis envy had always presented problems for psychoanalysis in terms of its phallocentrism and the assertion of feminine passivity and a weak superego. Lacan's privileging of the Phallus as the one indivisible master Signifier that anchors his whole system would seem to exacerbate this situation even further, so it may seem paradoxical that Lacan's work has been so influential for feminists. Crucially, Lacan has reformulated the notion of the phallus and castration as symbolic processes that affect both men and women. Unlike Freud, Lacan's Oedipus complex involves not only the frustration or satisfaction of the child's desire but also the recognition of the desire of the other. The child is forced to accept that the mother cannot satisfy its desire any more than it can fulfill the desire of the mother. The mother's desire is elsewhere. The phallus is the signifier of this rupture, or gap, it is not a thing-in-itself but a signifier of loss and lack and the giving up of the illusion that one's desire can be satisfied. The phallus, then, represents a moment of division and the recognition of a "lack-in-being" that reenacts the original splitting of the subject. Castration involves the symbolic process of the loss of *jouissance* (enjoyment) through the symbolic structuring of the body. In short, castration is not about the fear of losing one's penis but about giving up part of one's *jouissance*, and in this sense it applies to both men and women.

Sexual difference rests on the presence or the absence of the phallus, and every subject is faced with two potential positions: that of having or being the phallus. As the phallus is a signifier and not the penis as such, each position is theoretically open to both men and women and not restricted by biology, although men usually pretend to have the phallus, whereas women are seen to struggle to be the phallus. The point is that both masculinity and femininity in this account can be seen as forms of masquerade; men cannot possess the phallus any more than women can be it. Lacanian sexual difference is not anatomical difference, as in Freud, but it is anatomical difference that comes to represent or figure sexual difference in our culture. Lacan, therefore, suggests that the phallus has both an Imaginary function insofar as it is the object presumed to satisfy the mother's desire and a Symbolic function insofar as it is the signifier of lack.

Because the Symbolic order is constituted through lack, it can be said to be "phallic" insofar as the phallus is the primary Signifier of lack in the subject as well as sexual difference. For Lacan, sexual difference can only be understood in terms of the Symbolic, through which our subjectivity is structured, and the phallus is the signifier of that which cannot be accounted for by biology. As both men and women are subjects of the signifier and alienated through language, there can be no such thing as a sexual relationship because there is no "direct" relationship between men and women. Men and women are divided, split, within themselves and from each other: They do not interact with each other as men and women because there is always something that intrudes and disrupts that relationship; that is, the signifier. Men and women are not defined in relation to each other, as the opposite but complementary sex, but separately and in relation to a third term. According to Lacan, men and women are defined differently in relation to the Symbolic order. Men are completely determined by the phallic function, they are subject to symbolic castration and wholly alienated within language. Women, in contrast, are not wholly determined by symbolic order and castration. Thus, although men's *jouissance* (sexual pleasure, enjoyment, or more precisely, pleasure in pain) is limited and bound by the symbolic, that is, phallic, *jouissance*, women can also experience another form of *jouissance*, or something more than the phallic *jouissance*. Lacan likens this experience to a kind of ecstasy or mystical experience through which one is at once possessed and annihilated as a subject. Lacan's slogan, therefore, that "the woman does not exist," that she is not One, does not mean that women are any less complete, defined, or whole than men but, rather, that woman is "subjected" to the signifier differently. Woman does not exist as a whole, unified, category. Furthermore, woman has access to a surplus enjoyment that man is denied, although this surplus enjoyment cannot be spoken or symbolized.

The Borromean Knot

In the final decade of his life, Lacan's elaboration of the theory of sexuation became increasingly complex and relied ever more extensively on what he called "mathemes"; that is to say, mathematical formulas and diagrams that he believed could account for the logic of the unconscious. With a group of young mathematicians from the Ecole normale supérieure, Lacan attempted diagrammatically to represent the workings of the unconscious through knots such as the interlinking circles of the Borromean knot. As with his final interest in Joyce, it was as if Lacan were attempting to attain that impossible encounter with the Real of which he had so long theorized. His seminars and writings took on the style of Joyce's *Finnegans Wake*, the subject of one of his last seminars, which Roudinesco describes as the language of psychosis that remains intelligible (just) but utterly untranslatable. As Lacan's health declined, his seminar and clinical practice was reduced ever further to the most rudimentary element of his whole theoretical edifice, silence.

SEAN HOMER

See also **Louis Althusser; Jacques Derrida; Alexandre Kojeve; Claude Levi-Strauss; Maurice Merleau-Ponty; Ferdinand de Saussure**

Biography

Born in 1901, Lacan grew up in a comfortable middle-class Catholic family in Montparnasse, Paris, and attended the prestigious Catholic School, the Collège Stanislas. He studied medicine at the Paris Medical Faculty and specialized in psychiatry with a particular interest in psychosis. In 1932, Lacan published his doctoral thesis on *Paranoid Psychosis and Its Relations to the Personality*, based on the case of Aimée, a woman who had attempted to murder the actress Hugette Duflos and who had become something of a *cause celbré* among the Surrealist movement. In the early 1930s, Lacan associated with the Surrealists, publishing part of his thesis in their journals, and he began reading Freud. He entered analysis in 1932 with Rudolph Loewenstein, the most famous training analyst in the Société psychanalytique de Paris (SPP), which association was to last for six years. After protracted negotiations with the International Psychoanalytic Association, the SFP was refused membership in 1963, precipitating a further split within the SFP and Lacan forming his own school, the École freudienne de Paris. The break also necessitated moving his seminar, and at the invitation of Louis Althusser, Lacan delivered his fortnightly talk from 1964 to 1969 at the École normale supérieure. Finally, from 1969 to 1980, the seminar was delivered as a lecture at the École pratique des hautes études. Lacan was to dissolve the school in 1980, the year before his death, and a new school was founded, the École de la cause freudienne,

under the stewardship of his son-in-law, Jacques-Alain Miller. Throughout his life, Lacan remained suspicious of publication, or "poubellication" as he punned on it, and fearing plagiarism, his magnum opus, *Écrits*, was not published until 1966, when he was sixty-five years old. Thus, the core of Lacan's work is located in the seminar, which is now gradually being collated and published under the general editorship of Jacques-Alain Miller.

Selected Work

Écrits, 1966; as *Écrits: A Selection*, translated by Alan Sheridan, 1977a

Les Quatre Concepts fondamentaux de la psychanalyse: Seminar XI, 1964, edited by Jacques-Alain Miller, 1973; as *The Four Fundamental Concepts of Psycho-Analysis*, translated by Alan Sheridan, 1977b

Télévision, 1974; as *Television: A Challenge to the Psychoanalytic Establishment*, edited by Joan Copjec, translated by Denis Hollier, Rosalind Krauss, and Annette Michelson, 1990

Les Écrits techniques de Freud: Seminar I, 1953–54, edited by Jacques-Alain Miller, 1975; as *The Seminar of Jacques Lacan, Book I: Freuds Papers on Technique, 1953 54*, translated by John Forrester, 1988a

Le Moi dans la théorie de Freud et dans la technique de la psychanalyse: Seminar II, 1954–55, edited by Jacques-Alain Miller, 1978; as *The Seminar of Jacques Lacan, Book II: The Ego in Freud's Theory and in the Technique of Psychoanalysis 1954–55*, translated by Sylvana Tomaselli, 1988b

Les Psychoses: Seminar III, 1955–56, edited by Jacques-Alain Miller, 1981; as *The Seminar of Jacques Lacan, Book III: The Psychoses, 1955 56*, translated by Russell Grigg, 1993

L'Éthique de la psychanalyse: Seminar VII, 1959 60, edited by Jacques-Alain Miller, 1986; as *The Seminar of Jacques Lacan, Book VII: The Ethics of Psychoanalysis, 1959–60*, translated by Dennis Porter, 1992

Encore, Seminar XX, 1972–73, edited by Jacques-Alain Miller, 1975; as *The Seminar of Jacques Lacan, Book XX: On Feminine Sexuality, The Limits of Love and Knowledge, Encore, 1972–73*, translated by Bruce Fink, 1998

"Le stade du mirior comme formateur de la fonction du Je", 1949; as "The mirror stage as formative of the function of the I" in *Écrits: A Selection*, translated by Alan Sheridan, 1977

"Fonction et champ de la parole et du langage en psychanalyse", 1953; as "The function and field of speech and language in Psychoanaysis" in *Écrits: A Selection*, translated by Alan Sheridan, 1977.

Further Reading

Clark, Michael, *Jacques Lacan: An Annotated Bibliography*, 2 volumes, New York: Garland, 1998.

Derrida, Jacques, Le facteur de la vérité, in his *The Post Card: From Socrates to Freud and Beyond*, translated by Alan Bass, Chicago: University of Chicago Press, 1987

Evans, Dylan, *An Introductory Dictionary of Lacanian Psychoanalysis*, London: Routledge, 1996.

Feldstein, Richard, Fink, Bruce, and Jaanus, Marie (eds.), *Reading Seminar I and II: Lacan's Return to Freud*, Albany, New York: SUNY Press, 1996.

Feldstein, Richard, Fink, Bruce, and Jaanus, Marie (eds.), *Reading Seminar XI: Lacan's Four Fundamental Concepts of Psychoanalysis*, Albany, New York: SUNY Press, 1995.

Fink, Bruce, *The Lacanian Subject: Between Language and Jouissance* Princeton, New Jersey: Princeton University Press, 1995.

Fink, Bruce, *A Clinical Introduction to Lacanian Psychoanalysis: Theory and Practice*, Cambridge, Massachusetts: Harvard University Press, 1997.

Forrester, John, *The Seductions of Psychoanalysis: Freud, Lacan and Derrida*, Cambridge: Cambridge University Press, 1990.

Merleau-Ponty, Maurice, *Le Visible et l'invisible*, 1964 – posthumous; as *The Visible and the Invisible*, 1968

Michell, Juliet and Rose, Jacquline (eds.), *Feminine Sexuality: Jacques Lacan and the école freudienne*, Harmondsworth: Penguin, 1982.

Muller, John P. and Richardson, William J., *The Purloined Poe: Lacan, Derrida and Psychoanalytic Reading*, Baltimore, Maryland: John Hopkins University Press, 1988.

Nobus, Dany (ed.), *Key Concepts of Lacanian Psychoanalysis*, London: Rebus Press, 1998.

Roudinesco, Elizabeth, *Jacques Lacan*, Cambridge: Polity Press, 1999.

Žižek, Slavoj, *Enjoy Your Symptom: Jacques Lacan in Hollywood and Out*, London: Routledge, 1992.

Žižek, Slavoj, *Looking Awry: An Introduction to Jacques Lacan through Popular Culture*, Cambridge, Massachusetts: MIT Press, 1992.

LADURIE, LE ROY (EMMANUEL)
Historian

An eminent and renowned French historian, Emmanuel Le Roy Ladurie's works defy disciplinary boundaries. He seems as much at home in social anthropology, economics, sociology, linguistics, psychology, and geography as he does in social history. This is obvious and apparent not only in his selection of subject matter but also in the wide-ranging methods and forms of analyses and interpretation he employs towards the understanding of his topics. Whether it be a single town, as in the case of *Montaillou, village occitan de 1294 à 1324* (1975), an event such as *Le Carnaval de Romans* (1979), or a family as in *Le Siècle de Platter 1499 à 1628* (1995), one can always detect and discern an interspersing of ethnography, structuralism, semiotics, and historiography in his many and varied works. The end result is always a richly nuanced, highly detailed, and very often controversial and provocative account of the daily life of ordinary human beings and their social organization.

To that end, Le Roy Ladurie's prolific work exemplifies much of what is carried out in the Annales tradition. Probably the best-known member of the current third, and perhaps last, generation of *annalists* proper, Le Roy Ladurie is a leading expositor of the movement variously described as *la nouvelle histoire* ("new history"). Similar to his *annaliste* forbearers and contemporaries, his interest is in the continued revitalization of the way history is written in France and elsewhere. Rather than narrating political events and describing institutions from the "top down," Le Roy Ladurie is primarily concerned with "writing history from below," from a more human perspective in order to include, for example, peasants, transients, prostitutes, and heretics. This "pots and pans" approach to historical study derives out of a sensitive use of documentary and quantitative evidence from a wide variety of mostly government generated statistical sources, but also clerical records and hospital ledgers, to emphasize economic and social structures and trends. These generally large collections of data are then applied to what is arguably the overriding concern of *annalistes*, Le Roy Ladurie included: the study of the *longue durée* ("long time frame") in the most general sense of change, evolution, and development for the explicit purpose of uncovering the deeply embedded structural forces affecting, and sometimes determining, people's lives.

The distinctions between the "old" social history and the "new history" are elaborated by Le Roy Ladurie in many of the essays in his two-volume collection, *Le territoire de l'historien* (1973, 1978). This collection of essays, spanning a little more than a decade (1964–1976), includes his inaugural address entitled "L'Histoire immobile" ("History that Stands Still"), given at the Collège de France on November 30, 1973, when he succeeded Fernand Braudel. Here, in characteristic fashion, he suggested that European society had changed very little between 1300 and 1730 and that the "immobility" was largely due to zero population growth as well as to a stagnant agricultural technology that set the limits for the production of food. More importantly, however, in this essay, but also in many of the others in these two early volumes, Le Roy Ladurie admonishes the "old" traditional social history as being too impressionistic as well as for its largely uncritical reliance on positivist-inclined historiography, for which, curiously, the term is specifically meant to cover *histoire événementielle, histoire–raaecit*, biography, and political history, the four genres being virtually synonymous in their representation of the "old" historical school. More to the point, Le Roy Ladurie's hostility is aimed at the type of narrative or storytelling that believes it is entirely capable of making completely objective chronological sense of dramatic episodes in the areas of politics, war, and diplomacy, where the underlying motives and assumptions are that such procedures can provide a theory of knowledge as powerful and legitimate as the knowledge derived from laws or theories in the natural sciences. Conversely, for Le Roy Ladurie, the goal is to situate the seemingly static "event" within the "long term" and to analyze it not through narrative-based approaches, with their overreliance on qualitative material such as elite writings, novels, and other prose forms, but rather through a series of quantitative data that is more capable of identifying the latent structures underlying surface phenomena. In this way, events become truly worthy of study and approach scientific certainty when they serve as evidence for the history of broader structures through the posing of questions and the raising of hypotheses.

While Le Roy Ladurie was writing and publishing some of his essays on historical methods, he also managed to finish the monumental *doctorat d'Etat* with a project he would later publish as *Les Paysans de Languedoc* (1966), one of the great manifestos of the third generation of *annalists*. Strictly adhering to *annaliste* terminology throughout the thesis, he showed how, in the first of five sections, for example, climate exerted a powerful influence on human history in the preindustrial rural economy of Languedoc during the sixteenth and seventeenth centuries, while of course also attending to the material factors as the motor of any actual change such that the peasant is not a prisoner of class struggle but of the elements. Notably, grape growers in this region were imprisoned by a *"mentalite de longue durée,"* whereby grapes were consistently harvested too early in the season, thus making for a wine that was nearly undrinkable and unmarketable. It was not until the eighteenth century that it finally dawned on the farmers that letting their grapes hang on the vines a little longer would allow them to fully ripen, resulting in a substantial increase of their economic fortunes. Throughout the work, then, Le Roy Ladurie is concerned with why, in sixteenth-century Langeudoc, agricultural structures were mired in ancient Mediterranean practices and thus seemingly impervious to change. Through a combinatory approach to "structure" that borrows from Fernand Braudel and Claude Lévi-Strauss, Le Roy Ladurie considers geographic and material, as well as mental and psychological, factors to explain, for example, not only why grape harvesting finally occurred later in the season but also the population explosion during the sixteenth century. Both of these, but many other factors as well, were a result of capital accumulation and a form of *"psychisme inconscient."* The theme of climate is also important to the related work *Histoire du climat depuis l'an mil* (1967), in which he argued that climatic change in itself has had little or no significant consequence on food production in northwest Europe, as indicated by the temperature and climate in Europe, especially in France, since the year A.D. 1000.

Le Roy Ladurie's characteristic reliance on statistical sources, quantitative methodology, and long-term economic structures, but also his interest in agriculture and climate, are generally forgotten in his later and more famous works, with the exception that many of these works constitute what might best be described as a still photograph, an allusion to his earlier remarks on the "immobility of history." Although still attending to the analysis of structures, the history of varied and opposing voices, and collective movements and trends, Le Roy Ladurie in his famously popular and best-selling book, *Montaillou* (1975), shifted his focus to culture. Here he uses the Inquisition records of the southern French see of Pamiers as the basis for an absorbing anthropological reconstruction, or microhistory, of the mental and material world of Pyrennean peasants. These records (currently in the Vatican library) of the Latin *Registre* of Jacques Fournier, bishop of Pamiers and later Pope Benedict XII of Avignon, concerning the interrogation of people accused of Catharism, were originally extracted and compiled by Charles Molinier almost a century before Le Roy Ladurie eventually used them for his community study. The result for the reader is a total regional immersion into the early fourteenth-century mental, sexual, emotional, and religious life of Montaillou's inhabitants.

The enormous success of *Montaillou* was followed up with *Le Carnaval de Romans* (1979), a quintessentially ethnographic "thick description" of Romans, a little town lying about halfway between Grenoble and Valence in the Dauphine region. Here, Le Roy Ladurie focuses on a particularly violent episode that occurred in the town during the month of February in 1580. The annual carnival and its pre-Lenten excess during that year resulted in a revolt stemming from the high taxes and inflation that created animosities between the bourgeoisie, peasants, and nobles and that was further exacerbated by the ongoing conflicts between Huguenots and Catholics. Notable here is Le Roy Ladurie's turn to folklore and semiotics and his abiding concern with the symbolic meaning of events and a recovering or uncovering of its *structures mentales*. Yet here, too, gestures, rituals, and the *mentalité* surrounding this "total symbolic system" become most meaningful when applied to the *long durée* of other peasant uprisings during the course of the sixteenth century; for example, the St. Bartholemew's Day massacre of 1572. In the end, the revolt becomes a semiotic system, woven together with the aid of documents and the folklore embedded within them where, akin to the geologist, the underlying structure allows the randomness of the surface topography to become apparent or, in different terms, where the explicit ritual is made comprehensible through the implicit system of signs that govern it.

During the last twenty years of the twentieth century, Le Roy Ladurie continued his creative and imaginative forays into the minutiae of microhistory while at the same time keeping to the fundamental aspects of the Annales historiographic tradition. Although his preoccupation with primary sources, serial history, the history of group mentalities, and the history of material culture has not waned, his more recent works show a greater acceptance, if not respect, for political history and the history of events, both of which were vehemently rejected in earlier phases of the Annales movement. For example, his work, *Saint-Simon, ou le système de la Cour* (1997), in collaboration with Jean-François Fitou, recounts the court of Louis XIV and the politics of the regency, where the court of Versailles is depicted as the dwelling of a tribe with strange practices, obsessed with rituals, signs, and symbols. Similarly, *L'Argent, l'Amour et la mort en pays d'Oc* (1980) differs from his previous studies in that here his usual investigative skills include well-tempered techniques such as comparative folklore mixed with newer forms of structuralist literary analysis and linguistics.

Nonetheless, here, too, in *L'Argent, l'Amour et la mort en pays d'Oc*, Le Roy Ladurie continues using the peasant as the subject of his study, with the exception of *Carnival de Romans*, where he used a festival as his cultural sample; here, he uses a literary text. The study is situated in an eighteenth-century French village in a region known as the Pays d'Oc and is based on the short tale, *Jean-l'ont-pris* by Jean-Baptiste Castor Fabre (1727–1783), written sometime between 1756 and 1760. A masterpiece of Occitan literature, *Jean-l'ont-pris* is part of a corpus of sixty-five known fictions published in the Languedoc region between 1570 and 1790. Part of Le Roy Ladurie's book takes up the Indo-European variants of the folktale *Godfather Death* and its structural similarity to the canonical sequence found in *Jean-l'ont-pris*. In addition, Le Roy Ladurie scrupulously considers the Occitan commoners' way of thinking about marriage, money, mortality, and the supernatural to question many of the assumptions held by social anthropologists on marriage, dowries, endogamy, and bridewealth in the *ancien régime*. Le Roy Ladurie's extraordinary talent at combining literary analysis with historical anthropology is also apparent in *La Sorcière de Jasmin* (1983), a study of peasant beliefs about witchcraft. Important to note here is that Le Roy Ladurie continued to employ the written document as his data of choice: the diaries of the Duc de Saint Simon in *Saint-Simon*, the folktales in *L'Argent, l'Amour et la mort en pays d'Oc*, and here in *La Sorcière de Jasmin*, the discovery and use of the Gascon poem *Françouneto*, published in 1842 by the barber-poet Jasmin. Le Roy Ladurie's intent is that Jasmin's poem will help the reader to experience the world through the eyes of Gascon peasants of the *ancien régime*.

Le Roy Ladurie's most recent titles continue his career by building on the Annales global program of cooperation with the social sciences, namely, the transposing of Braudel's mostly temporal and quantitative categories into semiotic ones. This becomes apparent yet again with *Le Siècle des Platter 1499 á 1628* (1995), in which Le Roy Ladurie traces the lives of the Platter men—Thomas and his two sons, Felix and Thomas, Jr.—at the time of the European Renaissance and Reformation. True to form, Le Roy Ladurie unearths a wealth of detail about sixteenth-century life through the use of personal narratives, memoirs, diaries, and even menus to reconstruct the mentalities of early-modern European culture and society.

DENIS WALL

See also **Claude Levi-Strauss**

Biography

Emmanuel Bernard Le Roy Ladurie was born on July 19, 1929, in the village of Moutiers-en-Cinglais, located in the Calvados department of Normandy. At the age of sixteen, he was sent to the prestigious Lycee Henri-IV in Paris to prepare for the Ecole Normale Superieure but was soon expelled and forced to attend another lycee outside of Paris. Here he became interested in the politics of the extreme left, as represented by Mao Zedong's victory in China and also by his exposure to Marxism in the history classes of Jean Bruhat. On entering the Ecole Normale Superieure in September 1949, he joined the French Communist party (PCF) and devoted himself to militant activities on behalf of the party. In 1951, he completed his undergraduate degree but continued to work for the PCF, for which he undertook a statistical analysis of the Paris working class. After finishing a project on French policy in Indochina, he was awarded the *diplome des etudes superieures*. In 1952, he received France's most prestigious teaching diploma, the *agrege d'histoire*, and was subsequently appointed professeur at the Lycee Montpellier in 1953. His enthusiasm for Communism quickly dissipated after the death of Joseph Stalin in 1953, the 1956 shattering exposé of Stalin by Nikita Khrushchev, and the Russian invasion of Hungary. By 1963, he had completely severed all political ties. For three years (1957–1960), he held a research post at the National Center for Scientific Research. Turning his attention to history, after having again resumed his duties at the Lycee Montpellier, he began an exhaustive seven-year study of the region formerly known as Languedoc and carefully reconstructed the peasant society of that region from the late fifteenth to early eighteenth centuries. This was presented as the brief survey, *Histoire du Languedoc*

(*History of Languedoc*), published in 1962. The longer, 1,037-page version, *Les Paysans de Languedoc*, earned him a doctoral degree in letters from the Sorbonne in 1963 and was soon lauded as a masterpiece of Annales historiography. He taught at the Sorbonne (1970–1971) and at the University of Paris VII (1971–1973) before assuming his appointment at the Collège de France as chair of the History of Modern Civilization. From 1987 until 1994, he was the General Administrator of the Bibliothèque Nationale, thereafter assuming the title Président du conseil scientifique de la Bibliothèque Nationale de France, where he led, not without controversy, the debate and enactment of a more reader-friendly system of French libraries. He continues as Professeur honoraire at the Collège de France. Le Roy Ladurie is the consummate public intellectual, appearing frequently on state television and in the pages of the popular press and was previously a member of President François Mitterand's inner circle. In 1979, he collaborated with film director Daniel Vigne on a six-hour television documentary on French peasant life, entitled "Inventaire des Campagnes," awarded the Prix de la Critique and was later published in book form. Le Roy Ladurie is a chevalier of the French Legion of Honor. Above all, however, he is the model of the *historien-engage* whom Lawrence Stone, an eminent colleague, once called, "one of the most, if not the most, original, versatile, and imaginative historians in the world."

Selected Works

Les Paysans de Languedoc, 1294 à 1324, 2 volumes, 1966; as *The Peasants of Languedoc*, translated and with an introduction by John Day, 1974

Histoire du climat depuis l'an mil, 1967, 2nd edition, 1983; as *Time of Feast, Times of Famine: A History of Climate Since the Year 1000*, translated by Barbara Bray, 1971

Le Territoire de l'historien, 2 volumes, 1973, 1978; as *The Territory of the Historian*, translated by Ben and Siân Reynolds, 1979, and *The Mind and Method of the Historian*, translated by Siân and Ben Reynolds, 1981

Montaillou, village occitan de 1294 à 1324, 1975; as *Montaillou: The Promised Land of Error*, translated by Barbara Bray, 1978

Histoire économique et sociale de la France, vol. 1, *de 1450 à 1660*, and vol. 2, *Paysannerie et croissance*, 1976; as *The French Peasantry, 1450–1660*, translated by Alan Sheridan, 1987

Le Carnaval de Romans. De la Chandeleur au mecredi des cendres 1579 à 1580, 1979; as *Carnival in Romans*, translated by Mary Feeney, 1979

L'Argent, l'Amour et la mort en pays d'Oc, 1980; as *Love, Death, and Money in the Pays d'Oc*, translated by Alan Sheridan, 1982

La Sorcière de Jasmin, 1983; as *Jasmin's Witch*, translated by Brian Pearce, 1987

L'état royal, 1460 à 1610, 1987; as *The Royal French State*, translated by Juliet Vale, 1994

L'Ancien régime, 1991; as *The Ancien Régime: A History of France, 1610–1774*, translated by Mark Greengrass, 1996

Le Siècle des Platter 1499 à 1628, 1995; as *The Beggar and the Professor: A Sixteenth-Century Family Saga*, translated by Arthur Goldhammer, 1997

L'Historien, le chiffre et le texte, 1997

With Jean-François Fitou, *Saint-Simon, ou le système de la Cour*, 1997; as *Saint-Simon and the Court of Louis XIV*, translated by Arthur Goldhammer, 2001

Histoire de France des region. La Périphérie française des origines à nos jours, 2001

Histoire des paysans français. De la Peste noire à la Révolution, 2002

Further Reading

Burke, Peter, *History and Social Theory*, Ithaca, New York: Cornell University Press, 1992

Boyle, Leonard E., "*Montaillou* Revisited: Mentalité and Methodology," in *Pathways to Medieval Peasants, Papers in Medieval Studies* 2, edited by J. A. Raftis, Toronto: Pontifical Institute of Medieval Studies, 1981

Carrard, Philippe, "The New History and the Discourse of the Tentative: Le Roy Ladurie's Quotation Marks," *Clio*, 15,1 (1985): 1–14

Carrard, Philippe, *Poetics of the New History: French Historical Discourse From Braudel to Chartier*, Baltimore, Maryland: The Johns Hopkins University Press, 1992

Glidden, Hope H., "La Poésie du Chiffre: Le Roy Ladurie and the *Annales* School of Historiography," *Stanford French Review*, 3 (1981): 277–294

Hartigan, Francis X., "Montaillou," *Proceedings of the Annual Meeting of the Western Society for French History*, 21 (1994): 275–283

Mark, Vera, "In Search of the Occitan Village: Regionalist Ideologies and the Ethnography of Southern France," *Anthropological Quarterly* 60, 2 (1987): 64–70

Peters, Jan, "Das angebot der 'Annales' und das beispiel Le Roy Ladurie. Nachdenkenswertes über Französische sozialgeschichtsforschung," *Jahrbuch für Wirtschaftsgeschichte* 1 (1989): 139–159

Stone, Lawrence, "In the Alleys of Mentalité," *The New York Review of Books*, 26, 17 (8 November 1979): 20–24

LANGUAGE

Language was a preoccupation for twentieth-century thought in a manner in which it had not been in preceding centuries. Language, in the twentieth century, could no longer be understood as a transparent means of access to truth. Thought, whether in the domains of philosophy, linguistics, anthropology, or literary theory, turned its attention to the language of its own expression. Thought was understood not only to be mediated by the language in which it is formulated but also to be always dependent on it. All language came to be seen as meta-language; that is, language about language. Language is, inevitably, to some degree self-reflexive, in that it refers to other language and not directly and unproblematically to a referential world beyond. This preoccupation with the linguistic means of expression brought about an attentive analysis, or breaking down, of language and linguistic systems, sometimes declaring itself with a certain linguistic solipsism. The linguistic turn, as it has been termed, of twentieth-century thought, has not been a wholly French phenomenon, but many of its key practitioners have been French or French-speaking. Much thought on language in the twentieth century is inspired by the work of Friedrich Nietzsche (1844–1900), who famously drew attention to language as he demythologized the truth-seeking efforts of philosophic discourse: "What then is truth? A movable host of metaphors, metonymies and anthropomorphisms. . . . Truths are illusions which we have forgotten are illusions" ("On Truth and Lies in a Nonmoral Sense," p. 84). The analysis of language in the twentieth century has often been practiced with a demythologizing goal. The linguistic turn made an appeal to language, or to discourse (the extended use of language), as the limit point that philosophy could reach in its quest for knowledge. Philosophers would be misguided if they sought to render language more accurate by removing its ambiguities. The practitioners and inheritors of the linguistic turn tend to follow Ludwig Wittgenstein's (1889–1951) acknowledgement of the open multiplicity of "language games," in which meaning and intent are never fixed but are contextually determined.

One of the most influential early twentieth-century theorists of language was the Swiss linguistics scholar Ferdinand de Saussure. Saussure's work is of limited breadth in itself, and its influence has been spread by others through the elaboration of the potential within his work. His theory of language is set out in the *Cours de linguistique générale* (published posthumously in 1916), which in fact is not his own direct work, but was compiled after his death from the lecture notes taken by his students. In the *Cours*, Saussure develops his concept of the sign. Theories of the sign were not new: the Abbé de Condillac, for example, in the eighteenth century, had described how language grows out of a process of conventionalization of natural signs, positing three categories of sign: the accidental, the natural, and the arbitrary or institutional. It is this last aspect of language—the arbitrary nature of the sign— that is central to Saussure's linguistic analysis. For Saussure, the sign is composed of two basic elements: the signifier (*signifiant*) and the signified (*signifié*). The signifier is the spoken or written material of language, whereas the signified is the idea represented. Take the English word "cat," for example: the signifier would be the spoken or written form of the word, and the signified would be the idea of a cat in a person's mind. Neither the signifier nor the signified bear any intrinsic relation to the referent, which would be the actual physical feline furry animal. The referent, which might be a tangible object or an action such as running, is not part of the sign. This has led many Saussurians to assert that language has no connection with extralinguistic reality. It is certainly indicative of the fact that language is arbitrary or conventional. All language depends on social convention—a word functions only if more than one person understands it, which can only happen by convention. The relationship between a word and its meaning, between the referent (if there is one), the signifier, and the signified, is wholly arbitrary, and no natural or inevitable links obtain. For example, there is no essential reason why a dog should be called so because it is variously called *dog* in English, *chien* in French, and *Hund* in German. It might be objected that some signs do bear an essential link between the thing represented and the form of representation; onomatopoeia would be the obvious case. However, the relationship between onomatopoeic words and the noises they represent is more tenuous than it might at first seem—dogs in English go *woof*, whereas in French they go *ouah*, and in German they go *wau*. Signs that are not wholly arbitrary and that contain a natural element are termed "motivated." The arbitrariness of the relationship between the signifier and the signified might indicate that language represents a nomenclature for a set of universal concepts. One would simply replace a word in one language with a word in another to signify an identical concept. As any comparison between two different languages demonstrates, ideas cannot straightforwardly be transposed from the form of one language to the form of another. Signified concepts are, at least in part, generated by and dependent on the signifiers used to represent them. Saussure distinguishes between a synchronic study of language and a diachronic study. Synchronic linguistics would analyze language at a particular moment in time, without respect to historical context. Diachronic or historical linguistics would analyze the development of language or languages over time. Saussure tends to favor the synchronic but does not discount the diachronic. Linguistics before Saussure tended to get frustrated in the search for the historical origins of language. Synchronic linguistics enables language to be understood as a system. Meaning and identity are wholly functions of differences within the system. Consider the alphabet: there is no essential quality of "a-ness" in the letter "a." The letter is what it is by virtue of not being all the other letters of the alphabet. The utterance of the letter "a" immediately invokes the remaining letters of the alphabet. Similarly, with words, uttering a word invokes the linguistic system that enables that word to mean. Saussure terms an individual utterance of a meaningful linguistic unit a *parole*, and the abstract system of a language, its rules of combination and meaningful distinctions, he terms the *langue*. The *langue* is the general system passively assimilated by the individual, and the *parole* is an individual intentional act. Language has no logical essence, and the *langue* is the accumulation of so many particular *paroles*.

The linguistic paradigm established by Saussure has been applied to other areas of cultural analysis, both linguistic and nonlinguistic. Saussure can be credited with laying out the theoretical ground for semiology and structuralism. Semiology, a general science of signs, set out to study the life of signs within society. The rules of Saussurian linguistics were adapted as an explanatory paradigm for a broad range of cultural phenomena. Structuralism, much in vogue in French intellectual life in the 1960s and 1970s, developed Saussurian linguistics for the analysis of the implicit structures of discursive practices. One of the most influential semiologists and structuralists was the literary critic and cultural theorist Roland Barthes, who illustrated the theory and application of semiological analysis in works such as *Mythologies* (1957) and *Éléments de semiologie* (1964). In *Mythologies*, popular and bourgeois culture is understood as a kind of language to be decoded. Cultural artifacts (such as wine, cars, and wrestling) evoke connotations that function according to a grammar of cultural norms in which the historically contingent is passed off as natural. Barthes attempts to expose how the arbitrariness of the sign is masked by cultural habit. Saussure's linguistic model of *langue* and *parole* is adapted so that a particular cultural practice, such as the giving of a gift, is understood as an instance of *parole* invoking a preexisting cultural system of gift-giving, with its associated values and norms. The anthropologist Claude Lévi-Strauss (b. 1908) applied the methods of structural linguistics to the analysis of primitive societies and regarded language as an essential common denominator underlying cultural phenomena. In *Anthropologie structurale* (1958), he takes a formulaic approach to the analysis of cultural practices; for example, marriage regulations and kinship systems are a kind of language, a set of processes permitting the establishment, between individuals and groups, of a certain type of communication. Semiological and structuralist analyses decenter the individual speaking subject in relation to the language he or she uses. A person's discourse draws not so much on the ideas and feelings experienced as on the prescriptive rules of the language used. It is the resources and limitations of language that govern discourse as much as the intention of the speaker. The more a particular discourse attempts to evoke emotional or material reality, the more it is codified, both linguistically and culturally.

Saussure bequeathed an important binary model to postmodern theory. Language as a sign system could be understood as an operational code of binary oppositions, of which one of the most fundamental distinctions is between syntagmatic series and paradigmatic series. The syntagmatic dimension is the horizontal axis of combination in which sequences are formed by combining words in an intelligible order. A sentence is a syntagma of words. The paradigmatic dimension is the vertical axis of selection, marking a set of linguistic or other units that can be substituted for one another in the same position within a sequence or structure. Words sharing a similar grammatical function, for example, operate along the same paradigm. This binary contrast between combination and substitution offers a refreshed understanding of the figures of metaphor and metonymy when language is used symbolically. Metaphors involve a paradigmatic substitution based on a perception of similarity between two ideas. Metonymies involve a syntagmatic combination based on the perception of contiguity between contingently associated ideas. Syntagmatic combination is at work also in the figure of synecdoche (a particular form of metonymy) when a part is used to designate a whole ("all hands on deck," and so on). This linguistic model can also be applied to culture, where metaphoric and metonymic orders can be seen to operate along various axes of association. The problem with structuralist analyses is that they tend to be too formalist, working in a nondimensional space of abstraction. Although Saussure had stated that linguistics was part of a general science of semiology, the poststructuralist Barthes of the 1960s declared conversely that semiology is part of linguistics, which is to say that semiological analysis collapses back into language. Poststructuralist and postmodern approaches tend to blur any clear distinction between language and reality in a universal simulacrum where signs and referents operate on the same level. The idea of the simulacrum is developed by Jean Baudrillard (b. 1929) in *Simulacres et simulation* (1981).

The linguistic paradigm was adapted for psychoanalysis by Jacques Lacan (1901–1981), who stated aphoristically that the unconscious is "structured like a language." As Freud had seen the importance of linguistic associations in the working and interpretation of the unconscious, so Lacan takes the linguistic aspect of psychic functioning a considerable step further, describing the unconscious as constituted by a series of chains of signifying elements. Like an infernal translating machine, the unconscious translates words into symptoms, such that a symptom may be literally a word trapped in the body. To relieve the symptom, the repressed ideas need to be linked with the rest of the signifying chain. Methods of linguistic analysis are thus applied to psychoanalysis. The importance of language in the construction of the human subject is highlighted by Lacan's use of the term *infans* (in Latin, "one who cannot speak"), in his *Écrits* (1966). At the *stade du miroir* ("mirror stage") during a child's development, occurring between the ages of six and eighteen months, the *infans* is distinguished from the speaking subject: "L'assomption jubilatoire de son image spéculaire par l'être encore plongé dans l'impuissance motrice et la dépendance du nourrissage qu'est le petit homme à ce stade *infans*" (*Écrits*, p. 94), "The jubilant assumption of his specular image by the child at the *infans* stage, still sunk in his motor incapacity and nursling dependence" (*Écrits: A Selection*, p. 2). The mirror stage marks the child's transition from the "primordial forms" of the *infans* to the linguistic structure of the Symbolic order. The infant's accession to the Symbolic order of language marks a second birth as a human subject. The use of the linguistic simile, that the unconscious is structured like a language, would seem to imply that, for Lacan, language is the very condition of culture. As structural linguistics decenters the subject in relation to language, so Lacanian psychoanalysis dissociates words from identity. The words we use are used also by other people—must be used by other people to function—and consequently do not belong to us. Language extends beyond the subject because words can carry meanings that are outside the individual's conscious understanding or control. The other is the place of language, both internal and external to the speaker at the same time. With a gesture that would be described in cultural terms as postmodern, Lacan inverts the "depth model," which would privilege the signified over the signifier, thus giving priority to the signifier, the verbal element in psychic life.

The historian of ideas Michel Foucault (1926–1984) analyzes underlying changes in Western linguistic practices over several centuries in *Les Mots et les choses* (1966).

Foucault's position is antiempiricist, rejecting the notion of progressively revealed scientific truths and the transparency of language. Such a position allows him to see the blindness concomitant with the myth of transparency. Knowledge, on a Foucaldian model, is not a cumulative accretion of the ages, but an uncertain flux of ideas. Foucault describes how language, dating from the Middle Ages, has passed through functions of resemblance, representation, and historicity to a twentieth-century phenomenon that he terms the *heteroclite*, a disorder in which a number of possible orders of language live side by side. The domain of the heteroclite Foucault terms the *heterotopia*, a place where the apparent syntax and grammar of language are disturbed, where words and things cannot hold together: "Les *hétérotopies* inquiètent, sans doute parce qu'elles minent secrètement le langage, parce qu'elles empêchent de nommer ceci *et* cela, parce qu'elles bri-

sent les noms communs ou les enchevêtrent, parce qu'elles ruinent d'avance la « syntaxe », et pas seulement celle qui construit les phrases,—celle moins manifeste qui fait « tenir ensemble » (à côté et en face les uns des autres) les mots et les choses" (p. 9), "*Heterotopias* are disturbing, probably because they secretly undermine language, because they make it impossible to name this *and* that, because they shatter or tangle common names, because they destroy 'syntax' in advance, and not only the syntax with which we construct sentences but also that less apparent syntax that causes words and things (next to and also opposite one another) to 'hold together' " (p. xviii). Foucault's maverick approach to linguistic history may be both descriptive of a postmodern cacophony of language and a prescriptive expression of a poststructuralist will to de-structure. He is acutely alive to the figures of his own rhetoric. The privileged trope of the rhetorical panoply for Foucault is catachresis, which describes the fundamental inadequacy of language to fulfill the myth of its capacity to represent, to denote, or to signify objects in their particularity. The most literal appellation is already figural. The semantic slippages of catachresis describe the operations of all figural language and are the condition of all language-as-representation. There is not, and has never been, a proper name, a proper usage of language, or the correct application of a word to a thing. Metaphors are merely catachrestic movements in which the analogy is less immediately perceptible, marking the emptiness of the comparison with a putative substantiality.

The most broadly influential language-oriented philosopher of the latter part of the twentieth century, whose work has been accepted across a range of disciplines, is Jacques Derrida (b. 1930). Derrida's work emphasizes the instability of linguistic meaning, frequently using puns to illustrate semantic undecidability in the play of the signifier. No context is ever wholly saturable—meaning always goes astray somewhere, as for example, things may be gained as well as lost in translation. The analysis of language in Derrida's work can, at moments, seem like an end in itself. In his first significant work, *De la grammatologie* (1967), Derrida declares, "il n'y a pas de hors-texte." This statement can be interpreted from two angles. The more reductive interpretation would understand this to mean that there is no prelinguistic or extralinguistic reality, or that if there is, it is unknowable. A more expansive interpretation would understand this to mean that the text of language, in the broadest sense, appropriates all that it touches immediately and incorporates it into signifying systems. Both these interpretations represent a kind of negative theology of language and come around to the same point: that there is nothing of which we can be cognizant that is not articulated by language, there are no ideas independent of language, no pure signifieds, no transcendental essences. Derrida, like his structuralist predecessors, is using language as a metaphor and as an explanatory paradigm for philosophic ends to show that ideas exist only in their material and historical context. Derrida's key concept is based on a linguistic play: *différance*. *Différance* substitutes an "a" for an "e" in the traditional spelling of "différence." It is a nominalization of the verb "*différer*," meaning both to differ and to defer. Within *différence*, there is both difference and deferral, spacing and temporization, but the change of spelling is discernible only in writing and passes undifferentiated in speech. The difference between *différance* and "difference" is the difference within /difeRãs/. *Différance* is the abolition of a difference that presupposes identity. *Différance* is an active movement, the undecidable play of the trace in the obliterated origins of presence and absence. The sign unceasingly dislocates itself in a chain of differing and deferring substitution. In "La Pharmacie de Platon" in *La Dissemination* (1972), Derrida exploits semantic ambiguity around the word *pharmakon*, which is at once both poison and cure, both positive and negative, good and bad. Derrida uses linguistic analysis to deconstruct the stability of the notion of origins; for example, in his concept of "iterability," developed in the essays in *Limited Inc* (1990). "Iterability" is repetition in alterity—repetition of the same but not identical. "Iterability" derives from the Sanskrit "*itara*," meaning "other." As Rodolphe Gasché has observed in *The Tain of the Mirror* (1986), the Sanskrit etymology of "iterability" is doubtful. However, the speciousness or validity of Derrida's etymological claim, as an exclusively empirical datum, does not positively or negatively affect the theory of iterability. Indeed, it might be suggested that if the etymology is specious (as a number of Derrida's puns are), the term "iterability" itself becomes a performance of iterability—the illegitimate diffusion of the word detached from its origin in the play of the signifier. A first instance—an origin—cannot be a first instance unless there is a second instance to follow. It is only through the possibility of repetition in subsequent instances that the first instance becomes an instance at all. The "original" instance is always already differentially marked, or contaminated, with the traces of indefinite repeatability. A linguistic sign, or a system of signs, must be repeatable and detachable from the singular intention of its production. This dislocation of the original meaning of a word undermines the authority of the speaker in relation to the language they use. Another example would be the written signature, conventionally taken to be the mark of authentic individual intent, but even that, to make a claim to the very possibility of authenticity, must necessarily also be forgeable. Derrida's approach deconstructs the theory of speech acts developed by J. L. Austin (1911–1960) in *How to Do Things with Words* (1962). Austin makes a distinction between constative utterances, which state something, and performative utterances, such as vows or promises, which achieve something in the act of utterance. Derrida shows this distinction to be flawed and the assurance of the intention of the speaker to be a fallacy. The problem with Derrida's deconstructive approach is that the distinction between active and passive modes of intent on which it relies effectively recasts the intentional fallacy that it sets out to dispel. Following Rousseau's ideas in his *Essai sur l'origine des langues*, Derrida works on the assumption of the originary metaphoricity of language: "Il ne s'agirait donc pas d'inverser le sens propre et le sens figuré mais de déterminer le sens «propre» [du langage] comme la métaphoricité elle-meme" (*De la grammatologie*, p. 27), "It is not, therefore, a matter of inverting the literal [proper] meaning and the figurative meaning but of determining the 'literal' [proper] meaning of [language] as metaphoricity itself' (*Of Grammatology*, p. 15). Derrida's work on language, and most prominently his notion of *différance*, has been effectively carried over into many areas of analysis. Much theoretical discourse is concerned with the politics difference in one form or another (cultural difference, sexual difference, and so on), and Derrida's attention to the structures of language and his undermining of the systems of thought they underpin have proven to be a highly portable linguistic model.

MARTIN CALDER

See also **Roland Barthes; Jean Baudrillard; Jacques Derrida; Michel Foucault; Jacques Lacan; Claude Levi-Strauss; Ferdinand de Saussure**

Further Reading

Austin, John Langshaw, *How to Do Things with Words*, Oxford: Oxford University Press, 1975 (First published posthumously 1962).

Barthes, Roland, *Mythologies*, Paris: Seuil, 1957; as *Mythologies*, translated by Annette Lavers, St. Albans: Paladin, 1973.

Barthes, Roland, *Éléments de semiologie*, Paris, Seuil, 1964; as *Elements of Semiology*, translated by Annette Levers and Colin Smith, London: Cape, 1967.

Baudrillard, Jean, *Simulacres et simulation*, Paris, Galiléc, 1981; as *Simulacrum and Simulation*, translated by Sheila Faria Glaser, Ann Arbor: University of Michigan Press, 1994.

Culler, Jonathan, *Structuralist Poetics: Structuralism, Linguistics and the Study of Literature*, London: Routledge, 1975.

Derrida, Jacques, *De la grammatologie*, Paris: Minuit, 1967; as *Of Grammatology* (corrected edition), translated by Gayatry Chakravorty Spivak, Baltimore, Maryland: Johns Hopkins University Press, 1997 (First published in English 1976).

Derrida, Jacques, *La Dissémination*, Paris: Seuil, 1972; as *Dissemination*, translated by Barbara Johnson, London: Athlone Press, 1981.

Derrida, Jacques, *Limited Inc*, Paris: Galilée, 1990; as *Limited Inc.*, edited by Gerald Graff, translated by Samuel Weber and Jeffrey Mehlman, Evanston, Illinois: Northwestern University Press, 1988.

Descombes, Vincent, *Le Même et l'autre: Quarante-cinq ans de philosophie française (1933–1978)*, Paris: Minuit, 1979; as *Modern French Philosophy*, translated by L. Scott-Fox and J.M. Harding, Cambridge: Cambridge University Press, 1980.

Eco, Umberto, *A Theory of Semiotics*, Bloomington: Indiana University Press, 1979.

Foucault, Michel, *Les Mots et les choses: une archéologie des sciences humaines*, Paris: Gallimard, 1966; as *The Order of Things: An Archaeology of the Human Sciences*, translated by Alan Sheridan-Smith, London: Routledge, 1974.

Gasché, Rodolphe, The Tain of the Mirror: *Derrida and the Philosophy of Reflection*, Cambridge, Massachusetts: Harvard University Press, 1986, pp. 212–217.

Hewes, Gordon, *Language Origins: A Bibliography*, 2nd edition, 2 volumes, The Hague: Mouton, 1975.

Johnson, Christopher, *System and Writing in the Philosophy of Jacques Derrida*, Cambridge: Cambridge University Press, 1993.

Lacan, Jacques, *Écrits*, Paris: Seuil, 1966; as *Écrits: A Selection*, translated by Alan Sheridan, London: Routledge, 1980.

Lévi-Strauss, Claude, *Anthropologie structurale*, Paris: Plon, 1974 (first published 1958); as *Structural Anthropology*, translated by Claire Jacobson and Brooke Grundfest Schoepf, New York: Basic Books, 1963.

Lieberman, Philip, *On the Origins of Language: An Introduction to the Evolution of Human Speech*, New York: Macmillan, 1975.

Nietzsche, Friedrich, "On Truth and Lies in a Nonmoral Sense," in *Philosophy and Truth: Selections from Nietzsche's Notebooks of the Early 1870s*, edited and translated by Daniel Breazeale, Hassocks, England: Harvester Press, 1979.

Rousseau, Jean-Jacques, *Essai sur l'origine des langues*, in Œuvres complètes, eds Bernard Gagnebin and Marcel Raymond, Paris: Gallimard, "Bibliothèque de la Pléiade", volume 5, 1995, pp. 371–429; as *Essay on the Origin of Languages*, translated by John H. Moran, in *Two Essays on the Origin of Language: Jean-Jacques Rousseau and Johann Gottfried Herder*, Chicago: Chicago University Press, 1966, pp. 1–83.

Saussure, Ferdinand de, *Cours de linguistique générale*, 5th edition, Paris: Payot, 1960; as *Course in General Linguistics*, translated by Wade Baskin, New York: McGraw-Hill, 1966.

Sturrock, John, ed., *Structuralism and Since: From Lévi-Strauss to Derrida*, Oxford: Oxford University Press, 1979.

LAVELLE, LOUIS
Philosopher

During the first half of the twentieth century in France, the term "philosophy of mind" designated a reaction against the positivist tendencies of materialist or empiricist movements. The work of Louis Lavelle, as well as that of Bergson, René de la Senne, and Jean Norbert, belongs to the humanist orientation that characterized the so-called spiritualist thinkers. However, in opposition to Bergson and Brunschvicg, Lavelle's spiritualism does not attempt to assimilate the data of positive sciences, biology, or epistemology. His work is above all focused on a philosophy of consciousness. He was also one of the founders of the famous collection, "Philosophy of mind," of the Aubier publishing house.

The refinement and dialectical movement of his thought were constantly directed toward a moral, and not an epistemological, perspective. Ontology and metaphysics were actually the prerequisites of a reflection on the conditions of wisdom, which Lavelle modeled on ancient philosophy, with the significant addition of Christian themes. The main postulate of this reflection was the idea that the mind determines all our activities. However, Lavelle did not embrace a radical form of idealism because he insisted on the ceaseless dialectic movement that relates the mind to the world. Thus, the past is nothing outside the mind act that evokes it. The world enables the mind to actualize its powers. This explains why Lavelle's spiritualism became associated with the existentialist movements in France in the 1940s. Nevertheless, his ideal of freedom did not reside in political philosophy and the notion of engagement, as in Sartre's case, but in a conception of spiritual intimacy with oneself, capable of creating freedom. The emphasis on activity in Lavelle's ontology is reminiscent of the significance of action in Spinoza's system, according to which the mind can return to its rational essence through active comprehension of its passions.

Starting from his early ontological analyses, (his thesis, *La dialectique du Monde sensible* [The Dialectics of the Sensible World, 1922], and the study entitled *La Dialectique de l'éternel présent: de l'Être* [Of Being, 1928]), Lavelle went on to develop a theory of action and power, within which Being is the result of a constant spiritual activity. Far from representing something given, such as the trace of a sensory perception in a mechanical, physiological system (as it was the case with the Humian brand of empiricism), Lavelle's notion of Being derives from an act of consciousness. This act belongs to an absolute Act that posits Being in general and that is akin to the divine Act. In a similar manner to Le Senne, this strand of philosophy allows for a personal and eternal God who always remains present to man's spiritual activity. This postulate also ensures the possibility of validating the effort of finite and imperfect acts, which participate in the global Being of the universe. What are the implications of this metaphysics? Whereas knowledge, reflection, and thought are responsible for Being, inner life is wholly responsible for its destiny. Lavelle does not deny the irrational aspect of life, suffering, or misfortune within the historical or social orders, but according to him, the mind is supposed to transfigure these facts of life through its own movement of spiritualization.

From this point of view, the Act or Total Presence provides the horizon of man's spiritual activity, as well as the conditions of his inner freedom. This is why Lavelle's writing becomes increasingly concerned with the moral consequences of his spiritualism. Two essays best illustrate Lavelle's contribution to moral philosophy: *L'Erreur de Narcisse* (Narcissus's Error, 1939), and *Le Mal et la souffrance* (Evil and Suffering, 1951). The former insists on the need to rid oneself of arrogance and the delusions of vanity to create a happy relationship to the other. Ultimately, solipsism can only be defeated by the consciousness that rediscovers the act of participation into Being that is constituted by the other. Wisdom thus emerges as the constant struggle of the self against the temptations of Narcissus.

The implications of Lavelle's spiritualism are also particularly clear in *Evil and Suffering*, in which pain becomes assimilated to a process of enrichment, consisting of the liberation and the universalization of consciousness. The subjectivism derived from the selfishness and the self-centeredness of consciousness is therefore overcome. In a manner similar to Le Senne or Brunschvicg, the question of the evil finds a solution through the renewed trust in the universal creative power of the mind. It is this ascetic optimism that opposed Lavelle to the philosophies of the absurd that emerged at the end of the 1930s. It is not surprising to see that, in his *La Philosophie française entre les deux guerres* (French Philosophy between the two World Wars, 1942), Lavelle felt the need to differentiate his approach from the existential or existentialist movements, which considered the absurd aspect of the world to be a tragic and unsurpassable fact. Lavelle's theory of values further extended his moral optimism by emphasizing our participation in values.

Like Bergson, Lavelle believed that freedom cannot be thought without taking into consideration the question of time. It is actually through the activity of the mind, as part of the reintegration of the past within a signification process, that time really comes to be accepted. The past is not some isolated and immutable object, but something which is reappropriated by present thought and memory to become part of a new future. Therefore, far from being something to which one is subjected or something maddening, time appears as spiritual labor. The result of this activity frees the spirit, which thus acquires a kind of eternity.

Lavelle elaborated this perspective, which affirms the possibility of a new wisdom, in *Du temps et de l'éternité* (On Time and Eternity, 1945), during the Second World War, at a time when all the certainties of European humanism were turned upside down. His account of wisdom stood up against the excesses of materialism and the values upheld by a material civilization. It also brought along the consolations of inwardness and of faith in the creative potential of the mind in a world that was overwhelmed by the powers of war.

OLIVIER SALAZAR-FERRER

See also **Henri Bergson; Leon Brunschvicg; Rene Le Senne**

Biography

Louis Lavelle was born in 1883. Having obtained the *agrégation* in philosophy in 1909, Lavelle taught at the Sorbonne and then at the Collège de France from 1941 until his death in 1951.

Selected Works

La dialectique du Monde sensible, 1922
La Dialectique de l'éternel présent: de l'Être, 1928
De l'Acte. La Conscience de soi, 1933
La Présence totale, 1934
Le Moi et son destin, 1936
L'Erreur de Narcisse, 1939
Le Mal et la souffrance, 1940
La Philosophie française entre les deux guerres, 1942
Du temps et de l'éternité, 1945
Introduction à l'ontologie, 1947
Les puissances du moi, 1948
Le Traité des valeurs, 1951
De l'âme humaine, 1952.

Further Reading

Berger, Gaston, Louis Lavelle, Les Etudes philosophiques, *VI*, 2/3 (1951): 123–127.
Ecole, Jean, *Louis Lavelle Et Le Renouveau de La Metaphysique de L'Etre Au Xxe Siecle*, Hidesheim, Germany: Georg Olms Publishers, 1997.

LAW

The evolution of French law in the twentieth century is remarkable because it mirrors the tension in French culture and history between universalism and particularism. French law shifted away from particularism to become a major engine and inspiration for the European enterprise as well as a receptacle of European norms and a drive for European juridical integration. This form of integration, in turn, substantially contributed to the political integration of Europe and to the continuing move toward some form of "United States of Europe."

When it comes to French law, the twentieth century may be divided into two periods of roughly equal duration. In the first half of the century, the French legal system stood as a sovereign and autonomous body of laws typical of continental European democracies. In the second half of the century, the French system breathed life into a larger enterprise: the establishment of a constitutional legal order for Europe, the like of which was previously unknown to international law. In so doing, French law radically transformed itself, shifting from that of a sovereign nation into a legal system with the hallmarks of subordination that characterize polities that make up a larger Federation. In turn, this transformation paved the way for the incorporation into French law, through judicial and legislative harmonization, of norms similar to those of other European nations. The end result was a France that, at the dawn of the twenty-first century, delegated one of its Presidents to draft a new "Constitution of Europe."

The turning point for French law can be traced to a single day, May 9, 1950. On that date, France's Jean Schuman made the famous declaration that came to be named after him. The constitutional paradigm for Europe, he boldly announced, had to be changed. The unspeakable horrors of the first half of the twentieth century resulted, in his mind, from the failure to achieve a "united Europe." The answer lay not in the oppression of the defeated enemy but, rather, in bringing him into the fold of a "partnership" that would make war not only "unthinkable, but materially impossible." The seeds for the United States of Europe were planted, and they yielded over the next fifty years an entity transformed beyond any initial expectations that its individual component states may have harbored.

Although both phenomena were related, the integration of Europe into a legal partnership, unlike its political integration, was a smashing success. On the political scene, "democracy deficit," "malaise," and "opaque bureaucracy" came to characterize the integration of Europe. The core of the problem lay in how to ensure adequate representation for nation states, with a strong history of independence, into a European whole. The Parliament of Europe traditionally carried little, if any, power, being relegated to express a nonbinding opinion when asked to do so by the representatives of the executive branches of the European governments. The Brussels bureaucracy was mired in a sea of committees, each less transparent than the other and all vying for a democratic legitimacy that the Community never gained on the European street. Finally, at bottom, Europe faced the dilemma of how to give each member state a meaningful vote in adopting laws without paralyzing decision-making with unanimity requirements.

The legal world was experiencing a wholly different integration process. France, who with Germany, worked as a twin engine in the legal evolution of Eu-

rope, contributed to the establishment of a legal system that somewhat replicated its own. Europe borrowed from France a system of judicial review of administrative and government action, together with basic norms of jurisprudence. In turn, a series of rulings by the European court, characterized as "revolutionary," creating a "new legal order," or as plain "glorious," transformed French law from that of a sovereign nation into that of a quasi-State of Europe.

As scholars such as Joseph Weiler noted, the confluence of several factors, each of which may not have had such a great effect by itself, contributed to this constitutional metamorphosis. Through the doctrine of "direct effect," French law was forced to incorporate, without the necessity of any internal action on the part of its government, the norms of European law adopted by the Community. French courts were required to hear claims made under these norms of European law. When the European Court implied a "supremacy clause" into the European treaties, any rule of French law, however elevated, became subordinate to a conflicting norm of European law. To top it all, France accepted a state of affairs whereby its judges, even though the national constitution did not embody such a practice, had to invalidate acts of Parliament that negated the European norms. The upshot was a fundamentally transformed legal system where, instead of standing as a sovereign nation in an international organization, France became one component of a unified legal whole.

The transformation of French law was, as Weiler noted, the key trigger for the deepest constitutional crisis of Europe, a crisis that ironically salvaged the political future of the integration enterprise. In the mid-1960s, France threatened to walk out of the Community ostensibly on account of a feud over agricultural rules. As Weiler keenly observed, the true reason for DeGaulle's move was the planned shift from unanimity to majority (or qualified majority) voting in European lawmaking and its relationship to the constitutional transformation of French law. France did not anticipate that its constitutional system would be so transformed as to subjugate French law to a European bigger brother when it agreed that European decision-making would move to less-than-unanimity voting. Now that the law was so "strong," France's say in making it could not be diluted. Having witnessed the constitutional transformation helplessly, France had to salvage its decision-making power on the political realm.

Put simply, France was not ready to become New York or California, an important state, but one that would always have to bow to the will of a separate majority of the Union. So France balked until the Luxembourg Accords gave France a veto right over European lawmaking. French particularism triumphed in that De Gaulle made sure that although the transformed legal system bound France to Europe, the political process of lawmaking would be framed in such a manner as to preserve France's right to pick and choose the legislation that the constitutional system would impose on it.

However, the universalist constitutional framework that France had put in motion stayed in place. As Weiler observed, the irony is that the 1960s political crisis that the transformation of law engendered was resolved in a manner that preserved the constitutional system and that later contributed to the renewal of political integration and the emergence of universalism on the political front. The effect of constitutionalization on the French landscape, although deferred by De Gaulle's move, was irreversible. A couple of decades after the Luxembourg Accords, new Pharaohs ruled over France. They, unlike De Gaulle, had more willingness to accept the transformation of the normative landscape. Perhaps they had become more used to the process. Perhaps they perceived that the United States of Europe had to develop their common market faster if they were to stay competitive. In all events, they embarked in a new series of endeavors designed to make sure that France would truly, on a normative level and not just from a constitutional standpoint, become European: the harmonization process.

The constitutional changes had paved the way for the radical transformation of substantive French law brought about by the European harmonization process. Harmonization took place, of course, by legislative fiat, but also by decisions of the European Court of Justice that invalidated French law that ran afoul of European norms. Icons of French culture, such as cognac, lost their favored treatment through this process. France was directed to bring a wide array of laws, such as trademarks, banking, commercial, privacy, and environmental laws, in harmony with norms articulated by the Community. At the end of the day, although French law retains some of its unique characteristics, it joined that of the other European nations in so many fields of legal life as to resemble more that of a state in the United States of America than a classically sovereign nation.

Today, Europe undergoes constitutional conventions, adopts a new currency, and expands eastward. Europe also seeks to export its model of peace through rule-making and integration to embattled areas of the world, including the Middle East. French law, as an inspiration and as a receptacle of Europe, has much to do with how far Europe has gone.

ARI AFILALO

LE DŒUFF, MICHÈLE
Philosopher, Literary Critic

As is the case with many of her contemporaries, Michèle Le Dœuff writes on a surprising number of topics: Her research interests include the philosophy of science; the British Renaissance philosophy of Francis Bacon, Thomas More, and others; and the work of William Shakespeare. However, she is best known—particularly in the anglophone world—for her work on the importance of "the imaginary"—that is, of thinking in images—for the practice of philosophy. This work is explicitly feminist, antiracist, and anticolonialist in that it is inextricably bound up, for Le Dœuff, with a critique of what she sees as the dominance of philosophy by white European men. Indeed, Le Dœuff's corpus as a whole is characterized by her refusal of the notion, dear to the Western philosophical tradition, that women (and other marginalized groups) cannot think philosophically.

In her first published book, *Recherches sur l'imaginaire philosophique* (1980), Le Dœuff asserts that although Western philosophy traditionally prides itself on being consistently rational, it in fact relies on an extrarational use of images to maintain the illusion of rationality. Noting that such images typically are explained away as mere heuristic devices (inessential to the argument itself but necessary to convey the sense of the argument to nonphilosophers) or as residual traces of undeveloped thought, she argues that images function in philosophical argumentation to disguise those fundamental premises of the argument that cannot be justified in purely rational terms. Thus, these images conceal the fact that philosophical thought always contains within itself un-thought elements on which it depends. Moreover, philosophy's insistence that images are peripheral to its essential work leads to an emphasis on abstraction and universality that, as many other feminists have argued, effaces the recognition of particularity that is necessary for true ethical relationality. It is not surprising, then, that Le Dœuff goes on to show that many of the specific images prevalent in the history of philosophy express hostility toward women and various other groups—children, "common people," and so on—characterized as being outside of rational thought. In so doing, such images not only serve to maintain the myth of philosophy's exclusive claim to rational thought but also preserve philosophy as the domain of those white European men who, on philosophy's own terms, can alone demonstrate the ability to think rationally.

Le Dœuff finds a particularly riveting example of the often misogynist nature of the philosophical imaginary in the work of Sartre, for whom, according to Le Dœuff, women are always reduced to being (merely) sexed bodies, objects of male desire. This example is of special interest to Le Dœuff because of the relationship between Sartre and Simone de Beauvoir, whose *Le Deuxième sexe (1949)* was enormously important to the emergence of feminism in modern France. In *L'Étude et le rouet* (1989), Le Dœuff analyzes this relationship for what it reveals about the ways in which women are excluded from philosophy. Acknowledging that both Sartre and de Beauvoir agreed that Sartre was the philosopher of the couple, she points out that de Beauvoir was nevertheless successful in appropriating Sartre's existentialism for her own purposes, emphasizing its ethical and political potential and thereby making room within philosophy for the kind of open-endedness that is philosophy's greatest value. For Le Dœuff, in other words, de Beauvoir's project deviates from Sartre's precisely in its recognition of the specificity of the Other and in its insight that philosophical thought is intellectually and ethically obligated to otherness. This analysis, which asserts the value of particularity over universality, lays the groundwork for an articulation of Le Dœuff's concern with such pragmatic women's issues as contraception and abortion, as well as with the need to challenge the masculine dominance within the discipline of philosophy.

In *Le Sexe du savoir* (2000), Le Dœuff approaches the problem of women's exclusion from philosophy from yet another angle. Here she takes up the debate over whether men think differently from women not to settle the question but rather to insist that the question be abandoned. Examining philosophical discourses of women in the writings of both historical figures such as Plato and contemporary theorists of difference such as Jacques Derrida and Luce Irigaray, she attempts to articulate the possibility of a different kind of thinking, freed from the limitations of a rationality seen as exclusively masculine. In this connection—and borrowing a page from the feminism of sexual difference, of which she is otherwise critical—she invokes the body as a privileged indicator of the necessity for women to speak on their own behalf, as (rational) subjects in their own right, to win such basic political rights as access to abortion and contraception. She also further develops her earlier notion that it is essential to acknowledge the dependence of philosophical thought on the imaginary, the un-thought, so that dialogues might be established within philosophy that will open philosophy up to otherness.

Throughout her critique of the masculine dominance of philosophy, however, Le Dœuff stops short of arguing that philosophy is essentially patriarchal, and in this she diverges from the critiques of rationality and of the Western philosophical tradition developed by other French feminist theorists, including Irigaray and Hélène Cixous. Indeed, she summons what she sees as the strengths of philosophy—in particular, its reflectivity, its willingness to be self-critical—in her challenge of philosophy. In Le Dœuff's view, what is necessary is that philosophy abandon its notion of itself as a privileged meta-discourse, closed and inviolable, in favor of a recognition that philosophy is necessarily open-ended, incomplete, and dependent on otherness. Toward this end, she asserts the existence of a plurality of "rationalities," no one of which is or should be capable of exercising the kind of hegemony that has characterized the history of Western philosophy.

JUDITH L. POXON

See also **Simone de Beauvoir; Hélène Cixous; Jacques Derrida; Luce Irigaray; Jean-Paul Sartre**

Biography

Born in France in 1948, Michèle Le Dœuff received her Ph.D. in Philosophy in 1980 and has since taught at the Ecole Normale Supérieure at Fontenay and at the University of Geneva. Her written work is wide-ranging and driven by a passionate interest in the imagination, especially as it is implicated in and excluded from traditional Western philosophy. She has published studies and translations of such figures as Francis Bacon, Simone de Beauvoir, and William Shakespeare, but is perhaps best known in the Anglophone world for her second book, *L'Étude et le rouet. Des femmes, de la philosophie, etc.* (1989), in which she critiques the exclusion of women and "others" from the Western philosophical tradition.

Selected Works

Recherches sur l'imaginaire philosophique, 1980; as *The Philosophical Imaginary*, translated by Colin Gordon, 1989

L'Étude et le rouet, 1989; as *Hipparchia's Choice: An Essay Concerning Women, Philosophy, Etc.*, translated by Trista Selous 1991

Le Sexe du savoir, 2000

Further Reading

de Beauvoir, Simone, *Le Deuxième sexe*, Paris: Gallimard, 1949; as *The Second Sex*, translated by H. M. Parkshley, NY: Knopf, 1968.

Deutscher, Max (ed.), *Michèle Le Dœuff: Operative Philosophy and Imaginary Practice*, Amherst, New York: Humanity Books, 2000.

Gatens, Moira, "Le Dœuff," in *A Companion to Continental Philosophy*, edited by Simon Critchley, Malden, Massachusetts: Blackwell, 1998.

Grosz, Elizabeth, *Sexual Subversions: Three French Feminists*, Sydney: Allen & Unwin, 1989, Chapter 6.

Lechte, John, "Michèle Le Dœuff," in his *Fifty Key Contemporary Thinkers: From Structuralism to Postmodernity*, London: Routledge, 1994.

Matthews, Eric, "Recent French Feminists (Michèle Le Dœuff)," in his *Twentieth-Century French Philosophy*, Oxford: Oxford University Press, 1996.

Mortley, Raoul, "Michèle Le Dœuff," in his *French Philosophers in Conversation: Levinas, Scheider, Serres, Irigaray, Le Dœuff, Derrida*, New York: Routledge, 1991.

Saunders, Kerry, "Michèle Le Dœuff: Reconsidering Rationality," *Australasian Journal of Philosophy* 71,4 (1993): 425–435.

LE SENNE, RENÉ

Philosopher

The work of René le Senne belongs to the spiritualist movement in French academia that developed within a climate of relative indifference to foreign philosophies and psychoanalysis. Le Senne was among several French thinkers, including Lavelle, Dupréel, and Jean Nabert, who endeavored to elaborate a theory of values without any reference to phenomenology or to the Nietzschean revolution in philosophy. His ideological premises were, on the one hand, indebted to French post-Kantian thought and to Octave Hamelin's absolute idealism, but on the other hand, they drew on Bergson's Vitalist and spiritualist heritage.

Le Senne's spiritualism attempted to rationalize Christianism by interiorizing it and integrating it within a philosophy of values. During the first period in Le Senne's development, his work (such as his *Introduction à la philosophie* [Introduction to Philosophy, 1925]) tried to integrate the irrationality of psychological life and Kantian systematic thought without its categories, which Le Senne replaced by the "functions of the mind." He attributed particular significance to the contradictions of consciousness. Every contradiction involved suffering and overcoming. Suffering, therefore, possessed spiritual meaning, as it turned the finite subject toward the absolute subject and the infinite. From this point of view, contradictions and the imperfection of reason were not supposed to lead to nihilism. On the contrary, these aspects had to be guided by a moral imperative of the mind. Moreover, sacrifice provided the answer to the contradictions of moral life. The central Christian dimension inherent in spiritualism was thus highlighted by this line of argument.

Ontological skepticism itself had to be guided by the same moral imperative toward a duty to create being. The constructive attitude of the mind therefore confronted aestheticism and scepticism with the idea of "duty," which became the source of "all being and all action." This argument, which Le Senne elaborated in *Le Devoir* (On Duty, 1930), was derived from the constitution of the postulates of Kant's practical reason, which were then applied to the totality of man's spiritual life. From this perspective, one can say that Le Senne still upholds Hamelin's absolute idealism, which posits that consciousness creates its own conditions of experience. The idea of duty introduces a forceful guiding principle that ties up this idealism with the postulate of being: duty is therefore defined as "the idea which requires being."

Nonetheless, during a second period, Le Senne's idealism gradually turned toward a philosophy of values, which was reflected in the new edition (1939) of his *Introduction à la philosophie*. Far from being established by an act of the will, values were defined as emanations of the universal Spirit's transcendence manifested in us. Similarly, God, as absolute value, appeared as the source of all values. The transcendent character of value was defined with reference to its resistance to the individual and subjective attempts at appropriation (*Obstacle et valeur* [Obstacle and Value, 1934]). Moreover, the idea of Value divided into four main values, Truth, the Good, Beauty, and Love, which were then perpetually reassembled within specific situations. This axiology consisted of deriving particular values from the absolute Value. Through this axiology permeated by Platonicism, Le Senne's discourse led back to God, as the supreme value, in keeping with the classical ontological argument, which starts from the idea of God to arrive at God's existence. In *Obstacle et valeur* (1934), God possesses the function of an axiological foundation in the form of a sovereign person. It is He who attributes the possibility of being to the possibility of value. This theory of value, impregnated with metaphysics, was related to psychological studies (*Traité de caractériologie* [A Treatise of Characteriology, 1945]). In 1951, Le Senne attempted to bring together his theory of value and his research on the notion of character in *La Destinée personnelle* (Personal Destiny, 1951). He set out to elaborate a classification of characters according to criteria of emotivity, of activity, of the repercussion of impression, as well as the narrowness or width of the field of consciousness. This characteriology was supposed to improve self-knowledge and to lead to an accurate and efficient philosophical knowledge of the dialectical relationship that Le Senne established between character and value. The question at the heart of *La Destinée personnelle* concerned the choice between a passively experienced destiny (*destin*) and an appropriation of value through a personal act that represented a vocation (*destinée*). Le Senne develops a "psycho-dialectic," the function of which is to mediate between axiology and characteriology. Creation and acceptance, action and observation constitute the ever-present terms of this spiritualist dialectics.

As in the case of other spiritualist thinkers, such as Lavelle or Jean Nabert, Le Senne's theory situates the imperative of freedom and of the active and willful appropriation of freedom at the center of the argument. It is the respect of value that determined the happiness or the unhappiness of one's destiny. In fact, Le Senne's axiology proposes a form of spiritualist redemption whose means are exclusively philosophical (*Introduction à la philosophie*, 1939).

Spiritualism, as a doctrine according to which spiritual values need to be embodied in personal existence, is not very far from Emmanuel Mounier's personalism, with the exception of the political implications of personalism. The use of metaphysical concepts in axiology accounts for the rapidly fading interest in the spiritualist doctrine. Spiritualism was swiftly overshadowed, on the one hand, by the concepts of phenomenology and of French Existentialism and, on the other, by the emergence within critical discourse of the traditional concepts of the "self," of "freedom," of "reflection," and of "value" with reference to Nietzsche. It can also be said that the tendency of the spiritualist doctrine to employ metaphysical concepts without any attempt at analyzing the linguistic, semantic, and pragmatic constitution of the moral and the ethical discourses contributed to a large extent to the relatively rapid fall into oblivion of the movement. The Christian framework of spiritualism limited its ethical considerations. Nevertheless, the philosophy of effort and its relentless affirmation of spiritual values over historical and social forces left a powerful mark on prewar French thought.

OLIVIER SALAZAR-FERRER

See also **Henri Bergson; Louis Lavelle**

Biography

René le Senne was born in Elbeuf in 1882. He was a professor at the Sorbonne from 1929 to 1931 and from 1942 to 1952. With Louis Lavelle, he founded *Philosophie de l'esprit*. He died in Paris in 1954.

Selected Works

Introduction à la philosophie, 1925
Mensonge et caractère, 1930
Le Devoir, 1930
Obstacle et valeur, 1934
Introduction à la philosophie, 1939
Traité de caractériologie, 1945
Traité de morale générale, 1942
La Destinée personelle, 1951
La Découverte de Dieu, 1955

Further Reading

Berger, Gaston, "La vocation dans la philisophie de René Le Senne," *Giornale di Metafisica*, 10,3 (1955): 390–397.

Cadó, Valdemar, "L'esprit dans la philosophie de René Le Senne," *Laval Théologique et Philosophie*, 48,3 (October 1992): 343–350.

LECLERC, ANNIE
Writer

After four years studying philosophy at the Sorbonne in Paris and being taught by Deleuze and Derrida, writing about philosophy came naturally to Annie Leclerc, in the sense that philosophical thinking always remained for her coextensive with the intensity of living and was a prerequisite for an irrepressible quest for truth. Most important, however, philosophy was to give Leclerc the opportunity to practice her overriding passion: writing.

As for most French essayists in the tradition of Montaigne, and more recently Alain, philosophy for Leclerc remains principally based on observation, but more particularly in her case on a questioning of what is really entailed by the tradition of universality issuing from Descartes. Such an approach also relies, as do those of other contemporary French theorists, on a concomitant reclaiming of personal (female) experience. The influence of Jean-Jacques Rousseau, and a strong admiration for his writings, as expressed in her *Origines* (1988), was to be of prime importance in Leclerc's conception of philosophy. Her diverse writing, which ranges from autobiographical reflection on female experience (childbirth, menstruation, death of the mother) to texts addressing the meaning of philosophy, Descartes, the effect of reading, love for the other (gendered or not), violence, and war, constitutes by the unexpected contiguities of its subject matter a highly effective questioning of the laws and presuppositions of philosophical discourse. The variety of Leclerc's writing also represents a vital expression and fusion of poetic lyricism, philosophical thinking, cultural and social criticism, fiction, and autobiography, in which generic boundaries and conventions are constantly blurred and shifted.

Through the concept of "writing the body," Leclerc was to become an active proponent of feminine writing (*écriture féminine*). In contrast to Simone de Beauvoir, whose vision she perceived as tainted by masculine ideology, but in unison with other contemporary French theorists of sexual difference (Irigaray and, especially, Cixous, with whom she collaborated in *La Venue à l'écriture* [Coming to Writing, 1977]), Leclerc conceived "writing the body" as opening the door to a radically different and ideologically liberating type of knowledge and expression.

Her hugely successful best-seller *Parole de femme* (1974, *A Woman's Word*), followed by *Épousailles*

(1976, *Marryings*), were among the first texts to express "feminine" consciousness in the 1970s. Wary of dogmatism, Leclerc placed emphasis on life forces, love, exchange, and the relation to the other, and gave a different taste to the militancy of the time.

Parole de femme also quickly became the subject of controversy. In it Leclerc argues that women have been silenced by the dominant male language. In a world dominated by the male concern of "giving birth" to "man" (p. 7), ruled by a frightening obsession with property and death (p. 27), women have been excluded from its order, in which truth has been identified with man and his speech. Hence the necessity for women, for the sake of both genders, to invent a new language that speaks of women's difference, and through such discourse to revalue physical existence, as well as the textual musicalities and intensities habitually devalued by a male metaphysics of truth. Similar to Irigaray, Leclerc suggests that such language will bring a new pattern of relations between the self and the world, in turn engendering a liberatory "new world" of "life" (p. 89). Through a first-person subjective and passionate voice, the expressions of female bodily experiences, such as menstruation, pregnancy, breastfeeding, and most important, childbirth, constitute the most innovative parts of *Parole*.

In *Épousailles*, Leclerc articulates personal epiphanies and moments of insight that lead to privileged moments of *jouissance* (bliss), a concept also central to Julia Kristeva's psychoanalytic thinking. In Leclerc, the concept carries a sense of delight, sexual pleasure, and joy, coupled by the pragmatic meaning of being entitled to enjoy one's woman's rights. The privileging of the full presence of the body's pregnant speech is very close to the space of the metaphysics of presence that has since been defined by Derrida; for Leclerc, such *jouissance* or intensity of living underlies all philosophical thinking.

In the controversy that followed the publication of *Parole de femme*, Anglophone feminist critics saw the renewed value given to women's domestic life and childbearing function as politically and ideologically dangerous. Such critical positions against what was seen as "biological feminism," however, took Leclerc's writing at a primary level and ignored the fact that the female body of which Leclerc writes is necessarily fictional, a way of speaking of oneself rather than about oneself.

The critical temptation to assimilate Leclerc's writing with the tendency of *écriture féminine* to demonize men furthermore undervalued the driving force of her early writing, which endeavored to revalidate personal experience (at the time of *Parole de femme* and *Épousailles* a jubilatory bodily experience) to share it with the rest of the world.

More fundamentally, though, critics have also raised the question of whether "writing the body" as a new means of expression and a source of new knowledge can itself be exempt from (male) language. Leclerc was herself to take into account and address this undeniable difficulty some ten years later in *Hommes et femmes* (Men and Women, 1985). In the late 1980s, reflecting on the evolution of her thinking, Leclerc acknowledged a move toward a dialectical view of sexual difference, in which the latter is seen as originating in culture, mythology, and language rather than in the body itself (1993, Fallaize). In *Hommes et femmes* she focuses on the relationship between men and women, an aspect excluded from her early work. As with most of her writing, this essay constitutes an absolute valorization of both sexual and general love. In uncompromising fashion, in this time of radicalized feminism, Leclerc refuses to view men and women as irreconcilable opposites.

Origines (1988) further exemplifies Leclerc's position against gender separatism. The writing here, directly addressed to Rousseau, is couched in a language of love and intimacy and points out that it is an artificial exercise to separate men's writing from that of women. Even if the style of *Origines* is more controlled and the lyrical impulse is restrained, the text retains the strong autobiographical tone of Leclerc's early writing and the same episodic structure: reading notes, reflections on reading and writing, layered autobiographical fragments from both writers' lives. In her endless search for truth, Leclerc warns in *Origines* that love must not be consumed, that it can only exist in its deferment. Desire or the quest for what cannot be obtained is what life is all about, human love being always imperfect and only fulfilled in the humbleness of its humanity. An awareness of the paradoxical limitations and majesty of living is a constant feature of Leclerc's work, moreover, provided her with the irrepressible impulse to write. With *Clé* (Key, 1989), a fascinating little book that pursues a poetic self-analysis around the word *clé*, carried out through the childhood tale of Bluebeard, she explores further the experience of reading and its generic contamination of autobiographical writing.

The flamboyance, transparency, joy, even ecstasy of *Parole de femme*, *Épousailles*, *Hommes et femmes*, and *Origines*, texts that have been seen by some as four chapters of a single book written under the sign of a quest for origins to be found in writing, gradually gave place to the exploration of loss and lack in *Au feu du jour* (At the Light of Day, 1979)—a turning-point in her writing—*Le Mal de mère* (Mother Sickness, 1986) and *Exercices de mémoire* (Memory Exercises, 1992).

Exercices de mémoire is a long meditation on the nature of violence prompted by one of Leclerc's revelatory moments—the viewing of Claude Lanzmann's *Shoah* (1985)—which, as in her earlier writing, leads to the promise and the urge to write: a process typical of Leclerc's creative method. *Exercices* also reveals again some transgression of generic boundaries (here, historical writing on the Holocaust) in suggesting that historical consciousness can only be mediated by personal experience. In her evocation of intense personal experience mixed with references to the historical Nazi period, Leclerc argues against the good/evil binarism that she identifies as lying at the heart of conflict. Leclerc's distinctive voice reestablishes a balance in philosophical discourse, and the strength of her writing in *Exercices* primarily stems, in common with much other Holocaust writing, from the openness of the confessional mode that she adopts to explore this history of forgetting.

Although *Toi, Pénélope* (You, Penelope, 2001) is a poetic reflection around a reading of Homer's *Ulysses* with links to Leclerc's favored theme of gender difference in *Hommes et femmes, Éloge de la nage* (In Praise of Swimming, 2002) remains faithful to the fundamentally optimistic nature of Leclerc's thinking, returning to the exhilaration of her early work with an evocation of the sheer pleasure of living. This overriding optimistic sense of existence, beyond pain and suffering, appears to constitute a key element—indeed, a signature—in Leclerc's thinking and writing.

RAYNALLE UDRIS

See also **Simone de Beauvoir; Helene Cixous; Gilles Deleuze; Jacques Derrida; Julia Kristeva; Luce Irigaray**

Biography

LeClerc was born in 1940 in St. Sulpice Laurière (Limousin). She read Philosophy at the Sorbonne (Paris), where she graduated in 1964. In 1966 she married the Greek philosopher Nicos Poulantzas, with whom she had a daughter in 1970. From 1964 to 1985 she taught philosophy at the sixth-form level, with a sabbatical from 1976 to 1979 during which she focused on writing. From 1985 to 1996 she worked as a reader for her publisher, Grasset. Since 1986, she has run writing workshops in a School of Architecture and in prisons. Since 1998, LeClerc has been Vice-President of the Maison des Écrivains (House of Writers). She continues to devote the majority of her time to writing.

Selected Works

"Étoile-Nation," *Les Temps modernes*, 1967
Le Pont du nord, 1967
Parole de femme, 1974; republished 2001. Translated extracts appear in *French Connections: Voices from the Women's Movement in France*, edited by Claire Duchen (London: Hutchinson, 1987) and in *French Feminist Thought*, edited by Toril Moi (Oxford: Blackwell, 1987)
"Mon écriture d'amour," *Les Nouvelles Littéraires*, May 1976
"Communication," *Liberté*, 1976
"Je vais te manger," *Sorcières*, 1976
Épousailles, 1976
"Postface," in *Autrement dit*, by Marie Cardinal, 1977
"Si, pour changer, on laissait faire les femmes," *Le Sauvage*, 1977
With Madeline Gagnon and Hélène Cixous, *La Venue à l'écriture*, 1977
Au feu du jour, 1979
Hommes et femmes, 1985
Le Mal de mère, 1986
Origines, 1988
Clé, 1989
"Ces vérités enfouies dans les mains d'Hélène," *Le Magazine littéraire*, November 1992
Exercices de mémoire, 1992
"Moi mon silence," *Libération* ("Rebonds" section), March 2001
Toi, Pénélope, 2001
Éloge de la nage, 2002

Further Reading

Alzon, Claude, "Le Féminisme d'Annie Leclerc: 'Parole de femme' ou 'Propos d'homme'?" in *Femme mythifiée, femme mystifiée*, Paris: PUF, 1978
Anderson, Margaret, "La Jouissance—principe d'écriture," *L'Esprit Créateur*, 19 (Summer 1979): 3–12
Brewer, Maria Minich, "A loosening of tongues: from narrative economy to women writing," *MLN*, 99,5 (December 1984): 1141–1161
Brochier, Jean-Jacques, "Aimer Rousseau," *Le Magazine littéraire*, March (1988): 8
Cesbron, Georges, "Écritures au féminin. Propositions de lecture pour quatre livres de femme," *Degré Second*, 4 (1980): 95–119
Delphy, Christine, "Protoféminisme et anti-féminisme," *Les Temps modernes*, 30 (1976): 1469–1500; translated by Diana Leonard in *Close to Home: A Materialist Analysis of Women's Oppression*, London: Hutchinson, 1984
Gallop, Jane, "Annie Leclerc: Writing a Letter with Vermeer," *October*, 33 (1985): 103–118; reprinted and retitled as part of "Carnal Knowledge," in *Thinking Through the Body* by Jane Gallop, New York: Columbia University Press, 1988
Gelfand, Elissa, and Thorndike Hules, Virginia (eds.), *French Feminist Criticism: Women, Language and Literature. An Annotated Bibliography*, New York: Garland Publishing, 1985
Granjon, Marie-Christine, "Les Femmes, le langage et "l'écriture," *Raison Présente*, 39 (1976): 25–32
Horizons Philosophiques (special issue on Leclerc), 6,1 (Autumn 1995)
Hutton, Margaret-Anne, "Seeing but not believing: Annie Leclerc's Exercices de mémoire," *French Studies*, 51,4 (October 1997): 432–446
Powrie, Phil, "A Womb of one's own: the metaphor of the womb-room as a reading effect in texts by contemporary French women writers," *Paragraph*, 3,3 (November 1989): 197–213
Savigneau, Josyane, "Annie Leclerc et la passion de Jean-Jacques," *Le Monde des livres*, 4 March (1988): 4

Vilaine, Anne-Marie de, "Le Corps de la théorie," *Le Magazine littéraire*, January (1982): 25–28

LECOMTE DU NOÜY, PIERRE
Scientist

Pierre Lecomte du Noüy's intellectual life consisted of an increasing involvement in scientific research, followed by a growing interest in philosophy, theology, and the interpretation of the sciences. A representative of antimechanist and broadly religious trends in early twentieth-century French thought, he was in the end to attempt a synthesis in which science, value, and purpose each play significant roles.

Lecomte du Noüy's scientific work can be divided into five parts: cicatrization of wounds, absorption phenomena of surfaces, monomolecular layers, physicochemical characteristics of immunity, and molecular theory of plasma and serum. These projects involved new investigative techniques, for which he invented new instruments: the tensiometer, viscosimeter, ionometer, and infrared spectrophotometer. A member of many scientific societies and recipient of scientific awards, he published around two hundred scientific articles as well as several books. Lecomte du Noüy's most important contribution to the sciences is his study of the cicatrization (healing) of wounds, a study that he believed had philosophical implications and that lead him to propose the existence of a generalized biological time immanent in varying degree in all living organisms. Cicatrization involves, he discovered, two factors: the area of the wound and the age of the patient. On the basis of these factors, he worked out an "index of cicatrization" as part of an equation that allows prediction of the rate of healing of wounds. This equation was later extended to the description of healing in lesions other than simple skin wounds as well as to healing processes in warm-blooded as well as cold-blooded animals. (In the latter case, body temperature had to be added as a third fundamental factor.)

Though his original studies of cicatrization were completed in 1917, in *Time and Life* (1937) he was to extend and sum up this part of his work, arguing that the traditional division of temporality into two basic sorts, physical time and psychological time, is insufficient. To these must be added a third: physiological time, which differs in important respects from the other two. Physical (clock) time proceeds at a regular pace. In several respects, physiological time, though ordered, lacks this regularity. Physiological time proceeds at different rates depending on age. A wound heals five times more slowly for a man of sixty than the same wound would heal for a child of ten. It is thus not surprising that as one ages, time seems to pass more quickly as the organism's physiological time progressively slows. Inversely, a wound whose cicatrization is halted by infection will accelerate as if to recapture lost time after the infection is cured. Although physical time is the same everywhere, each living organism, Lecomte du Noüy speculates, embodies its own temporal rate.

The study of cytological time, undertaken by his mentor, Alexis Carrel (summed up in *Man, That Unknown*, 1937), both complemented and supported his own work and found subsequent corroboration in the discoveries of other biologists. Their insistence that the temporal ordering of the components of an organism must be studied to make possible the understanding of the organism made them forerunners of today's chronobiology.

Similar to Pierre Teilhard de Chardin, with whom he corresponded briefly, Lecomte du Noüy was influenced by Henri Bergson's ideas of temporality and evolutionary dynamics. In Lecomte du Noüy's case, however, the influence was indirect. It was Carrel, an avowed Bergsonian, who urged him to study physiological time without concern for any static substrate. It is very likely that many of the Bergsonian arguments in his writings came to him indirectly from Carrel. Carrel, Bergson, and Lecomte du Noüy agree that in its broadest temporal scale, evolution transcends mechanism and embodies a cosmic duration.

Lecomte du Noüy's scientific work is not based on some undercurrent of mysticism (a term hard to define in any case). It was undertaken at a period in his life when he was an agnostic and represents a thoroughly biophysical approach to life, an approach flatly rejected by many French biologists of his time. He rejected any vitalistic hypothesis and held that biological time is a purely chemical phenomenon. His researches did, however, rest on the assumption that he was dealing with a global phenomenon, which, though it has material components, could still be described on its own terms and as a whole. This was one of three factors that led him to attempt a nonreductionist and teleological explanation of biological evolution. The other two were his belief that chemistry and physics in his time did not have the ability to explain the origin of life or its development and his conclusion (based on the moral savagery of World War II) that science can not provide the basis for human moral development.

Lecomte du Noüy's interpretation of biological evolution is presented in *Human Destiny* (1947). Here, using figures derived from Charles E. Guye, he argues that the emergence of life must be due to "anti-chance." (Guye had calculated that the improbablity of a protein molecule coming emerging through the random coming together of atoms is on the order of 1:100160.) He also insists that the continuing evolution a life toward increasingly complex and more fully conscious creatures stands in sharp contrast with the second law of thermodynamics, which depicts nonliving matter's drift towards increasing randomness and disorder. A full accounting of the course of evolution must involve purpose. Lecomte du Noüy proposes the "telefinalist" hypothesis to explain what can be meant by evolutionary purpose. Purpose, he holds, can not be found in the individual organism, as some scientists have believed. Nor can it be found in the particulars of mutation and adaptation. A global phenomenon, it must be seen in its long-term effects, its overall trend.

These ideas, he believes, have important implications. They imply that man is not a machine driven by quasi-mechanical forces but a being with free will, capable of contributing to his own and the world's future. That evolution has purpose and tends toward moral and spiritual ends supports human freedom and gives humankind the will to persevere. The ultimate goal for humankind is to bring about a more harmonious, less destructive, more spiritual humanity. Thus, though he arrived at his views largely independently, Lecomte du Noüy's thought expressed many of the ideas and fundamental inspirations of French spiritualism dating back to Victor Cousin and Félix Ravaisson.

Lecomte du Noüy's writings have had little effect on either philosophy or theology. Though his spirited retelling of the course of biological evolution has been a favorite with the reading public and with apologists for religious orthodoxy, he has been roundly criticized for misinterpretations of probability, of thermodynamics, and of evolutionary theory. Such criticisms have undoubted force, but *Human Destiny* is a popular book, written for a very wide audience. A more objective assessment of his abilities and arguments could be obtained by reading, for example, *Between Knowing and Believing* (1967), a group of essays written between 1929 and 1945.

PETE A. Y. GUNTER

See also **Henri Bergson; Pierre Teilhard de Chardin**

Biography

Born in Paris in 1883, Lecomte du Noüy studied at the Lycée Carnot and then at the Sorbonne, where he received four degrees: B.S., 1900; Ph.B., 1901; Ph.D., 1905; and Sc.D., 1916. He was awarded an LL.B. at the Faculté de Droit in 1905. Descended from a long line of artists and authors (his mother was a successful novelist), he first tried his hand at drama, writing successful plays for the Paris stage and acting. During World War I, he served as lieutenant of infantry before being transferred to the laboratory of Alexis Carrel, where he worked on the problem of the healing of wounds. In 1923 he married an American, Mary Bishop Harriman. Between 1920 and 1927 he worked at the Rockefeller Institute for Medical Research (now Rockefeller University) in New York. In 1927 he established the first laboratory of molecular biophysics at the Pasteur Institute and in 1937 was named a director of the École des Hautes Études with a laboratory at the Sorbonne. During the German occupation, he escaped to the United States, returning briefly to France in 1946. He died in California in 1947.

Selected Works

Méthodes Physics en biologie et en médicine, 1933
Le Temps et la vie, 1936; as *Biological Time*, 1936, 1937
L'Homme devant la science, 1939; as *The Road to Reason*, 1948
L'Avenir de l'esprit, 1942
L'Homme et son destiné, 1948; as *Human Destiny*, 1947
Entre savoir et croire, 1964; as *Between Knowing and Believing*, translated by Mary Lecomte du Noüy, 1967

Further Reading

Carrel Alexis, *Man, The Unknown*, New York: Harper and Row, 1935
Huguet, Jean, *Rayonnement do lecomte du Noüy*, Paris: Vieux-Colombier, 1957
Lecomte du Noüy, Mary, *The Road to Human Destiny: A Life of Pierre Lecomte du Noüy*, New York: Longmans, 1955
Meyer, François. "Time and Finality According to Lecomte du Noüy in *Evolution in Perspective*, edited by G. N. Shuster and R. E. Thorson, Notre Dame, Indiana: University of Notre Dame Press, 1970, 108–116
Nagel, Ernest, "Pseudo-Science as a Guide to Human Destiny," in *Logic Without Metaphysics*, by Ernest Nagel, Glencoe, Illinois: Free Press, 1956, 419–422.
Wyckoff, Ralph W. G., "Lecomte du Noüy as a Biophysicist," in *Evolution in Perspective*, edited by G. N. Schuster and R. E. Thorson, Notre Dame, Indiana: University of Notre Dame Press, 1970, 172–183.

LEFEBVRE, HENRI
Marxist Philosopher

Unlike Althusser, who emphasized the later writings of Marx, or Sartre, who found inspiration in the early writings, Lefebvre was always concerned with Marx's thought as a whole. Indeed, this attempt to view a mediating position between two extremes could be said to characterize Lefebvre's entire career. In central early works such as *La conscience mystifiée* (written with Norbert Guterman, 1936) and *La materialisme dialectique* (1939), Lefebvre outlined a Hegelian Marxism that sought to challenge dogmatic, reductionist views of Marx and that aimed to capture the idealist elements retained in Marxist thought.

Central to Lefebvre's interest in Marx was the notion of alienation, which through his translations of the

1844 Manuscripts (again, with Guterman), in Morceaux Choisis (1934) de Karl Marx Lefebvre largely introduced to a French audience. For Lefebvre, the alienation resulting from capitalism needs to be taken beyond the economic sphere, as it can also be found in social and cultural interaction. The key event of the twentieth century, for Lefebvre, was the increased commodification of everyday life, as capitalism moved beyond the workplace, the domain of labor, in its domination of existence. The notion of everyday life, which Lefebvre himself believed to be his central contribution to Marxism, does not have the negative connotations of the term in Lukács and Heidegger. For Lefebvre, everyday life is worthy of celebration and is capable of being the site of resistance to capitalist appropriations. His analysis of everyday life can be usefully seen between the dominant strands of French thought in the period; it looks at the phenomenological subject, but within the structures of society. The concern with everyday life was central throughout Lefebvre's career, notably in the *Critique de la vie quotidienne* series (1947, 1958, 1961, 1981).

Lefebvre's writings on everyday life are studded with analyses of situations and places, from the French countryside of his birth to the new towns being built and the Paris he lived and worked in. This interest in the politics and sociology of the lived experience was found in numerous other works, including his detailed studies of *La vallée de Campan* (1963) and the *Pyrénées* (1965); but also particularly in a range of works concerned with the urban experience. Lefebvre felt that Marx, because of the time he was writing, had not taken into account the importance of the city or town. Lefebvre wrote widely on the politics and political economy of urban space, including *Le droit à la ville* (1968), *La révolution urbaine* (1970) and *La pensée marxiste et la ville* (1972). The works on the urban and rural were complemented by more general studies on the politics of location, including *Du rural à l'urbain* (1970), *Espace et politique* (1973), and especially *La production de l'espace* (1974).

This last work is probably the one for which he is best known today, at least in the English-speaking world. Lefebvre stresses the importance of the relation between the control of space and political struggles, the role of technology in producing spaces (the construction of buildings, town planning, the creation of tourist resorts, etc.) and the political economy of space. Rather than the oppositions of concrete material space or imagined mental space, Lefebvre outlines a theory of *l'espace vécu*, space as lived and experienced through the people who created, control, and live in it. Lefebvre's work moves beyond this initial position, however, demonstrating how understandings of space are historical and related to philosophical understandings. Against the predominantly historical emphasis of much Marxism, with a tendency to concentrate on the temporal, Lefebvre provides a valuable counterbalance.

Lefebvre's wide-ranging interests were not confined to everyday life, the urban and the rural and the question of space, for which he is best known today. Lefebvre wrote almost seventy books in his long career, ranging from scholarly discussions of figures in French literature (*Diderot*, 1949; *Rabelais*, 1955) and German thought (*Nietzsche*, 1939; *Marx*, 1964) through critiques of other trends in thought (*L'existentialisme*, 1946; *Au-delà du structuralisme*, 1971) to polemics against fascism (*Hitler au pouvoir*, 1938), and the bestseller of the *Que sais-je?* series (*Le marxisme*, 1948). Lefebvre outlined his most substantial philosophical vision in *Métaphilosophie* (1965), a complicated and multifaceted work. His vision of metaphilosophy seeks to go beyond or overcome (*dépasser*) philosophy. It seeks to bring a range of philosophies together, to relate them to the world and subject them to a radical critique and project them toward the future.

Nor should Lefebvre be looked at as a theorist of space alone. In works such as *Le somme et la reste* (1959), *La fin de l'histoire* (1970), and *Éléments de rythmanalyse* (1992) and later volumes of *Critique de la vie quotidienne*, he provides a number of insights into the question of time. Issues such as the moment, the linearity and purpose of history and the rhythms of the body and everyday life are discussed in ways that complement his work on space. It also trades on his long-standing interest in music.

Politically, Lefebvre was constantly engaged. His early career was within the French communist party, for which he briefly played the role of party intellectual. The polemics directed against Sartre in the 1940s were largely politically motivated, for example. Lefebvre left the party in 1958 in the aftermath of Khrushchev's denunciation of Stalin, but the difficulties between him and the party were apparent earlier, notably over the Lysenko affair and Zhdanorism. Lefebvre's principal political writing is the four-volume *De l'état* (1976–1978), in which he gives a historical overview of Marxist theories of the state, discusses the role of the state in the modern world, outlines a theory of the statist mode of production, and analyzes the relation between the state and society. Central among its themes is the analysis of the shift from nation-state to a world scale (*mondialisation*), with the extraction of surplus value not just from one class, but from one country to another. Here, earlier concerns such as alienation and the production of space are given more explicitly political readings. Equally, the notion of *autogestion*, a term usually translated as "self-management," but that has a sense of being "workers' control," is outlined as a possibility for radical democracy, with a move beyond mere representation, without a state focus, and with the return of power to local communities.

Lefebvre's interests thus range widely through sociology, philosophy, politics, and literary studies. In the Anglophone world, recent interest in his work has appeared in urban studies and geography. His writing style does not immediately endear him to readers, but the range of his ideas and their applicability beyond the constraints of their immediate context make likely a continued interest in his work.

STUART ELDEN

See also **Louis Althusser; Jean-Paul Sartre**

Biography

Henri Lefebvre was born in the Pyrenees in 1901 and was educated at the Sorbonne. In the early 1920s he was a member of a small group of left-wing students who founded the journal *Philosophies*, in which he published his first articles. Lefebvre associated with the Surrealists, drove a cab in Paris, and was involved in the Resistance. Although he taught in both lycées and Universities such as Nanterre and Strasbourg, he remained somewhat outside of the academic mainstream. His involvement with the Parti Communiste Français lasted from 1928 to 1958, and after leaving, he associated with Situationists, Maoists, and other leftist groups. Numbering Daniel Cohn-Bendit and Jean Baudrillard among his students, he had a profound effect on the events of May 1968, on which he wrote an important study. Writing until his death in 1991, Lefebvre produced almost seventy books and numerous articles.

Selected Works

With Norbert Guterman, *Morceaux choisis de Karl Marx* 1934
With Norbert Guterman, *La conscience mystifiée*, 1936
Hitler au pouvoir, 1938
La materialisme dialectique, 1939; as *Dialectical Materialism*, translated by John Sturrock, 1968
Nietzsche, 1939
L'existentialisme, 1946
Critique de la vie quotidienne, 3 volumes, 1947, 2nd ed., 1958, 1961, 1981; as *Critique of Everyday Life*, translated by John Moore, 1991, 2002, 2003
Le marxisme, 1948
Diderot, 1949
Rabelais, 1955
La somme et le reste, 1959
La vallée de Campan, 1963
Marx, 1964
Métaphilosophie: Prolégomènes, 1965
Pyrénées, 1965

Le droit à la ville, 1968; as *Right to the City*, translated by Eleonore Kofman and Elizabeth Lebas, in *Writings on Cities*, 1996
L'irruption, de Nanterre au sommet, 1968; as *The Explosion: Marxism and the French Upheaval*, translated by Alfred Ehrenfeld, 1969
Du rural à l'urbain, 1970
La fin de l'histoire: Épilégomènes, 1970
La révolution urbaine, 1970, as *The Urban Revolution*, translated by Robert Bononno, 2003
Au-dela du structuralisme, 1971
La pensée marxiste et la ville, 1972
La survie du capitalisme, 1973; excerpts as *The Survival of Capitalism*, translated by Frank Bryant, 1976
Espace et politique, 1973
La production de l'espace, 1974; as *The Production of Space*, translated by Donald Nicolson-Smith, 1991
Hegel, Marx, Nietzsche ou le royamme des ombres, 1975
De l'État, Four Volumes, 1976–1978
Le retour de la dialectique: 12 mots clefs, 1986
Éléments de rythmanalyse: Introduction à la connaissance de rythmes, 1992 as *Rhythmanalysis*, translated by Stuart Elden and Gerald Moore, 2004
Key Writings, 2003

Further Reading

Brenner, Neil, "Global, Fragmented, Hierarchical: Henri Lefebvre's Geographies of Globalisation," *Public Culture* 10 (1997): 135–167
Brenner, Neil, "The Urban Question as a Scale Question: Reflections on Henri Lefebvre, Urban Theory and the Politics of Scale," *International Journal of Urban and Regional Research* 24 (2000): 360–377
Brenner, Neil, and Elden, Stuart, "Special Issue: Henri Lefebvre in Contexts," *Antipode* 33 (2001): 763–825
Burkhard, Bud, *French Marxism between the Wars: Henri Lefebvre and the "Philosophies,"* Atlantic Highlands: Humanity Books, 2000
Elden, Stuart, "Between Marx and Heidegger: The Political and Philosophical Situation of Henri Lefebvre," *Antipode* 36 (forthcoming)
Elden, Stuart *Understanding Henri Lefebvre: Theory and the Possible* London: Continuum, 2004
Harvey, David, *Social Justice and the City*, Oxford: Basil Blackwell, 1973
Hess, Rémi, *Henri Lefebvre et l'aventure du siècle*, Paris: A. M. Métailié, 1988
Kelly, Michael, *Modern French Marxism*, Oxford: Basil Blackwell, 1982
Kofman, Eleonore, and Lebas, Elizabeth, "Lost in Transposition—Time, Space and the City." In Henri Lefebvre, *Writings on Cities*, Oxford: Blackwell, 1996: 3–60
Martins, Mario Rui, "The theory of social space in the work of Henri Lefebvre," in Ray Forrest, Jeff Henderson, and Peter Williams (eds.), *Urban political economy and social theory*, Aldershot: Gower, 1982
Maycroft, Neil, "Marxism and Everyday Life," *Studies in Marxism* 3 (1996): 71–91
Merrifield, Andy, "Henri Lefebvre: a socialist in space," in Mike Crang and Nigel Thrift (eds.), *Thinking Space*, New York: Routledge, 2000
Poster, Mark, *Existential Marxism in Postwar France: From Sartre to Althusser*, Princeton, New Jersey: Princeton University Press, 1975

Shields, Rob, *Lefebvre, Love & Struggle: Spatial Dialectics*, London: Routledge, 1999

Soja, Edward W., *Postmodern Geographies*, London: Verso, 1989

Soja, Edward W., *Thirdspace: Journeys to Los Angeles and Other Real-and-Imagined Places*, Blackwell: Oxford, 1996

LEFORT, CLAUDE
Political Philosopher

Throughout his long, distinguished career, not only has Claude Lefort convincingly argued for a revival of political philosophy, but his writings have served as an exemplar of how to conduct political philosophy itself. His analyses of the great political events of his day have been informed by the great works of philosophy both past and present, whereas his more philosophical work has been informed by the lessons of contemporary political events. From his youth as a Trotskyite to his cofounding with Castoriadis of the review *Socialisme ou Barbarie*, to his debates with Sartre in *Les Temps Modernes*, to the problems associated with the liberation of Eastern Europe, Lefort has not shied away from political events. However, Lefort has tried to dig beneath the ideologies of his day, and "clear a *passage* within the agitated world of passions" to understand the political.

The subject of political philosophy is the political (*le politique*) itself, as opposed to politics (*la politique*) or political activity, which is the focus of political science. Political philosophers should study how societies are ordered, or "the constitution of the social space, of the form of society, of what was once termed the 'city.'"

Lefort's writings can be viewed as a phenomenology of the political space and how it is represented. A society, to create a sense of unity, seeks to represent itself to itself and others in a unified fashion. The representation and the power of a society is staged (*mise en scène*) in different ways through different ideologies and different institutions, but this unified representation will never adequately represent all aspects of society. Thus, there is a fundamental conflict in the polis, between the society and its representation.

In describing the events of May 1968, Lefort finds a second type of "fundamental conflict" in society, between different groups and their interests. This conflict was more fundamental than the class divisions of Marx's philosophy: It was ubiquitous, against "oppressors" at all levels of society. Lefort finds a similar sentiment in Machiavelli's writings, especially Book IX of *The Prince*, and becomes convinced that conflict between nobles and people is not because of means of production but, rather, because of original desires or humors, and these conflicts will not dissolve in some communist utopia, they will always exist. In fact, Lefort sees the absence of struggle as one of the hallmarks of a totalitarian regime.

Lefort was one of the first left-wing intellectuals to criticize the Soviet regime as totalitarian. Totalitarianism, in his view, is characterized by its attempt to efface all social divisions. To do so, the regime must permeate all of society, and in a communist state the facilitator of the regime's power is the party. However, the party will never be able to control all aspects of society; the discretion of the bureaucrat will always remain. Further, those who oppose the state or party can never be completely eliminated. On the one hand, these dissidents play a positive role for the party because they will be branded as enemies of the people or Other, and this distinction between an "us" and a "them" will further unify the people. However, the continued existence of dissidents betrays the illusion that the representation of power coincides with the society itself.

Democracy, on the other hand, according to Lefort, best represents the original conflicts found in society. In one of his most famous formulations, he characterizes democracy as a form of government where power is an empty place. The political is not embodied in an individual, institution, party, or even the people themselves. In addition, the modern liberal state is one that no longer relies on any type of transcendental for its legitimacy. Instead, democracy is based on an endless struggle or debate; even the founding principles of liberalism, reason, the state of nature, and inalienable rights are fair game in this debate. Thus, democracy is based on uncertainty. "In my view the important point is that democracy is instituted and sustained by the dissolution of the markers of certainty. It inaugurates a history in which people experience a fundamental indeterminacy as to the basis of power, law, and knowledge, and as to the basis of relations between self and other, at every level of social life." Without any ultimate source of legitimacy, all "that remains is the legitimacy of debate or a conflict between separate interests."

Not only does democracy risk falling into a government based on self-interest, it also creates so much uncertainty that it makes totalitarianism enticing. Individuals will desire a transcendent foundation to reinforce their sense of community; thus, democracy is not merely the opposite of totalitarianism, it is a breeding ground for totalitarianism with its unifying themes. Totalitarianism fills a gap created by democracy and is very seductive because it is based on the representation of the "People as One." Oftentimes the place of power will be embodied in the person of the egocrat (Solzhenitsyn's term), just as under the *Ancien Regime* the power was embodied in the king.

What can serve as a check on this nascent totalitarianism that may be found within democracy itself? For Lefort a strong conception of human rights buffers the tyranny of the regime. Against Marx, who claimed that liberal political and civil rights serve merely to obfuscate property relations that bourgeois society requires, Lefort argues that the freedom of opinion, movement, and assembly allow for social interaction, or the expression of various interests. Thus, "a symbolic space comes into being, without definite frontiers and outside of political authority." Lefort notes that the Communist regimes of Eastern Europe were not so much against the ideas of the dissidents but tried to find a place for discourse.

Lefort also breaks with Marx's conception of ideology. For Lefort, ideology refers to the ways that modern societies attempt to represent themselves and attempt to cover up all social divisions without reference to any transcendental or other world. However, ideologies are precarious: There is always the possibility that they will be seen for what they are, symbolic discourse, and not the real. Bourgeois ideology, for example, attempts to anchor itself in terms such as humanity, science, or nation, but these terms only mask the fact that there is no point of certainty in bourgeois society. Lefort argues that bourgeois ideology and totalitarian ideology have recently been replaced by an invisible ideology that seeks to unify society through homogenization. Social divisions are masked by the intimacy of the mass media and through the creation of a unified consumer society, where all objects are reduced to being objects of consumption by any consumer.

Unlike Marx, Lefort does not find an underlying social reality beneath the predominant ideologies that can be discovered scientifically and reconciled with themselves. It is the duty of the political theorist to continuously descend into the cave and "and to explore it patiently" all the while knowing that "under the cavern there is another one, then still another."

WILLIAM PAUL SIMMONS

See also **Cornelius Castoriadis**

Biography

Lefort was born in Paris in 1924. He was a professor at the University of Nancy and then moved to the University of Caen. In 1964, he cofounded *Socialisme ou Barbarie* with Cornelius Castoriadis. He was formerly a researcher at the Centre National de la Recherche Scientifique and a professor at the University of São Paolo in Brazil, at the Sorbonne. At present, Claude Lefort is the Director of Studies (Emeritus) at the Ecole des Hautes Etudes en Sciences Sociales.

Selected Works

With Jean-Marc Coudray and Edgar Morin, *Mai 1968: la brèche*, 1968
Éléments d'une critique de la bureaucratie, 1971
Le Travail do l'œuvre: Machiavel, 1972
Sur une colonne absente. Écrits autour de Merleau-Ponty, 1978
Les Formes de l'histoire: essays d'anthropologie politique, 1978
L'Invention démocratique: les limites de la dominationtotalitaire, 1981
The Political Forms of Modern Society: Bureaucracy, Democracy, Totalitarianism, 1986
Essais sur la politique: XIXe–XXe siècles, 1986; as *Democracy and Political Theory*, translated by David Macey, 1988
Écrire: A l'épreuve du politique, translated by David Ames Curtis, 2000
"Human Rights Today" in *Human Rights and Chinese Values: Legal, Philosophical and Political Perspectives*, edited by Michael C. Davis, 1995
La complication: Retour sur le communisme, 1999

Further Reading

Caillé, Alain, "Claude Lefort, The Social Sciences and Political Philosophy," *Thesis Eleven*, 43 (1995):48–65
Dallmayr, Fred, "Postmetaphysics and Democracy," *Political Theory* 21 (February 1993): 101–127
Howard, Dick, *The Marxian Legacy*, Minneapolis: University of Minnesota Press, 1988
Marchart, Oliver, "Division and Democracy: On Claude Lefort's Post-foundational Political Philosophy," *Filozofski vestnik*, 21,2 (2000): 51–82
McKinlay, Patrick F., "Postmodernism and Democracy: Learning from Lyotard and Lefort," *The Journal of Politics* 60,2 (May 1998): 481–502
Poltier, Hugues, *Passion du politique. La pensée de Claude Lefort*, Geneva: Labor et Fides, 1998
Thompson, John B., *Studies in the Theory of Ideology*, Berkeley: University of California Press, 1984

LEIRIS, MICHEL
Poet, Autobiographer, Ethnographer, and Art Critic

Michel Leiris has contributed amply to twentieth-century French intellectual life. For Leiris, poetry is inseparable from revolution and authentic truth. Until 1939 and the publication of *L'Âge d'homme*, Leiris is seen as a poet who became an ethnographer. During the war, with the publication of some chapters of the first volume of *La Règle du Jeu* (1948–1976), Leiris became recognized as one of the most interesting writers of his generation. In 1929, Leiris interrupted his diary during his psychoanalysis and started to write *L'Âge d'homme* (1939). In this first autobiographical text, Leiris reveals himself, using a subversive mythologic staging of himself. Leiris seduces his reader, who becomes an accomplice in his sexual revelations. In

"De la littérature considérée comme une tauromachie," added to the reedition of *L'Âge d'homme*, he explains his intention to introduce danger in literature, and in a way, he answers Sartre and his notion of "littérature engagée." The greater the danger, the better the performance. Literature becomes an act in which the writer engages himself; the danger does not come only from the revelation, but from the difficulty in following the rule of authenticity (to tell the truth and to tell everything).

This rule of authenticity that Leiris imposes on himself presides over his future works (the four volumes of *La Règle du Jeu* [1948–1976]); Leiris never questioned the rule and never stopped writing obsessively about himself, exploring different forms of self revelation in the process of writing. The project of telling the truth slides toward the idea that truth appears in the process of writing, in interrogating the language itself, in changing the form of the writing, and in letting the words take the initiative. Leiris, hoping for the exactitude at the moment of remembrance, uses a data file, applying to literature the method of the ethnographer and the sociologist, but the content of the card index comes from memories.

After *La Règle du Jeu*, Leiris added three more books to his autobiography: *Le Ruban au cou d'Olympia*, *Langage tangage ou ce que les mots me disent*, and *A cor et à cri*. As the last two titles show, Leiris exploited language more and more consciously, as he did when he wrote his surrealist poems and especially *Glossaire, j'y serre mes gloses*, his own personal and subversive dictionary. This demonstrates the difficulty of drawing a line between autobiography and the other genres used by Leiris. His works were influenced by the sciences that developed during the century and are a demonstration that the self is expressed in all genres. Perhaps his works are, in fact, proof that in the twentieth century, the notion of literary genre became obsolete.

While doing archival work for the Mission Dakar-Djibouti (1931–1933), and with *L'Afrique fantôme* (1934), his diary of this trip, Leiris mixes ethnographic study and autobiographical writing. Claiming that with a maximum of subjectivity one can reach objectivity, he dared to bring the point of view of the observer into the scientific field. In 1945, Leiris accepted an official mission to the Ivory Coast and the British Gold Coast. This trip allowed him to express more clearly his anti-colonialism. He continued this critical thinking through January 1948, when he resided in Blida, Algeria, to discuss the responsibility of the writer and the artist in the debate on colonization. In 1948, Césaire asked Leiris to contribute his experience of ethnographer to help him formulate and uphold his concept of *négritude*.

From these trips and studies an important conference emerged. "L'Ethnographe devant le colonialisme" was presented by Leiris on March 7, 1950, at the Association of Scientific Workers. In the text, intended for students of ethnography, Leiris criticized the methods of ethnography he himself used during his first missions and advocated a more humanistic approach in which the ethnographer would be the spokesperson of colonized societies. The ethnographer should also help colonized people to know their own culture and identity. In *Race et civilisation* (1955), using both sciences and human sciences, he demonstrated that racial prejudice has a cultural origin and is a value judgment without an objective foundation. After his second trip to the Caribbean, he gathered his conclusions in an important book, *Contacts de civilisations en Martinique et en Guadeloupe* (1951), still considered a reference on Caribbean studies. In 1958, Leiris published *La Possession et ses aspects théâtraux chez les Ethiopiens de Gondar*, in which he demonstrated that theater and possession use the same founding process: In both cases, human beings are changed into something other than what they are originally. From this process, truth can emerge.

In the 1960s, he concentrated his work on African art, claiming that the objects brought from Africa or studied there should be considered as works of art.

Leiris always lived in close contact with artists and wrote numerous articles and monographs on twentieth-century artists, including Marcel Duchamp, Joan Miró, Elie Lascaux, and Henri Laurens. He wrote extensively on his artist friends Masson, Picasso, and Giacometti and, later in his life, on Francis Bacon. For Leiris, authenticity should also be at the center of the art object. In an article on the painting of Bacon, he explained that to be true or authentic, the work of an artist has to take as its subject current events or trends to give to the artistic creation "a shock value comparable to that of a singular event that concerns us" (*Au verso des images* [1980] 27–28). Similar to Picasso, who was also attracted by ethnology and realism, he was fascinated with the bullfight and Spain.

From 1946, he developed a love for opera. In 1956, he conceived of a book on opera: His 210 note cards were published after his death in a volume entitled *Operratiques*. Leiris selected some of his essays on literature and art and published them in a volume called *Brisées* (1966). This volume is a reflection of how Leiris lived in his time and how he was in close contact with all twentieth-century expressions and forms of modernity.

Michel Leiris became a member of the Communist Party in 1927. Convinced that he could not be a political militant, he left the party after a few months, in

1928, but remained a leftist, committed to the idea of the necessity of a revolutionary party.

In the journal *La Bête noire*, he spoke out against fascism and condemned the invasion of Ethiopia in 1935. At the beginning of World War II, Leiris was sent to sub-Saharan Africa. When he returned to Paris, he lent his support to the resistance group of the Musée de l'Homme and he wrote for the journal *Messages* founded by Jean Lescure, who also founded the Éditions de Minuit. As for Sartre, literature, for Leiris, is an act of resistance; in 1944 he cooperated in *Les Temps Modernes*. Leiris lent his support to Sartre against Camus when *L'Homme révolté* was published.

Leiris and Sartre were both anticolonialist and interested in writers associated with *négritude*, such as Aimé Césaire and Senghor. In 1956, he became a member of the antiracist movement, the MRAP, and in 1960 he signed, with 121 others, the Declaration on the Right to Insubordination during the Algerian war. Until 1969 he never stopped taking anticolonialist or antiracist positions in demonstrations or in conferences.

Leiris stayed in contact with all the leftist movements supporting the Cuban revolution, the antiwar movement in Vietnam, and the movement for equal rights for African Americans in the United States. He showed his support for the movement of May 1968 and continued to raise his voice against intolerance, injustice, and censorship until his death in 1990.

CATHERINE MASSON

See also **Maurice Blanchot; Aime Césaire; Leopold Senghor; Jean-Paul Sartre**

Biography

Michel Leiris was born in Paris on April 20, 1901, into a bourgeois Catholic family. In 1920, he recognized his vocation to be a writer. In 1923, Leiris wrote his first poem "Désert de mains" and published it in the journal *Intentions* in 1924. He joined the Surrealists in 1924. In disagreement with some of Breton's opinions, he ended his relationship with the surrealists in 1929. The same year he contributed articles to the journal *Documents*. In 1937 Leiris participated in the foundation of the Collège de Sociologie with Bataille and Caillois and presented in January 1938 a conference entitled "Le sacré dans la vie quotidienne" (The sacred in everyday life). The same year, he finished his diploma in ethnography from l'Ecole pratique des Hautes Études, defending his thesis *La Langue secrète des Dogons de Sanga*. He became a member of the Collège de pataphysique in 1955. He died on September 30, 1990.

Selected Works

L'Afrique fantôme, Paris, Gallimard, 1934 (reprinted 1951, 1968, 1981, 1988, 1996)
Miroir de la tauromachie, 1938
L'Âge d'homme, 1939; reprinted preceded by "De la littérature considérée comme une tauromachie," 1946, 1973
Haut mal, 1943
With Georges Limbour, *André Masson et son univers*, 1947
La Règle du jeu:
I. *Biffures*, 1948, 1991
II. *Fourbis*, 1955, 1991
III. *Fibrilles*. 1966, 1992
IV. *Frêle bruit*, 1976, 1992
La Langue secrète des Dogons de Sanga, 1948; reprinted, 1992
Contacts de civilisations en Martinique et en Guadeloupe, 1951
Race et civilisation, 1955, 1987, 1996
La Possession et ses aspects théâtraux chez les Éthiopiens de Gondar, 1958
Nuits sans nuit et quelques jours sans jour, 1961
Glossaire, J'y serre mes gloses in *Mots sans mémoire*, 1969
Brisées, 1966; reprinted, 1992
Mots sans mémoire, 1969
Au verso des images, 1980
Le Ruban au cou d'Olympia, 1981
Langage tangage ou ce queles mots me disent, 1985
A con et à chi, 1988
Pierres pour un Alberto Giacometti, 1991
Journal 1922–1989, edited by Jean Jamin, 1992
Operratiques, 1992
Francis Bacon ou la brutalité du fait, 1996

Further Readings

Armel, Aliette, *Michel Leiris*, Paris: Fayard, 1997
Hand, Sean, *Michel Leiris, Writing the Self*, Cambridge: Cambridge University Press, 2003
Kleiber, Pierre-Henri, *Glossaire. J'y serre mes gloses de Michel Leiris et la question du langage*, Paris: L'Harmattan, 1999
Lejeune, Philippe, *Lire Leiris. Autobiographie et langage*, Paris: Klincksieck, 1975
Masson, Catherine, *L'autobiographie et ses aspects théâtraux chez Michel Leiris*, Paris: L'Harmattan, 1995
Maubon, Catherine, *Michel Leiris: en marge de l'autobiographie*, Paris: Corti, 1994
Poitry, Guy, *Michel Leiris: dualisme et totalité*, Toulouse: Presses Universitaires du Mirail, 1995
Sermet, Joelle de, *Michel Leiris, poète surréaliste*, Paris: Presses Universitaires de France, 1997
Simon, Roland, *Orphée Médusé, Autobiographies de Michel Leiris*, Lausanne: L'Age d'homme, 1984
Yvert, Louis, *Bibliographie des écrits de Michel Leiris: 1924–95*, Paris: Jean-Michel Place, 1996

LEVINAS, EMMANUEL
Philosopher of Ethics

Emmanuel Levinas was probably the most influential and widely respected ethical thinker in France in the second half of the twentieth century. His early philosophical work was devoted to phenomenology. He collaborated on the first translation of Husserl's *Cartesian*

Meditations (1931), in 1930 he published the first full-length book in French on Husserl's thought, and in 1932 he published the first substantial article on Heidegger. Through the 1930s and 1940s, however, his dissatisfaction with his phenomenological forebears became increasingly apparent. In particular, he was troubled by what he regarded as the ethical shortcomings of phenomenology. He began to elaborate an anti-universalist, antifoundationalist, nonprescriptive ethics deriving from respect and responsibility for the Other. In postwar France, the dominance in intellectual circles of Marxism, structuralism, and early poststructuralism created an unfavorable climate for ethics. However, the interest of thinkers such as Blanchot (a friend from student days) and Derrida (who published the first substantial essay on Levinas in 1964) ensured that Levinas's importance as a philosopher was recognized even though ethics was out of fashion; and when, from the late 1970s onwards, poststructuralists attempted to counter the charge of irresponsibility by focusing more on ethical and political issues, they found in Levinas's work an ethics that shared their aspiration to break from some of the most deep-seated assumptions of the philosophical tradition. By the end of his life, Levinas had acquired the status of a landmark figure, and his two philosophical masterpieces, *Totalité et infini* (Totality and Infinity, 1961) and *Autrement qu'être ou au-delà de l'essence* (Otherwise than Being or Beyond Essence, 1974), are widely recognized as being amongst the most important works of philosophy written in French since the war.

Totalité et infini, first published in 1961, brought together the ideas that Levinas had been developing since the Second World War, and it formulated the terms and views for which he remains best known. The starting point of his philosophical trajectory lies in the apparently simple but powerful and far-reaching critique of Western philosophy as the history of the suppression of the Other (any idea, person or race that does not fit in with the dominant patterns of thought) by the Same (Being, essence, or the unity of Spirit): "Western philosophy coincides with the unveiling of the Other in which the Other, by manifesting itself as a being, loses its alterity. Philosophy is afflicted, from its childhood, by a horror of the Other which remains Other, an insurmountable allergy" (*En découvrant l'existence avec Husserl et Heidegger*, 1949, 188). Levinas would spend the rest of his career exploring this insight. The Other would become the key term of his thought and, indeed, of postwar French thought in general. The fundamental move of Western philosophy, Levinas suggests, is to make the Other an object of knowledge, something to be comprehended; the purpose of this is to reduce its strangeness, its constitutive alterity, and in the process to master the world by making it a knowable, controllable space of Sameness. Levinas's endeavor will be to think of the Other as Other, to preserve it in all its irreducibility to my own knowledge or powers. This Other is preeminently human, though in an important strand of his work Levinas also writes about the divine Other that eludes all knowledge and theology. The respect for alterity entails the attempt not to take the self, and its own restricted perspective, as the key to understanding everything that lies outside it.

Thus, the concern to preserve alterity is the basic issue of Levinasian ethics. Levinas's version of ethics is concerned neither with classic ethical questions regarding virtue, duties, or rights, nor with the formulation of moral principles, rules, or codes. Rather, Levinas focuses on the ethical significance of the encounter with the Other; that is, with an alterity that cannot be understood as a mere extension or reflection of myself, and that therefore also radically challenges both who I am and what I think. Through this encounter, I discover that I am not alone, that the universe is not subordinate to my needs and desires. The Other escapes me, and it confronts me with the unwelcome revelation that the world does not belong to me at all. Levinas uses perhaps one of his best-known terms, the face (*le visage*), to refer to the initial shock of this discovery of alterity. The face is a point of mediation between the real, living presence of another person and the transcendence of the Other, the fact that he or she is not a simple reflection of myself and does not belong to my world. In Levinas's writing, alterity is particularly associated with the feminine, which prompted the accusation by Simone de Beauvoir and others that Levinas was implicitly adopting a masculine perspective. Although some have sought to defend him by insisting that "feminine" should be understood metaphorically, Beauvoir's point is well made, and in his later writing, Levinas tended to avoid the implication that alterity is in any sense gendered.

The revelation of alterity is the key moment in Levinas's ethics. Levinas describes how the subject emerges out of the morass of what he calls the *il y a* (there is): brute anonymous existence before individual consciousness. The subject tears itself from the *il y a*, evading its chaotic senselessness to acquire a sense of individual existence, but this does not yet give it any ethical status. Without the presence of the Other, the world is my possession, I am at home in it, it responds to my needs. The Other shows me that I am not after all at home, that the very condition of my existence is that the world is shared with the non-me, that it is also inhabited by a radically alien presence that I can neither possess nor understand. It is easy to see that this revelation might be greeted with violence. The Other escapes my powers, but I can attempt to reassert my sovereignty by attempting to destroy it. "Murder," Levinas writes, "exerts a power over that which escapes power. . . . The Other is the only being that I can want to kill" (*Totalité et infini*, 1961, 216). I have no need to kill other beings because I can assimilate them in other ways—for example, by exercising my intellectual or physical superiority—but the Other is by nature recalcitrant to such assimilation. So the encounter with the face of the Other may provoke a violent response, I may attempt to master alterity by destroying it. Murder is, Levinas insists, simple and banal, "that most banal incident in human history" (*Totalité et infini*, 1961, 217); it corresponds to the desire of the subject to remain sovereign over a compliant world. However, murder, for Levinas, also inevitably fails to achieve its object. The face of the Other is infinitely vulnerable, it has no physical power over me, but neither can I destroy it by the exercise of my own physical power. This is because the face, in Levinas's sense of the term, is not simply a physical part of the body of another person, it is also a revelation of transcendence. It brings the irreversible realization that the world is not entirely my own. Levinas insists that, although violence is always possible, the face remains inviolable: "Neither the destruction of things, nor the chase, nor the extermination of living beings, can affect the face, which does not belong to this world" (*Totalité et infini*, 1961, 216). The reference to *extermination* here doubtless alludes to the extermination camps that haunt Levinas's thought although being only rarely explicitly mentioned in his writing. Levinas suggests that genocide can be understood as a violent attempt to suppress the Other, but it is a response which is doomed to failure. Killing other people may be a simple and banal event, but the Other cannot be killed because, as by definition it does not belong to my world, it escapes any power I might attempt to exercise over it. The Other opposes me with a resistance that cannot be measured in quantitative terms; this is what Levinas calls "the resistance of what has no resistance," and more precisely, "ethical resistance (*la résistance éthique*)" (*Totalité et infini*, 1961, 217). In a typically Levinasian paradox, although being infinitely weak, the Other is also infinitely strong; my acts of violence toward it will always fail because the face of the Other transcends my world. It may be little comfort to the actual victims of violence to know that the Other remains unharmed while they are suffering, but it is not Levinas's purpose to bring comfort. Rather, he is demonstrating the futility of violence by insisting that it can never achieve its true end: the eradication of the Other.

Levinas acknowledges that violence, warfare, or genocide are potential and indeed real responses to the encounter between self and Other, but violence entails a misunderstanding of the true significance of the encounter, which involves the discovery of the irreducible reality of the Other and, hence, the obligation to achieve a peaceful, or what Levinas call "nonallergic," coexistence with it (*Totalité et infini*, 1961, 218). This revelation of alterity serves as a fundamental moment through which the ethical subject comes into existence, and the various ramifications of Levinas's thought into areas such as language, communication, justice, society, religion, and sexuality can all be traced back to the concerted endeavor to preserve and respect the irreducible alterity of the Other. In his account of sexual desire, for example, Levinas breaks from the Platonic and Romantic tradition of erotic discourse, which envisages the desired person as a complement of the self, a missing part of one's own being. For Levinas desire, as distinct from need, is something that cannot be assuaged: It is provoked and sustained by the otherness of the Other rather than seeking to overcome it. The lover does not want fusion or oneness with the sexual partner but, rather, respects his or her alterity. Ethics is thus as much in play in erotic relations as it is in warfare. It does not consist of a set of rules or principles; it is rather the strenuous attempt to inhabit the space of alterity, to cohabit with the Other without diminishing its otherness.

In discussing the ethical encounter between self and Other, Levinas risks speaking of it as if it were an actual event that might occur within the biography of an individual. There is a clear potential for misunderstanding here. For Levinas, the encounter is not an empirical occurrence that may or may not happen and that takes place in chronological time; neither is there a "self" that exists before the encounter, and who might avoid the challenge posed by the discovery of alterity altogether. Rather, the encounter is an essential, originary moment through which the self comes into being. Using the terms that, with Derrida, following Heidegger, have come to form a central paradox of Continental thinking, the encounter has *always already* taken place. The self is constituted as self only as it also discovers the Other, and the encounter is not something that can be chosen or refused: It precedes freedom and determinism, action and passivity.

One of the crucial aspects of Levinas's philosophical endeavor is his interrogation of the language in which his enquiry is conducted. Levinas is aware that he must be vigilant if he is to counteract some of the implications of his own philosophical vocabulary. For Levinas, the language of philosophy is bound up with the privileging of Sameness that characterizes Western thought. It uses terms and concepts that identify, classify, and thus eliminate alterity. As the Other becomes an object of discourse and philosophical investigation, it is made to fit into the available patterns of language and thought. Even naming the Other entails violence against it. Levinas objects to theology on similar grounds: Theology constantly runs the risk of destroying the God it seeks to understand simply by talking about it. However, this inevitably puts Levinas in a difficult, perhaps insurmountable, position. His own philosophical terminology constantly risks reducing alterity to Sameness and thereby reproducing the very crime of which he accuses the philosophical tradition. Levinas's attempt to negotiate this problem, as he endeavors to write about the Other without making it an object of knowledge, gives rise to much of the difficulty that many readers encounter in his work. He strains to keep language flexible, open to strangeness; his terms are constantly changing, as they are redefined, adapted, or discarded. At all costs, he must resist a reification of his thought that would inevitably entail a violence against his overriding subject, the inassimilable Other.

One of the consequences of this is Levinas's intense self-consciousness toward his own textual performance. The strangeness, the openness to unexpected experiences and meanings, must seep into the philosophical text itself; it must be part of the experience of reading philosophy. As much as Levinas's writing attempts to describe and to account for the encounter with alterity, it also attempts to reproduce the shock of that encounter. Reading Levinas should thus also become an experience of something alien and unknown. For readers and commentators, this can be the source both of the fascination and the irritation of Levinas's writing. His texts tease by suggesting, but never achieving, a stable theoretical lens through which to view the Other. In a preface written originally for the German edition of *Totalité et infini*, Levinas acknowledged that his book remained tied to the language and patterns of thought that his own ethics of alterity was attempting to leave behind. His second major work, *Autrement qu'être* (1974), marks his dissatisfaction with his earlier text, a dissatisfaction that was in part a response to a long critique by Jacques Derrida that was first published in 1964. In this later work, the difficulty of the text is intensified. To an even greater extent than in his earlier writing, the very language of philosophy is engaged in a struggle against the philosophical traditions in which it is embedded. A whole new range of terms appear that were largely or entirely absent from *Totalité et infini*: proximity, approach, hostage, persecution, expiation, substitution, illeity, and enigma. Even the key word "Other" plays a less important role, being largely replaced by "the neighbor" (*le prochain*). Through this conceptual bombardment, Levinas displays a reluctance to establish and maintain a rigid theoretical framework. New terms are adopted, and familiar words are used in unfamiliar ways. Even

the typography of the text is bizarre: words are broken up by hyphens, usually to emphasize their etymology, as in "ex-pression" and "re-presentation"; they are partly italicized, as in "trans*parence*"; or neologisms are created, with nouns made by stringing words together with hyphens, such as "antérieur-à-tout-souvenir (prior-to-all-memory)" or "contre-mon-gré-pour-un-autre (despite-me-for-another)." Levinas is both dismantling the lexis and reconstructing it, disrupting his own prose both at the level of individual word and in larger syntactic units. Alterity has permeated the very textual practice of philosophy; it impedes easy comprehension and denies ready access to a firm set of philosophical propositions.

In this, however, Levinas is aware that he is fighting a losing battle against his own language. *Autrement qu'être* is a highly self-reflexive book that entails the ambitious project of disrupting philosophical language to find what might lie at the far side of thought. The title of the book refers to the attempt to exceed being, not to transform this "Otherwise" into a new Being. It rejects the language of ontology but remains aware that it must continue to use it, and it portrays this paradoxical stance as the very condition of a philosophy of transcendence. There can be no simple renunciation of the language and aims of ontology (other than silence or gibberish), as the power of the philosophical *logos* lies in its ability to absorb what interrupts it. Even so, Levinas strains to develop a practice of philosophy that can at least point toward an encounter with otherness beyond the constraints of language. If *Autrement qu'être* is, to say the least, a difficult book, it is in large measure because of its distrust of language that reduces the strangeness of the Other to themes and concepts. Levinas distinguishes between the Saying (*le Dire*) and the Said (*le Dit*). The latter is language reified into themes and information, whereas the former is an originary exposure to the Other that cannot entirely do without the Said, but that is always inevitably betrayed by it. Levinas's practice of philosophy endeavors to become a form of Saying, to respond to alterity without congealing into readily assimilated meanings.

In the light of this, Levinas weaves an intricate textual web in which terms are constantly revisited, renewed, amplified, or transformed. The vocabulary of *Autrement qu'être* mentioned above (hostage, obsession, persecution, substitution, responsibility, and expiation) is used by Levinas to describe the radical openness of the self to alterity, an openness that precedes all choice, decision, or action. I am *persecuted* by the Other, *hostage* to the Other, *accused* by the Other because it takes charge of and constitutes my selfhood before any decision I might have made; my responsibility for the Other is an *obsession* not a choice. Moreover, I am so little a self in the sense of a secure essence or identity, I am to such an extent constituted by the proximity of the Other, that I can be called on at any moment to occupy the position of the Other, to *substitute* for the Other, to *expiate* his or her actions and crimes. This notion of substitution is one of the cornerstones of *Autrement qu'être*, and it lies behind the exorbitant, excessive sense of responsibility for the Other that constantly surfaces in the text. This responsibility is not simply a concern for the Other or a duty of care. Levinas is describing a far more fundamental intermingling of self and Other, and this leads to one of the most radical and shocking moves in Levinas's thought: My responsibility for the Other is also a responsibility for his or her actions; I can expiate them, suffer for them, because they are in a sense my actions. In a footnote, Levinas explains, "My suffering is the focal point of all suffering—of all faults. Even of the fault of my persecutors, which comes down to undergoing the ultimate persecution, undergoing it absolutely" (*Autrement qu'être*, 1974, 186).

The position adopted here is uncompromising: I am even responsible for the crimes that my persecutors commit against me. Later, Levinas will play down some of the implications and possible consequences of formulations such as this, but they are clearly within the logic of his argument that the Other is an essential mystery, something that I cannot know or understand, but that, nevertheless, by its proximity constitutes me as a self. I am bound to it and responsible for it. This is at a far remove from what we might have expected from an ethics. Responsibility is limitless, there is no prospect of ever fulfilling it satisfactorily, the demands on the moral subject are stringent and unmeetable. Ethics offers no guidelines for a moral life, no definitions of virtue or goodness, no prospect of the good life or even of an easy moral conscience. Levinas's ethics have been described as postmodern. If this is fair, his thought belongs to the dark side of postmodernism. It is not the bright, playful celebration of difference and diversity but, rather, the anguished search for moral sense and a role for philosophy in a century of shattered consensus and extreme violence.

COLIN DAVIS

See also **Simone de Beauvoir; Maurice Blanchot; Jacques Derrida**

Biography

Emmanuel Levinas was born in Lithuania in 1906. In 1923 he went to the University of Strasbourg in France and soon began to concentrate on philosophy. He spent the academic year 1928–1929 in Freiburg, Germany, and attended the seminars of Edmund Husserl and Martin Heidegger. He became a French citizen in 1930 and began a teaching career. He was drafted into the French army in 1939, captured by the Germans in 1940, and spent the rest of the war in a prisoner of war camp. Many members of his family were murdered in the war. After the war, he became Director of the Ecole Normale Israélite Orientale and subsequently Professor of Philosophy at the Universities of Poitiers (1964) and Paris-Nanterre (1967) and the Sorbonne (1973). He died in 1995.

Selected Works

Théorie de l'intuition dans la phénoménologie de Husserl (Theory of Intuition in the Phenomenology of Husserl), 1930
De l'existence à l'existant (From Existence to the Existent), 1947
Le Temps et l'autre (Time and the Other), 1947
En découvrant l'existence avec Husserl et Heidegger (Discovering Existence with Husserl and Heidegger), 1949
Totalité et infini: Essai sur l'extériorité (Totality and Infinity: Essay on Exteriority), 1961
Difficile liberté: Essais sur le judaïsme (Difficult Freedom: Essays on Judaism), 1963
Quatre lectures talmudiques (Four Talmudic Readings), 1968
Humanisme de l'autre homme (Humanism of the Other Man), 1972
Autrement qu'être ou au-delà de l'essence (Otherwise than Being or Beyond Essence), 1974
Noms propres (Proper Names), 1976
Du sacré au saint: Cinq nouvelles lectures talmudiques (From the Sacred to the Holy: Five New Talmudic Readings), 1977
De Dieu qui vient à l'idée (Of God who Comes to the Idea), 1982
L'Au-delà du verset: Lectures et discours talmudiques (Beyond the Verse: Talmudic Readings and Discourses), 1982
Ethique et infini (Ethics and Infinity), 1982
Hors sujet (Outside the Subject), 1987
A l'heure des nations (At the Time of Nations) 1988
Entre nous: Essais sur le penser-à-l'autre (Between Ourselves: Essays on the Thinking-to-the-Other), 1991

Further Reading

Bernasconi, Robert, and Critchley, Simon (eds.), *Re-Reading Levinas*, London: The Athlone Press, 1991
Bernasconi, Robert, and Wood, David (eds.) *The Provocation of Levinas: Rethinking the Other*, London: Routledge, 1988
Critchley, Simon, *The Ethics of Deconstruction: Derrida and Levinas*, Oxford: Blackwell, 1992
Davis, Colin, *Levinas: An Introduction*, Cambridge: Polity, 1996
Derrida, Jacques, "Violence et métaphysique: Essai sur la pensée d'Emmanuel Levinas." In *L'Ecriture et la différence*, Paris: Seuil, 1967
Derrida, Jacques, *Adieu à Emmanuel Levinas*, Paris: Galilée, 1997
Husserl, Edmund, *Méditations cartésrennes: Introduction à la phéaoménologie*, translated by Gabrielle Peifer and Emmanuel Levinas, Paris: Vrin, 1986; first edition 1931

LEVI-STRAUSS, CLAUDE
Anthropologist

Claude Lévi-Strauss's theories have been fundamental to the renewal of modern anthropology, in particular the study of kinship systems, totemism, classification, and mythology. Throughout his works, he has sought to understand the functioning of so-called "primitive" modes of thought. In opposition to the theories formulated by influential predecessors such as Lucien Lévy-Bruhl, he has revealed that these "primitive" modes of thought are neither radically different (prelogical, prerational) nor fundamentally more archaic than our own "civilized" ways of thinking. Indeed, Lévi-Strauss is careful to present these "primitive" modes of thought not so much as the attribute of so-called primitive societies, but as an aspect of the way in which all human beings think.

Lévi-Strauss's influence, however, extends beyond anthropology into philosophy, literary criticism, psychoanalysis, and other areas. The dissemination of his ideas, in particular about the representation of historical time and the relationship between primitive ("cold") and Western ("hot") societies, gave rise to a number of debates with French philosophers, among them Jean-Paul Sartre (the last chapter of Lévi-Strauss's La Pensée sauvage [1962], entitled "Histoire et Dialectique," contains a virulent attack on Sartre's Critique de la raison dialectique), Paul Ricœur (see "Structure et herméneutique" in the special "pensée sauvage" issue of the journal Esprit published in November 1963), and Jacques Derrida (see, in particular, "La structure, le signe et le jeu dans le discours des sciences humaines" and "La Violence de la lettre: de Lévi-Strauss à Rousseau"). This dialogue (sometimes conflict) between anthropology and philosophy has played a major part in shaping contemporary French thought.

In the area of literary criticism, it was arguably Lévi-Strauss's influence on Roland Barthes, who in his early works used structuralist ideas to interpret literature, film, and fashion, that did the most for the constitution of a structuralist poetics. When, in 1964, Jacques Lacan gave his first seminar on "The Four Fundamental Concepts of Psycho-Analysis" at the École normale supérieure, one of the first questions that he raised was whether Lèvi-Strauss's notion of a pensèe sauvage could accommodate the unconscious as such (The Four Fundamental Concepts of Psycho-Analysis, 13). Lévi-Strauss himself borrowed and used concepts from many other disciplines (linguistics, mathematics, musicology, biology, and philosophy) and, in this respect, played a key role in demonstrating the value of the kind of interdisciplinary connections that are one of the distinctive features of contemporary French thought.

There is a fundamental ambiguity at the heart of Lévi-Strauss's works that resides in the way in which they combine scientific enquiry and metaphor, reasoning and poetic invention. In early essays, such as "L'Analyse structurale en linguistique et en anthropologie" or "Langage et société" (Anthropologie structurale, 1958), he expresses the ambition to elevate anthropology to a new level of scientificity by importing into anthropology the methodology of structural linguistics. It was this lateral connection between anthropology and structural linguistics that provided Levi-Strauss with the name for his method of anthropological enquiry: "structural anthropology." He forecast that the branch of modern linguistics founded by Ferdinand de Saussure and developed by his successors Roman Jakobson and Nikolai Trubetskoy (probably the three linguists who most influenced Lévi-Strauss) would revolutionize the social sciences in the same way that nuclear physics revolutionized the exact sciences. Part of what motivated Lévi-Strauss to turn to structural linguistics, and more specifically phonology, as a model for anthropology was that linguistics was the first social science to have succeeded in uncovering "necessary relations," normally the prerogative of the exact sciences (Anthropologie structurale, 40). And he thought that it might be possible for anthropology to follow in its wake.

However, it would be wrong to view Levi-Strauss's works in the light of this project alone, however important it may have been in his early works. In practice, it is doubtful whether one can accurately describe Lévi-Strauss's works as an application of the methods of structural linguistics to anthropology (even if this is often how he presents structural anthropology himself). The linguistic model often works more as the means of developing intricate metaphors or analogies—such as the one that he draws between "kinship systems" and "phonological systems" (the former guarantees the "circulation" of women, the latter the "circulation" of words)—that enable him to approach familiar material in an innovative way. Later, in the Mythologiques (1964–1971), his four-volume study of Amerindian mythology, Levi-Strauss was to identify Wagner (not Saussure, Jakobson, or Troubetskoï) as the founding father of the structural analysis of myths. What is his reasoning here?

One of the aims of Lévi-Strauss's structural method (this holds true of the whole of his work on myths, for example) is to show that seemingly different or dissimilar objects of study (let us say, two unrelated myths from two distinct populations) in fact share the same hidden armature or structure. Wagner often used musical motifs—in The Ring, the motif of the renunciation of love, for example—to establish connections between seemingly unrelated episodes in the stories that his operas tell. As Lévi-Strauss explained in an interview given on Canadian radio in 1977 (later published in *Myth and Meaning*, 1978), the musical motif of the renunciation of love first occurs in the *Rhinegold*, when Alberich learns that to conquer the gold he must renounce human love (which he does). However, subsequent uses of this motif do not coincide in any obvious way with events in the narrative that reflect this theme. It recurs in the *Valkyrie*, when, thanks to a sword buried in a tree, Siegmund initiates an incestuous relationship with his sister Sieglinde (here the hero has fallen in love, not renounced love), and it recurs in the *Valkyrie* when Wotan condemns his daughter Brunhilde to a long sleep surrounded by a ring of fire. Lévi-Strauss argues that these episodes share a common structural armature. In each case, "there is a treasure which has to be pulled away . . . from what it is bound to. There is the gold . . . stuck in the depths of the Rhine; there is the sword, which is stuck in a tree . . . there is the woman Brunhilde, who will have to be pulled out of fire" (*Myth and Meaning*, 48). From a structural point of view, Lévi-Strauss continues, "the gold, the sword and Brunhilde are one and the same." Said differently, they are structural variations of one another, and the uncovering of this hidden relationship between these three Wagnerian mythemes (in Lévi-Strauss's terminology, the mythical equivalents of phonemes, the elementary units of signification of myths) provides Lévi-Strauss with a more general key to the significance of Wagner's opera. Wagner uses the musical score in *The Ring* as the means of a structural analysis of the narrative sequences that form the libretto, and this is why Lévi-Strauss refers to Wagner as the father of the structural analysis of myths. In this context, it would appear that structuralism is better described as an application of the methods of operatic composition than of linguistic theory. Lévi-Strauss's many references to music and musicology in his analyses of the structure of myths underline the ambiguities and complexities involved in the structuralist approach to the interpretative act, which here appears more as an Orphic quest for concealed musical forms than the scientific application of an interpretative grid.

Furthermore, in the *Mythologiques*, Lévi-Strauss does not content himself with the role of critic or exegete. The *Mythologiques* is a complex, overdetermined work that, beyond its significance as a treatise on Amerindian mythology, constitutes Lévi-Strauss's attempt to create with mythical images the verbal analogue of a symphony. In this respect, it may be read as a mytho-poetic creation in its own right. Lévi-Strauss has commented on a number of occasions that he would have liked to have been a conductor (something for which, he says, he lacks the right genetic make up), and the *Mythologiques* are, in a sense, his way of fulfilling this childhood dream by other means.

Although his works are steeped in philosophy, Lévi-Strauss's decision to become an anthropologist was tied up, in part at least, with his rejection of philosophy. He studied philosophy (and law) at the Sorbonne in the 1920s and passed the *aggrégation* in 1931, but he abhorred the dialectical exercises that were the staple diet of the philosophy student of the day as well as the solipsistic fascination with the self that he saw as one of the traits of French philosophy. He characterized himself as having a "Neolithic intelligence" (which one may interpret, in part at least, as meaning that he has a propensity to think in metaphors). When he was offered a post as a lecturer in sociology at the University of São Paulo in 1934, he seized on the opportunity to expand his horizons.

In the 1930s, he carried out ethnographic field work in the Matto Grosso region of Brazil, in particular among the Bororo, the Caduveo, and the Nambikwara Indians. He was to give an account of these formative years of his life, as well as of his later escape from Nazi-occupied France to New York, some twenty years after the event in *Tristes tropiques* (1955). This book, his most personal, is at once an ethnographic treatise, a travelogue of sorts (or antitravelogue, as it starts with the sentence "I hate traveling and explorers"), a confession, and a series of meditations on the nature of anthropology, man's" relationship to his environment to history and to time. *Tristes tropiques* is also a profoundly ecological book. It is imbued with a pessimism that is born from the realization that the Amerindian populations that he studied were but the remains of far greater societies that have been all but decimated as a result of the European invasion of the New World. He could easily have echoed Paul Valery's comment, made in the aftermath of World War I, that "we now know that human civilizations are mortal." Western history, for Lévi-Strauss, is made up of a series of wrong turns. He is deeply skeptical of the excessive value that the modern world places on progress and of the event-driven conception of history that underpins the West's conception of time. He sees the inherent conservatism of "primitive" societies as an example of great wisdom. Their relationship to time is determined by their constant effort to minimize the effects of historical change so as to maintain their social institutions in a state of equilibrium. The order that exists in the present is conceived as a projection of an order that has existed since mythical times. One of the great modern ills is what Lévi-Strauss describes as an excess in the levels of communication that exist between populations. As a result, the world we inhabit is slowly establishing a global monoculture that, in the long run, will eradicate the very cultural differences that are the anthropologist's object of study. Travel itself, in any true sense of the term, will no longer be possible.

Lévi-Strauss's first major work, *Les Structures élémentaires de la parenté* (presented as a doctoral thesis in 1948 and first published in 1949), challenged the received wisdom that the nuclear family is the basic building-block of kinship systems. True to one of the fundamental insights of structuralism—namely, that the relationships between things matter more than the thing in itself—Lévi-Strauss argued that the elementary structures of kinship are to be found in the system of marital ties that link horizontally, as it were, one family to the next. For Lévi-Strauss, it is alliance, the system of relationships between families, that is the key to the constitution of kinship systems, not the nuclear family.

Marcel Mauss's influential essay *The Gift* (1925) played a key role in shaping Lévi-Strauss's ideas about kinship. Mauss developed a general theory about the role of gift exchange in human societies on the basis of his study of the Kula ring, a system of ceremonial gift exchanges developed by the Trobriand Islanders (the inhabitants of an archipelago lying off the Southeastern end of New Guinea). Lévi-Strauss proposed that marital alliances between groups took the classic form of a gift exchange relationship and that the gifts in this case were women. Drawing in particular on data from Australia, China, and India, he explained the many different forms of marital alliance as so many solutions to the problem of bringing about and regulating the exchange of women.

He argued that the rule that first set this system of exchange in motion, thereby instituting human society as we know it, was the incest taboo. The incest taboo forces individuals to form marital alliances outside of the immediate family group and hence to create broader social structures, an "international community." By bringing about exogamy ("marrying out"), the incest taboo sets in motion the multiple networks of "communication" that are the basis of human society (the communication of words, of goods and services, and of women). As such, the incest taboo may be viewed as the first social rule and the means by which early humans, living in a state of nature, first created culture (in a later work, Levi-Strauss was to emphasize that he viewed the nature/culture dichotomy more as a useful methodological tool for analyzing systems of representation than as an historically accurate concept).

Lévi-Strauss finally reduces the many different forms of marital alliances observed by anthropologists to three basic kinship structures that are constructed out of two types of exchange, which he terms "generalized" and "restricted."

Lévi-Strauss's reduction of all known forms of alliance to a much simpler system of underlying recurring patterns is characteristic of his structural method. It is a method that aims to go beyond the confusion and diversity of observed phenomena to uncover invariables, the structures that form the "deep grammar" of human society, and if one were to ask where these structures come from, Lévi-Strauss would doubtless answer, "the human mind (*l'esprit*)," by which he would mean the unconscious (although not in a Freudian sense). We are no more aware of the structures that determine social life than we are of the rules of grammar when we speak. These structures belong to the realm of an unconscious system, which Lévi-Strauss construes on the model of Saussure's concept of *langue* and that acts as a mediating term between self and other, individual and group. The existence of this unconscious system, akin to a matrix, is the very condition of social life, in the same way that the existence of what Saussure called *langue* (the deep grammar underlying linguistic competence) is the condition of meaningful speech.

In identifying and describing the elementary structures of kinship, whose logical template he formalized with the help of the mathematician André Weil, Lévi-Strauss is therefore also describing the functioning of the unconscious mind that generates them. The structural map of society is also, for Lévi-Strauss, a map of the functioning of the brain, which is one of the reasons why Lévi-Strauss said in *La Pensée sauvage* that "anthropology is a form of psychology." In the final stages of the interpretative process, structural analysis becomes a means of contemplating the functioning of the unconscious mind, whose mirror image is reflected in the "deep grammar" of human society. In the Lévi-Straussian scheme of things, this "mirroring effect," whereby the unconscious operations of the mind are unveiled, is a source of profound aesthetic emotion.

His later work, *La Pensée sauvage* (1962), is the description and analysis of an elemental mode of thought that subtends many different forms of cultural creation, from taxonomy to myth making. Put differently, it is a description of the structural unconscious. This mode of thought is what Levi-Strauss terms *pensée sauvage*. The expression is based on a pun: a "pensée" in French is both a thought and a kind of wild flower. La pensée sauvage is therefore a wild (in the botanical sense of the term) mode of thought and is to be understood in opposition to domesticated thinking, the specialized thinking developed by large-scale ("hot") societies for the purposes of productivity. What Levi-Strauss set out to show in *La Pensée sauvage* is that "wild thought" is, in many respects, the equal of domesticated thought and is certainly no less coherent or logical.

Levi-Strauss's critique of early anthropological theories about totemism illustrates this point well (see *Le Totémisme aujourd'hui*, 1962). Totemism is the custom of associating an individual or social group (usually a clan) with an animal species whose name it bears and with which it entertains a special relationship. In the past, totemism was thought to be based on the mystical identification of the members of a clan with their totemic animal. Totemism was construed as a remainder from a more archaic stage in human evolution (associated with animism) that existed before the emergence of rational thought. As such, it was the means of relegating "primitive" man not only to the ancient past but also to a realm closer to the state of nature than our own "civilized" societies.

Levi-Strauss's theory of totemism illustrates his very different view of the nature of *la pensée sauvage* and, hence, of primitive thought. For Levi-Strauss, totemism is essentially a classificatory tool, the means by which one social group encodes and signifies the resemblances and differences that form the basis of its relationship to another social group. Thus, the association of clan A with the totem Eaglehawk and clan B with the totem Crow should be read as the proposition that the relationship between clan A and clan B is analogous to that between the Eaglehawk and the Crow (clan A : clan B :: Eaglehawk : Crow). The system of resemblances and differences between Eaglehawk and Crow (both are carnivorous birds, but the first is a bird of prey, the second a carrion-eater) may be used, for example, to encode the relationships of friendship and competition, solidarity and opposition that bind these two clans. The institution of totemism is essentially a complex metaphor that a social group uses to express its view of itself.

The particularity of so-called "wild" modes of thought is that they function at a level of experience where "logical properties, as attributes of things, will be manifested as directly as flavors or perfumes" (*The Raw and the Cooked*, 14). It is a "logic of sensible properties," a "logic of the concrete." As such, it forms the basis of a primitive science or "science of the concrete."

How does such a primitive science based on "concrete logic" work? It constructs hypotheses and makes deductions about the properties of things on the basis of the observation of what seventeenth-century philosophers called their secondary qualities; in fact, those qualities of an object are perceived first, such as colors, odors, tastes, and textures. Although primitive science may not understand how the secondary qualities of any given object are related to its essential properties (as

does modern science), the gamble that there is a relationship between the two (e.g., that bitterness signifies toxicity) in practice pays off and enables the constitution of a form of speculative science. In this respect, what differentiates "primitive" or "concrete" science from modern science, according to Levi-Strauss, is not so much the types of mental operations that each presupposes (for Levi-Strauss, "man has always thought equally well"), but the fact that the former seeks to understand the natural world purely on the basis of the experience of sense perception, whereas the latter resorts to a plane of abstract formalization. The results of modern science are, of course, very different from those of primitive science. Nevertheless, Lévi-Strauss argues, they are both rooted in the same kinds of mental operations. What differ are the types of objects to which these operations are applied.

La pensee sauvage (concrete logic) is not only the basis of practical activities such as classification or primitive science but also the source of aesthetic and mythical creation. Nor are "wild" modes of thought the sole prerogative of "primitive" societies. In Western societies, "wild" modes of thought, Levi-Strauss says, continue to exist in, among other places, the "natural reserve" of art (in this respect, their status is that of an endangered species). What drives *la pensee sauvage* is a will-to-order that in many ways is common to art and science. The metaphor that Lévi-Strauss uses to describe the functioning of this mode of thought is that of *bricolage*, which one may loosely translate as "intellectual Do-It-Yourself." Given any set of heterogeneous elements, the role of the *bricoleur* is to find a way of fitting them together. The purpose of the bricoleur, whether myth-maker, artist, primitive scientist, or anthropologist, is to assemble the fragments of a puzzle into a coherent whole. As such, his or her victory is that of imposing order on disorder, meaning on incoherence. As an anthropological concept, *bricolage* refers to the process whereby we construct the many cultural schemas by which we give meaning and order to the world in which we live.

Another major aspect of Levi-Strauss's works is his theory of primitive mythology. He defines a myth as a logical tool for mediating a fundamental contradiction or paradox inherent to a given society. In "La Structure des mythes" (*Anthropologie structurale*), picking up on seemingly marginal features of the Oedipus story, such as references to "difficulties in walking straight and standing upright" contained in the names of a number of the characters (the name Oedipus itself may mean "swollen foot"), Levi-Strauss argued that this myth was concerned with the contradiction, inherent in Greek culture, between the belief that humans are born from the earth (autochthonous birth) and the knowledge that they are born from the union of a man and a woman. Lévi-Strauss interprets the Oedipus myth as a logical tool whose function is to relate the question, "Are humans born from one or from two?" to the derivative question, "Are they born from that which is different from them or that which is the same?" (*Structural Anthropology*, 216).

More generally, Lévi-Strauss saw primitive myths as being made up of a series of "superimposed" extended metaphors or analogies. Each myth encodes a set of problems or themes in terms of a series of interlocking analogies, the main purpose of the myth being to enable the conversion or translation of one analogy into the next. For example, there are a series of myths, discussed in *L'Origine des manières de table* (1968), that are about the origins of the alternation of day and night. They tell the story of how, in mythical times, divine or human actions put an end to the eternal day or eternal night that once existed on earth and brought about the regular alternation of day and night. Lévi-Strauss's interpretation of these myths is that they are about the institution of social order. More specifically, they are concerned with the problem of whom to marry. The myths warn against too equally dangerous extremes, that of an excessively close marriage (i.e., incestuous) or an excessively distant marriage (with a foreigner or enemy). The myths associate these undesirable forms of marital alliance with the equally undesirable astronomical extremes of "eternal night" or "eternal day," which occur when the moon and the sun are either too far apart or too close together. By contrast, the institution of the regular alternation of day and night signifies the ideal of a social order in which man and woman live at exactly the right distance from one another, one that is neither too close nor too far. What is unique about Lévi-Strauss's interpretation of this myth is not so much the unveiling of a coded message contained in the myth (a critical approach to myth that has existed at least since the "allegorical" interpretations practiced by the Ancient Greeks) but the fact that each code and its message always lead to other codes and other messages in such a way that we never reach a "final" or "original" meaning. The meaning of the myth disappears in a vanishing perspective of interlocking analogies. For example, the motif of the regular alternation of day and night may be related to another motif that exists in another series of myths that tell the story of how a river is magically made to flow in two directions. In other words, it is transformed into a river that could be traveled in both directions (upstream and downstream) in the same amount of time (in reality, the trip upstream would be much longer). The motif of the two-way river expresses in spatial terms what the motif of the alternation of day and night expresses in temporal terms. These motifs are combinatorial variations of one another and indeed of numerous other motifs. The point of Lévi-Strauss's analysis of myths is thus not so much to provide the key that enables the reader to decode the "hidden" meaning of the myth (although he does this too), but to trace the logic whereby one system of analogies (or mythical "codes") may be converted into another.

What interests Lévi-Strauss more than the "hidden" meaning of myths is their structure and genesis. As has already been indicated, the basic hypothesis underlying the *Mythologiques* is that myths come into being by a process of transformation of one myth into another. Each myth is the result of a kaleidoscopic type of rearrangement of elements, of a series of logical substitutions and permutations by virtue of which one myth is transmuted into another (the *bricoleur* metaphor applies here too). For Lévi-Strauss, myths do not have any meaning in themselves but only in relation to each other and therefore have to be studied in the course of their transformation from one into another to unlock their meanings.

The South American Gé tell the story of Botoque, who is taken by his elder brother-in-law to catch the young of a pair of macaws nesting on top of a steep rock (see "M7" in *Le Cru et le cuit*). Here is a fragment of that myth. Botoque is made to climb a makeshift ladder, but having arrived at the height of the nest, all he can find in it are two eggs. His brother-in-law asks for them. Botoque throws them down, but as they fall the eggs transform into stones which cut his elder brother's hands as he tries to catch them. Enraged, the latter removes the ladder and abandons Botoque. For several days, Botoque is stranded at the top of the rock. He is hungry and thirsty, and as he is becoming thinner he is forced to eat his own excrement. At last, he sees below him a spotted jaguar carrying a bow and arrow and all kinds of game. He wants to cry out for help, but fear of the jaguar renders him mute. The jaguar notices the shadow of Botoque on the ground. He tries, in vain, to catch it, then looks up, inquires after Botoque, replaces the ladder against the rock and invites the young boy down.

If one is to compare M7 to the other versions of this myth, one notices that a series of transformations have occurred. In M12, Botoque climbs the ladder to the nest of macaws but then lies to his brother-in-law, telling him that the nest is empty. The brother-in-law becomes impatient, so Botoque throws a stone at him (taken from his mouth, not the nest). And this stone transforms into an egg as it falls to the ground. In M7 and M8, Botoque, trapped on his rock, is forced to eat his own excrement; in M9, M10, and M11, Botoque is covered in the excrement of birds hovering around the nest. In M8, the jaguar climbs the ladder to help Botoque down; in the other versions he welcomes him at the foot of the ladder; in M9, M10, M11, and M12 the jaguar is given the macaws in exchange for his help, in M7 and M8 he is not.

As orally transmitted narratives, primitive myths are constantly being altered or transformed. This is why, to understand a myth, Lévi-Strauss starts by viewing it in the context of its many variants. In *Le Cru et le cuit*, he shows that the above Gé myth, a myth about the origin of fire (it concludes when Botoque steals fire from the jaguar and gives it to man), is in fact a transformation of a myth (M1) told by a neighboring population, the Bororo. The Bororo myth (M1) tells the story of the origin of rainwater, and Lévi-Strauss's argument is that it is, in fact, an inversion of the above Gé myth: It is a myth about the origin of fire metamorphosed into its opposite, a myth about the origin of water.

Lévi-Strauss's working method is to submit each myth to an analysis that reveals its transformational connections to other myths. These are progressively brought into the picture and in turn analyzed. Lévi-Strauss follows step by step the paths indicated by the myths themselves, which corresponded to the paths of their coming into being. As each myth is connected to the next, series of affiliated myths are integrated into broader units, and gradually the picture of a total system—compared by Lévi-Strauss to a nebula—emerges. In the process, the reader is taken on a journey from the tip of South Brazil to the Northwest coast of America.

Whatever the subject of Lévi-Strauss's anthropological inquiries, these often contain either an explicit or a veiled confrontation with the question, What is the nature of the aesthetic object? His work on Amerindian myth leads him to formulate, in his later work (*La Voie des masques*, 1975; *Le Regard éloigné*, 1983; *Regarder écouter lire*, 1993) a general theory of creation-by-transformation that anticipates later theories of intertextuality. Lévi-Strauss's transformation theory of creation provides a model for understanding art not so much in terms of the referential or mimetic function of art but in terms of the systems of internal connections that, beyond a work's "content," link it to other works of art (something that postmodern art has elevated to the rank of an overt counter-aesthetic). Lévi-Strauss's study of the mutations of Amerindian myths enabled him to formulate a transformational grammar that he put forward as a key to the functioning of the "structural unconscious" (in this respect, the *Mythologiques* are a continuation of his earlier project of elucidating *la pensee sauvage*). In essays such as "De Chrétien de Troyes à Richard Wagner" (*Regard éloigné*), or in the chapter devoted to Nicholas Poussin in *Regarder ecouter lire*, Lévi-Strauss sought to apply what he learnt from myths to other forms of creation, including Western art. His transformational model of creation anchors the act of creation in combinatorial logic. He finds the key to the relationship between one work of art and the next in a quasi-mathematical series of logical operations (inversions, reversals, substitutions, rotations, etc.) that account for the conversion of one work into the next. In this way, he establishes, for example, a subterranean transformational connection between a painting by Guercino, *Et in Arcadia Ego* (painted around 1621–1623) and two paintings by Poussin on the same theme, the first probably painted between 1629 and 1630 the other between 1638 and 1639. The conclusion one is invited to draw from this analysis is that Poussin thinks and creates in a way that is not entirely dissimilar from an Amerindian myth-maker. The value of Lévi-Strauss's interpretation of Poussin lies not only in his uncovering of the hidden transformations that, so he argues, link the above paintings but also in the very act of connecting such seemingly distant and dissimilar aesthetic objects. In viewing one of France's greatest and most classical painters through the lens of primitive myth, he invites us to question the hierarchy of aesthetic values that opposes Western art (one might have said "cooked" art) to primitive or "raw" art. His uncovering, in the *Mythologiques*, of deep structures within myth that resemble well-known musical forms such as the rondo or the sonata fulfils a similar function. If we follow this line of thought, we must also believe that these forms arise out the innate structures of the brain as opposed to having been shaped by history.

BORIS WISEMAN

See also **Roland Barthes; Jacques Derrida; Lucien Levy-Bruhl; Marcel Mauss; Paul Ricoeur; Jean-Paul Sartre; Ferdinand de Saussure; Paul Valery**

Biography

Claude Lévi-Strauss was born in Brussels, Belgium, in 1908 and brought up in the sixteenth arrondissement of Paris, rue Poussin. He studied law and philosophy and passed the a*ggrégation* in philosophy in 1931 (he studied for this exam alongside Maurice Merleau-Ponty and Simone de Beauvoir). He left for Brazil in 1935 to take up a post as a lecturer in sociology at the University of São Paulo. In the summer of 1935 and then later in 1938, Lévi-Strauss conducted ethnographic fieldwork in the Mato Grosso region of Brazil among the Caduveo and Bororo Indians and further west, among the Nambikwara. During World War II, he fled Nazi-occupied France for New York, where he attended the lectures of the Prague School linguist Roman Jakobson. Having returned to France, in 1950 he was elected to the chair in "Religions comparées des peuples non civilisés" (literally "Comparative Religions of Non-Civilized Peoples") at the École pratique des hautes études. He was later to have the title of the chair changed to "Religions comparées des peuples sans écriture" ("The Comparative Religions of Peoples without Writing"). In 1959, he was elected to the chair in social anthropology at the Collège de France and in 1973, he became a member of the Académie Française. In 1961, he founded (with Émile Benveniste and Pierre Gourou) the anthropological journal *L'Homme*.

Selected Works

Les Structures élémentaires de la parenté [The Elementary Structures of Kinship], 1949
Tristes tropiques [Tristes tropiques], 1955
Anthropologie structurale [Structural Anthropology], 1958
Le Totémisme aujourd'hui [Totemism], 1962
Le Pensée sauvage [The Savage Mind], 1962
Mythologiques [Introduction to a Science of Mythology], 4 volumes, 1964–1971: I. *Le Cru et le cuit* [The Raw and the Cooked]; II. *Du Miel aux cendres* [From Honey to Ashes]; III. *L'Origine des manières de table* [The Origin of Table Manners]; IV. *L'Homme nu* [The Naked Man]
Anthropologie structurale deux [Structural Anthropology 2], 1973
La Voie des masques [The Way of the Masks], 1975
Myth and Meaning, 1978
Le Regard éloigné [The View from Afar], 1983
Regarder écouter lire, 1993

Further Reading

Barthes, Roland, "Les Sciences humaines et l'œuvre de Lévi-Strauss," *Annales: économies, sociétés, civilisations*, 19 (1964)
Bellour, Raymond, and Clément, Catherine, ed., *Claude Lévi-Strauss*, Paris: Gallimard, 1979
Boon, James, *From Symbolism to Structuralism: Lévi-Strauss in a Literary Tradition* Oxford: Basil Blackwell, 1971
Clément, Catherine, *Lévi-Strauss ou la Structure et le malheur* Paris: Seghers, 1970
Derrida, Jacques, "La structure, le signe et le jeu dans le discours des sciences humaines," in *L'Écriture et la différence*, Paris: Seuil, 1967
Derrida, Jacques, "Structure, Sign and Play in the Discourse of the Human Sciences," in *Writing and Difference*, Routledge, 1978
Derrida, Jacques, "La Violence de la lettre: de Lévi-Strauss à Rousseau," in *De la grammatologie* Paris: Editions de Minuit, 1967
Derrida, Jacques, "The Violence of the Letter: From Lévi-Strauss to Rousseau," in *Of Grammatology*, Johns Hopkins University Press, 1976
Hénaff, Marcel, *Claude Lévi-Strauss and the Making of Structural Anthropology*, Minneapolis: University of Minnesota Press, 1998
Leach, Edmund, *Claude Lévi Strauss*, Harmondsworth: Penguin, 1976
Merquior, José Guilherme, *L'Esthétique de Lévi-Strauss*, Paris: Presses Universitaires de France, 1977
Pace, David, *Claude Lévi-Strauss: The Bearer of Ashes*, London: Routledge & Kegan Paul, 1983
Paz, Octavio, *Claude Lévi-Strauss: an Introduction*, London: Jonathan Cape, 1971
Ricœur, Paul, "Structuralisme et herméneutique," *Esprit*, 322 (1963): 596–627

LÉVY-BRUHL, LUCIEN
Ethnographer and Sociologist

Lévy-Bruhl wrote under the pseudonym of Deuzelle for *L'Humanité* before the newspaper became the property of the French Communist Party that was emerging from the split of the worker's movement that followed the Congress of Tours (1925). At that time, the French philosophical field (keeping in mind that Hegel was not yet translated and Marx was absent) was being split between the supporters of the spiritualist tradition, exemplified by the religious exegesis of Loisy, the immanence of Maurice Blondel, the intuitionism of Bergson, the spiritual evolutionism of Teilhard de Chardin, and the supporters of the positivism of Auguste Comte. The latter were fervent republicans striving to build, with an optimism characteristic of their time, a secular, socialist, and progressive morality, which would replace religious precepts and, therefore, be considered a science on the same basis as the others.

It is within this context that one has to understand why Lévy-Bruhl first turned to the translation of the Latin moralist Cicero (1881), then the commentary of Nicomachean Ethics by Aristotle (1882), and also wrote an essay titled "Darwin's Morality" (1883). The defense of his theses in 1884 still echoed this hope: *L'Idée de responsabilité* (The Notion of Responsibility, French thesis) and *Quid de deo Seneca senserit* (Latin thesis). In 1901, Levy-Bruhl published *La Morale et la science des moeurs* (Morality and the Science of Morals), which Durkheim summarized in laudatory terms in *L'Année Sociologique*.

After having examined the rationalist mystique of the Spinozist Jacobi (*La philosophie de Jacobi*, 1894) and the legacy of Auguste Comte (*History of Modern Philosophy in France*, 1899), whose correspondence with John Stuart Mill he edited (1899) and whose works he synthesized (*La Philosophie d'Auguste Comte*, 1900), Lévy-Bruhl became enthusiastic about psychology, which had reached France with the works of Bernard Perez, Pierre Janet, and Georges Dumas.

He soon became interested in another nascent science, ethnography. *Les Fonctions mentales dans les sociétés inférieures* (Mental Functions in Inferior Societies, 1910) was the first book that, based on the ethnographic data of the time (dealing mainly with Australian societies), revealed the specificity of what Lévy-Bruhl called "primitive mentality." The book used Durkheim's integrating notion that the type of social organization determines mental classifications and deduced from it that the identity principle follows a "law of participation" in the so-called "inferior societies." Thus the primitive mind would not be very sensitive to the contradiction principle. A prelogical mind is in opposition to rational thought (produced by civilized societies).

Lévy-Bruhl returned to classical philosophy after publishing this book and campaigned for Durkheim to be nominated for a position at the Sorbonne (which would occur in 1912).

Then came the First World War. Lévy-Bruhl wondered about the "causes of the European conflagration" (1915) and the armament industry (1916) before promoting the works and ideas of Jean Jaurès (1916, 1917, 1918). By 1919, he shared the ideas of Léon Blum, and it seemed that he would turn toward a more militant political engagement, but it was only as a specialist on the "primitives" that he would be invited to give a series of lectures in Germany, the United States, Belgium, and Britain.

He thus resumed his research on how attitudes of mind are constructed in different geographical and temporal spaces. In 1922, *La Mentalité primitive* (Primitive Mentality) provided a systematic exploration of how the so-called primitives would conceive the causality principle. In 1927, *L'Ame primitive* (The Primitive Soul) studied how the "primitives" see their own individuality when dealing with the group and discussed issues such as reincarnation and the state and status of the dead.

Simultaneously, there were many translations of his works. *Les Fonctions mentales* had first editions in Germany (1919), the United States (1925), and Great Britain (1926). *La Mentalité primitive* was translated in German in 1927 and in English in 1923. Still, the young American school of anthropology ignored him or reacted against his theses, as Paul Radin did by writing *Primitive Man as Philosopher* (1927). Even though Lévy-Bruhl gave the famous Herbert Spencer Lecture at Oxford University in 1931, the two new primary figures of British anthropology, Malinowski and Radcliffe-Brown, did not cite his texts. A third key figure, Evans-Pritchard, would devote his two first articles to him; his *Witchcraft, Oracles and Magic among the Azande* (1937) would pick up the problematic introduced by Lévy-Bruhl.

As early as the 1920s, Lévy-Bruhl was regarded as a figure of stagnant academia, rather than a contemporary and relevant thinker. Called an "appointed Sorbonnard" by Karady (1982, 18), he worked toward the creation of an Institute of Ethnology, which would open in 1925. He may have read the inaugural speech in front of Daladier, then Minister of the Colonies (who was financing the Institute), but it was Marcel Mauss and especially Paul Rivet who were the key architects of its creation. As he was thanking Lévy-Bruhl because he "did so much to popularize our studies," Mauss protested the radical opposition between mentalities, criticized the use of the word "primitive" for different peoples, and insisted on the lack of historical approach (1929).

Lévy-Bruhl took this into account. In *Le Surnaturel et la nature dans la mentalité primitive* (Supernatural and Nature in Primitive Mentalities), which explained how the "primitive" sees the supernatural where the "civilized" does not, and vice versa, he insisted less on the dualism between "primitive" mentality and "civilized" mentality than on the study of the former. His two following works, *La Mythologie primitive* (1935) and *L'Expérience mystique et les symboles chez les primitifs* (Mystical Experience and Symbols of the Primitives, 1938) followed along similar lines. The *Carnets Posthumes* (Posthumous notebooks), published in 1949, with a last entry dated February 2, 1939, completely rejected the primitive mentality in favor of the existence of two permanent structuring poles of the human mind. This thesis can be found in the works of the reverend Maurice Leenhardt, his main disciple and a specialist of Kanaka societies, who inherited the directorship of the study of primitive peoples from Mauss and who would be succeeded by Lévi-Strauss on his retirement.

Mary Douglas, the British ethnologist, reminded her audience during a lecture at the Collège de France in 2002 that the word "primitive" had become taboo following World War II and the horrors of the Holocaust. The distinction between "civilized" and "primitive" had to be challenged and erased. Lévy-Bruhl's work must be placed within the context of his time as well as contemporary reconsiderations of colonialism. His work must be seen first and foremost as an incredible synthesizing of the ethnographic data of the time, and so Evans-Pritchard's reference to his "extraordinary brilliance" (1934, 9) is understandable, even though same characteristic makes him difficult to read today. Lévy-Bruhl stated that social events are interdependent and that one type of society will necessarily have its own mentality, thus linking mentality or logical thought with environment. By doing so, Lévy-Bruhl dared to tackle the fundamental question of the other and his "essence," initiating a concern still pursued today by cognitive anthropology, which associates the ethnological approach with linguistics and neurosciences.

GÉRALD GAILLARD

See also **Emile Durkheim; Marcel Mauss**

Biography

Lucien Lévy-Bruhl was born in 1857. He attended the École normal supérieure. A member of the jury for the philosophy *agrégation* exams from 1892, Lévy-Bruhl was awarded the Chair of History of Modern Philosophy at the Sorbonne University in 1904.

In 1927, Lévy-Bruhl became the editor of the *Revue philosophique*, was accepted to the Academy of Moral and Political Sciences, and retired to devote himself to writing. He died in 1939.

Selected Works

La Philosophie de Jacobi, 1894
History of Modern Philosophy in France, 1899
La Philosophie d'Auguste Comte, 1900
La Morale et la science des moeurs, 1901
Les Fonctions mentales dans les sociétés inférieures, 1910
La Mentalité primitive, 1922
L'Ame primitive, 1927
La Mythologie primitive, 1935
L'Expérience mystique et les symboles chez les primitives, 1938
Carnets Posthumes, 1949

Further Reading

Cazeneuve, J., *Lucien Lévy-Bruhl: sa vie, son oeuvre, avec un exposé de sa philosophie*, Paris: PUF, 1963
Douglas, M., *Evans-Pritchard*, London: Fontana, 1980, 32
Evans-Pritchard, E. E., "Lévy-Bruhl," in *Theory of primitive religion*, edited by R. Needham, chap. 9 of *Belief, Language and Experience*, Oxford, 1965, 1979
Evans-Pritchard, E. E., "Lévy-Bruhl's theory of primitive mentality," Cairo, *Bulletin of the Faculty of Arts*, 2 (1943)
Goldman, M., "Raison et différence: à propos de L. Lévy-Bruhl," *Gradhiva*, 23 (1998): 1–21
Mauss, M., *Oeuvres* [Works], Vol. 2 (1969 [1929]): 131
Rivet, P., "Lucien Lévy-Bruhl," *JSA*, 9 (1939): 214–216

LINGUISTICS

Linguistics studies the sciences of language. At its core, it encompasses the study of phonology (sound patterns), morphology (internal structure of words), syntax (combination of words into sentences), semantics (meaning), and pragmatics (relationships among language, users, and context). These are the fields on which this article will focus. In a broader sense, linguistics also includes subcategories such as sociolinguistics (social functions of language variation), psycholinguistics (psychological mechanisms of the learning, production, and reception of speech), philology (study of language through written texts), dialectology (geographical or social dialects), lexicology (vocabulary), computational linguistics (statistical study of texts and mathematical modeling of the structure of languages), stylistics (linguistics applied to literature), and so on. Applied linguistics applies the theoretical findings of these language sciences to practical fields such as language teaching or speech recognition software. Most of the above domains were conceptualized in the course of the twentieth century, but nineteenth-century linguistics was dominated by philological and historical studies that compared specific forms in different languages to show how these languages were "genealogically" related and to reconstruct earlier stages of languages (e.g., French, Italian, and Spanish developed from Latin, which belongs to the family of Indo-European languages comprising Greek, Sanskrit, Celtic, and the like). Twentieth-century French linguistics persevered in that direction for a while but underwent a radical shift with the notion of language system introduced by Saussure.

The Swiss linguist Ferdinand de Saussure (1857–1913) was first known as a comparative and historical linguist (*Mémoire sur le système primitif des voyelles dans les langues indo-européennes*, 1879). He was a director of studies at the École des Hautes Études in Paris (1881–1891) before becoming professor of Indo-European linguistics and Sanskrit (1901–1913) at the University of Geneva. It is, however, for his teaching in general linguistics that he is now remembered, and more specifically for the three lecture courses he gave in Geneva between 1906 and 1911 that were published posthumously by two of his disciples, Charles Bally and Albert Séchehaye, as the *Cours de linguistique générale* (1916), on the basis of the notes taken by eight of the students who attended the courses.

The theory of language presented in the *Cours de linguistique générale* promotes the fundamental concept of language as a system in which all the elements fit together; that is, linguistic signs can only be identified in terms of the relations in which they stand to other elements within the system. This theory is articulated around four dichotomies: *Langue* is an abstract set of units and rules common to all the speakers of the same language that enables them to communicate with each other. As such, *langue* is seen as a social but abstract system that underlies and thus logically precedes *parole*, the individual and intentional production of language in a given context; that is, the actual utterances. Although the *Cours de linguistique générale* envisages the possible coexistence of a linguistics of *langue* and a linguistics of *parole*, it sees *langue* as being its primary object of study.

Second, the linguistic sign is a combination of a *signifiant* ("signifier," acoustic image, for example, the set of sounds [sör]) and a *signifié* ("signified," concept, for example, the semantic values associated to the word *soeur*). The connection between the signifier and the signified is arbitrary: It is not determined by extralinguistic facts but is entirely dependent on the linguistic system to which it belongs (here the system of contemporary French language) and is defined solely through its differences with other signifiers and signifieds, respectively.

Third, these differences depend on two kinds of relations that signs can enter into: "syntagmatic" (or horizontal) relationships between elements in a linear sequence and "associative" (or vertical, that is, paradigmatic) relationships when elements can substitute for each other in a given context.

Fourth, language can be studied from a synchronic perspective, that is, as a complete, independent system at a given point in time, or from a diachronic perspective, that is, in terms of changes over time. Contrary to some interpretations, Saussure did not entirely reject diachrony in favor of synchrony (after all, he was himself an historical linguist); but the *Cours de linguistique* stresses that before comparing elements belonging to various stages of the development of a language, one should first carry a synchronic description of the system of each of these stages, so that a synchronic approach logically precedes a diachronic one.

Approaches influenced by Saussure's concept of system are often presented under the label of structuralism. His theories did not only influence great French linguists such as Benveniste, Guillaume, or Martinet but had a wide effect on the study of linguistics in Europe (Prague School, Copenhagen School) and in the United States (Bloomfield, Chomsky). They also inspired French sociologists and anthropologists who, in turn, were very widely read outside France (Lévi-Strauss, Lacan).

Saussure's ideas were developed by his disciples of the Geneva School (e.g., Bally, Sechehaye, Frei) but were not immediately understood nor embraced in France. His colleague Antoine Meillet, in *Linguistique historique et linguistique générale* (1921, 1936), adopted his concept of system but remained a comparatist and defended a vision of general linguistic as a way to understand the causes of linguistic changes and to study how social structures determine specific linguistic structures, thereby favoring a diachronic approach and considering external factors rather than internal ones (his examples were mainly drawn from the evolution of vocabulary). He was a highly influential figure who taught many important French linguists, and his school of thought was sometimes called the "sociological school" because of its strong links to Durkheim's ideas.

Saussure's ideas started to spread in France through the theories advocated by the linguists of the Prague School (Jakobson, Karcevskij, Mathesius, and Trubet-

skoy). They combined the notion of functionalism with Saussure's concept of system and submitted that the structure of languages is determined by a number of specific functions, the main one being that of communication. Linguistic units are thus determined by their functions and by their distinctive features, which differentiate them from other units. Moreover, for the functionalists, language functions can be studied both synchronically and diachronically. Although their contribution touched all fields of linguistics (and even literary criticism), it was especially important in the field of phonology as, they helped shape the crucial notion of phoneme (the abstract representation of a sound). André Martinet, one of the main twentieth-century French linguists, participated in the Prague School discussions and developed his own brand of general linguistics (*A Functional View of Language*, 1962) and phonology (*Économie des changements phonétiques, traité de phonologie diachronique*, 1955). Georges Gougenheim also contributed to create a certain kind of French functionalism, working on phonology (*Éléments de phonologie française*, 1935), syntax (*Système grammatical de la langue française*, 1938), and vocabulary (*Etudes de grammaire et de vocabulaire français*, 1970). Incidentally, Martinet and Gougenheim were the first to offer a statistical analysis of a real corpus of spoken French (Gougenheim, 1956; Martinet, 1945). Other French functionalists are Mounin, D. François, F. François, and Mahmoudian; their journal is *La Linguistique*.

Émile Benveniste's work represents an interesting synthesis of the different trends outlined above because he was influenced by Saussure, was the successor of Meillet at the Collège de France, and collaborated with the Prague School. He was a comparatist (*Origines de la formation des noms en indo-européen*, 1935) as well as a specialist in general linguistics and semantics (*Problèmes de linguistique générale*, 1966, 1974). He defended a sociological conception of language seen as the locus of interaction in the human being between mental life and cultural life. In addition to his original views on semantics (notably challenging Saussure's arbitrariness of sign), his theories on discourse were instrumental for the development of the *théorie de l'énonciation*. Of particular importance were his studies of performative verbs (e.g., *je souhaite que*, "I wish that"; *je promets que*, "I promise that") and of the articulation of tenses and pronouns in narratives (opposing the objective mode of *histoire*, in the French *passé simple* and the third person, to the subjective mode of *discours*, in the present tense and the first person).

Apart from Saussure and a few other exceptions such as Benveniste, Meillet, or Martinet, French linguists have not influenced linguistic theories abroad nor offered general approaches to language, but have tended to develop their own idiosyncratic theories, mainly in terms of grammar. A grammar is a set of rules that govern the morphology and syntax of a language (the definition sometimes includes phonology and semantics as well). In linguistics, a grammar is always descriptive rather than prescriptive; that is, it describes the structure of language that native speakers know intuitively rather than prescribing a set of normative rules that speakers must use to speak or write their language correctly. That said, the normative tradition is very strong in France, notably because of the influence of the Académie Française, as can be seen by the multiple reeditions of books such as Grevisse's *Le bon usage*, or by the scandals generated by the various spelling reforms proposed during the twentieth century, or more recently, by the feminization of professional titles (e.g., *madame la ministre* versus *madame le ministre*).

The first grammars in the twentieth century envisaged the correspondence and interaction between thoughts and language forms. In *Des mots à la pensée. Essai de grammaire de la langue française* (7 volumes, 1930–1950), Jacques Damourette and Edouard Pichon argued against the arbitrariness of sign; their main aim in studying the structure of language was to understand the structure of thought. Ferdinand Brunot chose the opposite method in *La pensée et la langue, méthodes, principes et plan d'une théorie nouvelle du langage appliquée au français* (1936). By examining how general semantic concepts were expressed in a specific language, he submitted that the structure of thoughts helped to understand the structure of language. Gustave Guillaume concerned himself with the semantic content of grammatical classes. In his approach called "psychomecanics," he viewed thoughts as in a constant state of flux, operating both in psychological space and time. He studied how the different movements of thought combine to form a stable system (*langue*) before being produced as individual utterances into *discours*. Although linguistic units have a single virtual meaning in *langue* (*signifié de puissance*), they can be realized in a variety of actual uses in *discours* (*signifié d'effet*). Guillaume was especially interested in articles and tenses (*Le problème de l'article et sa solution dans la langue française*, 1919; *Temps et verbe. Théorie des aspects, des modes et des temps*, 1929) but his disciples in Belgium, Canada, and France broadened the scope of "guillaumism" toward many other topics in morphology and syntax (e.g., the subjunctive, pronominal verbs, etc.), both in synchrony and in diachrony (Imbs, Martin, Moignet, Pottier, Stefanini, Valin, Wagner, Wilmet, etc.).

Other French linguists were more interested in the structure of language as such than in the structure of thoughts. Lucien Tesnière in *Éléments de syntaxe structurale* (1959) offered an original view of syntax applicable to all languages. Instead of separating the sentence (*Pierre aime Marie*) between subject (*Pierre*) and predicate (*aime Marie*), he saw all elements as depending on the verb (*aime*) and represented these hierarchical relations as vertical graphs (*stemmas*). This grammar of "dependency" was adopted and developed by other linguists such as Fourquet, Galichet, and Zemb. In *Linguistique générale, théorie et description* (1964), Bernard Pottier offered a semantic approach inspired by functionalism and guillaumism that analyzed the level of elements forming the word up to that of the elements constituting the sentence. More recently, the *Groupe Aixois de Recherche en syntaxe* (GARS) has proposed a "pronominal approach" of grammar, which rejects the traditional notion of the sentence as the basic syntactic unit and identifies the syntactic functions of the various elements in the verb phrase by how they can be replaced by a pronoun (Blanche-Benveniste et al., *Pronom et syntaxe: l'approche pronominale et son application en français*, 1987).

Major linguistic theories developed in America have had some effect in France. Leonard Bloomfield (*Language*, 1933) advocated a behaviorist approach of language viewed as the set of utterances uttered by its speakers. His objectives were to identify the constituents of these utterances and to describe the distributional relations holding between them (i.e., in which environment they could or could not appear). Although many French linguists knew about Bloomfield's distributionalism, they mostly tended to criticize its tenets (particularly the rejection of semantic categories) while borrowing a few useful concepts rather than fully adopting it, with important exceptions such as the works of Dubois, Gross, and Salkoff. Noam Chomsky (*Syntactic Structures*, 1957; *Language and Mind*, 1968) has posited the innate existence of a native speaker's "competence" (unconscious knowledge of the language) and proposed the cognitive model of a generative grammar that would provide instructions for the production of the infinite number of grammatical sentences possible in a language, working from an underlying deep structure to a surface structure by means of specific instructions and, in some cases, transformations (e.g., going from an active structure to a passive structure: *Pierre aime Marie → Marie est aimée par Pierre*). Generativism was and still is popular with some French linguists (especially in the 1970s and 1980s), as illustrated in the works of Chevalier, Dubois, Dubois Charlier, Huot, Milner, Rouveret, and Ruwet.

In the last twenty years of the century, theories of "textual grammar" influenced by foreign linguists such as Halliday, Hasan, Givon, or Van Dijk have posited that linguistic regularities can also be discovered at the level of text formation and that the function of many linguistic elements such as personal pronouns, articles, demonstratives, and tenses can only fully be understood if one goes past the boundaries of the sentence (*phrase*) and studies the structure of the text as a whole (i.e., its discursive cohesion). Such preoccupations are reflected in the works of Adam, Apotheloz, Bronckart, Charolles, Combettes, Corblin, Coltier, Kleiber, Lambrecht, and Roulet. The field of textual grammar is often linked to the broader field of "discourse analysis," which not only examines the cohesion of sentences within the texts but also studies the relationships of the texts with their extralinguistic contexts (their coherence) and with preset discursive genres that dictate their formation (see Charaudeau and Maingueneau, 2002).

The field of discourse pragmatics is also strongly linked to that of *théorie de l'énonciation*, one of the main theoretical frameworks recently developed in contemporary French linguistics. It is inspired by the Anglo-Saxon philosophy of language (Austin, Grice, Searle, etc.) and by the works of linguists such as Bakhtin, Jakobson, Bally, and Benveniste, and it is based on the proposition that the utterances (*énoncés*) of a discourse inevitably contain traces of the locutionary activity (*énonciation*) that produced them, the context in which they were produced, and the subjectivity of the producer. On the one hand, "enunciation" can be described as an individual act, the result of which is a singular linguistic object; namely, the utterance (i.e., it pertains to Saussure's *parole*, not *langue*). On the other hand, it can be envisaged as a general phenomenon, namely a stable system that emerges from the multiplicity of all the individual acts of enunciation. Enunciation theory thus studies a set of specific mechanisms that govern the conversion by the locutor of the abstract system of *langue* into *discours* by identifying and interpretating the linguistic traces through which the act of speaking and the beliefs and attitudes of a speaker leave their imprint on the surface structure of the text: shifters (pronouns, tenses, and spatial and temporal deictics), presupposition, speech acts and performatives (e.g., to say *j'ordonne que* is to accomplish an act of command), connectives and "enunciative particles" (for example, *mais* "but," *puisque* "since," *eh bien* "so," *franchement* "frankly"), adverbs of scale and evaluative adjectives (e.g., *peu* "little," *un peu* "a little"), aspects (e.g., use of *imparfait* versus *passé simple*), modalities (e.g., use of conditional or adverbs like *peut-être* "maybe"), and reported discourse. Alongside very formal and almost mathematical approaches such as that of Culioli, we find more accessible ones such as that of Kerbrat-Orecchioni, who wrote a seminal book on the expression of subjectivity in language (*L'énonciation. De la subjectivité dans le langage*, 1980) and subsequently used enunciation frameworks to study topics such as conversation analysis, irony, and interrogation. Scholars such as Recanati and Berrendonner have kept to topics that were already well explored by language philosophers; namely, reference, speech acts, performatives, and presuppositions. Other authors such as Anscombre, Ducrot, Moeschler, and Roulet have tried to develop a more original theory of argumentation (i.e., rhetoric), looking specifically at the "chaining" (*articulation, enchaînement*) of utterances within the discourse. Finally, some scholars have applied these theories to specific discourse genres (e.g., literature for Maingueneau, the written press for Charaudeau, etc.), topics (reported discourse for Rosier), or periods (medieval French for Cerquiglini, Marchello-Nizia, Marnette, Perret).

There is a strong tradition of philological and historical studies in France, which have gradually been influenced by the idea that language evolution should be examined in terms of a succession of language states (or systems) and not through the atomistic view of one isolated element changing through time as was the case before Saussure (see the works of Antoine, Imbs, Gougenheim, Marouzeau, Martin, Moignet, Roques, Rychner, Wagner, and Wilmet and, more recently, Cerquiglini, Marchello-Nizia, Ménard, Perret, Picoche, Valli, Walter, and Zink). Studies on contemporary spoken French, initiated by linguists such as Bally, Bauche, Frei, Gougenheim, and Martinet have fully developed in the last quarter of the twentieth century, thanks to technological progresses, but also because spoken discourse is not viewed anymore as corrupted or substandard with regard to written discourse (see the works of Blanche-Benveniste and Gadet). Many of these historical and synchronic studies are now based on big language corpora, with the help of computer analysis.

SOPHIE MARNETTE

See also **Emile Benveniste; Emile Durkheim; Jacques Lacan; Claude Levi-Strauss; Andre Martinet; Ferdinand de Saussure; Structuralism**

Further Reading

Bally, Charles, and Albert Séchehaye, *Cours de linguistique générale*, Paris: Payot, 1916

Benveniste, Emile, *Origines de la formation des noms en indo-européen*, Paris: Adrien-Maisonneuve, 1935

Benveniste, Emile, *Problèmes de linguistique générale*, 2 volumes, Paris: Gallimard, 1966, 1974

Blanche-Benveniste, Claire, Deulofeu, José, Stefamimi, Jean, Eymde, Karel van den *Pronom et syntaxe: l'approche pronominale et son application en français*, 2nd ed., Paris: S.E.L.A.F., 1987

Bloomfield, Leonard, *Language*, New York: II. Holt and Company 1933

Brunot, Ferdinand, *La pensée et la langue, méthodes, principes et plan d'une théorie nouvelle du langage appliquée au français*, 3rd ed., Paris: Masson, 1936

Charaudeau, P., and Maingueneau, D., eds., *Dictionnaire d'Analyse du discours*, Paris: Seuil, 2002

Chomsky, Noam, *Syntactic Structures*, The Hague: Mouton, 1957

Chomsky, Noam, *Language and Mind*, New York: Harcourt Brace Jovanovich, 1968

Damourette, Jacques, and Pichon, Edouard, *Des mots à la pensée. Essai de grammaire de la langue française*, 7 volumes, Paris: d'Artrey, 1930–1950

Gougenheim, Georges, *Éléments de phonologie française*, Paris: Les Belles Lettres, 1935 Gougenheim, Georges, *Système grammatical de la langue française*, Paris: d'Artrey, 1938

Gougenheim, Georges, *L'élaboration du français élémentaire*, Paris: Didier, 1956

Gougenheim, Georges, *Etudes de grammaire et de vocabulaire français*, Paris: Picard, 1970

Grevisse, Maurice. *Le bon usage: grammaire française*. Paris, Gemblaux: Duculot, 1986. 12th ed.

Guillaume, Gustave, *Le problème de l'article et sa solution dans la langue française*, Paris: Hachette, 1919

Guillaume, Gustave, *Temps et verbe. Théorie des aspects, des modes et des temps*, Paris: Champion, 1929

Kerbrat-Orecchioni, Catherine *L'énonciation. De la subjectivité dans le langage*, Paris: Colin, 1980

Martinet, André, *La prononciation du français contemporain*, Paris: Droz, 1945

Martinet, André, *A Functional View of Language*, Oxford: Clarendon, 1962

Martinet, André, *Économie des changements phonétiques, traité de phonologie diachronique*, Berne: Francke, 1955

Meillet, Antoine, *Linguistique historique et linguistique générale*, 2 volumes, Paris: Champion, 1921, 1936

Pottier, Bernard, *Linguistique générale, théorie et description*, Paris: Klincksieck, 1964

Saussure, Ferdinand de, *Mémoire sur le système primitif des voyelles dans les langues indo-européennes*, Leipsick: Teubmer 1879

Tesnière, Lucien, *Éléments de syntaxe structurale*, Paris: Klincksieck, 1959

LIPIETZ, ALAIN
Political Ecologist

A leading member of the French Green Party and a representative in European Parliament, as well as a key figure in the Regulation School of political economy, Alain Lipietz is a prominent theorist of the post-Marxist Left in France. In wide-ranging and influential works, Lipietz poses key questions of political ecology and the development of green alternatives to traditional social movements, especially labor and socialism. For Lipietz, the labor movement, the historic social movement, and their great aspirations to socialism and communism no longer carry people's desires and hopes for a better world.

As with other postleftist theorists, Lipietz rejects the unity and centrality of the proletarian subject. He also rejects the thesis of the "unity of oppression," arguing that specific oppressions do not necessarily stem from capitalism. The Marxist unity of anticapitalist, proletarian, and communist was held together by the unity of the party and the state even when the components were threatening to separate from each other.

Lipietz also counters orthodox Marxist approaches in arguing for an ecologically informed critique of the all-powerful state and the growth of productive forces. He rejects the anthropocentrism of Marxism, which sees nature as "the inorganic body of humankind," or less. Society must be rebuilt through values of autonomy, solidarity, and respect and care for life, both natural and human.

Building on the work of Michel Aglietta, Lipietz has made important contributions to the Regulation School of political economy. The regulationist approach studies the reproduction of capitalist market economies through their various transformations and the political arrangements that allow accumulation to occur.

Transformations are regular for extended periods in which accumulation and economic growth are relatively undisturbed. This regular mode of transformation of production, distribution, and exchange Lipietz calls a "regime of accumulation," a macroeconomic regularity. This regime is based on a technological paradigm that includes principles of labor organization and the application of techniques.

Despite the apparent regularity, regimes of accumulation are always threatened by conditions of uncertainty. Regulatory mechanisms must therefore intervene to adjust individual expectations and behaviors to the general logic of the regime of accumulation. This "mode of regulation" provides the frame by which individuals might orient themselves to meet the conditions necessary for economic reproduction and accumulation. The establishment of a mode of regulation is not a given but rather the outcome of social and political struggles, victories, defeats, and compromises.

For Lipietz, social groups do not engage in endless struggle. Different social groups, dominant and subordinate, establish alliances and make concessions. Social bloc is the term he uses to designate a relatively stable system of relations of domination. A social bloc becomes hegemonic, in his account, when its interests correspond with those of a nation. The societal paradigm is the structuration of these interests and identities within political discourse.

The regime of accumulation, mode of regulation, hegemonic bloc, and societal paradigm each result from conflictual processes of historical development, and their mutual compatibility within a model of socio-economic development cannot be taken for granted or predicted. At the same time, their consolidation is undermined both by contradictions internal to the model of development and by forces repressed by, overlooked within, or excluded from the model.

Thus Lipietz identifies two forms of struggle that emerge in relation to any paradigm or model of development. The first involves struggles between social groups within the same paradigm, by those who uphold it, over differences concerning the distribution of benefits to be guaranteed within the regime of accumulation. These struggles are fought over perceptions of encroachments or anomalies and focus on the regulatory regime. The second form of struggle involves struggles against the hegemonic paradigm from the perspective of an alternative paradigm, identities, or interests based on or proposing a different conception of social life along with another regime of accumulation and different forms of regulation and composed of a different social bloc.

In the contemporary, post-Fordist, context, two societal paradigms are presently in conflict. These paradigms Lipietz terms the "liberal-productivist" and the "alternative." The values of each paradigm are compatible with a specific conception of democracy, which corresponds with specific economic bases.

Liberal-productivism is the neoliberal model of economics and politics that has become prominent globally over the last twenty years. Neoliberalism broke the Fordist link between technical progress and social progress. Accumulation, innovation, and competitive advantage become the only justifications required under liberal-productivism. Liberal-productivism offers a decentralized hierarchy in which democracy has retreated on every front. Debate and discussion are silenced by the omnipotent forces of the world market, and the proportion of humanity able to influence its own existence is reduced.

The alternative paradigm is exemplified in movements of ecology. Political ecology offers a new possibility: the convergence of social movements. This paradigm is similar to the red one in that it is based on a materiality of relations by opposing an "existing state of affairs," productivism most notably, which it analyzes that it might be opposed and in being based on a counter-system of values expressing "solidarity, autonomy, ecological responsibility, and democracy." Political ecology also proposes an alternative project of eco-development. Ecology offers a new movement capable of uniting those hopes for a new way of "living together," relating to each other, and defending the natural world as expressed in the new social movements.

The core of political ecology is not the environment, a background to human activity, but rather the complex totality of humans, their activities, and nature. Political ecology is focused on the mediations between humans and nature or, in other words, economy. Nature has become humanized. Everything from the acidity of water to the thickness of the ozone layer has become influenced by human activity. This means that humanity has become accountable for nature.

Ecology extends the respect for life beyond social democracy, the great achievement of the labor movement, to encompass international and intergenerational justice as well as justice between living species. In this way it moves justice beyond the purview of any specific state. Political ecology transcends social democracy, as social democracy transcended civil democracy, in recognizing new rights, entitlements, and subjects of rights.

Much like orthodox Marxists who posed the workers' movement as the agent of history, Lipietz presents the ecological paradigm as the privileged movement that encompasses the emancipatory aspirations of all movements and struggles. Although Lipietz propounds the autonomy and independence of social movements, he also sees this autonomy as facilitating "their possible future convergence in a Green paradigm." This convergence, in Lipietz's view, is not given by social forces, as in Marxist immiseration theories, but results from political and social constructions.

In the end, Lipietz's vision of how to implement his alternatives is a fairly limited reform of the welfare state. Lipietz, similar to other French political ecologists such as André Gorz, advocates a reduction in normal working time to an average thirty-hour week, with normal remuneration. Increasing free time and work sharing without loss of income are expressions of solidarity, as they imply a redistribution of income to be effective. This work sharing will only be accepted by those already employed if it leads to a growth of free time, which is a prerequisite for autonomy. Despite his stated preference for libertarian visions of socialism, Lipietz, like Gorz, offers a social democratic approach to the reduction of free time, in which it is only effected through state reforms, regulations, and taxation. Similarly, ecological and social conditions will be imposed on free trade through diplomatic means.

In other matters, Lipietz's approach is rather conservative. For example, he proposes the reintegration of unemployed workers through development of a third sector between the private and public sectors. This third sector would be subsidized by the government to provide socially necessary services while paying workers a normal wage and improved status. In his view, it expresses a move from the welfare state to the welfare community. However, this is merely a semantic shift because the third sector as described by Lipietz is still primarily funded and maintained by the state. Rather than a welfare community, it more closely resembles a workfare state.

JEFF SHANTZ

See also **Andre Gorz**

Biography

Alain Lipietz was born on September 19, 1947, and studied engineering at the École Polytechnique. Following two years working as a civil engineer after graduation, Lipietz has gone on to hold a number of diverse positions, including Chief Engineer with the Highway Department and Director of Research at CNRS. A former Maoist, Lipietz took part in a number of new left groups before becoming a candidate for the French Green Party in 1986. In 1992, he coordinated a study on the positions of various countries participating in the United Nations Conference on the Environment and Development (The Rio Conference). In 1997, he was made a member of the Conseil d'analyse économique by Prime Minister Lionel Jospin. Since 1999, Lipietz has been an elected representative of the Green Party in the European Parliament. In 2001, his election as Green Party candidate for the French presidential elections ended when controversy over public statements led the party to replace him with another candidate. Since 1973, Alain Lipietz has served as a researcher, currently as Director of Research, at CEPREMAP (Centre d'études prospectives d'économie mathématique appliquées à la planification) in Paris. His numerous writings on ecology and political economy have been widely influential among academics and activists alike.

Selected Works

Le Monde enchanté, 1983
L'Audace ou l'enlisement—sur les politiques économiques de la gauche, 1984
The Enchanted World: Inflation, Credit and the World Crisis, 1985
Mirages and Miracles: The Crisis of Global Fordism, 1988
Berlin, Baghdad, Rio, 1992
With G. Benko, *Les Régions qui gagnent*, 1992
Towards a New Economic Order: Postfordism, Ecology and Dmocracy, 1993
Green Hopes: The Future of Political Ecology, 1995
La société en sablier: le partage du travail contre la déchirure sociale, 1996
Coeditor with G. Benko, *La Richesse des régions. La nouvelle géographie socio-économique*, 2000
Coeditor with G. Benko and Pablo Ciccolella, *Economia y espacio: entre el mundo y la región*, 2001

Further Reading

Aglietta, M., "Capitalism at the Turn of the Century: Regulation Theory and the Challenge of Social Change," *New Left Review*, (1998) 232
Albritton, R., Itoh, Makoto, Westra, Richard, and Zuege, Alan, eds., *The Fortunes and Misfortunes of Post-Fordism*, London: Macmillan, 2001
Bonefeld, Werner, and Holloway, John, *Post-Fordism and Social Form*, London: Macmillan, 1991
Boyer, R., *The Regulation School*, New York: Columbia University Press, 1990
Clarke, S., "Overaccumulation, Class Struggle and the Regulation Approach," *Capital and Class*, (1988) 36
Clarke, S., "New Utopias for Old: Fordist Dreams and Post-Fordist Fantasies," *Capital and Class*, (1990) 42
Duménil, Gérard, and Lévy, Dominique, "Les Regulationnistes pouvaient-ils apprendre davantage des classiques? Une analyse critique de quatre modeles," *Economies et Sociétés*, 27,6 (1993): 117–155
Dunford, M., "Theories of Regulation," *Society and Space*, 8,3 (1990)
Graham, Julie, "Fordism/Post-Fordism, Marxism/Post Marxism," *Rethinking Marxism* 4,1 (1991)
MacLeod, Gordon, "Globalizing Parisian Thought-Waves: Recent Advances in the Study of Social Regulation, Politics, Discourse and Space," *Progress in Human Geography*, 21,4 (1997): 530–553
Robles, Alfredo C., *French Theories of Regulation and Conceptions of the International Division of Labour*, London: St. Martin's, 1994
Ruccio, David F., "Fordism on a World Scale: International Dimensions of Regulation," *Review of Radical Political Economics*, 21,4 (1989): 33–53
Rudy, Alan, "Nature, Labor and Gender: Marx, Lipietz and Political Ecology," *Capitalism, Nature, Socialism*, 11,2 (2000): 83–90
Tickell, Adam, and Peck, Jemic A., "Accumulation, Regulation and the Geographies of Post-Fordism: Missing Links in Regulationist Research," *Progress in Human Geography*, 16,2 (1992): 190–218
Whiteside, Kerry, *Divided Natures: French Contributions to Political Ecology*, London: MIT Press, 2002
Whiteside, Kerry, "Regulation, Ecology, Ethics: The Red-Green Politics of Alain Lipietz," *Capitalism, Nature, Socialism*, 7,3 (1996). 31–55
Whiteside, Kerry, "The Political Practice of the Verts," *Modern and Contemporary France*, 48 (1992): 14–21

LITERARY THEORY AND CRITICISM

French criticism and theory cannot be easily divorced from the overall intellectual climates that have waxed and waned throughout twentieth-century France. In fact, how we even categorize past developments and trends in France depends a great deal on recent historical perspectives. For example, from the vantage point of the 1950s, one might draw up the following short list of major figures to be considered: Marcel Proust, André Gide, Henri Bergson, Paul Valéry, André Malraux, Paul Claudel, Jean Cocteau, Gabriel Marcel, Jean-Paul Sartre, Simone de Beauvoir, and Albert

Camus. The surrealists, André Breton, Paul Eluard, and Louis Aragon, had already passed out of favor, and figures such as Guillaume Apollinaire, Antonin Artaud, Jean Genet, and Ferdinand Céline were viewed as more marginal exponents of avant-garde writing.

From the perspective of the 1970s, however, this canonical list had changed quite drastically, for by then, Gide, Claudel, Malraux, Cocteau, Camus, de Beauvoir, and Sartre had become far less fashionable. The new syllabus that replaced them included figures who had hitherto been quite obscure. They included Ferdinand de Saussure, Georges Bataille, Maurice Blanchot, Julien Gracq, Francis Ponge, René Char, Emmanuel Lévinas, Michel Leiris, Alexandre Kojève, Jacques Lacan, Maurice Merleau-Ponty, Roman Jakobson, and Claude Lévi-Strauss. Of course, these figures were very much the contemporaries of those they replaced, and when they did emerge, it was as if a whole generation of people, hitherto unnoticed, had suddenly stepped out from behind the shadows, even if many of them were already quite well established before World War II. Among these new faces were Bataille, Leiris, Lévinas, and Lacan. Moreover, it is significant that they came to prominence under the auspices of a younger generation of intellectuals whose careers were established in the postwar period: Roland Barthes, Paul Ricoeur, Michel Foucault, Jacques Derrida, René Girard, Julia Kristeva, Phillippe Sollers, Francois Lyotard, Gerard Genette, Jean Ricardou, and Gilles Deleuze. Yet another group, which included figures such as Hélène Cixous, Luce Irigaray, Philippe Lacoue-Labarthe, Felix Guattari, Jean-Luc Nancy, and Sarah Kofman, was to emerge shortly thereafter in the early 1970s. Together, these individuals form the better part of a list that today constitutes received opinion as to who the major French critics and theorists of the last four decades have been.

No doubt there is an argument to be made that these sorts of lists are problematic. For example, the Surrealists are really far more germane to 1960s thinking than one is usually led to believe, given that André Breton's well-known surrealist manifestos more than anticipate the Hegel–Marx–Freud conjunction that has been so central to Kristeva, Derrida, Foucault, Deleuze, and Guattari. Back in the late 1920s, Breton and other surrealists posited the idea of hysteria as a critical form of social contestation and saw it in terms of a revolt against gender oppression, something that more than slightly anticipated work by Foucault, Deleuze, Guattari, Irigaray, and Cixous. We have also not been encouraged to see that most of Lacan's ideas are really an amalgam of Jean-Paul Sartre's chapters on concrete relations with others (in *Being and Nothingness*) and Claude Lévi-Strauss's investigation of kinship rules in *Structures of Elementary Kinship*. In Lacan, there is

also the considerable influence of Breton, if not Dada/ Surrealism more broadly speaking, with its emphases on language, distortion, paranoia, foreclosure, the gaze, semblance, collage (or inmixing), *jouissance*, and acting out in public.

Deleuze, for his part, was open about his admiration for Bergson, though, oddly, Bergson seemed to have fallen from grace in the 1960s and the years that followed. Similarly, Gabriel Marcel has had enormous influence in the context of Paul Ricoeur's philosophical work (and, again, Lacan's thinking, as in the context of his remarks on *homo viator* in a late seminar), though Marcel's reputation also did not quite survive the intellectual revolution of the 1960s. Derrida's intellectual engagements with Valéry, and to some extent the Geneva School of literary criticism, tell a similar story.

Also problematic is the fact that the various syllabi are careful to avoid France's traditions of right-wing thinking. For example, it is not surprising that after World War II, existentialism would necessarily rise to prominence, given its political emphasis on freedom of choice, individuality, the rejection of totalitarianism, and the embrace of Otherness. It is also clear why figures like Proust and Gide might be emphasized, given their minority status as gay writers, and why individualists like Valéry—writing in the name of art—or religiously identified authors, men of moral decency like Paul Claudel might be privileged. In fact, however, these selections slant historical reality by excluding right-wing thinkers, if not fascist thinkers like Robert Brasillach, Maurice Bardèche, and Pierre Drieu la Rochelle.

The right-wing identification is especially problematic insofar as it was unstable. For example, Georges Bernanos started out as a writer in league with the infamous right-wing *L'Action Française*, but later repudiated the Catholic Church's collusion with Franco and Maurras and denounced the imposture of Vichy. Drieu la Rochelle apparently had both leftist and rightist leanings, and though he actively collaborated with Nazism during the war, he had also become disillusioned with fascism. He died in 1945 on his second suicide attempt and still remains a key figure for grasping what in France is called "la malaise moral" of a generation.

More nuanced political instability is illustrated in the case of Valéry, who had right-wing leanings and published his work in that context during the 1930s, though in essays like "Freedom of the Mind" (1939) it is hard to tell exactly where his allegiances lie.

The career of Maurice Blanchot has been much written about, and whatever one concludes, it is quite apparent that he occupied different political positions that cannot be reliably and clearly plotted, given the ambiguities and contradictions. Even someone like Sartre, who was opposed to fascism, managed to get his work staged and published during World War II, something that separates him from someone like Samuel Beckett, who lived in Provence, was active in the Resistance, and did not attempt to produce work publicly during that time. Similarly, one could contrast Lacan, who used World War II as a sort of study break (he studied Freud but also took courses in Chinese), to the poet René Char, who risked his life in the Resistance. Even Simone de Beauvoir's memoirs show that she was spending much of her time bicycling around Paris during the war, often to get to the Bibliotheque Nationale so that she could forget the war by means of immersing herself in Hegel's *Phenomenology of Mind*.

After the war, it was unacceptable to not be a leftist, and during the 1960s, leftism was the official politics of *Tel Quel*, the journal that printed the critically revolutionary writings of Barthes, Foucault, Derrida, Kristeva, Sollers, and so many others on the revised syllabus of the time (it was also the name of the group of writers associated with the journal). In fact, the political reality had been that as in the pre–World War II period, intellectuals after the war had been united by a sort of socialist mentality, in which leftist and rightist thinking actually overlapped to some degree.

This has been generally overlooked in Anglo-American receptions of recent French theory. For example, the Lacanian emphasis on the law of the father can be inflected from both the right (it is in tune with the patriarchy of *L'Action Française*) and the left (it satisfies Marxist theories of constructed identity). Similarly, Georges Bataille's fascination with violence and sacrifice engages with a mentality of vitalism and mass death that has strong analogies with the writings of fascist figures like Ernst Jünger, whom Bataille quotes in his *Oeuvres Complètes*. Indeed, Bataille's "La Part Maudit" is quite easy to read from a right-wing perspective as a fatalistic apologia for events like the Holocaust (that these sorts of events of horrific counterproductive expenditure are the rule, not the exception, in human societies, however appalling, and therefore, one cannot moralize). Again, Julia Kristeva's interest in Ferdinand Céline, which she took up in her book *Pouvoirs de l'horreur*, is quite politically ambiguous, because one does not quite know whether it condemns or apologizes for Céline. Kristeva's later writings on the maladies of the soul (i.e., of society) are in keeping with prewar right-wing complaints about the evils of capitalism (narcissism, lack of authority, despiritualization, political drift, sexual perversion). Complaining of democracy, Kristeva wrote in *The Sense and Non-Sense of Revolt*, "There are no longer laws but measures. (What progress! How reassuring for democracy!). . . . This means that, in the end, the new world

order normalizes and corrupts; it is at once normalizing and pervertible." Kristeva is quite in tune with Drieu la Rochelle when she argues that without laws, everything comes undone and values lose any efficacy. Derrida's ambiguous apologias for figures like Heidegger (who is perhaps defensible) and Carl Schmitt (who may well not be) is a far more subtle form of leaning to the right, one that Derrida dilutes considerably with what in recent years appears to be a liberal (rather than radical leftist) ideology, as in, for example, his writings on the freedom of the university. The writings of so-called New Philosophers, such as Henri Bernard Lévy and André Glucksmann, who reject both right- and left-wing politics, also hark back to a certain political ambiguity in French politics that Zev Sternhell tersely labeled, "neither left nor right," his point being that intellectuals of this sort are actually both and that such thinkers are easily seduced by fascism of some sort or other. How French Jews figure into all this (consider Bergson, Lévinas, Lévi-Strauss, Derrida, Finkielkraut, Lévy, and Glucksmann) is something that still requires sustained critical examination.

The history of French literary criticism threads its way through this rocky political and cultural history. What distinguishes French criticism, in particular, is the fact that so many of its great literary writers have also been enormously important literary critics and cultural commentators. One sees this already in late-nineteenth-century figures such as Charles Baudelaire and Stéphane Mallarmé, and in the early twentieth century, it is evident in the Surrealist movement, in which the difference between creative and critical writing is at times subverted or allowed to overlap. For figures like Breton, the writings of Freud on, for example, the dreamwork, were not examples of objective science so much as they were *de facto* surreal projects imagining another economy of mind whose laws had less in common with the stock market and the price of goods than with a counter-logic of creative (i.e. perverse) thinking that invalidated the primacy of reason and rationality. Moreover, this led the Surrealists to consider notions of marginality and to come to the defense of the socially marginalized. This points to the fact that much French criticism has been at war with what contemporary Germans now call the Enlightenment project, which had to do with standardization (or, conversely, strategic marginalization). Notions like reason and the self were obviously required for such a tactic to take place.

One sees the confrontation with Enlightenment thinking not only in the Surrealists but also in Bergson, Lévinas, Sartre, Lacan, and Derrida, whose writings on Rousseau and Kant demonstrate how much this battle is relevant even to the latter part of the twentieth century. This made certain right-wing thinkers, such as Heidegger or Schmitt, attractive in that they, too, were fighting against Enlightenment norms and forms of thinking. Not only did literary critics criticize the primacy of reason and the anthropology on which it rested (the primacy of Cogito or self), but some wrote literary texts that subverted Enlightenment (or "bourgeois") thinking. The writings of Jean-Paul Sartre, Maurice Blanchot, Julien Gracq, Michel Leiris, Alain Robbe-Grillet, Marguerite Duras, Michel Butor, and Philippe Sollers exemplify this trend.

No less striking is the group of French academic critics associated with phenomenological criticism, which included Gaston Bachelard, Georges Poulet, Jean-Pierre Richard, Marcel Raymond, Jean Rosset, and Jean Starobinski. In the prewar period, Gide and Valery took up diametrically opposed views: Gide argued that it was the genius and person of the author that concerned true creativity, whereas for Valéry, this had to do with the systematicity of the text itself. Phenomenological criticism married the two. It took the position that the systematicity of the text has something important to tell us about the consciousness of the one who wrote it. The key to phenomenological criticism was that its proponents imagined that the literary text is not a thing in itself but the trace of someone's consciousness that can be intuited by another: the reader. Albert Béguin, Charles du Bos, and Albert Thibaudet, who were critics active between the two world wars, had already laid some of the groundwork for this kind of approach insofar as they emphasized the personal sensibility of the critic and its self-reflexive elaboration. Du Bos is perhaps the most important precursor, in that he looked for a literary "milieu intérieur." This interior is qualitative and can be accessed through stylistic analysis. Evidently, Du Bos was searching for the soul of the work, its spiritual dimension, which was mediated by the self-consciousness and reflexivity of language. A work might therefore express a sluggish or lugubrious quality that wards off feeling, or it may be sprightly and lucid in ways that reflect a more affable soul. This is less naïve than it sounds. After all, works do affect us in a qualitative way that touches on sensation, something that recalls a thinker like David Hume, for whom perception and sensation cannot be divorced. Sensation is constitutive of cognition, and through sensation we come into close proximity with the quality of a work not just as a thing but as the expression of consciousness as a process of thinking in which the observer participates.

For the phenomenologal critic, the central point is that form animates the consciousness of the reader, who, in turn, intuits the consciousness of the form's source: that of the author. Phenomenological critics imagine the interlocution with the author's consciousness to be mediated if not determined by the form, shape, or structure that make up the text. It is this formal dimension of the literary work that concerned postwar critics, who were asking what thematic clues are revealed by the structure of the work insofar as understanding the consciousness of its source is concerned. This is where phenomenological and psychoanalytical forms of critical analysis merged, as in the case of Charles Mauron's *The Unconscious in the Work and Life of Racine*. It is also the juncture at which psychoanalysts entered into the game of literary analysis, as in the case of writings by Jean Laplanche and J. B. Pontalis.

Generally, phenomenologically oriented critics have looked for thematic invariants—for example, Jean-Pierre Richard's examination of depth (*profondeur*), George's Poulet's examination of circularity, or Gaston's Bachelard's examination of primary elements (earth, water, fire, air). These themes are not just literary devices, but existential clues to the workings of the text's founding consciousness—what in psychological terms might be called its complexes. The idea was not so much that finding these complexes would empirically answer questions about what a text definitively means but that they would help us better understand how the text complicates, defers, and disseminates meanings, even as they reveal something qualitative or particular to the text, say, Richard's observation of Baudelaire's "veiled" profundities versus Rimbaud's "superficial" depths.

In the 1950s, critics like Roland Barthes merged a phenomenological sensibility with specific attention to the so-called "sign." *Writing Degree Zero* was quite antiphenomenological in that it searched for a zero degree of qualitativeness or particularity in writing, because quality was always to be associated with questions having to do with the particularity of selfhood (in its bourgeois form as a personality with inimical properties particular to it). Still, in books like *Mythologies*, in which Barthes started reading popular culture as a semioclastic world, he drew from phenomenology in terms of making qualitative distinctions having to do with cars, groceries, events, and performances. For example, his juxtaposition of wrestling to boxing is qualitative, and however semiotic it may be, it still reveals a phenomenology of the touch (pressure and torsion in wrestling [which is supposedly Baroque and Catholic], hitting or battering in boxing [which is supposedly of the Enlightenment and typical of a Protestant phenomenology of distance]). Barthes's later interest in psychoanalysis (*jouissance* or pleasure) is also mediated by a phenomenology of the sign that is always countersigned by the consciousness of the critic. One detects something similar in Michel Foucault's writings on literature (e.g., his brilliant book on Raymond Roussel) and in Julia Kristeva's famous analysis of abjection in Céline.

Derrida's *Of Grammatology* of the late 1960s was an attempt to get beyond the gravitational pull of phenomenological analyses, and one can see in his formulation of the concept of *écriture* a bold attempt to divorce the sign from Cogito and consciousness. Sollers's novels of the period (e.g., *Nombres*) undertook a similar project: that of divorcing writing from expression. In literary criticism, this was echoed by the emergence of structuralist analyses by critics such as Tzvetan Todorov, Gérard Genette, and later, Michael Riffaterre, who rejected the phenomenological text/consciousness relation. Yet, in works like Derrida's *Glas*, we can see how even in the most brilliant attempt to divorce the sign from the consciousness of the writer, there is nevertheless a qualitative phenomenological recovery that takes place as tone: the death-knell of the text's style. Derrida's later autobiographical writings testify to this ultimate failure of getting beyond the pull of the phenomenology, as do texts by Irigaray and Cixous that are extremely lyrical and phenomenological in intent.

Given the advent of a phenomenologically oriented criticism in the 1950s, and its rejection by way of structuralist and semiotic approaches via Roland Barthes, Lévi-Strauss, Roman Jakobson, Tzvetan Todorov, Gerard Genette, Jacques Derrida, and Philippe Sollers, we can see from today's vantage point that the persistence of phenomenology has been much stronger and defiant than one could assume in the heyday of the structuralist analysis that followed on the heels of *nouvelle critique* (close reading). Notice that, of late, French intellectuals have begun appreciating and feting the work of Jean Starobinski, which deservedly merits a central place in one's consideration of recent French literary criticism, as it represents an audacious and balanced blend of phenomenology, biography, nouvelle critique, structuralist analysis, and psychoanalysis. Central to Starobinski's work has been the study of intersubjectivity and questions of opacity and transparency: the flight into literature to overcome the physical limitations of consciousness, an overcoming that is a spiritual journey into transparency (openness, freedom, the sublime). No doubt, the work of Louis Marin, Michel de Certeau, and Gilles Deleuze displays a similar ability to pull together diverse critical and philosophical strands in historical contexts like the Renaissance or late seventeenth century, and in such highly original ways as to not overlap. In recent years, Deleuze's writings have inspired younger theorists like Alain Badiou, and it is this line of influence that is now making itself felt abroad, particularly in North America, where Deleuze's enormously creative work is getting the renewed attention it justly deserves.

HERMAN RAPOPORT

See also **entries on the individuals mentioned in this entry**

Further Reading

Barthes, Roland, *Writing Degree Zero*
Barthes, Roland, *Mythologies*
Bataille, Georges, *Oeuvres Complètes*
Derrida, Jacques, *Glas*
Derrida, Jacques, *Of Grammatology*
Foucault, Michel, *Death and the Labyrinth*
Kristeva, Julia, *Pouvoirs de l'horreur*
Kristeva, Julia, *The Sense and Non-Sense of Revolt*
Mauron, Charles, *The Unconscious in the Work and Life of Racine*
Sartre, Jean-Paul, *Being and Nothingness*
Lévi-Strauss, Claude, *Structures of Elementary Kinship*
Sollers, Philippe, *Nombres*

LORAUX, NICOLE
Classicist

Nicole Loraux defined her research as an opening-up of classics to anthropology and to questions more specifically centered on Greek models of the *imaginaire*, which may be defined as a prediscursive level of experience that underpins culture; a set of images. Looking both at the possibilities of democracy and at the same time the cultural representations of sexual difference, Loraux invested Classical Greek studies with a reevaluation of the representation of citizenship and of the division of the sexes, taking into account the power of the *imaginaire* as well as the discourse of the normative.

In *Les Enfants d'Athéna* (1981), Loraux examines the apparent paradox inherent in the Athenian sense of identity. On the one hand, politics was predominantly a matter for men, and on the other, the city is named after a goddess, Athena. This opens the question of how the division of the sexes relates to Athenian ideas of democracy and citizenship—and the related question of the myth of origin—and the consequent view of the mother.

In *Façons tragiques de tuer une femme* (Tragic Ways of Killing a Woman, 1985) Loraux explores the specific forms of death reserved for women in tragedy. Death by another hand is as frequent for women as for men, but it is in the suicide of wives and the sacrifice of virgins that a distinction between the sexes is made, male suicide being rare. The specific location of the death-act in the body and the spectacular enactment of the killing of women are contextualized by Loraux as a representation-effect of the heroic code. *The Experiences of Teiresias* reflects on the centrality of the problematic feminine in the Athenian imaginary and on the problematic relationship between the feminine and the heroic.

In *Les Mères en Deuil* (Mothers in Mourning, 1990) Loraux looks at how the force of maternal grieving is given space in the theatre as if to channel its effect away from the public sphere. Hecuba laments the death of her daughter Polyxena by saying "Polyxena is my city." "The incommensurable character of the loss" of a child gives utterance to a maternal *menis* (wrath) that kills only sons, as it were in revenge on the father or husband.

In *L'Invention d'Athenes* (The Invention of Athens, 1993), Loraux studies the genre of the funeral oration, arguing that its function of praising the city in the names of its dead constituted an "invention" of the city, in that it placed the event in question against a background of myth and heroic exploits, thus maintaining Athens' claims to leadership. The funeral oration thus functioned in the social *imaginaire* as a kind of pre-Aristotelian discourse of democracy.

Né de la terre (Born of the Earth, 1998) looks at the myth of the foundation of Athens by Hephaistos, who, rejected by Athena, spilled his semen over the earth and so engendered Erichthonios, the mythical father of the Athenians. Loraux analyzes myths of origin in terms of the concept of founding alterity, as distinct from the reassuring celebration of like by like. The myth of origin of Athenian women is that of Pandora, constructed rather than engendered by the gods and sent as man's punishment for Prometheus's acquisition of fire from Heaven. Pandora then brings down on humanity the evils of the world through her curiosity. The "race of women" is thus constructed by the Athenians as a divine punishment; at the level of the *imaginaire* this gives a context to the exclusion of women from democracy.

In *La Cité divisée* (The Divided City, 1997), Loraux examines the use of forgetting as a political strategy in Athens, the "birthplace" of politics. After the defeat of Athens by Sparta in 405 B.C.E. and the subsequent return to democracy in 403 B.C.E., the city took an oath of forgetting: The citizens were to swear to forget the evils of the past. Loraux's reflection on this has an obvious bearing on contemporary history, particularly European history, which views remembrance rather as the gift of time and the guarantor of avoidance of past mistakes. At the same time, the Athenian amnesty (*Amnistie*, *démocratie*, as Loraux suggests) was seen not only as an enabling strategy for the restructuring of the city's integrity, a pragma of stability, but also as a generous forgetting of divisions, of *stasis*, and one of the first amnesties of Western civilization.

La Voix endeuillée (The Mourning Voice, 1999) considers the significance of mourning. Mourning is normally a delimited period during which the living participate ritually in death and the dead in life. This implies that once the ritual is accomplished, the separation of life from death will be enacted and life may proceed. Athens limited the expression of women's mourning, perceived as demoralizing in the public sphere. Loraux sees Electra's mourning as a refusal ever to separate from the father's death in a way that is antipolitical, against the *polis*.

The classicist Charles Segal, in his presidential address to the American Philological Association, gives just emphasis to the classicist's preoccupation with tangible correspondences between fact and theory, greater, in his view, than in the modern languages: "In literary criticism, for example, we tend to feel that interpretation should bear a reasonable resemblance to the normal and precise meanings of words and the standard usages of language." Loraux's unique contribution has been the recontextualization of the discourse of the normative in the discourse of the *imaginair*. As the classicist Froma Zeitlin writes, "Nicole Loraux's work throughout her career has been bold, original, and provocative. The subtlety of her thought and depth of knowledge established new standards for the interpretation of political and social institutions of the fifth-century Athens that have since become indispensable for our understanding of ancient Greece."

The growth of research on the construction of gender and civic identity in fifth-century Athens is a testament to the importance of her complex reading of the *imaginaire* of ancient Greek culture.

ANGELA RYAN

Biography

Nicole Loraux was born on April 26, 1943. She was named lecturer in the Department of History and Anthropology of the Greek Polis at the Ecole des hautes études en sciences sociales in Paris in 1975. She was eventually named director of research and was then made chair of department. In 1995, she was involved in a serious accident that left her unable to speak and with limited motor functions, although she remained lucid. She died after surgery on April 6, 2003.

Selected Works

Les Enfants d'Athéna, 1981; as *The Children of Athena: Athenian Ideas about Citizenship and the Division between the Sexes*, translated by C. Levine, 1993

Façons tragiques de tuer une femme, 1985; as *Tragic Ways of Killing a Woman*, translated by A. Forster, 1987

Les Expériences de Tirésias, 1990; as *The Experiences of Teiresias: the Feminine and the Greek Man*, translated by P. Wissing, 1995

Les Mères en Deuil, 1990; as *Mothers in Mourning: With the Essay of Amnesty and Its Opposite (Myth and Poetics)*, translated by C. Pache, 1998

L'Invention d'Athenes, 1993; as *The Invention of Athens: The Funeral Oration in the Classical City*, translated by Alan Sheridan, 1986

Territoires, frontières, passages, 1997

La Cité divisée: l'oubli dans la mémoire d'Athènes, 1997; as *The Divided City: Forgetting in the Memory of Athens*, 2002

Né de la terre, 1998; as *Born of the Earth: Myth and Politics in Athens*, translated by S. Stewart, 2000

La Voix endeuillée, 1999; as *The Mourning Voice: An Essay on Greek Tragedy*, translted by E. T. Rawlings, 2002

Further Reading

Zeitlin, Froma I., *Playing the Other: Gender and Society in Classical Greek Literature*, Chicago: University of Chicago Press, 1995

LUBAC, HENRI DE, CARDINAL
Catholic Theologian and Priest

From early in his professorial career an eclectic and prolific scholar, a courageous theologian who was forced to withdraw a book under threat of condemnation by name in a formal papal encyclical, a simple and humble priest of radiant sanctity, de Lubac was certainly the greatest French Catholic theologian of the twentieth century. Theologically, his towering achievement was to take the decisive step in disentangling a centuries-old confusion in the relationship between God and human beings, or, more technically, between supernatural grace and human rationality.

That confusion, which had separated rationality from orientation to a "union with God," implying justification on earth and salvation after death, had not only dominated Christian thought and Catholic theology since the thirteenth-century reaction of Duns Scotus to the "naturalism" of Thomas Aquinas, but was the major force powering the most irresolvable and bitter disputes among Christians, including the sixteenth-century schisms, over 600 years.

To some extent, de Lubac's solution had been overshadowed in the theological *Cahiers* of Joseph Maréchal and the work of Pierre Rousselot and one or two others, mostly associated with the review *La Nouvelle Revue théologique*. Essentially, de Lubac determined the theological means by which it became possible within the bounds of Christian orthodoxy to regard human rationality as naturally endowed with a supernatural finality. De Lubac was foremost a patristic scholar. The strength of his position lay in his return to the theology of the fathers of the Church, before the scholastics had attempted to define "supernature" to describe the effects of the redemption and what in human experience was extrinsic to the aspirations and exigences of human nature. Its weakness, which

caused the trouble consequent to his 1946 *Surnaturel* and was eventually remedied by his Jesuit colleague Karl Rahner, was a failure to confront high and postmedieval theology on its own scholastic terms.

De Lubac was born in Cambrai, entered the Jesuit order in 1913, and in 1917 suffered a war wound in the head that was to cause him serious headaches throughout his life. Insofar as the word can be used of anyone who lived close to the action in two world wars, who was suspended from teaching for suspected heresy, and who became a cardinal, de Lubac's career was outwardly normal. He was ordained priest in 1927, finished the routine stages of his Jesuit training, and was appointed professor of theology in 1935 at the Jesuit faculty of Fourvières, in Lyons. His first book, *Catholicisme*, appeared in 1938. Characteristically, *Catholicisme* concentrated on the social parameters of Christian commitment, which continued to be central to de Lubac's concerns, whether he was writing about the Eucharist as the sign of incorporation into the Christian community (*Corpus mysticum*, 1944), predicting the defeat of Feuerbach-type atheism (*Le Drame de l'humanisme athée*, 1944), showing the great strengths, but also the limitations of Buddhism (e.g., *Aspects du bouddhisme*, 1951, and *La rencontre du bouddhisme et de l'Occident*, 1952), repudiating anti-Semitism, or writing his formal works on patristic theology and exegesis (*Histoire et Esprit, L'intelligence de l'Ecriture d'après Origène*, 1950, and *Exégèse médiévale*, 1959 and 1964).

De Lubac was suspended from teaching in 1950. It was the price that had been negotiated by the Jesuits to avoid a condemnation by name of one of their number in the postwar encyclical of 1950 *Humani Generis*, by which Pius XII sought to curb some of the more radical rethinking of traditional theology that had emerged after the war. De Lubac moved to one of the Jesuit houses in Paris, producing the spiritually impressive *Méditation sur l'Eglise* of 1953 and a reworking of the 1946 *Surnaturel* in two volumes, published in 1965, *Le Mystère du surnaturel* and *Augustinisme et théologie moderne*.

He also wrote several works in defense of his close friend and Jesuit colleague Pierre Teilhard du Chardin (1881–1955). By 1960, de Lubac had been rehabilitated, and he was in that year appointed a formal theological adviser to the second Vatican Council, which John XXIII opened at Rome in 1962. De Lubac's pen has been detected in particular behind the pastoral constitution *Gaudium et spes*, issued on December 7, 1965, at the end of the fourth session of the Council under Paul VI.

De Lubac was also active in other areas, helping in 1941 to set up with Jean Daniélou the highly successful series of patristic texts with translations known as

"Sources chrétiennes," and in 1965 joining the board of the review *Concilium*, devoted to the interpretation, diffusion, and implementation of the council's doctrines. He was soon to leave the board, however, and in 1971, with Hans Urs von Balthasar and other members of the International Theological Commission, to found a number of journals under the general umbrella of the title *Communio*.

During World War II, de Lubac, still at Lyons, was at the forefront of those organizing help for colleagues threatened with execution by the Nazis, active as chaplains among the resistance workers in the Maquis, or organizing assistance for the needy in Lyons. He was an extremely well read individual, whose published works include books on Proudhon, Claudel, Péguy, and Pico della Mirandola as well as on his theological specialties.

In spite of the huge erudition, his mind, like his tastes, remained simple, kindly, and direct. It was impossible to coax from him an unkind word about those with whom he disagreed, even if they had done him some injury. De Lubac made a point of being especially helpful to younger colleagues. There is already an Association International Cardinal de Lubac, with an annual bulletin. Nothing serves his memory better than an accurate assessment of his position in the evolution of Catholic theology between the modernist generation of Loisy and the generation formed in the wake of the second Vatican Council.

ANTHONY LEVI

See also **Pierre Teilhard de Chardin**

Biography

Cardinal de Lubac was born in Cambrai in 1896. He studied law at the Facultés Catholiques in Lyon. In 1914, he joined the French army. He was involved in heavy fighting through 1917. After being discharged, he continued his studies at several institutions before joining the priesthood in 1927. In 1929, he was appointed Lecturer in Theology at the Facultés Catholiques. He moved to Paris in 1950. In the next year, he was named theological advisor to the archbishop of Lyon. He was inducted into the Institut de France in 1958. He worked as an expert advisor to the Vatican II council from 1962 until 1965. He was elevated to the Cardinalate in 1983. De Lubac lived in Paris until his death in 1991.

Selected Writings

Catholicisme, les aspects sociaux du dogme, 1938; as *Catholicism; a study of dogma in Relation to the Corporate Destiny of Mankind*, translated by Lancelot C. Sheppard, 1964
Corpus mysticum, 1944

Le Drame de l'humanisme athée, 1944; as *The Drama of Atheist Humanism*, translated by Edith M. Riley, 1949
Surnaturel, 1946
Histoire et Esprit, L'intelligence de l'Ecriture d'après Origène, 1950
Aspects du bouddhisme, 1951; as *Aspects of Buddhism*, translated by George Lamb, 1954
La rencontre du bouddhisme et de l'Occident, 1952
Méditation sur l'Eglise, 1953; as *The Splendour of the Church*, translated by Michael Mason, 1956
Exégèse médiévale, Les quatre sens de l'Ecriture, 4 volumes, 1959–1964
Augustinisme et théologie moderne, 1965; as *Augustinianism and Modern Theology*, translated by Lancelot Sheppard, 1969
Le Mystère du surnaturel, 1965; as *The Mystery of the Supernatural*, translated by Rosemary Sheed, 1967
L'Eternel féminin, étude sur un texte de Teilhard de Chardin, 1968; as *The Eternal Feminine*, translated by René Hague, 1971
Œuvres complètes, (50 vols. projected) Paris, Cerf, 1998–

Further Reading

Actes du Colloque du 12 octobre 1996, *Henri de Lubac et le mysrtère*, Etudes lubaciennes, 1
Association Internationale Cardinal de Lubac, *Bulletin annuel*
McPartlin, Paul, *The Eucharist Makes the Church. Henri de Lubac and John Zizioulos in Dialogue*, Edinburgh: Clark, 1993
McPartlin, Paul, "Eucharist and Church. The Contribution of Henri de Lubac," *The Month* 21 (1988)
Paxton, Nicholas, ed., *Essays in Memory of Cardinal de Lubac*, Salford: St Philip's, 1994
Redfern, Martin, *Henri de Lubac*, 1972
Russo, A., *Henri de Lubac*, Paris, 1994
The Theology of Henri de Lubac. An Overview, Tiber River, 1991
Wagner, Jean-Pierre, *Henri de Lubac, Bibliographie complète*, 2001

LYOTARD, JEAN-FRANÇOIS
Writer, Philosopher

Jean-François Lyotard was part of the postwar wave of twentieth-century French thinkers who were to have a deep and lasting influence across a wide range of academic subjects. Alongside such thinkers as Jacques Derrida, Gilles Deleuze, Jean-Luc Nancy, Michel Foucault, and Philippe Lacoue-Labarthe, many of whom he counted as friends, colleagues, and collaborators, Lyotard forged a reputation as the most philosophical thinker on postmodernity. His book, *La Condition postmoderne* (*The Postmodern Condition*, 1979), led to his international reputation and was the cornerstone of a series of debates on postmodernity, notably with the Frankfurt School through Jürgen Habermas and Manfred Frank and with American thinkers such as Richard Rorty and Frederic Jameson.

The main ideas of *The Postmodern Condition* mark the shift from modern to postmodern narratives. In particular, Lyotard argues that grand narratives and meta-narratives no longer hold sway over the way in which knowledge is sought, evaluated, and organized. This means that claims to historical, political, and scientific progress can no longer be judged according to a narrative that subsumes all others; for example, a Marxist narrative on the logical progress towards a postcapitalist society. Instead, there are many different language games with heterogeneous claims to validity. This state of irresolvable conflict between different claims to truth is the postmodern condition. It can be seen as open to diagnoses in terms of despair, in the sense that it seems doomed to violent and irrational resolutions of differences, for example, through the dominance of capitalist markets. It can also, however, be seen as a reason for jubilation, in the unmasking of false resolutions according to illegitimate grand narratives; for example, colonial narratives that simply ignore the values of the cultures they subsume.

The Postmodern Condition fails to resolve this opposition between hope and despair, because the book does not offer convincing arguments for the necessary end to grand narratives, nor does it provide a full account of how we should react to the new condition of postmodernity. The absence of such explanations can lead to summary dismissals of Lyotard's philosophy. However, these moves fail to take account of much more careful arguments developed in his essays on postmodernity, such as " 'what is postmodernism?' " (added as an appendix to the English translation of *The Postmodern Condition*). In these essays, Lyotard argues that the postmodern is not primarily to be thought in terms of epochs, as if the modern had to end for the postmodern to begin. Instead, the postmodern is part of the modern—its most valuable part, from the point of view of creativity and resistance to injustice. Thus, the reaction to the postmodern condition must be in terms of the production of postmodern works that testify to injustice and create new narratives of resistance against the homogeneity imposed by grand narratives. The correct interpretation of Lyotard's thesis with respect to the postmodern and to grand narratives is that the modern must include the postmodern to retain its productive power and that grand narratives have always been illegitimate.

The importance of *The Postmodern Condition* has been overdone, in terms of the philosophical grounds for resistance to injustice: Lyotard's politics and philosophy lie elsewhere. The three main books of his career are *Discours, figure* (1971), *Économie libidinale* (Libidinal Economy, 1974), and *Le Differend* (1983). These books are complemented by collections of essays such as *Des Dispositifs pulsionnels*, *The Inhuman*, and *Postmodern Fables*, all of which contain essays that are deeper and more carefully crafted than

The Postmodern Condition. The thesis of that book, though timely and influential, must be seen as dependent on, and secondary to, the development of Lyotard's central ideas in the three main books and in his inventive and beautifully crafted essays.

There is one central intuition that runs through all of Lyotard's work. Structures in the fields of knowledge, politics, aesthetics, ethics, and science depend on the intensity of feelings and emotions at work in forming, delimiting, and undoing them. A structure is nothing without those feelings, and yet they mark its internal and external limits. That is, structures matter to us because they carry feelings with them, but they do not have the capacity to tame those feelings, to bring them in as fully understood elements of the structures. Thus, in *Libidinal Economy*, Lyotard is interested in the way sexual desires and sensual feelings can be seen to be at work in economic relations. In *The Differend*, he is interested in the way the feeling of the sublime indicates a limit for particular structures defined as language games. The feeling of the sublime arises because there is such a limit; it is paradoxical combination of the pleasure taken in expanding a given language game and the pain felt in realizing that this expansion is not possible.

The interest in the internal and external limits of structures, where an internal limit marks a capacity of the structure to change that cannot be accounted for by the structure before the change, explain both Lyotard's success and unpopularity. His ideas are exciting in that they bring our attention to what he sees as insurmountable obstacles to the hegemony of forms of knowledge, political ideologies, aesthetic theories, and moral doctrines. However, the skepticism and, some would claim, pessimism implicit in such an interest in obstacles, not to mention the intellectual scandal of a limit that is claimed to be perceivable but not understandable, lead many commentators to be vehemently opposed to his ideas.

Lyotard himself suffers from this opposition in that his concern with politics and ethics is as an activist, particularly exercised by the need to do justice by those who have become excluded by systems and structures. Yet his philosophy does not provide him with the ideological and moral tools for positive, ultimate, or even partial progressive solutions to political and moral problems. His view is that new feelings and emotions will bubble up inside and at the borders of even the most just and comprehensive political systems, knowledge structures, and moral codes. This distrust of progress as allied to a logic or ideology explains Lyotard's longstanding anti-Hegelianism, expressed most forcefully in *Le Differend*.

The disbelief in metanarratives, in any totalizing account of historical progress in politics or morality, draws Lyotard toward marginal forms of politics, not at the expense of mainstream political action, but as a philosophical rider to the view that mainstream action is the highest form. Instead, he defends the view that, as philosophical and artistic thinkers, we have to work within structures in the name of what they cannot handle or exclude. So he maintains his interest in the modernism of Marx and Freud but refuses to give them the last word, preferring to keep that for the capacity of events to generate new and untreatable events. After *Discours, figure*, he qualifies this move as his drift away from Marx and Freud; not a final renunciation, but a skepticism with regard to absolute truths and final theories.

The tension that situates Lyotard between modernism and postmodernism, unwilling to embrace either as solutions to injustice, emerges in his early writings as an activist on the Algerian war of independence. He begins his essays on Algeria in line with the Marxist approach of the group, but gradually, he come to realize that the Algerian proletariat and bourgeoisie cannot be made to fit any given ideological structure so that the Algerian war of independence can be also be seen as a positive revolutionary force. Independence will occur, but revolution for the good will not. His arguments for this thesis are still positivist at this stage; that is, he gives an objective account of why the Algerian proletariat and bourgeoisie do not fit Marxist ideology. The former is too fragmented to constitute a revolutionary proletariat, the latter is too dependent on France, in regressive ways, to lead to the industrial revolution necessary for the constitution of that proletariat.

However, at the same time as he is making these positivist observations, Lyotard begins to ask whether this dissymmetry of structure and fact may not be necessary. He also begins to investigate ways in which he can show that this is the case. This leads to his interest in avant-garde art and literature, Freud and psychoanalysis, and structuralist linguistics. These are brought together in *Discours, figure*, Lyotard's doctoral thesis. For him, avant-garde art and literature do not correspond to any given epoch, but rather have the potential to be revolutionary for any epoch, because they leave a space for the eruption of new desires and feelings. Thus, using Freud's theses on the unconscious in conjunction with structuralist linguistics, Lyotard claims that avant-garde art combines structure with an exemplary openness to intense and transforming desires and feelings. This thesis provides him with an approach to works of art that feeds into a long series of essays on art, artworks, and artists that continues to his death. These essays have yet to be collected together, yet they are of lasting importance as works of criticism and keys to Lyotard's philosophy; see, for example, his wonderful essays on Monory, Cézanne,

or Buren. When they are viewed as a corpus, with *Discours, figure* at the core, it is clear that Lyotard was one of the most original and important art theorists of his age.

The theses developed in *Discours, figure* lead to two connected characteristics of Lyotard's next phase, his libidinal economics; these then come in and out of prominence over the remainder of his output. First, in terms of his own style and his writing on style and philosophy, Lyotard becomes an avant-garde philosopher; that is, a thinker who attempts to use stylistic innovations to make philosophy resistant to reductions in terms of matters of fact, knowledge claims, explicit theses about the world, and formal logical arguments. Instead, reading his works becomes an aesthetic experience similar to reading other great essayists rather than purely academic philosophers. He is a great innovator in terms of the styles of philosophy, constantly attempting to find the right style to make each of his works a work of art as well as a series of philosophical claims.

Second, in terms of the capacity for revolutionary transformations of avant-garde art, Lyotard comes to view all pursuits and things as potentially political. All things conceal within them the potential to become destabilizing events that show the internal and external limits of structures. *Libidinal Economy* and his last works, such as *Soundproof Room* (1998), take this capacity of resistance in all things most seriously, seeing any act that conceals intense feelings and desires, or intensities, in apparently settled structures as a form of political resistance. This leads to the distinction, in Lyotard's work, between politics, what we could call the macropolitics of parties and ideologies, and the political, the avant-garde work of shaking structures in the name of intensities.

This distinction can lead to an undue vilification of Lyotard's work, as if he turns his back on or attacks the benefits flowing from the "right" choices at the level of political parties and systems. At no point, though, can he be read as prescribing such a move. Rather, his view is that, alongside the right decisions in politics, for democracy and against repression, for example, comes a vigilance for that which even they necessarily exclude. His art and humor is often directed against the high seriousness, and hence blindness, of thinkers and structures that claim to embody the right and final political, and moral, solutions and choices. His ex-colleagues from *Socialism or Barbary*, such as Cornelius Castoriadis, are then correct in taking umbrage at the insults and shocking juxtapositions Lyotard deploys in *Libidinal Economy*, but they are wrong to assume that he is simply discounting politics in the name of a more passive attention to the intensities hidden in even the most deplorable structures, acts, and pursuits. Instead, his message is that they reveal the flaws and can also unlock values hidden within hegemonic structures or simple oppositions and hierarchies.

This sense of the political and the attention to that which becomes forgotten and hidden is an important resource for Lyotard's work on art and literature. It gives him a very sensitive eye and ear, but one that always maintains a wider sense of the political, ethical, and philosophical importance of creative moves in the arts. Few thinkers are capable of matching his sensitivity, allied to style and depth. This perhaps explains why his work has been more influential and more readily accepted in art and literature departments, where his work is taken as a way in, and an appropriate response to works, as opposed to departments of philosophy and politics, where his work can seem light and quirky or of marginal interest because of an irresponsible bent.

Yet Lyotard's third central book, *Le Differend*, was taken to be of philosophical and political importance, notably by his French contemporaries, Jean-Luc Nancy and Jacques Derrida. It often strikes readers as his most philosophical work, over and above *Discours, figure* and *Libidinal Economy*, because it avoids the earlier interest in the profusion of structures and intensities (in the way avant-garde art can make everyday objects and body-parts art objects, for example). Instead, Lyotard refines his concept of the event from earlier works through an encounter with Kant on the sublime and Wittgenstein on language games.

Events occur on the borders of language games. They are revealed by the feeling of the sublime that marks both the desire to extend the language game and its impossibility. In the presence of the feeling of the sublime, triggered by an event, we come to realize, for example, that the cognitive language game associated with the sciences reaches a limit on questions of ethics. Similarly, though, we come to realize that the language game of ethics or obligation can never cross over into the cognitive language game: We can never know the good, and what we feel obliged to do can never become a matter of knowledge.

Le Differend has many weaknesses as a systematic work on language games and is inferior to the works of Wittgenstein on which it draws, but it is arguable that this was never to be the core of the book, which instead was Lyotard's original and careful interpretation of Kant. This was to give rise to two more systematic works on Kant's political writings and concept of the sublime, *L'enthousiasme* and *Lessons on the Analytic of the Sublime*. The latter transcripts of Lyotard's lectures on Kant, in particular, show Lyotard as a cautious and scholarly teacher of philosophy, an approach that he must have deliberately eschewed in his more original works because of his sense of the necessity to carry intense feelings and desires and to bear witness to the event even in works of philosophy.

Many different arguments in *Le Differend* have come to prominence, nearly all with some degree of controversy. Manfred Frank, for example, draws attention to the apparent contradiction of an event that can be present and yet not known in any positive way. He also attacks the notion of a *differend*, that is, an irresolvable conflict based on the opposition of language games, claiming instead that it is possible to distinguish between different claims in a conflict; for example, through appeals to norms of truth. He develops these sharp critical points against what he assumes are Lyotard's claims that it is impossible to bear witness for the disappeared victims of the Holocaust except by bearing witness to that disappearance.

In fact, though, as Jacob Rogozinski argues, it is hard to see that Lyotard ever makes such a claim. His point is rather that over and above the right and proper legal and political forms of reparation, we should bear witness to the past and still-present threat of attempts to render others silent, in particular as it remains in the notion that everything can become an object of knowledge or understanding, or that we can at least posit and approach an horizon where misunderstandings and injustices diminish. Despite the fact that conflicts can and ought to be resolved, indeed through appeals to truth, Lyotard maintains that *differends* persist in these solutions and will continue to occur.

Jean-Luc Nancy and Jacques Derrida criticize Lyotard's definition of specific language games through the definition of their limits in the feeling of the sublime. They raise the possibility that Lyotard is instituting these language games as fixed categories in an illegitimate and inaccurate manner. Thus, Lyotard, despite his sense that the sublime can only reveal negative, unsurpassable, limits is giving rise to a new categorical judgment—one that, according to differing takes on deconstruction, perpetuates an injustice either in illegitimately categorizing things into categories they do not finally belong to or by excluding others from categories they do belong to. This criticism appears to have struck home, to the extent that Lyotard's work after *Le Differend* drifts away from language games and concentrates on a more speculative notion of that which comes to be undone by the feeling of the sublime.

After *Le Differend*, Lyotard's work becomes a prolonged experiment with the feeling of the sublime, not so much with its capacity to reveal events at the limits of language games, but with its capacity to undo the central principles of such games defined according to Kantian Ideas of Reason. For example, Lyotard seeks to undermine the Idea of Reason at the core of the modern political language game, that of perpetual technological progress, by setting it against the event of the inevitable destruction of this world and our search for another. Or again, he sets the Idea of the necessary presupposition of successful communication at work in any attempt to communicate linguistically with the events that reveal another person or thing as a presence we feel incapable of understanding.

Through the feeling of the sublime, we are drawn toward such an ungraspable otherness (the Other) for ethical or affective reasons. For example, the paintings of Barnett Newman are ethical in their appeal to the feeling of the sublime and in the way they allow otherness to come to the fore. Lyotard's essays on the sublime are collected in *L'Inhumain* (The Inhuman, 1988) and the later *Postmodern Moralities*. One of the most important of the essays is on Emmanuel Levinas, as it expresses Lyotard's closeness to Levinas on the subject of an ethics that comes out of a fundamental encounter with the Other. Yet the essay separates the two thinkers, in that Lyotard resists any idea that this ethical relation is fundamental in terms of realms outside those of ethical obligation—the understanding, for instance. He also resists the idea that this obligation is universal in any way: We may experience the feeling of the sublime in relation to the Other, though it is not necessary that we do.

Toward the end of his career, Lyotard combined his philosophy of the sublime with the more general work on different feelings, desires, and affects from his libidinal economics. He wrote a beautiful bibliography of Andre Malraux, balancing Malraux's sensitivity to feelings associated with nihilism and despair and his political activity and interest in the resistance to fascism and Stalinism. Lyotard is very moving on the connection between Malraux's emotional peaks and troughs, their relation to political moves, and his sensitivity to art works; for example, his *musée imaginaire*. Lyotard carries through these thoughts on aesthetic sensitivity, associated with the matter of art and expressed through our senses, to a further book on Malraux, *Soundproof Room*, and an unfinished, posthumous, book on Augustine. Lyotard's argument is that nihilism is the inevitable result of modern hopes, if these are not balanced by the stupefaction that accompanies a minute, but still sublime, sensibility to matter. Our senses can silence our cognitive and ethical thoughts and thereby counter their tendency to plunge us into despair when we face failure.

Lyotard was a great essayist, one of the most creative writers of his generation. As such, he leaves a rich legacy of provoking and inspiring pieces that will last through their capacity to trouble settled views and to generate new feelings with respect to familiar events.

JAMES WILLIAMS

See also **Cornelius Castoriadis; Gilles Deleuze; Jacques Derrida; Michel Foucault; Jean-Luc Nancy**

Biography

Jean-François Lyotard was born in Paris in 1925. He taught philosophy in secondary schools in France and Algeria, and then took up university posts at the Sorbonne and the French Universities of Nanterre and Vincennes. He was a member of the *Socialisme ou barbarie* group and a founder member of the Collège International de Philosophie in Paris. Later in his career, he taught at the University of California, Irvine and Emory University, Atlanta. He died in Paris in 1998.

Selected Works

Discours, figure, 1971
Économie libidinale, 1974; as *Libidinal Economy*, translated by I. Grant, 1993
La Condition postmoderne, 1979; as *The Postmodern Condition: a Report on Knowledge*, translated by G. Bennington and B. Massumi, 1984
L'Euthousiasme: la critique Kantienne de l'historie, 1986
Que peivdre? Adaml, Arakawa, Bureu, 1987
Le Différend, 1983; as *The Differend: Phrases in Dispute*, translated by G. Van Den Abeele, 1988
L'Inhumain: causeries sur le temps, 1988; as *The Inhuman: Reflections on Time*, translated by G. Bennington and R. Bowlby, 1991
Political Writings, edited by B. Readings and P. Geiman, 1993
Lessons on The Analytic of the Sublime, translated by E. Rottenberg, 1994
The Assasination of Experience by Painting, Uemory R. Bowlby, 1998
Postmodern Fables, translated by G. Van en Abeek, 1999
Soundproof Room, 1998; as *Soundproof Room*, translated by R. Harvey, 2001
La Confession D'Augustin, 1998; as *The Confession of Augustine*, translated by R. Beardsworth, 2000

Further Reading

Bennington, G., *Lyotard Writing the Event*, Manchester: Manchester University Press, 1988
Derrida, J., "Before the Law," in *Acts of Literature*, edited by D. Attridge, translated by A. Ronell, London: Routledge, 1992
Malpas, Simon, *Jean-François Lyotard*, London: Routledge, 2002
Nancy, J.-L., "Dies Irae," in *La faculté de juger*, edited by Jacques Derrida, Paris: Minuit, 1985
Readings, B., *Introducing Lyotard: Art and Politics*, London: Routledge, 1991
Williams, J., *Lyotard: Towards a Postmodern Philosophy*, Cambridge: Polity, 1998
Williams, J., *Lyotard and the Political*, London: Routledge, 2000
Yeghiayan, E., *Jean-François Lyotard: A Bibliography*, 2002; http://sun3.lib.uci.edu/indiv/scctr/Wellek/lyotard/index.html

M

MACHEREY, PIERRE
Philosopher

Pierre Macherey's reflections fall into three diverse philosophical fields. Macherey has contributed to the scholarship on particular philosophers such as Comte, Canguilhem, and most notably Spinoza (whose presence is felt everywhere in Macherey's works). He has been preoccupied with the problems of establishing and institutionalizing a history of philosophy in France. Finally, and perhaps most famously, he has reflected on the interaction between literature and philosophy.

Despite the seeming disparity of these interests, the metaphilosophical tenet that there is no single philosophy runs throughout Macherey's works. Drawing on Spinoza, Macherey rejects the idea that there could be a single, definitive philosophy and posits instead an infinity of philosophies that can only be evaluated *sub specie aeternitatis*. Thus, even the greatest deference for individual thinkers should never lead to a blind acceptance of their dogma, for which reason Macherey proposes to work with Spinoza rather than on him, as the programmatic book title indicates (*Avec Spinoza*, 1992).

If philosophy proposes no single system and therefore constantly exists in a process of becoming, the discipline is nevertheless not merely subjective. On the contrary, for Macherey, philosophy acquires its objectivity precisely by stretching beyond each individual philosopher and, in fact, by stretching beyond its own discipline and into others, such as literature, where thought may develop on equal terms. Thought does not belong to anyone in particular, but takes place in the works themselves, independent of the historical motivations of individuals. Each work, regardless of its form, intention, and discipline, thus contributes dynamically to a collective undertaking of defining and determining philosophy.

Macherey does not supply a formal definition of philosophy but, rather, refers to it as a practice. Within such a practice, any single philosophy contains gaps and inconsistencies and could never in itself constitute a closed system. Thus, Macherey distinguishes himself from most other poststructuralist thinkers, such as Deleuze and Guattari, by emphasizing the utility and necessity of dialogue in philosophy. If any philosophy is open-ended and inconsistent, it must naturally latch on to other philosophies and work with them to bridge inconsistencies. If such a metaphilosophy is dialectic, it is not teleological. Being a practice capable of producing effects in the world, philosophy must constantly modify itself simply to keep its effects up to date with the historical situation.

Despite an early spell with structural thinking in its Althusserian variant, Macherey's Spinozian instinct quickly led to an important critique of structuralism. As Spinoza fails to see Christian scripture as congruent and perfected, Macherey fails to see the literary or the philosophical work as unified and harmonious. In Macherey's most famous work, *Pour une théorie de la production littéraire* (A Theory of Literary Production, 1966), the literary work is treated as a diffuse and dense object that can only be explained by reference to its purely material production. Macherey thus rejects the New Critical viewpoint, which treats the work as a complete and coherent object ready for the critics' inspection. Simultaneously, structuralism stands accused of continuing the traditional hermeneutic search for rationality and unity by doing nothing but relocating the quest for unity to the level of a depersonalized and latent structure.

Macherey therefore attempts to turn the meaning of "structure" on its head. Structure could only be said to govern the work "in so far as it is diverse, scattered, and irregular" (*Literary Production*). Structure should therefore not serve to tie down the object of study and discard its dynamic and diachronic nature: "It is not a question of perceiving a latent structure of which the manifest work is an index, but of establishing that absence around which a real complexity is knit" (*Literary Production*). By withdrawing into the concept of structure, structuralism looks more like a formalism that closes the work as a system and here locates an interpretative center.

Macherey's early work, however, shares with structuralism the idea that the author himself is written by the work. Macherey's so-called production model wishes to do away with the romantic and bourgeois idea of the author as a self-governing creator. The author is merely a producer and is thus subject to a wide range of preexisting literary techniques and traditions. Other Marxist theorists (most notably Terry Eagleton) have accused this model of also being formalist, because of its consequent emphasis on craftsmanship. Macherey, however, sees literary production always as transforming discourse rather than reproducing reality: "Literary discourse . . . distorts rather than imitates." The text's ideology cannot be determined from the reality that the work supposedly depicts. Instead, ideology is seen as acted out in fiction and accessible only to the informed reader.

Contrary to a Marxist theorist like Lukács, Macherey adopts a model that avoids being normative; it does not try to tell us how a text should be and what reality it should depict. Criticism itself does not interfere at the level of the production of the text. Inspired by the Althusserian symptomatic reading, Macherey sees criticism as merely the science that acknowledges that any text necessarily has gaps and contradictions and attempts to elucidate the tension between the text itself and its ideological content. Whereas Macherey's early writing admitted literature's relative autonomy, Macherey's own interests soon turned away from the developed production model and toward literature's institutional position in the French educational system (cf. the preface "Présentation" co-authored with Balibar, 1974).

Literature's unique ability to shape thought thus remains an interest throughout Macherey's writing, and in the later *À quoi pense la littérature?* (The Object of Literature, 1990; translated 1999), Macherey rejects simply reading philosophy into literature. Acknowledging literature's ability to produce thought, Macherey favors developing a truly literary philosophy, which interweaves the two disciplines while first accepting that they are different domains in their own right.

NIELS BUCH-JEPSEN

See also **Louis Althusser; Etienne Balibar; Georges Canguilhem; Gilles Deleuze; Felix Guattari**

Biography

Born in Belfort in 1938, Pierre Macherey studied at the École normale supérieure in Rue d'Ulm from 1958 to 1963, where he participated in Louis Althusser's seminars that led to the publication of *Lire le Capital*. He was a lecturer at the Sorbonne from 1966 until 1992, when he became professor at the University of Lille–III.

Selected Works

With Althusser, Balibar, Establet, and Rancière, *Lire le Capital*, 1965

Pour une théorie de la production littéraire, 1966; as *A Theory of Literary Production*, translated by Geoffrey Wall, 1978

With Pierre and Etienne Balibar, "Presentation," in *Le Français national*, edited by Laporte and Balibar, 1974

Hegel ou Spinoza, 1979; 2nd edition, 1990

With Etienne Balibar, "On Literature as an Ideological Form," in *Untying the Text: A Post-Structuralist Reader*, edited by Robert Young, 1981

With Jean-Pierre Lefebvre, *Hegel et la société*, 1984

Comte—La Philosophie et les sciences, 1988

À quoi pense la littérature?, 1990; as *The Object of Literature*, translated by David Macey, 1995

Avec Spinoza—Etude sur la doctrine et l'histoire du spinozisme, 1992

"A Production of Subjectivity," *Yale French Studies*, 88 (1995): 42–52

In a Materialist Way—Selected Essays, translated by Ted Stolze, 1998

Further Reading

Barker, Francis. "Ideology, Production, Text: Pierre Macherey's Materialist Critics," *Praxis* 5 (1981): 99–108

Bennett, Tony, *Formalism and Marxism*, London, 1979

Eagleton, Terry, "Macherey and Marxist Literary Theory," in *Against the Grain: Selected Essays*, London: Verso, 1975; also in Parkinson, G. H. R., ed., *Marx and Marxisms*, Cambridge: Cambridge University Press, 1982

Eagleton, Terry, "Towards a Science of the Text," in *Criticism and Ideology—A Study in Marxist Literary Theory*, London: NLB, 1976, 64–101

Forgacs, David, "Marxist Literary Theories," in *Modern Literary Theory—A Comparative Introduction*, edited by Ann Jefferson and David Robey, London: B. T. Batsford, 1986, 134–69

Jameson, Fredric, *The Political Unconscious*, Ithaca, New York: Cornell University Press, 1981

Kavanagh, James H., and Lewis, Thomas E., "Interview with Etienne Balibar and Pierre Macherey," *Diacritics* 12 (1982): 46–51

Williams, Raymond, *Marxism and Literature*, Oxford, 1977

MÂLE, ÉMILE

Art Historian

Émile Mâle remains the most widely recognized of all French art historians, despite the fact that his theories are rooted firmly in nineteenth-century discourse. His major writings were survey volumes on the subject matter of religious art, rather than in-depth monographs treating individual works, or systematic stylistic analyses. Thus, his output has been branded both "popularist" and "relatively superficial." Although the first charge has substance, the second ignores both his scholarly milieu (he did a great deal of foundational study) and the raft of close analyses of individual works underlying each major publication. His professional agenda was complex; confessional bias, nationalism (he has been called a chauvinist), pedagogical zeal, and professional ambition variously inform his writings. Underneath it all, however, lies a profound personal engagement with the works he studied and a reciprocal concern with recovering their historical significance and preserving them for posterity. This is exemplified in the preface to his *Art et artistes du moyen âge* (1927).

Iconography—generally defined as the identification and classification of subject matter in representational art (some art historians stipulate a broader definition, and it may be applied to architecture as well)—forms the methodological basis of most of Mâle's writings. In specialized contexts, he also employed stylistic analysis (e.g., in his work on transmission of influences in architecture) and connoisseurship (e.g., in his recovery of the oeuvre of the late-medieval French Court painter Jean Bourdichon) but avoided engagement with Panofskian iconology and the formalism practiced by his younger colleague Henri Focillon. Accordingly, he is generally considered methodologically conservative, and it is common for critics to rate his intellectual contribution to the formation of his discipline relatively low. In his publications and teaching, he cast a wide net, covering aspects of European and near Eastern art and architecture from late Antiquity to the eighteenth century. At the core of his published output are four major iconographic studies, three on French religious art of the twelfth to the early sixteenth centuries, the fourth on Flemish, French, Italian, and Spanish Counter-Reformation art. The first of these to appear (in 1898) was *L'Art religieux du XIIIe siècle en France. Étude sur l'iconographie du moyen âge et sur ses sources d'inspiration* (hereafter *XIIIe siècle*), which was also Mâle's doctoral dissertation. From a conceptual point of view, this is his most interesting work and forms the basis of most appraisals of his scholarship.

XIIIe siècle is primarily an attempt to demonstrate how French medieval thought, which Mâle considered essentially unitary (and religious), is accessible through the investigation of the subject matter of cathedral imagery. Thirteenth-century religious art was chosen because Mâle believed it to represent the zenith of French aesthetic achievement (nonreligious art is ignored, a fact for which Mâle has justifiably been criticized). The methodology employed is literally iconographic because it treats imagery as a type of writing that has become opaque through ignorance and neglect, but whose meaning can be recovered if approached in the correct manner. "Medieval art is above all a form of sacred writing"; Mâle, Émile, *L'Art religieux du XIIIe siècle en France*, Paris, Ernest Leroux, 1898, p. 2 this is stated at the outset. This is not intended to suggest that cathedral imagery constitutes a self-contained semiotic system. "Writing" is not used in a metaphorical sense here. Rather, imagery is a straightforward translation of preexisting religious texts, or at least a vehicle for representing conventional symbolism that had already been elucidated in the writings of liturgiologists. Artistic license is countenanced only in the case of some "meaningless" and "innocent" marginalia. If the subject matter of a work of art is open to multiple interpretations, then this must also be true of its textual source. A cathedral such as Amiens, Chartres, or Rheims is no less than an encyclopedia of stone, glass, wood, and so forth (Vincent of Beauvais's mid–thirteenth-century encyclopedic work, the *Speculum maius*, along with the *Golden Legend* and the Bible, provides Mâle with a convenient model). Each image effectively represents a clause, sentence, or chapter, each cycle of images an individual book. Because (it is supposed) words are no more than thoughts, cathedral imagery also provides an index of thirteenth-century ideas. This index is apparently plenary, for not only does "every form clothe a thought" but "(even) the most abstract thought (was given) concrete form," Mâle, 1898 (as above), p. iii an opinion epitomized by a quote from Victor Hugo's *Notre-Dame de Paris* (1831) which appears in the conclusion: "Medieval man had no great thought that he did not write in stone." Mâle, 1898 (as above), p. 491 Mâle emphasizes that substantiating this point was the object of *XIIIe siècle*.

Obviously, Mâle was interested in more than straightforward explanation of the sources of thirteenth-century imagery (for which a descriptive catalogue relating artistic subject matter to texts would have sufficed). *XIIIe siècle* is not simply a lexicon of iconography, although it is occasionally classified as such. Its implications run much deeper. If thirteenth-century religious art, the greatest art of all, is no more than ersatz thought, then thirteenth-century thought, and by extension the thirteenth-century world in general, must also have represented a highpoint. The thirteenth century, in France at least, was a *saecula aurea* (elsewhere Mâle called its artists the "true inheritors of the spirit of ancient Greece"), Mâle, Émile, "L'Art chrétien du Moyen Age", *Revue bleue*, VII (2 février 1907), p. 174. (quoted in Therrien 1998, pp. 337–8, for which see "Further Reading" List). characterized not by individual brilliance (as was the Renaissance in Italy) but by a "diffused genius" Mâle, 1898 (as above), p. 5 of which even the most ignorant partook. This peculiarly French trait, elsewhere referred to as "theological will," quoted in Brush 1996, p. 72, for which see "Further Reading" List. both created the High Gothic cathedrals and rendered them universally intelligible. Art was didactic, the cathedrals catechists, and everyone was fit to receive the instruction they offered. Mâle's propositions do not actually entail a belief that the thirteenth century was generally (or even intellectually) superior to the age in which he lived. His intention was as much to impart glory to modern France through demonstration of an illustrious past as to extol the virtues of its medieval culture. It is to this pragmatic end that the concept of diffused genius resurfaces in Mâle's fiercely nationalistic *L'Art allemand et l'art français du moyen âge* (1917; reprinted 1940).

Such conclusions owe much to nineteenth-century Romanticism, as the quote from Victor Hugo suggests. Late eighteenth- and early nineteenth-century French architectural theory, which related buildings to language intimately, is also implicated. However, it would be wrong to suppose that because Mâle unavoidably inherited nineteenth-century assumptions and ideologies he produced nineteenth-century scholarship. Comparison of *XIIIe siècle* with Adolphe Napoléon Didron's *Iconographie chrétienne* (1843; English edition 1851, reprinted 1965), from which its methodology and even the encyclopedic notion derive, or with the writings of a true neo-Romantic art historian such as Henry Thode (1857–1920) demonstrates that Mâle's work represents a break with past traditions as much as a summation of them. His other major works, although maintaining the premise that subject matter in medieval representational art was basically translated text, do not show equal concern with recovering past *mentalités*. They are, however, distinguished by the same thematic consistency, depth of learning, and clarity of expression. This has ensured that although the rigidity

with which Mâle related imagery to texts is now generally questioned, his core writings are still widely translated, edited, and read for the large quantity of unquestionably valid and important information they do contain.

JULIAN M. LUXFORD

See also **Henri-Joseph Focillon**

Biography

Émile Mâle was born at Commentry in 1862, the son of a miner. He was educated at the Lycée de St.-Étienne, Lycée Louis-le-Grand (Paris), and the École normale supérieure (1883–1886). He taught literature at five secondary institutions successively from 1886 before becoming a lecturer in art history in December 1892. Mâle was professor of Medieval Archaeology (later Professor of Art History) at the Sorbonne from 1908. From 1927 he was director of the École Français in Rome; he retired in 1937, aged seventy-five. During his long career he belonged to many learned organizations, including the Society of Antiquaries, London. He was married, with one son and one daughter. Émile Mâle died at Chaalis in 1954, aged ninety-two.

Selected Writings

L'Art religieux du XIIIe siècle en France. Étude sur l'iconographie du moyen âge et sur ses sources d'inspiration, 1898; as *Religious Art in France: The Thirteenth Century: A Study of Medieval Iconography and Its Sources*, edited by Harry Bober, translated by Marthiel Mathews, 1984; as *The Gothic Image* and *Religious Art in France of the Thirteenth Century*, translated by Dora Nussey, 1913; latest edition, 2000

L'Art religieux de la fin du moyen âge en France. Étude sur l'iconographie du moyen âge et sur ses sources d'inspiration, 1908; as *Religious Art in France: The Late Middle Ages: A Study of Medieval Iconography and Its Sources*, edited by Harry Bober, translated by Marthiel Mathews, 1986

Quomodo Sibyllas recentiores artifices repraesentaverint, 1899

L'Art allemand et l'art français du moyen âge, 1917

L'Art religieux du XIIe siècle en France. Étude sur les origines de l'iconographie du moyen âge, 1922; as *Religious Art in France: The Twelfth Century: A Study of the Origins of Medieval Iconography*, edited by Harry Bober, translated by Marthiel Mathews, 1978

Art et artistes du moyen âge, 1927; as *Art and Artists of the Middle Ages*, translated by Sylvia Stallings Lowe, 1986

L'Art religieux après le concile de Trente. Étude sur l'iconographie de la fin du XVIe siècle, du XVIIe, du XVIIIe siècle. Italie, France, Espagne, Flandres, 1932

Rome et ses vieilles églises, 1942; as *The Early Churches of Rome*, translated by David Buxton, 1960

Les "Grandes heures" de Rohan, 1947

La Fin du paganisme en Gaule et les plus anciennes basiliques chrétiennes, 1950

Further Reading

Bober, Harry, "Editor's Foreword," in Mâle, Émile, *Religious Art in France: The Twelfth Century: A Study of the Origins of Medieval Iconography*, Princeton, New Jersey: Princeton University Press, 1978, v–xxiii

Brush, Kathryn, *The Shaping of Art History: Wilhelm Vöge, Adolph Goldschmidt, and the Study of Medieval Art*, Cambridge: Cambridge University Press, 1996

Camille, Michael, "Art History in the Past and Future of Medieval Studies," in *The Past and Future of Medieval Studies*, edited by John Van Engen, Notre Dame, Indiana: University of Notre Dame Press, 1994, 362–82

Didron, Adolphe Napoleon, *Christian Iconography* (2 vols), London: Bohn's Illustrated Library, 1851–86

Dilly, Heinrich, "Émile Mâle (1862–1954)," in *Altmeister moderner Kunstgeschichte*, edited by Heinrich Dilly, Berlin: Deitrich Reimer, 1990, 132–48

Émile Mâle et le symbolisme chrétien. Exposition organisée par la bibliothèque municipale de Vichy au Centre culturel et au Grand Casino de Vichy, 28 mai-20 juin 1983, exhibition catalogue, Vichy: Wallon, 1983

Grabar, André, "Notice sur la vie et les travaux de M. Émile Mâle," in *Institut de France, Académe des Inscriptions et Belles-Lettres. Comptes rendus de séances de l'année 1962*, Paris: Klincksieck, 1963, 329–44

Harvey, Jacqueline Colliss, "Mâle, Emile," in *The Grove Dictionary of Art*, volume 20, edited by Jane Turner, London: Macmillan, 1996, 189–90

Hugo, Victor, *Nôtre-Dame de Paris*, Paris: E. Renduel, 1836 (and subsequent editions)

Lambert, Élie, "Bibliographie des travaux de Émile Mâle," *Cahiers de Civilisation Médiévale*, 2 (1959): 69–84

Luxford, Julian M., "Émile Mâle (1862–1954)", in *Key Writers on Art: The 20ᵗʰ Century*, edited by Chris Murray, London: Routledge, 2003, 204–11

Sainte-Croix, Lucien, "Un grand historien de l'art au moyen âge: Émile Mâle," *Mercure de France*, 690 (15 July 1927): 324–350

Therrien, Lyne, *L'histoire de l'art en France. Genèse d'une discipline universitaire*, Paris: Éditions du C.T.H.S., 1998

MANDEL, ERNEST

Economist

Leader of the Trotskyist Fourth International for nearly fifty years, Ernest Mandel came to international prominence as a Marxist economist on the publication of his first major work, *Traité d'économie marxiste* (1962), which attempted "to start from the empirical data of the science of today . . . to reconstitute the whole economic system of Karl Marx." This early work, a project of recovery of classical Marxist political economy during a period of dominance by Stalinism and philosophical Marxism among the Western Left, was limited by its adherence to the mistaken orthodox Marxist identification of the postwar years as a period of capitalist decline despite unprecedented levels of growth.

In a substantial body of works which followed, Mandel turned his attention to theories of long waves of capitalist development, usually disregarded in Marxist theory, to explain the connection between trends such as the tendency of the rate of profit to fall and periodic crises. Long waves are generated by the ongoing capitalist need to replace human labor and expand development. This change in the composition of capital, especially through mechanization, in turn propels the declining rate of profit and economic crisis. Capitalism typically recovers from crisis through the elimination of inefficient capital, which restores accumulation on a more profitable basis, thus starting a new long wave of expansion. The fall of the rate of profit is not direct or linear but, rather, fluctuates over lengthy periods of time. These fluctuations establish a long wave, with its own specific expression of the laws of capitalist development. Each long wave then marks off its own distinct period of capitalist development.

Mandel attempted to analyze the specific form capitalism assumed after the Second World War, rather than to make abstract statements about capitalism in general. After World War II, capitalism entered a third historical phase (after the classic phase and imperialism) or third major long-wave period, which Mandel terms neocapitalism or the Third Technological Revolution, to emphasize the characteristic it shared with the other two expansive periods. Although other Marxist economists of the day had difficulties reconciling Marx's emphasis on the decline in the profit rate and the regularity of periodic crisis with the postwar economic boom, Mandel suggested that this process of rapid accumulation across several business cycles had been observed before in history and was about to end. Mandel noted that such waves of expansion were, in fact, limited, and eventually gave way to an extended period of decline and crisis.

His most important work on the third phase of capitalism was *Late Capitalism* (1975), which identified postwar capitalism as a period of great expansion of the powers of capital as noncapitalist spheres, especially services, are made subject to capitalist commodification. Production processes had been greatly transformed along with the organization of work itself through increasing mechanization, development, and spread of electronic and computer technologies and through commodification of agricultural and resource goods and processes. Class forces had been transformed as well, as a result of the rise of fascism, World War II, and the rise of the liberal state over the interventionist welfare state. Increasing employment levels and wages, along with the development of mass consumerism and the social safety net provided by the welfare state, brought capitalism an unprecedented legitimacy.

Although the expansive phase of the postwar long wave began with a growing rate of exploitation and low wages, related to the weakened position of the working class after the war, increased employment and greater working-class organization during the expansion worked to increase wages and slow the rate of exploitation. During the recessive phase, growing unemployment and stratification within the working class made workers vulnerable to capital's neoliberal ideological offensive.

Mandel disagreed with other theorists of long waves, such as Kondratieff, who viewed long waves as emerging solely from factors endogenous to the capitalist economy itself rather than as part of specific political conjunctures. Mandel linked long waves to "cycles of class struggle" and suggested that there was no necessity of recovery from a crisis. In his discussions, there is no guarantee of a return to a period of expansion, as bourgeois economists might argue. Coming out of a recessive long wave requires profound economic and social changes, for which class conflicts are decisive. Crisis alone will not lead to the collapse of capitalism. Only working-class self-organization and self-activity can resist the offensives of capital and end capitalist rule.

Mandel therefore devoted a large part of his writing to analyses of working-class organizations. Against the negative claims of social democratic, Stalinist, and bourgeois theories, Mandel's theory of bureaucracy asserted the possibility of democratic workers' organizations in contemporary society. For Mandel, the bureaucracy, rather than being the inevitable outcome of complex social orders or mass organizations, is the result of specific social relations and arrangements of production. Especially important in this regard is the division of labor between mental and physical work, which eventuates the institutionalization of a layer of experts with its own material interests and political practices that reflect its distinctness from the rest of the working class.

Working-class organizations become divided between layers performing different functions in which officials maintain a monopoly of knowledge. This occurs especially during long-wave growth periods, when workers are able to make substantial gains in living and working conditions even in the absence of heated mass struggles.

Concerned with the preservation of the organization above all, the officials work to contain, within manageable outlets such as electoralism or collective bargaining, any self-organization or activity of the rank-and-file, lest such activities threaten to render obsolete the officials and their organizational structures. This breeds passivity and disorganization within the rank-and-file, which has disastrous consequences for workers during long waves of stagnation, as has been the case since the 1960s. Giving up their most effective tools of struggle, the labor bureaucracies globally have been incapable of fighting neoliberal austerity measures since the 1980s.

At the same time, for Mandel, the bureaucracy's attempts to manage the relationship between workers and capital are regularly confounded by class struggle and capitalist profitability crises. From the class struggles, there emerges a core of militant workers and revolutionary socialists whose activities present possibilities for working-class development beyond the bureaucracies. Unfortunately, Mandel's discussion remains wedded to a vanguardist vision that views these developments in terms of the emergence of a workers' party, which centralizes the various organizations of working-class self-activity.

In other works, Mandel updates Trotskyist analysis of the Soviet Union and questions of the transition to socialism. Mandel rejected claims that the former Soviet societies were "state capitalist" based on the existence of commodity categories, such as wages and prices, because the means of production in those societies were not commodity based; planning was based on use-values, and money played a relatively passive role. In Mandel's view, a transitional phase between capitalism and socialism, which he insisted was a necessity, must maintain commodity markets, wage labor, and a state to ensure production and stimulate collective work. It must also maintain elements of bourgeois distribution. Such a period, which was not necessarily short term, would be characterized by a combination of the market and planned economy, especially as productive forces remained underdeveloped. Again, only workers' self-organization and self-activity could overcome both the market and bureaucratic planning.

Politically, Mandel made many mistakes. His pursuit of a stage theory of capitalist development remains teleological, undermining the emphasis on class struggle and working-class self-activity. In the late-1980s and early 1990s, he used the journals of the Fourth International to argue that capitalist restoration in the Soviet bloc countries was "completely impossible." Instead, he saw the main struggle of those times as being between an antibureaucratic political revolution or a return to Stalinism. Mandel presents class forces and class struggle as external factors that are important mainly because of their effects on the rate of exploitation and the rate of profit. This is criticized from Marxist perspectives, which present class forces as the central part of capitalist economies.

JEFFREY SHANTZ

Biography

Born in Belgium in 1923, Ernest Mandel began his lifelong commitment to revolutionary Marxism as a teenager. He participated in the underground sections of Leon Trotsky's Fourth International and attended the first European conference in 1938. As a member of the Belgian Trotskyist movement he was active in the resistance to the Nazi occupation and was twice arrested. After escaping Auschwitz following his first arrest, he was arrested again and deported to a prison camp in Germany in 1944. A key figure in rebuilding the Fourth International after the war, he was elected to its leadership body in 1946. He maintained his position as the political leader of the main organization of the Fourth International, the United Secretariat of the Fourth International, until his death in 1995.

Selected Writings

Introduction to Marxist Economic Theory, 1967

Marxist Economic Theory, 1968

The Formation of the Economic Thought of Karl Marx, 1971

Late Capitalism, 1975

The Second Slump, 1978

Trotsky: A Study in the Dynamic of His Thought, 1979

Long Waves of Capitalist Development: The Marxist Interpretation, 1980

With Alan Freeman, *Marx, Ricardo, Sraffa*, 1982

Delightful Murder: A Social History of the Crime Story, 1984

"What is the Bureaucracy?" in *The Stalinist Legacy*, edited by Tariq Ali, 1984, 60–94

The Meaning of the Second World War, 1986

Power and Money, 1992

Trotsky as Alternative, 1995

Further Reading

Achar, Gilbert, ed., *The Legacy of Ernest Mandel*, London: Verso, 2000

Chodos, Howard, "Theory and Metatheory in the Evolution of Marxism: A Review Essay," *Critical Sociology*, 24,1–2 (1998): 156–166

Day, R., "The Theory of the Long-Cycle: Kondratieff, Trotsky, Mandel," *New Left Review*, 99 (1976): 67–82

Elson, Diane, "Market Socialism or Socialization of the Market?" *New Left Review*, (1988): 172

Frank, André Gunder, "Inside Out or Outside In?" *Review*, 17,1 (1994): 1–5

Norton, B., "Epochs and Essences: A Review of Marxist Long-Wave and Stagnation Theories," *Cambridge Journal of Economics*, 12 (1988): 203–224

Norton, Bruce, "Late Capitalism and Postmodernism: Jameson/Mandel," in *Marxism in a Postmodern Age*, edited by Antonio Callari, Stephen Cullenberg, and Carole Biewener, New York: Guilford Press, 1995, 58–70

Nove, Alec, "Markets and Socialism," *New Left Review*, 161 (1987): 98–104

Postone, Moishe "Contemporary Historical Transformations: Beyond Postindustrial Theory and Neo-Marxism," *Current Perspectives in Social Theory*, 19 (1999): 3–53

Samary, Catherine, *Plan, Market and Democracy: The Experience of the So-Called Socialist Countries*, Notebooks for Study and Research, 7/8, Amsterdam: IIRE, 1988

Tylecote, Andrew, "On Inequality and the Rate of Profit in the Long Wave," *Economic and Industrial Democracy*, 7,1 (1986): 29–44

MARCEL, GABRIEL HONORÉ
Existential Philosopher, dramatist

Gabriel Honoré Marcel sought to discover an "authentic sense" to human life. He moved beyond the abstract rationalism of idealism, adopting the concrete approach of "incarnate being" and thus anticipating the personal-narrative and body-subject perspectives of postmodernism. Marcel admired Bradley, Hocking, and Royce for their examination of loyalty, community, and personal dignity. Other influences were Gustav Thibon and Charles Du Bos. Marcel in turn influenced Paul Ricoeur, Adenauer, Camus, Cocteau, and Malraux.

Eschewing university chairs and ponderous philosophic treatises, Marcel did not belong to a particular school of thought, nor did he encourage disciples. He was a respected drama critic, playwright, and author of philosophic journals and essays, which won him national and international literary prizes, membership in the Institute of France's Academy of Political and Moral Sciences, and world renown.

The appeal of Marcel's themes—interpersonal relations, commitment, "creative fidelity," community, and hope—and the lucidity of his insights characterize all his work. His legacy was encouragement to all to develop their own thought and forms of creative fidelity.

In both his dramatic and philosophic works, his approach was concretely realistic, conversational, and strikingly personal. In "Concrete Approaches to Investigating the Ontological Mystery," an essay of philosophical reflection written after "The Broken World," a four-act play, Marcel sketched the main lines of his worldview. Together, these two works form the keystone of his thought.

The drama and concrete description in the works evoke an "existential uneasiness." Busyness, distracting diversions, and superficial relations mask our attempts to avoid the sense of emptiness and alienation we experience in relation to ourselves and others. Like a musical composition, the essay develops through three movements. The first movement of the essay evokes the sense of an "ontological need," a need for "Being," or something that withstands all attempts to debunk it, something other, and more, than ourselves, yet something that can be present to us. Marcel warned that this ontological need can be repressed, denied, or ignored, but at a great cost. He suggests that a form of psychological analysis, one deeper and more sophisticated than that of Freud, may well discover the real significance of the ontological need. A world in which our identity is reduced merely to our social, political, and economic functions leaves us with a sense of emptiness and discontent. Something within us protests that we are other, and more, than our societal roles or history. Marcel formulates this ontological need as the question, "Who am I?"

The second movement clarifies the approach and method appropriate to deal with this question. Marcel introduces his now-famous distinction between problem and mystery. A problem is something outside us, separate, for which a completely objective explanation can be found. A mystery, in contrast, involves us; mystery is something that can be experienced only insofar as we welcome or are touched by the reality under investigation. A mystery, unlike a problem, requires the subject's active intervention to discover the meaning of the reality in question. So for Marcel, the question, "Who am I?" inquires into a mystery, and the method he proposes as appropriate for investigating this mystery is that of recollection and reflective clarification. "Recollection," Marcel writes, "denotes the act whereby I re-collect or gather what all is part of my life; yet it is also and at the same time an act of relaxation and abandon to . . . what is other and more than my self" (1933). Then reflective clarification, by a process of questioning and analysis, brings into focus the various essential aspects of the reality, critically reviews alternative interpretations of that reality, clarifies the available choice, and ultimately hopes for an authentic human existence.

In the third movement, various themes emerge that reveal the main lines of Marcel's response to the question, "Who am I?" The notion of presence is central to this whole reflection as Marcel explores the kind of presence appropriate to each of three realms of human experience.

Like most existential phenomenologists, Marcel recognized three distinctive regions or modes of being: the region of things or objects, the region of persons or subjectivities, and the region of the transcendent or the ultimate horizon of being. Marcel explores and notes the proper mode whereby each of these regions can be present to a human subject. He was extremely careful in his analyses, considering alternative conflicting interpretations and clarifying the attitudes from which these sprang.

Being incarnate situates us in the region of objects. One's attitude can determine whether it is "Being" or "Having" that characterizes one's experience of the presence of things. Objects may be present as things for having, things one can possess, collect, buy and sell, or pawn, but that remain outside the self. They can be overshadowed by others who have more or threaten to take them away. If one participates in the presence of things as extensions of one's incarnate being, that presence can enrich and uplift one's very being. To the extent that one relates to objects in terms of being, that is, participating in their uplifting and humanizing presence, the region of objects can provide fulfilling presence (*Être et avoir*, 1935).

In the second region of persons or "intersubjectivity," another distinctive mode of presence appears. Subjective attitudes determine the mode of presence of other persons to us. It is scandalous that some people relate to persons as objects; things that can be bought and sold, or manipulated like pawns. Genuine interpersonal relations are characterized by respect. The other person is an "other I." For the other person to become an intersubjective presence, the relationship between persons should occur through dialogue, initiated through one's appeal that another is with and for me.

Reflection on the realm of intersubjectivity shows that participation in interpersonal presence brings fulfillment to one's being. One cherishes the limitless value of the gift of another's presence. Marcel remarks that it is paradoxical that it is in giving oneself to others that one truly becomes oneself. His reflections, deepening his understanding of intersubjective being, continued in this essay and later formed two major books, *Du Refus à l'Invocation* (1940) and *Homo Viator* (1945).

He further pursued his reflections on intersubjectivity, clarifying the distinctive nature and requisite conditions for genuine commitment, or what he calls "creative fidelity." Persons who are self-possessed, who know who they are and what they want to live for, and who know who the other is and what the other loves and wants to live for, have the basis for authentic commitment. Such total commitment involves a being with, and for, one another that constitutes a *co-esse*, or a sharing of one another's being. Marcel emphasizes that openness and availability, as opposed to unavailability or being totally absorbed in ones self, are necessary conditions for this intersubjectivity of being.

When Marcel raises the issue of fidelity, he clarifies that fidelity is not mere compliance to routine repetition, nor conformity to a principle or promise. Fidelity is a response to a person, and to be genuine is always alive and creative. When, in the face of an unknown future, one pledges his or her fidelity to another, that act of will is spoken as a vow. Indeed, to Marcel a vow, or a life of fidelity, is in its depths rooted in hope, which finds its purest and most intense expression in the phrase, "I hope in Thee for us." Marcel adds that it is only through patient reflection that one discovers the link between the "us" and the "Thou."

Marcel's ongoing reflections on intersubjectivity bring to light his experience and understanding of transcendence, the third region. Marcel conceives of transcendence not as something remote and unrelated to us but as an "Absolute Thou," intimately present as a spiritual influx. Marcel recognizes that although transcendence is an "Other" mode of being, distinct from that of things or even that of incarnate human persons, still an "Absolute Thou" can be experienced as a trans-subjective presence with and for us in the same manner that an intersubjective presence occurs among people.

For Marcel, reflection on the presence of loved ones beyond death helped to clarify the possibility and nature of trans-subjective presence. Marcel's concrete reflections convey an experiential assurance of the presence of an "Absolute Thou" whose presence is there as part of one's being. He points out that to deny this would be a betrayal of that mystery, thereby reducing it to a mere problem, something outside the experience of the subject. He sees such betrayal as possible, and he specifies that despair, similar to fear and suicide, is an expression of the negation of being. Despair is a judgment that being as a whole is bankrupt. Despair or suicide precipitates the downfall one dreads. By contrast, the one who hopes affirms that there is, in being, something to which one can give credit. A genuine act of hope draws on the best of one's own resources, yet essentially is also based on the complicity of a force within being that is other and more than one's own.

Marcel's reflections illustrate that the transcendent is present for him as an "Absolute Thou," whose trans-subjective spiritual influx grounds and sustains personalizing acts of fidelity, hope, creativity, and love. He adds that the more one gives one's life over to this "Absolute Thou," the more one is truly oneself.

KATHARINE ROSE HANLEY

See also **Albert Camus; Paul Ricoeur**

Biography

Gabriel Honoré Marcel (1889–1973) lived most of his life in Paris, yet there was always an international dimension to his life. As a child, he spent two years in Sweden while his father was the French Ambassador there. Later, in life, as a renowned philosopher, Marcel was in demand worldwide as a public speaker. He was a respected Paris drama critic for forty years and served from 1952 until his death as a Member of the Institute of France, Academy of Political and Moral Sciences. He penned thirty plays that were performed in major theaters across Europe. As English translations appeared, Marcel plays have been performed by the BBC and staged in cities across the United States and Canada. He also authored some thirty philosophic works, whose style is conversational, inviting personal reflection on one's lived experience. He gave the Gifford Lectures at the University of Aberdeen in 1949–1950 and the William James Lectures at Harvard University in 1961–1962. Honors, including membership in the Institute of France, The National Prize for Literature, The Grand Prize of the French Academy, and The Goethe Peace Prize suggest the depth of his integrity and thought.

Selected Works

Le Seuil Invisible: "La Grace" et "Le Palais de Sable," 1914
L'Insondable, 1919
The Unfathomable, in *Presence and Immortality,* translated by Michael A. Machado, 1967
La Chapelle ardente, 1925; *Un Homme de Dieu,* 1922; and *Le Chemin de Crête,* 1935; as *Gabriel Marcel: Three Plays, "The Votive Candle," "A Man of God," and "Ariadne,"* 1952, translated by Marjorie Gabain (*"A Man of God"*) and Rosalind Heywood (*"The Votive Candle"* and *"Ariadne"*)
Journal Métaphysique, 1927; as *Metaphysical Journal,* translated by Robert Rosthal, 1952
Le Monde cassé, followed by the essay "Position et approches concrètes du mystère ontologique," 1933; as *The Broken World* followed by the essay "Concrete Approaches to Investigating the Ontological Mystery," translated by Katharine Rose Hanley, 1998
Être et avoir, 1935; as *Being and Having,* 1945
Le Dard, 1936; as *The Sting*
Le Fanal, 1938; as *The Lantern,* translated by Joseph Cunneen, 1958; revised by Katharine Rose Hanley, 1988
Du Refus à l'Invocation, 1940; as *Creative Fidelity,* translated by Robert Rosthal, 1964
Homo Viator, Prolégomènes à une métaphysique de l'espérance, 1945; as *Homo Viator, Introduction to a Metaphysic of Hope,* translated by Emma Craufurd, 1951
Théâtre comique: "Les Points sur les I," "Colombyre ou le brasier de la paix," "Le Divertissement Posthume," "La Double Expertise," 1947; as *"Dot the I"* and *"The Double Expertise,"* 1986 and 2001; as *Colombyre or The Torch of Peace,"* 1988, translated by Katharine Rose Hanley
Rome n'est plus dans Rome, 1951; as *Rome Is No Longer in Rome*
Les Hommes contre l'humain, 1951; as *Humanity against Mass Society,* translated by G. S. Fraser, 1952
Le Mystère de l'Être, 1951; *The Mystery of Being,* Vol. 1, *Reflection and Mystery,* 1950, Vol. 2, *Faith and Reality,* 1951, The Gifford Lectures
The Philosophy of Existentialism, 1956; contains "On the Ontological Mystery," "Existence and Human Freedom," "Testimony and Existentialism," and "An Essay in Autobiography," translated by Manya Harari
Paix sur la terre, 1965; as *The Philosopher and Peace,* translated by Viola Hermes Drath, 1965
La Dignité humaine et ses assises existentielles, 1965; as *The Existential Background of Human Dignity,* 1963, The William James Lectures
En Chemin vers quel éveil?, 1971; as *Toward The Awakening. The Autobiography of Gabriel Marcel,* translated by Peter S. Roberts, 2002
A complete listing of Gabriel Marcel's books in French and English, plus biblio-biographies, bibliographies, and other appendices are printed in *Gabriel Marcel's Perspectives on "The Broken World"* and are available online at http://www.lemoyne.edu/gms.

Further Reading

Cain, Seymour, *Gabriel Marcel's Theory of Religious Experience,* New York: Peter Lang, 1995

Gallagher, Kenneth T., *The Philosophy of Gabriel Marcel*, New York: Fordham University Press, 1975

Hanley, Katharine Rose, *Gabriel Marcel's Perspectives on "The Broken World,"* Milwaukee, WI: Marquette University Press, 1998

Miceli, Vincent, *Ascent to Being: Gabriel Marcel's Philosophy of Communion*, New York: Desclée, 1965

Michaud, Thomas, ed., *Gabriel Marcel and the Postmodern World, Bulletin de la Société Américaine de Philosophie de Langue Française*, Spring 1995

Moran, Denis P., *Gabriel Marcel: Philosopher, Dramatist, Educator*, Lanham, MD: University Press of America, 1992

Pax, Clyde, *An Existentialist Approach to God, The Philosophy of Gabriel Marcel*, The Hague: Martinus Nijhoff, 1972

Plourde, Simone, Parain-Vial, Jeanne, Davignon, René, and Belay, Marcel, *Le Vocabulaire Philosophique de Gabriel Marcel*, Montreal: Bellarmin, and Paris: Cerf, 1985

Randall, Albert, *The Mystery of Hope in the Philosophy of Gabriel Marcel, Hope and Homo Viator*, Lewiston, NY: Edwin Mellen Press, 1992

Schilpp, Paul A., and Hahn, Lewis E., *The Philosophy of Gabriel Marcel*, The Library of Living Philosophers, Volume 17, La Salle, IL: Open Court, 1984

Troisfontaines, Roger, *De L'Existence à l'Être, La Philosophie de Gabriel Marcel*, Leuven-Paris: Nauwelaerts-Vrin, 1968

MARIN, LOUIS
Philosopher, Cultural Critic

The work of Louis Marin was concerned with the theory and practice of representation, from the Bible up to postmodernism. A contemporary and colleague of Certeau, Derrida, and Lyotard, Marin worked mainly on seventeenth-century philosophy, literature, and art, but he also wrote on the *Quattrocento*, Thomas More's *Utopia*, Stendhal, and twentieth-century art.

Marin's work on representation was grounded in doctoral research on Arnauld and Nicole's *La Logique ou L'Art de penser* (1662–1683) and Pascal's *Pensées* (1670). Marin argues that the Port-Royal logicians' discourse about thought, ideas, and language attempted to cover up the element of fiction in its theory of the sign: the sign represents but it also hides the fact that it is impossible to produce a truthful representation. Marin considers the use made by the logicians of the Christian Eucharistic utterance, "This is my body." In his view, they only mention it as an example of their theory of the sign to deflect attention from its central importance; namely, that their whole system depends on the viability of that utterance. Marin revises the place given to the utterance and in fact posits it as the foundation of representation, as it represents the divine in language.

Marin explores how representation marks the violence and crisis at its foundation: Christ has been killed and his body is forever absent. Only a substitute can be put in place, through the words that perform the transubstantiation of the sacramental bread in the Eucharist. Representation is achieved but always carries with it a mark of its secret foundation, suppressed not so much to hide a weakness as to signal the pathos at the heart of language. Following Benveniste's analysis of subject positions and temporality, Marin emphasizes both the absence of the original source of the utterance and the reconstitution of that subject in the words "my body." A key discussion of these ideas can be found in the first chapter of *La Parole mangée* (1986), and a full exposition is provided in *La Critique du discours* (1975).

From this account of the representation of divine power in the Eucharistic utterance, Marin moves across to the political order by attending to the assertion of the absolute power of the monarch in the statement "L'Etat, c'est moi." Marin's discussions of royal representation in *Le Portrait du roi* (1981) address both the way power is represented and the rhetorical powers of representation. The countless literary and visual versions of the king demonstrate that royal power is carefully constructed and is an imaginary entity, an effect of representation. Marin discusses how the mediation of the king's power in histories and medals exploits both the symbolic order of writing and the imaginary order of spectacle. His focus on both message and medium is partly drawn from his reading of Pascal's *Pensées*.

Marin derives from his reading of Pascal several key ideas, which he applies to his study of verbal and visual representation: the impossibility of truth according to the notion of two infinities, the role of perspective in discourse, the relationship between the reason and the effects of power, the construction and alienation of identity in the social order, the function of the king's power as a figure, and the role of secrecy and digression in the discourse of desire and truth. Marin is one of a number of critics, from Sollers to Comte-Sponville, who are interested in the contemporary relevance of Pascal. When in 1984 Marin took part in the clandestine seminar in Prague organized by the Jean Huss Association, he chose the topic of Pascal and secrecy. Marin's later readings of Pascal may be found in the posthumous collection *Pascal et Port-Royal* (1997).

Marin was also interested in tensions in self-representation, particularly the question of fiction in relation to the self constructed in autobiography. Stendhal's *Vie de Henry Brulard* (1835) was the focus for Marin's research, the starting point being located in the autobiographer's question, "Quel œil peut se voir soi-même?" In *La Voix excommuniée* (1981), Marin investigates this question via the text's beginning and ending and through the accounts given of sexuality, memory, and trauma. He examines the crises experienced by the subject and the reproduction and reconstruction of that subject in writing. Invention, digression, quotation, and sublimation—with Raphael's *Transfiguration* playing a key role as the apotheosis of memory in *Brulard*—are all studied as the means to represent desire and identity in the text. Marin wishes to ground and embed his reading in the signs, rhetoric, and framework of the text under consideration. Rather than being uncritically immanent to the text, Marin recognizes the exposure of his discourse to the semifictitious status of autobiography. His reading performs a doubling of the text so as to reveal insights into the enigma of the textual reconstruction of the subject.

A fresh impetus to Marin's work on life-writing would come in the 1980s from the topic of conversion. He chose St. Augustine's *Confessions* as his case study, published in *Lectures traversières* (1992). Marin, similar to Derrida and Lyotard, notes that Augustine's personal crises and uncertainties do not end with his conversion, as this event can be read as a hiatus between the delaying before and the struggles after conversion. Marin tracks the rhetorical devices at work in Augustine's text to represent the turning-point of his conversion, including the reworking of other stories of conversion, and noting the hysterical symptoms, the phantasmal intensification of space and time, and finally the syncope or blind spot of the moment of conversion. The event of conversion becomes an important element in the theory of reading that Marin constructs in his last texts.

Over a period of twenty years, Marin made substantial contributions to the interpretation of Nicolas Poussin and Philippe de Champaigne. In the case of Poussin, he is best known for his application of semiotics to the Louvre version of the *Arcadian Shepherds* and the theory of reading a painting that he thereby constructs (*Détruire la peinture*, 1977). Throughout his work on Poussin, Marin focuses on the order of representation as both a mimetic and a self-reflexive process, looking at narrative techniques and subject positions. Marin is interested in the way Poussin's paintings both hide and reveal their representative methods. Rational perspective and third-person narrative establish the order, but gestures of looking at the spectator and disruptions to the temporal logic of a painting, detected in several key examples, betray the opacity of the system of representation.

Marin's exploration of the figure of the sublime in Poussin's landscapes has achieved a certain notoriety. According to Marin, *Landscape with a Calm* (Malibu, John Paul Getty Museum), *Landscape with a Storm* (Rouen, Musée des Beaux-Arts), and *Landscape with Pyramus and Thisbe* (Frankfurt, Städtisches Kunstinstitut) all indicate an impossible temporal or perspectival logic. In so doing, Marin argues, they indicate how that which cannot be represented can be mediated in a painting. Marin is again exploring how the limits of representation can be traced in the system of representation. He also points to the theoretical aporia confronting the spectator during the recognition of the sublime. In the context of modern French readings of the sublime, Marin sketches a prehistory of the Kantian sublime and offers points of comparison with the interpretations of Kant's *Critique of Judgement* proposed by Derrida and Lyotard.

Sublime Poussin (1995) was unfinished at Marin's death, although his plan for the remainder of the book is reproduced as an appendix. *Philippe de Champaigne ou la présence cachée* (1995) and *Des Pouvoirs de l'image* (1993) were also posthumously published, though in both cases they were effectively completed by Marin himself. His work on Champaigne since *Etudes sémiologiques* has been widely read in the field of French seventeenth-century religious painting. The Champaigne study is a remarkable document that looks at Champaigne's contact with Port-Royal. Marin constructs a multilayered discourse of ekphrastic description, political philosophy, biographical portraiture, and cautious theological investigation. By his example, Marin opens up the question of history in the interpretation of painting, urges caution in the assertion of doctrinal context, and returns continually to the issue of the effects of painting on the spectator.

Marin contends that Champaigne's canvasses depart from the norms of narrative representation to present instead the semiveiled path to conversion. As the artist of the hidden God of Port-Royal, Champaigne establishes the spectator as the decipherer of the signs of a painting. In Marin's view, the secret or even negative power of the representation can only be approached from the pole of the subject seeking the way through the signs of the picture. In his late work, and notably in the introductory essay in *Des Pouvoirs de l'image*, Marin relaunches discussion of a dual problematic: how to determine the powers of the image and how to assess the position of the subject-spectator.

NIGEL SAINT

See also **Emile Benveniste; Michel de Certeau; Jacques Derrida; Jean-Francois Lyotard; Jean-Luc Nancy**

Biography

Born in Grenoble in 1931, Marin studied philosophy at the École normale supérieure in Paris from 1950 to 1954. He then taught at lycées in Versailles, Morocco, and Tunisia and completed his military service at the Ministry of the Armed Forces in Paris. From 1961 to 1964 he worked as a cultural attaché in Turkey, helping to set up a hospital, a school, and a model farm. He was then Director of the French Institute in London for three years. He started teaching at the new Faculty of the University of Paris at Nanterre in 1967, and during the events of May 1968 he played a part in the negotiations between the students and the authorities, for which he was known as the "Archbishop." In the 1970s, Marin taught at the Universities of San Diego, California, and Johns Hopkins (Baltimore, Maryland), where there is now a Louis Marin Chair. From 1978 onward, Marin was a Director of Studies at the Ecole des Hautes Etudes in Paris. Throughout the 1970s and 1980s, Marin lectured and taught in many countries other than France and the United States, notably in Italy at the University of Urbino. Marin was instrumental in setting up the Centre de Recherches sur les Arts et le Langage (CRAL), a joint venture with the CNRS. He died in 1992.

Selected Works

Études sémiologiques: Écritures, peintures, 1971

Sémiotique de la passion: Topiques et figures, 1971; as *The Semiotics of the Passion Narratives*, translated by Alfred M. Johnson, Jr., 1980

Utopiques: Jeux d'espaces, 1973; as *Utopics: Spatial Play*, translated by Robert A. Vollrath, 1990

Chabrol, Claude, and Marin, Louis, *Le Récit évangélique*, Paris: Desclée de Brouwer, Aubier-Montaigne, 1974

La Critique du discours: Sur la "Logique de Port-Royal" et les "Pensées" de Pascal, 1975

Détruire la peinture, 1977; as *To Destroy Painting*, translated by Mette Hjort, 1995

Le Récit est un piège, 1978

"The 'I' as autobiographical eye: Reading notes on a few pages of Stendhal's *Life of Henry Brulard*," *October* 9 (Summer 1979): 65–79

La Voix excommuniée: Essais de mémoire, 1981

Le Portrait du roi, 1981; as *Portrait of the King*, translated by Martha M. Houle, 1988

"Writing History with the Sun-King," in *On Signs*, edited by Marshall Blonsky, 1985, 267–288

La Parole mangée et autres essais théologico-politiques, 1986; as *Food for Thought*, translated by Mette Hjort, 1989

"Transfiguration in Raphael, Stendhal, and Nietzsche," *Stanford Italian Review* 20 (December 1986), 67–76

"The Body-of-Power and Incarnation at Port-Royal and in Pascal, or of the Figurability of the Political Absolute," in *Fragments for a History of the Human Body*, edited by Michel Feher, 1989, 420–447

Opacité de la peinture: Essais sur la représentation au Quattrocento, 1989

"Rhetorics of Truth, Justice and Secrecy in Pascal's Text," *Argumentation* 4,1 (1990): 69–84

Lectures traversières, 1992; as *Cross-Readings*, translated by Jane Marie Todd, 1998

Des Pouvoirs de l'image: Gloses, 1993

"The Frontiers of Utopia," in *Utopias and the Millennium*, edited by Krishan Kumar and Stephen Bann, 1993, 7–16

De la Représentation, edited by Daniel Arasse et al., 1994; as *On Representation*, translated by Catherine Porter, 2001

Philippe de Champaigne ou la présence cachée, 1995

Sublime Poussin, 1995; as *Sublime Poussin*, translated by Catherine Porter, 1999

De l'Entretien, 1997

Pascal et Port-Royal, edited by Alain Cantillon, 1997

"L'Ogre de Charles Perrault ou le Portrait inversé du roi," in *L'Ogre historien: Autour de Jacques Le Goff*, edited by Jacques Revel and Jean-Claude Schmitt, 1999, 283–302

L'Écriture de soi, 2000

Further Reading

Arnauld, Antoine, and Nicole, Pierre, *La Logique ou L'Art depenser*, Paris: Hammanion, 1970

L'Atelier des Gobelins, "Table ronde sur *Des pouvoirs de l'image* de Louis Marin," *Littérature* 91 (October 1993): 82–104.

Chartier, Roger, "Pouvoirs et limites de la représentation: Louis Marin, le discours et l'image," *Au bord de la falaise*, Paris: Albin Michel, 1998, 153–170; as *On the Edge of the Cliff: History, Language, and Practices*, translated by Lydia G. Cochrane. Baltimore, Maryland: Johns Hopkins University Press, 1997, 90–103

Derrida, Jacques, "Louis Marin: By Force of Mourning," in *The Work of Mourning*, edited by Pascale-Anne Brault and Michael Naas. Chicago: University of Chicago Press, 2001, 139–164

Marin, Françoise, and Fabre, Pierre-Antoine, "Bibliographie de Louis Marin," *Littérature* 91 (October 1993): 105–126

Pascal, Blaine, *Pensées*, Ed. Louis Lafuna. Paris: Seuit, 1963

Reiss, Timothy J., "Sailing to Byzantium: Classical Discourse and its Self-Absorption," *Diacritics* 8 (June 1978): 34–46

MARITAIN, JACQUES
Catholic Philospher

Jacques Maritain may have been the world's last major self-declared disciple of Thomas Aquinas, the last truly neo-Thomist philosopher basing a core metaphysic on an analogical hierarchy of being, and the last believer in the *philosophia perennis* that so dominated orthodox Catholic thinking during the century preceding World War II. His role as a political philosopher was less prominent, but is proving more durable and was, from the beginning of World War II, more important.

Like so many students of his generation, he was attracted to the only available coherent metaphysic, which was Spinoza's, and then by the philosophy of Henri Bergson, known as vitalism or intuitionism, whose lectures at the Collège de France Maritain attended in 1903–1904 with Charles Péguy.

He had fallen in love with a Russian Jewish immigrant, Raïssa Oumansoff, not quite a year his junior, after meeting her in 1901, and they made a pact to commit suicide in a year if they did not find a solution to what they considered to be the arid rationalism favored by the French academic establishment. It was the discovery of Bergson that saved them, and they married in November 1904. Under the influence of Léon Bloy, they then both became Catholics.

In 1914, Maritain published his first book, *La Philosophie bergsonienne: études critiques*, which was heavily critical of his earlier mentor. He began to become known as a philosophical apologist for Catholicism, outside France as well as within it, apparently ignoring the major theological constraints on Aquinas's thought and concentrating his arguments on defending the rationality of Aquinas's principles. His metaphysical thought was Catholic in that Maritain's metaphysic called for both a revelation and a mystical fulfillment for rational human beings, making it necessarily hostile to all forms of materialism and to all philosophies of human self-sufficiency.

When Maritain converted to Catholicism, the Church was under pressure both from external forces of anticlericalism and the internal rise of modernism, springing chiefly from Renan and Loisy, but also from such peripherally important figures for France as von Hügel, Bremond, Tyrell, and Döllinger. Maritain was not a historian, and he rejected post-Cartesian thought for the primacy he thought it gave to epistemology over metaphysics, erroneously seeing Aquinas's thought as pristine in its concern for a truly cosmic philosophy of modes of being. The famous five ways of proving God's existence, so near the center of Maritain's thought, may have served Catholic apologetics very well for the century between the two Vatican councils, but they were scarcely more than an aside for Aquinas himself.

Chronologically, and it is generally supposed also logically, Aquinas started from his critique of knowledge, which for Maritain was primarily just a part of metaphysics rather than the analysis of the human spiritual functions that have always been held to have been simultaneously its center and its starting point. Whatever its demerits, however, such a philosophy filled a Catholic need to prove the rationality of belief in a revelation and to counter both incipient scientific rationalism and Kantian idealism, both of which Maritain linked to the medieval nominalist view, rejected by Aquinas and others, that there was no foundation outside the mind for universal concepts.

For Maritain, the individual object of knowledge is apprehended and recreated in the mind in an immaterial way, so that the mind, through an *esse intentionale*, identifies itself with the object of its knowledge. Such a view restores the role assigned by Aquinas, himself unaware of the Arabic glosses on Aristotle on which he was in part drawing, to the passive and active functions of the intellect in receiving sense impressions and turning them into knowable mental concepts.

The seven degrees of knowledge for Maritain result from the different sorts of objects of human knowing, starting from scientific knowledge, demanding the construction of universal objects, their connections and causes. The other degrees of knowing involve objects increasingly independent of individually existing extramental objects, first quantity and extension, then substance and qualities, and so on up the ladder of increasing immateriality and intelligibility. The higher forms of knowledge have objects that transcend the observable and the measurable.

There are also degrees of "suprarational knowledge," whose objects are revealed truth, which can be known only with the help of faith, and mystical knowledge of the deity whose mode is "suprahuman and supernatural," a knowledge by "connaturality" that can be inchoately obtained through mystical contemplation and is morally elevating. Maritain was to refine his theory of degrees of knowledge, most notably in the 1953 *Approches de Dieu*, but it is to distinguish sorts of knowledge of and about God that he puts such emphasis on the proofs of God's existence, which obviously result in something less than knowing God, whether positively, negatively, or analogically.

Maritain's moral and political philosophy is much easier to approach. There is a "natural" law derived from divine rationality inscribed on human nature itself, a proposition that may seem simple, but that means that divine law, however promulgated, is in accordance with human moral aspirations, but also that it is possible to construct a complete ethic without any explicit reference to God at all, working purely from the natural order, as notoriously Grotius was to do, followed in the eighteenth century by Montesquieu.

It follows for Maritain that human beings have a natural right to realize their moral and spiritual fulfillment, the fundamental basis for his liberal views on human rights. Individuals may be related to a society that may impose obligations on them, but they are also persons and must be treated as having inalienable rights in the moral and spiritual orders. As beings capable of intellectual activity and freedom, they cannot be subordinated to common goals, as they are in fascist, communist, and all other secular humanisms. Maritain's Christian humanism here comes quite close to Mounier's personalism, although it has a more clearly religious orientation.

Maritain realizes the need to establish a relationship between democracy and Christianity (*Man and the State*, 1951). His attempt centers on the view that democratic ideals are inspired by belief that the primary source of all authority is God, but the argument is not strong, and Maritain's political theory reflects more his sensitivity to ambient values than his high powers of logical argument. He was writing in English in the United States in the earlier years of Senator Joe McCarthy's nefarious activities.

There can be little argument about Maritain's importance. He has been translated into about twenty languages, and his stand on human rights has been echoed in major U.N. declarations, as well as in the papal statements of both Paul VI and John Paul II. It is probable that de Gaulle incorporated his thinking into the preamble to the 1946 constitution of the Fourth Republic. Much of what he published was intended for a readership outside the circles of professional philosophers or other academics. There is an English-language edition of his works as well as the French one, at least two reviews devoted largely to his thought, and some twenty national associations, as well as the Institut International Jacques Maritain.

ANTHONY LEVI

See also **Henri Bergson; Leon Bloy**

Biography

Maritain was born in 1882. He studied philosophy and the natural sciences at the Sorbonne. In 1904, he married Raïssa Oumansoff. They both converted to Catholicism in 1906. He took a teaching position at the Collège Stanislas in 1912. In 1914, he was appointed to an assistant professorship in the history of modern philosophy at the Institut Catholique. After a brief period of war service, he was appointed to a professorship at the Institut Catholique in 1921. In 1928 he was named chair of the logic and cosmology department, a position he held until 1939. During World War II, he taught at Princeton (1941–1942) and Columbia (1941–1944). He led France's delegation to UNESCO and helped author the United Nations Declaration of Human Rights. In 1948, he resigned from international diplomacy to teach moral philosophy at Princeton. Maritain died in 1973.

Selected Works

The Collected Works of Jacques Maritain, 20 volumes.
La Philosophie bergsonienne: études critiques, 1914; as *Bergsonian Philosophy and Thomism*, 1955
Art et scolastique, 1920; 1927 edition, as *Art and Scholasticism* translated by Joseph W. Evans 1962
Eléments de philosophie, 2 volumes, 1920, 1923; as *An Introduction to Philosophy*, translated by E. I. Watkin, 1944; as *An Introduction to Logic* and *Formal Logic*, 1937
Trois Réformateurs: Luther, Descartes, Rousseau, 1925; as *Three Reformers: Luther, Descartes, Roiusseau*, 1929
Le Docteur angélique, 1930; as *St Thomas Aquinas*, translated by F. J. Scanlan, 1931
Distinguer pour unir: ou, les degrés du savoir, 1932; as *Distinguish to Unite: or, The Degrees of Knowledge* translated under the supervision of G. B. Phelan, 1959
Humanisme intégral: problèmes temporels et spirituels d'une nouvelle Chrétinté 1936; as *True Humanism*, translated by

M. R. Adamson, 1938; as *Integral Humanism*, translated by Joseph W. Evans, 1968
Les Droits de l'homme et la loi naturelle, 1942; as *The Rights of Man and Natural Law*, translated by Doris C. Anson, 1943
Christianisme et démocratie, 1943; as *Christianity and Democracy*, translated by Doris C. Anson 1944
Man and the State, 1951
La Philosophie morale, 1960; as *Moral Philosophy*, 1964
Œuvres complètes de Jacques et Raïssa Maritain, 15 volumes, 1982–

Further Reading

Allard, Jean-Louis, and Germain, Pierre, *Répertoire bibliographique sur la vie et l'œuvre de Jacques et Raïssa Maritain*, Ottawa, 1994
Allard, Jean-Louis, *A Philosopher in the World*, Ottawa: University of Ottawa, 1985
American Maritain Association, *Selected Papers from Seminar on Jacques Maritain's "The Degrees of Knowledge,"* St. Louis, 1981
Daly, Mary F., *Natural Knowledge of God in the Philosophy of Jacques Maritain*, Rome: Catholic Book Agency, 1966
DiJoseph, John, *Jacques Maritain and the Moral Foundation of Democracy*, Lanham: Rowman and Littlefield, 1996
Dunaway, John M., *Jacques Maritain*, Boston: Twayne, 1978
Evans, Joseph W., ed. *Jacques Maritain, the Man and His Achievement*, New York: Sheed and Ward, 1963
Fecher, Charles A., *The Philosopher of Jacques Maritain*, Westminster: Newman, 1953
Jung, Hwa, *The Foundation of Jacques Maritain's Political Philosophy*, Gainsville: University of Florida, 1960
Nottingham, William J., *Christian Faith and Secular Action: An Introduction to the Life and Thought of Jacques Maritain*, St. Louis: Bethany 1968

MARXISM

Both among well-known thinkers and in intellectual life more generally, the influence of Marxist thought in the twentieth century was substantial. The quality and popularity of debates within historical materialism reached their height in the three decades following the Second World War, and the reputation of prominent individuals such as Louis Althusser and Jean-Paul Sartre spread well beyond France. With a strong tradition of revolutionary caesura in the realm of political practice, neither liberalism nor social democracy had properly taken root, and both broader political developments and intellectual life itself were dominated by bodies of thought that emphasized such notions as emancipation, salvation, and total change. For a time, Marxism seemed to be in almost perfect harmony with socioeconomic and political reality on the one hand, and the world of ideas on the other.

Historical Context

The Dreyfus Affair is often cited as the point at which intellectual commitment to politics, or *engagement*, first appeared, and it is important for an understanding of the combative tradition that prepared the ground for the widespread acceptance not only of the Marxist method but also its later repudiation. In January 1898, the novelist Emile Zola accused the War Office of a judicial crime in his public letter *J'Accuse*, after Captain Alfred Dreyfus was convicted of espionage. Intellectuals on the left defended Dreyfus in what seemed like a case strongly motivated by anti-Semitism, and intellectuals on the right, such as the anti-Semitic Catholic writer Charles Maurras, attacked Dreyfus with equal vigor in a cause which became so divisive that the Third Republic seemed at one point in danger of collapsing.

To understand the nature of the left in the twentieth century, including the intellectual left, it is necessary to point to an earlier event, namely, the bloody repression—by the Thiers government—of the popular uprising and experimentation with direct democracy that constituted the Paris Commune of 1871 by which Marx himself was so interested and heartened. This repression pushed the nascent labor movement further to the left, much of it into anarcho-syndicalism, laying the ground for a later flowering of Marxism among intellectuals. This contrasted with intellectual life in Britain, for example, which was influenced by social democracy and liberalism, in part reflecting the relative peace between labor movement, capitalist class, and successive governments. The crushing of the Commune and other examples of state repression, ironically combined with a modernization of formal political institutions in the Third Republic from 1870 onward through formal championing of the insurrectionary role of ordinary people in state republicanism, also meant that the tradition of an ideology of emancipation was reinforced, and it was a relatively small step from this republicanism (at least in its left variants) to Marxism.

Indeed, the tradition of regime change through revolution and, more generally, sudden, total change instead of gradual political reform had been established in 1789 and compounded not only by subsequent revolutions in 1830 and 1848 but also by coups d'etat in 1799 and 1852 and regimes ended by war in 1814 and 1870. This type of turbulence would stretch well into the twentieth century, with invasions in 1940 and 1944, a quasi–coup d'état in 1958, and an uprising in May 1968. Such a political climate had already encouraged the emergence of socialist writers such as Auguste Blanqui (1805–1881) and the writers whom Friedrich Engels criticized as being utopian rather than scientific socialists; in particular, Comte de Saint Simon (1760–1825) and François-Charles Fourier (1772–1837), who exerted an important influence on the earlier stages of French socialism, including through experiments with direct forms of democracy and cooperative living. Pierre-Joseph Proudhon (1809–1865) was a key influence on the early labor movement, particularly in its anarcho-syndicalist form.

In 1920 came another landmark for understanding of the reception of Marxism among intellectuals in the twentieth century, when large numbers of French socialists left the Second International to join the *Parti Communiste français* (PCF) as part of the Third International, established to defend the Russian Revolution of 1917 and facilitate the struggle against capitalism elsewhere in the world. This left the ranks of the Socialists depleted and made the PCF by far the biggest French political party for much of the rest of the twentieth century, both in terms of membership and in terms of votes at many national and local elections. It was the role of Communists in the Resistance against Nazi occupation from 1941 to 1944, however, and the subsequent division of the world into two competing political and military spheres, that finally established Marxist thought as the giant it became after the Second World War. From then until the 1980s, the PCF itself was home to many Marxist intellectuals, whereas other nonmembers were either broadly sympathetic to it or wary or hostile toward the activities of the party itself but encouraged in the exploration of Marxist thought by the existence of a large, predominantly working-class party on French soil whose main ideological influence was historical materialism.

Moreover, event after event seemed to continue to confirm the legitimacy of a world view that condemned the activities of the ruling class and that sought to wholly replace the existing order rather than gradually reform it: these included the struggle against fascism and fascist ideology in the 1930s and the labor movement's pushing the Popular Front government toward more radical reforms in 1936, widespread strikes in 1947 (which led to the exclusion of Communist ministers from the government of reconstruction), the violence of the French state in its desperate and chaotic attempts to retain Algeria as part of France in the late 1950s, Gaullist authoritarianism between 1958 and 1969, and the student and workers' uprising and general strike of May 1968.

The heyday of intellectual Marxism between the end of the Second World War and the mid-1970s seems, in retrospect, to have followed on logically from left-wing resistance against Nazi occupation. By 1944, the dominant view was that it was both morally correct and illegal to have fought collaboration with Germany by the Vichy regime, and the capitalist state and its political representatives were thoroughly discredited among many intellectuals. Not only were right-wing, collaborationist intellectuals greatly marginalized after the war, but the established order in general was called into question.

Spheres of Influence

It was in this climate, where for many people profound socioeconomic and political transformation of some kind (rather than piecemeal reform) still seemed necessary and possible, that well-known intellectuals of the left came to have a tremendous influence. In the immediate postwar period, Jean-Paul Sartre became the archetypal committed intellectual of the twentieth century, declaring in the first issue of *Les Temps Modernes* in 1945 that "[w]e place ourselves on the side of those who wish to change both man's social circumstances and the conception he has of himself. Also, with regard to social and political events, our journal will take a stand in every case." Speaking out publicly on countless issues, signing innumerable petitions and addressing large crowds during the events of May 1968, Sartre came to epitomize left-wing intellectual *engagement*. His appeal was enhanced because he was by no means a traditional Marxist but, instead, adapted his own brand of existentialism to Marxism, in particular with the publication of a substantial attempt to reconcile existentialism with Marxism, which culminated in *Critique de la Raison dialectique* (1960). The book was a landmark both because of the clarity of the belief in the usefulness of Marxism from such a central figure and because of its level of abstraction; as a work of philosophy, it was to have a substantial influence on other spheres of intellectual activity. Sartre was to remain both an important figure working in the defense of Marxism among intellectuals and a writer who distanced himself from any form of orthodoxy most of the time. Tension between him and the PCF ebbed and flowed; after the war, the party attacked his existentialism, and Sartre—for example, in his *Matérialisme et révolution* (1946)—attacked the PCF's Stalinism, but in the 1950s he became a fellow traveler without ever becoming a member of the party. In the 1970s, he became editor of the banned Maoist newspaper *La Cause du Peuple* and worked for several years with *Gauche Prolétarienne*.

It is also important to single out Louis Althusser, who held a post at the Ecole Normale Supérieure, who was a member of the PCF from 1948, and who from the mid-1960s became one of the most important French intellectuals of the twentieth century. Developing a structuralist interpretation of Marxist theory that asserted that the economic is determining only in the last instance and that other spheres develop in a semiautonomous fashion, in *Pour Marx* and *Lire le Capital*, Althusser rejected the notion that Marxist thought was a continuation of Hegel's philosophy, arguing that there

was an "epistemological break" between Marxism and previous forms of thought. There was, he argued, a clear line of divide between Marx's early writings and the mature writings. Influenced among others by the anthropologist Claude Lévi-Strauss and psychoanalyst Jacques Lacan, he published a seminal essay in 1970 titled "Idéologie et appareils idéologiques d'Eta," in which he explores aspects of the formation of the individual's relationship with class structures as mediated by the capitalist state. Althusser's popularity can be explained not only by his intellectual rigor but also by his political credibility as a long-time member of the PCF, while maintaining some distance from the more dogmatic and uncritical aspects of the PCF's intellectual life. In 1978, he confirmed the dissidence within the PCF with the publication of his essay, "Ce qui ne peut plus durer dans le parti communiste."

The Communist Party itself was home to numerous intellectuals, and although some toed the line to such an extent that they made little contribution to the exploration of Marxist thought, others produced truly scholarly works. In addition to Althusser, it is worth mentioning Paul Nizan, Georges Politzer, Jacques Decour, Jacques Solomon, and Henri Mougin—all of whom died during or just after the Second World War—and in the postwar period, Roger Garaudy, Henri Lefebvre, Auguste Cornu, René Maublanc, Jean-T. Desanti, Maurice Caving, Victor Leduc, Jean Kanapa, and Georges Cogniot. There were PCF members working in a number of academic disciplines, including Albert Soboul, who held the Chair of the History of the French Revolution at the Sorbonne (Georges Lefebvre, who had held the same post, was also inspired by Marxism to a certain extent).

Indeed, in virtually every sphere of intellectual activity, Marxism has left its mark. In many cases, protagonists have espoused a form of structuralism combined with historical materialism, including Maurice Godelier, Lucien Sebag, and Emmanuel Terray in anthropology; the early Roland Barthes and Julia Kristeva in semiology; Michel Pêcheux and Françoise Gadet in discourse analysis; and Lucien Goldmann, Pierre Macherey, and Christian Metz in literary and film theory. Paradoxically, with the exceptions of some of the work of Etienne Balibar and Nicos Poulantzas, the analysis of politics has on the whole attracted the attention of non- and often anti-Marxists.

If we take on board, as we should, the importance of broader intellectual activity in the dissemination, critique, and therefore perpetuation of ideas, we must consider the role of countless anonymous individuals in consolidating the influence of Marxist thought. Such "organic" intellectuals (in Antonio Gramsci's terms) were to be found in particular in trade unions such as the Communist-oriented Confédération Générale du

Travail, the Confédération Française Démocratique du Travail (especially in the 1970s, when it was recognized as being a *marxisant* laboratory of ideas), and in the Parti Socialiste Unifié. The Parti Socialiste (PS) was also influenced by Marxism right up until the election of François Mitterrand as President of the Republic in 1981; the Marxist-leaning CERES wing of the party was very much involved in writing the program for that election, at a time when the PS was still talking of a "rupture avec le capitalisme."

It is also worth mentioning the Trotskyist new left, which grew in the years after May 1968, in part because of the PCF's less-than-enthusiastic attitude toward the events of May, particularly in the first days, but also because of the gradual discrediting of the Soviet Union not only among famous intellectuals but also among many politically aware students and workers. Publishing houses with distance from PCF orthodoxy, such as Maspéro, La Brèche, and Syros, did well, bringing out new editions of Gramsci, Mao, and Trotsky and publishing other theory that was often within a new left framework.

Decline

The decline of Marxism among French intellectuals in the last quarter of the twentieth century was also closely connected with political developments. The post-Gaullist era of the 1970s brought reforms that made French society seem more in step with other advanced capitalist countries such as Britain, West Germany, and the nordic countries, where the fruits of economic success had been distributed more evenly, where the *patronat* had been more willing to make concessions to the labor movement, and where the state had been less heavy-handed. After coming to power in 1981 on the strength of a left-social democratic program and with support from the PCF, the Socialists quickly abandoned much of their radicalism and implemented an austerity program, deciding that a center-left, pragmatist approach was the best way to remain in power. The Communists who had joined the government in 1981 remained until 1984, by which time they were also associated with measures that seemed to make the working class pay for increasing social and economic problems, including rapidly rising unemployment. This, together with the cumulative effect of the gradual discrediting of the whole Soviet project, followed by the breakup of the Eastern bloc from 1989, helps explain why the PCF entered the twenty-first century with little prospect of being more than a marginal influence on national politics. Just as the existence of a large Communist Party had played an important part in the earlier widespread interest in Marxist thought, its decline contributed to the discrediting of

Marxism among many individuals. Indeed, true to the bipolar intellectual heritage of the Dreyfus affair, the backlash against Marxism from the late 1970s onward was as thorough as had been intellectuals' embracing of it in the postwar era.

This reaction took various forms, including the headlong attack by the so-called New Philosophers in the 1970s, who included several former Marxists such as Bernard-Henri Lévy, André Glucksmann, Christian Jambert, and Guy Lardreau. Although the movement was short-lived, its protagonists were significant in that they set a trend for defense of human rights in a very general way (which in practice often simply meant anti-Communism), and this was to become a theme right up to the beginning of the twenty-first century.

More significant, perhaps, was the attempt in the 1980s and beyond by another anti-Marxist, liberal-leaning group of political philosophers, historians, social theorists, and anthropologists who set out to consolidate such liberal tradition as there was in France, to rework areas that had hitherto been largely the preserve of left intellectuals, to import ideas from abroad, and generally to create on the intellectual plane an ongoing, sympathetic discussion of French political liberalism that was in harmony with the dominant political and economic practices of the time. These individuals include François Furet, Marcel Gauchet, Pierre Rosanvallon, Luc Ferry, Alain Renaut, Jacques Julliard, Blandine Kriegel, and Phillipe Raynaud. One of the most important areas to assert or reassert liberal ideas and meet the influence of Marxism head-on was history, most notably via the historiographical revisionism of the former PCF member François Furet. He argued that, as with the 1917 Russian Revolution, the revolution of 1789 had inevitably been followed by countless numbers of directly related deaths. The general message was that it was time for the French to cease to glorify revolution, both in the past and in the present.

In the meantime, death or tragedy took its toll on individuals who had famously been Marxists or influenced by Marxism: Sartre and Barthes died in 1980, Lacan in 1981, and Beauvoir in 1986. Poulantzas committed suicide in 1979, and Althusser was confined to a mental institution after killing his wife and died in 1990.

In the realm of French thought as it evolved after 1968, there was certainly in structuralism a shift from the more conventional combative and activist Marxist framework. Claude Lévi-Strauss, Roland Barthes, Jacques Lacan, Michel Foucault, and Jacques Derrida, although each partly influenced by Marx, did not hold with the idea that class struggle was the motor of history and that class was the dominant influence in structuring societies. Emancipation of the working class (and arguably, ultimately, of other classes as well) via the overthrow of the bourgeoisie and socialization of the means of production were certainly not central to any of their intellectual projects and usually did not appear at all. Louis Althusser, of course, did work within Marxism throughout his career and was a long-serving member of the PCF. However, if much structuralist analysis was "political" in some senses, and helped underpin both a distance from liberalism and aspects of the post-1968 counterculture, it could also (with the important exception of Althusser) be interpreted without an emphasis on the importance of agitation for social change. This contrasted with the nonstructuralist variants of Marxism in particular, including even Sartre's Marxism, which were nothing without the unity of theory and practice.

There is no clear line of divide between structuralism and poststructuralism, and Foucault arguably straddles the two. However, Jean-François Lyotard is perhaps one of the most clearly poststructuralist French intellectuals, arguing famously in *The Postmodern Condition* (1984) that we were witnessing the decline of grand narratives; that is, the decline of the relevance of theories that claim to explain phenomena as part of total systems and in terms that had universal relevance. Poststructuralism was thus a reaction against the legacy and tradition of the Enlightenment in terms of philosophy and against the twentieth-century movements of emancipation, which apparently drew inspiration from the Enlightenment tradition, including, in particular, Marxism. This, together with the disillusionment of the generation of 1968, helps explain why poststructuralism's skepticism with regard to "grand narratives" and the relativity of its approaches in various areas of intellectual activity struck such a chord for a certain period in French intellectual history.

Reemergence?

Despite all of this, the single most prominent public intellectual during the 1980s and 1990s was the sociologist Pierre Bourdieu, who was firmly on the left and was strongly influenced by Marxism in some respects. In particular, he borrowed from Marx the notion of Capital and extended from the economic to other, cultural spheres. At the turn of the twenty-first century there were other signs that there was a certain renewal of the Marxist heritage, with, for example, Althusserian Marxists Alain Badiou and Jacques Rancière working within a framework influenced by historical materialism. The prolific activity by the Trotskyist philosopher Daniel Bensaïd to an extent mirrored the renewed radicalism on the ground after 1995 in the form, for example, of the radical new trade union SUD and new social movements around illegal immigrants and

homeless people. It is also worth mentioning Luc Boltanski and Eve Chiapello's *Le Nouvel Esprit du capitalisme*, published in 1999.

It would be wrong to conclude, then, that at the end of the twentieth century the influence of Marxism in France had disappeared altogether. In addition to new works by individuals, the publishing venture *Raisons d'agir*, started by Bourdieu, has done much to promote activism, and although not strictly Marxist, it is certainly influenced broadly by this tradition. The fact that roughly ten percent of all votes at the Presidential elections of 2002 went to candidates who were openly Trotskyist indicates that Marxism is far from falling on entirely deaf ears, even if some of those votes were cast to express strong opposition to governmental policies and to the increasing proximity of mainstream left and mainstream right.

NICK HEWLETT

See also **entries on individuals mentioned in this article**

Further Reading

Anderson, Perry, *Considerations on Western Marxism*. London, Verso, 1976.

d'Appollonia, Ariane Chebel, *Histoire politique des intellectuels en France 1944–1954*, 2 volumes, Paris: Editions complexe, 1991

Benton, Ted, *The Rise and Fall of Structural Marxism: Althusser and His Influence*, London: Macmillan, 1984

Bidet, Jacques, and Kouvélakis, Eustache, eds., *Y a-t-il une pensée unique en philosophie politique?* Paris: Presses Universitaires de France, 2001

Dews, Peter, *Logics of Disintegration. Post-structuralist Thought and the Claims of Critical Theory*. London: Verso, 1987

Drake, David, *Intellectuals and Politics in Post-War France*, London, Palgrave, 2002

Elliott, Gregory, *The Detour of Theory*, London: Verso, 1987

Flood, Christopher, and Hewlett, Nick, eds., *Currents in Contemporary French Intellectual Life*, London: Macmillan, 2000

Hazareesing, Sudir, *Intellectuals and the French Communist Party: Disillusion and Decline*, Oxford: Oxford University Press, 1991

Julliard, Jacques, and Winock, Michel, *Dictionnaire des Intellectuels français*, Paris: Seuil, 1996

Kelly, Michael, *Modern French Marxism*. Oxford: Blackwell, 1982

Leymarie, M., *Les Intellectuels et la politique en France*, Paris: Presses Universitaires de France, 2001

Ory, Pascal, and Sirinelli, François, *Les Intellectuels en France. De l'Affaire Dreyfus—à nos jours*, Paris: Armand Colin, 1992

Ross, George, "Intellectuals Against the Left: the case of France," in *Socialist Register 1990*, edited by Ralph Miliband and Leo Panitch, London: Merlin Press, 1990

Winock, Michel, *Le Siècle des Intellectuels*, Paris: Seuil, 1999

MASSIS, HENRI
Essayist, Literary Critic, Literary Historian,
Political Writer

Elected to the Académie Française in 1960, Henri Massis is today remembered not so much as a first-rank producer of literary works but rather as an eloquent witness of literary, cultural, and political life predominantly in the first half of twentieth-century France.

Massis's multifaceted writing career found an early expression during his university days, when he published a study on Zola, *Comment Zola composait ses romans* (How Zola Composed His Novels, 1906), *Le Puits de Pyrrhon* (Pyrrho's Well, 1907), and a book on *La Pensée de Maurice Barrès* (The Thought of Maurice Barrès, 1909), whom he had met in 1906. Fundamental ideas, such as his adherence to patriotic nationalism and to traditional cultural and Catholic values, started emerging and were to remain part of his credo throughout his life.

Massis attracted public attention in 1911 when he published, along with his friend Alfred de Tarde and under the pseudonym of Agathon, his assessment of the state of the French university system, entitled *L'Esprit de la nouvelle Sorbonne* (The Spirit of the New Sorbonne). Criticizing new scientific methods that he saw as a German threat to French university teaching, Massis was a fervent defender of the liberal arts education. He warned against "a progressive debasement of general culture . . . and the formation of a new kind of person: not the *honnête homme* of the Renaissance tradition but the *esprit spécialiste*" (Fraser, 1986, 141). Two years later, in 1913, his second survey as Agathon, *Les Jeunes Gens d'aujourd'hui* (Young Men of Today) revealed that the students of the pre–World War I years tended to be anti-intellectual, patriotic, and Catholic.

Massis converted to the Catholic faith in 1913. His passion for Catholicism and his defense of the values of order and morality fuelled all of his literary, journalistic, and political endeavors. A follower of his friend Charles Péguy, he launched attacks against writers such as Anatole France, Romain Rolland, Henri Bergson, and above all, André Gide. Massis had hoped for a return to spirituality among the postwar generation and denounced both Gide as a corruptor of youth and his growing influence as a violation of all morality. As early as 1914, Massis wrote a feuilleton in the *Éclair*, entitled "The Perversity of André Gide," in which he condemned the writer's attempts at legitimizing sin and integrating it into a private morality. In 1929, the attack was renewed in "La faillite d'André Gide" (The Failure of André Gide). Massis never deviated from his stark judgement: Gide, for him, represented a person possessed by the devil, a *démoniaque*. In contrast, Massis approved of Marcel Proust, as the Proustian fictional world did not attempt to destroy the moral universe. In *Le drame de Marcel Proust* (The Drama of Marcel Proust, 1937), he tried to uncover the writer's psychology. Massis's interest in these authors culminated in his 1948 book *D'André Gide à Marcel Proust*.

Having come to admire Charles Maurras, leader of the *Action française*, and adhering to his concept of "integral nationalism," Massis was to become one of his confidants without, however, ever joining Maurras's organization. In 1919, Massis's widely read manifesto, "Pour un parti de l'intelligence" (For a Party of Intelligence), was signed by fifty-four major French writers and artists. In the aftermath of World War I, the manifesto, reflecting numerous convictions held by the *Action française*, claimed the restoration of the French spirit and state and the Catholic Church, a renewal of intellectual life in France, and a national and metaphysical reconstitution of France as the guardian of civilization. This was well received by the conservative intelligentsia and ultimately led to the creation of the *Revue universelle* in 1920. Funded by Jacques Maritain and Maurras, the review's publisher was Jacques Bainville; Massis was the editor. Its ambitious program was to create an intellectual federation of the world, led by French thought.

In the climate of France's neo-Thomist revival, led by Jacques Maritain, the collection "Le Roseau d'or" was published by Plon from 1925 to 1932, with Massis acting as one of its directors. His preoccupation with the perceived dangers of Bolshevism, Germanism, and Asiatism towards the West is the basis of his *Défense de l'Occident* (The Defense of the West, 1927), published in the collection. Beyond political and ideological differences with the East, Massis saw the ultimate threat in the radical opposition between Western and Eastern spirituality: only France, as spiritual leader of the West, steeped in its Catholic tradition, would ensure that scientific progress maintained an authentic human spirit by achieving an "integral restoration of the principles of the Greco-Latin civilization and of Catholicism" (Toda, 1987, 265). This central theme was taken up again in 1935, when Massis published the "Manifeste des intellectuels français pour la Défense de l'Occident et la paix en Europe" (October 4; Manifesto of French Intellectuals for the Defence of the West and Peace in Europe), a document that garnered more than 850 signatures. There Massis marshaled two arguments to defend Italy's annexation of Abyssinia: Italy's supposed superior cultural influence would benefit the African country, and an attack by Western countries on Mussolini might send Italy into Bolshevic arms.

Massis's encounters with Mussolini in 1933 and Spain's General Franco and Portugal's President Salazar in 1938 were related in *Chefs: Les Dictateurs et nous* (Leaders: The Dictators and Us, 1939). Seeing a chance to rebuild the old France, he was at Marshal Pétain's side when the country, occupied by Germany in World War II, was run by the Vichy government. After the war, Massis was released after only one month of internment as, true to his convictions, he had never made the slightest ideological concession to Hitler and the Nazi movement and had refused collaborationist activities. Also in 1941, Massis had published *Les Idées restent* (The Ideas Remain), in which he had set the French spirit clearly apart from the German mentality. As pronounced as his rejection of Germany and Nazism was his dislike of Russia and Bolshevism. *Découverte de la Russie* (Discovery of Russia, 1944) reads like a sequel to his former *Défense de l'Occident*. Ultimately, for Massis, France's choice was not so much between different political ideologies, such as Communism and Capitalism, but between the "monde moderne" (modern world) and the "monde chrétien" (Christian world).

Henri Massis was especially influential during the 1920s: According to Chenaux, the Roman Occidentalism of someone like Massis represents a strong current of the European Catholic conscience of that period (Chenaux, 1999, 227). His rich literary output includes literary essays, criticism, and monographs on writers such as Alain, Bernanos, Claudel, Psichari, and Cocteau. Moreover, his keen observations are invaluable when studying the intellectual development of twentieth-century France. It may be surmised that Massis's political ideas, with their marked sympathy for Charles Maurras and his *Action française*, and his espousal of traditional values and the orthodox tenets of the Catholic Church are somewhat echoed today in the principles of the *Front National*, which tries to capitalize on this particular historical inheritance.

ASTRID HEYER

See also **Alain; Henri Bergson; Georges Bernanos; André Gide; Jacques Maritain; Charles Maurras**

Biography

Massis was born in Paris on March 21, 1886. He was a student at the Parisian Lycées Condorcet and Henri IV (where Alain taught him) and at the Sorbonne. He married and had one son. From 1905 he served in the military and fought in World War I. From 1911 to 1914, he was subeditor of *L'Opinion*. In 1913, Massis converted to Catholicism. He was both editor (1920–1939) and director (1939–1944) of *La Revue universelle*. In 1929, he was awarded the Académie Française Grand Prize for Literature. He was founder and editor of *1933*, a newspaper, from 1929 to 1934. Dur-

ing World War II, he served under the Vichy Government. After the war, he worked for the publishing house Plon in Paris. In 1960, he was elected to the Académie Française. Massis died in Paris on April 16, 1970.

Selected Works

Comment Émile Zola composait ses romans, 1906
Le Puits de Pyrrhon, 1907
La Pensée de Maurice Barrès, 1909
With Alfred de Tarde (jointly as Agathon), *L'Esprit de la nouvelle Sorbonne*, 1911
With Alfred de Tarde (jointly as Agathon), *Les Jeunes Gens d'aujourd'hui*, 1913
"The Perversity of André Gide", 1914
Romain Rolland contre la France, 1915
La Vie d'Ernest Psichari, 1916
"Pour un parti de l'intelligence" 1919
Jugements, 2 volumes, 1923–1924; revised edition, 1929
Jacques Rivière, 1925
Œuvres de Blaise Pascal, 1926
En marge de "Jugements": Réflexions sur l'art du roman, 1927
Défense de l'Occident, 1927
Avant-Postes (chroniques d'un redressement), 1910–1914, 1928
"La faillite d'André Gide" 1929
Évocations, souvenirs, 1905–1911, 1931
Dix Ans après: Réflexions sur la littérature d'après guerre, 1932
Débats, 1934
"Manifeste des intellectuels français pour la Défense de l'Occident et la paix en Europe", 1935
Les cadets de l'Alcazar, 1936
Notre ami Psichari, 1936
L'Honneur de servir, 1937
Le Drame de Marcel Proust, 1937
Chefs: Les Dictateurs et nous, 1939
With Robert Brasillach, *Le Siège de l'Alcazar*, 1939
La Guerre de trente ans, 1940
Les Idées restent, 1941
Découverte de la Russie, 1944
D'André Gide à Marcel Proust, 1948
L'Allemagne d'hier et d'après-demain, 1949
Portrait de M. Renan, 1949
Maurras et notre temps, 2 volumes, 1951
L'Occident et son destin, 1956
L'Europe en question, 1958
Visages des idées; À contre-courant; Thèmes et discussions, 1958
De l'homme à Dieu, 1959
Salazar face à face, 1961
Barrès et nous, 1962
Au long d'une vie, 1967

Further Reading

Baudin, Frédéric, "Littérature et christianisme. Les années 20: un âge d'or?" *La Revue Réformée*, 209 (September 2000), Tome LI, http://www.unpoissondansle.net/rr/0009/baudin.html
Chenaux, Philippe, *Entre Maurras et Maritain*, Paris: Cerf, 1999

Fraser, Theodore P., *The French Essay*, Boston: Twayne, 1986

Gerbod, Françoise. "Mounier, lecteur de Péguy, face à Henri Massis," *L'amitié Charles Péguy*, Bulletin d'Informations et de recherches, 89 (Janvier–Mars 2000): 5–12

Griffiths, Richard, *The Reactionary Revolution: The Catholic Revival in French Literature 1870–1914*, New York: Ungar, 1965, and London: Constable, 1966

Julliard, Jacques, Winock, Michel, *Dictionnaire des intellectuels français. Les personnes. Les lieux. Les moments*, Paris: Éditions du Seuil, 1996

Leitolf, Otto, "Die Gedankenwelt von Henri Massis," *Romanische Studien* 53,1940: 1–118

Peyre, Henry, "East and West in Recent French Literature (1927)," *Revue André Malraux Review*, Edmonton, Alberta, 24,1–2 (1992–1993): 127–132

Poulet, Robert, *Le Caléidoscope*, Lausanne: L'Âge d'Homme, 1982

Toda, Michel, *Henri Massis: Un Témoin de la droite intellectuelle*, Paris: La Table Ronde, 1987

Weber, Eugen, *L'Action française*, Paris: Stock, 1962; as *Action Française*, Stanford, California: Stanford University Press, 1962; reissued by Éditions Fayard, 1985)

Winock, Michel, *Nationalisme, antisémitisme et fascisme en France*, Paris: Seuil, 1982; as *Nationalism, Anti-Semitism, and Fascism in France*, translated by Jane Marie Todd, Stanford, California: Stanford University Press, 1998

MAURON, CHARLES
Literary Critic, Theorist

Though he was the founder of his own brand of psychoanalytic literary criticism called *psychocritique* (psychocriticism), Charles Mauron was not a psychoanalyst or even a trained literary scholar. Educated as a chemist, it was only his failing eyesight and fortuitous encounters with members of the English literary and artistic circle known as the Bloomsbury Group that led to his turn to things literary. His blindness and his late and (thanks to his friends) very British, rather than French, aesthetic education are directly responsible for the idiosyncratic form of his psychological theory of creation.

Mauron's first two books, *The Nature of Beauty in Art and Literature* (1927) and *Aesthetics and Psychology* (1935), developed his view of aesthetics as an empirical psychological science. Mauron was attracted to the theories of Sigmund Freud earlier than most French critics, but he always wanted to add to the psychoanalytic topography of the psyche some higher spiritual reality that would account for the creation of art better than the libidinal unconscious. What did appeal to him in psychoanalysis was how it opened the door to expressive and affective approaches to literature that valued intuition and subjectivity as ways to knowledge. By 1950, when he published *L'Introduction à la psychanalyse de Mallarmé* (Introduction to the Psychoanalysis of Mallarmé), Mauron had found a way to reconcile what he called the subjective and the objective aesthetics and psychology.

In this work, he chose to present himself as the "man of science" he had been trained to be and called his method an experimental one. As a mode of literary analysis, *psychocritique* focuses on certain literary structures whose origins are attributed to what is called the "unconscious personality" of the author. This is not to say that Mauron denied the importance (or existence) of textual structures that might be consciously intended and deliberately elaborated, but these were not where his interest lay. He acknowledged three variables in the poet's free act of creation: milieu, language, and the artist's personality. It was the latter that fascinated Mauron. Working from Freud's concept of the unconscious, latent source of the manifest content and form of the work of art, Mauron sought the hidden (and therefore more significant) unity to be found beneath the surface unity of a text. This was clearly a very formalist kind of adaptation of psychoanalysis to literary ends, but it was premised on the belief that "scientific psychology" offered important insights into imaginative fantasies, the creative process, and also ego-object relations.

Psychocritique never confused the work of art with a dream or symptom of the artist; this was psychoanalysis adapted, not adopted. It brought together what Mauron saw as the advantages of a patient's free associations (when conscious control was voluntarily suspended) and the analyst's careful attention to repetition. The method he devised was very much the product of a man who had lost his sight and could no longer read, but who relied on his prodigious memory and aural reminders (as people read aloud to him). The "psychocritic" had to know the poems being analyzed by heart and superimpose them in (in this case) his mind before letting his conscious attention float; coincidences would then suggest themselves, though in no conscious or chronological order. If the coincidences could not be explained by the formal surface unities of the text, then they were considered unconscious and latent—and therefore significant. Grouped together in what Mauron called "obsessive metaphors," these networks of associations "resonated" within the author's psyche. The work of Melanie Klein was important to Mauron's thinking of these networks as attempts to create a unified vision of the inner fragmented world.

Klein's insistence on the dynamic nature of psychic interrelations and, in particular, her theories of projection and of the internalization of desired objects allowed Mauron to move from this idea of static associative networks to a more dynamic model. In *Des Métaphores obsédantes au mythe personnel* (From Obsessive Metaphors to the Personal Myth, 1964), he posited a psychic "forcefield" created by those networks of images, a site of conflicts and defenses that gradually became polarized into mythic figures that acted out certain dramatic roles representing Kleinian internalized objects and identifications. This was the personal myth, the obsessive fantasy, beneath the recurring images. This dynamic model made possible the psychocritical move from lyric poetry (which was easy to memorize and superimpose mentally) to larger dramatic and epic works, as in *L'Inconscient dans l'oeuvre et la vie de Racine* (The Unconscious in the Work and Life of Racine, 1969). Mauron's investigation of the work of Molière, however, forced him to consider two new things: the role of genre and the function of the unconscious of the audience. When that French dramatist's personal myth turned out to be the same as the formal structures of comedy in general, Mauron tackled the genre as a whole in *Psychocritique du genre comique* (Psychocriticism of the Comic Genre, 1964), supplementing Klein's work with the theories of Freud on jokes, Carl Jung on the collective unconscious, and Anna Freud on defense mechanisms.

Aesthetics and psychology (the words that make up the title of his second book) continued to be the twin poles of Mauron's thinking. *Psychocritique* revealed a constant tension between his formalist desire to study the structures of the work of art itself and his interest in the psyche of the creator. It was not surprising that, for a brief time in the 1960s, Mauron would become involved in the famous battle in France over the *nouvelle critique*—that is, over the importing of the insights and methods of the social sciences into literary criticism. Today his work tends to be considered out of date, though occasionally there are valiant, if strange, efforts to reread him, say, in Lacanian terms. His contribution to critical methodology and to the interpretation of individual authors has been sufficient, however, to keep the term *psychocritique* reserved in French for this particular—and very peculiar—brand of thinking psychoanalytically about the creative process.

LINDA HUTCHEON

Biography

Born in St. Rémy de Provence in 1899, Charles Mauron trained as a chemical engineer in Marseille, but his increasing blindness (from detached retinas) made him rethink his career. It was a friend, the British art critic Roger Fry, who urged him to try his hand at translating. With the aid of his first wife, he translated E. M. Forster's *A Passage to India*, which this would prove to be the first of many translations from English to French, including the works of Laurence Sterne, Virginia Woolf, T. E. Lawrence, D. H. Lawrence, and Katherine Mansfield. He began publishing his specifically psychocritical work after the Second World War. As the mayor of St. Rémy from 1945 to 1959, he was engaged both politically and culturally, lending his

strong voice to the cause of the retention of Provençal culture and language. He finally received his *doctorat ès lettres* from the Sorbonne when he was sixty-four years old and taught briefly at the Université d'Aix before his death in 1966.

Selected Works

The Nature of Beauty in Art and Literature, translated by Roger Fry, 1927
Aesthetics and Psychology, translated by Roger Fry and Katherine John, 1935
Mallarmé l'obscur, 1941
Introduction à la psychanalyse de Mallarmé, 1950; as *Introduction to the Psychoanalysis of Mallarmé*, translated by Archibald Henderson, Jr., and Will McLendon, 1963
Des Métaphores obsédantes au mythe personnel: Introduction à la psychocritique, 1964
Psychocritique du genre comique, 1964
Le Dernier Baudelaire, 1966
L'Inconscient dans l'oeuvre e la vie de Racine, 1969
Le Théâtre de Giraudoux, 1971

Further Reading

Clancier, Anne, "Charles Mauron," in her *Psychanalyse et critique littéraire*, Toulouse: Privat, 1973
Cruickshank, John, "Psychocriticism and Literary Judgment," *British Journal of Aesthetics*, 4 (1964): 155–159
Hutcheon, Linda, *Formalism and the Freudian Aesthetic: The Example of Charles Mauron*, Cambridge: Cambridge University Press, 1984
LeSage, Laurent, "Charles Mauron in Retrospect," *L'Esprit Créateur*, 14 (1974): 265–276
Mehlman, Jeffrey, "Entre psychanalyse et psychocritique," *Poétique*, 1 (1970): 365–383

MAURRAS, CHARLES
Essayist, Poet, Political Journalist, and Activist

A staunch opponent of the Third Republic, the reactionary nationalist and monarchist Charles Maurras leveled the most sustained assault on its values and institutions. Targets of his attacks ranged from the French Revolution itself to criticisms of democracy as a form of government and a social system. He was driven by what he feared was a decline of France as a great nation and its descent into decadence. Maurras's writings, with their preoccupation with the nation's decline as a world power coupled with a concern over its internal instability, reveal a prefiguring of the complex of issues that would soon engulf Europe in violence.

Maurras was not merely a critic of the failings of democracy, he attacked its very essence. In his view, the appearance of democracy in a state marked its descent into barbarism, a condition in which everything was subordinated to the individual. Democracy meant the rule of hedonism and profit that valued the present at the neglect of the past and the future, which simultaneously provided necessary breaks on consumption and spurred innovations in production. The democratic ideal was an affront to nature because it subjected greatness to mediocrity, the superior to the inferior, quality to quantity. Its laws destroyed customs and instincts that emerged from natural tendencies.

Maurras offered an elitist theory intended to reach an active minority that might found a monarchist regime. The masses could not understand the complex interests of France. The Third Republic was suffering under the rule of people who lacked any special gifts or talents. The decay of aristocracy, that group of families supposedly committed to national interest, in France made a powerful and united republic impossible. A new aristocracy, naturally suited to rule France, was required.

In his reading of history, there had never been a positive example of progress that had been initiated or carried through by the masses. History revealed to him the opposite: Enterprise and will were expressions of a minority that possessed the necessary characteristics of virtue and strength. Maurras took for granted that a coherent group possessing these qualities actually existed. Moreover, he saw this group as part of a fixed hierarchy and was inattentive to changes in the composition of elites, which theorists such as Mosca and especially Pareto had emphasized.

Maurras showed only contempt for institutions such as the electoral system, which allowed "the people" any voice in politics. The electoral system was for him another outgrowth of individualism and could not account for the general interest of the nation. Individual interests took precedent over general interests, which were far to complex to be grasped by the masses. An electoral regime inevitably came under the rule of a class of opportunists who looked only toward the next election and held no concern for the future.

The masses lacked the appropriate faculties of reflection and historical memory, and this meant that the elected were subjected to the ignorance of public opinion. Public opinion, vague and shifting, could not form a basis for durable institutions and practices. In contrast to electoralism, which undermined authority, Maurras idealized hereditary authority, which he saw as allowing for order and stability. In an elite regime, the state could act for the general interest despite opposition by public sentiment.

Maurras also viewed liberty as a false principle that was counter to nature. Ideas of liberty for all violated the laws of nature, reason, and the state. These are the real laws that must rule the citizen. Because people were not equal, liberty could only be the privilege of the few.

Liberty proposed the sovereignty of the individual, which Maurras rejected. In his view, the nation or state always took primacy of position, and this primacy could not yield to the individual. The individual had no natural rights, only duties to society. Individual liberties were insignificant in relation to the sovereignty of the nation and the maintenance of its traditions. Furthermore, the basic element of society was not the individual but the family. True liberty rested not in the individual but in the restoration of the power of the family.

Ideas of equality were also counter to nature for Maurras. Laws that asserted the equality of all members of society were false, as, in reality, all societies exhibited an unequal distribution of liberties. Increased division of labor and the diversity of social roles meant difference and assured functional inequalities. Equality meant turning governance over to the mass of inferiors, which would necessarily lead to the rule of incompetence.

Maurras was thoroughly opposed to the Revolution. In his view, it was so much the product of foreign ideas that it could not properly be called French. The Revolution was not the product of contradictions or defects in the *ancien régime* but arose from the influence of individualism, Calvinism, and the teachings of Rousseau. Maurras's opposition to the Revolution was complete, and he rejected all of its aspects, which he saw as anti-French. The Revolution had taken France from its natural course of development, exacerbating the divisive effects of atomism and individualism. The decadence of the Third Republic dated from the Revolution itself. The Revolution had destroyed the local institutions, great families, and social authorities on which the power of France was based.

The Revolution had also denied France its place as the inheritor of the Greek and Roman civilizations. Maurras desired the revival of the classical spirit based on authority, hierarchy, and inequality. Traditional values were being threatened by romanticism, which Maurras saw as part of a barbarian invasion of France by outsiders. Maurras spoke out against modernist developments in culture, decrying impressionism and other forms of "degenerate romanticism." A defender of classicism, he chastised the bourgeoisie for its lack of appreciation of the classics.

According to Maurras, the Third Republic was a foreign regime and needed to be replaced by one that was truly French. The organized foreigners who threatened France were made up, for Maurras, of four *Etats Confédérés:* masons; Swiss, English, and German Protestants; Jews; and *métèques,* a word coined by Maurras for recently naturalized "guests" or their children. A virulent anti-Semite, his most consistent attacks were leveled against Jews, whom he viewed as a foreign element in France and the source of harmful values. In Maurras's view, these four estates controlled all of France's political life.

Maurras stood at the forefront of the counterrevolution in twentieth-century France. Overturning the practices of the Revolution required a counterrevolution that upheld authority rather than liberty, hierarchy rather than equality, family rather than the individual, duty rather than rights. The vehicle through which he waged the counterrevolution was the *Action Français* movement, which became the condensation point of the extreme Right. Maurras realized that *Action Français* would not gain power through regular constitutional channels. The group was an organized conspiracy to prepare the groundwork for a *coup d'état*. The group would develop the organization and disseminate the ideas that would make a coup successful. This groundwork included violence, and the *Action Français* regularly fought its political battles in the streets. The end of this planned coup would be the installation of the monarchy and the rule of hereditary elites.

JEFFREY SHANTZ

Biography

Born in Martigues in 1868, Charles Maurras left Provence for Paris in 1885. In 1899, Maurras, along with Henri Vaugeois, founded the extremist *Action Français* group, which, under Maurras's influence, espoused a monarchist nationalism supported by campaigns of violence. During the 1930s, Maurras expressed admiration for both Mussolini and Franco. Under the Nazi Occupation in World War Two, Maurras, a virulent anti-Semite, supported Marshal Pétain and collaborated with the Vichy regime. For this he was sentenced, in 1945, to life imprisonment and removed from the Académie Française, to which he had been elected in 1938. In 1951, he was transferred from prison to house arrest at a private clinic at Troyes, where he died in 1952.

Selected Writings

Jean Moréas, 1891
Le Chemin de paradis: mythes et fabliaux, 1895
Trois idées politiques: Chateaubriand, Michelet, Sainte-Beuve, 1898
L'Avenir de l'Intelligence, 1905
Anthinéa: d'Athènes à Florence, edited by Librairie Honoré and Edouard Champion, 1913 [1901]
L'Action Française et la religion catholique, 1913
Quand les Français ne s'aimaient pas, chronique d'une renaissance, 1890–1905, 1916
Les Chefs socialistes pendant la guerre, 1918
Les Idées royalistes sur les partis, l'état, la nation, 1919
Le Chemin de paradis: contes philosophiques, edited by E. de Boccard, 1921

Kiel at Tanger, 1895–1905: la République français devant l'Europe, 1905–1913–1921, 1921
Mademoiselle Monk ou la génération des événements, 1923 [1905]
La Musique intérieure, 1924
L'Allée des philosophes, 1925
Barbarie et poésie, 1925
Enquete sur la monarchie, 1925 [1901]
Romantisme et révolution, 1925 [1922]
L'Avenir de l'intelligence, 1927
Corps glorieux ou vertu de la perfection, 1928
Quatre nuits de Provence, 1930
Les Principes, 1931
Au signe de Flore: la fondation de l'Action française, 1898–1900, 1931
Méditations sur la politique de Jeanne d'Arc, 1931
Dictionnaire politique et critique, 5 volumes, 1931–1934
Napoléon avec la France, ou contre la France?, 1932
Le Mont de Saturne: conte moral, magique et policier, 1950
Maitres et témoins de ma vie d'esprit: Barrès, Mistral, France, Verlaine, Moréas, 1954
Oeuvres capitales: essais politiques, 1954
Critique et poésie, 1968
Mes idées politiques, 1986 [1937]

Further Reading

Buthman, William Curt, *The Rise of Integral Nationalism in France: With Special Reference to the Ideas and Activities of Charles Maurras*, New York: Columbia University Press, 1939

Chiron, Yves, *La Vie de Charles Maurras*, Paris: Perrin, 1991

De Leonibus, Gaetano, "Conspiracy: An Aesthetic Value in Charles Maurras's Political System," in *Repression and Expression: Literary and Social Coding in Nineteenth-Century France*, edited by Carrol F. Coates, New York: Peter Lang, 1996

Griffiths, Richard, *The Reactionary Revolution: The Catholic Revival in French Literature 1870/1914*, New York: Frederick Ungar, 1965

Joseph, Roger, and Forges, Jean *Nouvelle Bibliographie de Charles Maurras*, 2 volumes, Aix-en-Provence: L'Art de voir, 1980

Jouanny, Robert A., "Maurras et les débuts de l'école romane," *Etudes maurrassiennes*, II (1973): 107–116

Maritain, Jacques, *Une opinion sur Charles Maurras et le devoir des catholiques*, Paris, 1926

Osgood, Samuel M., *French Royalism Under the Third and Fourth Republics*, The Hague: Martinus Nijhoff, 1960

Péguy, Charles, *Notre patrie*, Paris, 1915

Sternhell, Zeev, *Ni droite, ni gauche: l'idéologie fasciste en France*, Paris: Editions du Seuil, 1983

Talvart, Hector, *Fiche de Charles Maurras*, La Rochelle, 1930

Talvart, Hector, *Maurras religieux et suscitateur de foi*, La Rochelle, 1930

Vandromme, Pol, *Maurras, léglise de l'ordre*, Paris: Editions du Centurion, 1965

Vandromme, Pol, *Maurras entre le légiste et le contestataire*, Paris: TEQUI, 1991

MAUSS, MARCEL
Ethnographer

The father of French ethnography, Marcel Mauss greatly influenced social sciences and left an exceptionally rich intellectual legacy. He is naturally identified with Emile Durkheim (1854–1917), his uncle and mentor.

Marcel Mauss accomplished his first great work in collaboration with his friend and colleague Henri Hubert (1872–1927) on "Sacrifice: Its Nature and Function" (1899). The article was published in *L'Année Sociologique* (The Sociological Year), founded by Durkheim in 1898. Responsible for the sociology of religion section, Mauss became one of its most active contributors. He succeeded Léon Marillier at the École Pratique des Hautes Études in 1901, where he was put in charge of teaching the "History of Religion of Non-Civilized Peoples." Mauss's research was essentially comparative and thoroughly documented and fell within a program that aimed to study the ritualistic manifestations of religious life and intended to develop a theory of the sacred. His work quickly expanded beyond the sociology of religion to touch on the theory of knowledge as shown in *Quelques formes primitive de classification* (A Few Primitive Forms of Classification), which he wrote with Durkheim in 1903. Followers of Durkheim do not hesitate to say that sociology is a collective psychology, the purpose of which is the study of collective representations.

The main debate raised by Durkheim's first books at the end of the nineteenth century revolved around the opposition of the individual and society. One of the problems sociology faced at its beginning was its own specificity and its relationship with other disciplines, especially psychology. Not only did this debate oppose Durkheim to his adversaries, including Gabriel Tarde, it also divided his associates, as can be seen in the first volumes of *L'Année Sociologique*. Célestin Bouglé, who, with his friend Paul Lapie, was somewhat ambivalent with regards to Durkheim's problematics, acknowledged the individual's place and, looking to go past the individual/society dichotomy, spoke of interaction, association between individuals, and communication between consciences.

Very early on, Mauss attempted to diminish the obvious dogmatism of Durkheim. In a text titled "Sociology," co-authored with Paul Fauconnet in 1901 for *La Grande Encyclopédie*, he highlighted the psychological aspect of social life, beliefs, and collective feelings. He wrote, "The intimate base of social life is an ensemble of representations." He added, "Thus in this light, one could say that sociology is a psychology." It is of course a psychology that is distinctive from individual psychology. In 1904, Mauss published with Henri Hubert in *L'Année Sociologique* an important "General Theory of Magic" that showed that the laws of collective psychology broke those of individual psychology. Mauss and Hubert wrote, "It is the opinion that creates the magician and the influences that emanate from

him." The use of the concept of *mana* as the founding idea of magic would spark a long controversy.

During World War I, Mauss volunteered and was assigned to work as an interpreter. The war was a tragedy for him and took away Durkheim, his son André, and several associates from *L'Année Sociologique*. Afterward, Mauss took over Durkheim's work and tried to restart *L'Année Sociologique*, but only two volumes would be published in 1925 and 1927. Mauss remained, however, extremely politically active. He started to write a great work on the Nation and, after the publication of his "Observations on violence" in *La Vie Socialiste*, started to plan a book on Bolshevism. Then, bolstered by a new interest in the "exotic" that stirred interest in ethnography, Mauss, with Lucien Lévi-Bruhl and Paul River, created the *Institut d'Ethnologie de Paris* (Paris Institute of Ethnology) in 1925. A school developed from the Institute, producing students and researchers (Jeanne Cuisinier, Alfred Métraux, Marcel Griaule, Georges Dumézil, Denise Paulme, Michel Leiris, Germaine Dieterlen, Louis Dumont, André-Georges Haudricourt, Jacques Soustelle, and Germaine Tillion) that would devote themselves to much field work, mostly in Africa, and that organized the first great ethnological expeditions.

Endowed with great intellectual curiosity and an exceptional erudition, Mauss took his research in various directions, from magic to body techniques and the notion of person. He corrected his uncle's antipsychologism by establishing "Real and practical relationships between psychology and sociology" in a text he published in 1924 in *Journal de Psychologie*; the following year he published his "Essai sur le don. Forme et raison de l'échange dans les sociétés archaïques" (The Gift. The Form and Reason for Exchange in Archaic Societies).

Never before had Durkeim's nephew followed with such interest the works of psychologists. He took part in the activities of the *Société de Psychologie*, of which he became the president in 1923. Among his friends were Blondel, Dumas, and above all, Ignace Meyerson, who worked in an editorial capacity at the *Journal de Psychologie Normale et Pathologique* (Journal of Normal and Pathological Psychology). Mauss wrote, "Sociology, psychology, and physiology, it all must blend." The focus is to be on the object of the "complete, concrete man" and to analyze "phenomena of totality." In 1926, again in the *Journal de Psychologie*, he published a study on the "Physical effect on the individual of the idea of death suggested by the collectivity." Mental confusion, inhibition, delirium, and hallucination greatly interested Mauss but, unlike psychologists, he did not see them as pathological manifestations.

His writings were first compiled by Claude Lévi-Strauss in 1950 in *Sociologie et Anthropologie* (Sociology and Anthropology) and in 1969 in three volumes by Victor Karady, titled *Oeuvres*. His political writings, which were numerous as Mauss was an active socialist militant, would only be compiled by Marcel Fournier in 1977. Mauss's political work includes many observations and precious "appreciations" that combine, as he himself acknowledged, the ardor of the scientist and the politician. He did not hesitate to promote some traditional values in the conclusion of his "Essai sur le don" (The Gift), such as almsgiving, and proposed a morality based on solidarity and reciprocity.

MARCEL FOURNIER

See also **Maurice Blondel; Georges Dumezil; Emile Durkheim; Claude Levi-Strauss; Lucien Levy-Bruhl**

Biography

Born in Epinal in 1872 in a family of merchants and rabbis, Mauss studied philosophy in Bordeaux under Durkheim. After he gained his *agrégation* in philosophy in 1895, he abandoned classical studies for the sociology of religion. At the Ecole Pratique des Hautes Etudes, and during a mission in the Netherlands and England, he acquired a solid knowledge of philology, history of religions, and ethnology. Mauss was already politically active in college, siding with the socialists; he wrote for *Mouvement Social* and helped start the *Société nouvelle de librairie et d'édition* (New Bookselling and Publishing Company) with Lucien Herr and Charles Andler. Once he became a professor, Mauss remained active within the mouvement coopératif and the socialist party, publishing many articles in *L'Humanité*, a newspaper he helped create. Marcel Mauss was elected in 1930 to the *Collège de France* and was appointed to the Chair of Sociology. Marcel Mauss died on February 11, 1950; he was seventy-seven years old.

Selected Works

Écrits politiques, edited by Marcel Fournier, 1997
Essais de sociologie, 1969
Ouvres, 3 volumes, edited by Victor Karady, 1968–1969
Sociologie et anthropologie, edited by Claude Lévi-Strauss, 1950

MEDIA

Media in France since the nineteenth century have been very much a focal point for the intellectual life and for the development and discussion of thought, but the recent developments of mass media are marked by a shift away from traditional forms of communication and exchange and toward a complete revolution of the relationship between intellectuals and creators with their public. Indeed, the media have been one of the main reasons why the status of the intellectual, and especially the "committed intellectual," has changed dramatically in the last three decades.

This is especially the case with television and more recently the Internet and other forms of electronic communication. Whereas up to the beginning of the 1980s, there were only three TV channels in France, all State-controlled, and four main radio stations, the number of satellite or cable channels controlled mostly by large conglomerates has now exploded, as well as the number of radio stations of all kinds, operating in a fiercely competitive market in which the main rule is the *audimat* (audience ratings). Similarly, the offer of printed titles in the press has multiplied under the form of specific interests magazines, whereas the more traditional opinion press (mostly newspapers) has at best stagnated, if not entered a long-term crisis. The role of the State in the media sector is nevertheless still prominent, although it has changed nature and justification. There is still a significant offering of public sector TV and radio, which is getting a large chunk of the total audience, and the public administration also closely regulates (and in some cases subsidizes) the market, including the types of products that have to be offered to the media consumers. The main justifications for this strong public intervention are to guarantee the diversity of offerings and opinion that markets would not maintain, to sustain production and creation at a national level, and to prevent the "commodification" of cultural goods in the hands of international markets. The level of regulation is an important debate at French and European levels, and it has to be understood in the context of globalization and growing control of media supports and products by large international firms. The politics of "cultural exception," defended by successive governments since the 1980s, and the resulting conflicts in the international trade arena such as the World Trade Organization (especially with the United States), are seen as a way of maintaining and promoting cultural diversity.

The Printed Media: Press in Crisis?

Although until the 1970s the print media—newspapers, magazines, and reviews—were the most potent way for intellectual debates to take place in France, this has changed dramatically in the last three decades. Indeed, one could speak of a crisis, not so much of the printed media as a whole, but of the traditional role of such media. Newspapers and traditional reviews have suffered a real decline in their audience and popularity, whereas magazines of all sorts have proliferated and developed niche markets that usually have more to do with specific hobbies or personal interests than the diffusion of ideas and debates.

If there is a crisis, it mostly affects newspapers. The number of titles has fallen dramatically since the beginning of the twentieth century. For instance, the number of daily newspaper titles published in Paris (the so-called national papers), which had reached eighty in 1914, had fallen to eight in the mid 1990. The readership has slowly eroded, with only thirty-six percent of the French in 1997 reading a newspaper every day, against fifty-five percent in 1973. The French now read fewer newspapers than their neighbors—15 for 100 people per day, against some 30 in Great Britain and Germany. In particular, they read fewer national newspapers (i.e., Paris-based, nationally distributed ones). These do not have a very wide direct audience, although they are often at the center of the news and where national debates still take place, alongside television. Among those considered quality national newspapers, *Le Monde*, the highly respected so-called reference newspaper, only prints around 400,000 copies a day (no more than *L'Equipe*, the sports national daily), with *Le Figaro* coming just behind but *Liberation* trailing at some 170,000 copies. These are ridiculously small print runs compared, say, with those of the main British morning paper, *The Sun*, reaching 3.5 million copies a day among popular dailies (the main French daily, *Le Parisien-Aujourd'hui*, prints some 550,000 copies only) and those of the main quality paper, *The Daily Telegraph*, running at around 1 million copies a day. Some minor dailies survive because of their specific audience—*L'Humanité* is the Communist Party voice, and *La Croix* is a Catholic newspaper. Many historical titles have either disappeared (such as *L'Aurore*, or *Combat*), or are just surviving (*France-Soir*).

Indeed, French people mostly read regional broadsheets, the most important of them being *Ouest-France*, distributed from the north of Normandy to the whole of Atlantic cost regions down to Aquitaine, with multiple local editions, and printing an average of 800,000 copies a day. In other regions, a wide range of papers can be found, although groups such as the Hersant group controls an important number of regional papers such as *Le Progrès* as well as national ones such as *Le Figaro*. Sunday papers are not developed in France, but in a way, weekly news magazines (comparable to Time or Newsweek) take their place, and these have a wide readership—from the classic *Paris-Match* (700,000 copies per issue), a mix between Life and a celebrity gossip magazine, renowned for its picture pages, to the trendsetting, Paris-centered *L'Express* and *Le Nouvel Observateur*, each running at a readership of around half a million, and other, less popular titles such as *Le Point* or *Marianne*.

The economic situation of the press, and especially newspapers, is not healthy—not only do they have to rely on cover price more than, say, their British or American counterparts because of limited advertisement resources now directed more toward television (advertising accounts for only forty-nine percent of daily newspapers' income, against sixty-two percent in the United Kingdom and eighty-seven percent in the United States). Indeed, newspapers are receiving subsidies from the State to maintain sufficient competing titles and diversity of opinion. Papers are clearly politically oriented. For instance, *Le Figaro* is clearly identified as a conservative paper, whereas *Liberation* is seen as being on the left. Similarly, news magazines are either oriented toward the left or center-left (*Le Nouvel Observateur, Marianne*) or center-right (*L'Express*) or are clearly conservative (*Le Point, Valeurs Actuelles, Le Figaro Magazine*).

The last twenty years have seen the complete reorganization of the magazine publication sector. There are now thousands of new titles, mostly monthly and often associated with international and European titles, catering for all tastes and areas of life, from women's magazines (including the original and world-famous *Elle*) to teen fashion ones, from specialized sports to computing, from do-it-yourself to biking, often belonging to stables owned by large press conglomerates that can be as well French (Hachette) as European (Beterlsman, EMAP, and so on). These new offerings, which see a flow of titles constantly appearing and disappearing, contrasts with the more traditional intellectual reviews, which manage to maintain their presence and are still central to the intellectual and social debates, but with a very limited readership. Historical titles such as *Esprit* and *Les Temps Modernes* jostle alongside more contemporary reviews such as *Le Débat* (center-left) or *Commentaires* (liberal right). However, literary reviews such as the celebrated *NRF (Nouvelles Lettres Françaises)* are now occupying a niche market.

A specificity of French media is the structure of the book publishing business. Although most of the great historical publishing houses (such as Larousse, Grasset, Le Seuil, Fayard, Minuit, and so on) have now been incorporated into larger media conglomerates (*Presses de la Cité*, Hachette, and the like), there are some significant businesses that have managed somehow to keep their independence. First and foremost is Gallimard, the family business which has the most prestigious list of authors in its catalogue. It is still the main competitor every year for the literary prizes season, in which the *Prix Goncourt* occupies a central place, with the *Renaudot* and *Médicis* prizes also particularly coveted. Among the myriad of other independent publishing companies, some occupy a preeminent place in literary life, such as *Actes-Sud*, which in a few years managed to become a major player, especially in the publication of translated works.

Television and Radio: An Explosion of New Choices

As in other European countries, the daily life of French people is largely organized around TV viewing—although it developed at a slightly slower pace than in the United Kingdom. In 1973, only sixty-three percent of French people were watching TV every day, but this number has now increased to nearly eighty percent. On average, each person watches it some twenty-two hours per week, five hours more than in 1973. It is interesting that French people are very fond of their radio stations: they listen as much to radio as they look at TV per week on average. Long-wave radio stations still benefit from the strongest audience (the main public national station, *France-Inter*, is the most popular, offering a mix of news, debates, variety, and music, followed by stations such as *Europe 1, RTL*, and *RMC*). At the same time, the explosion of FM stations since 1982 has created an enlarged audience, with intense competition among music, locality-based, community, or specialized interests stations.

General TV channels are dominated by privately owned TF1, which, because of its populist programming (sports, hit films, variety, reality shows) regularly gains up to a third of the national audience. It is followed by the two main State-controlled channels, FR2 and FR3. Other popular channels are the Canal+ encrypted paid subscription channel and M6, a youth-oriented channel that introduced France to the pleasures of reality shows (with *Loft*, equivalent to the Dutch and British *Big Brother*, a clear favorite). Some general channels are quite original, such as the States-funded Franco-German Arte channel, devoted to art and ideas, and broadcast in the two languages. At the same time, the development of cable TV has paralleled that of satellite-based offerings. The two so-called digital bunches (*bouquets numériques*) of Canal Satellite and TPS offer a mix including general channels and thematic channels and subscription ones (mostly films and sports).

The staple of TV programs offered to the French viewers is not that different from that in other European countries. The most frequent program offered (especially on TF1, Canal+, M6 and a number of bundled channels) are U.S. series. Sports programs, films and dramas, variety shows, and "reality" shows obtain the highest ratings. However, some other types of programs can attract a considerable audience and become

social events; this was the case of the literary and ideas programs *Apostrophes* and then *Bouillon de Culture*, anchored by Bernard Pivot, which, from 1975 to 2001, were the main outlets for giving an audience or a readership to an author, an intellectual, or an artist and for launching a debate of ideas. The *Nouveaux Philosophes* movement, for instance, benefited crucially from *Apostrophes* exposure in the 1970s.

Mass Media and Intellectual Life

The mass media have become so central to the life of the French that in itself it has become a frequent subject of reflection and controversy. Two interrelated issues, especially, have been widely debated in the last two decades. The first one is the place of the committed intellectual as a central figure in French social life, and the second debate concerns the role of the media in constructing and organizing the view of the world held by viewers.

The ways in which the *intellectuel engagé* (the committed intellectual) has operated socially have been closely attached to the way the press (but also, in the recent decades, radio and television) operate. The emblematic event of Emile Zola having the full text of *J'Accuse* published on the front page of the daily newspaper *L'Aurore* in 1898 only epitomizes the constant use of the press by academics, literary authors, and other intellectuals during the nineteenth and twentieth centuries—in fact, since the pre-Revolutionary days of the Enlightenment. Many central figures from Victor Hugo to Camus or Mauriac and Sartre have used the press as their main sounding board, and indeed, the constant debate about the role of the intellectual in French society is closely intertwined to that of the power of the media in the French democracy—the so-called fourth estate.

Indeed, a whole debate in the columns of *Le Monde* in the late 1980s was devoted to the possible demise of the socio-political role of the "intellectual" as a leader of opinion orchestrating socio-political debates. A common view then expressed was that the traditional intellectual figure was now replaced by that of the ever-present media professionals such as anchors, program managers, journalists, and variety show hosts. Well-known hosts and journalists, such as François de Closets, Patrice Poivre d'Arvor, and Michel Drucker, to name a few, not only have become household names, but now write the best-sellers to be found in bookstores and supermarkets and replace the traditional intellectuals in the social debate. It is interesting to note that figures such as Sartre, Aron, Camus, or Mauriac, for instance, or more recently Bourdieu, had the reverse trajectory: It is as already well-known intellectuals and authors that they went to journalism or article writing (e.g., Camus becoming the editor of *Combat*, first published during the war as an organ of resistance).

The Media, the State and Forces of Globalization: A French Debate

There has been a long tradition in France of the State seeking to control directly or indirectly the mass media. The systematic censorship of the press during the nineteenth century lasted up to the end of Second Empire in 1870, and freedom of expression in the media only got fully established through the 1881 law on press freedom. Even later, numerous expressions of direct censorship occurred. The totalitarian regime imposed on media by the Vichy regime during the occupation was to be expected, but it was symptomatic of the relationship between the media and the State that some newspapers and magazines got censored on a regular basis during the Algerian war (1954–1962), for instance, for criticizing the Army for violent behavior against civil population or for the practice of torture. Another feature of French media that has been frequently noted (and that derives from the historically fraught relation with the political power) is the tendency for self-censorship of media in relation to figures of power. A well-known case is the way in which important aspects of the late President Mitterrand's personal life were left hidden from the French public for decades.

Another aspect of the close links between the State and media has been that the development of the new media of radio and television has occurred through state companies since their inception. Indeed, there was a State monopoly for radio and television broadcasting from the French territory up to the early 1980s. It is symptomatic that the public radio stations and TV channels (grouped up to 1974 into a single body, the ORTF) were managed directly from the Ministry of Information and Government Speaker: Government public relations and public broadcasting were indeed seen during the 1960s as a single task. The French State often even had a controlling stake in the major radio stations that were broadcasting from outside the national territory (such as Europe 1). It is the socialist government that deregulated radio in 1982, and the following conservative government that sold the main TV channel (TF1) to the private sector (to the main construction engineering company Bouygues) in 1987. Deregulation, followed by the development of new media opportunities such as satellite broadcasting, opened up the field irreversibly in the late 1980s.

However, these developments do not signify the end of the involvement of the State in the media. First, the public broadcasting channels and stations are still very much a feature of the so-called *Paysage Audiovisuel Français* (PAF: an expression to designate the whole framework of TV and radio broadcasting in France). Second, the State has now constituted a proper regulation framework for the whole sector. The main institution is the CSA (*Conseil Supérieur de l'Audiovisuel*), which controls the operations of radio and television broadcasting companies. A number of rules concerning corporations are applied to avoid overbearing concentration—for instance, no company can control more than thirty percent of publications in a segment of the press.

A third aspect of State intervention is the continued support, especially in terms of public subsidies, given to media industries. Typical of those terms are the supports to film industry either for the distribution of *Arts et Essais* films or for the production of French films that could not attract sufficient funding from a production company. Similarly, daily newspapers receive subsidies (tax exemptions, distribution costs reductions, and so on) to maintain sufficient diversity and independence of the press.

Finally, a feature of recent debates in France concerning media industries (and, more generally, all cultural goods industries) is the growing importance of the theme of "cultural exception." This concept appeared in the context of the negotiations of the GATT (General Agreement on Trade and Tariffs) and, more recently, the World Trade Organization (WTO), which replaced it. Although the debate can appear arcane, it is of utmost importance and has provoked considerable opposition between France and the United States. The basic idea behind it is that cultural goods (including media) cannot be considered as any other good in the context of the general deregulation of trade of services across the world because this would endanger and in the long term eliminate cultural diversity and national or regional cultures. This is the result of the evaluation that the media industries of the United States are in a dominant position, being able to make a profit on their domestic market and then to dump their production across the world at a low price, undercutting national media industries. As a consequence, there is, for instance, in France a system of quotas—a proportion of music and songs played on France-based stations must be in French, and a proportion of TV and radio programs from France and the European Union must be broadcast by each station or channel.

However, the French media are themselves increasingly part of conglomerates that seek an international profile—increasingly, there is an Europeanization, if not a globalization, of the largest of media groups operating in France. Groups such as Hachette or Havas now make a majority of their profits outside France. Indeed, the recent saga of the Vivendi International group, born out of a utilities company in the 1980s and finally acquiring the status of global player after the acquisition of Universal Studios, is particularly revealing. In 2001, Jean-Marie Messier, the CEO of Vivendi International, started a polemic in the columns of *Le Monde* stating that cultural exception and cultural diversity policies were outdated remnants of a bygone age and that international conglomerates were now able to provide cultural and opinion diversity by competing at global level. This view provoked an outcry, and the reactions proved the strength of the cultural diversity ideology in French society. A few months later, Vivendi International collapsed because of financial overexposure.

FRANÇOIS NECTOUX

See also **Raymond Aron; Pierre Bourdieu; Albert Camus; Jean-Paul Sartre**

Further Reading

d'Almeida, Fabrice, and Delporte, Christian, *Histoire des médias en France de la Grande Guerre à nos jours*, Paris: Flammarion, 2003

Bourdieu, Pierre, *On Television*, New York: New Press, 1998

Bertholus, Jean-Jacques, *Les Médias-maîtres. Qui contrôle l'information?* Paris: Le Seuil, 2000

Debray, Regis, *Media Manifestos*, London: Verso Books, 1996

Donnat, Olivier, *Les Pratiques culturelles des Français*, Paris: La Documentation Française, 1998

Johnson, Jo, and Orange, Martine, *The Man Who Tried To Buy The World: Jean-Marie Messier & Vivendi Universal*, London: Viking, 2003

Kuhn, Raymond, *The Media in France*, London: Routledge, 1996

Ramonet, Ignacio, *La Tyrannie de la Communication*, Paris: Gallimard, 2001

MERLEAU-PONTY, MAURICE

Philosopher, Writer

Merleau-Ponty had a typical French academic career, apart from a brief period at the beginning of the Second World War, when he served as an infantry officer. But, like many French intellectuals, especially of his time, he was actively involved in wider cultural, social, and political life. Although he did not, like his friend Sartre, write novels and plays, his writings extend far beyond technical philosophy, including essays on painting, literature, cinema, and current political events. It is, however, as a philosopher that he made his greatest contribution, and even his writings on the arts and politics are informed by his philosophical reflections.

The single most important influence on Merleau-Ponty's philosophy was the phenomenological movement initiated by the German philosopher Edmund Husserl (1859–1938). By "phenomenology," Husserl meant the description, without theoretical assumptions, of "phenomena," that is, the way things actually appear to consciousness, with a view to uncovering their essential structures. He held it to be before empirical science, which takes these essential structures for granted and constructs detailed explanations of the workings of the world on that basis.

Merleau-Ponty first discovered Husserl's thought as a student at the École normale supérieure, but it was only later, when he encountered the later writings of Husserl, that phenomenology came to dominate his own philosophical thinking. In these later writings (most of which were only published after his death) Husserl developed phenomenology in a more "existential" direction: The somewhat austere and quasiscientific analyses of his earlier period were replaced by much more concrete reflection on actual human experience in response to what he saw as a crisis of the European sciences. This was, at least, the way Merleau-Ponty interpreted the works he read in the newly founded Husserl Archive in Louvain in the late 1930s. The phenomenology that appealed to Merleau-Ponty was existential phenomenology, which he saw as an attempt to get back to the roots of abstract theorizing in the direct human contact with the world in ordinary experience. Phenomenology for him was not so much a doctrine as a style of thinking: Unlike the sciences or traditional philosophy, it aimed not to explain our experience of the world, but simply to describe it. The aim of this description was to increase our understanding of the world in which we are necessarily involved. The world for us is not an object of contemplation, but the place in which we live.

Merleau-Ponty's word for our direct involvement with the world is "perception," and the description of the world as we perceive it must be at the heart of any truly phenomenological philosophy. (Hence the title of his major work, *Phénoménologie de la perception* [Phenomenology of Perception, 1945].) "Perception" can, however, be a misleading term for anyone familiar with traditional philosophy or psychology. In the tradition of Western philosophy, perception tends to be treated simply as a form of cognition, a way of becoming aware of truths about objects and their properties. It is in this sense that, with empiricist thinkers at least, perception is regarded as the source of objective knowledge about the world, as in the sciences. Merleau-Ponty's concept of perception is much broader: It refers to our whole relation to the world around us, including the cognitive relation, but also, more important, to our active and emotional relations with objects. Human beings "perceive" the world not simply in the sense of taking in information about it through their senses, but in the sense of moving about in it, handling it, using it, responding emotionally to it, and so on. The world as we perceive it is not the value-free, purely "objective," world of science, but a world that has meaning for us in virtue of its relation to our active purposes and our emotions. The world is always "my" world for each individual human subject, but this is not idealism, the view which treats reality as in some sense created by the mind, as part of the world's meaning for anyone is its sheer inexhaustibility, the impossibility of ever discovering its full reality or meaning.

Empiricist philosophers, because of their preoccupation with knowledge or cognition, thus misrepresent perception as we actually experience it. Because perception is, for them, simply the ultimate source of our scientific knowledge of objects and their properties, they are bound to regard it as made up of atomistic "sense-data" or "sensations," each corresponding to, and caused by, one discrete property of each object. The perceiver is then just the passive recipient of these sense-data. But this leaves unexplained the unity and meaningfulness of our perceived world. "Intellectualist" philosophers (as Merleau-Ponty calls them, referring to such thinkers as Kant) try to explain these features of our world by saying that our own minds actively impose them on the passive data of perception. But even to do this is implicitly to accept the empiricist assumption that perception in itself is not unified or meaningful. It is this very assumption that a phenomenological description of perception calls in question. If we try to get back to what perception is actually like for us, without making any theoretical assumptions about what it must be like if science, for example, is to be possible, then we shall see, Merleau-Ponty thinks, that perception is intrinsically unified and meaningful. We perceive things differently, for instance, against different backgrounds or in different contexts; we see other people as people, to whom we can relate in various ways, rather than simply as collections of meaningless sense-data. Similarly, we experience the place where we live as "home," a familiar collection of streets, houses, shops, cafés, and so forth.

In this way, phenomenological description acts as a corrective to the tendency in our culture to think of the objective, scientific account of reality as fundamental, and so of any thought of meaning or value as derivative and "purely subjective." For Merleau-Ponty, this reverses the proper order: We can understand the scientific view of the world only when we see it as an abstraction for certain purposes from the much richer and more fundamental experience of the world that he calls "perception." This is not in any sense meant to be antiscientific: Merleau-Ponty shows by his careful discussion of findings from many branches of science, especially physiology, that he has considerable respect for science. His intention is not

to denigrate science but to understand it better as a human activity. There is, nevertheless, a problem for Merleau-Ponty here, whose force he himself came to feel, particularly in the posthumously published writings of the last ten years of his life. To describe experience already involves some detachment from the experience itself: It requires the use of language, and so of general concepts, and in this sense an element of theoretical interpretation. It is one thing, however, to say that phenomenology uncovers the roots of scientific theorizing in concrete human experience and another, much less impressive, thing to say that it uncovers the roots of scientific theory in another theoretical interpretation of experience. Merleau-Ponty never succeeded in finding a solution to that fundamental problem for phenomenology, though in his later and unfinished writings we can see him hinting at the possible outline of such a solution in a view of language and representation based more on artistic creativity than on more literal-minded thought.

Short of finding a solution to this problem, phenomenology becomes in effect the assertion of the priority of ordinary, commonsense, ways of understanding our experience and the world we experience over the attempt by science to transcend any such purely human viewpoint. Science aims to achieve the complete objectivity of a description of the world that is not relative to any particular perspective—what has been called the "God's-eye view," Such "objectivism," to use Merleau-Ponty's term, is anyway incoherent, as scientists themselves are clearly not Gods, but human beings, so that anything they say must be said from a human point of view. To the extent that objectivism permeates our culture, phenomenology performs a useful service, even if it cannot get back all the way to the fundamental layer of direct, concrete, theory-free experience to which it aspires. Being as free as possible at least of the assumptions of "objective thought," phenomenological description can reinstate the importance of the ordinary human ways of thinking about the world that even scientists must take seriously when they are simply living their lives rather than engaging in abstract theorizing.

Phenomenology so interpreted clearly implies a certain view about our own relation to the world that we experience, which Merleau-Ponty expresses by means of another of his key concepts, that of "being-in-the-world" (the hyphens are essential to the linguistic expression of the concept, both in French and in English; the German term, *Inderweltsein*, is able to dispense with hyphens because of the German conventions for forming such nouns from noun-phrases). This was a concept that both Merleau-Ponty and Sartre borrowed from the German philosopher Martin Heidegger (1889–1976). Heidegger had been a student of Husserl's but took phenomenology in new and quite un-Husserlian directions. Although Merleau-Ponty took over the concept from Heidegger, however, it plays a very different role in the context of his philosophy from that it has played in Heidegger's. For Merleau-Ponty, to say that human being is being-in-the-world is to say both that we cannot think of ourselves as disembodied subjects, existing outside the world, and that we cannot think of the world apart from our subjective view of it. This marks a radical departure from the tradition of modern French philosophy, and indeed modern Western philosophy as a whole, which starts from Descartes's conclusion that the subject of experience and of rational thought could, in principle, exist even if there were no world at all. In his "method of doubt," Descartes had sought certainty by rejecting everything in our present ways of thinking that was open to doubt, even of the flimsiest and most bizarre kind. The most extreme doubt of all was based on the supposition that we might be radically deceived by an evil demon, so that all our beliefs, even the very basic belief that there is a world apart from ourselves, might be open to doubt. Even that extreme supposition could not, however, cast doubt on our own existence as thinking subjects, as we had to exist in order to be deceived. Thus, our existence, Descartes concluded, is logically distinct from the existence of the world. It is this conclusion, and its implications, that are called in question by Merleau-Ponty's contention that human being is necessarily being-in-the-world.

The implications are far-reaching. Above all, if we are Cartesian subjects who exist apart from the world, then it must be possible, in principle at least, to achieve a view of the world from a perspective that is detached from the world itself: a "God's-eye view," as it was earlier described. It is the possibility of achieving such a view, however, that is presupposed in modern scientific objectivism. That is, bizarre though it may sound, the modern scientific view of the world rests ultimately on Descartes's argument from the possibility of extreme doubt. Equally clearly, to reject Descartes's conclusion and to insist that human being is being-in-the-world is also to reject scientific objectivism and all that it implies. It is to replace human experience at the center of all that we can say about ourselves and the world we live in. This in turn implies important conclusions about our nature as human beings. We cannot, Merleau-Ponty argues, think of ourselves from the outside, as nothing but objects in the world like any other, the meeting-place of various intersecting causal chains governed by timeless scientific laws. We are indeed such objects, but we are also much more: We are subjects who experience the world from our own individual point of view, determined by our particular position in space and time, living in a particular society at a

particular time in its history. This is the sense in which Merleau-Ponty's phenomenology is "existential" and an instance of "existentialism." It does not treat human beings as creatures of pure reason who gain their dignity by virtue of their capacity for transcending the limitations of their finite existence to achieve universality. On the contrary, it sees them as worthy of respect precisely because they are concrete individuals who have to deal with the world as they find it and cannot escape from the limitations of their position within time, space, and history.

This has consequences for Merleau-Ponty's view of the role of philosophy itself. Philosophy obviously cannot be, as it was traditionally conceived, the quest for eternal truths of reason that will hold universally in all times and places. Philosophers too are human beings, who can only aspire to such truth as is available to them from the perspective of their particular time and location. In questioning the conventional assumptions of their own time, philosophers necessarily step somewhat beyond their own time, and in that sense make an advance in rationality, but what they achieve thereby is not some permanent truth but only a revisable view of what might be more rational to believe about the world and humankind. Philosophy is radical reflection on the human situation, but it is not an attempt to step outside the human situation entirely. In this respect, Merleau-Ponty's philosophy, especially in the less "phenomenological" form in which it appears in his last writings, marks an important stage in the process of undermining the whole modern, or Enlightenment, project of "humanism." This process was taken further by his successors, in the structuralist, poststructuralist, and postmodernist movements (some of whom, interestingly, had been his students). By "humanism," these thinkers meant the conviction that underlay European culture from Descartes onward and that was most fully expressed in the Enlightenment, of the absolute centrality of the individual human subject and of the capacity of that subject to have access to universal truths of reason, whether in science, morality, or conceptions of social organization.

Merleau-Ponty's rejection of the idea of philosophy as the science of pure reason was clearly an opposition to "humanism" in this sense. However, at least in *Phenomenology of Perception* and his other earlier works, he remained profoundly humanistic in a wider sense. The whole theme of his thought there is (in the title of one of his essays) "the primacy of perception"; that is, the centrality of individual human experience to our understanding of the world and of our place in it. The world remains essentially a human world, and even the world of nature has to be experienced through human concepts of what is "natural." This is so even though human beings cannot escape their human limitations and even though, as mentioned above, we necessarily experience the world as being inexhaustible by our experience, as always containing more that is still to be known and understood.

The perspectival character of human experience, of our being as being-in-the-world, suggests another of Merleau-Ponty's key concepts, that of the "body-subject." To say that each of us necessarily perceives the world from our own individual point of view is to imply that we are not disembodied, for a disembodied perceiver could not be located in any particular point in space (only physical objects have spatial locations). Similarly, to say that our being is being-in-the-world, that the world is not merely something we contemplate, but the place that we inhabit and with which we interact, implies that we must be embodied, as it is hard to see how a disembodied being could have that kind of active engagement with its surrounding milieu. At the same time, as argued above, we are not in the world in the way that mere physical objects are, as the passive plaything of forces. We are embodied, but we are embodied subjects, beings who are able to be conscious of their world and to interact with it in the light of that consciousness. The notion of being-in-the-world is thus opposed not only to Cartesian objectivism but also to the Cartesian mind–body dualism that is necessarily associated with it—the idea that what we are essentially is disembodied or purely spiritual subjects, who just happen to be connected, in this life at least, to a physical body. For Descartes, the material part of us, the body, was just like any other part of matter, subject in its behavior to the laws of physics and chemistry and fully intelligible in terms of those laws, whereas the essential part of us, the mind or soul, was not part of the physical or spatial world at all and not governed by its laws. Even traditional materialists who opposed Descartes were influenced by him, at least in their view of our physical nature as a purely mechanical or physico-chemical system, and differed from him only in denying that there was anything more to us than that physical nature.

The notion of the body-subject enables Merleau-Ponty to propose a view of human beings that avoids both Cartesian dualism and traditional mechanistic materialism. For if our subjectivity is essentially embodied, and our embodiment is that of a subject, then we are neither just another type of physical object (as in traditional materialism) nor a peculiar amalgam of something mysterious and nonphysical with such a physical object (as in Cartesian dualism). What we are is human beings; that is, living creatures who are fully physical, but who are also conscious of and interact with their worlds by means of their embodiment (e.g., by means of their senses and the movements of their limbs). Whereas for Descartes the essence of subjectiv-

ity was "I think" (as in his famous "I think, therefore I am"), for Merleau-Ponty it is "I can." In other words, our subjectivity consists not primarily in intellectual contemplation of the world, but in active engagement with it. Equally, human behavior (and even to some extent the behavior of nonhuman animals) has to be seen not as a composite of two processes, one "inner" consisting of subjective thoughts and one "outer" consisting of bodily movements, but as a single process of purposive bodily actions. Still less is it to be reduced, in the style of behaviorism, to the outward bodily movements alone. Merleau-Ponty's first major work, *La Structure du comportement* (The Structure of Behavior, 1942) is largely devoted to a critique of behaviorism along these lines, claiming it to be inadequate even as a basis for a truly realistic science of psychology. As he argues there, as well as in *Phenomenology of Perception*, human behavior (and much animal behavior, too) can only be fully understood in the light of the behaver's intentions and purposes, even when those intentions and purposes may not be explicitly conscious. Embodied subjectivity implies that when we act, we act with some intention, but that we necessarily realize that intention by making certain bodily movements; for instance, I grasp the cup in my hands and raise it to my lips because I want to drink from it. The ways in which my hands move in performing this action are governed by laws of physics: Indeed, the physical constraints on how the human body can move set limits to the kinds of intention (as opposed to wish) that human beings can form. Nevertheless, to explain my action in the example simply in terms of the physical laws governing bodily movements clearly leaves something vital out. It does not answer the question, "Why did you raise the cup to your lips in that way?" The explanation of my action as such requires reference to my intention, or purpose, or motivation, in acting in this way on this occasion.

If so, then the sciences of human behavior (history, sociology, psychology, and all their derivatives) must take this into account. To make sense of human behavior, it is not enough to grasp the causal antecedents of the mechanisms by which we perform our actions (though these mechanisms are an essential background to human activity), we must understand the significance of what is done for those who are doing it. We make sense of, say, a politician's actions in terms of the policies that he is pursuing, his underlying political values, his need for reelection, his rivalry with other politicians, and so on. All of these purposes, motives, and so forth have a history: He has developed his political values in the course of his past experience, as he has developed the political ambition that leads him to want reelection. His rivalry with other politicians probably springs in large part from some deeper competitive trait in his personality, which also has a history. In short, to see human behavior as intelligible in this way is to see a human life, and a particular human self, as developing over time, as having a past that influences the present and so the future. Merleau-Ponty discusses Freudian psychoanalysis at length from this point of view. He does not interpret it in the way that Freud's own language often implies, as a theory about the influence of unconscious biological forces on the "conscious mind." Rather, he sees it as a method of understanding present behavior as given meaning by past experiences that are not consciously remembered, but "sedimented" (to use his own word) in bodily habits of response to situations that may even be in conflict with our conscious intentions. Crucial to Freud's account, of course, is that these past experiences are essentially sexual in nature. Merleau-Ponty believes, however, this can readily be accommodated if we see sexuality as part of our human mode of being-in-the-world. That is, sexuality should be seen neither as a matter of thought alone, nor as a purely mechanistic response to external stimuli, but as a kind of "atmosphere" that permeates the world of most human beings because of the nature and constitution of human bodies. If so, then there will be an inescapable sexual dimension to most human experiences and, thus, to the shape and meaning that they give to our subsequent actions. In some unfortunates with sexual problems, as in the famous case of Schneider, discussed at length in *Phenomenology of Perception*, the problem will consist in the loss, perhaps because of physical injury or disease, of this aspect of human being-in-the-world.

If our past conditions the meaning of our present actions, then human freedom to act will not be absolute: its degree will depend on the extent to which we can become conscious of our past experiences and so modify their influence on our present behavior. In some cases, it may be almost impossible to escape from our past in this way; for example, when we have long-standing and deeply entrenched habits of behavior or response. Unlike Sartre, who always inclined toward an absolutist view of freedom, Merleau-Ponty is much more aware of the constraints on our freedom imposed by our situation. We are not always free in any real sense. If we were, then the word "free" would lose its meaning because of the lack of a contrast. A fundamental part of our situation is social: Human beings exist not as isolated individuals, but along with others. This follows from the fact that our being is being-in-the-world. We are not disembodied subjects, but subjects in relation to a world, a world that also includes other subjects. We are what we are in part in virtue of our relations to each other. The world that we inhabit is as a result a social world, a world that includes not just physical objects, but items of a social

or human significance: towns, streets, buildings, furniture, and so on, and this society, which is in a sense part of ourselves, like ourselves has a history that gives meaning to its present. We cannot make sense of societies, any more than of individuals, except by taking into account their pasts and the way in which those pasts have developed into their presents.

This view of society and history underlies the humanistic Marxism that dominated Merleau-Ponty's political thinking for much of his life. Merleau-Ponty was always politically left-leaning, seeking a more humane and rational society. In the 1930s, he came to believe that the Hegelianized form of Marxism that was then becoming intellectually fashionable (based on the recently rediscovered early writings of Marx) offered the best theoretical framework for left-wing politics. This type of Marxism fitted well with Merleau-Ponty's general philosophical positions as outlined above. Unlike the "Marxism-Leninism" that predominated in the Soviet Union and in the Communist Parties that paid allegiance to the USSR, Merleau-Ponty's Marxism did not treat Marxism as "scientific socialism," an account of social development that aimed to be scientific in the sense of emulating the natural sciences. Scientific socialism claimed to have discovered the economic law of development of modern society, from which, as from the laws of classical physics, it was possible to predict future developments. The form of Marxism that appealed to Merleau-Ponty, in contrast, did not speak of "laws" in this sense, but saw social development as the outcome of intelligible human solutions to the problems created by the past and its legacy. The nature of the problems of course constrained the kinds of solutions that could be offered, so that, as Marx himself had said, human beings make their own history, but not in circumstances chosen by themselves. Similar to individuals, societies have freedom to choose their own future, but this freedom is not absolute: It is limited by the historical situation in which they find themselves. The existence of even some degree of freedom, however, contradicts any belief in historical inevitability of the kind that is so characteristic of orthodox Soviet Marxism. More than one solution to any problem is possible. There can be no guarantee, therefore, that, for instance, people who are "objectively" working-class will see a socialist transformation of society as the only solution to their problems.

Given this overall theory of politics and history (and no doubt also given his personality), it is not surprising that Merleau-Ponty had a difficult relationship with the French Communist Party. During and immediately after the Second World War, he was broadly sympathetic to the Party, in view of its professed ultimate aims and its importance to the French working class. (This feeling was not entirely reciprocated, and he came under attack from the Communists, especially when he criticized the Soviet Union in works such as *Humanisme et Terreur* [Humanism and Terror, 1947].) He always had reservations, however, which intensified as more information became available about the Soviet show trials, labor camps, and persecutions of dissident groups. While refusing to be an anticommunist, and so side with the French bourgeoisie and U.S. Cold War attitudes, he found it increasingly impossible to be procommunist. The outbreak of the Korean War, which he saw as an example of Soviet aggression, brought about a final break with Soviet communism. It also marked the beginning of his rift with Sartre, who took a more pro-Soviet stance. In his work *Les Aventures de la dialectique* (Adventures of the Dialectic, 1955), he traced the way in which the idea of a "dialectical" Marxism (i.e., roughly speaking, a Marxism that did not model itself on classical mechanics) had progressively been lost and replaced by the idea of Marxism as "scientific socialism." In the long final chapter, Merleau-Ponty launches an attack on Sartre as an "ultrabolshevist," defending support for the Communist Party not on the basis of a genuinely dialectical understanding of history, but simply on the pragmatic grounds that it was perceived by the French working class as its representative. For the rest of his life, Merleau-Ponty, although remaining emotionally on the left, took a much less active role in politics, and his interventions were motivated more by a general radical humanism than by any attachment to Marxist theory.

Maurice Merleau-Ponty was thus a complex and many-sided figure. His thought was always engaged with the real world: Indeed, the attraction of phenomenological philosophy for him was that it promised, in Husserl's slogan, to bring us back "to the things themselves." As Merleau-Ponty interpreted that slogan, it meant that phenomenology could reinstate ordinary human experience as the starting point in our account of the world. We do not need to follow the traditional tendency in European philosophy and culture, especially since Descartes, to start from the general theories that we construct, above all in the sciences, to explain that experience. The world is essentially a human world, and the meanings that we find in it through living in it are just as much a part of the reality of things as the properties identified by science. Human beings themselves cannot be regarded simply from the outside, as another species of objects: We have to understand ourselves, our behavior, and our institutions from the inside, in terms of our human purposes and values. Because we cannot transcend our humanity, however, there is no possibility of a final understanding of our existence or of the world in which we exist. This essentially humanist way of thinking permeates what Merleau-Ponty has to say on philosophical method, on the nature of psychological explanation, on the mind–body problem, on the relation of individuals to each other and to society, on history, on politics, and on the arts. It enables him to say things about all these topics that have the ring of truth about them, or at the very least that suggest promising lines of thought of a kind not to be found in exactly this form in any other philosopher. Merleau-Ponty does not offer a "system": Indeed, it would be quite contrary to the whole spirit of his thought to do so. What he does offer is a connected set of thoughts about a very wide range of human concerns. This alone would be enough to justify the claim made by another leading French thinker, Paul Ricoeur, that Merleau-Ponty was one of the outstanding philosophers of the twentieth century.

ERIC MATTHEWS

See also **Paul Ricoeur**

Biography

Maurice Merleau-Ponty was born March 14, 1908, in Rochefort-sur-Mer (Charente Maritime). He studied at the Lycée Janson-de-Sailly and Lycée Louis-le-Grand, Paris, and at École normale supérieure, Paris, from 1926 to 1930. He taught at the Lycée de Beauvais from 1931 to 1933 and would continue to teach at the lycée level at intervals up until 1945. Merleau-Ponty was a reserve officer in the French army from 1939 to 1940. He was Professor of Philosophy at the University of Lyon, 1945–1949; editor in chief and political editor of *Les Temps modernes*, 1945–1952; and Professor of Psychology and Pedagogy at the Sorbonne, 1949–1952. He was a Professor at the Collège de France, Paris, from 1952 until his death in Paris on May 3, 1961.

Selected Writings

La Structure du comportement, 1942; as *The Structure of Behaviour*, translated by A. L. Fisher, 1963

Phénoménologie de la perception, 1945; as *Phenomenology of Perception*, translated by Colin Smith, 1962

Humanisme et Terreur, 1947; as *Humanism and Terror*, translated by John O'Neill, 1969

Sens et non-sens, 1948; as *Sense and Non-Sense*, translated by Hubert L. Dreyfus and Patricia A. Dreyfus, 1964

Éloge de la philosophie, 1953; as *In Praise of Philosophy*, translated by J. Wild and J. M. Edie, 1963

Les Aventures de la dialectique, 1955; as *The Adventures of the Dialectic*, translated by J. Bien, 1973

Signes, 1960; as *Signs*, translated by Richard C. McCleary, 1964

Le Visible et l'invisible, 1964; as *The Visible and the Invisible*, translated by Alphonso Lingis, 1968

Résumés de cours, Collège de France, 1952–60, 1968; as *Themes from the Lectures at the Collège de France 1952–60*, translated by John O'Neill, 1970

La Prose du monde, 1969; as *The Prose of the World*, translated by John O'Neill, 1973

Further Reading

Dillon, M. C., *Merleau-Ponty's Ontology*, Bloomington, IN: Indiana University Press, 1988

Edie, J. M., *Merleau-Ponty's Philosophy of Language: Structuralism and Dialectics*, Washington, D.C.: University Press of America, 1987

Langan, Thomas, *Merleau-Ponty's Critique of Reason*, New Haven, CT: Yale University Press, 1966

Langer, Monika, *Merleau-Ponty's Phenomenology of Perception: A Guide and Commentary*, London: Macmillan, 1989

Madison, Gary, *The Phenomenology of Merleau-Ponty: A Search for the Limits of Consciousness*, Athens, OH: Ohio University Press, 1981

Mallin, Samuel B., *Merleau-Ponty's Philosophy*, New Haven, CT: Yale University Press, 1979

Matthews, Eric, *The Philosophy of Merleau-Ponty*, Chesham: Acumen Publishing Limited, 2002

O'Neill, John, *Perception, Expression, and History: the Social Phenomenology of Maurice Merleau-Ponty*, Evanston, IL: Northwestern University Press, 1970

Priest, Stephen, *Merleau-Ponty*, London: Routledge, 1998

Whiteside, K. H., *Merleau-Ponty and the Foundations of an Existential Politics*, Princeton, NJ: Princeton University Press, 1988

METZ, CHRISTIAN

A prominent French film theoretician, Metz worked alongside Barthes, Genette, Todorov, and Greimas at the prestigious Ecole pratiques des hautes études, during the Structuralist revolution in linguistics. He applied linguistic theory and semiotics (the study of signs and symbols) to the analysis of film. His early research was inspired by the semiological study of literary narrative, which Roland Barthes had pioneered. Metz set out to provide a full taxonomy of the signs and principles that govern the syntax of film. His essay on the *grande syntagmatique* of film, first published in 1966 in a special issue of *Communications* devoted to the Structuralist analysis of the narrative, argued that cinematographic language could be analyzed in terms of syntagmatic components and syntagmatic relationships. This approach produced an initial classification of the segments of film narrative into six main types: the autonomous shot, the scene, the sequence, the descriptive syntagma, the alternating syntagma, and the frequentative syntagma.

The division of the last two types into three subcategories each reflected the Structuralist drive of Metz's classification, which proceeded from overarching categories to ever smaller components through oppositions and distinctions based on a system of bifurcating subtypes. It was, nonetheless, precisely the last two categories (the alternating and the frequentative syntagmas) that continued to pose difficulties and gradually began to expose the practical and theoretical limitations of Metz's taxonomy, despite successive amendments.

Throughout the late 1960s and early 1970s, Metz repeatedly emphasized the need for further refinement of his model. One particular set of problems, relating to the emphasis on narrative in Metz's *grande syntagmatique*, was highlighted by the New Wave experimentation in French cinema, beginning in the late 1950s. The syntagmatic analysis of the image-track can most usefully be applied to traditional or modern cinematographic practices, which privilege sequential ordering, in the sense of plot with action and characters. The relevance of the syntagmatic model is, however, less definite outside the bounds of a certain period in the historical development of cinema (which Metz himself situated between the stabilization of sound, or 1933–1935, and the moment preceding the first New Wave films; that is, roughly, 1955).

The fundamental analogy of cinema and language in Metz's work capitalized on the achievements of Saussure's linguistic theory and, in particular, on his distinction between *langue* (language-system) and *langage* (language). However, the photographic realism of film, or the literal meaning of images such as, for example, the image of a train, excluded what semiotics calls "the double articulation" of any language-system (*langue*), which is the necessary use of material sounds or letters to designate an object such as "train." Moreover, as a one-way mode of communication that uses no invariant arbitrary signs (because each image, unlike words, is unique), cinema failed to qualify as *langue*, but displayed the qualities of a *langage*, such as the capacity of articulating images in a purposeful and intelligible manner.

Metz's initial aspiration had been to provide a phenomenological foundation to his conception of film narrative, although he strived to avoid the identification of his language-inspired methodology with a normative science, such as grammar. His ideological sources situated him in a direct lineage with the Russian formalists (e.g., Vladimir Propp) and with the French narratologists (Greimas, Barthes, and Bremond, whose work Metz acknowledged in the "Notes towards a Phenomenology of Narrative," 1996). The phenomenological and formalist thrust of Metz's view of cinema as language can be said to be responsible for the reductive account of film narrative in terms of logical, unilinear chronology. Further difficulties arise from the alleged primacy of denotation within film language: "It is first of all by its denotative procedures that the cinema is a specific language" (Metz wrote in his essay on film, in 1966). This position implied that connotation was derivative, a mere supplement to narrative denotation. The difference between the two types of signification also referred to the presence or absence of a temporal signified (the former corresponding to denotation and the latter to connotation).

Resulting ambiguities and possible confusions between denotative and connotative segments, as well as between diegetic and nondiegetic elements, were identified and, in most cases, successfully dealt with by Metz himself or by later practitioners of his method. Nevertheless, the secondary place assigned to connotation prompted criticism of Metz's account of visual aspects and issues of mise-en-scène, which seemed either relegated to derivative status or reduced to denotation.

Despite its acknowledged imperfections, Metz's *Essai sur la signification au cinema* (Vol. 1, 1968; Vol. 2, 1972) almost instantly became the landmark reference work for European and American film specialists. The English translation, *Film Language. A Semiotics of Cinema* (1974), had a lasting effect on Anglo-American film theory. The reaction to Metz's conception was initially polarized following, on the one hand, the sustained attacks (led by Brian Henderson) in *Film Quarterly* (1970–1977) and, on the other, the influential attempts at applying the syntagmatic method to the Anglophone cinematic production (Peter Wollen, Stephen Heath). Later works, such as *Langage et cinema* (Larousse, 1971), which was translated into English as *Language and cinema* (1974), had a similarly mixed reception, although Metz altered his theoretical stand to make room for more cultural and historical considerations.

The most important addition to Metz's original project occurred as he began incorporating psychoanalysis into his study of film language. *Le Signifiant imaginaire: psychanalyse et cinema* (1977), published in English translation in 1982 (*Psychoanalysis and Cinema. The Imaginary Signifier*) highlighted the fundamental role tht psychoanalysis played, alongside linguistics, in the understanding of processes governing the constitution of language-systems as well as of nonverbal sign-systems, such as cinema. Jacques Lacan's reinterpretation of Freudian theory from the perspective of semiotics and linguistics provided the basic theoretical framework of Metz's conception of the imaginary signifier. In analyzing the relationship between the spectator and the cinema screen, Metz relied on the Lacanian account of the formation of the ego through identification with his or her mirror reflection to argue that the "voyeurism of the spectator has to do with the primordial experience of the mirror." However, starting from this primary level of the imaginary, as defined by Lacan, Metz proceeded to analyze the second, symbolic stage of signification, which he considered to be the codified or formalized articulation of cinematic language. His earlier work on the "grande syntagmatique" was thus extended to include the sociological and psychological implications of "cinematic fiction as a semi-dreamlike instance." Metz's awareness of the complex interaction between the iconic and verbal dimensions of film narrative underscored his language-based search for an integrated theoretical discourse. The importance of Metz's revised conception of the cinema resides precisely in the attempt at dealing with the previously neglected iconic aspects through the Freudian and Lacanian interpretations of subconscious processes and of dream symbolism. After Metz's untimely death in 1993, his methodology continued to be applied to visual communication outside cinema, with particularly notable and perceptive results in media studies and the analysis of television commercials.

RAMONA D. FOTIADE

See also **Roland Barthes; Gerard Genette; Algirdas Greimas; Jacques Lacan; Ferdinand de Saussure; Tzvetan Todorov**

Selected Works

Essais sur la signification au cinéma, Vols. 1 and 2, 1968–1972; new edition, 1975–1976
L'analyse des images, 1970
Langage et cinéma, 1971
Film language: a semiotics of the cinema, translated by Michael Taylor, 1974
Language and cinema, translated by Donna Jean Umiker-Sebeok, 1974
Psychanalyse et cinéma, 1975
Le signifiant imaginaire: psychanalyse et cinéma, 1977
A seminar with Christian Metz: cinema – semiology, psychoanalysis, history, introduced and edited by John L. Davies, 1982
Psychoanalysis and cinema: The Imaginary Signifier, translated by Celia Britton, Annwyl Williams, Ben Brewster, and Alfred Guzzetti, 1982
"Notes towards a Phenomenology of Narrative," *Revue d'esthétique*, 3–4, 1996

Further Reading

Altman, C. F., "Psychoanalysis and cinema: the imaginary discourse," *Quarterly Review of Film Studies* 28,3 (1977): 251–272
Andrew, Dudley, "Film analysis or film theory: to step beyond semiotics," *Quarterly Review of Film Studies*, 2,1 (1977): 33–41
Durgnat, Raymond, "The death of cinesemiology (with not even a whimper)," *Cineaste*, 10,2 (1982): 10–13
Durgnat, Raymond, "Through the looking sign," *Quarterly Review of Film Studies* 9,4 (1983): 267–282
Henderson, Brian, *A Critique of Film Theory*, New York: EP Dutton, 1980
Heath, Stephen, *Questions of Cinema*, London: Macmillan, 1981
Michel, Marie, ed., *Christian Metz et la théorie du cinema*, Paris: Klincksieck, 1990
Stam, Robert, Burgoyne, Robert, and Flitterman-Lewis, Sandy, eds., *New Vocabularies in Film Semiotics. Structuralism, Post-Structuralism and Beyond*, London: Routledge, 1992

Wollen, Peter, *Signs and Meaning in the Cinema*, London: Secker and Warburg, 1969

MODERNISM AND POSTMODERNISM

Jean-François Lyotard coined the term "postmodernism" in his book *La Condition postmoderne* (1979), immediately giving rise to a heated philosophical debate on the project of modernism among contemporary French philosophers. As a result, not only has the "postmodern" become a hugely controversial and confusing name for a particular epoch, but it is also a category under which all strains of poststructuralism or "difference-thinking" may be subsumed.

It is impossible to understand the real issue at stake in this discussion so long as postmodernism is taken as a distinct philosophical movement or as the name for a "new age" following the "end" of modernism. "Postmodern" strategies of thought acquire their innovative power by the critical way in which they review the hidden structures of the enterprise of modernism. Current debates relating to modernism and postmodernism primarily concern the question of what theory is best used to tackle the problems of a functionally differentiated society of knowledge. For Lyotard, postmodernism is certainly not something that comes after modernism: "On the contrary, postmodernism is already implicated in modernism because modernism contains a moving force to overcome itself in the light of a self-different state of affairs." Considering the many conflicting opinions on this issue, Lyotard characterizes postmodernism as a revision of modernism. Bruno Latour exaggerates this idea by entitling his essay on symmetrical anthropology: "Nous n'avons jamais été modernes" (cf. bibliography). It is not a question, therefore, of overcoming or dismissing modernism, but rather of intensifying the capacity for self-criticism that is inherent to modernism in the sense of a rational pluralism.

What is at stake philosophically in the controversy between modernism and postmodernism? Authors as varied as Jürgen Habermas and Gilles Deleuze may be consulted in an attempt to answer this question. In short, postmodern thinking can be seen to reject a certain ("modern") subject-theoretical model of rationality that found its paradigmatic expression in Hegel's idealistic thought on history. Following Hegel, history is assumed to be a logical process by which freedom and criticism are dialectically related to each other in such a way as to ultimately relieve humanity from its dependency on opaque (political, religious, etc.) structures. The integration of diverse types of discourse (logical, aesthetic, theological, etc.) into one "big" unifying concept (a "narrative," as Lyotard puts it)

concerning the becoming and revelation of the spirit indicates the most crucial point of conflict in the discussion. For Hegel's vast narrative not only turns out differences, it also mediates these differences in a problematic manner. According to this idea of mediation, the narratives of metaphysics or Christianity provoke permanent suspicion: Postmodern thinkers suspect that these concepts perform abstract and presumptuous explanations—the same critique applies to competing enterprises such as emancipation, capitalism, socialism, and technology.

In *Différence et répétition* (1968), which is no doubt one of the most significant books within the French philosophy of difference, Gilles Deleuze defines the modern world (following Nietzsche) as a world of simulacra or illusions. This world maintains—in a simplified version—the primacy of difference in relation to identity:

> All these signs can be ascribed to a generalized anti-Hegelianism. Difference and repetition have substituted the identical and the negative, identity and contradiction. Only insofar as difference is subordinate to the identical does difference implicate the negative and lead to contradiction. The primacy of identity defines the world of representation. But modern thought arises from the failure of representation, the loss of identities and from the discovery of all those forces that effect the representation of identities from below. The modern world is a world of simulacra.

The modern thought propagated by Deleuze goes against the so-called "world of representation" and against the primacy of identity and its dialectical presuppositions. In this view, modernism itself is seen to be inclined toward transcending its own achievements insofar as they result from a problematic blockade of thought. Eminently modern thought is thus necessarily postmodern.

One question that remains is whether "postmodern criticism" falls back into premodern fantasies of origin and unity or whether it really is able to undermine the set of notions that characterize modernism (and that may be responsible for the social hierarchies that define postwar capitalism). Does it make sense, from a philosophical point of view, to coordinate into more extensive and comprehensive narratives the discourses of the social system that are dispersed into heterogeneous language games? Or is it preferable to radicalize these differences and reaffirm their disagreement? Moreover, does the discourse of enlightenment, which is traditionally directed toward subjective autonomy, guarantee an increase of freedom, or is it what led to the catastrophe of Nazi concentration camps? This is how the question that divides the opposing parties into two groups could possibly be reformulated.

This short introduction already suggests why the strict opposition between "modernism" and "postmodernism" is not sufficient. In fact, there are not only many intersections between the more modern and more postmodern positions but also a plurality of ways of thinking. It makes no sense to reduce this plurality to two extreme positions called modernism and postmodernism. Polemicists against the postmodern (Habermas) or against the logocentric (Derrida) stand in the way of concrete reflection on the critical implements of the rejected theories. An example for this is the omnipresent discussion on the death of the subject and the end of man.

Most of the so-called postmodern philosophers strongly criticize the model of representation within a metaphysics of the subject, yet they still hold on to a transformed version of subjectivity. In contrast, advanced directions within modern analytical and pragmatic philosophy tend to undermine a representational theory of consciousness. It is not sufficient to state reliance or release of the subject. The need for a nonrepresentational theory of subjectivity still remains.

A good starting point from which to reconstruct the complex problems that concern modernism is perhaps the classical theory of society. From this point of view, the secularization process of Western culture is simultaneously conceived as a differentiation process of social structures, with enlightenment as its moving force. This is why the claim that old-fashioned religious and metaphysical ideas are to be rationalized or demystified in a process of *Entzauberung* (Max Weber) goes hand in hand with tendencies that institutionalize capitalistic corporations and the public administrative organization. The modernization of the *Lebenswelt* is an attempt to compensate the loss of a comprehensive religious conception of the world and its authoritative obligation. The social situation of modernism can thus be described as producing normative content out of itself. If it is correct to define modernism by an increasing devaluation of universal doctrines, then it seems to be helpful to consider the new, emerging post-metaphysical theories as only provisional and temporary compensations. In this respect, nihilism (something like a postmodern question mark that is inscribed in the center of modernism) is taken into account.

To begin with, a form of "metaphysical homelessness" (Lukacz) was discovered in the context of art and art criticism. The notion of modernism was developed in the eighteenth century, *Querelle des Anciens et des Modernes*. The "modernists" were considered "modern" because they refused to accept antique prototypes and standards. Instead, they proclaimed the beginning of a new, modern epoch. Characteristic of the experience of this modern time was its essential openness to the future. The future—in the modern sense of the word—is that which cannot be foreseen. This is why modernity disrupted the established structures that claimed eternal validity, and it also explains why the notion of modernism is profoundly characterized by a self-assessment of avant-garde art and its unique experience of time, at least since Charles Baudelaire.

The concepts of modernism and progress are closely linked. The adjective "modern" designates a new regime, a break, a mobilization of capacities or a revolution of time. Words like "modern" and "modernization" are necessarily defined in contrast to a stable and archaic past that is constantly in the process of being lost. The improvement of life conditions is one of the main topics of modernism. Progress is related to a utopian or visionary schema that may be realized step by step, in accordance with a teleological model of history—or the utopian idea situated at the beginning of future, always before the concrete proceedings because its peculiar modus of being cannot be represented.

The oft-cited Dialectics of Enlightenment (developed by Horkheimer and Adorno of the Frankfurt School) prove that reason-guided emancipation from structures of mythical power manifests a compulsive and mythical domination of nature. The scientific deconstruction of metaphysics is therefore metaphysical itself, so long as it depends on a logic of instrumental reason. Hence, the modern idea of progress presumes an epistemological notion of truth that is derived from the new empirical sciences. The destiny of Western civilization culminates in the abandonment of reflection about those regions of being that cannot be grasped in patterns of knowledge. Adorno and Horkheimer seem to dismiss the project of modernism when they state that the process of social modernization gains a catastrophic degree of independence; that is, loses its affiliation with reason and freedom, the resources of enlightenment. As soon as modernism reaches the point when the claim of continual improvement is no longer trustworthy, the whole project of modernity is questioned.

Heidegger shares this devastating vision of the achievements of human science in seeing at work in the domination of technology an expression of the modern will to power and, thus, of the totally unleashed figure of modern subjectivity. Modern times are portrayed as a disaster that humanistic rationalism can do nothing to avoid. The unalterable destiny that condemns man (in the technological age) to conceive only representational, calculable, and practical objects within the realm of the given stands in stark contrast to an ontological experience that is able to explore the depths of the essential structures of technology that cannot be justified by finite reason. As a result, it is impossible to control the anonymous fatality of the "history of being." Heidegger's proposal is to adopt an attitude of calmness and self-possession that turns away from superficial constraints and obligations. From this point of view, only real and authentic works of art are able to express the "other side" of the present structures of decline. Following Heidegger, it remains the philosopher's task to explain these aesthetic figures. Art is thus seen to emerge as a counterforce to the problems that accompany the development of the modern age.

This tone of cultural pessimism is brought to an end in the works of Foucault and Deleuze and other French thinkers of the "school" of phenomenology and structuralism. They do maintain central motifs from Heidegger and the German critical theory of sociology (the Frankfurt School) with regard to the rejection of the metaphysical primacy of identity. Transcendental structures of philosophy cannot therefore be completely elucidated, and man's politico-economic, biologic, or linguistic structures and conditions of life cannot be fully comprehended by human understanding. The separation of different spheres of value at least since Kant—empirical sciences, autonomous arts, the realm of justice and morals—means not only a loss of traditional normative standards in favor of comprehensive structures of instrumental reason but also a transformation of culture and tradition including techniques of living and principles of value.

It is this cultural transformation that Nietzsche had in mind when in his last productive years he called for a "revaluation of values" (*Umwertung der Werte*) to help mobilize antinihilistic forces. Inspired by George Bataille, Pierre Klossowski, and others, many French thinkers of the 1960s adopted this Nietzschean formula directed against the strategies of thought that negate life on behalf of superior (moral-theological) values. According to them, the categorical concepts of ordinary dialectical or transcendental logic fall short because they evaluate life from a nontemporal and transcendent position, acting like the last guardians of universality. Eager to avoid transcendent aspirations, postmodern theoreticians seek to conceive philosophical notions as singularities which by no means determine *a priori* the conditions of possible knowledge.

Authors such as Michel Foucault or Jean-François Lyotard developed a theory of language that does not subjugate different types of discourse under a general rule but allows real and contingent relationships to be analyzed, in contrast to theories that are subjectively based on categorical principles incorporating multiple and inhomogeneous discourses into one universal catalogue. In contrast to Jürgen Habermas, Lyotard seeks to invent a philosophy that accommodates dissent, misunderstanding, and disagreement, and prefers therefore a theory based on insoluble conflict (*le différend*) than

one that is primarily concerned with understanding and harmony. Connected to this is the idea that discourses are based on techniques of power and that they are at the same time preconditions for the exercise of power. Foucault's method of genealogy sets itself the task of studying these constellations of power relations and arrangements of knowledge.

With the critical devaluation of modern individualism, the autonomy of practice and reflexivity of experience in favor of a discipline-power, control-power, and bio-power, it might seem as if we have stumbled into another hopeless evil. But this diagnosis is misleading: In *Histoire de la sexualité* (1976), Foucault develops a conception of existence techniques that, because of its aesthetic attributes, is able to draw lines of resistance or lines of flight between territorialities and concentrations of power. This resistance is not so much organized on behalf of lasting political forces and identities or established authorities as under the pretext of "bodies and pleasures" within the immanence of life suffering or else escaping from the influences of disciplinary practices. What Foucault or Deleuze provide is not a political program, but a political morality and a conceptual apparatus that allows one to identify and define processes favoring a certain kind of politics beyond the Marxist theory of class struggle. It is apparent from explicit remarks as well as from the authors' own political engagements that they are sympathetic to the marginal movements that have been the principal force behind recent developments on the left in Europe.

At this point, we enter another region of problems and themes with regard to postmodern theories: their preference for traditionally neglected subjects such as the phenomenology of sensibility (emotions, perception, imagination, etc.). That which the norm of modern thinking rejects as marginal and strange promises to reveal the functioning of the process of normalization to illuminate the real intensity of that which is excluded as abject or vile. This accounts for an increased interest in the phenomenon of insanity (from paranoia to schizophrenia), following Jacques Lacan and his structurally inspired critical psychoanalysis, and for a new philosophy of literature and art. At the end of the twentieth century, art (the "anti-nihilistic counter-power *par excellence*," according to Nietzsche) emerges as the central paradigm of a philosophy (ontologically based on virtual, differential, and contingent structures) that comes to terms with the disappearance of objectivity, an ideal objectivity that pretends not to be affected by historical imagination.

The heated debate between hermeneutics and deconstruction constitutes one of the most contentious issues within the field of aesthetic questioning. In *Marges de la philosophie* (1972), Jacques Derrida sharply criticizes traditional hermeneutics, which is based on a dialogue model of communication, for failing to consider the extent to which any act of understanding (especially of literature) necessarily depends on the given context. As Derrida suggests, hermeneutic theory tends to rely on ideological assumptions because it starts from the typical example of successful understanding under symmetrical conditions, excluding hierarchical power-relationships in principle, as if meaning is substantially independent of context. In contrast, the advocates of hermeneutics (at least in its Gadamer version) hold Derrida guilty of recklessly squandering the aesthetic content of art to the extent that it is not used in the context of an existential effort to improve human self-understanding but to favor metaphysical dispersion, historical uprooting, and educational amnesia.

Heidegger's attempt to renew ontology, which was to intensify the modern tendency toward a generalization and subjectification of temporality, not only underlies this conflict of interpretations but his radicalized approach to temporality in fact constitutes one of the main motifs of postmodern thought. Time becomes the parameter of a kind of philosophical thinking that draws the finality of being, which can only appear in the horizon of time, to its most far-reached conclusion. What is of primary importance is not the content of time, not what goes on in time, which develops in accordance with the inner logic of time, but the duration of time as such, time in its temporality and in relation to which all elements of content lose their eternal value and separate themselves into differential components or singularities. The special emphasis on temporality as the ontological form of endless repetition not only breaks with the dominant idea of an identical and unchangeable form of subjectivity or with the importance of a teleological model of history, but opens the way for an application of genetic methods to the realm of structuralism. Fundamentalist principles of any philosophy of science dissolve in the face of the abyss of temporality.

Lyotard's report on the condition of knowledge in highly developed societies draws on Wittgenstein's conception of language games (*Sprachspiele*), which clearly turns away from the positivist program of the Vienna Circle (*Wiener Kreis*) around Schlick and Carnap. Based on a physicalist language of observation, the purpose of this program is to carry out a logical construction of the world or to outline a verifying theory of scientific statements. In fact, Wittgenstein's reflections in the *Philosophical Investigations* (1952) concerning the plurality of discourse-types are easily compatible with developments in the realm of the history of science since Thomas S. Kuhn and his groundbreaking work *The Structure of Scientific Revolutions* (1962). Kuhn shows that progress in science does not merely amount to an accumulation of knowledge within a certain frame of established norms and rules but also in extraordinary (revolutionary) cases as a shift of paradigm. This arrangement corresponds to a displacement or modification of the idea of scientific reason: the principle of universal metalanguage is replaced by a plurality of formal and axiomatic systems that are able to demonstrate denotative statements.

This tendency connects with a further thesis concerning the far-reaching change in the structure of hard science in the last century. With reference to the French school of epistemology (founded by Gaston Bachelard), historians of science such as Michel Serres or Bruno Latour claim that the previously declarative order is currently being substituted by a process-logical order of knowledge. Not only does the progressive technicalization of society lead to a global network of electronic databases, but at the same time it leads to an alteration of the hierarchical structures in the system of education. The process by which power expands and legitimizes itself is increasingly being ruled by available modes of information production and storage, accessibility, and operationality. Databases storing an overflow of information that anyone can access but that exceed the concrete capacities of each user are the encyclopedias of the future. In accordance with the antiquated or obsolete status of man concerning his personal memory, power seems to have switched to the administration of externalized electronic memory banks. French media-philosophers such as Paul Virilio or Jean Baudrillard, theoreticians of "la post-histoire," have focused on the concept of simulation to analyze the effects of new communication technologies on people's perception of reality. In their view, the aestheticization of life as a consequence of new technology practices has already advanced to such a degree that references to reality only occur through signs, images, and symbolic representations that are constructed within the technological system.

Recent theories on gender difference unfolded by Luce Irigaray, Hélène Cixous, and Julia Kristeva—to mention only some of the best-known philosophers in this field—have drawn attention to the close relationship between recent French philosophy and the underlying principles of feminist theories. Thinking difference allows one to reconstruct genealogically the absence of women in language, to begin to understand their role in the evolution of Western discourse, and to develop new feminist figurations of female subjectivity. As Lacan pointed out in his seminars at the beginning of the 1970s, learning how to speak takes place in conformity with the "law of the father," which codifies desire and goes hand in hand with excluding the specificity of female experience.

In the light of feminist theory in particular, it is clear that so-called postmodern philosophy certainly does not speculate on the end of history or modernism. Quite the contrary: Postmodern thinkers set out to conceptualize the power of history in a philosophically adequate way. The fact that we cannot predict what is to come means that we must take the future into our own hands in the best way possible. Paul Feyerabend's ill-reputed formula "anything goes" does not mean that it is satisfactory to embrace apathy and avoid critical engagement. As stated in *Against Method* (1975, §1):

> If a person turns to consider the rich material that has emerged throughout the course of history, and if his or her purpose is not to dilute that material in order to satisfy the lowest human instinct, which is a craving for mental security in the form of clarity, precision, "objectivity" and "truth," then that person will recognize that there is only one principle that applies to all circumstances and to any state of human evolution. The principle is: Anything goes. (first sentence, § 1 of German edition, p. 35)

Perhaps we may consider Gilles Deleuze as appropriately responding to this (in a Nietzchean undertone) when he insists that there can only be one ontological proposition that states the unity of being and thus commits it to the multiplicity of differences within the unpredictable processes of becoming.

MARC RÖLLI

See also **Gaston Bachelard; Georges Bataille; Jean Baudrillard; Helene Cixous; Gilles Deleuze; Jacques Derrida; Michel Foucault; Luce Irigaray; Pierre Klossowski; Julia Kristeva; Jacques Lacan; Jean-Francois Lyotard; Michel Serres**

Further Reading

Abel, Günter (ed.), *Französische Nachkriegsphilosophie. Autoren und Positionen*, Berlin: Berlin-Verlag, 2001

Adorno, Theodor W., and Horkheimer, Max, *Dialektik der Aufklärung. Philosophische Fragmente*, Frankfurt: Fischer, 1969 (1944); as *Dialectic of Enlightenment. Philosophical Fragments*, ed. by Gunzelin Schmid Noerr Stanford University Press, 2002

Baudrillard, Jean, *L'échange symbolique et la mort*, Paris: Gallimard, 1976

Bauman, Zygmunt, *Modernity and ambivalence*, Cambridge: Polity Press, 1991

Bauman, Zygmunt, *Postmodernity and its discontents*, Cambridge: Polity Press, 1997

Benhabib, Seyla et al., *Feminist Contentions. A philosophical exchange*, New York: Routledge, 1995

Deleuze, Gilles, *Différence et répétition*, Paris: Epimethée, 1968; as *Difference and Repetition*, Columbia University Press, 1995

Derrida, Jacques, *Marges de la philosophie*, Paris: Editions de Minuit 1972; as *Margins of Philosophy*, Chicago: University of Chicago Press, 1984 transl. by Alan Bass

Eagleton, Terry, *The illusions of postmodernism*, Oxford: Blackwell, 1996

Feyerabend, Paul, *Against Method*, London: Atlantic Highlands, 1975

Foucault, Michel, *Les mots et les choses. Une archéologie des sciences humaines*, Paris: Gallimard, 1966

Foucault, Michel, *Histoire de la sexualité*, 3 volumes, Paris: Gallimard, 1976–1984; as *History of Sexuality* I–III, New York: Vintage Books, 1990

Giddens, Anthony, *A critical theory of late modernity*, Stanford: Stanford University Press, 1991

Habermas, Jürgen, *Der philosophische Diskurs der Moderne. Zwölf Vorlesungen*, Frankfurt/Main: Suhrkamp, 1985; as *The Philosophical Discourse of Modernity*: Twelve Lectures. MIT Press, 1990 transl. by Frederick G. Lawrence

Jameson, Fredric, *Postmodernism, or, The Cultural Logic of Late Capitalism*, Durham, NC: Duke University Press, 1992

Kuhn, Thomas S., *The Structure of Scientific Revolutions*. Chicago: University of Chicago Press, 1962

Latour, Bruno, *Nous n'avons jamais été modernes. Essai d'anthropologie symétrique*, Paris: Editions La Découverte, 1991

Lyotard, Jean-François, *La condition postmoderne: rapport sur le savoir*, Paris: Editions de Minuit, 1979; as *The postmodern condition: a report on knowledge*, Minnesota University Press, 1985 translated from the French by G. Bennington and B. Messumi

Nicholson, Linda (ed.), *Feminism/Postmodernism*, New York: Routledge, 1990

Seidman, Steven (ed.), *The Postmodern Turn: New Perspectives on Social Theory*, Cambridge: Cambridge University Press, 1995

Silverman, Hugh J. (ed.), *Postmodernism—Philosophy and the arts*, New York: Routledge, 1990

Sokal, Alan, and Bricmont, Jean, *Imposture intellectuelles*, Paris: Odile Jacob, 1997

Turner, Bryan S. (ed.), *Theories of Modernity and Postmodernity*, London: Sage, 1990

Wellmer, Albrecht, *Zur Dialektik von Moderne und Postmoderne. Vernunftkritik nach Adorno*, Frankfurt/Main: Suhrkamp, 1985

Welsch, Wolfgang, *Unsere postmoderne Moderne*, Berlin, Akademie-Verlag 2002

Wittgenstein, Ludwig, *Philosophical Investigations*, translated by Elizabeth Auscombe. Oxford: Blackwell Publishers, 1953

MONOD, JACQUES (LUCIEN)
Scientist, Philosopher

Monod made significant contributions to biology, philosophy, and the socialist movement in twentieth-century France. His professional training was in biochemistry. In 1965, he shared the Nobel Prize with André Lwoff and Francois Jacob for groundbreaking research on protein synthesis and the discovery of a previously unrecognized category of genes that regulate the functioning of other genes. In 1961, Monod laid foundations for later advances in genetic science when he proposed the existence of messenger RNA (ribonucleic acid), by which the components of DNA are identified and transported to a sugar-phosphate base for replication. The mechanism by which DNA codes are transmitted was thereby explained, opening up new avenues of investigation. Within this framework, Monod and his associates further hypothesized the existence of operator genes that regulate the activity of protein synthesizing genes by specific chemical sequences determining the manufacture of messenger RNA.

Beyond his impressive scientific discoveries, Monod was also active in philosophical reflections on the concept of life, processes of natural selection, and evolutionary theory. His 1970 book *Le hasard et la nécessité: essai sur la philosophie naturelle de la biologie moderne* (*Chance and Necessity: An Essay on the Natural Philosophy of Modern Biology*) was influential in promoting the role of random probability in the development of living things, including human beings. The title of Monod's work, as he indicates, is taken from a fragment popularly attributed to the ancient Greek materialist philosopher Democritus of Abdera, according to which "Everything existing in the universe is the fruit of chance and of necessity."

These two factors, chance and necessity, are described by Monod as determining the course of nature generally and more particularly the development of all living things. There is no insurmountable opposition in these contrary forces, as Monod understands them, and no contradiction in his belief that they jointly govern all natural phenomena. His ruling concept, which has come to be widely appreciated if still controversial in the philosophy of science, is one in which causally necessary laws operate on chance variations in nature to effect change. The application to biology in Monod's theory fits the Darwinian model of the evolution of species through natural selection. According to this account, statistically random but still causally necessitated genetic mutations are molded by law-like natural selection pressures for survival and reproduction into the incremental variations that eventually produce new species. In conformity with this evolutionary image, Monod regards every aspect of biology as the result of the combined effect of chance distributions of matter and variations in their properties transformed by necessary causal principles, a view by which he opposes vitalism and animism in previous philosophical explanations of the concept of life.

Monod considers the microstructures of living things to be mechanical, in what he refers to as their "microscopic cybernetics." Within this explanatory system, Monod accommodates new experimental findings in microbiology, including the synthesis of enzyme-proteins, from the simplest of organic compounds and organisms through the history of evolution, including the complications of human biology. He interprets information in the genetic code as a fundamental invariant of life that is nevertheless subject to modification through spontaneous random associations of protein subunits, first in microscopic and then macroscopic morphogenesis.

The difficult question for Monod's philosophy involves the nature and limits of chance. If chance is merely as a name for unknown or unrecognized enormously complicated necessities, then there is no fundamental metaphysical difference between necessity and chance. What we then call random or chance genetic mutations are presumably as much the result of necessity functioning at the microphysical level on the molecular and atomic constituents of chromosomes as more obviously deterministic macrophysical phenomena. The implication in that case is that chance simply reduces to hidden physical necessities, that there is no separate force of chance operating in the universe, and that chance only disguises our ignorance of underlying causal necessity. Although Monod does not directly discuss the problem, it appears that he favors a reductive concept of chance while preserving its explanatory value, and that in this way he proposes to demystify the origin of life as accidental rather than a product of intelligent supernatural design.

Monod had a considerable effect on contemporary French thought in both its scientific and philosophical dimensions. His humanistic and ultimately Marxist socialist worldview grew out of his understanding of the conditions of life and the place of human beings in the larger evolutionary scheme. Moreover, he believed that science properly understood would provide a sounder model of knowledge than the "blind faith" of religion. The prestige of Monod's scientific research provided him with a forum for his political ideals and thereby placed him in the vanguard of French socialist intellectuals. His participation in public demonstrations and frequent letters to the editorial columns of Paris newspapers afforded him an opportunity to denounce social injustices. It is possible to project a continuum of implications from Monod's concept of chance and necessity from biology to politics. The effect of Marxist economic laws acting on random conditions of birth and distributions of resources in a materialist-historical framework can account for societal factors just as they do in the evolution of species. Monod evinces a classical education in his writings, in which he relates the most modern discoveries of biology and physics to the founding ideas of ancient Greek philosophy and world literature. Monod's importance is as much a factor of his poetic sensibilities and social concern as of his lasting contributions to rigorous biological science.

DALE JACQUETTE

Biography

Jacques Lucien Monod was born in Paris on February 9, 1910. His family moved to the south of France in

1917. Monod was educated at the Lycée de Cannes, and in 1928 began advanced biological studies in Paris at the faculté des sciences, where he earned a science degree in 1931 and a Ph.D. in natural sciences in 1941. He lectured at the faculté in 1934 and conducted research at the California Institute of Technology as a Rockefeller Fellow in 1936. Monod later joined the Institut Pasteur as laboratory director and was made Director of the Cell Biochemistry Department in 1954. In 1959 he was appointed Professor of the Chemistry of Metabolism at the Sorbonne; in 1967 he became Professor at the Collège de France, and in 1971 Director of the Institut Pasteur. During his career, Monod published numerous books and more than 110 articles in scientific journals, and received many prestigious international awards, including among others the Montyon Physiology Prize of the Academie des Sciences (Paris, 1955), Honorary Foreign Member of the American Academy of Arts and Sciences (1960), and Foreign Member of the Royal Society (London, 1968). Monod died in Cannes on May 31, 1976.

Selected Works

Reserches sur la croissance des cultures bactériennes, 1942
From Biology to Ethics, 1969
Le hasard et la nécessité: essai sur la philosophie naturelle de la biologie moderne, 1970
Chance and Necessity: An Essay in the Natural Philosophy of Modern Biology, translated by Austryn Wainhouse, 1971
Coeditor, *Of Microbes and Life*, with Ernest Borek, 1971
Selected Papers in Molecular Biology, edited by André Lwoff and Agnès Ullmann, 1978
Pour une éthique de la connaissance; textes choisis et présentés par Bernardino Fantini, 1988

Further Reading

Debré, Patrice, *Jacques Monod*, Paris: Flammarion, 1996
Lwoff, André, and Ullmann, Agnès, eds., *Origins of Molecular Biology: A Tribute to Jacques Monod*, New York: Academic Press, 1979
Quagliariello, Ernesto, Bernardi, Giorgio, and Ullmann, Agnès, eds., *From Enzyme Adaptation to Natural Philosophy: Heritage from Jacques Monod: Proceedings of the Symposium on Jacques Monod and Molecular Biology, Yesterday and Today*, Amsterdam: Elsevier Science, 1987
Soulier, Jean-Pierre, *Jacques Monod: le choix de l'objectivité*, Paris: Frison-Roche, 1997

MOUNIER, EMMANUEL
Catholic Philosopher and Editor

Emmanuel Mounier is significant above all for having developed the influential Christian social philosophy of Personalism during the 1930s and for being the founder and first editor of the Paris-based review *Esprit*.

He started to develop his thinking on social philosophy as a member of an informal group of nonconformist Christians. Close at first to the Catholic theologian Jacques Maritain, who sought to renew Church thinking from a Thomist perspective, Mounier was strongly influenced by Charles Peguy, about whom he cowrote an essay in 1929 with Jacques Izard. Another source of inspiration, as for many Christians attempting to reflect on modernity, was the 1891 encyclical *Rerum Novarum* of Pope Leo XIII, which rejects socialism and communism as solutions to the alienation of human life in the modern world, but that also vigorously denounces liberalism and capitalism as exploiting and alienating workers. The 1929 Wall Street crash and the Great Depression that followed, which exemplify the dysfunctional nature of modern capitalism, were crucial moments in the formation of Mounier's thinking.

In 1932 he abandoned his teaching career and launched the review *Esprit*, which soon become one of the main conduits of intellectual debate in France, and that is still a recognized and vital part of it. The first issue included the personalist manifesto. The result of a collective reflection about the practice of the Christian faith in the midst of the burning socioeconomic and political controversies of the day, including the deep ideological and political divide between socialism and capitalism, personalism is defined by Mounier as a "break with the established disorder." It denounces the individualist materialism and consumerism of capitalism, which negates the human spirit, alienating ("dehumanizes") and exploiting workers, and also the totalitarian collectivism of communism and fascism. Both are seen as "reductive" of the person, who, though an "absolute," is also present in the world through society. Mounier therefore attempts to define a form of humanist engagement for the transformation of society, using a "third way" between capitalism and communism, what he calls "a philosophy of engagement . . . inseparable from a philosophy of the absolute or of the transcendence of the human model." This engagement is to be within the world—the "revolution" that Mounier calls for is both "personalist and communalist." Society is seen as a community of persons, as opposed to a collective as well as a mere collection of individuals.

During the 1930s, Mounier and *Esprit* were often at the forefront of the many conflicts of the period—strongly opposing Hitler from the start, protesting against the nonintervention of European democracies such as France and Great Britain in defense of the Republic in the Spanish Civil War; and condemning the infamous 1938 Munich Agreement among Hitler, Chamberlain, and Daladier. At the same time, Mounier further developed his philosophy, which attracted a wider audience, publishing *Manifeste au service du personalisme* in 1936. After the defeat of France, Mounier chose to continue to edit *Esprit* up to late 1941, when it was forbidden by the authorities, and he maintained a critical dialogue with elements of the Vichy regime (especially the École d'Uriage, a school [1940–1941] that sought to train young people for leadership and that in fact produced a number of men who played a leading role in the Resistance). In 1942, Mounier was arrested for participation in the nascent *Combat* resistance movement, but he was acquitted. He went into hiding for the duration of the war, contributing to clandestine publications and writing.

After the Liberation, *Esprit* joined the Seuil publishing stable, and the team was reinforced by a number of people from the Resistance (such as J.-M. Domenach) and a number of philosophers, including Etienne Borne, Jean Lacroix, and Paul Ricoeur. During the Cold War, *Esprit* strove to act as a bridge in the ideological conflicts that threatened to tear French society apart. Mounier himself opened up to communists, although he was sharply critical of regimes in Eastern Europe, and wrote frequently on issues such as the Cold War, decolonization, totalitarianism, and Franco-German reconciliation, but without ever neglecting the importance of spirituality in his approach of the person within the contemporary society. The influence of personalism persisted long after the death of Mounier in 1950. A number of groups and associations took their inspiration from it, notably the Christian progressive group La Vie Nouvelle, which stressed the importance of a practical experiences of community life, and from which a number of influential people came (such as Jacques Delors, Finance Minister of the 1986 government, and a forceful President of the EC commission from 1985 to 1994). During the 1960s, a number of political associations (such as Clubs Jean Moulin or Citoyens 60) that sought the modernization of a noncommunist left were also strongly influenced by Mounier's personalism.

In the early 1990s, a debate arose in French intellectual circles about Mounier's position during the Second World War, the argument being that personalism (defined as a "third way" before the war) was close to various forms of French neofascist political thought that also defined themselves as a "third way." This thesis, defended especially by the "New Philosopher" Bernard Henri-Levy and by Zeev Sternhell, has been laid to rest by a renewed analysis of Mounier texts from the prewar and war period.

FRANCOIS NECTOUX

See also **Jacques Maritain; Charles Peguy; Paul Ricoeur**

Biography

Emmanuel Mounier was born in 1905 into a well-to-do Grenoble family with rural roots. He studied philosophy under Jacques Chevallier before going to Paris in 1927 and receiving his *agregation*. He became a teacher of philosophy, but abandoned teaching in 1932 when he founded the review *Esprit*. Mounier died in 1950.

Selected Writings

Manifeste au service du personalisme, 1936
Personalism, 1970
The Character of Man, 1956

Further Readings

Amato, Joseph A., and Sallomone, William, eds., *Mounier and Maritain—A French Understanding of the Modern World*, University of Alabama Press, 1975
Hellman, John, *Emmanuel Mounier and the New Catholic Left 1930–1950*, University of Toronto Press, 1981
Kelly, Michael, *Pioneer of the Catholic Revival: the Ideas and Influence of Emmanuel Mounier*, London: Sheed and Ward, 1979
Rauch, R.W., Jr., *Politics and Belief in Contemporary France: Emmanuel Mounier and Christian Democracy 1932–1950*, Aspen Publishers, 1972
Winock, Michel, *Esprit, des intellectuels dans la cité 1930–1950*, Paris: Le Seuil, Points-histoire, 1996

MUDIMBE, VALENTIN YVES
Writer

Valentin Yves Mudimbe occupies a central position in contemporary African literature and thought. Mudimbe is a prolific polymath whose works have been deeply shaped by his experience of colonial rule in the former Belgian Congo and the aftermath of decolonization. As he is a former Benedictine monk, the effect of Catholicism on central Africa plays a key role in his writings (poetry, novels, essays). This intellectual production, written not only in French but also in English, is characterized by interdisciplinarity (philosophy, anthropology, art and literary criticism, and linguistics) and an ability to break the boundaries between the essay and the novel.

As a novelist he came first to prominence with *Entre les eaux* (1973). This novel, published by the pan-African and anticolonialist publisher Présence africaine (Paris), is an indirect reflection of Mudimbe's own conflicts as an African intellectual. Pierre Landu, the main protagonist, is a Black African cleric, who, in an endeavor to reconcile the universalist principles of Catholicism and Marxism, abandons his parish and joins a Marxist guerilla armed group. Landu's syncretic attempt results, however, in failure as he realizes his inability to be accepted as anything but a representative of a quintessentially non-African and bourgeois tradition.

In his three subsequent novels, *Le Bel immonde* (1976), *L'Écart* (1979), and *Shaba deux* (1989), Mudimbe further illustrates this difficult search for an African paradigm in a world in which interdependency is a synonym for Western hegemony. From Cheikh Hamidou Kane to Sembene Ousmane or Ahmadou Kourouma, this commitment to explore the very hybrid nature of postcolonial sub-Saharan Africa is at the core of Francophone literature. Mudimbe is undoubtedly part of this tradition. With his novels, however, he manages to distance himself from the latter's ethnographic realism. His spatially and temporally fragmented narratives are reminiscent of the *Nouveau Roman*'s phenomenological move toward a more subjective, self-reflexive, and therefore disjointed—albeit erudite and intertextual—treatment of reality.

In his essays, Mudimbe offers an even more explicit picture of the ambivalent situation of postcolonial Africa. *L'Autre face du royaume* (1973) and *L'Odeur du père* (1982) provide critical analyses of North-American and European (what he commonly refers to as "eur-américain") ethnocentrism and its neocolonial effect on Central Africa. Engaged in a radical poststructuralist critique of anthropology, Mudimbe, deeply influenced by the Foucaultian approach to cultural hegemony, not only reiterates the collusion between this discipline and colonialism, but also explores and deplores Central Africa's inability to think and verbalize itself outside this imported epistemological framework. He advocates, therefore, the development of a truly African "third way" that would enable the enactment of a symbolic parricide and liberate the former colonial subject from "l'odeur du père" ("the father's odor").

In spite of this commitment to promote African values, Mudimbe remains throughout his *œuvre* very critical of *négritude* and Afrocentrism. He dismisses as too essentialist Cheikh Anta Diop's Egypt-centrist attempt to define black Africans through the Pharaonic legacy. His third way is more cosmopolitan, and less inclined to emphasize the purported uniqueness of the Negro-African identity. Similar to other African philosophers, such as Kwame Appiah or Paulin Hountondji, he regards sub-Saharan Africa as a fundamentally hybridized space in which "Africanness" is challenged by the "eur-américain" categories and procedures of thought.

His critique of Western imperialism and of its underlying "ethnological reason" is further developed in *The Invention of Africa* (1988). This very influential essay (the effect of which on Postcolonial Studies can be compared to Edward Said's *Orientalism*) investigates and deconstructs the historical, cultural, and religious factors behind the emergence of Africanism as an autonomous field of study. In this discussion, Mudimbe shows that Westerners, be they travelers, missionaries or professional anthropologists, fashioned an idea of Africa, what he also refers to as the "Colonial Library," that is more revealing of the observers than of the "objects" under their scrutiny. Focusing, as in former and subsequent essays, on his native Congo, Mudimbe describes the context in which Catholicism became the major central African faith. In this discussion, explored along similar lines in his 1994 collection of essays, *The Idea of Africa*, he shows the importance of the epistemological reversal of the 1920s. This significant shift from evolutionism to a more sympathetic (he talks of *Einfühlung*) and relativist approach of the "other" had a major influence on anthropological practices and, conversely, on Christianization. As a consequence of this reversal, the Belgian missionaries (and particularly the ethno-philosophical vein promoted by Father Placide Tempels and his disciples) gradually relinquished the "Theology of Salvation" for a "Theology of Indigenization." Although a tactical and hegemonic move (in reference to this shift, Mudimbe refers to "Tactics and Strategies of Domestication" [*The Idea of Africa*, 114–29]), this new approach on the part of the missionaries also reveals the existence of a "third space of enunciation" as Homi K. Bhabha put it in *The Location of Culture* (1994), in which the colonized subjects and their "masters" jointly redefined the faith. This notion of religious "inculturation" (i.e., the culture-sensitive "transplantation" of Catholicism in central Africa) remains central in *Les Corps glorieux des mots et des êtres* (1994) and *Tales of Faith* (1997). *Les Corps glorieux* is an autobiographical essay in which Mudimbe reflects, against the rich, multilingual and cosmopolitan background of his personal trajectory as a writer and an academic, on colonization and the (religious, linguistic, political) conflicts of memories that it generated in contemporary Congo.

Finally, this ability to blur the limits between genres, most prevalently demonstrated by these last two books, constitutes Mudimbe's method of asserting the stateless (*apatride*) nature of his creative freedom: "Here I am on the margin of margins: Black, African, Catholic, yet agnostic; intellectually Marxist, disposed towards psychoanalysis, yet a specialist in Indo-European philology and philosophy" (*Parables and Fables*, 1991, 13).

PIERRE-PHILIPPE FRAITURE

See also **Cheikh Anta Diop**

Biography

Valentin Yves (a.k.a. Vumbi Yoka) Mudimbe was born in 1941 in Likasi, Congo Kinshasa. After a short-lived but significant career as a monk in Rwanda, he resumed his studies. From 1966 to 1971, he was a lecturer at the universities of Lovanium (Congo), Paris-Nanterre, and Leuven, where he was awarded a doctorate in 1970. In 1971, he was appointed to a Chair in Compared Literature and Linguistics at the University of Lubumbashi (Zaire). As a result of his political opposition against the Moubutu-led Zairian dictatorship, he was forced into exile and immigrated to the United States in 1981. Since 1988, Mudimbe has been Newman Ivey White professor in Literature at Duke University (North Carolina). He has taught (at Duke and the University of Stanford) a wide range of topics including Structuralism, Phenomenology, and African philosophy. He is also a noted classicist. In 1997, he was made Doctor Honoris Causa at the University of Paris VII. Mudimbe is the author or editor of twenty-one books. He is the general secretary of SAPINA (the Society for African Philosophy in North America).

Selected Works

Entre les eaux. Dieu, un prêtre, la révolution [*Between Tides*], 1973

L'Autre face du royaume. Une introduction à la critique des langages en folie, 1973
Le Bel immonde, 1976
L'Écart, 1979
L'Odeur du père. Essai sur les limites de la science et de la vie en Afrique Noire, 1982
Shaba deux. Les Carnets de Mère Marie Gertrude, 1988 (89?)
The Invention of Africa. Gnosis, Philosophy, and the Order of Knowledge, 1988
Parables and Fables: Exegesis, Textuality, and Politics in Central Africa, 1991
Coeditor, *The Surreptitious Speech: Présence africaine and the Politics of Otherness, 1947–1987*, 1992
Coeditor, *History Making in Africa*, 1993, with Bogumil Jewsiewicki
Les Corps glorieux des mots et des êtres. Esquisse d'un jardin africain à la bénédictine, 1994
The Idea of Africa, 1994
Tales of Faith: Religion as political Performance in Central Africa, 1997
Coeditor, *Nations, Identities, Cultures*, 1997

Further Reading

Mouralis, Bernard, *V.Y. Mudimbe ou le discours, l'écart et l'écriture*, 1988
Kasende, Jean-Christophe Luhaka, *Le roman africain face aux discours hégémoniques: étude sur l'énonciation et l'idéologie dans l'œuvre de V.Y. Mudimbe*, 2001
Gbanou, Sélom Komlan, and Mukala, Kadima-Nzuji, eds., *L'Afrique au miroir des littératures. Nomen est omen. Mélanges offerts à Valentin-Yves Mudimbe*, 2002

N

NANCY, JEAN-LUC
Philosopher

Jean-Luc Nancy's thought takes place in a context of the withdrawal of transcendent meaning, or of the absence of sense both as a philosophical and a historical event, the condition of our time. His thought is thus a thought of finitude, which asks: How are we to think our relation to the world, to existence, in the absence of already established meaning? The absence of sense implies here a withdrawal of transcendence, but "being" is not, for all this, left with a character of empirical fact. A series of related terms that scan Nancy's writing from the early 1970s to the present communicate the sense of a transcendence operative within the heart of immanence; that there is no transcendental meaning to existence does not mean that existence is devoid of sense, is meaningless. This is to say that being or existence is not thought of in relation to a transcendent notion of presence; its presence is rather thought of as an exposure, sharing, offering or abandonment. Nancy's work may thus be situated in the context of deconstructive thought from the 1960s onward that critically and analytically undermines metaphysical notions of presence or transcendental sense, to then rethink the disjunctive relation of presence to itself, the exposure to itself at its very heart, on its threshold or at its limit. Nancy's writing is resolutely critical of the exercise of sublation, the *Aufhebung*, which appropriates or idealizes the materiality or naked existence of being, but that also consistently refuses either to idealize this materiality in its turn or to be content with the dissolution of metaphysical concepts. To refute transcendental categories in the name of empirical principles such as "the body," "the text," and so on is to replace one transcendent sense by another. Nancy attempts rather to think of the transcendence of immanence.

A singular quality of Nancy's work is his insistence on the relation between thought and, what might, for want of a better word, be called materiality. Thought is irreducibly tied to its event, its site (*lieu*), and its weight (*le poids*), and thus to the singularity of existence. Nancy's thought may be termed poststructuralist if this designates a critical attitude toward the abstraction of language and meaning from the singularity of their taking place, or from concrete existence. Meaning has a necessary relation to the world, which is not thought in terms of reference or the absence of reference, but as affect, weight, and touch. The concept of exscription, among others, names this relation whereby writing exceeds itself and spills over itself into affection or weight, where it touches existence. Rather than thinking the disjunctive relation between meaning and the real in exclusively negative terms, Nancy seeks to explore the singular site at the limits or at the heart of meaning where it touches existence, the birth to presence or the creation of a world. His philosophy, although it is resolutely critical of transcendental ideals, is profoundly a philosophy of generosity and charity toward "the world."

Nancy's thought emerges in a context in which, in the 1960s and early 1970s, the materiality of the signifier or the instance of the letter are proposed as strategies for the dissolution of the transcendental subject. His thought partakes of a deconstructive strategy in that it seeks to show how these strategies cannot do without the transcendental notions or philosophical concepts they seek to dissolve, and thus reinstitute them in their very discursive and rhetorical movement. Thus, in *Le titre de la lettre; une lecture de Lacan* (1972), coauthored with Philippe Lacoue-Labarthe (a collaboration that was also to produce *L'absolue littéraire* [1978], *Le mythe nazi* [1991], and some related articles), the authors show how Lacan's insistence on the instance of the letter or on the preeminent role of the signifier ends up philosophically re-inscribing the subject it is intended to dissolve. This, however, is not intended explicitly as a criticism of Lacan, as an exercise of critical judgement, but rather an a certain kind of reading, a strategy of reading that underlines the ambivalence of any systematic or totalizing claim. Nancy and Lacoue-Labarthe achieved a kind of notoriety when Lacan, in 1975, recognized their book as the best and the only attempt to read him.

If a series of figures of thought that punctuate Nancy's writing may be seen as corporeal (touch, weight, heart), his thought is not one that posits the body as ultimate signifier or as unique point of reference. To do so would be to construe the body as transcendental signified. Rather, in *Corpus* (1992), Nancy shows how "the body itself" (*le corps proper*) expels and annihilates that which it purports to name, and the body is rather to be thought in terms of its global multiplicity, as bodies, and in terms of the plurality of its modes of touch, the singular sites of the body's contact. Nancy's philosophy is thus as attentive to the banalities and to the current political miseries of existence as to philosophical systems.

The critique of transcendental appropriation and the demand to think the political condition of the present and the last centuries have led Nancy to address the issue of community. Working with the thought of Bataille, among others, Nancy proposes the term community to designate the inherent exposure of man to the other, as the openness of a relation rather than the closure of that relation in a unity (a communion), or in an atomistic conception of the individual. Here again, in an explicitly political sense, Nancy's thought analytically disarticulates the principles that appropriate the exposed and open nature of being in relation to a totality.

In common with other philosophers of his generation (e.g., Derrida, Lacoue-Labarthe, Sarah Kofman) Nancy has importance as a writer on literature and to a lesser extent on the visual arts (painting and film). The concern with literality, and with a writing that *exscribes* itself informs a number of texts in which Nancy addresses the particularity of poetry. However, literature and poetry are not posited either as a form of language that would represent or inscribe the ineffable or as the "beyond" of philosophy. The options of absolute literality and of the ineffable mystery are resisted in favor of an approach to literature that emphasizes, again, the exposure of meaning to existence, and vice versa. Moreover, in an early work with Philippe Lacoue-Labarthe on the German Romantics around the *Atheneaum*, Nancy addressed the relation of literature to philosophy through a consideration of the becoming-theory of literature; it is the relation of literature to truth and to totality that is at stake here. As totality is construed as an infinity or as an excess, literature's only access to truth becomes the fragment.

Nancy's recent work has sought to address our contemporary social and political condition. Already, *La communauté désœuvrée* (1986) and *Corpus* (1992) were concerned with the politics of community and of population. The essay *La création du monde ou la mondialisation* (2002) confronts in its title the potential contrast between a philosophy that, after Heidegger, concerns itself with the coming to presence of existence, and a social and political context of the dominance of technique. Nancy's thought, however, is not characterized by a nostalgia for the lost narratives that may have enabled a sense of communion or of history; the withdrawal of the Gods, otherwise speaking of transcendent principles, leaves existence and history to their own finitude, and this finitude itself demands to be thought and enables the chance or the decision of existence.

PATRICK FFRENCH

See also **Georges Bataille; Jacques Derrida; Jacques Lacan**

Biography

Born in Bordeaux in 1940, Jean-Luc Nancy is now Professor of Philosophy at the University of Strasbourg, where he has lived and taught for over twenty years, and a Visiting Professor at the Universities of Berlin and Berkeley, California. As a student he was taught at the Sorbonne by Georges Canguilhem and Paul Ricoeur. His initial interests were around questions pertaining to religion and theology; early texts by Nancy appeared in the Catholic review *Esprit* in the 1960s. It is with Philippe Lacoue-Labarthe, however, that he coauthored his first publication, in book form, *Le titre de la lettre*, in 1972. Also with Lacoue-Labarthe, Nancy wrote the definitive analysis and translation of the fragments of the German Romantic journal the *Atheneaum*, and with Lacoue-Labarthe, he has contributed to work on Nazism and on the Holocaust with *Le mythe nazi*. Nancy has been involved, with Derrida, Lacoue-Labarthe, and Sarah Kofman, with the collection *La philosophie en effet'* of Editions Galilée. He has published as single author over thirty books, from the studies of Hegel and Kant, *La remarque spéculatif* and *L'impératif catégorique*, respectively, to short essays such as *Corpus, Le partage des voix,* and *L' "il y a" du rapport sexuel.* Among the most significant books are *La communauté désœuvrée* (1986), *Corpus* (1993), and *Etre singulier pluriel* (1996). His writing is not limited to philosophy, and he has written influential articles on Bataille, Leiris, Rimbaud, and Baudelaire, among other writers, as well as, more recently, texts on film (*L'évidence du film*) and on painting (*Le regard du portrait,* 2000). A recent text, *L'Intrus* (2000) is an essay concerning the global market in human organs, the question of transplantation and intrusion, biological and social, which draws on Nancy's own experience of a heart transplant operation.

Selected Works

With Philippe Lacoue-Labarthe, *Le titre de la lettre,* 1972
La remarque spéculative, un bot mot de Hegel, 1973
With Philippe Lacoue-Labarthe, *L'absolu littéraire,* 1978
Ego sum, 1979
Le partage des voix, 1982
La communauté désœuvrée, 1986
L'expérience de la liberté, 1988
Une pensée finie, 1990
Le poids d'une pensée, 1991
With Philippe Lacoue-Labarthe, *Le mythe nazi,* 1991
Corpus, 1992
Le sens du monde, 1992
Etre singulier pluriel, 1996
Le regard du portrait, 2000
L'intrus, 2000
La pensée dérobée, 2001
L' "il y a" du rapport sexuel, 2001
La création du monde ou la mondialisation, 2002

Further Reading

Jacques Derrida, *Le toucher,* Paris: Galilée, 2000
Paragraph, 16,2 (July 1993), *On the work of Jean-Luc Nancy,* edited by Peggy Kamuf
On Jean Luc Nancy: The Sense of Philosophy, edited by Darren Sheppard, Simon Sparks, and Colin Thomas, London: Routledge, 1997

NIZAN, PAUL-YVES
Writer, Journalist

It might not have become clear before he died in 1940, a casualty of World War II, that Paul Nizan would never define French political and philosophical thought so completely as his close friend Jean-Paul Sartre. Nizan had by the early 1930s become established as a leftist political thinker of stature. The breadth of his works, including poetry, novels, theater, scenarios, literary criticism, pamphlets, philosophical

writings, prefaces, translations, and most important, political journalism, allowed him to reach a wide audience, not all of whom may have had an immediate sympathy for the views of this militant leftist intellectual. Nizan's sphere of influence would moreover extend well beyond his lifetime; his works continue to serve as a model of rebellion against the establishment.

Nizan's first work to achieve a major critical success, *Aden-Arabie* (1931), introduced him to the world of French intellectuals beyond his circle of friends. Prompted by his own indecision as to his future, the text is based on his experiences while he served as a tutor for a merchant's son in Aden (1926–1927). Nizan's formative experience resulted from this interlude, in which his contact with the bourgeois colonial world left him with little but disgust for its culture and its institutions. On his return to Paris, he joined the Communist Party and soon published the text inspired by his stay. The text depicts the illusory nature of travel, a false romantic means of escape. Further, Nizan not only elaborated a vision of France steeped in the aftermath of the war but, more important, he sketched out the portrait of *Homo economicus,* slave to capitalism, clearly inspired by Nizan's affiliation with Marxism. In essence, *Aden-Arabie* was a declaration of war on the bourgeoisie, enemy of "l'homme réel." Much of the impact of the text comes from the anger that infuses it. That Nizan remains one on the archetypal angry young men is a testimony to the force of the text.

Perhaps as a result of the depreciation of capitalism as an economic system, the period after the stock market crash of 1929 saw a rise in the value placed on the object. Nizan's writings evidence this significant ideological shift from the period of his collaboration on *La Revue Marxiste.* In literary terms, what Henri Lefebvre would later categorize as a program to "retrieve the object," this stance signals a shift from the primacy of the word and from literary interiority as seen in the works of Marcel Proust, Joyce, and Virginia Woolf. Nizan's works echoed the sentiments of Emmanuel Berl's *Mort de la morale bourgeoise* (1929), a book he reviewed positively for *Europe*: "the bourgeois . . . can believe himself to be blessed and protected by the inventions, myths and promises of his vocabulary."

Published in 1932, Nizan's *Chiens de garde,* a political pamphlet against philosophic idealism, was a devastating attack on the bourgeoisie, its culture, and its institutions, and this work would became one of the founding texts of engaged literature. Its immediate success was also a *succes de scandale.* Nizan attacked those who sought to preserve the establishment. He asserted that the bourgeois did "not have any contact with real objects." In effect, the bourgeoisie was a class that existed without any class consciousness; it existed as an imaginary class, cut off from the real. This work announced Nizan's commitment to Communism and Stalinism, a commitment that would later be betrayed by Stalin's treaty with Hitler.

A year later, Nizan published *Antoine Bloyé*, a novel rooted in his family tree, which would explore in fictional terms the indictment brought against the bourgeoisie in *Chiens de garde*. Although the character of Antoine Bloyé is inspired by Nizan's father, he serves not so much as a retelling of the personal but as a figure of the working class that slowly becomes part of the bourgeoisie, replete with all the moral compromises and ultimate alienation that it entails. Nonetheless, Nizan's work is not simply an example of socialist realism; rather, it is, to paraphrase the words of André Malraux, a privileged means of expression of the human tragedy. Similar themes are explored in his *Le Cheval de Troie* (1935), dealing with the life of a high school instructor in the provinces who would become engaged in a strike.

The most developed rendering of Nizan's political landscape was to have found its literary expression in a series of novels treating communism in the 1930s. When Nizan died at Dunkerque, the manuscript of the second volume that he had been working on was lost. Of this project, only the first volume, *La Conspiration* (1938) was completed. This novel won for him the Prix Interallié (beating out Sartre's *La Nausée*). As an example of autobiographical fiction, the novel portrays, analyzes, and judges the generation of intellectuals of which Nizan himself was a member. Nonetheless, *La Conspiration* reflects a more complex view of politics and of the role of the individual. Part of the appeal of *La Conspiration* to its public was the distance that Nizan was able to establish between the autobiographical and the universal. Many readers could recognize themselves, yet few would recognize Nizan's ironic detachment. The world he depicts is no longer made of black and white extremes, a realization that will ultimately lead to Nizan's defection from the Communist Party. His *Chronique de septembre* (1939) reveals Stalin's betrayal and Nizan's disillusionment with Communism, precipitated by the Nazi–Soviet treaty at the onset of World War II.

Two decades after his death, Nizan would once again become a figure of resistance in the 1960s and early 1970s when both *Aden-Arabie* and *Chiens de garde* were reissued. Jean-Paul Sartre's introduction to the 1960 reprinting of *Aden-Arabie* elevated Nizan's work to cult status in the 1960s. In a period troubled by the Algerian War and the collapse of the French colonial empire, Nizan's angry young man fuelled the imagination of the generation of May 1968 and still inspires that of the French leftist intellectual. That ef-

fect can be seen in, for example, Serge Halimi's *Les Nouveaux chiens de garde* (1997), which criticizes the media as forces of the establishment. Thus, Nizan's example continues to provide a viable and effective model for political engagement.

EDITH BENKOV

See also **Jean-Paul Sartre; Henri Lefebvre**

Biography

Paul Nizan was born February 7, 1905, in Tours. His father worked for the French national railroad. Nizan attended the Lycée Henri IV in Paris and became close friends with Jean-Paul Sartre in 1922. His first essays and poems were published in *Valeurs* and *Revue sans titre*, 1923–1924. Nizan enrolled in the ENS in 1924, left in 1926 for Aden, returned to ENS in 1929, and entered the Ecole Normale Supérieure that year. He taught philosophy in Bourg-en-Bresse, 1931–1932. Nizan was a member of Communist Party from 1927 to 1939 and a legislative candidate for the Communist Party in Ain in 1932. He spent a year in the Soviet Union with his wife in 1934. Nizan contributed over 100 articles of literary criticism for the major leftist and Communist newspapers and magazines, including *Monde, Vendredi, Europe, La Revue marxiste, Russie d'aujourd'hui, L'Humanité*, and *Ce Soir*, 1932–1939. His first literary success, *Aden-Arabie*, appeared in serial form in *Europe*. He was a political columnist for *L'Humanité*, 1935–1936, and head of international politics section of *Ce Soir*, 1937–1939. Nizan died at the Battle of Dunkerque on May 23, 1940.

Selected Works

Aden-Arabie, 1931; with a preface by Jean-Paul Sartre, 1960; as *Aden, Arabie*, translated by Joan Pinkham, 1968

Les Chiens de garde, 1932; as *The Watchdogs; Philosophers of the Established Order*, translated by Paul Fittingoff, 1971

Antoine Bloyé, 1933; as *Antoine Bloyé*, translated by Edmund Stevens, 1973

Le Cheval de Troie, 1935, as *Trojan Horse*, 1937

La Conspiration, 1938; as *The Conspiracy* translated by Quintin Hoare, 1988 *Chronique de septembre*, 1939

Complainte du carabin qui disséqua sa petite amie en fumant deux paquets de Maryland et Hécate ou la méprise sentimentale, 1982

Paul Nizan, intellectuel communiste. Articles et correspondance 1926–1940, edited by Jean-Jacques Brochier, 1967

Further Reading

Alluin, Bernard, and Deguy, Jacques, *Paul Nizan écrivain*, Presses universitaires de Lille, 1989

Arpin, Maurice, *La Fortune littéraire de Paul Nizan. Une analyse des deux réceptions critiques de son oeuvre*, Berne: Lang, 1995

Cohen-Solal, Annie, *Paul Nizan, communiste impossible*, with Henriette Nizan, Paris: Grasset, 1980

Ishaghpour, Youssef, *Paul Nizan. Une figure mythique et son temps*, Paris: Le Sycomore, 1980

Kershaw, Angela, "Gender, Sexuality, and Politics in Paul Nizan's *La Conspiration, Modern Language Review*, 98,1 (January 2003):27–43

King, Adèle, *Paul Nizan, écrivain*, Paris: Didier, 1976

Leiner, Jacqueline, *Le Destin littéraire de Paul Nizan et ses étapes successives. Contribution à l'étude du mouvement littéraire en France de 1920 à 1940*, Paris: Klincksieck, 1970

McCarthy, Patrick, "Sartre, Nizan and the Dilemmas of Political Commitment," *Yale French Studies*, 68 (1985):191–205

Ory, Pascal, *Paul Nizan. Destin d'un révolté*, Paris: Ramsay, 1980

Redfern, Walter David, *Paul Nizan. Committed Literature in a Conspiratorial World*. Princeton, New Jersey: Princeton University Press, 1972

Schalk, David L, "Professors as Watchdogs: Paul Nizan's Theory of the Intellectual and Politics," *Journal of the History of Ideas*, 34 (1973):79–96

Scriven, Michael, *Paul Nizan. Communist Novelist*, Houndsmills, Basingstoke, Hampshire and London: The MacMillan Press, 1988

Steel, James, *Paul Nizan un écrivain conformiste?* Paris: Presses de la fondation nationale des sciences politiques, 1987

Suleiman, Susan, *Paul Nizan: Pour une nouvelle culture*, 1971

P

PAULHAN, JEAN
Editor, Writer

Jean Paulhan was best known as the director of the *Nouvelle Revue Française* during its illustrious interwar years, a role that, along with his many editorial activities through which he encouraged and published the best of a generation of French writers, earned him the reputation as the *éminence grise* of modern French literature. The story of his contribution to contemporary French thought remains untold and difficult to assess, perhaps because of the sheer heterogeneity of his *oeuvre*, as well as the playful, elusive nature of his writings on the practice and theory of literature, what Henri Meschonnic termed, "an anti-theoretical theoretical writing." (*Le signe et le peène*, 1975) The direction of Paulhan's early thinking owed much to his father, Frédéric Paulhan, a well-known philosopher in France whose works were a blend of philosophy, linguistics, and the scientific psychology of the period. Paulhan studied literature and philosophy at the Sorbonne, during which time he made the acquaintance of the anarchist Jean Grave. He was also introduced to the Russian and Polish émigré community in Paris, where he met Sala Prusak, who would eventually become his first wife. The powerful attraction anarchism held for Paulhan would be evident later, reappearing in the book with which he is most strongly associated, *Les Fleurs de Tarbes* (The Flowers of Tarbes, 1941), under the guise of what he termed literary "Terror," or the endless necessity of writing against the literature and language of one's predecessors. Between 1908 and 1910, Paulhan went to Madagascar, where he taught at the island's first French high school. While there, he learned Malagasy and became fascinated by the function and inexplicable power of proverbial language. He wrote a number of essays on Malagasy proverbs, a linguistic phenomenon that was eventually transformed into Terror's opposite term in *Les Fleurs de Tarbes*, namely, "Rhetoric," or conventional language, commonplaces, and literary clichés.

Paulhan's ideas on language develop through his many short, occasional essays but also in his book reviews and the *chroniques* written in the Nouvelle Revue Française under the pseudonym Jean Guérin. His ideas are synthesized in *Les Fleurs de Tarbes*, which scans a truly encyclopedic and eclectic range of mostly French literary references. These are all invoked, however, to illustrate a deceptively simple thesis: the eternally recurring conflict between "terrorists" (those who see innovation as a rejection of preexisting models) and "rhetoricians" (those who believe creativity is only possible by working within the necessary limits of conventional forms). Even though the book is in some sense situated within the broader French intellectual context of the opposing ideological trends of abstract rationalism and a Durkheimian sacred violence, for Paulhan these are not distinctly contrasting positions, because when pushed to their limits, they turn out to be two sides of the same (literary and linguistic) coin. As he notes, it is ultimately impossible to determine whether a given word or expression is "original" or not.

This undecidable aspect at the heart of language, and Paulhan's focus on the rhetorical dimension of literature, have led to the view of his work as prefiguring literary critics such as Gérard Genette, Roland Barthes, Paul de Man, and Jacques Derrida. Paulhan shared with de Man a keen attention to the epistemological and ethical consequences of taking the rhetorical uncertainties of language and literature seriously and an understanding of the impossibility of apprehending the world with a nonlinguistic innocence. Where Paulhan diverged radically with de Man was in his unshakeable belief in the possibility of privileged moments of "sacred" experience, or of "mystery," what Maurice Blanchot, in talking of Paulhan, termed his "passion for the One."

Paulhan's interest in various mystical philosophies (Taoism, Buddhism, and Zen) grows increasingly apparent toward the end of his life, but one can in fact trace it back through all of his writing, in particular his short prose pieces, or *récits*, which are often autobiographical in origin and have as their setting his time in Madagascar and the First World War. If his theoretical texts are motivated by a patient and unremitting search for the "secret of language," his fictional texts usually end with a startling and paradoxical resolution. This takes the form of a sudden revelation, or shift in perspective, which is a reversal of the way things seemed up to that point. In *Progrès en amour assez lents* (Progress in Love on the Slow Side, 1968), for example, it is the narrator's failing, or inability to do the things he is supposed to do as a lover, that end up, to his surprise, being his most attractive quality. The reversal, or transformation, in which apparently opposite and antagonistic terms fuse together and are overtaken by the experience itself, is what Paulhan elsewhere describes as the "precise figure of mystery" (*Clef de la Poésie*, 1944). Once we can understand the subtle dynamics of his *récits*, this in turn illuminates the rhetoric of his essays, which can be read performatively as well as thematically. One of these, *Clef de la poésie* (Key to Poetry, 1944), is on one level an attempt to define a rigorous "law" that could apply to all poetic expression, but on another is a kind of parody of a logical argument that participates in the process it attempts objectively to describe. This has the consequence of undermining the very epistemological oppositions (true/false, subjectivity/objectivity, poetic language/rational language) it uses to construct its argument.

To attempt to fit Paulhan into any philosophical context, or to situate his writing within a historical progression of ideas, is thus a frustrating exercise. Although he was extremely well acquainted with the intellectual and political developments of his time, such as Saussurean linguistics, Freudian psychoanalysis, Marxism, German philosophy, ethnology, and phenomenology, he was as free-ranging and open-ended in his philosophical references (e.g., including Duns Scotus, Vailati, Lao-Tseu, and the ancient Greeks) as he was in his literary allusions. In fact, he often went against the grain of prevailing opinion or ideology with a certain calculated perversity, famously defending blacklisted collaborationist writers in the literary purge after the Second World War, when he had been one of the most prominent of *Résistants* during the war. As politically dubious as it may appear, Paulhan's polemic in fact argues passionately in favor of the need to respect democracy at a very fundamental level. Paulhan was also one of the champions of Cubist painting and of *informel* artists such as Fautrier and Dubuffet, publishing several books in this field. Modern art in many ways represented for him an aesthetic version, and an intensely successful one at that, of the immediacy and purity of expression he sought for so long in the literary and linguistic domain. Cubism and *papiers collés* in this sense served almost as artistic templates for him. The singular rearrangement of commonplace elements, and the exuberant painterly presence of a Braque or Picasso painting, for example, are analogous to the stylistic and intellectual uniqueness of Paulhan's own thinking and writing. Indeed, even though Paulhan was writing in the midst of the modernist revolution in art and literature, the ironic self-consciousness of his texts, and their performative reenactment of the rhetorical and intertextual dynamics they describe, place them more firmly in the postmodern era.

MICHAEL SYROTINSKI

See also **Roland Barthes; Maurice Blanchot; Jacques Derrida; Emile Durkheim; Ferdinand de Saussure**

Biography

Paulhan was born 1884 in Nîmes. He earned a degree in literature and philosophy at the Sorbonne in 1904. He taught at a French lycée in Madagascar, 1908–1910, and the following year (1911) taught Malagasy at the Ecole des Langues Orientales. That same year, he married Sala Prusak. Paulhan served in the French army, and was wounded in action in 1914. He became secretary of the *Nouvelle Revue Française* in 1920 and succeeded Jacques Rivière as chief editor in 1925. He left *NRF* in 1941, when it was taken over by Drieu la Rochelle. Paulhan received the Grand Prix de Littérature in 1945 and the Grand Prix de la Ville de Paris in 1951. He was the director of the relaunched *NNRF* from 1953 to 1963. Paulhan was elected to the Académie Française in 1965. He died in Neuilly on October 9, 1968.

Selected Writings

Les Hain-Tenys mérinas, 1911
Le Guerrier appliqué, 1917

Jacob Cow le pirate ou Si les mots sont des signes, 1921
Le Pont traversé, 1921; as *The Crossed Bridge*, translated by Christine Laennec and Michael Syrotinski, 1994
La Guérison sévère, 1925; as *The Severe Recovery*, translated by Christine Laennec and Michael Syrotinski, 1994
L'Expérience du proverbe, 1925
Entretien sur des faits divers, 1930
"Les Fleurs de Tarbes," serialized in *NRF*, 1936
La Rhétorique renaît de ses cendres, 1938
La Demoiselle aux miroirs, 1938
Les Fleurs de Tarbes, ou La Terreur dans les Lettres, 1941
Aytré qui perd l'habitude, 1943; as *Aytré Who Gets Out of the Habit*, translated by Christine Laennec and Michael Syrotinski, 1994
Clef de la poésie, 1944
Braque le patron, 1945
F.F. ou le critique, 1945
La Métromanie ou les dessous de la capitale, 1946
Guide d'un petit voyage en Suisse, 1947
A demain la poésie, 1947
De la paille et du grain, 1948
Fautrier l'enragé, 1949
Les Causes célèbres, 1950
Le marquis de Sade et sa complice, 1951
Petite préface à toute critique, 1951
Lettre aux directeurs de la Résistance, 1952
La preuve par l'étymologie, 1953
Du bonheur dans l'esclavage, 1961
Oeuvres complètes, 5 volumes, 1966–1970
Progrès en amour assez lents, 1968; as *Progress in Love on the Slow Side*, translated by Christine Laennec and Michael Syrotinski, 1994
Carnet du jeune homme, 1977
Le clair et l'obscur, 1983
Traité du ravissement, 1983
Essai d'introduction au projet d'une métrique universelle, 1984
Choix de lettres I: 1917–1936. La Littérature est une fête, 1986
Choix de lettres II: 1937–1945. Traité des jours sombres, 1992
Choix de lettres III: 1946–1968. Le Don des langues, 1996

Further Reading

Badré, Frédéric, *Paulhan le juste*, Paris: Grasset, 1996
Blanchot, Maurice, *Comment la littérature est-elle possible?* Paris: Corti, 1942
Dhôtel, André, *Jean Paulhan*, Lyon: La Manufacture, 1986
Dieudonné, Julien, *Les récits de Jean Paulhan*, Paris: Champion, 2001
Jean Paulhan: Cahier du centenaire (1884–1984), publié sous la direction d'Yvon Belaval, Paris: Gallimard, 1984.
Jean Paulhan le souterrain: Actes du colloque de Cerisy-la-Salle 1973, Direction et introduction par Jacques Bersani, Paris: 10/18, 1976.
Judrin, Roger, *La Vocation transparente de Jean Paulhan*, Paris: Gallimard, 1961
Lefebve, Maurice-Jean, *Jean Paulhan, une philosophie et une pratique de l'expression et de la réflexion*, Paris: Gallimard, 1949
Paulhan, Jean, *La Vie est pleine de choses redoutables: Textes autobiographiques*, edited and annotated by C.P. by Claire Paulhan, Paris: Seghers, 1989
Paulhan, Jean, *Progress in Love on the Slow Side*, Récits by Jean Paulhan, with an essay by Maurice Blanchot, translated by Christine Moneera Laennec and Michael Syrotinski, Lincoln: University of Nebraska Press, 1994
Paulhan, special issue of *L'Infini*, 55, Autumn 1996
Paulhan: Le Clair et l'obscur: proceedings of conference at Cerisy-la-Salle 1998, edited by Claude-Pierre Perez, Paris: Gallimard, 1999
Syrotinski, Michael, *Defying Gravity: Jean Paulhan's Interventions in Twentieth-Century French Intellectual History*, Albany: State University of New York Press, 1998

PHENOMENOLOGY

Edmund Husserl (1859–1938) is rightly recognized as the founder of phenomenology. Dermot Moran notes that phenomenology is, "a movement which, in many ways, typifies the course of European philosophy in the twentieth century . . . announced by Edmund Husserl in 1900–1901 as a bold, radically new way of doing philosophy." It sought "to bring philosophy back from abstract metaphysical speculation wrapped up in pseudo-problems, in order to come into contact with the matters themselves, with concrete living experience" (*Introduction to Phenomenology*, 2000, xiii). No area of human experience was to be excluded from phenomenological investigation, yet it was only in the late 1920s and early 1930s that Husserl and the phenomenological project became known in France, mainly through the work of Emmanuel Levinas, both as translator and commentator, and it was only in the 1950s that Husserl's main corpus became available in French translation. Spiegelberg notes that "[t]here can be little question that after the early thirties the centre of gravity of the Phenomenological movement has moved to the French Philosophical world" (*The Phenomenological Movement*, 1984, 425). Moran echoes this sentiment: "Phenomenology also translated into different philosophical climates, most notably in France, where Emmanuel Levinas began a tradition of exploration of phenomenology" (Moran, 2000, xiv). Significant figures in this French "tradition" would be Emmanuel Levinas, Gabriel Marcel, Jean-Paul Sartre, Maurice Merleau-Ponty, and Paul Ricoeur. Jacques Derrida might also be considered an interlocutor. Yet phenomenology in France has not remained a self-contained and isolated discipline, but has become a dialogical partner (at times obscured) with other trends in French philosophy, not least Marxist critiques, literary theory, deconstruction, feminist thought, and perhaps most recently, religion.

Perhaps phenomenology in France can best be distinguished by its particular style and concern. Its style tends to reflect the literary and cultural milieu of French writing; in contrast to the apparently more scientifically rigorous style of German phenomenologists, French phenomenology tends to be more narrative and discursive. Consider, for example, how Marcel and Sartre develop their ideas not only through the medium of plays and novels; the "metaphysical novel" and the "theatre of ideas" are brought together. This makes phenomenology in its French expression both more accessible to the reader and more nuanced and evasive, as, in its existential focus, it would seem to make it less rigorous in its expression. Human existence, as embodied, affective, social, and cultural, tends to subvert and surprise a phenomenology inclined solely toward scientific rigor.

Husserl's Phenomenology, and Its Significance in France

Husserl, following Brentano, laid stress on the "intentional inexistence" of objects. The object appearing in consciousness—the phenomenal object—is the real object. Phenomenology sought to give a critical and scientifically rigorous account of mode and the meaning of the object appearing in consciousness. Husserl's key works are *Logical Investigations* (1900–1901), *Ideas for a Pure Phenomenology and Phenomenological Philosophy* (1913), *Introduction to the Phenomenology of Internal Time-Consciousness* (1928), and *Méditations Cartésiennes* (first published in French in 1931), an extended version of Husserl's lectures delivered in Paris in 1929, and translated and coedited by Levinas, whose own doctoral study on *The Theory of Intuition in Husserl's Phenomenology* had been published "in French" in 1930.

The sciences, for Husserl, seemed to display a rigor in the pursuit of certainty, but remained in themselves uncritical and unfounded. The evidence that they offer is circumscribed by the confines of their own particular discipline. Sciences such as physics, biology, and psychology "make use of a certain number of fundamental notions whose meaning the sciences themselves do not clarify—for example, memory, perception, space, time, etc. . . . [yet] . . . [t]hese notions determine the necessary structure of different domains of being and constitute their essence" (Levinas, 1995, 3). Husserl's phenomenological project is to contest the "natural" attitude that the sciences betray by developing a phenomenological method that gives foundation to all other methods. The "world of the sciences"—what Husserl calls "regional ontologies"—are founded on more basic notions that need to be exposed through a phenomenological reflection and reduction.

What then are the key themes in Husserlian phenomenology, particularly with regard to its French development?

First, the "natural attitude" and the "phenomenological attitude"; the natural attitude is inadequate to the reality of the perceived object. Perception does not embrace the object in its entirety. For example, the arborologist may look at the cherry tree that blooms each spring in my garden and assign it its place in the arboretum, and in the "world of trees" that arborologists inhabit, the forester may look on it and perceive it as being out of place in his managed forest, the gardener may view the tree as a focal point of the garden, the cabinetmaker may view it as useful in his craft of cabinetmaking, and for me the cherry tree is a delight to look at and may conjure up Chekhov and his world. Whose tree is the tree in my garden? The "fact" is that the reality of the tree correlates with my apperception of it. Consciousness is meaning-bestowing, and the bestowing of this meaning gives access to the object of intended. The natural attitude is inadequate to its object. What is required is a phenomenological attitude.

What Husserl contests here is a Cartesian dualism that would separate the known object from the knowing subject and the consequent epistemological and ontological dilemma of the adequation of knowing and known. Because the phenomenal object is the real object, the question of its independent ontological status will need to be "bracketed" in a "pheomenological epoché." The Cartesian dimension is significant for the reception of Husserl's phenomenology in France. For example, Léon Brunschvicg, writing in the 1920s and 1930s, portrayed a Cartesian understanding of consciousness. Husserl's *Paris Lectures* had taken Descartes's "Meditations" as a point of departure.

Second, there is the notion of intentionality. Consciousness is always a consciousness of something. It intends or directs itself to particular objects and directs itself in various ways, whether as perceiving, remembering, desiring, and so forth. In the terminology of Husserl's *Ideas*, every *noesis* (act of consciousness) has a corresponding *noema* (object of consciousness), both of which are correlated. Thus, "every perception is a perception of the perceived, every idea an idea of an ideate, every desire a desire of a desired, every emotion an emotion of something moving" (Levinas, 1979, 122). These various ways of intending an object presume, according to Husserl, thought's ability, in the midst of a manifold of possible meanings, to reduce the "idea" of the object, or to pursue an "eidetic reduction." Thus, despite the many possible apperceptions of the cherry tree that blooms in the garden, consciousness is able to abstract a core idea: I have the essential idea of a tree, the meaning of which can be multiple and diverse.

Implicated in this notion of perception as always "perception of an object as" is the absolute existence of consciousness, or "the transcendental ego." Indeed, Levinas will note that "attributing absolute existence to concrete conscious life" and transforming its very notion is "the fundamental intuition of Husserlian philosophy" (1995, 25). Consciousness is not dependent on, nor does it approximate to, the external world;

rather, "the world of transcendent *res* necessarily depends on [*ist angewiesen an*] consciousness" (Husserl, *Ideen*, 49).

Third, the question of the adequacy of evidence: Husserl's complaint against the sciences had been that the evidence they offered was prejudiced, partial, uncritical, and unfounded. Perception, at any given moment, cannot embrace its object in a comprehensive gaze. It presumes other aspects or perspectives, the evidence for which can only be fulfilled, for example, by my walking around the tree. Robert Sokolowski's example of a "cube" is helpful. From one aspect, a cube presents itself as a two-dimensional square, from another aspect as a pyramid viewed from above. The perception of a cube as a cube is a complex process, which implies not only the ability of consciousness to link together its various perspectives but also to retain these through time (Sokolowski, 2000). Said otherwise, intentions are both empty and fulfilled, and evidence is both adequate and inadequate. Empty intentions await fulfillment, and evidence tends toward ever-greater adequacy. "The aspects which we see at any given moment always indicate further aspects, and so on. Things are never known in their totality; an essential character of our perception of them is that of being inadequate" (Levinas, 1995, 21–22).

Fourth, not only is the evidence represented in consciousness inadequate, perception as representation itself is also inadequate. At any given moment, perception does not embrace the object in its entirety, nor is the object adequately embraced by perception alone. French phenomenologists tend to focus on the inadequacy of representational consciousness as giving access to an object. Husserl himself had acknowledged that consciousness was concrete. Although transcendental, it was nonetheless consciousness of a world, and implicated engagement with a world. "While asserting the primacy of theory for Husserl . . . his essential thesis consists in locating being in concrete life. This is why practical and aesthetic life also have an intentional character and the objects constituted by them also belong to the sphere of being" (Levinas, 1995, 158). Nonetheless, Husserl's phenomenology, in its French development, would be recognized as being overly theoretical, privileging consciousness as representation, failing to address adequately concrete lived experience in its historical, sociocultural, and intersubjective situation. It is this lacuna that will become the main point of criticism of Husserl by his French followers, and it is also the void that they will seek to fill.

A fifth area merits mention: the phenomenology of internal time consciousness. Intentional objects are not only extended in space, like the cube, but also in time. In 1905, Husserl delivered a series of lectures on "The

Phenomenology of Internal Time Consciousness," which Heidegger prepared for publication in 1928. Consciousness has not only a retentive phase whereby each successive event flows from a previous event but also a protensive aspect. For example, in a musical composition, no individual note (or period of rest, for that matter) stands in isolation; the present moment in the work builds on, and retains, past notes, phrases, and structure. For example, take the structure of a fugue: the recurrent, and at times reversed, fugal themes depend for their effect on the ability of consciousness to retain the past in order that the present might have the significance that it has. So too, each moment in the piece is going somewhere; it is not only retentive but protensive. In listening to the fugue piece, what comes next is anticipated (often according to the rules and grammar of an established musical canon). This protensive element is most often overlooked, but it is thrown into relief when the music diverges from, and refuses, an anticipated resolution. As Bergson would argue in *Le Temps vécu* (1933), and Husserl would attempt to account for phenomenologically, time is duration.

The Reception and Development of Phenomenology in France

Spiegelberg identifies two phases of French phenomenology, "a mainly receptive period," involving such as Levinas and Gabriel Marcel and his *Metaphysics Journal* (1927), and a "predominantly productive phase." Sartre's *Transcendence of the Ego* (1936–1937), perhaps the first properly phenomenological work in France, marks the crossover. Sartre acknowledges his indebtedness to Levinas for his exposure to phenomenology. He had discussed Husserl and German phenomenology with Raymond Aron and realized that phenomenology offered a way of overcoming the opposition between idealism and realism, of being able to bring together philosophy and lived experience, of connecting consciousness and the world as we find it. Having read Levinas's study on Husserl, Sartre began his own phenomenological writings. In *The Transcendence of the Ego*, he contests the notion of a transcendental ego. Consciousness of the self is only ever given with consciousness of a world: "consciousness is purely and simply consciousness of being conscious of that object" (Sartre, 1936–1937, 90). Sartre's phenomenological writings continued with *L'Imagination* (1936), *L'Imaginaire* (1940), and *L'Étre et le Néant* (1943), perhaps reflecting the influence of Heidegger's *Sein und Zeit* (1927)—originally dedicated to Husserl, though the dedication was subsequently removed following Heidegger's turning to National Socialism—and translated into French in 1938 by H. Corbin. Corbin's translation is significant not only for its effect on French phenomenology and the existential force it gives to phenomenology, but also for subsequent reception of key phenomenological and existential terms in the English-reading world. Thus, for example, *Dasein* becomes *réalité humaine*, and *Eigentlich* becomes *authenticité*, which becomes in English "authenticity."

The Productive Phase of Phenomenology in France

The existence of the human person in the world was indicated as the characteristic and diverse concern of phenomenology in France; thus the emphasis on role of the body, affectivity, the social world, culture, intersubjectivity, and ethics. Husserl's phenomenological enterprise had given emphasis to the theoretical and the cognitive. Representation was the decisive notion. French phenomenologists both acknowledged and took distance from this, recognizing that phenomenological access to reality was not limited to the theoretical and the cognitive. The life-world in which the conscious subject *lived* was an existential world, and implicated in this existential was history, culture, and the fact of other people. In addition, consciousness was also embodied.

Thus, with regard to the body, we find Sartre beginning to address the phenomenological significance of the body in *Being and Nothingness*. Consciousness is not disembodied: the body is not something apart from me. I am my body. Merleau-Ponty will take up and develop this theme in *The Phenomenology of Perception* (1945). Before ever we begin to perceive things, we are already in the world. The body is the condition of the epistemic, or knowing, subject. We are "body-subjects," and it is as "body-subjects" that we encounter and interact with the world in a meaningful way. The "body-subject" is a precondition of perception. For example, although perception is always perception of an object, the ability to gain a perceptual perspective on an object presupposes the ability to shift perspective, and the ability to shift perspective presupposes the ability to move around. This emphasis on the body as a center of meaning marks a move away from the Cartesianism that, paradoxically, might be considered one of the factors that contributed to Husserl's reception in France.

With its interest in the embodiment of the subject, phenomenology finds significant points of encounter with other strands of French philosophical thought. The embodied subject is a social construct. The body becomes the site of pleasure and pain. Thus, in Michel Foucault's archaeological and genealogical analysis of the body in *History of Sexuality*, as also in feminist critiques such as those of Luce Irigaray and her interlocution with Lacan, phenomenology and wider interests meet.

The emphasis on a body-subject, or an embodied consciousness, further opens on to the stress on affectivity and aesthetics and the cultural environment. In his study on Husserl's theory of intuition, Levinas had drawn attention to the strictures of Husserl's overly theoretical and cognitional approach. Ricoeur, for his part, draws attention to the hermeneutical task: existence comes to expression, meaning, and reflection only through interpreting the various objectified significations that arise in the social, institutional, and cultural environment in which it finds itself. One comes to one's self through the appropriation of meanings that precede the subject. The body, too, becomes the locus of intersubjectivity and sociality, in which are implicated politics, justice, and sexuality. Life in the world is not solitary. There are others also, with whom a world of meaning and culture are constructed, a world in which phenomenology opens on to the social, the cultural, and the ethical.

However, the rejection of Husserl's transcendental ego, first seen in Sartre, has the wider consequence of placing in question the subject itself. Not only is the embodied subject a social construct in need of deconstruction, but it is on the verge of oblivion. This can be seen in especially in literary theorists and in the debate regarding the relationship between text, author, and reader. Sean Burke rightly notes that the death and absence of the author in French literary theory "is inseparable from the massive reaction in France to the resuscitation of the Cartesian cogito in Husserlian phenomenology" (Burke, 1992, 163). Thus Foucault can write of Maurice Blanchot that, "So far has he withdrawn into the manifestations of his work . . . [that he is] . . . not hidden by his texts, but absent from their existence" (Foucault, *Maurice Blanchot*, 1990, 19). The author remains "outside" and absent. His or her mind and intention is hidden and inscrutable. All that is available, as Derrida will say, is the text: "there is nothing outside the text of grammatology, 158." The primacy of the text, and the question of both the reader-critic and the author's relation to it, remains an area of philosophical reflection and debate.

This is seen no more so than in the characteristic interest in the nature and structure of language displayed by the Geneva School, with whom the names of Jean Starobinski, Jeanne-Pierre Richard, George Poulet, and Jean Rousset are associated, but whose influence can be said to extend to such as de Saussure, Lévi-Strauss, Barth, Althusser, Lacan, Foucault, and Derrida. The author-subject and the reader-subject, which are in danger of deconstruction and disappearance, return and find a point of encounter in the text.

Literary criticism opens onto a phenomenology of reading. J. Hillis Miller comments that criticism, "has a beginning and an end in the coincidence of the mind of the critic and the mind of the author" (*The Geneva School*, 1966, 468–69). George Poulet will stress, again with phenomenological significance, the affective reader response that the text will evoke and the mutually constructive interaction of critic and text. The text critiques the reader, who, in his critical reading, gives the text new meaning and life. Similar to Penelope's work, there is a constant weaving, unpicking, and reweaving.

Derrida perhaps marks the current state of development of phenomenology in its French guise in its interaction with other strands of thinking, whether literary and textual, ethical, social, or religious. Phenomenology in France is part of a complex process of thinking and rethinking that, continues its attempt at an adequate account of lived human experience.

MICHAEL PURCELL

See also **Louis Althusser; Raymond Aron; Maurice Blanchot; Leon Brunschvicg; Jacques Derrida; Michel Foucault; Jacques Lacan; Claude Levi-Strauss; Emmanuel Levinas; Gabriel Marcel; Maurice Merleau-Ponty; George Poulet; Paul Ricoeur; Jean-Paul Sartre; Ferdinand de Saussure**

Further Reading

Bernet, R., Kern, I., and Marbach, E., *An Introduction to Husserlian Phenomenology*, Evanston, IL: Northwestern University Press, 1999

Burke, S., *The Death and Return of the Author*, Edinburgh: Edinburgh University Press, 1992

Derrida, J., *Of Grammatology*, Baltimore: Johns Hopkins University Press, 1976

Foucault, M., *History of Sexuality (3 vols)*, Harmondsworth: Penguin, 1988, 1990, 1998

Foucault, M., *Maurice Blanchot*, New York: Zone Books, 1990

Heidegger, M., *Being and Time*, Oxford: Blackwell, 2000; (German original, 1927; French translation (Corbin), 1938)

Husserl, E., *Logical Investigations*, London: Routledge, 2001

Husserl, E., *Ideas*, London: Routledge, 2002

Levinas, E., *The Theory of Intuition in Husserl's Phenomenology*, Evanston, IL: Northwestern University Press, 1995, (French original, 1930)

Levinas, E., *Discovering Existence with Husserl*, Evanston, IL: Northwestern University Press, 1998

Levinas, E., *Totality and Infinity*, The Hague: M., Nijhoff, 1979

Merleau-Ponty, M., *Phenomenology of Perception*, London: Routledge, 2002

Miller, J. H., *Geneva School*, Virginia Quarterly Review, 1967, 465–68

Moran, Dermot, *Introduction to Phemenology*, London: Routledge, 2000

Poulet, G. *The Phenomenology of Reading* in Adams, H., *Critical Theory*, New York: Harcourt, 1971

Sartre, J-P., *Transcendence of the Ego*, New York: Noon Day, 1970

Sokolowski, Robert, *Introduction to Phenomenology*, Cambridge: Cambridge University Press, 2000

Spiegelberg, Herbert, *The Phenomenological Movement*, The Hague: M., Nijhoff, 1984

PHILOSOPHY

French philosopher Henri Bergson stated in *La Philosophie française:* "France's role in modern philosophy is quite clear: France has been the great initiator. Elsewhere, no doubt, great philosophers have emerged, but nowhere has there been as in France an uninterrupted continuity of original philosophical innovation." (Bergson 1915, 236) Other philosophers might take issue with Bergson's claims, as indeed with his statement that "all modern philosophy is derived from Descartes." His panoramic view of French philosophy provides nonetheless a model for appraisal of philosophy in the French sphere, in terms of the extent to which it may be said to have achieved these aims.

The precise extension of the term "philosophy" is not less problematic than that of the term "French": there is no uncontroversial definition of the set "French Philosophy." Certain highly original French thinkers such as Bourdieu are sometimes included, sometimes excluded. French philosophy and literature are often connected: the impossibility of entirely separating thought from its language medium is evident in earlier cases such as Montaigne (1990, 1595) and Montesquieu (1995 [1758]), and no less so for Bourdieu (1986) or Cixous (1994). The epistemological approach to literary theory of Antoine Compagnon (1998) is essentially philosophical in its use of Aristotelian and Platonic categories. Philosophy was traditionally transnational: If Abelard's place in French philosophy is clear, how can the importance of Aquinas's teaching in Paris to medieval philosophy be set aside, and if Aquinas, why not Albertus Magnus, who taught him? In more recent times, one of the effects of the 1968 cultural revolution on subsequent thought is the emergence, or reemergence, of a common metalanguage for such disciplines as philosophy, anthropology, feminism, literature, linguistics, psychoanalysis, sociology, theory of culture, and theory of theory (see Starr, 1995). The attempts of Sartre (Sartre, 1943, see also Anderson, 1993), Camus (1946, 1946, 1957), or Derrida to renew the central questions (What? How can I know? What is I?) in a world in which traditional belief systems have proved inadequate, constitute the thought-event that defines the philosophical process.

The interpenetration of contemporary epistemological systems is a paradigm for the essentially universal characteristic of the philosophical frame of reference, which not only predates but would tend to critique and undermine modern notions of national–cultural boundaries. One statement that may safely be made, bearing out Bergson's point, is that it is most unlikely that French philosophers have ever seen themselves as doing French philosophy but, rather, as doing philosophy. Further, philosophy as a profession has not been as split in France from philosophy as a way of living, as might be the case elsewhere. This is still evidenced by, and in part to the result of, the teaching of philosophy in second-level education and the continued existence of the dissemination of philosophical ideas to the general (ideally, universally educated) public by, for example, the *nouveaux philosophes* in the 1970s, André Comte-Sponville (1995), and even, at another level, the fashionable *cafés philosophiques* or the televised debates of Bernard Pivot. These practitioners see themselves as a defense against *inculture* or the new barbarism (Glucksmann 1977; Lévy 1977, 1987), and might well claim descent from the Encyclopédistes, who addressed themselves to an educated public rather than to each other. Any effort to impose external categories on French philosophy or to try to divorce it from its inseparables, language, literature, and the human sciences, and the general *imaginaire*, must result in a reductive view.

The profession of philosopher in France is articulated around such processes as the all-important *agrégation de philosophie*, teaching at second-level and in the Universities or the parallel *grandes écoles*; mediatization to the general public; participation or not in a *maître-élève*-type structure of professional mentoring; being read mainly in France or mainly elsewhere. These are some of the specificities of philosophy's embedding in French-speaking culture: They sometimes lead to writers, whose thought might be seen as distinctively French and original, being recategorized by foreigners as not "really French," or not "really philosophers," or not uninfluenced by their predecessors elsewhere, as if to put an intellectual *cordon sanitaire* around the domain. As A. Phillips Griffiths says in his excellent *Contemporary French Philosophy*, nothing can be representative of contemporary French Philosophy except French Philosophy itself. Even modernity is not a simple category: Lamarckism, out of favor as Darwinism gained acceptance, has regained a certain level of relevance to new studies of memetics, and medieval philosophy has regained a level of interest that could not be reflected in Bergson's panorama. This article will examine some possible conceptual or methodological specificities, some salient personalities, some important moments of philosophy in France or in French.

Bergson cited three aspects of philosophy in France as being characteristic. The first is *la simplicité de la forme*, or clear and simple language; the second is his idea that philosophy in France has tended to be closely linked to science (in the wider French extension of the term, knowledgeable investigation), and the third, *le goût des philosophes français pour la psychologie, leur penchant à l'observation intérieure* or their taste for psychology, their tendency toward interior observation.

Aspect 1: A Clear and Simple Language

The first idea may amaze readers of Lacan, Derrida, or Cixous. Some of the problem of the cultural transfer of French theoretical writing lies in the inevitable limits of the translation process: Because a text is read in context, there is a sense in which a French philosopher, once translated, "becomes" an Anglograph philosopher and may appear puzzling, especially in the modern era when absolute belief in essential meanings is no longer tenable, or even be absorbed into the target tradition, imperceptibly changing meaning (Ryan 2003). Bergson's point, however, related to the public addressed, rather than the style of philosophical writing (though French philosophers tend to give exceptional attention to style): "there is no philosophical idea, however profound or subtle, which may not and ought not be expressed in the language of all. French philosophers do not write for a limited circle of initiates, but for all humanity." What is foregrounded here is a general preoccupation with language as the stuff of philosophy. Many writers have philosophized in a variety of textual forms: in the case of Hélène Cixous, this variable geometry of expression is a vital function of her project.

Gaston Bachelard famously wrote *Ecrire c'est se cacher* (writing is hiding oneself). Many of Bachelard's works studied the metaphoric way in which language expressed thought, using the archetypal and universal metaphoric and metonymic chains of air, water, fire, or dreams. In thus analyzing the processes of the human mind, he emphasized the centrality of affectivity in engaging even with apparently "objective" concepts. Perception of the phenomenological was prescientific and imaginary before becoming systematized at more conscious levels. This idea bears on certain modern theories of cognition, such as Morin's *pensée complexe* and Grice's implicature.

Ferdinand de Saussure's (1857–1913) legacy to philosophy lies in his rethinking of the relationship between language and meaning. Post-Saussurians are interested in the interrelationship between units and the rules by which units can be put together. Meanings can vary widely, but only those meanings that are agreed on and sanctioned within a particular language will appear to name reality. These relations are mainly relations of difference. This conceptualization of the function of language has been important for later philosophies of difference.

Maurice Merleau-Ponty, similar to Husserl, emphasized the importance of the phenomenological reduction, or *epochè*, that opens access to the immanent "essences" of the consciousness of *vécu*, or "lived experience." This does not deny the natural world but emphasizes consciousness and embodied experience, which is what perception is. The perceiving subject is always changing: there is no subject in general. Merleau-Ponty opposed Descartes's *cogito*: "I perceive" is not "I think" and is not universal. Merleau-Ponty's attention to language and reading of Saussure inspired early structuralism: He highlighted two Saussurian principles, that meaning in language arises through a diacritical relationship between signs, and that a diachronic study of language cannot explain usage. However, *langue* is the system that enables *parole* or speech, and in focusing on the level of *parole* as embodied language, phenomenology has found it difficult to cope with the general problem of otherness. Having rejected the unconscious, phenomenology treats every subjective instance as present to itself.

Roland Barthes, whose theory related primarily to the literary text, articulated the "death of the author" theory, which has been more comfortably received by literary critics (who saw it a liberating) than it might be by philosophers, who have nonetheless been influenced by Barthes's analysis in addressing the predicament of the writing subject.

Algirdas Julien Greimas was born in Lithuania and settled in France. His first works (Greimas 1966, 1970) were influenced by Propp's investigation of stories and by structural linguistics. He proposed a "modèle actanciel" used in *Maupassant, la Sémiotique du texte* (1976). Borrowing from Propp the concept of "actants," he saw them as syntactic functions (*sujet, objet, destinateur, destinataire, opposant, adjuvant*). He studied the shifts in the logical structure underlying the syntagmatic dimensionality of narrative. In *Sémiotique des passions* (1991), he applied semiology to passions: this work has been compared to Barthes's *Fragments d'un discours amoureux*.

Claude Lévi-Strauss's contribution to thought lies principally in his structural analysis of myths (*La Pensée sauvage*) and of behavior codes (*Le Cru et le cuit*) as well as social structures themselves (*Anthropologie structurale*) as systems of signs.

When Pierre Bourdieu argued (Bourdieu 1986), albeit in very long sentences, that the discourse of authority derives that authority not from any inherent qualities, but from the belief the audience invests in the speaker, he is not honing elaborate tools of philosophy on examples too minute to matter to people; he is, on the contrary, seeking to engage public consciousness on vital issues of the public space. His syntax is complex, but decodable to the patient reader. Masculine domination is seen by Bourdieu (2000) as still so profoundly anchored in our unconscious that we do not see it. It is more necessary that ever to examine the symbolic structures of the androcentric unconscious that survives in men and women. Bourdieu also analyzes the *habitus*, or power-invested behavior and language systems of different power groups in society (Bourdieu, 1996), and explores the fundamental relationship between language and power (Bourdieu, 1986) His thinking owes a debt to structuralism, in the way it decoupled language and essential meaning, opening the space in which the arbitrary, political, poetic, or other imbrications of language and meaning might be articulated in creative expression and unpacked by self-aware readers.

Hélène Cixous grew up in the background of French-colonial Algeria and in the cultural space of an Austro-German Sephardic Jewishness and the persecutions of World War II. Cixous is preoccupied with power and justice at all levels. She strives to locate the origins of repression and the articulation of exclusion. A seminal text, *La Jeune née* (Cixous, 1975, translated as *The Newly Born Woman*, 1986), explores in a poetic form the egregious trend of human discourse to binary oppositions, which distort our view of the dual, for example, humanity as women and men, and end always in a construction of opposition and hierarchy. The fundamental underlying opposition is always man/women, with man somehow on top. This is a highly original construal: It points to the significance of how humanity, though dual from its earliest existence, has apparently no concept of "more than one-ness" that is not instantly hierarchized. Her reading of Joyce and Shakespeare, and indeed the extraordinary range of her reading and her sensitivity to nuances of discourse, gives her writing an exceptional referentiality that repays close and patient reading. It is at once poetic and reflective, moving seamlessly between creative expression and philosophical thought and theory. She has played a part in a renewal of the academic space, with her role in founding the experimental Université de Paris VIII-Vincennes-Saint Denis; the Centre de Recherches en Etudes Féminines, which she chairs; and the review *Poétique*, which she founded with Tzvetan Todorov and Gérard Genette. She has published over fifty novels and plays, as well as theoretical essays. Her writing always involves issues of liberation in the personal and the collective, and her association with the woman's cause, the Third World (expressed in her interest in Clarice Lispector and Nelson Mandela and her plays on Cambodia or India), German and Russian death camps (in Paul Celan, Ossip Mandelstam, Marina Tsvetayeva, and

Anna Akhmatova), the philosophical texts of Jacques Derrida, and her encounters with Antoinette Fouque and Ariane Mnouchkine, with whom Cixous collaborates. Her writing positions itself as a kind of renewed cosmography, or originating scripture, a source for the renewal of life. She expresses the need for a feminine, and in some cases maternal, economy, one based on the gift, a new form of exchange between the self and the other. *Ecriture féminine* is the idea of such an economy in linguistic exchange—without which there can be no social change.

Jacques Derrida, influenced by Husserlian phenomenology, published a translation of Husserl's *The Origin of Geometry* in 1962. Derrida's writing focuses on the relation between philosophy and language, and his concept of deconstruction aims to unmask and overcome hidden conceptual or theoretical privilege in text. Key concepts used in texts suppress an opposite concept that they presuppose. Reason, the transcendent, the male, and the sacred are linked to and presuppose passion, the empirical, the female, and the profane, although without the latter the former do not make sense. Priority genuinely rests with the suppressed concept, as it is presupposed to the privileged one. Thus, the primacy of a concept is undermined, or privilege is replaced by equality at a later stage, where the conflicting claims to privileged status are resolved by a new concept that can incorporate the two former opposites.

Working on the concept of *différance*, Deleuze and Derrida (drawing on Nietzsche, Heidegger, and Freud) have sought to displace the traditional metaphysics of identity in favor of a metaphysics of difference. Derrida argues that a conception of the world in which difference is the primary term requires not only that we reconceptualize identity and similarity as secondary notions but that the difference in identity itself must be reconfigured. Because *différance* refers to the quasi-transcendental conditions of consciousness, conceptuality, or linguistic meaning as such, Derrida insists that it is neither a word nor a concept nor any kind of being in the traditional sense. It is his avowedly paradoxical name for the primordial movement or "play" of being that gives rise to differences. *Différance* may be translated in various ways: *deferment, deference, deferral* (Lyotard's *différend* is a related though distinct concept). *Différance* is that which constitutes signs as signs because signs are not that to which they refer. They differ, opening a space from that which they represent, and they defer, opening up a temporal chain; following Sassure's argument, signs "mean" by differing from other signs. The coinage "différance" refers at once to the differing and the deferring of signs. At an ontological level, the differing and deferring of signs from what they mean means

that every sign repeats the creation of space and time; that *différance* is the ultimate phenomenon in the universe, both active and passive, that which enables and results from Being itself.

Jean Baudrillard engages with all forms of cultural production: He is the semiologist of postmodernity, of the proliferation of images and the delirium of communication. His exporting of theory into the world of images and plastic forms has gone beyond accounting for artistic expression to influence its practice. His reflections on the paradoxes of communication, the power of the media, terrorism, consumerism, and the death of politics are seen almost as prophetic by his most assiduous readers, as if reality were a metonymy of his theoretical vision. He quotes Michaux in *le Crime parfait* (Baudrillard) "the artist is the person who resists at all costs the elemental desire to leave without a trace."

Aspect 2: A Link to Science

Bergson's second idea is that philosophy in France has tended to be linked to other aspects of knowledge, specifically what he calls positive science: "Philosophy in France has always been closely linked to positive science. Elsewhere . . . the two talents or habits of mind have come together only in exceptional cases. . . . French philosophy, however, has positioned itself in an essential relationship to science." Both the term "positive science" and its reception have shifted ground significantly since Bergson's time; his point remains relevant, however, from two points of view. First, most French philosophers have continued to link their philosophical thinking to other aspects of knowledge, in a kind of collective neo-Aristotelianism: philosophy of science, with Le Doeuff; literature and creative expression, as in the case of Bachelard, Sartre, Camus, and Barthes; linguistics and derived methods of formal analysis, as with Derrida, Lévi-Strauss, Saussure, Greimas, and Bourdieu; political issues, including freedom, women's condition, and body politics, as with de Beauvoir, Irigaray, Cixous, Kristeva, Foucault, Bataille, Levinas, Lyotard, and Althusser; the management and mediation of human relations, as with Lacan, Deleuze, and Guattari; and in the tradition of the spiritual in French philosophy, Teilhard de Chardin, Weil, and Ricoeur.

Second, there is the effect on French thought of the political, racial, and class conflicts of the twentieth century, particularly those conflicts that led to and derived from the two great wars. The history of the influence of those periods on the ethics and politics of sociology, medicine, education, gender, and ethnic issues has only begun to be written; it may not yet be possible fully to address all the issues engaged. The aftermath of World War II and the mediatization of the worst horrors of oppressive social engineering (in more European countries than one might think) was the period of a total change in thinking about human rights, the rights of the mentally ill, and of different ethnic or religious groups, as well as of women. Sartre, Beauvoir, Camus, Foucault, Lévinas, Deleuze, and Cixous are examples of thinkers profoundly influential in reflection on the ontology and epistemology of freedom, having in different ways encountered the limits and paradoxes of ethical systems that might heretofore have seemed, in hindsight, relatively comfortable to the *vécu* or lived reality of most philosophers, by definition educated and privileged people.

Reflection on freedom, not only its nature but how it is to be maintained and constructed for a global humanity—one that can see the consequences of its actions in the immediacy of modern telecommunications—is by no means confined to twentieth-century French philosophers. At the same time, France's experiences of their relativities of oppression and freedom, their causes and consequences, have been unique in certain crucial respects, and this might explain Gutting's statement that "The concern with individual freedom as a concrete, lived reality has, more than anything else, maintained the distinctiveness of French philosophy throughout the century" (Gutting, 380). The lived experience and the complex ethics of combat or noncombat; of occupation and its varied narratives of guilt and responsibility; of liberation and postwar rhetorics of justice and right; of suffering, exclusion, survivor guilt; these issues are present in the French imaginary as in personal and inherited narratives. Many have yet, if ever, to be related, and affect French thought in many spheres. The simple human-rights model of post–World War II received narratives is adequate to account neither for the unimaginable experiences of the individuals, nor for the reductive interpretation of French mentalities in relation to present-day world issues. The attempts by Sartre to construct a post-humanist ethics as suggested in *L'Etre et le néant* (Sartre, 1943) or Camus's representations of flawed heroes (Camus, 1948, 1954) attempting to live some kind of situated ethics within human systems disillusioned about the possibility of Enlightenment universal justice, provide foreground for a crucial fact: The ethical systems by which we judge cultural narratives are themselves originally cultural narratives.

For Jean-Paul Sartre, existentialism, embracing among other things a theory of the self, and ethics, are driven by a preoccupation with freedom and agency. Systems of essential belief having failed, the individual is an isolated island of subjectivity: that being the case, what are we to value and what is to value us? Our value can only be internal. We are radically free, and we create our nature and our value through the choices we make. No doubt the period fostered the sensibility that the world was indifferent, giving the existential condition its characteristics of anxiety, despair, and uncertainty in the absence of reliable human systems. However, existentialism is not determined merely by the despair associated with conflict and loss of faith in belief-systems: We are more than our external determining forces, and we can make of ourselves what we will. The values we construct for ourselves cannot be overthrown by others, so long as we act with what Sartre calls "good faith," avoiding acting with *mau vaise foi*. To be free, we must respect the freedom of others. In Sartre's creative writing, it may be noted that human psychology comes into play in a rather less arbitrary, but more entropically, determined sum of forces than this ethical system would suggest. Unconscious, tribal, and other archaic impulses are best mediated—if at all—through the acceptance, more or less, of some form of value-ethics. At the same time, the ethical issues, for example, those to do with France's involvement in World War II and its occupation, are perhaps more starkly polarized than in reality. Sartre attempts to articulate freedom as the fundamental truth of human existence, consciousness acting from inside and not from external determinations. This ought not mean too wide a scope for random action, because we act from a fundamental project that we create in our choices, and in a situation wherein we encounter obstacles or resistances. Sartre later attributed his statement, "whatever the circumstances, and whatever the site, a man is always free to choose to be a traitor or not," to his experiences of the war. As Gary Gutting says, "Sartre's experiential examples expand from the hyper-individuality projected onto is objects by the *flâneur* disinterestedly observing café life, to the commitment of a situated agent struggling with the natural and historical worlds." (Gutting, 151).

On the one hand, no fundamental project is really available to the truly dispossessed; on the other, humans with some level of agency, however situated, cannot escape the responsibility of consequences. In *Critique de la raison dialectique*, Sartre went on to say that an account of praxis (action) solely in terms of its prior conditions is possible only if we first have an understanding of the praxis in terms of its overall purpose or meaning.

For Albert Camus, human existence is absurd. His writing is permeated by conflicts of the period: the Algerian civil war and Nazi occupation. A central preoccupation is responsibility, guilt, and innocence in the face of tragedy. How can one be innocent in an absurd world? His flawed heroes embody original guilt.

Simone de Beauvoir's most influential work was *Le Deuxième sexe* (Beauvoir, 1949), in which she famously stated, "One is not born a woman but becomes one." This work, extremely controversial at the time, is an existential examination of the female condition in which Beauvoir constructs a model of male–female relations as a struggle in subjectivity, man compelling woman to assume the status of the Other. Some aspects of it—her theories of female bodily sexuality, her rejection of motherhood, and marriage—have been criticized by later feminists. At the same time, her work is seen as pioneering and enabling for later progress in feminist thought. She is still celebrated today as a founding figure of French feminism, with widespread influence on more recent writers, and also of philosophy in general. Her role in the evolution of Sartre's thought has been given a much-needed reevaluation. She later reworked the implication of *Le Deuxième sexe* that women had to refuse the feminine other. Her engagement in the cause of women was lifelong and involved her in the polemic over the decriminalization of pregnancy termination. In *The Ethics of Ambiguity* (Beauvoir, 1947), she distinguished two types of freedom and recognized that existential subjectivity does not mean that personal freedom is not bound up with that of others—a philosophical question she had already examined in depth in her fictional writing.

Michel Foucault's thought falls into three phases. In *Les Mots* and *L'Archeologie du savoir*, he finds the conditions of knowledge in anonymous historically emergent epistemes, the modern episteme emerging at the end of the eighteenth century and making possible the emergence of the subject. In the second phase, in *Discipline and Punish* and the *History of Sexuality*, he locates discourse in a larger context of nondiscursive practices, especially those of power. Discipline is a set of techniques for controlling humans. The third phase analyzes subjectivity, especially the practices of the self. We are to act in our "true selves." There is always resistance to freedom—we can refuse what we are. The self is not discovered but created, in the invention of new ways not caught up in the disciplinary order: This is the work of freedom.

Louis Althusser, a Communist, integrated Marxism with structuralism. He saw the social agents, whether economic, political, or ideological, as structures united within structures of structures. This meant in effect that the subject was displaced from any central role in the historical process.

This adds to the resonance of Jean-François Lyotard's later rejection of the ethical "we" in *la Condition postmoderne:* History has transmitted to us an ethically centered "we," who proved to be in fact the subject inscribed in the political discourses of those dominant races, classes, or cultures privileged as the sole addressors of normative claims. At the same time, the modern existential "we" is no less guilty of excluding the disempowered, whose voice, because they have no access to the discourse of normative justice, is not heard. Discourse is the system of conceptual structures that we use to represent the world. The phrase, or unit of linguistic meaning as uttered, posits a human system of addressor (speaking), addressee (spoken to), the sense or *sens* of the claim made, and the referent of this sense. As an example, the claim that gas chambers existed in Nazi Germany might be unprovable before a tribunal (addressee) that required proof from an eyewitness who is, necessarily, dead. The sense of the phrase making the claim is embedded in the sense of justice sought in the present for the past and from judges with their own frame of reference to the past; nor is it clear how the narrative and the ethical system may rejoin each other in language, even assuming allround good faith. These limits and entropies of the relationship between language and power were never absent, but humanity was forced to confront them in particular ways, to find narratives to explain and address these issues during these conflicts and their aftermath.

Lyotard borrows from Wittgenstein the idea that the meaning of a term, a phrase or a sentence, is in how it functions in human interaction. The fundamental unit of communication is a "phrase." "To learn names," he says, "is to situate them in relation to other names by means of phrases" (Lyotard, 44). A specific referent achieves its meaning in and through its linkage with other phrases: It can be located within different networks of names, and the linkages between phases are not "right" nor "wrong," but rather useful or superfluous, meaningful, or senseless. The statements of a witness to Auschwitz cannot defeat the revisionism of Faurisson; it is not a matter of making him submit to the verificationist game, because Auschwitz is a political and ethical issue. A phrase can take many forms and follow different regimens: storytelling, commanding, prescribing, questioning, convincing, scientific proof, within different genres of discourse. There is no judgment-stance outside the agonistic struggle of the *différend.* Phrases always present a possible world; the subject is situated by the phrase, and the phrase both is and signifies that something is taking place. One cannot not phrase, for even silence or refusal is a phrase. The real problem is the hierarchy of one phrase over another: exclusion, ruling out, invalidating, denial, displacement, and negation. Nazism is precisely such a denial; this, for Lyotard, is terror in its purist form.

Emmanuel Levinas, of Lithuanian and French-Jewish origin, studied in Freiburg with Husserl and Heidegger, and his first works show their influence

(Levinas 1930, 1947, 1949). After his wartime experience of captivity, he went on to elaborate a philosophy of ethics, looking at the question of the Other and the Face. Levinas rejects the idea that we can encounter the Other simply as a principle; rather, it is the other person as an ethical imperative. The self as the focus of meaning "lives off" (*vivre de*) external objects. When we encounter the Other through its face (*visage*) and speech (*parole*), it is not an object that can be absorbed into our interiority, but an epiphany, which engages our responsibility to respect it: "To expose myself to the vulnerability of the face is to put my ontological right to exist into question" (Kearney 60). The virtue-ethics requirement of the Face is a condition of freedom because freedom is the reaction to the Other's demand for respect.

Gilles Deleuze in *Différance et repetitions* (1968) critiques the philosophy of representation that has dominated European thought since Plato. For him, experience is not the representation of a transcendental object by means of intuitions and concepts, but the expression and or actualization of Ideas by means of a complex process of differentiation. Metaphysics is grounded only in the repetition of ideal problems, themselves defined in terms of differences.

Michèle Le Doeuff continues the long French tradition of philosophy of science, taking it into the contemporary critique of phallocentric subjectivity. Her work establishes a feminist epistemology and explores the *Imaginaire*, imaginary or set of images that underlie conceptualization. Her work, like that of Gilbert Durand, in *Structures anthropologies de l'imaginaire*, and also Lacan and Irigaray, investigates the prediscursive level of experience that underpins culture as well as individual psychic development. The imaginary is sexed, she says, the male imaginary characterized by unity, individuation, stable form, and identity whereas the female imaginary is characterized by plurality, fluidity, and mobility or formlessness.

Aspect 3: A Taste for Psychology

Bergson's third characteristic of French philosophy is the *goût des philosophes francais pour la psychologie*. Here there is no lack of more recent examples, both in relation to psychoanalysis and to different theories of the self. Jacques Lacan's work as a psychoanalyst and teacher has always reflected an engagement with world-explanatory discourse that is not always apparent to the readership of his dense and highly referential style. Though in a different mode, he attempts similar to Cixous and Derrida to convey a totality of meaning, at the unconscious as well as the conscious level, and his discourse carries with it a semantic and semiotic undertow drawing on his wide reading as well as on constant linguistic play. His assertion that the unconscious is structured like a language would have obvious and fundamental implications for many aspects of philosophy. His relation of the Freudian hermeneutic techniques of condensation and displacement to *métaphore* and *métonymie* (this more specific concept chosen over the more generic *synecdoque*) engages subjectivity as a process in the reversal of power that Freud's articulation of the unconscious has already partially achieved. Lacan's model goes further to displace the subject from control over language in any of its spheres of activity. He explores how being is constituted, how language is acquired, how sexual difference is constituted in such a way as to give rise to culture. "Males and females . . . pay a price for being constituted as social creatures, each sex cohering as an identity only by losing something. This certainly related the problem of the Other, so present in contemporary French philosophy: woman becoming a symptom for men of Otherness, of the outside, while women avoiding confusion with a phallic signifier for difference, are subversive of patriarchal closures" (Wright, 1992, 201–207). Lacan's redefinition of psychic disorder as located in language has had great influence on the profession and in particular on the work of Françoise Dolto, whose work with children and young people has been groundbreaking, and whose ideas on communication with children, including unconscious body-image and symbolizing castration, have been widely disseminated through her radio programs and her writing for parents, educators, and carers (Dolto).

Luce Irigaray, a practicing analyst, has focused on psycholinguistics, dissenting from Lacan's views on female sexuality (and expelled from his school). *Speculum de l'autre femme* (Irigaray) is a critique of the discourse of Western philosophy as the master discourse that excludes the feminine and the maternal. She attempts to construct a version of feminine subjectivity "speaking as" woman, using the strategic and symbolic positioning of women as Other. She writes increasingly in an allusive and lyrical style, and indeed, attention to style is a characteristic of French writing.

Julia Kristeva, writer, philosopher, and analyst, brings together Marxist theory and Russian formalism with structuralism and psychoanalysis in an interdisciplinary approach to questions concerning subjectivity. Her writing on semanalysis, polylogue, women-centered desire, time, and sensibility in Proust all attest to a theoretical framework for reading that links the "knowledge" of the unconscious, a sensitivity to the poetic nature of all languaged expression, and an understanding of the forces at work in human communication, derived from the encounter of two discourses that is psychoanalysis.

Georges Bataille's writing is preoccupied with guilt, especially as a linking of the body, phallocentric sexuality, and violence. His fiction, *Histoire de l'oeil*, explores bodily functions and parts in a way that appeared transgressive at the time. His imaginary is influenced by Nietzsche, Sade, and Gilles de Rais and has a certain obsession with pain and death. From the point of view of recent feminist body politics, the transgressive aspect would appear to be the representation in writing of these bodily realities, the politics of the body having tended to associate it with the feminine, the female, or woman, and to denigrate it as weak, immoral, unclean, or decaying—hence the phallocentric pleasure of inflicting pain on it. Bataille founded journals related to his interests in sociology, religion, and literature and was the first to publish Barthes, Foucault, and Derrida.

A different uniting of personal quest to world view was that of Pierre Teilhard de Chardin, who theorized human evolution as moving from the biological to the noological: "Is evolution a theory, a system or a hypothesis? It is much more: it is a general condition to which all theories, all hypotheses, as systems must bow and which they must satisfy henceforth if they are to be thinkable and true. Evolution is a light illuminating all facts, a curve that all lines must follow" (Chardin, 1961, 219). Evolution has developed from geogenesis to biogenesis and has ended up as noogenesis. An evolution conscious of itself could also direct itself. Noogenesis moves ever more clearly toward self-direction; it is now something we determine: "Not only do we read in our slightest acts the secrets of [evolutions] proceedings; but for an elementary part we hold it in our hands, responsible for its past to its future" (Chardin, 1961, 226).

Another thinker in the French tradition of the spiritual, albeit in the much more restricted space allowed to women, is Simone Weil. Philosopher, social activist, and religious searcher, she published little during her lifetime, but her posthumous works in sixteen volumes earned her reputation for original thought. She was preoccupied with the nature and possibility of individual freedom, deciding in the end for liberalism rather than socialism: "What a country calls its vital economic interests are not the things which enable its citizens to live, but the things which enable it to make war. Gasoline is much more likely than wheat to be a cause of international conflict" (Weil, 1949). She alternated teaching philosophy with manual labor because she believed writing should be based on experience.

Paul Ricoeur has written on hermeneutics, theology, psychoanalysis, and aesthetics applied to a variety of philosophical, social, religious, and cultural topics, from the paradoxes of political power to the relationship between life and art and life and death. A "son of a victim of the First World War," Ricoeur was captured and imprisoned by the Germans during World War II. His relationships with twentieth-century philosophers included Heidegger, Jaspers, Eliade, and Jacques Lacan. Ricoeur has expressed admiration for the work of Levi-Strauss, Foucault, and especially the narratologist Algirdas-Julien Greimas. This reflects Ricoeur's pursuit of models of interpretation: Much of his work attempts to mediate between different theories of linguistics, hermeneutics, and criticism. Working with both phenomenology (which gives emphasis to the cognitive archaeology of symbolic interpretations) and structuralism (which tends to privilege internal structures of signification), Ricoeur's thought, although by no means confessional in a reductive sense, retains a turn toward some possibility of entelechy, some space for a relationship between meaning, subjectivity, and truth.

The variety of the philosophical enquiries mentioned bears out in its turn Bergson's idea that philosophy in France refuses to constitute itself into a single system, which is its strength, in his view, and its particularity: "It is a philosophy which follows closely the contours of external reality, such as the physicist might envisage them, and closely also the contours of internal reality, such as they appear to the psychologist. By this very fact, it usually avoids taking on the form of a *system*. It rejects extreme dogmatism and also radical criticism: its method is as far from Hegel as from Kant" (Bergson).

This is not always understood as the quality Bergson saw. The reception of philosophy has tended to distinguish the so-called continental style of philosophy from the analytic, the first being seen as language-based and the second associated with the Anglo-American sphere. Analytic writers, in their attention to logic, language, and conceptual questions, are sometimes accused of concentrating on relatively unimportant matters, of being more interested in perfecting philosophical tools than in using them to address fundamental questions. Although French theoretical writers are viewed by some as overly ambitious and difficult to read, their preoccupation with difficult, complex, and even painful, but universal, human issues in the contemporary condition is worthy of attention.

ANGELA RYAN

See also **entries on the individuals mentioned in this article**

PHILOSOPHY OF SCIENCE

In addition to scientists, who devote themselves to improving sciences directly, we can consider three other categories of people as holding an interest in science: historians, epistemologists, and philosophers. Historians study sciences from a chronological point of view. Epistemologists concentrate on how scientific theories are elaborated and how knowledge. Of course, the difference between these three types is often blurred: Being an epistemologist or a scientist does not prevent one from forming opinions as to what science can or could tell us that is somehow metascientific.

The term "epistemology"—"the science of knowledge" if we refer to the ancient Greek (*logos* and *episteme*)—was coined in 1854 by a Scottish metaphysician, James Frederick Ferrier (1808–1864), and appeared for the first time in France in a French translation of Bertrand Russell's *Essay on the Foundations of Geometry*, published in 1901.

The notion of the philosophy of science is older, having been used for the first time by the French philosopher Auguste Comte (1798–1857) in 1830, four years before André-Marie Ampère, to whom the expression is often wrongly attributed. The term crossed the Channel with the help of William Whewell, a professor at Cambridge, who used it in his book *The Philosophy of Inductive Sciences, Founded upon their History* (Whewell, 1840). As Dominique Lecourt puts it, it is reasonable to posit that the term's initial usage was "linked to attempts to classify sciences while respecting their diversity as well as showing their unity" (Lecourt, 2001, 14) and was designed to give mankind the key to a philosophy freed from metaphysics, especially in regards to Comte.

It is interesting to question the emergence of these different fields of study. Both the nineteenth and the start of the twentieth centuries comprised a time characterized by a profound reshaping of mathematics toward formalization and an enduring interest in logic. Men such as George Boole (1815–1864) and Gottlob Frege (1848–1925) in particular played an important role in this attempt to give a new foundation to reasoning and mathematical language. Indeed, thanks to an innovative and indispensable work on the concept of the infinite, Boole and Frege gave birth to part of the symbol-alphabet on which science is based today. This is why specialists like Roland Omnès use the word "break" to qualify our time; that is, a "formal break" (as opposed to a "classical" time). In his words, our time is defined by "the loss of the spontaneous representation of the world from which all thoughts came from, the dismantling of common sense and the precious flowers which are its philosophical principles, [and] the peculiar primacy of abstraction, formalness" (Omnès, 1994, 138–139). Another part of the answer is sociological: the nineteenth century was the period during which the strong emphasis put on the democratization of education forced the teaching world to agree

on a symbolization accessible to all, from Lille to Toulouse and Rennes to Strasbourg, to facilitate communication.

Since the Industrial Revolution, the number of sciences and specializations has greatly increased, so much so in fact that in each of the main scientific branches such as physics, biology, and mathematics, the scientific community states that it is probably impossible to get hold of one person able to know not only sciences as a whole but his or her own branch in its totality. Even if some recent discoveries have allowed scientists to make connections between different areas (see the proof of Fermat's last theorem by Andrew Wiles), because of the ever-increasing number of research laboratories, Ph.D. students, and researchers—each working to further his or her own subject—the situation does not show any signs of change.

This context partly explains the rise of the philosophers of science. In the eighteenth century, for instance, a thinker who was not renowned for being a scientist could introduce to his contemporaries (and therefore himself understand) the discoveries of the great scientists of his time (Voltaire popularized Newton's results, for instance). This is because of the fact that, until that time, science was linked to philosophy: Philosophers were scientists and vice versa; Pythagoras, Descartes, Leibniz, Aristotle, and Pascal all exemplify this figure. Today, given the degree of technical expertise and the profusion of ideas that characterize the sciences, the relationship between the two fields has inevitably evolved. The nineteenth century therefore naturally saw the birth of the philosophy of science, the branch of philosophy dedicated to the study of a subject that had lost its clarity with respect to the reasonably educated man. In addition to a strong training in the history of philosophy, philosophers of science had to have an equally strong education in sciences, without which it was no longer possible for them to comprehend the evolutions and philosophical implications of science.

Their role, therefore, became more isolated from the traditional schools of philosophy because of the relatively unharmonious relationship between philosophy and science, as the latter pretended (or supposedly pretended, according to some philosophers) that it can sufficiently explain and solve everything. In reaction to this partly misunderstood ambition, philosophy often ostracized or discredited those who could speak both languages, so to speak, or who wanted to give their opinion on both subjects.

However, this division of powers has not prevented French intellectuals from appropriating to scientific concepts. Indeed, it caused a great stir in 1997 when Jean Bricmont and Alain Sokal's *Impostures intellectuelles* (1997) was published, in which the poor thought and outright nonsense in some of Lacan, Kristeva, Baudrillard, and Deleuze's pseudo-science was analyzed.

No matter what its status, the philosophy of science has been very active in the twentieth century, especially with the so-called chaos theory at work in meteorology, quantum physics, and fluid mechanics. This theory was quite a popular success and indirectly allowed a few philosophers, such as Clément Rosset in France, to rethink the concept of chance.

The evolution of mathematics in the second half of the nineteenth century convinced many that it was possible to set up a flawless system of logic. In other words, at one point some believed there was a formal way to reach truth and that a thought, on the condition that it followed a precise path, could be irreproachable; that is, true. Furthermore, Russell and Whitehead tried to subjugate the entire field of mathematics to this logic in their *Principia Mathematica* (1910–1913).

It is with this background in mind that we must read the claims of logical positivism, developed in 1929 in the *Manifeste de la conception du monde*, which united scholars and philosophers (otherwise referred to as the Vienna circle), among which can be cited Moritz Schlick (1882–1936), Carnap (1891–1970), and Otto Neurath (1882–1945). They wanted to make Leibniz's dream come true and assimilate the problems of philosophy into mathematical ones, influenced by Russell and Whitehead's aforementioned *Principia Mathematica*, *Les fondements de l'arthmétique* by Frege (1969), and Wittgenstein's *Tractatus logico-philosophicus* (1922). Because mathematics were thought to be capable of attaining the highest degree of perfection, philosophy too was believed to encompass the solutions to all conceptual and intellectual problems. At this point, science takes over and sets philosophers the task of renewing philosophy: Renewing, because instead of expecting logic to answer the old philosophical questions already posed by the Presocratics (which would of course have been nonsensical), the Vienna circle—thereby following the "first" Wittgenstein (as opposed to the "second," who wrote the *Philosophical Investigations*, Wittgenstein's thought seen as being two-fold)—redefined the very concept of philosophy. This was done by extracting the pseudoproblems from philosophy, that is, problems that cannot be observed, which meant eliminating metaphysics (*meta physis* in ancient Greek: what comes after, what is beyond nature, therefore beyond the observable). Language, called into question in the *Tractatus*, is blamed for a great deal of our conceptual confusions, and it is because of this that philosophy must be a "criticism of language" (Wittgenstein, 1922, 4.112).

From this point, the philosophy of science took a turn that was to divide specialists for several decades.

Being mainly of European origin, especially from Austria and Germany, many of the logic positivists emigrated to America as the Second World War loomed larger.

In France, this movement, which evolved in the philosophy of language, was not well received. First, we must note along with Dominique Lecourt and others that most of the French logicians who could have followed and furthered Whitehead's, Frege's, and other logical positivists' work died before they came to maturity. Louis Couturat, a friend of Russell, died at the age of forty-six, Jean Nicod at thirty-eight, and Jacques Herbrand at twenty-three.

This is not the only explanation for this French opposition to a "logical" philosophy, however. Indeed, Auguste Comte founded positivism, but it is with quite a different approach that the Vienna circle understood the notion. For Comte, what prevailed in positivism was not empiricism but speculation, which means that an observation relies on a theory, even a minimal one. This difference is significant and partly explains their two separate orientations. Second, the French philosophers rejected the idea that logic could provide them with a flawless methodology. This rejection can once again be related to Comte, for whom science was auxiliary but in no way whatsoever a foundation, and was famously developed by Henri Poincaré, who considered that formal logic could not explain mathematics, as intuition, the necessary unknown, could.

These conceptual options also had an important influence on the very methodology they used. The logical positivists progressively stripped their interrogations of any historical aspect to reflect only on very specific problems such as induction, falsification, or the unity of science. This clearly shows the disinterest of English and German philosophy in diachronic matters and, hence, their subsequent drift toward epistemology.

In France, however, the situation was completely different. As early as the mid-nineteenth century, history and the philosophy of science have been closely linked. From Comte to Michel Foucault (1926–1984), and with Antoine Augustin Cournot (1801–1877), Gaston Bachelard (1884–1962), and Georges Canguilhem (1904–1995), the questioning of what sciences "tell" us has never been envisaged without consideration of their evolution. It is because of this particular approach to the history of science that specialists speak not so much of a French school but of a French trend in the philosophy of science.

Without doubt, Bachelard, Canguilhem, and Foucault are among the most cited names both in and outside France for their contribution to this "French trend." It is interesting to note that each one of them reflected on the philosophy of science from a different domain: Bachelard from the point of view of mathematics and physics, Canguilhem from medicine and biology, and Foucault from social sciences.

Gaston Bachelard was a Republican legend: born in 1884 in a small village of Champagne called Bar-sur-Aube to tobacconist parents, the grandson of a cobbler, he started his working life as a postman. Studying during his free time, he earned a degree in mathematics in 1912 and became a secondary school math teacher. He then did advanced work in philosophy, wrote his Ph.D., and held the chair of History and Philosophy of Science at the Sorbonne. In addition to being a famous philosopher of science, he was an influential literary critic. Bachelard developed a "historical epistemology" (expression first used by D. Lecourt) and, influenced by his teaching experience, reflected on what hampers scientific knowledge, which he called "epistemological obstacles":

- First experience: A preconceived idea built up with time
- General knowledge: The general ideas we have on the basis of unfounded analogies
- Unitarian and pragmatic knowledge: The first one sees a unity at work in nature, the latter a utility for mankind
- Substantialism: The idea that what is inside is explanatory, as in the case of alchemy
- Animism: Transposes the body into science; for example, when the digestive process was used to explain chemical reactions
- Libido: Sexualized chemical reactions or electricity
- Quantitative knowledge.

Bachelard stressed the notion of "epistemological rupture," by which he meant that science evolves in an irregular way, devoid of continuity. This is why, in *The New Scientific Spirit* (1985) and *La philosophie du non* (1940), he tried to highlight the ruptures or breaks caused by Lobatchewsky (non-Euclidean geometry), Einstein (general relativity), and de Broglie (wave mechanics) and the idea that the "non" in these expressions did not imply that these new theories negated those which preceded but, rather, encompassed them.

Georges Canguilhem was a doctor and a philosopher, and he illustrated the advantages of the mixing of epistemology and the history of science with his concept of "recurrent history," inherited from Bachelard's discontinuism. Through it, he wanted to highlight the history of an idea as much as the different meanings and justifications it gained along the way. Vitalist in a new way, he refused the traditional dichotomy between mechanism and animism (the living is either a machine or a spirit) and proposed to revise the concept of the living in the light of its true originality;

that is, life. By doing so, he showed what was metaphysic in mechanism and was therefore able to criticize its methodology to put forward his own, which he named and developed at length in *A Rational Vitalism*.

Canguilhem is especially renowned for his Ph.D. Dissertation, *The Normal and the Pathologic* (1991), in which he stressed that normality is second to deviation and that the ordinary notion of the norm as a statistic obscures the evidence of fundamental and individual specificities. Therefore, medicine is not as much a science as an art. He also insisted on the fact that the pathologic is not the opposite of normality, "since life in a pathologic state is not an absence of norms but the presence of other norms" (1965, 166). In other words, a pathology is not abnormal. Discontinuist in the history of science, he is therefore also discontinuist in the way he conceives normality and pathology, contrary to François Broussais, Auguste Comte, or Claude Bernard, whose continuism he analyzes pertinently, showing how it constituted another type of epistemological obstacle.

Michel Foucault, in the field of social sciences, worked toward an "archaeology of knowledge." The expression is Foucault's reply to the implications of anthropology, whose fundamental claim is that there is one human nature and whose aim is to gather from all human civilizations the essential and universal. He strongly disagreed with Hegel's account of a linear history and was classified as a structuralist. His "archaeology of knowledge" implies the understanding of the context in which knowledge arises or, in his own terms, the *épistémé* of a given period: "the subterranean configuration of knowledge that makes any scientific discourse possible" (Baraquin and Laffitte, 2000, 117). What makes Foucault's ideas interesting is that he does not try to account for the puzzle of knowledge throughout its history, to render its unity, its essence, but to study how each period manages to give birth to knowledge, what it relies on and in what way it is justified. These hidden pieces of the puzzle do not give us more information about the "truth" of an object but offer more details about what constitutes the basis of our current relationship to the world.

Of course, the French philosophy of science does not end with these three names. Since Foucault, Canguilhem, and Bachelard, many specialists have entered the field, such as Granger, Dagognet, Desanti, Latour, Omnès, and Lecourt, but none has yet influenced the field as much as these three. Paradoxically, in the last few years, France has shown itself to be opening up to the ideas of logical positivism, and even more to the philosophy of language. Jacques Bouveresse, for example, who always kept his distance from the Marxist–structuralist frenzy of the 1960s and 1970s and was elected to the chair of Philosophy of Language and

Knowledge at the Collège de France in 1995, has published widely on Wittgenstein and has played an important role in introducing his work in France.

DENIS LEJEUNE (TRANSLATED WITH THE HELP OF ALEX NEEDHAM)

See also **Gaston Bachelard; Jean Baudrillard; Georges Canguilhem; Gilles Deleuze; Michel Foucault; Julia Kristeva; Jacques Lacan**

Further Reading

Alquié, Ferdinand, *La philosophie des sciences*, La Table Ronde, 2001

Andler, Daniel and Fagot-Largeault, Anne, *Philosophie des sciences*, Paris: Gallimard, 2002

Bachelard, *The New Scientific Spirit*, Houston, TX: Beacon Press, 1985

Bachelard, *La philosophie du non*, Paris: PUF, 1940

Barberousse, Anouk, Kistler, Max, and Ludwig Pascal, *La philosophie des sciences au XXè siècle*, Flammarion, 2000

Baraquin, N., and Laffitte, J., *Dictionnaire des philosophes*, Paris: Colin, 2000

Bouveresse, Jacques, *Le philosophe et le réel*, Paris: Hachette, 2000

Bricmont, Jean, and Sokal, Alain, *Impostures intellectuelles*, Paris: Odile Jacob, 1997

Canguilhem, Georges, *La connaissance de la vie*, Paris: Vrin, 1965

Canguilhem, Georges, *The Normal and the Pathologic*, New York: Zone Books, 1991

Comte, Auguste, *Philosophie des sciences*, Paris: Gallimard, 1996

Desanti, Jean-Toussaint, *Les Idéalités mathématiques*, Seuil, 1968

Frege, *Les fondements de l'arthmétique*, Paris: Seuil, 1969

Koyré, Alexandre, *Etudes d'histoire de la pensée scientifique*, Paris: Gallimard, 1973

Lecourt, Dominique, *Dictionnaire d'histoire et philosophie des sciences*, Paris: PUF, 1990

Lecourt, Dominique, *Philosophie des sciences*, Paris: PUF, 2001

Omnès, Roland, *Philosophie de la science contemporaine*, Paris: Folio Essais, 1994

Popelard M. D., and Vernant D., *Les grands courants de la philosophie des sciences*, Paris: Seuil, 1997

Popper, Karl, *La quête inachevée*, Calmann-Lévy, 1989

Prigogine, Ilya, and Stengers, Isabelle, *La nouvelle alliance*, Paris: Gallimard, 1997

Russell, Bertrand, *Histoire de mes idées philosophiques*, Paris: Gallimard, 1988

Russell, and Whitehead, *Principia Mathematica*, Cambridge: Cambridge University Press, Vol. 1, 1910; Vol. 2, 1912; Vol. 3, 1913

Serres, Michel, *Eclaircissements*, Flammarion, 1993

Thompson, Mel, *Philosophy of Science*, Hodder & Stoughton, 2001

Whewell, W., *The Philosophy of Inductive Sciences, Founded upon their History*, Parker, 1840

POETRY

The painter Paul Degas once lamented that he could not write, even though he did not lack ideas. According to Paul Valéry in *Degas danse dessin*, Mallarmé answered that, "one does not write with ideas but with words." Following Mallarmé's example, in this as in many other things, twentieth-century poets in French have refused the reduction of poetry to ideas with a vigor equal to that of philosophers and scientists when they oppose their work to what they understand poetry to be. One could even say that modern poetic writing is a continuous attempt to break the link between thought and poetry. From positions as opposed as those of the Surrealists and of Valéry through to *Tel Quel* writers and recent work influenced by mathematics and linguistics, poets have insisted that language creates rather than expresses meaning. Some have considered that poetry, like music, does not have to refer to a world beyond signs, or more precisely, significance or "meaning" (taken as a verb), or that it is ultimately an autoreferential game.

Yet, as Michel Deguy, a poet well aware of the formal experiments of the century, noted, if poetry is not philosophy, and could even be defined by its distance from philosophy, what makes a poet or a work "great" can hardly be defined in any other way than by reference to thought, the crucial point being that not all thought is expressible in philosophical or scientific categories. This does not mean that poetry should express depths of emotion or personal subjectivity. In fact, the origins of this position are the reflections of Bergson and then Heidegger on the irreducibility of determinations of time and space within consciousness to conceptual determinations. Like modern painting, poetry, a nonconceptual reflection on the experience of a consciousness situated in the world, becomes an essential form of thought. René Char's 1955 meeting with Heidegger became emblematic for many subsequent writers, among them Yves Bonnefoy, who insisted that poetry is connected to a real beyond the text. If poetry's role is not to express subjectivity, neither is it to simply describe or celebrate the existing world; rather, through its use of sound, rhythm, and silence, poetry is somehow able to approach "Being" in its singularity and productivity, without claiming to contain a truth in either of the classical senses of the correspondence of a concept to a reality, or of the coherence of a proposition within a system.

This constant hesitation as to the nature of poetry derives from the oddity of an art that consists of intimately marrying sound and meaning; that is, to combine constraints belonging to the musical and to the rational, as Valéry called them, two radically heterogeneous orders. So the only common ground between the two positions is perhaps to see in poetry a productivity or *poiesis* (according to the etymology recalled by Valéry in his *First Lecture on Poetics* of 1937) and not a way of expressing or illustrating a predefined content, emotions, facts, or ideas, which another form of writing could convey, though, of course, the thoughts by which it has been influenced, and which in turn it has helped to develop, encompass a wide range of concerns. History and politics have been central, but technological transformations, psychoanalysis, phenomenology, and various manifestations of structuralist and poststructuralist ideas are also important.

In addition, poetry always reflects and reacts to earlier poetic writing. Thus, the early poetry of the century responds to movements such as Symbolism, and the development of a more metaphysical approach to poetry after the Second World War is a reaction to Surrealism and a return to the inspiration of Pierre Reverdy. Most poets of the first half of the century are linked to some degree to movements—Dadaism, Futurism, Surrealism, Négritude—that consider poetry as a force or an instrument not so much for celebrating the given, man or nature, as for questioning the assumptions and attitudes embedded in common sense, in particular through its reliance on categories fixed by an unreflected use of language. As a consequence, all the traditional forms of poetic writing are questioned, and the boundaries of poetry with other arts and with action are blurred. If the period of the Second World War sees a resurgence of traditional forms (in particular lyrical or epic poetry), aimed at carrying a message, at expressing suffering or representing history, this is soon superseded by movements and individuals that again see in poetry an original experience or act, whether from the point of view of a phenomenology of a presence to the world or through formalist plays on linguistic constraints, taken as prime generators of meaning, in lieu of intentions of signification. The first tendency is that of a return to things as well as a reflection on modes of apprehending space; the second leads to the work of the poet-mathematicians of the OuLiPo school, or to the techniques of cut-up or collage of fragments of preexisting discourse, in the more recent "objectivist" poetry.

This general suspicion vis-à-vis traditional objects and forms of poetry carries with it a number of consequences concerning the nature of writing, the notion of the poetic image, and the status of the poet as subject.

The poetry of the period puts an unprecedented emphasis on *writing* taken as the physical (in particular visual) existence of the poem. For instance, rare are the major poets of the century who have not taken part in the production of a *Livre d'Artiste*, a collaboration between a poet and an artist, which consists of a formal dialogue or counterpoint rather than the illustration of a content, a tradition initiated by the collaboration of Mallarmé and Manet that flourished in works uniting poets and "abstract" artists (e.g., in 1913, *La Prose du Transsibérien* by Blaise Cendrars and Sonia Delaunay, or, in 1948, *Le Chant des morts*, by Pierre Reverdy and Pablo Picasso). Since the disposition of the poem on the page, the use of all sorts of typographical or graphical means and of blank spaces within lines, becomes essential, the traditional structures of the verse are either abandoned or played with. This does not mean that by losing rhyme and fixed meter, poetry has lost its links with orality and the arts of memory but, rather, that texts meant to be read are now often conceived as a form of drawing in the aural spectrum, as writing is perceived as the production of shapes in the visual one. In other words, from Dada to the voice poets of the 1960s and 1990s, the inflections of the voice, the arrangement of the printed words, are not punctuations of meanings but games with the traditional instruments of the act of meaning or what the literary critic Roland Barthes called *signifiance*, "significance," as opposed to "signified" and to "reference." Although previously, poetic structures in writing (meter, rhyme, alliteration, assonances) were notations of vocal patterns, which in turn served memory, it now seems that oral and written forms are simply parallel ways of experiencing the significance that is lost into the meanings themselves in the ordinary use of language.

Just as verse undergoes a major transformation, so does the poetic image. It was previously the instrument of a reference; that is, a relation between the text and an "outside." A particular event, situation, character, or emotion needs to be visualized to acquire the memorable presence of the real. This was the purpose of the image: Ulysses is a fox, Achilles a lion. Now, the text signifies by referring to an experience, a tradition, or a knowledge beyond it. The transformation of the poetic image consists of keeping the singularity, the presence of the real referent, while refusing the metaphorical relationship of analogy or comparison. Identity at a distance rather than closeness is what is now researched, to the point that Pierre Reverdy declares that provided the relationship is exact (*juste*), the further away the elements of the poetic image, the stronger the image is (a definition André Breton sees as a catalyst of his thought, in his first *Manifesto of Surrealism*). The word "like" is banished, the relationship is now interior to the image, and immediately an extraordinary productivity of images become possible. This was of course the hallmark of the Surrealist period, but the interiorization of the imaginary link could be traced to the works of Rimbaud and Lautréamont, among others, and is perhaps at its greatest in Apollinaire. Thus, his famous evocation in *Alcools*, of street lights seen through the fog one evening in the docks of London, as "wounds on the blood-dripping fog." ("La Chanson du mal-aimé") It generates a series of images connected to the flight through the Red Sea and in turn a whole world, organized by the tensions and contradictions of states of mind: the suffering of an abandoned lover that it would have simply illustrated in previous uses of the poetic image. When the image turns from analogy to internalized difference or even contradiction, what counts is *poiesis*, creation, more than reference.

This in turn questions the status of the poet. If he is not the artist in charge of depicting a given world, exterior or interior, using language as a tool, he seems to be the product of the generative process of the *poiesis* itself. Well before Structuralism and, so to speak, from the inside of the creative process, the reflection of poets such as Breton and the Surrealists or, again, Valéry, questioned the notion of authorship and gave chance a crucial and legitimate role in art. Poetry is work, and often arduous work, on forms and conventions, but it aims at an encounter with a singularity that cannot be expressed in concepts, be it a specific sensation, a state, or a presence. The conscious work we can do is largely aimed at transforming our perception of a language to which we do not pay attention in its free and practical usage. Sometimes, by chance, in this process, what was hoped for but could not be defined in advance occurs. In the end, when the idea of an intention against which the text could be measured has disappeared, the very distinction between writing and criticism, poetry and poetics vanishes. The poem is a reflection on the causes and conditions of its own genesis.

Avant-Gardes

The dada movement was created by performers at the Cabaret Voltaire in Zurich in 1916. In their experimental readings, performance was emphasized by the use of masks and stage décor, while the words were often rendered meaningless: sound and phonemes aimed at surprising, shocking, and exhilarating the audience rather than communicating with it. Dadaists including Hugo Ball, Tristan Tzara, the Janco brothers, Raoul Hausmann, and Richard Huelsenbeck made spontaneity, destruction, and provocation the goals of their work, using chance or marginal forms of expression in highly sophisticated compositions, in their resistance to logic and art in their accepted forms.

Surrealism aimed at continuing dada's revolt, although abandoning its destructive nihilism. As a movement, under the direction of André Breton, its key figure, it dominated the arts in the 1920s. Breton's 1924 *Manifesto of Surrealism* is considered the central theoretical text of the movement, but he also wrote poetry and the influential *Nadja*, an unclassifiable prose text at the confluence of the travel diary (with photo-

graphs), the dream narration, and the medical case study. Surrealism is notable for fusing poetry, prose, and the visual arts. More than simply literature, art was necessary to life: It was life.

Among the poets associated with surrealism were Robert Desnos, Antonin Artaud, Philippe Soupault, and Benjamin Péret, as well as Paul Éluard and Louis Aragon. The Surrealists were influenced by nineteenth- and early twentieth-century poetry; they looked especially to Rimbaud for his description of the poet as seer, to the German Romantics, and to Reverdy for his work on the image, and they considered Sade, Fourier, Nerval, Lautréamont, and Jarry to be their precursors. While philosophers rediscovered presocratic and Medieval philosophy, they studied and collected primitive Western art, naïve art, or traditional arts, in particular from Africa, Oceania, and the Far East (the most interesting writers from this point of view are Leiris and Artaud). These primordial proliferations of forms and transformations were a clearer expression of the productivity of the mind than the subsuming of form to the transcendence of an ideal in classical Western art. They also read works on dreams and desire by Freud and later psychoanalysts, but Surrealism is not so much a celebration of dream in itself as of the mental activity or "surreality" it reveals. Ultimately, art mirrors this activity: Breton defines Surrealism as "pure psychical automatism." Above all, they loathed all literature that reinforced, in its very form, the illusion that the existing social order is a natural reality (hence their rejection of the traditional forms of the novel), and that "common sense" is the natural operation of the mind. Several of these writers (Breton and Aragon, in particular, who had a medical training) had firsthand experience of the First World War, a war that cast doubt on the sanity of the ruling classes. Their professed aim was revolutionary, not only to change society but, in the words of Rimbaud in *Une Saison en Enfer*, to "change life." Many joined the Communist Party or other left-wing organizations, and the movement itself operated as a political group, with factions and exclusions (e.g., Artaud, Soupault, and Vitrac).

Freedom and love were proclaimed central to Surrealist poetry. Desire and the demand for sexual freedom were expressed in texts in which woman was a desired muse, a mediator of nature, or a natural poetic catalyst (great examples being Gisèle Prassinos, who was published by the Surrealists when she was fourteen, or later on, Joyce Mansour). The unconscious was seen as a powerful subversive force, in particular in its unexpected effect on language, so techniques included automatic writing, hypnosis, dream narratives, and collective writing. Hence the large number of important Surrealist reviews, including *Littérature*, *Le Surréalisme au service de la revolution*, and *Minotaure*.

For the Surrealists, exploring the unconscious and the world around them allowed for a synthesis between the real and the imaginary that was the surreal. In poetry, this was expressed and explored in the image. These verbal images, which have their counterparts in surprising, even shocking, visual images in collage, painting, and of course, film (a unique medium, in which a new reality is constantly born of the editing and assemblage of images) are perhaps the most influential and enduring aspects of their work.

Poets of Négritude

As a movement, Surrealism died with the Second World War, but it survived to some extent in the work of writers or thinkers who had been initially associated with it—Artaud, Bataille, Lacan, and Michaux, for instance—and it also reverberated in literatures that had been considered so far as marginal or minor, but of which it recognized and revealed the importance. This is in particular the case of the poetry of Négritude, discovered by Breton in the work of the Martiniquais poet Aimé Césaire, one of the most celebrated poets in French in the century. The Surrealist project was very close to that of the poets of Négritude, namely, to voice the rebellion of that part of the human that had been crushed by the development of the Western world, in particular through a reappraisal of the culture and experience of those who had been the most cruelly oppressed, the *nègres*. Césaire's poetry, however, perhaps more than that of his friend the Senegalese poet Léopold Sedar Senghor and that of other members of the extraordinarily productive black diasporas from Africa, America, and the Caribbean living in Paris in the 1920s and 1930s, is not so much a poetry of cultural roots as of the absolute loss of rootedness in the experience of forced displacement. Césaire's famous *Notebook of a Return to the Native Land* (1939) could be read as a reflection on what is lost from one's own nature when one has lost the sense of belonging to any site and when one is dispossessed of the experience of one's own duration. He is thus perhaps the only poet of that stature who straddles both halves of the century, readable as a Surrealist, in his truly unique proliferation of images and verbal transformations and, at the same time (especially in his later poetry), as a poet of the presence to a place. The tellurian (or volcanic) presence of Césaire should not diminish the originality and importance of other poets of the Caribbean or Africa, however. Senghor, in his landmark *Anthology of the new Negro and Malagasy Poetry in French* of 1948, revealed many of these voices. Many others have appeared since, for instance, Edouard Glissant in the Caribbean, who produced at the same time an important body of work on a "poetics of relation" and on the ideas of margins and minorities, seeing in modern poetry a key to the understanding of the constitution of identities in a time of generalized *métissage*.

Resistance

Poetry in general had a greater readership during the Second World War than before or afterward, and poets of the Resistance were widely read at the Liberation. Less interested in the productivity of the imaginary, many poets at this time aimed at telling life as it should be, although former poets of the Surrealist group were also important. Significant writers emerged during that period—René Char, Jean Cassou, Pierre Emmanuel, Jean Cayrol, Eugène Guillevic, and Jean Tardieu, for instance but the most popular were Louis Aragon and Paul Éluard. Aragon, who was a prominent member of the Communist Party and who had been at the forefront of the antifascist fight during the Spanish Civil War, fought the German invasion, and took part in the Resistance, in particular with writers including Pierre Seghers and Jean Paulhan. The poetry he wrote during this period, in works such as *Le Crève-Cœur* and *Les Yeux d'Elsa*, seems retrospectively nationalist, both in content and in form, but this is to celebrate the historical construction of the nation as opposed to the myth of racial purity. Similarly, through the *Elsa* cycle, he concentrates on values of love, femininity, and freedom in contrast to the theme of virility. During the war, Éluard gradually moved to writing clandestinely, particularly in the illegal *Lettres françaises*. He collected Resistance poetry for the anthology *L'Honneur des poètes*, published in 1942 by Les Éditions de Minuit (itself founded secretly in 1941). Benjamin Péret, perhaps the most anarchist of the Surrealists, in his *Le Déshonneur des poètes* (published in 1945 in Mexico), attacked them and other writers for their sudden return to nationalism and lyricism and for their neoclassicism. Other poets published openly and were subject to censorship, in such reviews as the *Nouvelle Revue Française*, under the direction of Drieu la Rochelle from 1940 to 1943. *Poésie*, run by Seghers as means of communicating and defending poetry, was published openly but urged its contributors to express their opposition by writing "contraband language."

Worlds and Objects

Poetry composed in the second half of the century is hard to classify, partly because its unifying characteristics are a recognition of the failure of ideologies, a suspicion of unifying points of view, and a fascination for the singular. Char is a classic example of a poet who detached from Surrealism in favor of a return to the reality of a particular landscape, his native Provence, and an almost oracular style. Poets now focus on the world around as much as on states of mind, and their awareness of the power of language—so great that it goes unnoticed in its ordinary use, when we assume reality to be ordered according to its categories—encourages the dramatization of a conflictual relationship with words.

The prose poems of Francis Ponge are notable for the central role accorded to things: *Le Parti pris des choses*. His careful descriptions of them became *objeux*, a term invented to designate texts that exploited etymologies and sounds to create new ways of looking at the most familiar of things. When successful, these give correlative pleasure called *objoies*.

The illogical and dreamlike atmosphere of Henri Michaux's poems appears to testify to the influence of Surrealism, but above all, his work (poetic as well as pictural) is an extremely precise, methodical, sometimes scientific account of the turbulent workings of the mind when exploring fantasy, outlandish places, and mind-altering drugs.

Saint-John Perse's poetry, often disguised under an ironic grand style, starts from the displacement constitutive of the culture of his native Caribbean as an opportunity to question the apparent coherence and naturalness of the places and times we inhabit. Later on, Pierre Oster Soussouev celebrated place and examined the irreducible multiplicity present in landscape in a similar way.

These works can all be compared in one crucial sense: the work of the poet is indirect. Not only are these singular facts or objects detached from the chains of causes, functions, and circumstances that, to us, might have brought them about, but they have no perceptible value or significance in themselves that could define them as exceptional by contrast with a type, a rule, or an expectation. That is precisely their poetic value: The composition is such that we perceive them as odd insofar as we cannot immediately relate them to the usual abstractions we use unthinkingly to cope with the mass of singularities we constantly experience in the world. Poetry here is a continued consciousness attentive to the effort of world-making through language.

Words and Things

This paradoxical attempt at conveying the irreducibility of the real to the forms used to identify it is at the heart of works that have been more directly inspired by philosophical thought. Char's poetry displayed the important influence of modernist poetry, such as Rimbaud's *Illuminations*, as well as that of pre-Socratic thought as reread by Heidegger. One of the early texts by Bonnefoy is entitled *Anti-Platon* (1947). It contains

a criticism of the concept and prefaces his first major work, *Du mouvement et de l'immobilité de Douve*. "Douve" is both proper and common name, naming different realities, signifying perhaps above all a limit of words and world. For many poets whose writing careers have spanned the second half of the twentieth century, an interest in philosophy entails a constant refusal of theories. Such work is an attempt to regain the reality of the world around, in the singularity of all its elements.

Jean Follain, for instance, examined the simplest things and the duality between ephemeral events and permanence in an effort to find out the "secret of the world." Eugène Guillevic, with whom Follain founded the *École de Rochefort*, privileges the link with objects through sensation and reveals the silence of things as active. This of course always involves a delicate balance between the effacing of the word in favor of the thing and the primary role required of language.

Later on, contact with a much more elemental world motivated the work of Jacques Dupin and André du Bouchet. Dupin's style is abrupt, and creation must mimic the violence of the bare mineral in its splintered presence. Dupin, du Bouchet, and Bonnefoy, along with Michel Leiris and Louis-René des Fôrets, edited *L'Éphémère*, an important review that from 1967 to 1972 published poetry, art, and poetic criticism while refusing to take a theoretical stand. Here, poetic language is constantly exploring its limits, even when this leads to silence. Bernard Noël, another important poet of that generation, focuses on the transformation of the physical conditions of the perception of the poem, from orality to vision, and the corresponding mental spaces. From his earliest texts, Du Bouchet, playing with gaps in the layout of the page, makes silence as important as words. Desert becomes a strikingly common setting for poets such as Perse, Jabès, or Lorand Gaspar, whose work focuses on the matter in the world from which the mystery of life emerges.

At the same time, however, now that poetry has turned away from transcendence (be it interior or exterior) and rediscovered presence through an exploration of the difference (or, more precisely, in the terms of Derrida's studies of Mallarmé and of Jabès, *differance*) of sign and void, poets are bound to confront the question of creativity. Michel Deguy insists that the destruction of the grand illusions of ideology and theology of a substantial presence of meaning must be accompanied by a work that sees in finitude the source for creativity. A move toward the real world is therefore inseparable in Deguy's work from the constant defense and renewal of poetic language.

From that point of view, a number of schools, more interested in the processes of this language itself, have emerged during that period, slowly taking over from the more ontological approach. Movements such as Lettrisme (founded by Isidore Isou in 1946), Cobra (Christian Dotremont published the *Petit Cobra* manifesto in 1949), and OuLiPo (founded in 1960 by Raymond Queneau and the mathematician François Le Lionnais) explored the physicality and plasticity of writing. Queneau, for instance, using formal constraints, proposes a meta poetry and the invention of rules able to generate a vast potential literature, as in his *Cent Mille Milliard de Poèmes*, a collection of ten sonnets conceived in such manner that each line (usually printed on a separate strip of paper) can replace any other line, enabling 10^{14} different poems to be read, a work so large that no human being could write or read the totality of its virtual instantiations. These formal explorations of the resources of language have among their sources Mallarmé's great work, *Un coup de Dés jamais nàbolira*, but their aim is no longer to return to a purer usage of language or to recover an original experience of nomination but, rather, more modestly but with a great sense of irony, to introduce a play in the vast flood of texts that constantly submerges us.

Several contemporary groups explore in their own ways this abandonment of all illusions of transcendence (of the real, or of the self) to the text. Christian Prigent and the writers of the group TXT reinvented oral poetry, using the material substance of the text when read aloud in very specific ways to reflect intensities associated with its own genesis. Emmanuel Hocquard, founder of the group and publishing house Orange Export Ltd., reread the method of the American objectivists (Retznikov in particular) from the point of view of Wittgenstein's reflection on language, abandoning all lyricism and all claim to a specificity of poetic writing, and developing instead techniques of three-dimensional collage. The important point is that when existing texts, even the most ordinary, are thus disarticulated, fragmented, and recomposed, a distance or a "hole" is created in which the poet can breathe. Writers such as Olivier Cadiot and Pierre Alferi applied Hocquard's *méthode du blaireau* (shaving the shaving-brush and gluing back each filament) to great ironic effect and theorized it further in the first issue of their influential Revue de Littérature Générale on *La Mécanique Lyrique*, a work that can be considered the manifesto of some of the most innovative writing in French today.

It is impossible to summarize a history that is probably the most productive in innovations and styles the history of French writing, but it seems clear that if poetry is considered as a reflective exercise of thought in the present, this exercise is conceived as an operation on subjectivity, not as an expression or exploration of it—as a meditation, for instance, would be. If, however, it is considered as an instrument for the production of specific objects, these objects are only important as points of application of processes of transformation. Thus in the end, poetry remains different: It always attempts to be life, not to show it.

JEAN KHALFA and EMMA WAGSTAFF

Further Reading

Aragon, Louis, *L'Oeuvre poétique*, 7 volumes, Paris: Livre Club Diderot, 1989–1990

Bancquart, Marie-Claire, *La Poésie en France du surréalisme à nos jours*, Paris: Éditions Ellipses, 1996

Bancquart, Marie-Claire, *Poésie de langue française 1945–1960*, Paris: Presses Universitaires de France, 1995

Bishop, Michael, *The Contemporary Poetry of France: Eight Studies*, Amsterdam: Rodopi, 1985

Bonnefoy, Yves, *Du Mouvement et de l'immobilite' de Douve*, Paris: Gallimard, 1970.

Bonnefoy, Yves, *Entretiens sur la poésie*, Paris: Mercure de France, 1990

Breton, André, *Oeuvres Completes*, 3 volumes, Paris: Gallimard, 1988–1999.

Cardinal, Roger, ed., *Sensibility and Creation: Studies in Twentieth-Century French Poetry*, London: Croom Helm, and New York: Barnes and Noble, 1977

Caws, Mary Ann, *The Presence of René Char*, Princeton, N.J.: Princeton University Press, 1976

Cendrars, Blaise and Delaunay, Sonia, *La Prose du Transsibérien et de la petite Jehanne de France*, Paris

Césouire, Aimé, *La Poésie*, Paris: Le Sevil, 2000

Cohen, Jean, *Structure du langage poétique*, Paris. Flammarion, 1966

Collot, Michel, *La Poésie moderne et la structure d'horizon*, Paris: Presses Universitaires de France, 1989

Collot, Michel, *La Matière-émotion*, Presses Universitaires de France, 1997

Deguy, Michel, *La poésie n'est pas seule*, Paris: Le Seuil, 1988

Esteban, Claude, *Critique de la raison poétique*, Paris: Flammarion, 1987

Éluard, Paul, *Oeuvres Complètes*, Paris: Gallimard, 1990–1995

Frontier, Alain, *La Poésie*, Paris: Belin, 1992

Glissant, Édouard, *Introduction à une poétique du divers*, Paris: Gallimard, 1996

Jaccottet, Philippe, *La Semaison, carnets 1954–1979*, Paris: Gallimard, 1984

Jarrety, Michel, *Dictionnaire de poésie de Baudelaire à nos jours*, Paris: Presses Universitaires de France, 2001

Khalfa, Jean, ed., *The Dialogue Between Painting and Poetry: Livres d'Artistes 1874–1999*, Cambridge: Black Apollo, 2001

Mallarmé, Stéphane, *Oeuvres Complètes*, Paris: Gallimard, 1998

Noël, Bernard, *Qu'est-ce que la poésie?* Paris: Éditions J.M. Place, 1995

Péret, Benjamin, *Oeuvres Complètes*, 7 volumes, Paris: José Corti, 1969–1995

Pinson, Jean-Claude, and Thibaud, Pierre, eds., *Poésie et Philosophie*, Tours: Farrago, 2000

Prigent, Christian, *Ceux qui merdrent*, Paris: Éditions POL, 1991

Queneau, Raymond, *Cent mille milliards de poèmes*, Paris: Gallimard, 1961

Reverdy, Pierre and Picasso, Pablo, *Le Chant des Morts*, Paris: Tériade, 1948

Rimbaud, Arthur, *Oeuvres Complètes*, Paris: LGF, 1999

Rothenberg, Jerome and Clay, Steven (eds.), *A Book of the Book*, New York: Granary Books, 2000

Senghor, Léopold Sédar, *Anthologie de la nouvelle poésie nère et malgache*, Paris: Presses Universitaires de France, 1948

Stamelman, Richard, *Lost Beyond Telling: Representations of Death and Absence in Modern French Poetry*, Ithaca, New York: Cornell University Press, 1990

Valéry, Paul, *Oeuvres*, 2 volumes, Paris: Gallimard, 1957

POLITICAL MOVEMENTS AND DEBATES

Political life in France throughout much of the twentieth century was often stormy and passionate. This was a century whose undoubted progress was punctuated by world wars, periodic economic crises, acute ideological conflict, the Cold War, wars of decolonization, and a difficult process of modernization. However, France's political turbulence—at least until the latter part of the century—must also be attributed to the depth of the divisions that were inherited from the Revolution of 1789 and were added to in the course of the nineteenth century. The principal dividing lines ran successively between absolute and constitutional monarchists, between liberal-conservative constitutionalists (who opposed the extension of the suffrage) and republicans, between Catholics and republicans, between conservative "opportunist" republicans and radical purist republicans, and toward the end of the century, between radical republicans, with their attachment to individual rights, and collectivist socialists, who until the Dreyfus Affair were mistrustful of the "bourgeois republic."

The Dreyfus Affair (1894–1899) arose out of a disagreement concerning the innocence or guilt of an army officer in an espionage case. Defenders of Dreyfus's innocence claimed he had been scapegoated and convicted by the Army because he was Jewish. The Affair escalated into a conflict between those who defended what the Republic represented (the universal rights of the individual, regardless of origin) and the twin pillars of the "old" France, the Army and the Catholic Church, with their adherence to the principles of hierarchy and submission to authority for the good of that organic community which is the Nation. Defense of the Republic prevailed over its enemies, and this led to the separation of Church and State in 1905. The Affair also contributed to a realignment of political forces into what would become their modern configuration.

Convinced by Jean Jaurès that socialism could be achieved by the extension of republican rights to the social and economic fields, Socialists joined with Radicals in the defense of the regime. This *rapprochement* created the basis of the twentieth-century left. In contrast, conservative republicans, fearful of the rise of a revolutionary labor movement, joined with anti-Dreyfus Catholics who had rallied to the Republic and formed a conservative right. Owing to the Republic's rough treatment of the Church, this *ralliement* was at first lukewarm, but shared sacrifice in the First World War; and France's victory over Germany in 1918 convinced many Catholics that the Republic was solid enough to defend the nation and was, therefore, worthy of allegiance. Catholic conservatives thus became the major component of the parliamentary right. Between them and the left lay the Moderates, liberal-conservative republicans who were the main representatives of business interests. Although in religious matters they inclined toward alliance with the secularist Radicals, their social conservatism inclined them toward the right.

This overall picture was further complicated by a greater degree of party-political fragmentation than it is possible to examine here and by the existence of extremes that were not integrated into the republican consensus. Thus, in the interwar period, it was difficult to sustain stable coalitions, and governments came and went in rapid succession, even between elections. The rules of the political game seemed particularly opaque and, to a large extent, excluded public involvement. This did little to reconcile certain antiliberal milieus to the parliamentary republic. Unstable coalitions and the functioning of the constitution—which tipped the balance of power in favor of the legislature, rather than the executive branch—made decisive government virtually impossible and fuelled criticism that the regime was, at best, weak and leaderless and, at worst, open to corruption and manipulated by a narrow, self-serving political elite with scant regard for the real national interest.

Antiparliamentarianism was, indeed, one of the characteristics of the nationalist extreme right, whose nationalism was chauvinistic and usually accompanied by virulent anti-Semitism. Other characteristics were authoritarianism, the cult of the great leader, hostility to modern individualism and capitalism, and a preference for a hierarchical and corporatist society. A common theme was that France was threatened by moral decadence and that this was aided and abetted by the parliamentary republic in league with Protestants, Jews, Freemasons, and parasitical foreigners. However, there was not one extreme right, but two. One-the one hand, there was a counterrevolutionary, monarchist right, galvanized from 1905 on into the *Ligue de l'Action Française* by Charles Maurras. Its youth wing, the *Camelots du Roi*, was active in street agitation in the 1920s. On the other hand, there was a national-populist right, which was exemplified at the turn of the century by Déroulède's *Ligues des Patriotes* and in the 1920s and 1930s by the *Jeunesses Patriotes*. This tendency wanted to impose a constitutional revision (by force if necessary) that would establish an authoritarian presidency, responsive by dint of referenda to the people ("real" democracy), and put an end to parliamentary flummery.

The interwar period provided fertile ground for the growth of extreme nationalism. A generation of disillusioned war veterans provided a captive audience for nationalists who condemned successive governments for not doing enough to make defeated Germany pay and ensure, by firmness, that there would be no future German threat. This situation was exacerbated by the economic slump that, in the wake of the 1929 Wall Street crash, affected France durably from 1932 on and called liberal capitalism into question. In addition, in Europe, the First World War and its sequels had given form to two new extreme ideologies: Communism and Fascism, each of which either fascinated or repelled French intellectuals. Anticommunism and antifascism became the main types of intellectual commitment.

All of these factors contributed to the instability of the 1930s and led to the formation of new antiregime movements. Among these was the *Ligue des Croix-de-Feu*, which had grown out of a veterans' association and was characterized by antistatist traditionalism and Catholic conservatism. However, movements such as *Solidarité française* and the *Parti franciste* espoused a much more totalitarian right-wing ideology. This raises the question of whether France had a homespun fascism that posed a real threat in this period. Historians are divided on the matter, although most French historians reject the idea. Be that as it may, the parties of the left certainly believed in the existence of a domestic fascist threat at the time. Their response was to form an antifascist alliance, which led to the *Front Populaire* government of 1936. This alliance included the French Communist Party (PCF) and brought about its integration into the French republican tradition and the national political community after years of isolation.

The PCF was born of an historic schism within the Socialist Party in 1920, when the majority tendency accepted Lenin's conditions for membership of the recently created Communist International. These effectively subordinated the new party to the Moscow line and imposed its conversion into a strictly disciplined, semiclandestine machine bent on the overthrow of the bourgeois order using all available means. Having started out from a strong base, the PCF lost much of its membership in the course of the 1920s, owing to its dogmatism and internal purges. It devoted much of its effort to attacking the Socialist Party's supposed betrayal of the working class. By 1930 it was at risk of becoming a marginalized sect. However, it was saved from this fate by its involvement in the *Front Populaire*.

After the 1920 split, the Socialist Party recovered, but it found itself in a difficult posture in the interwar period. On the one hand, it continued to declare itself revolutionary, but because of PCF competition, it had difficulty attracting working-class members. On the other hand, it had become an important parliamentary party but could not agree on an economic and social reform program with its republican ally, the Radical Party. This ambiguity was severely put to the test in the 1936 Blum government, which achieved significant social reforms but was dogged by economic problems and the vexed question of what France's official position should be on the Spanish Civil War. Some Socialists and the PCF inclined toward helping the Spanish republicans, but the British pressured Blum into accepting a position of neutrality. Within a year, disagreements between Socialists and Radicals over social legislation put an end to France's first experience of a Socialist-led government. The period was also overshadowed by the growing prospect of another European war, as Hitler annexed Austria and trampled over central Europe.

Even in the late 1930s, the memory of the carnage of the First World War remained painful enough to sustain a strong current of pacifism, which did not prepare France well for the impending war. However, pacifism was espoused for different reasons by different camps. Although the Parliament ratified the conciliatory 1938 Munich agreement, the vote was perhaps misleading. The conservative right was divided between its traditional anti-German nationalism and anti-Communism (Munich would give Hitler a free hand in the East to check Bolshevism). The extreme right voiced noisy approval of Munich (arguing that authoritarian regimes were needed to stop the spread of Communism). The Moderates were largely appeasers: with France's alliances looking ineffectual, their wishful thinking led them to hope that an accommodation could still be reached with Hitler. The Radicals were divided between appeasers and advocates of firmness. In the Socialist Party, there was a substantial minority that did not follow Blum's conversion to firmness and clung to unconditional pacifism. However, with the escalation of German aggression, the climate of opinion moved toward resignation to war. But there were no mobilizing themes as in 1914 (recovery of the lost provinces, an immediate threat to French territory), and many still hoped for an accommodation.

Distinct from the rest, the PCF zigzagged in line with changes in Soviet policy. Following Stalin's 1934 line, it was antifascist and condemned Munich. However, when news of the German–Soviet pact of nonaggression broke in August 1939, it was wrong footed and adopted a disconcerted neutrality. After Hitler's invasion of Poland and French mobilization, the PCF supported extra military spending, but when the USSR in turn invaded Poland, the party was outlawed by the French government and went underground. However, the German invasion of the USSR in June 1941 freed the PCF to engage in wartime resistance.

Thus, in the early stages, Resistance networks were organized by individuals and not by the parties. In any case, after France's defeat, the Occupation and Vichy suspended the activity of the political parties. They did not begin to play a political role again until General de Gaulle, the leader since 1940 of the Free French and France's postwar leader in waiting, brought them into the National Resistance Council in May 1943. That said, the PCF had a head start in resistance activity and was able to present itself as the patriotic party *par excellence*. Despite the fact that many Socialists were active in the Resistance, their party (only reconstructed in spring 1943) missed the boat with regard to outstanding resistance credentials.

At the Liberation (1944–1945), the prewar parties of the center and right were tainted by their acceptance of capitulation in 1940. In addition, the national mood was left-leaning. The Resistance had spawned a desire for political renewal beyond traditional party frameworks, which would bring together energetic reformers, be they Catholic or Socialist. However, this aspiration soon evaporated. The Socialist Party, threatened by the new popularity of the PCF, reaffirmed its Marxism and closed in on itself, whereas progressive Catholics formed a new Christian Democrat party, the *Mouvement Républicain Populaire*. The political scene was thus dominated by these three parties, which, briefly in coalition, squabbled over what kind of constitution France should have. Deeply opposed to their parliamentarian views, France's provisional leader, the acclaimed "Liberator" de Gaulle, quit the scene in the hope that the folly of the parties would soon provoke popular demand for his return as a strong leader in a presidential system of his own making. Nevertheless, by the end of 1946, France had a new constitution, but one whose chaotic procedures would soon resemble those of the prewar years.

The Fourth Republic (1946–1958) is remembered chiefly for its chronic governmental instability, which rendered it incapable of dealing effectively with intractable problems, notably the thorny and divisive question of decolonization in Indochina and Algeria. Its achievements were largely overshadowed by its failings. After the sense of shared purpose in the Resistance, postwar France saw the reappearance of deep political divisions. These were exacerbated by two fac-

tors: on the one hand, the Cold War and the presence of a strong Communist Party and, on the other, constant pressure from the Gaullists for constitutional revision. Although these two forces, at either ends of the political spectrum, could simultaneously make life difficult for governments, they could not join together to offer an alternative.

After the self-imposed expulsion of the PCF from government in 1947, "Third Force" coalitions (involving variously Socialists, Christian Democrats, Radicals, Moderates, and liberal conservatives, with little in common except the defense of the regime) struggled on from crisis to crisis. This inglorious period was, however, the heyday of the PCF. Despite its political isolation after 1947, the party was not marginalized. It belonged to a vast geopolitical Communist space. Party activists could accept temporary setbacks in their own country in the knowledge that they were marching with history toward universal proletarian emancipation. In addition, the PCF was unlike any other party in France. It was, indeed, a counterculture. It controlled the major labor union, the CGT, and administered a large number of municipalities. In addition, it had an abundant press, youth movements, women's and veterans' associations, and sports and leisure clubs. The fact that throughout the late 1940s and 1950s one voter in four (one in five in the 1960s and 1970s) voted communist was therefore only one indication of the party's strength.

The immense popularity of the PCF owed a great deal to its status as "the patriotic party of the Resistance." Individuals who had not been in the Resistance could have a vicarious connection with it through their party activism, which provided them with a sense of belonging and solidarity with a great and infallible cause. This was also true of intellectuals, who were undoubtedly attracted more by the idea of fraternizing with an idealized proletariat and communing with the universal than with the intricacies of Marxist philosophy. Although the party exploited the prestige of its intellectuals to the full, the endorsement of fellow travelers, such as Jean-Paul Sartre, was equally useful because they had the appearance of independence. A sphere of activism particularly favored by intellectuals was the Communist-controlled Peace Movement, which regularly mounted campaigns against American "imperialism" and presented the USSR as the dove of peace.

However, cracks began to appear in this edifice when three years after the death of Stalin, the leaked 1956 Kruschev report revealed that the adulated Soviet hero had in fact been a murderous tyrant. This was soon followed by the repression of the Hungarian revolution by Soviet tanks. Around the same time, the PCF's opposition to France's own atrocities in the Algerian War (1954–1962) was strangely muted. The support of intellectuals for the PCF began to wane, and in the 1958 elections that followed de Gaulle's return to power at the height of the Algerian crisis, the party lost over one-fifth of its electorate. However, what is perhaps in retrospective as curious as the postwar appeal of the PCF is the length of time it took for critiques of its Stalinism to have much effect. The erosion of the party's intellectual credibility and cultural relevance was gradual, and it was not until the 1980s that this was translated into irreversible electoral decline and political futility.

Another aspect of French "exceptionalism" was de Gaulle's *Rassemblement du Peuple Français*, launched in 1947. The strategy assigned to this movement was to get enough members of Parliament elected to force constitutional revision and enable de Gaulle's return to power. However, in 1951 the number of Gaullists elected fell short of fulfilling this strategy, and within a short time, they were absorbed into the routine of Third-Force politics. Thus, it was not the existence of a structured Gaullist movement that recalled de Gaulle to power in 1958, but the threat of civil war, brought about by the revolt of the French army in Algeria against a government in Paris suspected of giving in to the armed struggle of the Algerian Nationalist Liberation Front (FLN) for independence. The bulk of the political class reluctantly looked to de Gaulle to save the situation and bring the army back into line. His condition for accepting power was, of course, the drafting of a new, presidential, constitution. It was in these dramatic circumstances that France's present regime, the Fifth Republic, was born.

From 1958 until Algerian independence in 1962, the political parties shied away from hampering de Gaulle's attempts to reach a solution to the conflict. Opposition to the war therefore came from the intellectual and student left. Notable here was the activism of the students' union, the UNEF, of the small dissident socialist party, the PSU, of left-wing catholic organizations, and of the *Manifeste des 121*. The latter was a public petition associated with Sartre and the pro-FLN writer Francis Jeanson. It condemned the torture practiced by the army in Algeria and called on national servicemen to desert. Some of its signatories were subsequently subjected to repressive measures in this period of severe State censorship.

As president, de Gaulle pursued a policy of *grandeur*, intended to restore France's international prestige after years of drift. Foreign and defense policy was therefore given priority, although attention had to be paid to the modernization of the economy to pay for this ambition. France in the 1960s therefore underwent a somewhat authoritarian process of modernization. At the same time, the regime maintained an atmo-

sphere of solemnity, which was in keeping with its ethos of national duty, but increasingly out of tune with the sociocultural changes that postwar economic expansion was producing.

This mismatch was visible in the events of May 1968, which began in student anti–Vietnam War protests and deep, perhaps anomic, dissatisfaction with an archaic university system and then escalated to a *contestation*, not merely of the Gaullist state, but of the entire staid social order over which it presided. The libertarian themes of the students struck a chord with workers, especially those who were subjected to dehumanizing production-line work, exacerbated by an authoritarian style of management. Within a matter of weeks, student demonstrations and police brutality had sparked off a massive strike movement that brought the normal life of the country to a standstill and provoked a political crisis. The government recovered from this, but de Gaulle's confidence was durably shaken, and he voluntarily departed the scene the following year.

Paradoxically, in this increasingly prosperous consumer society, the social critique of the May movement was couched in terms remembered from the past; that is, in terms of revolutionary class struggle. However, it is significant that the youth movement did not look to the traditional herald of revolution, the PCF, and that it gave rise in the following years to social movements not based on economic class but on identity and "life space" issues (feminism, ecologism, regionalism, and the antinuclear and gay rights movements).

By the time the tide of post-1968 radicalism had ebbed, François Mitterrand had resurrected the Socialist Party (PS) and taken it into a strategic alliance with the PCF. Although the assertion of Valéry Giscard d'Estaing (president, 1974–1981) that France wanted to be governed from the center corresponded to a not unreasonable sociological intuition, in terms of political logic, its time had not yet come, and the 1970s saw the high point of left/right polarization of politics. Giscard's dream of an "advanced liberal society" was also soured by the onset of a post–oil crisis recession because semi-*dirigiste* France was not ready to accept an unfettered market economy and forego the protections offered by the State.

Although Mitterrand and the PS were able to sweep to victory in the 1981 elections, it was less because the electorate wholeheartedly embraced their program than because, after twenty-three years in government, the right was weary and divided and the left had been generous with its promises. The PS promised a "break with capitalism" and, more straightforwardly, a significant reduction of unemployment. In fact, the Socialists achieved neither of these goals. While the public resented the massive increase in unemployment, left-wing activists viewed the Socialist's 1983 U-turn and reluctant acceptance of market forces as a betrayal.

As for left-wing intellectuals, they had largely fallen silent as soon as the left had come to power. However, the roots of this "silence of the intellectuals" went back to the intellectual crisis of Marxism, and of its last redoubt, Third-Worldism, in the 1970s. Emblematic of this was the 1978 campaign to help the Vietnamese "Boat People," which brought about a reconciliation between Sartre and his long-standing liberal adversary, Raymond Aron. More than this, the very model of the committed intellectual disappeared. This reflected not so much a rejection of intellectuals as such, as of their authority. The claim of a particular class of individuals to possess unquestionable legitimacy and authority on all matters was no longer tenable in the media age. Besides, novelty was now in the other camp.

In the 1980s the leadership of the right fell to Jacques Chirac, who embraced the neoconservative "revolution" launched in the United Kingdom by Margaret Thatcher and in the United States by Ronald Reagan. Accordingly, Chirac developed an economic program based on market deregulation and privatization, which he put into practice when the right was again in government in 1986. Popular enthusiasm for this policy took a knock, however, after the 1987 Stock Market crash, and the right had to retreat from doctrinal economic liberalism. This narrowed the gap between the economic outlook of the left and the right. In addition, after 1983, all French governments were committed to the monetary constraints imposed by the European Monetary System. They could not, therefore, increase spending and reflate the economy to reduce unemployment, which continued to rise, producing a deep sense of insecurity in the country and the impression that governments were powerless. Disaffection with mainstream politicians was further fuelled by the implication of a number of them in financial scandals.

The above factors facilitated the reemergence of the extreme right. Its contemporary incarnation, the Front National (FN) led by Jean-Marie Le Pen, is the heir of the extreme nationalist tendencies seen above. Its originality is, first, to have federated these within a single movement and, second, to have constructed a modern and effective organization capable of contesting elections at all levels. To this we can add the appeal of a leader who manipulates the media with considerable skill and rails against the "establishment," which is "betraying" the people. Central to the FN's popular appeal, however, is its exploitation of anti-immigrant sentiment. Le Pen has managed to convince a sizeable proportion of the electorate that their national identity is threatened by the presence of foreigners on their soil. The FN's electoral success began in the mid-1980s and has best been illustrated by Le Pen's presence in the

second-round run-off against the incumbent president, Chirac, in the 2002 presidential election.

Since the 1990s, there have been a number of trends that are not identifiable with any one party. One of these is concern about loss of national sovereignty. Although this has typically manifested itself in hostility to further European integration, it can be argued that it also lay behind President Chirac's refusal to back the U.S. and U.K. military intervention in Iraq in 2003. A second theme is the continuing hostility of a large proportion of the French to economic liberalism. This is sometimes expressed in antiglobalization movements but is most visible in strike movements in defense of public services, which in 1995 and 2003 paralyzed the public sector. The debate is still open as to whether such collective action is merely a corporatist defense of safe jobs, or whether it speaks, more universally, in defense of a particular socioeconomic model.

After this review of a stormy century, we can perhaps conclude that, despite France's political "normalization" since the 1980s, there remain traces of a sometimes cherished, sometimes deplored, French "exception."

LAURENCE BELL

Further Reading

Flood, C., and Bell, L., *Political Ideologies in Contemporary France*, London: Pinter, 1997

Hazareesingh, S., *Political Traditions in Modern France*, Oxford: Oxford University Press, 1994

Judt, T., *Marxism and the French Left*, Oxford: Oxford University Press, 1986.

Lévêque, P., *Histoire des Forces politiques en France*, Paris: Armand Colin, 1997

Sirinelli, J.-F., Vandenbussche, R., and Vavasseur-Desperriers, J. *La France de 1914 à nos jours*, Paris: Presses Universitaires de France, 1993

Winock, M., *La France politique*, Paris: Seuil, 2003.

POLITZER, GEORGES (AKA FRANÇOIS AROUET; FÉLIX ARNOLD)
Communist Writer

While studying at the Sorbonne, Georges Politzer met other philosophy students, including Pierre Morhange, Henri Lefebvre, and Norbert Guterman. Together they founded the group Philosophies in 1924, which was also the name they gave to the review their group published (1924–1925). Intended to be the review of a *mouvement littéraire*, Politzer and his colleagues were opposed to Henri Bergson's and Léon Brunschvicg's philosophy, and appealed to a *révolte de l'esprit*.

Georges Politzer's thought was rooted in his familiarity with the work of Freud, which was rare at that time. One of his first articles in *Philosophies* was titled "Le mythe de l'anti-psychanalyse." During the Rifs' War (in Morocco), *Philosophies* joined Henri Barbusse's call with the reviews *Clarté* and *La Révolution surréaliste*. Their rapprochement was followed by the writing of the manifesto "La Révolution d'abord et toujours," published in *L'Humanité* in 1925. Shortly thereafter, Georges Friedmann joined the group and they published a new review, *L'Esprit*; only two issues appeared, in May 1926 and January 1927. In 1926, Politzer published the translation of Schelling's *Recherches philosophiques sur l'essence de la liberté humaine*, with a preface by Henri Lefebvre.

Politzer continued his research in psychology and psychoanalysis, and in 1928 he published the *Critique des fondements de la psychologie*, in which he elaborated on the idea of a concrete psychology. This book was intended to be the first volume of a series of books called *Matériaux pour la critique des fondements de la psychologie*, but the project never came to fruition. He published another book in 1929 under the pseudonym François Arouet, titled *La Fin d'une parade philosophique : le bergsonisme*, in which he attacked Bergson's thinking with vehemence. He took part that same year in the *Revue marxiste*, patronized by Charles Rappoport, with his old partners from the group Philosophies: Morhange, Lefebvre, Friedmann, and Guterman. Paul Nizan contributed to this creation, and it is through his impetus that some of them, like Politzer, became members of the Communist party. *La Revue marxiste* published Marx and Engels's earliest texts, and Politzer (under the pseudonym Félix Arnold) wrote an article about Lenin, *Matérialisme et Empiriocriticisme*. The review was funded by Georges Friedmann's father, who also provided funds for the foundation of the publishing house Les Revues. They published the *Revue de pyschologie concrete*, edited by Politzer, who analyzed the crisis of psychology and psychoanalysis and called for the "recherche d'une psychologie positive." These two reviews were shortlived because their funds were gambled away by Morhange. Politzer informed the Communist Party of this event, after which Morhange and Guterman were expelled from the party.

This episode shows that Politzer submitted to the Communist party's decrees. In 1930, he was appointed to the Confédération Générale du Travail Unifiée's Bureau de Documentation. His task was to write reports on individuals of whom the party was suspicious. Then he was placed in charge of the group's economic commission. Politzer gave up his psychology research, and from this point he was only dedicated to political economy and to popularizing Marxism. He published numerous economic papers in the party's review, *Les Cahiers du Bolchevisme*, and in the Communist daily newspaper, *L'Humanité*. Renouncing his intellectual past and at his old interests, he argued against any association between Marxism and psychoanalysis, and he even attacked the "freudo-marxisme" in *Commune*, the review of the Association des Ecrivains et des Artistes Révolutionnaires, of which he had once been a member.

Apart from these various activities, he taught philosophy at the Université Ouvrière. From August 1935, he taught courses in Communist Party schools, first in Genevilliers's Ecole élémentaire, then at the Ecole Centrale of the Party (in Arcueil). His courses on Marxism were published posthumously in 1948 under the title *Principes élémentaires de philosophie*. He took part also, in 1937, in the Communist party's tribute to Descartes for the tercentenary of *Discours de la Méthode*. In December 1936, he signed the Déclaration des intellectuels républicains au sujet des événements d'Espagne, published in *Commune*.

In 1938, he translated the *Dialectique de la nature* of Engels, with the Communist physicist Jacques Solomon, and took part in the foundation of the Groupe d'études materialists with the physicist Paul Langevin, which studied Marxism's contribution to the sciences. He contributed logically to the review *La Pensée*, "revue du rationalisme moderne" (1939), launched by the same group through the impetus of Paul Langevin and Georges Cogniot. He wrote, most notably, an article about the death of psychoanalysis.

He was called up to military service in 1939 and was a corporal in a Supply Corps based in military school. Demobilized in August 1940, he decided to gather Communist professors, and it is very likely that he wrote the manifesto called "Aux intellectuels du Parti" in November 1940. He founded *L'Université libre* with Jacques Decour and Jacques Solomon and continued to secretly lead *La Pensée* with them.

Living clandestinely (under the names of Jean Aguerre and Jean Destruges), he was arrested at his home in February 1942 as a member of the now-forbidden Communist Party. Delivered to German authorities in March, he was jailed and tortured. He was shot as a hostage May 23, 1942, at Mont-Valérien (near Paris), the same day as Jacques Solomon and Jacques Decour.

ANNE MATHIEU

See also **Henri Bergson; Leon Brunschvicg; Jean Grenier; Henri Lefebvre**

Biography

Georges Politzer was born in Nugyvarad in 1903. He studied philosophy at the Sorbonne. In 1924, he cofounded the group Philosophies and the journal of the same name. In 1929, he became associated with the *Revue marxiste*. Throughout the 1903s, he was an active member of the Communist Party, publishing articles in its official publications and teaching courses on communism in the party's schools. In 1939, he was called to military service. In 1942, he was arrested for his involvement with the Communist Party, and in May of that year he was executed.

Selected Works

Critique des fondements de la psychologie, as François Arouet, Tome I, 1928
La Fin d'une parade philosophique: le bergsonisme, 1929, 1967
Principes élémentaires de philosophie, 1948 (numerous editions)

Further Reading

Lefebvre, Henri, *La Somme et le reste*, 2 volumes, Paris: La Nef de Paris, 1959
Ory, Pascal, *Paul Nizan, destin d'un révolté*, Paris: Ramsay, 1980
Racine, Nicole, "Georges Politzer," in *Dictionnaire biographique du mouvement ouvrier français*, edited by Jean Maitron
Robrieux, Philippe, *Histoire intérieure du parti communiste*, Tome IV, Paris: Fayard, 1984
Trebitsch, M., "Les mésaventures du groupe 'Philosophies,'" *La Revue des revues*, 3, 1987

POSTSTRUCTURALISM

Poststructuralism is a difficult, rather diffuse, and often highly misunderstood category used to refer to developments within the broader field of French structuralist criticism and theory that occurred toward the end of the 1960s and throughout the 1970s. It is important to note that the French, unlike the English-speaking world, tend not to differentiate between structuralism and poststructuralism, but view developments in the late 1960s and early 1970s in a continuum with what went before, albeit in terms of a notion of structure that is more historically contingent, decentered, and open-ended. There is much to justify this refusal to identify a radical break between structuralism and the various ruptures it undergoes during the late 1960s in the work of the *Tel Quel* group (most importantly in Barthes's shifting critical thinking or in Kristeva's work on the semiotic and intertextuality) and in the work of philosophers such as Jacques Derrida, Gilles Deleuze, and Jean-François Lyotard. This is not only because the seminal work of some of these figures (e.g., Derrida and Deleuze) dates back to the early 1960s or late 1950s, when structuralism was rising to

an ascendant position, but also because many of the motifs associated most closely with post-structuralism are, to a degree, already present in what one might call high structuralist thinking. The emphasis on the decentering of structure, on its open-endedness and incompleteness, can be seen already in Lacan's conception of the symbolic order as it develops in the late 1950s, whereas the emphasis on the historical finitude of structure devoid of any transcendental foundation or guarantee is clearly present in the early work of Michel Foucault (e.g., *Histoire de la Folie*). Likewise, structuralist narratology incorporates some categories that point to an open-ended and diffuse notion of structure; for example, Gérard Genette's use of the term "archi-texte." Nevertheless, it is true that these various moments, which are important aspects of broadly structuralist thinking, are more decisively articulated and more radically foregrounded in what the Anglo-Saxon community has come to know as poststructuralism. This can best be indicated in the light of two key essays published in 1967: Derrida's famous "La structure, le signe et le jeu dans le discours des sciences humaines" (1967) and Deleuze's less well-known "A quoi reconnaît-on le structuralisme?" (1967).

The year 1967 was a key turning point within the history of French structuralism. In "La structure, le signe," Derrida alludes to what he calls an "event" in the history of the concept of structure and suggests that this event takes the form of a rupture but also a reintensification of this concept. Before this event, Derrida argues, the concept of structure has been centered or firmly anchored on a fixed point of origin or moment of presence. If various elements within a structure of thought are articulated by way of a system of differences forming an interrelated whole, then that whole itself has a fixed center that grounds the whole and regulates its differential relations in a relatively stable and determinable manner. This center has always functioned like a transcendental signifier guaranteeing the identity and self-presence of the system and has taken on various names throughout the history of European thought: essence, existence, substance, subject, transcendence, consciousness, God, man, and so on. This moment articulates one of Derrida's most famous theses, namely, that of the history of European thinking as a history of *logocentrism* and, after Heidegger, the determination of being as presence. The event of rupture that Derrida attempts to describe here is a historical moment in which contemporary thought and understanding finds itself, a moment that cannot be reduced to any one individual philosopher but that, nevertheless, is most radically expressed in the work of certain key thinkers: the Nietzschean critique of metaphysics, the Freudian critique of the subject, and most important for Derrida, the Heideggarian destruction of the tradition of onto-theology. In all cases, what is articulated is the loss of any founding or transcendental signifier that centers the structuring power of structure on a point of origin or moment of presence. It is in this context that a key category of much poststructuralist, and subsequently postmodern, thinking emerges: the category of discourse. Once deprived of any foundational or transcendental signifier that would ground a signifying system within an economy of presence and self-identity, a structure knows no point of fixity or anchorage that escapes the dynamic of differential relations to articulate its existence as structure. The transcendental signifier is now no longer a structuring principle but is itself caught up within or looped down into the finite economy of structuration. One of Derrida's most controversial, and perhaps most misunderstood, terms, that of play or *jeu*, takes on a key role here.

The phrase "free play of the signifier" has often been taken to refer to a kind of semantic relativism where, in the absence of any "real" meaning, signifiers can mean anything at all, as they essentially mean nothing. It is important to note that, for Derrida, this is not, nor ever was, the case. The term "play" (*jeu*) implies simply that signification occurs as an effect of differential relations within a signifying system. Play is far more like the space or "give" between mechanical cogs that allows them to turn than it is a principle of total arbitrariness. Derrida's point is that, in the absence of any transcendental signifier, the entire field of signification is subject to a certain slippage, indeterminacy, or contamination within the differential play of the signifying system. This slippage or play is what allows meaning to be produced as an effect of the signifying system, but that, at the same time, prevents the system from grounding itself as self-present or self-identical (Derrida's term *différance* articulates this generalized movement). The absence at the heart of any signifying system or structure is not, for Derrida, a principle of arbitrariness whereby anything can mean what one wants it to mean. Rather, meaning itself is produced within a movement of substitutions within the signifying system (x means y, y means z, etc.), which endlessly supplements the underlying absence of a transcendental signifier. Because of this, the movement of signification will never come to rest nor know any limit or final term. In Derrida's thinking, therefore, the system or structure is finite, but the play of signification it produces is open-ended or infinite.

It is interesting to note that Derrida devotes much of "La Structure, le signe" to uncovering this open-ended system of signification at work in the structural anthropology of Claude Lévi-Strauss. This indicates once again that the distinction one might make between structuralism and poststructuralism is by no means watertight or secure. Derrida's argument that the concept of structure needs to be thought in an open-ended way and in the absence of any founding or transcendental term is closely echoed in Deleuze's essay "A quoi reconnaît-on le structuralisme?" (1967). Deleuze's 1967 account of structuralism is, in many ways, similar to that given by Derrida, even if the terms he deploys are at times quite different. Deleuze invokes a number of figures to describe the structuration and dynamic movement of signifying systems: virtual and actual, serial and, above all, the "case vide." He makes the point that all the elements, relations, and values of a structure coexist as a whole and that as differential elements or relations, they exist in a manner that is complete and perfectly determined. However, as a perfectly determined whole, a structure exists only virtually. That which presents itself to us, that which is actualized within a virtual structure, are only specific relations or values that make manifest specific phenomena. For Deleuze, we have no language that would articulate, make present, or determine the entirety of any structure, as the language we have is necessarily a fragmentary, and very specific, actualization of an always virtual totality. This means that structure, so far as we can determine it, is always indeterminate, open-ended, and infinite (hence, an attempt to produce a grammar or syntax of any structural system would be futile). The actualization of differential and signifying relations occurs, according to Deleuze, in series of singular signifying moments. A structure actualizes its specific symbolic elements when its differential relations organize themselves in these series; structure is then, for Deleuze, serial or multiserial. Such signifying chains would be, for instance, those symbolic series articulated around phonetic or morphological differential relations, or those series of signification organized around certain domains of meaning: linguistic, economic, biological, and so on. The emphasis here is very similar to that of Derrida in "La Structure, le signe": In the absence of any foundational term which would transcend the serial structuring movement of the system, each series is open-ended and knows no closure.

Derrida's emphasis on play and on the absence of any transcendental signifier is repeated in a different way in Deleuze's use of the term "case vide." For his own reasons (relating to his conception of immanence and of Being as univocal), Deleuze is reluctant to use words such as "absence," and the term "empty" here designates a gap or undetermined space within any structure or series that allows the signification or sense to be produced (echoing Derrida's logic of supplementarity). It is this empty space that allows the movement or passage of sense to be articulated along signifying chains in a process of symbolic substitution (what Deleuze terms "object = x"). As a kind of primary indeterminacy, the "case vide" operates as a third term that disrupts the binary relations of symbolic structure (which, left intact, would render the whole static and closed in on itself) and allows sense or signification to emerge as a dynamic movement of production.

A number of key points emerge from Derrida's and Deleuze's 1967 recasting of the notion of structure. First, they are foregrounding elements that, they insist, have always been present in classical or high structuralism. Second, they both place a key emphasis on that which escapes symbolic or structural determination. In Derrida's case, what is absent is any transcendental signifier or instance that could found the whole in an economy of presence; in Deleuze's, it is the "case vide," the empty space that, as a primary indeterminacy, allows for symbolic exchange to occur and produces signification in series or chains of signifiers. In both cases, structure is seen as finite, but infinite in the movement or play of signification it produces and hence decentered, open-ended, and non–self-identical. It is worth noting that, even though poststructuralism has been conventionally associated with textual or symbolic play, with the celebration of indeterminacy and absence of origin, it has, from its earliest formulations in these essays, placed a key importance on that which exceeds symbolic determination or ontological disclosure. This excess, which has most often been designated in the category of the "real," always works as the third term that ungrounds or decenters structure. For all the emphasis on textual play, then, poststructuralist thought has, from the outset, attempted to account for and take responsibility for the excess of thought and meaning, an excess that, these thinkers would hold, makes thought and meaning possible in the first instance. In both cases, what is at stake is not meaning as absence, void, or simple arbitrariness; rather, it is meaning as production, as effect of a limitless process of signification.

All these issues were taken up in the "turn" of Barthes work, which was marked by the publication of *S/Z* (1970) and *Le Plaisir du texte* (1973) in the 1970s. In the earlier "Introduction to the Structural Analysis of Narrative," Barthes emphasizes the function of the *index*, which he describes as "a more or less diffuse concept which is nevertheless necessary to the meaning of the story: psychological indices concerning the characters, data regarding their identity, notations of atmosphere and so on." *Image Music Text*, p. 9. This might indicate that for Barthes, even in his structuralist moment, the notion of structure being deployed does not imply an entirely self-enclosed formal entity but, rather, structure whose integrated planes and levels also open out onto wider and more diffuse webs of cultural signifiers. The index has, if you like, a con-

notative function that relies on a whole range of cultural contexts and associations with which the reader will probably be familiar. The openness and more diffuse character of the index is radicalized in the structural analysis of Balzac's short story that Barthes undertakes in his 1970 work, *S/Z*. Here Barthes does not use Benveniste's notion of levels of description or analysis, as he did in the earlier essay. Nor does he seek to identify units that will combine on or between levels distributionally and relationally in the way that a sentence is built up according to the rules of grammar and syntax. Rather, he cuts the whole of Balzac's short story up into short bits of text that he calls *lexias* (*lexies* in French). The division of these short contiguous fragments is arbitrary and is only, as Barthes says, "l'enveloppement d'un volume sémantique," the enclosure of a semantic volume. The key point to note here is that any notion of an enclosed or integrated formal structure seems to have gone straight out of the window. "The text," Barthes writes, "in its mass, can be compared to the sky, flat and deep at the same time, smooth, without edges, and without points of reference" (*S/Z*, p. 20). This seems to be a dramatic departure from the project announced only four years earlier in "Introduction to the Structural Analysis of Narrative." The lexia, as a semantic unit, is Barthes tells, us traversed by codes, of which he identifies five: the hermeneutic code, described as the totality of elements relating to the posing, resolving, or answering of specific questions within narrative; the semantic code, which indicates specific meanings and function much like the earlier index; the symbolic code (displacements and associations of meaning), the proaïretic code (sequences of action), and the cultural codes (which refer to wealth of cultural references as knowledge). The key point to note here is that for Barthes, these codes are not units that combine according to a syntax of narrative. The terms he uses are terms like *tissu*, implying that the narrative is woven in a more plural and heterogeneous way from all these codes (echoing Deleuze's use of the term "series"). The codes form a multiplicity of cultural meanings or voices that traverse each lexeme. The text is a work of multiple strands, and if it is a structure at all, it is a highly diffuse and open-ended structure that is not centered on itself or self-identical in any way but is internally plural, different from itself and without identity. In this sense, for the Barthes of *S/Z* and after, structure has become subject to finitude. It is an open-ended, spatiotemporally finite multiplicity that is coextensive with the untotalizable totality of human culture itself, a generalized writing that is the condition of possibility for all writing and all narrative. One can see clearly here the manner in which the poststructuralist Barthes has adapted his literary critical thinking to the recasting of the concept of structure undergone in the seminal essays of Derrida and Deleuze discussed above.

Poststructuralism, such as it can be seen to emerge in the 1967 essays of Derrida and Deleuze and then manifest itself in the shifts undergone in Barthes's critical thinking, signals the looping down of the concept of structure into the multiplicity and difference of spatial and temporal finitude. This, in turn, implies an infinitization of the process of signification itself, which is seen in terms of a dynamic and open-ended process of production. As has been indicated, far from being purely a gesture that affirms symbolic free-play and semantic equivocation, poststructuralism attempts to break open the concept of structure and place it in relation to its own excess. It is in this context that the body and issues of embodiment become an important point of focus in the very late 1960s and throughout the early 1970s. This can be seen in Barthes's discourse on the body of this period and on the notion of libidinal economy taken up and developed by Lyotard and Deleuze in their texts of the 1970s. The body becomes a site of excess, a space of libidinal drives and affects, forces that both bear the inscriptions of signifying systems in unconscious traces but that are at the same time resistant to any structured codification of meaning. In Barthes's *Le Plaisir du texte* (1973), Lyotard's *L'Économie libidinale* (1974) and *Discours Figure* (1971), Deleuze's *Anti-Œdipe* (1972–1973), as well as in Kristeva's work around the category of the "semiotic," the body is a site of rupture, a space of finitude in which codes are fragmented, a site that is itself so radically singular it cannot be coded. The double emphasis placed here on signification as infinite process of production, and on the body as a site of this production, provides the most fruitful perspective within which texts gathered under the term poststructuralism can continue to be read. Above and beyond the attempt to rethink structure in a more finite and open-ended fashion, poststructuralism's emphasis on excess and on the relation of signifying systems to an always effervescent "real" took French thought beyond the formalism and abstraction of structuralist thinking that dominated the human sciences throughout much of 1950s and 1960s.

IAN JAMES

See also **Roland Barthes; Emile Benveniste; Gilles Deleuze; Jacques Derrida; Michel Foucault; Gerard Genette; Julia Kristeva; Claude Levi-Strauss; Jean-Francois Lyotard; Structuralism**

Further Reading

Barthes, R., "Introduction to the structural Analysis of narrative" "The Death of the Author" and "From Work to Text" in *Image Music Text*. London: Fontanna, 1977
Barthes, R., *S/Z*, Paris: Seuil, 1970; translated by R. Miller, Oxford: Blackwell, 1990
Barthes, R., *Le Plaisir du texte*, Paris: Seuil, 1973; translated by R. Miller, New York: Noonday, 1975
Barthes, R., *Roland Barthes par Roland Barthes*, Paris: Seuil, 1975; translated by R. Howard, London: Macmillan, 1977.
Deleuze, G., *Différence et répétition*, Paris: 1968); translated by P. Patton, London: Athlone, 1994
Deleuze, G., *Logique du sens*, Paris: Minuit, 1969; translated by M. Lester, London: Athlone, 1990
Deleuze, G., "A quoi reconnaît-on le structuralisme?" in *La Philosophie au XXième siècle*, edited by F. Châtelet, Paris: Hachette, 1973
Deleuze, G., and Guattari, F., *L'Anti-Œdipe*, Paris: Minuit, 1972–1973); translated by R. Hurley, M. Seem, H. Lane, London: Athlone, 1984
Deleuze, G., and Guattari, F., *Mille Plateaux*, Paris: Minuit, 1980; translated by B. Massumi, Minneapolis: University of Minnesota Press, 1987
Derrida, J., *La Voix et le phénomène*, Paris: Presses Universitaires de France, 1967
Derrida, J., *De la grammatologie*, Paris: Minuit, 1967; translated by G. C. Spivak, Baltimore, Maryland: Johns Hopkins University Press, 1997
Derrida, J., "La Structure, le signe et le jeu dans le discours des science humaines," in *Écriture et la différence*, Paris: Seuil, 1967; translated by A. Bass, Chicago: University of Chicago Press, 1978
Derrida, J., *Marges de la philosophie*, Paris: Minuit, 1972; translated by A. Bass, Brighton: Harvester Press, 1982
Foucault, M, *Histoire de la Folie*, Paris: PLON, 1961
Kristeva, J., *La Révolution du langage poétique*, Paris: Seuil, 1974; translated by M. Waller, New York: Columbia, University Press, 1984
Lyotard, J.-F., *Discours Figure*, Paris: Klincksieck, 1971
Lyotard, J.-F., *L'Economie Libidinale*, Paris: Minuit, 1974

POULANTZAS, NICOS
Communist Intellectual and Academic

Nicos Poulantzas was a Greek intellectual who spent his most productive years teaching and researching in France. A committed member of the Greek Communist Party of the Interior, he was also active and influential in theoretical and political debates on the French left. He held various academic posts in Paris—his last being that of professor of sociology at Vincennes University—but his work defied disciplinary boundaries in its concern to critique contemporary capitalism. While remaining faithful to the basic tenets of Marxism, Poulantzas was an innovative thinker who changed his position on the state and political strategy several times in response to theoretical debates and political events. This is reflected in his intellectual and political development over the twenty years of his active engagement in theoretical and political issues until his suicide on October 3, 1979. During this time, he became the most influential postwar Western Marxist theorist of the state. Outside France he was best known for his analysis of the relative autonomy of the capitalist state and, subsequently, for his analysis of the state as a social relation. Most influential in this regard was his debate over several years, in *New Left Review*, on the nature of the capitalist state with another Marxist theorist, Ralph Miliband. This led to the translation of all of his most important books into English and several other languages and to continuing critical engagement with his work by social scientists as well as political activists.

Following his successful pursuit of a law degree in Greece, which gave him the chance to study political science and sociology, Poulantzas's intellectual career began with studies in Marxist legal philosophy and legal theory from a Sartrean perspective. This was the topic of his doctoral dissertation (completed in 1965) and several other studies in the early 1960s. He then turned toward political theory and began to develop a view of the capitalist type of state and political struggle that owed much to Antonio Gramsci, the Italian communist activist and theorist, and to postwar Italian Marxist thought. In particular, Poulantzas seized on Gramsci's analysis of hegemony as the exercise of political, intellectual, and moral leadership as the defining feature of class power in advanced capitalist democracies that were based on possessive individualism economically and on individual citizenship in a national state politically. He also highlighted Gramsci's emphasis on the key role of the state apparatus in a broad sense in mediating and organizing the hegemony of a power bloc (a durable coalition of dominant economic and political class forces) as well as in disorganizing the subaltern classes. This view was soon integrated into a broader perspective on the role of the state in capitalist societies influenced (not always to the good) by the structural Marxism of Louis Althusser and Étienne Balibar. The most developed account of this stage in his thought is his book, *Pouvoir politique et classes sociales* (1968).

Shortly thereafter, Poulantzas embarked on a slow retreat from the immobilizing implications of a structural Marxist view and displayed increasing concern with strategically relevant theoretical issues, such as the nature of fascism and military dictatorships, the changing contours of imperialism and social class relations, and the role of parties and social movements in modern capitalism. This productive period of study and struggle is well represented in his three books on *Fascisme et dictature* (1972), *Classes sociales dans le capitalisme d'aujourd'hui* (1974), and *La Crise des dictatures* (1975). In his final studies, he increasingly addressed problems posed by the self-evident crisis in European Marxism as social theory and as a guide to practice, taking on board some of Foucault's arguments about the ubiquity of power as a social relation and Henri Lefebvre's ideas on space and spatiality,

critiquing the *nouveaux philosophes*, and engaging in debates about representative and direct democracy. His last and greatest work was *L'Etat, le pouvoir, le socialisme* (1978), in which, according to his own immodest claim, he finally outlined the key ideas of the hitherto unfinished Marxist theory of the state. The key to this theory was the notion that the state is a social relation (rather than a thing or subject) and that state power is therefore best interpreted as the material condensation of the changing balance of forces. In addition, this text provides rich and insightful comments on the spatiality and temporality of the capitalist state, the mental-manual division of labor and official discourse, the changing political forms of the capitalist type of state, new forms of state intervention, and arguments about the necessity of a democratic transition to democratic socialism.

Politically, Poulantzas was initially committed to democratic politics, then converted to Marxism-Leninism, subsequently became a left Eurocommunist, and eventually, subscribed to a radical democratic politics that committed to cross-class alliances and was favorable to an independent role for social movements. These later commitments are particularly clear in *L'Etat, le pouvoir, le socialisme* (1978). The driving force behind this political as well as intellectual development was, above all, political events in Greece and France. Poulantzas was concerned about understanding how changes in imperialism affected national states and class struggles in Europe; analyzing the prospects of left European Communism and the Union de la Gauche in France; addressing the pressing problems of a democratic transition to democratic societies after the crisis of the Greek, Portuguese, and Spanish dictatorships in the mid-1970s; understanding the emerging crisis of state socialism; and identifying and contesting the trend toward authoritarian statism in northwestern Europe. As he observed these events and participated in them, he often found his theoretically derived expectations about broad trends in economic and political development confirmed, but he was also caught unawares by surprising shifts in political conjunctures. These included the events of May 1968 in France and their aftermath, the Greek *coup d'état* in 1969, the collapse of the Greek junta in 1974 under the weight of its own internal contradictions and the stresses induced by struggles at a distance from the dictatorship, and the collapse of the *Union de la Gauche* at the prompting of the French Communist Party in 1977. These events prompted him to reevaluate the possibilities of class struggle, the nature of normal and exceptional capitalist states, the character of the state as a social relation, the leading role of the vanguard communist party and the working class in the struggle for socialism, the contributions to revolutionary change of popular-democratic struggles and new social movements. In this way, he was forced to rethink both his basic theoretical ideas and his applied theoretical-strategic concepts, and in so doing, he eventually developed his distinctive theoretical account of the state as a social relation and his distinctive strategy for a democratic transition to democratic socialism.

BOB JESSOP

See also **Louis Althusser; Etienne Balibar; Henri Lefebvre; Jean-Paul Sartre**

Biography

Nicos Poulantzas was born in Athens on September 21, 1936. He obtained a law degree in Athens, and then studied briefly in Germany before moving to Paris in 1960, where he settled permanently. He had a varied academic career, holding several posts at universities in Paris. His last position was Professor of Sociology at Vincennes University. Poulantzas committed suicide on October 3, 1979.

Selected Works

Pouvoir politique et classes socials, 1968
Fascisme et dictature, 1972
Classes sociales dans le capitalisme d'aujourd'hui, 1974
La Crise des dictatures, 1975
L'Etat, le pouvoir, le socialisme, 1978

Further Reading

Jessop, B., *Nicos Poulantzas: Marxist Theory and Political Strategy*, Basingstoke: Macmillan, 1985

POULET, GEORGES
Critic

A philosophically oriented literary critic, Georges Poulet marks an important phenomenological turn in the discipline. Emphasizing the dynamic nature of the reading process, Poulet's "criticism of consciousness" sees a literary work as essentially a verbal reflection or manifestation of the author's mind. Ontologically speaking, a text is thereby seen as a mental object that allows the reader to enter in contact with the writer's preceding mental experience.

Poulet's criticism is hence founded on a principle that, strictly speaking, bears little relation to literary studies. Focusing on unveiling the mind manifested in the text, language in fact threatens to be the very veil that the critic is challenged to undo. To be receptive to the subjective apprehension of the writer's mind, the critic must momentarily annihilate the formal features of the work: He or she must reveal what the work is before it takes its objective form.

For that reason, Poulet's criticism characteristically pays little regard to formal boundaries such as genre notions and disciplines; philosophy and literature merge, and any textual manifestation—including journals, letters, and fragments—become part of the author's oeuvre. Only a comprehensive corpus will encompass all facets of a comprehensive mind that therefore must be studied in its totality—without, however, resorting to strictly biographical observations.

Yet if language is taken to obstruct the apprehension of the writer's subjectivity, a methodological difficulty lies in wait. Reaching behind the formal aspects of the work, the critic can no longer rely on the structure of language, and left simply with an intangible and amorphous inner world, criticism stands in danger of being equally lacking in structure and, hence, of being merely impressionistic.

To address this methodological problem and its critical *impasse*, Poulet reverts to the notion of the cogito. Refining Marcel Raymond's use of this Cartesian concept, Poulet takes the cogito to be the "point of departure" on that itinerary of the author's mind that the critic is subsequently to run through and map out (cf. the title *Le Point de depart* [1964]). With the literary work becoming a field for self-discovery, the cogito is to be located in the moment when the author first apperceives his self and comes to awareness of his own being, which explains Poulet's fascination with the literary theme of awakenings. Once this initial moment is located, literature can be approached as a continual reintroduction of the author's consciousness into his work.

The moment of awareness establishes duration, and the cogito can henceforth be situated within a temporality. The experience of temporality in the literary work has therefore been one of Poulet's principal occupations, as the title of the central work *Studies in Human Time* indicates. Time, however, takes an almost spatial form, with the cogito at the center suspended in its temporal, spatial, and causal relations with the world. These categorical relations mark the "interior distances" that both separate the subject from the world and, through awareness, allow engagement with it (cf. the title *The Interior Distance* [1952]). By closing in on an expanding consciousness through these categorical relations, Poulet's criticism thus becomes methodical by reverting to a traditional subject–object relation as its structuring principle.

The cogito thus marks the starting point on the author's mental journey and therefore gives a unique key to the identity of the author's oeuvre. The cogito unites an author's production by showing internal coherence and similarity within a great variety of textual material. Yet with the cogito as the common denominator in all literary oeuvres, literature now seems reduced to a monotonous collection of cogitos that the critic is then left to compile systematically. The cogito, however, serves not just as an *identifying* but also as a *differential* principle: It renders each oeuvre unique and sharply differentiable from other authors'. Ideally, oeuvres should therefore be studied in their difference much more than in their similarity (cf. *La Poésie éclatée: Baudelaire/Rimbaud* [1980]).

Furthermore, the critic cannot approach the cogito passively but must retrieve an author's cogito through his own inward experience. Only through a process of awareness similar to that previously experienced by the author can the critic hope to efface his or her own self's specificity and prepare his or her critical sensitivity for apprehending that other consciousness. Criticism is therefore essentially a "consciousness of consciousness," as Poulet's intellectual disciple and heir, J. Hillis Miller, describes it.

Consequently, the reading process does not move linearly from the unfamiliar to the familiar in the light of further interpretation. Rather, reading is a phenomenon by which intersubjective recognition surfaces from the depths of the reader's own consciousness, allowing momentary fusion to take place between author and reader. When this fusion is ordered into a narrative, it becomes literary criticism.

This unity of the perspectives of the critic and the writer, a feature otherwise typical of most modernist criticism, has earned Poulet's method the label of "criticism of identification" in conjunction with the more commonly used "criticism of consciousness." "Identification," however, is potentially misleading. The critic does not simply "identify" with the author: No less than an identical self to that of the author must have operated within the critic if his criticism is at all to be successful.

Around these critical principles of consciousness and identification, a number of prominent thinkers gather as "the Geneva School." Mainly an invention of Poulet's, this metahistorical and metaformalistic school of criticism has never produced a manifesto or jointly edited a review. Yet it clearly comprises, in addition to Poulet himself, Marcel Raymond, Albert Béguin, Jean Rousset, Jean-Pierre Richard, and Jean Starobinski.

Poulet distinguishes himself within this school by a more absolute obedience to the principle of disinterestedness. The identification with the other consciousness that takes place in the reading process never becomes a means to any further end, not even a means to obtaining indirect access to himself (as may be the case in Starobinski). The identification of critical thought with the criticized thought should take place exclusively for the sake of the author.

This disinterestedness is a consequence of Poulet's idealism by which nothing comes before consciousness and everything follows from it. Although it is not always clear (as Paul de Man has pointed out) whether the critic should understand the cogito as an origin or a center of the textual oeuvre, the cogito itself stands as a sort of mental "big bang" with an ensuing infinite expansion of the author's mental universe.

However, if each author's oeuvre stands for a unique and isolated mental universe, one must ask how a critic can approach and apprehend several authors: How could his critical consciousness coincide with a whole collection of unique minds? The question is important because the Geneva School stands accused of disregarding literary history that precisely attempts to group authors according to objective criteria. In his later criticism, Poulet has therefore attempted to apply the cogito metahistorically by allowing a historical period to be conceived of as a closed unity of consciousness (cf. *La Pensée indéterminée* [1987]). History can thus be approached, not linearly, but as a system of concentric spheres of consciousness that allows the critic to leap from one sphere to another.

Poulet's criticism has had a considerable effect on Anglophone criticism, in particular through the writings of J. Hillis Miller. However, American New Critics such as René Wellek have resisted Poulet's method on the grounds that the ensuing criticism remains impressionistic and, moreover, unjustifiably presupposes consciousness to be a unitary concept. Nevertheless, Poulet's work remains close to all criticism of interpretation in its impulse to structure the literary work through a cohesive and nonideological critical narrative.

NIELS BUCH-JEPSEN

See also **Albert Beguin; Marcel Raymond**

Biography

Born on November 29, 1902, in Chênée, Belgium, Georges Poulet studied at the University of Liège and received Ph.D.s in both law and literature. From 1927, he taught at the University of Edinburgh, and from 1952, he taught at Johns Hopkins University in Baltimore, Maryland, where he was the editor of *MLN* and where, in 1953, he met his new colleague, J. Hillis Miller. Four years later, Poulet became professor of French at the University of Zürich, and from 1968, he held the same post at the University of Nice. As a young man, he had published articles, poems, and a novel under the *nom de plume* of Georges Thialet, but his career only really began in 1949 with the publication of the first volume of *Studies in Human Time*, which won him the Prix Sainte-Beuve. He died in Brussels on December 31, 1991.

Selected Writings

Etudes sur le temps humain, 1949; as *Studies in Human Time*, translated by Elliott Coleman, 1956
La Distance intérieure—Etudes sur le temps humain II, 1952; as *The Interior Distance*, translated by Elliott Coleman, 1959
Les Métamorphoses du cercle, 1961; as *The Metamorphoses of the Circle*, translated by Carley Dawson and Elliott Coleman, 1966
L'Espace proustien, 1963; as *Proustian Space*, translated by Elliott Coleman, 1977
Le Point de départ—Etudes sur le temps humain III, 1964
Trois essais de mythologie romantique, 1966
"Une critique d'identification," in *Les Chemins actuels de la critique*, edited by Georges Poulet, 1967: 7–22
Mésure de l'instant—Etudes sur le temps humain IV, 1968
Benjamin Constant par lui-même, 1968
Quatre conférences sur la nouvelle critique, 1968
Qui était Baudelaire? 1969; as *Baudelaire: The Artist and his Work*, translated by Robert Allen and James Emmons, 1969
"Phenomenology of Reading," *New Literary History* 1 (1969): 53–68
La Conscience critique, 1971
"Poulet on Poulet—the Self and the Other in Critical Consciousness," *Diacritics* 2 (1972): 46–50
Entre moi et moi—Essais critiques sur la conscience de soi, 1976
La Poésie éclatée—Baudelaire/Rimbaud, 1980; as *Exploding Poetry: Baudelaire/Rimbaud*, translated by Françoise Meltzer, 1984
With Marcel Raymond, *Correspondance 1950–1977*, 1981
La Pensée indéterminée I De la renaissance au romantisme, 1985
La Pensée indéterminée II—Du romantisme au début du XXe Siècle, 1987
La Pensée indéterminée III—De Bergson à nos jours, 1990

Further Reading

Alexander, Ian W., *French Literature and the Philosophy of Consciousness: Phenomenological Essays*, Cardiff: University of Wales Press, 1984
de Man, Paul, "Vérité et méthode dans l'œuvre de Georges Poulet," *Critique*, 25 (1969): 608–623
Jeanneret, Michel, "L'École de Genève?" *Revue d'Histoire Littéraire de la France*, 95 (1995): 54–64
Miller, J. Hillis, "The Literary Criticism of Georges Poulet," *MLN* 78 (1963): 471–488
Miller, J. Hillis, "The Geneva School: The Criticism of Marcel Raymond, Albert Béguin, Georges Poulet, Jean Rousset, Jean-Pierre Richard, and Jean Starobinski," in *Modern French Criticism, from Proust and Valéry to Structuralism*, edited by John K. Simon, 1972: 277–310
Miller, J. Hillis, *Others*, Princeton, New Jersey: Princeton University Press, 2001
Wellek, René, "Poulet, Du Bos, and Identification," *Comparative Literature Studies* 10 (1973): 173–193

PRÉVOST, JEAN
Novelist, Biographer, Critic

Jean Prévost did not systematize his works into a logical whole. Not that the material was insufficient: Prévost's work includes numerous essays, novels, biographies, and articles published in journals and magazines, not to mention his thesis *Sur la creation chez Stendhal*. This heritage, collected, would comprise about twenty volumes of original and creative thought. Killed by the Nazis in 1944, Prévost did not have time to bring his work to a conclusion; perhaps, though, Prévost would have never tried to propose a systematic philosophy anyway, as, very much like his teacher Alain, he belonged to that group of thinkers for whom theory only makes sense if it is based on life experience and who test their theories through the prism of their own lives.

Starting in 1924, Prévost wrote on a regular basis in *N.R.F., La Nouvelle Revue Française*, one of the most prestigious and influential French journals of the time, as well as *La Revue Européenne* and *Europe*. Prévost published articles on a broad variety of subjects, including politics, history, and philosophy. The central problem that Prévost explored at the time was the search of self. In *Tentative de Solitude* (1925), the protagonist cultivates his proud spirit to the point where his whole existence can be reduced to pure thought, which results in a symbolic annihilation of the self when the hero is killed by a train. In *Brûlures de la Prière* (1926), the main threat is religious mysticism, rather than intellectualism: It is only when the protagonist abandons religion and connects his spirit to his body that he acquires his self. Thus, Prévost's thought progresses in the vein of Alain's constructive intellectualism, proclaiming introspection a moral danger. Developing his ideas as part of contemporary philosophical polemicists, Prévost nevertheless turns to his predecessors and publishes the articles "La Sagesse de Descartes" (1925) and "Réfutation du Pari de Pascal" (1926), in which he addresses the philosophical thinking of these great thinkers of the past to summarize his own philosophical ideas and expand on them.

Plaisirs des Sports (1925), published in connection with the Olympic Games of 1924, serves as an original conclusion to Prévost's philosophical research. Sports, for Prévost, are a means to understand the self, as it is only in reunification of the spirit and the body that harmony can be attained. Likewise, according to Prévost, intellectual exercise cannot be separated from physical exercise; thus, perfection can only be achieved by cultivating both. Parallels between ancient and modern, as well as the connection between the past and the present, characterize Prévost's thought and writing and emphasize his reliance on culture as a guide for humanity. Although Prévost's ideas on sports clearly draw on the Greeks, their importance consists of opposing contemporary presentations of sports only as competition and theatrical performance for the public.

Following Alain, Prévost develops ideas of harmonious self into a philosophy of happiness. Unlike Alain, though, Prévost does not connect happiness and virtue; rather, he contends that the goal of human development is not virtue but happiness. Happiness can be achieved by the individual who, in search for self, discovers and follows his personal rules, the process leading to achieving the state of happiness. Notably, Prévost opposes any attempt to socially impose systems of value: Their discovery during the pursuit of happiness should be the result of an individual effort.

An enemy of any form of oppression and empowerment, Prévost sees the remedy in the naturally good qualities of human characters as well as in culture. Thus, his philosophy opposes Freudian ideas on the importance of the sexual drive in human beings and on the relative independence of the subconscious. That is not to say that for Prévost everything is subject to intellect: He accepts passions and instincts that contribute to the individual's search of self. However, their force should be controlled by the intellect, which alone can channel the passions into a moral path. Thus, Prévost admires Napoleon for his energy but refuses him grandeur, reserving it for the people and the moral ideas of the Great French Revolution. According to Prévost, the self cannot achieve greatness if it is devoid of generosity and loyalty.

Although the 1920s were for Prévost years of great productivity (he wrote and published essays, autobiographical articles, a novel, research on esthetics, and critical articles on literature), in the 1930s the sociopolitical reality forces Prévost to shift the emphasis of his writings to political and historical issues. In 1932 he published *L'Histoire de France depuis la guerre*, which, in essence, represents a study of historical events leading to the contemporary crisis in France. Although politically Prévost sided with the left, his historical views are less straightforward than are the Marxists', so that he does not accept economic determinism and assigns a more important role to ideologies, culture, and individuals. Likewise, Prévost reveals deep political insight in criticizing the left for its disagreements in the face of the increasing fascist threat, the politics that will have drastic consequences. The essay also reflects Prévost's disillusionment with the bourgeois democracy in France, which he calls a mere right of people to elect lords and change them at certain periods (1932, 220–221).

The late 1930s witnessed another turn in Prévost's political engagement: Considering himself a writer in the first place, he tried to reach objectivity by withdrawing from everyday political activity. His last political essay, "La Terre est aux hommes" (1936), is a study of demographic processes in Europe and Asia and, at the same time, an attempt at popularization of sociological knowledge. Whatever the scientific value of this research, it clearly demonstrates Prévost's views on a writer's duty as an educator and cultural mediator. Not surprisingly, Prévost's language, without being simplistic, is simple and accessible. Aiming at clarification and elucidation of complex philosophical and sociopolitical matters for a nonprofessional reader, Prévost consistently avoids vague philosophical terms and jargon, viewing the language as a medium to facilitate rather than obfuscate communication.

Written at a time when justification of violence, both on the left and on the right, and dehumanization of society become part of philosophical as well as sociopolitical development, Prévost's work affirms its position within the humanist tradition of French thought. Its intrinsic value consists of its defense of the free construction of self for any individual, as well as reaffirmation of the moral choice for honesty and justice. Shot to death at the age of forty-three years by the Nazis, Prévost demonstrated by his heroic death and in his life how thinking and self-interrogation culminate in living honorably and dying with dignity.

MARIA MIKOLCHAK

See also **Alain**

Biography

Born in 1901 into a family of educators, Prévost was a student first at Lycée Henri IV, 1918–1919, where his teacher was Alain, and then at the École Normale Supérieure, 1919–1924. He joined the Socialist Revolutionary Students in 1919 and was briefly imprisoned for his political activity. He started his journalist career in 1924 and wrote for *L'Œvre*, *N.R.F.*, *Revue Européenne*, and *Intentions*, at the same time trying his hand as a writer of novels. In 1929, he published his first literary criticism. Drafted in 1939, Prévost fought in World War I; he was wounded and demobilized in 1940. He defended his doctoral dissertation, *La Creation chez Stendhal*, in Lyon in 1942. Prévost joined the Resistance in 1943. He was shot and killed by the Nazis on August 1, 1944.

Selected Writings

Plaisirs des Sports. Essay sur le corps humain, 1925
Tentative de Solitude, 1925
Brûlures de la Prière, 1926

La Pensée de Paul Valéry, 1926
Essai sur l'Introspection, 1927
Le Chemin de Stendhal, 1929
Les Frères Bouquinquant, 1930
Les Epicuriens francais; Trois Vies exemplaires: Hérault de Sechelles, Stendhal, Sainte-Beuve, 1931
Histoire de France depuis la guerre, 1932
La Terre est aux hommes, 1936
La Chasse du matin, 1937
Maîtrise de son corps, 1938
Usonie. Esquisse de la civilisation américaine, 1939
La Création chez Stendhal. Essai sur le métier d'écrire et la phychologie de l'écrivain, 1942
Baudelaire. Essai sur l'inspiration et la création poétiques, 1953

Further Reading

Prevost, Mme Jean & Mme Rouvière, eds., *Atrocités Allemandes. Vercor. Documents authentiques recueillis par Mmes Jean Prévost et Rouvière*, Paris: Editions S.F.N., 1945
Bertrand, Marc, "Jean Prévost disciple d'Alain," *ML Baltimore* 80 (1965): 618–622
Bertrand, Marc, *L'oCEvre de Jean Prévost*, Berkeley: University of California Press, 1968
Marie, Jean Noel, "L'Invention de 'Stendhal' d'après Jean Prévost," *Colloque de Cerisy-La-Salle* (June 30–July 10, 1982)

PRICE-MARS, JEAN
Haitian Writer and Intellectual

The 1915 landing of the United States Marine Corps in Haiti, and the subsequent occupation of the country, were deeply traumatic events for the Haitian ruling class. Many of its members reacted by reaffirming and strengthening their cultural and affective ties with France. The language of the former colonial metropole, its relative lack of color prejudice, its elegance of fashions, sophistication of manners, and refined way of life were called on as weapons of resistance against "Anglo-Saxon" materialism, vulgarity, and racist brutality. At the same time, as they tried to understand the root causes of the nation's catastrophe, some Haitian intellectuals began to question their traditional glorification of the French and urban component of the country's culture and collective personality, coupled with the rejection of its African and rural one.

Foremost among these intellectuals was Jean Price-Mars, who soon became their mentor and spokesman. Before the landing of the Marines, he had published short stories and articles on pedagogic questions in various Port-au-Prince newspapers. He now began to lecture on topics that, for all intents and purposes, had previously been ignored by Haitian intellectuals. First, under the form of talks before society audiences, then of periodical articles, and later of books, he articulated ideas that seemed revolutionary at the time and that are still being debated in Haiti today.

Price-Mars's main contention was that Haitians suffered from "collective bovarysm," which the French psychologist Jules de Gaultier (1858–1942) had defined as the determination to see oneself as other than one is. Price-Mars chided his elite countrymen for wanting to believe that Haiti was part of France, not politically, to be sure (Haitians were rightly proud of having attained independence by defeating Bonaparte's armies), but culturally. They had convinced themselves, he argued, that their sensitivity, sense of propriety, idiosyncrasies, qualities, and even defects were no different from those of the French, and that consequently it was right and proper that their country's contributions to literature and the arts should follow Parisian fashions blindly. Michelet's assertion that Haiti was "a little black corner of France" was taken as a compliment.

In no way did Price-Mars denigrate the French element of "Haitian-ness." or aspire to replace it. His argument was that this facet of a dual reality should not cancel or even obscure the other; that is, the contribution of the silent, illiterate, rural majority of Haitians, who were generally of pure African descent, did not speak French but only Créole, were often practitioners of voodoo, had their own social organization and customs, and found the European lifestyle of the mostly light-colored (*mulâtre*) elite quite irrelevant.

Affirming the respectability of the majority's culture was disturbing to Price-Mars's readers not only because it put their self-image in question but because it challenged their self-proclaimed superiority and consequent right to all economic and political power. Price-Mars even accused the elite of sharing European color prejudice and being unwilling to embrace the African heritage that all Haitians have in common. He quipped, in *Ainsi parla l'Oncle* (1928, 45) that a Haitian would rather be told that he resembled an Eskimo, a Samoyed, or a Tungus than be reminded of his Guinean or Sudanese ancestry.

Price-Mars's most important contribution was to redefine Haitian authenticity by studying the customs and "folklore" of the Haitian peasantry and revealing them to the educated Haitians, by whom they had consistently been ignored. They were particularly disturbed by his assertion that voodoo was not, as they assumed, a hodge-podge of primitive superstitions, but a full-fledged African-American religion deserving respect. In fact, Price-Mars was the first scholar to publish a description and evaluation of the popular religion of Haiti. To add insult to injury, he claimed that, despite its best efforts, the elite's *Weltanschauung* was not as different from that of the masses as it wanted to believe, and that some members of its best families were secret devotees of the voodoo spirits.

Price-Mars encouraged writers to depict the life of their rural countrymen. His call was answered by a host of young authors, who considerably expanded the range and depth of Haitian letters. Jacques Roumain's 1931 novel *La Montagne ensorcelée* (to which Price-Mars wrote an Introduction) was the first of the Haitian "peasant novels." The masterpiece of this new genre was Roumain's 1944 *Gouverneurs de la rosée* (translated into English [in 1947 by Langston Hughes and Mercer Cook as *Masters of the Dew*], and into seventeen other languages to date). Many poets began to draw inspiration from the beauty and suffering of the despised masses, wrote panegyrics to the voodoo spirits, and began to compose in Créole. Some years later, a vibrant school of untutored "naïve" painters of rural landscapes and peasant life would attain worldwide recognition.

Price-Mars inspired anthropologists to study the lore of the Haitian rural folk. With his disciple Jacques Roumain, he founded in 1941 the Institut d'ethnologie, the first Port-au-Prince academic institution to offer courses in the discipline. He was also a respected historian: His *La République d'Haïti et la République dominicaine* (1953), published simultaneously in French and Spanish versions, was a seminal study of the relations between the two countries.

It is hard to overestimate the effect of Price-Mars's thought on twentieth-century Haitian intellectuals. Although his argumentation was unfailingly courteous and he took great care to soothe the ruffled feathers of his readers, there is no doubt that, in their time and place, his ideas were truly revolutionary. Price-Mars was and is, even by those who disagreed with him, the most admired thinker in the nation's history. The fact that he became one of the few Haitian intellectuals to receive recognition and praise from the international community further enhanced his stature.

Part of Price-Mars's strategy in his efforts to force Haitians to come to terms with their dual heritage was to acquaint his readers with the geography, history, religions, and customs of ancestral Black Africa. Many of his lectures and articles, as well as three of the eight chapters of *Ainsi parla l'Oncle*, deal exclusively with this material. Price-Mars's knowledge of the subject was secondhand (he only visited Africa once, when he was ninety years old), but he introduced his readers to the works of the French anthropologists and ethnographers whose scholarship, along with those of other social scientists, was forcing a revision of the traditional European image of sub-Saharan Africa as a "dark" continent of primitive savagery. His insistence that his elite compatriots recognize and show pride in their African roots was one of the first expressions of the worldwide movement that came to be known as Negritude. One of its founders, the poet and future president of independent Senegal, Léopold Sedar Senghor, testified that during his student days in Paris he read Price-Mars and was deeply inspired and influenced by his works; President Senghor proclaimed Price-Mars "the father of Negritude."

When Price-Mars turned eighty years old, an international collective work entitled *Témoignages sur la vie et l'œuvre du Dr Jean Price-Mars 1876–1956* (Paul and Fouchard, 1956) was published in his honor in Port-au-Prince, with contributions from a most distinguished group of Haitian and foreign anthropologists, poets, historians, and linguists. That same year, Prince-Mars went to Paris to attend the first *Congrès des écrivains et artistes noirs* (whose organ was the influential bilingual journal *Présence africaine*). Three years later, he presided over the *Deuxième Congrès* in Rome. He was *commandeur* of the Légion d'honneur and recipient of a long list of distinctions from governments and universities all over the world.

LÉON-FRANÇOIS HOFFMANN

See also **Leopold Senghor**

Biography

Jean Price-Mars was born October 15, 1876, in Grande Rivière du Nord, Haiti. After completing secondary education in Cap-Haïtien and Port-au-Prince, he studied medicine in Port-au-Prince and Paris, where he also became interested in anthropology. From 1900 to 1915 he served in his country's diplomatic service in Berlin, Washington, and Paris. Back in Haiti he taught, lectured, published, and became active in politics. He served in the Senate and, in 1930, ran unsuccessfully for the presidency. Price-Mars was named Minister of Foreign Affairs and later Minister of Education in 1946–1947 before being sent as Ambassador to the Dominican Republic, and heading Haiti's delegation to the United Nations. He was Ambassador to Paris from 1957 to 1959 and continued writing and publishing until his death in Port-au-Prince on March 1, 1969, at the age of ninety-three.

Selected Works

La Vocation de l'élite, 1919
Ainsi parla l'Oncle, 1928; as *So Spoke the Uncle*, translated by Magdaline W. Shannon, 1983
Une étape de l'évolution haïtienne, 1929
Formation ethnique, folklore et culture du peuple haïtien, 1939
La République d'Haïti et la République dominicaine, 1953
Lettre ouverte au Dr René Piquion: Le préjugé de couleur est-il la question sociale? 1967

Further Reading

Paul, Emmanuel C., and Fouchard, Jean, eds., *Témoignages sur la vie et l'œuvre du Dr Jean Price-Mars 1876–1956*, Port-au-Prince, Imprimerie de l'État, 1956

Cornevin, Robert, "Présentation," *Ainsi parla l'Oncle*, 3rd ed., Montreal: Leméac, 1973, pp. 11–42

Antoine, Jacques C., *Jean Price-Mars and Haiti*, Washington, D.C.: Three Continents Press, 1981

Shannon, Magdaline W., "Introduction," *Ainsi parla l'Oncle (So Spoke the Uncle)*, translated by Magdaline W. Shannon, Washington, D.C.: Three Continents Press, 1983

Shannon, Magdaline W., *Jean Price-Mars, the Haitian Elite and the American Occupation, 1915–1935*, New York: St. Martin's Press, 1996

Roumain, Jacques, *Gouverneurs de la rosée*, Port-au-Prince, Imprimerie de l'État, 1944

Roumain, Jacques, *La Montagne*, Port-au-Prince, Imprimerie de l'État, 1931

PROUST, MARCEL
Writer

Proust is the author of *A la recherche du temps perdu* (In Search of Lost Time, 1913–1927). This work is considered one of the supreme achievements of world literature. It was written between 1908 and 1919 and is made up of seven different volumes. Proust has had an enduring influence not only on twentieth-century novelists but also on other artists and philosophers. This work was a point of reference for various phenomenologists such as Sartre and Merleau-Ponty and for structuralists or poststructuralists like Levy-Strauss, Barthes, or Deleuze as well as for the German philosophers Adorno and Benjamin. His novel assimilates many of the philosophical theories of his time, from the spiritualism of Alphonse Darlu and in some sense of Bergson (his cousin by marriage) to the aesthetic theories of Ruskin, W. Pater, and the French Schellingian G. Séailles.

In a letter to Jacques Rivière dated February 7, 1914, he confesses that his book is less a search for time past, than a search for truth. Even if the resurrection of the past, as narrated at the beginning of the novel in the famous passage about the *madeleine*, has become one of the most famous symbols in French literature, it only plays a role within the larger enterprise of discovering "real life." Thus, the notion of "time past" not only refers to the passing away of human existence but also to the sterile existences of those who, failing to discover the true nature of reality, waste away their lives in high society, at the salons, in conversations. In the last volume, *Le temps retrouvé* (Time Regained, 1927) the narrator confesses that his whole life (and the novel itself) might be summed up under the title, "A Vocation." Proust's major "philosophical" ambition is to account for the real nature of art. From the beginning of the novel, he describes how some events and "obscure impressions" symbolize "a call" and solicit the attention of the narrator (Marcel) who will only be able able to "decipher" them once he has discovered his task as writer: to answer to their call appropriately is to create a work of art (Time Regained, translated by C. K. Scott Moncrieff and T. Kilmartin, Penguin Books, 1989, p 972). This revelation makes it obvious that in life (i.e., in Proust's novel, the major part of the *Recherche*), words are often presented as inappropriate reactions and are far removed from the impressions we have. For instance, when he crossed the bridge over the Vivonne, the shadow of a cloud upon the water had made him cry "Gosh" and jump for joy. This reaction is not art: One can never trust the spontaneity of one's expressions to be an adequate reflection of what one feels. That kind of spontaneity, which is life itself, characterizes the "bachelor of arts" (*célibataires de l'art*) who stops at sterile and inappropriate reactions to artworks or "calls": Their "expressions" are only of an artificial excitement and are not objects of laborious and "inward-directed study." Nevertheless, in their ludicrous and snobbish behavior, they represent "the first attempts of nature in her struggle to create artists" (Time Regained, o.c., p. 927).

However, Proust's novel is not an experimental application of aesthetic theories but, rather, an articulation of philosophical insights into the nature of life, subjectivity, experience, and the self. In this respect, the narrator's task of the "clarification of his experiences" reflects an interesting philosophical problematic that is motivated by the quasi-religious conviction that one has a real task in life; namely, the quest for truth. This task is nourished by the conviction that the true character of our existence and experiences only come to light once they have been "clarified" in a work of art. Life itself contains a truth insofar as it announces the creation of art in which it has to be raised. Love, friendship, and mundane affairs are all forms of abdication wherein one turns aside from writing. Only in writing do impressions come into truth. As a consequence, Proust's novel has a circular construction, which must be understood from this aesthetic task: The book the narrator has to write preexists in him. It is the inner book of his experiences and memories. Art is not a decadent evasion of reality, nor is it a hedonistic and aesthetic attitude toward life, but it is a "translation" of that "inner book." Furthermore, the task of the writer is experienced as being the real life only because life itself announces it. Life, as Proust abundantly seems to suggest, prefigures the work of art.

This prefiguration is often illustrated by the experience of "family resemblance" between scenes of life and existing monuments of arts; for instance, with the description of a butcher's shop in terms of Rogier Van der Weyden's "Last Judgment," or in the description of Balbec as if it were a painting of Elstir. The novel also includes literary pastiches and intertextual references to Barbey D'Aurévilly, Flaubert, Baudelaire, Madame de Sévigné, and Racine, among others. It is as if life had already accomplished a latent translation-process that the writer had only to render explicit.

In this respect, in the attention Proust pays to the task of "clarifying impressions," he points to an aspect of the self that seems very relevant for philosophical exploration and that exceeds the models of the thinkers by whom he seemed influenced. His conception of self is not that of a Bergsonian totality or duration. Rather, it combines the idea of a pure "multiplicity" with that of an insisting identity. That identity, however, does not coincide with any inner personal continuity; it precisely breaks it into shards. What strikes Marcel at the end of his quest and at the occasion of the famous revelation in the courtyard of the Guermantes mansion, tripping over the uneven cobblestones, is not simply the revelation of his task or his vocation. The sensation itself fulfils him with happiness, and it is that same happiness that at various times in his life had been given to him by the sight of the trees in Hudimesnil, by the view of the twin steeples of Martinville, or by the flavors of a madeleine dipped in tea. Even before he is able to understand the meaning of that emotion, he is captured by the consciousness of its sameness, and it is precisely the experience of that identity that finally resolves him to search for more profound reasons and causes. This identity has an insistence in the impression and is something that, although being "common both to the past and to the present, is much more essential than either of them." (Time Regained, o.c., p. 943). This is what Proust will finally call "essences." Between impression and expression, life and art, these essences insist on and compel the narrator's devotion of his life to understanding and seizing them, meaning to create a work of art. Therefore, Art is the most "austere school of life" and the only way to account for the truth of life: "For when it is a question of writing, one is scrupulous, one examines things meticulously, one regrets all that is not truth. But when it is merely a question of life, one ruins oneself, makes oneself ill, kills oneself all for lies." (Time Regained, o.c., p. 947).

ROLAND BREEUR

See also **Roland Barthes; Henri Bergson; Gilles Deleuze; Claude Levi-Strauss; Maurice Merleau-Ponty; Jacques Riviere; Jean-Paul Sartre**

Biography

Marcel Proust was born in Anteuil in 1871. Proust studied at the Ecole des Sciences Politiques, taking *licences* in law (1893) and in literature (1895). Long before he began to publish fiction, he was already able to attract some of the most sought after people of his day and became a *habitué* of the bourgeois "salons" and of the most exclusive drawing rooms of nobility. In 1896, he wrote *Les plaisirs et les jours*; from 1895 to 1899 he wrote *Jean Santeuil*, and translated John Ruskin's *Bible of Amiens* and *Sesame and Lilies*. Only from 1909 did he begin his real masterpiece, *A la recherche du temps perdu*. Proust died of pneumonia in Paris in November 1922, before the publication of the last three volumes of his masterpiece.

Selected Works

A la recherche du temps perdu, 3 volumes, edited by P. Clarac and A. Ferré, 1954; 3 volumes, 1987; 4 volumes, edited by J.-Y. Tadié, 1988–1990; 1988–1990; 1 volume, 1999; 3 volumes, translated by C. K. Scott Moncrieff, revised by T. Kilmartin, further revised by D. J. Enright. London

Further Reading

Albaret, C., *Monsieur Proust*, Paris: Laffont, 1973

Beckett, S., *Proust*, London: Grove Press, 1931

Bowie, M., *Proust among the Stars*, London: Harper Collins, 1998

Breeur, R., *Sujet et singularité, Une lecture phénoménologique de Proust*, Grenoble: Millon, 2000

Curtius, E. R., *Französischer Geist im zwanzigsten Jahrhundert*, Bern: Francke Verlag, 1953

de Lattre, A., *La doctrine de la réalité chez Proust*, 3 volumes, Paris: José Corti, 1979–1985

Deleuze, G., *Marcel Proust et les signes*, Paris: PUF, 1964

Descombes, V., *Proust, philosophie du roman*, Paris: Minuit, 1987

Henry, A., *Marcel Proust, théories pour une esthétique*, Paris: Klincksieck, 1981

Henry, A., *La tentation de Marcel Proust*, Paris: PUF, 2000

Jauss, H.-R., *Zeit und Erinnerung in Marcel Prousts "A la recherche du temps perdu,"* Heidelberg: Winter Heidelberg, 1970

Painter, G. D., *Marcel Proust*, 2 volumes, Chatto & Windus, 1959–1965

Poulet, G., *L'espace proustien*, Paris: Gallimard, 1963

Richard, J.-P., *Proust et le monde sensible*, Paris: Le Seuil, 1974

Rivière, J., *Quelques progrès dans l'étude du coeur humain*, Librairie de France, 1927 and Paris: Gallimard, 1985 Paris

Robert, P.-E., *Marcel Proust lecteur des Anglo-Saxons*, Paris: Nizet, 1976

Shattuck, R., *Proust's Binoculars*, Alfred A. Knopf, 1963 1992

Shattuck, R., *Proust*, Fontana, Collins, 1974 1984

Tadié, J.-Y., *Proust et le roman*, Paris: Gallimard, 1971

Tadié, J.-Y., *Lectures de Proust*, Paris: Colin, 1971

Tadié, J.-Y., *Proust*, Paris: Gallimard, 1996

PSYCHOANALYTIC THEORY

Psychoanalytic theory in France is the product of this country's creative and continuing response to Freud's work. The theory has arguably developed most fully in France, where Sigmund Freud studied for a time under the neurologist Jean Charcot. Psychoanalytic theory has transformed the categories and methodology of many of the most productive intellectuals in France, enabling a break with a dominant Cartesian past.

The theory has significant ramifications throughout Europe and the Americas in many disciplines, both old and new. In literature, French psychoanalytic theory, following Freud's own frequent references, has produced provocative readings of classic texts from Marie Bonaparte to Serge Doubrovsky and Claude Richard, perhaps because this medium gives voice to the psychological. Bonaparte introduces a Freudian approach into the French reading of Poe, begun by the Symbolistes, in her *Edgar Poe: Etude psychanalytique* (1933). Doubrovsky's book on Proust in 1974 brings psychoanalysis and existentialism to bear on *In Search of Lost Time*. Doubrovsky demonstrates how the novel, born out of angst and alienation, ultimately calls into question the sense of identity created by autobiographical writing.

Psychoanalytic theory has also had an effect on the interdisciplinary fields of cultural, feminist, and gay studies in Britain and the United States. In France, publishers and universities often designate such interdisciplinary areas *Sciences Humaines*, a broad category including the humanities and social sciences, as they are known in English, but normally excluding the natural sciences with the exception of the philosophy of science. Adhering to a rationalist, "objective" methodology dominated by the physical experiment, the natural sciences frequently attempt to remain within the boundaries of their disciplines, unaffected by psychoanalytic theory. Theorists have, however, examined their positivistic, pragmatic approach from a psychoanalytic perspective. Thus, psychoanalytic theory has to some degree contributed to the contemporary understanding of science as well.

Psychoanalysis has indelibly marked two areas of contemporary French thought: Feminist Studies, a branch of identity politics, and Film Studies, a relatively new form of knowledge production. Although psychoanalytic theory is very important to producing new knowledge in these fields, some critics, often part of the left-Hegelian tradition, allege that psychoanalysis undermines a necessary consideration of history and of concepts of class, value, and capital. Other critics, especially American psychologists, object that psychoanalysis and the disciplines influenced by it are no longer viable branches of knowledge.

Some argue for more historical analysis from psychoanalytic theory; for example, in Julia Kristeva's controversial book *About Chinese Women* or in Doubrovsky's study of Proust. In general, however, psychoanalytic theorists in France do display an awareness of historical conditions and the ways psychic formations interact with other events in the public sphere. Kristeva's analysis of Hannah Arendt and totalitarianism is a clear instance of such historical awareness.

Marx's contributions inform psychoanalytic theorists, but they often do not accept his belief that economic and class conflict is the major influence on the distribution of power in contemporary societies. For example, although accepting Marx's framework early in her writing, Kristeva has come to focus on the psychic formations that help shape the economic. Lacan, to cite another example, has discussed the role of the signifier in Marx's view of the commodity fetish. In fact, beyond these two cases, psychoanalytic theory in French frequently engages with Marxist thought. The theory is not incompatible with Marx's ideas, as Franz Fanon's (*Les Damnés de la terre*, 1907) and Louis Althusser's (*Pour Marx,* 1965) work makes clear.

Psychoanalysis contests the French tradition of Cartesian rationalism. Briefly put, according to the Cartesian tradition, the subject is primarily conscious and able to understand the object free of sense distortion. The subject is an entity distinct from the object it analyzes, the truth of the object being valid across time and place. French rationalism continues as a strong influence in eighteenth-century Enlightenment social theory (e.g., Montesquieu), in Structuralist linguistics and anthropology (Ferdinand De Saussure, Roman Jakobson, and Claude Lévi-Strauss), and in current discussions of neoliberalism, as Zygmunt Bauman suggests in *Intimations of Postmodernity*. It is also present in Existentialist thought in the notion of an autonomous self that surfaces in Sartre's rereading of Descartes. The positivism underlying the physical sciences described earlier is built on a similar notion of the self, one whose sense perceptions provide evidence of the material world.

The single most significant French psychoanalytic theorist, Jacques Lacan, builds on Freud's seminal work, using his discovery of the unconscious to transform this concept of the self and the dominant rationalist worldview shaped by Western metaphysicians since at least the seventeenth century. A key marker of French psychoanalysis is language, showing the rationalist inheritance via, for example, Roman Jakobson's linguistics, but especially Lacan's modifications of this inheritance. For Jakobson, language is the set of rules governing a particular idiom. His work on aphasia led him to see metaphor and metonomy in the condensation and displacements Freud describes in his *Interpretation of Dreams*. Influenced by Jakobson's work, Lacan builds his theory in part on Freud's discoveries of language's effect on psychic formations and of the Father's authority as expressed in and through language. Language becomes, for Lacan, what gives shape to the subject's existence, the form making the subject and the Father's authority knowable. The mind does not transcend the body in its efforts to know the object. Instead, it makes itself known in language, understanding the world in concert with sense data and bodily memories, especially of the Father.

Writing in dense and passionate prose, Lacan frequently lectures to psychoanalysts in training and incisively analyzes the work of other psychoanalytic theorists, building on their contributions and ridiculing their weaknesses. In one of the most widely discussed essays of the 1950s, initially delivered as one of his seminars, "Function and Field of Speech and Language in Psychoanalysis," Lacan indirectly defines the subject as the entity constituted by the dialogue of self and other, of analyst and analyzed. His theory is based in part on his psychoanalytic practice: In an effort to enable patients to create a less alienated and more continuous consciousness and personality, he employs Freud's "talking cure" to identify later events in their lives that shape and help interpret earlier episodes. Lacan talks with his patients to uncover the unconscious in his or her history and to understand how they may have become caught in harmful behaviors and subject to severe emotional distress. A therapeutic purpose underlies his theory of the nature of the subject's existence and the ways in which it is shaped by the Father's authority as expressed in and through language.

Like Freud, Lacan demonstrates that the paternal authority underlying the social contract creates severe internal conflicts. "On a Question Preliminary to any Possible Treatment of Psychosis," another influential seminar from the 1950s, revisits one of Freud's patients, Judge Schreber. Lacan reveals Schreber's painful delusions and increasing inability to speak: He becomes a woman attempting to make love to a withdrawing God. In the process, he suffers slow speech, a stammer, and in the worst throes of his illness, a catatonic stupor. Eventually he is able to master language and to live with his homosexuality within the patriarchal structures of family life and society.

More than a theory of individual psychic formations, Lacan's writing studies how the Father's authority plays a role in producing knowledge and shaping power structures within disciplines and institutions. He has demonstrated psychoanalysis' usefulness and legitimacy in revealing the psychological, social, and linguistic processes by which authority and truth are constructed, not only for an individual like Schreber but also for a science like psychology and, in so doing, radically transforms the Cartesian perspective. At the same time, Lacan mounts a critique of the alienating effect of positivism in the experimental sciences and in American psychology. In "Function and Field of Speech and Language," he refers, for example, to the pioneering work of the first interpreters of Freud as the "recreation of human meaning in an arid period of scientism." Ignoring the dialectical structure of language, experimental science "objectifies" (or, more accurately, constructs a myth of the objective) to such a degree that the subject loses his or her meaning, forgetting existence and, ultimately, forgetting death.

Lacan's convincing critique of positivism ironically highlights the reason psychoanalysis has been attacked by psychologists, especially in the United States, as outdated and scientifically untenable. From early in his writing ("The Mirror Stage," 1949), he takes issue with the same positivistic/pragmatic models American psychologists often consider truer, more "objective," and more advanced than those of psychoanalysis.

Lacan analyzes three topics fundamental to language and to the production of knowledge: intersubjective logic, temporality, and the history of the symbol. Using the talking cure as his model, Lacan suggests that its intersubjective logic provides insight not only into an individual's psychological difficulties but also into experimental science as a dangerous social construction denying subjectivity and, in that sense, existence itself. Intersubjective logic provides a proper foundation for legitimate scientific inquiry that, unlike the physical sciences, will be life-affirming. He explains that the analyst leads the analyzed individual to study the relation between the latter's ego and the "I" of his discourse. Analyst and patient identify with each other, producing a two-way transference allowing the patient's id to become that of the analyst. Throughout his theory, as in the conclusion of "Function and Field of Speech and Language," Lacan focuses on language as interaction between self and other, an interaction marked by the linked desires to live and to die, by biological and cultural causes, and by the change brought about by the compulsion to repeat. Lacan's theory has given legitimacy and context to the psychoanalytic thinkers who have followed in his wake, including Julia Kristeva.

An expatriate, as are several other major psychoanalytic French theorists (e.g., Algerian-born Hélène Cixous), Julia Kristeva, like Lacan, has helped bring about a wider recognition of the crucial role of language as dialectical process. Arriving in Paris from her native Bulgaria in the early 1960s to study, she quickly became a controversial, prolific writer. She has had most of her theory and novels published in excellent English translations by Columbia University Press, exerting considerable influence on many other intellectuals in and outside of France. Like Cixous, her novels, certain volumes of her theory (e.g., *Strangers to Ourselves* on the status of the immigrant and *In the Beginning Was Love* on religion), and frequent visits to the United States to lecture have made psychoanalytic theory accessible to a larger audience despite its complexity.

Kristeva uses the sociolinguistic constructions Lacan has theorized, the Name-of-the-Father, and the Symbolic Order, for example, to identify psychic formations in texts and in her patients. The Name-of-the-Father is the idea that the Father is the principal authority figure underlying society and language. As Freud had explained, the Father must be "killed" for the subject's psyche to advance through the oedipal stage, to master language, and to assume the social role of Father in his or her own right. The mastery of language enables one to exist in the Symbolic Order. Lacan includes signifiers and speech along with language in his theory of the Symbolic, understanding language as communication, governed by the set of laws familiar to a group of speakers, as Jakobson explains. Following Lacan (Mikhail Bakhtin after Freud is another important precursor here), Kristeva sees literature and the other arts as texts giving shape to a speaking subject inherently multiple. Unlike Lacan, however, she gives significant attention to Freud's discovery that the woman must identify with the Mother early on, rejecting the feminine role later to assume a social function. Kristeva has also returned to Freud's concept of the "Father of individual pre-history," an androgynous figure fleetingly described in his *Group Psychology*. Thus, using many elements from their work, Kristeva moves beyond Freud and Lacan and their emphasis on the Father to describe an alternation of identifications with Father and Mother. She assigns great value to forms of language that are associated with the Mother and that resist the rules of communication, creating the category "Semiotic" to describe these forms. Kristeva shifts Freud's and Lacan's emphasis on the Father, the Symbolic, and reason to the Mother, the Semiotic, and affect. At the same time, Kristeva retains a significant role for the Father and thus makes the case for the political effect of speech: It communicates at the same time that it resists communication. Briefly put, in her theory, the search for the lost object that is the Mother brings on a depression that is stimulating, potentially creative, and revolutionary (e.g., in *Soleil noir*, 1987).

Kristeva's recent work focuses on two intellectuals in a series of volumes entitled "Feminine Genius": Hannah Arendt, the German-born philosopher who emigrated to the United States, and Melanie Klein, the Austrian-born psychoanalyst who wrote much of her work in London. A forthcoming book is devoted to Colette, the French novelist. Writing critical biographies describing and analyzing their lives and work, Kristeva places Arendt and Klein in the context of psychoanalytic theory. She examines the psychic forma-

tion underlying Arendt, demonstrating the ways in which the philosopher transforms melancholy into the writer's job of work, enabling herself to be reborn in her texts. For Arendt, writing is a form of political action whose ultimate goal is a kind of miraculous beginning. Examining her most influential work, *The Origins of Totalitarianism*, Kristeva describes totalitarianism in Arendt as the death drive that destroys the public space enabling dialogue. Hitler's and Stalin's regimes eliminate political activity as a dialectic that makes people human, as an interaction between self and other with the potential to bring about radical change. Kristeva shows how Arendt's examination of totalitarianism, despite her rejection of psychoanalysis, reveals the psychic formations underlying Nazi and Soviet tyranny: perversion, hysteria, and death drive. Arendt in fact uses the first two concepts herself in describing tyranny. In this way, *The Origins of Totalitarianism* constitutes a form of group psychology (p. 226) in Kristeva's theory.

Although the methods and concepts of psychoanalytic theory are well-illustrated in Lacan and Kristeva, feminist or women's studies and film reveal its effect, for example, on identity politics and emergent fields of study. Many feminists, especially in the Anglophone world, reject Freud's work and the ways it has been used in psychoanalytic theory; others, especially in France, find the theory helpful. It was arguably Lacan who, after Freud, identified gender as a fundamental category of thought in his elaboration, for instance, of the Name-of-the-Father. Although American feminists frequently reject his focus on male sexuality and the inevitable association of the Father with the social contract, French feminists, including Julia Kristeva, Hélène Cixous, and Luce Irigaray, do not. Kristeva has, it is true, rejected the "feminist" label and has called attention to the potentially reactionary role of motherhood, but her theory fits the category if feminist thought is broadly conceived as work that analyzes the status of the concept of woman to contribute to knowledge production and to undercut damaging hierarchical structures. Instead of rejecting it, these writers use psychoanalytic theory to examine people and texts in an effort to understand the gendered hierarchies of contemporary life and to bring about change. This is clear in Kristeva's series on feminine genius, described above.

The single most useful contribution of psychoanalytic theory to Feminist Studies is perhaps the notion that gender inflects the psychic formations shaping attitudes and behavior. It does so in a manner that is linked to biology but not by the necessity of cause and effect. Men and women retain and develop associations with both Mother and Father that influence sexual identity and virtually every aspect of life. In short,

Freud's concept of the Father of individual prehistory, as elaborated in Julia Kristeva's work, for instance, is a figure with both male and female characteristics. According to this theory, the woman, like the man, identifies with an androgynous figure, enabling her both to recognize authority, the male, and reason and to accede to rebellion, the female, and affect. Psychoanalytic theory does not see male and female as essences that are part of a deterministic model but rather as internal associations guiding development and behavior. Kristeva, Cixous, and Irigaray, to take these three as examples, have produced an impressive variety of texts exploring especially literature, philosophy, religion, and social institutions in a broadly conceived feminist framework.

Psychoanalytic theory also lies at the heart of many theoretical debates in film studies. This is not surprising given the complexity and visual intensity of both film and dreams. In *Sexuality in the Field of Vision*, 1986, Jacqueline Rose analyzes a common ground in psychoanalytic theory, feminism, and film to the extent that ideology is linked to gender in all three domains. In his *Language and Cinema* (1971), Christian Metz, a pioneer in French film theory, speaks of film in Lacanian terms as a form of subjectivity in which all previous films taken as a whole shape meaning. At the same time, the subjectivity within the film has the power to change the context provided by previous movies. He states, "Every film shows us the cinema and is also its death" (See Stephen Heath's analysis of Metz in *Questions of Cinema*.) For Metz, film (like language for Lacan) calls attention to the ways in which subjectivity and meaning are created: The subject is not a given, but instead constructs himself or herself in many ways. In realist, narrative, or fiction film, according to Metz, signifiers deny this construction and multiplicity, much as the subject of science described above denies the construction of objectivity. A movie resists coherence and communication even as it conveys meaning.

Finally, film testifies to the Father's authority at the same time that it constitutes a search for the lost object that is the Mother. As in Lacan's analysis of the mirror stage, when the child recognizes his or her body as an image, film theory sees the movie as fundamentally voyeuristic, as the place of the "look" where the real may be represented in the screen illusion of narrative film, where the look is primarily that of the characters. Cinematic codes, however, like the signifiers of verbal language, may shift the look, thereby creating a variety of perspectives resisting communication while also moving toward a unified image of the self. The codes may take the form, for example, of the camera's look as it records, or the audience's as it watches, as Laura

Mulvey explains in an early example of film theory inspired by Lacan.

The effect of French psychoanalytic theory is clear in many fields including Literary, Film, and Feminist Studies. It has convincingly argued for an understanding of the subject as a dialogue of self and other and for a recognition of the role of a gendered language in producing knowledge and institutions. Psychoanalytic theory studies psychic formations as part of a larger project to explore the imagination and to produce radical change. Its notion of language's shifting perspectives has proven to be creative, liberating, and therapeutic, "restoring our belief in the world" as Giles Deleuze, another influential French psychoanalytic theorist, says of film (*Cinema 2*).

CAROL MASTRANGELO BOVÉ

See also **Louis Althusser; Helene Cixous; Gilles Deleuze; Fritz Fanon; Luce Irigaray; Julia Kristeva; Jacques Lacan; Claude Levi-Strauss; Ferdinand de Saussure**

Further Reading

Althusser, Louis, *Pour Marx*, Paris: Maspero, 1965; as *For Marx*, translated by Ben Brewster, London: New Left Books, 1969

Bonaparte, Marie, *Edgar Poe: Etude psychanalytique*, Paris: Denoel & Steele, 1933

Cixous, Hélène, *L'Exil de James Joyce ou l'Art du remplacement*, Paris: B. Grasset, 1968; as *The Exile of James Joyce*, translated by Sally A. J. Purcell, London: John Calder, 1976

Doubrovsky, Serge, *La Place de la madeleine: écriture et fantasme chez Proust*. Paris

Mercure de France, 1974; as *The Place de la Madeleine: Writing and Fantasy in Proust*, translated by Carol Mastrangelo Bové, Lincoln: University of Nebraska Press, 1986

Fanon, Franz, *Les Damnés de la terre*, 1907; as *The Wretched of the Earth*, translated by Constance Farrington. New York: Grove Press, 1968

Irigaray, Luce, Paris: Editions de Minuit, 1985; as "Is the Subject of Language Sexed?" translated by Carol Mastrangelo Bové, *Hypatia*, 2, 3

Kristeva, Julia, *Soleil noir: dépression et mélancolie*, Paris: Gallimard, 1987; as *Black Sun: Depression and Melancholia*, translated by Leon S. Roudiez, New York: Columbia University Press, 1989

Kristeva, Julia, *Hannah Arendt*, Paris: Fayard, 1999; as *Hannah Arendt*, translated by Ross Guberman, New York: Columbia University Press, 2001

Kristeva, Julia, *Melanie Klein*, Paris: Fayard, 1999; as *Melanie Klein*, translated by Ross Guberman, New York: Columbia University Press, 2002

Lacan, Jacques, "Fonction et champ de la parole et du language en psychanalyse," in *Ecrits*, Paris: Seuil, 1953; as "Function and Field of Speech and Language in Psychoanalysis," in *Écrits: a Selection*, translated by Alan Sheridan, New York: Norton, 1977

Lacan, Jacques, "Sur un sujet préliminaire à tout traitement possible en psychose," in *Ecrits*, Paris: Seuil, 1953; as "On a Question Preliminary to any Possible Treatment of Psychosis," in *Écrits: a Selection*, translated by Alan Sheridan, New York: Norton, 1977

Metz, Christian, *Langage et Cinéma*, Paris: Larousse, 1971; as *Language and Cinema*, translated by Donna Jean Umiker-Sebeok, The Hague: Mouton, 1974

Mulvey, Laura, "Visual Pleasure and Narrative Cinema," *Screen*, 16, 3

Richard, Claude, *Lettres américaines*, Paris: Éditions Alinéa, 1987; as *American Letters*, translated by Carol Mastrangelo Bové, Philadelphia: University of Pennsylvania Press, 1998

PSYCHOLOGY

Modern psychology in France has its roots in the Enlightenment and in the idea inherent in the Western philosophical tradition that appropriate knowledge of the world and the self can lead to greater happiness. During the eighteenth century, when knowledge and representation were still tied to a totalizing framework of thought, the dominant model of the natural sciences seemed perfectly adaptable to the study of the human mind or spirit, as it was then called. In *De l'esprit* (1758), Claude Helvetius could confidently envisage the possibility of treating the moral being of man according to the measure of experimental physics and propose the construction of an "experimental ethics," but French naturalism also had a long tradition, going back to Descartes's mechanistic physiology, that is clearly echoed in La Mettrie's *L'Homme Machine* (1748). Far from being a simple automaton, a puppet in the hands of its divine maker, a human being according to La Mettrie, was moved by its own self-generated vitality, which could also be transformed according to the logic of survival. La Mettrie's proto-evolutionary idea was important in creating a bridge between a mechanistic, static form of materialism and an idealist, temporal view of the spirit that could support the concept of a dialectical development of the mind, which finds its exemplary expression in Hegels's *Phenomenology of the Mind* (1807).

The German physiologist Wilhelm Wundt, who worked under the guidance of the physicist Wilhelm von Helmholtz at the University of Heidelberg, is generally recognized as the founder of "empirical psychology," a new science that quickly found support in France. In his *Dictionnaire raisonné des sciences, des arts et des métiers* (1765), Diderot borrowed Wundt's term, *psychology*, to define the branch of philosophy concerned with the study of the human soul, and divided it, following Wundt, into experimental or empirical psychology and rational psychology. However, France also had its own empirical school, represented among the *philosophes* by Condillac, whose *Essay on the Origin of Human Knowledge* (1746) drew heavily on Locke's idea according to which human knowledge is the fruit of experience. In his *Treatise on Sensations*

(1754), Condillac went even further, asserting that knowledge could be reduced to sensation alone and demonstrating his argument by the famous example of the statue whose mental activities are stirred into being by the stimulation of the various sense organs. Condillac resisted, however, the term *psychology*, because the word had an unpleasant metaphysical flavor associated with the philosophical repertoire of the Ancien Régime.

Irrespective of these terminological quibbles, Diderot's (or rather Wundt's) distinction between an empirical and a rational or spiritualist psychology is important for understanding the development of this emerging science in nineteenth century France. The distinction clearly helps in situating Théodule Ribot as the representative of the empirical, scientific approach to the human mind, whereas Maine de Biran exemplifies the opposite spiritualist pole that gives precedence to internal examination (or introspection) over external observation. As some historians have argued (see Woodward and Ash, 1982, Introduction), however, this distinction breaks down under close analysis. Even more, according to the same author, it would be difficult to sustain, judging by the evidence, that psychology achieved real disciplinary autonomy in the nineteenth century, in spite of the appearance of professionalization, produced by the creation of institutional enclaves, and specialized laboratories and journals.

Although in *The Order of Things* (1966), Foucault has argued in favor of the emergence of a new episteme at the beginning of the nineteenth century, which in his view brings a historical, compartmentalized approach to the study of nature and its objects (including the relatively new topic of human nature), it appears that the reality was much more confused. What we have instead, in the case of psychology, according to Woodward's argument, is "the problematic emergence and gradual self-definition of one discipline among others" (*The Problematic Science*, Introduction). Moreover, this emerging discipline is one that constantly trespasses on other disciplinary boundaries. In discussing the conceptual foundation of psychological thought in the nineteenth century in the different domains of philosophy, biology, and physics, Woodward observed, "Each foundation grew into a tradition that cut across disciplinary lines, challenging existing categories of thought and leading to reformulations of discourse about mind. . . . Psychobiology, psychophysics, child psychology, social psychology, and anthropometry each stand for a fluctuating boundary of the new scientific discipline" (*The Problematic Science*, p. 2).

Going back to the previous distinction between a materialist, deterministic approach to the human mind and a spiritualist, voluntarist approach to the same subject, it is interesting to note that Maine de Biran, usually associated with the spiritualist school and the proponent of introspection or self-reflection as a method of investigating the mind, did not exclude external observation, physiology, or psychopathology. Victor Cousin (1792–1867), de Biran's student, continued the spiritualist tradition with an emphasis on intuition as a synthetic faculty. The concept of a distinct self (*moi*), accessible through the powers of introspection, plays an important role in the later philosophy of Henri-Louis Bergson, who proposed a synthesis between reason and experience, through the import of evolutionary ideas. In Bergson's works, the notion of a fluid self, corresponding to a fluid sense of time (*durée*), is opposed to the spatialized notion of time and memory favored by reason. This dynamic and yet unstable notion of the self informs Proust's *À la recherché du temps perdu*, which, alongside Freud's *Interpretation of Dreams*, constitutes one of the most significant examples of self-analysis in twentieth-century literature.

Proust and Freud, as Malcolm Bowie has shown, have a lot in common. Impelled by desire (which is itself a path to knowledge), the two have pored over every nook and cranny of the human psyche in search of an ever-elusive truth. If Freud turned the study of the unconscious into a science (or pseudoscience, as some critics might argue), the practice of "depth psychology" (*psychologie des profondeurs*), that is, the exploration of the submerged layers of the mind, was by no means the prerogative of psychoanalysis alone. In his first *Manifesto of Surrealism* (1924), André Breton, the founder of the surrealist movement in France, made the unconscious the prime source of inspiration for a new generation of writers, who chose to define the "modern spirit" through that which escaped its conscious control, while using a deliberate, experimental approach ("automatic writing") for its discovery and creative use. In spite of Breton's acquaintance with some of Freud's major texts and his training in psychiatry during his early years, it is clear that the surrealist conception of the unconscious he promoted was far from passing scientific muster. Freud himself was unimpressed when he received Breton's gift copy of the *Communicating Vessels* (1932) and made no effort to disguise his lack of interest during the brief exchange of letters that ensued.

Breton's medical knowledge did not prevent him from falling under the spell of "unscientific" notions of the mind, such as those advocated by the spiritualist movement, which in the nineteenth century reacted to the materialist, positivist approach advocated in France by Auguste Comte. Although Comte more or less ignored psychology altogether and despised the very idea of introspection for its absurd pretense of investigating a nonfactual object (i.e., the mind), the parapsycholo-

gists, with Franz Mesmer and Frederic Myers, went to the other extreme. Mesmer posited the existence of an ineffable fluid that permeated both the universe and the human body that could be manipulated through its electromagnetic properties to achieve miraculous cures. Myers, on his part, believed in a spiritual continuum between life and death and, before Freud, defined the concept of the subliminal self, which escaped the conscious control of the patient.

Again, as Woodward has argued in his Introduction to *The Problematic Science* (1982), psychology in the nineteenth century was far from being a well-defined discipline. It fluctuated not only between various disciplinary boundaries, but also between scientific and unscientific thought, between theory and fiction, for as Woodward warns us, "We must not assume that the criteria of today's science are the same as those of yesteryear" (*The Problematic Science*, Introduction). It may seem quite normal for the period that Myers's *Human Personality and Its Survival of Bodily Death* (1903) would be warmly received by William James, the psychologist, who had also presided over the Society of Psychical Research in the United States. No less surprising, perhaps, would be the fact that the first international meetings of psychologists before the First World War gathered side by side clinical psychologists, parapsychologists, and philosophers. Théodule Ribot, the founder of "scientific" psychology in France, and the first to occupy the newly created position in experimental psychology at the Sorbonne, was also the main editor of the *Revue philosophique de la France et de l'étranger* (1876). More important perhaps, the links between psychology and psychopathology (or psychiatry), especially strong in France, were not free from some of the "unscientific" influences coming from parapsychology.

In effect, the understanding of hysteria, this cultural invention that was crucial nonetheless to the development of the psychiatric institution in France, relied, in a first phase at least, on the practice of hypnosis, which served to reenact the patient's symptoms. Hypnosis also was not too far removed from the presuppositions connected with the "unscientific" practices proposed by Mesmer, but Jean Martin Charcot, whose name is now linked to the study of hysteria and who was in his time a famous physician and distinguished neurologist, did not hesitate to present his findings on hypnosis to the Academy of Sciences in Paris. Freud, who came from Vienna to study with Charcot in the winter of 1885–1886, was clearly impressed by the master's hypnotizing talents, which the latter practiced at the Salpêtrière, mainly on responsive female patients, and by Charcot's powerful arguments in favor of viewing hysteria as a real disease, which in the absence of an organic etiology may be caused by a sexual factor (*la chose sexuelle*).

Freud's *Studies on Hysteria* (1895), published with Joseph Breuer, clearly took into account Charcot's teachings, and the idea of recovering the patient's traumatic experience through hypnosis ("the cathartic method") exposed in this study is no doubt indebted to Charcot's "unscientific" methods of exploring a psychiatric condition. Although Freud soon abandoned hypnosis in favor of the "talking cure," which became psychoanalysis, he did not forget Charcot's suggestions about the possible sexual origin of neuroses, including hysteria. The importance, moreover, of recognizing the existence of a submerged zone of the psyche outside the accessibility of consciousness or the control of reason was upheld even by those who rejected hypnotism as a dubious method, such as Pierre Janet (1859–1947), and embraced an experimental methodology. Janet's doctoral thesis, *L'automatisme psychologique* (1889), comes close to Freud's later theoretical theses by ascribing certain unusual or abnormal mental states (automatisms) to unconscious factors.

The "unscientific" ideas related to suggestibility and hypnosis were not abandoned altogether at the turn of the nineteenth century, however. In fact, they made a certain career in the discipline of "crowd psychology" (*psychologie des foules*) represented in France by Gustave Le Bon and Gabriel Tarde, and were used to explain the origins and manifestations of social aggression. As Alexandre Métraux has pointed out in his article, "French Crowd Psychology: Between Theory and Ideology" (see (*The Problematic Science*, pp. 276–290)), crowd psychology developed in France in reaction to the perceived threat posed by the so-called dangerous classes (i.e., labor), which, in parallel with developments in industrial production and the intensified demands on workers, were also finding ways to organize themselves against the forces of capital.

Although the proponents of crowd psychology were trained mainly in sociology, and criminology in Tarde's case, they clearly benefited from the notion of suggestion, which had played an important role in Charcot's understanding of hysteria. On the basis of the observation that mass behavior is different from that of a public, they tried to explain the subtle psychosocial changes that accounted for the difference. Tarde resorted to the model of imitation, which in his opinion explained how an individual could mimic another's behavior even at a distance. Le Bon was more skeptical of a positive explanation of suggestion or suggestibility in crowd behavior, although admitting its effects, and had to concede that suggestion was still a "mysterious mechanism." As Métraux has argued, it was Alfred Binet's understanding of perception in hypnotized patients that offered a psychiatric model for crowd psychologists.

Binet and other French psychologists at the end of the nineteenth century, such as Ribot and Janet, were heavily influenced by associationism, a philosophical doctrine developed in England by John Stuart Mill and popularized in France by Hyppolite Taine. On the basis of experiments on visual perception, created by the association of sensations and images, Binet argued that perception could be modified under hypnosis. The resulting hallucinatory effects obtained in a hypnotized, hysterical subject could be seen to be analogous to the polarization and distortion of affect in the individuals that formed a crowd. Suggestion thus acquired a certain scientific respectability, and it is interesting to see that even as late as 1921, in *Group Psychology and the Analysis of the Ego*, Freud started his discussion of mass behavior with a review of Le Bon's theses. Although Freud subsequently adopted a different explanation for Le Bon's observations on the hypnotic effects that a leader can have on a crowd, he nonetheless takes into account the idea that the behavior of a social aggregate can be analyzed on the model of an individual response.

In addition to his experiments in perception, Binet is perhaps best remembered for his study of intelligence, the development of experimental methods or tests for measuring it, and the foundation in 1895 of the first specialized journal entirely devoted to psychology, *L'Année Psychologique*. Binet also had a durable influence in America on the development of standardized tests that are still in use today, no doubt because of the propensity of American psychologists for quantifying statistical methods for measuring even such complex psychological phenomena as intelligence. It is certainly true that as elsewhere in the world, psychology in twentieth-century France became increasingly assured of its scientific status and branched out into several subdisciplines, such as clinical psychology, cognitive psychology, genetic psychology (most notably with the work of the Swiss psychologist Jean Piaget, devoted mainly to child learning), or social experimental psychology (with P. Fraisse and J. Piaget). Equally true, however, is the fact that more than most other places, and certainly more than in the United States, psychology in France has retained strong ties to philosophy, which may also explain why, as a scientific discipline, psychology is still willing to entertain questions (and doubts) about its object (i.e., human behavior and the mind).

Although philosophy clearly bears an imprint on many a French psychologist's work—Piaget's evolutionary notions of the development of the mind through assimilation and adjustment can also be related to Hegel's dialectic understanding of the contradictions pertaining to the spirit (*Geist*)—the reverse is also true. French philosophers in general, from Descartes on, and twentieth-century philosophers as well have clearly shown a keen interest in psychological issues. Henri Bergson's work, *Essai sur les données immédiates de la conscience* (1907), belongs as much to philosophy as it does to psychology. The same may be said of Gaston Bachelard's work, *La Dialectique de la durée* (1936), Jean-Paul Sartre's *L'Imaginaire* (1940), or Merleau-Ponty's *Phénoménologie de la perception* (1945). As a cultural historian, Michel Foucault has demonstrated an extensive knowledge in psychiatry, which he put to interesting use in his revisionist, genealogical approach to cultural phenomena, especially in his *Folie et déraison. Histoire de la folie à l'âge classique* (1961) and in *Naissance de la clinique. Une archéologie de la perception médicale* (1963).

The most interesting, and controversial, synthesis of philosophy and psychology in twentieth-century French literature is represented no doubt by the works of Jacques Lacan. Lacan arrived late to psychoanalysis, after a long apprenticeship in psychiatry, which resulted in his doctoral thesis, *De la Psychose paranoïaque dans ses rapports avec la personnalité* (1932). Here the influence of nineteenth-century notions of psychopathology, such as they appear in Ribot's work, *Les maladies de la personnalité* (1885), or Janet's work *Névroses et Idées fixes* (1898), is clearly visible. Even in this early study, however, Lacan's tendency to move beyond and between disciplinary boundaries is equally marked. His very use of the concept of "personality" suggests the epistemological ambition of reaching outside the physical, neurological description of a sick brain into larger psychological and sociocultural considerations. It seems, therefore, normal that in his discussion of "personality," Lacan should refer to such notions as Lévy-Bruhl's ethnographic concept of "primitive mentality" or to the historical-materialist concept of "person," derived from the "concrete psychology" of Georges Politzer and Henri Wallon.

Even more dazzling is the evolution of Lacan's thought after the Second World War, an evolution in which the lessons of Alexandre Kojève's lectures on Hegel are fertilized through a new, structuralist reading of language and human behavior, resulting in Lacan's magisterial reinterpretation of Freud's psychoanalysis. Although viewed with suspicion by the scientific community of psychoanalysts, both in France and in the United States, Lacan's theories of the subject modeled on a speculative understanding of psychosis (rather than neurosis, as in Freud's case) have nonetheless proved to be productive in a whole area of cultural studies and continue to inspire literary scholars on both sides of the Atlantic, proving to some extent the advantage of fuzzy disciplinary boundaries, even when it comes to twentieth-century thought. What Woodward had argued in the case of psychology, a "problematic science" in the nineteenth century, could be said to hold for some developments in French psychological/ psychoanalytical thought in the twentieth century; namely, that in a paradoxical way, the reflective tendencies of psychology as a discipline have perhaps contributed to a reconsideration of some of the conceptual presuppositions in a number of human sciences and in such different fields as ideology, communication, or sexuality. It would be hard to imagine that a narrowly conceived discipline, such as clinical psychology, in spite of its specific relevance, could produce such wide epistemic effects, and one can only welcome the thinkers who are willing, even as modern scientists, to venture outside their territorial spheres into hazier, but possibly productive, philosophical considerations.

ALINA CLEJ

See also **entries on individuals mentioned in this article**

Further Reading

Benjamin, L., ed., *A History of Psychology: Main Sources and Contemporary Research*, New York: McGraw-Hill, 1996

Bringmann et al., eds., *A Pictorial History of Psychology*, Chicago: Quintessence, 1996

Danziger, K., *Constructing the subject: Historical Origins of Psychological Research*, Cambridge: Cambridge University Press, 1990

Ellenberger, H. F., *The Discovery of the Unconscious*, New York: Basic Books, 1970

Gay, Peter, *The Enlightenment: An Interpretation*, 2 volumes, New York: Knopf, 1969

Knight, I. F., *The Geometric Spirit: The Abbé Condillac and the French Enlightenment*, New Haven, CT: Yale University Press, 1968

McGrath, W. J., *Freud's Discovery of Psychoanalysis: The Politics of Hysteria*, Ithaca, NY: Cornell University Press, 1986

Macey, David. *Lacan in Contexts*, London and New York: Verso, 1988

Mengal, Paul et al., eds. *Les origines de la psychologie européenne (16e–19e siècles), Revue d'histoire des Sciences Humaines*, Presses Universitaires du Septentrion, 2000

Mueller, F.-L., *Histoire de la psychologie. De l'Antiquité à nos jours*, Paris: Payot, 1960

Ricoeur, Paul, *Freud and Philosophy*, translated by B. Savage, New Haven: Yale University Press, 1970

Robinson, Daniel, *An Intellectual History of Psychology*, New York: Macmillan, 1981

Sternberg, Robert, *Metaphors of Mind. Conceptions of the Nature of Intelligence*, Cambridge: Cambridge University Press, 1990

Vergnaud, Gérard, ed. *Les Sciences cognitives en débat*, Paris: CNRS, 1991

Webb, J., *The Occult Underground*, La Salle, IL: Open Court, 1974

Woodward, William, and Ash, Mitchell, eds. *The Problematic Science: Psychology in Nineteenth-Century Thought*, New York: Praeger Special Studies, 1982

R

RANCIÈRE, JACQUES
Philosopher

As Alain Badiou has aptly pointed out, Jacques Rancière's work does not belong to any particular academic community, but rather, it inhabits unknown intervals "between history and philosophy, between philosophy and politics, and between documentary and fiction." His unique methodology, eclectic research habits, and voracious propensity for assimilating European intellectual and cultural history are comparable perhaps only to the unclassifiable work of Michel Foucault, an author with whom he himself acknowledges certain affinities. If his voice has yet to be heard in full force in the English-speaking world due to a lack of translations and sufficient secondary literature, it is perhaps attributable to what Rancière himself has called the partition of the sensible (*le partage du sensible*), or the system of divisions and boundaries that define what is visible and audible within a particular political regime.

Although closely affiliated with the group of neo-Marxists working around Althusser in the 1960s, Rancière's virulent criticisms of the latter after 1968 served to distance him from the author with whom he had shared the common project *Lire le Capital* in 1965. As Rancière explained in the preface to *La Leçon d'Althusser* (1974), the theoretical and political gap separating his work from Althusserian Marxism was instigated by the events of May 1968 and the realization that Althusser's school was a "philosophy of order" whose very principles anesthetized the revolt against the bourgeoisie. Uninspired by the political options proposed by thinkers such as Deleuze and Lyotard, Rancière saw in the politics of difference the risk of reversing Marx's statement in his "Theses on Feuerbach": "We tried to transform the world in diverse ways, now it's a matter of interpreting it" (1974, p. 14). These criticisms of the response by certain intellectuals to the events of May 1968 eventually led him to a reexamination of the social, political, and historical forces operative in the production of theory.

In the first two books to follow the collection of essays on Althusser, Rancière explored a question that would continue to preoccupy him in his later work: from what position do we speak and in the name of what or whom? Whereas *La Nuit des prolétaires* (1981) proceeded via the route of meticulous historical research to unmask the illusions of representation and give voice to certain mute events in the history of workers' emancipation, *Le Philosophe et ses pauvres* (1983) provided a conceptualization of the relationship between thought and society, philosophic representation, and its concrete historical object. Both of these works, along with *Le Maître ignorant* (1987), contributed to undermining the privileged position usurped by philosophy in its various attempts to speak for others, be it the proletariat, the poor, or anyone else who is not "destined to think." However, far from advocating a populist stance and claiming to finally bestow a specific identity on the underprivileged, Rancière thwarted the artifice at work in the discourses on the singularity of the other by revealing the ways in which they are ultimately predicated on keeping the other in its place.

With the more recent publication of *Aux Bords du politique* (1990) and *La Mésentente* (1995), Rancière has developed a politics of democratic emancipation, which might best be understood in terms of its central concepts. To begin with, the *police* is defined as "a symbolic constitution of the social," that establishes a partition of the sensible or a law that divides the community into groups, social positions, and functions. This law implicitly separates those who take part from those who are excluded, and it therefore presupposes a prior aesthetic division between the visible and the invisible, the audible and the inaudible. The essence of *politics* (*la politique*) consists in interrupting the partition of the sensible by supplementing it with a part of those who have no part (*une part des sans-part*), thereby modifying the very status of what is visible and audible. It is partially for this reason that Rancière defines *the political* (*le politique*) as relational in nature, founded on the intervention of politics (*la politique*) in the police order rather than on the establishment of a particular governmental regime. Moreover, politics in its strict sense never presupposes a reified subject or predefined collection of individuals such as the proletariat, the poor, or minorities. On the contrary, the only possible subject of politics is the *people* (*dēmos*), or the supplementary part of every account of the population. Those who have no name, who remain invisible and inaudible, can only penetrate the police order via a mode of *subjectivation* that is the very instantiation of politics: *democracy*. Understood neither as a form of government nor as a "style of social life," democracy is strictly speaking for Rancière the exceptional incursion of *equality* that disrupts the fixed hierarchies of the established order.

From his publication of *Les Mots de l'histoire* (1992) and *Mallarmé* (1996) up to his most recent work, Rancière has repeatedly foregrounded his longstanding interest in aesthetics while at the same time analyzing its conjunction with both politics and history. In positioning himself against the Sartrean preoccupation with *engagement* and the more recent hegemony of the Tel Quel group, Rancière presents his reader with a unique account of aesthetics as well as an innovative description of its dominant regimes. According to the genealogy he has undertaken, the *ethical regime* of images characteristic of Platonism is primarily concerned with the origin and destination of imagery in relationship to the ethos of the community. The *representative regime* is an artistic system of Aristotelian heritage that liberates imitation from the constraints of ethical utility and establishes a normatively autonomous domain with its own rules for fabrication and criteria of appreciation. The *aesthetic regime* of art puts this entire system of norms into question by abolishing the dichotomous structure of *mimesis* in the name of "an immanence of thought in sensible matter." It thereby provokes a transformation in the partition of the sensible leading from the primacy of fiction to the primacy of language, from the hierarchical organization of genres to the equality of represented subjects, from the principle of appropriate discourse to the indifference of style with regard to the subject matter presented and from the ideal of speech as act and performance to the model of writing.

Rancière's critical genealogy of artistic regimes and political forms, dominated as it is by a logic of contradiction and a Kantian concern for conditions of possibility, has also dealt extensively with the emergence of history as a unique discipline and, more recently, with psychoanalysis and film. In all three cases, the argument is similar in nature: the historical conditions of possibility for the appearance of these practices are to be found in the negotiations between the representative and aesthetic regimes of art. Thus continuing to work in the intervals between politics, philosophy, aesthetics, and historiography, Jacques Rancière will undoubtedly leave his own indelible mark on one of his privileged objects of study: the partition of the sensible.

GABRIEL ROCKHILL

See also **Louis Althusser; Alain Badiou; Roland Barthes; Gilles Deleuze; Jacques Derrida; Michel Foucault; Julia Kristeva; Jean-Francois Lyotard; Jean-Paul Sartre**

Biography

Born in Alger, Algeria, in 1940, Jacques Rancière was a student at the École Normale Supérieure in the early 1960s. He taught at the University of Paris VIII (Vincennes-Saint Denis) from 1969 to 2000, occupying the Chair of Aesthetics and Politics from 1990 until his retirement. He was one of the driving forces behind the journal *Révoltes logiques* from 1975 to 1986, and served as a Director of Programs at the *Collège international de philosophie* from 1986 to 1992. An active member of the Paris intellectual and political community, he has been a dynamic participant in shaping post–May 1968 political theory and is currently elaborating one of the most significant contributions to aesthetics that is comparable in scope to the earlier endeavors of such authors as Adorno, Sartre, and Barthes. He is the author of numerous philosophical works, the most important of which span the following domains: political theory (*Le Philosophe et ses pauvres*, 1983; *La Mésentente*, 1995), historiography (*Les Noms de l'histoire*, 1992), literary criticism (*La Parole muette*, 1998), and film theory (*La Fable cinématographique*, 2001).

Selected Works

La Leçon d'Althusser, 1974

La Nuit des prolétaires, 1981; as *The Nights of Labor: The Worker's Dream in Nineteenth-Century France*, translated by John Drury, 1989

Le Philosophe et ses pauvres, 1983; as *The Philosopher and His Poor*, translated by John Drury, Corinne Oster, and Andrew Parker, forthcoming

Le Maître ignorant: Cinq Leçons sur l'émancipation intellectuelle, 1987; as *The Ignorant Schoolmaster: Five Lessons in Intellectual Emancipation*, translated by Kristin Ross, 1991

Aux Bords du politique, 1990; as *On the Shores of Politics*, translated by Liz Heron, 1995

Courts Voyages au pays du peuple, 1990; as *Short Voyages to the Land of the People*, translated by James Swenson, forthcoming

Les Noms de l'histoire: Essai de poétique du savoir, 1992; as *The Names of History: On the Poetics of Knowledge*, translated by Hassan Melehy, 1994

La Mésentente: Politique et philosophie, 1995; as *Disagreement: Politics and Philosophy*, translated by Julie Rose, 1999

Mallarmé: La Politique de la sirène, 1996

"Dix Thèses sur la politique," in the 1998 edition of *Aux Bords du politique*; as "Ten Theses on Politics," translated by Davide Panagia, *Theory and Event*, 5:3 (2001)

La Chair des mots: Politiques de l'écriture, 1998

La Parole muette: Essai sur les contradictions de la littérature, 1998

Le Partage du sensible: Esthétique et politique, 2000; as *The Politics of Aesthetics*, translated by Gabriel Rockhill, forthcoming

La Fable cinématographique, 2001; as *Film Fables*, translated by Emiliano Battista, forthcoming

L'Inconscient esthétique, 2001

Further Reading

Badiou, Alain, "*Rancière et la communauté des égaux*" and "*Rancière et l'apolitique*," in his *Abrégé de métapolitique*, Paris: Éditions du Seuil, 1998

Campion, Pierre, "Mallarmé à la lumière de la raison poétique," *Critique*, 53 (1997): 467–480

Cingolani, Patrick, "Modernité, démocratie, hérésie," *Critique*, 53 (1997): 446–460

Farge, Arlette, "L'Histoire comme avènement," *Critique*, 53 (1997): 461–466

Dosse, François, "La Sous-détermination," in his *L'Empire du sens: L'Humanisation des sciences humaines*, Paris: Éditions La Découverte, 1995

Guenoun, Solange, "Jacques Rancière: Literature, Politics, Aesthetics: Approaches to Democratic Disagreement," *SubStance: A Review of Theory and Literary Criticism*, 29 (2000): 3–24

Guenoun, Solange, "Interview with Jacques Rancière: Cinematographic Image, Democracy, and the 'Splendor of the Insignificant,'" *Sites: The Journal of 20th-Century Contemporary French Studies*, 4 (2000): 249–258

Michaud, Yves, "Les Pauvres et leur philosophe: La Philosophie de Jacques Rancière," *Critique*, 53 (1997): 421–445

Morlock, Forbes, "The Story of the Ignorant Schoolmaster," *Oxford Literary Review*, 19 (1997): 105–132

Panagia, Davide, "Dissenting Words—A Conversation with Jacques Rancière," *Diacritics: A Review of Contemporary Criticism*, 30 (2000): 113–126

Ross, Kristin, "Rancière and the Practice of Equality," *Social Text* 9 (1991): 57–71

SubStance: A Review of Theory and Literary Criticism 103 (2004), Special Issue on Jacques Rancière (contributors include: Arlette Farge, Michèle Garneau, Eric Méchoulan, Jacques Neefs, Michel Pierssens, and Gabriel Rockhill)

Žižek, Slavoj, "Badiou, Balibar, Rancière," in his *The Ticklish Subject*, London: Verso, 1999

RAYMOND, MARCEL
Literary Critic

The work of Marcel Raymond mainly belongs to the renewal of literary criticism linked to the Geneva school of critical theory. His Swiss nationality placed him, from the outset, at the crossroads of French and German influences. His early writings on Ronsard in Paris (*The Influence of Ronsard on French Poetry, 1550–1585*, published in 1927), were still marked by the erudite, analytical, and comparative approach of French academia. Raymond attempted to provide a detailed analysis of Ronsard's stylistic influence on his contemporaries, such as Montaigne and d'Aubigné.

Following these studies, Raymond's conception was shaped by French critics such as Jacques Rivière and Charles du Bos, as well as by Bergsonian theorists and German thought, which gradually made him move away from the literary positivism of his beginnings. Moreover, in between 1926 and 1928, Raymond was profoundly influenced by Dilthey's theories and by Heinrich Wölfflin. In 1927, he translated the latter's *Fundamental Principles of Art History*. The role that Dilthey attributed to *Erlebnis*, or lived experience, in the process of creation and in the reception of the work of art, but, more importantly, the place he assigned to comprehension as the transfer of the interpretative subjectivity to the consciousness of the interpreted author also played a significant part in Marcel Raymond's conception. His notion of "penetrating sympathy" or, indeed, the "state of profound receptivity" extended Dilthey's idea of comprehension to the study of contemporary literature. It is equally certain that, under the impact of Bergsonism, Raymond's theory was guided to the consideration of the evolution and of the singularity of the work of art. The dialectical play between life and forms, which Georg Simmel described in *The Tragedy of Culture*, comes up in Raymond's account of the difficulties posed by the interpretation of literary texts. At the same time, Dilthey placed a greater emphasis on the ideas of connection and totality of the work of art in the constitution of the units of meaning. In fact, Dilthey attributed fundamental significance to the anthropological function of art as the expression of a particular existence and of a particular consciousness that represented the totality of the soul: feelings, will, and intellect. The method thus articulated around the concepts of "receptivity" and "totality" could then be applied to works of literature and, in particular, to poetry.

It is with Raymond's *From Baudelaire to Surrealism* (1933) that this method enjoyed considerable success. Its approach involved sidetracking formal or purely objective analyses of the poetic work to make room for the reconstitution of the writer's personality, with his or her own intentional aims. As part of this process, the commentator's intuition plays a role that is situated between exegesis and comprehension, whereas formal analyses are constantly referred to the central intuition of the commentator. This constitutes the central thesis, which comes to light in *The Meaning of Quality* (1948). Raymond therefore does not reject the requirement of objectivity placed on scholarship, on stylistics, and on the analysis of prosodical and rhythmical patterns of the work, all of which vouch for the scientific character of literary criticism. He integrates these elements within a wider "identification" with the work and with the artist's world. "The global intuition, which looks for a vital center in the work, needs to be checked, adjusted at every step through the most lucid examination of the detail, of the linguistic, rhythmical and stylistic specificity" (*The Salt and the Ashes*).

Truth and Poetry (1964) reiterates this understanding of the humanistic aim of the literary work of art as world and meaning for dwelling. Ultimately, Raymond's criticism belongs, to a great extent, to the prewar existential movement, represented by Jean Wahl, Benjamin Fondane (*False Treatise of Aesthetics*, 1938), and Léon Chestov. This is true at least in as much as one can say that the existential horizon of reading opens up a confrontation with the transcendent and the mythical dimensions. To understand the relevance of this position, one needs to be reminded of the controversy concerning the value of poetry as mystical knowledge, which raged among intellectuals at the time when *From Baudelaire to Surrealism* was published. Following the Abbé Bremond's study, *Poetry and Praying*, the debate over the analogy between religious or mystical states, on the one hand, and poetic experience, on the other, had been kept alive by a host of prestigious interlocutors such as Jacques Maritain, de Renéville, Paul Claudel, Benjamin Fondane, Georges Blin, Marcel Raymond, and Albert Béguin. This same controversy resurfaced, under a different guise, in *Truth and Poetry*, in which Raymond discussed Yves Bonnefoy's considerations on the essence of poetry.

In *From Baudelaire to Surrealism*, Raymond introduced a new manner of using citations: the quoted text becomes incorporated in and extended by the commentary. The familiar questioning of the poet was accompanied by the critic's familiar address to the reader, which willingly took on the tone of confidences and personal questions. Scientific distancing made room for literary intimacy. Apparently unrelated analyses of modern poets, such as Baudelaire, Rimbaud, Jean Moréas, de Noailles, Apollinaire, Mallarmé, Cendrars, alongside other nowadays forgotten authors, were linked together by the concern to define modern poetry. And, according to Raymond, modern poetry had to avoid the trappings of spiritualist as much as sensorial tendencies, mysticism as much as immediacy. In defining poetry as "metaphysics made perceptible to the heart, and expressed through images," Marcel Raymond strives all along to keep the two imperatives of sensibility and spirituality together. This explains his marked reservations to poetic irrationalism and surrealist experimentation. The investigation of the unconscious, of dreams, hallucinations, and narcotics, which formed an inherent part of literary experiments during the 1920s and 1930s, seemed at the time just another danger to be avoided. This explains the reason why Raymond's interest in the post-Romantic exploration of dreams never went as far as the suspension of one's lucidity. "Why is it that the hope of discovering always further away in the shadow, in the silence, the glimmer of some surreality, is more often than one would hope accompanied by the preliminary dismissal of the mind, which is supposedly unable to face present reality, and render it transparent and meaningful?" asked Raymond, when confronted with André Breton's position. Ascesis and abandonment alternated to open up a path to the text, but reflection and intellectual reintegration constituted the final word of this sympathy-based critical analysis.

Whereas the work represented an integral and self-sufficient world for the "participative" approach, it nonetheless lay within the framework of the intersubjectivity between the artist and the reader-commentator. Its scope was therefore always humanistic; it involved understanding oneself through a work of art. Marcel Raymond's students or his successors, such as Albert Béguin, Georges Poulet, Jean Starobinsky, and Jean-Pierre Richard, would, in their turn, develop this conception of literary criticism with reference to the aim of self-knowledge or, indeed, with reference to ontological and philosophical explorations, which pointed to religious concerns. In 1946, when he questioned Paul Valéry's intellectualist conceptions, Raymond's argument equally served to distance him from the ambitions of the intellect (*Paul Valéry and the Temptation of the Mind*, 1946).

The interest in reflection and autobiography is also reflected in Marcel Raymond's choice of editorial and critical works. He prepared the critical edition of Jean-Jacques Rousseau's writings with Bernard Gagnebin for the Pléiade collection. Rousseau provided Raymond with the opportunity to explore the notion of reverie and the orientation of literature toward self-discovery (*Rousseau: The Quest for the Self and Reverie*). Raymond became involved in a controversy with Henri Gouhier concerning the place of Rousseau's philosophical works, as the former had assigned central importance to the *Confessions and Reveries of a Solitary Walker*. According to Raymond, as well as Albert Béguin, reverie constitutes the privileged experience of the suspension of borderlines between memory and fiction, between the objective and the subjective, the subject and the object. This topic allowed him to investigate the polarity of modern poetry: the quest for the self (*soi*) and the dissolution of the "I" (*moi*). He thus came back to the question of the inherent "magic idealism" of poetry. As contrasted to the classical hero's aspiration to self-control, the romantic hero was open to the creative and cosmic powers of self-expression. In similar fashion to Albert Béguin, Raymond analyzed the power of dreams with reference to German romanticism and highlighted the connection with the exploration of the unconscious. This approach can also be said to account for Raymond's significant contribution in making surrealism aware of its links with German romanticism.

Whether Raymond explored the work of Sénancour (*Sénancour, sensation and revelations*, 1965), or that of Fénélon, his analysis was guided by the same type of interrogation. Hence, the autobiographical orientation of his last works comes as no surprise (*Chronicles*, 1965; *The Salt and the Ashes*, 1970; *Memories of a Good Child*, 1976). Marcel Raymond's diary, memoirs, and poetic works represent the stylistic variations of a consistent existential conception of literary criticism. These works most often give expression to a feeling of melancholy and postromantic longing, while also continuing the investigation of dreams and the beyond, which Raymond constantly pursued through the study of German romanticism and surrealism. The disappearance of the loved woman, the religious questioning over the certainty of faith, the sources of writing, and the limits of intellectualism constitute recurrent themes that illustrate the continuity between Raymond's criticism and his personal writings. It is only natural that the critic should become a poet and publish in later life works of simple, confidential nature (*Poems for the Absent One*, 1966; *Beyond Dark Waters*, 1976; *Text at Sunset*, 1980). The analytical quality already present in his criticism has become to some extent detached and autonomous in relation to his other writings.

Ultimately, no assessment of Marcel Raymond's work would be complete without a mention of his influence as a professor at the University of Geneva, where he contributed, through his teaching, to the foundation of the Geneva school of critical theory. Moreover, his correspondence with contemporary poets and his friendship with members of poetic circles, such as Maurice Chappuz, for example (Marcel Raymond, *The Shadow Eye, Correspondence, 1944–1981*, 1997), have added a social and historical dimension to his work, which had a considerable impact in its own time. The numerous exchanges of letters and debates with Albert Béguin (*Albert Béguin and Marcel Raymond, Letters, 1920–1957*, 1976), with Georges Poulet (*Marcel Raymond-Georges Poulet, Correspondence*, Corti, 1981), or with Henri Gouhier testify to a prolific intellectual life that remained in touch with its time. The other members of the critical school of Geneva, such as Albert Béguin, Georges Poulet, Jean Starobinsky, or Jean Rousset, continued Raymond's enterprise of defining poetry, at times through theoretical opposition. Georges Poulet explored, for example, the temporal dimension that characterizes every work and emphasized the identification with the author. Jean-Pierre Richard (*Poetry and Depth*, 1955) focused on outlining the sensorial world pertaining to each poet. These further developments and debates themselves finally provide the most eloquent indication of the perennial significance of Marcel Raymond's work.

OLIVIER SALAZAR-FERRER

See also **Albert Beguin; Henri Bergson; Yves Bonnefoy; Jacques Maritain; Georges Poulet; Jacques Riviere; Paul Valery; Jean Wahl**

Selected Works

L'influence de Ronsard sur la poésie française, 1550–1585, 2 vols., E. Droz, 1927

De Baudelaire au surréalisme, Corréa, réed. J. Corti, 1933

Paul Valéry ou la tentation de l'esprit, La Baconnière, 1946, réed. 1964

Le Sens de la qualité, La Baconnière, 1948

Baroque et Renaissance poétique, J. Corti, 1955

Jean-Jacques Rousseau, La Quête de soi et la rêverie, J. Corti, 1962

Vérité et poésie, 1964

Poèmes pour l'absente, 1966

Être et dire, La Baconnière, 1970

Par-delà les eaux sombres, 1976

Le Trouble et la présence, L'Âge d'homme, 1977

Écrit au crépuscule, L'Âge d'homme, 1980

RICOEUR, PAUL
Philosophical Theologian

It is difficult to place Paul Ricoeur among the thinkers who populate the intellectual history of the last century. Neither strictly a philosopher nor a theologian, his work has ranged over subjects as diverse as human freedom, the problem of evil, phenomenology, psychoanalysis, and narrative discourse. Certainly, though, he must be considered, along with Martin Heidegger and Hans-Georg Gadamer, as one of the central figures in the development of what can be understood as a contemporary hermeneutic philosophy. The origins of Ricoeur's own hermeneutical method can be traced to the point where he first articulated his opposition to the "immediacy," "adequation," and "apodicticity," of the Cartesian and Kantian "I think." Ricoeur set out to define this opposition by way of his exploration of what he called the "absolute involuntary" in his "first substantial philosophical work," *Freedom and Nature: The Voluntary and the Involuntary*, published in 1950. In this work, Ricoeur laid out the foundational elements of what was to be a sweeping philosophical exploration of the human will. Ricoeur conceived this Philosophy of the Will as an inquiry that would move from *Freedom and Nature* through the two-part project *Finitude and Guilt*, comprised of the texts *Fallible Man* and *The Symbolism of Evil*, finally arriving at a "poetics" of the "experiences of creation and recreation pointing toward a second innocence." This last has never appeared.

In *Freedom and Nature*, Ricoeur argued that an exploration of the will must begin eidetically because an understanding of the most profound possibilities of the voluntary subject emerges only out of a descriptive analysis of the involuntary. Thus, the eidetics of *Freedom and Nature* are linked to the phenomenology of Edmund Husserl and, more specifically, to the noetico-noematic analyses of his work during the time of the *Ideas* and the *Logical Investigations*. Ricoeur had been introduced to the work of Husserl in the 1930s and ultimately went on to translate his *Ideas* from the German in the 1940s. At the time of *Freedom and Nature*, what Ricoeur found so compelling about Husserl's analyses was that they sought to understand the voluntary, or "willing," subject and the correlative structures of the subject's intentionality before going on to describe the existential dimensions of intending itself. But from the first, Ricoeur extended the "eidetic analysis of the operations of consciousness to the spheres of affection and volition," weaving an existential thread through the fabric of the Husserlian phenomenology he had adopted. In so doing, Ricoeur was following the lead of Gabriel Marcel, whose famous "Friday" seminars he had attended in the 1930s, and

attempting to define a new phenomenology that would disclose a "living being which from all time has, as the horizon of all its intentions, a world, the world," and not merely "an idealist subject locked within its system of meanings."

What is revealed by understanding this "living being," said Ricoeur, is the "no of my contingency," the specter of my own nonbeing, the enigma of my "brute existence," which "secretes the most radical negation—the absence of aseity." In linking radical negativity to the impossibility of independent human existence, Ricoeur was beginning to form what became a career-long connection to the philosophy of Hegel, one that remains extremely ambiguous and yet vastly important within his work. As Ricoeur makes clear, in Hegel's philosophy the subject is characterized as an entity that comes to understand its existence only through the dialectical encounter with its own utter negation. It is this idea of negation, says Ricoeur, that makes Hegel's philosophy fundamentally different from the eidetics of Husserl's.

Because of what he takes to be the phenomenological and existential dimensions of Hegel's philosophy, it is easy to understand why Ricoeur is drawn toward the Hegelian methodology as he attempts to rethink the eidetics of Husserl. But Ricoeur turns away from the "all too enticing Hegelian negativity," claiming that although it adds a "tragic tone" to his own phenomenological analysis, its call for an absolute mediation of negation acts to cover over the existential experiences that are originally disclosed by way of Hegel's dialectical method. The Hegelian negativity, argues Ricoeur, because it necessarily emerges within the synthetic boundaries of the absolute, is "not yet negation," but merely an expression of otherness: "There is only the distinction between this and that."

What is at issue, then, as he began to write *Fallible Man*, the first of the two volumes of *Finitude and Guilt*, was Ricoeur's attempt to define what he understood to be the necessary existential bond between the self and the other without lapsing into a naïve Hegelianism. Thus, Ricoeur suggested that in *Fallible Man* he sought to demonstrate that evil is not simply one of the "limit-situations implied by the finitude of a being submitted to the dialectic of acting and suffering," but a "contingent structure" of what he had been calling the "absolute involuntary." In this way, *Fallible Man* moved a step beyond even the extended, more existential, eidetic inquiry of *Freedom and Nature*. Where the phenomenology of *Freedom and Nature* disclosed the "weakness of a being exposed to evil" and capable of "doing wrong," the phenomenological inquiry of *Fallible Man* explored the actuality of "being evil."

In attempting to understand the actuality of evil in *Fallible Man*, Ricoeur again lifted up the idea of fragility he had first detailed in *Freedom and Nature*. Now, though, he defined fragility as the "constitutive disproportion" of the subject necessarily located between the opposing poles of the infinite and the finite. It may be that the origins of this idea of disproportion are already to be found in Ricoeur's appropriation of Hegel's phenomenology at the time of *Freedom and Nature*. But again, the goal in the first volume of *Finitude and Guilt* was to supersede Hegel's phenomenological act of synthesis, something Ricoeur sought to do in *Fallible Man* by adjusting his ontology of disproportion to Kant's "brilliant discovery" of the transcendental imagination. What Ricoeur found so important about the transcendental reflection performed in the first *Critique* is Kant's placing of the imagination at the "crossroads of the receptivity specific to sensibility and the spontaneity characteristic of understanding." The significance of this Kantian discovery for Ricoeur is that after *Freedom and Nature* it seemed to offer him a notion of a necessary phenomenological synthesis defined by the epistemological limits of disproportion without having to make a Hegelian move toward a sublative absolute.

Thus, as Ricoeur moved from *Fallible Man* to the second volume of *Finitude and Guilt*, he had delineated what might now be properly called a phenomenology of disproportion and begun to define what he took to be his own unique non-Hegelian reflexive philosophy. With this in mind, in *The Symbolism of Evil* he again took up the problem of the immediacy of the *Cogito*. By way of his long "detour through symbols," Ricoeur attempts to demonstrate that the subject does not know itself directly, but "only through the signs deposited in memory and in the imagination by the great literary traditions." What this means is that the "I" of the *Cogito* is always a ciphered entity, one in need of a process of interpretation. Here, Ricoeur is setting out his first "definition of hermeneutics," what he describes as a grafting of the hermeneutical onto phenomenology.

In the 1960s, this hermeneutic was conceived of as a "deciphering of symbols," which themselves were understood as "expressions containing double meanings." Ricoeur claims that what was lacking in his own hermeneutic during the 60s was a willingness to adopt at least one dimension of the system of "structural analysis" that had emerged at this time, that which would require an "objective" treatment of all sign systems. Although in a sense this is true, and although Ricoeur would go on to extend his hermeneutical method in the 1970s and 1980s by way of an examination of metaphor and narrative, something else seems to be at stake in his hesitancy to move beyond an analysis of symbols in the 1960s.

In *The Symbolism of Evil*, Ricoeur argued that the double meaning of symbols is revealed in the "literal, usual, common meaning" pointing the way to virtually "unveiling" a second meaning. This second, deeper meaning is disclosed because the "symbol gives rise to thought," it sets us thinking by way of what Ricoeur understands as a spontaneous hermeneutics. What this allows for, says Ricoeur, is a certain interpretive process of reflective "restoration," by which the "surplus of meaning" contained in the symbol is recovered. Admittedly, it is difficult to know what Ricoeur means by a hermeneutics of restoration, as this notion appears at once both too Cartesian and too Hegelian for him to accept. It does seem, however, that this spontaneous process of interpretation represents the dialectical counterpoint to fragility in Ricoeur's conceptualization of a reflexive philosophy as it is articulated at the time of *Finitude and Guilt*.

This will all be called into question, though, as once he finished *The Symbolism of Evil*, Ricoeur entered into a long and exhaustive examination of Freud in *Freud and Philosophy: An Essay on Interpretation*. This endeavor caused him to redefine what he understood the general hermeneutical process to be. In his amazing reading of the texts of the "great Viennese master," arguably the best ever performed, Ricoeur discovered that the Freudian hermeneutic proceeds differently from the one that he himself articulated in *The Symbolism of Evil*. Instead of unfolding as a restorative process by which the most primordial meanings of subjectivity are disclosed, Freud's process of analytic interpretation functions as a suspicious "hermeneutics," exposing the ciphered, distortive, dissimulative quality of subjectivity.

As Ricoeur makes clear, fundamental to Freud's hermeneutics of suspicion is the notion that the "whole of consciousness" is a false consciousness. In this way, the work of Freud reminds Ricoeur of his own resistance to the claim for the immediacy of the *Cogito*. For although, like Descartes, Freud argued that everything that makes its way into consciousness must be called into question, he did not maintain that consciousness itself is the great "Archimedean point" that grounds subjectivity, but instead argues that along with the objects of consciousness, consciousness itself must be doubted.

Honest and superb reader of texts that he is, Ricoeur left himself in a precarious position after his examination of Freud's metapsychological systematization of psychoanalysis in *Freud and Philosophy*. Ricoeur says that this examination of the Freudian metapsychology is concerned with disclosing the "epistemological problem in Freudianism," what he takes to be the ambiguous "structures of psychoanalytic discourse." The major difficulty in understanding the psychoanalytic epistemology, suggests Ricoeur, is that Freud's texts present themselves as a "mixed discourse," at times seeming to speak of the "conflicts of force subject to an energetics" and at other times seeming to speak of the "relations of meaning subject to a hermeneutics." The purpose of Ricoeur's examination, then, is to "overcome the gap between the two orders of discourse" and to arrive at the point where "one sees that the energetics implies a hermeneutics and the hermeneutics disclose an energetics." For Ricoeur, it is at this exact dialectical point where an energetics and a hermeneutics come together that the "positing or emergence of desire manifests itself in and through a process of symbolization."

This would seem to be familiar territory for Ricoeur, as it appears that at this point in *Freud and Philosophy* he has again arrived at a place where a reflective process of interpretation will allow for the "unveiling" of the deeper meaning of symbols. But this would be to misrepresent Freud; for as Ricoeur himself argues, in bringing an energetics and a hermeneutics together by way of his metapsychological description of desire, Freud is exposing only the fragility of the subject and not the possibility of a restorative moment within which this fragility is overcome. Again, the Freudian hermeneutic is not Ricoeur's hermeneutic.

Oddly, at the end of *Freud and Philosophy*, Ricoeur attempts to overcome the Freudian problematic of desire by way of Hegel's phenomenology. This would seem to be the last place to which he would turn in an effort to redefine his own hermeneutical method. But Ricoeur says that what Hegel offers him at this point is a restorative teleology that he can place over against Freud's archeologylike hermeneutics of suspicion. Here it appears that Ricoeur is attempting to recast Freudian desire as Hegelian negation and then to go on to argue that this desire is fulfilled in a synthetic movement toward the absolute. But this is something that Ricoeur will not allow himself to do; and thus, in the end, he shifts Hegelian negation, as desire, back within the epistemological boundaries of Kant's critical philosophy, claiming that although "desire is revealed as *human* desire only when it is desire for the desire of another consciousness," it is never desire absolutely fulfilled.

It may be argued that it is his reading of Freud that ultimately convinces Ricoeur that his admittedly "Hegelian-style" attempt to totalize the mediations of disproportion revealed by his own phenomenological inquiry will never be successful. This is something that he does not address, though, because after he finished *Freud and Philosophy* he turned his attention to the "second front" of his "conflict of interpretations" with other philosophical systems. This second thrust of the conflict will be waged against "structuralism," the ov-

erarching title Ricoeur gives to the "vast linguistic current stemming from Ferdinand de Saussure." What he finds problematic about structuralist thinkers is their attempt to question subjectivity, not by way of a hermeneutics of suspicion, but by reducing language to the "functioning of a system of signs without any anchor in a subject. For Ricoeur, the limitation of this analysis is to be found in its notion of signs as differential units functioning within a system made up only of internal relationships. What has been missed, according to Ricoeur, is the fact that the 'primary unit of meaning' in language is not the sign but the sentence," what he calls the "instance of discourse." Here, Ricoeur has shifted his phenomenological argument from symbols to the wider problem of language. It remains the same argument, however, being Kantian in its articulation: Meaning emerges in the mediative moment when "someone says something to someone about something."

The careful reader of the texts of Ricoeur that appear during the late 1960s, especially of the articles gathered together in *The Conflict of Interpretation: Essays on Hermeneutics*, will notice his continued attempt to delineate a nontotalizing yet sublativelike system of interpretive restoration that will allow him to overcome what he takes to be the nihilating experience of a subject haunted by the "productions of the unconscious" and the "immense empire of signs." Because, as Ricoeur himself says, this attempt began to seem ever more "vain and suspect," he might have made a religious turn at this point in his career, as he does become extremely interested in the work of certain theologians at this time, but he remains true to his promise not to mix discourses, and thus the material of the 1970s and 1980s remains philosophical in its orientation.

Ricoeur extends his examination of the problem of language in what he takes to be the "twin texts" *The Rule of Metaphor* and the three-volume *Time and Narrative*, which ground his work in the 1970s and 1980s. Continuing the discussions of *The Conflict of Interpretations*, in the first of these "texts" Ricoeur sought to define the subject in relation to the "semantic innovations" of metaphor. In the 1970s Ricoeur argued that what makes metaphors so powerful is their ability to drive language beyond the limits of its prosaic boundaries and into an "extralinguistic" place of poetic creativity. This was clearly Ricoeur's attempt at a phenomenological response to the structuralist argument that there is no "outside" of language, one that again sounds very Hegelian in its expression. By the time he wrote the three volumes of *Time and Narrative* in the 1980s, though, he seemed aware of the limitations of *The Rule of Metaphor*. In particular, he understood that he has not adequately defined his notion of the link between the intentionality of metaphorical statements and the subject that receives them in an experiential "act of reading."

Although Ricoeur again took up this issue in the articles gathered together in *From Text to Action: Essays on Hermeneutics, II*, it is really in the three volumes of *Time and Narrative* in which he addressed this problematic in depth. It seems clear that what makes *Time and Narrative* so innovative, and thus so important, is not its extension of the problem of language from metaphor to narrative but its exploration, by way of a reading of Augustine and Aristotle, of the "aporias of time." For Ricoeur, the aporetic nature of time, especially as it is understood through the juxtaposition of the reflexive visions of Augustine and Aristotle, would seem finally to offer a way to define the elusive non-Hegelian phenomenology of disproportion that he has been seeking after for so long. But in the end, Ricoeur must concede that in turning toward Augustine, he has once again made a Hegelian move: the temporal aporias of finitude, like his own fragile moments of disproportion, are always already swept up within the perfection of the divine. Ricoeur understands the problem here perfectly: Augustinian time is simply Hegelian negation seen through theological eyes. Thus, as he writes *Oneself as Another*, the last great work to appear so far in his long and distinguished career, it may be that Ricoeur has come to the point where he must admit that

> . . . one does not know and cannot say whether [the] Other, the source of the injunction, is another person whom I can look in the face or who can stare at me, or my ancestors for whom there is no representation, to so great an extent does my debt to them constitute my very self, or God— living God, absent God—or an empty place. With this aporia of the Other, philosophical discourse comes to an end. (Ricoeur, *Oneself as Another*, 355)

PHILIP C. DIMARE

See also **Ferdinand de Saussure**

Biography

Paul Ricoeur was born February 27, 1913 and is a philosopher, phenomenologist; recipient of numerous awards, including the Hegel Prize from Stuttgart in 1985, the Karl Jaspers Prize from Heidelberg in 1989, the Grand Prize of the French Academy for Philosophy in 1991, the Nietzsche Prize from Palermo (Italy) in 1987, and the Dante Prize from Florence (Italy) in 1988; is the holder of honorary doctorates from more than thirty leading academic institutions in thirteen different countries; and has been made a member of the learned societies of seven different countries, including the Académie Royale des Lettres, des Sciences, et des Arts de Belgique, American Academy of Arts and Sciences (Boston), and Académie Royale Néerlandaise des Sciences.

Spanning a wide range of topics, including the history of philosophy, phenomenology, hermeneutics, psychoanalysis, Marxism, biblical narrative, and meditations on guilt and evil, his vast collection of writings is made up of landmark texts such as *Gabriel Marcel et Karl Jaspers: Philosophie du mystère et philosophie du paradoxe* (1948), *Philosophie de la volonté I: Le volontaire et l'involontaire* (1950), *Historie et vérité* (1955), *De l'interprétation: Essai sur Freud* (1965), *Le conflit des interprétations: Essais d'herméneutique* (1969), *Le métaphore vive* (1975), *Temps et récit, Tome I, II, III* (1983, 1984, 1985), *Soi-même comme un autre* (1990).

A teacher after completing his university studies in 1935, he married and became a father during the years before the war. Drafted, he became a combatant and a prisoner of war before returning to Chambon-sur-Lignon with his family in 1945. Holder of academic positions at the University of Strasbourg between 1948 and 1957, the Sorbonne between 1956 and 1967 (where he shared a seminar with Jacques Derrida), and, beginning in 1970, the University of Chicago. He gave the prestigious Gifford lectures in Edinburgh in February of 1986. Retired from formal teaching positions, Ricoeur continues to lecture and publish.

Selected Works

Philosophie de la volonté, I: Le volontaire et l'involontaire, 1950; as *Freedom and Nature: The Voluntary and Involuntary*, translated by Erazim V. Kohak, 1966

Histoire et vérité, 1955; as *History and Truth*, translated by Charles A. Kelbley, 1965

Philosophie de la volonté. Finitude and Culpabilité, I: L'homme fallible, 1960; as *Fallible Man*, translated by Charles A. Kelbley, 1965

Philosophie de la volonté. Finitude and Culpabilité, II: La symbolique du mal, 1960; as *The Symbolism of Evil*, translated by Emerson Buchanan, 1967

De l'interprétation: Essai sur Freud, 1965; as *Freud and Philosophy*, translated by Denis Savage, 1970

Le conflit des interprétations: Essais d'herméneutique, 1969; as *The Conflict of Interpretations, Essays in Hermeneutics*, translated by Don Idhe, 1974

La métaphor vive, 1975; as *The Rule of Metaphor: Multi-Disciplinary Studies of the Creation of Meaning in Language*, translated by Robert Czerny, with Kathleen McLaughlin and John Costello, 1978

Temps et récit, Tome I, 1983; as *Time and Narrative, Vol. I*, translated by Kathleen McLaughlin and David Pellauer, 1984

Temps et récit, Tome II, 1984; as *Time and Narrative, Vol. II*, translated by Kathleen McLaughlin and David Pellauer, 1985

Temps et récit, Tome III, 1985; as *Time and Narrative, Vol. III*, translated by Kathleen Blamey and David Pellauer, 1988

Du texte à l'action: Essais d'herméneutique, II, 1986; as *From Text to Action: Essays in Hermeneutics, Vol. II*, Kathleen Blamey and John B. Thompson, 1991.

Soi-même comme un autre, 1990; as *Oneself as Another*, translated by Kathleen Blamey, 1992.

Further Reading

Bourgeois, Patrick L., *Extension of Ricoeur's Hermeneutic*, 1975

Dicenso, James, *Hermeneutics and the Disclosure of Truth: A Study in the Work of Heidegger, Gadamer and Ricoeur*, 1990

Dornisch, Loretta, *Faith and Philosophy in the Writings of Paul Ricoeur*, 1990

Gerhart, Mary, *The Question of Belief in Literary Criticism: An Introduction to the Hermeneutical Theory of Paul Ricoeur*, 1979

Ihde, Donald, *Hermeneutic Phenomenology: The Philosophy of Paul Ricoeur*, 1971

Lowe, Walter, *Mystery of the Unconscious: A Study in the Thought of Paul Ricoeur*, 1977

Rasmussen, David M., *Mythic-Symbolic Language and Philosophical Anthropology: A Constructive Interpretation of the Thought of Paul Ricoeur*, 1971

Reagan, Charles E., *Studies in the Philosophy of Paul Ricoeur*, 1979

RIVIÈRE, JACQUES
French Critic, Essayist, Catholic Apologist

Until his premature death from typhoid fever at the age of thirty-eight, Jacques Rivière, who has been described by Henri Peyre as "one of the most complex literary sensibilities of the last two hundred years," published a range of penetrating essays for the influential *Nouvelle Revue française* (*NRF*) on literature, music, and painting. A prisoner of war from the earliest days of World War One, he would become an important commentator on the controversial Franco-German question. His Sorbonne dissertation for the *diplôme d'études supérieures* was on Fénelon's theodicy, and he was one of a number of French writers and intellectuals to be received (or received back) into the Catholic Church in the opening decade and a half of the century. His highly introspective spiritual journey gave rise to further essays devoted to the question of religious faith, with his notes toward a Christian apologetics being published posthumously under the title *A la trace de Dieu*. Within his Catholicism, Rivière negotiated a path between the Thomist rigor of a Claudel and the extremes of the modernist tendency, while nevertheless displaying more of an affinity with the latter's emphasis on *inquiétude*. It was the difficulty of belief that attracted him. His deep-seated need to accommodate a commitment to an individualism that was at odds with the orthodox demand for purity (which he insisted was beyond his capabilities) required some subtle, but

strikingly honest, argumentation. All his writings are characterized by an uncompromising concern with sincerity, an avowedly demanding ideal that is given its most explicit exploration in the essay of 1912 entitled "De la sincérité envers soi-même." Though not a philosopher as such, he maintained a devotion to the life of the mind and to what he defined as his "passion for general ideas," while preserving himself from intellectual aridity through his delight in beauty. He maintained that he *felt* his ideas and, on one occasion, described himself as motivated by a "mystical cult of truth."

In the early days of the *Nouvelle Revue française*, the young Rivière contributed some of the most distinctive literary and artistic criticism to appear in its pages, as the essays collected in his 1911 volume of *Etudes* (on such diverse figures as Ingres, Wagner, Cézanne, and Bach, as well as Baudelaire and Debussy) are there to show. His highly personal and sympathetic criticism reveals a rare ability to identify with what Hofmannsthal, in the special memorial number of the *NRF* devoted to Rivière, would later describe as the "spiritual coming into being of a poem or work of art." He himself would refer to his gift for "seeing into the creative artist's mind," a perception that allowed his fellow *NRF* critic, Ramon Fernandez, to compare his stance to Bergson's emphasis on the intuitive. Yet despite the influence of the symbolist school on his early preferences, his concern was never solely with the realm of aesthetics. Instead, he developed a preoccupation with the nature of French cultural identity and reflected on its function in relation to the cultural and political turmoil of the age. He professed a deep-seated, but skeptical, attachment to the priority accorded within the French tradition to lucid intelligence, which led him to extol the merits of a new form of classicism. His *maîtres*, he claimed, were Descartes, Racine, Marivaux, and Ingres, figures that, for him, were united by their common denial of all that was "shadowy." He nevertheless made no pretense at a system of thought, preferring to tease out the tensions and inadequacies within any single idea or belief, especially when it offered much that was attractive or felt by him to be conducive to the preservation of the essential tenets of civilization. His friend and contemporary, Charles du Bos, duly referred to his resolve always to "think against himself."

As editor of *La Nouvelle Revue française* when it resumed publication after the First World War, Rivière was responsible for the review developing a new identity that allowed it to exert a broader influence in French culture and politics than its distinctive, but more narrowly literary, prewar numbers had been concerned to achieve. The *NRF* could easily have fallen victim to internal dissent in the years after 1919. Its preservation was almost entirely due to an editorial strategy that bore the hallmark of Rivière's entire intellectual life, namely his commitment to negotiating compromises that were not only susceptible of scrupulous intellectual justification but represented a genuine new direction rather than a watering-down of the component parts. As a young man, he had come under the divergent sway of André Gide's philosophy of individualism and Paul Claudel's uncompromising Catholicism. If the friendship between Gide and Claudel failed to survive the former's burlesque treatment of religion in his novel *Les Caves du Vatican* (1914), Rivière remained close to them both, managing the improbable feat of securing contributions from both for the same number of the review. For all his championship of classicism, he penned for the *NRF* an article on Dada that, despite its surface irony, was not unsympathetic to the movement, thereby causing the intransigent André Breton to place his erstwhile allies beyond the pale. Antonin Artaud, theorist of the theatre of cruelty, was another unlikely figure to have engaged his attention; they exchanged a number of letters. Rivière was also an early disciple of Freudian psychoanalysis, which had been slow to find adherents in France. One of his essays on Freud appeared in T. S. Eliot's *Criterion*, which had been founded in part as an English equivalent to the *NRF*. (Before the war, Rivière had been introduced to Eliot in Paris by his closest friend and brother-in-law, Alain-Fournier, the author of *Le Grand Meaulnes*, who was giving the poet French conversation lessons.) It was Rivière, too, who retrieved Proust's great novel for the *NRF* following Gide's infamous rejection of *Du côté de chez Swann*. His essays on Proust show an unrivaled appreciation of the novelist's modernist aesthetic. His only completed novel, *Aimée* (1922), was dedicated to him.

In *L'Allemand* (1919), Rivière allowed himself to give vent to a deeply held antagonism toward the German national character, but characteristically, he made a strenuous and sophisticated contribution to French postwar efforts to promote Franco-German relations. In *NRF* circles he provided a valuable counterbalance to those inclined to ally themselves with the proponents of cruder forms of nationalism.

Rivière's unduly modest status in the history of French intellectual life is partly attributable to his early death. Much of his production was only published, or collected, posthumously. A full awareness of the values he sought to promote and of the unique quality of his intellectual and spiritual life is dependent on familiarity with the letters he exchanged with leading literary figures of the period, many of which have remained unpublished until of late. Few of his writings have been translated into English.

MICHAEL TILBY

See also **Andre Gide**

Biography

Jacques Rivière was born in Bordeaux on July 15, 1886. He was educated at the Lycée de Bordeaux, Lycée Lakanal, Paris and University of Bordeaux (*licence-ès-lettres*, 1907); twice failed his *agrégation*. He formed a close friendship at Lakanal with Henri Fournier (Alain-Fournier, author of *Le Grand Meaulnes*), whose sister Isabelle he married in 1909. He began a lifelong correspondence with Paul Claudel (under whose influence he embarked on a career of theological enquiry) in 1907. He began a lasting friendship and collaboration with André Gide in 1908. He taught literature and philosophy at École Saint-Joseph des Tuileries and Collège Stanislas, Paris, from 1909 to 1911. He earned a *Diplôme d'études supérieures* in philosophy at the University of Paris (with a thesis on Fénelon) in 1911. That same year, he was named secretary of the *Nouvelle Revue française*. He was called up as a sergeant in the 220th Infantry in 1914 and taken prisoner in the battle of Eton on August 24, 1914. He was a prisoner of war in Germany from 1914 to 1917. He was named editor of the *Nouvelle Revue française* in 1919. Rivière died of typhoid in Paris on February 14, 1925.

Selected Works

Etudes, 1911 (4th enlarged edition, 1924) [*Studies*]
L'Allemand, souvenirs et réflexions d'un prisonnier de guerre, 1918 [*The German, Memories and Reflections of a Prisoner of War*]
A la trace de Dieu, 1925 [*The Path to God*]
Quelques progrès dans l'étude du coeur humain (Freud et Proust), 1926 [*Progress in the Study of the Human Heart (Freud and Proust)*]
De la sincérité envers soi-même. De la foi, 1927 [*On Sincerity towards Oneself On Faith*]
Le Français, 1928 [*The Frenchman*]
Carnets 1914–1917, edited by Isabelle and Alain Rivière, 1974 [*Notebooks*]
Rimbaud; dossier (1905–1925), edited by Roger Lefèvre, 1977
Etudes. L'Oeuvre critique de Jacques Rivière à "La Nouvelle Revue française," edited by Alain Rivière, 1999 [*Studies. Jacques Rivière's Critical Writings in the "Nouvelle Revue Française"*]

Correspondence

Artaud, Antonin, *Correspondance avec Jacques Rivière*, Paris: Nouvelle Revue française, 1927
Paul Claudel-Jacques Rivière, *Correspondance 1907–1924*, edited by Auguste Anglès and Pierre de Gaulmyn, Paris: Gallimard, 1984 (Cahiers Paul Claudel, 12)
André Gide-Jacques Rivière, *Correspondance 1909–1925*, edited by Pierre de Gaulmyn and Alain Rivière, Paris: Gallimard, 1998
François Mauriac-Jacques Rivière, *Correspondance 1911–1925*, edited by John E. Flower, University of Exeter Press, 1988

Marcel Proust-Jacques Rivière, *Correspondance 1914–1922*, edited by Philip Kolb, new enlarged edition, Paris: Gallimard, 1976

Jacques Rivière-Alain-Fournier, *Correspondance 1904–1914*, edited by Alain Rivière and Pierre de Gaulmyn, 2 vols., Paris: Gallimard, 1991

Jacques Rivière-Charles du Bos, *Correspondance*, edited by Jean-Pierre Cap, Lyons: Université de Lyon II – Centre d'études gidiennes, 1990

Jacques Rivière-Gabriel Frizeau, *Correspondance (1906–1922)*, edited by Victor Martin-Schmets, Biarritz: Atlantica, 1998

Further Reading

Beaulieu, Paul, *Jacques Rivière*, Paris: La Colombe, 1956

Cap, Jean-Pierre, *Decadence of Freedom: Jacques Rivière's Perception of Russian Mentality*, Boulder: Colorado University Press, 1984

Charlot, Pierre, *Jacques Rivière. Une vie ardente et sincère*, Paris: Bloud et Gay, 1934

Cook, Bradford, *Jacques Rivière: A Life of the Spirit*, Oxford: Blackwell, 1958

Coquoz, François Marie, *L'Evolution religieuse de Jacques Rivière*, Fribourg: Editions universitaires, 1963

Fernandez, Ramon, "Jacques Rivière et le moralisme," *Nouvelle Revue française*, 28 (1927), 279–82

Gide, André, *Incidences*, Paris: Nouvelle Revue française, 1924

Jans, Adrien, *La Pensée de Jacques Rivière*, Brussels: La Cité chrétienne, 1938

Lacouture, Jean, *Une adolescence du siècle: Jacques Rivière et la NRF*, Paris: Seuil, 1994

Levy, Karen, D., *Jacques Rivière*, Boston: Twayne, 1982

Maritain, Jacques, "L'Apologétique de Jacques Rivière," *La Revue universelle*, 26 (1926), 101–09

Naughton, Helen Thomas, *Jacques Rivière: The Development of a Man and a Creed*, The Hague: Mouton, 1966

O'Neill, Kevin, *André Gide and the "Roman d'aventure,"* Sydney: Sydney University Press, 1969

Raymond, Marcel, *Etudes sur Jacques Rivière*, Paris: Corti, 1972

Rey-Herme, Yves (ed.), *Jacques Rivière: une conscience européenne (1916–1924)*, Paris: Gallimard, 1992

Stolpe, Sven Johan, *Den Kristna falangen Franske essayer*, Stockholm, 1934

Suffran, Michel, *Jacques Rivière ou la conversion à la clarté*, Paris: Wesmael-Charlier, 1967

Tolzien, Waldemar, *Jacques Rivière, seine Entwicklung und die Problematik seiner Geistesart*, Hamburg: Seminar für romanische Sprachen und Kultur, 1931

Turnell, Martin, *Jacques Rivière*, Cambridge: Bowes and Bowes; New Haven: Yale University Press, 1953

ROBBE-GRILLET, ALAIN
Writer

The foremost practitioner and theoretician of the French *nouveau roman*, or new novel, which rejected the anthropocentric humanism practiced and theorized by Jean-Paul Sartre and Simone de Beauvoir in favor of a new approach to realism and the novel, was Alain Robbe-Grillet. Perhaps because of the degrading wartime occupation that Robbe-Grillet's generation had endured, the traditional humanistic faith in the power of mankind to comprehend nature and impose moral and political order on society began to seem naively overconfident. Robbe-Grillet's novels refuse all analysis of ideas and deny his characters the power to even understand, much less to master and transform, their circumstances. Instead, he limits his narratives almost exclusively to meticulous and apparently objective descriptions of the superficial appearance of generally mundane objects, leaving the interpretation of their significance almost entirely to the reader.

Sartre's view of the novel, at least as it came to be characterized with respect to Robbe-Grillet's work, claims that its primary function is to present aspects of reality in language, along with authorial messages about the nature and value of that reality. Sartre draws a distinction between prose, which uses a relatively transparent language to communicate philosophical and political ideas, and poetry, which relies on a relatively opaque and self-referential language, focusing not on reference to the real world, but on its own form as an aesthetic object. The novel would thus be a vehicle for social change and political commitment, usually called "engagement" in this implicitly left-wing context. The timing of Robbe-Grillet's early works made him the perfect test case for a new way of thinking about language and literature. This movement, which came to be known as structuralism, claimed that all texts are poetry in Sartre's sense; they are primarily and fundamentally formal structures that refer not to the people and events of the real world but to other words and texts. Literary works do not communicate the author's political agenda but rather construct a space in which the reader is free to create a wide range of interpretations, none of which are constrained by the author's intentions or by realistic correspondence to the outside world of social issues. Roland Barthes, who would become among the most famous and influential of structuralist thinkers, virtually began his career (as well as Robbe-Grillet's) with a 1954 essay on *Les Gommes* (The Erasers), "Littérature objective" (the literature of objects). Barthes argued that the detailed descriptions of objects that fill Robbe-Grillet's books are not representations of reality but rather verbal structures that relate to each other rather than the world outside the book. The structuralist critic Gérard Genette, in an essay published with *Dans le Labyrinthe* (In the Labyrinth), demonstrated that Robbe-Grillet's novels combine sets of formal elements into paradigms that are then altered, expanded, and contradicted by reference to themselves rather than to any outer reality. Robbe-Grillet's rejection of Sartre may itself be understood as a political rather than purely artistic strategy.

A generation that had lived through Hitler and Stalin might be expected to reject "totalitarian" theories in which authors control and direct language and meaning and to welcome a theory that "liberates" writing from that control. As Robbe-Grillet remarked in his autobiographical *Le Miroir qui revient* (Ghosts in the Mirror), if Fascism and Communism represented order and political engagement, "there's no doubt I would choose disorder."

The handful of early novels that brought Robbe-Grillet's work to critical attention are all distinctive, but share enough common ground technically and thematically that one example may suffice to illustrate their major characteristics. *La jalousie* (Jealousy), probably his best-known novel, opens with a detailed description of the precise form and location of a shadow cast by one of the pillars supporting the roof of a porch, followed by a similar description of a brief conversation between two women, then descriptions of the balustrade on the porch railing and of the geometrical arrangement of a field of banana trees. The descriptions are all equally impersonal and objective, suggesting that we can see other people's exteriors just as we see those of inanimate objects, but that the psychological interiority of their thoughts and feelings and motives are just as opaque to our understanding as is the psychology of the trees. We can observe their appearance and follow their positions as they move, but can never know or comprehend them.

Robbe-Grillet adopts a number of formal techniques to match this thematic emphasis, including the effacement of the narrator and the abandonment of chronology. There are no descriptions of the narrator and no references to his thoughts; indeed, the word "I" never occurs, typically replaced by impersonal constructions. The pervasive reliance on the present tense and the frequent repetition of incidents—often with minute variations from one instance to another—leave the impression of a fragmented world with no meaningful order underlying its inscrutable surface. Despite these obstacles, the reader can recuperate a skeletal plot, in which the jealous narrator obsessively scrutinizes his wife and neighbors in an effort to confirm his suspicion that his wife is having an affair with his neighbor. His equally obsessive scrutiny of his inanimate surroundings is usually seen as evidence of his need to suppress and control his nearly hysterical jealousy. Thus Robbe-Grillet's novels are often said to have deferred psychology and interpretation rather than eliminating them, making the reader construct the characters and plot from a series of carefully selected details rather than on the basis of authorial direction and aid. For most readers, these apparently objective works turn out to be thoroughly subjective invitations to in-depth psychological analysis.

Robbe-Grillet's reputation rests primarily on the four novels of the 1950s, and his work since then is generally regarded as adding little of significance to the early breakthroughs in subject and technique. He has also earned a degree of critical, if not popular, success with a series of projects in which he adapts the themes and techniques of the novels to experimental films, making particular use of disordered and contradictory chronologies and characters whose actions and motives resist explanation. He has published several of his screenplays together with still photographs as what he calls "ciné-romans," or "cine-novels." He has also worked on a number of "assemblage" books that feature his own texts accompanying photographs or paintings by other artists, including *La Belle Captive* (The Beautiful Captive), which juxtaposes his text with surrealist paintings by René Magritte. For many critics, the cinematic work is of markedly less interest than the early novels, and the writings of the 1970s are little more than cliché-ridden soft pornography. Nevertheless, the highly original early novels marked a clean break with any previous fiction, serving as a model and an inspiration for a generation of creative writers and as a productive challenge for a generation of literary theorists.

WILLIAM NELLES

See also **Roland Barthes; Simone de Beauvoir; Gérard Genette; Jean-Paul Sartre**

Biography

Robbe-Grillet was born on August 18, 1922, in Brest, France. In 1942 he passed the entrance examination for the prestigious National Institute of Agronomy, but his studies were interrupted by a year of forced labor for the German government as a lathe operator in a tank factory. He graduated in 1945 and worked as a statistician, engineer, and agronomist from 1945 to 1951 in Paris, Bulgaria, Morocco, Guinea, Guadeloupe, and Martinique. He wrote his first novel, *Un Régicide*, in 1949, while still employed as an agricultural scientist, but in 1951, while convalescing from a work-related illness, he began writing full time and gave up his career in agronomy. After publishing four novels, Robbe-Grillet shifted his focus again and began his third different career, this time in the cinema, first as a screenwriter for French director Alain Resnais, then as writer and director of his own films.

Selected Works

Les Gommes, 1953, novel; as *The Erasers*, translated by Richard Howard, 1964
Le Voyeur, 1955, novel; as *The Voyeur*, translated by Richard Howard, 1958

La Jalousie, 1957, novel; as *Jealousy*, translated by Richard Howard, 1959

Dans le Labyrinthe, 1959, novel; as *In the Labyrinth*, translated by Richard Howard, 1960

L'Année dernière à Marienbad, 1961, cine-novel; as *Last Year at Marienbad*, translated by Richard Howard, 1962

Instantanés, 1962, stories; as *Snapshots*, translated by Bruce Morrissette, 1968

L'Immortelle, 1963, cine-novel; as *The Immortal One*, translated by A. M. Sheridan Smith, 1971

Pour un Nouveau Roman, 1963, essays; as *For a New Novel*, translated by Richard Howard, 1965

La Maison de rendez-vous, 1965, novel; as *La Maison de rendez-vous*, translated by Richard Howard, 1966; as *The House of Assignation*, translated by A. M. Sheridan Smith, 1970

Projet pour une révolution à New York, 1970, novel; as *Project for a Revolution in New York*, translated by Richard Howard, 1972

Glissements progressifs du plaisir, 1974, cine-novel

La Belle Captive, 1975, text with illustrations

Topologie d'une cité fantôme, 1976, novel; as *Topology of a Phantom City*, translated by J. A. Underwood, 1977

Un Régicide, 1978, novel (written in 1949)

Souvenirs du triangle d'or, 1978, novel; as *Recollections of the Golden Triangle*, translated by J. A. Underwood, 1984

Djinn, 1981, novel

Le Miroir qui revient, 1984, autobiography; as *Ghosts in the Mirror*, translated by Jo Levy, 1988

Angélique, ou L'Enchantement, 1988, autobiography

Les Derniers Jours de Corinthe, 1994, autobiography

Further Reading

Fletcher, John, *Alain Robbe-Grillet*, New York: Methuen, 1983.

Heath, Stephen, *The Nouveau Roman: A Study in the Practice of Writing*, London: Elek, 1972.

Jefferson, Ann, *The Nouveau Roman and the Poetics of Fiction*, Cambridge: Cambridge University Press, 1980.

Leki, Ilona, *Alain Robbe-Grillet*, Boston: Twayne, 1983.

Morrissette, Bruce, *Intertextual Assemblage in Robbe-Grillet from Topology to the Golden Triangle*, Fredericton, New Brunswick: York Press, 1979.

Morrissette, Bruce, *Les Romans de Robbe-Grillet*, 1963, translated as *The Novels of Robbe-Grillet*, Ithaca, New York: Cornell University Press, 1975.

Stoltzfus, Ben, *Alain Robbe-Grillet: The Body of the Text*, Rutherford, New Jersey: Fairleigh Dickinson University Press, 1985.

ROUGEMONT, DENIS DE
Writer

Denis de Rougemont is not a thinker who with hindsight one could see as a major intellectual figure of the twentieth century. He is the author of an influential book on love in medieval culture (*L'amour et l'occident*, 1939) and is also perhaps known in association with various groupings claiming the philosophy of *personalism*, a doctrine largely superseded by the existentialism of Sartre and others, with which it shares some characteristics. This lack of historical profile, however, is linked to the nature of de Rougemont's thought, which is polemical and acutely tied to its moment. If one takes account of the plurality of de Rougemont's interventions across a series of different contexts, a picture emerges of a consistent critical enemy of totalitarian politics, a militant federalist (*L'un et le Divers*, 1970), a resolute European, an exemplar of the committed intellectual, and an encyclopedic thinker (*Vingt-huit siècles d'Europe*, 1961). De Rougemont might also be characterized as a Swiss, rather than a French, thinker, in that Switzerland played a significant role in his thought and was also in some instances the specific object of his writing (*La Suisse ou l'histoire d'un peuple heureux*, 1965).

Born in 1906, Denis de Rougemont belonged to the intellectual generation of the 1930s and to the vague grouping categorized after the event as the "nonconformists of the 30s," that is, as intellectuals who were neither orthodox Marxists nor advocates of bourgeois liberalism, nor fascists. De Rougemont was initially an important contributor to the "personalist" review *Ordre Nouveau* and a member of the group of that name, founded by Arnauld Dandieu and Robert Aron in early 1930s, and he was also later a prominent voice in the expression of the philosophy of personalism centered around Emmanuel Mounier and the journal *Esprit*. Personalism, in the form that it takes in de Rougemont's writings, is a rigorously antideterminist philosophy that prefigures existentialism in its emphasis on the realization of humanity, of the freedom of man, through action. De Rougemont's *Penser avec les mains*, for example, of 1936 affirms the necessary link of thought and action and calls for a thought through action, for a conception of thought as an act. Personalism for de Rougemont is a philosophy based on an affirmation of the person, as a creative vocation or in other senses a becoming, rather than on the atomistic individual, the basis, for de Rougemont, of a necessarily totalitarian politics. Personalism is vigorously critical of fascism and of capitalism as denials of the values of integrity and freedom of the person, whereas it was critical of Marxism for its overemphasis on man as producer and for its overdeterministic and objective philosophy. The manifesto of *Ordre nouveau* of 1932, for example, affirms the three principles of personalism, antiproductivist communism, and regionalism, in which "personalism" is defined as affirming the person insofar as they act or are engaged in a creative struggle. An economic doctrine is founded on this conception of man, which is critical of the productivist nature of Marxism, whereas a rigorously antistate, federalist or communist politics also derives from the philosophy of man realizing and liberating himself through creative action. De Rougemont's militant personalism is oriented toward a revolution with a Christian or Kierkegaardian flavor, rather than Marxist one. His references were to Kierkegaard and Proudhon, rather than Hegel and Marx.

De Rougemont's personalism is thus a militant humanism, pitched against philosophies of determinism. His thought is unremittingly affirmative as regards the commitment of the intellectual and argues against Benda's disinterestedness. His prewar writings are polemical interventions, manifestos almost, for *Ordre nouveau* and *Esprit*. But his thought also has an analytic element. "Man" in the contemporary world of which de Rougemont writes had become objectified, fragmented, and dehumanized. Such a degradation of the value of humankind was to be countered by a demystificatory critique of contemporary myths of humanity and by the personalist revolution.

This imperative to analyze the myths that dehumanize man and prevent the liberation of the person inform de Rougemont's most successful book of the twenty or so he wrote, *L'amour et l'occident* of 1956, in which he analyzed passion since the Middle Ages as a myth or as a symbolic fable. The myth, according to de Rougemont, acts as a kind of framing device in which society regulates its violence or symbolizes evil. De Rougemont treated passion (as it is represented in medieval texts and from that period to the present) as a historically determined factor, linked to a particular Christian heresy. His thesis developed to state that as love becomes democratized, war tends to take on the role that passion had played and passion seeks other forms in which to invest its "errant libido." This developed disastrously in the twentieth century into the politics of the mass, qualified as the extension of war, passion transposed to the level of the collective.

De Rougemont's thought is profoundly antinationalist. In both the prewar writings and *L'amour et l'occident*, the politics of the state are seen as virtually equivalent to totalitarian politics. De Rougemont was thus resolutely affirmative of federalism and of the importance and value of Europe, as a series of publications in the 1970s bear out. His last book, *Lettre ouverte aux Européens*, underlines the political and cultural value of Europe as a dynamic tension of unity and diversity and calls again for a federalism that would confirm this.

PATRICK FFRENCH

See also **Julien Benda**

Biography

Denis de Rougemont was born in Neuchatel in 1906 and educated there before moving to Paris in 1930. In the 1930s he was closely involved with the foundation of the personalist movement around the group and journal *Ordre nouveau* with Arnaud Dandieu and Robert Aron and then the journal *Esprit* with Emmanuel Mounier. He spent the year 1935–1936 in Germany at the University of Frankfurt, producing as a result the book *Journal d'Allemagne*, a condemnation of Nazism. At the outbreak of the war, De Rougemont was in Switzerland mobilizing resistance against Hitler. Apparently sent away in 1940 because of this, he spent the war in New York, where he joined a number of other European exiles. After a critical essay on atomic weapons (*Lettres sur la bombe atomique*, 1946) he returned to Europe in 1947, where he was involved with efforts toward a unified federalist Europe. He participated in the foundation of the *Centre Européen de la culture* in Geneva in 1950 and was its first director. From 1952 to 1966, as President of the *Congrès pour la liberté de la culture*, de Rougemont was a critical voice against Stalinist and Zhadnovite cultural policy. In the latter years of his life he was involved in the creation of the international dictionary of federalism, which was completed after his death in Switzerland in 1985.

Selected Works

Politique de la personne, 1934
Penser avec les mains, 1936
Journal d'Allemagne, 1938
L'amour et l'occident, 1939; revised 1956, 1972
La Part du diable, 1942
L'aventure occidentale de l'homme, 1957
Journal d'une Epoque, 1968

Further Reading

Ackermann, Bruno, *Denis de Rougemont: une biographie intellectuelle*, Geneva: Labor and Fides, 1996
Saint-Ouen, François, *Denis de Rougemont: introduction à sa vie et son oeuvre*, Geneva: Georg, 1995

S

SARTRE, JEAN-PAUL
Philosopher, Writer

Jean-Paul Sartre is undoubtedly the best-known French philosopher of the twentieth century. Associated primarily with existentialism, but also with phenomenology and later with Marxism, Sartre's brilliance as a writer and thinker was manifest not only in his philosophical writings but also in his novels, dramas, essays, literary criticisms, biographies, and autobiography. He was a polymath whose work transcended boundaries of both genre and discipline. His 3,000-page study of Gustave Flaubert, for example, published in the early 1970s, was, in his own words, a "roman vrai," a "true novel," which, in its attempt to answer the vast question "What can we know of a man today?" drew on psychoanalysis, structuralism, Marxism, philosophy, and literary theory. If Sartre's work has had varied fortunes, its synthetic and eclectic approach and its difficulty of classification have certainly contributed to the unease of the academic establishment with respect to its place in the philosophical and literary canon. Simultaneously lionized as a liberator of thought and feared as a moral iconoclast in the 1940s, Sartre came to be recognized as France's major philosopher in the 1950s and early 1960s, only to be eclipsed by the vogue for structuralism, about which he harbored serious philosophical reservations, in the 1960s, and deconstruction in the 1970s. Since his death in 1980 Sartre's star has been once again in the ascendant, in particular in the wake of the current revival of interest in questions of ethics and of subjectivity. Indeed, the peculiar ambivalence of Sartre's attitude to human-

ism, which he both mocks and celebrates by turns, seems more in accord with the mood of the new century than any simpler or more straightforward position.

Sartre is a philosopher of freedom and a philosopher of paradox. His conception of the relationship between liberty and situation, according to which the human being is always and only free within and with respect to his or her situation, allows him to talk of "the necessity of liberty," to envisage freedom as something to which we are "condemned" and, in the later years of his life, to maintain that we are simultaneously free and predestined. The development of his ideas can be traced through their relationship to his understanding of freedom.

In the earliest phase, in the 1930s, Sartre's work focused primarily on questions of the nature of the self, the status of the emotions, and the role of imagination in human consciousness. In *The Transcendence of the Ego* (1936), Sartre argued against Husserl that the ego is transcendent, not transcendental. By this he meant that the ego, or self, is not a constituting, unifying core from which actions, choices, and personality derive. It is not what Sartre called an "X pole," which would support psychic phenomena. It is not a real totality of consciousnesses. It is rather a construct, a product of reflection, an ideal unity of states and actions, brought into being by the synthetic unity of our representations. Consciousness may be constitutive, and Sartre agrees with Husserl that transcendental consciousness constitutes the world we live in, but he differs from Husserl on the question of the transcendental ego. In 1936, Sartre even argued that consciousness is not, initially at least, personal. It is the reflexivity of consciousness that personalizes it. The unifying and individualizing role attributed to the ego by phenomenology was, in Sartre's view, entirely false. It puts the cart before the horse. It is, on the contrary, consciousness that makes possible the unity and personality of the I (or ego). The transcendental ego is not only redundant but would be positively harmful, entailing the death of consciousness insofar as it would provide a center of opacity within the translucency of consciousness. There is no " 'I' " prior to the reflexivity of consciousness. Nor is the ego the direct unity of reflective consciousnesses. Such a unity is immanent and is simply the flux of consciousness. The ego is, rather, an indirect and transcendent synthetic unity of states, qualities, and actions. For this reason the ego cannot be intuited directly by introspection: There is no self in consciousness to be intuited, and all attempts to do so are doomed to disappointment as they encounter only a deceptive mirage.

Moreover, the very reflexivity of consciousness itself militates against capturing the ego. Not only is the ego external to consciousness, it is not even permanently present to consciousness. The ego can only ever be glimpsed obliquely, out of the corner of one's eye, so to speak (indeed, Sartre later wrote of the ego in terms of a blind spot). For, paradoxically, reflexivity kills off the very object it seeks: Once I turn my attention away from what I am doing onto the "I" who is doing it, my consciousness shifts from the unreflexive mode in which the ego was engaged, and the ego disappears. "The Ego appears only when we are not looking at it. . . . By its nature the Ego is fleeting" (70). If I turn my attention away from the intentional object of my behavior—the picture to be hung, or the tire to be mended, for example—there is necessarily no longer any "I" who is hanging the picture, and therefore no "I" for my intuition to apprehend. Consciousness has shifted from a simple reflexive mode to a complex but nonetheless nonreflexive mode that tries futilely to concentrate on an object that has already disappeared. This means that I can never know myself in any privileged sense: My knowledge of myself comes not from intuition but rather from observation and analysis, much like my knowledge of other people. However, this apparent failure is, as so often in Sartre, in fact a source of radical freedom: If my self could be pinned down and objectified this would, Sartre argued, entail "the death of consciousness" (23). The ego is not so much the owner of consciousness as its object. Consciousness itself is radically free and cannot slough off this freedom even to a transcendental ego.

In *Sketch for a Theory of Emotions* (1939) Sartre's analysis of human liberty explores the degree to which we are free with respect to our emotions. He distinguishes between emotions proper and sentiments or passions, which are, like the ego, transcendent syntheses of repeated experiences. Love, for example, is not strictly speaking an emotion at all but rather an amalgam of emotions, like Proust's "intermittences of the heart." Emotions in their brute state are irrational ways of apprehending the world, which aim to transform it, as if by magic. They are temporary responses to situations that appear to go beyond my ability to deal with them. Sartre's examples are predominantly negative: I burst into tears because I cannot bear to confess the harm I have committed; I become angry because I cannot win an argument; I tear up the paper on which a difficult mathematical problem is written because I cannot solve it. Nothing has changed but I have the momentary illusion of having escaped the difficult situation. Positive examples are less numerous, but tears of joy, or explosions of excitement, can equally well fit the model offered. The irrationality of emotion does not mean, however, that it is necessarily insincere: Insincerity is always possible; I may feign a joy or an anger that I do not in fact feel, but most of the time emotion is no less sincere than any other mode of human behavior. We undergo emotion, but once it is underway we may find it hard to stop; we are in the thrall of the consequences of our own construction, victim of our own trap.

This analysis provides a good example of the complexity of Sartre's understanding of freedom. His conception of human liberty is radical, but it is not facile. The choices we make, be they in terms of self-construction or of emotional response, do not leave us unchanged. We are always implicated by the decisions and actions we have taken previously. Our freedom is not *ex nihilo*, but rather operates from the basis of our situation. The same is true even of imagination, the primordial example of the freedom of consciousness, which it in fact constitutes. In *L'Imaginaire* (1940) Sartre showed the ambivalence of imagination, as both the essence of freedom in the world and yet also offering the possibility of escaping from the world into an unreal realm. Just as he argued that the ego was not *in* consciousness, so Sartre argued that images are not in consciousness, indeed nothing is in consciousness, consciousness is rather a way of relating to the world through one of its two major modes, imagination and perception. In imagination I posit the imagined object as absent, unreal, or nonexistent; in perception I posit it as real and as present, I can observe it, and I cannot change it. It is rather through imagination that I can bring about change. Indeed, imagination is the key not only to change but also to all kinds of freedom; it is through the imagination that I view the world as a coherent totality, rather than as a simple, contingent sum of its parts. Through the imagination I impose order and pattern on the world and view it in terms of temporality, spatiality, cause and effect, and so on. But if the imagining consciousness is free, this does not mean that it is arbitrary. Like all consciousness it is intentional; that is to say that it is always of something, and it negates the real only from a position in the real. As in the case of emotion, imagination does not act in a void, nor does it leave things unchanged: imagination has its effects in the real world, often mediated through the body. To take a simple example, sexual imagination may cause physical excitement, disgusting images can provoke nausea and even vomiting. Imagination is "the whole of consciousness as it realizes its freedom" (236), but it is not free from the consequences of its own activity.

In *Being and Nothingness* (1943) Sartre gave his most extended account of the nature of consciousness, of the relationship between consciousness and world, and between one consciousness and another. Consciousness is *pour-soi*, for itself, that is to say it is self-conscious, divided in itself by its self-awareness. It is, as we have seen, always intentional, and its intentional object may be the *en-soi*, the in itself, the solid world of being, of all that is not conscious; or its object may be *autrui*, other people and their consciousnesses; or it may take itself as its own object. *Being and Nothingness* has been described as devoting 600 pages to Nothingness and only a dozen to Being, and this quip is not far off the mark. Sartre's concern is primarily to describe how consciousness operates by negating or nihilating being, that is not of course to say "annihilating" it, but rather introducing an imaginary negation of the real into being, and thereby both, as we have seen, constituting it as a "world" and also recognizing that it is something other than consciousness. Indeed, consciousness is pure negativity; it negates not only the world but also itself: its past self, which it is no longer, its present self, which has no being or stability and is thus indefinable, and its future self, which it is not yet. Consciousness is only ever defined paradoxically as "a being which is what it is not and which is not what it is" (97). This lack of an essence is what constitutes the inalienable and inescapable freedom of consciousness; it has no positivity, no plenitude, and no self-identity.

Being and Nothingness carries further Sartre's reflections on the self in the section entitled "Le circuit d'ipseite" ("The circuit of selfness"). It describes for the first time what Sartre understood by the subject (rather than the self), for the only appearance of the subject in *The Transcendence of the Ego* was a negative one: "Absolute consciousness, when it is purified of the 'I', has nothing of a subject about it" (*TE*, 87). In *Being and Nothingness*, Sartre still rejected the notion of a transcendental subject and maintained that consciousness is rather "a transcendental field without

a subject" (291), but he did discuss both the subject and subjectivity in non-Husserlian terms. Subjectivity is defined as "consciousness (of) consciousness" (29), and the "instantaneous cogito" (89). That is to say, subjectivity is the spontaneous reflexivity of consciousness when it is directed toward something other than itself; in other words, when I am concerned to hang the picture or change the tire, not when I am self-consciously attempting to watch myself do so. It is the spontaneous reflexivity of consciousness, then, the very way in which consciousness is *pour-soi* that personalizes it. But of course, reflexivity does not only personalize consciousness, it also divides it: consciousness is only *pour-soi* because it is not *soi*, only for itself because it is not itself. The *pour-soi* of consciousness is by definition riven, present to itself and thereby separated from itself, constituted by its own self-division. Its self-presence is precisely "a way of not coinciding with itself, of escaping identity" (119). "The subject," wrote Sartre, "cannot be itself. If it is present to itself, that means it is not completely itself" (120). Nor can the subject really know or understand itself, despite the transparency of consciousness. (Self)-consciousness is no guarantee of self-knowledge. In the first place it is because, as we have seen, the self is a construct that cannot be identified with either consciousness or the subject, and understanding of it is more likely to come from observation and analysis than from introspection. Secondly, our very feeling that the self is innate may provide a further hurdle to understanding: Insofar as I attempt to attribute my behavior to my self rather than see my self as, in part at least, a product of my behavior, I reverse the order of cause and effect and interpret my actions with inadvertent but inevitable bad faith. However, insofar as I may have either an intuitive or indeed a theorized existential attitude toward human freedom, I run a third paradoxical risk in my attempts at self-knowledge: I may fail to recognize the extent to which I am bound, in fact if not in theory, by the self I have spent my life constituting and by the expectations of other people. I have, it is clear, no privileged understanding of my self.

All this is equally true, of course, of the consciousnesses of other people, but my consciousness cherishes its sovereignty and is unwilling, indeed arguably unable, to share it with others. One of the main stumbling blocks impeding the peaceful human coexistence derives precisely from the way in which consciousness constitutes the world: other consciousnesses also constitute the world, they constitute the world with me in it, they constitute me, see me as an object in their world, not as a free constituting subject. In Sartre's terms they "steal" the world from me. I, in return, view them as objects, try to deny their freedom, which threatens my autonomy, try to turn them into the mere objects in my world, objects of my gaze. Mutual support and recognition does not figure in *Being and Nothingness* except to be denied; all human relations involve sadism and masochism: Love itself is a battleground for supremacy, even apparent tolerance is part of an inescapable power struggle. "Respect for the freedom of the other is an empty expression" (480), Sartre concluded.

In consequence, we spend much of our time denying what we know to be true: denying our own inescapable freedom, which is so overweening that it causes us anguish, and denying the freedom of others, which we find threatening to our independence. Sartre called such denial of the truth "mauvaise foi," or bad faith, and its forms are manifold. *Being and Nothingness* itself contains many famous examples of it: the café waiter who is so taken up in his role as waiter that he forgets he is any more than his job; the homosexual who denies that his homosexual behavior means that he *is* a homosexual, and indeed also his friend, who insists that it *does* (both have a false but convenient view of the way in which behavior relates to selfhood); or again the example of the girl out on a date who equally conveniently "forgets" to notice her hand when her suitor is holding it. But most of the examples of freedom, its relationship to situation, and its denial in various forms of bad faith come from Sartre's literary works, both fiction and drama.

The relationship of freedom to situation is a very complex one. In the first place, human freedom is always necessarily situated, rather than being an abstract, disembodied liberty. It is situated in time and place, but also more intimately with respect to personal characteristics, such as age, race, gender, and class of origin, characteristics that Sartre refers to as "facticity." In Sartre's novels and plays, situation and facticity are shown as simultaneously permitting and restricting the exercise of freedom. Roquentin in *la Nausee* discovers both the contingency of the material world and ultimately his own freedom with respect to it; he discovers that his historical biography of the Marquis de Rollebon cannot give his life meaning and justification, but also that he is free to cease work on it; that the small-town pettiness of Bouville is oppressing and depressing him, but also that he is free to leave. But it is his work on Rollebon that he abandons, his hometown that he decides to leave. His freedom is both total and yet very closely specified. Similarly, in *Les Mouches*, Orestes decides to return to his hometown of Argos and avenge his father's death by killing his mother, Clytemnestra, and her lover, Egistes, who carried out the assassination. His choice is freely made, but only he could make it, and what is more, his specific situation meant that many choices were necessar-

ily unavailable to him, such as a peaceful homecoming to the bosom of a loving family. By the extremity of his situation, Orestes provides a powerful demonstration of the interdependence of liberty and situation. His status as a mythological figure with a destiny also makes him a particularly paradoxical example of freedom in action. *Les Mains sales* offers another example of the complex relationship between liberty and situation: Hugo is a left-wing intellectual who decides to join the Communist party but finds himself unable to escape his social background, both because it determines how he is perceived by his fellow party members and because it has been so strongly formative of his choice of self and values. Hugo's bourgeois idealism ultimately prevents him from embracing the pragmatism necessary to productive political action. He makes the painful discovery of the truth of Sartre's view that radical change (or "conversion") is always possible but never easy: "I could have acted differently, of course, but at what cost?" as he asks in *Being and Nothingness*. The cost is a thoroughgoing reappraisal of one's life-choices, which cannot be merely tinkered with piecemeal.

In the 1950s Sartre's main activities were political rather than literary or philosophical, though in 1951 he published his biographical and psychoanalytical study of the novelist Jean Genet and in 1959 his last major play, *Les Sequestres d'Altona*. The difference between the two works shows clearly the degree to which Sartre's ideas had evolved during the decade. *Saint Genet* is a literary and philosophical study that, although going much further than his essay on Baudelaire of 1947, nonetheless devotes little time to the political or historical issues that may underlie Genet's background as a foster child who grew up to feel thoroughly alienated from bourgeois society. Genet opted to become a homosexual, a thief, and finally a writer of works of extraordinary power and perverse but lyrical beauty celebrating treachery, violence, and murder. Sartre's analysis is said to have stunned Genet to the point where he could no longer write for several years, but its power clearly lies in its acuity as existential rather than political analysis. *Les Sequestres*, on the other hand, is an overtly political play: Set ostensibly in postwar Germany, its evocation of the torment and guilt of Frantz the torturer, youngest son of the von Gerlach family, alludes transparently to the Algerian question and the issue of torture of the Algerian terrorists/freedom fighters, which has returned so poignantly in recent years to haunt the collective French conscience. Frantz is still free in an existential sense, but the domain within which he can exercise his freedom seems dramatically reduced. Frantz is indeed at liberty to come down from the room in which he has for so many years attempted to deceive himself about Germany's postwar fortunes. But when he does come down, it is to drive off with his father, a wealthy businessman who also collaborated with the Nazis, in a double suicide pact. Franz and his father certainly make a choice: There is no suggestion of coercion, still less of some kind of causality or determinism, but it is hard to see what other options were open to them if they were to cease their self-delusion and accept the reality of their wartime activities. The von Gerlach family remains arguably free within their situation, but their room for maneuver seems tiny when compared, for example, with that of Orestes, another political figure, some fifteen years earlier.

Les Sequestres d'Altona was first performed a year before the publication of Sartre's second major philosophical work, the *Critique de la raison dialectique* (1960), and it prefigures many of its most significant preoccupations. The *Critique* represents Sartre's most serious and large scale attempt to come to terms with Marxism. After the war he had participated in a short-lived attempt to forge a non-Communist left-wing alliance, the RDR or Rassemblement democratique revolutionnaire. In the 1950s during the Cold War he had drawn closer to Communism, in part in reaction to the excesses of McCarthyism, but the rapprochement, which survived the revelations about the Gulags, was eventually halted by Sartre's horror at the Soviet repression of the Hungarian uprising in 1956. It was in any case a very one-sided affair because the French Communists wanted little to do with the existentialist intellectual who wished to ally his philosophy of freedom with their politics of necessity. Sartre therefore went his own way alone, and in both *Questions de methode* (1956) and in the *Critique* to which it eventually served as theoretical introduction, he attempted to find a way of reconciling the insights of Marxism with its analysis of social conditioning and political forces, with the corollary truths of existentialism, with its understanding of the role and importance of the individual in history, and of the interaction of individual freedom with historical situation.

Sartre claimed in the *Critique* to be returning to the ideas of Marx himself, which had been overlaid by the doctrinaire rigidity of contemporary Marxism in a way that would bring about the death of the movement if its sclerosis were not reversed. Marx, he argued, always recognized that if History makes men, it is equally true that men make History: "Men make History on the basis of what History has made of them." Contemporary Marxism, Sartre believed, had lost sight of the dialectical nature of this truth and had become reductive, narrow, and fatally inimical to individual freedom. The *Critique* aimed to offer a new perspective on issues such as social conditioning, historical progress, the class struggle, the role of the individual

in history, scarcity, and revolutionary activity by taking into account the way in which freedom operates within social movements, the way in which human beings interact in group situations, and the complex power struggles that had been analyzed philosophically in *Being and Nothingness*. Indeed, Sartre's analyses of questions of scarcity, praxis and the practico-inert, and colonialism remain highly relevant today and are in fact just now being rediscovered by political philosophers who had previously pigeonholed Sartre within his early phase, which focused primarily on questions of individual freedom. The description of the practico-inert, for example, which shows how all human action inevitably produces unintended side effects and tends to ossify, can be fruitfully used as a tool in the ecological analysis of the "greenhouse effect," though Sartre's own examples were rather in terms of deforestation and economic issues.

The last phase of Sartre's philosophical career centered on autobiography and biography: *Les Mots* (1966), Sartre's brief, witty, and beautifully written account of his childhood, and *L'Idiot de la famille*, his rambling, dense, and difficult three-volume analysis of Gustave Flaubert. When asked in what way he could justify spending so much of his time on a French nineteenth-century novelist, Sartre replied that he saw his work as profoundly political insofar as it was an experiment in anthropology and methodology. How fully can we understand a human being when we bring to bear all the tools of contemporary knowledge: psychoanalysis, sociology, history, Marxism, aesthetics, and of course, philosophy? Sartre's question goes to the heart of epistemological enquiry: Can we ever synthesize the different domains of human knowledge to produce a viable totalization, or are we doomed to remain with discrete fragments? Sartre's wager was that totalization may be possible, but more importantly he believed that it is of prime importance to make the attempt. Failure would teach as much about the conditions of knowledge as success. In a sense, *Les Mots* and *L'Idiot* represent the two poles of the same enterprise: the one, an attempt to understand the self, as it were, from the outside, using not intuition and introspection, but rather a dry, ironic narrative that appears to draw nothing from personal sentiment or intimate self-knowledge; the other, an attempt to understand another person as closely as possible from the inside, using letters, diaries, personal accounts, and a form of radical empathy that, like all phenomenological inquiry, attempts to enter intuitively into the experience described. Hence the apparently paradoxical brevity of the autobiography and the exorbitant length of the biography. Again, both texts can be seen as complementary ways of dealing with the question of the relationship between freedom and situation, Sartre's autobiography, providing an ironic account of a life lived as a kind of destiny within the "family comedy," and the biography of Flaubert, a primarily serious attempt to disentangle the complex nexus of choices and conditioning within an individual life, taking the family not as stage but rather as mediator of the forces of social, cultural and political history on the one hand, and psychoanalytic and even somatic drives on the other.

Sartre has yet to find his eventual position in the hierarchy of twentieth-century French thought. The uncertainty still surrounding his work would be a likely source of pleasure to the man who refused the Nobel Prize, who gave away his money and manuscripts to friends and strangers in need, who harangued the workers at the gates of the Renault factory in Paris in 1968, who visited the Baader-Meinhof terrorists in prison, and who accepted the nominal editorship of a Maoist newspaper in the 1960s. Sartre was always a loose canon rather than part of the canon, antiestablishment, be that social, philosophical, or literary. The venom with which he was attacked by certain proponents of structuralism in the 1960s (never by the truly original thinkers such as Deleuze, Foucault, Barthes, or Lacan, but rather by their followers) illustrates the power of his thought and the sway it still had even at the height of its unpopularity. Today, in the wake of the demise of Marxism, the attrition of structuralism, and the disaffection with postmodernism, Sartre may yet again be taken with the philosophical seriousness his paradoxical (anti)humanism deserves.

CHRISTINA HOWELLS

See also **Roland Barthes; Gilles Deleuze; Michel Foucault; Jacques Lacan**

Biography

Jean-Paul Sartre was born in Paris in 1905, where he attended the Lycee Montaigne, the Lycee Henri IV, and the Lycee Louis-Le-Grand, apart from three years in La Rochelle (1917–1920) after his mother's remarriage. From 1924 to 1929 he attended the École Normale Superieure, where he failed the *agregation* in philosophy in 1928, only to come first in it a year later. It was there that he met his lifelong partner Simone de Beauvoir. In the 1930s, Sartre did his military service, taught philosophy in Le Havre, and studied in Berlin. He also published *La Transcendance de l'ego, L'Imagination, La Nausee*, and *Le mur*. He was conscripted in 1939, captured, and taken to a series of prisoner-of-war camps in 1940, from which he escaped in 1941. The forties were a time of travel, theatrical productions, and extensive publication of fiction, drama, and philosophy. The fifties saw Sartre's activities become increasingly political, as he traveled to the Soviet Union and China, gave lectures and speeches, and signed manifestos against the Cold War. In 1956 he condemned the Soviet intervention in Hungary and in 1957 protested against French involvement in the war in Algeria. From then on there was a further decrease in literary production (only *Les mots* was published in the sixties), but an increase in political and philosophical writing. In 1968 Sartre supported the student movement of May and condemned the intervention of Soviet troops in Czechoslovakia. His huge study of Flaubert was interrupted in the early seventies by ill health and blindness, but he continued to give interviews, to make tapes, to sign manifestos and petitions, and to travel widely for political purposes, in particular in attempts to help the Middle East peace initiatives. He died on April 19, 1980, and is buried in Montparnasse cemetery.

Selected Works

La Transcendance de l'ego, 1936
L'Imagination, 1936
Esquisse d'une theorie des emotions, 1939
L'Imaginaire, 1940
L'Etre et le neant, 1943
Critique de la raison dialectique, 1960
Critique de la raison dialectique, vol. II, 1985
L'Idiot de la famille, vols. I to III, 1971–1972

Further Reading

Aronson, R., *J-P Sartre. Philosophy in the World*, 1980
Caws, P., *Sartre*, 1979
Schilpp, P., *The Philosophy of J-P Sartre*, 1981
Goldthorpe, R., *Sartre: Literature and Theory*, 1984
Howells, C., *Sartre: The Necessity of Freedom*, 1979
The Cambridge Companion to Sartre, 1992
Fell, J., *Heidegger and Sartre*, 1979

SARRAUTE, NATHALIE
Novelist, Literary Critic, Playwright

Nathalie Sarraute developed a style and mode of thought that occupies a singular place in French intellectual history. Although often associated with the nouveau roman, she preferred to work independently of the contemporary critical eye, always refusing to define her writing by literary labels. Her novels successfully embody her critical perspective, and her criticism functions as an extension of her novels.

Tropism, Sarraute's signature notion, is the conception that provides the unifying thread for her entire oeuvre. The term, borrowed from biological science, refers to the involuntary response of an organism as it moves toward or away from external stimuli such as light, heat, moisture, or electricity. She applies the scientific to the psychological: Sarraute's tropisms are the involuntary inner movements of the mind. As a plant would move toward or away from the sun, the inner human movements respond unintentionally to external situations that occur in everyday life. Although practically imperceptible, tropisms govern all behavior. They are everything in life that happens but cannot be expressed in words. As such, Sarraute highlights those fleeting moments between thought and action, the involuntary response to our environment, which is transmitted only by sensations. It is in probing this silence that we discover the insecurity, tension, jealousy, violence, or cruelty that is at the base of all human relations.

Sarraute tried to capture the millisecond of a moment between responding to our environment and consciously or not so consciously choosing an action, an idea she compared to abstract painting. A modern painter reflects upon and treats classical forms differently, producing a completely unrecognizable object, which is manifested on the canvas by the distortion of shape, incomplete figures, odd mixes of colors, and nontraditional use of shadow and light. Stylewise, the painting offers nothing familiar to the viewer. More like a secret puzzle, it obliges the spectator to decode the arcane and fragmented picture for meaning. Sarraute sees this not as exclusion or elitism, but as an invitation to learn that figures and forms in the contemporary world can communicate something beyond their classical contexts.

In the same way the abstract artist manipulates a paintbrush to lead the viewer to understand the erratic life of sensations in classical facades, an author plays with language and literary techniques to unmask the presence of tropisms to the reader. In undermining the conventional construction of words, punctuation, and syntax, Sarraute seeks to reveal a secret order of language, one that incarnates her vision of these psychological movements. In her novels, such as *Tropismes* (1939), *Portrait d'un inconnu* (1948), *Martereau* (1953), *Le Planétarium* (1959), and *Les fruits d'or* (1963), she employs repetition, omits names and proper nouns, sometimes even adds a foreign word, and places ellipses and hyphens in the middle of words as ways to show the ever-changing possibilities of language. Likewise, she distorts chronology, gives no apparent depth to her characters, applies shifting narrative points of view, and presents only a partial plot in which repetitive fragments explain the events. Like the viewer in front of an abstract painting, this subversion of the traditional framework of the novel calls on the reader to piece together meaning.

One of her chief concerns is dialogue. Spoken and thought words belong to the same language, thus dialogue should not be separated from the rest of the nar-

ration. All words are efforts to express inner feeling, whether it is a character's exclamation or a reflection of the narrator. Sarraute sought to break barriers between these different usages of language and between languages themselves. In turn, barriers collapse among reader, author, narrator, and characters. In *L'usage de la parole* (1980) and *Ici* (1995), she blurs dialogue, foreign words, and narration, which turns into a guessing game between the reader and author. Similarly, in plays like *Le silence* (1967) and *Pour un oui ou pour un non* (1982), the movement of her language in the script corresponds to character movements on stage.

Although Jean-Paul Sartre wrote the introduction to *Portrait d'un inconnu*, applauding it as an antinovel, Sarraute was ignored by critics in the thirties, forties, and fifties. Even today, what remains extraordinary about her first work, *Tropismes*, is its neglected precocity. In 1939, she was dealing with fundamental characteristics of the nouveau roman more than ten years before the appearance of novels by Alain Robbe-Grillet, Claude Simon, Michel Butor, Robert Pinget, and other known authors included in this wave of experimentalism. By the time Robbe-Grillet's *Pour un nouveau roman* was published in 1961, it was clear that the nouveau roman conveyed a variety of theoretical premises, all identifiable in *Tropismes*. Cycles of interwoven images and figures, which sabotage the reliability of the omniscient narrator and the stability of the characters, are the primary examples.

Sarraute gained more understanding in 1956 with her most important critical contribution, *L'ère du soupçon*. After the publication of only three novels, she remodeled literary theory with this collection of four essays: "De Dostoïevski à Kafka" (1947), "L'ère du soupçon" (1950), "Conversation et sous-conversation" (1956), and "Ce que voient les oiseaux" (1956). Like *Tropismes*, critics still overlook its astuteness. It was the first theoretical analysis on the nouveau roman, published five years before Robbe-Grillet's well-known treatise on the movement. Sarraute's innovative analysis of Russian, French, British, and American authors evolves from one question: What is the state of the novel in 1956 and where is it going? As she wrote in the introduction, the project originated vis-à-vis a curiosity in her own experimental writing and how it related to the novels of Dostoïevski, Kafka, Camus, Joyce, Proust, and Virginia Woolf. She situated tropisms in the history of literature and thought in the nineteenth and early twentieth centuries, a history of continuing evolution. She condemned critics who refused to consider authors after Balzac and Flaubert as participants in this history. She explained that she, along with modern writers, were experimenting with style and trying to revolutionize language just as Balzac and Flaubert were doing in the 1800s. She showed that contemporary novels were not disintegrating literature but adhering to the natural continuation of its ever-changing history.

Other critical writings, such as "Paul Valéry et l'enfant d'éléphant" (1947) and "Flaubert le précurseur" (1965), further demonstrated her competence as a novelist and a critic of both fiction and poetry. Although practically unknown until the late 1990s, Sarraute gave lectures on literature in England, the United States, and Russia, always focusing on her principal idea of tropisms. Sarraute's theoretical and artistic contributions anticipated the more famous works of the nouveau roman; they continue to offer us an opportunity to analyze the incommunicable aspects of language and, ultimately, the hidden realities of human relations.

JENNIFER ORTH

See also **Albert Camus; Alain Robbe-Grillet; Jean-Paul Sartre; Claude Simon**

Biography

Nathalie Sarraute was born on July 18, 1900, in Ivanova, Russia. From the age of eight, she lived in Paris and was schooled at the Sorbonne in law. She spent one year at Oxford and then continued her studies of legal science in Berlin. She gave up practicing law to become a full-time writer around 1940. As a Jew, she was forced to go into hiding during the Nazi occupation of France, posing as a governess for her three daughters. When she was over eighty, she published an autobiographical work, *L'enfance* (1983), which describes her childhood in Russia and France. She died on October 19, 1999.

Selected Works

Tropismes, 1939 (Tropisms)
"Paul Valéry et l'enfant d'éléphant," 1947 (Paul Valéry and the child of the elephant)
Portrait d'un inconnu, 1949 (Portrait of an unknown)
Martereau, 1953
L'ère du soupçon, 1956 (The Era of Suspiscion)
Le Planétarium, 1959 (The Planetarium)
Les Fruits d'or, 1963 (Golden Fruits)
"Flaubert le précurseur," 1965 (Flaubert, the Precurser)
Le Silence, 1967 (play) (Silence)
Le Mesonge, 1967 (play) (Lie)
Entre la vie et la mort, 1968 (Between Life and Death)
Vous les entendez?, 1972 (Do you hear them?)
Isma ou ce qui s'appelle rien, 1973 (play) (Isma or which is called nothing)
C'est beau, 1975 (play) (It's beautiful)
disent les imbéciles, 1976 (Say the imbeciles)
Elle est là, 1978 (play) (She is there)
L'usage de la parole, 1980 (Usage of Speech)
Pour un oui ou pour un non, 1982 (play) (For a yes or For a no)
L'Enfance, 1983 (Childhood)

Nathalie Sarraute, qui êtes-vous?, 1987 (with Simone Benmussa) (Nathalie Sarraute, who are you?)
Tu ne t'aimes pas, 1990 (You don't love yourself)
Ouvrez, 1997 (Open)

Further Reading

Asso, Françoise, *Nathalie Sarraute. Une écriture de l'effraction*, Paris: Presses Universitaires de Paris (PUF), 1995
Benmussa, Simone, *Entretiens avec Nathalie Sarraute*, Tournai, Belgium: La renaissance du livre, 1990
Critique, Tome LVIII, 656–657, *Nathalie Sarraute ou l'usage de l'écriture*, Paris: Les Editions de Minuit, 2002.
Jefferson, Ann, *The Nouveau Roman and the Poetics of Fiction*, Cambridge: Cambridge University Press, 1981
Minogue, Valerie, *Nathalie Sarraute and the War of the Words*, Edinburgh: Edinburgh University Press, 1981
Pierrot, Jean, *Nathalie Sarraute*, Paris: José Corti, 1990
Robbe-Grillet, Alain, "Le Réalisme, la psychologie et l'avenir du roman," *Critique*, 111–112 (1956): 695–701
Sontag, Susan, "Nathalie Sarraute and the Novel," in *Against Interpretation and Other Essays*, London: Eyre and Spotiswoode, 1967
Watson-Williams, Helen, *The Novels of Nathalie Sarraute: Towards an Aesthetic*, Amsterdam: Rodopi, 1981

SAUSSURE, FERDINAND DE
Linguist

Widely acknowledged as the founder of modern linguistics, Ferdinand de Saussure revolutionized the scientific study of language. He broke with the reigning philological tradition of his day, which emphasized historical and comparative approaches. Against this diachronic perspective, Saussure championed a synchronic point of view in which language is analyzed as a system. His theories helped to build methodological trends that established linguistics as an independent science, focusing not on history or psychology but on the linguistic system itself.

Paradoxically, Saussure's legacy derives to a large extent from a book that he never wrote. The posthumous *Cours de linguistique générale* (1916) was compiled by his successors, Charles Bally and Albert Sechehaye, based on students' notes from lectures Saussure gave at the University of Geneva during the period 1907–1911. The *Cours* presents a range of key concepts, among the most important of which are *langue, parole*, and *langage*. For Saussure, *langue* was the linguistic code, the set of conventions one learns when acquiring a language. It is independent of any individual's conscious attempt to modify the linguistic system. Saussure considered *langue* to be the true object of linguistics. *Parole* refers to the collectivity of all linguistic utterances made by speakers of a certain language. That is, *parole* is the dynamic expression of *langue*. Whereas *langue* is social, *parole* is individual, and the two together comprise what Saussure calls *langage*.

One of Saussure's fundamental insights is that language operates thanks to relations and the differences they reveal. For Saussure, any language is composed of two types of relations: syntagmatic, on the one hand, and associative, or paradigmatic, on the other. The syntagmatic category deals with the ways in which various linguistic elements may be combined to form utterances. The paradigmatic category groups together elements that could conceivably be substituted for one another, including sounds at the level of the word (as in get/let/set) and words at the level of the sentence (as in rapidly/steadily/slowly).

Perhaps the most characteristic aspect of Saussure's thought is his profoundly influential definition of the sign. The Saussurian sign has a bilateral structure made up of the signifier, or sound-image, and the signified, or concept. Saussure illustrated the inseparability of the signifier and the signified by comparing them to two sides of a single sheet of paper. Saussure's mentalistic conception of the sign excludes the notion of reference, and so the sign is not defined as referring to some object or concept in the real world. Rather, signs have a strictly relational meaning, signifying by virtue of their difference from other signs. As Saussure stated famously, in language there are no positive values, but only differences. To illustrate this principle, Saussure proposed the example of a game of chess. While playing chess, one may use most any object to represent the king, the queen, the pawn, and so on, as long as each piece is distinguishable from the others.

Related to the uncoupling of sign and referent is Saussure's emphasis on the linguistic sign's arbitrariness. On the one hand, this means simply that there is no necessary, pregiven link between a signifier and its signified. More crucially, the principle of arbitrariness illustrates that languages sort the world into concepts in different ways. For example, the English *house* and *home* are both *maison* in French, whereas the French *fleuve* and *rivière* have only one corresponding word in English, *river*. According to Saussure, not only is language the most advanced of all sign systems, one whose elements may be recombined to form an infinite variety of utterances, but it also boasts of the highest degree of arbitrariness.

For Saussure, language offers the best model for understanding what he termed *sémiologie*, a general science of signs in the context of social life. Although Saussure only hinted at the development of such a science, many theorists, inspired in part by his theories, have since developed various forms of what is now commonly called semiotics. Thinkers such as Roland Barthes, Umberto Eco, and Algirdas Julien Greimas number among the most notable examples.

Within the field of linguistics, Saussure's considerable influence has been likened to that of Sigmund Freud in psychoanalysis or that of Émile Durkheim in sociology. The three main trajectories of Saussurian-inspired linguistic thought, in addition to the Geneva school, are associated with the Prague school of functional linguistics, including Roman Jakobson; the Copenhagen school of glossematics, led by Louis Hjelmslev; and the descriptive linguistics of Leonard Bloomfield in the United States. More recently, Saussure's deemphasis of linguistic evolution in favor of states of language has significantly influenced the thought of renowned linguist Noam Chomsky.

Beyond those thinkers who devoted themselves to semiotics or to linguistics per se, beginning in the 1960s a whole generation of theorists in the human sciences adopted a structural approach inspired by Saussure. Although Saussure himself did not appear to have used "structure" in a technical sense, he is considered the source of the theoretical system known as structuralism. As the impetus for this widespread intellectual movement, Saussure's work wielded considerable influence over a variety of fields, including anthropology (Claude Lévi-Strauss), philosophy (Louis Althusser, Jacques Derrida, Michel Foucault), literary theory (Gérard Genette), and psychoanalysis (Jacques Lacan). Saussure's presence continues to be felt throughout the contemporary human sciences, bringing new generations of readers to his work.

The *Cours de linguistique générale* has been translated into over a dozen languages. To date there have been two English translations of the *Cours*. Although the more recent translation by Roy Harris (1983) presents a number of useful innovations, the terminology used in Wade Baskin's earlier translation (1959) has remained the standard usage, as in his choice of *speaking* for *parole*, *language* for *langue*, and *human speech* for *langage*. In 1996, previously unknown manuscripts of Saussure were discovered in his family home in Geneva. These texts, assembled and published for the first time in 2002 as *Écrits de linguistique générale*, may well open a new chapter of research on the thought of this deeply original and influential thinker.

HEIDI BOSTIC

See also **Louis Althusser; Roland Barthes; Jacques Derrida; Emile Durkheim; Michel Foucault; Gérard Genette; Algirdas Greimas; Jacques Lacan; Claude Lévi-Strauss**

Biography

Born in Geneva on November 26, 1857, to a distinguished family that included several generations of natural scientists, Ferdinand de Saussure demonstrated interest in language study from an early age. He began his career endeavoring to reconstruct the Proto-Indo-European vowel system. The brilliant 1879 *Mémoire* that resulted, the work for which he was most widely known during his lifetime, posited the existence of a purely hypothetical sound. Saussure's hypothesis would be confirmed only in 1927, following the decipherment of Hittite and its identification as an Indo-European language. Saussure went on to defend a dissertation on Sanskrit in 1880. He became Maître de conférences at the École des Hautes Études in Paris, where he would remain for ten years before returning to the University of Geneva. He published an important article on Lithuanian accentuation in 1896. Saussure also pursued literary research on medieval German legends, as well as a project that hypothesized the presence of anagrams of proper names in Latin poetry. The results of both of these projects remained unpublished during Saussure's lifetime and were discovered only in the 1970s. Saussure remains best known for the posthumous *Cours de linguistique générale*. He died at Château Vufflens near Geneva on February 22, 1913.

Selected Works

Cours de linguistique générale, 1916; as *Course in General Linguistics*, translated by Wade Baskin, 1959; new translation by Roy Harris, 1983

Mémoire sur le système primitif des voyelles dans les langues indo-européennes, 1879

"Accentuation lituanienne," *Anzeiger* of *Indo-germanische Forschungen*, 6 (1896): 157–166

Recueil des publications scientifiques de F. de Saussure, 1922

Écrits de linguistique générale, edited by Simon Bouquet and Rudolf Engler with Antoinette Weil, 2002

Further Reading

Badir, Sémir, *Saussure: la langue et sa représentation*, Paris: L'Harmattan, 2001

Benveniste, Émile, "Saussure After Half a Century" in *Problems in General Linguistics*, translated by Mary Elizabeth Meek, Coral Gables, Florida: University of Miami Press, 1971

Bouquet, Simon, *Introduction à la lecture de Saussure*, Paris: Payot and Rivages, 1997

Cahiers Ferdinand de Saussure, Geneva: Droz, 1941–

Culler, Jonathan, *Ferdinand de Saussue*, revised edition, Ithaca, New York: Cornell University Press, 1986

Godel, Robert, *Les Sources manuscrites du* Cours de linguistique générale *de F. De Saussure*, Geneva and Paris: Droz, 1957

Harris, Roy, *Reading Saussure: A Critical Commentary on the Cours de linguistique générale*, LaSalle, IL: Open Court, 1987

Harris, Roy, *Saussure and His Interpreters*, Edinburgh: Edinburgh University Press, 2001

Koerner, E. F. K., *Bibliographia Saussureana, 1870–1970*, Metuchen, NJ: Scarecrow Press, 1972

Koerner, E. F. K., *Saussurean Studies/Études saussuriennes*, Geneva: Slatkine, 1988

Matthews, Peter, *A Short History of Structural Linguistics*, Cambridge and New York: Cambridge University Press, 2001

"The Two Saussures," *Semiotext(e)*, special issues 1/2 (1974); 2/1 (1975)

Thibault, Paul J., *Re-reading Saussure: The Dynamics of Signs in Social Life*, London and New York: Routledge, 1997

SAYAD, ABDELMALEK
Writer

The core of Sayad's work is an exploration of the idea that migration always has to be viewed in terms of the double dimension of emigration/immigration. In other words, an individual who migrates is at one and the same time, both an *emigré* and an *immigrant*. Consequently, migration has necessarily to be read simultaneously in terms of the social, political, economic, and cultural conditions in the emigration country and the immigration country. Sayad's work also needs to be seen in the context of the relationship with Pierre Bourdieu that began in Algeria during the time of the Algerian War of 1954 to 1962. This relationship is exemplified by the fact that their early publications were joint, most notably their study of the role of French colonialism and more especially the Algerian War on the reordering of social relations in agriculture in Algeria with its consequent impact on the Algerian rural peasantry: *Le Déracinement: La crise de l'agriculture traditionnelle en Algérie*. It was also a relationship that would continue after Bourdieu's return to France and Sayad's emigration there in 1963. In 1968, Bourdieu founded the Centre for European Sociology and in 1975, the journal, *Actes de la Recherche en Sciences Sociales*, which would provide the base within which Sayad would develop his analysis of the dual character of migration as both emigration and immigration and apply this to the development of a more profound understanding of the situation of the Algerian emigrant/immigrant in France. In his earlier work, Sayad was concerned with exploring what it felt like to be an emigrant/immigrant and in what ways particular aspects of the colonial history of Algeria meant that the condition of the Algerian emigrant/immigrant in France was reflective of this. Later, he would argue that each emigrant/immigrant, both individually and collectively, had to be read in terms of the specificities of their "field" of migration.

Sayad sought, using conceptual categories shared with Bourdieu, to find a way to comprehend emigration as a process that said something about the social world that extended beyond the individual condition of the *emigré*. In his writing, he paid much attention to the precise use of words and their often ambiguous meanings, hence his insistence on the duality of the migrant condition as reflective simultaneously of the paradigm of emigration/immigration. However, his focus, like the work of the CES collective, progressively evolved into a discussion of the relationship between fields. For Sayad, this meant the field of emigration/immigration on the one hand, and on the other, the development during the nineteenth century of the idea of nation and its attachment to the constitution of the state, as he argued that the ambivalence in the situation of the emigrant/immigrant was because their nation of original belonging was left behind by emigration, whereas in the nation to which they came, they could not belong because the sole reason of their presence was the condition of work. The centrality of work in the definition of the emigrant/immigrant was then a major factor in their own consideration and the consideration by others of their temporary (*provisoire*) status. In reality, of course, the idea that emigration/immigration is temporary is an illusion because the conditions that engender it, namely, the triumph of globalization and the generalization of capitalism, do not disappear so that emigration/immigration must necessarily continue.

Although it was Algeria and therefore the particular contexts of emigration/immigration from Algeria that preoccupied him (such as the conditions of life in the 1950s and 1960s in the *bidonville* that grew in Nanterre on the periphery of Paris), his later work, although it still retained its focus on Algeria, was also an exploration of the use and, in particular, the imprecise use of language. For example, in an article published in 1994, he discussed how problematic the primary terms of the policy-makers are: adaptation, assimilation, insertion, integration. Sayad argued that these ought rather to be seen as expressions of state ideologies (*pensée d'Etat*) that represent both a field and a relationship between fields, so that if one examines any of them, one will gain insights into the way in which a particular state is thinking about emigration/immigration. This shift in his work from a focus on the position of the Algerian emigrant/immigrant also led him to an exploration of what are the matrix of ideas that underpin processes of naturalization, drawing on the work of legal theorists such as Hans Kelsen and John Gilissen. This enabled him to extend his theoretical framework to a consideration of processes for the inclusion of the emigrant/immigrant and therefore the limitations of the options that are available in most states, more particularly the ambiguous state of naturalization, ambiguous because of its implicit link with a concept of nature and the natural and therefore of it as a state of the unnatural. The corollary of that is a translation of the emigrant/immigrant into an apparent threat to both the state within which they have settled and the one that they have left. It is to counter this presumed threat

that it is necessary for both the state from which the emigrant leaves and the state to which the emigrant goes to view the condition of emigration/immigration as a temporary (*provisoire*) phenomenon. To do otherwise would mean that both states would have to accept the universal character of emigration/immigration, something that the nation–state is reluctant to do, preferring instead to view the emigrant/immigrant as marked metaphorically and even physically by their position in a hierarchically ordered social, political, and economic world. The extent and range of Sayad's explorations of the condition of the emigrant/immigrant are important because they allow one to step outside the somewhat mechanical view of emigration/immigration engendered by normative state policies. However, much of his argument for why emigration/immigration occurs depends on a reading of the origins of capitalism as an exclusively northern and western European engendered phenomenon.

KAY ADAMSON

See also **Pierre Bourdieu**

Biography

Sayad was born in the mountain village of Aghbala in Little Kabylia in 1933. He attended school both there and in Bougie and then the Teachers' College at Bouzaréa. His first teaching post was at a school in the Casbah of Algiers. He met and teamed up with Pierre Bourdieu at the University of Algiers shortly afterward. However, like many others, he left Algeria in 1963, one year after independence, for France. Associated with the Centre for European Sociology, founded by Pierre Bourdieu in 1968, he also later became Director of Sociological Research at the CNRS and a member of the École des Hautes Études en Sciences sociales. His relatively early death in 1998 followed a long illness. Among his other collaborators were Gabrielle Balazs, also a member of CES, and Eliane Dupuy of *Peuples meditérranéens*.

Selected Works

Le Déracinement. La crise de l'agriculturelle traditionnelle en Algérie (with P. Bourdieu), 1964
Un Nanterre algérien, terre de bidonvilles (with E. Dupuy), 1995.
"A Displaced Family," in The Weight of the World. Social Suffering in Contemporary Society, edited by Pierre Bourdieu et al., 1999
La double absence. Des illusions de l'émigré aux souffrances de l'immigré, 1999
"Institutional Violence" (with Gabrielle Balazs) in The Weight of the World. Social Suffering in Contemporary Society, edited by Pierre Bourdieu, 1999

SENGHOR, LÉOPOLD (SÉDAR)
Poet, Politician, Essayist

Senghor reflected that he would rather be remembered as a poet than as a politician. At the time of his death, both of these roles were evoked. Few alluded to his definitions of "négritude" as it inflected his poetry, politics, and life. In 1988 he retraced the evolution of Negritude from the defense and promotion of the "values of black civilization" to a fight to free Africa from "cultural colonization" and finally to a "new humanism." His insistence on intuition was inspired by Henri Bergson, in correlation with this philosopher's 1889 reflection on consciousness (*Liberté 3*, p. 97). In 1964 he reminisced about 1949, when German ethnologues (Frobenius, Westernmann, Bauman, Jensen) were describing African culture. This brought decisive help to African intellectuals whose culture was erased to the benefit of their French education, under the pretense that no African civilization preexisted French colonization. Negritude called for an effort to record and gather a tradition of African thought, as did Alassane Ndaw in 1983. It led to the record of history from an African perspective (*Liberté 3*, p. 405ff). As a form of humanism, Negritude paved the way for African socialism.

In the 1930s, Senghor estimated that African students in Paris were inspired by the *Revue du monde noir*, a joint enterprise involving people from Martinique and Haiti. Negritude had predecessors since 1915 in Haiti, where a spirit of resistance against U.S. domination arose. Senghor also mentioned the Harlem renaissance, with Claude MacKay as its leader. Seeking antecedents to Negritude, Senghor found inspiration in Paul Claudel and Charles Péguy, in what he called the "Revolution of 1889," which corresponded to a rejection of literary "naturalism" and the idea that people are products of their time, place, and surroundings. Instead, the soul and supernatural or surreal spheres were evoked. Senghor returned to the Catholic faith after a brief hiatus. Arthur Rimbaud's *Illuminations* and Saint-John Perse are often considered influential to Senghor's poetry. Conversely, the Dadaists, the surrealists and the cubists were strongly influenced by African arts and amicable to African artists. As André Breton called Césaire a "surrealist," Senghor found in surrealists "Negro poets."

Political orientation distinguished the founders of *L'Etudiant noir* (Aimé Césaire, Léon Gontran Damas, Senghor) from the Marxist group of *Légitime Défense* (Etienne Léro, René Ménil, and Jules Monnerot). The proponents of *Negritude* were socialist, and they considered that slavery derived first and foremost from cultural despise. In fact, culture always came before politics and economics for Senghor, the one leading the two others. Cultural critic Edward Said repeated the same idea in 1988 ("Yeats and Decolonization" p. 72).

Senghor's initial 1930s' Negritude was racist (*Liberté 5*, p. 106). In 1971 Jacques Louis Hymans provokingly underlined the odd conformity between Senghor's ideas when seduced by Barrès's and Hitler's "blood and soil." The collective image of the black man was determined by "the color line," to quote W. E. B. Du Bois (1903), who defined it as the problem of "the twentieth century," when pigmentation took precedence over human reality. African intellectuals reacted with calculated or imprudent narcissism. The enterprise of reversal from a negative to positive value can be measured in Césaire's word *négritude*, vindicating what had been denigrated. It presented the risk of reaffirming the worst of European ideologies even in negation.

Senghor's life is a symbol of the rectification of the humanities, sciences, and politics from within French culture, stressing its African debt and making room for African specificity. His detractors depicted him as a French puppet because he fell short of systematically opposing France. From his perspective, he always remained true to his 1930s discourse to the Chamber of Commerce of Dakar to the effect that he aimed to "assimilate but not be assimilated." Senghor's adherence to a project of "universal culture" did not allow for the pitfalls of a cultural "purism," which he rejected consistently after Nazism revealed some of its potential developments. In the domain of politics, Senghor was against division and "Balkanization." He always emphasized the idea of cultural harmony. He also rejected the "spirit of Fachoda," alluding to French and English struggles over their respective politico-economic influence. Senghor remained a man of cultural dialogues, whereas "post-Negritude" theoreticians may allude to "split codes" impossible to reconcile (Henry Louis Gates) or to breaches of communication in the nonverbal dimension (Edouard Glissant). The newer generations may be deemed "militant," eager to sever cultures, when Senghor's Negritude had more to do with self-discovery and with the fact of being black in a white world of self-declared supremacy.

Hence, Senghor's conception of "francité" (symmetrical to Negritude but less geographically "rooted") and *francophonie* started with cultural openness to foreign thought, to "métissage," which he hoped would eventually lead to "universal culture." The founders of "universal culture" are many: Senghor cited Pierre Teilhard de Chardin, as well as the cultural program proposed under General de Gaulle in the *Jeanney report* (July 18, 1963). The latter proposed French civilization as a particularly happy blend of cultures fundamentally available for further "métissage." The idea that "francité" led to a "universal culture" rested on an evaluation of French language that Senghor attempted as a linguist, anthropologist, and humanist, all the while surveying the African participation in civilization from prehistory to the present. He favored French language as a precise tool of communication. "Francité" as French culture was a historical part of Senegalese identity that had already engaged his country toward a "universal culture," and should be controlled positively, lest it turn into an imperialist competition to impoverish all cultures with the global imposition of a single one—probably Anglo-American.

Originally, Senghor sympathized with leftist Christians gravitating in the circles of the journal *L'Esprit* and Emmanuel Mounier. Negritude valued African beliefs, and in Marx's early writings Senghor saw no serious opposition to religion. Nor did Senghor support a theologically determined government and philosophy. He prized humanism as in the probing thought of Montaigne.

In 1965 Ezekiel Mphabele worried about the potential application of Negritude as a monopoly of static African identity, censoring any social criticism in the context of an idealized Africa. Senghor was aware of flaws; his political speeches clearly denounce Senegalese "nepotism," for instance. Mphabele feared Negritude was a stifling standard of literary performance for black writers. Thus he proposed that Negritude be "left as a historical phase." Senghor considered Negritude as a dynamic evolving to answer to the needs of blacks in various conjunctures. Indeed, Senghor admitted he had come to realize that there existed many African cultures, and he could not speak for all blacks.

Senghor's Negritude is contested as a concept, or as a philosophy, but not as a powerful rallying force that gave strength to pre- and postindependence Africans. Senghor located the debate of "post-Negritude" between politicians with ideologies at the service of specific imperialists on the one hand and "people of culture" on the other hand. William Kluback evaluated Senghor as "the lonely poet of international cooperation" and as the cultivator of "the creative possibilities of the human spirit."

SERVANNE WOODWARD

See also **Maurice Barrès; Henri Bergson; André Breton; Aimé Césaire; Edouard Glissant; Pierre Teilhard de Chardin**

Biography

Senghor was born in Joal, Senegal, in October 1906. He studied at the Mission Catholique of Ngasobil from 1914 to 1920. He graduated from the regular secondary high-school system in 1928 and entered the Lycée Louis-le-Grand. He taught literature and grammar at the Lycée Descartes of Tours (1935–1938), when he took courses in African linguistics from Lilias Homburger at the École pratique de hautes études and from Paul Rivet, Marcel Mauss, and Marcel Cohen at the Institute of Ethnology in Paris. He held a position in African language and civilization at the École Nationale de la France d'Outre-Mer (1944–1960). He accepted Lamine Guèye's selection to become deputy at the French National Assembly (1945, served 1946–1961). Married to Ginette Eboué, daughter of the Governor General of French Equatorial Africa (two sons). He founded an alternative to the socialist party, the Bloc Démocratique Sénégalais (1948). He contributed to Alioune Diop's journal, *Présence Africaine*, and was promoted as major theoretician of *Négritude* in Sartre's preface to Senghor's *L'Anthologie de la nouvelle poésie nègre et malgache de langue française* (1948). He divorced and was elected mayor of Thiès (Sénégal, 1956). In October 1957 he married Colette Hubert. In 1960, he was elected president of Senegal (reelected 1963, 1968, 1973, 1978). Resigned in 1980 in favor of his prime minister since 1969, Abdou Diouf, and retired in Normandy. He was elected a member of the French Academy in 1983. Senghor died at home in Verson (Normandy) on December 20, 2001.

Selected Works

Essays and Related Prose
Pierre Teilhard de Chardin et la politique africaine, 1962
Liberté 1: négritude et humanisme, discours, conférences, 1964
Les Fondements de l'africanité ou négritude et arabité, conference pronounced at the University of Cairo, 16 February 1967, 1967
Liberté 2: nation et voie africaine du socialisme, discours, conférences, 1971
La Parole chez Paul Claudel et chez les négro-africains, 1973
Pour une relecture africaine de Marx et Engels, 1976
Liberté 3: négritude et civilisation de l'universel, discours, conférences, 1977
La poésie de l'action, conversations avec Mohamed Aziza, 1980
Liberté 4: socialisme et planification, discours, conférences, 1983
Discours de réception à l'Académie française, 1984
Ce que je crois. Négritude, Francité et Civilisation de l'universel, 1988
Liberté 5: le dialogue des cultures, 1992

Further Readings

Ako, Edward O., "Langston Hughes and the Negritude Movement: A Study in Literary Influence," *College Association Journal*, 28/1 (1984): 45–56
Barrett, Lindsay, "Negritude: As Developed by Léopold Sédar Senghor and Aimé Césaire," *Books*, 10 (1972): 14–17

Biondi, Jean-Pierre, *Senghor ou la tentation de l'universel*, Paris: Deno'l, 1993

Blair, Dorothy S., "Léopold Sédar Senghor, poète bicontinental: La présence française dans l'œuvre de l'apôtre de la Négritude," *L'Information littéraire*, 28 (1976): 160–69

Condé, Maryse, "Négritude césairienne, Négritude senghorienne," *Revue de littérature comparée*, 48 (1974): 409–19

Hymans, Jacques Louis, *Léopold Sédar Senghor: An Intellectual Biography*, Edinburgh: Edinburgh University Press, 1971

Kesteloot, Lilyan, *Négritude et situation coloniale*, Yaoundé: Clé, 1970

Kluback, William, *Léopold Sédar Senghor. From Politics to Poetry*, New York: Peter Lang, 1997

Mbom, Clément, "Senghor, Césaire, Fanon. Un univers, trois visions," *Afrique littéraire*, 79 (1986): 3–29

Moore, Gerald, "Assimilation or Negritude," in *Twelve African Writers*, Bloomington: Indiana University Press, 1980

Spleth, Janice (editor), *Critical Perspectives on L. Sédar Senghor*, Washington, D.C.: Three Continents, 1994

SERRES, MICHEL
Writer, Philosopher

Michel Serres, a prolific and sometimes provocative thinker, has often baffled and bemused the intellectual world with his use of relational concepts, myth, and narrative, along with his conflation of the archaic and contemporary, in his diverse writings on science, culture, and time. Serres considers the more than twenty books that have evolved from his life work as a series based on his lifetime project—the construction of a philosophical system that is compatible with contemporary global society.

Serres's philosophy is based on a theory of relations, his goal being the movement *between* objects and ideas, rather than departure from a unique point of interpretation. Through his writings the stagnancy of historical monuments and myths take on a luminous glow, radiating fluidity of thought and inventiveness.

Having worked his way diligently through academia, Serres found his eventual lightness and freedom of thought in an interdisciplinary space, far from the space of criticism and textual commentary. Acutely aware that a philosophical system based on exact concepts is redundant when trying to express the fluid nature of time and history, Serres has often been criticized for his lack of scientific rigor, but particularly for his use of poetical and allegorical language.

Serres himself has said in conversation with Bruno Latour that he was formed intellectually by science's "internal revolutions," particularly by the emergence of quantum mechanics and information theory, and philosophically by the relationship—internal and external—between science and violence, the political experience of Hiroshima forming the basis of his political and philosophical ideas. Serres acquired his philosophical training from outside the mainstream intellectual movements of that time, resulting in a hybridization of literature and the sciences in much of his work. The separation of the sciences and literature within the academy has meant, according to Serres, that ideas destined for both disciplines have been poorly received. What he proposed, rather, was a "new" scientific spirit, in which all hierarchical systems are excluded.

The theme of invention is taken up by Serres, but for him invention emerged from randomness and chaos, from chance and other possible realities. Serres once said that perhaps what he has been writing all along has been a sort of *angelology*, a study of knowledge based on "relational bodies," on the "message-carrying" angel, or linguistically, the preposition. Serres said that for every angel, he imagines a preposition: preposition, that which existed before positions or concepts have been formulated. For Serres, angels represent freedom from the constraints of theory, where the form of narrative becomes the ideal method of communication. However, angels are more than just message carriers, they also serve to mark possible networks and confluences: "A preposition does not transport messages; it indicates a network of possible paths, either in space or in time." In *Angels, a Modern Myth* (1995), Serres clarified why the concept of angels should be of such importance to contemporary life, representing "a philosophy of communication, traversed by systems of networks and interferences, and demanding, in order to be able to establish itself, a theory of the multiplicities, of the chaos, hubbub and noise, that come before all theory." His desire to return to a "pretheory" state is reflected in his interest in the philosophy of the communication of ideas, or the rapport between concepts and ideas, which he often finds more interesting than the ideas and objects themselves.

Always a philosophical voyager through history and mythology, Serres uses poetic narrative to open up to the unexpected, making surprising links between places and objects. Arguing, for instance, that the work of Lucretius anticipates the framework of modern physics, particularly in relation to chaos theory, Serres resurrects ideas, thinkers, events, and monuments from the past, relegating them the same standing and influence as more contemporary thinkers, an activity that has been often criticized. The importance of history, for Serres, is in its possible resurrection and application for the present and future of humanity. In *Le Tiers-Instruit*, the Harlequin, a common French cultural trope, becomes a model for fractal dimensions. As Assad outlines in *Reading with Michel Serres*, he has become "Serres's epistemological model for a strange attractor."

One of the main themes running through his works is the concept of time and particularly how this is constructed in contemporary society. Opposed to the idea of time as being merely a succession of events, Serres considers it as a far more complex, fluid, and inventive process. In fact, all our difficulties with the theory of history, according to Serres, arise from the fact that we think of time in this inadequate way. Once again, we find in the work of Lucretius a "global theory of chaos and turbulence, holding out the hope of a "chaotic theory of time." Time, according to Serres's intuitiveness, does not flow, but, rather, percolates: "In a filter one flux passes through, while another does not." In the development of history, and from this concept of time, objects and ideas that seem quite distant can, in reality, come together, which Serres calls "folded" or "crumpled" time, something he feels is necessary to the formation of inventive thought. Chaos theory and certain mathematical concepts can also help clarify Serres's concept of "folded" time.

> A certain theory of numbers reorders their sequence in such a way that near neighbours become very distant, while, inversely, distant numbers come closer. (*Conversations on Science, Culture, and Time*, 1995)

In the *Hermes* series, Serres explored the concept of "noise," which is then developed through to *Genesis*, where it is used to elucidate his theory on time and the "multiple." For Serres, noise is a necessary part of communication; like the pretheory space occupied by the hubbub of angels, it cannot be eliminated from the communication process. Noise makes a reading of the message more difficult, yet there is no message without resistance. Serres recalls in *The Parasite* that "parasite" also means noise in French, a noise in a channel of communication. "Was this noise really a message? Wasn't it, rather, static, a parasite?" Also, and as John Lechte has remarked, *noise* represents the "unknown," that which one must venture into necessary to the constitution of knowledge and the formation of new knowledge. In *Genesis*, a new philosophical object, the "multiple," became Serres's model for a new concept of time. Serres attempts to reclaim the multiple as a conceptual practice, an idea that may only perhaps be sounded, lost as it becomes in its translation into language, and as a conceptual tool. Abstract though it may seem or appear to the naked eye, it lends itself quite readily to the auditory senses.

In her discussion of *The Parasite*, Maria Assad argues that there is the overriding notion of the excluded middle (*le tiers exclu*) built into the very concept of *noise* in Serres's work, without which the entire logical structure of Western thought is unthinkable: "the excluded third insinuates him/it-self into a given system only to become, in turn, the system per se." This excluded third or middle is a recurring trope in Serres's work, to reappear as the philosophy of the excluded middle, a philosophy for the third and fourth worlds. Harari and Bell's commentary of *le tiers exclu* emphasizes that the most suggestive aspect of *The Parasite* is the problem of human relations.

In *The Natural Contract*, which he himself calls a "global fable," Serres explored the future relationship between humankind and planet earth, between nature and culture. The physical world of nature bursts into the spectacle of history, as he explores the possibility of humankind making a contract with the earth. Serres's project has long been to construct a philosophy that reflects the changing world in which we live, the world of innovations in science, medicine, and new technologies, in a mutual exchange between the local and the global. His latest work *Hominescence*, following on somewhat from *The Natural Contract*, engages with the changing nature of the human being in relation to identity, the global environment and new technologies, in an attempt to seize the seeds of a new humanity. In it Serres argues that new technologies finally give us the power to change the world and ourselves, depending on how we choose to master these changes, and most importantly, without excluding, or indeed, without the total destruction of, the third and fourth worlds.

DENISE B. WHITE

Biography

Michel Serres was born in 1930 in Agen, France. After a brief stint at Naval College, Serres concentrated on studying philosophy to become one of the world's most innovative scholars in the history of science, social sciences, and the humanities. He submitted his doctorate thesis on Leibniz entitled "Le Systèm de Leibniz et ses modèles mathématiques" in 1968, and Leibniz was to prefigure in much of his philosophical work from that point onward. He has taught at Clermont-Ferrand, the University of Paris VIII (Vincennes), and the Sorbonne. He was elected to the Académie Française in 1990, has served as visiting professor at Johns Hopkins University, and has been a faculty member of Stanford University since 1984. He holds the Chair of the History of Science at the Sorbonne, and he has been a full Professor at Stanford University since 1984. Prior to 1984, he taught at the University of New York at Buffalo, the University of California at Irvine, the University of Montreal, the University of Sao Polo, and John Hopkins University at Baltimore.

Selected Works

Hermès. Vol 1. La Communication, [Communication] 1969
Hermès. Vol 2. L'Interférence, [Interference] 1972

Hermès. Vol 3 La Traduction, [Translation] 1974

Esthétiques sur Carpaccio, [Carpaccio's Aesthetics] 1975

La naissance de la physique dans le texte de Lucrèce, Lucretius [The Birth of Physics in the Works of Lucretius] 1977

Hermès. Vol 5. Le Passage du nord-ouest, 1980; as *Hermes: Literature, Science and Philosophy* (selected essays from *Hermes*, Vols. 1–5), edited by Josué V. Harari and David F. Bell, 1982

Hermès, Vol 4: La Distribution, [Distribution] 1981

Genèse, 1982; as *Genesis*, translated by Genevieve James and James Nielson, 1995

Le Parasite, 1980; as *The Parasite*, translated by Lawrence R. Schehr, 1982

Détachement: apologue, 1983; as *Detachment*, translated by Genevieve James and Raymond Federman, 1989

Rome: le livre des fondations, 1983; as *Rome, the Book of Foundations*, translated by Felicia McCarren, 1991

Les cinq sens: philosophie des corps mêlés, [The five Senses: Philosophy of mingled bodies] 1985

"Corruption The Antichrist: A Chemistry of Sensations and Ideas," *Stanford Italian Review*, 6:1–2 (1986): 31–52

L'hermaphrodite: Sarrasine sculpteur, [The Hermaphrodite: Sarrasine the sculptor] 1987

Eléments d'histoire des sciences, sous la direction de Michel Serres, 1989; as *A History of Scientific Thought: Elements of a History of Science*, 1995

Statues: le second livre des fondations, [Statues: the second book of Foundations] 1989

Le Contrat naturel, 1990; as *The Natural Contract*, translated by Elizabeth MacArthur and William Paulson, 1995

Le Tiers-instruit, 1991; as *Troubadour of Knowledge*, translated by Sheila Faria Gloser and William Paulson, 1997

Légende des anges, 1993; as *Angels, A Modern Myth*, translated by Francis Cowper, edited by Phillippa Hurd, 1995

Les origines de la géométrie: tiers livre des fondations, [The Origins of Geometry: third book of foundations] 1993

Atlas, [Atlas] 1994

Eclaircissements: cinq entretiens avec Bruno Latour, 1994; as *Conversations on Science, Culture, and Time* (with Bruno Latour), translated by Roxanne Lapidus, 1995

Eloge de la philosophie en langue française, [in praise of French language philosophy] 1995

Nouvelles du monde, [News of the World] 1997

Hominescence, [Hominescence] 2001

Further Reading

Assad, Maria L., *Reading with Michel Serres: An Encounter with Time*, Albany, NY: State University of New York Press, 1999

Connor, Steve, "The Five Senses" Conference Paper available at http://www.bbk.ac.uk/eh/eng/skc/5senses.htm

Crahay, Anne, *Michel Serres: La Mutation du Cogito: Genèse du Transcendental Objectif*, Bruxelles: Editions universitaires: De Boeck Université, 1988

Gleick, James, *Chaos: Making a New Science*, New York: Viking Penguin, 1987

Harari, Josué V. and David F. Bell, *Hermes: Literature, Science, Philosophy*. Baltimore: John Hopkins University Press, 1982

James, Geneviève, "Entretien avec Michel Serres," *The French Review*, 60.6 (May 1987): pp 788–796

Latour, Bruno, "The Enlightenment Without the Critique: A Word on Michel Serres' Philosophy," In *Contemporary French Philosophy*, edited by A. Phillips Griffiths, New York: Cambridge University Press, 1987

Lechte, John, *Fifty Key Contemporary Thinkers*, London: Routledge, 1994

Pierre, Nadia, *"Hominescence," l'Humanité*, (October 2001): available online at http://www.humanite.presse.fr/journal/2001/2001–10/2001–10–08/2001–10–08–074.html

SEXUALITY

One of the major epistemological shifts the twentieth century has seen is the pluralization and democratization of our understanding of the meaning of sexual identity and behavior. Sexuality as an object of study entered the sphere of science in the late nineteenth century with the rise of clinic-based psychology. The branch of medicosocial discourse known as sexology, popularized mainly in Germany by Karl Ulrichs (1826–1895) and Richard von Krafft-Ebing (1840–1902), found parallels among French and Belgian medical practitioners and social theorists such as Joseph Guislain (1797–1860) and Alfred Binet (1857–1911). Sexology favored a descriptive, taxonomical method of classification and interested itself in all types of sexuality that deviated from "the norm." The resulting catalogue of inversions and perversions was accompanied by an investigation of the physiological, environmental, and psychological factors that purportedly contributed to sexual perversion and degeneration. Early psychoanalytic writings, such as the first of Freud's *Three Essays on the Theory of Sexuality* (1905), are heavily indebted to nineteenth-century sexology.

Although commonly associated with the *fin-de-siècle* European climate that produced it and in which it flourished, the sexological method, exemplified by taxonomy, the case study, and an obsession with the nature/nurture debate, persists today, though its key proponents are no longer found in northern Europe but in North America. Over the past fifty years, developments in Continental thought and critical theory, often produced in the French tradition, have begun to dismantle the assumptions about sexuality perpetuated by the positivistic and pathologizing discourse of sexual science.

Of all the trends affecting French intellectual life and the university discipline of critical theory in the late twentieth and early twenty-first centuries, the conceptualization of sexuality as a critical paradigm is among the most significant and wide-ranging. Recent theoretical approaches to sexuality intersect, on the one hand, prominent late twentieth-century debates regarding the constructed status of identity in the modern world (the deconstruction of the unified subject as a bourgeois fiction) and, on the other, discussions of the disruptive and revolutionary potential of marginalized or undertheorized sexual identities and practices (feminist, gay, etc.). Theorizing sexuality, then, is a paradoxical business, which at once disrupts the assumptions of the personal and the individual traditionally associated with sexual life while, at the same time, necessarily inflecting thinking and reading practices with subjective considerations.

Thinkers on sexuality in the field of French thought differ considerably in their ideological and political standpoints, from Lacan's structuralist reworking of Freud, through Deleuzian critiques of psychoanalytic method, to the demystifying processes of Foucauldian discourse analysis. This said, most branches of thought that accord central import to sexuality do share a common aim, albeit one they attempt to achieve via radically different methods. This aim can be summarized as an attempt to denaturalize and demystify the assumptions about the "nature" of sexuality that had previously influenced (and continue, critical theory notwithstanding, to influence) both commonsense thinking about sex and gender and regulatory medicolegal discourses. This multifaceted attempt to dismantle prejudices about the "natural" status of sexuality cannot be separated from the broader agenda of 1960s and 1970s poststructuralist thinking, heralded and exemplified by Roland Barthes's *Mythologies* (1957), which sought to bring to light the tacit ideological codes subtending all cultural products and practices.

The psychoanalysis of Jacques Lacan (1901–1981) occupies a pivotal and paradoxical place in modern thought on sexuality in France and elsewhere. It stands first as an authority discourse, a meaning-making system grounded in the diagnostic epistemologies of clinical reality. Yet, it has also provided an imaginative critical framework with which even politically dissident thinkers can conceptualize gendered and sexually-determined reading and viewing practices. Much feminist film criticism, for example, including Laura Mulvey's canonical 1973 article, "Visual Pleasure and Narrative Cinema," is heavily dependent on Freudian concepts such as scopophilia (perverse voyeurism) and fetishism and on Lacan's theory of the mirror stage.

The considerable renown enjoyed by Lacanian theory in the field of the theoretical humanities is largely attributable to the prominent place accorded in his theory to language and the processes of signification. Abstracting from the aspects of Freud's thought that are indebted to biology and taxonomical sexology, Lacan's return to Freud consists of an elaboration of those elements of Freud's opus that focus on the significance of language in constructing the subject of desire. Writing against any trace of humanism in Freud, Lacan replaced his system of drives with a system of signs, heavily influenced by the linguistics of Ferdinand de Saussure (1857–1913) and the structural anthropology of Claude Lévi-Strauss (1908–). Desire, for Lacan, no

longer belongs to the seething mass of inchoate drives in the Freudian unconscious; rather, it runs along the chain of signification that is the language of Lacanian unconscious.

A prominent tenet of this linguistic theory of sexuality is the contention that desire operates with reference to the law. Freud's Oedipal configuration and the internalized parental superego are replaced with the "name of the father" (*nom/non du père*), a symbolized interdiction in the field of speech. The law of the father is the law of sexual difference (the structural version of Freud's castration), which is a primarily linguistic difference. To accede to the order of language and the possession of a name, the subject must sacrifice the prelinguistic bond with the mother. This sacrifice is then marked for the subject by the experience of lack in desire. Adult human beings—the subject of speech—are henceforth haunted by the alienating gap between the primary loss of the maternal object and the signifying processes with which they must navigate and negotiate future desires.

The privileged signifier in Lacan's symbolic order is the phallus, an abstract version of the penis whose presence or absence is so significant for the Freudian child. It is in relation to the phallus that masculinity and femininity are delineated: the masculine subject believes (in vain) that he has the phallus, whereas the feminine subject seeks to be the phallus (see especially *Le Seminaire, Livre V: Les formations de l'inconscient* [1957–1958]. In Seminar XX (1973), Lacan posits highly speculatively and intriguingly that there may be a *jouissance* outside of the phallus, to which women, with their more distant connection to the Symbolic order as man's other, may have privileged access.

Lacanian concepts of desire and the Other owe much to Lacan's exposure to Alexandre Kojève's teaching and interpretation of the Hegelian master–slave dialectic. Due in part to its prominence in Lacanian theory, the Other is a term with significant import in modern French thought, shared by two of its privileged fields: sexuality and ethics. One area in which these two concerns come together is that of feminism. The term *French feminist theory* refers to a highly disparate corpus of texts by names such as Luce Irigaray (1932–), Julia Kristeva (1941–), and Hélène Cixous (1937–). These names are united, however loosely, by some principal concerns. First, they seek to highlight the significant silence regarding the phenomenology of sexual difference within the Continental philosophical tradition. Secondly, they try to establish a theory of the desiring female body.

The work of feminist philosopher Luce Irigaray attempts to elucidate a particular blind spot in Western thought, by illustrating, after Simone de Beauvoir, that woman is always already constructed as the "other" of the desiring (masculine) subject of philosophy and psychoanalysis. Picking up on Lacan's speculative concept of the *jouissance* outside the phallus, Irigaray attempts to conceive of a feminine imaginary characterized by plurality and an opening onto maternity, in contradistinction to what she sees as the dominant masculine imaginary, which is destructive and reductive (see especially *Speculum de l'autre femme*, 1974). Her theory of an ethics of the sexual relation also draws on the work of Emmanuel Lévinas (1905–1995). Lévinas's influential theory of alterity constructs the ethical challenge posed by the encounter with the Other as one of unconditional respect for irreducible otherness. Lévinas sees the erotic relationship as a primarily ethical site, in which the subject is called to "caress" rather than to "possess" the loved one, whose integrity and difference must be preserved (see *Totalité et infini*, 1965).

French feminists commenting on the male-authored Western philosophical tradition have taken issue with the concept of logocentrism—the privileging of rational thought and "objective" knowledge. Rebaptizing it "phallogocentrism," they argue that this is not a universal or neutral philosophical principle, but a gendered one. Concerned with linear thinking and intellectual mastery, it is revealed as a fantasy of the phallic economy. In a parodic critique of the workings of "phallogocentrism," Irigaray uses images of female genitalia—plural lips that constantly caress and address each other—to suggest the polymorphous plurality of female sexuality and subjective experience (see especially *Ce sexe qui n'en est pas un*, 1977). One criticism of Irigaray's strategy is the difficulty one encounters when trying to interpret the status of these images. Just as the phallus in Lacanian theory transcends—while simultaneously recalling—the mere fleshy penis, Irigaray's self-caressing lips are charged to mean beyond metaphor. However, the decision to privilege genital morphology means that Irigaray risks reducing the gamut of female subjectivity (political, emotional, libidinal) to the perceived workings of a set of genitals, and thereby tying women firmly back to ideas of biological determinism.

Kristeva's corpus of writing to date is extremely varied in its focus and approach, bridging semiotics, psychoanalysis, philosophy, and cultural analysis. Of particular relevance to the conceptualization of sexuality, her *Révolution du langage poétique* (1974) considers the written text as a symbolic body, through the surface of which disturbing libidinal desire (the "semiotic") may erupt. For Kristeva, the source of the semiotic is the pre-Oedipal, prelinguistic relation to the maternal, which is denied and foreclosed by the entry into language. She terms this realm of nondifferentiation the *chora*. Kristeva suggests that the subject never to-

tally abandons a connection with the semiotic, and that deviations, experiments, and distortions in certain experimental literary forms, such as writing by Mallarmé and Joyce, exemplify the ongoing power and pleasure of the maternal realm, offering the reader a nonphallic *jouissance*.

Cixous shares Kristeva's interest in the experience of writing from a position of marginality and in the power of the erotic to disrupt the linguistic order. She is principally known as the exponent of the theory of *écriture féminine*, a form of writing that would allegedly emerge spontaneously from the plurality and fluidity of feminine sexual and bodily experience, if only the writing subject could free herself from the thought-traps of linear patriarchal discourse (see particularly "Le Rire de la Méduse," 1975; *La Jeune née*, 1975; and "La Venue à l'écriture," 1977). Critics of *écriture féminine* object to its overtones of essentialism, but it must be remembered that for Cixous, *feminine* and *biologically female* are not one and the same (though, problematically, in the French language *feminin(e)* is commonly used to mean both). Indeed, her experiments in writing parallel those of the late Barthes, which privilege the corporeal and posit the possibility of a polymorphous sexual textuality, which encourages reading and writing practices that eschew the phallic (see especially *Le Plaisir du texte*, 1973).

Although the feminists discussed earlier engaged in an uncomfortable but intimate relationship with the psychoanalytic tradition (Irigaray and Kristeva are practicing analysts as well as detractors of the psychoanalytic institution's masculine bias), an alternative strand of theory on sexuality was produced in the 1960s and 1970s from the Marxist-Materialist tradition, which wholly opposed the psychoanalytic perspective. The most prominent member of the Marxist group, whose activities centered around the journal *Questions Féministes*, was the radical separatist feminist Monique Wittig (1935–2002). Wittig's writing, particularly her philosophical fiction (*Les Guérillères*, 1969; *Le Corps lesbien*, 1973) demonstrates impatience with the contemporary fashion for psychoanalysis and repudiates the concept of the unconscious. Wittig's writing constitutes an attack on the essentialism and biological determinism, which she espied in the writings of feminists such as Irigaray and Cixous, who went under the banner of *Psych. et Po. (Psychanalyse et politique)*. Wittig asserts that women are oppressed as a class owing to male political domination, and not because of unconscious sexual repression. Her refreshingly iconoclastic and aggressive vision is epitomized by the Wittigian sound bite "Lesbians are not women," which summarizes her belief that the class of person designated "women" must be understood as an effect of the patriarchal tradition that constructs it, not as a "natural" group. Wittig calls for a powerful reimagining of society based on a female–female sexual relation, which is creatively announced in her polemical fiction by a play with the very language of subjectivity. In *Les Guérillères*, the generic plural "ils" becomes "elles"; (whereas) the first-person pronoun in *Le Corps lesbien* incorporates a split ("j/e," "m/a," etc.), suggesting a subjectivity that is both cut off from the masculine order and that is always already self-reflexive regarding the conditions of its construction.

A Marxist critical perspective and a dissatisfaction with deterministic psychoanalytical models of sexuality are also found in the collaborative work of philosopher Gilles Deleuze (1925–1995) and radical anti-Freudian analyst Félix Guattari (1930–1992). Their influential *L'Anti-oedipe* (1972) argues against the pervasive influence of Freud's paradigm of the family romance. It contends that the Oedipal dynamic is a myth that creates a fictional subject of desire produced by a repressive law and fixes desire in a triangular structure. By shoring up the Oedipal configuration, linchpin of the nuclear family, psychoanalysis is charged with a conservative *bourgeois* agenda that serves the interests of capitalist models of production rather than sexual liberation.

Deleuze and Guattari's work also constitutes a forceful renunciation of the presupposition that underlies much thought about sexuality from Plato, through Freud and Lacan, to the sometime surrealist philosopher, Georges Bataille (1897–1962): the notion that desire operates in an economy propelled by lack. In *L'Érotisme* (1956), Bataille echoed (without fully acknowledging his debt) the dynamics of Freud's model of the Life Drive and the Death Drive expounded in *Beyond the Pleasure Principle* (1920). Bataille argued that sexuality is the sphere of human life in which excessive, chaotic, and murderous impulses surge up and risk disrupting the system of economic circulation in which the subject is habitually held in check. For Bataille, the excess of death-dealing energy in eroticism is transgressive rather than reactionary, as it operates in a dialectical relation to taboo, which it does not destroy but intensifies. Bataille argued, for example, in a politically problematic gesture, that women may only achieve orgasm because they make themselves believe they are being raped.

In an imaginative polemical response to Plato, Freud, and Bataille, then, *L'Anti-Oedipe* seeks to upend the widely-accepted notion that desire equals lack. Replacing the latent humanism of even Lacan's structural psychoanalysis with metaphors of "desiring-machines," Deleuze and Guattari sought to show that the psychoanalytic model effectively short-circuits the productive nature of desire, which does not lack objects but rather accrues them greedily in an unstoppable libidinal flow.

In the companion volume, *Mille Plateaux* (1980), Deleuze and Guattari used a complex metaphorical language that substitutes the rhizome (a root with multiple, multidirectional filaments) for the hierarchical or linear "arborescent structure," in order to suggest the wrong-headedness of theories that confine desire to the subject–object relation. Heavily influenced by the antipsychiatry movement, this work valorizes the schizophrenic position, rather than relegating it to the realms of pathology. The "schizo," who operates according to a principle of pleasurable multiplicity, rather than being reduced to a narrow hydraulic and anatomy-bound model of libido, becomes a radical desiring being, sharing certain similarities with Monique Wittig's reconstructed lesbian subject.

If Deleuze and Guattari's project represents a Marxist-influenced attempt to think against the discursive constraints of the psychoanalytic tradition, Michel Foucault's analysis of the way in which power functions in the field of sexuality seeks to contest both Freudian and Marxist assumptions. *Histoire de la sexualité* (1976) comprises three volumes of which the first, *La Volonté de savoir*, is by far the most influential. It sets out to redefine the history of sexuality via a critique of existing epistemologies of power. Foucault (1926–1984) argues that it is a fallacy that modern culture represses sexuality. Conversely, he claims, the subject is constantly interpellated by a demand to confess the nature of his "true" sexual self. Sexuality has not been underdiscussed since the nineteenth century, then, but overarticulated, in what Foucault describes as a proliferation of discourses about desire.

Foucault shows that the psychological-medical discourses responsible for naming and cataloguing sexuality at the end of the nineteenth century (sexology; psychoanalysis) have created "perversions" as categories of behavior and "perverts" as categories of person. Foucault interprets this as a replacement of the Christian church's belief that sexual acts are something immoral that you might *do* with the taxonomical creation of typologies of person that you are charged to *be*. The confession thus acts to define the subject (who is the subject *of* discourse and subject *to* power in language). Power for Foucault, then, operates discursively rather than repressively.

In the final years of his life, Foucault was particularly interested in formulating strategies for avoiding the regulation, through knowledge, of dissident sexual behaviors and relationships. Taking the gay subcultures of 1980s San Francisco as his inspiration, he argued that it is by engaging in activities and desiring dynamics that avoid aping heterosexuality and socially-sanctioned coupledom that dissident pleasure may be liberated from normative discourse. With its conscious and playful mimicking of power structures, sadomasochism was seen as a particularly rich source of subversion. For Foucault, gay sadomasochistic ghettos were paradigmatic communities that escaped regulatory cultural mechanisms by organizing themselves around principles of pleasure and performativity.

The idea that the pleasures of gay sexuality are a source of potential social and discursive disruption was shared by the political activist Guy Hocquenghem (1946–1988), founder of the *Front Homosexuel d'Action Révolutionnaire* and author of the polemical article *Le Désir homosexuel* (1972). Straddling politics and theory, Hocquenghem was both a gay liberationist and a demystifier of the concept of fixed homosexual identity. His position thus blurs the boundary between identity politics (gay and lesbian experience as a marker of shared, marginal oppression, rooted in notions of definable identity and communality) and the strand of thought known as queer theory, which privileges plurality and the mobilization of discourses of meaning. Queer theory is more prevalent in the Anglo-American academy than in the French context, perhaps because of the considerable influence of the American gender theorist Judith Butler. This said, Foucault's and Hocquenghem's writings are landmark texts in the development of queer theory, even if much Anglo-American writing fails to acknowledge its movement's European roots. Butler herself is an exception, as she addressed a direct response to French thinkers Lacan, Wittig, Deleuze, and particularly Foucault in her landmark text *Gender Trouble: Feminism and the Subversion of Identity* (1990).

Foucault's neo-Nietzschean project of genealogical reading has marked a significant turning point in modern debates on sexuality. Although heavily criticized for its masculinist bias (by feminist thinkers such as Sandra Lee Bartky and Kate Soper) and its white European bias (by Ann Laura Stoler and Sander Gilman), it stands nonetheless as the precursor of much theoretical work, which takes as its focus a critical rereading of cultural history from the perspective of sexually and ethnically marginalized groups. In a broader context, Foucault's work in the mid-1970s may be seen to prefigure the shift that has taken place over the past twenty years in critical debates from a focus on high theory (poststructuralism; Derridean deconstruction) to revisionist historiography.

In the contemporary moment, debates in sexuality are intensified and lent complexity by the growing field of postmodernist thought and the theories and possibilities offered by cyberspace and virtual communication media. The foregrounding in queer theory of the liberating potential of gender fluidity, drag, performativity, and playfulness in the field of sexuality announces the possibilities of the virtual and the imaginative over the discursive certainty of fixed bodily narratives. Whether sexuality, extended beyond the perimeters of the stably gendered body, will remain a critical category and whether the abandonment of a body of knowledge on sexuality will constitute the longed-for Foucauldian turn to "bodies and pleasures" both remain to be seen.

LISA DOWNING

See also **Roland Barthes; Georges Bataille; Simone de Beauvoir; Hélène Cixous; Gilles Deleuze; Jacques Derrida; Michel Foucault; Felix Guattari; Guy Hocquenghem; Luce Irigaray; Alexandre Kojeve; Julia Kristeva; Jacques Lacan; Claude Lévi-Strauss; Emmanuel Levinas; Ferdinand de Saussure; Monique Wittig**

Further Reading

Bartky, Sandra Lee, "Foucault, Femininity, and the Modernization of Patriarchal Power," in *Feminism and Foucault: Reflections on Resistance*, edited by Irene Diamond and Lee Quinby, Boston: Northeastern University Press, 1988

Bersani, Leo, *Homos*, Cambridge, Massachusetts and London: Harvard University Press, 1995

Boothby, Richard, *Death and Desire: Psychoanalytic Theory in Lacan's Return to Freud*, New York and London: Routledge, 1991

Bowie, Malcolm, *Lacan*, Cambridge, Massachusetts: Harvard University Press, 1991

Braidotti, Rosi, *Patterns of Dissonance: A Study of Women in Contemporary Philosophy*, Oxford: Polity, 1991

Bristow, Joseph, *Sexuality*, London and New York: Routledge, 1997

Burke, Carolyn, Naomi Schor, and Margaret Whitford (editors), *Engaging with Irigaray: Feminist Philosophy and Modern European Thought*, New York: Columbia University Press, 1994

Butler, Judith, *Subjects of Desire: Hegelian Reflections in Twentieth-Century France*, New York: Columbia University Press, 1987

Butler, Judith, "Variations on Sex and Gender: Beauvoir, Wittig and Foucault," in *Feminism and Critique*, edited by Seyla Benhabib and Drucilla Cornell, Cambridge: Polity, 1987

Butler, Judith, *Gender Trouble: Feminism and the Subversion of Identity*, New York: Routledge, 1990

Dollimore, Jonathan, *Death, Desire and Loss in Western Culture*, Harmondsworth: Penguin, 1998

Gilbert, Harriet (editor), *The Sexual Imagination from Acker to Zola: A Feminist Companion*, London: Jonathan Cape, 1993

Gilman, Sander L., *Difference and Pathology: Stereotypes of Sexuality, Race and Madness*, Ithaca, NY: Cornell University Press, 1985

Halperin, David M., *Saint Foucault: Towards a Gay Hagiography*, Oxford: Oxford University Press, 1995

Hand, Seàn (editor), *The Lévinas Reader*, Cambridge, MA and Oxford: Blackwell, 1989

Marshall, Bill, *Guy Hocquenghem: Theorizing the Gay Nation*, London: Pluto, 1996

Mitchell, Juliet and Jacqueline Rose (editors), *Feminine Sexuality: Jacques Lacan and the École freudienne*, Basingstoke: Macmillan, 1982

Moi, Toril, *Sexual/Textual Politics: Feminist Literary Theory*, London: Methuen, 1985

Moi, Toril (editor), *The Kristeva Reader*, Cambridge, MA and Oxford: Blackwell, 1986

Moi, Toril (editor), *French Feminist Thought: A Reader*, Cambridge, MA and Oxford: Blackwell, 1987

Rosario, Vernon A., *The Erotic Imagination: French Histories of Perversity*, Oxford: Oxford University Press, 1997

Schor, Naomi, "Dreaming Dissymmetry: Barthes, Foucault and Sexual Difference," in *Men and Feminism*, edited by Alice Jardine and Paul Smith, New York: Methuen, 1987

Sellers, Susan (editor), *The Hélène Cixous Reader*, London: Routledge, 1994

Shiach, Morag, *Hélène Cixous: A Politics of Writing*, London: Routledge, 1991

Soper, Kate, "Productive Contradictions," in *Up Against Foucault: Explorations of Some Tensions Between Foucault and Feminism*, edited by Caroline Ramazanoðolu, London: Routledge, 1993

Spargo, Tamsin, *Foucault and Queer Theory*, Cambridge: Icon books, 1999

Stambolian, George and Elaine Marks (editors), *Homosexualities and French Literature: Cultural Contexts/Critical Texts*, Ithaca, NY and London: Cornell University Press, 1979

Stoler, Laura Ann, *Race and the Education of Desire: Foucault's History of Sexuality and the Colonial Order of Things*, Durham, NC: Duke University Press, 1995

Whitford, Margaret (editor), *The Irigaray Reader*, Cambridge, MA and Oxford: Blackwell, 1991

Wright, Elizabeth, *Lacan and Postfeminism*, Cambridge: Icon books, 2000

SIMON, CLAUDE
Novelist

The late 1950s saw the emergence of an important and identifiable, if loose, grouping of French novelists known as the *nouveau roman*. This group included Michel Butor, Claude Mauriac, Claude Ollier, Robert Pinget, Jean Ricardou, Alain Robbe-Grillet, Nathalie Sarraute, and Claude Simon. In contrast with several of the other members of the original nouveau roman group and, in particular, with Ricardou, Butor, Robbe-Grillet, and Sarraute, who all published fully developed critical or theoretical essays that explicitly articulated their aesthetic views, Claude Simon has published no extended declarations of principle. His statements about literature and art are scattered throughout his many interviews, his various colloquium interventions, the preface to *Orion aveugle*, the texts that figure in his two volumes of photographs, and his Nobel acceptance speech. Correlation of these comments reveals, however, a substantial number of recurring preoccupations. Chief among these are the following: the *décalage* between the instantaneity of perception and the linearity of the linguistic expression; the role of cultural baggage in our perception of the world; the discontinuity of perception; the selectiv-

ity of memory; the intrinsically distortive nature of storytelling; the promotion of the associative and suggestive potential of language; the aesthetic—as opposed to logical, chronological, or psychological—coherence of the work of art; and the relationship between word and image.

Although wary of abstraction and reluctant to be drawn into unfamiliar theoretical territory, Simon has, nevertheless, found echoes of his own preoccupations in both Russian formalism (which was being "rediscovered" by French intellectuals and publishers in the 1960s) and in contemporary French structuralist theory. His allegiance to formalism has been remarkably consistent, with citations of Chklovski, Tynianov, Eichenbaum, and Jakobson regularly punctuating his aesthetic comments since the early sixties. For Simon, as for the formalists, art is unable to change the world, but it does have the power to change our perception of it. Art does not render reality easier to assimilate; it defamiliarizes and makes reality more difficult to assimilate through the deployment of aesthetic devices, which check or impede habitual responses. Thus, in Simon's fiction, the situations in which his protagonists find themselves—war, the breakdown of relationships, illness, travel—interrupt routine, suspend perceptual habits, and even subvert commonsense assumptions about the world, the exposure to physical or psychological risk, and the concomitant impairment of faculties and emotional trauma serving to throw into sharp relief previously unnoticed features of the immediate physical environment. Ultimately, formalism appeals to Simon not because of its theoretical sophistication—indeed, its taxonomic grid is much less refined that those offered by structuralism—but because it accommodates referential sensory experience and, in particular, corresponds closely to Simon's own emphasis on perceived experience at the expense of "knowledge."

The influence of structuralism on Simon's thinking is rather more piecemeal. Although he occasionally cites discrete ideas derived from Barthes and Lacan, it is Lévi-Strauss's concept of "bricolage" that has made the most enduring mark on his thinking. In particular, "bricolage" fits well with Simon's argument that the "creative" urge stems from a very basic human desire "to make something." "Bricolage" also sums up the processes by which Simon turns various types of "found material" into an aesthetically coherent structure. Like the "bricoleur," Simon works with preexisting materials—memory images, family documents, and various cultural items (literary and nonliterary intertexts, images drawn from high and low culture)—and his task consists, by and large, in the production of an "ensemble," which transcends the specific functions of the original materials and objects and whose coherence derives from the formal interdependence of its components.

Consistent with these formalist and structuralist influences is Simon's resolutely anticommitment stance. Although reluctant to engage in theoretical debate and political or philosophical polemics, Simon's astringent criticism of Sartre and Camus, the occasional open letters published in the press, and his often humorous but acerbic critique in *L'Invitation* of the 1986 Issyk-kul Forum testify to his hostility toward any conception of literature that would define it in terms of ideological commitment. However, though quick to dismiss the concept of committed literature, Simon does acknowledge the importance of historical context. The history of the twentieth century—two devastating world wars, the Nazi and Soviet camps, Hiroshima—has, according to Simon, been a significant contributory factor in the development of certain types of literature and visual art, which, by their eschewal of the abstract and their common desire to return to the concrete, acknowledge the bankruptcy of Western humanist thought. However, as his analysis of Picasso's *Guernica*, in "Deux écrivains répondent à Jean-Paul Sartre," demonstrates, the relationship between historical context and the artwork is oblique, the event acting as stimulus, the limits and potential of the medium, and the formal demands of composition determining the outcome. By the same token, his novel *Le Palace* should not be read as an account of the Spanish Civil War; rather, it is a literary construction resulting from the confused impressions and fragmentary memories that were rushing through Simon's consciousness as he put pen to paper a quarter of a century later.

Simon's conception of the relationships between life and art, between autobiography and fiction mirrors that of his conception of the relationship between historical circumstance and artwork. Although he has regularly condemned biographical approaches, he has, with equal regularity, insisted on the biographical nature of his raw material. Simon's resistance to biographical criticism has its origins in a personal aesthetic that, on many points, accords both with formalist theory and with the "party line" of the nouveau roman, but which derives, largely, from his reading of the work of other writers, notably Montaigne, Dostoïevski, and Proust. The concept of self as a coherent, evolving, unique identity is alien to Simon. The self is not a homogeneous stable personality, but a composite and often volatile phenomenon that is composed of a multitude of disparate sensations and memories. Moreover, for Simon, the biographical reading simply misses the point. Once "literariness" is defined in terms of the internal aesthetic coherence of the artwork rather than in terms of verisimilitude, as soon as a distinction is

made between the incidents of the writer's life and what takes place at the moment of writing, biographical facts and documents lose their status as interpretative "keys." However, if their psychological interest is undermined, they remain important as evidence of the experiential data that stimulated the production of a given work. In Simon's fiction, from *L'Herbe* to his most recent novel *Le Tramway*, the role of life experience as fictional stimulus is everywhere apparent. However, amidst the wealth of verifiable autobiographical data, the reader encounters numerous warnings against naïve biographical interpretations, as well as more positive metafictional indicators regarding the aesthetic principles underlying the composition of the text. Thus, many of the countless *mises en abyme* that punctuate Simon's novels and the various biographical extracts relating to other writers, painters, and various historical figures that appear in several of his novels (notably, *Histoire, La Bataille de Pharsale, Les Géorgiques*, and *Le Jardin des Plantes*) serve both to indicate the limits of (auto)biography and the perils of biographical readings and to highlight—through the creation of intertextual contrasts and correspondences—the contrapuntal and associative procedures on which Simon's art is based.

JEAN H. DUFFY

See also **Roland Barthes; Albert Camus; Jacques Lacan; Claude Lévi-Strauss; Revolution; Alain Robbe-Grillet; Jean-Paul Sartre**

Biography

Claude Simon was born on October 10, 1913, in Tananarive, Madagascar. Educated at the Collège Stanislas in Paris, Simon went on to study painting under André Lhote, though he subsequently abandoned his ambitions to become a painter. In 1936 he went to Barcelona, where he was involved in gunrunning for the Republicans. During the Second World War, Simon served as a cavalry officer in the 31st Dragoon Regiment. Captured at the Battle of the Meuse in 1940, he was sent to a POW camp in Saxony, but escaped during transfer to another camp and spent the rest of the war in hiding, first in Perpignan and then in Paris, where his flat served as an information centre for the Resistance. Although in the course of the 1940s and early 1950s Simon published three novels and an autobiographical text (*La Corde raide*, 1947), it was with the publication in 1957 of *Le Vent* that his mature writing career was launched. In 1960 *La Route des Flandres* was awarded the Prix de l'Express and, in 1967 *Histoire* was awarded the Prix Médicis. Simon was awarded the Nobel Prize for Literature in 1985.

Selected Works

Le Vent, 1957; as *The Wind*, translated by Richard Howard, 1959

L'Herbe, 1958; as *The Grass*, translated by Richard Howard, 1961

La Route des Flandres, 1960; as *The Flanders Road*, translated by Richard Howard, 1962

Le Palace, 1962; as *The Palace*, translated by Richard Howard, 1964

Femmes, 1966 ("Women")

Histoire, 1967; as *Histoire*, translated by Richard Howard, 1969

La Bataille de Pharsale, 1969; as *The Battle of Pharsalus*, translated by Richard Howard, 1971

Orion aveugle, 1970 ("Blind Orion")

Les Corps conducteurs, 1971; as *Conducting Bodies*, translated by Helen R. Lane, 1975

Triptyque, 1973; as *Triptych*, translated by Helen R. Lane, 1977

Leçon de choses, 1975; as *The World about Us*, translated by Daniel Weissbort, 1983

Les Géorgiques, 1981; as *The Georgics*, translated by Beryl and John Fletcher, 1989

La Chevelure de Bérénice, 1983; as *Bérénice's Golden Mane*, translated by Simon Green, 1998

Discours de Stockholm, 1986 ("Stockholm Speech", i.e. Simon's Nobel Prize acceptance speech)

L'Invitation, 1987; as *The Invitation*, translated by Jim Cross, 1991

Album d'un amateur, 1988 ("Album of an *amateur*")

L'Acacia, 1989; as *The Acacia*, translated by Richard Howard, 1991

Photographies, 1937–70, 1992 ("Photographs, 1937–1970)

Le Jardin des Plantes, 1997; as *The Jardin des Plantes*, translated by Jordan Stump, 2001

Le Tramway, 2001; as *The Trolley*, translated by Richard Howard, 2002

Further Reading

Bertrand, M., *Langue romanesque et parole scripturale: Essai sur Claude Simon*, Paris: Presses Universitaires de France, 1987

Birn, R., and Gould, K. (eds), *Orion Blinded: Essays on Claude Simon*, Lewisburg: Bucknell University Press, 1981

Brewer, M. M., *Claude Simon: Narrativities without Narrative*, Lincoln and London: University of Nebraska Press, 1995

Britton, C., *Claude Simon: Writing the Visible*, Cambridge: Cambridge University Press, 1987

Calle, M. (ed.), *Claude Simon: Chemins de la mémoire*, Sainte-Foy: Griffon d'argile, 1993

Carroll, D., *The Subject in Question: the Languages of Theory and the Strategies of Fiction*, Chicago: Chicago University Press, 1982

Dällenbach, L., *Claude Simon*, Paris: Seuil, 1988

Duffy, J. H., *Reading Between the Lines: Claude Simon and the Visual Arts*, Liverpool: Liverpool, University Press, 1998

Duffy, J. H. and A. Duncan (eds), *Claude Simon: A Retrospective*, Liverpool: Liverpool University Press, 2002

Duncan, A. B. (ed.), *Claude Simon: New Directions*, Edinburgh: Scottish Acadmeic Press, 1985

Duncan, Alastair, *Claude Simon: Adventures in Words*, Manchester and New York: Manchester University Press, 2003 (first edition, 1994)

Evans, M. J., *Claude Simon and the Transgressions of Modern Art*, Basingstoke: Macmillan, 1987

Ferrato-Combe, B., *Ecrire en peintre: Claude Simon et la peinture*, Grenoble: ELLUG, 1998

Genin, C., *L'Expérience du lecteur dans les romans de Claude Simon: lecture studieuse et lecture poignante*, Paris: Champion, 1997

Laurichesse, J.-Y., *La Bataille des odeurs: l'espace olfactif des romans de Claude Simon*, Paris: L'Harmattan, 1998

Loubère, J.A.E., *The Novels of Claude Simon*, Ithaca: Cornell University Press, 1975

Mongin, P., *L'Effet d'image: essai sur Claude Simon*, Paris: L'Harmattan, 1997

Orr, M., *Claude Simon: The Intertextual Dimension*, Glasgow: University of Glasgow French and German Publications, 1993

Revue des lettres modernes, Série Claude Simon 1: À la recherche du référent perdu, 1994, edited by Ralph Sarkonak

Revue des lettres modernes, Série Claude Simon 2: L'Écriture du féminin/masculin, 1997, edited by Ralph Sarkonak

Revue des lettres modernes, Série Claude Simon 3: Lectures de "Histoire", 2000, edited by Ralph Sarkonak

Ricardou, J. (ed.), *Claude Simon: Colloque de Cerisy*, Paris: Union Générale d'Editions, 1975; reprinted as *Lire Claude Simon*, Paris: Les Impressions Nouvelles, 1986

Roubichou, G., *Lecture de "L'Herbe" de Claude Simon*, Lausanne: L'Age d'homme, 1976

Sarkonak, R., *Claude Simon: les carrefours du texte*, Toronto: Paratexte, 1986

Sarkonak, R., *Les Trajets de l'écriture: Claude Simon*, Toronto: Paratexte, 1994

Starobinski, J, G. Raillard, L., Dällenbach, and R. Dragonetti, *Sur Claude Simon*, Paris: Minuit, 1987

Sykes, S., *Les Romans de Claude Simon*, Paris: Minuit, 1979

Thierry, F., *Claude Simon: une expérience du temps*, Paris: SEDES, 1997

Thouillot, M., *Les Guerres de Claude Simon*, Rennes: Presses Universitaires de Rennes, 1998

SOCIOLOGY

Did the French invent sociology? Most think so because Auguste Comte coined the term around 1835, and Émile Durkheim wrote the famous manifesto of the discipline in 1895, *Les Règles de la méthode sociologique* (The Rules of the Sociological Method). The answer is both less satisfying for French jingoism and more complex. The interest in social phenomena may go all the way back to Aristotle and Plato, but it is in the European (French and English) nineteenth century that, without a doubt, sociologists first undertook empirical and systematic study. Between 1880 and 1914, and almost simultaneously, French, British, and German researchers gave sociology a scientific program, outlining its rules and its first concepts. As Durkheim was working on the *Rules* and applying them to the study of the social causes of *Suicide* (1897), H. Spencer was publishing his *Principles of Sociology* (1874–1896), F. Tönnies was opposing *Gemeinschaft und Gesellschaft* (1887), G. Simmel was presenting his *Soziologie* (1908), and M. Weber was undertaking a masterful and gigantic analysis of the relationship between religion and economics (*Die Protestantische Ethik und der Geist des Kapitalismus*, 1904). Also as the Americans were opening up to the new discipline, their first scholars (L. Ward, F. Giddings, W. Sumner, A. Small) were essentially inspired by the Europeans.

The question, however, cannot be settled on historiographical grounds only because, as soon as it emerged, sociology was torn by theoretical and institutional conflicts in which the French played a key role. Durkheim's ambition and, more broadly, the ambition of the French positivistic current was in fact to turn the new discipline into a full science, that is, a science modeled after natural sciences, and thus to fulfill Comte's prophesy of a "queen of all sciences" that would sit at the top of the pyramid of knowledge. Such an ambition not only excluded any compromising with a psychology that was deemed unworthy of the status of science, but also—as the Germans noted—any epistemological specificity. Sociology, being a positive discipline, had to break away from the speculations of philosophy and from the solipsism of nonexperimental psychology. It had to rule over all social sciences, henceforth reduced to the rank of vassals subject to the rules of the sociological process. Although this program was, fortunately, never fully applied, it still had numerous and serious consequences. All at once, the entire German spiritualist (Dilthey) or neo-Kantian (Rickert, Weber, Simmel) tradition was nullified, and the Anglo-Saxon sociographic tradition was downgraded to the rank of valet of the governments.

In fact, Durkheim very carefully ensured that the "School" he had founded around the journal *L'Année sociologique* (The Sociological Year, 1898) remained closed to German influences, even though it was molded after it. The French public would not meet German sociology until R. Aron (*Sociologie allemande contemporaine*, 1939) opened it to new and rich perspectives. Even in France, Durkheim dismissed without any scruples the original and evocative thought of G. Tarde (*Les Lois de l'imitation* [The Laws of Imitation], 1890) and of R. Worms, the French authority on Spencerian organicism and the influential, active founder of the *Revue Internationale de sociologie* (1893).

Therefore, the only academic sociology that the French invented at the turn of the nineteenth century—and it is quite a magnificent invention—was the Durkheimian sociology. This school would dominate French sociology with almost no competition up to the eve of World War II, as the reader will see in this work's article on Durkheim. On the other hand, the French can be proud to count among their ranks Montesquieu and his *Esprit des lois* (The Spirit of Laws, 1748). According to R. Aron (1968), Montesquieu was the most authentic precursor of the discipline, who ear-

lier had created sociological analysis and one of its most promising methods: the typological method.

Sociology owes the place it occupies in the French intellectual landscape to the conditions under which it appeared and developed as well as to the political and social stakes with which it was involved. If one can state, as does J. Duvignaud (1966), that sociology is a "daughter of the Revolution," one must not forget to specify that it is both a political (democratic) revolution and an economic (industrial) revolution.

There is no need to go back to Saint-Simon, to whom we owe the concept of "industrial society," to be convinced that there are close ties between a nonactivist social thought and the political and social upheavals of the French Revolution; one needs only consider sociology's debt toward the analyses of de Tocqueville. Aside from the openly reactionary (but theoretically evocative) thinking of J. de Maistre and L. de Bonald, who both highlighted the role of intermediary institutions (or "body") between the power of the state and the individuals, the works of de Tocqueville were particularly instrumental in the creation and development of a sociopolitical thought on the democratic and industrial societies. The famous author of *L'Ancien Régime et la Révolution* (1856) was not only a brilliant historian, but first and foremost a powerful conceptualizer of democracy as well as of the social and political conditions of collective mobilization (through a concept expressed in modern sociology as "relative frustration"). With *De la démocratie en Amérique* (Democracy in America, 1835–1940), he showed himself to be the first relevant sociologist of modernity.

A few decades later, Durkheim still was aiming to study the conditions for the stability of the Republican system and the consequences of industrialization when he was writing *De la division du travail social* (1893) or analyzing *L'Éducation morale* (1952, posth.). Tocqueville feared the creation of new aristocracies, but Durkheim was more in line with the nineteenth-century authors who were concerned by the subversive potential of the working classes on the bourgeois democratic order. In this respect, France can be compared to England and the efforts it made very early on to alleviate the workers' misery and remedy it without upsetting the social order in the process. France also had its "*Mélioristes*" with two prominent precursors of empirical sociology.

L. Villermé, a philanthropic physician won over by reformative ideas, was the most significant personality in this new trend of social survey. The author of an important paper on prison reform (1820), he also led a pioneering survey on the moral and physical conditions of the workers in the textile mills (1840). This would be pursued on a larger scale by F. Le Play, an engineer who devoted himself to the study of the social status of European workers (1855) with a focus on the analysis of family budgets. His hypothesis was that the state of a society could only be grasped through the study of smaller units; he thought that the family unit was a microcosm in which the tensions and contradictions of the global society were reflected. A Catholic conservative, he is thus known as the creator of the *monographic* method, which is based on factual observation and interviews, and as the initiator of a network of local observatories across the region—the *Unions pour la paix sociale* (Unions for social peace), whose works would allow to be drawn the first realistic portrait of the French working class. It is significant that later some of his most important disciples would be recruited in England. French sociology can thus claim to have come from a long tradition of empirical studies on social facts and social change, which, by contrast, highlighted the need for a nonexistent theorization.

When founding "his" sociology, however, Durkheim gave it more a conceptual, theoretical orientation than an empirical program. This sociology, being more concerned with analyzing "collective representations" than facts of "social morphology" (which it left to ethnology that would be led in France by M. Mauss, Durkheim's nephew), was seduced by the trappings of ambitious synthesizing and of the philosophy of history. Its favorite problematics—education, morality, religion—intended first and foremost to study and state the social conditions that would promote the stabilization of a social order based on republican values, which were still being threatened. Thus Durkheimianism may have seemed to many of its contemporaries to be a militant sociology—which it certainly was, but it is impossible to reduce it to just that. The fact is that between the two world wars, French sociology, wrapped into itself, anemic and deaf to the political and social debates of the time, was dying. M. Halbwachs gave it new life by opening it to the Anglo-Saxon world and new problematics in the fields of economics (with F. Simiand), social psychology (1938), and human geography. Still, this second wind came too late to allow the Durkheimian tradition to survive. The time had not come yet for the end of French sociology; it was only the end of a certain way of thinking and practicing it.

It is only after 1945 that French sociology started to look like our modern sociology—but not quite yet like our actual sociology. It emerged not only from a partially destroyed society, but also from the programmed destruction of the Durkheimian tradition. As soon as the Liberation, it would benefit from a period of reconstruction that would (re)place it at its highest and best level. Better yet than reconstruction, one should speak of new construction. Indeed, the new

"leaders" of the discipline all voted for a modernization that would penalize Durkheimianism. J. Stoetzel, who was presiding from Bordeaux over the destiny of the Institut Français d'opinion publique (Institute of French Public Opinion, IFOP, created in 1939) and then over the newly created Centre d'études sociologiques (CES), used American methodology (specialized, empirical, and quantitative) and asked his colleagues to "forget Durkheim!" The philosophical landscape of the time, meanwhile, united Sartrists and Marxists in a rejection of positivism—the former not accepting that social facts could be seen "as things," the latter doubting that there could be social sciences other than historical materialism.

Thus at first French sociology prudently kept away from the sociophilosophical debates of the time, restricting itself to an "empiricism" with which it could implement the process and methods young researchers had brought back from their stays in American Universities. It would be the birth of the Fifth Republic—and the revolutionary students of May '68 probably did not know it—that would allow sociology to become a full discipline in France. Starting with the creation of a bachelor's degree in 1958 and through the following decade, many research centers and journals were created (notably *Sociologie du travail* [Sociology of Work] and *Revue française de sociologie*). Meanwhile, sociology became a trade that could be learned and practiced. Orders and public funding increased, thanks essentially to planning authorities who were not only addressing economists (INSEE—Institut national de la statistique et des études économiques), political economists (FNSP, Fondation Nationale des Sciences Politiques), and demographers (INED, Institut national d'études démographiques), but also specialists in social issues. The fields most often studied were work (under the leadership of G. Friedmann), the city (P.-H. Chombart de Lauwe), the school system (P. Bourdieu), leisure (J. Dumazedier), rural life (H. Mendras), and administrative organizations (M. Crozier). Thanks to competent teams and efficient methods, the true portrait of French society could start to be drawn—something that until then had been done through ideological speculation. One study synthesizing work is notable in this regard—*Le Partage des bénéfices* (Sharing Profits, 1966)—which its editors concluded with "The sociology of small true facts and social philosophy which, set on another level, pretends to grasp social phenomena and all their aspects, have in common the masking and dissimulation of absence as well as the urgent need for a theory of the social system."

The events of May 1968, which legendarily began in the Sociology Department at the University of Nanterre, would bring great visibility to the discipline. It would in turn earn prestige in the eyes of the national intelligentsia, prestige that would draw intellectuals from all sides. At the same time, sociology sent its own researchers to explore other fields in the humanities and social sciences. The sociologists' infatuation with the works of M. Foucault or L. Althusser demonstrated a "sociologization" of philosophical problematics, unless it was a philosophical intellectualization of sociology's problematics, which would be rendered through a *theoricism* as abstruse as dogmatic. It comes as no surprise, then, that French sociology would thus become fragmented in several more or less diverging theoretical trends. By the end of the twentieth century, there were four main trends, each headed by a "leader" solidly anchored in one academic institution or another.

The first trend was built around A. Touraine, who very early on had inaugurated a first new paradigm with his *Sociologie de l'action* (1965). Touraine then turned to the problematic of producing "social historicity" by the collective agents that are the "social movements" and of which he would become a leading theoretician (1978). The second trend, led by M. Crozier, ruled over the sociology of organizations with the definition of theoretical and methodological frames of a strategy analysis that agents formulate depending on the freedom and power granted to them by a social system's "zones of uncertainty" (1977). A third trend, with close theoretical and conceptual orientations to the second, was initiated by R. Boudon. This trend developed and formalized an original "methodological individualism" (1977), whose unit of reference was the "intentional and rational" agent. The agent's behaviors were defined by the structure of the "interaction systems" to which they belonged and whose "aggregation" made up the essential matter of social reality (1979). Lastly, a fourth trend, under the leadership of P. Bourdieu, analyzed social practices as a result of both the interiorization of cultural schemas of action (habitus) and permanent strategies of opposition and distinction (1979) within "fields" of positions of power structured by the spread of "capitals" (1980). Until the late 1980s, these trends structured a French sociology that was widely opened to the most diverse philosophies and, at the same time, careful to tie theory and empiricism, order and change, agents, and structures.

As of this writing, French sociology is in all respects considered a major scientific discipline. Its academic institutionalization is provided by laboratories (part of which belong to the Institut de recherche sur les sociétés contemporaines, IRESCO [Research Institute on Modern Societies] and to the Maison des sciences de l'homme, MSH [House of Human Sciences in Paris]). It is also provided by diplomas (in particular those granted by the École des hautes études en sciences sociales, EHESS [School of Higher Education for So-

cial Sciences]) as well as international journals and a still timid but real professionalization. The social recognition of French sociology is made evident by an ever-growing number of students, substantial research funding, and steady demand for expertise. It is nowadays open to all fields of social life, which have their own specialists, and it has not neglected any of the theoretical orientation, process, or technique that constantly enrich the discipline. It is diverse, and its branches are growing in various ways, some more pertinently and rapidly than others. The great ideological and epistemological conflicts have somewhat abated, leaving room for theoretical and methodological debates that are substantial and often lively.

If one wanted to point out, on a theoretical level, some of today's most innovative and prolific areas of work, one would especially need to mention the research done in the fields of sociology of experience (Dubet, 1994) and sociology of the mind (Boudon, 1990 and 1999), as well as the study of social networks (Castells, 1996), domination (Bourdieu, 1993), and moral discourse (Boltanski and Thévenot, 1991). What best characterizes French sociology over the last decade, however, is the interest from all sides—as if in reaction to the "hyper-structuralism" of the '70s—for the observation and analysis of the metasocial stimuli of individual behaviors. The growing number of works, theorethical and empirical, on the rationality of the agent (Boudon 2003), the formation of subjectivity (Dubet and Wieviorka, 1995), or the plurality of the self (Lahire, 1998), show today's existence of a French "sociological pendulum" (Cuin, 2002) that keeps alternating the way social issues are approached.

Beyond the theoretical and institutional restructurings that occur within any scientific discipline and prove their vitality, French sociology has kept to this day the characteristics that show its place within a national intellectual tradition and grant it a certain specificity compared to other sciences. Three such characteristics should be noted because they allow discussing French sociology in the singular, in spite of its diversity. First, a constant interest for theoretical elaboration differentiates it from the generalized empiricism of the discipline. Second, a strong concern about taking into account structures and agents, micro- and macrosocial levels, and stability and change prevents it from being reduced either to a social philosophy or a collective psychology. Third, a measured and reflective sympathy for popular social movements allows it to be neither indifferent to nor alienated from collective stakes (except recently for P. Bourdieu and some of his disciples).

Is French sociology paying the price for this relative wisdom by no longer being considered a field open to any speculation, if not any utopia, but as a science (almost) "like any other"? As it has become through its process and its highly technical language more demanding for the mind and harder to read, it has today yielded a great part of its editorial field to neighboring disciplines that are more easily attractive: philosophy (especially moral), history (in particular that of "the present time"), or anthropology (in particular that of everyday life). Is this because French sociology has found its true place within the division of intellectual work, or on the contrary, because it has let itself be dispossessed of some of its problematics? That is the question one may ask about sociology today.

CHARLES-HENRY CUIN

See also **Louis Althusser; Raymond Aron; Joffre Dumazedier; Emile Durkheim; Jean Duvignaud; Michel Foucault; Maurice Halbwachs; Marcel Mauss**

Further Reading

Aron, Raymond, *La Sociologie allemande contemporaine*, 1935, reprinted Paris: P.U.F., 1981

Aron, Raymond, *Les Étapes de le pensée sociologique*, Paris: Gallimard, 1968

Boltanski, Luc and Laurent Thévenot, *De la justification*, Paris: Gallimard, 1991

Boudon, Raymond, *Effets pervers et ordre social*, Paris: P.U.F., 1977

Boudon, Raymond, *La Logique du social*, Paris: Hachette, 1979

Boudon, Raymond, *L'Art de se persuader*, Paris: Fayard, 1990

Boudon, Raymond, *Le Sens des valeurs*, Paris: P.U.F., 1999

Boudon, Raymond, *Raison, bonnes raisons*, Paris: P.U.F., 2003

Bourdieu, Pierre and Jean-Claude Passeron, *Les Héritiers*, Paris: Minuit, 1964

Bourdieu, Pierre, *La Distinction*, Paris: Minuit, 1979

Bourdieu, Pierre, *La Misère du monde*, Paris: Minuit, 1993

Bourdieu, Pierre, *Le Sens pratique*, Paris: Minuit, 1980

Castells, Manuel, *La Société en réseau*, Paris:

Chombart de Lauwe, Paul-H., *Des Hommes et des villes*, Paris: Le Seuil, 1965

Clark, Terry N., *Prophets and Patrons: The French University and the Emergence of Social Science*, Cambridge, MA: Harvard University Press, 1973

Cuin, Charles-H., "Le balancier sociologique français: entre individus et structures," *Revue européenne des sciences sociales*, XL, 124 (2002): 253–262

Cuin, Charles-H. and François Gresle, *Histoire de la sociologie*, 2 vol., Paris: La Découverte, 2002.

Crozier, Michel and Erhard Friedberg, *L'Acteur et le système*, Paris: Le Seuil, 1977

Crozier, Michel, *Le Phénomène bureaucratique*, Paris: Le Seuil, 1964

Darras (Coll.), *Le Partage des bénéfices*, Paris: Minuit, 1966

Dubet, François, *Sociologie de l'expérience*, Paris: Le Seuil, 1994

Dubet, François and Michel Wieviorka (editor), *Penser le sujet. Autour d'Alain Touraine*, Paris: Fayard, 1995

Dumazedier, Joffre, *Vers une civilisation des loisirs?*, Paris: Le Seuil, 1962

Durkheim, Émile, *De la division du travail social*, 1893, reprinted Paris: P.U.F., 1973

Durkheim, Émile, *L'Éducation morale*, 1925, posth., reprinted Paris: P.U.F., 1963

Durkheim, Émile, *Le Suicide*, 1897, reprinted Paris: P.U.F., 1960

Durkheim, Émile, *Les Règles de la méthode sociologique*, 1894, reprinted Paris: P.U.F., 1986

Duvignaud, Jean, *Introduction à la sociologie*, Paris: Gallimard, 1966

Friedmann, Georges, *Le Travail en miettes*, 1956, reprinted Paris: Gallimard, 1964

Halbwachs, Maurice, *Esquisse d'une psychologie des classes sociales*, 1938, reprinted Paris: Librairie M. Rivière, 1964

Lahire, Bernard, *L'Homme pluriel*, Paris: Nathan, 1998

Le Play, Frédéric, *Les Ouvriers européens*, Paris: Imprimerie impériale, 1855

Leclerc, Gérard, *L'observation de l'homme. Une histoire des enquêtes sociales*, Paris: Le Seuil, 1979

Marcel, Jean-Ch., *Le Durkheimisme dans l'entre-deux-guerres*, Paris: P.U.F., 2001

Mendras, Henri, *Comment devenir sociologue, ou les mémoires d'un vieux mandarin*, Paris: Actes Sud, 1995

Mendras, Henri, *La Fin des paysans*, Paris: A. Colin, 1967

Montesquieu, Charles-L., *L'Esprit des lois* (1748)

Mucchielli, Laurent, *La Découverte du social. Naissance de la sociologie en France (1870–1914)*, Paris: La Découverte, 1998

Saint-Simon, Claude-H. de, *La physiologie sociale. Oeuvres choisies*, introduction and notes by G. Gurvitch, Paris: P.U.F., 1965

Tarde, Gabriel, *Les Lois de l'imitation*, 1890, reprinted Paris: Slatkine Reprints, 1979

Tocqueville, Alexis de, *Œuvres complètes*, 18 vols., Paris: Gallimard, 1952

Touraine, Alain, *La Voix et le regard*, Paris: La seuil, 1978

Touraine, Alain, *Production de la société*, Paris: La seuil, 1973

Villermé, Louis, *Tableau de l'état physique et moral des ouvriers employés dans les manufactures de coton, de laine et de soie*, Paris: Renouard, 1840

SOLLERS, PHILIPPE

Novelist

Between 1960 and 1982, Philippe Sollers was a leading figure of the avant-garde group and review *Tel Quel* at the Éditions du Seuil, defending the *nouveau roman* [new novel] (in an initial move that lasted until 1964), as well as promoting Ponge, Artaud, and Bataille's works. He embraced the "structuralist revolution" and elaborated a "*[t]héorie d'ensemble*" together with Roland Barthes, Jacques Derrida, Julia Kristeva (whom he married in 1967), and Jacques Lacan. Sollers participated in the 1968 Revolution, in an ambiguous oscillation among Marxism, Chinese Taoism, and Cultural Revolution, and a strategic cooperation with the French Communist party that led to contacts with Genet and Althusser. He translated into French a number of poems by Mao Tze Tung; published a volume on Mao, Lenin, and Marxism entitled *Sur le matérialisme*; made an official trip to China (as part of a *Tel Quel* delegation); and finally separated from the then-current "scholasticism" of the "*Église marxiste*" [Marxist church] in 1976.

Beginning in 1982, Sollers, who had converted from agnosticism to Catholicism in 1979 and was then mostly interested in the Bible, the Vatican's political influence, and the connections between human eroticism and the arts, replaced *Tel Quel* with the review *L'Infini*, published by Gallimard. Sollers's oeuvre, still in full progress, at this writing comprises five nonfigurative novels (*Le parc; Drame, Nombres; Lois; Paradis*), over ten autofictional novels aimed at a larger audience, numerous essays on literature and the arts (some of them published nowadays in *Le Monde* or *Le Monde des Livres*), an autobiography (*Portrait du joueur*), and a diary (*L'année du Tigre*).

Although rejecting "everything that says 'we' " and the very idea of an intellectual "mission," Sollers did not abandon intellectual action. He has denounced the Spectacle (in Guy Debord's sense); the global *"grande Tyrannie"* [big Tyranny] of *"Leymarché Financier"* [The financial market] that manipulates bodies, merchandise, spirits, and limits; *"la parole sur le sexe et la parole sur la parole"*; [Speech on sex and speech on speech] the "planetary culture" in the making, with its rampant *DPI* (*Détérioration Psychique Irréversible*) [Irreversible Psychic Deterioration] and its efficient *Bureau des Communications Négatives*, [Bureau for Negative Communications] *GSI* (*Gestion des surfaces imprimées, imagées*), [management of printed surfaces] and *Bureau des Divertissements Nuls* [Bureau of Null Entertainment]. At the same time he has systematically promoted *"une analyse permanente des crédulités"* [a permanent analysis of credulities], a struggle against *"la pavlovisation générale"* [general Pavlovization], and explored the forms of artistic, religious, or erotic dissidence to be used by individuals who commit the *"délit de vie distincte"* [delict of distinct life] to preserve their freedom. Among those, commitment to critical thinking, guided by a dialogue with exceptions, is crucial.

The exceptions Sollers has in mind are writers, works, and artists such as Homer, the Bible, *La Chanson de Roland*, Dante, Machiavelli, Sade, Casanova, Mozart, Fragonard, Poussin, Proust, Lautréamont, Rimbaud, Joyce, Céline, Cézanne, high moments of the universal conscience such as Taoism with its logic of the body and sex, Jesuit art with its "penseurs de l'éducation raffinée," [thinkers of refined education] the Counter-Reformation or Baroque style, the eighteenth century, whole cultures (such as the Chinese culture with its special symbolic economy, the *culture d'exception française* with its high if not highest concentration of great writers), and whole religions (such as Catholicism with its lack of fanaticism and lucid treatment of sexuality). Sollers prefers the Church to the State, Notre-Dame de Paris to the Panthéon, the eighteenth to the nineteenth century. What the excep-

tions can mainly teach us is that art has *une fonction d'exultation* [a function of exultation], that books are magical instruments indicating at the right moment to the right person the way to follow and annihilating, if well read, *la propagande du malheur* [the propaganda of misfortune], that writing represents *la présence à soi sous une autre forme* [the presence to oneself in a different form], a positioning in the absolute heart of time, the confirmation of Duns Scotus's affirmation that only the ultimate endpoint of the individual is real.

Sollers distinguishes between three types of novels: (1) those in which the narrator, Proust, for example, in *À la recherche du temps perdu*, is searching for a truth that he or she does not possess but will reach at the end of the story; (2) those in which the narrator, Nabokov at times, claims to be searching for truth but does everything possible to know nothing about it; and (3) those in which the narrator knows everything in advance and therefore goes straight to truth (the writer's body, sexuality, his or her interactions with other bodies and discourses), without the tiresome psychology of the nineteenth-century family saga. The third is the type of novel Sollers has chosen to write lastly. It leads to fantastic or autobiographical forms of oral narrative, with oblique encounters (epiphanies) inscribed in a substantial and playfully meditated duration by a *"stratège de la vie privée"* [strategist of private life] that is fully aware of the sensual and sexual presence of one's body into one's thinking (*"Audio ergo video. Audio-video cogitando, ergo sum"*). [I hear, therefore I see. I hear-see while thinking, therefore I am]. This third type also leads to novels that always are an *histoire du bonheur* [a story of happiness?].

Although he values Bataille's work, Sollers rejects his view of eroticism as the approbation of life even into death. Sexual negativity should be eliminated, sexual experimentation has to result in an expansion of reason, thus avoiding subliminal esoteric references or repressive desublimation (that is, pornography). Sexuality and the consciousness of pleasure are for Sollers a domain in which writing can go the furthest nowadays and in which language is liberated as well, even if French is *"une langue qui meurt"* [a language that is dying].

According to Sollers, there is no sexual community inasmuch as no two sexualities are alike. Accepting the dichotomy homosexual/heterosexual amounts to proclaiming as a decisive criterion that of the "manipulated object," instead of subjective desire. Men, women, and children do not belong to the same species. Male femininity has nothing in common with female masculinity. In one of his recent novels, eroticism comes to be defined as an exchange of their childhoods, outside the *"roman familial-social,"* between autonomous adults.

To feminists who call into question patriarchal hierarchy and the symbolic paternal function, masculinist Sollers reacts by calling into question motherhood, "*la langue maternelle*" [the maternal language], the archaic Mother, and the Catholic belief in the Blessed Virgin that leads to an ideal Catholic womanhood and a corresponding idealism projected by males. Maternal love, says Sollers, is a fiction invented by mother and child together; men play a role in it both as children and as parents. The reaction is partial (it does not consider women's role in the fiction of patriarchal hierarchy), but openly presented as such in most of the cases because Sollers is definitely an *autreur* [otherer] type of author, a relaxed chronicler of the thinking habits, vices, and discourses of a vast multitude of Others, the builder of a unique and humorous database of contemporary voices we all recognize.

Sollers once presented the development of his oeuvre as the gradual building of a "château baroque" [baroque castle] made of words and meant not so much for his readers, as for being *habité par l'auteur* [inhabited by the author]. We now can perceive the main lines of the structure and feel, at times, the almost welcome guests of an essentially clandestine and recluse thinker and writer.

SANDA GOLOPENTIA

See also **Louis Althusser; Antonin Artaud; Roland Barthes; Georges Bataille; Jacques Derrida; Julia Kristeva; Jacques Lacan**

Biography

Novelist and essayist Philippe Joyaux (who adopted, in 1957, the pseudonym Sollers) was born on November 28, 1936, in Talence. He went to school in Bordeaux and at the Sainte-Geneviève Jesuit school in Versailles (from which he was expelled for "*indiscipline chronique et lecture de livres défendus*") [chronical indiscipline and reading of forbidden books] and abandoned, after two years, the École supérieure des sciences économiques et commerciales, where he was expected to prepare for directing the family business. From 1957, when he published his first text (*Le défi*) shortly followed by an acclaimed Proustian novel (*Une certaine solitude*), Sollers has dedicated his life to writing and the intellectual pursuits that could nourish and exalt it.

Selected Works

Novels, Diary

Une curieuse solitude, 1958, as *A Strange Solitude*, translated by Richard Howard, 1959 *Le Parc*, 1961, as *The Park*, translated by A. M. Sheridan Smith, 1968

Drame, 1965, as *Event*, translated by Bruce Benderson and Ursule Molinaro 1986
Nombres, 1968
Lois, 1972
H, 1973
Paradis (vol. I), 1981
Femmes, 1983, as *Women*, translated by Barbara Bray, 1990
Portrait du joueur, 1984
Paradis II, 1986
Le Coeur Absolu, 1987
Les Folies françaises, 1988
Le Lys d'or, 1989
La Fête à Venise, 1991, as *Watteau in Venice*, translated by Alberto Manguel, 1994
Le Secret, 1992
Studio, 1997
L'année du Tigre (Journal 1998), 1999
Passion fixe, 2000
L'étoile des amants, 2002

Essays

L'Intermédiaire, 1963
Logiques, 1968
Théorie d'ensemble (with others), 1968
L'Écriture et l'expérience des limites, 1971, as *Writing and the Experience of Limits*, translated by Philip Barnard with David Hayman, edited by David Hayman, 1983
Sur le matérialisme: De l'atomisme à la dialectique révolutionnaire, 1971, 1974
Théorie des exceptions, 1986
Les surprises de Fragonard, 1987
De Kooning, vite, 1988
Carnet de nuit, 1989
Improvisations, 1991
Le Paradis de Cézanne, 1995
Le Cavalier du Louvre, Vivant Denon, 1995
La Guerre du Goût, 1996
Picasso le héros, 1996
Casanova l'admirable, 1998
(with others) *De Tel Quel à l'Infini: l'avant-garde et après*, 1999
Le Divin Mozart, 2001
Éloge de l'Infini, 2001
Illuminations à travers les textes sacrés, 2003

Interviews

Entretiens de Francis Ponge avec Philippe Sollers, 1970
Délivrance: Maurice Clavel et Philippe Sollers face à face, 1977
Vision à New York: Entretiens avec David Hayman, 1981
Voies et détours de la fiction (interviews with Louis-René des Forêts from 1962), 1985
Le rire de Rome: Entretiens avec Frans de Haes, 1992
La divine comédie: Entretiens avec Benoît Chantre, 2000

Works Edited

Artaud, 1973
Bataille, 1973
Rodin: Dessins érotiques (with Alain Kirili), 1987
Photos licencieuses de la Belle Époque, 1987
Sade contre l'Être Suprême, 1992

Further Reading

Barthes, Roland, *Sollers écrivain*, Paris: Éditions du Seuil, 1979, as *Writer Sollers*, translated by Philip Tody, Minneapolis: University of Minnesota Press, 1987

Champagne, Roland A., *Philippe Sollers*, Amsterdam and Atlanta, GA: Editions Rodopi B.V., 1996

Clément, C., *Sollers, La Fronde*, Paris: Julliard, 1994

de Cortanze, Gérard, *Sollers ou La volonté de bonheur*, Éditions du Chêne, 2001

Derrida, Jacques, *La Dissémination*, Paris: Éditions du Seuil, 1972, as *Dissemination*, translated by Barbara Johnson, Chicago: University of Chicago Press, 1981

Forest, Philippe, *Philippe Sollers*, Paris: Éditions du Seuil, 1992

Forest, Philippe, *Histoire de "Tel Quel,"* Paris: Éditions du Seuil, 1995

Kristeva, Julia, *Recherches pour une sémanalyse*, Paris: Éditions du Seuil, 1969

Kristeva, Julia, *Les Samouraïs* (a novel), Paris: Fayard & Gallimard, 1990

Kurk, K.-C., *Consummation of the Text: A Study of Philippe Sollers*, Lexington: University of Kentucky Press, 1979

Louvrier, P., *Philippe Sollers mode d'emploi*, Paris: Éditions du Rocher, 1996

Le Magazine littéraire (special issue: *Philippe Sollers and Tel Quel*), 65 (June 1972)

Pollard, M., *The Novels of Philippe Sollers*, Amsterdam and Atlanta, GA: Editions Rodopi B.V., 1994

Pleynet, M., *Le Voyage en Chine*, Paris: POL, 1980

Van der Poel, I., *Une révolution de la pensée: maoïsme et féminisme à travers Tel Quel, Les Temps modernes et Esprit*, Amsterdam and Atlanta, GA: Editions Rodopi B.V., 1992

Thibaudeau, Jean, *Mes Années Tel Quel: Mémoire*, Montreal: Écriture, 1994

SOREL, GEORGES
Writer, Political Theorist

Georges Sorel is a perplexing and contentious figure whose political positions, especially, varied wildly, and much space would be required to encompass the great diversity of his thought. From revisionist Marxist to revolutionary syndicalist, through flirtations with monarchist nationalism and sympathies for Leninism and fascism, Sorel's writings engage with most of the crucial currents of social thought in the first decades of the twentieth century.

Most of his thought is concerned with the emergence and development of the socialist movement as a vital ethical as well as political force. Based on the significance of his influential book, *Reflections on Violence*, Sorel is regarded primarily as a theorist of revolutionary syndicalism. His interest in syndicalism, however, was predominantly motivated by his belief that it was the movement that held the greatest prospect for an ethical regeneration of society.

Sorel, because of his emphasis on ethics, was perhaps the most inventive and tenacious of the many critics of Marxism during the time of the Second International, and he provided the most creative reinterpretation of Marxist theory. In his view, it was wrong to view Marxism as a total theory, as many Marxists did, because any analysis is necessarily partial. No historical movement can be captured in its totality, and no theory can express the complexity of historical processes.

Throughout his work, Sorel grappled with the collapse of theoretical certainty and problems of political unity, especially in relation to socialist theory. For Sorel, the social was indeterminate, and social unity was constructed through action dependent on will. Determinism, in Sorel's view, had no place in social science. Sorel preferred to emphasize the spontaneous, nonrational character of social action and was perhaps the first to shift the emphasis in Marxism from economics to culture, rethinking Marxism not as science but as "social poetry." In doing so he replaced the logic of necessity in Marxism with a logic of contingency. Marx had offered only a working hypothesis, one that was incomplete and emotion laden. Sorel, unlike other commentators, embraced the combination of emotional and "scientific" aspects in Marx's thought. His conclusion was that Marxism needed to be redefined, and all attempts to make it a science must be abandoned.

Sorel began by drawing an important distinction between what he termed "natural nature" and "artificial nature" or the social constructions by which we impose our own voice on a nature that confronts us as silence. In Sorel's view, the natural is fluid, chaotic, mysterious, infinitely complex, and obscure; the artificial reflects a striving after order and simplicity (and thus engages in acts of violence against subtlety, ambiguity, complexity, chaos, and flux in nature). Complexity could be grasped by taking individual elements out of their surrounding context and examining them. This simplifying process Sorel called *diremption*. In his view, the character of certain elements of events can be understood by isolating them, by examining them apart from their broader connections to a totality. This intellectual technique allows for an understanding of a reality, which is otherwise incommensurable with human intellect. The *diremption* is similar to what Max Weber would later call "ideal types" or abstract models to which real objects might be compared.

For Sorel, an element of artificiality was introduced into all analyses, including the scientific, by what he termed an "expressive support," which is necessary for their constitution. These expressive supports bridge the gaps in discourse. Marked by sentimentalism and laden with emotion, they provide the appeal of social movements. Expressive supports work as the elements around which social blocs can form. Any unity, then, is recognized (against the hopes of the Marxists) as fictive, or at least as resulting from expressive supports, which may include fictions.

Against this background, Sorel devised his conception of social myth as a means to escape the limitations of determinism and materialism. In Sorel's work one sees a rejection of any efforts to trace historical progression through dialectic, emphasizing instead the myths by which agents actively organize to undermine a political status quo. Social myths are the crucial aspects in all social movements. Myths help participants to understand the present, explain efforts for social change and point to the desired future society. Unity is achieved not through centralized organizations or political representation but through myth. The myth provides the ensemble of images powerful enough to bring the diverse elements of the movement together in common action. The myth constitutes what Proudhon had termed "a profound unity of consciousness." Of these myths, none was more important to Sorel than the myth of the "General Strike" by which workers would realize their heroic capacities and unite to enact the great social regeneration. For Sorel, the myth of the General Strike served as a point of unification for proletarian identity in a social context in which that identity was diverse and lacking unity.

The myth is more than a *diremption* because it represents a complex of images of reality at more than one point rather than a single isolated element. In allowing for the irrational and nonlogical, the myth is closer to the fluidity of reality than the logical abstractions of social theory. Unlike the logical abstractions of theory, which do not inspire people to act, the myth motivates actions. In saying this, Sorel is not advocating irrational movements over rational ones, as some critics have claimed, but drawing attention to the mythic aspects of all movements.

Sorel's work is devoted to an attempt to discover the connection, missing in the writings of socialists, including Marx, and sociologists alike, between the character of social blocs and their political activity. Marx, for example, had failed to understand the character of working class association and the institutional and psychological aspects of class action. One's position as a member of a class cannot account for an individual's actions. Sorel sought to understand what mediates between one's status and one's actions. Because, in his view, class identities rely primarily on local associations rooted in specific experiences, Sorel contended that it is these connections that provide the basis for new social relations and give socialism its significance.

Through his analysis of social myth, Sorel also came to reject notions of a universal ethic that transcended class divisions. Different movements draw their strength from unique symbols and experiences and not from doctrines of Truth or Justice shared by all. The socialist order would be built on the associations and ties that were essential in industrial work. This view encouraged Sorel's rejection of politics and parties and led to his insistence that the working class

separate itself from bourgeois culture and morals and develop modes of living that resisted compromise and co-optation. Only in constant opposition to the bourgeoisie could the working class develop its own ethic suitable for socialism. Political separatism, what Sorel called *scission*, the constitution of a strict demarcation between the institutions of the proletariat and those of the bourgeoisie, is a necessity for socialism. Revolutionary syndicalism provides the appropriate strategy for change because it upheld autonomous associations of workers organized in a nonhierarchical manner, which allowed for local initiative, crucial for a decentralized social order.

JEFFREY SHANTZ

Biography

Georges Sorel was born in Cherbourg in 1847 and graduated from the College of Cherbourg in 1864. Upon graduation he moved to Paris to attend the École Polytechnique. In 1867 he began work as an engineer with the Bureau of Bridges and Highways, working in Corsica and Albi until taking an early retirement in 1892. In recognition of his efficient and dutiful civil service, Sorel was made a Chevalier of the Legion of Honour in 1891. After his retirement, Sorel moved to Paris and began his second life as a writer. From the late 1890s until his death in 1922, Sorel dedicated himself to an engagement with social struggles and movements in an attempt to understand the forces that might revive society from its bourgeois decline.

Selected Works

Le Procès de Socrate, 1889
La Ruine du monde antique, 1901
Introduction à l'économie moderne, 1902
Le Système historique de Renan, 1905
Réflexions sur la violence, 1908; as *Reflections on Violence*, translated by T. E. Hulme, 1961
Les Illusions du progrès, 1908; as *The Illusions of Progress*, translated by John Stanley and Charlotte Stanley, 1969
La Révolution dreyfusienne, 1909
La Décomposition du marxisme, 1908; as *The Decomposition of Marxism*, translated by Irving Louis Horowitz, 1961
Matériaux d'une théorie du prolétariat, 1919
De l'utilité du pragmatisme, 1921
D'Aristote à Marx, 1935

Further Reading

Andreu, Pierre, *Notre Maitre, M. Sorel*, Paris: 1953
Beetham, David, "Sorel and the Left," *Government and Opposition*, (1969): 308–323
Berlin, Sir Isaiah, "Georges Sorel," *Times Literary Supplement*, 31 (1971): 1617–1622
Horowitz, Irving L. *Radicalism and the Revolt Against Reason*, Carbondale: Southern Illinois University Press, 1968

Kolakowski, Leszek, "Georges Sorel: Jansenist Marxist," *Dissent*, winter (1975): 63–80

Laclau, Ernest. *New Reflections on the Revolution of Our Times*, London: Verso, 1990

Laclau, Ernesto and Chantal Mouffe. *Hegemony and Socialist Strategy*, London: Verso, 1985

Meisel, James H. *The Genesis of Georges Sorel*, Ann Arbor: University of Michigan Press, 1951

Portis, Larry, *Georges Sorel*, London: Pluto Press, 1980

Roth, Jack J. "Revolution and Morale in Modern French Thought: Sorel and the Sorelians," *French Historical Studies*, (1963): 205–223

Talmon, J.L. "The Legacy of Georges Sorel," *Encounter*, February (1970): 47–60

Vernon, Richard, *Commitment and Change: Georges Sorel and the Idea of Revolution*, Toronto: University of Toronto Press, 1978

STAROBINSKI, JEAN
Writer

In interviews, Jean Starobinski defines himself as a sedentary person, but his constant concern has always been with movement, a notion that structures and gives form to his work. One quote by Thomas Aquinas in *Action and Reaction* (1999) could serve as an epigraph to his complete works: "tout ce qui est mû, est mû par un autre," "anything that is moved is moved by an alterity." His attraction to Rousseau and Montaigne, the eighteenth century, or philology, as well as melancholia or the image of the clown, is always moved, in both senses of the term, by the same fascination for change, versatility, and its inseparable opposite, immutability, as one can observe from titles like *Jean-Jacques Rousseau: la transparence et l'obstacle* (1957), *Montaigne en mouvement* (1982), *Les mots sous les mots: les anagrammes de Ferdinand de Saussure* (1971), or *Action et réaction. Vie et aventure d'un couple* (1999). His critical practice revolves around the identification of points of tension in a text, which serve as a springboard to the study of motion both as a creative energy and a structuring paradigm.

His comparatist and interdisciplinary approach to a text, an author, a period, or a work of art is marked by a limpid style that avoids jargon and is nourished by the encyclopedic knowledge of an old-school humanist. As in Montaigne, references abound, and arguments advance with the support of clearly identified voices. Like Diderot (a recurring presence in his work), Starobinski mirrors in his critical studies the variety and order of motion of the object of his attention. From the early *Transparence* until his latest works, a single concern with deepening the process of interpretation constantly returns. Starobinski's method and critical point of view is poles apart from deconstruction because for him meaning does not escape from interpretation in a vacuum of sense. Loyal to the ideas of the Geneva school, there is no predetermined grid of interpretation to his studies. A sympathy to the work (*L'Oeil vivant*), nuanced with the idea of a "confused interest" and an "embarrassment" experienced in the encounter with the text, gives his work its first sparkle. Then comes the time of analysis, a journey through the object of study and an illumination through cross studies and juxtaposition of sources requiring what he terms a "regard surplombant," which is neither totally empathetic nor separated from the work by the screen of a deterministic critical theory. Finally, the work of art is unveiled, allowing the reader a glimpse of meaning without considering it as a revelation. Like Stendhal, who finds in the fact of appearing and disappearing "complementary attitudes" (*L'Oeil vivant*, p. 204), meaning in Starobinski's work maintains its elusiveness, without frustrating the critic or the reader as it enhances the nature of their relation to works of art.

Starobinski's critical work focuses on a vision of life that never imposes itself as sovereign or definite. He starts with a text, with what is given to read, progressing toward the unknown. If his entire work is developed through variations on a theme (Rousseau, Montaigne, Racine, Corneille, La Rochefoucauld, Diderot and Voltaire, Stendhal, Valéry, Saussure, Freud, and so on) and on perspectives of approach (history, history of ideas, philosophy, psychoanalysis, psychiatry, medical sciences), his goal remains the same: creating an intimacy with the text or the work of art or the period and questioning it in a fruitful manner, bringing sense to the pattern that structures it in its formal, rhythmic, or symbolic way. For instance, in *Montaigne en mouvement*, he captures the three stages of Montaigne's *Essays*: the rejection of a world based on appearances, the quest for the essence of the self, and the ultimate recognition of the necessity of those same appearances.

Starobinski's work creates poetry and depth: depth of analysis, of reading, of care for meaning; poetry, etymologically, as a construction of meaning for his reader. Starobinski never forgets that what is at stake is a game of glances between the author and the reader, and his erudite investigations are more invitation than exclusion. Interdisciplinary analyses of changes in the eighteenth century that lead to new values in *L'Invention de la liberté: 1700–1789* reward equally the specialist and the general reader. His interest for that period can be explained by the way he defines it in *Action and reaction*: "constantly moving on to meet the world, experiencing new stimulation, trying to wake up from its boredom" (Interview with Isabelle Rüf, "domaine parlé," Radio Suisse Romande, 2000). Starobinski's critical work is entirely moved by this desire for an encounter with a piece of work and with humanity. His attraction to contemporary artists led him to collaborate with Nicolas Bouvier, Claude Garache, and Yves Bonnefoy.

His sustained interest in the figure of the other is reflected in the three main axes of his studies: representation of human body, melancholia, and the order of the day. These three leitmotifs are intrinsically related to the fundamental tension between appearance and being, between moments of plenitude and emptiness. In his *Histoire du traitement de la mélancolie* (1960), he concentrated on retrieving the movement from physical sensation to form, then from form to meaning. How can bodily language and sensations, which to Starobinski are the most authentic form of expression of the self, find a form of expression that breaks away from a solipsist prison? For this reason, the texts' silences do not represent for the critic repression or void, but merely another expression of the subject, split between his desire for transparency and authenticity and his attraction to the mask. Melancholia heightens tension between opposites, between the highest exhilaration and the deepest "spleen." Quoting Baudelaire's study of the painter Constantin Guys, Starobinski defined the modernity of tension he sought: "transitoire, fugitif, contingent, la moitié de l'art, dont l'autre moitié est l'éternel et l'immuable" (*Les Cheminées et les clochers*).

ELISE NOETINGER

See also **Yves Bonnefoy**

Biography

Jean Starobinski was born in Geneva in 1920. He studied classics then medicine at the University of Geneva. He was a lecturer in French Literature at the University of Johns Hopkins in Baltimore (1953–1956), at the University of Basle (1959–1961), and then at the University of Geneva, where he also taught the history of ideas and the history of medicine.

Selected Works

Jean-Jacques Rousseau: la transparence et l'obstacle, 1957; as *Jean-Jacques Rousseau: Transparency and Obstruction*, translated by Arthur Goldhammer, 1988
L'Oeil vivant, 1961; as *The Living Eye*, translated by Arthur Goldhammer, 1989
L'Invention de la liberté, 1964; as *The Invention of Liberty*, translated by Bernard C. Swift, 1987
La Relation critique, 1970
Portrait de l'artiste en saltimbanque, 1970
Les Mots sous les mots: les anagrammes de Ferdinand de Saussure, 1971; as *Words upon Words*, translated by Olivia Emmet, 1979
1789: Les Emblèmes de la raison, 1973; as *1789: The Emblems of Reason*, translated by Barbara Bray, 1982
La Mélancolie au miroir. Trois lectures de Baudelaire, 1990

Montaigne en mouvement, 1982, *Montaigne in Motion*, translated by Arthur Goldhammer, 1985
Action et réaction. Vie et aventure d'un couple, 1999

Further Readings

Bonnet, Jacques (editor), *Pour un temps: Jean Starobinski*, 1985.
"Jean Starobinski," *Magazine littéraire*, 280 (1990):
Ender, Evelyne, "Jean Starobinski," *The Johns Hopkins Guide to Literary Theory and Criticism*, 1997
Ender, Evelyne, "The Geneva School," *The Johns Hopkins Guide to Literary Theory and Criticism*, 1997
Gagnebin and Savinel, *Starobinski en mouvement*, 2001

STRUCTURALISM

In the broadest sense of the term, structuralism is not a specific movement, but rather a historically diffuse tendency that is decisive for developments within knowledge throughout the twentieth century. It influenced the growth of the social sciences in general, and was important for the development of a wide number of disciplines in particular: sociology, linguistics, anthropology, psychoanalysis, philosophy, economics, political theory, and even mathematics and biology. Within this wider context, structuralism can first and foremost be identified with the attempt to achieve scientific rigor in the analysis of social multiplicity or of complex systems, and is principally characterized by the tendency to privilege the whole of a system over its individual elements. More specifically, one could broadly label as structuralist any discipline that aims at the mathematical formalization of the relations existing between the individual elements that form a system or structure.

The development of the structuralist movement in France can be traced from its earliest influences in the thought of nineteenth- and twentieth-century writers such as Emile Durkheim and Edmund Husserl, through to its grounding in the work of the Swiss linguist Ferdinand de Saussure and that of the Russian formalist school, and then to the flowering of French literary structuralism in the 1960s. In this context structuralism can be identified specifically with the privileging of language as a paradigm and with the tendency to deploy the terms, categories, and methodology of modern linguistics within other domains, primarily anthropology, psychoanalysis, and literature but also within, among other areas, philosophy and sociology.

The term *structure* first appeared in a significant way in 1895 with the publication of Emile Durkheim's *The Rules of Sociological Method*. Durkheim, like many other nineteenth-century thinkers, saw society as a whole that cannot be reduced to the sum of its parts; a key emphasis of the nascent discipline of sociology was the interdependence of society's various elements and on the totality that structures the relations between them. Durkheim was not alone in privileging the notion of system or structure here, and what occurred in sociology at this time occurred elsewhere, reflecting an increasing will toward scientificity in a number of disciplines, for instance, economics, linguistics, and biology. The birth of structuralism can be situated between 1900 and 1925, specifically in the work of Swiss linguist Ferdinand de Saussure, in that of the Russian Formalist school, but also in the subsequent work of the Prague School of Linguistics, founded in 1926. In fact Saussure used the term *structure* very infrequently in his seminal *Cours de linguistique générale*. Although he is generally acknowledged to be the founding father of structural linguistics, the birth of structuralism proper occurred in the work of the Prague school.

The *Cours de linguistique générale*, published in 1916, is based on the notes of students who attended three courses between 1906 and 1911. If Saussure is the father of structuralism, it is perhaps primarily because of the distinction he introduced in this work between *langue* and *parole, language* and *speech.* Saussure insisted that language be considered as "a self-contained whole and a principle of classification," a unique relational structure comprising distinct units, which combine together according to strict laws. Within the infinitely multiple and varied acts of speech, certain invariable structures can be determined and classified, and these form the system of *langue*, which makes any act of speech possible. These invariable structures constitute the rules of grammar, the articulation of syntax, and a series of systematized phonetic differences. For Saussure it is this system or structure of *langue* that was the object of study for linguistics. This represents the archetypal structuralist gesture: the search for invariables and constants that form a relational whole and that act as a condition of possibility for individual acts of production. The upshot of this within Saussure's *Cours* was a series of formalized dichotomies around which the system of *langue* can be described, for example the distinction between synchronic and diachronic states of language, between form and substance, between syntagmatic and paradigmatic relations, and famously, the distinction within the verbal sign between signifier and signified. He also developed the doctrine of the arbitrary nature of the sign, which holds that the relation of signifier to signified is purely conventional and emphasizes the differential nature of phonetic and semantic elements such that language can be seen as a system of differences or differential values that are without positive content.

The *Cours de linguistique générale* laid the foundation for modern structural linguistics both in Europe and America. In Europe it was decisive for the work of earlier linguists such those of the Prague school (principally Roman Jakobson and Nikolai Trubetskoy), but also for the later research of the Copenhagen school (headed by Louis Hjelmslev) and for the work of French structural linguists such as Emile Benveniste, André Martinet, and Algirdas-Julian Greimas (who, although of Lithuanian origin, was trained in France). Despite all their differences and disagreements, what unites the varying strands in structural linguistics is the tendency to view the meaning and distinctive sound of a word as a function of its relationship with other words and to view language as a whole as a network of functional relationships, which articulate distinct categories or classes of linguistic elements (grammatical, phonetic, lexical, and so on).

Saussure also laid the foundation of the structuralist enterprise outside linguistics by speaking of semiology, the study of sign systems in general. Language for Saussure was comparable to systems of writing, the alphabet of deaf-mutes, symbolic rites, polite formulas, or military signals. With this, Saussure set the stage for the privileging of linguistics and the linguistic model within the wider domain of structuralism as it came to be applied to other fields of knowledge in later years. Any form of social phenomena, and even for the psychoanalyst, Jacques Lacan, the human unconscious, can be seen as a system of symbols or signs and thus "structured like a language." Linguistics and the linguistic method became the pilot science of structuralism and the means by which scientific rigor was introduced into other disciplines.

This happened from the earliest stage in the attempt to define "literariness" undertaken by the Russian formalists and in particular in the work of Roman Jakobson. Jakobson was a central figure in the development of French structuralism. Of signal importance here is his work within Russian formalism, within the Prague School of Linguistics, and then particularly the influence he exerted on Claude Lévi-Strauss in the early 1940s. Based around the *Linguistic Circle of Moscow* (founded 1915) and *Opoyaz* (St. Petersburg society for the study of poetic language founded in 1917), Russian formalist theory attempted to define the specificity of literary language. Their work involved the search for an immanence in the literary text, for an internal coherence that would make the whole greater than the sum of its parts and did so with reference to linguistic categories. Their explorations were then radicalized in work of the Prague School, which unified the formalist attempt to identify "literariness" with Saussurian linguistics. For his part, Jakobson insisted that the poetic work is above all a "verbal structure" and that "since linguistics is the global science of verbal structure, poetics must be regarded as an integral part of linguistics."

Addresser	→	Emotive function
Addressee	→	Conative function
Context	→	Referential function
Code	→	Metalingual function
Contact		Phatic
Message		Poetic function

Figure 1. Jakobson's communication model.

The communication model (Fig. 1) developed by Jakobson ascribes different functions to a linguistic message. These functions, such as emotive, conative, referential, and metalingual, are determined according to which aspect of the linguistic message is foregrounded or emphasized. Thus an emphasis on the addresser articulates an *emotive* function, on the addressee a *conative* function, on the context a *referential* function, and so on. For Jakobson, a focus on the message is the primary function of *poetic* language. The aim of his poetics, therefore, will be to analyze individual poems or narratives in the light of their verbal structure in order to discern their specifically "literary" characteristics in linguistic terms. Unlike later literary structuralists in the 1960s, Jakobson did not seek an overarching structural typology of literature or of narrative but looked at each individual work structurally, as a kind of a structure. Within the context of Jakobson's communication model of primary importance is the category of the code (corresponding to the *metalingual* function). It is a central thesis of structuralism that the code (or structure) precedes the message and acts as an independent principle that governs the possibility of its production. More importantly, in its exclusive concern with the code, structuralist poetics avoids all recourse to the consciousness of a speaking subject and emphasizes the prevalence of the structure as an essentially unconscious phenomenon. Structure, here, is conceived of as an ideal form—atemporal and invariant, and structuralism is generally characterized by the tendency to search for constants and invariable elements within complex and variable phenomena.

An important influence for Jakobson here is the work of the German philosopher Edmund Husserl and in particular Husserl's early two-volume work of phenomenology, *Logical Investigations* (1900 and 1901). Husserl's attempt to identify the essential and necessary logical structures that underpin human consciousness and govern its ability to constitute meaning (and more generally categories of knowledge), had, as Jakobson himself acknowledged, a decisive impact on the development of his researches within linguistics. Although it is widely recognized that structuralism in France eclipsed the dominance of (predominantly Sar-

trian) phenomenology in the late 1950s, the importance of Husserl's thinking for its early development is less well documented. The general tendency of structuralism to think of structure in an abstract, universalist, and idealizing manner owes much to the influence of Husserlian phenomenology. Both share a tendency to remove from the field of inquiry, or "bracket off," the empirical referent in an attempt to determine its condition of possibility in terms of a more abstract relational or logical field. The key difference between them lies in the fact that although phenomenology (at least in its Husserlian guise) lays an important emphasis on consciousness (the phenomenological ego), structuralism brackets off individual consciousness along with the empirical referent. The overarching *intersubjective* structure is always and exclusively the primary focus.

This is exemplified most clearly in the structural anthropology of Claude Lévi-Strauss. Trained in philosophy and influenced by a prevalent neo-Kantianism, Lévi-Strauss moved into ethnology in the 1930s via his readings of Emile Durkheim and Marcel Mauss. He began his work in anthropology proper with a reaction against Durkheim, who used published written sources only and did not rely on fieldwork. Although Durkheim remained an important point of reference, the impact of Mauss on Lévi-Strauss's work was decisive. Mauss defined social life as "a world of symbolic relationships" and developed the concept of the *total social fact*. He stressed the need, within anthropology, to move beyond social atomism to the social totality, the need for an anthropology that accounts for all modes of behavior and aspects of experience simultaneously, whether physical, social, or psychological.

The key breakthrough in Lévi-Strauss's work occurred as a result of meeting Roman Jakobson in New York in 1942. His friendship with Jakobson in the early 1940s was decisive for the adoption of structural linguistics as a model for the study of anthropology. This can be seen in Lévi-Strauss's first major work, *Les Structures élémentaires de la parenté* (The Elementary Structures of Kinship, 1949). Significantly, he abandoned any analysis of kinship based on the primacy of blood ties or filiation and specifically rejected biological accounts or explanations of the incest taboo. For Lévi-Strauss the joining of the sexes and the prohibition of incest is above all a socially regulated transaction—a cultural and symbolic fact. The incest taboo is not negative, therefore, but is rather productive of social links and of the social structure as a whole insofar as it is an exogamous principle—generating alliances, links, and bonds outside the family unit. Through this notion of the incest prohibition as a productive principle of social relations the whole kinship system came to be analyzed as part of an arbitrary system of representation. Anthropology is freed from the natural sciences and moved into the realm of cultural signs or symbols that can be studied within a wider semiology whose scientific rigor is underwritten by the structural linguistic model. Lévi-Strauss identified the incest taboo as a universal constant, implying that the structure uncovered by anthropology is not spatially and temporally specific to one culture but has a universal, atemporal status.

A further key development within French structuralism occurred with the adoption by Lacanian psychoanalysis of the Lévi-Straussian notion of symbolic structure and the recourse to Saussurean and Jakobsonian distinctions to theorize the formal structure of the unconscious. Although Jacques Lacan stressed the need for a "return to Freud" in his famous Rome Address (1953), one might debate how far his account of the unconscious is really like Freud's because it explicitly took over the notion of a symbolic order from Lévi-Strauss. Where the Freudian unconscious implies, to a large degree, a singular substructure proper to the individual in which traces of past experience or trauma are repressed or displaced, the Lévi-Straussian symbolic is transpersonal, intersubjective, and foreign to individual affects, to content, and to historical determination. As a formal structure the symbolic function is, in a sense, an empty site without individual content.

The Lacanian symbolic unconscious is, more than anything, an intersubjective formal structure rather than a subjective one; it is social rather than personal, an inside, which in fact exposes the human subject to the exteriority of an impersonal network of signification. This explains Lacan's constant reference to formalized schema (of desire, of intersubjective recognition) and his tendency in his later period toward the mathematization of unconscious and intersubjective relations. In the 1950s it is his borrowing from linguistics, which is decisive along with his tendency to develop formal schema for the unconscious using linguistic categories. First and foremost is his transformation of Saussure's signifier and signified distinction and the emphasis he placed on the slippage of the one under the other. This supersedes and overturns Saussure's analogy of the signifier and signified being like the two sides of a piece of paper. Lacan also drew on Jakobson's distinction between metaphor and metonymy, which he assimilated to the figures of condensation and displacement used by Freud to describe the dream-work in the *Interpretation of Dreams*. Just as Lévi-Strauss treated kinship relations as a structural whole using the linguistic model as a template, so Lacan, in a very similar move insisted, famously, that the unconscious is structured "like a language."

However, a key difference in emphasis between the Lévi-Straussian and Lacanian concept of the symbolic and of the unconscious subject must be highlighted. One needs to take into account the influence on Lacan's work of Alexandre Kojève's reading of Hegel. Of particular importance here is his formalization of the unconscious intersubjective relation in terms of a dialectic of desire and recognition. Kojève's seminar on the *Phenomenology of Spirit* was given throughout the 1930s and had a great impact on a whole generation of French writers and thinkers. Lacan's emphasis on a break within the Hegelian/Kojèvian dialectic of desire, on its impossible fulfillment, its absence of closure, and its endless repetition, led him to a notion of structure that is far more open-ended, decentered, and disseminated than the universal constant of the Lévi-Straussian symbolic order, implying as it does a structure that is closed, centered on itself, and forming some kind of coherent totality. This fragmentation of the symbolic order, as the site of constant lack, of metonymic slippages and displacements, heralds the future of poststructuralism as it developed in the late 1960s and early 1970s.

As structuralism became a dominant influence in linguistics, anthropology, and psychoanalysis throughout the 1950s, it also began to take a firm foothold within the domain of literature and of literary criticism and theory. This is best seen in the trajectory taken by Roland Barthes, who in many ways represents the key figure of French structuralism in literature throughout the 1950s, 1960s, and 1970s. Barthes's writing perhaps most clearly represents the developments and shifting tendencies of structuralism in France throughout this period. His 1957 work *Mythologies* can be seen as a foundational text. In this work various aspects of French bourgeois culture are dissected, satirized, and subjected to careful analysis of their signifying structure, including beef-steak and chips, margarine adverts, wrestling, the health benefits of red wine—the whole realm of cultural clichés and received ideas that provide the ideological glue of French bourgeois society. In *Mythologies* Barthes looked at the formal structure of these cultural phenomena but did so in order to diagnose ideological forms of meaning, in order to dissect the way in which certain mass media messages "invert culture into nature" as he put it. By this he meant the turning of ideological historical forms into apparent natural and timeless essences. Barthes borrowed from the Saussurean model of signification, which bases itself on the relation between signifier and signified, but introduced another level of signification allowing social sign systems to be formalized in a broader manner. In the seminal theoretical essay, which brings together the pieces of *Mythologies*, "Le Mythe Aujourd'hui," Barthes outlined a structure (Fig. 2) whereby the initial signifier and signified of a cultural message (a linguistic or visual sign) together form a signifier that combines with a further ideological signified to form a mythological sign. By doing this, he showed the way in which a strictly linguistic system can be integrated into and act as the building block for wider cultural sign systems and provided the basis for the analysis of such systems in the discourse of semiology.

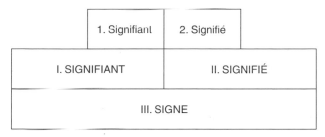

Figure 2. Barthes's analysis of myth.

This gesture is extended into the domain of literary analysis in a number of Barthes's texts published throughout the late 1950s and 1960s, culminating with the publication of *Critique et Vérité* and "Introduction à l'analyse structurale des récits," published in 1966. In the latter text Barthes attempted to formulate an underlying "grammar" of narrative, which would act as a governing law, or structure, for the production of narratives in general. With narrative, Barthes writes, we are confronted with a heterogeneity of forms and examples, just as Saussure was confronted with the heterogeneity of speech acts when he came to develop the concept of general linguistics. Barthes, like Saussure, was searching for the *langue* that would govern the production of individual narratives (the *parole* of each literary text). The structural analysis of literature must therefore seek a combinatory scheme, an implicit system of rules and units that make narrative possible in its most general and universal self.

In order to pursue, this Barthes borrowed from structural linguistics, specifically that of Emile Benveniste, and took over the concept of levels of description. Where the linguist talks about phonetic, phonological, or grammatical levels of analysis, so in the study of narrative Barthes talks of narrative levels and of relations between elements on the same level (known as distributional) as well as relations between elements on different levels (known as relational). Barthes identified three levels within narrative, that of *functions*, of *actions*, and of *narration*, and proceeded by breaking narrative down into units (i.e., segments of the story), which can then be isolated to show the way in which they combine with other elements. Crucially Barthes posed the question of how units combine both distributionally and relationally to build up narrative in the same way as a sentence is built up from its respective units. He identified a number of different functions: *nuclei*, *catalyzers*, *indices*, and *informants*. *Nuclei* articulate primary points of the narrative, which set chains of events off; *catalyzers* give momentum and carry the story forward; *indices* correspond to elements that signify or connote more diffuse cultural meanings; and informants simply supply general information. Barthes's formalization of narrative structures here betrays the influence of a number of key structuralist figures whose work he brings together in a broader synthesis, figures such as Emile Benveniste, previously mentioned, but also Algirdas-Julian Greimas and Tvetan Todorov. This attempt to outline an overarching structural typology of narrative is developed much further in other works, in particular by Todorov and by Gérard Genette, both of whom offer much more highly developed and sophisticated accounts in texts such as *Poétique de la prose* (Todorov, 1971) and *Figures I, II*, and *III* (Genette, 1966, 1969, 1972).

The fate of structuralism within the wider intellectual field (for example, the disciplines of philosophy, sociology, and political theory) is much more diffuse and much less reliant on the importation of specific categories and distinctions from linguistics. The French historian of structuralism, François Dosse, identifies a broader category, aside from developments in literature, anthropology, and psychoanalysis, which could be termed *historical* or *epistemic* structuralism and which would include, among others, the work of Louis Althusser, that of the sociologist Pierre Bourdieu, and of philosophers such as Michel Foucault and Jacques Derrida. It is important to note that the French, unlike the English-speaking world, tend not to differentiate between structuralism and poststructuralism but view developments in the late 1960s and early 1970s in a continuum with what went before, albeit in terms of a notion of structure that is more historically contingent, decentered, and open-ended.

The work of Foucault most clearly exemplifies the difficulty of situating philosophical developments within the domain of structuralism proper or within any clear distinction between structuralism and poststructuralism. Foucault's early work on madness (*Histoire de de la Folie* [1961]) bears the mark of manifold influences, for example, his training in philosophy, where the importance of Hegel, Nietzsche, Husserl, and Heidegger are paramount, or indeed his interest in literature and literary–philosophical experimentation, in particular the writing of Raymond Roussel and above all that of Maurice Blanchot. The specifically structural aspects of his work on madness have their roots in his early admiration for the psychoanalysis of Jacques Lacan and, in particular, owe much to the work on myth carried out by Georges Dumézil (a figure whose writing on myth is explicitly structural but who consistently remained at a distance from developments within linguistics). In *Histoire de la folie* Foucault gives a history of Western European culture and thought in which madness appears, not as an autonomous phenomenon, as an independent entity or substance, but rather as a function of a complex and historically contingent series of discourses, in which the principle of reason is valorized and unreason or the irrational is devalorized, marginalized, and excluded. History, here, unfolds as a series of discursive (or as Foucault will later say, "epistemic") shifts in which madness and reason function interdependently and in which specific historical developments (for example, the incarceration of the mad within institutions) can be seen as a product of these broader discursive shifts. Crucially, Foucault's aim is to historicize the valorization of reason in Western culture, to displace the claims it makes to universality and generality, and through this to revalorize all that has been marginalized and excluded within this tradition.

Foucault's work has been explicitly associated with the development of structuralism in France, insofar as it put an end to the hegemony enjoyed by Sartrian existentialism throughout the 1950s and more generally marked the end of phenomenology as the dominant tradition within French philosophy. Yet it is clear that the emphasis his work on madness places on the historical contingency of discursive structures, and on all that these structures exclude or marginalize, prefigures to a very large degree the developments of poststructuralism.

The history of structuralism in France, from its origins in sociology, phenomenology, and linguistics, to its dominance in the domains of anthropology, psychoanalysis, literary theory, and philosophy, is both diffuse and complex. A clear movement can be discerned, however, from the emphasis on structure as an universal, invariant, and atemporal condition of possibility, to one that is far more diffuse, disseminated, and historically finite. Often controversial in the way in which it brackets off both individual experience and reference to an empirical world, structuralism has nevertheless been one of the most influential forms of thought in the twentieth century.

IAN JAMES

See also **Louis Althusser; Roland Barthes; Emile Benveniste; Maurice Blanchot; Jacques Derrida; Georges Dumezil; Emile Durkheim; Michel Foucault; Algirdas Greimas; Alexandre Kojeve; Jacques Lacan; Claude Lévi-Strauss; Marcel Mauss**

Further Reading

Barthes, R., "The Death of the Author" and "From work to Text," in *Image Music Text*. London: Fontana, 1977

Barthes, R., *S/Z*, Paris: Seuil, 1970; as translated by R. Miller, Oxford: Blackwell, 1990

Barthes, R., *Le Plaisir du texte*, Paris: Seuil, 1973; The pleasure of the text as translated by R. Miller, New York: Noonday, 1975

Barthes, R., *Roland Barthes par Roland Barthes*, Paris: Seuil, 1975; Roland Barthes by Roland Barthes as translated by R. Howard, London: Macmillan, 1977

Deleuze, G., *Différence et répétition*, Paris: P.U.F., 1968; Difference and Repetition translated by P. Patton, London: Athlone 1994

Deleuze, G., *Logique du sens*, Paris: Minuit 1969; Logic of sense translated by M. Lester, London: Athlone, 1990

Deleuze, G., and F. Guattari, *L'Anti-Œdipe*, Paris: Minuit, 1972/73; Anti-œdipus as translated by R. Hurley, M. Seem, and H. Lane, London: Athlone 1984

Deleuze, G., and F. Guattari, *Mille Plateaux*, Paris: Minuit, 1980; A Thousand Plateaus as translated by B. Massumi, Minneapolis: University of Minnesota Press, 1987

Deleuze, G., "A quoi reconnaît-on le structuralisme?" in *La Philosophie au XXième siècle*, edited by F. Châtelet, Paris: Hachette, 1973

Derrida, J., *La Voix et le phénomène*, Paris: P.U.F., 1967

Derrida, J., *De la grammatologie*, Paris: Minuit, 1967; of grammatology as translated by G. C. Spivak, Baltimore and London: Johns Hopkins University Press, 1997

Derrida, J., "La Structure, le signe et le jeu dans le discours des science humaines," in *Écriture et la différence*, Paris: Seuil, 1967; writing and difference as translated by A. Bass, Chicago: University of Chicago Press, 1978

Derrida, J., *Marges de la philosophie*, Paris: Minuit, 1972; Margins of Philosophy as translated by A. Bass, Brighton: Harvester Press, 1982

Kristeva, J., *La Révolution du langage poétique*, Paris: Seuil, 1974; Revolution in poetic language as translated by M. Waller, New York: Columbia University Press, 1984

Lyotard, J.-F., *Discours, figure*, Paris: Klincksieck, 1971

Lyotard, J.-F., *L'Economie Libidinale*, Paris: Minuit, 1974

SUARÈS, ANDRÉ
Poet, Novelist, Essayist

The work of André Suarès is permeated by an aesthetic aristocratism, which has for a long time confined it to a specialist readership. Suarès was a contemporary of Claudel, Gide, and Francis Jammes. However, his symbolist-inspired style was saturated with metaphors, like Saint Pol-Roux's poetry. The sustained intensity of his writing required the reader to make a constant effort of concentration. For Suarès, art was an absolute vocation that burned and consumed its author's life. His motto was: "To write is to put oneself on trial." Hence, Suarès often postured as the heroic man of letters, who was proud, poor, solitary, fiery, and an inveterate traveler. In his work, the feeling of not being understood by his contemporaries was coupled with the idea of belonging to an illustrious genealogy, which included Pascal, Tolstoy, Cervantès, Nietzsche, Dostoevsky, and Goethe. This adulation stemmed on the one hand from the romantic cult of the genius and, on the other, from the Nietzschean apology of the Superman, which accounts for Suarès's truly religious account of energy, in the guise of passion, more often than not. André Gide remarked in his diary: "Our great-nephews will be amazed at the silence that our time managed to maintain or impose around him."

Despite his isolation, Suarès lavishly published his works at the beginning of the century, and his articles were well received by the mainstream French literary press. Charles Péguy published him in the *Cahiers de la Quinzaine*. Suarès's first works still reflected a symbolist sensibility, tinged with mystical accents: *Images de la grandeur* (Images of greatness) (1901), *Le Livre de l'émeraude* (The Emerald Book) (1902), and *Sur la mort de mon frère* (On my Brother's Death) (1904). In the poet's imagination, Brittany appeared as a postromantic land, already marked by a sense of tragic nihilism. Suarès's poetry displayed a great range of symbolist features. Heavily adorned at times, his poetic writing would often veer to the prose poem or adopt the epistolary form, as in *Caprices* (1977). The publication of *Bouclier du zodiaque* (Shield of the Zodiac) in 1907 first established his reputation as a poet, although his prolixity and effervescent style made Suarès more comfortable with the prose of essay writing. At some point he was tempted to adopt a Celtic identity and publish under the pseudonym of Caërdal. Further isolated by the war, he corresponded with Jean de Boschère and Henri Dommartin. The latter published a monographic study of Suarès as early as 1913. The poet was already fascinated by notions of suffering, contradiction, and self-pride. Art to him was a sacrifice and an act of sainthood.

Like Barrès, Suarès was a great portrait and landscape painter. As a visual artist, he produced a vast array of sketches, travel diaries, letters, and articles on his favorite haunts: Brittany, Italy, and Provence. In this vein, *Marsiho* (1931), devoted to Marseille, provided a baroque and colorful description of the city, which resembled the author and in which he had spent his childhood. The incursions into the geography of the city, its working-class districts, and its history combined to create a paradoxical and vibrant vision. Suarès's daring, his sensuality, and his eroticism stood out in sharp contrast to the reserved style of the classical writers of his time.

In fact, the excessive and intense nature of Suarès's writing was splendidly suited to his subject. *Provence* (1925) and *Temples grecs, maisons des Dieux* (Greek Temples, Homes of the Gods, 1937) revealed a more intimate and more confidential narrator, who had remained passionate, but also showed a great stylistic mastery of the French language. Mythology was always present in his descriptions of Provence or of Italy. Whether he happened to be in Arles or in Aix-en-Provence, Suarès pursued his long declaration of love to the Greek and Latin Provence, while nevertheless looking for the traces of Van Gogh's and Gauguin's passage through Arles. Even if his gaze was clearly guided by the antiquity, Suarès possessed the qualities of a surprising and lucid observer, someone who paid attention to the transformations of his time and was a great naturalist and a connoisseur of the plant world. The paradox of the ancient and the modern runs through his works. Suarès cannot be confined to the framework of the Mediterranean writers. He was also the author of an essay on Paris, *Cité, nef de Paris* (The Cité, the Nave of Paris, 1933), which enjoyed a very good reception at the time and displayed the same stylistic mastery as his writings on Provence.

Sketches of great personalities were another recurrent topic of Suarès's work. The literary essay provided Suarès with a renewed opportunity to create tortured and passionate artists' portraits, in which he put a lot of his own personality. In *Trois hommes (Pascal, Ibsen, Dostoïewski)* (Three Men: Pascal, Ibsen, Dostoevsky), published in 1913 and, much later, in *Trois grands vivants (Pascal, Tolstoï, Baudelaire)* (Three Great Living Artists: Pascal, Tolstoy, Baudelaire), published in 1938, Suarès gave free rein to his vision of the tragic and passionate genius. These portraits reveal his fascination with Christian asceticism and the devastating impact of Dostoevsky's nihilistic ideas. Suarès's admiration for Pascal can be said to correspond to an aesthetics of suffering that would remain a constant feature of his work. Fortunately, however, starting with 1911, when Suarès discovered Italy, the Mediterranean sensuality gave new impetus to his writing and became the source of inspiration for his book, *Vers Venise* (Towards Venice), 1911, which marked the beginning of a series of essays: *Fiorenza* (Florence) and *Sienne la bien-aimée* (Sienna, the Beloved), eventually collected in *Le Voyage du condottiere* (The *Condottiere*'s Journey or The Mercenary's Journey), published in 1932. Suarès's view of Italy was colored by his immense historical and artistic erudition. Suarès's Italy, like Taine's, is a country of monuments and museums. Nevertheless, his point of view belongs to the tradition of travel writing on Italy, which had been launched by Montaigne, inasmuch as Suarès adopts the position of a Renaissance aesthete. Throughout his journeys from Bâle to Ravenne, which took him to Milan, Cremona, Pavia, Sienna, Verona, Parma, Mantua, and Venise, the "Condottiere of beauty" saw contemporary Italy as reflected by the great figures of painters, sculptors or musicians—Holbein, Leonardo da Vinci, Monteverdi, Corregio. This baroque and sumptuous Italy offers the traveler an opportunity for self-discovery. Art and civilization are but mirrors of the self. They provoke and excite the poet's soul. Each city corresponds, in fact, to a spiritual and metaphysical posture. Suarès's work reminds one of Barrès's lyricism as much as of Nietzsche's Italian writings, but the author of *Le Voyage du condotierre* saturated his text with a wealth of materials that rendered his passionate vision difficult to follow at times. His cult of energy and grandeur excluded any moments of rest or pauses in the narrative. The exalted view of Sienna, where the Condottiere encounters his master, Guido Riccio, confirms the impression that Suarès's aesthetics reflected the transformation of a Christian sensibility. In fact, his style is heavily indebted to the baroque mentality and its excesses. Steeped in history, he represents a mannerism in French literature. It is therefore only natural that Suarès discover his elective affinity with sixteenth- and seventeenth-century Italy. The Condottiere is both a saint of aestheticism and a sensual observer who takes spirituality for passion. *Sienne la bien-aimée* (Sienna the Beloved) praises the reconciliation between the Condottiere and the world. The historical figures of Saint Francis of Assisi and of Catherine of Sienna show the way to charity and plenitude. Beauty responds to the expectation of love. The self-realization within silence, serenity, and harmony becomes manifest in this city and in Guido Riccio's teachings. It would be fair to say that the trilogy of the *Voyage du condottiere* ultimately contains the meaning of Suarès's entire work.

But Suarès was an equally engaging moralist writer. A fervent admirer of Pascal, he was tempted by the fragmentary, swift, and lively form of the aphorism. The author's intelligence was relentlessly exercised, as it applies to psychology as well as to cultural, political, or geographical issues. However, the analysis never became objective. Suarès lets himself be guided by his passions and his sensuality. This duality of intelligence and sensuality in Suarès's perception of the world provided the inspiration for his work, *Hélène chez Archimède* (1949) (Helena at Archimedes's). Helena comes to tempt Archimedes with her beauty and charm. The dialogue between the scholar and the young woman leads to an elaborated analysis of beauty, of its limits, and of the ultimate superiority of intelligence. As a moralist, Suarès increasingly tended to adopt the position of a religious thinker without religion, which involved a religious attitude to spirituality and love. Throughout his life, Suarès continued to reflect on Pascal's work (*Puissance de Pascal*, The Power of Pascal, 1923). This was the theme of his great unfinished work, which he started writing after the war: *Paraclet*, posthumously published in 1998.

It is perhaps difficult to avoid the impression of a thoroughly anachronistic work, given Suarès's fascination with history and his deliberate turning away from modernity and the twentieth-century technical revolution. A contemporary of Cendrars and Apollinaire, he illustrated the opposite reaction to the general admiration that accompanied the advent of technical ingenuity and the emergence of the industrial landscape. Suarès's physical appearance resembled that of a nineteenth-century character or of a musketeer whose long hair and wide-brimmed hat never failed to amaze. However, just like his contemporaries, Julien Benda and Romain Rolland, Suarès was a great European. He published *Le principe Européen* (The European Principle) in 1897. It is from this perspective that he declared his admiration for Goethe and Wagner. But he did not share Rolland's pacifism, and as early as 1934, he started writing violent pamphlets against Hitler, in which he anticipated the dangers of Hitler's Germany. This is the spirit that animates his *Vues sur l'Europe* (Perspectives on Europe) and his *Chroniques* (regular newspaper column) in the *NRF* (*Nouvelle Revue Française*). Suarès's *Vues sur l'Europe* was among the most violent anti-Hitler writings published in the French press. The author provided a lucid analysis of *Mein Kampf*, warning European democracies of the danger of giving in to Hitler. But his impassioned remarks did not find support in the position of the majority of the editors of the *NRF*, whose main concern was not to deepen the political rift between France and Germany.

Suarès continued to denounce the abuses of totalitarian systems and attacked Mussolini's regime, while nevertheless exalting the heroic grandeur of the antifascist struggle. But he never stopped defending the idea of a united Europe, which could integrate national specificities within a distinctive cultural community. His courageous position situated him in the first line of fire when the German troops occupied Paris. His name was included in the Otto lists, which banned the publication of Jewish writers, and of those opposed to the Nazi regime. Under threat following the German military presence in France, Suarès had to leave Paris in 1940 and confront the insecurity of a way of life that would only change after the end of the war. Despite his situation, he never became anti-German. On the contrary, he remained a staunch defender of European unity after the war, launching an appeal to general reconciliation and forgiveness, greeting with emotion Karl Jaspers's dignified personal acknowledgment of the heavy burden of German responsibility.

Suarès's published correspondence forms an important part of his work. The volume that gathers Suarès's correspondence with Claudel and Romain Rolland (*Correspondance André Suarès-Paul Claudel*, 1951), as well as the letters he exchanged with André Gide, Henry Dommartin, Jean de Bosschère, and Jean Paulhan, shed light on the author's personality, who was, at times, overshadowed by an unjust reputation of arrogance and misanthropy. Suarès, in fact, maintained a lifelong relationship with the artistic milieu of his time, in particular with musical circles (as proves his range of works on this topic, *Debussy*— 1922; *Musique et poésie* (Music and poetry)—1928; *Musiciens* (Musicians)—1931. He was one of the first to remark on the value of works by Fauré, Stravinsky, and Roussel. He mounted a vigorous defense of Bach's work, when the public had turned away from him at the beginning of the century. In the domain of visual arts, Suarès collaborated with the sculptor Antoine Bourdelle, as well as with the painters Georges Rouault and Maurice Denis, for the illustration of some of his works. Suarès was also one of the first to defend Picasso's work.

The author of approximately 100 published volumes, as well as of an important unpublished posthumous work, André Suarès deserves to be read and rediscovered by present-day audiences. Although in France he was awarded Le Grand Prix of Paris, he remains a largely unknown writer. Poet, moralist, novelist, essayist, and political writer, Suarès could be rightly considered as a great writer of the twentieth century.

OLIVIER SALAZAR-FERRER

See also **Maurice Barres; Julien Benda; Andre Gide; Jean Paulhan**

Biography

Suarès was born in Marseille on June 12, 1868. He authored nearly 100 books during his life and was awarded Le Grand Prix of Paris. He died in Saint-Maur-des-Fossés on September 7, 1948.

Selected Works

Airs, Cinq livres de poèmes, 1900
Images de la grandeur, 1901
Le livre de l'émeraude, 1902
Sur la mort de mon frère, 1904
Bouclier du zodiaque, 1907
Dostoiewski, 1912
Cressida, 1913
Trois hommes (Pascal, Ibsen, Dostoiewski), 1913
Cervantès, 1916
Puissance de Pascal, 1923
Provence, 1925
Haï Kaï d'Occident, 1926
Art de vivre, 1928
Musique et poésie, 1928
Vues sur l'Europe, 1929
Marsiho, 1931
Le voyage du condottiere, 1932
Cité, nef de Paris, 1933
Le Crépuscule sur la mer, 1933
Vues sur Napoléon, 1933

Temples grecs, maisons des Dieux 1937
Cirque, 1939
Hélène chez Archimède, 1949
Présentation de la France, 1950
Caprices, Poèmes inédits, 1977

SUBJECT (SELF AND SUBJECTIVITY)

The question of the subject marks one of the central concerns of French thought in the twentieth century. Over the years, the concept of the subject has been interrogated, dislocated, deconstructed, and repositioned according to myriad different theoretical frameworks. This critique has taken many different forms and has been directed toward different aspects of the subject. It has contested the mastery of the subject in relation to authorship and writing, deconstructed its metaphysical primacy in the field of meaning, interrogated the omnipotence of self-consciousness and reason, and undermined its role as historical agent. As a consequence, it has been suggested that the subject has been obliterated or dissolved by an antihumanist discourse, its constitutive function now transferred to the nonsubjective structures of language, discourse, and power. Has the question of the subject now been erased "like a face drawn in the sand at the edge of the sea," as Foucault concluded in his study of the human sciences' preoccupation with the figure of the subject? Or might such a viewpoint ignore the many ways in which contemporary discussions continue to pose the question of the subject anew, bringing forth new figures of thought and being? Contemporary thinkers understand the problem not in terms of an antihumanist gesture, which, as is often claimed, dissolves the subject, but rather with an attention to the paradox of the subject that sustains the problem of the construction of the subject, even when it is deemed absent.

One of the clearest indications of twentieth-century French thought's continued regard for the subject can be found in Jean-Luc Nancy's philosophical project, "Who comes after the subject?" In February 1986, Nancy sent a letter containing this question to nineteen French philosophers, inviting each to respond. The resulting volume of essays presents a wide range of perspectives encompassing not only philosophical ones, but also feminist, psychoanalytic, linguistic, literary, ethical, and political perspectives (Cadava et al., 1991). When we extend our focus beyond a regard for the contemporary, moreover, we find that much of twentieth-century French thought, from Bergson and Marcel, to Sartre and Merleau-Ponty, also presents powerful formulations of self and subjectivity and exhibits a strong regard, in the case of the existentialism and phenomenology of the latter two thinkers, for the embodied existence of the subject and an ontology of social being.

Setting the Scene

In a very general sense, the French preoccupation with rethinking the subject is united in its rejection of the paradigmatic modern formulation of the subject as *subjectum*, namely as the objectifying ground for knowledge and as the foundation for all possible being. Here, the subject appears to serve primarily an epistemological function, delineating the field of intelligibility, appropriating what lies outside itself, and bringing everything within the purview of its own self-consciousness. Although most twentieth-century philosophers would agree that the subject is now a site of inherent rivalry and contestation, it is clear that the construction of a modern, rational subjectivity was inaugurated by the Cartesian thinking subject (underscored by the well-known formulation: *ego cogito ergo sum*, I think therefore I am) and the Kantian transcendental subject of knowledge. Both positions considered the conditions of possibility for knowledge to be antithetical to the particulars of immediate experience and the body, hence establishing a dualism between the affective, embodied life of the subject and the rational capacity of cognition and the intellect.

We can observe the imprints of these twin philosophical positions in French thought in the early decades of the twentieth century, particularly in the idealist philosophy of Lanchelier and Brunschvicg (see Gutting, 2001, for an overview). It was against this intellectualization of the subject, where knowledge resulted not from any sense of lived experience or historical consciousness but from the closed interior of the mind, that the emerging school of existentialism in the 1930s developed its regard for lived subjectivity. Finding their own philosophical heritage of idealism and positivism glaringly insufficient, thinkers such as Sartre and Merleau-Ponty turned toward the phenomenology of the German philosophers Edmund Husserl and Martin Heidegger to find their fundamental reference point for a philosophy of existence. Husserl's efforts to free phenomenology of a naive subjectivism and empiricism and develop a transcendental subjectivity, together with Heidegger's reflections on man as being-in-the-world, offered the groundwork for a new philosophy of the concrete. Later, this regard for Husserl would be augmented by a renewal of Hegelian studies in France introduced by Jean Hyppolite's 1946 translation of the *Phenomenology of Spirit* and particularly by the lecture course of Alexandre Kojève (1933 and 1939). This seminar was, at various points, attended by Jacques Lacan, George Bataille, Pierre Klossowski, Andre Breton, Sartre, Merleau-Ponty, and Raymond Queneau, who transcribed and edited the lecture course (Kojève, 1980). Kojève's prioritizing of the master–slave dialectic in Hegel's *Phenomenology*, his emphasis on an anthropological conception of history, and his incorporation of Heideggerian notions of death and finitude introduced a view of the subject of desire, immersed in the world of history and action and requiring recognition by others to develop self-consciousness and knowledge. Thus, it was initially through an engagement with German philosophy that the concept of the subject was configured.

The Worldly Subject

The contribution of Jean-Paul Sartre to the question of the subject cannot be underestimated. In *The Transcendence of the Ego* (1936), Sartre claims that Descartes had ignored the prereflective life of consciousness, instead identifying consciousness or ego with the reflective act of thought. Following Husserl, Sartre argued that consciousness is not in itself some *thing* or substance with clear attributes or properties; it is always intentional and directed toward objects outside it. In this way, consciousness exists primarily as a form of awareness of the way in which it relates to the world and to others. We first know something of our self not through an act of self-reflection but through our awareness of objects in the world. Consciousness thus implies an internal relation with itself, but it cannot really be known in itself. Knowledge is the result of engagement with objects as they become objects *of* consciousness rather than being the result of reflection of consciousness upon *itself*. In *Being and Nothingness* (1943), Sartre pursued the phenomenological implications of this formulation of consciousness, and in *Existentialism and Humanism* (1946) the ethico-political implication are set out. Individuals do not have a predetermined nature or essence that defines them prior to their engagement in the world: "Man first of all exists, surges up in the world—and defines himself afterwards." Sartre's radical subjectivism requires that every individual be free to choose what they will become and take responsibility for this choice without conditions. This existential condition is one that all human subjects have in common. Man, in short, is radical freedom, and his reality is human action. The authentic existential subject is one who embraces its own freedom as the fundamental truth of human existence and as the ultimate goal of an authentic life.

Sartre's attempt to rescue the subject from a purely epistemological function and place it firmly within the world of experience still maintains a sharp distinction between subject and object, whereby even the other is objectified by the singular subject and remains radically distinct. With this dualism, and the notion of radical choice (or free will) underpinning his subjectivism, many of Sartre's commentators identify a residual Cartesianism in his conception of the subject. It was not until the structuralist movement, particularly through the call for the "dissolution of man" presented by Lévi-Strauss, and Althusser's rejection of Sartre's bourgeois human subject and the development of a notion of history as a "process without a subject," that Sartre's thought would finally fall out of favor. However, most of the damage was already done by 1946 when Heidegger presented French philosophers with his "Letter on Humanism." Here he attempted to distance his perspective from that of Sartre, claiming that the revival of anthropological humanism (aided by Kojève's reading of Hegel and Heidegger) remained metaphysical. By equating human subjectivity with human existence, Sartre reified *Dasein* (Being) and its ontological relation to the act of thinking and to language, both of which open a path to Being. The function of the subject as foundation and origin of thought and action is not called into question; neither is its continued attachment to an ontotheological framework, where Man ultimately replaces God as the omnipotent being of radical freedom. Unsurprisingly, Heidegger's "Letter" would later add considerable fire to the structuralist call to "dissolve man" and free the human sciences from the metaphysics of the human subject, as well inspire the poststructuralists' decentering of the subject and their genealogical accounts of its formation. Many aspects of structuralist and poststructuralist thought are prefigured in Merleau-Ponty's phenomenological approach to the subject. Merleau-Ponty points to the limits of dualist ontologies like Sartre's, although his starting point of stressing the inextricable relation between consciousness and world is quite similar. He also rejects the idealist tendencies of Husserl who, by isolating subjectivity from the world through the phenomenological reduction, draws his analysis away from our bodily being in the world from which the subject cannot be unshackled. In *The Phenomenology of Perception* (1945), Merleau-Ponty argues that it is prepredicative bodily perceptions that structure the objects of experience rather than the intuitions of a transcendental subjectivity. The task of an existential phenomenology is to locate and express this primordial rationality of embodied perception as an aspect of our intersubjective experience. In the posthumously published notes *The Visible and the Invisible*, this dimension of immanent, embodied perception is attached to Nature, an anonymous, prereflective field of forces that Merleau-Ponty describes as "the Flesh" or "raw Being." Imbued with the property of genesis or becoming, the Flesh inscribes the subject into the world; both self and other

are embodiments of Nature. Thus there is a unity or a reversibility within and between body and mind and between subject and nature or Flesh. Does Merleau-Ponty here establish an anonymous collective mind, an impersonal subject that comes to stand in for the metaphysical subject? Or should we rather view his later insistence on an incarnate structure of being, a *Logos* of language from which all creative expression stems and as his high regard for Lévi-Strauss's science of mythology, as diverse attempts to seal the constitution of intersubjectivity within nonsubjective structures?

The Death Knell of Subjectivity?

By introducing aspects of structuralism into his mature philosophy, Merleau-Ponty was mobilizing those very authorities that were to be invoked against all forms of phenomenology after 1960 (Saussure, Lévi-Strauss). It is also at this point that we can note the decline of interest in Hegel and a turn to Nietzsche, and for some, Spinoza. Both philosophers could be viewed as anticipating the antihumanist gesture of structuralism that translates the constituting power of the human subject into a complex system of differential relations or anonymous forces, be they language, power, ideology, or discourse. No longer the origin of linguistic form and expression, the active *praxis* of history, the source of power, or the foundation of truth and certainty, structuralist antihumanism questions the metaphysical properties of the subject and reconfigures its form and status.

The tidal effects of structuralism extend far into the human sciences, from philosophy to literature, semiology to politics and psychoanalysis. One element that can give unity to this interdisciplinary venture of the 1960s is the focus on language as a structure with its own rules of operation, application, and modes of signification such that the constitution of language and the sign required no recourse to an enunciating subject as author of speech. No longer can language be viewed as easily manipulated and its content determined by the creativity of consciousness; instead the imprint of consciousness on language is faint and without weight. The structural linguistics of Saussure turned to focus on the division between signifier (sound-image) and signified (the concept) within signification itself, finding no natural, pregiven relationship between them. For Saussure, language is an arbitrary system, based on the difference rather than the simple coincidence between signifier and signified. If Benveniste continued to focus on the role of subjectivity in language, his analyses drew attention to the role and function of linguistic rules in the constitution of pronouns. The foundation of subjectivity is really built on its *position* in language, specifically its position in the I-You polarity and their relation to the third person (the neutral or "middle voice"). Benveniste recognized that the instance of discourse (as the *practical enactment* of language) allowed for infinite variety in content and interpretation, thus lending language its fictive or ironic dimension.

The influence of these reflections on language (which also extend to the Heideggerian concern for the relation of language to being) can be seen in the writings of Maurice Blanchot, Roland Barthes, and Jacques Lacan, where the authorial subject is dissolved and a new regard for the agency of language is established. In *The Space of Literature* (1955), a work that was to be of profound influence on the early Foucault, Blanchot's regard is for the limits of language and for a poetic space that may efface the presence of authorial identity and personality. Here, language circles the author, who must give up the claim to expressive writing in the first person and enter the anonymous field of language. Kafka, Blanchot tells us, entered literature only when he replaced the I with the neutral, intransitive "he." Roland Barthes also rejects the idea of the text as the expression of authorial intention; writing is dispersed amidst the multiple discourses that make up the text. It is the reader, rather than the writer, who unifies the text by taking up a position in relation to it, a reader who is not merely constituted by the ideological and cultural codes in a given society (as Althusser claims of the subject of ideology). In *The Pleasure of the Text* (1973), Barthes describes a transgressive experience of the text, *jouissance*, where language exceeds all representational limits and the subject, as reader, disappears in the aesthetic experience of the text.

Both of these perspectives indicate the effects of the structuralist repositioning of the subject in relation to language, but it is the conjoining of psychoanalysis with structural linguistics in the writings of Jacques Lacan that has had greatest influence. Irigaray, Kristeva, and Castoriadis, for example, each developed conceptions of subjectivity out of their critical disengagements with the controversial Lacanian school (Roudinesco 1997). In common with many French philosophers, Lacan decenters the Cartesian *cogito*, a form of selfhood he associates with the birth of the modern ego. His early essay, "The Mirror Stage," distinguishes between the subject as ego or I (*moi*) and the primordial being of the subject (*je*), which lies beyond the ego and may be approached through analysis. There is no thinking subject prior to the ego's identification with an image. The event of the mirror stage offers the discordant being its first apprehension of bodily unity. It allows the fragmented being to become an I and to be harnessed to an ontological structure according to

which it may think, perceive, and recognize itself as a permanent, coherent structure. This event, however, really situates the instance of the ego in a line of fiction where it misrecognizes the split or discordance (*Spaltung*), which characterizes its formation and renders its experience one of profound lack. Whereas the imaginary ego may try to solder this discordance and fill out the void created within itself by seeking out the objects of its desire, plenitude and fulfillment remain impossible goals to achieve. Lacan's subject is first and foremost a speaking being, and the conditions of possibility for speech are given by the *symbolic* order of language. Unlike Saussure, Lacan describes a relation of noncorrespondence between word and thing such that the signifier may become polysemic and resistant to meaning. Most cultural signs do reflect the dominant meanings of the community, but the signifying chain also allows signifiers the possibility of mobility and transgression. It is here, within the gaps in meaning that the unconscious finds expression. It haunts the subject who is reduced to being a signifier by taking up a place in the symbolic order, and its language is able to make present the absence of being and the lack of the subject. It is this linguistic aspect of his account that Lacan's critics have rejected, claiming that it gives scant regard for the affective life of the subject (Kristeva, Castoriadis), and that the scopic economy on which the mirror stage is founded is a masculine model that ignores the distinct emergence of feminine subjectivity (Irigaray).

The Paradox of the Subject

This attention to the realm of language and the ontological status of subjectivity continues in the writings of Jacques Derrida, although here there is no attempt to establish a theory of the subject. Rather, the project of deconstruction is one of strategically questioning the foundations of language and the conditions governing the possibility of conceptualization. Deconstruction does not simply break with the discourse of the subject but tries to locate and scrutinize that which remains excluded in the construction of the subject. Through its vigilant readings and critiques, deconstruction seeks to undo forms of discourse that center the subject in relation to knowledge using the metaphysical qualities of self-presence, transparency, and identity to confirm its authorship. Such representational thinking is built on the suppression of difference and alterity. Yet it is difference (*différance*) that produces the very possibility of philosophical discourse (Derrida, 1981). It envelops the subject, forever preventing and stalling its attempts to *become* a subject and ensuring that the moment of closure or containment of subjectivity (as ego, as *subjectum*) never quite arrives. In this way, the deconstruction of the subject recognizes that the subject's condition of possibility is also the condition of its *impossibility*. A paradox thus lies at the heart of the subject: the gesture that summons it into existence and gives it form is also one that establishes its eccentric existence. The subject only persists through a certain ceasing to be.

This paradox at the heart of subjectivity can now be expressed more clearly. On the one hand, contemporary theorists of subjectivity wish to undermine, dislocate, and deconstruct the subject and, on the other hand, to attend to its insistence and ineluctable significance in order to reconfigure it in some way (for example, recall Nancy's question: "Who comes *after* the subject?"). Such a paradox must not, however, be confused with the desire on the part of the human sciences to discover and name the innermost recesses of subjectivity and hence restore its centrality and stability. Such an epistemological project is doomed from the start, as Foucault reminds us in *The Order of Things*, with the image of the subject as an empirico-transcendental doublet (at once an empirical subject and a transcendental object of knowledge) trying to gain self-knowledge when its stability and self-certainty are open to question. Are we to understand *all* the strategies to (dis)locate and (de)construct the subject advanced by the human sciences (including those set out earlier) as merely attempts to fill out the subject to a state of plenitude of meaning once again? Are all reflections on the subject to founder and fall back into this kind of metaphysical subjectivism?

In the case of the writings of Michel Foucault, the answer must be a resounding "no." As with Derrida's strategic questioning of the constitutive power of the subject, we do not receive any clear solutions. In his early archaeological analyses, Foucault describes an anonymous order of discourse where the rules governing statements create the conditions for sense and impose certain limits on speech, thought, and action. Nonetheless, if (following structuralism) the subject here becomes an effect of discourse, it is not wholly determined. Instead, a struggle for subjectification occurs, and the subject must be made to occupy and function according to these discursive rules. The body must inscribe within itself the principle of subjection. As Foucault's writings change their emphasis to a genealogical analysis of the body and power, this aspect of struggle as resistance and transgression accompanies the hollowing out of an interiority and may also be a site of transformation and possibility: a becoming other of the subject. In this way, Foucault offers us no clear account of the subject. Neither constitutive nor constituted; without the power of determination, and yet not quite determined effect of discourse, structure, and

power, the subject must live out this paradox or vacillation, which takes the place of its constitutive power.

Each of the perspectives considered previously point to the subject as an ineluctable philosophical problem. Consequently, the subject cannot simply disappear or dissolve with the antihumanist gesture of structuralism. This humanist antihumanist dichotomy, which is so often used to characterize debates around the problem of the subject, is an unhelpful one. Such a principle of reversal: *either* constitutive origin *or* determined effect, cannot recognize that the continued relevance of the subject does not issue in its delayed return or resurrection. The subject is not simply recuperated by contemporary French thought; instead, it endures or persists in the radical problematization of its conditions of existence and possibility. It is in such acts of questioning that the disruptive effects of the subject can be found.

CAROLINE WILLIAMS

See also **Louis Althusser; Roland Barthes; Emile Benveniste; Henri Bergson; Maurice Blanchot; Leon Brunschvicg; Cornelius Castoriadis; Jacques Derrida; Michel Foucault; Luce Irigaray; Alexandre Kojève; Julia Kristeva; Jacques Lacan; Claude Lévi-Strauss; Gabriel Marcel; Maurice Merleau-Ponty; Jean-Luc Nancy; Jean-Paul Sartre; Ferdinand de Saussure**

Selected Works

Barthes, Roland, *Selected Writings*, edited by Susan Sontag, 1983

Benveniste, Emile, *Problems in General Linguistics*, translated by Mary Elizabeth Meek, 1971

Blanchot, Maurice, *The Space of Literature*, translated by Ann Smock, 1982

Derrida, Jacques, " 'Eating Well,' or the Calculation of the Subject: An Interview with Jacques Derrida" (conducted by Jean-Luc Nancy), in *Who Comes After the Subject?*, translated by Peter Connor and Avital Ronell, edited by Eduardo Cadava, Peter Connor, and Jean-Luc Nancy, 1991

Derrida Jacques, *Positions*, translated by Alan Bass, 1981

Derrida Jacques, *Margins of Philosophy*, translated by Alan Bass, 1982

Foucault, Michel, *The Archaeology of Knowledge*, translated by Alan Sheridan, 1973

Foucault, Michel, "The Subject and Power," in *Michel Foucault: Beyond Structuralism and Hermeneutics*, edited by Hubert Dreyfus and Paul Rabinow, 1982

Heidegger, Martin, "Letter on Humanism," in *Basic Writings*, translated by David Farrell Krell, 1977

Irigaray, Luce, *This Sex Which Is Not One*, translated by Catherine Porter with Caroline Burke, 1977

Kojève, Alexandre, *Introduction to the Reading of Hegel*, translated by James Nichols, 1980

Lacan, Jacques, *Écrits: A Selection*, translated by Alan Sheridan, 1989

Merleau-Ponty, Maurice, *The Phenomenology of Perception*, translated by Colin Smith, 1962

Merleau-Ponty, Maurice, *The Visible and the Invisible*, translated by Alphonso Lingus, 1968
Sartre, Jean-Paul, *The Transcendence of the Ego*, translated by Forrest Williams and Robert Kirkpatrick, 1957
Sartre, Jean-Paul, *Existentialism Is a Humanism*, translated by Philip Mairet, 1948
Saussure, Ferdinand de, *Course in General Linguistics*, translated by Wade Baskin, 1974

Further Reading

Butler, Judith, *Subjects of Desire: Hegelian Reflections in Twentieth Century France*, New York: Columbia University Press, 1987
Cadava, Eduardo, Peter Connor, and Jean-Luc Nancy, *Who Comes After the Subject?* London: Routledge, 1991
Critchley, Simon and Peter Dews, (editors), *Deconstructive Subjectivities*, Albany, NY: SUNY Press, 1996
Descombes, Vincent, *Modern French Philosophy*, translated by L. Scott-Fox and J.M. Harding, Cambridge: Cambridge University Press, 1980
Gutting, Gary, *French Philosophy in the Twentieth Century*, Cambridge: Cambridge University Press, 2001
Macksey, R. and E. Donato, (editors), *The Structuralist Controversy: The Languages of Criticism and the Sciences of Man*, Baltimore: The John Hopkins University Press, 1972
Rockmore, Tom, *Heidegger and French Philosophy: Humanism, Antihumanism and Being*, London: Routledge, 1995
Roth, Michael, *Knowing and History: Appropriations of Hegel in Twentieth-Century France*, Ithaca, NY: Cornell University Press, 1988
Roudinesco, Elizabeth, *A History of Psychoanalysis in France 1925–1985*, translated by Jeffrey Mehlman, London: Free Association Books, 1990
Silverman, Hugh, *Questioning Foundations: Truth/Subjectivity/Culture*, London: Routledge, 1993
Williams, Caroline, *Contemporary French Philosophy: Modernity and the Persistence of the Subject*, London: Athlone Press, 2001

SURREALISM

Surrealism was a literary and artistic movement originating in Paris in the early 1920s. It rejected social, moral, and logical conventions and sought to revolutionize art, literature, and life in the name of freedom, desire, and revolt. It emerged from the social upheaval of post–First World War Europe (the term was invented by Apollinaire in 1917) and more especially from Dadaism, founded in Zurich in 1915, which rejected traditional Western values and promoted the irrational and the absurd through a series of "antiartistic" events based on provocation and profanation. In 1922, a group around Breton broke with the negative tactics of Dada, whose scandals were running the risk of becoming institutionalized, in order to explore a positive form of revolt. The year 1924 marked the official launch of the movement, with Aragon's *Une vague de rêves* (A Wave of Dreams) that charts the activities of the group, Breton's first *Manifeste du surréalisme* (First Manifesto of Surrealism) that defines its philosophical principles, and the launch of the surrealist journal *La Révolution surréaliste* (The Surrealist Revolution). Combining Rimbaud's injunction to "Change life," Marx's "Transform the world," and the Marquis de Sade's libertarian ethos, the surrealists sought the liberation of the individual and the transformation of society. They were active in the fields of art, literature, film, philosophy, and politics. Above all, however, they formed "a community of ethical views" (Toyen). The mostly male group was made up of writers (Aragon, Artaud, Cahun, Desnos, Eluard, Péret, Soupault, and others) and artists (including Dali, Ernst, Magritte, Malkine, Miró, later Dominguez, Matta, Paalen), although its membership fluctuated with ideological and personal conflicts and crises, leading to defections and exclusions, as well as new directions for the group. In the 1930s it gained an international dimension with groups in countries such as Belgium (Magritte, Delvaux), Czechoslovakia (Styrsky, Toyen), Egypt (Henein), England (Nash, Penrose), Latin America (Paz), Martinique (Césaire), and Yugoslavia (Ristich). The "heroic period" (Nadeau) of surrealism lasted until 1940, when several of its members, including Breton, went into exile to escape occupied France, although surrealist activities continued during the war years in New York, Mexico, and Paris. The group was re-formed after 1945 with a new generation of members (including Bédouin, Mansour, Pierre, and Schuster). Following Breton's death in 1966, the group was "auto-dissolved" in 1969. Surrealist groups continue to be active, however, in cities like Paris, Prague, Sao Paulo, and Chicago.

From the outset the surrealists stressed the experimental and scientific character of their activities. They set up a "Bureau des recherches surréalistes," run by Artaud, and researched the unconscious (automatism, hypnosis, dream) in order to explore the "real functioning of the mind" (Breton). The journal *La Révolution surréaliste* (1924–1929), edited by Artaud then Breton, published collective texts, poems, surveys (on suicide, sexuality), as well as drawings, photographs, and paintings.

Surrealist theoretical declarations can appear paradoxical, contradictory, and diverse. The surrealists rejected the notion of a school with a fixed body of doctrine. Surrealism was considered as an open quest continuously redefining itself in terms of a project ("Surrealism is what will be," 1947). Hence, in his 1924 *Manifeste*, Breton first defined the surrealist quest as "the future resolution of these two states of dream and reality, seemingly contradictory, into a kind of absolute reality, a surreality," drawing on the work of Freud to affirm the continuity and interaction between waking life and dreams. Underlining the scientific nature of his text, he gave a dictionary-like definition of surrealism grounded in psychiatry: "Surrealism, *noun, masc.*: pure psychic automatism by which it is proposed to express, either verbally or by writing, or by any other means, the real functioning of thought. Thought dictated outside any control by reason or any moral or aesthetic consideration." As medical students during the 1914–18 war, Aragon and Breton had received psychiatric training and were influenced by Janet's concept of psychic automatism, Myer's "subliminal self," and Freud's theories of the unconscious and its relation to dreams. However, although the surrealists and Freud shared an interest in the unconscious, their aims differed radically. Freudian psychoanalysis, considering the manifest content of dreams as symptoms that allow the analyst to recover their latent content and hence the source of the neurosis, has a therapeutic aim, the reintegration of the individual into society. The surrealists, on the other hand, were interested in dreams and free association as a means of freeing the individual's creative powers, and they exploited the manifest dream material for poetic and artistic ends. Breton also presented automatism as a praxis, even providing instructions on how to write an automatic text, a method designed to free the mind from all rational or pragmatic considerations and liberate the voice of the unconscious and the language of desire through free associations. Surrealist automatic texts include Breton and Soupault's *Les Champs magnétiques* (1920; The Magnetic Fields), Breton's *Poisson soluble* (1924; Soluble Fish) (to which the *Manifeste* was originally published as an introduction), and Breton and Eluard's *L'Immaculée conception* (1930; The Immaculate Conception). Although Breton later admitted to the relative failure of automatism ("Le Message automatique" [1933; "The Automatic Message]), poetry and prose texts were written using part-automatic processes, by Breton himself (*Clair de terre*, 1923), Desnos (*Corps et biens*, 1930), Eluard (*Capitale de la douleur*, 1926), whereas artists such as Masson, Miró, and Ernst experimented in graphic automatism.

In his *Second Manifeste du surréalisme* (1929; Second Surrealist Manifesto), a polemical text in which he reassessed his earlier definition of surrealism, Breton elaborated on the concept of the surreal as the resolution of opposites, grounding his definition in Hegelian dialectical thought. Surrealism was defined as the search for "un certain point de l'esprit d'où la vie et la mort, le réel et l'imaginaire, le passé et le futur, le communicable et l'incommunicable, le haut et le bas cessent d'être perçus contradictoirement" (a certain mental point where life and death, the real and the imaginary, the past and the future, the communicable and the uncommunicable, high and low, cease to be perceived as contradictory"). Breton's "point de l'esp-

rit" is situated in the past or future, in the nostalgia for a lost pre-Oedipal unity (present in the myth of childhood and the androgyne myth) or the messianic myth of a future totality, identified for a while with the Marxist myth of reconciliation. The surreal is thus considered essentially as a project or possibility. Breton claimed that the dialectical method could be applied to resolve not only social questions, but also the problems of love, madness, and art. Bataille, leader of a dissident group of surrealists, which included Desnos and Leiris, and editor of the journal *Documents* (1929–30), attacked Breton's concept of the dialectic, claiming it was premised on an idealized notion of (romantic) unity. He countered Breton by arguing in favor of an engagement with material or "base" reality and positing a dynamic dialectical process that maintains contradiction between elements. In *Les Vases communicants* (1932; Communicating Vessels), Breton brought together Marx and Freud in his elaboration of dialectical materialism, claiming to have resolved certain contradictions in surrealist doctrine. He also explored the notion of "hasard objectif" (objective chance), based on Hegelian thought and defined as the point of intersection between inner desires and external reality (*Position politique du surréalisme* [1935; Political Position of Surrealism]). During the 1940s and 1950s Breton developed an interest in analogical thought, based on the work of Fourier, alchemy, and the elaboration of a new myth (*Arcane 17*, 1945). Alchemy was the central theme of the 1947 surrealist Paris exhibition, conceived as an initiatory space, and articles linking surrealism with alchemical thought were published in the surrealist journal *Médium* (1952–55). This self-questioning and ferment of surrealist thought testify to its refusal to be retrieved by a single, globalizing definition and to its character as a quest rather than a doctrine.

The surrealists' political position was grounded in their desire to reconcile individual revolt with the needs of the social revolution ("Nous sommes les spécialistes de la révolte" [1924; We are the specialists of revolt]). In their collective declarations and tracts, they denounced all forms of oppression—state, church, family, fatherland, colonialism. After their initial anarchist stance, inherited from Dada, the group adopted Marxist ideology and joined the French Communist Party in 1927. In 1930 their journal, *La Révolution surréaliste*, was superseded by *Le Surréalisme au service de la révolution* (1930–33), marked by a shift toward a more visible political engagement, publishing more political articles and fewer automatic texts and poems and reaffirming positions that were antimilitarist (Char, "Les porcs en liberté" [1930; Pigs in freedom]), anticlerical (Ernst, "Danger de pollution" [1931; Danger of pollution]), and anticolonial ("Ne visitez pas l'Exposition Coloniale" [1931; Don't visit the Colonial Exhibition]). Bunuel and Dali's film *L'Age d'or* mocked church, family, and state, provoking controversy and violent reactions from the Right when first shown in 1930. In spite of their radical positions, the surrealists' relations with the Communist Party were uneasy because they refused to subordinate the surrealist concept of global revolt to the social revolution, which led to charges against them of counter-revolutionary activity. Aragon and Sadoul, however, adopted the party's line on proletarian literature after the Congress of Kharkov (1930) and denounced surrealism as incompatible with dialectical materialism, thus breaking with Breton's group. In *Les Paris sont ouverts* (1934; Place your Bets), Claude Cahun vehemently attacked Aragon's position, advocating the freedom of art against the constraints of socialist realism. Breton's "Limites non frontières du surréalisme" (1936; "Limits not frontiers of surrealism") confirmed the group's adherence to dialectical materialism and the necessity of social revolution, while defending the freedom of "la grande aventure mentale" (the great mental adventure) of poetry and art. In 1935–36 Breton and Bataille collaborated in the Contre-Attaque group of revolutionary antifascist intellectuals, which opposed the reformist policies of the Popular Front and, turning to eighteenth-century revolutionary models, as well as Hegel and Nietzsche, sought a position outside the discourse of Marxist revolutionary thought. In 1938 in Mexico Breton and Trotsky (whose biography of Lenin had first attracted Breton's interest in communism in 1925) wrote a manifesto titled "Pour un art révolutionnaire indépendant" (For an Independent Revolutionary Art), attacking Hitler, Stalin, and bourgeois ideology and defending the freedom of artistic activity: "Ce que nous voulons: l'indépendance de l'art—pour la révolution; la révolution—pour la libération définitive de l'art" (What we want: the independence of art—for the revolution; the revolution—for the definitive liberation of art). In 1938 the surrealists joined the F.I.A.R.I. (Fédération internationale de l'art révolutionnaire indépendant), founded by left-wing intellectuals who sought to steer a revolutionary path free of totalitarianisms of Right and Left. Although the group around Breton retreated from political action during the war years in New York, the surrealists who stayed in Paris were actively involved in Resistance activities (Aragon, Eluard, the Main à Plume group). On the group's return from New York in 1946, Breton, criticized for his nonparticipation in Resistance activities (Tzara, "Le Surréalisme et l'après-guerre" [1947; Surrealism and the Postwar Period]), was politically marginalized. Surrealism as a major movement had been superseded by existentialism, and Sartre and Camus attacked Breton's idealist position. However,

the surrealist group, revitalized in the postwar period by the participation of younger artists and writers, collaborated with revolutionary syndicalist and anarchist groups and continued to support opposition movements against the war in Indochina ("Liberté est un mot vietnamien" [1947; Freedom is a Vietnamese word]), Soviet intervention in Hungary ("Hongrie, soleil levant" [1956; Hungary, rising sun]), and the Algerian War ("Déclaration sur le droit à l'insubordination dans la guerre d'Algérie" [1960; Declaration on the right to insubordination in the Algerian War]).

Surrealism is generally considered primarily as an artistic movement, as testified by the large international surrealist art exhibitions (London, 1936; Paris, 1938, 1947, 1959, and 1965; Mexico, 1940; and New York 1942), its glossy art journal *Minotaure* (1933–39), and the art collections of its members (Breton, Eluard, and Péret had important collections of Oceanic, African, and North American Indian masks and objects). Although visual art was given one footnote in Breton's first *Manifeste, La Révolution surréaliste* reproduced paintings, drawing and photographs. In its pages Max Morise and Pierre Naville initiated a debate questioning the existence of surrealist painting. Breton settled the argument with the publication of "Le Surréalisme et la peinture" (1925–27; Surrealism and Painting), where he rejected the imitation of external reality and favored the exploration of a "purely internal model," that of dream, hallucinatory or fantastic images. Art was considered not as an end in itself—whence Breton's disdain for pictorial techniques or his discussion of painting in terms of poetry (Baudelaire, Rimbaud), the search for a mode of expression "au-delà de la peinture" (beyond painting) (Ernst), or Miró's desire to "assassiner la peinture" (assassinate painting)—but as a means of liberation, thereby seeking to annex the group's artistic activities to surrealism's global liberatory project, beyond purely artistic considerations. The surrealists rejected the pictorial conventions of realism ("l'art à l'école du perroquet" [art parrot-fashion]), turning to non-European art forms, art naïf, the art of the insane, mediumnistic art that, they claimed, are free from the restrictions of established codes and express fundamental impulses.

Surrealist aesthetics—based on the nineteenth-century writer Lautréamont's image "Beau comme la rencontre fortuite, sur une table de dissection, d'un parapluie et d'une machine à coudre" (Beautiful as the chance encounter on a dissecting table of a sewing machine and an umbrella), and on Pierre Reverdy's definition of the image as "une création pure de l'esprit" (1918; a pure creation of the mind)—was first defined in terms of the verbal or visual image as the bringing together of heterogeneous elements, creating a new reality through the collision or *étincelle* (spark)

(Breton) of their encounter. This was later developed in the more radical theory of "la beauté convulsive" (convulsive beauty), a concept of aesthetic paradox rather than dialectical fulfillment, where the copresence of contradictory elements (becoming and being, movement and stasis) is foregrounded (Breton, *Amour fou*, 1937 [Mad Love])

Surrealist art is characterized by a diversity of forms of expression: painting, drawing, photography, collage, objects, sculpture, found objects; and of styles: automatism, the precise portrayal of dream(like) scenes, collage, and assemblage. In the 1920s artists such as Masson, Miró, and Ernst developed a form of graphic automatism that sought to eliminate any conscious control and a preconceived subject and develop the spontaneous generation of images, open pictorial signs often with erotic connotations, inviting the active participation of the spectator. In the mid-1930s automatism was explored further through techniques of *decalcomanie* (Dominguez), *fumage* (Paalen), or *grattage* (Frances). During the surrealists' exile in New York, artists such as Matta and Donati worked in the space between figuration and abstraction, influencing the young abstract expressionist painters. In Paris in the 1950s a younger generation of artists, including Hantaï, Loubchanski, and Reigl, practiced a form of automatism promoted by Breton, Pierre, and others as "abstraction lyrique" (lyrical abstraction), and exhibited in the Etoile Scellée Gallery, of which Breton was director. A second group of artists, "calqueurs de rêve" (dream copiers), used traditional pictorial techniques to reproduce hallucinatory, fantastic, or oneiric images (Dali, Magritte, Tanguy). Dali claimed his paintings were "la photographie de l'esprit" (photography of the mind), the projection of precise obsessions or dream images (explicit sexual imagery, soft dissolving forms). By contrast, Magritte and others reproduced dreamlike images staging the dream mechanisms of condensation (in composite bodies) and displacement (in fragmented bodies). A third group of artists developed techniques of collage (Ernst, Hugnet, Breton), consisting of the cutting and pasting of disparate images, which produced monstrous configurations. Artists also experimented in three-dimensional assemblage as a conjunction of heterogeneous objects (Bellmer, Miró, Oppenheim). Although Dali elaborated his paranoiac-critical method to interpret his paintings, defined as "un délire d'interprétation imaginatif" (a delirium of imaginative interpretation), inspired by the Freudian model, the majority of surrealist artists sought to create enigmatic, mysterious, or fantastic images: "I want to create a mystery, not to solve it," claimed Magritte. The aim of surrealist art, based on the effect of *dépaysement* (defamiliarization), was to counteract the automatization of the gaze and renew the viewer's perception of the world, making her see images emerging from the unconscious, "de l'autre côté de l'oeil" (the other side of the eye) (Dali).

In all their activities, whether philosophical, political, or artistic, the surrealists endeavored to reconcile artistic freedom and ideological commitment without compromising their ethical position in relation to the revolutionary transformation of society and the individual. Their influence can be seen, for example, in the revolutionary theory of the Situationist International group (1957–68), in the *Tel Quel* group's defense of poetic revolt (Rimbaud) and libertarianism (Sade), and in the anarchist declarations of the May 1968 student revolt in Paris, which reiterate the essential surrealist values of revolt, desire, and freedom. Their legacy among French intellectuals and artists is evident in continuing debates, on the dialogue between Marx and Freud, on transgression and desire, on the links between collective and individual freedom.

ELZA ADAMOWICZ

See also **Antonin Artaud; André Breton; Aimé Césaire**

Further Reading

Alquié, Ferdinand, *Philosophie du surréalisme*, Paris: Flammarion, 1955; as *The Philosophy of Surrealism*, translated by Bernard Waldrop, Ann Arbor: University of Michigan Press, 1969

Alquié, Ferdinand (editor), *Entretiens sur le surréalisme*, Paris: Mouton, 1969

Biro, Adam and René Passeron (editors), *Dictionnaire général du surréalisme et ses environs*, Paris: Presses Universitaires de France, 1982

Breton, André, *Oeuvres complètes*, 3 vols., Paris: Seuil (Pléiade), 1988, 1992, 1999

Davis, Helena, *Dada Turns Red. Surrealism and Politics*, Edinburgh, Scotland: University of Edinburgh Press, 1990

Nadeau, Maurice, *Histoire du surréalisme*, Paris: Seuil, 1964; as *The History of Surrealism*, translated by Richard Howard, London: Cape, 1968

Pierre, José (editor), *Tracts surréalistes et déclarations collectives 1922–1969*, 2 vols., Paris: Le Terrain Vague, 1981

La Révolution surréaliste (1924–29), reprinted Paris: Jean-Michel Place, 1975

Richardson, Michael and Krzysztof Fijalkowsi (editors), *Surrealism Against the Current. Tracts and Declarations*, London and Sterling, Virginia: Pluto Press, 2001

Rosemont, Franklin (editor), *André Breton. What Is Surrealism?* London: Pluto Press, 1978

Le Surréalisme au service de la révolution (1930–33), reprinted Paris: Jean-Michel Place, 1976

T

TEILHARD DE CHARDIN, PIERRE
Priest, Theologian, Anthropologist

A Roman Catholic priest and paleoanthropologist, Teilhard advocated a doctrine of cosmic evolution that, he believed, is consistent with fundamental Christian teaching. His many writings (the best known of which is *The Phenomenon of Man*, 1959) are a mixture of science, philosophy, and theology with an admitted admixture of mysticism. He might almost be regarded as an ultra-Augustinian, starting from a profound faith to fully understand the phenomenon of evolution, which, on his terms, embodies the progressive embodiment of the cosmic Christ.

For Teilhard, evolution is all embracing, extending well beyond the world of living things. Long before life appeared, the basic stuff of the world was undergoing irreversible change. This process embodies a fundamental tendency in nature for all things to become more complex, a tendency that he terms "complexification" and that, he urges, embodies a universal Law of Complexity. (This is often termed the Law of Complexity-Consciousness by Teilhard scholars, because he treated the rise in the level of complexity as commensurate with a rise in level of consciousness.) Complexification—a term now used by many complexity theorists—accounts for the emergence of atomic and molecular structure and, ultimately, for the emergence of life.

In his belief that life has arisen through the increasing complexity of matter, he appeared to accept a straightforward mechanistic and materialistic explanation of evolution. This is certainly misleading in one respect, however. Matter as he understood it is far from mechanical. Like all things in nature it has both an "outside" and an "inside." From the outside it exhibits quantitative connections and measurable dimensions, which science has so far studied with great success. But from the inside matter is qualitative, is active, and possesses some degree of consciousness. It is scarcely an automaton, because it embodies the possibility of endless creativity. Because it contains primitive consciousness, it contains the seeds for the emergence of ever higher levels and types of awareness. Teilhard, like Alfred North Whitehead and other process philosophers, thus accepted a "panpsychist" outlook. It is not surprising that a "Hymn to matter" should appear in his *Hymn of the Universe* (1961). Theologians, he taught, have wrongly condemned matter as an obstacle to spirituality and a negative form of being. In truth, it is a means to spirit and is heavily laden with profound potentialities.

A purposive concept of evolution is a natural outgrowth of this concept of matter. We find in evolution, he stated, not merely random drift but orthogenesis, the tendency to develop organisms in specific developmental directions. That is, each branch in the tree of evolution embodies the fulfillment of particular orders of biological possibility and excludes others. All major evolutionary achievements are dependent on this directed and cumulative thrust.

In a broad sense, for Teilhard the concept of evolution already applies to the earth, prior to the appearance and development of life. The possibility of biogenesis and of evolution depends on a threefold planetary succession, beginning with the lithosphere (one of his specialties was stratigraphy), proceeding to the hydrosphere (initially, the oceans), and then to the atmosphere, divided into the atmosphere *per se* and the stratosphere. To these is then added the biosphere: the web of life that comes to cover the planet.

Part of the difficulty in assessing Teilhard's account of the emergence and evolution of life is the twofold nature of his explanation. He argued, first, that categories like complexification and orthogenesis are necessary if the real significance and character of life are to be understood. To these broad quasi-metaphysical notions he added another, that of "radial energy," which he traced to the inside of matter, and which he contrasted with "tangential energy," the expression of the external character of materiality. At other times he suggested purely scientific explanations.

In his discussion of scientific conceptions of life he often contrasts Lamarckian theories with Darwinian theories, noting the disagreements concerning them in the science of his time. As a rule, however, he came down on the side of Lamarckianism, the view that evolution proceeds through the inheritance of acquired characteristics. This is unfortunate, because today very few biologists take Lamarckianism seriously. (Some contemporaries, like Edward J. Steele, do make a case for a limited role for Lamarckian inheritance, but in an essentially Darwinian context.) That Teilhard pays so little attention to either Mendelian genetics or neo-Darwinian theory is a real weakness in his thought. A contemporary follower of Teilhard might argue that whatever scientific notions of evolution might be adduced, none could satisfactorily explain the full scope of life, which depends on the inherent—one might almost say superabundant—activity of matter and the presence of orthogenetic order. Such an argument would satisfy few contemporary scientists.

Most scientists and philosophers have stressed the divergent character of evolution, with its continual production of diverse life forms in increasing conflict with one another. But as is evident from his axiom, "Everything that arises converges," he took the alternative view. The most marked character of evolution for him is convergence, the bringing of disparate elements into unity—ultimately into total planetary unity. Though he conceded that the general direction of life prior to the emergence of man had been to produce a ramified tree of divergence of species, each of these branches of each species on each branch of this tree must be seen to involve the coming together of parts into unity. But with the appearance of man, there is clearly an inescapable movement toward the unity of the human species. This movement and the factors that immediately precede it are termed by him "hominization." Hominization involves the upwelling of new possibilities and values, most notably the central value, love.

With the appearance of man, Teilhard argued, evolution had come to be characterized more by cultural than by biological or genetic change. As he realized, and as contemporary scientists believe, human cultural change, far from being Darwinian, is Lamarckian throughout. That is, it consists in the passing on of both patterns of behavior and new knowledge ("memes," in the terminology of Richard Dawkins) to succeeding generations. If the emergence of life was a threshold after which evolution took on a significantly new character, hominization is a threshold that presages still more dramatic transformations. The new psychosocial level inevitably leads to novel alternatives and higher levels of organization. With these come new thought patterns, new organizations of awareness, and new patterns of cooperation. The end result is a world in which humanity is increasingly less isolated, increasingly more interconnected. The course of human evolution thereby gives rise to a "noosphere," a worldwide collective awareness based on increasingly effective means of communication. Though still dependent on the biosphere, the noosphere crowns the earth with a planetary consciousness. But this process is in no way completed. It has a still more ultimate goal.

If for him everything that arises converges, it becomes clear with the development of his thought that the ultimate point of convergence is more than a biological or even a social goal. The ultimate goal (which he was sure could be reached) is Point Omega: a state in which spirituality and matter, soul and body, nature and supernature, science and faith find their ultimate unity. Often identified by him as the Second Coming of Christ, the Omega Point is the ultimate goal toward which all existence on this planet has tended. It will be, he believed, the triumph of love.

Teilhard's concept of Point Omega is inevitably obscure, precisely because it is a mystical vision. It might be tempting to identify it with God. It is clear, however, that it is God insofar as he determines the direction and goal of cosmic history. The integration of all consciousness at Omega represents the spirit of Christ at work in nature.

Summing up a vision at once so sweeping and yet so heavily weighted with detailed knowledge is difficult. Writers dealing with his thought have thus stressed particular aspects of his voluminous writings while leaving others less well explored. The outline of his phenomenology of evolution just presented therefore can make no claim to formal completeness. Moreover, if the difficulties of presenting a satisfactory descriptive tableau of his system are quite real, the problem of giving a just assessment of the value and the defensibility of a corpus of thought that has been so roundly condemned and so extravagantly admired are even more pronounced. Their resolution requires an analysis of both the valuable and the questionable in his writings.

In one respect Teilhard (many of whose essential writings date back to the 1920s and 1930s, though they were not published until the 1950s and still later) is seen to be well ahead of his time. Today we are still struggling to come to grips with a planetary civilization. Economics has become globalized; it overflows the boundaries of once self-sufficient nation-states to create an international web of trade and manufacture. This would have not been in the least surprising to him, nor would the rise of the Internet. His grasp of "planetization" and its implications is undeniable. Similarly, the way in which he described biological evolution in planetary terms, stressing the mutual togetherness of the biosphere with the planet, bears more than a passing resemblance to ideas subsequently brought together under the aegis of the "Gaia hypothesis" according to which the world can be seen as a single organism, responsive to itself and capable of response to stress.

These insights and the processes they point to, however important they are for understanding our present situation, seem to have a negative side that he did not recognize, or which in any case he did not choose to stress.

Julian Huxley, in his excellent introduction to the English translation of *The Phenomenon of Man*, points out that Teilhard does not seem aware that the increasing homogeneity of the planet that he describes is marked by the disappearance of cultural variety, and that this might itself impoverish any ultimate synthesis at the Omega Point. Similarly, nowhere in his writings is there any suspicion that overpopulation might provoke social and political conflicts, including the most dangerous of these, war. Nor do his writings mention either environmental degradation or species extinction: problems that on his terms could undermine progress toward or even the possibility of an ultimate harmonious unity.

Besides what might be termed the social and naturalistic consequences of Chardin's position, there are innumerable theological questions to which his standpoint gives rise. These have been widely, often heatedly debated.

Perhaps the central theological problem in Teilhard is the question of whether or to what extent he is a pantheist, one who makes God into a nature deity, in his case presumably making God into an evolutionary phenomenon. Another way of putting this point is to argue that in his synthesis his supernaturalism is sacrificed for the sake of his naturalism. Clearly this will always remain a point of contention. One way of distinguishing Christianity from any pantheist doctrine is to stress God's creation of the world, an act that establishes in some sense His independence from it. On this point Teilhard is strangely silent, describing the sudden coming into existence of matter in the form of elementary particles. The source of this explosive appearance, however, is nowhere discussed. One way of defining Teilhard's putative pantheism is to say that for him evolution, or even any one of the orthogenetic branches of which it consists, is God. But nowhere in Teilhard's writings does one find this sort of theological reductionism. If God guides the process of evolution, it does not appear that he can be, literally, contained in any part it. But though he states clearly that God is both "preexistent and transcendent" (an orthodox theological definition of God's relation to nature) his actual explanations seem to show only that God transcends any particular aspect of evolution, not that he transcends the physical universe as such. As noted earlier, the question of his preexistence of nature is in practice left open.

Another major theological problem in his system (the one that caused the initial and early negative response of the church) is his treatment of evil. In no way does he deny the reality of evil, which he regards as omnipresent in nature and in human existence. Nor does he seem to treat it as unreal or illusory. The difficulty for more orthodox theologians is that he understands it as essentially an unavoidable by-product of evolution at every step. It is impossible to have evolutionary advance, with its components of contingency and creativity, and not have disorder and destruction as concomitant factors. Not every evolutionary possibility can result in success. Many—the majority—we know must be failures. To the extent that life proceeds, it is accompanied at every level by disorder, failure, decomposition, isolation, and anxiety. This should not dissuade us from seeing the immense, superabundant good of the process itself.

In taking this standpoint he is open to two opposed criticisms. From the side of the skeptic he can be condemned for a presumed willingness to gloss over the amount of evil in the world and to claim the fundamental goodness of the process of evolution on the basis of a presumed excellence or of its ultimate results without proof. Any reply must rest on Teilhard's mystical vision, for which the overwhelming value of the process and its presumed absolute culmination is a given. From the side of the faithful, the problem lies in Teilhard's refusal to distinguish natural evil from human evil. It is not clear that vicious, destructive acts by human beings are simply by-products (costs, so to speak) of the creative advance of nature or even that many of them have any relevance to the overall development of life at all. Nor is it clear whether or how these are to be ransomed by the culmination of the Omega Point, or by any other aspect of Teilhard's system.

Interest in his ideas, intense and widespread particularly during the 1970s and 1980s, has abated in part, though it shows no sign of disappearing. Poet of a vision of purposeful evolution, he has inspired many readers with his insights, even where many so inspired have not concurred with his theology. The sociologist of planetary man, he has drawn attention in an unmistakable way to the global situation in which humankind now finds itself and has made it clear that the human future depends on the ability to deal with it in wise and humane terms. Deeply immersed in Roman Catholic doctrine and tradition, his insistence that these require to be rethought in terms of modern knowledge and the modern situation even when it has drawn opposition has struck a profound cord with progressive Catholics and breathed new life into both practice and theological outlook.

PETE A.Y. GUNTER

Biography

Born in Sarcenat, France, in 1881, Teilhard entered the Society of Jesus (the Jesuit order) in 1899 and was ordained priest in 1911. In 1912 he began higher studies in paleontology, in which he received his doctorate at the Sorbonne in 1922. His attempt to unite Christian doctrine with biological evolution resulted in his being expelled in 1926 from the Catholic Institute in Paris. From that time until 1946 he was largely exiled to China, where, among many other activities, he was involved in the paleontological research that lead to the discovery of Peking man. During this period he completed his major work, *The Phenomenon of Man*, which in spite of several entreaties to the Vatican he was not allowed to publish. During this time he also completed stratigraphic and paleontological studies in China and elsewhere in the Orient. Though several of his theological writings were circulated in manuscript during his lifetime, none of these were published until after his death, in New York, in 1946. These were to give rise to heated controversies both inside and outside the church. In 1962 the Holy Office, though casting no doubt on his spirituality or his sincerity, issued a monitum, or simple warning, against uncritical acceptance of his ideas.

Selected Works

La Phenomène humaine, 1956; as *The Phenomenon of Man*, 1959

L'Apparition de l'homme, 1956; as *The Appearance of Man*, 1965

Le Groupe zoologique humain, 1956; as *Man's Place in Nature*, 1966

Lettres du voyage (1923–1939), 1956; as *Letters From a Traveller*, 1962

La Vision du passé, 1957; as *The Vision of the Past*, 1966

Le Milieu divin, 1957; as *The Divine Milieu*, 1960, 1961

Hymne de l'univers, 1962; as *Hymn of the Universe*, 1962, 1965

L'Activation de l'énergie, 1964; as *The Activation of Energy*, 1970

Comment je crois, 1969; as *Christianity and Evolution*, 1971

Le Coeur de la Matière, 1976; as *The Heart of the Matter*, 1979

Further Reading

Cowell, Sion, *The Teilhard Lexicon*, Brighton: Sussex Academic Press, 2001

Cuénot, Claude, *Teilhard de Chardin: A Biographical Study*, London: Burns and Oates, 1965

Dodson, Edward O., *The Phenomenon of Man Revisited; A Biological Viewpoint on Teilhard de Chardin*, New York: Columbia University Press, 1984

Galleni, Ludovico, "Is the Biosphere Doing Theology?" *Zygon*, 36, no.1 (2001): 33–48

Grau, Joseph A., *Morality and the Human Future in the Thought of Teilhard de Chardin*, Rutherford, New Jersey: Fairleigh Dickinson University Press, 1976

Haught, John F., *Chaos, Complexity and Theology*, New York: Anima, 1994

King, Ursula, *Towards a New Mysticism: Teilhard de Chardin and Eastern Religions*, New York: Seabury Press, 1980

McCarthy, Joseph M., *Pierre Teilhard de Chardin: A Comprehensive Bibliography*, New York: Garland, 1981

O'Connor, Catherine R., *Woman and Cosmos: The Feminine in the Thought of Teilhard de Chardin*, Upper Saddle River, NJ: Prentice Hall, 1971

Provençal, Yvonne, *The Mind of Society*, Amsterdam: Gordon and Breach Publishers, 1998

Steele, Edward J., et al., *Lamarck's Signature*, Reading, MA: Perseus Books, 1998

Wolsky, Alexander, "Teilhard de Chardin's Biological Ideas," *Teilhard Studies*, no. 4 (spring 1981): 1–20

THEOLOGY AND RELIGIOUS THOUGHT

Although the origins of modern French theological and religious thought are elusive, it may not be inappropriate to trace them to the work of the seventeenth-century philosopher René Descartes. Descartes's use of "clear and distinct ideas" and his insistence on the alliance between philosophical reflection and the sciences have been extremely influential for the French intellectual tradition in general, but his connection to the theological and religious thought of France has more to do with his attempt to establish an absolute, self-grounded epistemological system, a so-called first philosophy. Clearly, the notion that philosophical inquiry should be the foundation on which all other knowledge is built extends back to the beginnings of philosophy itself, but it takes its modern form in Descartes's *Meditations on First Philosophy*, the work in which he most explicitly sought to delineate his own irrefutable basis for all knowledge. In the *Meditations*, Descartes argued that "first philosophy" should take as its point of departure an epistemological examination of the human entity: What is it, he asks, that we can know with absolute certainty? He attempted to answer this question by initially calling into doubt everything of which he was unsure, using only that which cannot be doubted in order to establish what is philosophically certain. In short order, he stripped away the apparent reality of the physical world, including the idea of the body, leaving himself only with the *Cogito*, the thinking subject.

Using elements of Anselm's ontological argument, woven together with his own conception of the human subject as an imperfect being, Descartes argued from the *Cogito* back to the necessary existence of God. The significance of this argument for the *Cogito* itself is important to note; for even though Descartes's meditative inquiry moves from the *Cogito* back to God's existence, God was still conceived to be *ontologically* prior to human beings. Given that his first philosophy turns on the idea that the human being is an intermediate entity, something between "God and nothing," this conception of God's ontological primacy was essential to Descartes. As the contemporary philosophical theologian Paul Ricoeur says: ". . . God confers on the certainty of myself the permanence that it does not hold in itself."

The Cartesian attempt to fuse the imperfect self with the perfection of the divine gave rise to an ongoing debate by the heirs of Descartes. Malebranche, for example, and to an even greater extent Spinoza, noting Descartes's projection of an infinite point of arrival back onto a finite point of origin, identified the *Cogito* as no more than an abstract and empty truth. For the whole tradition of idealism extending through Kant, Fichte, and Husserl, the *Cogito* came to be understood not as a foundational "first truth" on which a second, third, and fourth truth could be built, but only as the "ground that grounds itself, incommensurable with all propositions, not only empirical ones but transcendental ones as well." In twentieth century France, the dispute over the *Cogito* would begin to take shape as a philosophical conflict between Jean-Paul Sartre and Gabriel Marcel. It is of interest that Sartre suggested, like Descartes in the *Meditations*, that the starting point of philosophical inquiry must be the "subjectivity" of the human subject, and that the fundamental truth of that subjectivity is the *Cogito, ergo sum*. He even went so far as to argue that "[t]here can be no other truth to take off from than this: *I think; therefore, I exist*." But Sartre did not limit himself to the Cartesian *Cogito*. Rather, he defined an existentialist subject that has the power to choose how it will participate in the world. Sartre's philosophy is predicated on the notion that life has no predetermined meaning, that "existence precedes essence." Deeply influenced by the work of Mar-

tin Heidegger, Sartre followed the great German thinker by arguing that "existence" is characterized by the human subject being "thrown," without its assent, into a world that seems to lack any sense of cosmic purpose or guidance. This position was not unique to Sartre, as it can certainly be seen in the work of a thinker like Nietzsche, or perhaps more importantly in regard to Sartre, in the work of the Danish religious philosopher Søren Kierkegaard. Like Sartre, Kierkegaard also believed that the senselessness of the world could fill us with feelings of hopelessness and despair. Kierkegaard, though, believed that if one were willing to take an "absurdly" courageous "leap of faith," one would come to understand that the things that occurred in the world were part of God's eternal plan. Sartre found this position naïve, claiming not only that God did not exist, but that authentic existentialism is grounded on the notion of the nonexistence of the divine.

Although he did not believe in God, Sartre resisted any idea that God should be abolished "with the least possible expense." Rather, said Sartre, the existentialist "thinks it is very distressing that God does not exist, because all possibility of finding values in a heaven of ideas disappears along with Him." If God does not exist, then everything is possible; there is nothing that human beings are constrained to be, they are free. Indeed, as Sartre says, without God, humanity is "condemned to be free"; condemned "because he did not create himself . . . because, once thrown into the world, he is responsible for everything he does." For Sartre, the brute facticity of our thrownness and our freedom leads to a profound sense of existential "anguish." In fact, insists Sartre, humanity "is anguish."

Although Marcel was a Christian thinker whose philosophy was infused with the notion of God, it was not Sartre's atheism that he found most troubling. Rather, what disturbed Marcel above all else about Sartre's existentialism was the latter's idea that the "essence of the relations between consciousnesses is not the *Mitsein*; it is conflict." What Sartre is suggesting by giving expression to this ominous proclamation becomes clear if one calls to mind an oft-quoted story found in *Being and Nothingness*. Sartre asks us to imagine that a man is kneeling outside a door, peering through the keyhole and attempting to eavesdrop on what is going on inside. Intent on what he is doing, he does not hear the approach of another person until it is too late; looking up, he realizes that he has been caught, the other stands watching him. According to Sartre, in the "gaze" of this other I become aware of myself as an "object" of another consciousness as subject. In an almost violent sense, says Sartre, the other's consciousness invades mine; I experience the other as a free subject making me into an object for another.

As Marcel suggests, there is perhaps "nothing more remarkable in the whole of Sartre's work than his phenomenological study of the 'other' as looking and of himself as exposed, pierced, bared, petrified by his Medusa-like stare." Marcel believed, though, that this part of Sartre's work was too often misunderstood. Returning to the story of the man caught in his act of deceit, Marcel says that it is not by chance that this example is chosen by Sartre. As he points out, the act of eavesdropping is something not ordinarily "pursued in public"; we expect that we will be alone, hidden away from prying eyes. But, argues Marcel, it remains to be seen whether this sense of being alone is "true of human life as a whole." Clearly it is for Sartre, insists Marcel, as the awareness of others cannot be separated from the "shock of the encounter" with my existential freedom, an "alien freedom" that is ultimately "adverse and threatening." Caught by the gaze of the other, I am confined within the being-in-itself: "I bend down to peep through the keyhole in exactly the same way as a tree is bent by the wind."

Marcel believes that Sartre's existentialism leaves us with no possibility for the intimacy of the communal, whether we are speaking of friends, of life partners, or of God. For Marcel, Sartre's analysis of the interaction between the self and the other necessarily leads to a wholly negative conclusion. The goal of the relational act becomes merely a way of achieving "absolute value" in the eyes of the other, a way of transforming the objectifying gaze that had "previously passed through me or had immobilized me in an in-itself." To be sure, Marcel admits that Sartre's existentialist conclusions may seem appropriate in a mid–twentieth-century world where the "sense of the ontological," of being at its deepest levels, is lacking. Indeed, Marcel sounds more than a bit like Sartre when he says that the modern world is characterized by a sense of "brokenness," that as the world has become more and more technologically advanced, the individual has become increasingly fragmented, divided into a diffuse mass of what Marcel calls "vital" and "social" "functions": consumer, churchgoer, parent, citizen, and so on. For Marcel, as it is for Sartre, this "functionalized" world is empty and devitalized. Unlike Sartre, though, who Marcel claims has offered up a philosophy that "rests upon the complete denial of *we* as subject, that is to say upon the denial of communion," he believes that we are in the presence of a great ontological mystery that manifests itself in the communal moment between the self and the other.

It becomes more obvious what Marcel means by the notion of the communal if his discussion of the idea of the "gift" is examined. Turning back to *Being and Nothingness*, Marcel draws our attention to what he takes to be the "astonishing interpretation of giving" presented by Sartre. As Marcel points out, Sartre tells us that: "Gift is a primitive form of destruction . . . a form of destructive appropriation." Ultimately, "to give is to enslave." As might be expected, Marcel rejects this characterization of the gift, claiming that it merely reveals Sartre's inability to "grasp the genuine reality of what is meant by *we* or of what governs this reality, that is precisely our capacity to open ourselves to others." Marcel, of course, is not naïve enough to believe that there is no such thing as a "pathology of giving," or that there are not "cases of moral suicide" in which a person "abdicates and annuls himself completely for the benefit of another." This is not what he means by the notion of the gift, though, as for Marcel, "to give oneself is to devote or consecrate oneself to another, and no doubt simply to consecrate oneself."

Marcel reveals more about his claim for the consecrating character of self-giving when he considers the act of giving from the perspective of the beneficiary of the gift. In regard to this, Marcel suggests that if one is to be certain that something has been given, and not simply lent, one needs a "formal assurance." According to Marcel, this assurance comes by way of words, either spoken or written, which "may appear as constituting the gift as such." This at least is the case for particular things, which can be "designated as gifts" and "whose possessor can be identified," says Marcel. But does it hold true for the ". . . infinitely more important thing, the fundamental gift: the gift of life, that is, the fact, with all its concrete applications, of being in the world?" For Marcel it does hold true because, for him, we cannot be in the world without "being fitted into it in conditions which are fixed to a certain point or extent in the vast human adventure." The essential gift of life, then, is bestowed on us by way of God's ultimate act of creative consecration, and this special gift is constituted as such by the revelation of the Word in the midst of the communal moment.

The explicitly religious ideas of Marcel lead the discussion to the work of Paul Ricoeur. Although like Marcel, Ricoeur places himself firmly within the Christian tradition, he has struggled his entire career to pursue an "autonomous, philosophical discourse," one that would allow him to bracket out the "convictions" that "bind [him] to biblical faith." Initially, one can see in this struggle Ricoeur's desire to rethink the existentialism of Sartre without resorting to what he understands to be a "naïve faith." Toward this end, Ricoeur seeks to reformulate Sartre's idea of the "nihilation of being-in-itself" by arguing that the process of negation functions on two unique but interrelated levels: On a primary level, negation is the constitutive element that gives rise to the differences between and among the things-of-the-world; on a secondary, or existential level, however, negation acts as a "denegation," as the application of the "not" to the primal negativity of objective differentiation. Sartre's philosophy, says Ricoeur, does not allow for this secondary denegation of ontological difference because it defines being as a "brute fact": The subject is simply a thing-in-the-world. Because of this, the "value" that "introduces a *need-to-be* into being can only be lacuna or lack," and thus "all possibility of grounding nihilating acts in a higher affirmation is ruled out under the penalty of falling back into the initial ensnarement. Being can no longer be a refuge, it is a trap. . . ."

What Ricoeur is claiming here, sounding very much like Marcel, is that on an existential level, negativity represents a moment of transgressive denegation, which marks the point at which the subject seeks to overcome the fragility of existence by *affirming* the relational bond between the self and the other. At this point, Ricoeur appears to have left himself somewhere between Sartre and Marcel, between what he himself understands as a nihilating withdrawal from the other and the "first faith of the simple soul," which is constituted in the revelation of the Word. Ricoeur seems well aware of this, especially as he shifts the focus of his "conflict of interpretations" from Sartre to other thinkers in the French tradition.

Although he does not write specifically about Jacques Lacan, it may be argued that in a certain sense Ricoeur's monumental work, *Freud and Philosophy*, is a response to the ideas of the great psychoanalyst. Lacan, following Freud, posits the resolution of the Oedipus complex as the crucial moment in the formation of subjectivity. What so many have found especially intriguing about Lacan's notion of subjectivity is his linguistic interpretation of the Oedipus stage and in particular his suggestion concerning the human being's access to language. Lacan argued that this accession involved the "casting of original desire into the abyss of the unconscious." Desire cannot be signified directly because it does not happen in language, but before language. What we are left with, then, are the traces of desire, made manifest by way of metaphoric and metonymic signifiers forever pointing beyond themselves to a realm of the signified lost.

Again, Ricoeur does not write specifically about Lacan, but he at least alludes to his ideas in *Freud and Philosophy* when he defines his own notion of a "hermeneutics of suspicion." According to Ricoeur, interpretation as an act of suspicion can be linked to the work of Freud, Nietzsche, and Marx. Ricoeur suggests that fundamental to all of these thinkers is the idea that we must "look upon the whole of consciousness as a 'false' consciousness." In this way, the work of Freud, Nietzsche, and Marx once again reveals the problematic of Cartesian doubt. Everything that makes its way into consciousness must be called into question. The three masters of suspicion broaden this Cartesian aporia, though. Where Descartes doubted the objects of consciousness but maintained that consciousness itself was the great Archimedean point that grounded subjectivity, Freud, Nietzsche, and Marx not only doubted the objects of consciousness, but they also doubted consciousness itself.

If Ricoeur remained on the side of a hermeneutics of suspicion he could more easily be aligned with figures like Sartre and Lacan and ultimately with postmodern thinkers such as Jean-François Lyotard and Jacques Derrida. But in *Freud and Philosophy* he proposed to overcome suspicion with what he calls a hermeneutics of restoration. Oddly, although he says that he wants to keep the discourses of philosophy and religion apart, he grounds his restorative hermeneutics on faith. Admittedly, he does claim that this is a faith that has "undergone criticism," a "post critical faith," as Ricoeur terms it. Nevertheless, it is still faith. It seems, then, that for Ricoeur, the "other is the necessary path of injunction," that with the "aporia of the Other, philosophical discourse comes to an end."

In a rather ironic way, Ricoeur's allusion to the end of philosophical discourse connects his work to that of Lyotard, who sees the "postmodern condition" as one in which "grand legitimating narratives" are breaking down. Lyotard claims that these narratives first emerged as stories told by humans in order to define a cultural identity. In each culture, says Lyotard, certain of these stories began to take on a special meaning; they became the "legitimizing" narratives that identified a culture as unique, giving it a sense of justification and worth. According to Lyotard, the current condition of Western society is one in which we no longer accept the grand narratives of our cultural history as legitimate. The negative effect of this, contends Lyotard, is that capitalism and its discourses have been able to dominate in the late twentieth century. The positive effect, though, is that the possibility has been opened up for the articulation of a whole series of small narratives and practices.

An example of one in this series of "petite narratives" is the work being done by French feminist thinkers such as Luce Irigaray and Julia Kristeva. It is important, and interesting, to note that both of these thinkers have defined their own work within, and against, the psychoanalytic framework marked out by Lacan. Calling attention to the fact that in the foundational place of the Oedipal stage the "mother appears only as a shadowy figure" and the "daughter's development is parasitic upon what is essentially a drama played out between the son and the father," Kristeva and Irigaray seek to enter the psychoanalytic discussion at the precise point where the "woman is missing."

It may be argued that Irigaray lays out her feminist themes in opposition to the masculine boundaries imposed by Lacan's linguistic order. For Lacan, the order of language, what he calls the "symbolic order," is formed during the Oedipal stage; because the Oedipal stage is primarily masculine, the symbolic is essentially a male ritual. Beyond this, though, the symbolic is also an order of "identity," a linguistic and masculine attempt to reduce everything to sameness and solidification. Because of this, says Irigaray, the symbolic order is resistant to changeable, flowing, and adaptable modes of experience. Irigaray contrasts this masculine rigidity with feminist expressions of the corporeal, the fluid, and the tactile. This can be seen in works like *This Sex Which Is Not One*, in which she attempts to overcome the inflexibility of theoretical articulation by the use of tropes, double-entendres, poetic prose, and questions that continually unfold back upon themselves.

Although she also wishes to enter the discussion of psychoanalysis at the point where the woman is missing, one might make the case that Kristeva is not as wary about the symbolic order, about the order of language, as is Irigaray. Where Irigaray contrasts her feminism with the masculine elements of psychoanalysis, Kristeva seeks to discover the feminine that has been repressed within its margins; or, put another way, she attempts to allow the symbolic to reveal what is nonsymbolic in it. Kristeva terms the nonsymbolic the "semiotic." She defines it as a prelinguistic, preverbal, archaic dimension of language that is bound to the drives of the child toward the mother, before the moment of the father's interference. The importance of these semiotic drives, says Kristeva, is that they have the power to disrupt the overwhelming influence of the symbolic from within the symbolic order itself.

In a powerful sense, the treatments of religion offered up by both Irigaray and Kristeva grow out of their critiques of psychoanalysis, and finally of the Western intellectual tradition as a whole. Irigaray's references to religion tend to be fleeting, and thus are somewhat hard to trace. It may not be inaccurate, though, to say that for Irigaray, religion is like the Oedipal moment, rigidly reducing everything to the same: "the Other . . . as yet manifest through his creation (the Father), present in his form (the son), mediator between the two (spirit)." This God, though, asks Irigaray, "Are we capable of imagining it as a woman? Can we dimly see it as the perfection of our subjectivity?" As one might expect, Irigaray answers no to these questions. What is needed for woman to emerge from the shadows, says Irigaray, is "God in the feminine." Provocatively, Irigaray posits Jesus as this possible ground of feminist expression. Of course, for Irigaray, this is not the "ethereal Jesus of the pulpit," but the bodily Jesus

of the Gospels who suffered and died on the cross, the Jesus who Christianity has attempted to "disincarnate," from whom it has sought to "tear away the flesh," the Jesus it has been intent on "defeminizing" since the first century.

As with the threat of the symbolic, Kristeva seems less suspicious about religious discourse than does Irigaray. Although she does maintain that it can "all too easily take the form of an institutionalized discourse," she also believes that it can "manifest the subversive power of the semiotic." This latter notion can be seen in her discussion of the Virgin Mary in her oft quoted essay, "Stabat Mater." Writing at once as a scholar and a poet, Kristeva weaves together discussions of the complex interconnection between language and subjectivity, ruminations on the role of the Virgin Mary in the Catholic tradition, and on her own experience of the maternal. Presented in parallel columns, which push and strain against each other, the essay is focused on maternity throughout. In this way, Kristeva is seeking to reveal the "physical doubling of a woman's body during pregnancy that allows her to be, quite literally, both one and other." It is this experience of radical alterity, says Kristeva, that the dominant male culture has attempted to cover over. Kristeva argues that this can be seen quite clearly in the Catholic vision of the Virgin Mother: by way of giving prominence to Mary's Immaculate Conception, her perpetual virginity, and her ascension into heaven, the Church has sought to "erase the bodily traces of actual birth." For Kristeva, this effacement of the body has deprived the figure of the Virgin Mother of her power of subversion, deprived her of the possibility of being understood as the "split and fluid" feminine obverse of the masculine Trinity.

Although he has written very little about religion, it is perhaps appropriate to give the last word on this subject to Derrida: "*How 'to talk religion'? Of religion? Perhaps one must take one's chance in resorting to the most concrete and most accessible, but also the most barren and desert-like, of all abstractions.*" This is Derrida delaying, "deferring" as he would say, his discussion of religion, a deferral that has extended over some forty years. It is an example of his peculiar negative or apophatic theology. Characteristic of Hellenistic, Jewish, and Christian mystical traditions before and after the beginning of the common era, apophatic theology uses "negating concepts" to define what God is by saying what he is not. The power of this type of theological articulation, especially for someone like Derrida, is that it exposes the inadequacy of human language to speak about God in the very moment that it gives expression to concepts that are applied to God. This act of apophatic doubling appears to be much like Derrida's own deconstructive doubling. Indeed, in his

Margins of Philosophy, Derrida himself admits that the "detours, locutions, and syntax" within which he "will often have to take recourse" will look very much like those of negative theology, occasionally even to the point of "being indistinguishable from negative theology." For Derrida, "this difference, this negativity in God is our freedom, the transcendence and the verb which can relocate the purity of their negative origin only in the possibility of the Question."

PHILIP C. DiMARE

See also **Jacques Derrida; Luce Irigaray; Julia Kristeva; Jacques Lacan; Jean-François Lyotard; Gabriel Marcel; Paul Ricoeur; Jean-Paul Sartre**

Further Readings

The Bible and Culture Collective, *The Postmodern Bible*, Yale University Press, 1995

Derrida, Jacques and Gianni Vattimo (editors), *Religion*, Stanford University Press, 1998

Derrida, Jacques, *Writing and Difference*, The University of Chicago Press, 1978

Descartes, René, *Meditations on First Philosophy in Which the Existence of God and the Distinction of the Soul from the Body Are Demonstrated*, Hackett Publishing Company, 1979

Irigaray, Luce, *This Sex Which Is Not One*, Cornell University Press, 1985

Joy, Morny, Kathleen O'Grady, and Judith Poxon, *French Feminists on Religion*, Routledge 2002

Kristeva, Julia, *Desire in Language: A Semiotic Approach to Literature and Art*, Columbia University Press, 1980

Kristeva, Julia, *Powers of Horror: An Essay in Abjection*, Columbia University Press, 1982

Lacan, Jacques, *Ecrits*, Norton, 1977

Lyotard, Jean-François, *The Postmodern Condition: A Report on Knowledge*, University of Minnesota Press, 1984

Marcel, Gabriel, *The Mystery of Being*, Vols. I and II, Henry Regnery Company, 1950 and 1951

Marcel, Gabriel, *The Philosophy of Existence*, Philosophical Library, 1949

Ricoeur, Paul, *The Conflict of Interpretations: Essays in Hermeneutics*, Northwestern University Press, 1974

Ricoeur, Paul, *Freud and Philosophy: An Essay on Interpretation*, Yale University Press, 1970

Ricoeur, Paul, *Oneself as Another* The University of Chicago Press, 1992

Sartre, Jean-Paul, *Being and Nothingness: A Phenomenological Essay on Ontology* Simon and Schuster, 1956

Saussure, Ferdinand de, *Course in General Linguistics* New York: McGraw-Hill, 1959

THIBAUDET, ALBERT
Philosopher, Critic

Often included among the greatest French literary critics of the twentieth century, Albert Thibaudet occupies a central place in the development of modern criticism. Thibaudet left evaluation conclusively behind and, instead, worked explicitly with critical methods and reading strategies, adopting, for instance, Bergsonian psychology as a theoretical approach and not refraining from political and philosophical reflections (*Les Idées politiques de France*). Several of his works, however, directly dissect the nature of the critical discipline, thereby inaugurating the French emphasis on metacriticism (*Physiologie de la critique*, *Réflexions sur la critique*). With important monographs on Mallarmé, Flaubert, Stendhal, and Valéry, Thibaudet's method remains largely author based, but contrary to previous critical paradigms (e.g., Sainte-Beuve's school), it keeps its focus on the works rather than on the personalities. The individual authors' literary capacities are rather studied as they combine with history, politics, and society, determining larger literary orientations, which the critic is to compare and classify.

Thibaudet's first major work, *La Poésie de Stéphane Mallarmé* (1912), renewed a fading interest in Mallarmé by explicating his difficult poetry, not through biographical facts, but through a penetration into the poet's "logic" as reflected through artistic choices. In his later monographs, in particular *Gustave Flaubert* (1922), Thibaudet employed sympathy with the author as a methodological tool, hereby anticipating the later identificatory principles of Charles du Bos and the emerging Geneva school of Poulet, Raymond, Starobinski, and Béguin. However, to Thibaudet methodic sympathy never cancels out the differences among the authors themselves. Literary history is, rather, a dynamic field of contrasts and conflicts, allowing the critic to establish opposing pairs of authors, such as Voltaire and Rousseau, that propel history forward.

If life does serve as a model of understanding, the critic should approach it only in its encompassing continuity and transformation. The life of a person thus turns out to be a window to the "life" of a whole period, as reflected in the title *La Vie de Maurice Barrès— Trente ans de vie française II* (1921). Thibaudet's perception of time and duration thus proves heavily influenced by Bergsonian philosophy. Having been a young student of Bergson at Lycée Henri IV, Thibaudet later declared that no contemporary thought had a more profound impact on him. In 1923, when turning to a mature study of Bergson, Thibaudet let this philosophical system define a whole generation (*Le Bergsonisme— Trente ans de vie française III*). However, the overall faithfulness to Bergsonian thought is at times questionable. Bergson's creative concept of *élan vital* holds a natural attraction to a critic interested in innovation and renewal. Thibaudet, however, intentionally employed this concept to define and justify the new role of the critic. By never falling prey to dialectic refutations, the critic in fact holds a clear advantage over the philosopher when situating a particular thinker in the overarching *élan vital* of thought.

While embracing philosophical reading strategies, Thibaudet exerted himself to avoid potential dogmatism. Doctrines can serve the critic, but the critic should not serve doctrines. The definitions of genre and other critical categories should therefore not tempt the critic to stipulate rules for creation: "The genre is behind the artist not before him." With a Bergsonian respect for the genius, creation happens along a trajectory that is unpredictable as life itself. Thibaudet therefore hailed the freedom and volatility of the novel as a literary equivalent of life (*Le Liseur de romans*, 1925). Although Thibaudet devoted long studies to Greek culture and had reservations about the literary value of movements like dadaism, his critical impulse thus remained otherwise reconcilable with modernist literature's preference for the new and innovative.

Even if Thibaudet unremittingly scrutinized the role of the critic, his *Physiologie de la critique* (1930) serves as his most consistent work of metacriticism. Partly an exposition of existing critical methods and partly a methodological manifesto, the *Physiologie* marks an important modern confidence in the creativity of the critic. Having first demarcated three types of criticism: "spontaneous criticism," "professional criticism," and "criticism of the Masters," Thibaudet himself appears to be transcending all three categories. The "professional criticism" that "introduces logic and discourse into the literary coincidences" is indicative of the professorial critic in Thibaudet who appreciates an author in his or her historical position. Yet, Thibaudet's emphasis on sentiment as an indispensable associate of rationality drives him toward the "spontaneous" criticism traditionally encountered in journalism or in the *Salons*. Finally, the third kind of criticism, "criticism of the Masters," which occurs when great writers comment on great writers, involves a kind of sympathy with genius, something Thibaudet had already proved himself capable of doing.

By moving in and out of these three categories, Thibaudet himself established a critical method equally based on construction and creation. Critical construction takes place whenever a book is ordered according to an idea, whether of genre, tradition, generation, or nationality. Creation, however, is more rare and rests on the critic's ability to fall into the duration of the author. The critic must "live" his author in the way that an author lives his character. Thus following the work's own creative course, Thibaudet's method of construction and creation becomes a life criticism.

Although numerous contributions to journalism and politics indicate a certain qualitative limit in the range of the critic, Thibaudet's theoretical reflection brought literary periodization to the fore. As a contributor to *Nouvelle Revue Française* from 1911 to 1936, Thibaudet established his fame more in the capacity of "professional" critic who is precisely to compare, classify, and define. Reprinted posthumously as volumes of *Réflexions*, these literary articles reconcile his own philosophically motivated emphasis on renewal and duration with the journal's ambitions of locating a modern way of writing.

Naturally interested in the possibility of situating authors historically, Thibaudet launched in the *NRF* of 1921 the idea of grouping authors according to generations. Having already worked with the idea of such sequences in the *Trente ans de vie française* series, Thibaudet noticed how "one generation typically reacts against the preceding one." Despite the admitted arbitrariness of any ordering sequence, the notion of generations therefore remains productive as it "coincides more reliably with the unpredictable change and the living duration" of literature as a human activity. Thibaudet's last major work is thus a comprehensive history of French literature classified according to the generations of 1789, 1820, 1850, 1885, 1914, a division that highlights both literary and political transformations (*Histoire de la littérature française de 1789 à nos jours*, 1936, completed by Jean Paulhan). Although often caught in a dilemma between the constructive urge to classify and the creative quest for the *élan vital*, Thibaudet's method anticipates modern criticism as the crossroads of all disciplines.

NIELS BUCH-JEPSEN

See also **Albert Beguin; Henri Bergson; Georges Poulet; Marcel Raymond; Paul Valery**

Biography

Born on April 1, 1874, in Tournus in the Saône-et-Loire, Albert Thibaudet completed his secondary education at the *lycées* of Lons-le Saunier, Louis-le Grand, and Henri IV, where Henri Bergson was his philosophy teacher. Having completed his philosophical *licence* from the University of Dijon in 1893, he taught in several *collèges* around France until in 1908 he completed the *agrégation* in history and geography and began teaching at the *lycées* of Annecy, Grenoble, Besançon, and Clermont-Ferrand. After serving France during World War I, he taught at the universities of York and Uppsala before in 1924 becoming professor of French at the University of Geneva, where he taught until his death in 1936. In 1897 he had published a piece of drama in prose and verse, *Le Cygne rouge*, and from 1908 he began reviewing books for *La Phalange*. An article on André Gide from October 1909 brought him to the attention of the *Nouvelle Revue Française*, and from 1911 he contributed to this latter review, soon under his own famous rubric *Réflexions sur la littérature*.

Selected Works

La Poésie de Stéphane Mallarmé—Étude littéraire, 1912, final edition, 1926

Les Heures de l'Acropole, 1913

Les Idées de Charles Maurras—Trente ans de vie française I, 1920

La Vie de Maurice Barrès—Trente ans de vie française II, 1921

Gustave Flaubert. Sa Vie. Ses romans. Son style, 1922, final edition 1935

La Campagne avec Thucydide, 1922

Le Bergsonisme—Trente ans de vie française III, 1923

Paul Valéry, 1923

Intérieurs: Baudelaire—Fromentin—Amiel, 1924

Le Liseur de romans, 1925

Étranger ou Études de littérature anglaise, 1925

Les Images de Grèce, 1926

La République des professeurs, 1927

Amiel ou La Part du rêve, 1929

L'Acropole, 1929

Physiologie de la critique, 1930, final edition 1948

Mistral—ou La République du soleil, 1930

Stendhal, 1931

Les Idées politiques de France, 1932

Histoire de la littérature française de 1789 à nos jours, 1936; as *French Literature from 1795 to Our Era*, translated by Charles Lam Markmann, 1968

Réflexions sur la littérature, 1938

Réflexions sur le roman, 1938

Réflexions sur la critique, 1939

Réflexions sur la littérature II, 1941

Further Reading

Bergson, Henri, "Quelques mots sur Thibaudet critique et philosophe," *Nouvelle Revue Française* (July 1936)

Compagnon, Antoine, "Curtius et les critiques français: Brunetière, Thibaudet, Du Bos," in *Ernst Robert Curtius et l'idée d'Europe*, edited by Bem and Guyaux, Paris. Champion, 1995

Davies, John C., *L'Œuvre critique d'Albert Thibaudet*, Genève: Droz, 1955

Davies, John C., "Thibaudet and the Problem of Literary Generations," *French Studies*, 12 (1958): 113–124

Glauser, A., *Albert Thibaudet et la critique créatrice*, Paris: Boivin, 1952

Rambaud, Henri, "Vues sur Albert Thibaudet," *L'Esprit Créateur*, 14 (1974): 163–171

Rousset, Jean, "Albert Thibaudet: La Passion des ressemblances," *Bulletin de l'Académie Royale de Langue et de Littérature Françaises*, 65, no. 1 (1987): 70–78

TODOROV, TZVETAN

Literary Theorist, Essayist

On arriving in France in 1963, Tzvetan Todorov joined the structuralist movement, which at that time was dominant. His thesis, supervised by Roland Barthes and published in 1967 under the title *Littérature et signification*, offered an analysis of the poetics of Laclos's *Les liaisons dangereuses* (Dangerous Acquaintances) that announced its aspirations in the very first sentence: "The following work claims a place in the context of a science of literature or, as we shall prefer to call it, poetics."

Given his background and his ability to read Russian authors in the original, Todorov was very familiar with the Russian formalists. He introduced the first translations of their work in France, which he collected in 1965 under the title *Théorie de la littérature. Textes des formalistes russes*. Theory of literature. (Texts of Russian Structuralists). As such, he represented a vital link between the linguistic circles of Prague and Moscow and the French structuralist school, which he enriched with the writings of Roman Jakobson, Vladimir Propp, and Mikhaïl Bakhtin. This collection of articles was to have a decisive influence on the "Tel Quel" group led by Philippe Sollers and on the theorists of structuralism.

In 1968 he was invited to write the section on poetics in the joint work *Qu'est-ce que le structuralisme?* (What's the Structuralism?) by virtue of the fact that he was the first literary theorist in France to attempt to establish a theoretical project for the critical analysis of literary texts. In 1969, he invented the term *narratology*, which was subsequently popularized by Gérard Genette. He joined forces with Genette to found the review *Poétique* in 1970. The first period of Todorov's critical work, which has been distinguished overall by both its quantity and its international impact, was set against the backdrop of this semiotic and structural movement. During this first period, from 1963 to the late 1970s, he was primarily interested in literary forms and genres. Initially, he emphasized a descriptive and analytical approach (the culmination of which is found in the *Dictionnaire encyclopédique des sciences du langage*, edited with Oswald Ducrot), becoming interested later on in literature's historical aspects and its social significance.

Todorov describes poetics as "an approach to literature that is both 'abstract' and 'internal.' " The subject of poetics is not the literary work itself: what poetics considers are the properties of a particular discourse, namely literary discourse. The individual work is then considered purely as the manifestation of a much more general abstract structure of which it constitutes just one possible permutation." This abstract property defines the singularity of the "literary fact," its "*littérarité*" (literariness). As a theorist, Todorov draws simultaneously on Aristotle's *Poetics*, on Jakobson, and on Paul Valéry. His work is thus distinct from literary criticism, which comments on individual works, in that he seeks to construct a theoretical model of the literary discourse itself. Despite these conceptual distinctions, Todorov has always engaged in lively debate with both literary critics and the advocates of humanist and classical academic criticism. However, Todorov acknowledged in 1973 that poetics "is therefore called on to play an eminently transitional role," albeit without denying the relevance of structural relations and research into the formal organization of texts.

Whereas formalists such as Jakobson have often based their poetics on the analysis of poetry or short texts (such as fairy tales, in the case of Propp), Todorov is characterized by his focus on the study of narrative forms and the novel. He thus attempts to define the specific narrative characteristics of particular genres, such as the detective novel or the fantasy novel. He provides his own definition of fantasy, based on the notion of uncertainty and hesitation between natural laws and the sudden occurrence of apparently supernatural events. He points out that this kind of text, which has become canonical for genre theorists, already implies interpretation on the part of the reader, who has to identify with a character and share their hesitations. The structural approach to genre is thus not confined to its specific formal structure, but automatically takes account of the effects of reading that are created by the text. The study of genre must also make allowance for abstract theory and for a confrontation with existing texts at the same time. This enables Todorov to distinguish between historical genres (classical tragedy exists because works were published in seventeenth-century France that laid claim to this literary form) and theoretical genres (based on an *a priori* model, such as the opposition established by Todorov between the fantastic and the marvelous). Again, though, he acknowledges that the system of genres is in a state of continual evolution, and that theory is rooted in history.

Todorov seeks to construct a grammar of the narrative, a narratology, which he will then be able to use to study nonliterary narratives: eyewitness accounts, whether these date from the Spanish conquest of Mexico or from the concentration camp prisoners of the Second World War. Gradually, his thinking outgrew a structural approach, within which he had never wished to be confined, to take an interest in the meaning and interpretation of texts. His two works on the symbol bring to a close the first phase of his work and presage a move toward anthropology. Todorov thus established a link between the romantic conception of the symbol and the view of poetry as an end in itself advanced by the Russian formalists. The romantics posited Beauty and Art as ends in themselves, and they were later joined in this by the intransitive view of poetry championed by Jakobson. He believes that the poetic text exists as an end in itself and is simply a language game. Todorov goes back to the works of St. Augustine on allegory and symbol and seeks to uphold a more open interpretation of the symbol as a universal phenomenon that is naturally comprehensible to all.

The question of meaning and of value now becomes crucial, as in 1984 Todorov stated his view, in *Critique de la critique*, that "we today have a conceptual apparatus that is sufficient (despite its obvious imperfections) to describe the structural properties of literature and to analyze its historical significance." In this book, he adopted the model of dialogue-based criticism, inspired by the work of Bakhtin, and thus turned to "la question de l'autre" ("the question of the Other"), to quote the subtitle of *La conquête de l'Amérique*. Otherness became one of the central themes of the second period of a body of work that rediscovers human values: "Literature is concerned with human existence, it is a discourse (those who are afraid of big words) that focuses on truth and morality. Literature is a revelation of man and the world, said Sartre, and he was right" (Critique de la critique, p. 788). Todorov is now concerned less with technique than with meaning itself, shifting the focus of his work toward the history of ideologies and toward moral and political values.

At the same time, by contrast with a formalism based on the death of the subject, he argues that the human sciences should take account of the human dimension of the object of study and integrate the researcher's personal experience. In *Nous et les autres*, he set out the defining characteristics of this scientific discipline: ". . . the community of subject and object, and the inseparability of facts and values. Here, thinking that is not based on the researcher's personal experience quickly degenerates into scholasticism, giving satisfaction only to the researcher himself or to bureaucratic institutions, which are partial to quantitative data." However, this development does not represent a break with, still less a repudiation of, Todorov's earlier work. For Todorov, semiotic analysis cannot be conducted without taking account of the relationship with the Other, and the study of other cultures is based on the interpretation of their signs. Thus, semiotics, hermeneutics, and ethics interpenetrate one another.

Rereading Dostoyevsky in the original, Todorov takes up and disputes the interpretations of Bakhtin to show how forms and meanings are interdependent and must be understood in the light of the philosophical and symbolic preoccupations that underlie the Russian writer's work. Analysis of the linguistic type, as conducted by the structuralists, must be combined with a moral reflection that takes account of the diversity of the human being and his relationship with others, because "the human being is irreducibly heterogeneous, existing only in dialogue: the Other is found within the being" (*M. Bakhtine. Le principe dialogique*). For Todorov, the semiotic approach is inconceivable taken in isolation from the relationship with the Other.

Todorov extended this line of thinking on the tension between identity and otherness within each individual to the intercourse between cultures, by considering the discovery of the Other that is made via narratives of exploration and conquest. In *Nous et les autres*, he first argues that "the intercultural is a component of the cultural" and goes on to attempt an evaluation of the values inherent in each culture, asking whether they are relative or not. Initially, he says in *Les morales de l'histoire*, a dialogue is established between the identity of the researcher and that of the foreign work under study, with each side emphasizing its own values. This dialogue-based confrontation brings out the relativity of viewpoints, but in a way that leads to the abandonment of "the prejudice that consists of imagining that one may abandon all prejudices (. . .): the 'I' remains distinct from the Other." Finally, "through interaction with the Other, my categories are transformed, so that they become meaningful for the two of us, and—why not?—for third parties too."

This interest in otherness can obviously be traced back to Todorov's personal background, as a foreigner who chose to use the French language and who therefore looks at literature as an outsider. Bakhtin already believed that one culture could only be fully revealed in the eyes of another, and Todorov agreed with this theory when he subjected the view of other peoples taken by French writers such as Montesquieu, Diderot, and Rousseau to a rereading in *Nous et les autres*. Thus, a foreigner judges the way French writers talk about foreigners.

This confrontation between researcher and studied work does not rule out the possibility of judgment either—judgment of both an aesthetic and ethical nature. Because of his avoidance of dogmatism and relativism, he is free to pronounce on authors such as Jean-Jacques Rousseau, politicians such as Benjamin Constant, and some of the most tragic strands of contemporary history such as Nazism and Stalinism. "Censure is undesirable," he says in *Les morales de l'histoire*, "but no more so than the total impunity of discourse." The critic thus has the right to judge the writings of Sade and to condemn sexist or racist statements.

The third part of his work could be categorized under the heading of "exemplary narrative." In his final works, Todorov often takes as his starting point a real-life experience: a trip to Warsaw, a newspaper article he has read, a childhood memory. All are real-life narratives that raise moral questions. Just as Spinoza wanted to abolish the distinction between sacred texts that were held to be absolutely true and other texts that were open to dispute, so Todorov seeks to subject all narratives, literary and otherwise, to the same critique, in order to derive a moral teaching—if not the truth—from them. In addition, this use of anecdote is also based on a determination on the part of the critic to become involved in his books and to reject a pose of objectivity.

The question of evil is often central to these narrative-cum-commentaries, which relate to the tragedies of the twentieth century: the concentration camps, for example, or the victims of communism, a phenomenon of which he had firsthand experience in his native Bulgaria. In *Face à l'extrême*, he holds that "moral life was not extinguished in the camps. In fact, it is even possible that we may find something there on which to base an everyday morality that is appropriate for the present age." Rejecting Adorno's assertions about the impossibility of continuing to produce literature after Auschwitz and Hiroshima, Todorov considers that although "art for art's sake" may no longer be really possible, literature may serve to bear witness. The exemplary narratives of concentration camp survivors can lend a meaning to history and act as moral guides. And where narratives do not exist, Todorov patiently pieces together accounts, after painstaking ethnological enquiry, in order to reconstruct as accurately as possible one such extreme situation, in *Une tragédie française. Eté 1944*.

Thus, finally, throughout his research, Todorov defined himself as a mediator: "[my role] is the role of the critic, mediating between authors and readers, and the role of the immigrant, mediating between two cultures" (Verrier, 1995). He started by acting as an intermediary between the Russian formalists and the French structuralists; he then sought to understand what a literary text is by creating tools for formal analysis. Later, having examined the thought of the main French and European writers, he wished to understand how one culture can encounter another, even in periods of war and extreme violence. He then reflected on real-life narratives by ordinary people in order to transmit them to as many people as possible, using the arsenal of interpretative techniques supplied by dialogue-based criticism and anthropology. In his view, formalism has never ignored the question of literature's contents, which raise fundamental questions about existence. The continuity in his work thus lies in an attempt to capture four centuries of European cultural history (from Montaigne to the Nazi camps) via specific moments and authors: Rousseau, Constant, the conquest of Mexico by the Spanish, the praise of the everyday in the Netherlands of the seventeenth century. However, he does not seek to build up these analyses into a system: rather, he prefers the path of narrative, a course that is steered between the past and the present (especially in *Les abus de la mémoire*), between France and foreign cultures, between oneself and others.

MARC LITS

See also **Gerard Genette; Paul Valery**

Biography

Born in Sofia, Bulgaria, in 1939, Tzvetan Todorov emigrated to France in 1963, after completing his degree at the Faculty of Literature in Sofia. He submitted his Ph.D. in literature in 1966, under the supervision of Roland Barthes. He was then involved in the research into literary theory and semiotics associated with the École Pratique des hautes Études in Paris, working with Barthes, Greimas, Genette, and Lévi-Strauss. He founded the review *Poétique* with Gérard Genette in 1970. He was appointed a member of the CNRS, where he became director of research. He is also a visiting professor at several American universities.

Selected Works

Littérature et signification, 1967 Literature and meaning

Grammaire du Décaméron, 1969 Grammar of the Decameron

Introduction à la littérature fantastique, 1970; as *The Fantastic: A Structural Approach to a Literary Genre*, translated by Richard Howard, 1973

Poétique de la prose, 1971; as *The Poetics of Prose*, translated by Richard Howard, 1977

Dictionnaire encyclopédique des sciences du langage (with Oswald Ducrot), 1972; as *Encyclopedic Dictionary of the Sciences of Languages*, translated by Catherine Porter, 1979

Poétique, 1973; as *Introduction to Poetics*, translated by Richard Howard, 1981

Théories du symbole, 1977; as *Theories of the Symbol*, translated by Catherine Porter, 1982

Symbolisme et interprétation, 1978; as *Symbolism and Interpretation*, translated by Catherine Porter, 1982

Les genres du discours, 1978, as *Genres in Discourse*, translated by Catherine Porter, 1990

Mikhaïl Bakhtine. Le principe dialogique, 1981; as *Mikhail Bakhtin: The Dialogical Principle*, translated by Wlad Godzich, 1984

French Literary Theory Today: A Reader, translated by R. Carter, (not published in French), 1982

La conquête de l'Amérique. La question de l'autre, 1982; as *The Conquest of America; The Question of the Other*, translated by Richard Howard, 1984

Critique de la critique. Un roman d'apprentissage, 1984 Criticism of the criticism. An education novel

Frêle bonheur. Essai sur Rousseau, 1985; as *Frail Happiness: An Essay on Rousseau*, translated by John T. Scott and Robert D. Zaretsky, 2001

Nous et les autres. La réflexion française sur la diversité humaine, 1989; as *On Human Diversity: Nationalism, Racism, and Exoticism in French Thought*, translated by Catherine Porter, 1993

Les morales de l'histoire, 1991; as *The Morals of History*, translated by Alyson Waters, 1995

Face à l'extrême, 1991; as *Facing the Extreme: Moral Life in the Concentration Camps*, translated by Abigail Pollak and Arthur Henner, 1996

Eloge du quotidien. Essai sur la peinture hollandaise du XVIIe siècle, 1993 Praise of everyday life. Essay on the Dutch painting of the XVIIth century.

Une tragédie française. Eté 1994: scènes de la guerre civile, 1994; as *A French Tragedy: Scenes of Civil War, Summer 1944*, translated by Mary Byrd Kelly and Richard J. Golsan, 1996

La vie commune. Essai d'anthropologie générale, 1995; as *Life in Common: An Essay in General Anthropology*, translated by Katherine Golsan and Lucy Golsan, 2001

Les abus de la mémoire, 1995 The abuses of memory

L'homme dépaysé, 1996 The disoriented man

Le jardin imparfait. La pensée humaniste en France, 1998; as *Imperfect Garden: The Legacy of Humanism*, translated by Carol Cosman, 2002

Benjamin Constant, la passion démocratique, 1997; as *A Passion for Democracy: Benjamin Constant*, translated by Alice Seberry, 1999

Eloge de l'individu, 2000 Praise of individual

Mémoire du mal, tentation du bien, 2000 Memory of evil, Temptation of good

Further Reading

Verrier, Jean, *Tzvetan Todorov. Du formalisme russe aux morales de l'histoire*, Paris: Bertrand-Lacoste, 1995 From the Russian Formalism to the morals of History

Verrier, Jean, "La notion de 'récit exemplaire' chez Tzvetan Todorov," *Recherches en communication*, 7 (1997):89–104 The notion of "exemplary story" by T.T.

TOURNIER, MICHEL
Novelist, Essayist

Tournier's hyperbolic, kaleidoscopic, incandescent, and disconcerting novels compare favorably to the works often designated as "magic realism," particularly the work of the Latin American authors Gabriel García Márquez, Isabel Allende, and Jorge Luis Borges. However, because of the grand scope of his fiction and the ingenious methods by which paradoxical plots unravel and coalesce, Tournier has also been associated with Thomas Mann, Leon Tolstoy, and Robert Musil. His ability to provoke controversy by presenting relatively straightforward narrations teeming with subversive content (as the Bible does, he would argue), places him in a parallel mode with authors like Thomas Pynchon, Italo Calvino, Patrick Süskind, and V. S. Naipaul. Thus, it comes as no surprise that critics representing both left- and right-wing ideology have assailed him for creating fiction that, although intellectually and linguistically stimulating, is overly dramatic, sensual, symbolic, and perverse. Liberals see evidence of a fascism that constrains human behavior and contradicts a benevolent interpretation of world order; whereas conservatives lament any kind of moralizing impulse, and both parties are reluctant to praise the accomplishments of a successful French novelist who has managed to distance himself from the fashionable theories of deconstructionists and practitioners of "le nouveau roman," while at the same time exploiting the parameters of traditional narratology in order to shock and titillate. Tournier would defend himself by articulating a position "between scarcity and synthesis" and by reminding critics that many of his works were first conceived as theatrical performances ("le théâtre en jeu") or "mimesis"; hence, they are meant to be intellectually visible and open to public scrutiny as working documents. In the tradition of Samuel Beckett, Tournier has more often than not relied on an ironic detachment from his own creations to maintain a self-deprecating and irrepressible sense of humor (what he calls "le rire blanc," an absolute form of cosmic, Rabelaisian laughter), even in the face of catastrophic, nightmarish conditions.

Tournier's non-fiction (*Le Vent Paraclet, Le Vol du vampire, Le Coq de bruyère, Le Crépuscule des masques, Le Tabor et le Sinaï, Le Miroir des idées*) offers a tantalizing collection of intertextual ideas and philosophical thoughts in which he crosses the boundaries between autobiography, history, travelogue, and social psychology in order to give greater resonance to his novels and short stories. Most of his essays are whimsical—inspired by the gifts of the Holy Spirit: "la subtilité" (subtlety), "le faste" (pomp), and "la drolêrie" (jesting); he once quipped, "The more I laugh, the less I joke." In the 1980s and early 1990s, he cultivated a media personality that was flamboyant, provocative, narcissistic, self-mythologizing, and Machiavellian. Nevertheless, several recurrent intellectual patterns and preoccupations can be identified: the importance of questioning dominant ideologies; the child as absolute outsider who learns, through a series of rites of passage, the extent to which personal freedom is compromised by normative social values; the ambiguity of all texts and translations—semantic slippage allows, however, for endless rewritings and interpretations, what he calls a "hermeneutic quest"; historical research is a literary endeavor by which scrupulous documentation of subjects and objects (selective facts) leads to uncanny revelations; literature represents an antidote for the poison of political power, which imposes beliefs, by presenting alternative strategies that should be discussed; the New Millennium will be characterized by a form of pan-sexualism—the end of masculine and feminine stereotypes; Spinoza's three kinds of knowledge (passion, the scientific method, direct intuition of essence) allows a philosophical novelist to give concrete weight to intangible objects—"a lie in the direction of truth"; the *Image* (all visual media including painting and sculpture) is impure—condemned by Islamic fundamentalists but enshrined in Western culture—only the *Sign* is pure (written and spoken language).

Le Miroir des idées contains fifty-eight essays in the form of dichotomies (for example, "The Soul and the Heart," "Apollo and Dionysus," "Memory and Habit," "The Primary and the Secondary") representing Tournier's "key concepts or categories." Like the parables of the Gospels, these essays are elliptical and edifying, pose more problems than provide answers, and perform what he calls "a recuperative function." Tournier's protean mask can seem impenetrable and his playfulness can seem disconcerting; he once referred to himself as "un petit Tarzan métaphysique." He includes himself as a reference under the epithet "the angel of Choisel"—Choisel is the name of his home. Twice he refers to Edward Reinrot ("pure red" in German); "Reinrot" is "Tournier" backwards without the "u". In another cryptic allusion, he cites Ibn Al Houdaïda—"Houdaïda" means "to turn" (Tournier) in Arabic.

Tournier's ultimate goal is to invert hierarchical relations in order to sustain what he calls "progrès à rebours" (subversive progress). Like Friday—"Robinson Crusoe's dancing god"—there is an innocence, or at least a neutrality, in Tournier's worldview. Like some Harlequin before God, he approaches the absolute by means of laughter, living for the moment without any trace of nostalgia or apprehension of the future.

With such a theatrical disposition grounded in philosophy, Tournier implores the reader to respond as a cocreator of new ideas, rooted in myth and allegory, the only possible defense against the malaise of postmodernity. Therefore, his works can be summarized as steps toward transcendence through a series of initiation rites at different levels of consciousness, much like Scheherazade's thousand and one tales. Tournier emphasizes that Gustave Flaubert and Émile Zola had a profound influence on him, not only because of the scientific rigor associated with their fiction, but also because each was willing to take major emotional and philosophical risks—as true avatars of romanticism—by presenting history and mythology as the sublimation of power and creativity. Tournier can best be seen as a natural philosopher and etymologist, as someone who questions the status of all categories, who implies that phenomenology and experience overwhelm ethical theory, as someone who attempts to aestheticize day-to-day existence, and who practices a continuous ordering of reality through correctness of detail in the philosophical tradition established by Gottfried Leibnitz, Friedrich Hegel, Immanuel Kant, Baruch Spinoza, and Arthur Schopenhauer.

Tournier's most clearly delineated characters (Robinson Crusoe in *Vendredi ou les limbes du Pacifique*; Abel Tiffauges in *Le Roi des aulnes*; Jean, Paul, and Alexandre in *Les Météores*; and Gilles de Rais in *Gilles et Jeanne*) represent a fusion of psychological, literary, and cultural types, on which Tournier has drawn from numerous sources; there is a long trail of semiotic references, Freudian infantile behaviors, anthropological signs and symbols (Tournier studied with Claude Lévi-Strauss), Foucault-like constructions of madness, "angst" and hermetic subjectivity from Jean-Paul Sartre and Friedrich Nietzsche, and idols and icons from Carl Gustave Jung. Thus, Robinson Crusoe is a hero of exotic solitude, of personalized premodern civilization, of a narcissistic internal labyrinth. Abel Tiffauges, the archetypal fetishist, is also a surrogate savior who inhabits a world of biological and sadomasochistic metaphors and circumstances. Gilles de Rais is like a moth hypnotized by the flames of his own debauchery. He cannot reconcile himself to the loss of his mentor, Joan of Arc, who personifies the Cardinal Virtues; hence, he commits himself to self-destruction through the Seven Deadly Sins. Jean and Paul—positive and negative images of each other and of escape to and from deviance and insanity—lure their uncle into a series of pilgrimages in honor of some kind of androgynous, unisex, polymorphous sensuality at the margins of society in Iceland, Canada, Casablanca, Japan, Venice, and Berlin. For Tournier, the desert is one of his most compelling motifs because it represents loss of intimacy, attachment, and affection, and those who inhabit the deserts of society are "secondary characters" encapsulated by contexts established by authority figures and forever marginalized, like the African immigrants in France who appear in *La Goutte d'or*. Tournier seems mesmerized by what he calls "bricolage" or "détournement," a process by which the odds and ends of culture act like a centrifugal force that pushes outward to capture the "otherness" of vagrants and of vagabonds. Like Charles Baudelaire, Tournier remains fascinated by the monstrous appearance of fringe types and desert dwellers who have little to offer except their unquenchable thirst for the supreme wonder of the human condition. Tournier's fiction and essays, despite their unique and obsessively formalized logic in which objectivity is pushed to the point of hallucination, represent a nostalgia for a lost wholeness, for a fresh look at origins and endings, and for the pure joy of questioning, exploring, and discovering new gardens that break through the wall of complacency and indifference. As he once observed, "Le secret d'un livre c'est la patience"; Tournier's open secret is mystical, mythic, and adventurous.

ROBERT FRAIL

Biography

Born in Paris, he grew up in a bilingual French-German household, and he often spent childhood summers with an uncle in Germany. Sickly as a child (he lived briefly in a Swiss sanitarium), his sporadic schooling was mostly in private Catholic schools. He received the baccalauréat in philosophy (1941), then a master's degree in philosophy, a certificate in psychology, and an advanced degree ("licence") in law (1946) from the University of Paris. For four years, he studied at the University of Tübingen, Germany (1945–49), but upon returning to Paris, he failed to obtain the "agrégation" in philosophy, which would have qualified him as a teacher. For the next twenty years he worked as a journalist, editor, and translator in publishing houses and for radio and television productions. Since 1962 he has lived in a former vicarage twenty miles south of Paris, where he has devoted himself to the creation of highly imaginative works of fiction, children's literature, and sociopolitical essays. His total output represents works translated into twenty languages, with millions of copies sold. He is a skilled photographer, and he has given numerous interviews in various media since the publication of his first two novels: *Vendredi ou les limbes du Pacifique* (1967), winner of Le Grand Prix du Roman, and *Le Roi des aulnes* (1970), the only book unanimously approved for Le Prix Goncourt by the Académie Goncourt, to which he was elected in 1972.

Selected Works

Vendredi ou les limbes du Pacifique, 1967; as *Friday, or the Other Island*, translated by Norman Denny, 1969
Le Roi des aulnes, 1970; as *The Ogre* (U.K. *The Erl-King*), translated by Barbara Bray, 1972
Vendredi ou la vie sauvage, 1971; as *Friday and Robinson: Life on Esperanza Island*, translated by Ralph Manheim, 1972
Les Météores, 1975; as *Gemini*, translated by Ann Carter, 1981
Le Vent paraclet, 1977; as *The Wind Spirit*, translated by Arthur Goldhammer, 1988
Le Coq de bruyère, 1978; as *The Fetishist*, translated by Barbara Wright, 1984
Pierrot ou les secrets de la nuit, 1979; as *Pierrot, or the Secrets of the Night*, translated by Margaret Higonnet, 1985
Gaspard, Melchior et Balthazar, 1980; as *The Four Wise Men*, translated by Ralph Manheim, 1982
Le Vol du vampire: notes de lecture 1981 Flight of the Vampire (Notes from Readings)
Gilles et Jeanne, 1983; translated by Alan Sheridan, 1987
La Goutte d'or, 1985; as *The Golden Droplet*, translated by Barbara Wright, 1987
Le Médianoche amoureux: contes et nouvelles, 1989; as *The Midnight Love Feast*, translated by Barbara Wright, 1991
Le Miroir des idées, 1994; as *The Mirror of Ideas*, translated by Jonathan Krell, 1998
Éléazar ou la source et le buisson, 1996 Eleazar or the source (of water) and the Bush

Further Reading

Bevan, David, *Michel Tournier*, Amsterdam: Rodopi, 1986

Bouloumié, Arlette, *Michel Tournier, le roman mythologique*, Paris: Jose Corti, 1988

Cloonan, William, *Michel Tournier*, Boston: Twayne, 1985

Davis, Colin, *Michel Tournier: Philosophy and Fiction*, Oxford: Clarendon Press, 1988

Gascoigne, David, *Michel Tournier*, Washington D.C. and Oxford: Berg, 1996

Koster, Serge, *Michel Tournier*, Paris: Henri Veyrier, 1986

Krell, Jonathan, *Tournier Élémentaire*, West Lafayette, IN: Purdue University Press, 1994

Merllié, Françoise, *Michel Tournier*, Paris: Dossiers Belfond, 1988

Petit, Susan, *Michel Tournier's Metaphysical Fictions*, Amsterdam and Philadelphia: John Benjamins, 1991

Roberts, Martin, *Michel Tournier: Bricolage and Cultural Mythology*, Saratoga, CA: Stanford University Press, 1994

Shattuck, Roger, "Locating Michel Tournier," in his *The Innocent Eye: On Modern Literature and the Arts*, New York: Farrar Strauss Giroux, 1984

Vray, Jean-Bernard, *Michel Tournier et l'Écriture seconde*, Lyon: Presses Universitaires de Lyon, 1997

Worton, Michael (editor), *Michel Tournier*, London and New York: Longman, 1995

V

VALÉRY, PAUL
Poet

Although Valéry considered artistic creation the supreme human activity, he insisted his poetry was subordinate to a concern with understanding the workings of the human mind. In the eyes of the author of *La Jeune Parque* (1917) and *Charmes* (1922), poetry demanded the rigorous monitoring of a state of heightened self-consciousness in which mind, body, and world were united in a unique moment of perception that gave access to a reality that preceded language and thought. It was with this realm of "prethought" that this deeply rational being, who was nonetheless attracted to the mystical, was concerned in all his writings. Whereas the latter are testimony to his unrivaled intellectual range, taking in the physical sciences, mathematics, philosophy, history, politics, and economics as well as art, music, linguistics, and poetics, Valéry was not concerned to make a contribution to any particular discipline but, rather, to trace the interdependent shifts discernible in the perceiving self and the reality that was the object of the latter's perception. Though in itself a disinterested pursuit, it was a form of inquiry that possessed radical implications for any intellectual activity that took its conventional basis in language for granted. Valéry himself was consistently dismissive of any theoretical explanation he regarded as dependent on a use of language that lacked a basis in objective reality.

Valéry was in his early twenties when he began his investigation into the human intellect in two important works, *Introduction à la méthode de Léonard de Vinci* (1895) and *La Soirée avec Monsieur Teste* (1896). These were followed in 1921 by his Socratic dialogues *Eupalinos ou l'Architecte* and *L'Ame et la danse*, which were conceived as exploratory celebrations of the "pure" arts of architecture, music, and dance. A third dialogue, *L'Idée fixe*, in which the two figures, Moi and Le Docteur, explore the relationship between the intellect and the experimental sciences, appeared in 1932. In parallel with these works, Valéry pursued his intellectual inquiry in a range of occasional lectures and essays, and above all, in the remarkable posthumously published notebooks, or *Cahiers*, that together occupy almost 27,000 pages. This "travail de Pénélope" as he termed it, was initially inspired by the notebooks of Leonardo and consisted of the investigations into the cognitive processes of the mind he conducted at daybreak throughout a period spanning some fifty years. With a view to their eventual publication, Valéry spent the latter years of his life organizing these myriad fragments in accordance with a system that employed thirty-one headings and 215 subheadings.

Leonardo, like Goethe, represented for Valéry universal man, an ideal to which he unapologetically aspired. Alongside such revered figures, however, he created the imaginary persona of the (overly) cerebral Monsieur Teste who, in the manner of his creator, pursues an intense concentration on the intellect to uncommon lengths, illustrating the requirement for intellectual processes to refine themselves through their own self-conscious activity. Valéry would return periodically throughout his life to this *alter ego* he referred to as his *croquemitaine* (bogeyman), and whose oft-quoted declaration "La bêtise n'est pas mon fort" ("stupidity is not my strong point") is less straightforwardly immodest than Edmund Wilson and certain other critics have sometimes supposed.

Broadly speaking, Valéry may be regarded as a rationalist and a skeptic committed to the questioning of received ideas and the form in which they are expressed. In his insistence on his method, he aligned himself with Descartes, Pascal being his *bête noire* as a result of his readiness to abandon rationality and embark on a crucial leap of faith. His thinking has been related to eighteenth-century materialism and was undoubtedly marked by nineteenth-century scientific ideas. There is, in his work, sympathetic engagement with Freud and Einstein. Resemblances between his thinking and that of Nietzsche and Bergson have been the subject of detailed debate. His overriding concern with perception suggests a parallel with Merleau-Ponty and other phenomenologists. Yet in the end, his obsession with the intellect for its own sake remains distinct from the activity of any systematic philosopher.

Valéry indeed disclaimed the title of philosopher, maintaining that he had never read Hegel and once suggesting, only half-humorously, that what he practiced was "Misosophy." By this should be understood a hostility to all systems of thought and a respect for the way reality is in a state of perpetual evolution. (Régine Pietra has referred appropriately to his "negative philosophy": see Gifford and Stimpson, 1998, chapter 5). Opposed to any kind of absolute, his commitment was to an espousal of total relativity. He was committed to avoiding the definitive, while equally declaring himself to be the enemy of the vague. His method was rooted in a disciplined self-detachment. Even the prescience he showed in his political analyses (in spite of being on the "wrong" side in the Dreyfus affair) has been attributed by his son, François, to his having "applied to the political field a method of observation and analysis tried out on himself."

The publication of the *Cahiers* made possible for the first time an appreciation of the profound originality of Valéry's intellectual endeavor, rendering previous studies of his thought, which had been obliged to work in terms of fully fashioned ideas rather than the actual form of the investigation, seriously incomplete. The multiple fragments emerge not as preliminaries to the published essays, but as manifestations of the author's inquiry in a more advanced form. Highlighting the originality of his diverse and eclectic jottings, Valéry was dismissive of his published work, maintaining that it was these studies that represented falsification, in that they "eliminated the provisional and the non-reiterable, the instantaneous, the medley of pure and impure, order and disorder." In order to convey an authentic trace of the human consciousness at work in its most inchoate state, it is necessary for him both to allow language and syntax to be strained to the limits and to respect rudimentary expression. Prose poems exist alongside abstract analysis in which the author has recourse to mathematical equations to describe the processes at work. Aphorisms, together with other seemingly categorical statements describing his method and his observations, are, in this work that is grounded in a mistrust of ideas, frequently subversive of the conventional form they appear to respect, revealing themselves instead to be part of an endless process of self-refinement. Not the least original dimension of the *Cahiers* is the way in which apparently straightforward formulations subtly question their own lucidity. At all times, the mind, for Valéry, has to be in a state of readiness for new and surprising discoveries.

Valéry's place in twentieth-century French thought is difficult to determine. Although he may be regarded as a precursor of "la nouvelle critique," with the "Tel Quel" school, for example, deriving its very name from one of his works, he can neither be assigned to a particular philosophical movement nor regarded as having produced disciples. It is significant that, unlike many other French thinkers of his period and later, he was never himself a teacher of philosophy. On the other hand, through both his poetic practice and his prose writings, he has exerted a widespread influence on successive generations of readers, who have found themselves seduced into participating in his creative exploration of human consciousness. At the turn of the twentieth century, the concentration by scholars on elucidating the significance of the *Cahiers*, both at the fundamental level of their form and in relation to their profound implications for the human sciences, promises to establish Valéry as one of the most original thinkers of his age.

MICHAEL TILBY

See also **Henri Bergson; Maurice Merleau-Ponty**

Biography

Valéry was born in Sète on October 30, 1871, and educated at the Lycée de Montpellier and University of Montpellier. He earned a law degree in 1894. He was employed as a translator and editor by Cecil Rhodes' British South Africa Company in London in 1896. He became a contributor to *The New Review* in 1897. Valéry married Jeannine Gobillard, niece of painter Berthe Morisot, in 1900. He worked as the private secretary to Edouard Lebey, managing director of Havas News Agency, from 1900 to 1922. Valéry was elected to the French Academy in 1925. He was awarded an honorary doctorate from the University of Oxford in 1931. He was named Chair of Poetics at the Collège de France in 1937 and Director of the French

Academy in 1941. Valéry died in Paris on July 20, 1945.

Selected Works

Introduction à la méthode de Léonard de Vinci, 1895; as *Introduction to the Method of Leonardo da Vinci*, translated by Thomas M. McGreevy, 1929

La Soirée avec Monsieur Teste, 1896; as *An Evening with Monsieur Teste*, translated by Jackson Mathews, 1947

"La conquête allemande," "The German Conquest" 1897

"The Crisis of the Mind," 1919

Eupalinos ou l'architecte, 1923; as *Eupalinos, or the Architect*, translated by W.M. Stewart, 1932

L'Ame et la Danse, 1923; as *Dance and the Soul*, translated by Dorothy Bussy, 1951

Variété, 1924; as *Variety*, translated by Malcolm Cowley, 1927

Variété II, 1929, as *Variety*, second series, translated by William Aspenwall Bradley, 1938

Pièces sur l'art, 1931 *Writings on Art*

Regards sur le monde actuel, 1931; as *Reflections on the World Today*, translated by Francis Scarfe, 1948

L'Idée fixe, ou deux hommes à la mer, 1932; as *Idée fixe. A Duologue by the Sea* translated by David Paul in *The Collected Works of Paul Valéry*, vol. 5.

Oeuvres, edited by Jean Hytier, 2 vols., 1957, 1960

The Collected Works of Paul Valéry, edited by Jackson Mathews, 15 vols., 1956–75

Cahiers, 29 vols., 1957–61

Cahiers, édition établie, présentée et annotée par Judith Robinson, 2 vols., 1973–74

The "Cahiers/Notebooks" of Paul Valéry, translated and edited by Brian Stimpson, Paul Gifford, and Robert Pickering, 5 vols., 2001–

Further Reading

Blüher, Karl-Alfred and Jürgen Schmidt-Radefeldt (editors), *Valéry und die Philosophie (Forschungen zu Paul Valéry*, 5), Kiel: Forschungs- und Dokumentationszentrum Paul Valéry der Universität Kiel, 1992

Crow, Christine M., *Paul Valéry and Maxwell's Demon: Natural Order and Human Possibility*, Hull, England: University of Hull, 1972

Crow, Christine M., *Paul Valéry: Consciousness and Nature*, Cambridge: Cambridge University Press, 1972

Cruickshank, John, "Valéry and the Great War" in *Baudelaire, Mallarmé, Valéry. New Essays in Honour of Lloyd Austin*, edited by Malcolm Bowie, Alison Fairlie, and Alison Finch, Cambridge: Cambridge University Press, 1982

Cruickshank, John, *Variations on Catastrophe. Some French Responses to the Great War*, Oxford: Clarendon Press, 1982

Derrida, Jacques. "Qual quelle. Les Sources de Valéry" in *Marges de la philosophie*, Paris: Editions de minuit, 1972 (first published in MLN, 87 (1972), 563–599); as *Margins of Philosophy*, translated by Alan Bass, Brighton. Harvester, 1982

Gifford, Paul, *Paul Valéry—le dialogue des choses divines*, Paris: Corti, 1989

Gifford, Paul, and Brian Stimpson (editors), *Reading Paul Valéry: Universe in Mind*, Cambridge: Cambridge University Press, 1998

Ince, W. N., *The Poetic Theory of Paul Valéry: Inspiration and Technique*, Leicester: Leicester University Press, 1970

Kluback, William, *Paul Valéry: Philosophical Reflections*, New York: Peter Lang, 1987

Kluback, William, *Paul Valéry: The Search for Intelligence*, New York: Peter Lang, 1993

Kluback, William, *Paul Valéry: Illusions of Civilization*, New York: Peter Lang, 1996

Kluback, William, *Paul Valéry: The Continuous Search for Reality*, New York: Peter Lang, 1997

Reinstate Judith Robinson's very important 1963 study: *L'Analyse de l'esprit dans les "Cahiers" de Valéry* Paris: Corti, 1963

Robinson, Judith, *L'Analyse de l'esprit dans les "Cahiers" de Valéry*, Paris: Corti, 1963

Robins, Ruth and Julian Wolfreys, "In the wake of . . . Baudelaire, Valéry, Derrida" in *The French Connections of Jacques Derrida*, edited by Julian Wolfreys, John Brannigan, and Ruth Robins, Albany, New York, State University of New York Press, 1999

Robinson, Judith, "Language, physics and mathematics in Valéry's *Cahiers*," *Modern Language Review*, 55.4 (October 1960): 519–536

Schmidt-Radefeldt, Jürgen, "Valéry et les sciences du langage," *Poétique*, 31 (1977): 368–385

Signorile, Patricia, *Paul Valéry, philosophe de l'art: l'architectonique de sa pensée à la lumière des "Cahiers,"* Paris: Vrin, 1993

Stimpson, Brian, "The Writing 'I': Subject, Voice and Language in the Work of Paul Valéry," An Inaugural Lecture, London: Roehampton Institute, 1995

Suckling, Norman, *Paul Valéry and the Civilized Mind*, London, New York, and Toronto: Oxford University Press, 1954

Valéry, François (editor), *Paul Valéry et la politique*, Paris: Gallimard, 1984

Whiting, Charles G., *Paul Valéry*, London: Athlone Press, 1978

VERNANT, JEAN-PIERRE
Classicist

Antifascist activist on the left bank in the 1930s, famed resistance fighter "Le colonel Berthier" during the second world war, philosophy professor at a *lycée* in Toulouse after the war, then *Directeur d'Études à l'École Pratique des Hautes Études*, and finally Professor at the *Collège de France*, holding a chair in the Comparative Study of Ancient Religions, Jean-Pierre Vernant has done more to revitalize the study of the Greek world than any other figure of postwar France, and perhaps in the entire Western World. His broad intellectual and personal experience has helped move the study of archaic myth from a narrow categorizing perspective to an attempt to reconstruct the history of the subject and its social constitution. As he acknowledged in a 1998 interview, he has remained throughout his career a resolute "utopian," who dreamed of "groups united by friendship on an equal plane" (http://www.ombres-blanches.com/pages/bulletin/octnov1998/vernant.html). He has continued to be an active voice against the forces of the extreme right in France, as represented by the National Front of Jean-Marie Le Pen, in their attempt to appropriate the heritage of Greece as a model for their dream of an ethnically pure, "western" and ultimately Indo-European society (http://www.vacarme.eu.org/article92.html).

The politics of Vernant's encounter with the Greek world, however, are anything but simple and seldom explicit. What his work has done most crucially is to elaborate a unique multidisciplinary method for the study of the ancient Greek world. It seeks through what he terms historical psychology to construct a structural model of Greek man's self-conception in a strictly delimited symbolic universe. Vernant's chief intellectual influences are widely acknowledged: Louis Gernet, the first French Hellenist to use anthropological methods to study Greek history; Georges Dumézil, the founder of modern comparative Indo-European mythology; Émile Benveniste, who used comparative linguistic data to elucidate the history and meaning of social institutions; and Claude Lévi-Strauss the theorist of the structural study of myth.

Less well known, but clearly of great personal and intellectual importance to Vernant, is the work of Ignacy Myerson. Myerson developed a school of psychology that examined the historical determination of specific cognitive faculties. The relation of this work to the historical study of *mentalités* is evident, but Vernant rejects that concept, derived from the *Annales* school, as too global and too general to be of use for the true historical psychologist who involves himself or herself in the study of "particular functions like memory, imagination, person or will" (*Mortals and Immortals*, 1991). Thus in an article defending his reading of Hesiod's myth of the five races in terms of Dumézil's model of the three basic social functions of Indo-European ideology (sovereignty, warfare, and material production), Vernant notes that time as conceived by the archaic and classical Greeks was not the abstract continuum of modern thought but a logical succession of stages. For Vernant, then, notions such as the Greek "discovery" of reason, the individual, and science—all truisms of the humanist tradition—are problematic if not to be rejected outright. Even such seemingly self-evident categories as "memory" are to be rigorously historicized and contextualized within the larger structures of archaic and classical Greek civilization. Greek science and philosophy cannot be disassociated from the rise of the *polis* as the chief political unit in Greece, the advent of a money economy, and the development of city planning based on concepts of strictly delimited geometrical space and abstract equality before the law.

Vernant, then, is a philosophical antihumanist. He may not reject the subject or its experience as a meaningful category, but he does reject both concepts when used as abstract universals possessing meaning outside specific historical and material contexts. Philosophical antihumanism, although widely acknowledged in structuralism and poststructuralism, is most closely associated with the work of the Marxist philosopher Louis Althusser. Vernant does not mention Althusser in any of his major publications, but the influence of Marx on his work and his continuing engagement and debate with the French Communist Party is one of the least-appreciated parts of his anglophone reception. From his 1956 essay "Psychological Aspects of Work in Ancient Greece" to his 1995 introduction to *The Greeks*, Marx's economic thought is a constant influence on Vernant's own. In the former essay, there is a subtle analysis of the psychological impact of the priority of use value over exchange value in Greek thought. Vernant demonstrates that inasmuch as labor was conceived not in terms of either an abstract force or the production of commodities for exchange but in terms of the use value it produced, the form of the object of production was conceived as preexisting the act of production. "The material cause is not really productive: it plays the role of a means by which a pre-existing form actualizes itself in matter." The importance of this observation is not to be underestimated. Vernant has given us here nothing less than the economic basis of Plato's theory of forms, though he is much too subtle to make so brash a claim. In *The Greeks*, he quotes directly from Marx's *Holy Family* to argue against the humanist notion that "if historians managed to reconstruct perfectly the décor in which the ancients lived, they would have accomplished their task, and in reading their work, each of us would find ourselves standing in the sandals of Greek." Subjectivity, in short, is not portable. Far from being a crude dialectical materialist, Vernant explicitly rejects the model of culture as a reflection of a preexisting material substructure. He argues instead that the rise of philosophical reason was inextricably tied to the monetary and political changes that marked Greece during the sixth and seventh centuries B.C.E., but was not their reflection, a position that recalls Althusser's notion of structural causality.

Vernant offers us a way of understanding antiquity through the comparative study of models of thought, memory, and perception that are profoundly different from our own. The interpreter's job, he argues, is to reconstruct the contexts that made those models operative in sufficient detail and with sufficient conceptual rigor to allow them to be compared to other models. While acknowledging the dependence of this type of interpretive work on the kind of positivist and philological fact collecting that had characterized the study of antiquity in France prior to World War II, he rejects such piecemeal "index card" models of thought as insufficient to the task at hand. His own methods have been widely influential in France, in part through his founding of the Centre Louis Gernet, a research center that attracts scholars from all over the world. His name is associated with those of the most important and innovative Hellenists in France today, including Marcel Detienne and Pierre Vidal-Naquet. Vernant's influence is widely recognized by anglophone Hellenists as well.

PAUL ALLEN MILLER

See also **Louis Althusser; Emile Benveniste; Georges Dumezil; Claude Lévi-Strauss**

Biography

Jean-Pierre Vernant was born January 4, 1914, in Provins. He began his academic career as a student at the Sorbonne in the 1930s, where he was also an antifascist activist in the Latin Quarter. He received his *agrégation* in philosophy in 1937. Throughout the Second World War, he was active in the Resistance, winning fame under the code name Colonel Berthier. Director of Hautes Etudes, at the École Pratique des Hautes Études from 1957 to 1975, he was elected to the Collège de France in 1975. He was also the founder and director of the Centre de Recherches Comparées sur les sociétés anciennes (Centre Louis Gernet) from 1964 to 1985. He remains an active scholar in his nineties.

Selected Works

Les origines de la pensée grecque, 1962; as *The Origins of Greek Thought*, 1982
Mythe et société en Grèce ancienne, 1974; as *Myth and Society in Ancient Greece*, translated by J. Lloyd 1980
Les ruses de l'intelligence. La métis des Grecs (with Marcel Detienne), 1974; as *Cunning Intelligence in Greek Culture and Society*, translated by Janet Lloyd, 1978
Mythe et pensée chez les Grecs. Études de psychologie historique, 1985, revised third edition
Mythe et tragédie en Grèce ancienne, 1972 (with Pierre Vidal-Naquet); as *Tragedy and Myth in Ancient Greece*, translated by J. Lloyd, 1988
Travail et esclavage en Grèce ancienne (with Pierre Vidal-Naquet), 1988
Oedipe et ses mythes (with Pierre Vidal-Naquet), 1988
L'individu, la mort, l'amour. Soi-même et l'autre en Grèce ancienne, 1989
Mythe et religion en Grèce ancienne, 1990
Figures, idoles, masques, 1990
La Grèce ancienne 1. Du mythe à la raison (with Pierre Vidal-Naquet), 1990
Mortals and immortals. Collected essays (F. Zeitlin, editor), 1991
La Grèce ancienne 2. L'espace et le temps (with P. Vidal-Naquet), 1992
La Grèce ancienne 3. Rites de passage et transgressions (with P. Vidal-Naquet), 1992
L'Homme grec (J.-P. Vernant, editor), 1993; as *The Greeks*, translated by Charles Lambert and Teresa Lavender Fagan, 1995

Further Reading

Benamou, Georges-Marc, *C'était un temps déraisonnable: les premiers résistants racontent*, Paris: Laffont, 1999
Brisson, Jean-Paul, Jean-Pierre Vernant, and Pierre Vidal-Naquet, *Démocratie, citoyenneté et héritage gréco-romain*, Paris: Liris, 2000
Di Donato, Riccardo, *Per una antropologia storica del mondo antico*, Firenze: La nuova Italia, 1990
Loraux, Nicole, Gregory Nagy, and Laura Slatkin (editors), *Antiquities. Postwar French Thought*, Volume III, New York: New Press, 2001
Poikilia: études offertes à Jean-Pierre Vernant, Paris: Éditions de l'École des hautes études en sciences sociales, 1987
Zeitlin, Froma I. (editor) "Introduction," *Mortals and immortals. Collected essays* Princeton, New Jersey: Princeton University Press, 1991

VIDAL-NAQUET, PIERRE
Historian

An historian specializing in antiquity, Pierre Vidal-Naquet has contributed to renewing the understanding of classical Greek society. He is also an engaged intellectual who fought for human rights, especially during the Algerian War, at which time he protested against torture practices of the French army, and in the 1990s, during which he produced critical work refuting revisionist theories of the Holocaust.

Although he started his career as a historian of the ancient world (mostly Greece), he has also used the historical method to assess and comment on the contemporary world. A member of the Paris group of historians characterized by a use of anthropology and critical sociology methods in the analysis of historical evidence and by a cultural criticism approach, he is close to figures such as Vernant or, from North America, Finchley (of whose work he organized translations in France). He published his first major work, *Cleisthenes the Athenian*, in 1964, but the study that established him as a leading historian is *Myth and Tragedy in Ancient Greece*, cowritten in 1972 with Jean-Pierre Vernant. Starting from a rigorous historiography investigation that seeks to avoid anachronistic interpretation, Vidal-Naquet put the discourse or the evidence into its anthropological, behavioral and sociopolitical context. His aim is often to identify and give a presence to the powerless and the excluded (women, slaves, craftsmen, foreigners) who are either absent or taken for granted in the historical texts as well as in the official history. He defines himself as a history "traitor" who aims at debunking the official or accepted historical discourse.

But Pierre Vidal-Naquet is also an intellectual "engaged with his time"—and he has been principally known as a leading figure in human rights and civil liberties protests. From the late 1950s he denounced the widespread practice of torture by the French Army in the Algerian War. Obviously inspired by his family experience, he wrote: "The idea that the same tortures could be inflicted first in Indochina and Madagascar, then in Algeria by French Army officers or policemen horrified me. . . . In a way, (my reaction) is patriotism." Further, what was at the root of his reaction was not only torture itself (of which everybody was aware) but the fact that it had become a "State institution" corrupting and perverting democracy: ". . . fifteen years after the collapse of Hitler's order, French militarism . . . had managed to restore torture—making it again a kind of institution in Europe." His first intervention was the creation of the Marcel Audin Committee in 1958, from the name of a Communist teacher in Algeria who "disappeared" in the hands of the Army, presumed tortured to death. A fervent critic of colonialism, he was also one of the writers and signatories (alongside Sartre, Duras, and others) of the so-called "Manifesto of the 121" that in 1960 supported the members of the Jeanson network arrested for helping the Algerian independantists of the FLN, asserting the right of "insubordination" and "treason" as a condition for the respect of truth and freedom.

In the 1980s and 1990s he became a leading intellectual figure in the fight against the rise of revisionist history. He used his expertise as an historian to denounce such well-known figures as Faurisson for either negating or questioning the extent of the Holocaust or some of its specific aspects, such as the existence of gas chambers. In this context, he was involved in a number of controversies about the extent of freedom of expression, especially with Noam Chomsky. He has also been active for the defense of immigrants without documentation (the "sans papiers").

It is interesting that Vidal-Naquet views his historical research and his work on contemporary society as both dealing with issues of discourse falsification. On ancient texts, the issue is to reconstruct the existence of outsiders in the silent discourse; whereas on contemporary issues, such as revisionist theories of the Holocaust, his aim is to deconstruct the falsified discourse in order to recover the underlying evidence.

FRANÇOIS NECTOUX

Biography

Pierre Vidal-Naquet was born into a liberal Jewish bourgeois Paris family in 1927 and was still in school when the Second World War broke out. His parents are arrested in 1944, his father tortured by the Gestapo in Marseilles, and both were deported to Auschwitz, never to return. A graduate of the prestigious École Normale Supérieure, he specialized in the study of Antiquity, especially Greece. In 1969 he became a Director of Studies at the École des Hautes Études en Sciences Sociales (Vth Section) in Paris. From 1984 to 1997 he was director of the Centre Louis Gernet, a joint CNRS/EHESS research center devoted to comparative research on ancient cultures.

Selected Works

Tragedy and Myth in Ancient Greece (with Jean-Pierre Vernant, 1972
Assassins of Memory: Essays on the Denial of Holocaust, 1987
The Black Hunter: Forms of Thought and Forms of Society in the Greek World, 1981
The Jews: History, Memory and the Present, 1991
Cleisthenes the Athenian: An Essay on the Representation of Space and Time in Greek Political Thought, 1964
La Torture dans la République, 1972
The French Student Uprising November 1967–June 1968: An Analytical Record (with Alain Schnapp), 1969

VIRILIO, PAUL
Academic, Writer, Military Historian

Paul Virilio is one of the few French thinkers to have replaced philosophical and sociological discourse with a discourse on war and the "militarization" of social structures. He has written extensively on such related themes as the "archeology" of the bunker, the relationship between speed and politics, the virtualization of political and cultural life, and the influence of the discourse of war in many areas of contemporary life. Having studied phenomenology with Merleau-Ponty at the Sorbonne, his earlier writings focused on urbanism and spatial politics, whereas later on he was to write on a wide variety of cultural topics, centering around his key concepts of speed and the acceleration of cultural life, the politics of vision, and the discourse of war.

Virilio's critique of technology, politics, and society provides an illuminating insight into the political and social implications of advances in technological and communication industries, particularly that of the cinema. His interest in cinema is more of a materialistic and political nature than an aesthetic concern, and he discusses cinema in relation to the aesthetics of war and of the "sight machine," the cinematic apparatus as a colonizing force.

One of Virilio's central arguments is the importance he places on the military–industrial complex in relation to the spatial organization of the city and of cultural life in general. In *Speed and Politics*, Virilio offers a critique on war and speed in relation to the development of modern urban culture and society. Here, Virilio argues that the modern urban conglomeration is based on the "immobile" fortified town of the feudal system, where the role of the city's engineer is to fight against this inertia and to facilitate and modulate the movements of armies and indeed the urban masses. Virilio coined such concepts as "militarization of space," "dromology" and the "aesthetics of disappearance," and much of his work stems from a phenomenological cultural background, using such thinkers as Husserl and Merleau-Ponty, while also drawing on Eastern military theorists, such as Sun Tse and Mao Tse-tung. Interspersed among his writings on urban space and the culture of war are his numerous and influential writings on the cultural and communications industries and the dangers of new technologies of reproduction, such as *The Aesthetics of Disappearance* (1991), *War and Cinema* (1980), *Polar Intertia* (1999), *The Information Bomb* (2000), and more recently, *Art and Fear* (2003).

In his excellent introduction to *The Virilio Reader* (1988), James Der Derian acknowledges that Virilio is not the first theorist to discern the "dark side to the Enlightenment" and the ways in which this is manifested in the possible perils of technological and military advances. He argues that Walter Benjamin anticipates Virilio's linking of technologies of acceleration and war in "Art in the Age of Mechanical Reproduction," and in his usage of the Italian Futurist Filippo Marinetti, Der Derian argues that Guy Debord's *Society of the Spectacle*, in its study of the spectacle and the fetishization of the image, equally provides a critical basis for Virilio's own critique of materialist interpretations of modernity. He also puts forward a strong argument for the links between Virilio and his contemporaries in cultural theory, citing Foucault's critique of war and the technologies of control in *Panopticism* and Baudrillard's hyperreal politics in his *Simulations*.

Writing from a similar vantage point of war and conflict to that of his contemporaries, Michel Serres, Foucault, Deleuze, and Derrida, Virilio has pointed out in an interview with Der Derian that war has been his university, from which everything else has proceeded: "I am a victim of war, a 'war baby.' As a child I lived through the horrors of the Second World War, through the reign of technology as absolute terror. . . . These are the traumatizing events which shaped my thinking." He continues in the interview that his primary interest in cinema and cinematics was the "putting into movement of images," an interest he shares with Deleuze in his *Cinema I Movement Image*. He argues that cinema has changed the nature of war itself (a concept that is borne out by the news coverage of the recent wars in the Persian Gulf, Afghanistan, and Iraq), the nature of which changes with the "logistics of perception."

The military lookout-post offers the invader an all-encompassing viewpoint not only over the military environment but also over the social environment. Similarly, the camera's peephole of the military airplane becomes a sighting device complementing the weapon itself: "the eye's function being the function of the weapon." This logistics of military perception forms the basis of *War and Cinema*, where a war of images replaces the war of military objects. Here, Virilio's concept of the "aesthetics of disappearance" questions the nature of nuclear deterrence, where Stealth equipment "can only function if its existence is clouded with uncertainty." In *The Possessed Individual* (1992) Kroker points out that Virilio's *War and Cinema* is a postmodern bible of the Gulf War, where war *becomes* cinema. Elsewhere, Virilio argues that when distinctions between mental and visual images collapse, virtual reality overrides reality, where real time has priority over spatial considerations, coterminus substitutions of reality begin to "war with one another," and a "war of images" ensues.

One of Virilio's key concepts, and one that runs through most of his texts, is that of "chronopolitics" or speed, a state encouraged by the militarization of society and of cultural life. In *Speed and Politics*, for instance, Virilio cites the example of the historical conflict over control of the oceans as an example of pure speed in operation. Speed as a pure idea without content comes from the sea, he argues, and "the right to the sea creates the right to the road of modern States, which through this becomes totalitarian States." No longer is it a question of crossing a continent from one city or shore to the next, but "the fleet in being creates a new dromocratic idea: the notion of displacement without destination in space and time." Elsewhere, Virilio argues that in the hands of the militarists, the speed of the various means of communication and destruction is "the privileged means for a secret and permanent social transformation."

Following on somewhat from *Aesthetics of Disappearance*, where he suggests that modern vision and the city are both dominated by time-based cinematic technologies of disappearance, Virilio's most recent work to be published in English is *Art and Fear*, where he uncovers the dangers of the disappearance of representational art in the contemporary state of "presentational" art, an art dominated by the mass media and communication industries, one in which the speed of light is replaced by the speed of sound, and where the politics of silence becomes a grave issue in light of historical political atrocities. Here, Virilio warns contemporary artists of the dangers inherent in forgetting Auschwitz and the realities of war. In "A Pitiless Art," he attacks the multimedia art world, and particularly "body artists" such as Orlan and Stelarc, for their Nietzschean antihumanism. As stated in the introduction to *Art and Fear*, Virilio believes that the mutism intrinsic to contemporary body art paves the way for the terrorization of the real body by the virtual body. Virilio coins the term *pitiless art* for art where real-time effaces duration, where the contraction of time and the immediacy of the present is privileged over a representational art that is allowed to unfold over time. Once again, the field of perception becomes a battle-field. In "Silence on Trial," he makes a scathing commentary on the introduction of "talkies" and on the "harmful" effects of the soundtrack on the "image track" in contemporary cinema.

DENISE BRIDGET WHITE

See also **Jean Baudrillard; Guy Debord; Gilles Deleuze; Jacques Derrida; Michel Foucault; Michel Serres**

Biography

Paul Virilio was born in Paris in 1932 and grew up in the northern coastline of Brittany. During Hitler's *Blitzkrieg* he was evacuated to the town of Nantes, directly experiencing its bombardment. He converted to Christianity in 1950 at the age of eighteen, and he was later drafted to fight in the Algerian War of Independence (1954–1962), after which he studied phenomenology with Merleau-Ponty at the Sorbonne in Paris. Along with Claude Parent, he founded the *Architecture Principe* group and journal in 1963 and was later named Professor, General Director, and President at the École Spéciale d'Architecture in Paris. He also helped to found the International College of Philosophy. He actively contributed to the journals *Esprit, Cause Commune*, and *Traverses*, as well as numerous international journals, and in 1979 he founded *Radio Tomate* with Felix Guattari. He has worked with the *Foundation Cartier pour l'art contemporain* on several exhibitions, the first being *La Vitesse* in 1991. After his long and diverse career spanning teaching, philosophy, urban studies, film, military history, and city planning, he now works with the homeless in Paris.

Selected Works

Bunker Archeology, 1975
Speed and Politics: An Essay on Dromology, 1977
The Aesthetics of Disappearance, 1980
Pure War: Revised Edition, 1983
War and Cinema: The Logistics of Perception, 1984
The Vision Machine, 1988
Polar Inertia, 1990
"L'Ecran du desert: chroniques de guerre," 1991
The Art of the Motor, 1993
Open Sky, 1995
The Information Bomb, 1998
Strategy of Deception, 1999
Art and Fear, 2000
Ground Zero, 2002

Further Reading

Armitage, John, "Art and Fear: An Introduction," in *Art and Fear*, translated by Julie Rose, London: Continuum Books, 2003
Armitage, John (editor), *Paul Virilio: From Modernism to Hypermodernism and Beyond*, London: Sage, 2000
Baudrillard, Jean, *Simulations*, New York: Semiotexte, 1983
Clausewitz, Von C., *On War*, Ware: Wordsworth Editions, 1997
Deleuze, G. and F. Guattari, *A Thousand Plateaus: Capitalism and Schizophrenia*, London: The Athlone Press, 1988
Der Derian, James, "Introduction," in *The Virilio Reader*, Blackwell, 1998
Der Derian, James, "Is the Author Dead?" An Interview with Paul Virilio by James Der Derian in *The Virilio Reader*, Blackwell, 1988
Kroker, Arthur, *The Possessed Individual, Technology and Postmodernity*, London: Macmillan, 1992

VOVELLE, MICHEL
Historian

Michel Vovelle is arguably France's foremost historian of mentalities, a discipline that he has defined as "the study of the mediations and of the dialectical relationship between the objective conditions of human life and the ways in which people narrate it, and even live it" (*Ideologies and Mentalities*, Cambridge: Polity 1990). Vovelle has studied in particular the mentalities of French revolutionaries, Western attitudes toward death, the decline of Christianity, and popular festivities. His corpus of material extends to include images, epitaphs, and the written fragments left by marginal and forgotten figures. Individual case studies are balanced with quantitative ones, whereas narrative is rehabilitated as a source of historical information. This approach to historiography is seen by Vovelle as a continuation of the work by his mentor Ernest Labrousse and Georges Lefebvre, among others.

Vovelle recognizes the inertia and durability that characterize mentalities: the *longue durée* is held responsible for conditioning the practice of French revolutionary violence, which was heir to a double tradition of street and state violence. The failures of progressive politics, including those reversals experienced by Vovelle in his own militant life, spurred him on to studying the rigidities and complexities of popular attitudes. However, Vovelle is interested above all in the revelatory impact of moments of crisis. Vovelle asks: Are there breaks or phases of sudden maturation in the domain of mentalities? Is it really possible, as with the French Revolution, to change the way human beings think in the space of ten years? Or are there in collective mentalities crises that have been developing over a long period, but which are likely to express themselves suddenly in the context of a revolutionary upheaval? In *L'Irrésistible ascension de Joseph Sec, bourgeois d'Aix* (The Unstoppable Rise of . . ., Bourgeois of Aix; Aix: Edisud, 1975), the epitaph of an obscure Jacobin self made man opens the door onto a mental universe where the revolutionary period inaugurates a new age of the hero, whether individual or collective and anonymous. The French Revolution gives birth to a new idea of civic heroism, the construction of a pantheon and, with this "transferral of sacrality," accelerates the long-term process of de-Christianization. Festivals display the hierarchy and the dreams, the said and the unsaid, of a society at a given moment: their revolutionary transformation is traced by Vovelle in *Les métamorphoses de la fête en Provence (1750–1820)* (Metamorphoses of the festival in provence Paris: Flammarion, 1975). In his monumental study, *La Mort et l'Occident* (Death and the West; Paris: Gallimord 1983), Vovelle shows how death, as the inescapable end point of any human adventure, constantly reveals the mentality of a period.

Around the Bicentenary of the French Revolution, Michel Vovelle, a lifelong Marxist and one of the French Communist Party's last prominent intellectuals, was confronted with the crisis of Communism and a challenge, notably by François Furet, to the Jacobin orthodoxy then dominating the historiography of the Revolution. Vovelle's first published book had been an edited volume of Jean-Paul Marat's writings, and he remained proud to be a "Robespierrist" and successor to Lefebvre and Albert Soboul as Sorbonne Professor of the History of the French Revolution. However, Vovelle's emphasis on mentalities aimed to steer a course between a "vulgar Marxist" history that explained the events of 1789 solely in terms of economics and social structures (the overthrow of feudalism by a rising bourgeoisie, the Jacobin alliance between the progressive bourgeoisie and the proletarian *sansculottes*) and a revisionist current that gave decisive autonomy to the political and saw 1789 as a victory for liberal democracy, the Terror of Year Two as protototalitarian (see François Furet, *Interpreting the French Revolution*, Cambridge: C.U.P. 1981). That the great history colloquium of the Bicentenary, organized under Vovelle's auspices, was devoted to "Images of the French Revolution" bore out this desire to break with dogma and stereotype. Although this change of focus from the "cellar" of the infrastructure to the "loft" of the superstructure pleasantly surprised ex-Marxist historians like Emmanuel Le Roy Ladurie, Vovelle's stated aim was to refine rather than renounce a Marxist approach to history. Unlike in the work of Philippe Ariès (e.g., in *Hour of our Death*, Harmondsworth: Penguin 1983), who has theorized a "collective unconscious" that obeys its own rhythms and causalities, mentalities are not given autonomous or timeless characteristics: they do not sit on a "cushion of air" but rather have a complex relationship with the rest of historical reality. For example, Baroque representations of death are seen by Vovelle as one expression of a social climate, of which absolutism is a political translation. The emphasis on the macabre in the late Middle Ages and the late nineteenth century does not bear a crude correspondence to demographic change, but can be related to other forms of social upheaval. The history of mentalities, therefore, does not dispense with the concept of ideology, but rather seeks to make it more complex, revealing what Louis Althusser called, in *Lenin and Philosophy* (London: New Left Book, 1971), the "interlacing of historical time," an expression understood by Vovelle as "both inertia in the diffusion of key ideas and coexistence, at various stratified levels, of models of behavior inherited from different traditions" (*Ideologies and Mentalities*). Vovelle's theorization of "mentality" could be seen as a welcome return to the original subtleties of Marx's concept of "mode of production" or as its final dissolution in the myriad explanatory causes of human behavior.

GAVIN BOWD

See also **Louis Althusser; Philippe Aries; Emmanuel Le Roy Ladurie**

Biography

Michel Vovelle was born in Eure-sur-Loir in 1933. He was educated at the Lycée Louis-le-Grand and then the École Normale Supérieure de St-Cloud. He was professor of history at the University of Aix-en-Provence before being nominated to the Chair of History of the French Revolution at the Sorbonne, which he occupied until 1993. He was president of the commission appointed to organize academic commemorations of the Bicentenary. Vovelle is the former president of La Société des Études robespierristes, and he is currently honorary president of La Société des Amis de L'Humanité.

Selected Works

The Fall of the French Monarchy (1787–1792), Cambridge: Cambridge University Press 1984
Religion et Révolution: la déchristianisation de l'an II, Paris: Hachette, 1976 Religion & Revolution: The Dechristianisation of Year Two
Theodore Desorgues ou la désorganisation, Paris: Seuil, 1984

La mentalité révolutionnaire, Revolutionary Mentalities Paris: Seuil, 1985

Les Aventures de la raison. Entretiens avec Richard Figuier, The adventures of reason, interviews with Paris: Belford, 1989

La Révolution française The French Revolution Paris: Nathan, 1992

Combats pour la Révolution française Struggles for the French Revolution Paris: Messidor, 1993

"Histoire et représentations," 1993 pp. 66–81.

Further Reading

Boureau, Alain, "Pour une histoire restreinte des mentalités," *Annales ESC*, 6 (November/December 1989): pp. 2–35

Kaplan, Steven L., *Farewell Revolution: The Historians' Feud, France 1789/1989*, Cornell: Cornell University Press 1995

Lefebvre, Georges, *The Great Fear of 1789: Rural Panic in Revolutionary France*, London: New Left Books, 1973

Lloyd, Geoffrey, *Demystifying Mentalities*, Cambridge: Cambridge University Press, 1990 Cambridge

WAHL, JEAN
Poet, Philosopher, Teacher

Celebrated by Levinas for his "marvelous pointillism," while Guéroult called him "the Monet of philosophy," Wahl may be the most intuitive and didactic of Bergson's students. A poet himself, he crossed over from philosophy into poetry and back in order to fashion a phenomenological reflection on existence, starting from the metaphysical experiences of "thinker-poets," such as Hölderlin and Hegel, Kierkegaard and Rimbaud, Lequier and Blake.

Within the philosophical establishment Wahl was an anticonformist thinker of unusual reach. Almost single-handedly he launched the Hegelian renewal of the 1930s so crucial to poststructuralism, and forty years thence he organized and responded to Derrida's first "*Différance*" lecture. Yet rather than crafting or promoting his own philosophies, Wahl dedicated himself to the works of a multitude of philosophers and poets—often noncanonical—and to his own colleagues and students.

Wahl contested the view of the philosophical task as amounting to either a hermeneutics of the history of philosophy (the partial project of Bergson and Heidegger) or a neo-Kantian rationalism in the vein of Brunschvicg and Lalande. More in keeping with Husserl's injunction to turn "to the things themselves" (although his phenomenology was unknown in France until the 1930s), for Wahl existence emerged out of the direct sensible encounter of thought with experience, and philosophy must look "towards the concrete," the title of his 1932 book on James, Whitehead,

and his lifelong friend, Gabriel Marcel. Wahl's challenging spirit informed his 1920 dissertation, as he chose within French philosophy the perennial figurehead, Descartes, for a covert dialogue with his mentor, Bergson, the reigning figurehead. Borrowing from the latter the notion that metaphysical intuition shapes a philosopher's worldview, he boldly proposed that the finite instant, the very negation of Bergson's duration, is the core intuition of Descartes's philosophy. He argues that because Descartes's cogito needs be restated "each time" it is to serve as foundation to truth, the temporality of Cartesian certainty must be discontinuous. Reason and presence thus flicker between finite instants of lived certainty, and only the creative act of iteration, not time's inherence to subjectivity, can unify thought. A heterodox and not particularly well received thesis, it is nonetheless emblematic of Wahl's thinking style, and it reveals his central philosophical concern: the tearing of experience by finitude is also advent, creation, and poetry.

Following Deleuze's homage to Wahl in *Difference and Repetition*, we may approach his two better-known works as rereadings of Hegel's difference and Kierkegaard's repetition. With the pioneering 1929 *Le Malheur de la conscience dans la philosophie de Hegel*, Wahl circumvented both theological and logicist recuperations of the Hegelian dialectic in order to reinscribe it within German Idealism (the *Phenomenology of Spirit* was then not in vogue). For Wahl, what motivates Hegel's sublation (*Aufhebung*) isn't a rational need for a synthetic device but, as for Schelling, Novalis, or Hölderlin, a "mystical intuition" that, sundered from experience, consciousness despairs from, yet also finds a new dynamic basis in, this sundering. Unlike negativity, which is a notion, despair has the "affective warmth" of an emotion: without this embodying of the rational into lived experience, neither the dialectic nor the conciliation of the real and the rational within an absolute Concept would be possible. The Hegelian system rests, therefore, on the mystical insight of the reversible valence of despair, and Wahl translates this reversibility into a critique of philosophy. If a system always converses with its basis in experience, and without falling into biographical reductionism, philosophy isn't self-posited and Idealism is subverted.

Wahl was understandably led towards antisystematic post-Hegelians like Nietzsche and especially Kierkegaard. He gave a reading of the entire corpus of the latter in the voluminous 1938 *Études kierkegaardiennes*, using the best secondary literature available in German, English, and French. Deepening his interest for despair, discontinuity and becoming, with Kierkegaard Wahl took up a paradoxical thought of ethics, faith, and poetry, which constantly resorts to deferral, repetition, and leap to negotiate the intensified subjection of consciousness to immediate experience. Leaving Hegel's "intellectual dialectic" behind while devoting a long chapter to Heidegger, Wahl concluded the book on Kierkegaard's "existential dialectic," steeped in the unresolved contradictions of "lived ideas" or transcendental realism. In the important 1939 essay "Poésie et métaphysique," (in the war journal *Messages*) this existential dialectic is generalized as "metaphysico-poetic Truth" in Blake, Hegel, Schelling, Keats, Rimbaud, and late romantics. Wahl thereby inaugurated a broad study of the interregion between poetry and philosophy, which, although it has fascinated German thinkers since Schlegel, entered French letters late (and via Heidegger) with Blanchot, Deguy, Lacoue-Labarthe, and Nancy or the recent ontopoetology of Dastur and Escoubas.

After the publication, in 1944 and 1948, of collections of essays representative of his trajectory, *Existence humaine et transcendance* and *Poésie, pensée, perception*, Wahl's writings continued formulating (sometimes monumentally, as in the 700-page *Traité de métaphysique*) a poetic thinking of existence weaving Jaspers with Van Gogh and Traherne. In parallel, he kept writing free verse in both French and English: after a first collection published in 1938, *Connaître sans connaître*, comes a collected edition in 1945 including poems written in the concentration camp of Drancy. Many of his later poems remain unpublished.

Wahl's anti-intellectualist work defies summation: no architectonic, no hierarchy in the spheres of existence, no overarching methodology can stand for his versatile interrogations on the metaphysical experience of experience. Besides the leitmotivs identified earlier, Wahl has nonetheless a central and original preoccupation: transcendence. Neither Kantian transcendentalism, nor the Husserlian bracketing of experience, nor Heidegger's transcendence into *Dasein's* finitude, transcendence for Wahl devolves from the subject's intermittent engagement with the sensible. Oscillating between concrete adherence to and abstract coherence of its object, transcendence becomes the dynamic instability of embodied thought. But instead of an aporia or malaise, this rhythm opens an original avenue that "consists in transcending transcendence, that is to say, falling back into immanence." Levinas, whose belated academic career is almost entirely owed to Wahl's friendship, recognized in this return to immanence, or "*transdescendance*," a crucial piece of the puzzle by which the "*transascendance*" of eschatology toward the godhead may be countered, so that ethical responsibility to the other, unescapable and obsessive, remains within or replaces the subject: "The beyond of the self is the unicity of the self, the new identity of what is beyond compare, the tip of metaphysical experience having pierced the *order* of universal identity . . ." (Levinas, 1976). Although Wahl's work isn't thematically about ethics, a constant concern with alterity underlies and illuminates his readings and his philosophy. His ultimate legacy, Levinas surmised, may well be his boldness, which "prepared in France a new type of reader and writer in philosophy and a new manner [*facture*] for the book" (Levinas, 1976).

CHRISTOPHE WALL-ROMANA

See also **Georges Bataille; Henri Bergson; Maurice Blanchot; Gilles Deleuze; Jacques Derrida; Emmanuel Levinas; Jean-Luc Nancy**

Biography

Wahl was born in Marseille in 1888. He joined ENS in 1907, gaining the *agrégation* in 1910, in first place. After three years at the Fondation Thiers, he taught in *lycées* in Nantes, Tours, and le Mans. He became a university professor in Provence and then at the Sorbonne, where he obtained a chair in 1936. In December 1940, together with other academics of Jewish descent, he was expelled from the Sorbonne. In 1941 he was arrested by the Gestapo and sent to the concentration camp of Drancy, from which he was eventually freed through the intervention of friends. In July 1942 he arrived in New York at the New School for Social Research, and soon after Mount Holyoke College offered him a teaching appointment. In 1945, he returned to France, married Marcelle Sicard, and was reinstated at the Sorbonne, accepting in subsequent years visiting positions at the universities of Chicago, Berkeley, and

Tunis. In 1946 he founded the Collège Philosophique and was named President of the Société Française de Philosophie. Wahl died in 1974.

Selected Works

Les Philosophies pluralistes d'Angleterre et d'Amérique, 1920; as *The Pluralist Philosophies of England and America*, translated by Fred Rothwell, 1925

Du Rôle de l'idée de l'instant dans la philosophie de Descartes, 1920 *The Role of The Idea of The Instant in Descartes's Philosophy*

Le Malheur de la conscience dans la philosophie de Hegel, 1929 *The Unhappiness of Consciousness in Hegel's Philosophy*

Étude sur le "Parménide" de Platon, 1930 *Study on The Parmenides of Plato*

Vers Le Concret—Études d'histoire de la philosophie contemporaine; trois articles sur W. James, Whitehead et le "Journal métaphysique" de Gabriel Marcel, 1932 *Toward the Concrete: Studies on the History of Contemporary Philosophy, three articles on W. James, Whitehead and the "Philosophical Journal" of Gabriel Marcel*

Études kierkegaardiennes, 1938 *Kierkegaardian Studies*

Connaître sans connaître, 1938 (poetry) *Knowing Without Knowing*

Existence humaine et transcendance, 1944 *Human Existence and Transcendence*

Poèmes de circonstance, 1944 (poetry) *Occasional Poems*

Poèmes, 1945; (selection) as *Voices in the Dark: Fifteen Poems of the Prison and the Camp*, translated by Charles Guenther, 1974

Tableau de la philosophie française, 1946 *Overview of French Philosophy*

Petite Histoire de l'existentialisme (suivie d'un appendice: "Kafka et Kierkegaard"), 1947 *A Short History of Existentialism (with an appendix on "Kafka and Kierkegaard")*

Poésie, pensée, perception, 1948 *Poetry, Thought, Perception*

Jules Lequier, 1948 (selection)

The Philosopher's Way, 1948

Thomas Traherne, *Poèmes de la félicité*, 1951 (translation) *Poems of Felicity*

La Pensée de l'existence, 1952 *The Thought of Existence*

Traité de métaphysique, 1953 *Metaphysical Treatise*

Les philosophies de l'existence, 1954; as *Philosophies of Existence: An Introduction to the Basic Thought of Kierkegaard, Heidegger, Jaspers, Marcel, Sartre*, translated by F.M. Lory, 1969

Vers La Fin de l'ontologie—Étude sur L'introduction de la métaphysique de Heidegger, 1956 *Toward The End of Ontology: A Study on Introduction to Metaphysics by Heidegger*

L'Expérience métaphysique, 1964 *The Metaphysical Experience*

Further Reading

Darras, Jacques (editor), *Jean Wahl, le poète, In'hui*, 39 (1992)

Levinas, Emmanuel, "Jean Wahl, sans avoir ni être," in *Jean Wahl et Gabriel Marcel*, edited by Jeanne Hersch, *Bibliothèque des archives de philosophie*, 21, Paris: Beauchesne, 1976

Levinas, Emmanuel, "Jean Wahl et l'émotion," *Cahiers du Sud*, 331, (1955); as "Jean Wahl and Feeling," in *Proper Names*, translated by Michael B. Smith, Stanford, California: Stanford University Press, 1996

Jarczyk, Gwendoline, "Jean Wahl, I—Le malheur de la conscience: de Jean Wahl à Hegel," and Labarrière, Pierre-Jean, "Jean Wahl II—Le Hegel de Jean Wahl: un philosophe de l'existence," in *De Kojève à Hegel, 150 ans de pensée hégélienne en France*, Paris: Albin Michel, 1996.

Luyat-Moore, Anne, "Wallace Stevens and Jean Wahl," in *Strategies of Difference in Modern Poetry: Case Studies in Poetic Composition*, edited by Pierre Lagayette, Madison, New Jersey: Fairleigh Dickinson University Press, 1998

Stallknecht, Newton P., "Beyond the Concrete," *Review of Metaphysics*, 8 (1954): 144–155

Worms, Frédéric, "D'un instant à l'autre: Descartes, Bergson, Jean Wahl et nous," in *Du Rôle de l'idée de l'instant dans la philosophie de Descartes*, edited by Jean Wahl, Paris: Descartes & Cie, 1994

WEIL, SIMONE
Writer, Philosopher

Simone Weil was one of the most perceptive, enigmatic intellectual figures in twentieth-century France. A philosophical inheritor of neo-Platonism and Kant, a social activist who drew heavily on Marx's materialist critique, and a Christian mystic whose ascetic faith kept her outside the Roman Catholic Church, Weil lived a commitment—even before her conversion experience while reading George Herbert's poem "Love"—to preserve the sacred she discerned at the core of every human being. She believed in the spirituality of human work, attempting to revalue both the activity and the worker by engaging in the former and educating the latter. Much of her work appeared after her premature death, edited by Albert Camus, Simone Pétrement, and others. The complexity of her work, melding the spiritual and the political, has drawn generations of admirers and critics.

Reflecting the influence of her teacher Alain, Weil, from her earliest notebook entries (*Notebooks of Simone Weil*, 1956), philosophical lectures (*Lectures on Philosophy*, 1978), and essays (*Intimations of Christianity among the Greeks*, 1957), embraced a science with a metaphysical origin that, in order to preserve the importance of human agency and its obligation to the divine, she describes as decreation. In the act of creation, God abdicated a part of Himself, that is, a part of being, before withdrawing. The abdicated part of being—a renunciation by love—is the created reality we inhabit. Created reality, the object science takes for itself, is governed by the laws of force, matter, and motion. Weil's epistemology cautions that the objects taken by science do not exhaust reality. She criticized a science that lost sight of the metaphysical origin of all that is, openly doubting the value of a science that did not bring us closer to God. Weil's thought depends on the spiritual assumption that God has been here but withdrawn, leaving human beings to act on the part of the divine we experience through grace.

Weil's neo-Platonism prompted her to conceive of the human soul as having two parts roughly corresponding to the two levels of reality: the decreated and the created. The decreated is the divine, uncreated part of the soul, the residue of God's presence in the act of creation. It forms the core of our being and is the locus of the supernatural in human beings. The decreated part of the soul is the potential receptacle of grace. The second, more prominent part is the natural, created part of the soul. This is the carnal part of the soul that sins and is susceptible to the "gravity" of created existence. For Weil, the two parts of the soul coexist in a difficult, but necessary tension. If the created part of the soul attends to its own experience, Weil argued, it experiences sin as suffering, which yields the opportunity to know the decreated, the ethical, the Good. Suffering becomes an invitation to an authentic form of spiritual freedom. The human soul is the source and possibility of an ethical way of being in the world. Her difficult ethic derives from negotiating the tension between the created and decreated parts of the soul. We negotiate this tension through knowing, which for Weil is a question of distinguishing between *Gravity and Grace* (1952). She intentionally described the movements of the soul using terms familiar to science. Gravity, the unbearable weightiness of created being, is only effectively countered by the presence of grace, that is, the perspective one gains by attending to the decreated part of being. The tension is between the weight of the stuff of our daily lives, our culture, and its values and our lucidity, attention, and the understanding that gives them meaning. The pull of gravity preoccupies the soul with the mundane and can be inexorable. Grace, an openness to the supernatural available only through the decreated part of the soul, yields an insight making a balance possible.

Weil appreciated science's valuation of sense experience. The senses, through the intermediary of the body, can restore the balance between the two parts of the soul. Through the body, the attentive being knows the created world and recognizes the self as part of it. Weil disputed the modern liberal notion of the autonomous self that values the individual before others and alienates us from nature. For Weil, attending to the decreated and recognizing our interconnectedness are necessary preludes to letting go of the autonomous self (the "I"). She invoked Hindu mysticism to argue that an individual mindful of the integration of body and soul, of the created and the decreated, can no longer consider the self autonomous. Autonomy implies a distance from the rest of creation that allows what evil there is in the world. Evil, Weil suggested, is the distance between the two parts of the soul, between God and creature, between human being and human being. It is a distance to be suppressed only through the death of the autonomous self.

Human beings function in an environment of what Weil calls necessity. Weil fleshed out this idea in her essay "On the Pythagorean Doctrine." Characterized by movement and gravity, necessity is the underlying order, the interconnected wholeness existent among the elements of the natural world with which the human mind tries to cope. Although the movements of necessity suggest the mutual interdependence of all things, necessity also manifests itself in the natural world as volatility. Refusing to concede to this volatility, the human mind tries to protect itself through knowledge claims, by making it intelligible and predictable. Science discerns tendencies, which it posits as laws and maxims. Similarly, theoretical justifications for political order and the institutions that embody them are also intended to shield human beings from the volatility of (human) nature. Ordering matter—or human beings—Weil understood meant a kind of coercion that reality and human beings resist. Trying to overcome the contingency of the natural world placed human beings in a conflict that it could not win, the psychological seeds of the perpetual conflict that Weil discerned in contemporary politics.

Weil's politics depended on these epistemological assumptions. In her early work, *Oppression and Liberty* (1934), she drew heavily on Marx for her analysis of the oppression embedded in power structures. It is the materialist critique and the general spirit of Marx's project that Weil found compelling. She never abandoned Marx's initial diagnosis that a human spirit cannot reside in or as a unit of production. Weil appreciated the mythopoeic impulse in Marx's work, identifying a nearly religious faith lurking in his understanding of power relationships. Parts of Marx's work moved the deeply spiritual Weil, but by the 1930s, the theoretical inadequacies of Marxism and the atrocities committed in its name were impossible to ignore. Although Weil understood that Marx's motive had been a yearning for liberty and equality, she also knew that his work constituted a materialist religion more akin to utopian socialism. Marx so desired to transform material reality into a less oppressive form that he put his faith in that material transformation as the only way to save human beings from themselves. Marx's materialistic religion, Weil argued, succumbed to temptations similar to those found in liberal capitalism, abandoning the very human spirit he intended to preserve.

Marx, Weil argued, subjected himself to the same materialist form of power that had become the substance of all political interactions. But Weil understood that a political analysis focused only on power—let alone a political vision dependent on power—failed to account for human agency and, therefore, the needs of human being. Her own political analysis, influenced by her spiritual awakening, suggested that force was the real stuff of human activity. After all, she suggested, power was little more than the ability to command others' use of force. Force—that influence that each of us exerts by virtue of being human—is the real substance of human action in the world. Weil interrogated the possibilities and abuses of force in her important essay *The Iliad, or the Poem of Force* (1956). Against the understanding of force as simply the capacity to coerce, Weil saw force as both the coercive power that a human being can exert over another and the creative potential possessed by each human being. Force is the unknown factor of human relationships, the use of which determines their value. We necessarily exert force, consciously or not, for ends either productive or destructive of the human. Weil argued that attending to the divine in the other is to recognize the force we exert and to self-consciously use it for creative, productive ends.

Authentic human interaction, Weil believed, requires that we be conscious of both our subjection to and possession of force. How we use the force we possess, therefore, is critical: the more we have, the more accountable we are. When we consciously subject others to force, we objectify them, treat them as if they were things. The human as thing is a contradiction for Weil—a soul could not exist in a thing. In response, Weil embraced the Kantian aspiration always to treat human beings as ends-in-themselves. She sought a way to hold social actors responsible for the way they use the force they possess. To this end, she found hierarchies useful. In her last work, *The Need for Roots* (1952), Weil argued that social hierarchies are didactic, inevitable, and even necessary. Hierarchies represent a natural order of things. But hierarchies do not represent differences in kind. Their existence acknowledges inevitable differences in means, talents, or stations among individuals. Greater status yields not greater license, but greater responsibilities. When those responsibilities are obscured by the gravity of appearance, the integrity of human action and the possibility of the grace that bears witness to our humanity are compromised.

Force can objectify the human being subjected to it, but there are similarly dire consequences for the spirit of the oppressor. The power of life and death exists only to replicate itself. The exercise of this force perpetuates the cycle of conflict and resistance. One cannot lord life and death over another human being for long and hope to remain human. The intoxication of force causes human beings to forget their limitations, and they overreach, as the Greeks Weil loved knew so well, sowing the seeds of their own destruction. The objectification of the human is a violation of

the sacred that characterizes the environment of the *Iliad* and found reflection in Weil's world. In these environments of unrelenting force, the life of the human loses its sacrality, its decreated nature is ignored, and biological existence is all that remains. The human thing is all but stripped of the capacity to take responsibility for its existence. Preoccupied with imminent death, or with its unworthiness to live, there is neither time nor energy to give meaning to or to make human this being's existence.

It did not take her experience in Spain or in the Second World War for Weil to identify the soul-deadening effects of a force not limited by a concern for the human soul. She found them in the structure and relationships of the factory. The physical and spiritual degradation of modern labor was a constant source of concern in Weil's thought. In the collection later called *Lectures on Philosophy*, Weil encouraged her students at Roanne in 1933 to know the experience of the laborer by sharing his burden. She embraced this classroom rhetoric by working a number of factory jobs in Paris from late 1934 until late summer 1935. A self-consciously undertaken experiment, the impact of this experience on Weil's thought cannot be overstated. Throughout the period, Weil, as frail and weak of constitution as she was perceptive and determined, kept a journal in which she jotted down her observations and feelings during and after her fourteen-hour days collected as *La Condition ouvrière* (1951). She also wrote a series of letters that reflected her journal and in which she added further insight into her experience collected in *Seventy Letters* (1965). Work, for Weil, was the application of the mind as a tool to the matter that makes up created reality. Through work, that is, through the methodical action of reason and the body, human beings bring usable order to matter. Weil initially found that immersion in factory life liberated her from abstract formulations. But she came to experience the factory as an environment rationally organized with little regard for human needs. Its organization swallowed up the human. What went on in the factory was not work, but rather an oppressive and spiritually deadening repetition of mechanical movements. The fixity of one's attention on a minute fragment of the process, Weil found, denied the worker any sense of engagement, accomplishment, or completion. The emphasis on efficiency, more pieces finished in less time, compounded the problem because any increase in efficiency was met only by demands for more efficiency. The factory organized work to maximize the output of what Weil called the collective but did so at the expense of the humanity of labor.

Weil's single most important essay, "Human Personality," asserts a conception of the human against the conditions she found in the factories and in the world around her. Modernity sacrificed the sacred in human beings: the possibilities inherent in individual human beings, their will and capacity to know the good, their creative energy, and their intelligence. Written in the last year of her short life, this essay makes a crucial distinction between the personal and the impersonal. For Weil, everything that is personal is error and sin. Saying "I" or taking the collective signification "We" as the source of one's identity unduly distinguishes the I or We from the rest of humanity. Weil's idea of the impersonal defied the nihilistic conception of the personal. The impersonal in human beings is sacred, evidence of the presence of decreated being. It signals a capacity for reflective distance that allows love for others in themselves rather than through some conception we impose on them. Seeing others from this reflective distance, which Weil called attention, allows us to see the intrinsic value of the other. The detachment required by the impersonal, however, is not a distance on the other, but a distance on the self. It is the requirement of selflessness in reference to the other simply because the other is a site of decreated being. Our primary ethical obligation is to respect and nourish the sacred presence that is each individual other.

The expectation to be treated according to the good rather than evil is evidence of the sacred in human beings, a theme Weil fleshed out in *Gravity and Grace* and in the spiritual meditations in *Waiting for God* (1951). As we are tossed about by necessity, the inevitable confrontation with evil—the awareness of the distance between ourselves and God—always surprises, producing a startled cry of outrage. Out of this outrage come protective devices like governing institutions for which we create the theoretical justifications she addresses in her essay, "The Power of Words." These structures provide comfort, but they generate their own necessity and work their own injustices. Moreover, the comfort they provide is a security in our autonomous selves and a function of the personal. They represent a dangerous evasion of our responsibilities to the impersonal, privileging the carnal over the sacred. The discipline of the impersonal is Weil's ethical counter to this temptation to comfort. The impersonal, valuing attentive detachment, requires removing from social and political institutions whatever is detrimental to the growth of the impersonal in its members. It means attending to the good, known through the decreated part of the human soul. Drawing on the good in our actions requires a stillness that modern civilization does not allow. To know the good, Weil suggests, human beings need silence and warmth. What they get instead is "icy pandemonium."

The icy pandemonium of modern life obscures the fact that what we share is life in a state of affliction.

For Weil, affliction is the true state of human being, a device for pulverizing both soul and pride. Engaging affliction—and recognizing our own—is the first requirement of action in accordance with the good. The modern business of living, replete with noise and indifference, shields busy human beings from affliction. Only those who are materially deprived or those who consciously seek the good know their affliction. Most people avoid confronting their own affliction by concentrating on busyness or pointing out the sins of others. Both are strategies for ignoring the afflictions of self and other. Embracing the impersonal requires recognizing affliction as our commonly shared state of being. It is imperative to put oneself in the place of the afflicted, recognizing one's own sin before another's, and recognizing their suffering as part one's own. The awareness required for this recognition is grace that alone can so orient a soul to make it capable of attending to affliction and thus knowing truth. Weil's requirement that ethical action in the world be grounded in love means attending to affliction that one can do only from the space of the impersonal, the core of ethical action in the world.

Modern humanity's inability to attend to its own affliction, Weil believed, reflected the absence of a sense of grounding, its uprootedness. Written in London during the last year of her life, Weil's book-length *The Need for Roots* is her meditation on *deracinèment* or uprootedness. The willingness of uprooted Europeans to destroy their environment confirmed for Weil the inadequacy of that environment as home. Weil described rootedness as a natural sense of mutual belonging, an identity of interest, between an individual and his or her milieu. It means a recognition that cultural values should not only have weight (gravity), but also meaning and coherence (grace). She first diagnosed uprootedness in her study of the effects of modern working conditions, but her findings there were substantiated during the war as she considered the modern nation–state. The modern forms of both work and nation deprived human beings of what they should provide—a sense of belonging, meaning. The nation–state, Weil suggested, had become the single most significant collectivity in modern human existence, the source and fount of all human identity, the sole object of the otherwise ennobling human attributes of loyalty and sacrifice, the most significant repository for human meaning. Yet, at the apex of its influence, the nation–state had decomposed, uprooting humanity, leaving it stunned and confused as to its identity and its source of meaning. Reclaiming roots meant recapturing the spontaneity of life, which she believed was the source of a community's strength. To that end, she wrote to her Resistance colleagues, the postwar governance of France must encourage the creative expression that gives voice to a community's sense of itself. The vital medium—the spontaneous expression of a country's inhabitants, where a community finds its life—is Weil's alternative to the modern nation–state. France must be reconstituted—physically and spiritually—as a vital medium, distinct from but no better than other vital media. All communities are shaped by causes good and evil, just and unjust, and so are invariably flawed. Nonetheless, rootedness meant that a country should be worth treasuring for the meaning it holds and the people it sustains. The institutions of the state exist to protect the vital forces that create the country.

Weil recognized that some form of collective identity, some form of belonging, was necessary to the human spirit. The need for a spiritual component, the connectedness and stillness necessary to access the decreated, suffused Weil's work. Only a genuinely spiritual way of life could arrest the course of totalizing politics. The beautiful, commonly shared and recognized as home, is that in the vital medium that was to be loved, preserved, and protected. Fashioning the political and spiritual terms in which a just and livable human order could be built in *The Need for Roots* required an enumeration of the needs of the soul. Ignoring the needs of the soul created the hopeless and destructive human beings of the twentieth century. The needs of the body (i.e., food, sleep, and warmth) should be the minimum provided by a vital medium. The needs of the soul, which she identified in a list of seemingly antithetical pairs, were more fragile and less easily met than those of the body: order/liberty; obedience/responsibility; equality/hierarchism; honor/punishment; security/risk; private property /collective property; and freedom of opinion/truth. The pairings, which she claimed were necessary in *The Need for Roots* but which she actually executed in "Draft for a Statement of Human Obligations," are a useful device that Weil owes to her neo-Platonic background. Each pair forms a dialectical whole, that is, each pairing speaks to a need of the human soul that can barely be articulated outside the pairing. Each need is utterly essential but reaches its fruition and its limit in its mate. In this way, Weil articulated the tensions that make up human beings and, thus, underlie human social and political existence. These tensions must be negotiated mindfully by every individual because the impact that formal social and political institutions (collectivities) can have on them must always be limited by what Weil calls consent.

Weil's understanding of consent—which requires us to recognize the divine source of all obligation—entails obedience to necessity. Consent means opening the self to the divine without using that openness disingenuously to justify all manner of acts. Consent must be identifiable as an aspiration to the good. Human

beings, she argued, find their only true freedom in this kind of obedience. Her enumeration of the needs of the soul provides a picture of the just political order. Justice is not a series of principled statements, but rather is made possible by the creation of conditions for the exercise of a certain kind of human freedom. A political order that does not create the conditions necessary to meet these needs can expect neither love nor consent and will not survive. In preserving the individual by seeing that the needs of the soul are met, Weil hoped for the emergence of a new form of collectivity deriving its legitimacy from a climate of justice rather than from its structures. A commitment to meeting those needs will mandate just as opposed to arbitrary structures. None of the needs she enumerated can be met by the solitary self; they require the authentic human interaction that modern political order made impossible and that Weil hoped to foster.

Weil's is an intimate conception of human interaction. She made of empathy a decisive ethical value. She valued a distance on the self (the "impersonal") as requisite to entering into the suffering of another. The ethical actor must be free of all self-interest except as it is understood as being bound up in the well-being of the other. For Weil, only this distance on the self creates the possibility of the intimate spiritual interaction with the other that must characterize human existence. Even this interaction is not wholly interpersonal. There is always the presence of a third, the divine presence. Acting on the impersonal is acting on the divine within, the residue of decreation, and bringing that divine to the encounter. The creative component of this response is its form, which calls for discerning the source of the suffering and addressing it in a way that will not dehumanize the sufferer even further. The creative effort is to bring the other into fellowship with the actor, to reintegrate the other into the community. Though in her own life, she struggled to find a community, her theoretical grasp of communal meaning is part of her enduring appeal. There is beauty in constructively acting on suffering in the presence of the divine. In the just community this individual ethical imperative, this commitment to the possibilities within the afflicted other, is the primary social and spiritual value. The value of empathy colors the self-understanding of this community, the structures of this community, and every exercise of force within the community.

JOHN RANDOLPH LEBLANC

See also **Alain; Albert Camus**

Biography

Simone Adolphine Weil was born in Paris on February 3, 1909. After excelling in her baccalauréat preparation, she entered the Lycée Henry IV in 1925, where she spent three years studying under Alain (1868–1952). Placing first in her entrance examinations for the École Normale Supérieure in 1928, she completed her dissertation *Science and Perception in Descartes* in 1930, successfully passing her *agrégation* in philosophy in July 1931. Weil traveled to Berlin in 1932 where she witnessed the ascension of Hitler. In 1934, despite her always fragile health, Weil took several factory jobs in and around Paris. In 1936, she took her pacifism to Spain, where she worked briefly in an anarchist militia. Events forced Weil to abandon her pacifism in 1939, and after the war began, she sought a way to intervene against Nazi aggression. In her search for agency she traveled from Vichy to Marseilles to New York and finally back to London in 1943, where she was employed in the Ministry of the Interior for the Commissariat of Action upon France. Ongoing poor health forced Weil to resign from her post in July. She was admitted to Grosvenor Sanatorium in Ashford. While in the hospital, Weil refused to take more food than those starving in occupied France were receiving. She died of starvation and pulmonary tuberculosis on August 24, 1943.

Selected Works

La Pesanteur et la Grâce, 1947; as *Gravity and Grace*, translated by Arthur Wills, 1952

L'Enracinement, 1949; as *The Need for Roots*, translated by Arthur Wills, 1952

L'Attente de Dieu, 1950; as *Waiting for God*, Translated by Emma Craufurd. New York: Putnam, 1951

La Connaissance surnaturelle, 1950 (Supernatural Understanding)

La Condition ouvriére, 1951 (The Condition of the Working Class)

L'Iliade ou le poème de la force from *La Source Greque*, 1953; as *The Iliad or the Poem of Force*, translated by Mary McCarthy, 1956

Letter to a Priest, translated by Arthur Wills, 1954

Oppression et Liberté, 1955; as *Oppression and Liberty*, translated by Arthur Wills and John Petrie, 1973

Venise Sauvé, 1955 (Venice Saved)

The Notebooks of Simone Weil, 2 volumes, translated by Arthur Wills, 1956

Écrits de Londres et dernières lettres, 1957 (London Writings and Last Letters)

Intimations of Christianity among the Ancient Greeks, translated by E.C. Geissbuhler, 1957

Leçons de Philosophie, 1959; as *Lectures on Philosophy*, translated by Hugh Price, 1978

Écrits historiques et politiques, 1960 (Historical and Political Writings)

Pensées sans ordre concernant l'amour de Dieu, 1962 (Disorderly Thoughts Concerning the Love of God)

Selected Essays, 1934–1943, translated by Richard Rees, 1962

Seventy Letters, translated by Richard Rees, 1965

On Science, Necessity and the Love of God, translated by Richard Rees, 1968

First and Last Notebooks, translated by Richard Rees, 1970

Gateway to God, translated and edited by David Raper, 1974

The Simone Weil Reader, edited by George Panichas, 1977

Simone Weil: An Anthology, edited by Sian Miles, 1986

Formative Writings 1929–1941, translated by Dorothy McFarland and Wilhelmina Van Ness, 1988

Further Reading

Allen, Diogenes, *Three Outsiders: Pascal, Kierkegaard, Simone Weil*, Cambridge: Cowley Press, 1983

Allen, Diogenes and Eric O. Springsted, *Spirit, Nature, and Community: Issues in the Thought of Simone Weil*, Albany, NY: State University of New York Press, 1994

Andrew, Edward, "Simone Weil on the Injustice of Rights-Based Doctrines," *The Review of Politics*, 48 (1986): 60–91

Bell, Richard, *Simone Weil: The Way of Justice as Compassion*, Totowa, NJ: Rowman and Littlefield, 1999

Bell, Richard, *Simone Weil's Philosophy of Culture: Readings Toward a Divine Humanity*, Cambridge: Cambridge University Press, 1993

Blum, Lawrence and Victor Seidler, *A Truer Liberty: Simone Weil and Marxism*, London: Routledge and Kegan Paul, 1989

Cabaud, Jacques, *Simone Weil, A Fellowship in Love*, New York: Harvill, 1965

Camus, Albert, "La Condition ouvrière de Simone Weil," *L'Express* (December 13, 1955), reprinted in Camus, *Essais* ("Essays") (1965), 1700–1702

Camus, Albert, "Extract from letter to Mme. Selma Weil," *L'Express* (February 11, 1960), reprinted in Camus, *Essais* ("Essays") (1965), 1699

Camus, Albert, Preface to *L'Enracinement*, reprinted in Camus, *Essais* (1965): 1700–1702

Davy, Marie-Magdalene, *The Mysticism of Simone Weil*, Boston: Beacon Press, 1951

Dietz, Mary, *Between the Human and the Divine: The Social and Political Thought of Simone Weil*, Totowa, NJ: Rowman and Littlefield, 1989

Dunaway, John, *Simone Weil*, Boston: Twayne Publishing, 1984

Fiori, Gabriella, *Simone Weil: An Intellectual Biography*, Atlanta: University of Georgia Press, 1989

Hellman, John, *Simone Weil: An Introduction to Her Thought*, Waterloo, Ontario: Wilfrid Laurier University Press, 1982

Little, Janet, *Simone Weil: Waiting on Truth*, Oxford: Berg, 1988

Lukacs, John. "Resistance: Simone Weil," *Salmagundi*, 85–86 (1990): 106–118

McFarland, Dorothy, *Simone Weil*, New York: Ungar, 1983

McLellan, David, *Utopian Pessimist: The Life and Thought of Simone Weil*, New York: Poseidon Press, 1990

Merton, Thomas, "Pacificism and Resistance in Simone Weil", in *Faith and Violence: Christian Teaching and Christian Practice*, Notre Dame, Indiana: Notre Dame Press, 1968

Nevin, Thomas, *Simone Weil: Portrait of a Self-Exiled Jew*, Chapel Hill: University of North Carolina Press, 1991

Perrin, J. M., and Gustave Thibon, *Simone Weil as We Knew Her*, London: Routledge and Kegan Paul, 1953

Pétrement, Simone, *Simone Weil: A Life*, translated by R. Rosenthal, New York: Pantheon, 1976

Pirruccello, Ann, "Interpreting Simone Weil: Presence and Absence in Attention," *Philosophy East and West*, 45 (1995): 61–72

Rees, Richard, *Simone Weil: A Sketch for a Portrait*, Oxford: Oxford University Press, 1966

Rosen, Fred, "Labour and Liberty: Simone Weil and the Human Condition," *Theoria to Theory*, 7 (1973): 33–47

Springsted, Eric, *Christus Mediator: Platonic Mediation in the Thought of Simone Weil*, Chico, CA: Scholars Press, 1983

Springsted, Eric, *Simone Weil and the Suffering of Love*, Cambridge: Cowley, 1986.

Teuber, Andrews, "Simone Weil: Equality as Compassion," *Philosophy and Phenomenological Research*, 43:2 (1982): 221–237

Tomlin, Eric, *Simone Weil*, New Haven, CT: Yale University Press, 1954

White, George (editor), *Simone Weil: Interpretations of a Life*, Amherst: University of Massachusetts Press, 1981

WITTIG, MONIQUE
Writer, Feminist Theorist

Monique Wittig's success began with the 1964 novel *L'Opoponax*, considered at the time a *nouveau roman*. Her subversive fictitious work delivers a theoretical slant, especially a Marxist feminist one that sees women as an oppressed class. Wittig focused her theoretical work primarily on the larger political system behind women's plight, which she designated as heterosexuality. Much of her fiction narrates lesbianism as antithetical to the heterosexual power structure. The theory of the female lesbian subject that she espouses is apparent in the fiction she creates and raises "woman" and "lesbian" to a position of the desiring subject.

Wittig has explained that heterosexuality as a system of power categorizes sex into essential parts, primarily in order to ensure the very notion of "difference," a philosophical notion based on One and its Other, or "sameness" and "difference." Because sexual difference is based on essentialism, women are often connected to notions of nature in a heterosexual society. These ideologies perpetuate the notion that women are "natural," "essential," "submissive," and "weak." Heterosexual societies insist that women remain visibly sexed at all times, as if a constant social reminder of their supposed essentialism. Wittig argued that this categorization of sex socially ensures women's subjugation and social powerlessness. Female homosexuality—or female love of "same," in lieu of "difference"—has long been concealed or even destroyed, because, according to Wittig, lesbianism breaks down the cultural and social glue of the heterosexual power structure.

Because of women's inferiority, they are comparable to the proletarian "class." Adhering to a Marxist feminist position, Wittig aligned women to "class" by showing that the heterosexist social structure positions women in the role of the worker. However, what in fact is to be recreated is not the working economy, but heterosexuality, the ideology based on dominator and dominated ("difference"). Wittig explained that the dominant heterosexist ideology socially enables women's oppression, especially in the institution of marriage, where women submit to a free-labor contract (reproduction, cooking, and housework). Thus, compulsory heterosexuality is the basis for the reproduction of a "heterosexual economy"; furthermore, the subjugation of women is necessary for its continuation and perpetuation.

Under the power structure of heterosexuality, women live in a state of Marxian false consciousness. Unaware of the regime that controls them, women consequently yield to all heterosexist propaganda. Wittig showed that heterosexuality as an ideology socially preserves women's oppression by controlling both their mental activity and their physical body that must at all times be "seen (and made) sexually available to men." Like any oppressive ideology, a political system cannot perpetuate itself for long if the subjects become aware of the source that oppresses them.

The method to end oppression so that women can "exist" requires the obliteration of sexual categories that constrain women and any system that perpetuates these categories. The destruction of the category of sex as the basis of power would involve revolutionary war of some sort, and consequently, a utopia would result. In her 1969 novel *Les Guérillères*, Wittig developed this desire for a complete dissolution of the larger power structure by depicting a Sapphic society of women who wage war against men, a fictitious annihilation of heterosexism and its male perpetrators. Combining theory and praxis, the author refused heterosexual writing conventions and penned a lesbian—feminist corpus of fiction that forces the reader to confront her own labels of sexuality, womanhood, and writing (as in *L'Opoponax, Les Guérillères, Le Corps lesbien*, and *Virgile, non*).

Expounding on Simone de Beauvoir's notion that "woman" has been socially constructed from myths (*Le Deuxième sexe*, 1949; as *The Second Sex*, translated by H. M. Parshley, 1953), Wittig affirmed that not only is "woman" associated with various social myths; indeed, the notion of "woman" is a myth. The "Myth of Woman" is an idea that is wholly constructed by these falsified sexual categories, in which "woman" is a fabrication by man whose design is on her subservient oppression. As a consequence, the mythified construct is believed as fact: "[...] they are seen as women, therefore, they are women. But before being seen that way, they first had to be made that way" ("One is not Born a Woman" in *The Straight Mind and Other Essays*, 1992). The fabrication of "woman" is a heterosexual cultural myth that insists on the individual oppression of every "woman." Therefore, believing that "sex" is a natural and biological category insists on believing the myth and buries women further in oppression.

Language as an institution also culturally enables the construction of sexual difference, according to Wittig. Unlike the gender-neutral "je," woman as a speaking or writing subject must always display her gender through language to continually remind her audience of her inferiority and oppression (for example, adjectives and certain past participles in French must always mark gender: "Je suis française" or "Je suis partie"). Female gender marks consequently never permit woman to speak from the genderless, universal position of the speaking "je." Instead, woman must always particularize herself "in a crablike way" when trying to speak. Because she is publicly denied authorial speech, she can only mimic the sounds and speech of men and thereby mimic subjectivity. Linguistic control forces woman to deny herself subjectivity and likewise forbids her access to philosophy, politics, or other abstract elements of the "social body." The linguistic structure is therefore fundamental in woman's oppression as it publicly denies her subjectivity and universality; it is also instrumental in the maintenance of the heterosexual social contract. Due to linguistic gender oppression, Wittig purposefully employed the feminine plural pronoun, "elles," as the subject of her utopian novel *Les Guérillères* (1969) and split the first-person subject to create a purely feminine subject, "j/e," in *Le Corps lesbien* (1973).

Gender in language provides a base for women's oppression and consequently depends heavily on the meaning of difference, or binary opposition (as in Wittig's "Homo Sum," located in *The Straight Mind and Other Essays*, 1992). Poststructuralist feminists, like Wittig, claim that binaries have no referent other than in an opposition to a universal masculine concept; whereas the masculine side of the binary claims universality, the opposite term asserts feminine particularity. Thus, the universality of man depends on the negation of the lesser other term, "woman," which, as Wittig showed, is a cultural fabrication. Man's subjectivity depends on the objectivity of "woman," a concept deeply embedded in language and society that perpetuates women's oppression.

The lesbian exists outside this heterosexual paradigm as a subject who has "escaped" heterosexist oppression and the subsequent discourse of "the straight mind." Wittig's notion of the lesbian is someone who refuses oppressive heterosexist gender types and chooses not to adhere to the myth of woman. In refusing to "become heterosexual" and support her own political heterosexualizing, the lesbian places herself outside the cultural obligation of heterosexuality and man's oppression; in a heterosexual mind frame, "lesbians are not women." As a "not-woman," the lesbian is an "escapee" because she stubbornly refuses to submit to the economy, politics, or ideology of heterosexuality. Hence, in Wittigian terms, the lesbian is a political warrior subject, a *guérillère*, who initiates the revolution to utopia.

KRISTI L. KRUMNOW

See also **Simone de Beauvoir**

Biography

Born in the region of Alsace, France, in 1935, Monique Wittig became a student in the 1960s at the Université de Paris. Her first attempt at writing earned her the Prix de Médicis in Literature for *L'Opoponax* (1964), a story of budding sexuality between two young women. Though very active in the May 1968 student riots and the developing women's groups, Wittig managed to find time to write *Les Guérillères* (1969), another success. After these successful publications about women, Monique Wittig's interest in women's situation continued to develop on the social level. In the summer of 1970, she began to recognize the full political and active potential of her fictional works. In order to awaken the dormant public to the oppression of women, she, along with other members of the Mouvement de Libération des Femmes (MLF), demonstrated on the sights of various Parisian monuments, making passers-by think about signs that read, "There is one who is even more unknown than the Soldier: his wife." In the same time period, Wittig's writing unceasingly confronted lesbianism in works such as *Le Corps lesbien* (1973) and *Brouillon pour un dictionnaire des Amantes* (1975). In 1976, Wittig moved to the United States, where her work continued in the theoretical vein. She published several essays in the 1980s, all of which convey her feminist thought and many of which have been conveniently published in the collection *The Straight Mind and Other Essays* (1992). Most of these essays originally appeared in the French journal *Questions féministes* and were translated by Wittig herself in English for the journal *Feminist Issues*. Wittig's interest in feminism and lesbianism often converges on a theoretical, social, cultural, and political plane. Although sometimes known as a "radical feminist" or a "lesbian separatist," her unique methodology contributes significantly to the ongoing debates in Gay and Lesbian Studies and Queer Theory. After having completed a Ph.D. in 1986 from the Université de Paris-Sorbonne, Monique Wittig began a position in 1990 at the University of Arizona in Tucson, where she was a professor of both French and Women's Studies. During that time, she continued to lecture at Gay and Lesbian Pride events in both France and the United States. She passed away on January 3, 2003.

Selected Works

L'Opoponax, 1964; as *The Opoponax*, translated by Helen Weaver, 1966

Les Guérillères, 1969; as *Les Guérillères*, translated by David Le Vay, 1971

Le Corps lesbien, 1973; as *The Lesbian Body*, translated by David Le Vay, 1975

Brouillon pour un dictionnaire des Amantes (with Sande Zeig), 1975; as *Lesbian Peoples: Material for a Dictionary*, translated by Monique Wittig and Sande Zeig, 1979

"Paradigm," translated by George Stambolian, in *Homosexualities and French Literature*, edited by Elaine Marks and George Stambolian, 1979

The Constant Journey (with Sande Zeig), 1984; as *Le Voyage sans fin*, translated by Monique Wittig and Sande Zeig, 1985

Virgile, non, 1985; as *Across the Acheron*, translated by David Le Vay and Margaret Crosland, 1987

The Straight Mind and Other Essays, 1992; as *La pensée straight*, translated by Monique Wittig, 2001

Paris-la-Politique et autres histoires, 1999

Further Reading

Birkett, Jennifer, "Sophie Ménade: The Writing of Monique Wittig," in *French Erotic Fiction: Women's Desiring Writing, 1880–1990*, edited by Alex Hughes and Kate Ince, Oxford and Washington D.C.: Berg, 1996

Brée, Germaine, "Experimental Novels? Yes, But perhaps 'Otherwise': Nathalie Sarraute, Monique Wittig," in *Breaking the Sequence: Women's Experimental Fiction*, edited by Ellen G. Friedman and Miriam Fuchs, Princeton, NJ: Princeton University Press, 1989

Butler, Judith, "Monique Wittig: Bodily Disintegration and Fictive Sex," in *Gender Trouble: Feminism and the Subversion of Identity*, London and New York: Routledge, 1990

Farwell, Marilyn R., "The Lesbian Narrative: 'The Pursuit of the Inedible by the Unspeakable,' " in *Professions of Desire: Lesbian and Gay Studies in Literature*, edited by George E. Haggerty and Bonnie Zimmerman, New York: The Modern Language Association of America, 1995

Günther, Renate, "Are Lesbians Women? The Relationship between Lesbianism and Feminism in the Work of Luce Irigaray and Monique Wittig," in *Gay Signatures: Gay and Lesbian Theory, Fiction and Film in France, 1945–1995*, edited by Owen Heathcote, Alex Hughes, and James S. Williams, Oxford and New York: Berg, 1998

Hale, Jacob, "Are Lesbians Women?" *Hypatia*, 11/2 (spring 1996). 94–121

Martel, Frédéric, *Le Rose et le noir: Les homosexuels en France depuis 1968*, Paris: Éditions du Seuil, 1996; as *The Pink and the Black: Homosexuals in France since 1968*, translated by Jane Marie Todd, Stanford, CA: Stanford University Press, 1999

Ostrovsky, Erika, *A Constant Journey: The Fiction of Monique Wittig*, Carbondale: Southern Illinois University Press, 1991

Shaktini, Namascar, "A Revolutionary Signifier: *The Lesbian Body*," in *Lesbian Texts and Contexts: Radical Revisions*, edited by Karla Jay and Joanna Glasgow, New York and London: New York University Press, 1990

Whatling, Clare, "Wittig's Monsters: Stretching the Lesbian Reader", *Textual Practice*, 11/2 (Summer (1997): 237–48

Notes on Contributors

Adamowicz, Elza.
Department of French, Queen Mary, University of London, United Kingdom. Entry: SURREALISM.

Adamson, Kay.
Glasgow Caledonian University, United Kingdom. Entries: MOHAMMED ARKOUN, ABDELMALEK SAYAD.

Afilalo, Ari.
Department of Law, Rutgers University, New Jersey. Entry: LAW.

Ahearne, Jeremy.
Department of French Studies, University of Warwick, United Kingdom. Entry: MICHEL DE CERTEAU.

Angermueller, Johannes.
Department of Sociology, Otto-von-Guericke University of Magdeburg, Germany. Entry: INTELLECTUALS.

Aspley, Keith.
Department of French, University of Edinburgh, United Kingdom. Entry: ANDRÉ BRETON.

Azérad, Hugues.
Department of French, Cambridge University, United Kingdom. Entries: JULIEN BENDA, LÉON BLOY.

Baudry, Hervé.
Faculdade de Letras – IEF, University of Coimbra, Portugal. Entry: GÉRALD HERVÉ.

Baugh, Bruce.
University College of the Cariboo, Canada. Entry: INFLUENCE OF GERMAN THOUGHT.

Bell, Laurence.
Department of Linguistic, Cultural, and International Studies, University of Surrey, United Kingdom. Entry: POLITICAL MOVEMENTS AND DEBATES.

Benkov, Edith J.
Program in French and Francophone Studies, San Diego State University, California. Entries: GEORGES DUBY, PAUL NIZAN.

Berry, David.
Department of European & International Studies, Loughborough University, United Kingdom. Entry: DANIEL GUÉRIN.

Bignall, Simone.
Department of Philosophy, University of Sydney, Australia. Entries: FÉLIX GUATTARI.

Bolt Rasmussen, Mikkel.
Department of Art History, University of Aarhus, Denmark. Entry: GUY DEBORD.

Bostic, Heidi.
Department of Humanities, Michigan Technological University. Entries: ALGIRDAS JULIEN GREIMAS, LUCE IRIGARAY, FERDINAND DE SAUSSURE.

Bové, Carol M.
Department of Modern Languages, Westminster College, Pennsylvania. Entries: FEMINISM, PSYCHOANALYTICAL THEORY.

Bowd, Gavin.
Department of French, University of St. Andrews, United Kingdom. Entry: MICHEL VOVELLE.

Boyman, Anne.
Department of French, Barnard College, New York. Entry: KNOWLEDGE AND TRUTH.

Breeur, Roland.
Hoger Instituut voor Wijsbegeerte, Katholieke Universiteit Leuven, Belgium. Entries: ANTONIN ARTAUD, MARCEL PROUST.

Breitenbauch, Henrik østergaard.
Watson Institute for International Studies, Brown University, Rhode Island. Entry: RAYMOND ARON.

Buch-Jepsen, Niels.
Department of Comparative Literature, Cornell University, New York. Entries: MIKEL DUFRENNE, PIERRE MACHEREY, GEORGE POULET, ALBERT THIBAUDET.

Calder, Martin.
Department of French, University of Bristol, United Kingdom. Entry: LANGUAGE.

Cazenave, Odile.
Department of Foreign Languages and Literatures, Massachusetts Institute of Technology. Entries: CALIXTHE BEYALA.

Chadwick, Kay.
Department of French, University of Liverpool, United Kingdom. Entry: CATHOLICISM.

Chambers, Angela.
Director, Centre for Applied Langauge Studies, University of Limerick, Ireland. Entry: AIMÉ CÉSAIRE.

Clej, Alina.
Department of Romance Languages and Literatures, University of Michigan. Entries: MAURICE BARRÈS, FRENCH THOUGHT IN THE UNITED STATES, PSYCHOLOGY.

Cooper, Nicola.
Department of French, University of Bristol, United Kingdom. Entry: FRENCH COLONIAL THOUGHT.

Cooper, Sarah.
Department of French, Cambridge University, United Kingdom. Entry: JULIA KRISTEVA.

Cuin, Charles Henry.
Department de sociologie, Université de Bordeaux II, France. Entries: ÉMILE DURKHEIM, SOCIOLOGY.

Davis, Colin.
Department of French Studies, University of Warwick, United Kingdom. Entries: ALBERT CAMUS, EMMANUEL LEVINAS.

DiMare, Philip C.
Department of Humanities and Religious Studies, California State University, Sacramento. Entries: PAUL RICOEUR, THEOLOGY AND RELIGIOUS THOUGHT.

Downing, Lisa.
Department of French, Queen Mary and Westfield College, United Kingdom. Entry: SEXUALITY.

Duffy, Jean.
Department of French, University of Edinburgh, United Kingdom. Entry: CLAUDE SIMON.

Egéa-Kuehne, Denise.
College of Education, Louisiana State University. Entry: EDUCATIONAL THEORY.

Elden, Stuart.
Department of Geography, University of Durham, United Kingdom. Entry: HENRI LEFEBVRE.

Elevitch, Bernard.
Department of Philosophy, Boston University, Massachusetts. Entries: ALAIN (ÉMILE-AUGUSTE CHARTIER), LÉON BRUNSCHVICG.

ffrench, Patrick.
Department of French, King's College London, United Kingdom. Entries: GEORGES BATAILLE, HISTORICAL SURVEY: 1968-, JOURNALS AND PERIODICALS, JEAN-LUC NANCY, DENIS DE ROUGEMONT.

Fitzgerald, Kevin S.
Independent Scholar. Entry: MAURICE BLANCHOT.

Forsdick, Charles.
Department of French, University of Liverpool, United Kingdom. Entry: COLONIAL AND POSTCOLONIAL EXPERIENCE.

Fotiade, Ramona D.
Department of French, University of Glasgow, United Kingdom. Entries: CHRISTIAN METZ.

Fournier, Marcel.
Département de sociologie, Université de Montréal, Canada. Entry: MARCEL MAUSS.

Frail, Robert J.
Director of International Studies, Centenary College, New Jersey. Entry: MICHEL TOURNIER.

Fraiture, Pierre-Philippe.
French Department, Oxford Brookes University, United Kingdom. Entries: VALENTIN MUDIMBE.

Fullbrook, Edward with **Kate Fullbrook.**
Independent Scholars. Entry: SIMONE DE BEAUVOIR.

Gaillard, Gérald.
Université de Lille 1, France. Entries: ANTHROPOLOGY, LUCIEN LÉVY-BRUHL.

Garfitt, Toby.
Department of French, Oxford University, United Kingdom. Entry: JEAN GRENIER.

Goffey, Andrew.
Brighton, United Kingdom. Entry: BARBARA CASSIN.

Golopentia, Sanda.
Department of French Studies, Brown University, Rhode Island. Entries: ÉMILE BENVENISTE, ROGER CAILLOIS, PHILIPPE (PHILIPPE JOYAUX) SOLLERS.

Goodhart, Sandor.
Department of English, Purdue University, Indiana. Entry: RENÉ NOEL GIRARD.

Gratton, Johnnie.
Department of French, Trinity College, Dublin, Ireland. Entry: AUTOBIOGRAPHY.

Guiney, M. Martin.
Department of Modern Languages and Literatures, Kenyon College, Ohio. Entry: RENÉE BALIBAR.

Gunter, Pete A. Y.
Department of Philosophy and Religion Studies, University of North Texas. Entries: PIERRE LECOMTE DU NOÜY, PIERRE TEILHARD DE CHARDIN.

Hallward, Peter.
Department of French, King's College London, United Kingdom. Entries: ALAIN BADIOU, GILLES DELEUZE.

Hanley, Katharine Rose.
Department of Philosophy, Le Moyne College, New York. Entry: GABRIEL HONORÉ MARCEL.

Han-Pile, Beatrice.
Department of Philosophy, University of Essex, United Kingdom. Entry: MICHEL FOUCAULT.

Hewitt, Nick.
Department of French, The University of Notttingham, United Kingdom. Entry: CULTURE.

Hewlett, Nick.
School of Arts and Humanities, Oxford Brookes University, United Kingdom. Entry: MARXISM.

Heyer, Astrid.
Department of Modern Languages, Brescia University College, United Kingdom. Entry: HENRI MASSIS.

Hiddleston, Jane.
Department of French, University of Warwick, United Kingdom. Entry: ABDELKEBIR KHATABI.

Hoffmann, Leon-François.
Department of French and Italian, Princeton University, New Jersey. Entry: JEAN PRICE-MARS.

Homer, Sean.
City College Thessaloniki – Sheffield University, Greece. Entries: HUMANISM/ANTI-HUMANISM, JACQUES LACAN.

Howells, Christina.
Department of French, Oxford University, United Kingdom. Entry: JEAN-PAUL SARTRE.

Humphreys, Matthew.
Department of Law, University of Surrey, United Kingdom. Entry: FRANÇOIS GÉNY.

Hutcheon, Linda.
Department of English, University of Toronto, Canada. Entry: CHARLES MAURON.

Ippolito, Christophe.
Department of French and Italian, Dickinson College, Pennsylvania. Entry: JOFFRE DUMAZEDIER.

Jacquette, Dale.
Department of Philosophy, Pennsylvania State University. Entry: JACQUES (LUCIEN) MONOD.

James, Ian.
Faculty of Modern and Medieval Languages, Cambridge University, United Kingdom. Entries: PIERRE KLOSSOWSKI, POST STRUCTURALISM, STRUCTURALISM.

Jessop, Robert.
Department of Sociology, Lancaster University, United Kingdom. Entry: NICOS POULANTZAS.

Judaken, Jonathan.
Department of History, University of Memphis, Tennessee. Entries: FRENCH-JEWISH INTELLECTUALS, HOLOCAUST IN FRANCE, THE JEWISH QUESTION.

Kellner, Douglas.
Social Sciences and Comparative Education, University of California, Los Angeles Graduate School of Education & Information Studies. Entry: JEAN BAUDRILLARD.

Kelly, Debra.
Department of French, University of Westminster, United Kingdom. Entry: ASSIA DJEBAR.

Khalfa, Jean.
Department of French, Cambridge University, United Kingdom. Entry: POETRY.

Kitson, Simon.
Centre for European Languages and Cultures, University of Birmingham, United Kingdom. Entry: HISTORICAL SURVEY: 1939-1968.

Kotowicz, Zbigniew.
Department of Historical and Cultural Studies, Goldsmiths College, United Kingdom. Entry: GASTON BACHELARD.

Krumnow, Kristi.
Department of French and Classics, University of South Carolina. Entry: MONIQUE WITTIG.

Lane, Jeremy.
Department of French, The University of Nottingham, United Kingdom. Entry: PIERRE FÉLIX BOURDIEU.

Laroussi, Farid.
Department of French, Yale University, Connecticut. Entry: FRANTZ FANON.

Layton, Robert.
Anthropology Department, University of Durham, United Kingdom. Entries: HENRI BREUIL, ARNOLD VAN GENNEP.

LeBlanc, Randy.
Department of Social Sciences, University of Texas at Tyler. Entry: SIMONE WEIL.

Lejeune, Denis.
Paris, France. Entries: YVES BONNEFOY, PHILOSOPHY OF SCIENCE.

Leonard, Miriam.
Department of Classics and Ancient History, University of Bristol, United Kingdom. Entry: CLASSICS.

Levi, Anthony.
Chipping Norton, United Kingdom. Entries: LUCIEN FEBVRE, ETIENNE HENRY GILSON, PAUL HAZARD, HENRI DE LUBAC, JACQUES MARITAIN.

Lits, Marc.
Département de communication, Observatoire du récit médiatique, Louvain-la-Neuve, Belgium. Entries: ÉMILE MICHEL CIORAN, TZVETAN TODOROV.

Luxford, Julian.
Clare College, United Kingdom. Entries: HENRI-JOSEPH FOCILLON, EMILE MÂLE.

Majumdar, Margaret.
London, United Kingdom. Entry: LA FRANCOPHONIE.

Markus, György.
Department of Philosophy, University of Sydney, Australia. Entry: LUCIEN GOLDMANN.

Marnette, Sophie.
Boston, Massachusetts. Entry: LINGUISTICS.

Marshall, Bill.
Department of French, University of Glasgow, United Kingdom. Entries: GUY HOCQUENGHEM, HOMOSEXUALITY.

Masson, Catherine.
French Department, Wellesley College, Massachusetts. Entry: MICHEL LEIRIS.

Mathieu, Anne.
Nantes, France. Entries: GEORGES POLITZER.

Matthews, Eric.
Department of Philosophy, University of Aberdeen, United Kingdom. Entry: MAURICE MERLEAU-PONTY.

McKellar, Kenneth S.
Department of Modern Languages, King's College at The University of Western Ontario, Canada. Entry: GEORGES BERNANOS.

McKinnon, Andrew.
Department of Sociology, University of Toronto, Canada. Entry: JACQUES ELLUL.

Merine, Katia.
Centre for Translation and Comparative Cultural Studies, Warwick University, United Kingdom. Entry: PATRICK CHAMOISEAU.

Mikolchak, Maria.
Department of Foreign Languages, St Cloud State University, Minnesota. Entries: JEAN PRÉVOST.

Miller, Paul Allen.
Department of Comparative Literature, University of South Carolina. Entries: GEORGES DUMÉZIL, JEAN-PIERRE VERNANT.

Mills, Catherine.
Philosophy Program, Australian National University, Canberra. Entry: GEORGE CANGUILHEM.

Mullarkey, John.
School of Humanities and Social Sciences, University of Sunderland, United Kingdom. Entry: HENRI BERGSON.

Munro, Martin.
Department of Liberal Arts, University of the West Indies, Trinidad and Tobago. Entry: RENÉ DEPESTRE.

Nectoux, François.
Faculty of Human Sciences, Kingston University, United Kingdom. Entries: ECONOMICS, ROGER GARAUDY, HISTORICAL SURVEY: 1918–1939, MEDIA, EMMANUEL MOUNIER, PIERRE VIDAL-NAQUET.

Nelles, William.
Department of English, University of Massachusetts, Dartmouth. Entries: GÉRARD GENETTE, ALAIN ROBBE-GRILLET.

Noetinger, Elise.
Department of French, Cambridge University, United Kingdom. Entry: JEAN STAROBINSKI.

Norris, Christopher.
Philosophy Section, University of Cardiff, United Kingdom. Entries: PIERRE DUHEM, ALEXANDRE KOYRÉ.

Orth, Jennifer.
Université Paris VII, France. NATHALIE SARRAUTE.

Oventile, Robert.
English and Foreign Languages Division, Pasadena City College, California. Entry: JACQUES DERRIDA

Oyallon, Monique.
Department of Languages and Literature, Mansfield University of Pennsylvania. Entry: MARC BLOCH.

Pollard, Patrick.
Department of French, Birkbeck College, United Kingdom. Entry: ANDRÉ GIDE.

Poxon, Judith.
Department of Humanities and Religious Studies, California State University, Sacramento. Entries: HÉLÈNE CIXOUS, MICHÈLE LE DOEUFF.

Purcell, Michael.
Faculty of Divinity, University of Edinburgh, United Kingdom. Entry: PHENOMENOLOGY.

Rapaport, Herman.
Department of English, University of Southampton, United Kingdom. Entry: LITERARY THEORY AND CRITICISM.

Robinson, Christopher.
Oxford, United Kingdom. Entry: TONY DUVERT.

Rockhill, Gabriel.,
Centre Parisien d'Etudes Critiques, Paris, France. Entries: JEAN LUC GODARD, JACQUES RANCIÈRE.

Rölli, Marc.
University of Marburg, Germany. Entries: ALEXANDRE KOJÈVE, MODERNISM AND POST-MODERNISM.

Rushton, Peter.
School of Health, Natural and Social Sciences, University of Sunderland, United Kingdom. Entry: PHILIPPE ARIÈS.

Ryan, Angela.
Department of French, National University of Ireland, Cork. Entries: NICOLE LORAUX, PHILOSOPHY.

Sachs, Leon.
Department of French, Davidson College, North Carolina. Entry: HISTORIOGRAPHY.

Saint, Nigel.
Department of French, University of Leeds, United Kingdom. Entry: GEORGES DIDI-HUBERMAN, LOUIS MARIN.

Salazar-Ferrer, Olivier.
Alliance français de Glasgow, United Kingdom. Entries: ALBERT BÉGUIN, MAURICE BLONDEL, RENÉ HUYGHE, VLADIMIR JANKÉLÉVITCH, LOUIS LAVELLE, RENÉ LE SENNE, MARCEL RAYMOND, ANDRÉ SUARÈS.

Salhi, Kamal.
Department of French, University of Leeds, United Kingdom. Entry: CHEIKH ANTA DIOP.

Schouest, Scott J.
Department of Music, Central Michigan University. Entry: OLIVIER MESSIAEN.

Senior, Matthew.
Department of French, University of Minnesota, Morris. Entry: BODY, MICHEL HOULLEBECQ.

Shantz, Jeffrey.
Department of Sociology, York University, Canada. Entries: ANDRÉ GORZ, DANIEL HALÉVY, JEAN JAURÈS, ALAIN LIPIETZ, ERNEST MANDEL, CHARLES MAURRAS, GEORGES SOREL.

Sherman, David Lloyd.
Department of Philosophy, University of Montana, Missoula. Entry: EXISTENTIALISM.

Shields, James.
Department of French Studies, University of Warwick, United Kingdom. Entries: MAURICE BARDECHE, DRIEU LA ROCHELLE.

Simmons, William Paul.
Social and Behavioral Sciences, Arizona State University – West. Entries: GEORGES GURVITCH, CLAUDE LEFORT.

Spoiden, Stéphane.
Department of Humanities, University of Michigan, Dearborn. Entry: RÉGIS DEBRAY.

Stafford, Andy.
Department of European Languages and Cultures, Lancaster University, United Kingdom. Entries: ART HISTORY, CRITICISM, AND AESTHETICS; ROLAND BARTHES; JEAN DUVIGNAUD; ANDRÉ GLUCKSMANN; EDGAR MORIN.

Syrotinski, Michael.
Department of French, University of Aberdeen, United Kingdom. Entry: JEAN PAULHAN.

Thomas, Bonnie.
Mt. Hawthorn, Australia. Entry: EDOUARD GLISSANT.

Tilby, Michael.
Department of French, Cambridge University, United Kingdom. Entries: JACQUES RIVIÈRE, PAUL VALÉRY.

Udris, Raynalle.
Department of Modern Languages, Middlesex University, United Kingdom. Entry: ANNIE LECLERC.

Vassallo, Helen.
Paris, France. Entry: JEANNE HYVRARD.

Notes on Contributors

Wall, Denis.
*Department of Sociology, University of Toronto, Canada.
Entries: Maurice Halbwachs, Emmanuel Le Roy Ladurie.*

Wall-Romana, Christophe.
*Department of French, University of California, Berkeley.
Entries: Jean Wahl.*

Wandel, Torbjorn.
*Division of Social Science, Truman State University,
Missouri. Entry: Historical survey: 1870–1918.*

Webb, David.
*Department of Philosophy, Staffordshire University, United
Kingdom. Entry: Jean Cavaillès.*

White, Denise Bridget.
*Department of English, Birkbeck College, United Kingdom.
Entries: Michel Serrès, Paul Virilio.*

Williams, Caroline.
*Department of Politics, Queen Mary and Westfield College,
London, United Kingdom. Entries: Louis Althusser,
Cornelius Castoriadis, Subject (self and subjectivity).*

Williams, James.
*Department of Philosophy, University of Dundee, United
Kingdom. Entry: Jean-François Lyotard.*

Winter, Yves.
*Department of Rhetoric, University of California, Berkeley.
Entry: Étienne Balibar.*

Wiseman, Boris.
*French Department, University of Durham, United Kingdom.
Entry: Claude Lévi-Strauss.*

Woodward, Servanne.
*Department of French, University of Western Ontario,
Canada. Entries: Léopold (Sédar) Senghor.*

Wright, Alan.
*Department of Theatre and Film Studies, University of
Canterbury, New Zealand. Entry: André Bazin.*

Index

Index

Index

Index

Index

Index

Index

Index